The Art of Top Cow

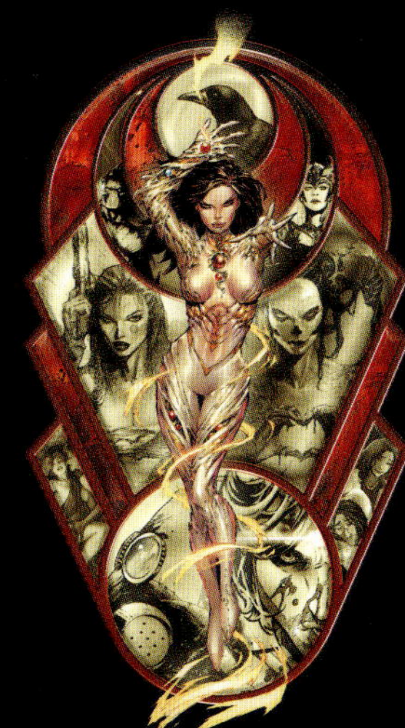

Legacy

published by
Top Cow Productions, Inc.
Los Angeles

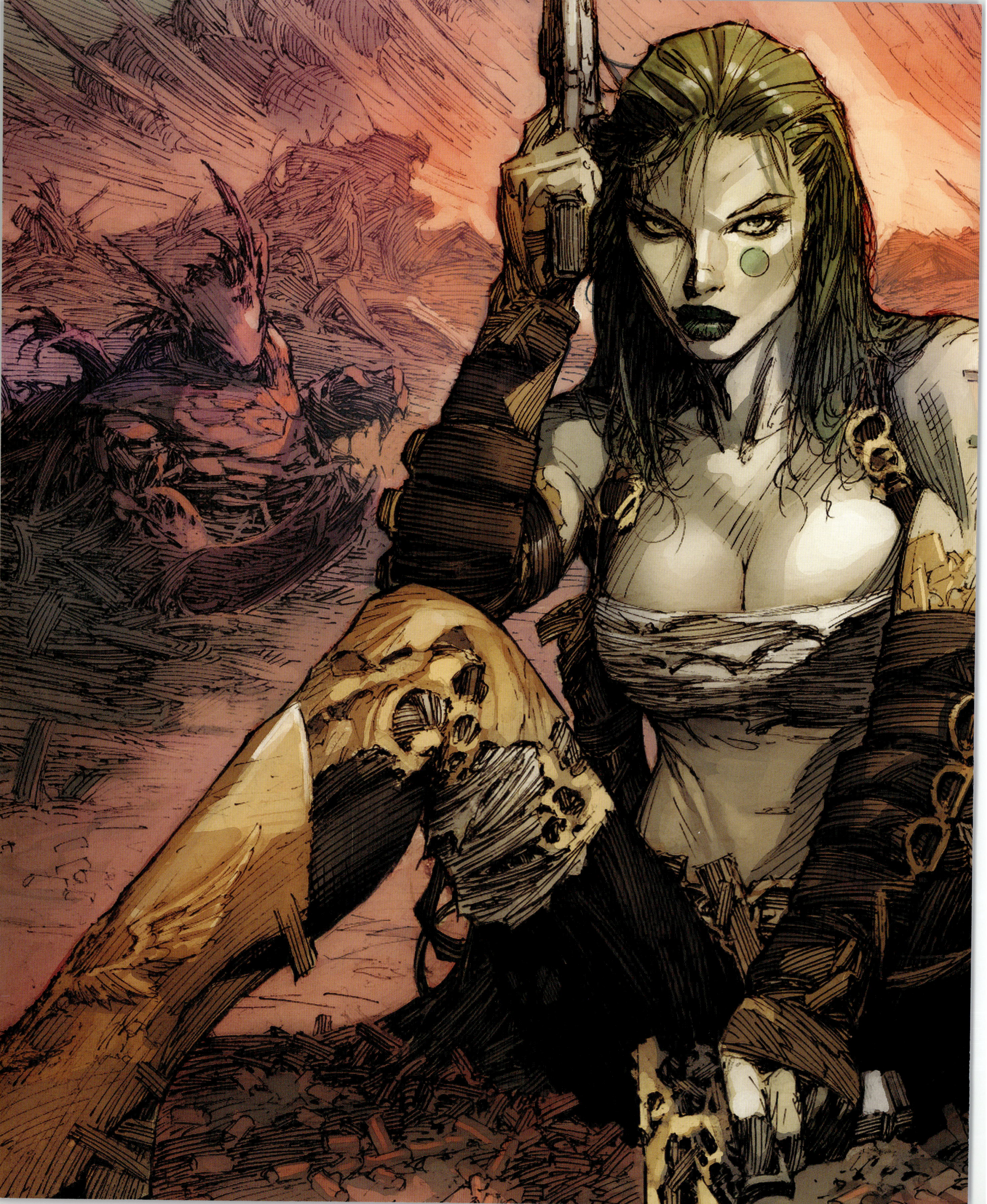

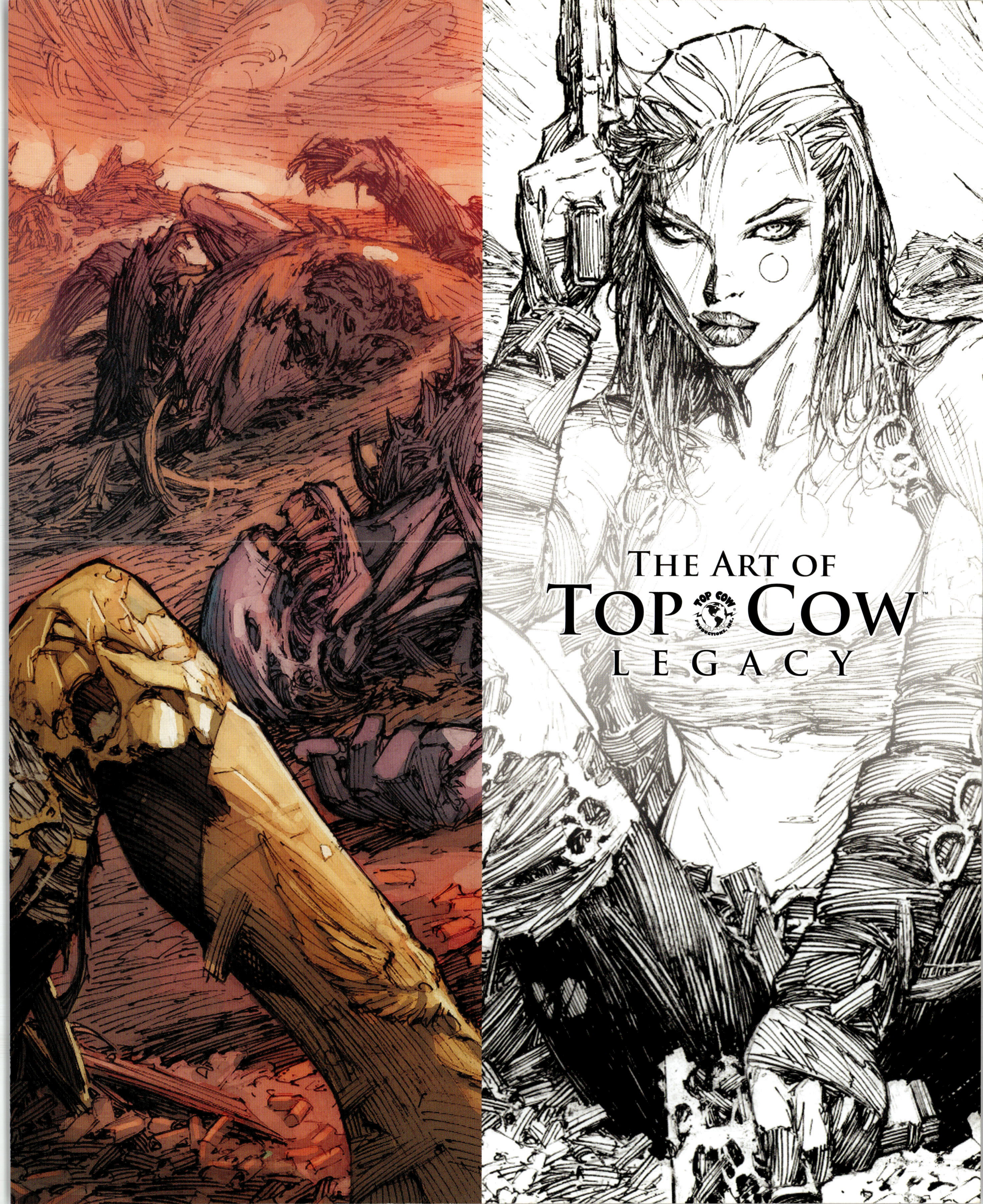
THE ART OF
TOP COW™
LEGACY

THE ART OF TOP COW™ LEGACY

For Top Cow Productions, Inc.
Marc Silvestri - CEO
Matt Hawkins - President & COO
Vincent Valentine - Director of Special Projects
Phil Smith - Edits, Design and Production
Lisa Y. Wu - Marketing Director
Want more info? Check out:
www.topcow.com
for news & exclusive merchandise!

IMAGE COMICS, INC.
Robert Kirkman – Chief Operations Officer
Erik Larsen – Chief Financial Officer
Todd McFarlane – President
Marc Silvestri – Chief Executive Officer
Jim Valentino – Vice President
Eric Stephenson – Publisher & Chief Creative Officer
IMAGECOMICS.COM

The Art of Top Cow: Legacy, Art Collection
July 2025. First printing. Published by Image Comics, Inc. Office of publication: PO BOX 14457, Portland, OR 97293. Printed in China. For international rights, contact: matt@topcow.com. Hardcover ISBN: 978-1-5343-3093-1. Softcover ISBN: 978-1-5343-2816-7.

for this edition,
Book Design, Layout
and Edits by
Phil Smith

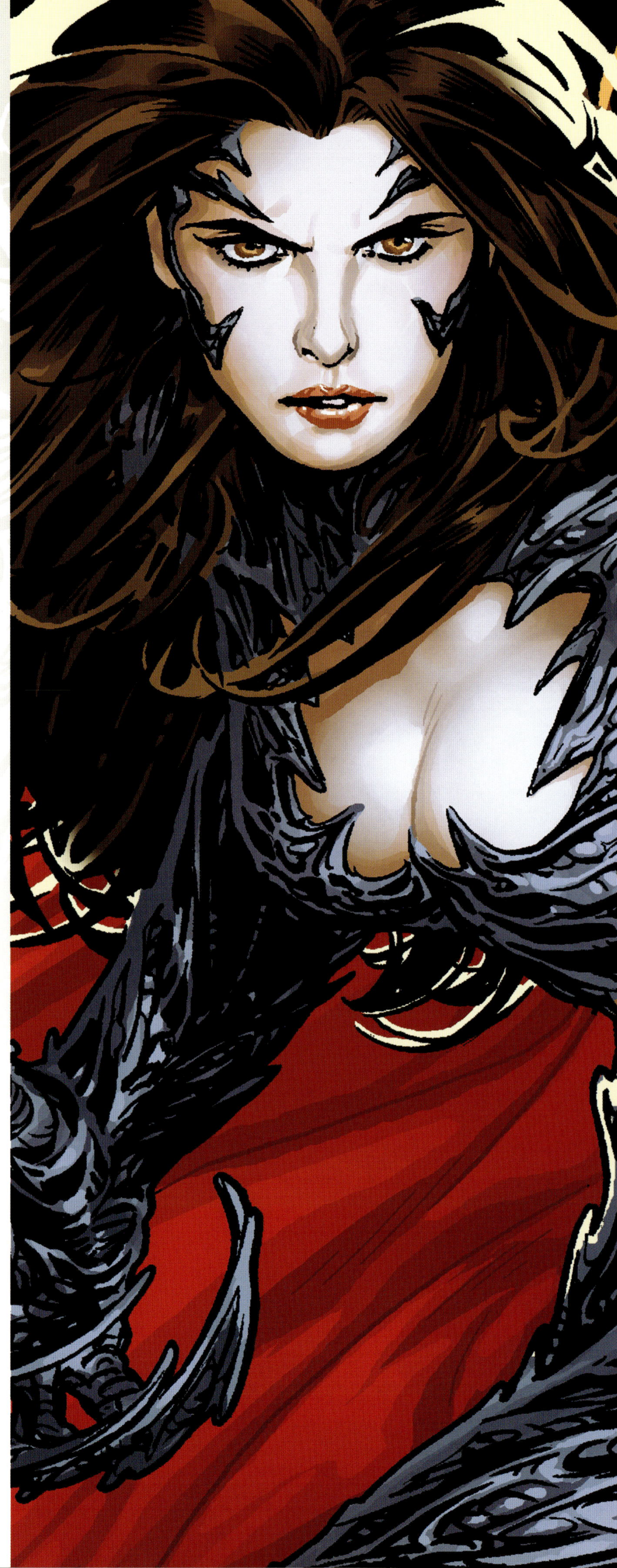

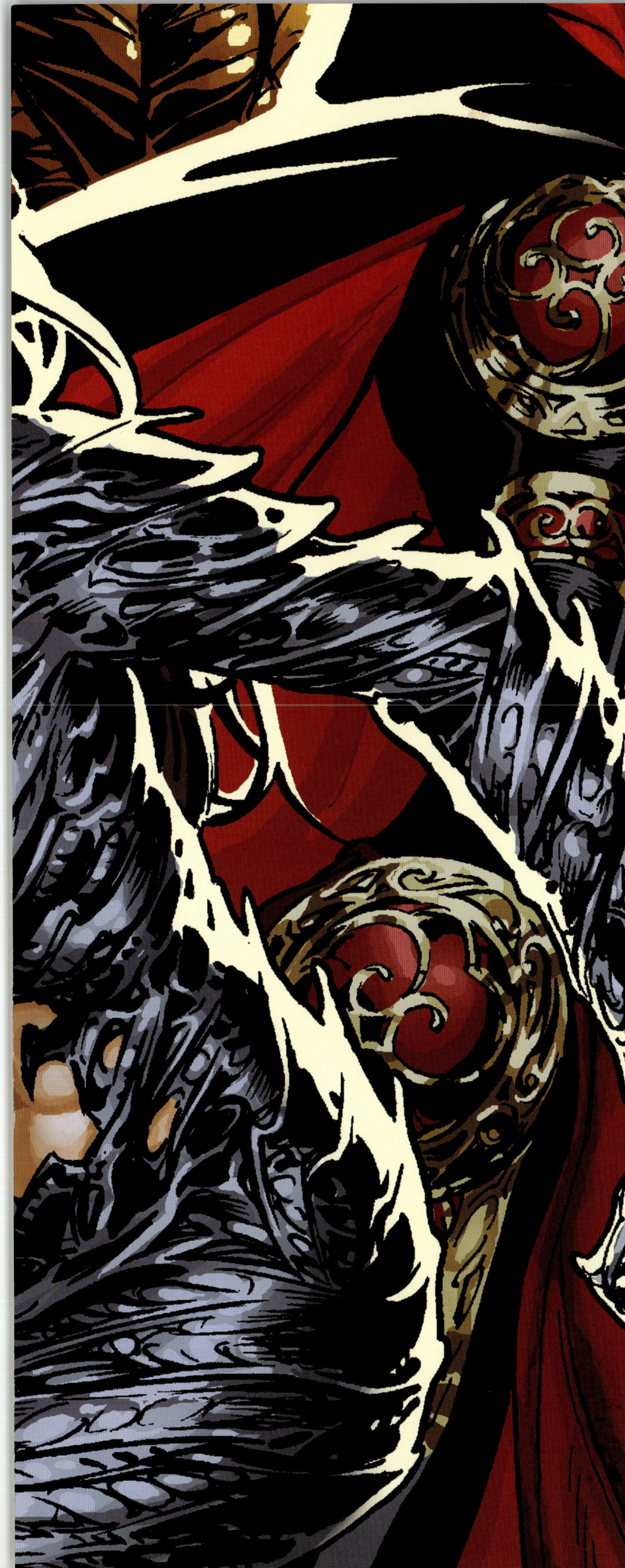

TABLE OF CONTENTS

TOP COW UNIVERSE

TOP COW SHOWCASE

This spread. *Artifacts* issue #2 cover A,
pencil, ink, and color art by: Ryan Sook

Overleaf. *The Art of Top Cow* [2009] cover,
art by: Marc Silvestri and Steve Firchow

Hardcover edition Endpapers.
Front leaf, art by: Stjepan Sejic
Back leaf, art by: Brett Booth and Thomas Mason

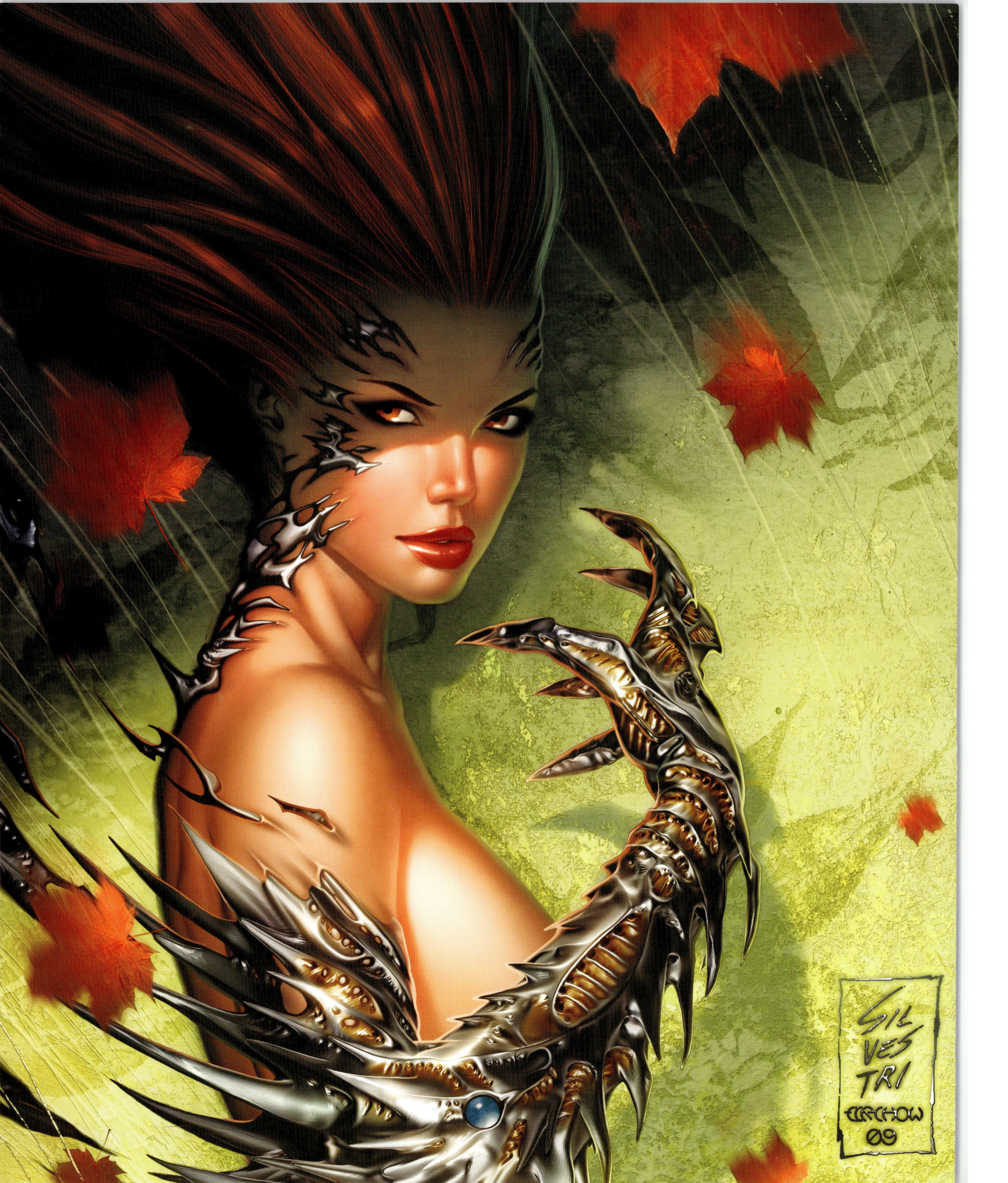

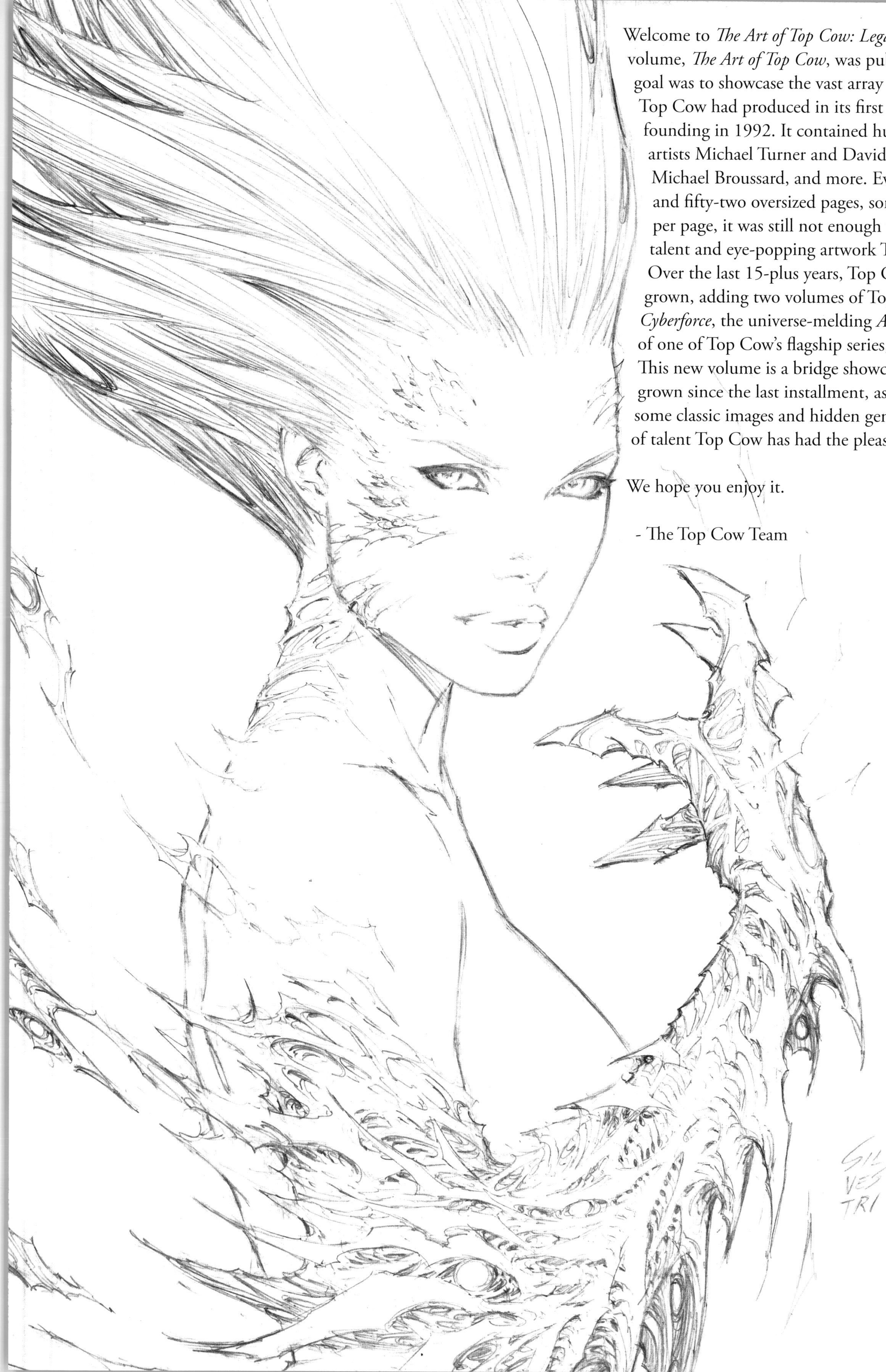

Welcome to *The Art of Top Cow: Legacy*. When the original volume, *The Art of Top Cow*, was published in 2009, the goal was to showcase the vast array of artists and artwork Top Cow had produced in its first 17 years since its founding in 1992. It contained hundreds of images from artists Michael Turner and David Finch to Stjepan Sejic, Michael Broussard, and more. Even with three hundred and fifty-two oversized pages, some with over five images per page, it was still not enough to cover the breadth of talent and eye-popping artwork Top Cow had to offer. Over the last 15-plus years, Top Cow's library has only grown, adding two volumes of Top Cow's original series *Cyberforce*, the universe-melding *Artifacts*, and the relaunch of one of Top Cow's flagship series, *Witchblade*, and more. This new volume is a bridge showcasing how Top Cow has grown since the last installment, as well as a look back at some classic images and hidden gems from the vast library of talent Top Cow has had the pleasure of working with.

We hope you enjoy it.

\- The Top Cow Team

{WITCHBLADE}
Series Covers • Selected Works

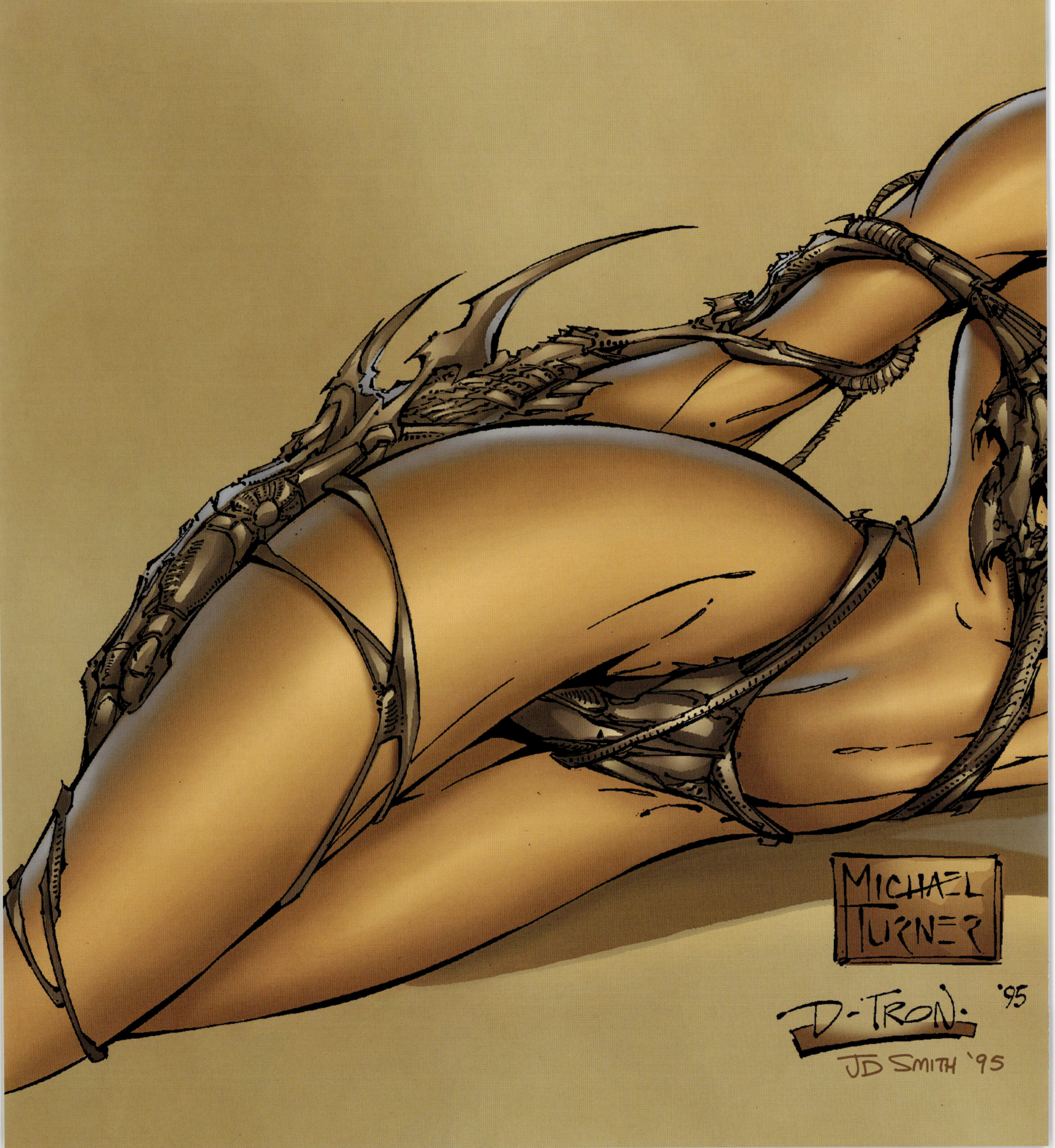

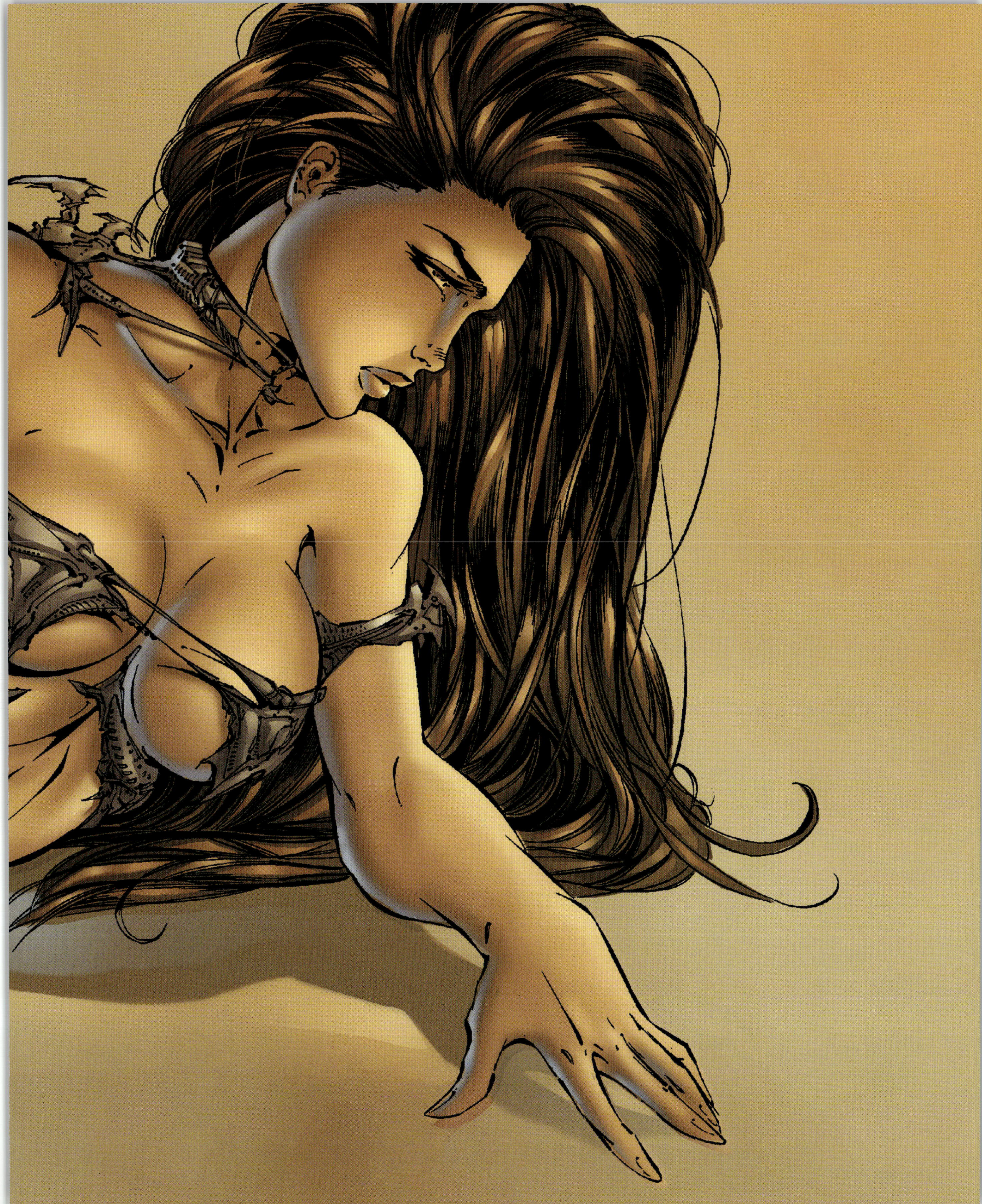

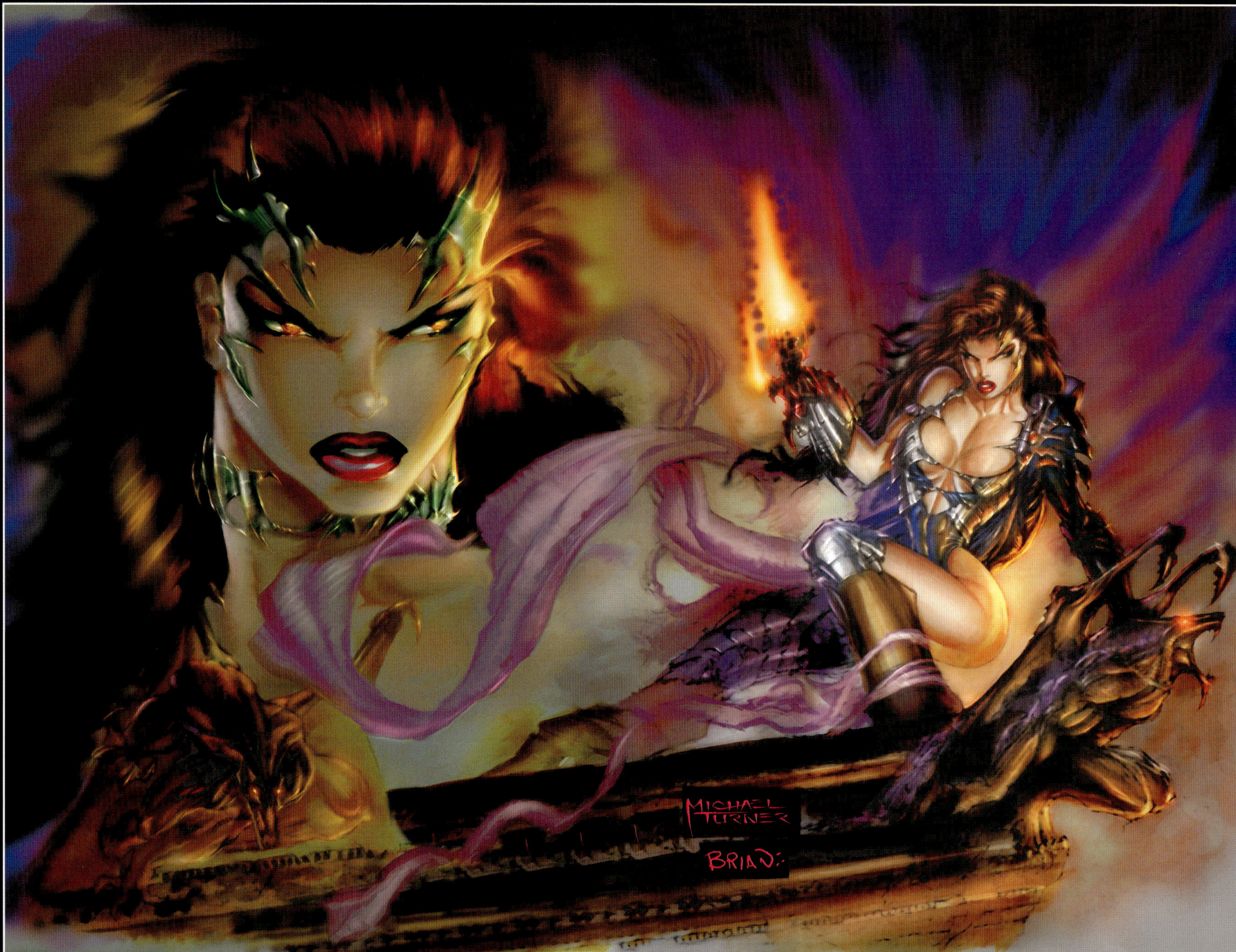

Witchblade created by
Marc Silvestri, David Wohl, Brian Haberlin & Michael Turner

*Witchblad*e was first published in October 1995-November 2015. The series returned in 2017 and relaunched in 2024 and remains one of the core titles of the Top Cow Universe. The following gallery begins with the most current iteration, ushering in an exciting new era of *Witchblade!*

If this is your first time hearing about *Witchblade*, in a nutshell: New York City Police Detective Sara Pezzini is the latest in a long line of bearers of the Witchblade, a mysterious artifact that takes the form of a deadly and powerful mystical gauntlet. Bound by destiny, the Witchblade chooses one woman in a generation who must stand between the forces of Light and Dark and preserve The Balance.

Over the years, the Witchblade has chosen several bearers, including Sara Pezzini, Danielle Baptiste, Alex Underwood, and more across the ages.

Above. *Witchblade* issue #1 cover,
art by: Michael Turner and Brian Haberlin

Previous page. *Witchblade* 1995 poster,
art by: Michael Turner, D-Tron, and Jonathan D. Smith

Facing page. *Witchblade* issue #17 cover,
art by: Michael Turner, D-Tron, and Jonathan D. Smith

Currently Sara is back, relaunched in 2024 with the creative team of writer **Marguerite Bennett**, artist **Giuseppe Cafaro**, colorist **Arif Prianto** and letterer **Troy Peteri.**

On the following pages, we look at some of the fantastic artists and artwork that have kept the series a fan favorite across eras.

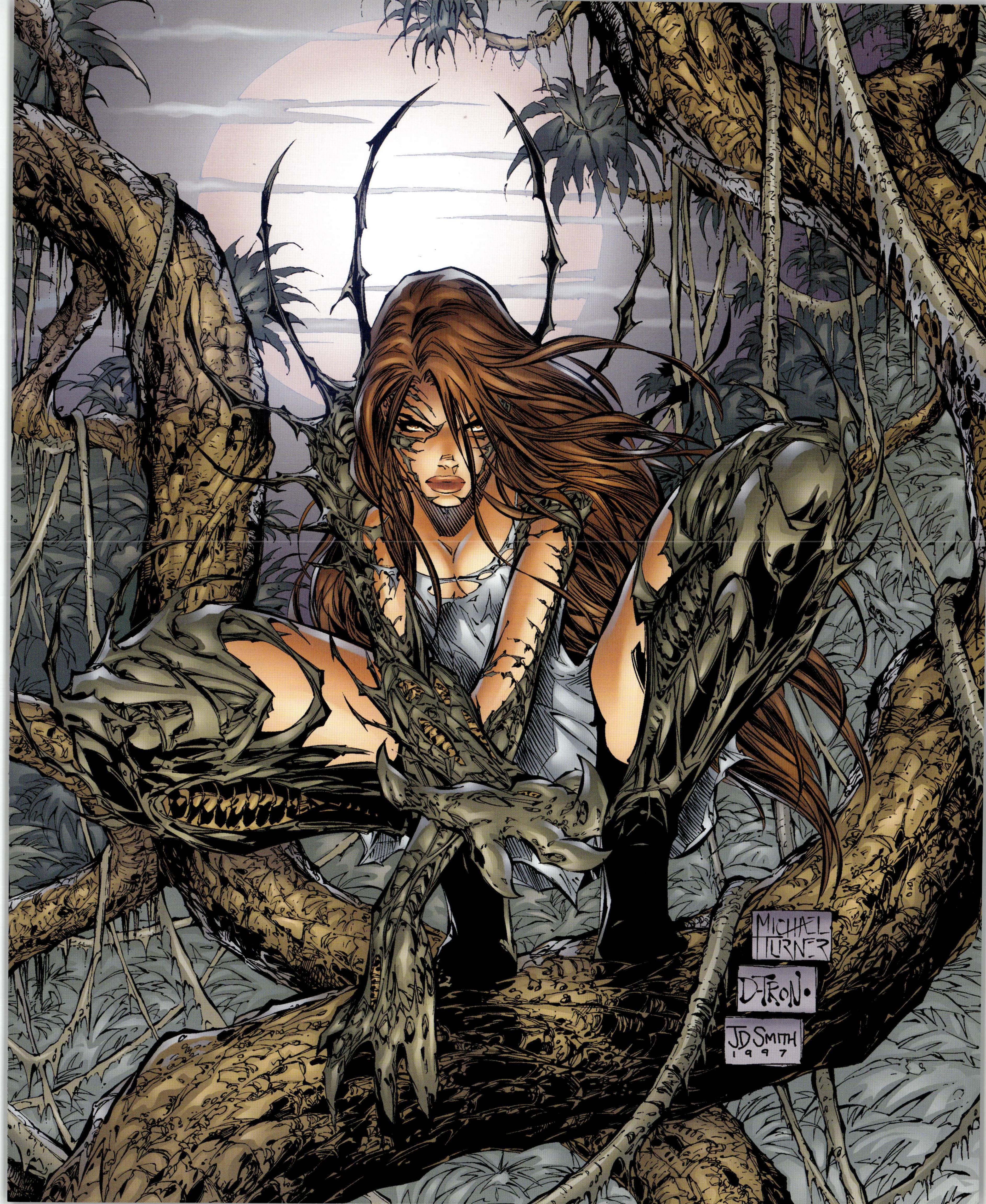
MICHAEL TURNER
D-TRON
JD SMITH
1997

Witchblade logo c1995

Witchblade logo c1996

Witchblade television series logo c2001

Witchblade anime and Takeru manga series logo c2006

Witchblade logo c2007 designed by **Todd Klein**

Witchblade logo c2017 for the second series.

Witchblade logo c2024

In advance of the 2024 relaunch of *Witchblade,* Top Cow looked at all iterations of past logos ('90s, '00s, TV, Anime/Manga, and the 2007 redesign). There were great elements to them all. We decided to go back to the beginning and do a simpler update on the original logo. The idea was to keep the big '90s energy but clean and keep the iconic W.

Facing page. *Witchblade* first appearance in *Cyblade/Shi* issue #1,
line art by: Marc Silvestri and Matt "Batt" Banning

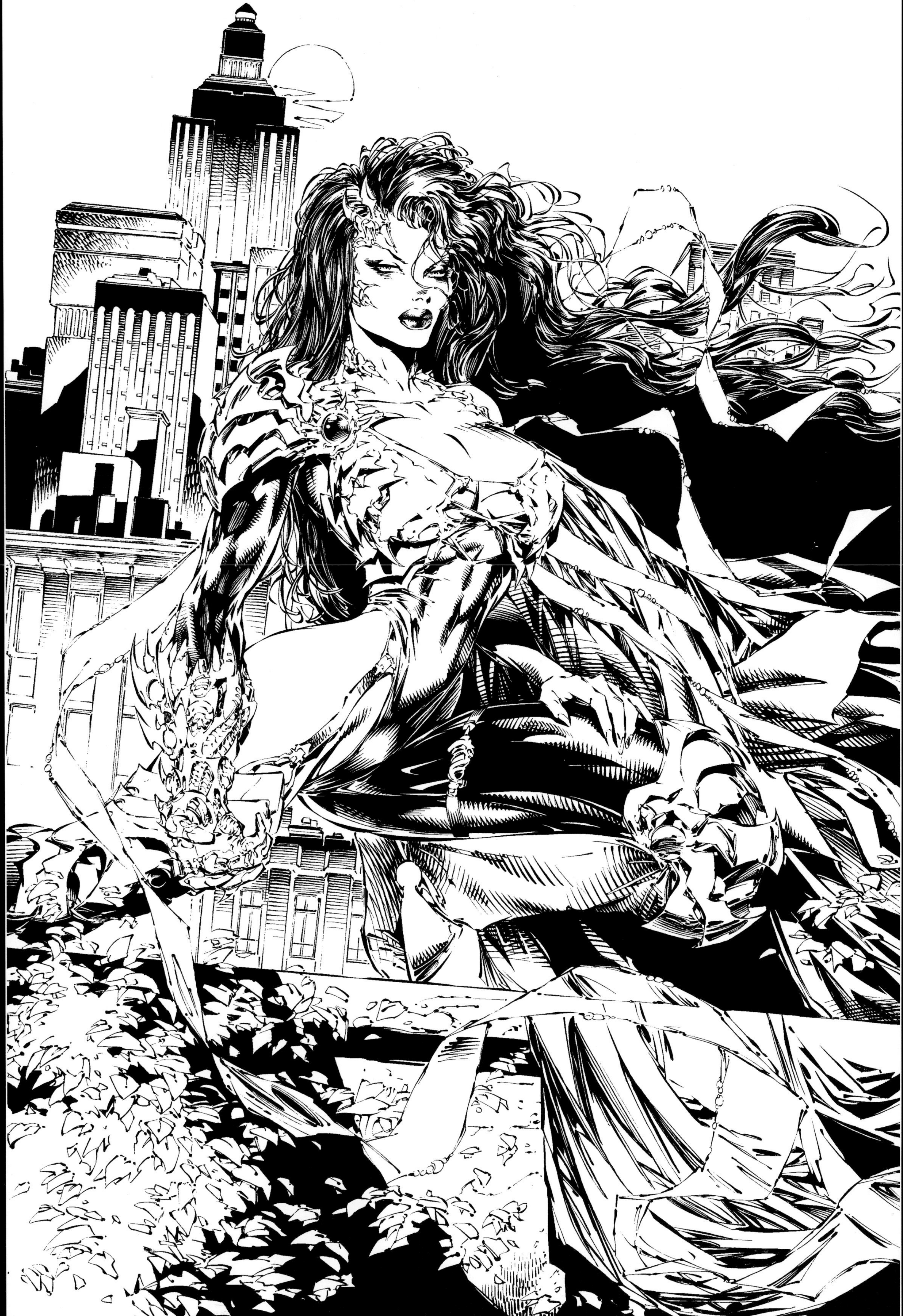

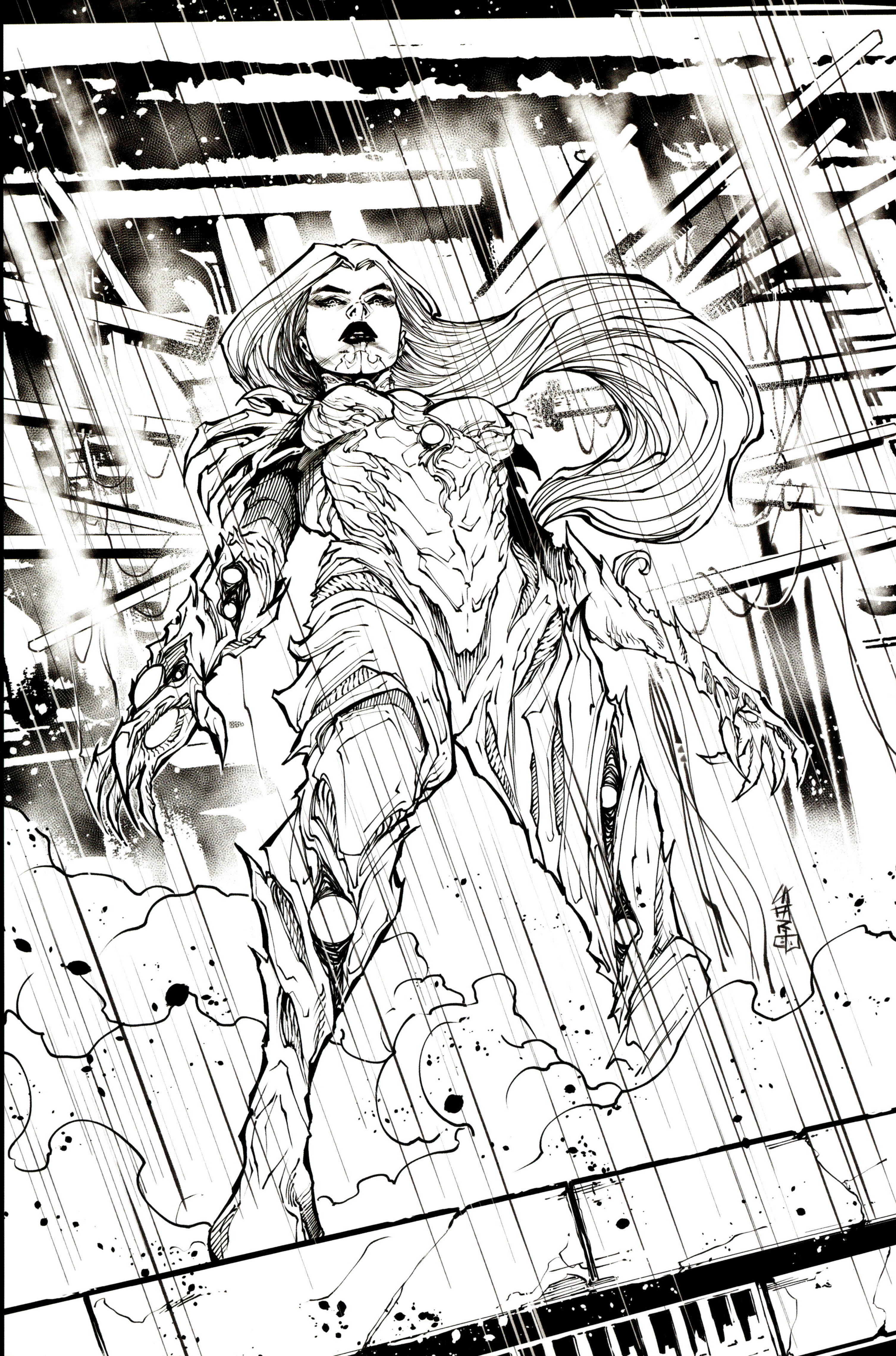

Witchblade #1 [2024] advance cover concept,
line art by: Giuseppe Cafaro.

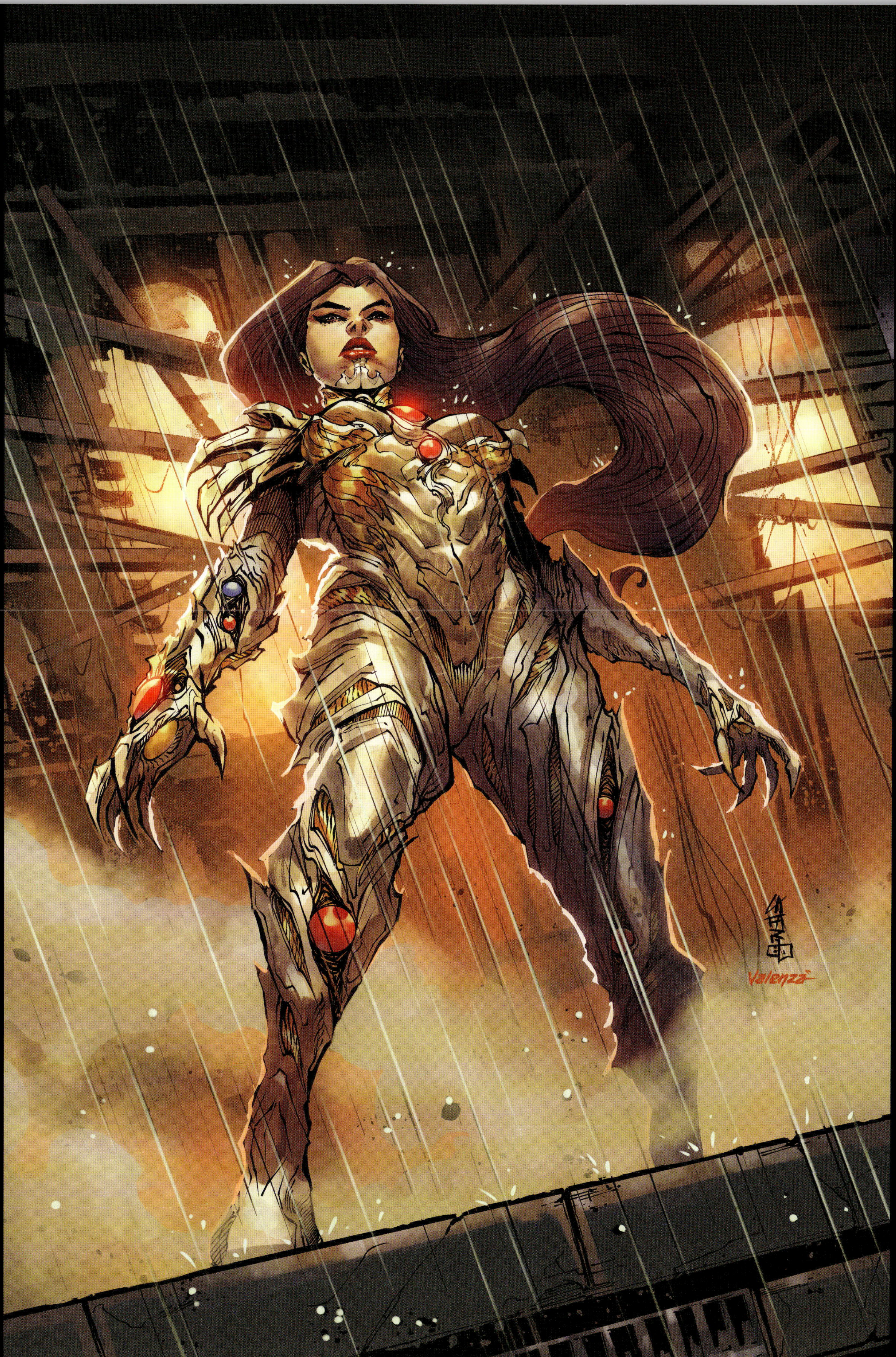

Witchblade #1 [2024] advance cover concept,
art by: Giuseppe Cafaro and Bryan Valenza

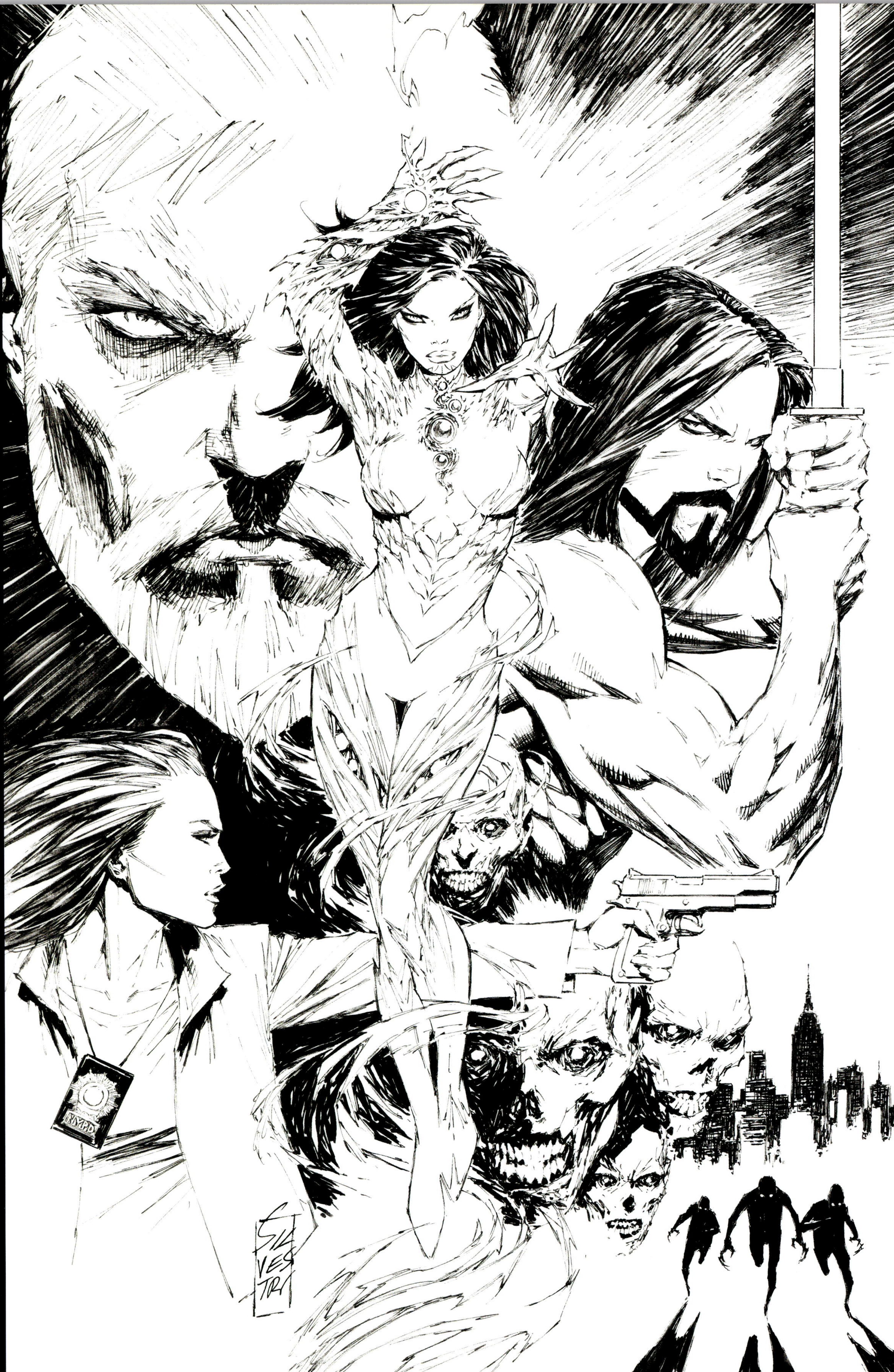

Witchblade #1 [2024] cover A, E, H, and I,
line art by: Marc Silvestri

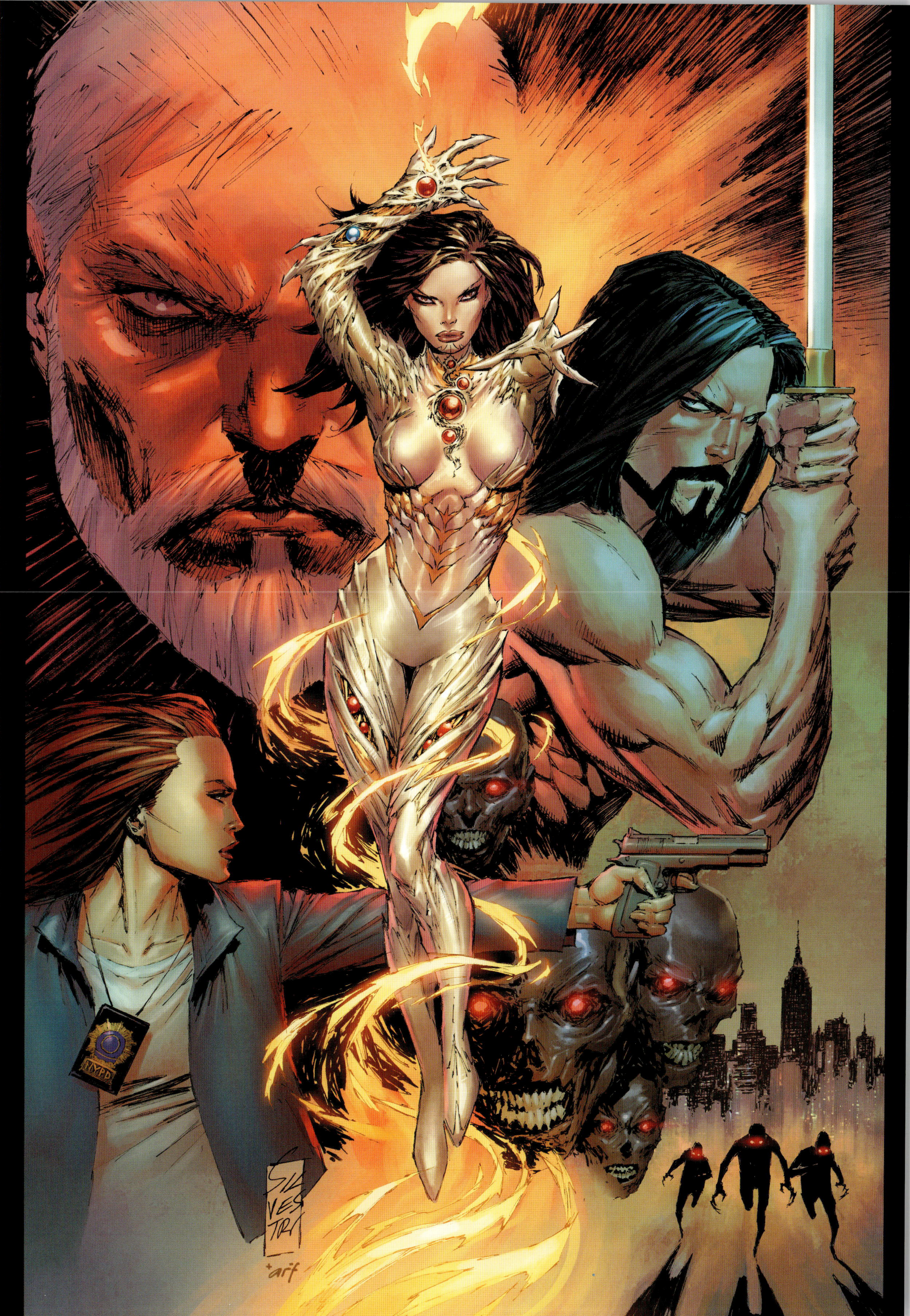

Witchblade #1 [2024] cover A, E, H, and I,
art by: Marc Silvestri and Arif Prianto

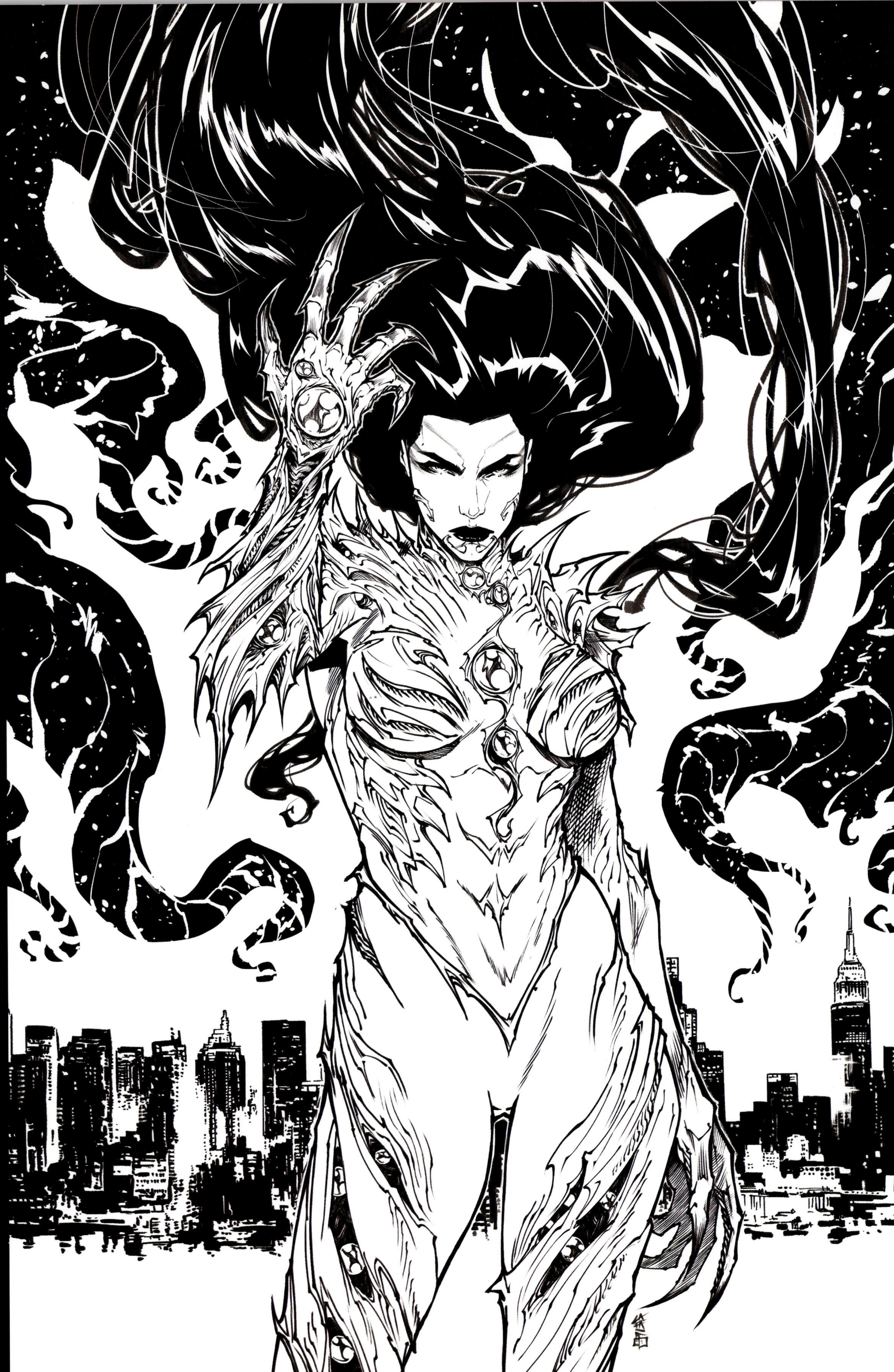

Witchblade #1 [2024] cover B,
line art by: Giuseppe Cafaro

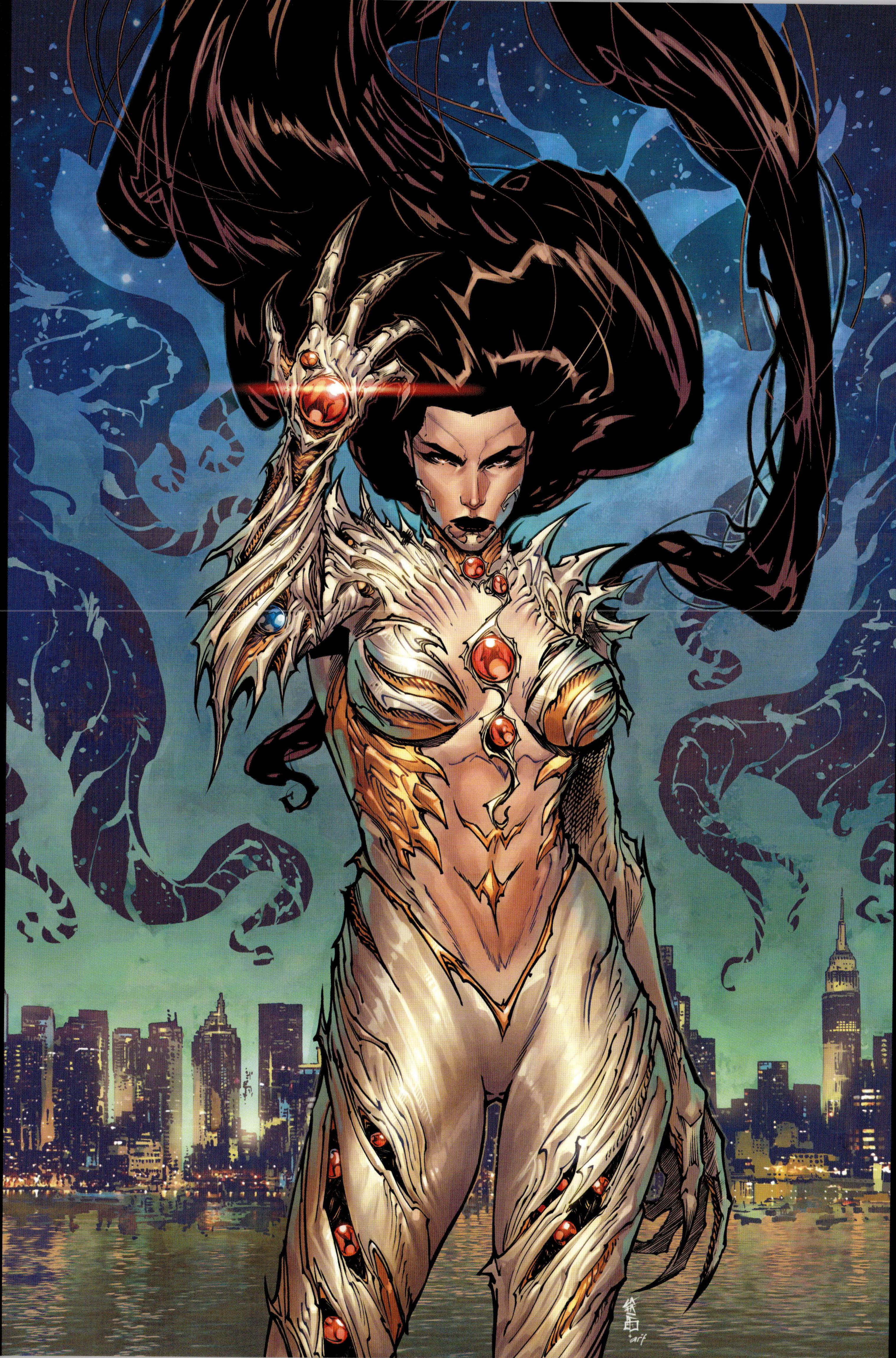

Witchblade #1 [2024] cover B,
art by: Giuseppe Cafaro and Arif Prianto

Witchblade #1 [2024] cover D,
line art by: Dani

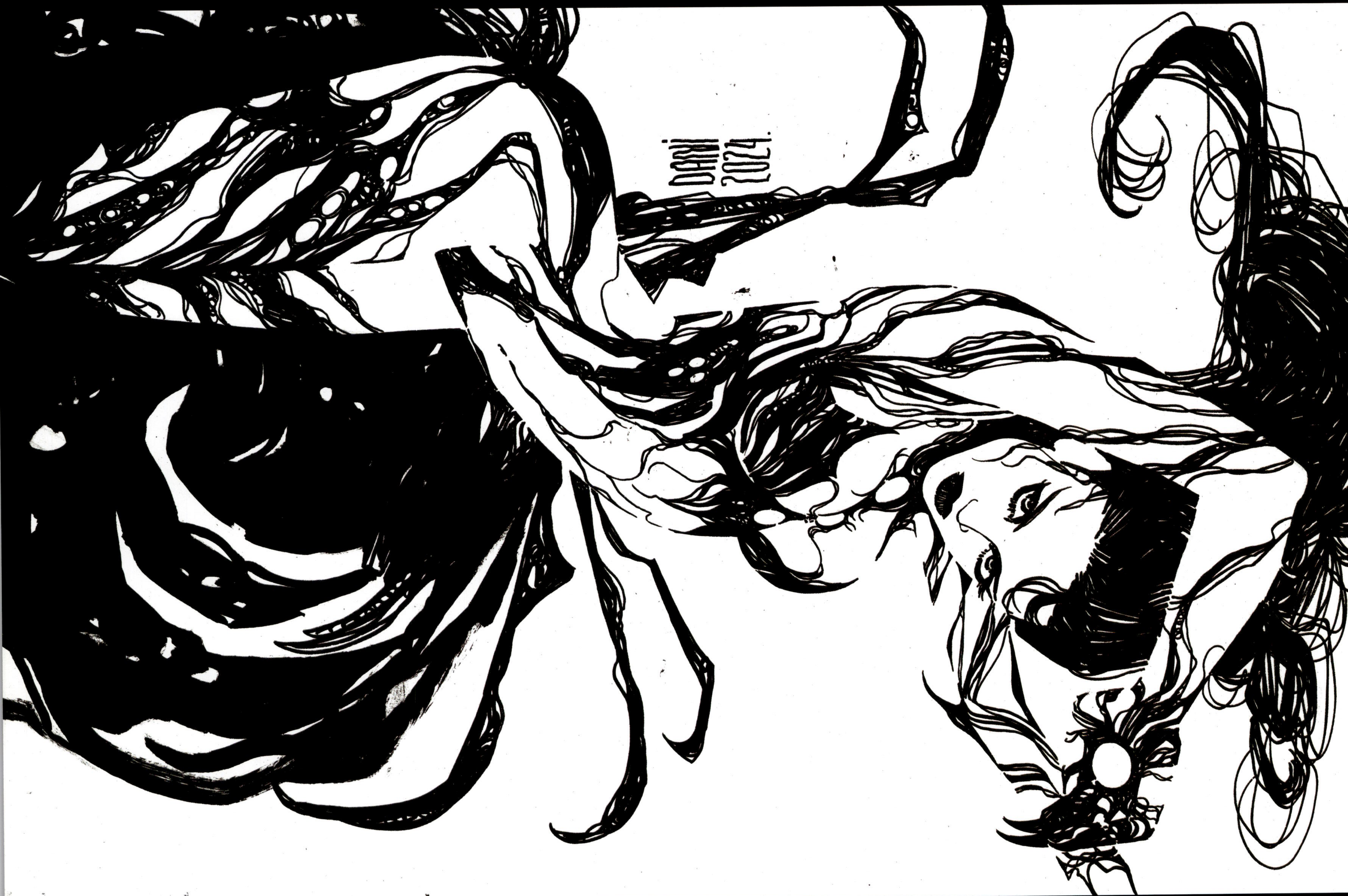

Witchblade #1 [2024] cover D,
art by: Dani and Brad Simpson

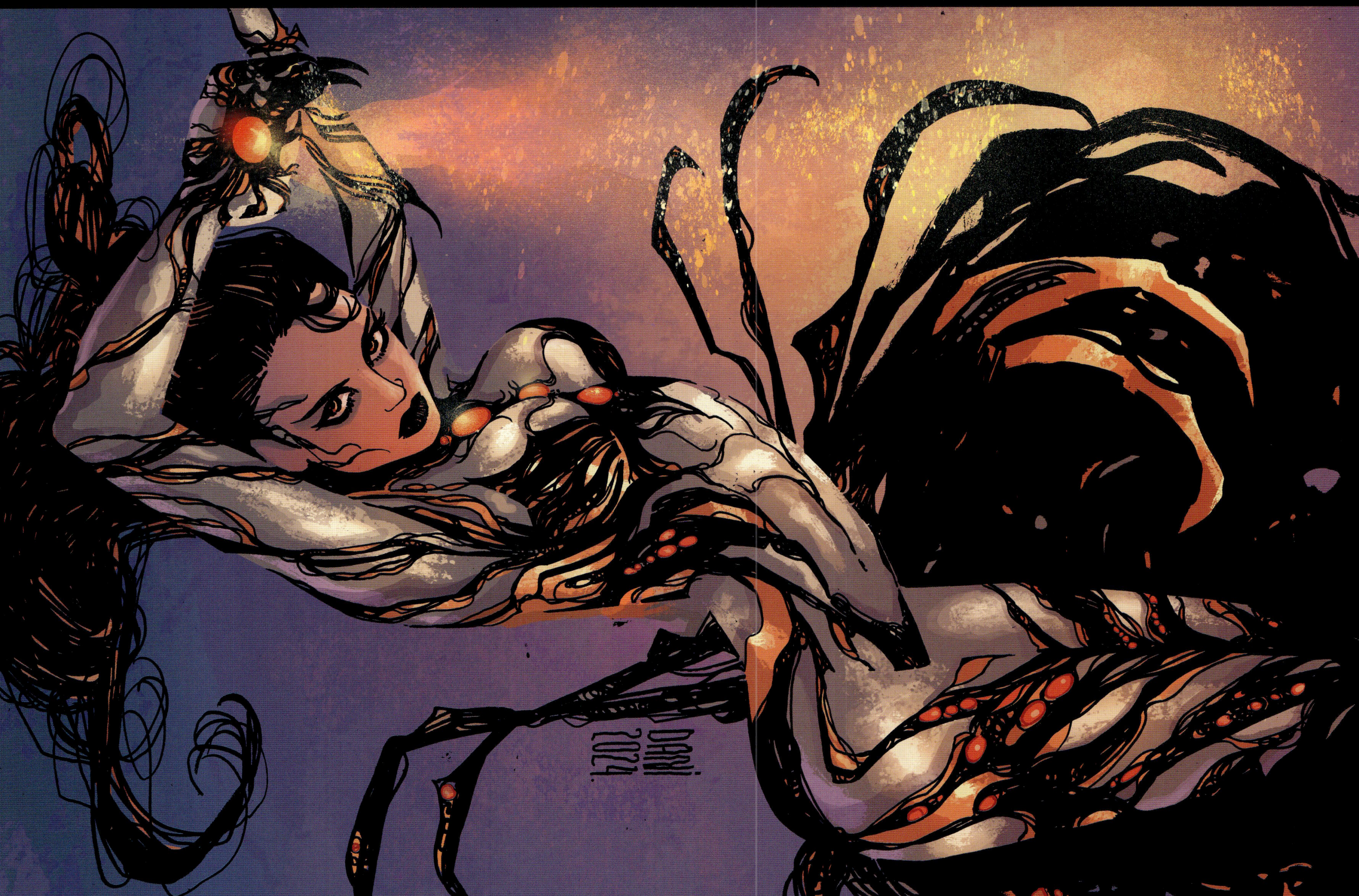

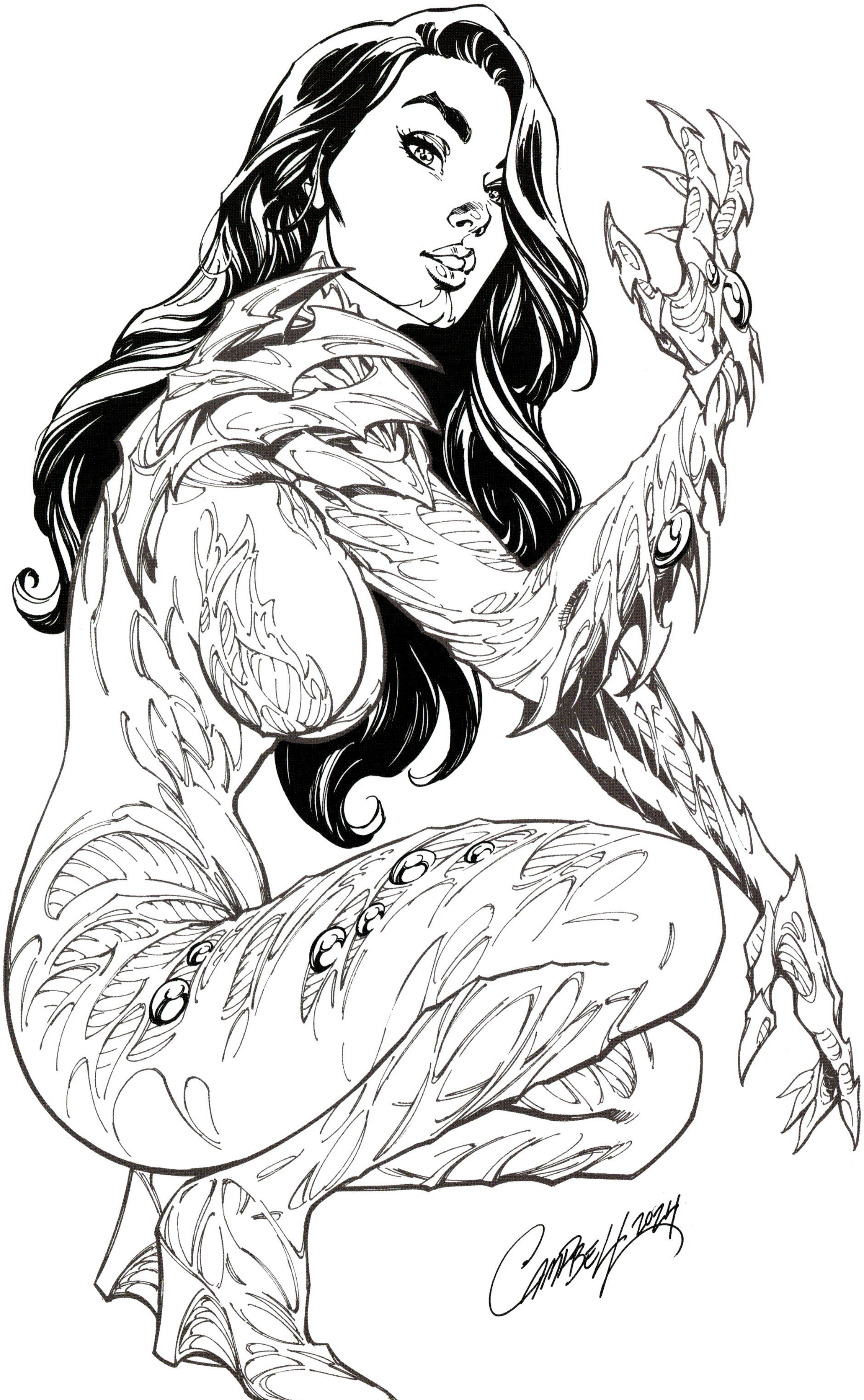

Witchblade #1 [2024] cover F and J. Scott Campbell Exclusive,
line art by: J. Scott Campbell

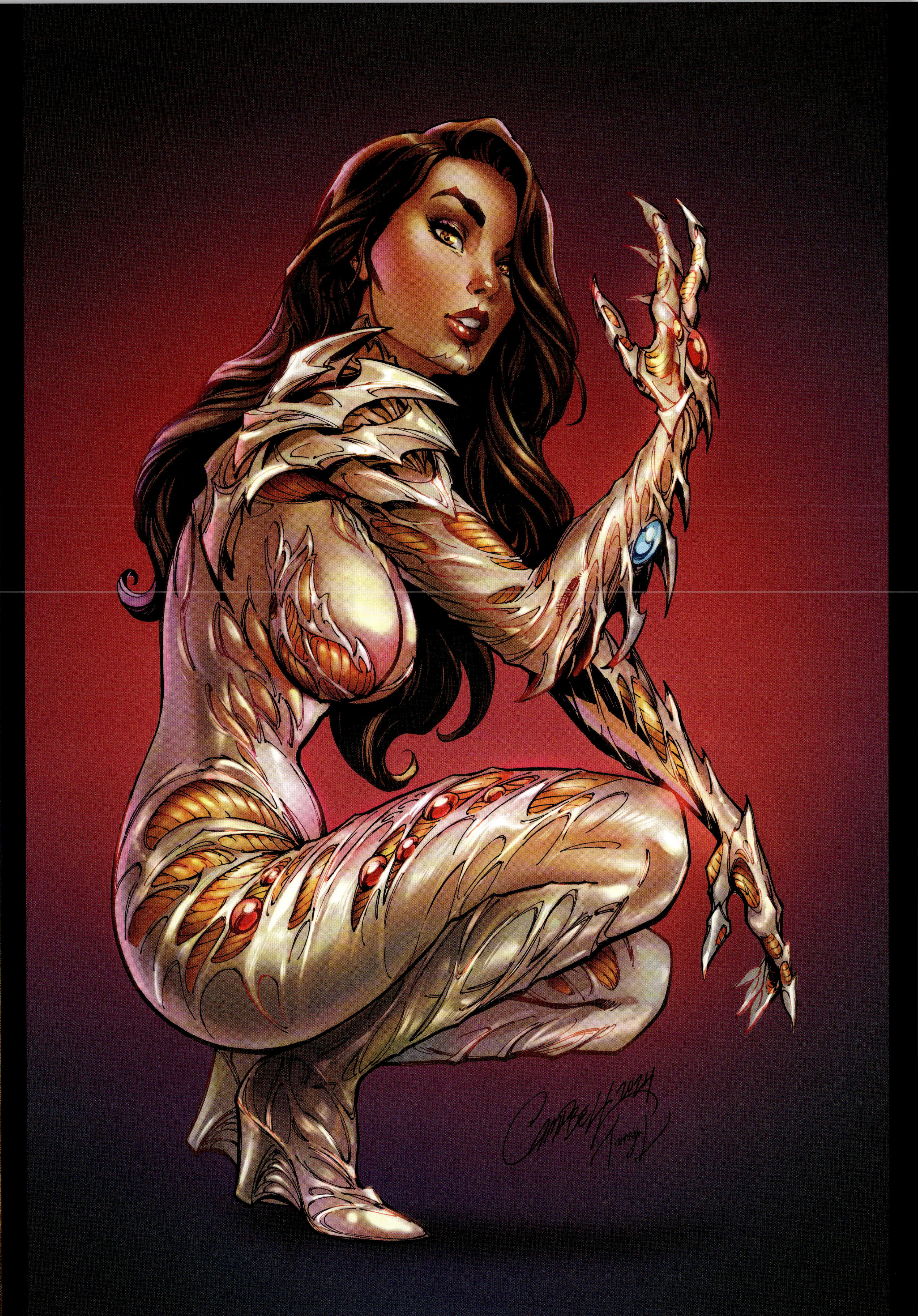

Witchblade #1 [2024] cover F,
art by: J. Scott Campbell and Tanya Lehoux

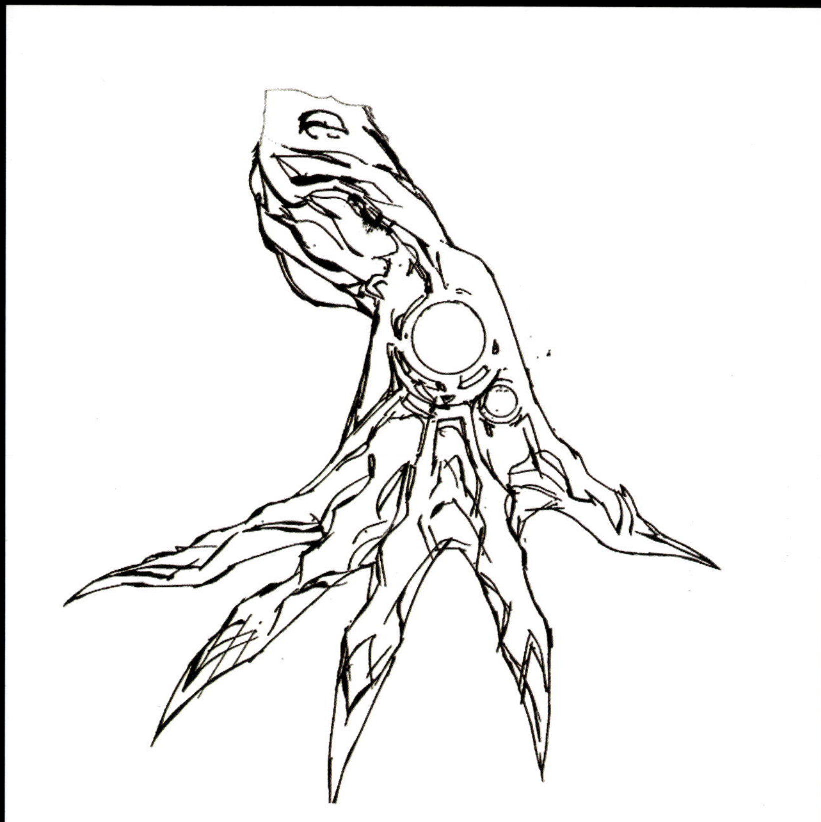

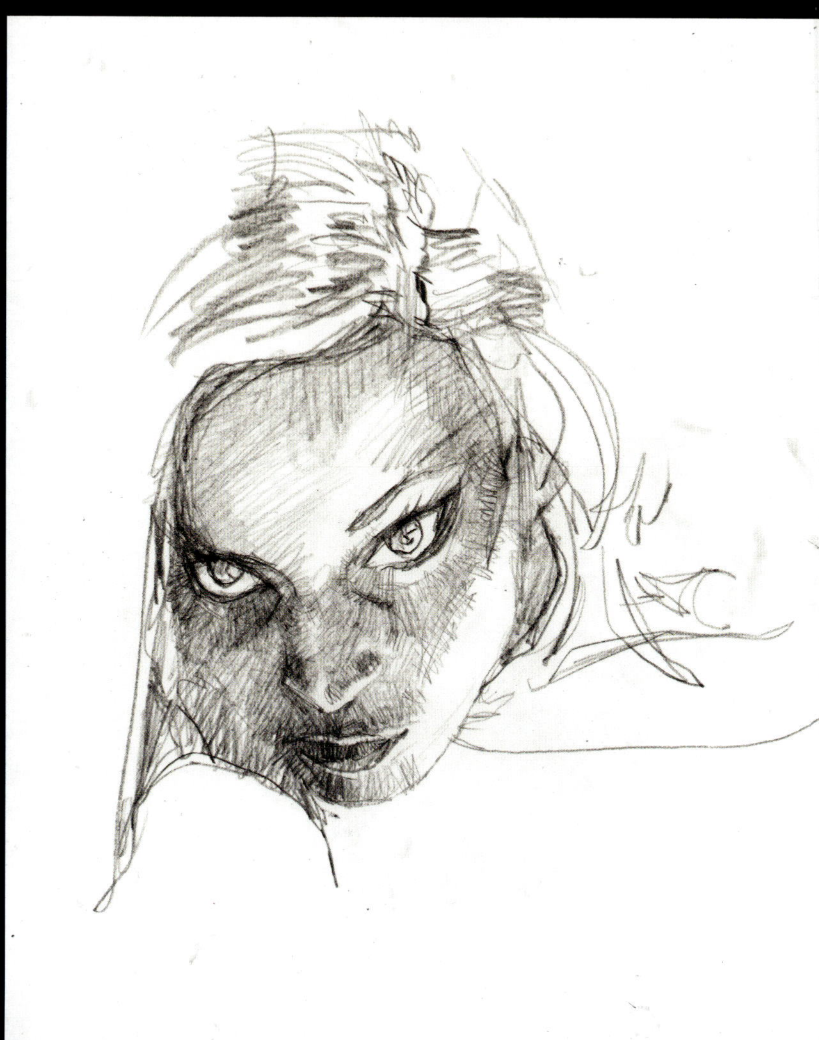

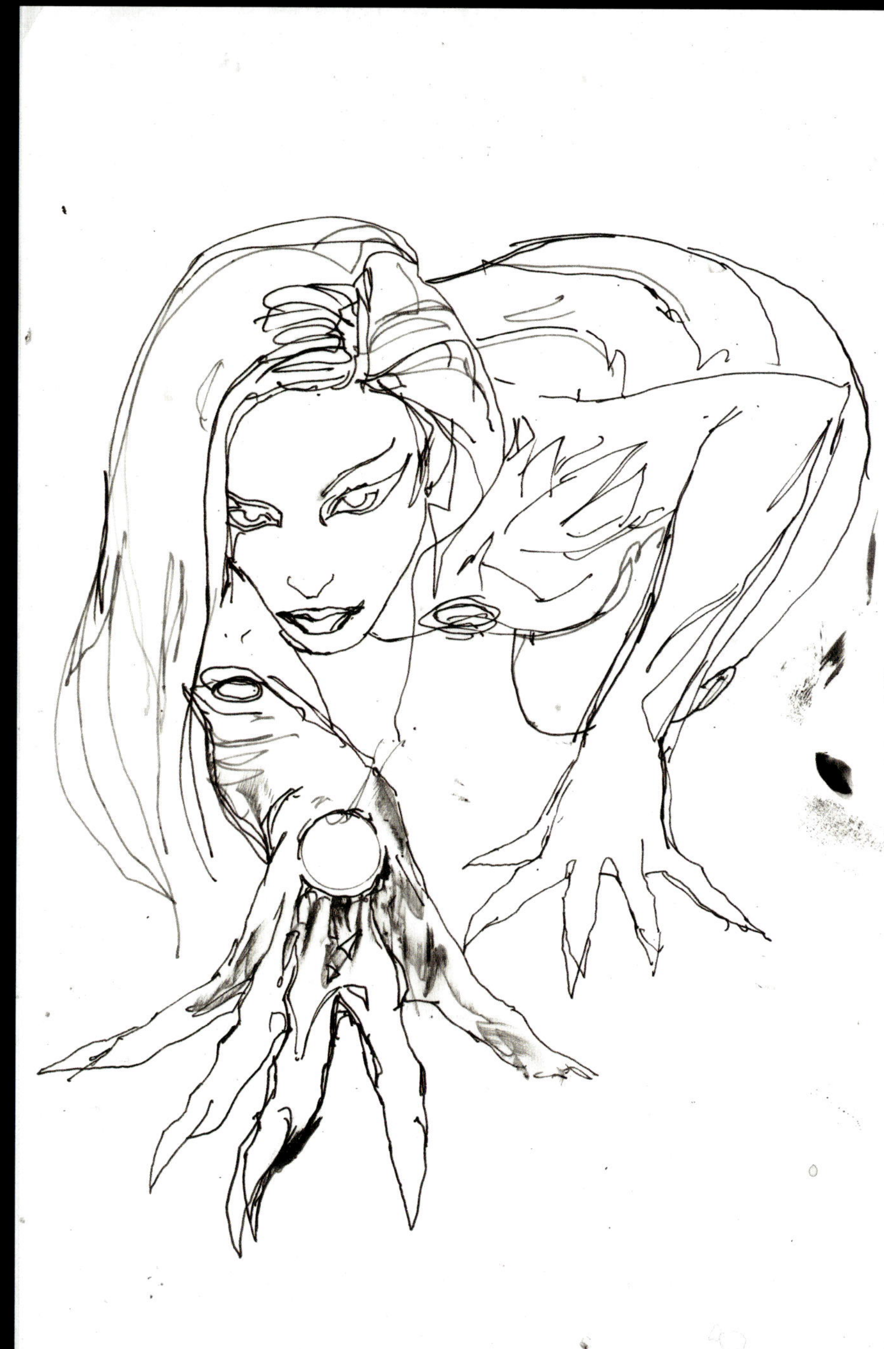

This page. ***Witchblade*** **#1 [2024] cover G, "prelims" by: Bill Sienkiewicz**

Bill Sienkiewicz is an artist's artist. His style has transformed over the years from an energetic line art style to highly experimental. When given the chance to commission him for a *Witchblade* cover we (the royal we) jumped at the chance and this image has become a fan-favorite collectible and an iconic addition to the legacy of the series.

Facing page. ***Witchblade*** **#1 [2024] cover G, art by: Bill Sienkiewicz**

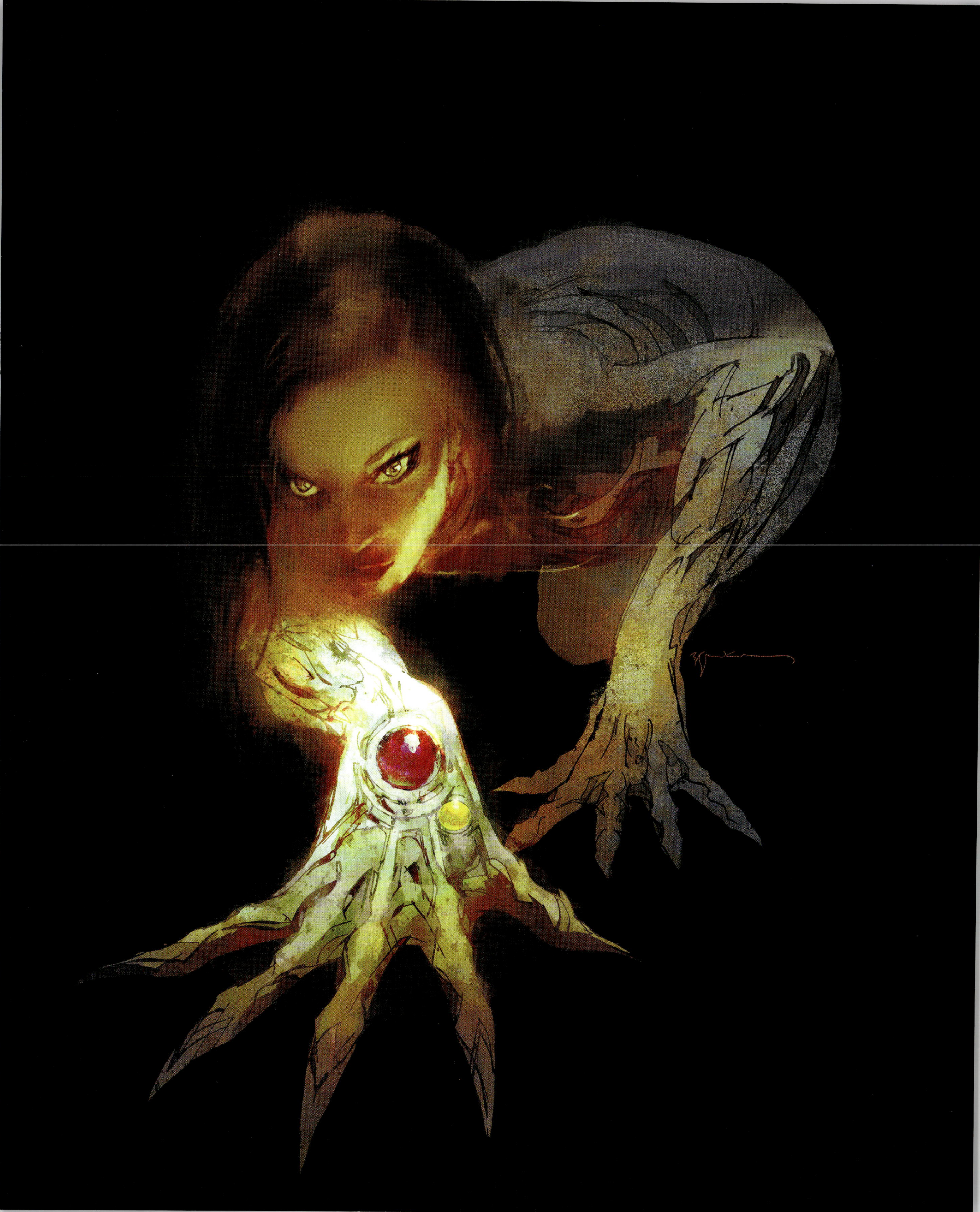

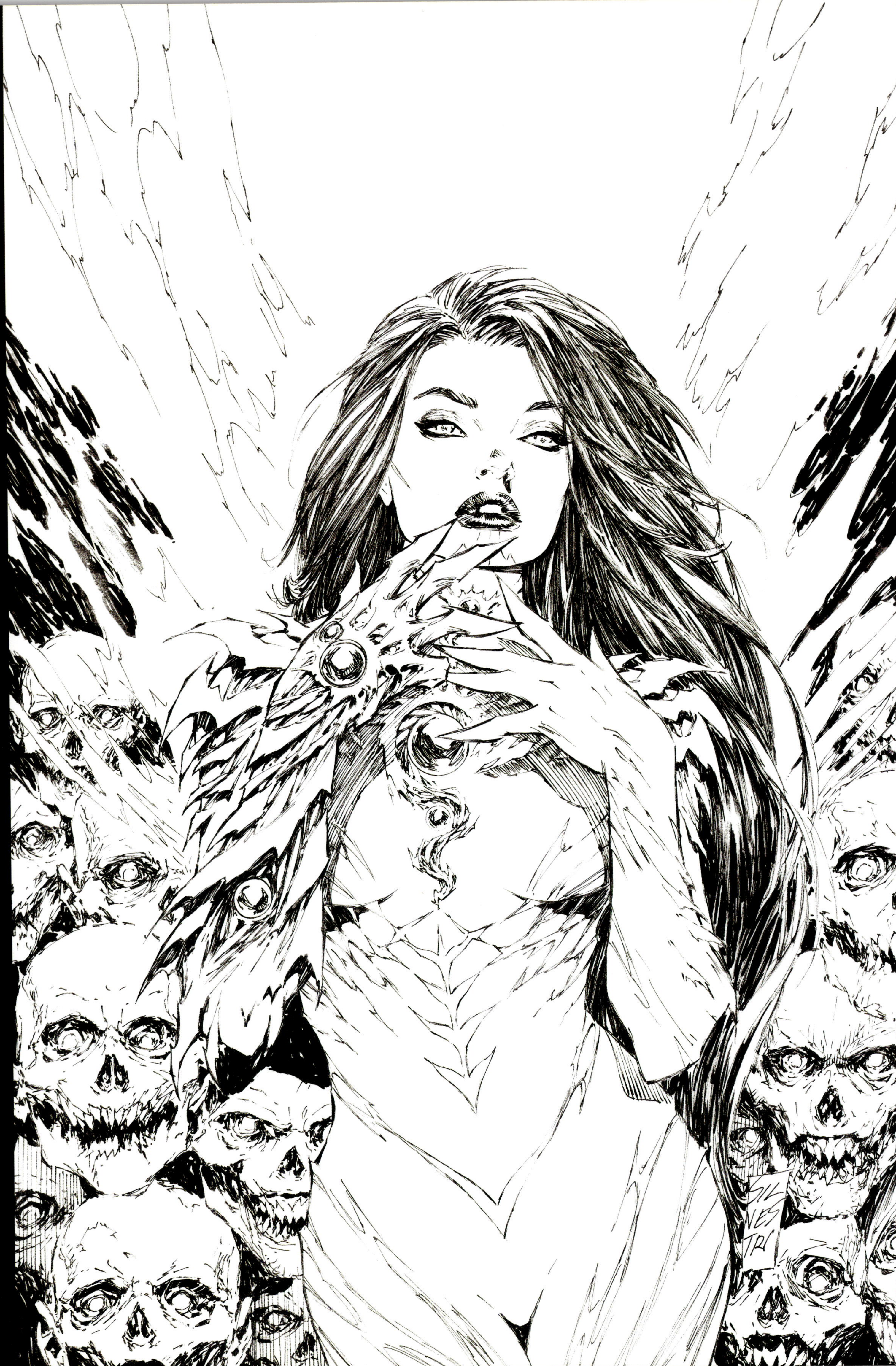

Witchblade #1 [2024] Convention and Top Cow Store Exclusive,
line art by: Marc Silvestri

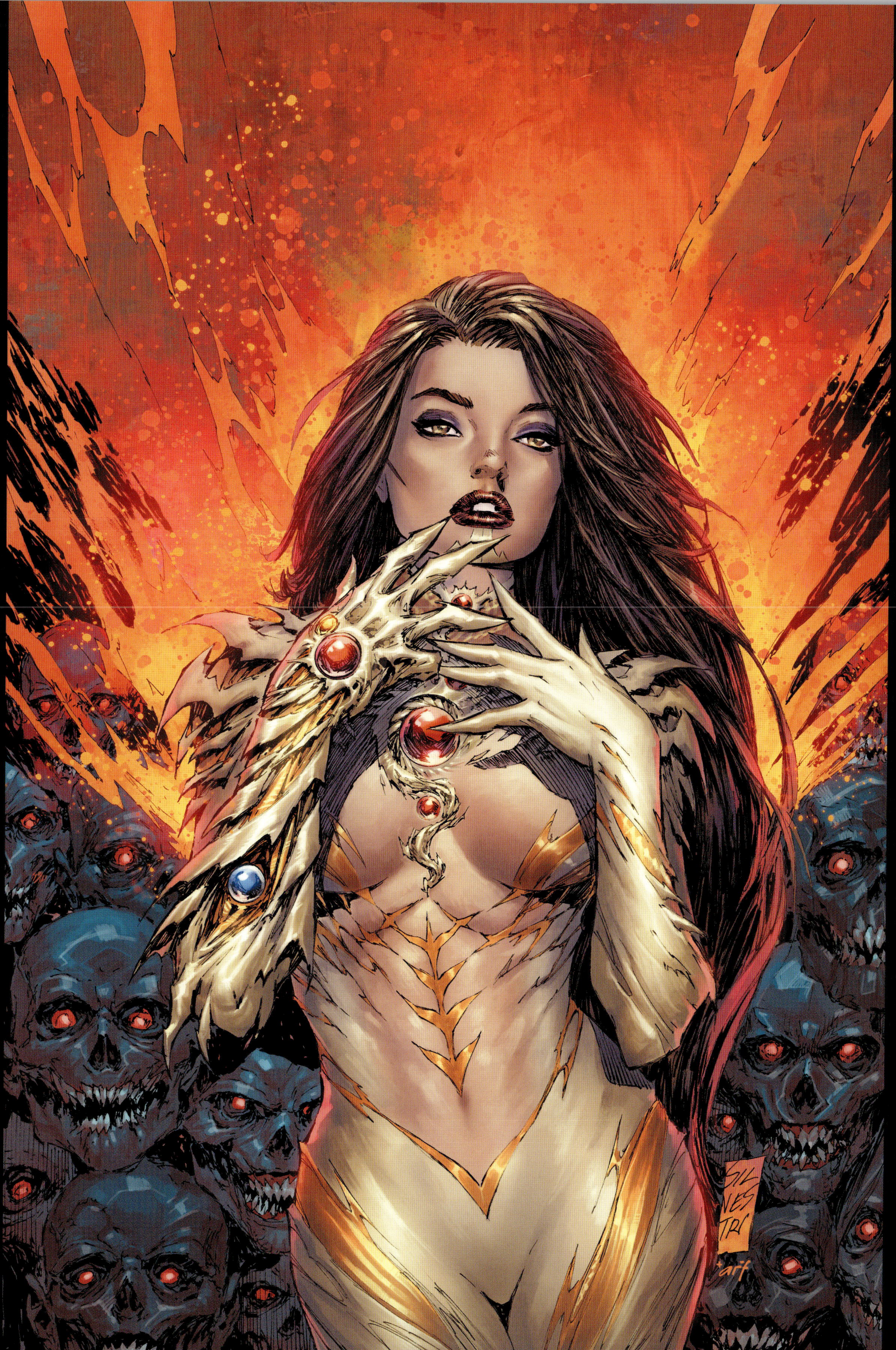

Witchblade #1 [2024] Convention and Top Cow Store Exclusive,
art by: Marc Silvestri and Arif Prianto

Scenes from *Witchblade* #1 [2024], inks and colors by **Giuseppe Cafaro** and **Arif Prianto.**

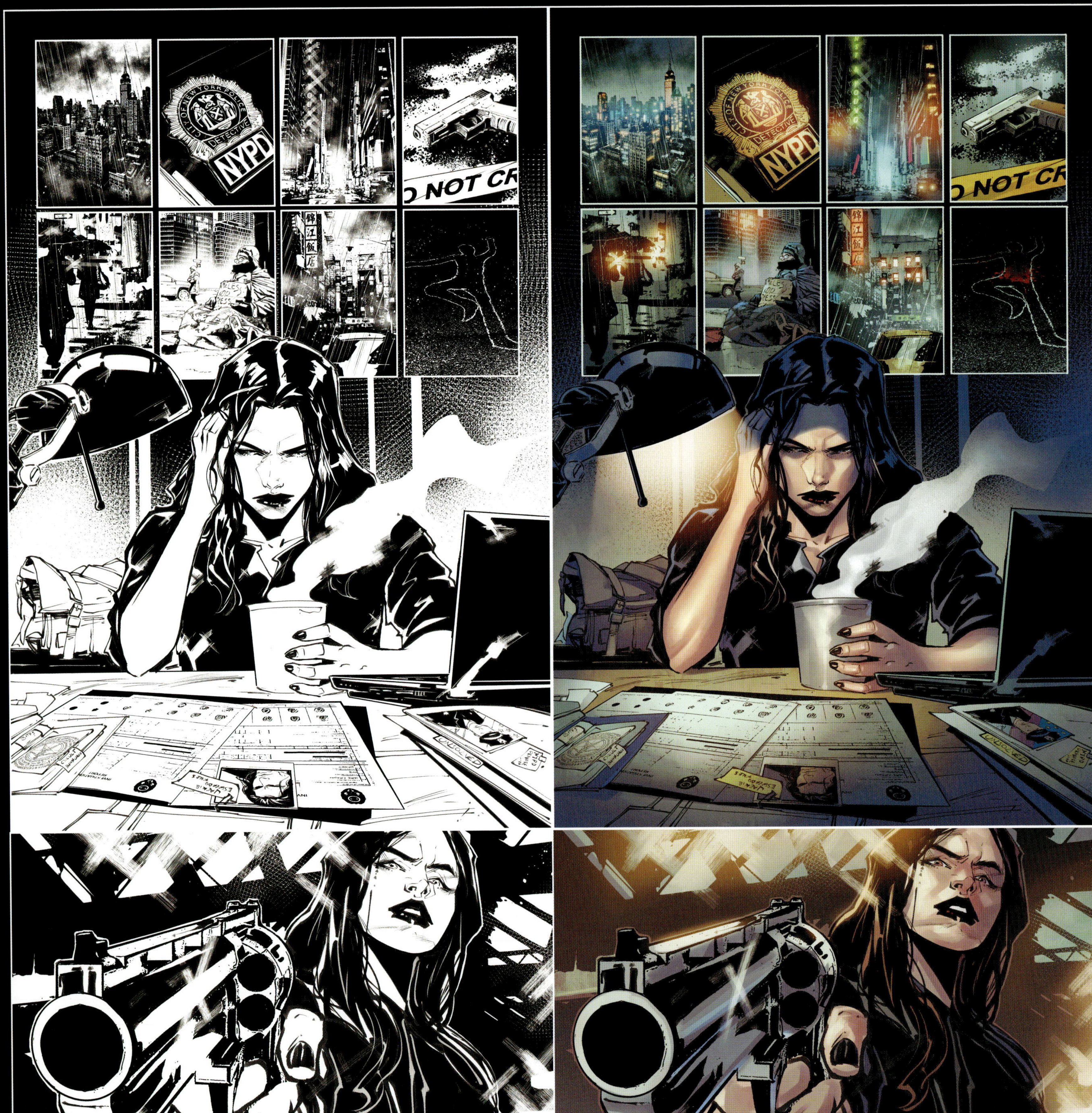

Giuseppe Cafaro's bold lines, mixed with the craft of colorist Arif Prianto, takes mundane scenes and makes them extraordinary.

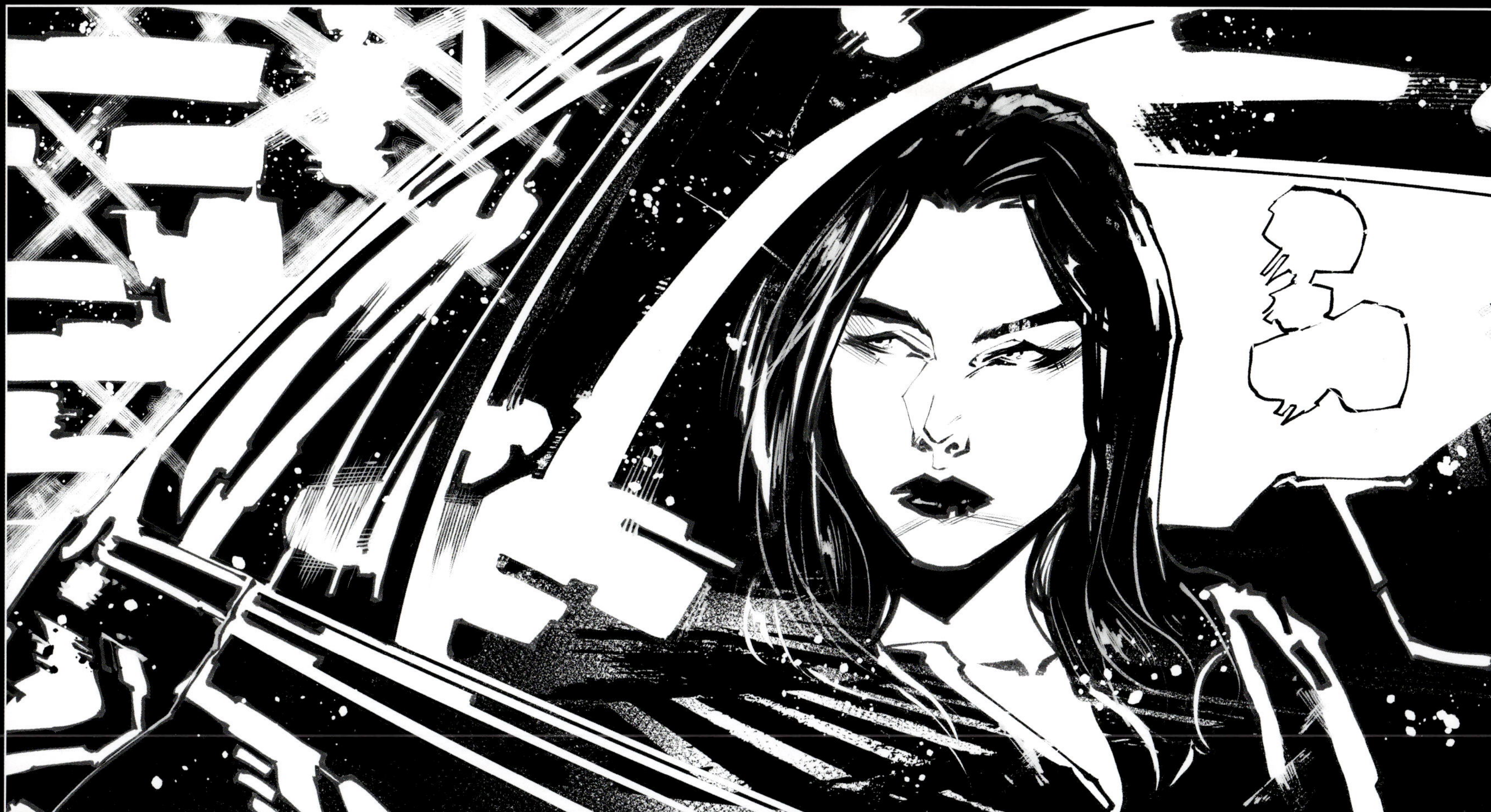

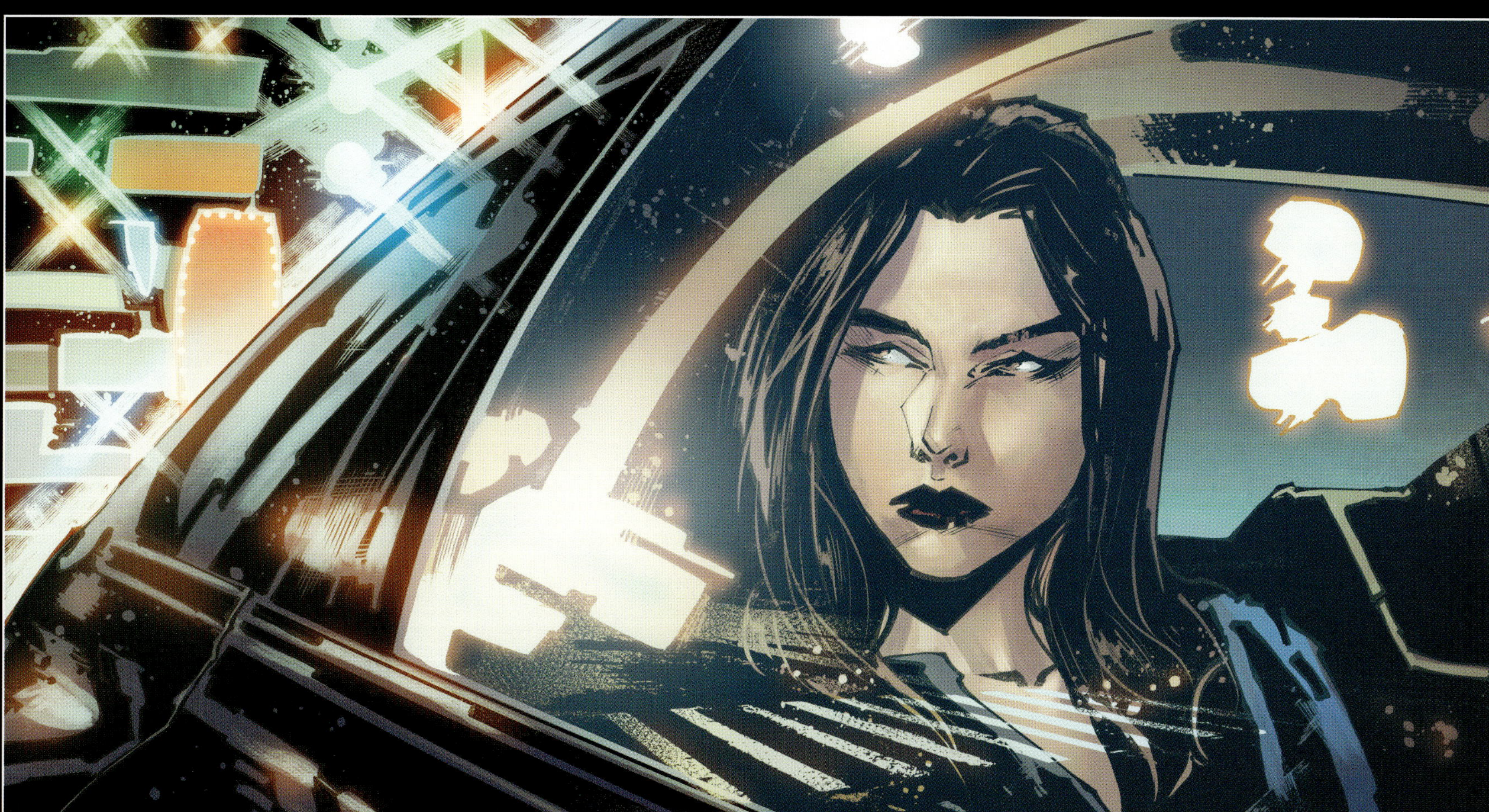

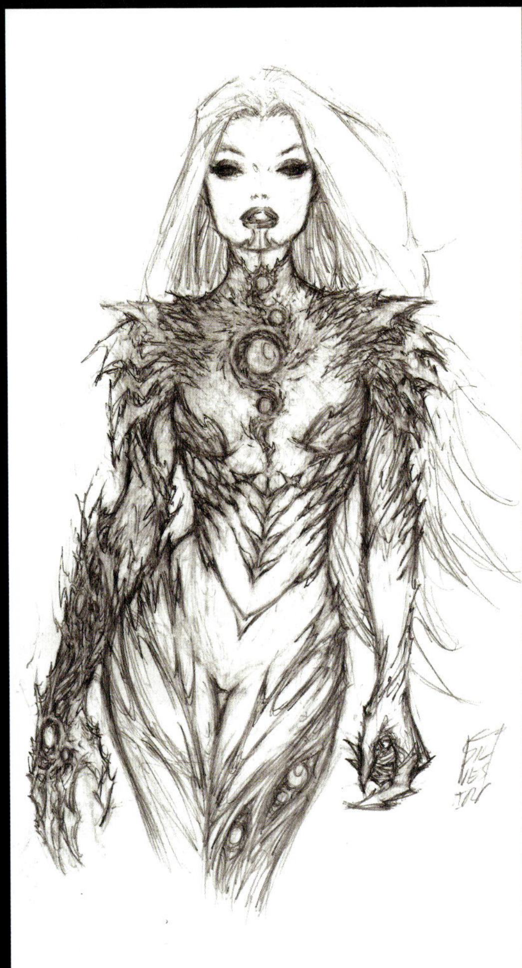

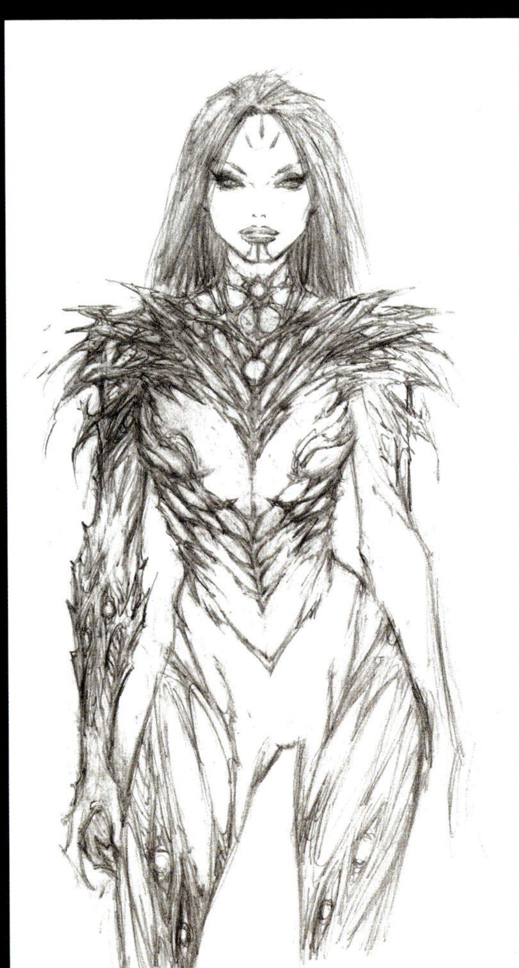

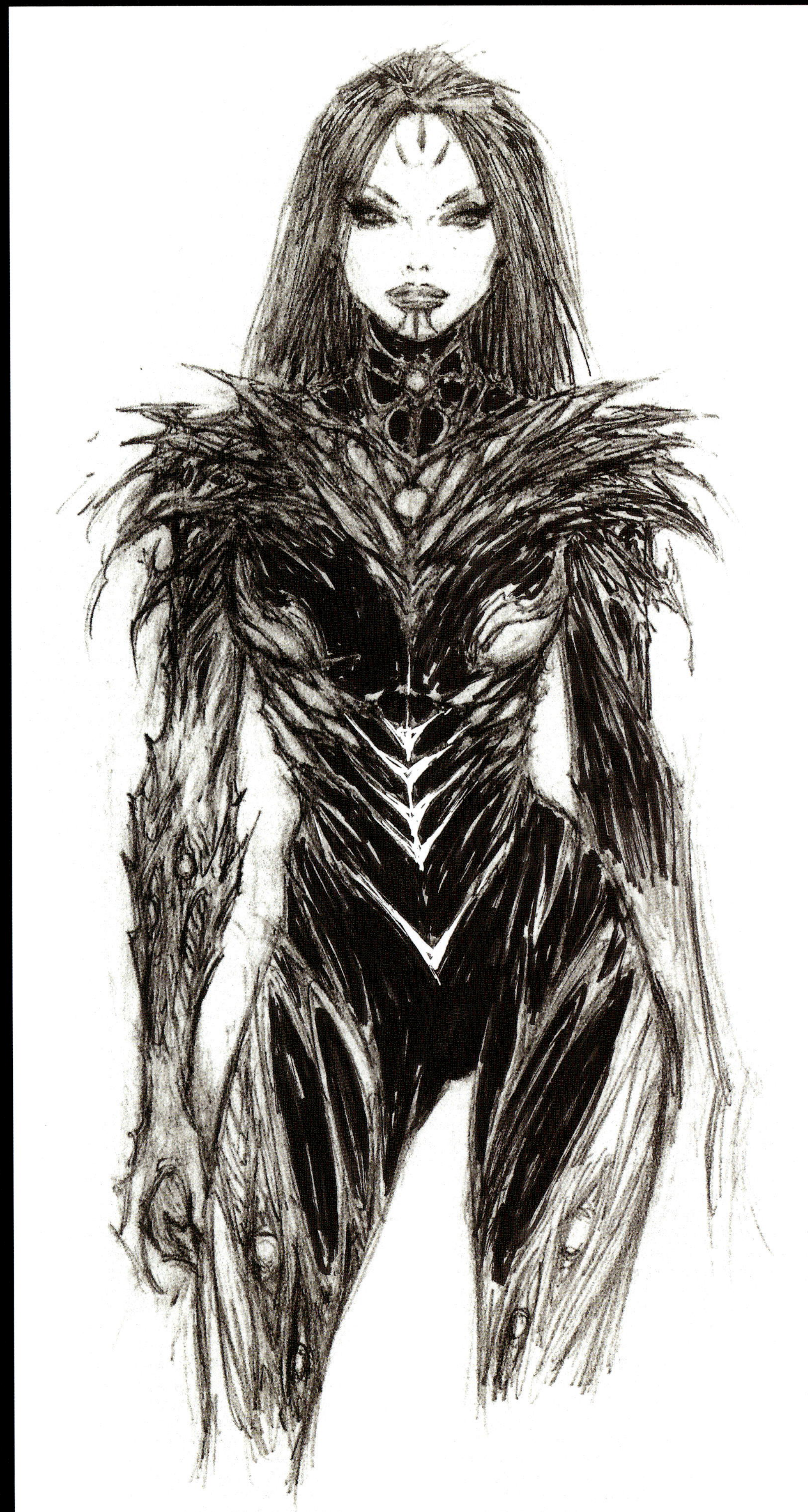

Early Witchblade armor redesign sketches for the newest series by **Marc Silvestri**

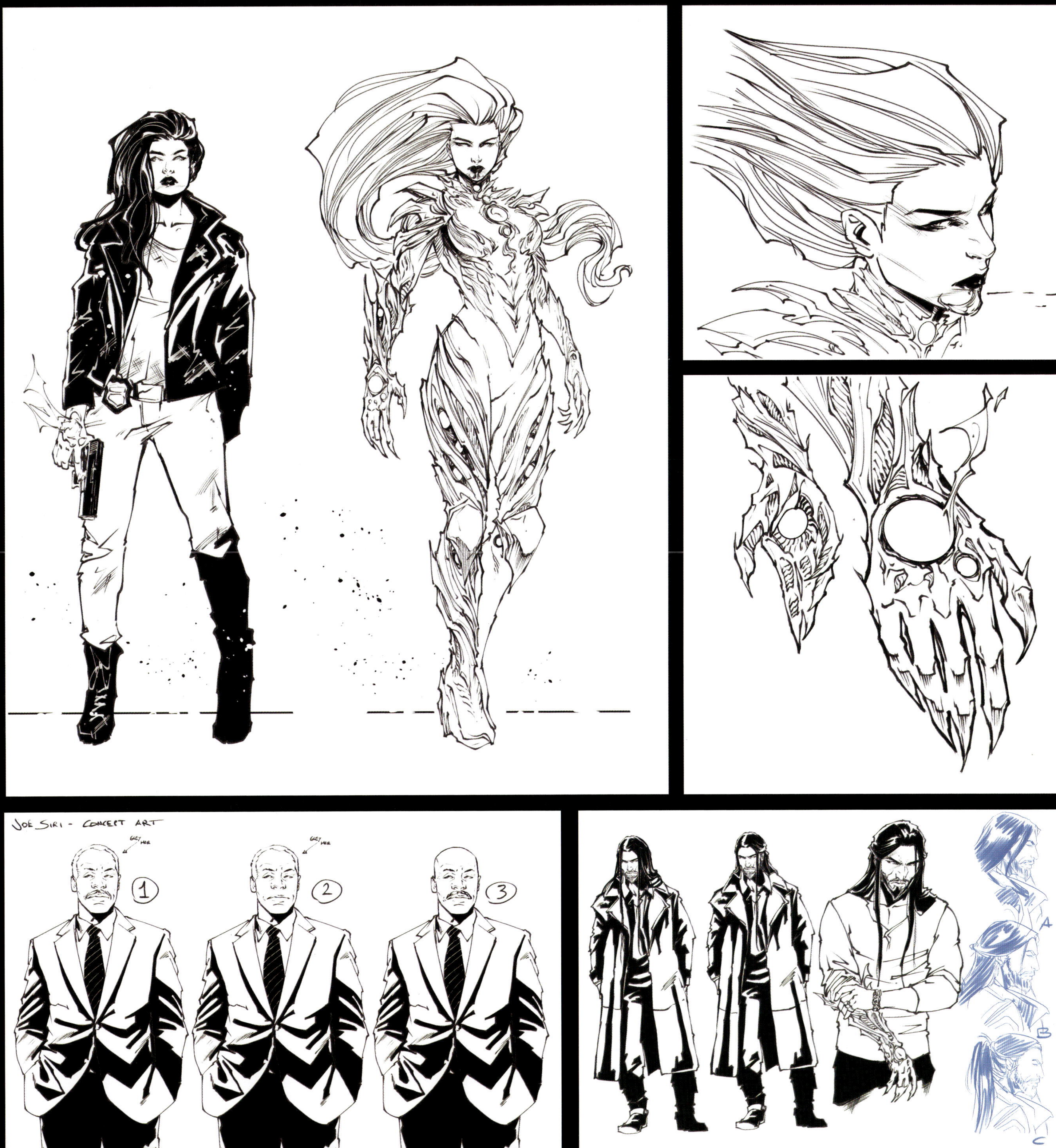

Character Designs by **Giuseppe Cafaro** of Sara, the Witchblade armor, Captain Joe Siri and Ian Nottingham.

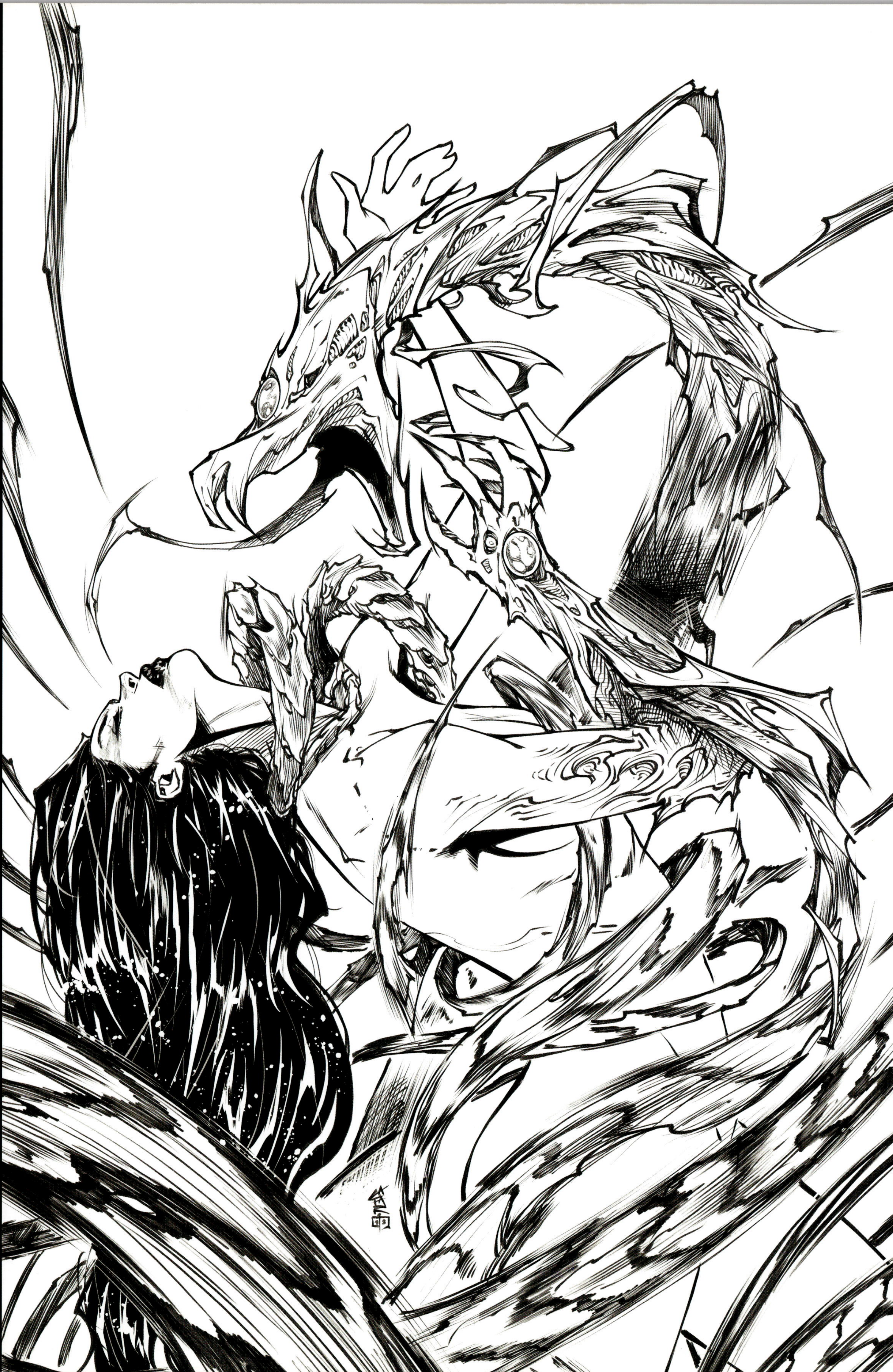

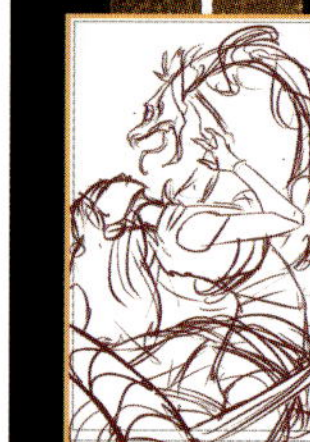

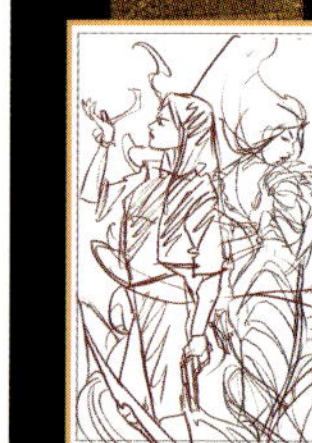

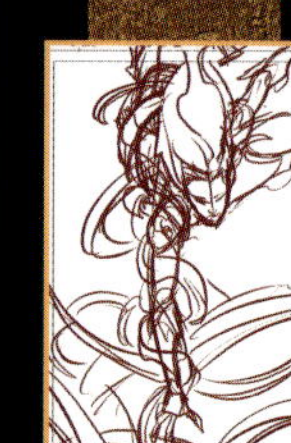

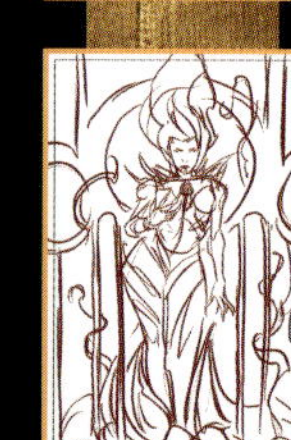

Witchblade #2 [2024] cover A, thumbnails and line art by: Giuseppe Cafaro

Witchblade #2 [2024] cover A,
art by: Giuseppe Cafaro and Arif Prianto

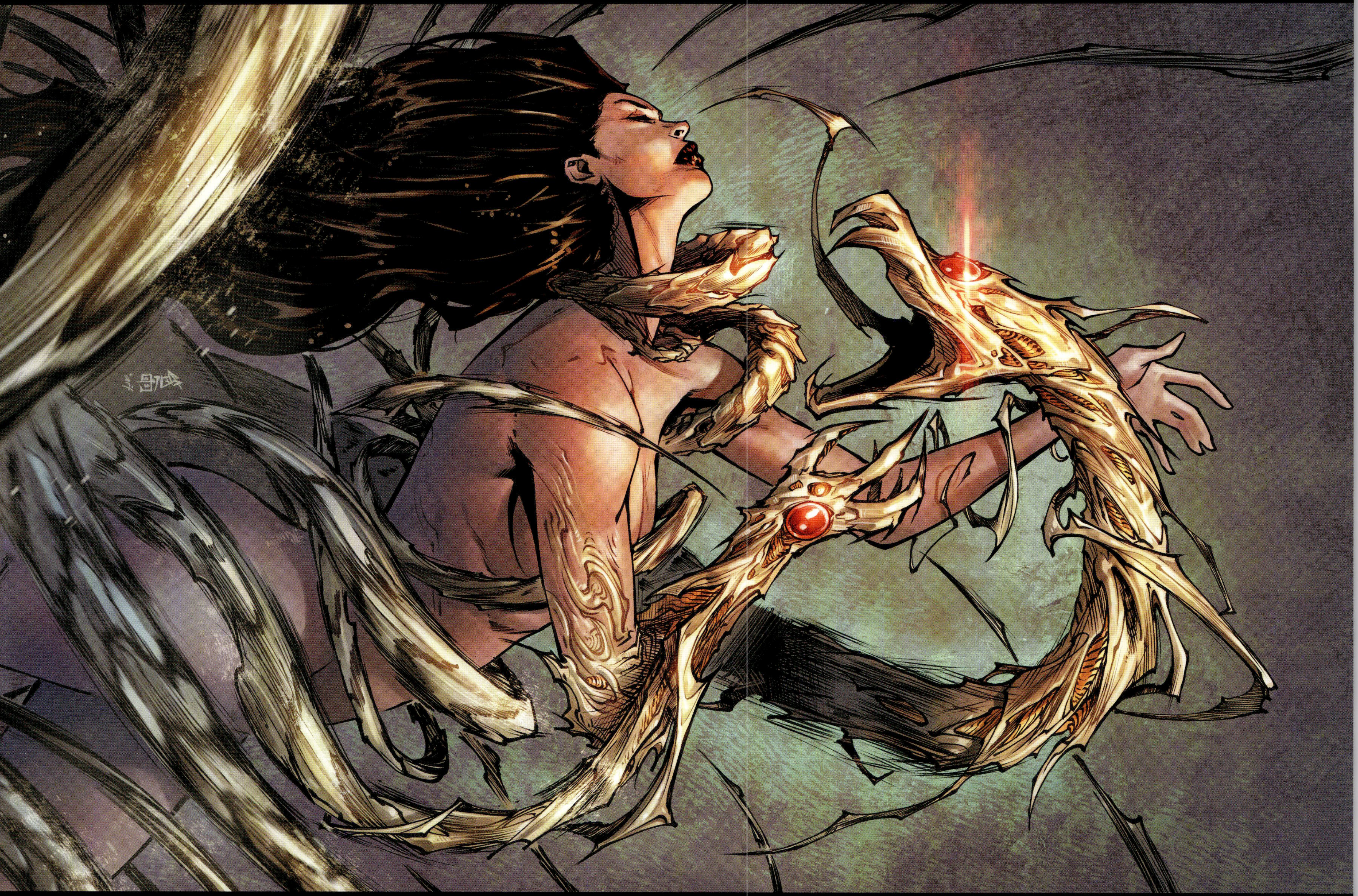

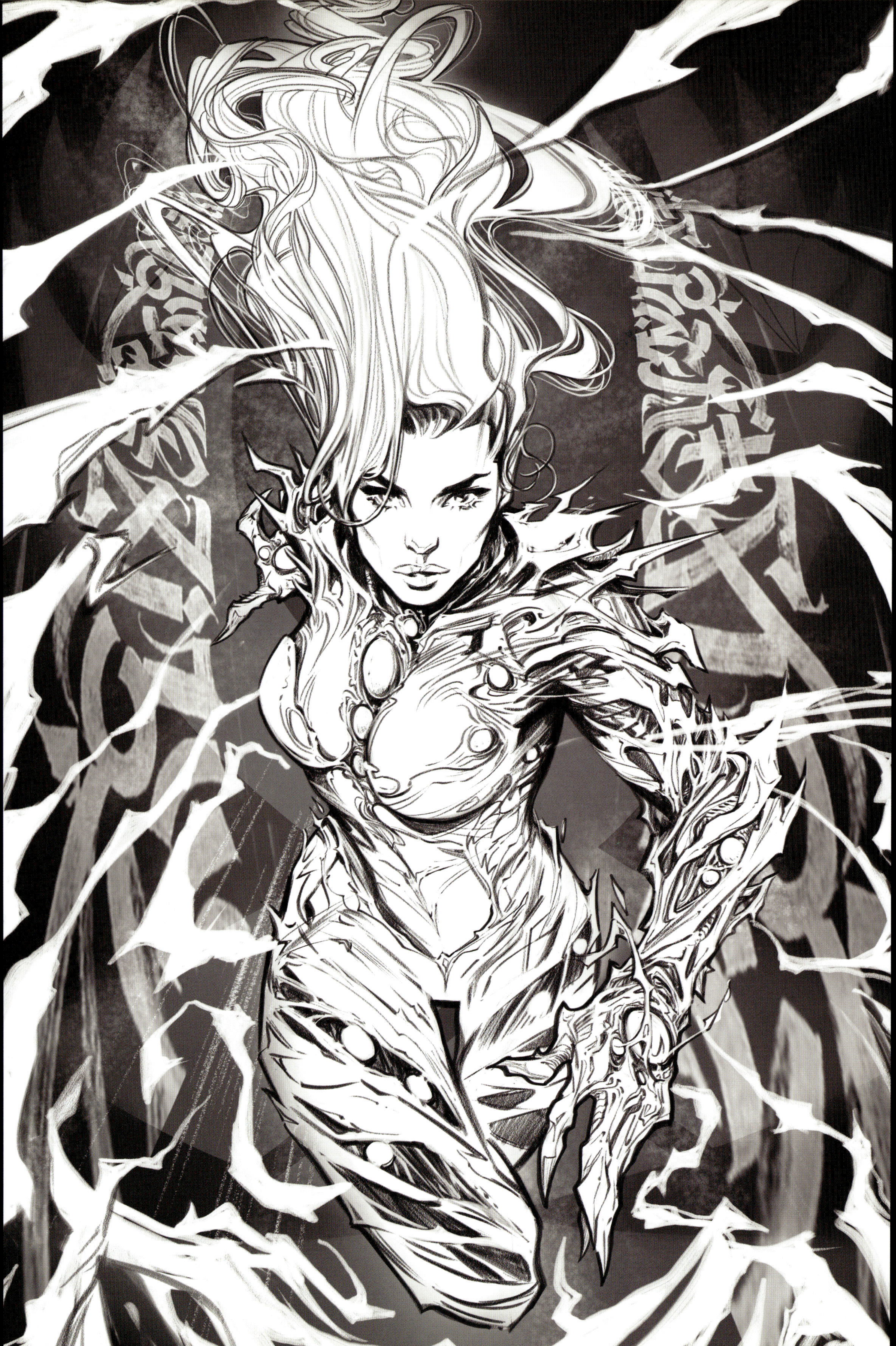

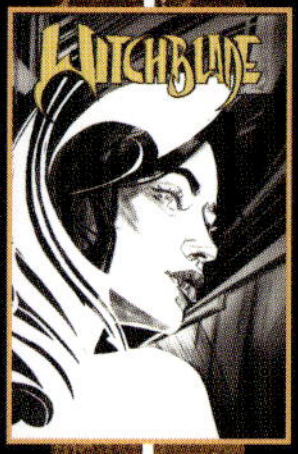

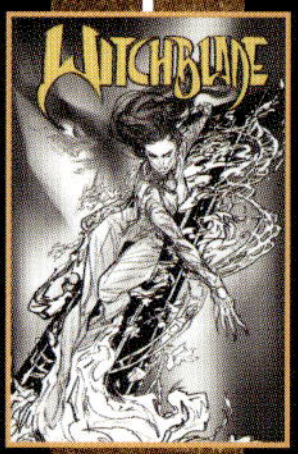

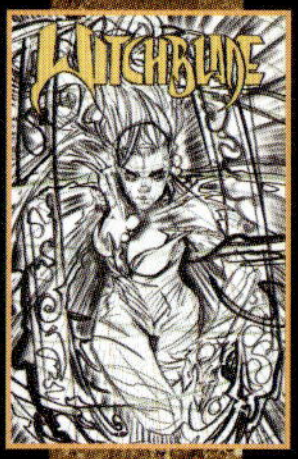

Witchblade #2 [2024] cover B, thumbnails and line art by: Joëlle Jones

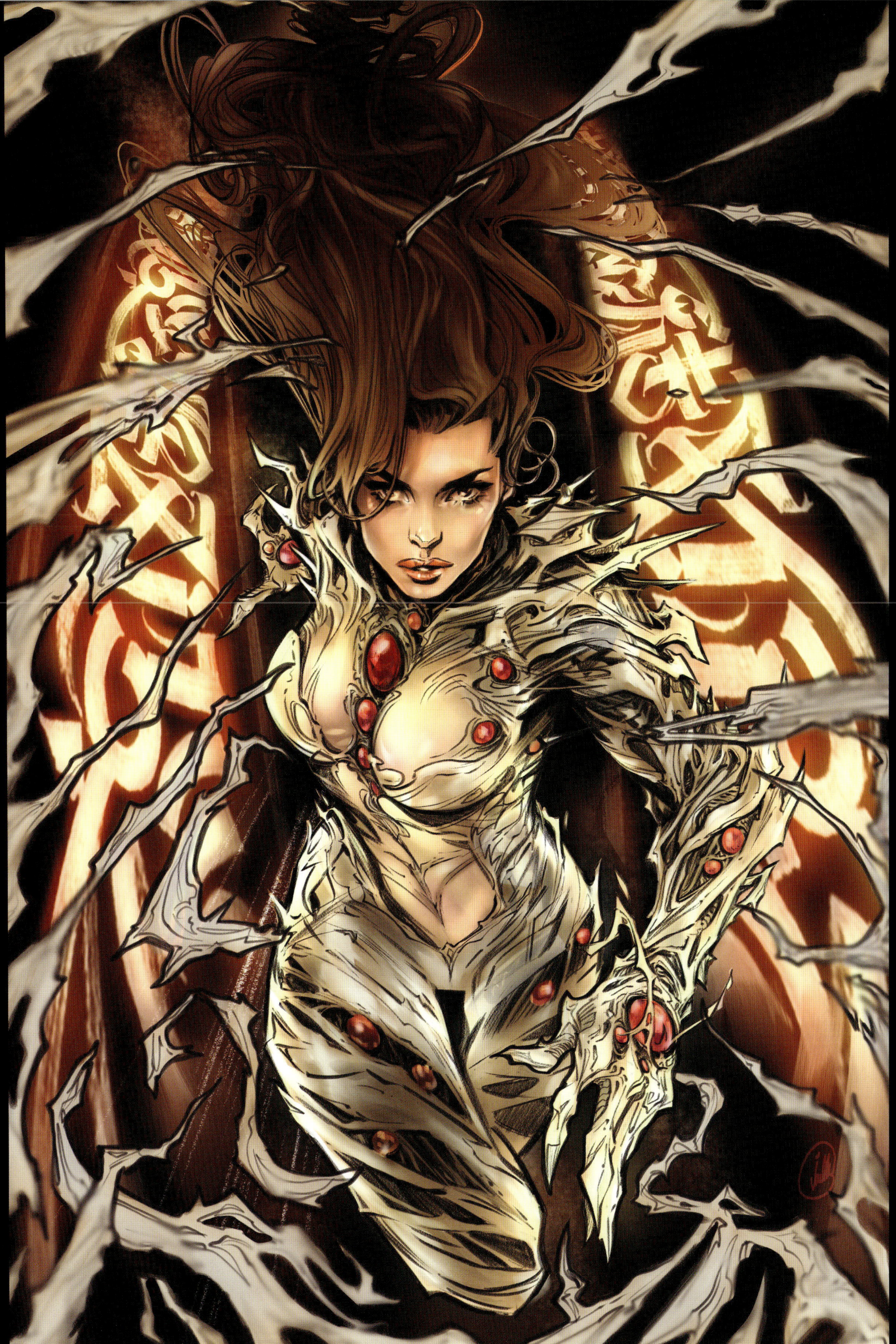

Witchblade #2 [2024] cover B,
art by: Joëlle Jones

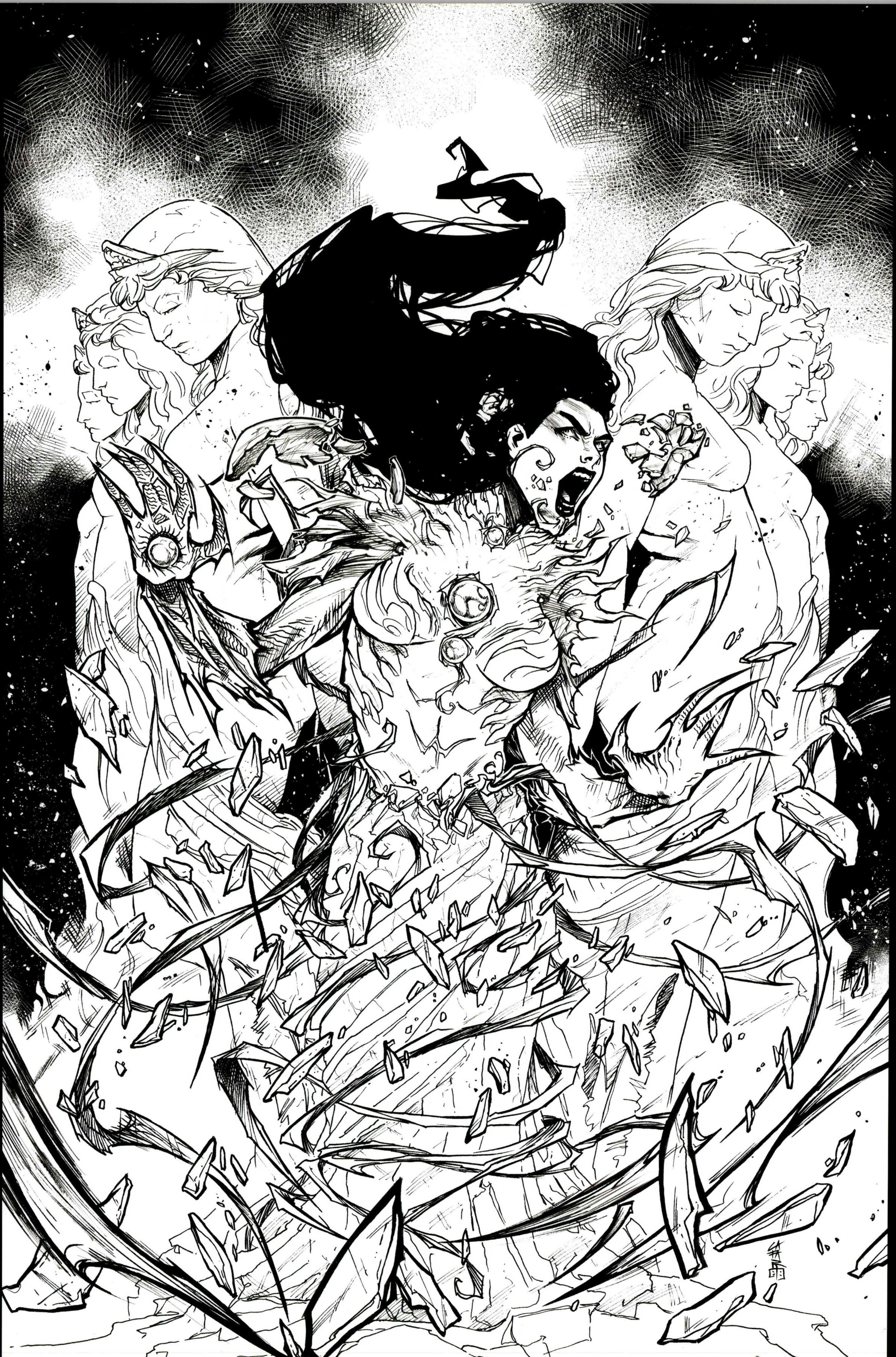

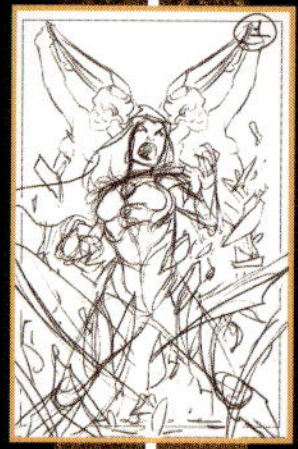

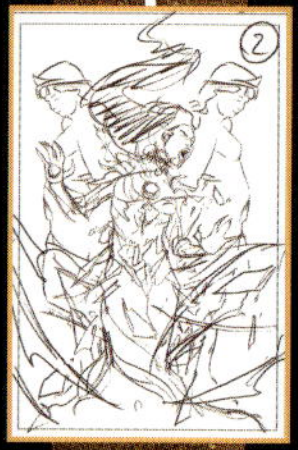

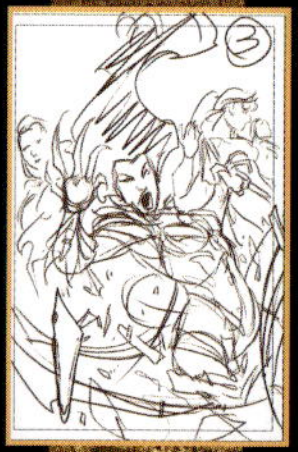

Witchblade #3 [2024] cover A, thumbnails and line art by: Giuseppe Cafaro

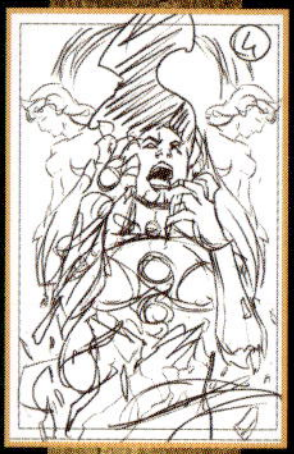

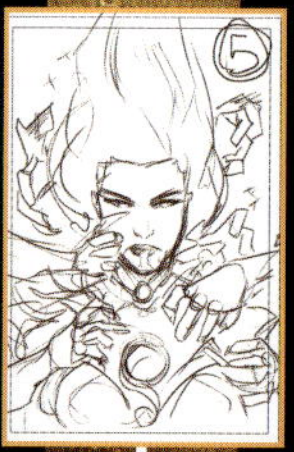

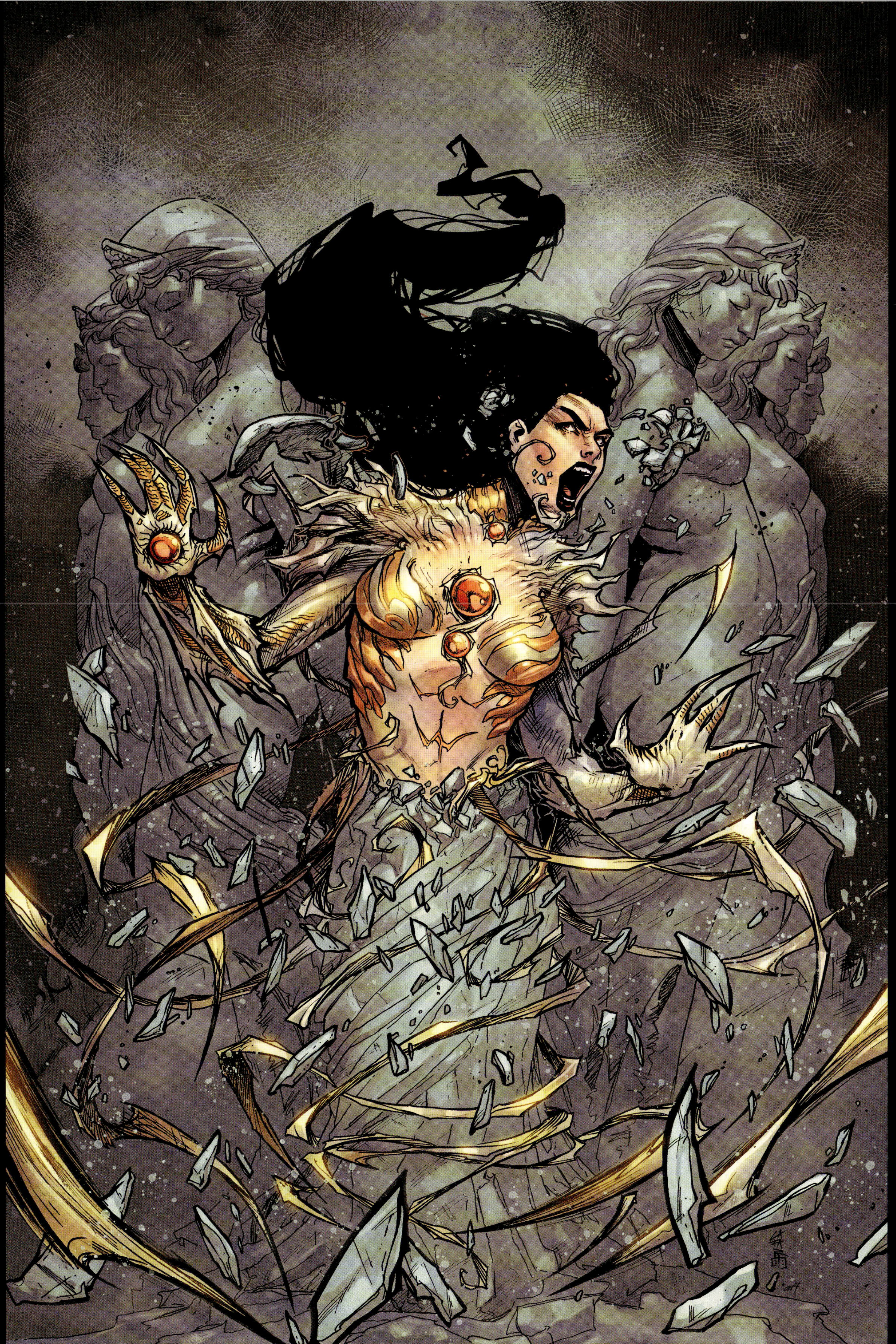

Witchblade #3 [2024] cover A,
art by: Giuseppe Cafaro and Arif Prianto

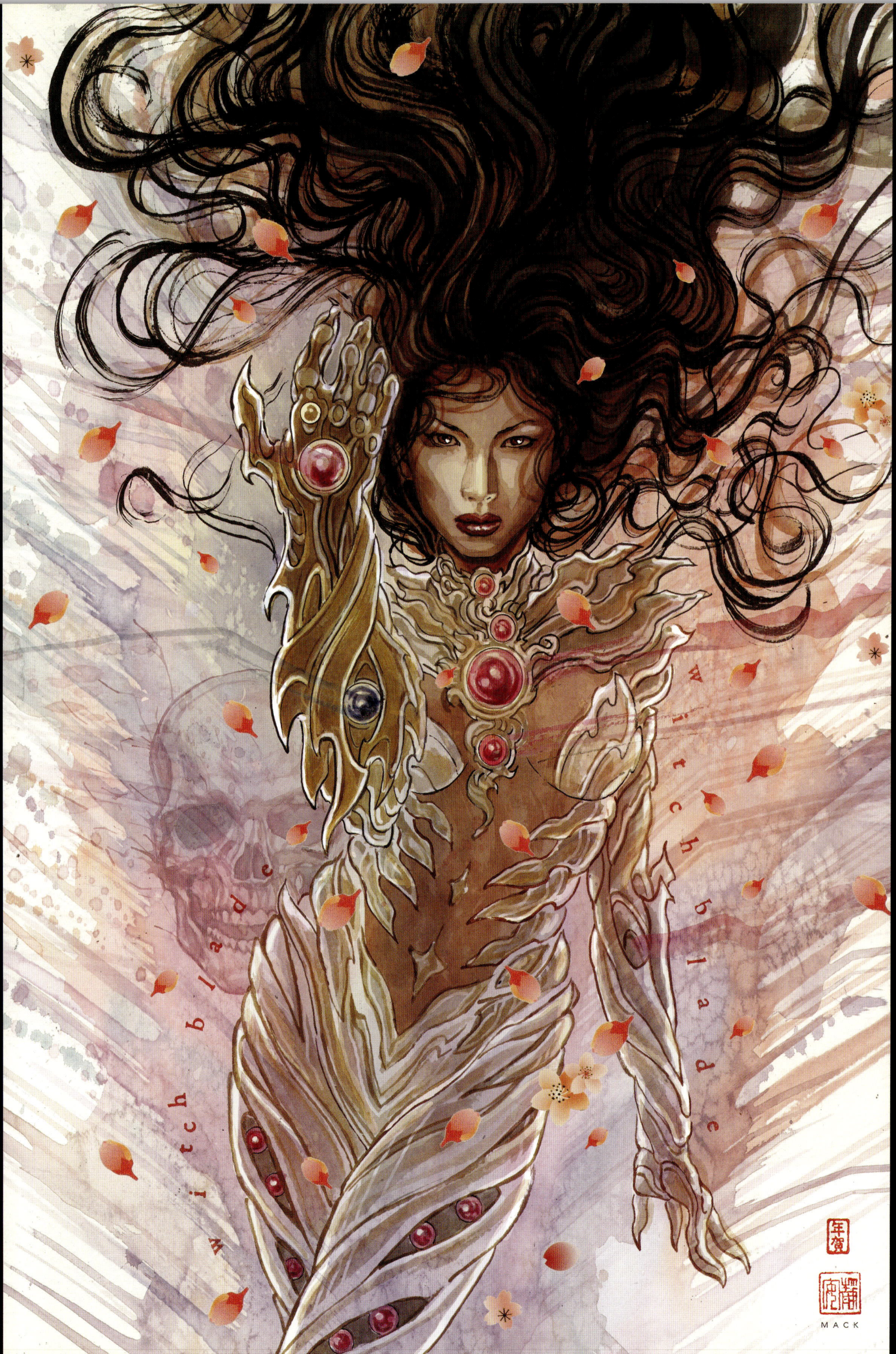

Witchblade #3 [2024] cover B,
art by: David Mack

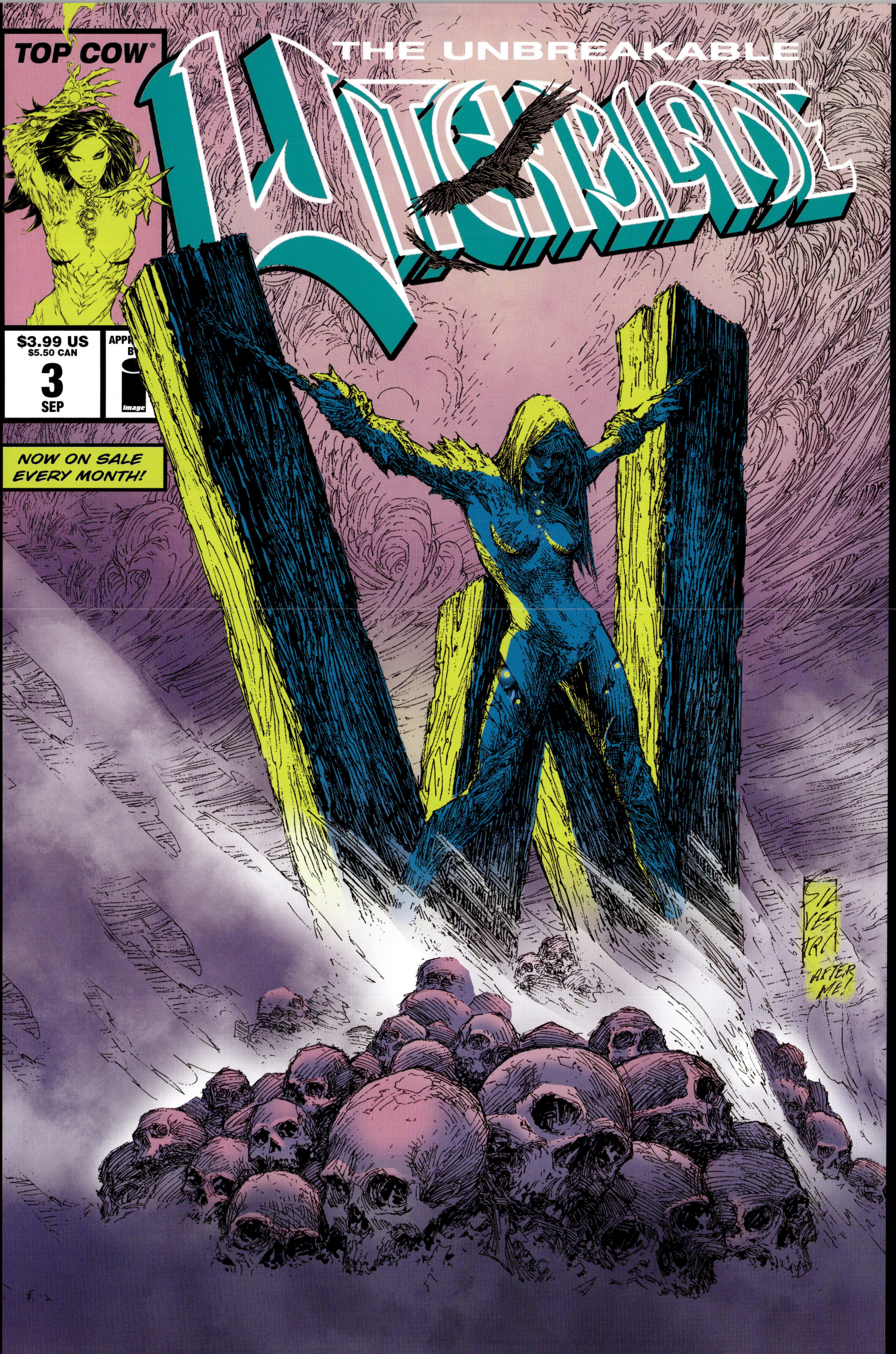

Witchblade #3 [2024] cover C and D* Homage Variants,
art by: Marc Slivestri and Phil Smith *Cover D, Original printing with fluorescent ink

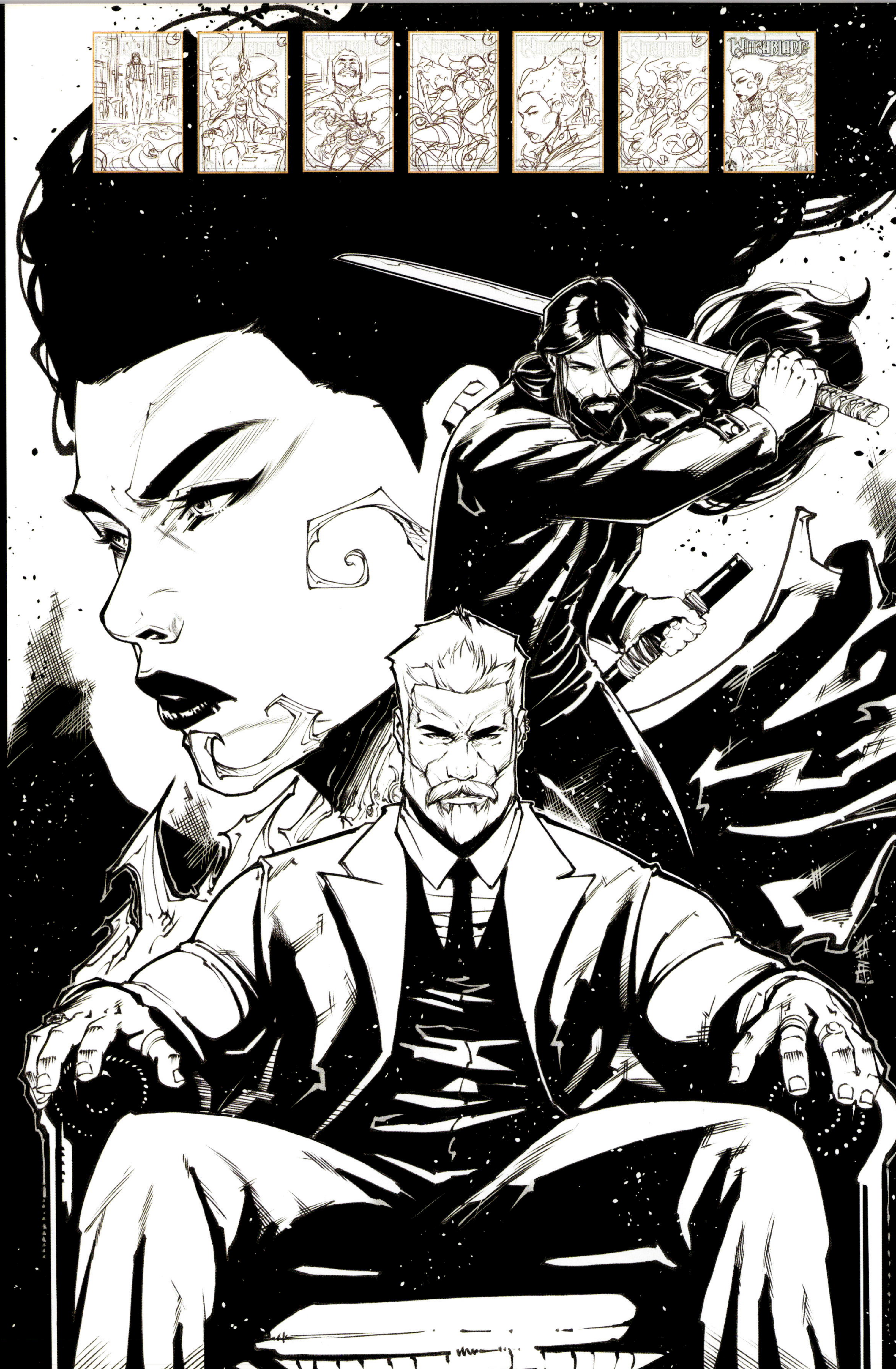

Witchblade #4 [2024] cover A,
thumbnails and line art by: Giuseppe Cafaro

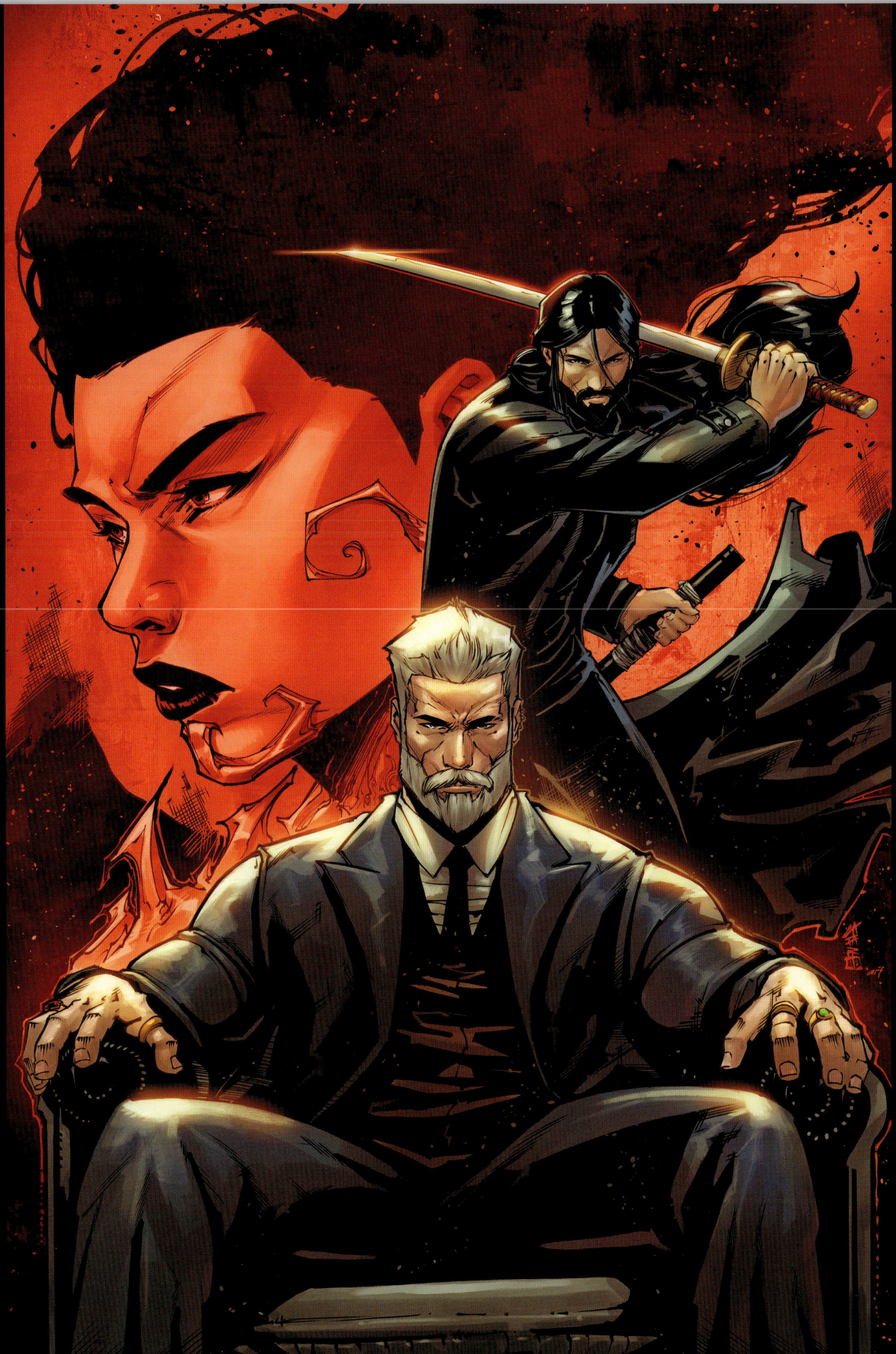

Witchblade #4 [2024] cover A,
art by: Giuseppe Cafaro and Arif Prianto

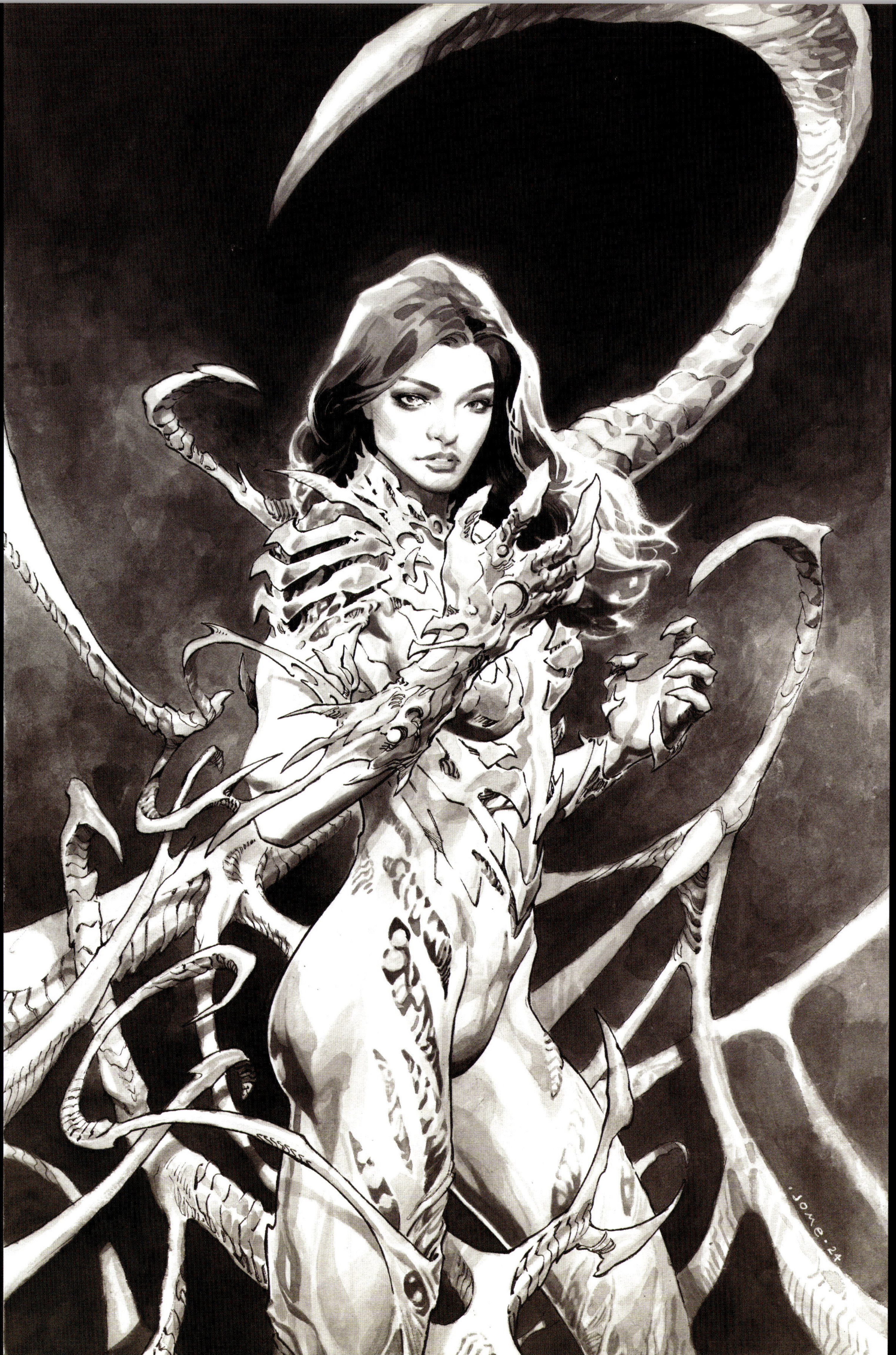

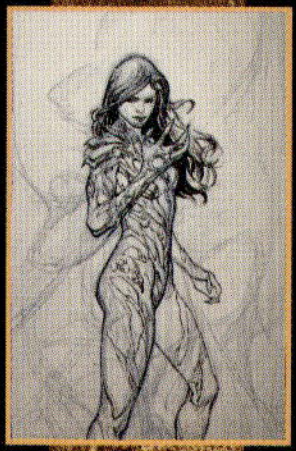

Witchblade #4 [2024] cover B, thumbnail and line art by: Jerome Opeña

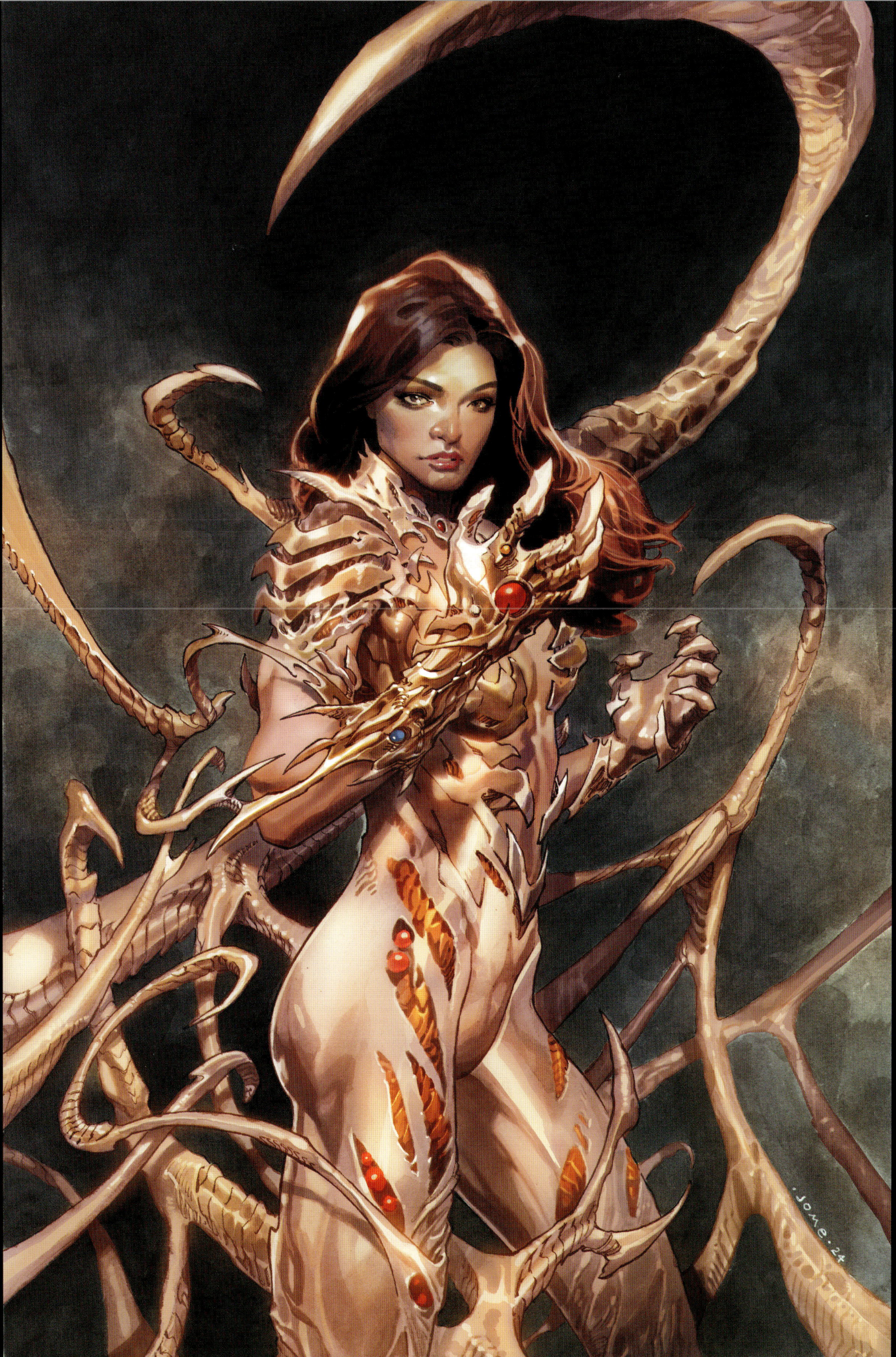

Witchblade #4 [2024] cover B,
art by: Jerome Opeña and Sunny Gho

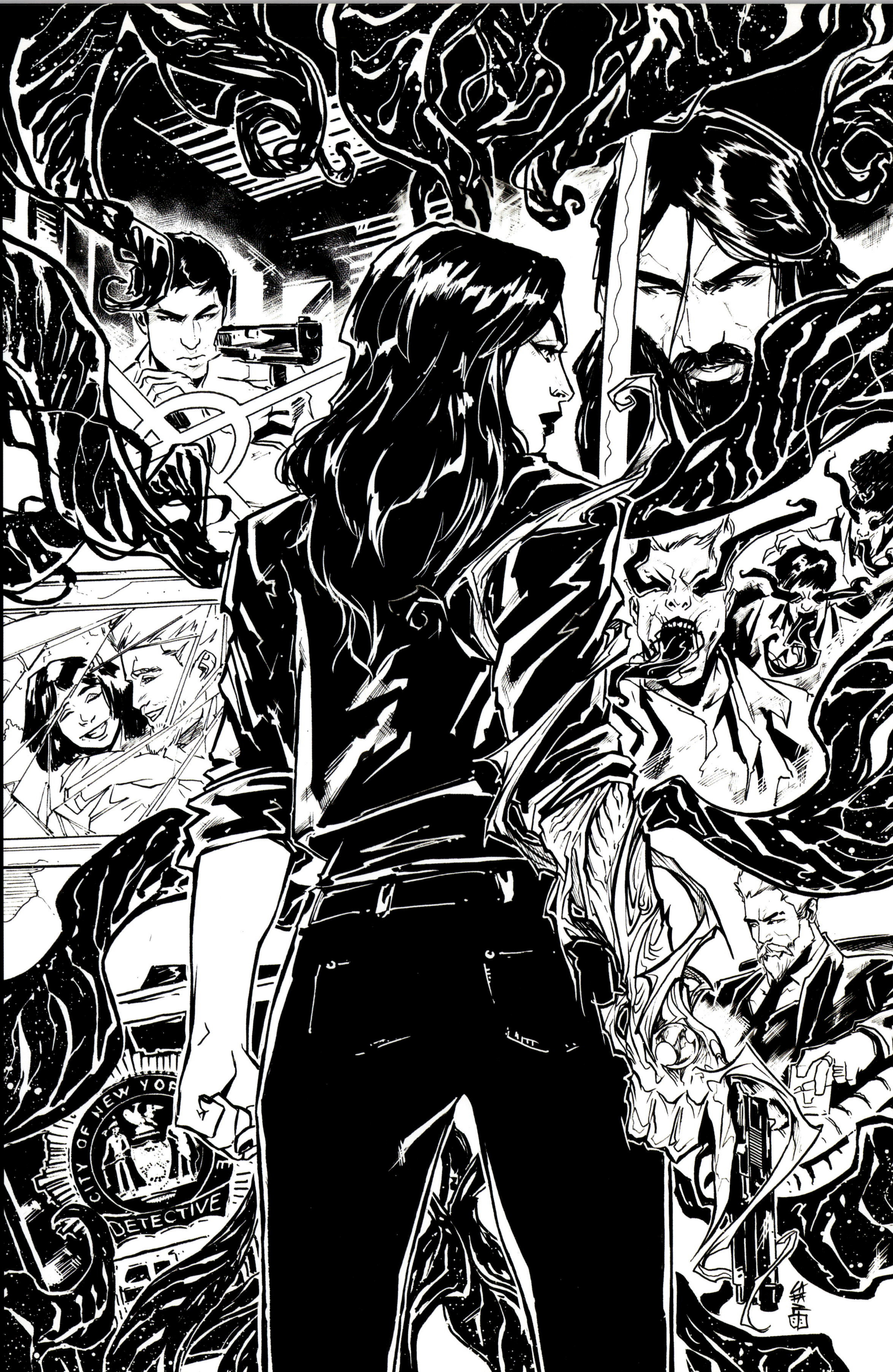

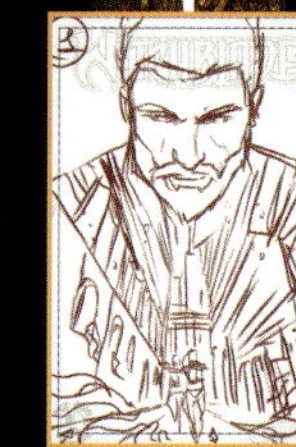

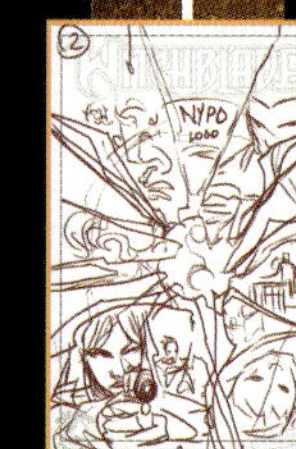

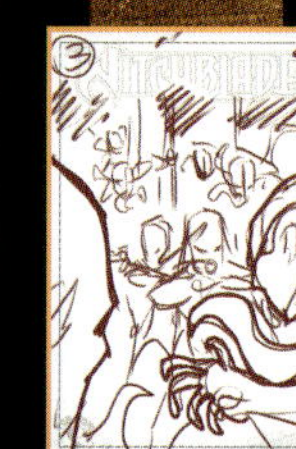

Witchblade #4 [2024] cover A,
thumbnails and line art by: Giuseppe Cafaro

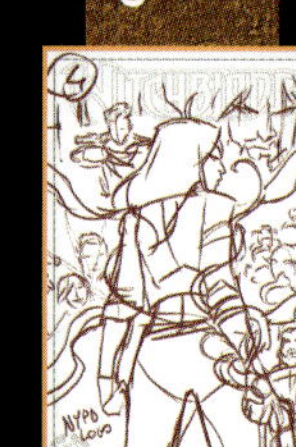

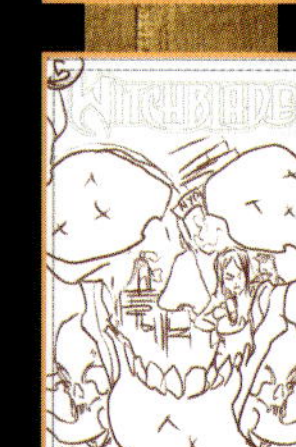

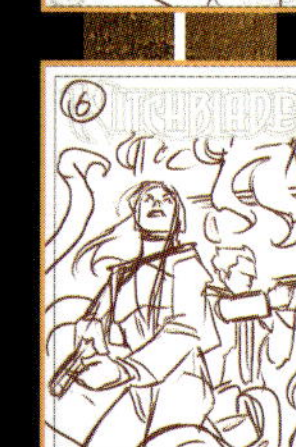

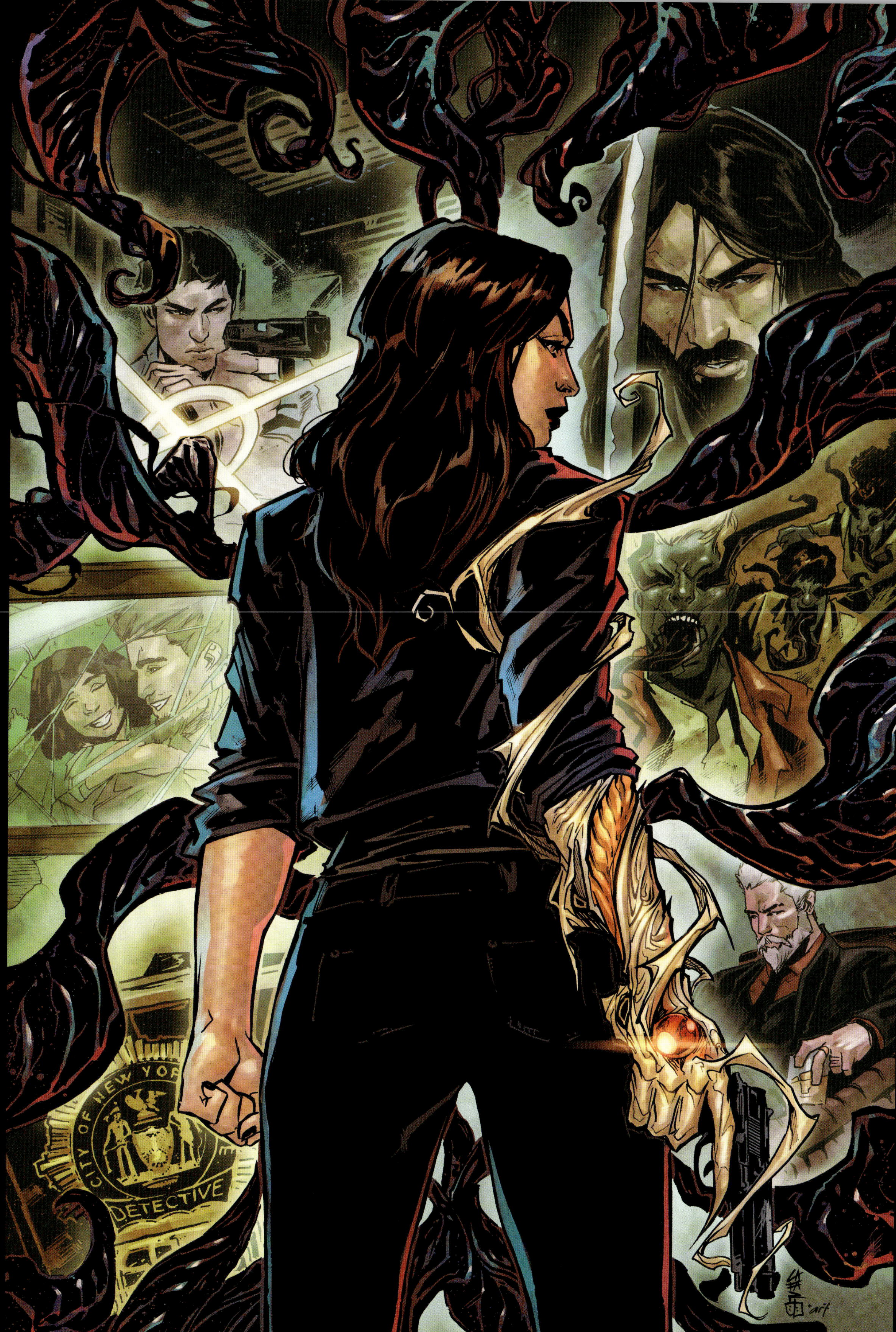

Witchblade #5 [2024] cover A,
art by: Giuseppe Cafaro and Arif Prianto

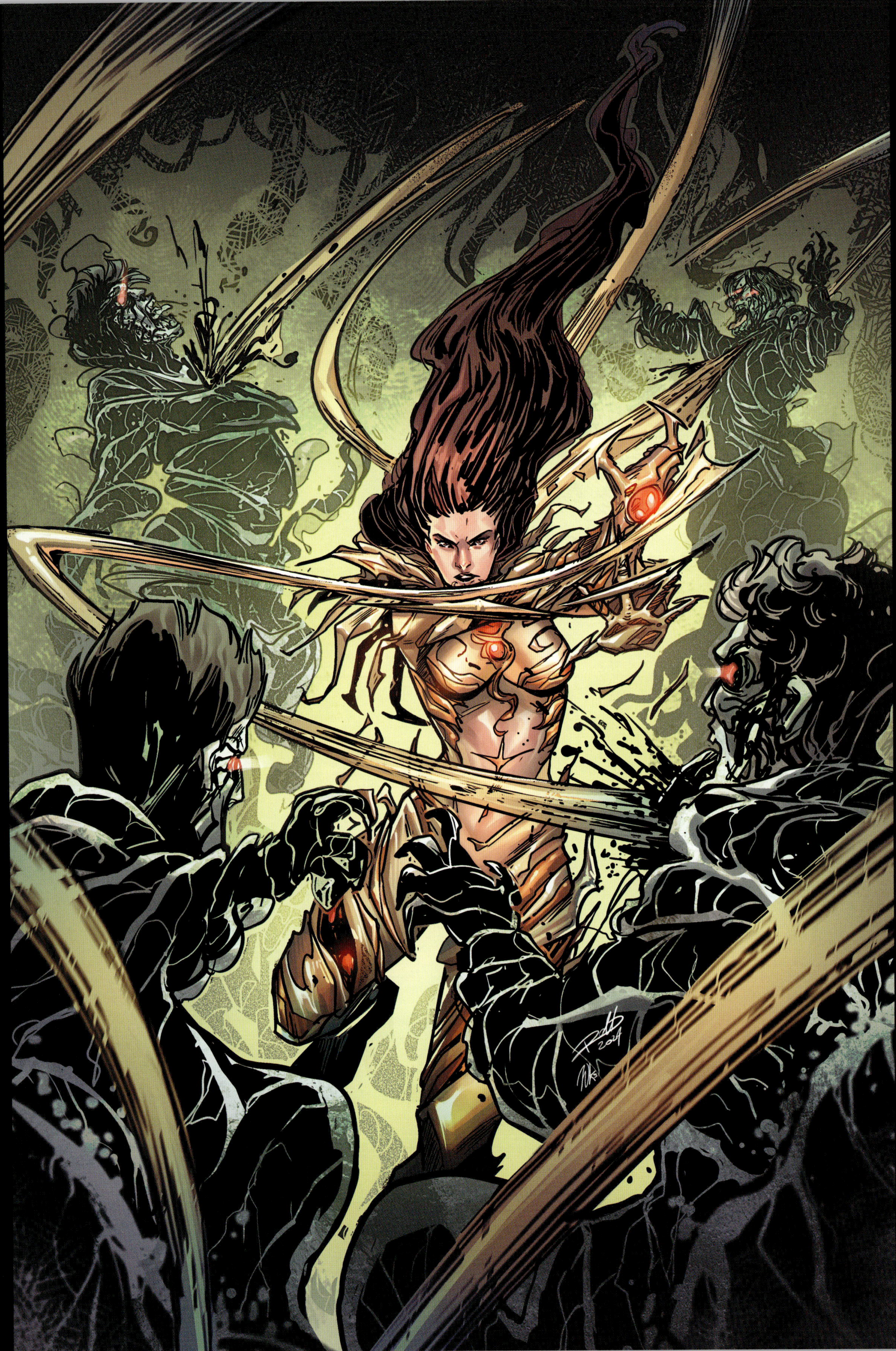

Witchblade #5 [2024] cover B,
art by: Roberta Ingranata and Warnia Sahadewa

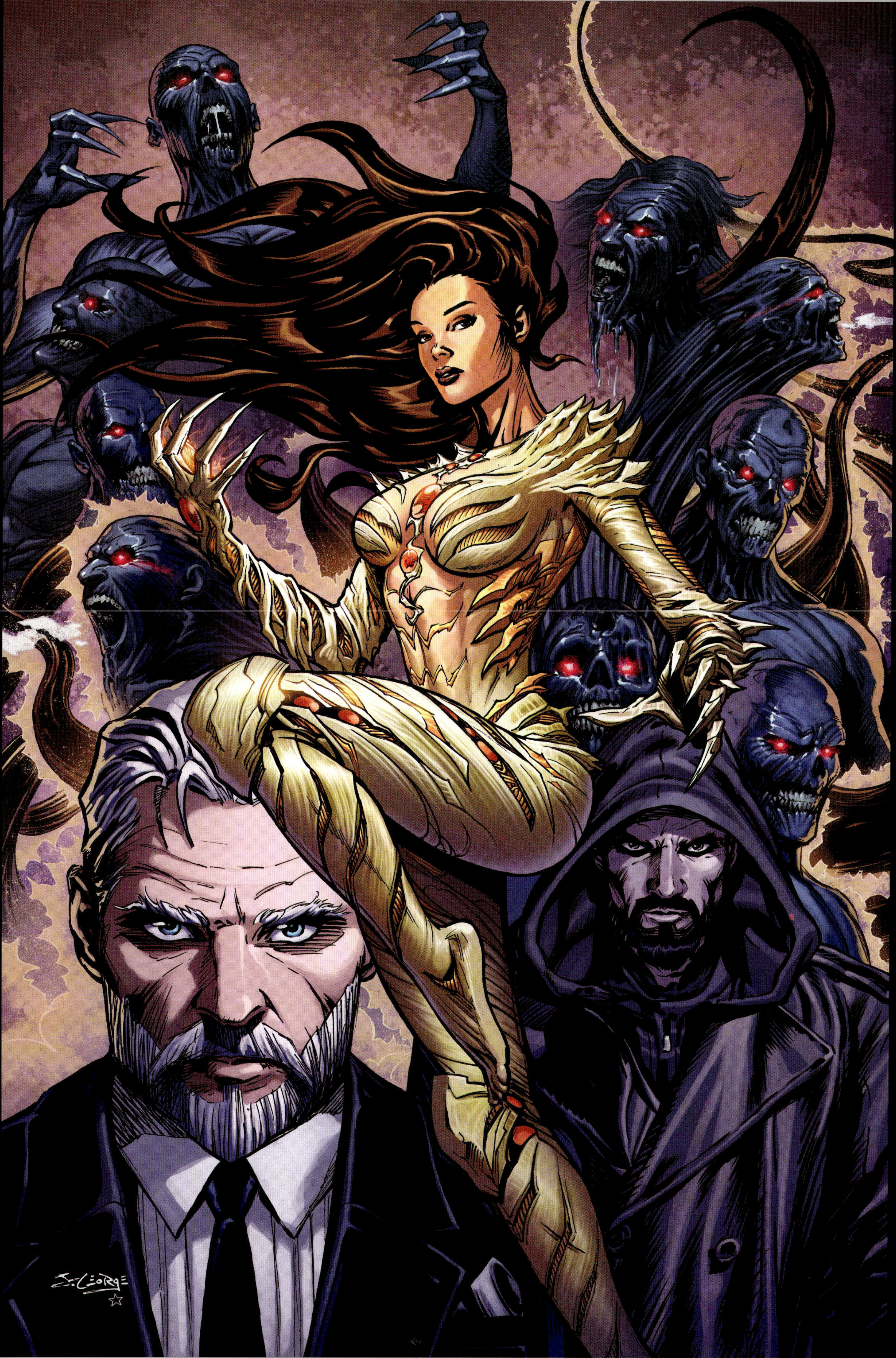

Witchblade #6 [2024] cover B,
art by: Joshua George and John Starr.

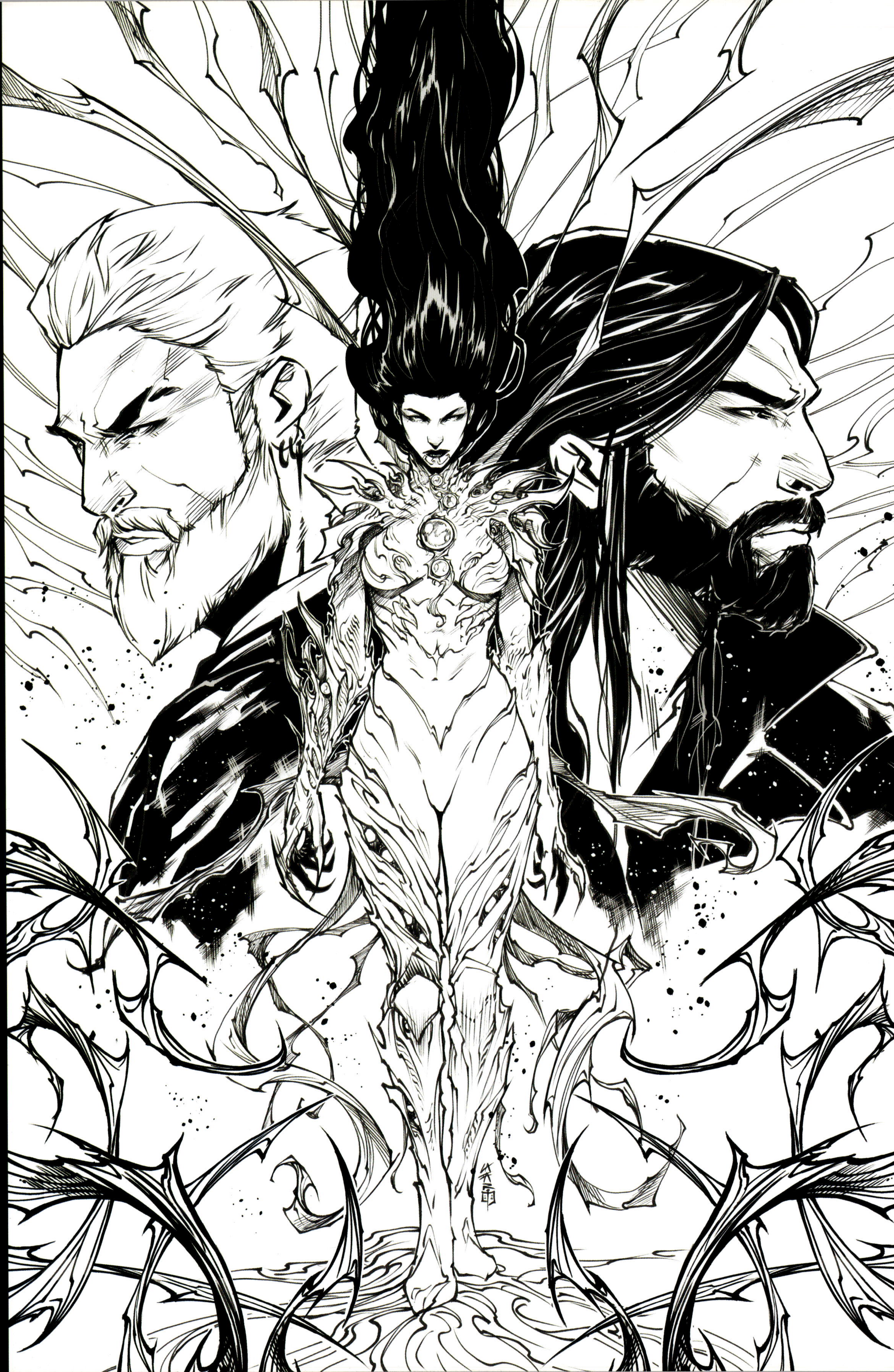

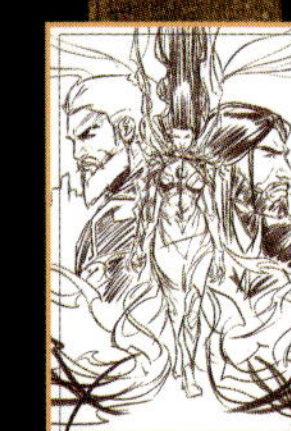

Witchblade #6 [2024] cover A, thumbnail and line art by: Giuseppe Cafaro

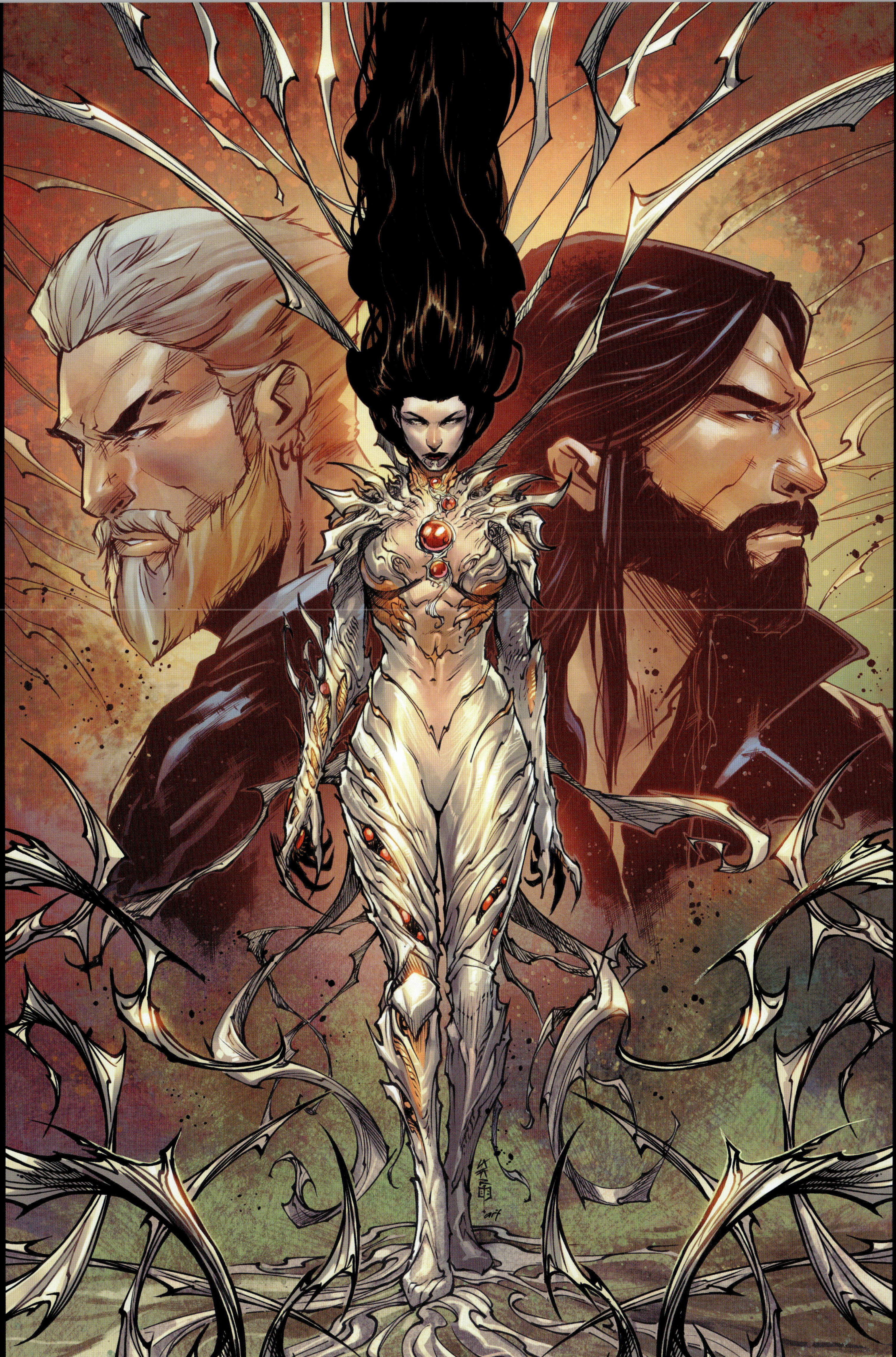

Witchblade #6 [2024] cover A,
art by: Giuseppe Cafaro and Arif Prianto

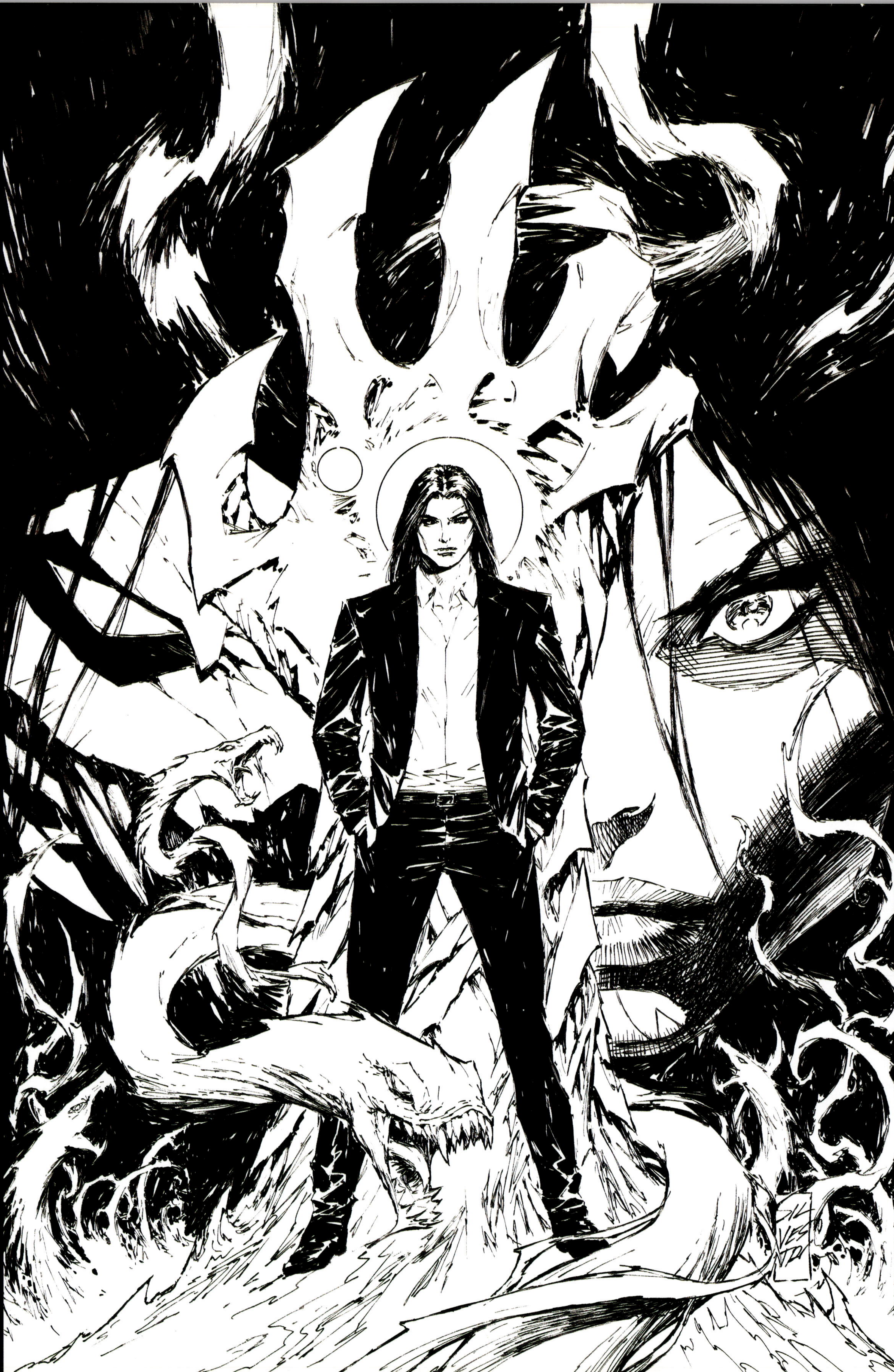

Witchblade #7 [2024] cover A,
line art by: Marc Silvestri

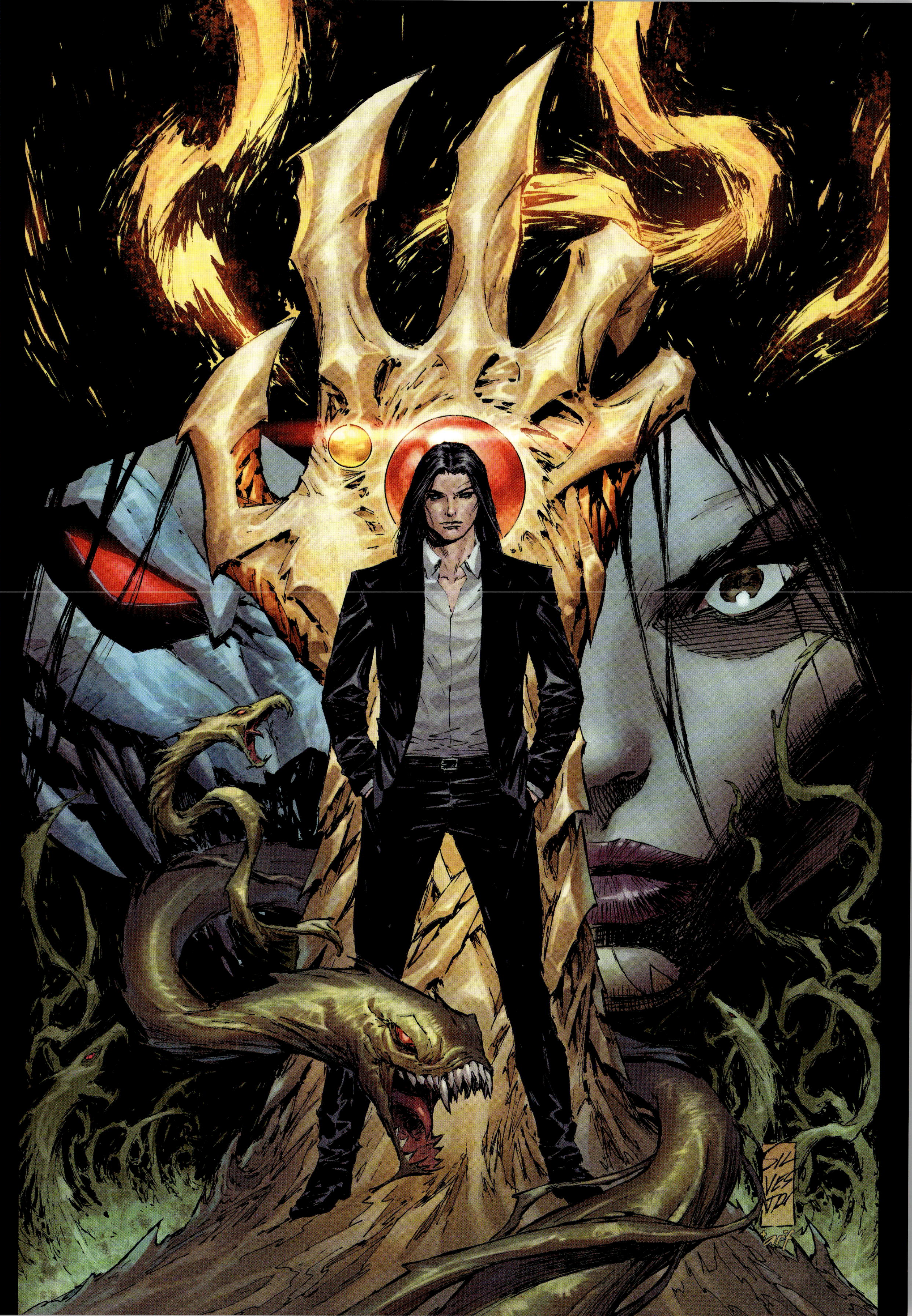

Witchblade #7 [2024] cover A,
art by: Marc Silvestri and Arif Prianto

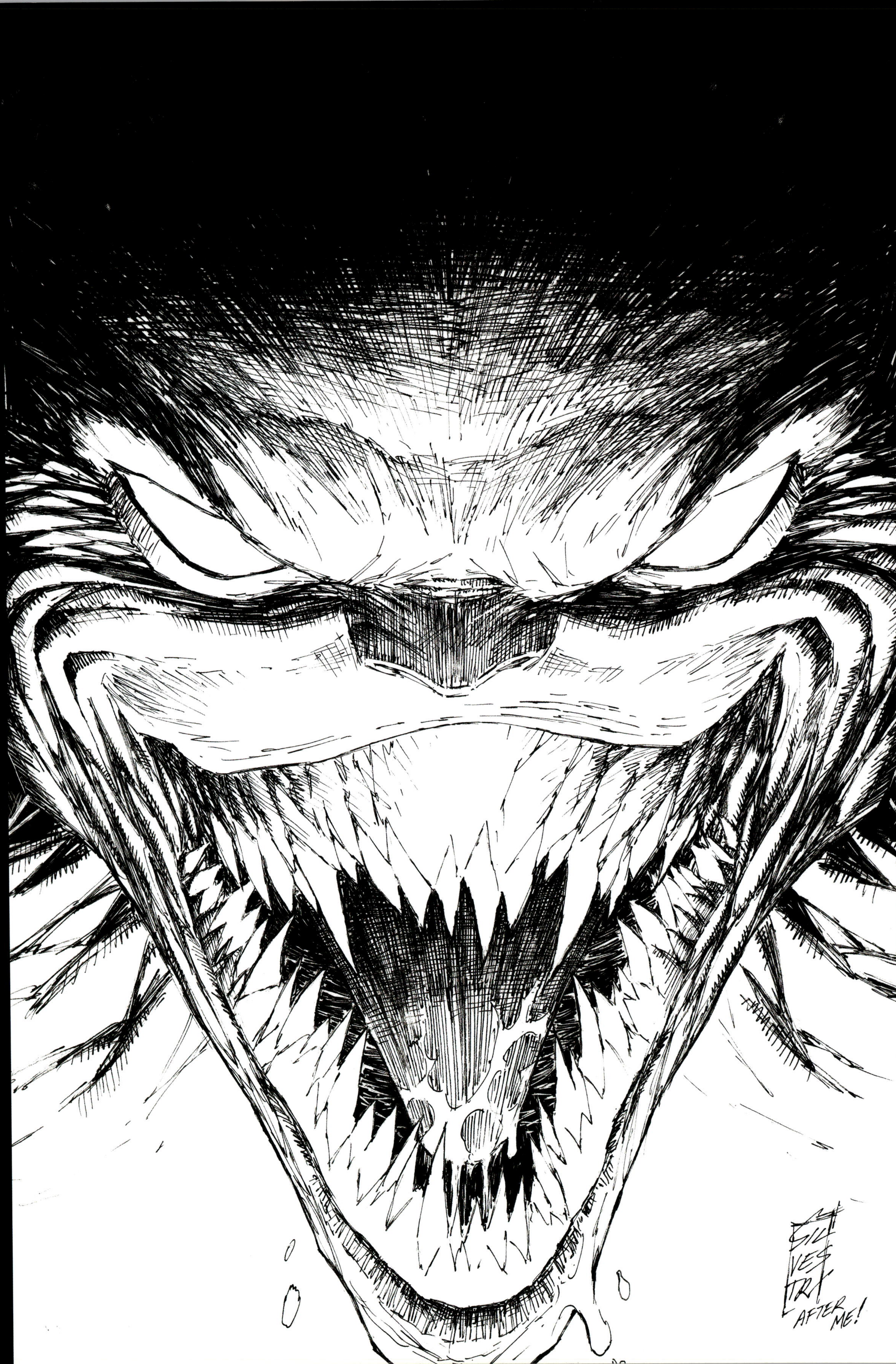

Witchblade #7 [2024] cover C, Homage Variant,
line art by: Marc Silvestri

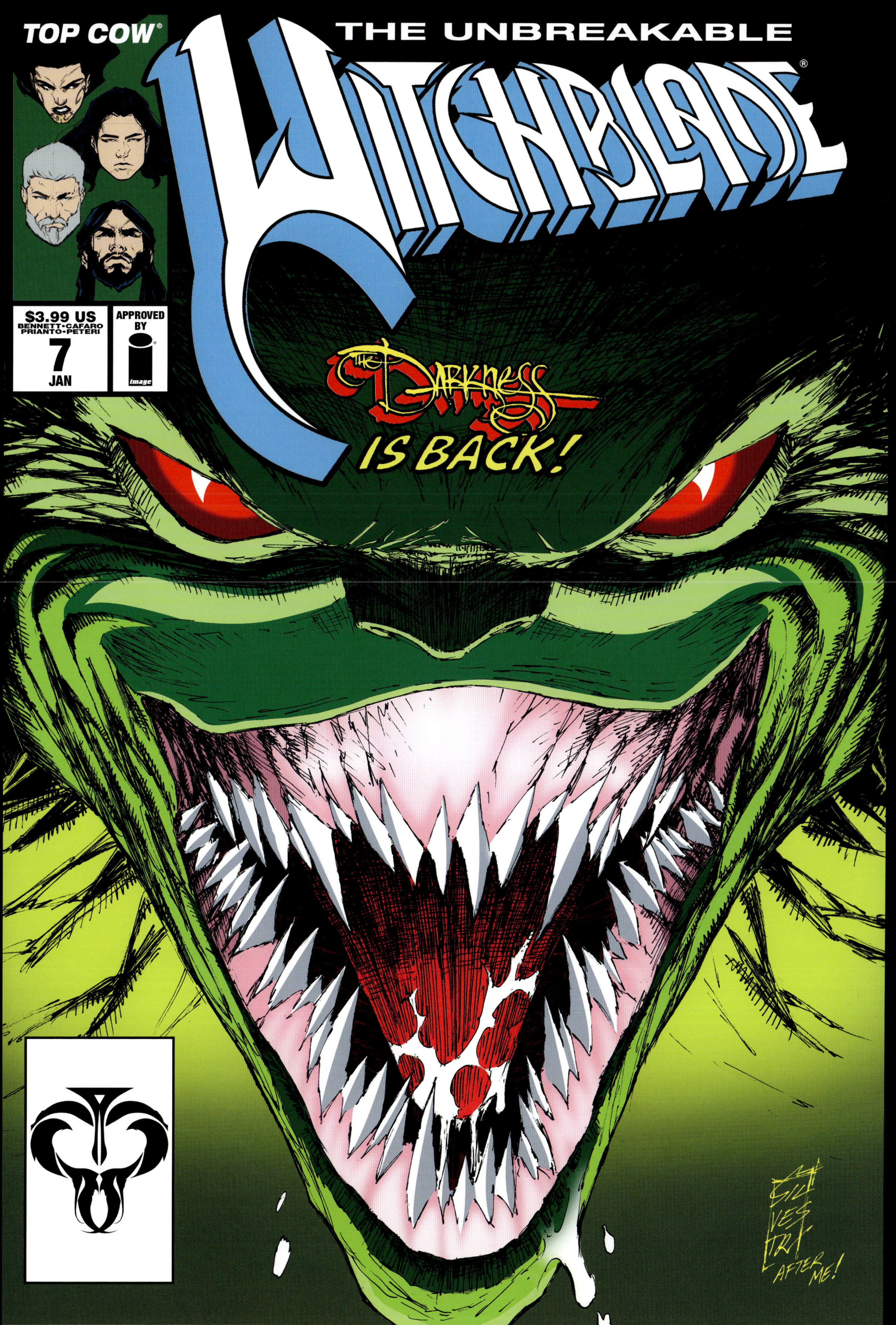

Witchblade #7 [2024] cover C, Homage Variant,
art by: Marc Silvestri and Phil Smith

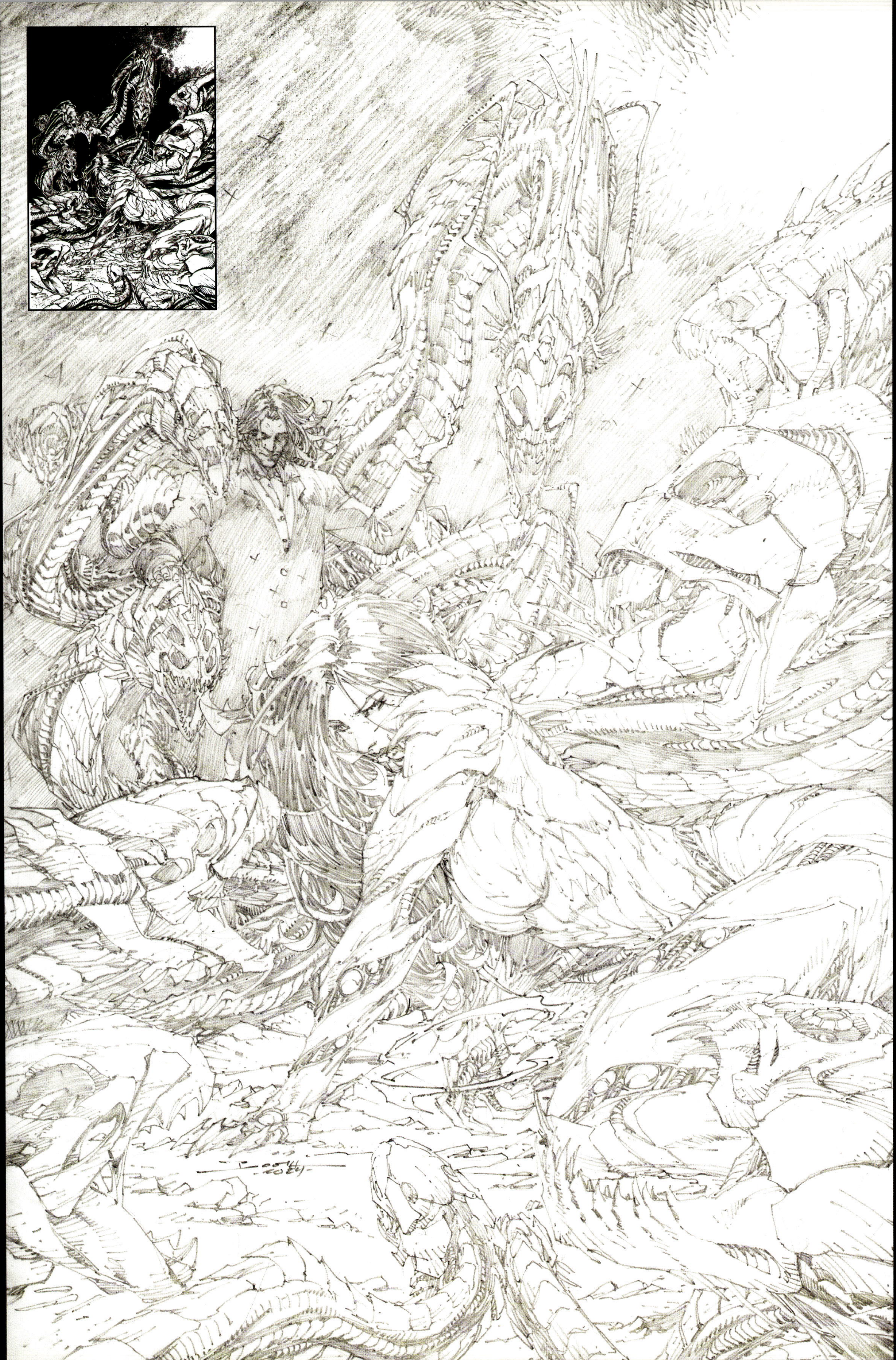

Witchblade #7 [2024] cover D,
line art by: Brett Booth and Sal Regla

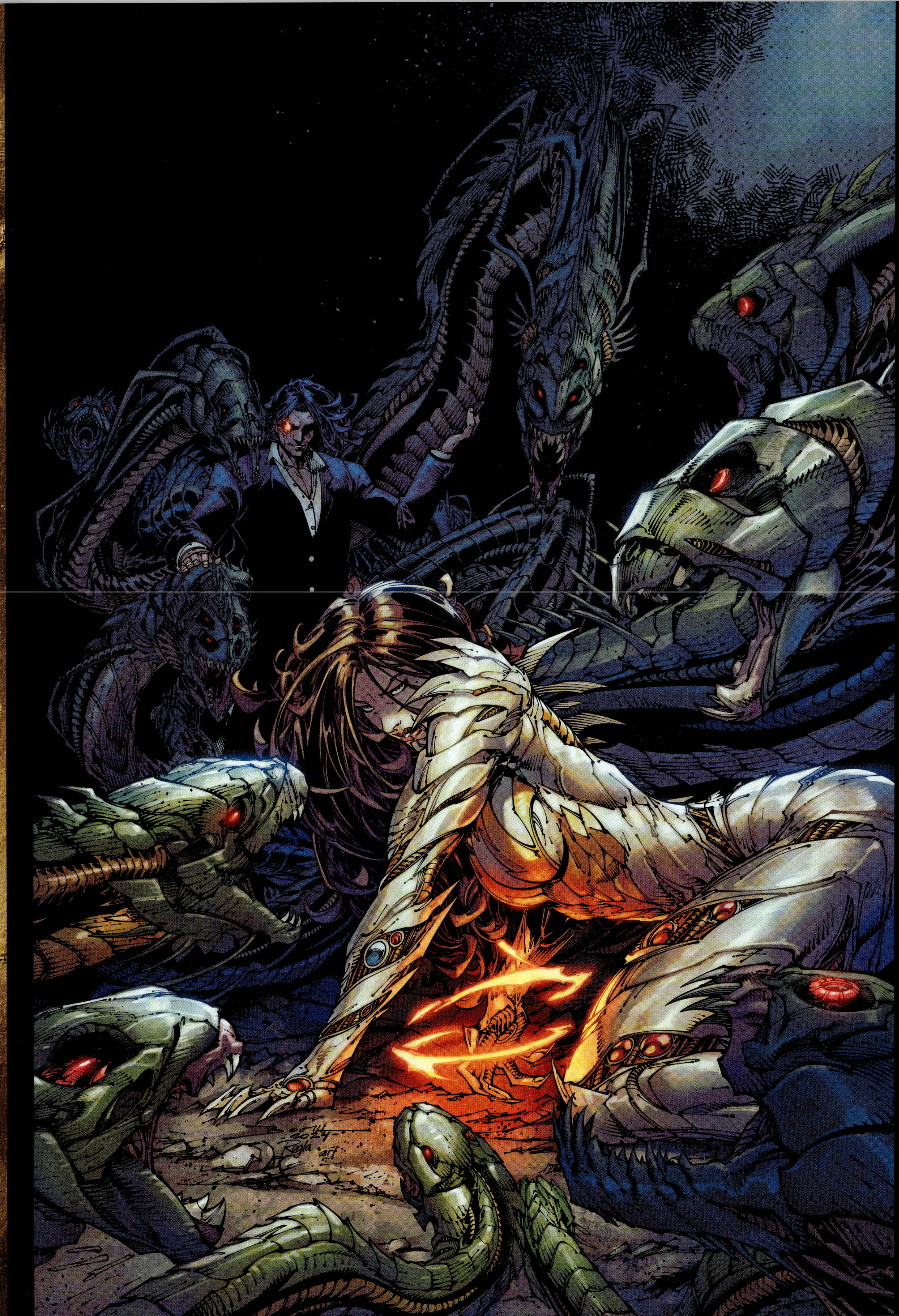

Witchblade #7 [2024] cover D,
art by: Brett Booth, Sal Regla, and Arif Prianto

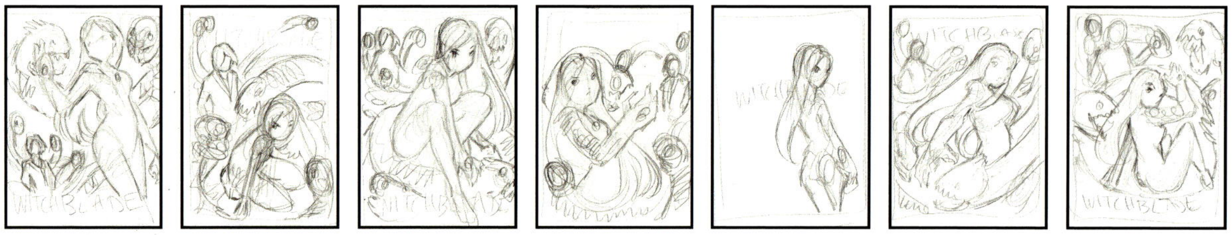

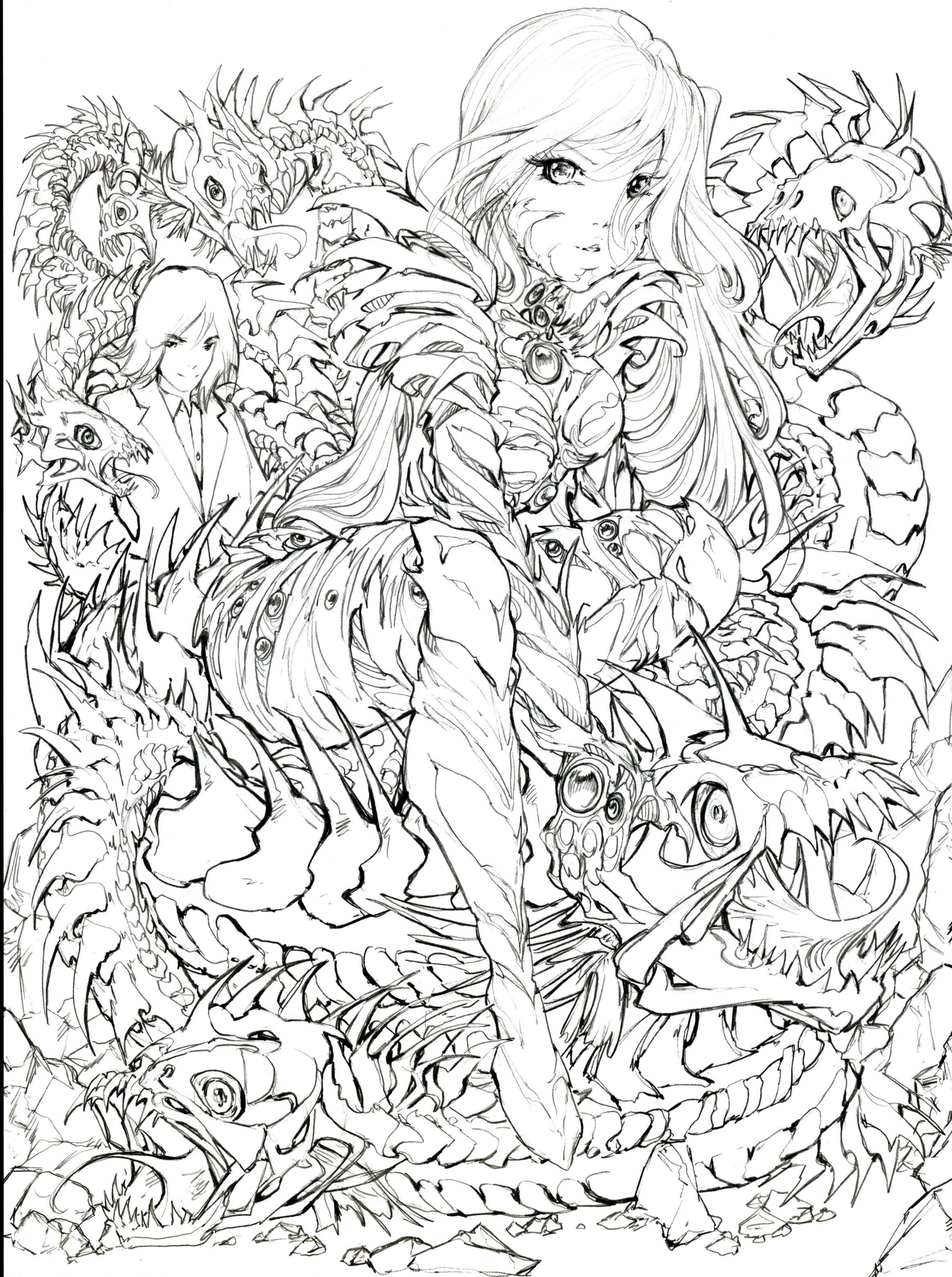

Witchblade #8 [2024] cover B,
thumbnails and line art by: Camilla d'Errico

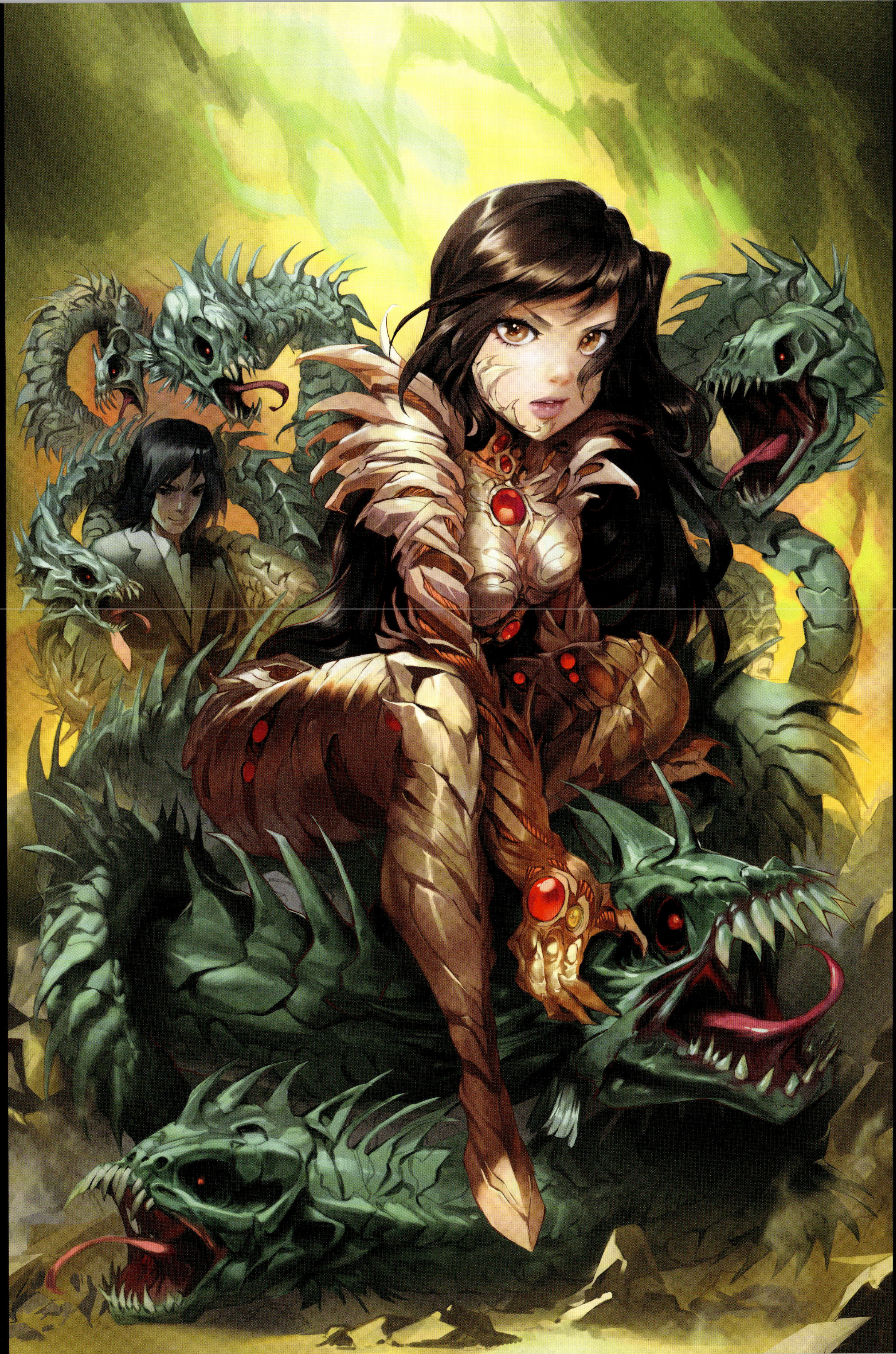

Witchblade #8 [2024] cover B,
thumbnails and line art by: Camilla d'Errico and Asuka111

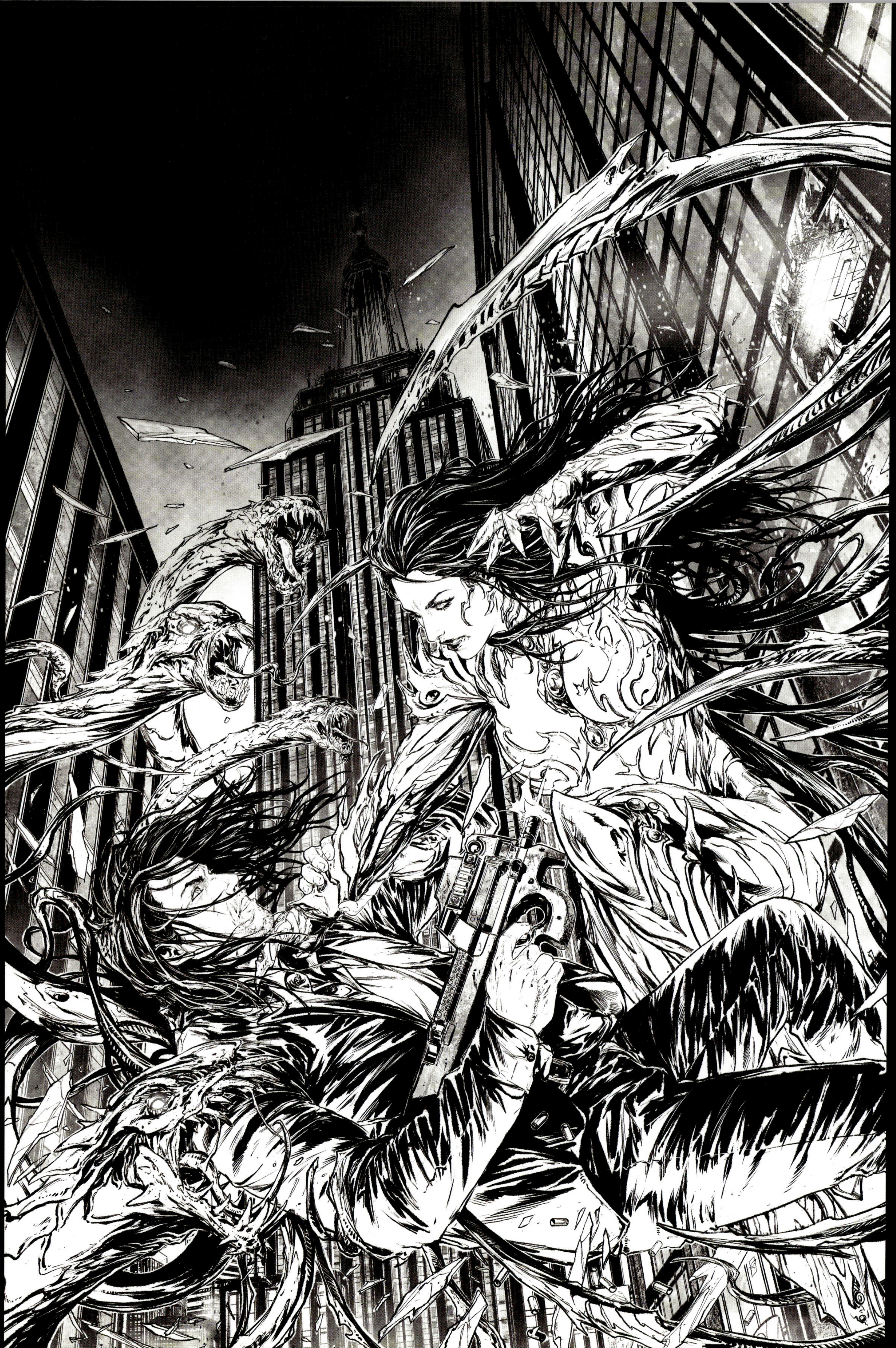

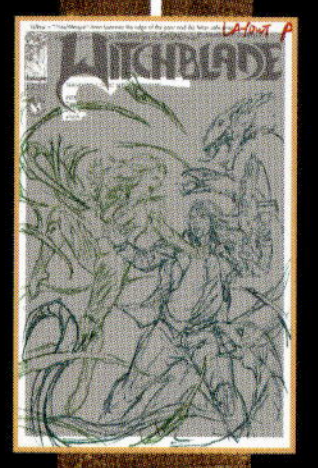

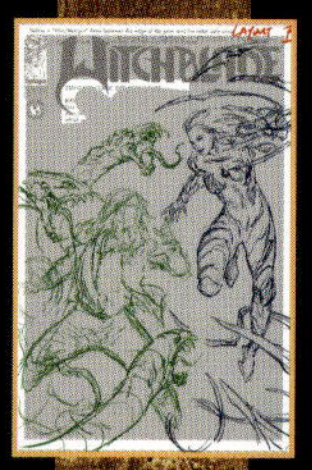

Witchblade #9 [2024] cover B, thumbnails and line art by: Raymond Gay

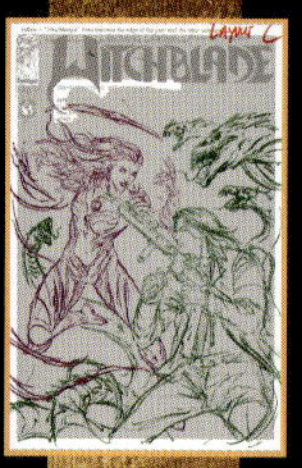

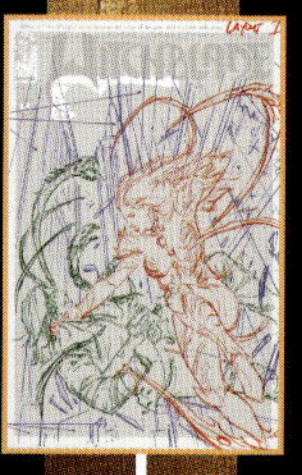

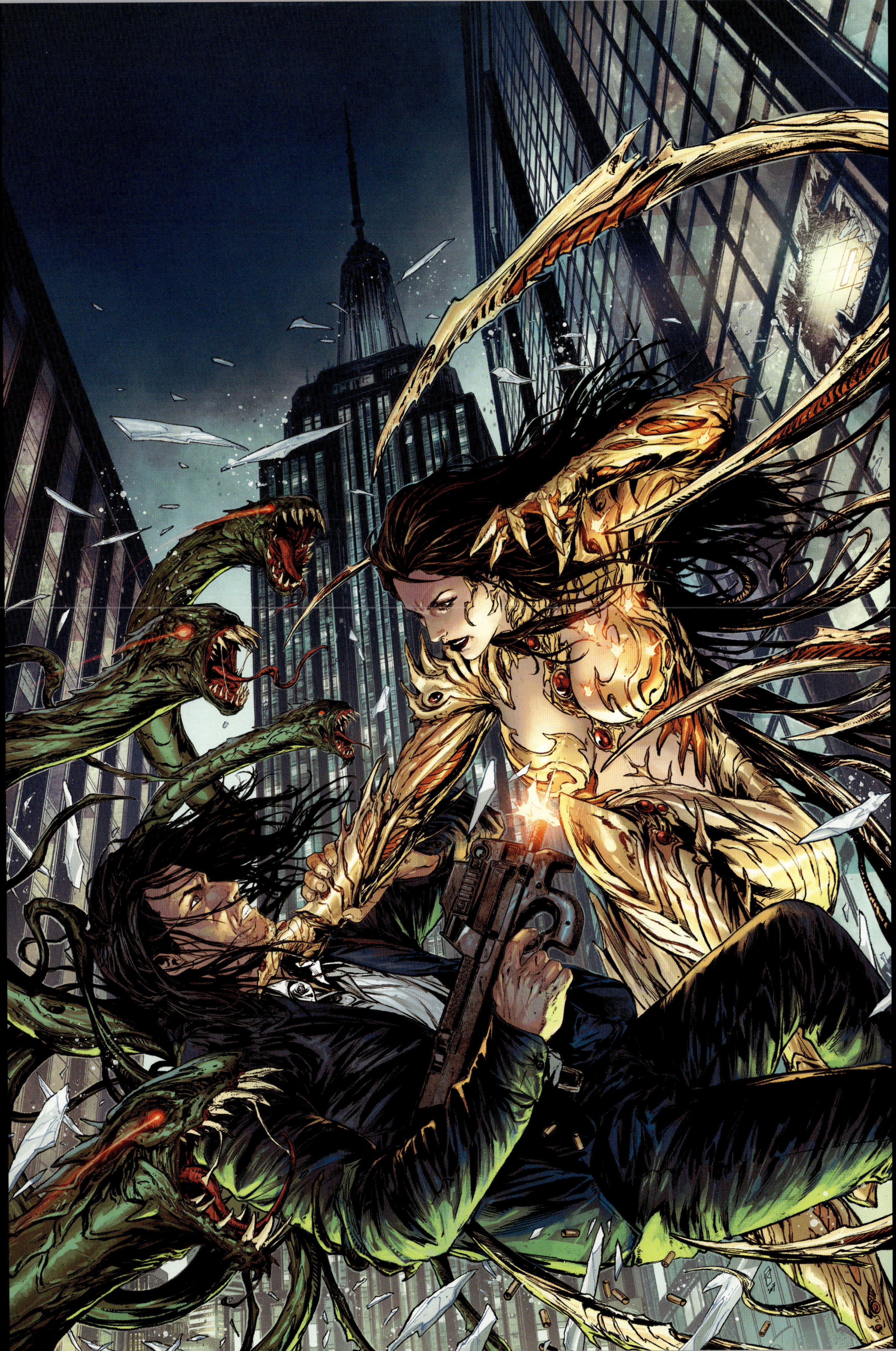

Witchblade #9 [2024] cover B,
art by: Raymond Gay and Arif Prianto

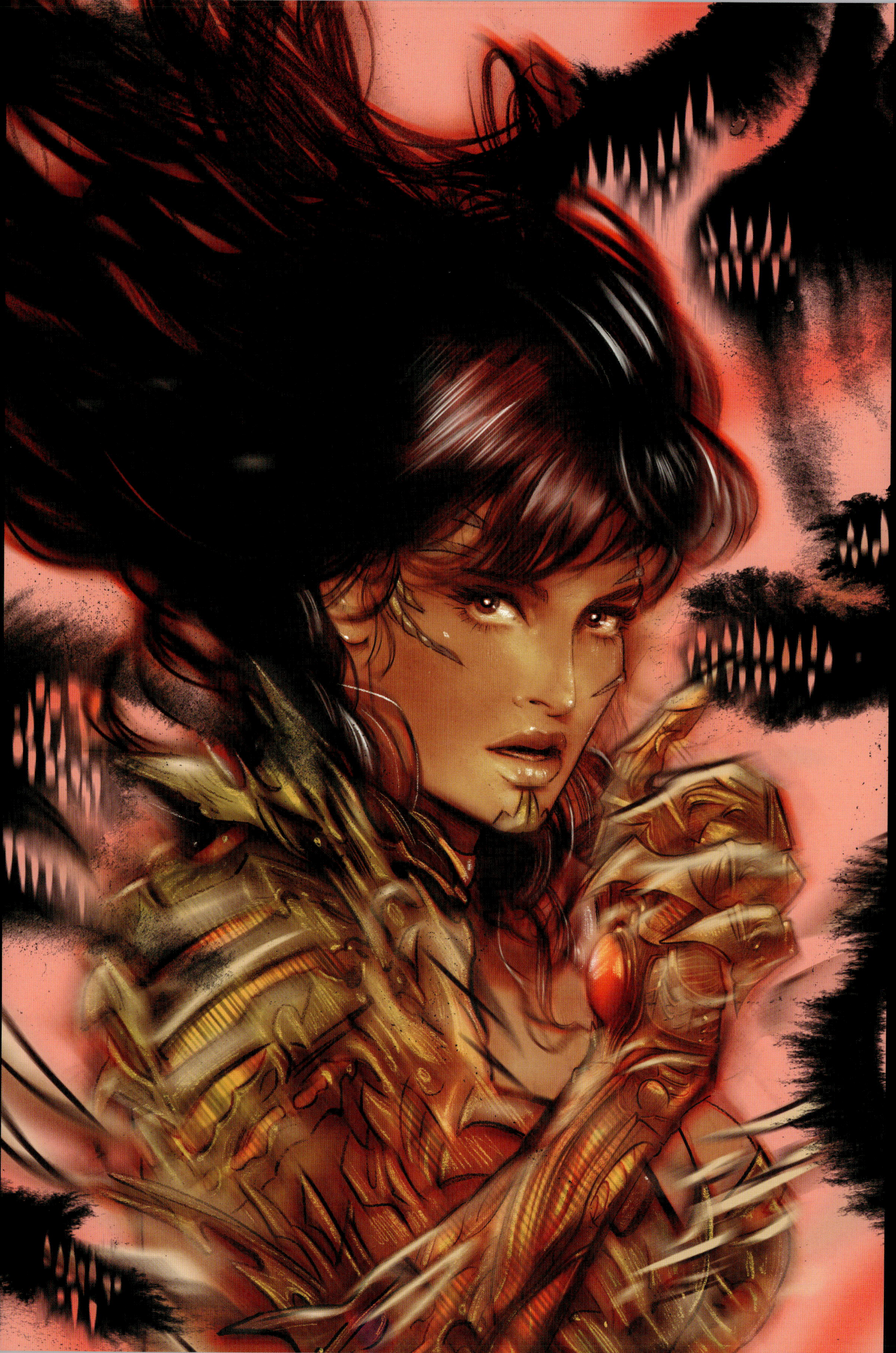

Witchblade #10 [2024] cover B,
art by: Tula Lotay

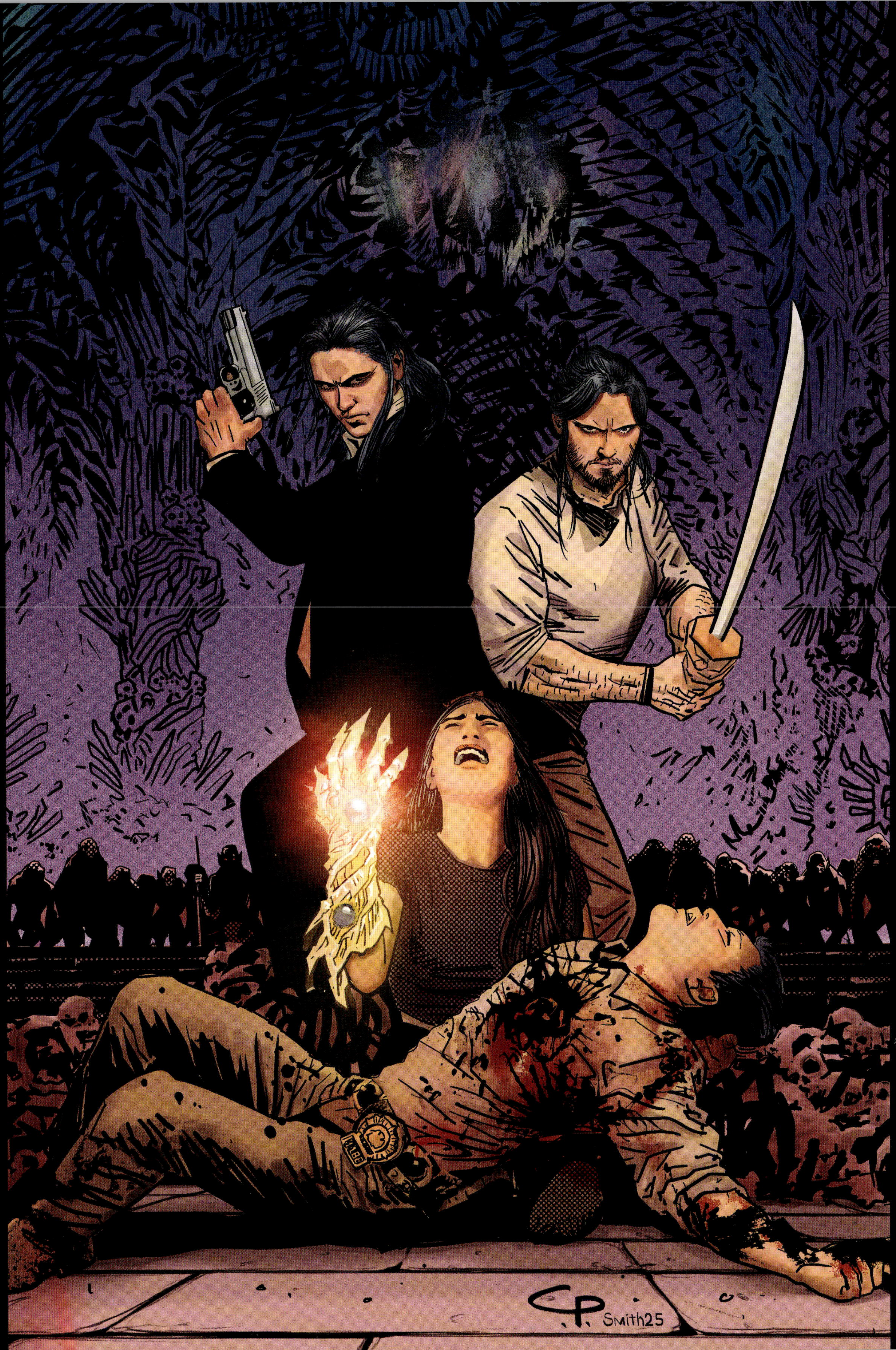

Witchblade #11 [2024] cover B,
art by: C.P. Smith

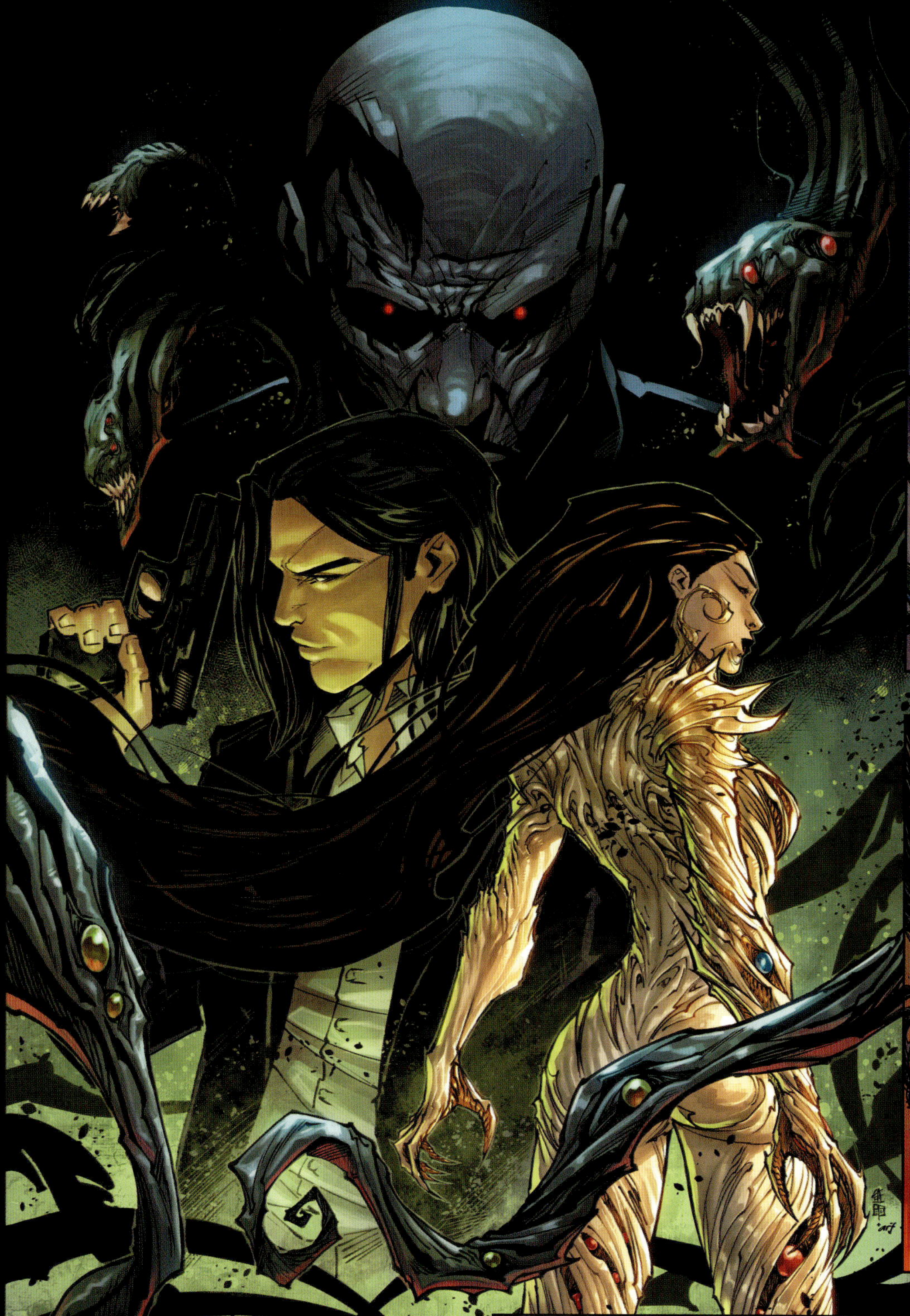

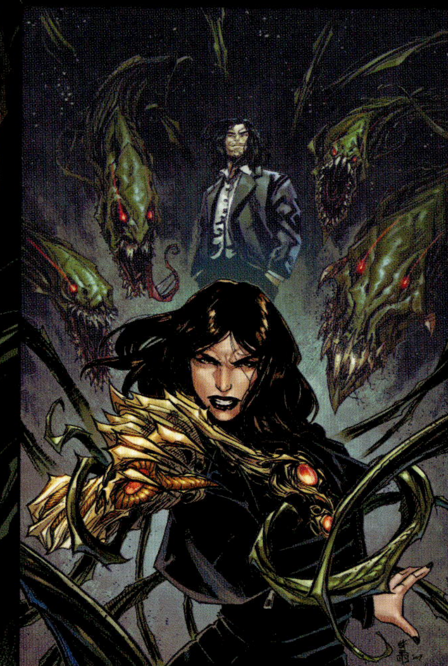

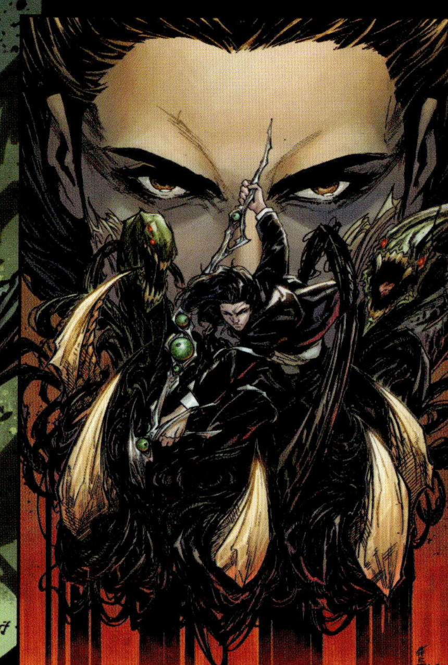

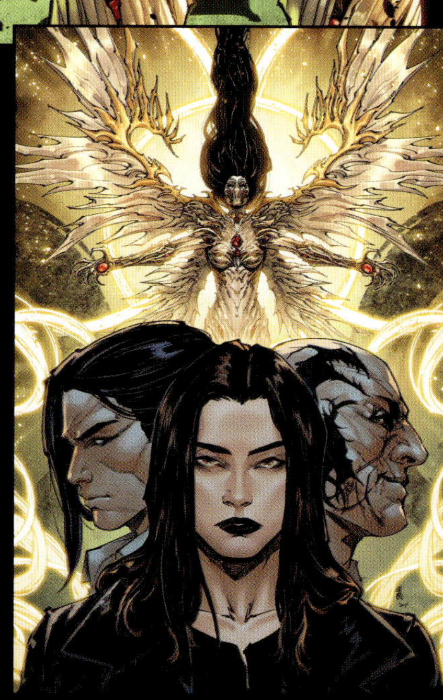

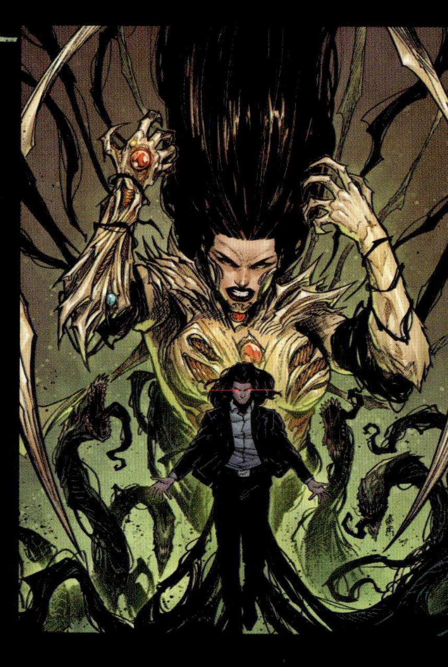

This page, clockwise from above.

Witchblade #10 [2024] cover A,
art by: Giuseppe Cafaro and Arif Prianto

Witchblade #7 [2024] cover A,
art by: Giuseppe Cafaro and Arif Prianto

Witchblade #8 [2024] cover A,
art by: Giuseppe Cafaro and Arif Prianto

Witchblade #9 [2024] cover A,
art by: Giuseppe Cafaro and Arif Prianto

Witchblade #11 [2024] cover A,
art by: Giuseppe Cafaro and Arif Prianto

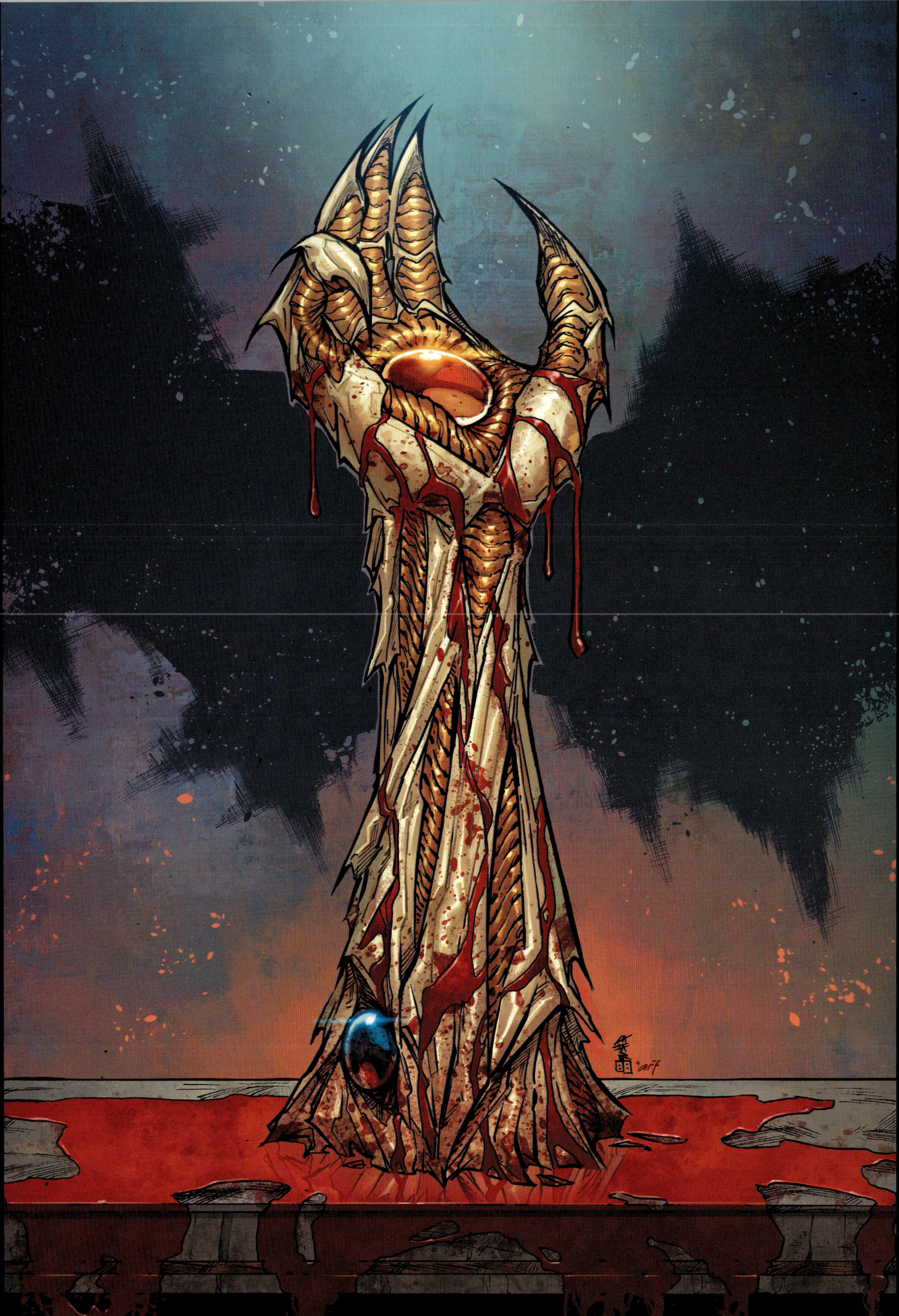

Witchblade #12 [2024] cover A,
art by: Giuseppe Cafaro and Arif Prianto

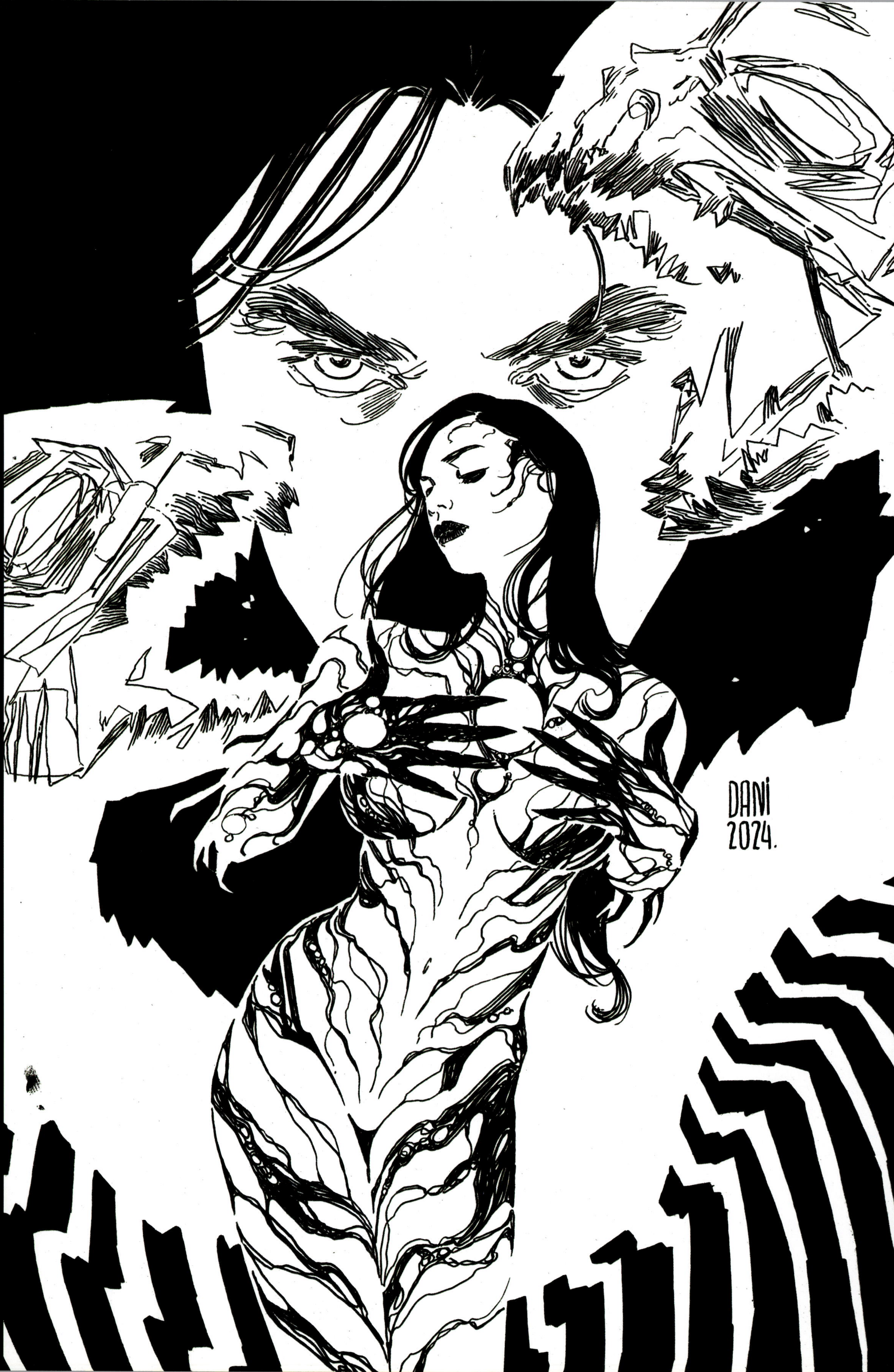

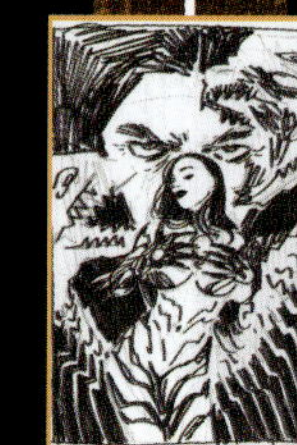

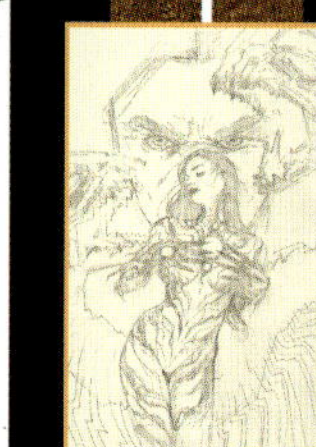

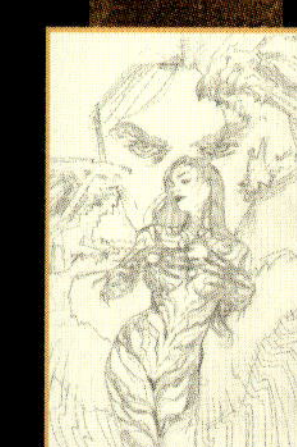

Witchblade #12 [2024] cover B, thumbnails and line art by: Dani

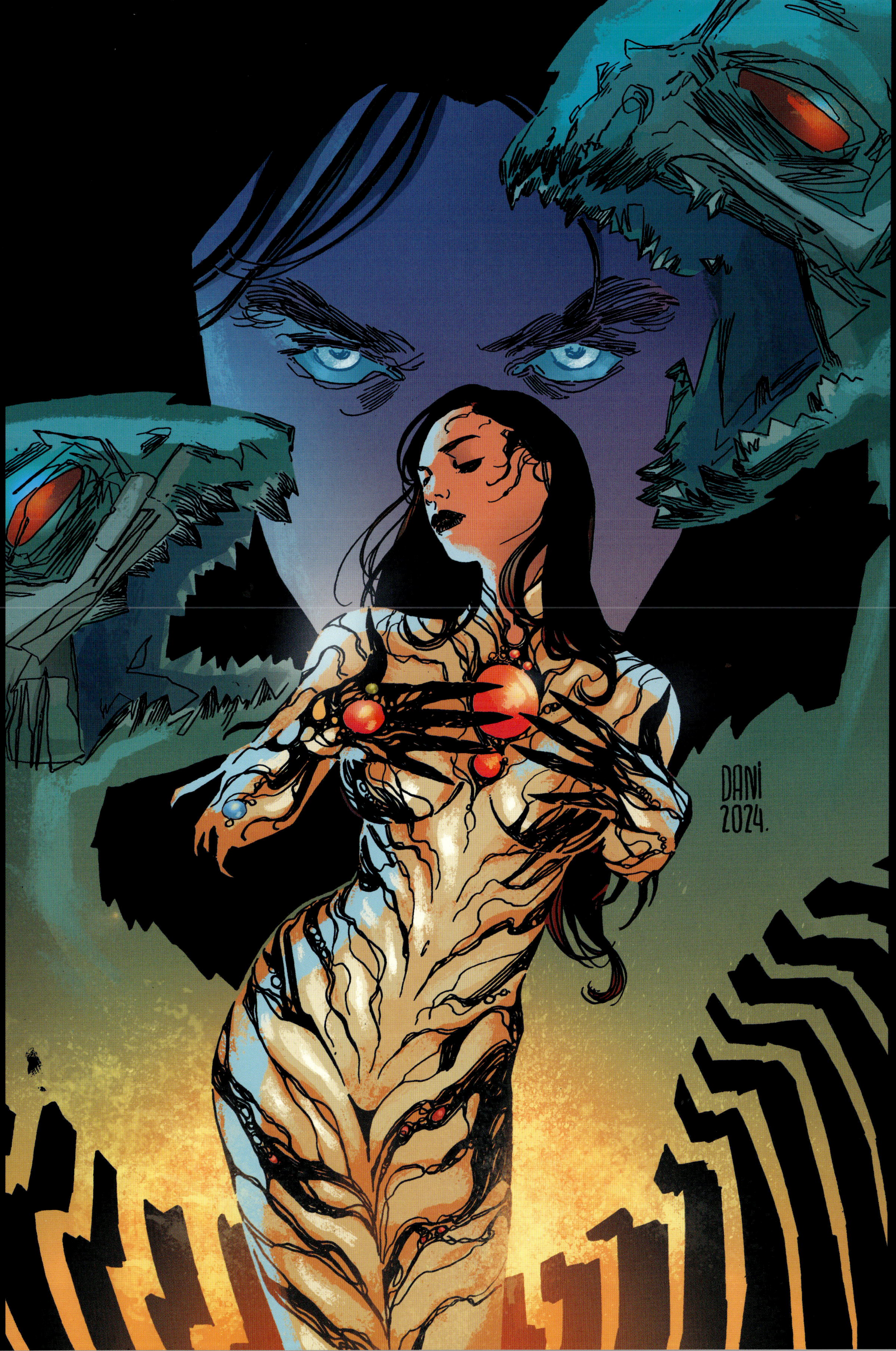

Witchblade #12 [2024] cover B,
art by: Dani and Brad Simpson

Witchblade, interview with
MARGUERITE BENNETT

Edited by ELENA SALCEDO.

"ELENA SALCEDO: I think it's amazing that you have been in this industry less than a decade and you've had the chance to work on some high-profile characters and comics. Normally, you have to write indie books to write a title like *Batwoman*. But you're going the other direction, which points to a close-knit, passionate audience that has a lot of love for *Witchblade*. But this feels like a class of its own. How did it feel to get that phone call from Marc?

MARGUERITE BENNETT: Well, first off, thank you so much for the kind and generous introduction! And I can say I'm happy to head in that direction because I am also a member of that close-knit and passionate audience, hahaha!

Funnily enough, it wasn't a call but an Uber ride – Marc and I shared a car from the airport on the way to a convention in Minneapolis in the fall of 2019, and he told me I was one of the people he was hoping to speak to that weekend. We talked about *Witchblade*, and it was such an honor; I grew up watching that TV show and weaving in and out of the comics. I don't know if y'all have had the pleasure, but I love talking to Marc. He's so gracious, thoughtful, patient, and charming. I've adored working with him, and I'm humbled to have his trust on the project.

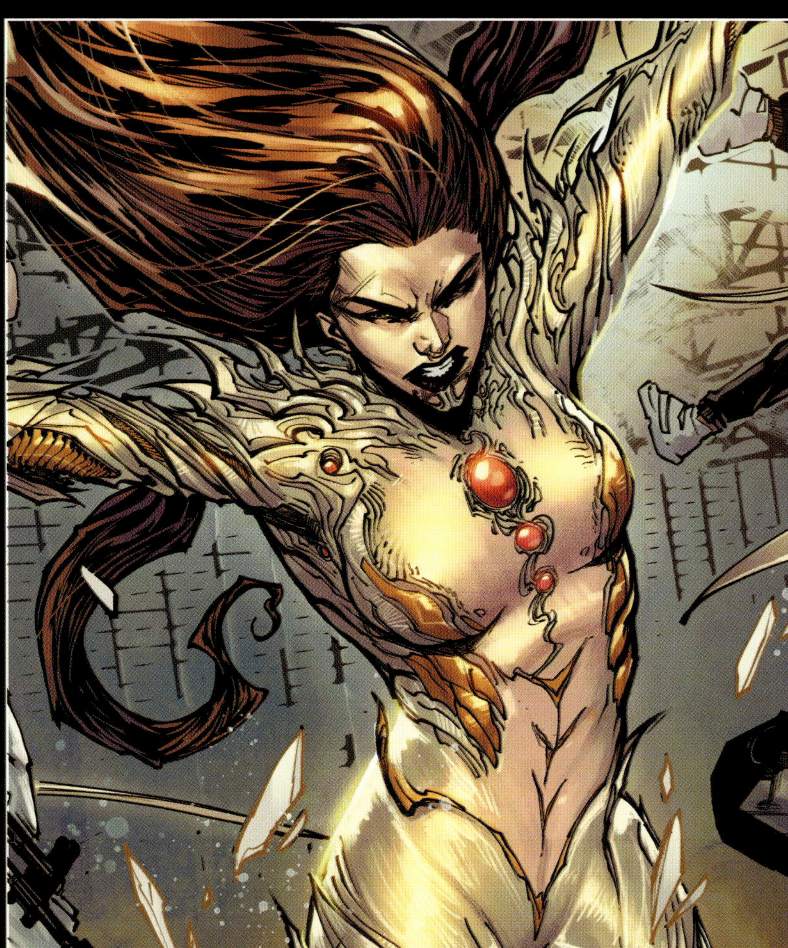

SALCEDO: There's a lot of nostalgia attached to *Witchblade*. You're no stranger to that in your work. But how do you keep an established audience happy while fulfilling yourself as a storyteller? Who are you writing for when you are working on something that isn't your creator-owned idea?

BENNETT: I have a lot of genuine enthusiasm for the core of *Witchblade*—women, power, mythology, sexuality, revenge, fantasy, history—and we're going to be heading back to basics in a big way. It's been decades since the series debuted, and I wanted to make faithful and passionate readers happy, as well as throwing open the doors to new readers who haven't yet had to the chance to meet Sara in all her glory.

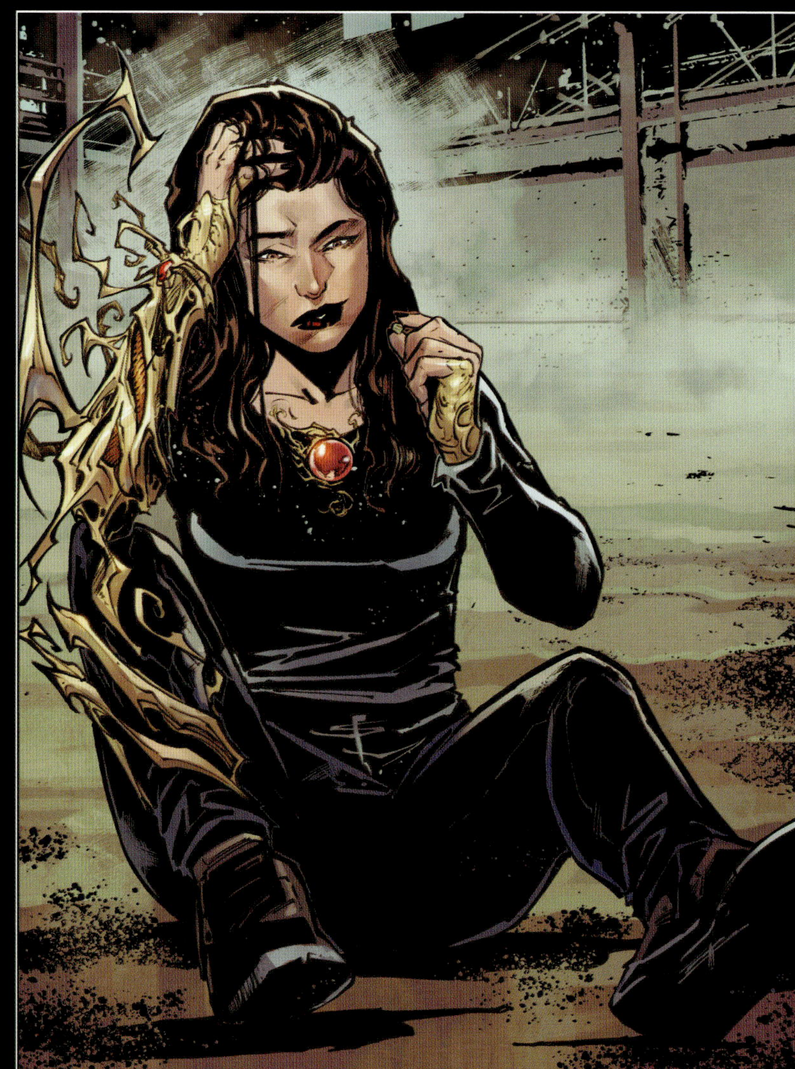

SALCEDO: How are you connecting with Sara? There are so many issues to choose from. Do you have any storylines or runs you're drawing from?

BENNETT: Our relaunch is such a major jumping-on point, I'm trying to flatten the playing field and roll out the richest, rawest, reddest carpet I can. If you've never read *Witchblade*, never even heard of it, you'll have a great time in this series—provided you're on board with horror, fantasy, sexuality, and some real big weirdness.

In terms of inspiration, I'm really focusing on the first three years of the book and bringing in that cast of characters. There's a lot to love.

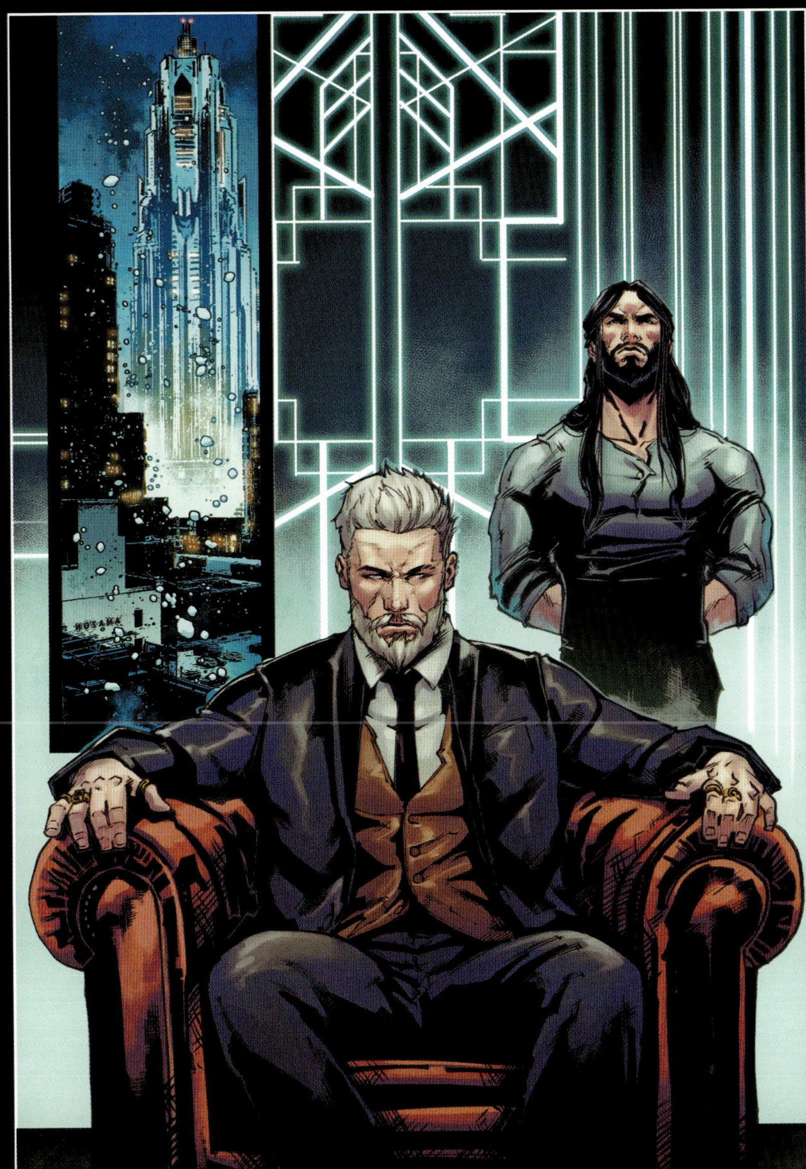

SALCEDO: What is it that you want to say with this first arc? Is there a theme or feeling you want to convey to *Witchblade* fans who have been craving more Sara for nearly seven years?

BENNETT: The Witchblade (I don't believe it's a spoiler to say) is a tool sent to bring justice to a world out of balance.

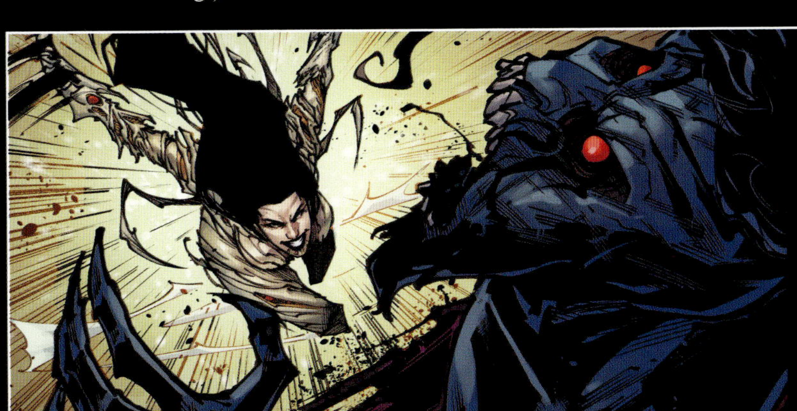

But that tool requires an avatar to wield it, and that avatar is always a woman. So, does this woman wield the Witchblade, or does the Witchblade wield the woman? If your strength lies in being turned into a tool, a vessel, an object, what does that say of your agency, your identity, your power? What is your power? What do you do with it?

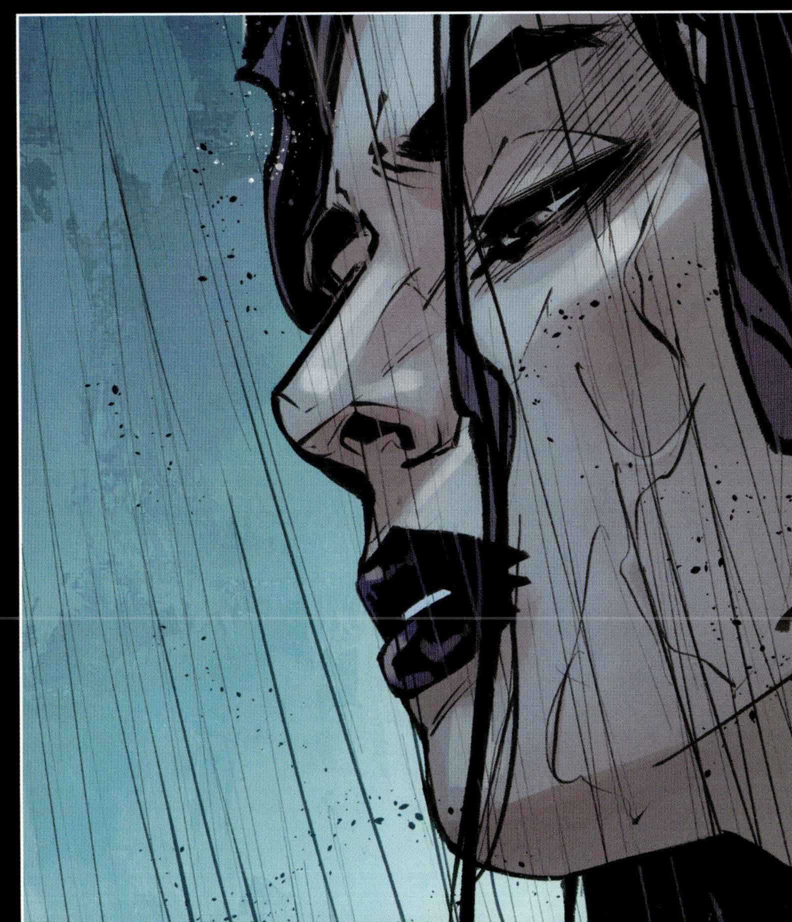

Before the Witchblade's arrival, Sara's world is harsh, gray, bleak, and sharp. She lives by her wits and her willpower, slat-ribbed as an alley cat, stalking her prey in a shadow game of not-quite-good and absolutely evil, a chess match of lies and deceit.

When the Witchblade comes, it comes like a comet. It is an obliterating experience.

Suddenly, the world is bursting with color, overflowing with sensory input. Every nerve in her body is electrified with knowledge and power and will, everything rich and abounding with life. It's Eve and the apple. Her mind has changed. Her body has changed. Sara sees and knows the world as she never has before and understands what she can be and do within that magnificent Eden threatened by chaos and corruption on all sides.

Oh, yeah, and also, it's gonna be real fun.[1] ”

1 Salcedo, Elena, ed., "Witchblade, interview with Marguerite Bennett," in *Witchblade* #1/2 (August 2021): 16-17.

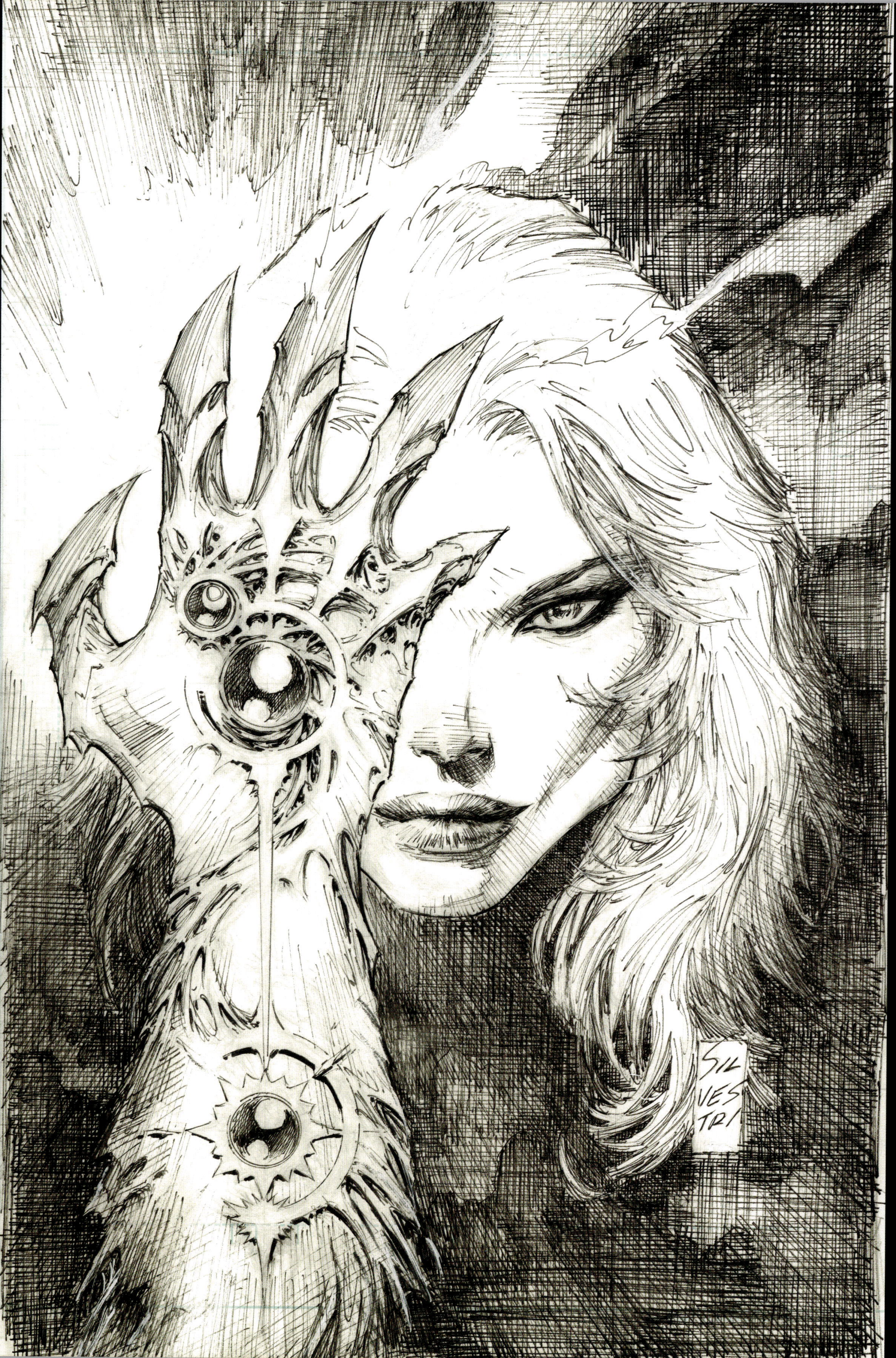

Witchblade #1/2 (2021) cover A,
line art by: Marc Silvestri

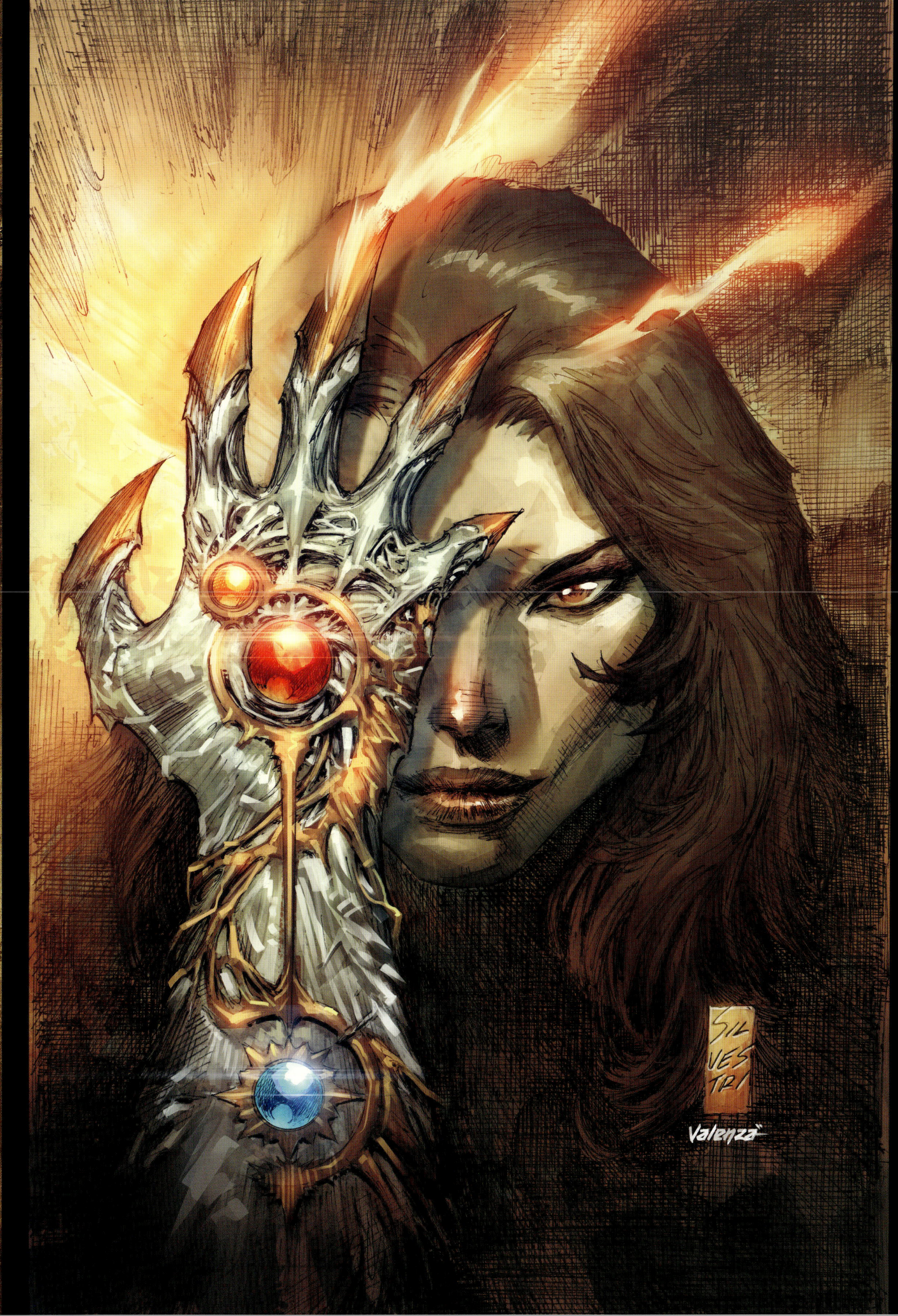

Witchblade #1/2 [2021] cover A,
art by: Marc Silvestri and Bryan Valenza

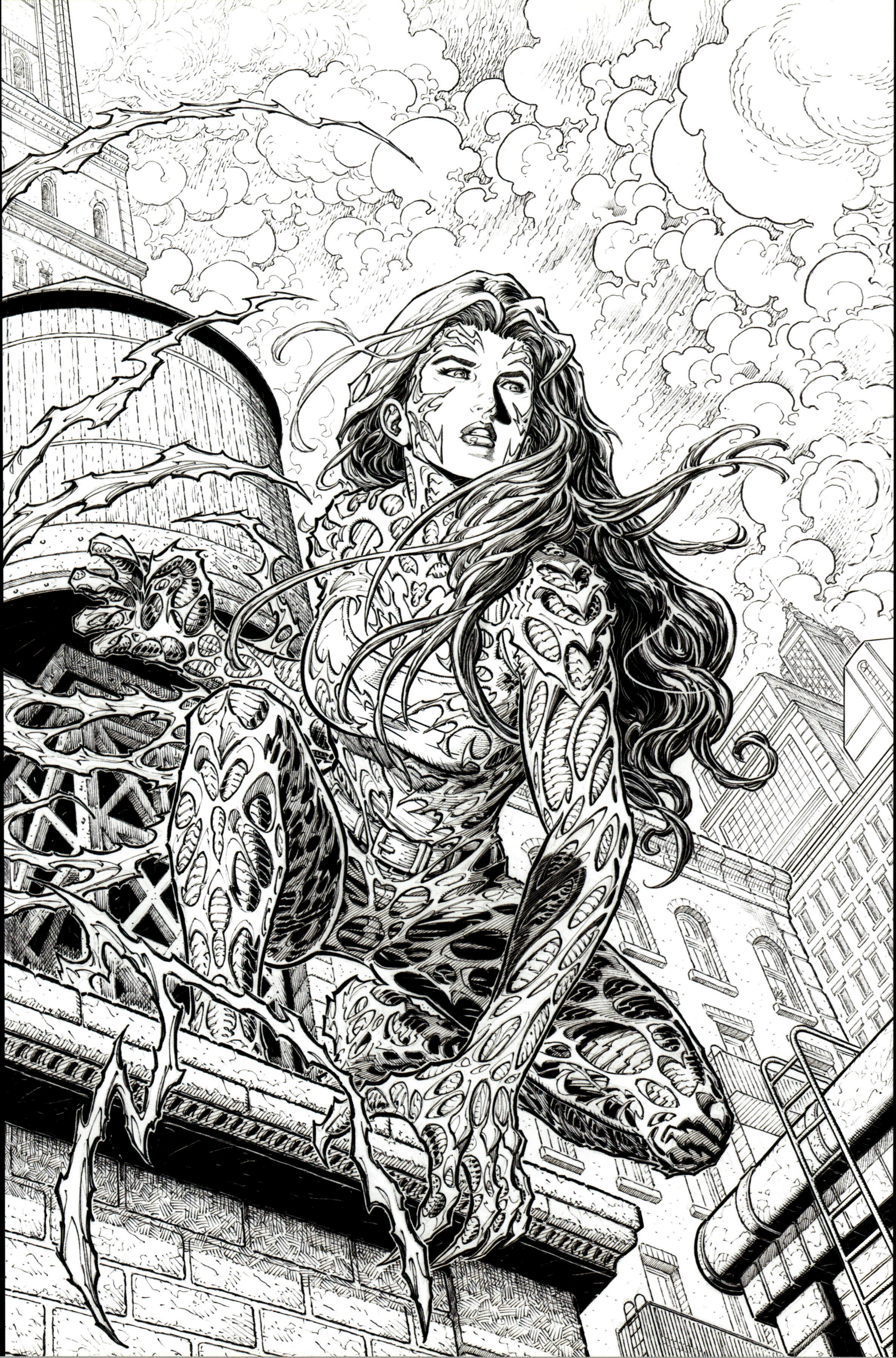

Witchblade #1/2 [2021] cover B,
line art by: Ian Churchill

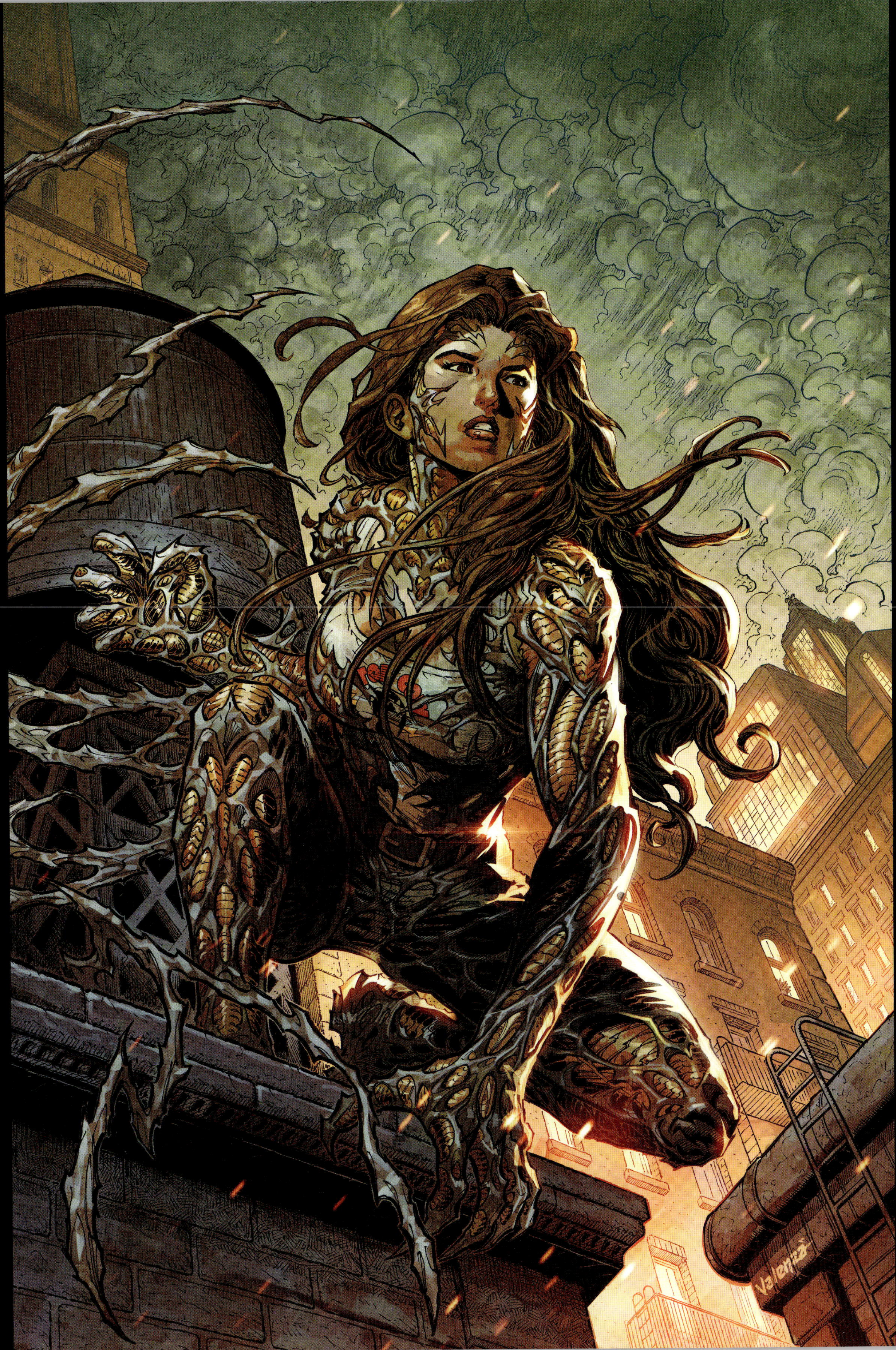

Witchblade #1/2 [2021] cover B,
art by: Ian Churchill and Bryan Valenza

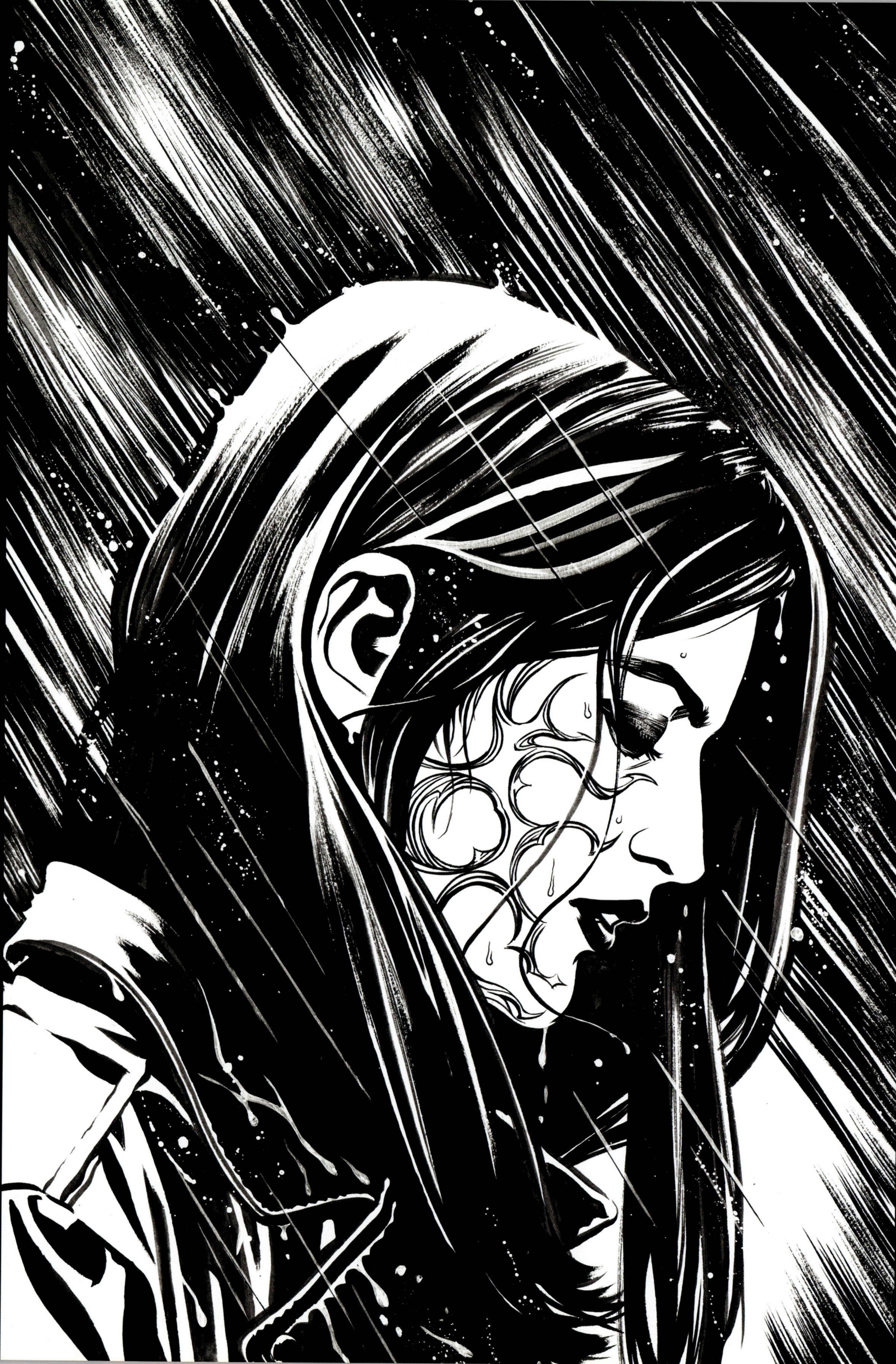

Witchblade #1 Kickstarter preview cover A,
line art by: Francesca Ciregia

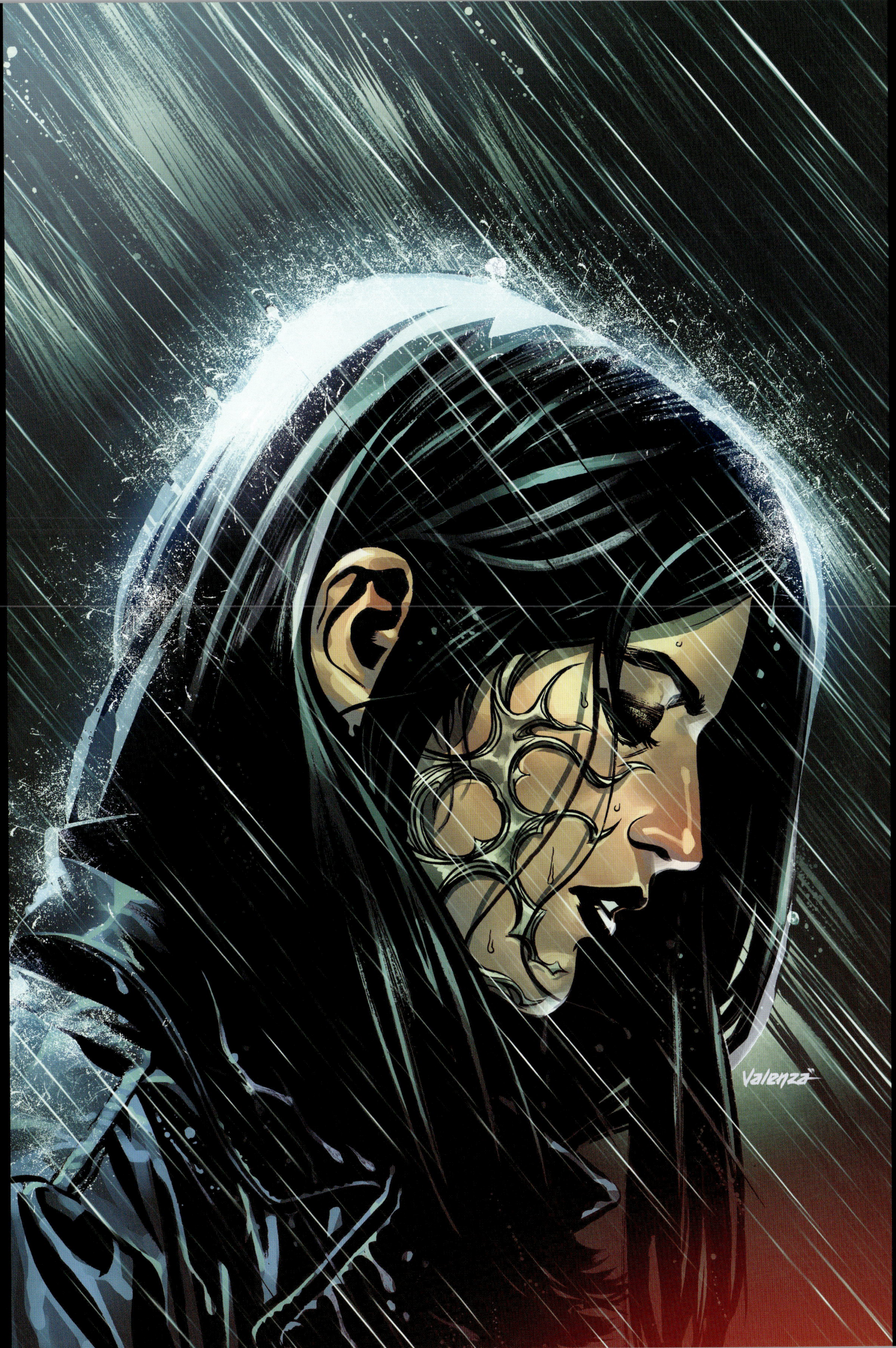

Witchblade #1 Kickstarter preview cover A,
art by: Francesca Ciregia and Bryan Valenza

Witchblade Fan Questions, with creators **MARC SILVESTRI**, **BRIAN HABERLIN** and **DAVID WOHL**.

Edited by **ELENA SALCEDO** and **MATT HAWKINS**.

“ **@streetbreakerX2: How did you come up with the inspiration for *Witchblade?***

MARC SILVESTRI: Back in the mid-nineties, there was a big gap in female-led superhero comics and the mainstream publishers had little interest in filling it. We, at Top Cow, were of course all too happy to do it for them! There had been some successes like Billy Tucci's *Shi* (in fact, the *Cyblade/Shi* crossover introduced Sara to the world), but not many others were giving it a real go. Brian Haberlin and David Wohl came to me with the idea of doing a female hero loosely based on the Excalibur mythology but set in modern day. I immediately loved the concept, and we started fleshing it out. Michael Turner was doing incredible work for us at the time, and we were looking for his next project. *Witchblade* was the perfect fit and the rest is history! We put all of our creative and marketing muscle behind it and to this day I think it was one of the better title launches in all of comics.

BRIAN HABERLIN: It was the time when Shi and Lady Death were top comics, and we had the hubris to think we could do better. That and David and I were always fans of Michael Moorcock and his hero's weapons that weren't always well behaved.

DAVID WOHL: Yeah, the sentient weapon element was a big part of it at first. Along with the idea that it has existed for thousands of years and had many different wielders. Always women who were strong willed and heroic. Then, at the same time, we wanted it to be grounded and gritty, so having it end up in the hands of young NYPD detective–who was trying to just live her life while trying to deal with these amazing abilities–seemed like a perfect fit.

@DarthDeverell: What's it like to see the legacy of this series that's been going for over two decades? Would you like to see it make the leap to other media again as it did with the Yancy Butler TV series?

MARC: It was a thrill beyond belief that we managed to get a non-Marvel or DC comic character on television, let alone one with a female lead! Comic adaptations were rare back then and good ones even rarer, but we managed to do it. Now as everyone knows, comics are king in other media so keep your eyes peeled because we're always looking to pop up in other media. And since *Witchblade* is such an evergreen character, don't be surprised when she does!

BRIAN: I'm sure it will be again.

DAVID: Yeah, I definitely believe there is a place for it out there. It still has fans, and the subject matter is still resonant today.

@mystic_azure: Was Ian Nottingham originally going to be related to Jackie? And in *Witchblade* #500 Since it was vague who the father of Sara's twins was, did you intend Nottingham to be the dad or were you leaving it open for a future character?

MARC: That was always a fun “maybe” for us and the fans. We'll see what happens together!

BRIAN: I'll leave that one to David.

DAVID: We definitely played with the idea of the two men being connected. But I think we ultimately decided that they'd be better off staying in their own lanes since they were both such cool, distinct characters. And good call on *Witchblade* #500 because we were laying groundwork for the Jackie/Sara union. And who knows–maybe that one is still on the horizon!

@fargokraken: What do you think is the key element that's made *Witchblade* so popular since its creation?

MARC: I think that the cool concept of a character having a power struggle with a semi-sentient weapon of peace or war will always be appealing. That kind of power struggle will always cause the hero to step up and do the right thing. Plus adding in the burden of it being the wielder's destiny whether they want it or not is just so ripe for a hero's journey. Toss in a great, relateable real-world character like Sara Pezzini and you have a winning combination!

BRIAN: Well...Mike Turner was on fire at the time, and I think the character was believable...she had weird strange problems but also the same problems everyone has as well...so she was also relateable.

@furyroseillustrations: If you could choose a classic *Witchblade* cover art image to be made into a statue, which would you pick?

MARC: Not to be coy, but that's an impossible question for me to answer! We've been blessed with having the best artists in comics do their take on Sara and I honestly think they all deserve a statue! I think the sculptors better get busy!

BRIAN: I always liked the issue 8 cover as long as the stained glass window could be with the sculpt.

DAVID: Either the *Witchblade* #5 cover, where she has her arms crossed with the Witchblade on one hand and a gun in the other, or issue 4, with the big gauntleted hand behind her.

@brandon_hooper88: Which actress do you see playing Sara on the big Screen?

MARC: There are so many talented actresses out there that would be perfect for Sara. And in today's world of comic-driven tent-pole movies, who wouldn't want the chance to be the lead of a franchise with such a strong character as its heart? Plus, I was told years ago by someone pretty big in the movie business that it was bad luck to say who you'd dream cast in your film!

DAVID: Well, I don't want to jinx anything, but Jennifer Lawrence, Saoirse Ronan or Florence Pugh would be cool. And they'd all have very distinct takes, I imagine.

@graphicpolicy: The character debuted in a very different era. What do you think holds over from then and how each decade has impacted the character and her world?

MARC: I think the fact that Sara is a very human character tasked with basically protecting mankind will always resonate. She is the classic case of picking up a mantle she never asked for and wielding it despite the great personal cost. She didn't grow up wanting to be the wielder of The Witchblade, but when she came to the realization that she was born to be, she owned it…for us.

@jamesbauer5: What were your favorite stories that you worked on during your time on *Witchblade?* And, are there any series you'd be interested in having a *Witchblade* crossover in the future?

DAVID: I really enjoyed the first story arc, because we were able to create so much mythology as we were doing it. And between Brian, Marc, Michael Turner, Christina Z and I, as well as all the other fertile minds we had at Top Cow at that time, it was so exciting to build this world that would lay the groundwork for other Top Cow series as well. Also, getting to work with Pat Lee on two *Witchblade/Dark Minds* books was very special to me, and I felt like we created a really compelling story. Lastly, I loved doing *Witchblade/Wolverine*, part of our “Devil's Reign” crossover with Marvel. We did this whole alternate story where Mephisto was messing with Sara's mind, and that was a lot of fun–especially seeing Michael draw Mephisto and Wolverine along with our regular Witchblade cast.

I think the book still has a lot of resonance today because at its essence it's just a story about a heroic figure trying to find her way in a world that is very different than she originally believed it to be. It has interpersonal drama, lots of suspense, action, fantasy and horror. Probably a lot of superficial elements will change to make it relevant for today, but the underlying themes and characters are timeless.

@bread_pirate: What has the experience been like creating and writing for a character that would stand the test of time?

DAVID: It's been one of the most fulfilling aspects of my career, and I always look back on the time of its creation fondly. I'm so thankful to Marc that I had the opportunity to be part of *Witchblade's* history, and I'm still proud of the work I did on it.

Brendan O'Moore: What has been your favorite part of working on *Witchblade*, and what stories would you recommend to new readers?

DAVID: I guess I'm biased, but I have to recommend the original storyline, but I'd also say the runs by writers Ron Marz and Paul Jenkins both took the series to new, cool places that really expanded on our original material in very interesting and surprising ways. They also worked with some amazing artists that picked up the torch from Michael–like Mike Choi, Francis Manapul, Stjepan Sejic and many others![2] ”

2 Salcedo, Elena, ed., and Matt Hawkins ed., “Witchblade Fan Questions,” in *Witchblade* #1 Preview (May 2023): 16-17.

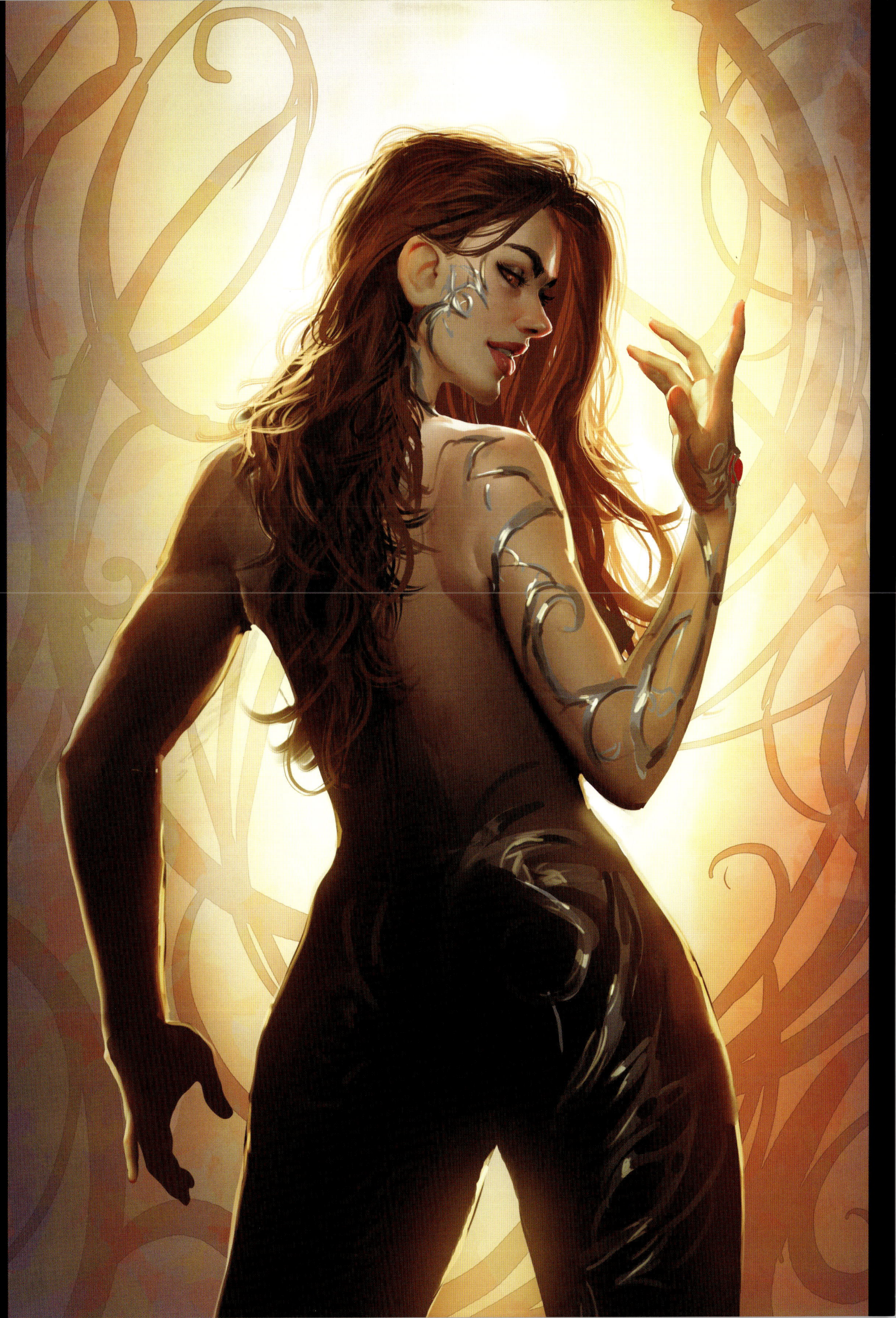

Witchblade #1 Kickstarter preview cover B,
art by: Stjepan Sejic

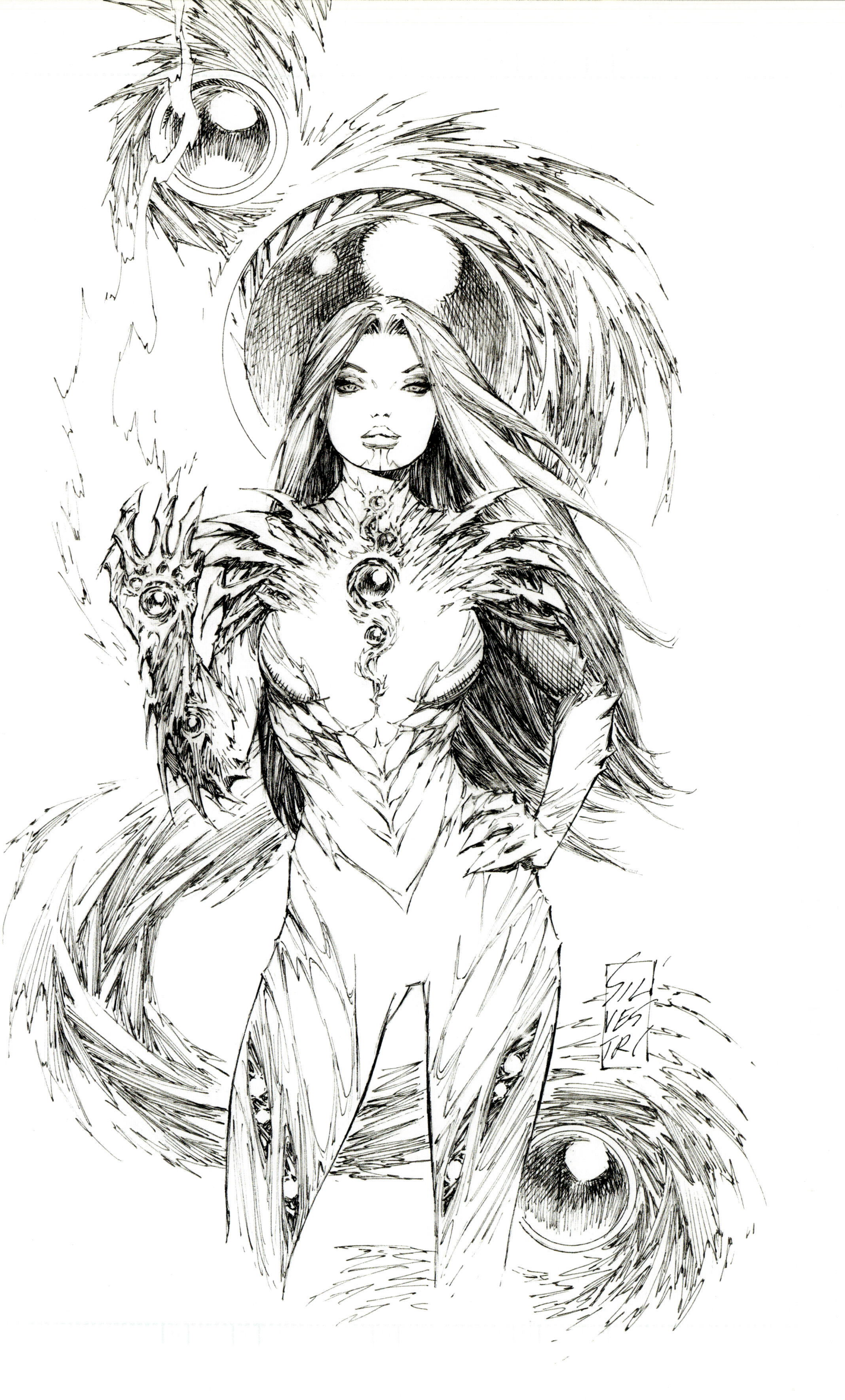

Witchblade #1 Kickstarter preview cover D,
line art by: Marc Silvestri

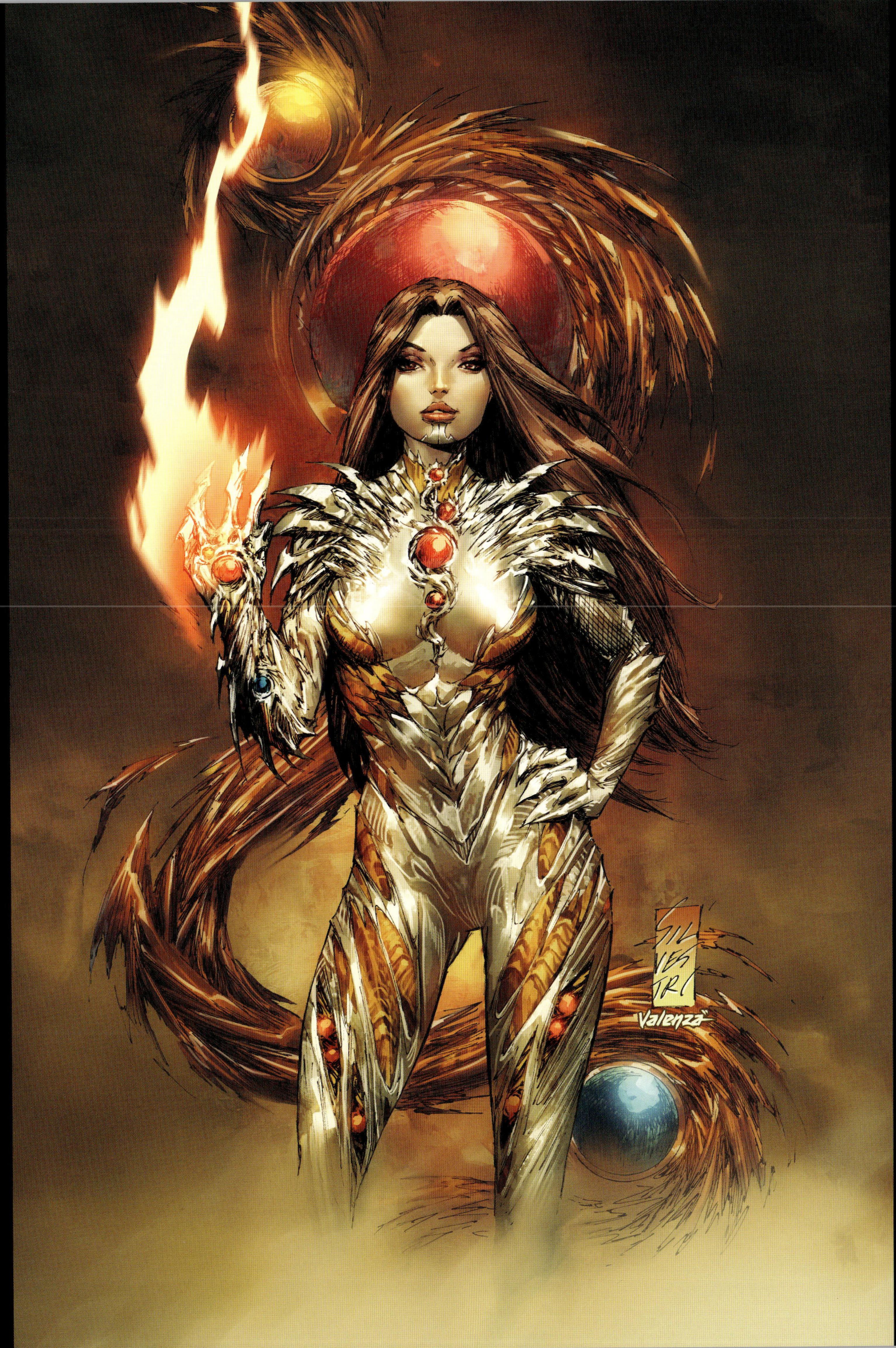

Witchblade #1, Kickstarter preview, cover C,
art by: Marc Silvestri and Bryan Valenza

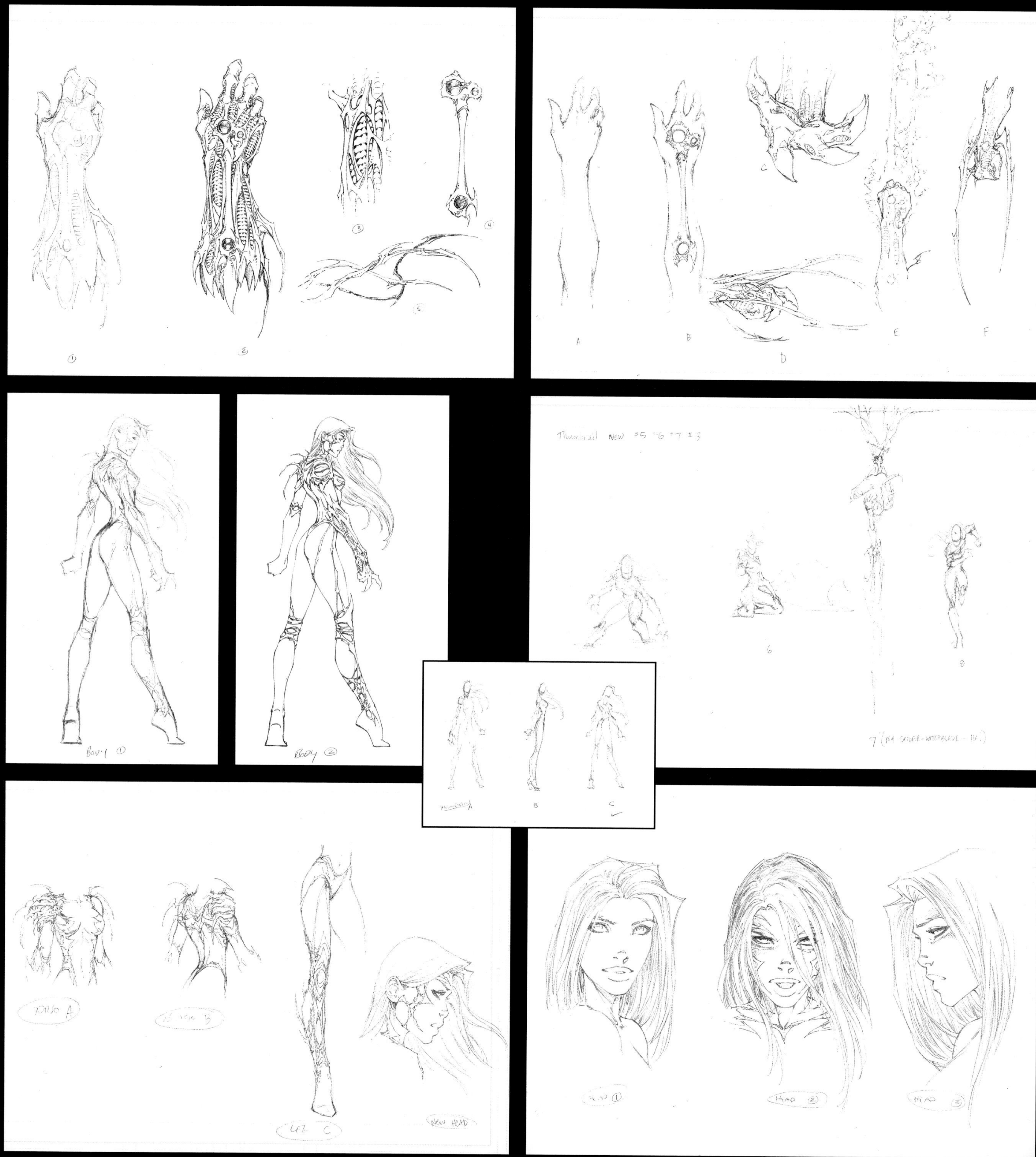

Above. Original sketches from *Wizard Witchblade Special* #1 [1998] "How to draw Witchblade by Michael Turner," art by: Michael Turner

In 1998, *The Wizard Witchblade Special* #1 [1998], featured a 6-page art tutorial on "How To Draw Witchblade" by **Michael Turner** himself! Special thanks to Top Cow supporter **Jens Schlicht** for sharing re-scans of the original art for this collection.

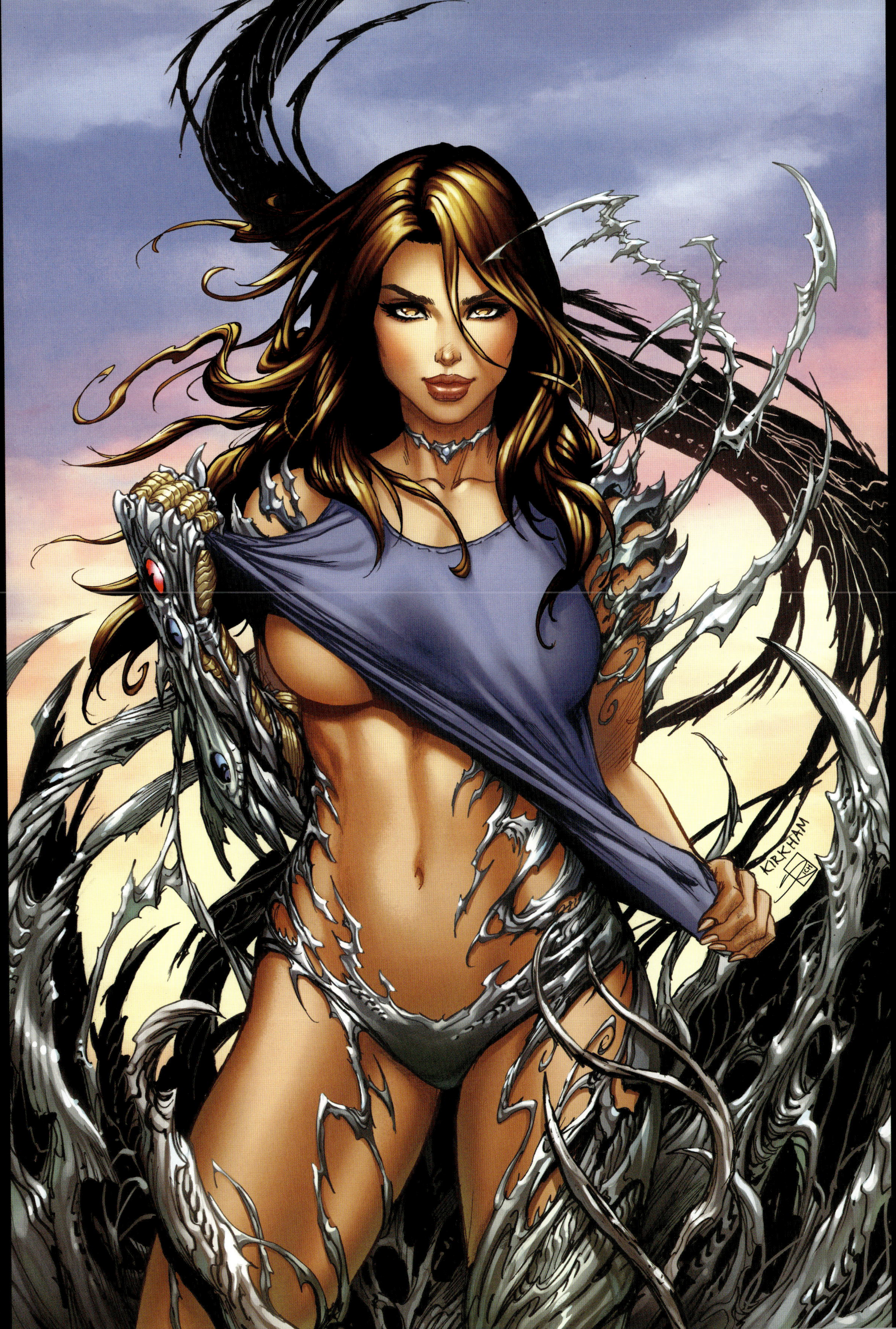

Witchblade issue #1, 25th Anniversary Top Cow Store Exclusive variant, art by: Tyler Kirkham and Sabine Rich

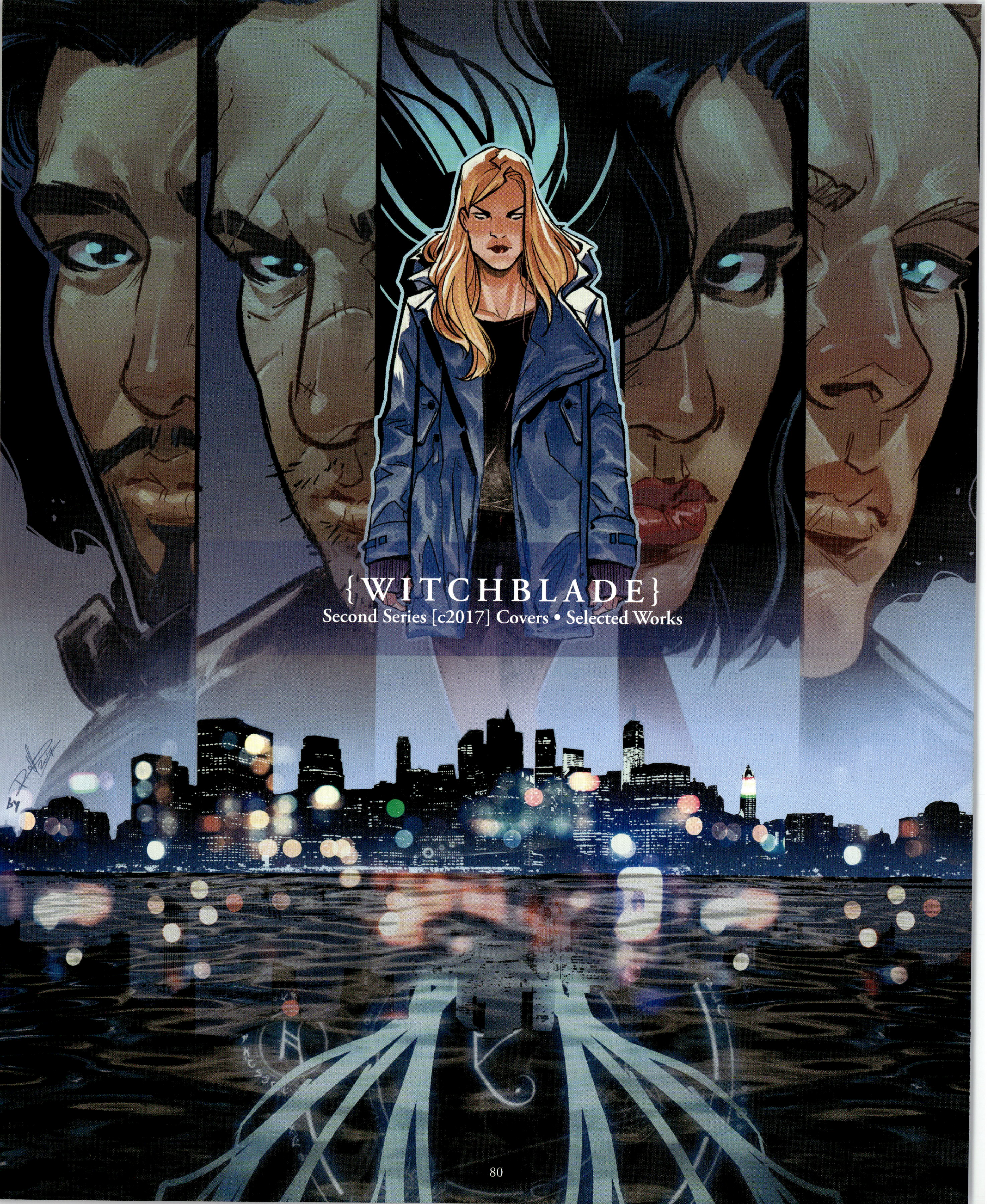

{WITCHBLADE}

Second Series [c2017] Covers • Selected Works

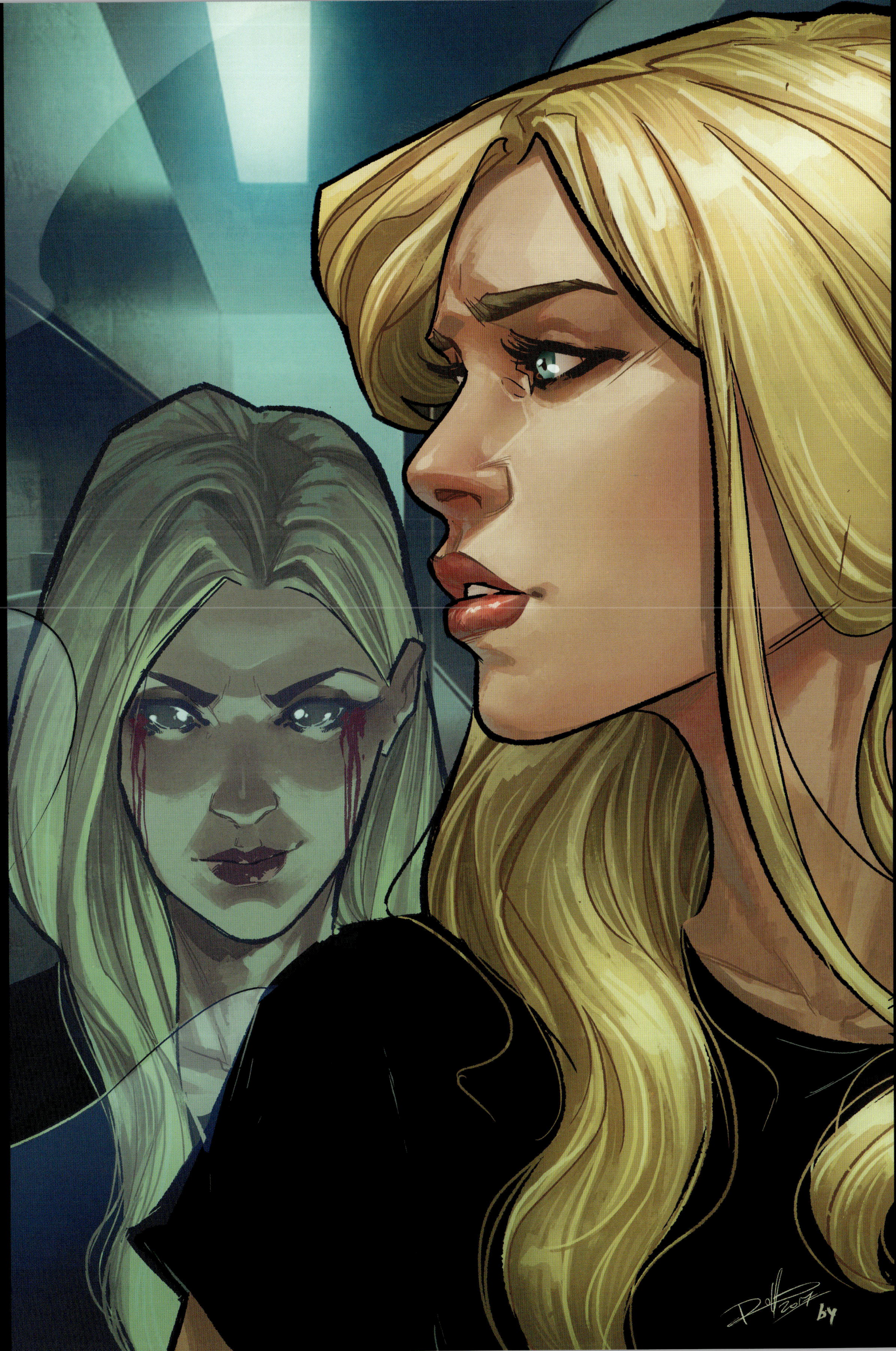

Witchblade #1 [2017] cover A,
art by: Roberta Ingranata and Bryan Valenza

Witchblade's second series was launched in 2017 with the stellar creative team of writer **CAITLIN KITTREDGE** and artist **ROBERTA INGRANATA**. Below is an excerpt from a behind-the-scenes interview by **BRITTANY MATTER**.

“Kittredge & Ingranata Raise Witchblade's Gauntlet
INTERVIEW BY **BRITTANY MATTER**

BRITTANY MATTER: After two years without *Witchblade* in circulation, and a 20-year history to live up to, how are you two pushing the legacy forward? What was it about this story that made both of you want to work on it?

CAITLIN KITTREDGE: I feel like we have a unique opportunity to offer a modern feminist take on the book, both by respecting the soul of the source material and by introducing a new set of characters and a new updated story that will appeal to Image's current audience. I'd read *Witchblade* on and off as a teenager, but I haven't kept up with the book as an adult, so I'm coming to it with totally fresh eyes.

It's pretty much everything I like in a comic—a flawed protagonist, mystical backdrop for the story, kick-ass worldbuilding, and a ton of directions to go as the project evolves. I've never worked on an established property before, just my creator-owned projects, and so it's a new frontier for me personally, and I'm looking forward to learning as I go.

ROBERTA INGRANATA: I'm a very big fan of *Witchblade*, so when I was called to draw it, I was shocked and completely overwhelmed. It's such an honor for me to work on this series for so many reasons. I read all of Caitlin's *Witchblade* pitches last year, and I've been falling in love with it since then. Caitlin is an amazing writer. I love her cinematic style and her great ability to convey characters' feelings. Her sensitivity made me say, “Yes! We're going to be a great team.”

BRITTANY: What can die-hard fans and newcomers look forward to? Will it pick up right after issue number 185?

CAITLIN: This *Witchblade* is a total reboot, with a new heroine, new continuity, and a new backstory for the Witchblade itself. Basically, the previous volume is Patrick Stewart's *Star Trek*, and our book is J.J. Abrams's *Star Trek*. It's the same source material but a totally new take on the interpretation. I had a really great experience reworking the existing world to fit in with our new cast and the story we're telling.[3] ”

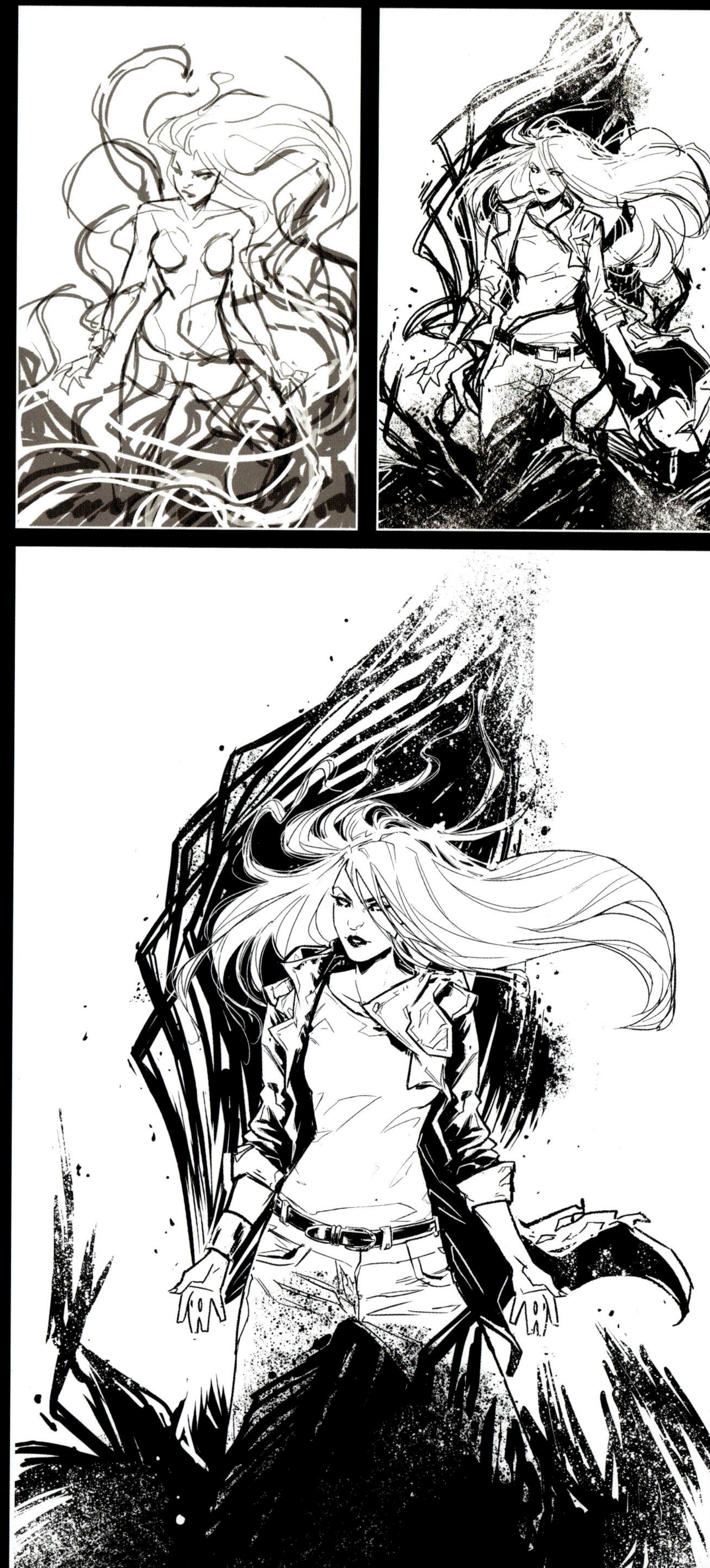

Above. *Witchblade* #2 [2017] cover A, thumbnail to line art process, art by: Roberta Ingranata

3 Matter, Brittany. “Kittredge and Ingranata Raise Witchblade's Gauntlet,” in *Witchblade* #1 [2017] (December 6, 2017): 28-31.

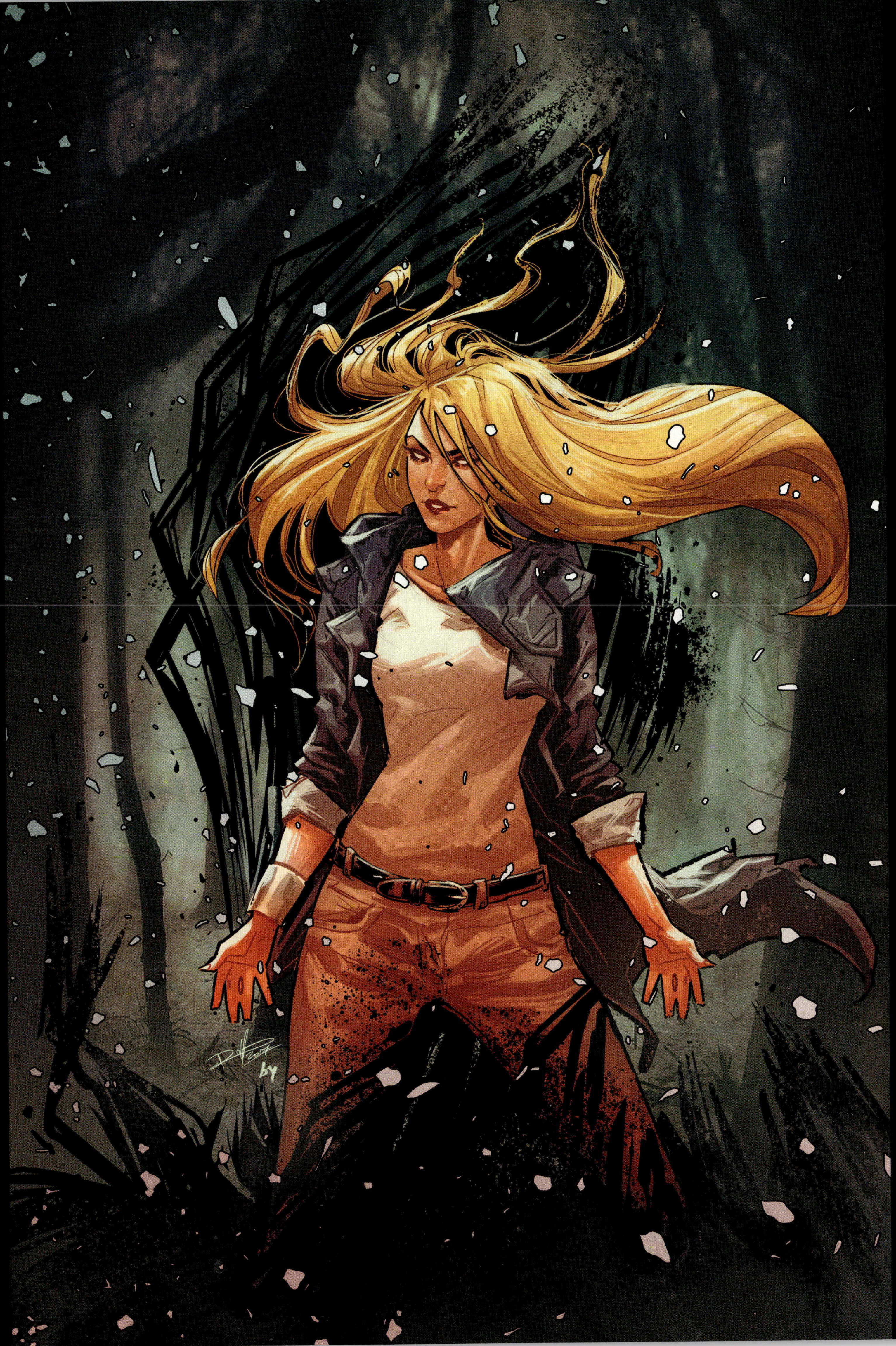

Witchblade #2 [2017] cover A,
art by: Roberta Ingranata and Bryan Valenza

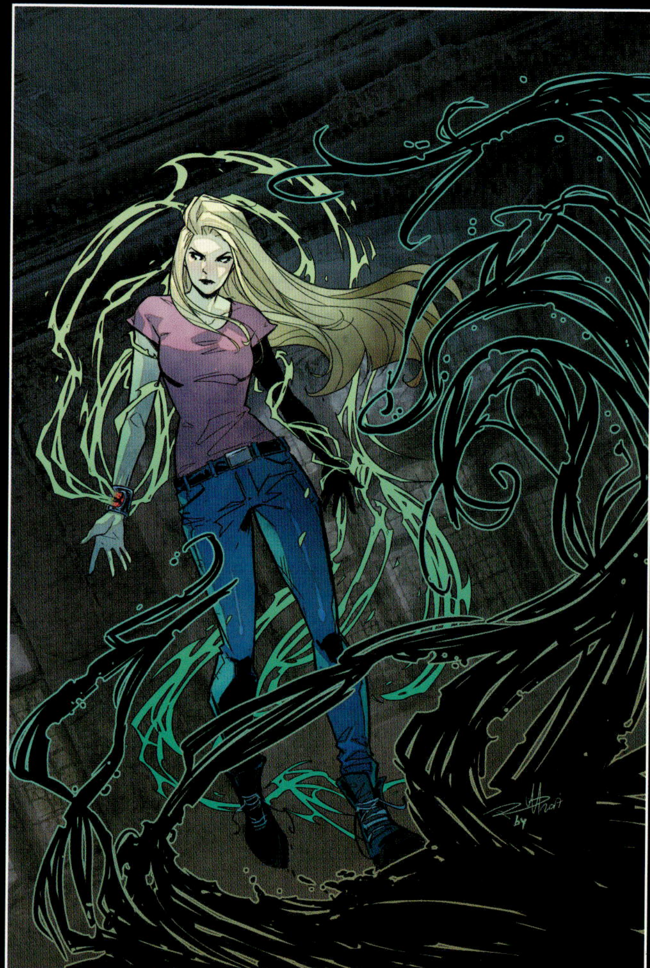

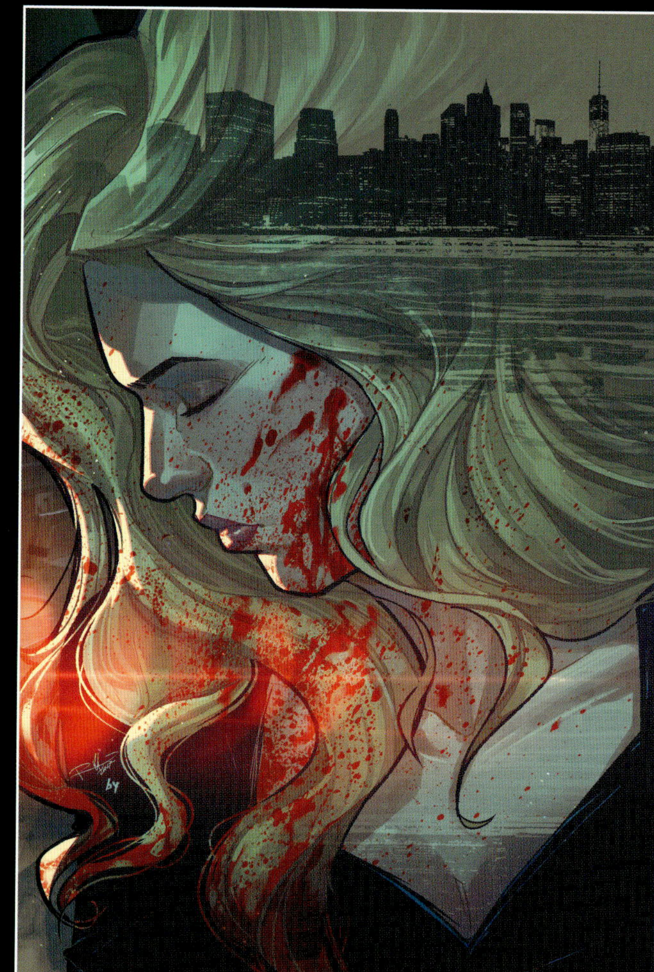

Far left. *Witchblade* #3 [2017] cover A,
art by: Roberta Ingranata and Bryan Valenza

At left. *Witchblade* #4 [2017] cover A,
art by: Roberta Ingranata and Bryan Valenza

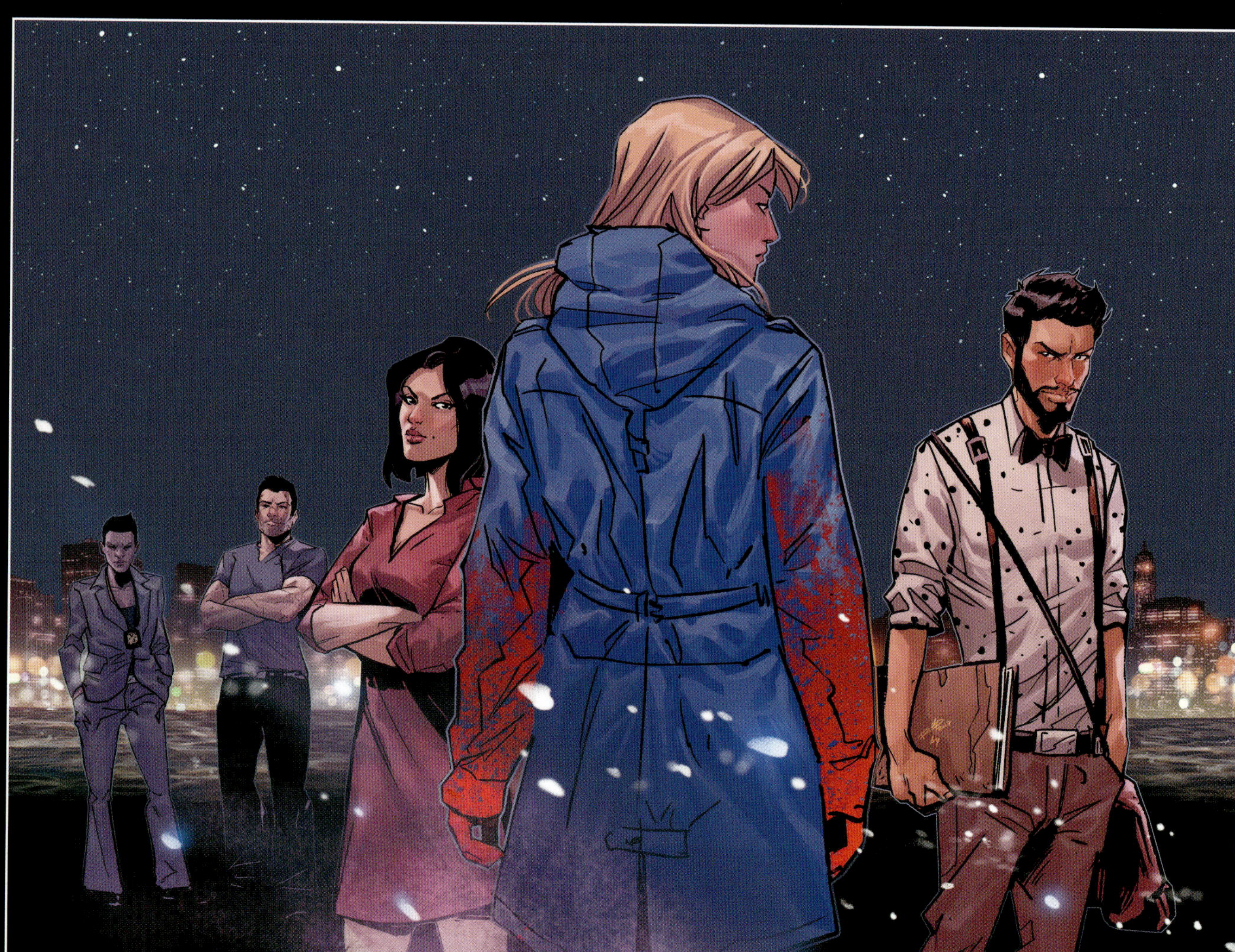

At left. *Witchblade* #4 [2017] cover B,
art by: Roberta Ingranata and Bryan Valenza

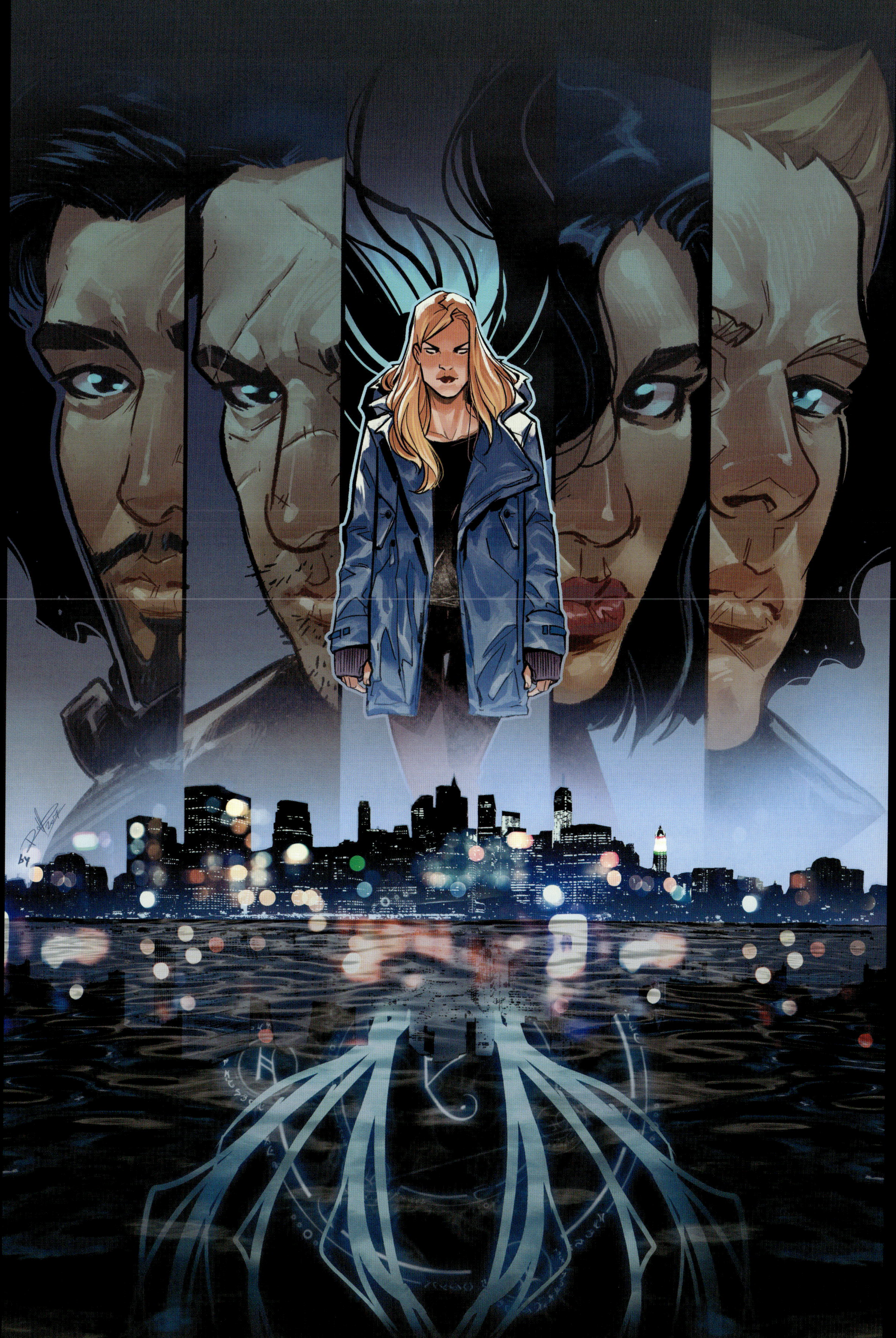

Witchblade #5 [2017] cover A,
art by: Roberta Ingranata and Bryan Valenza

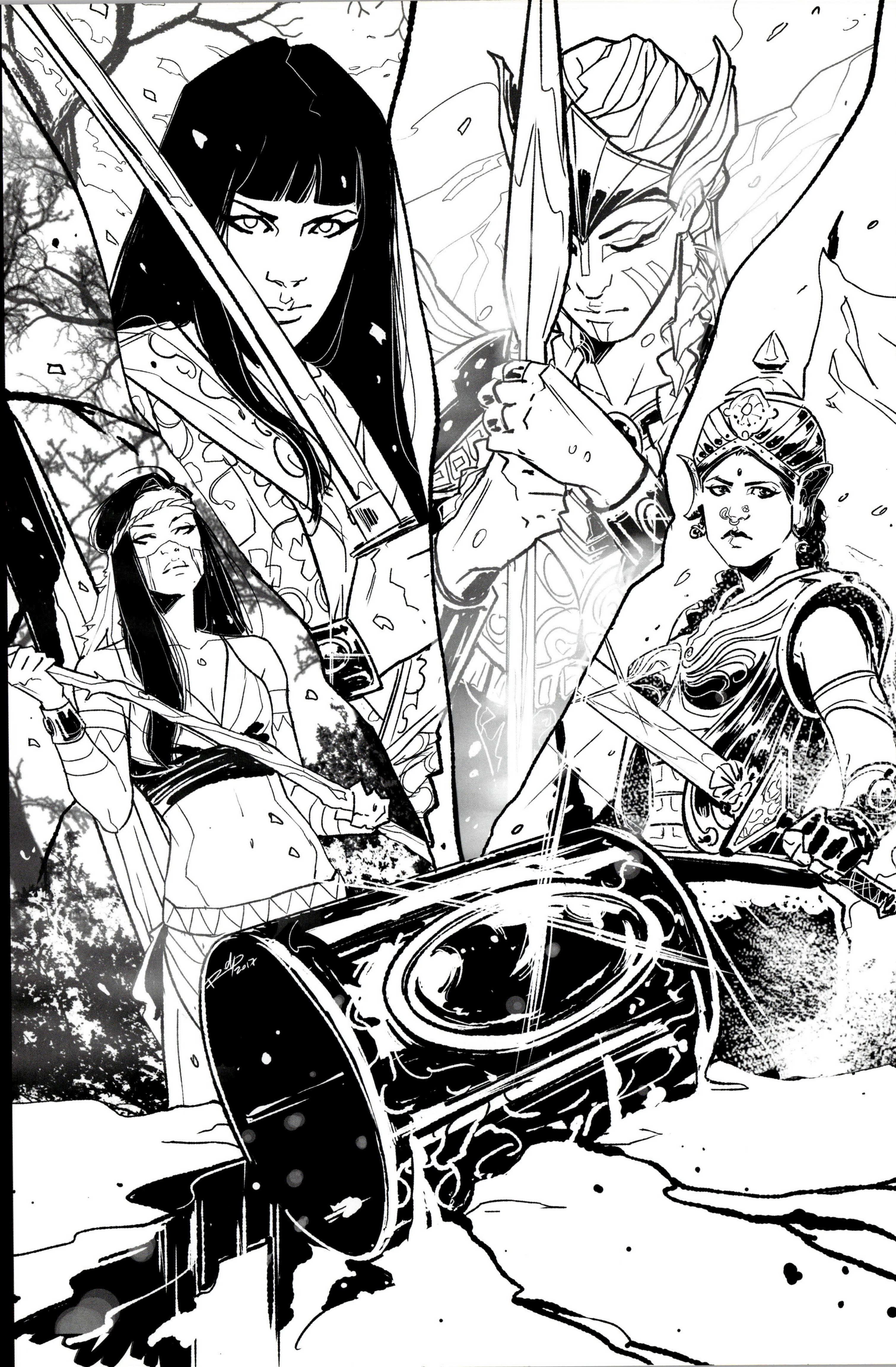

Witchblade #6 [2017] cover,
line art by: Roberta Ingranata

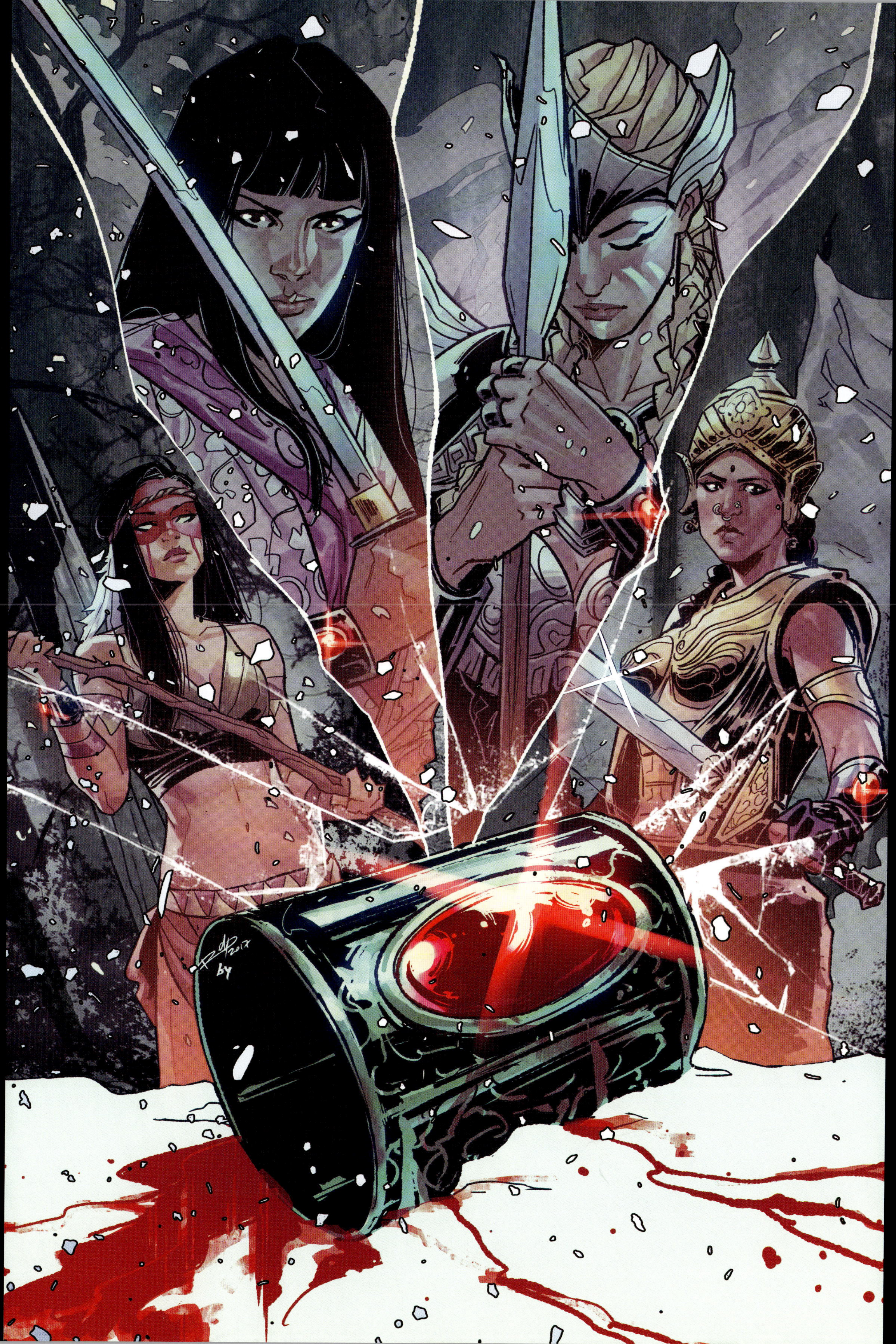

Witchblade #6 [2017] cover,
art by: Roberta Ingranata and Bryan Valenza

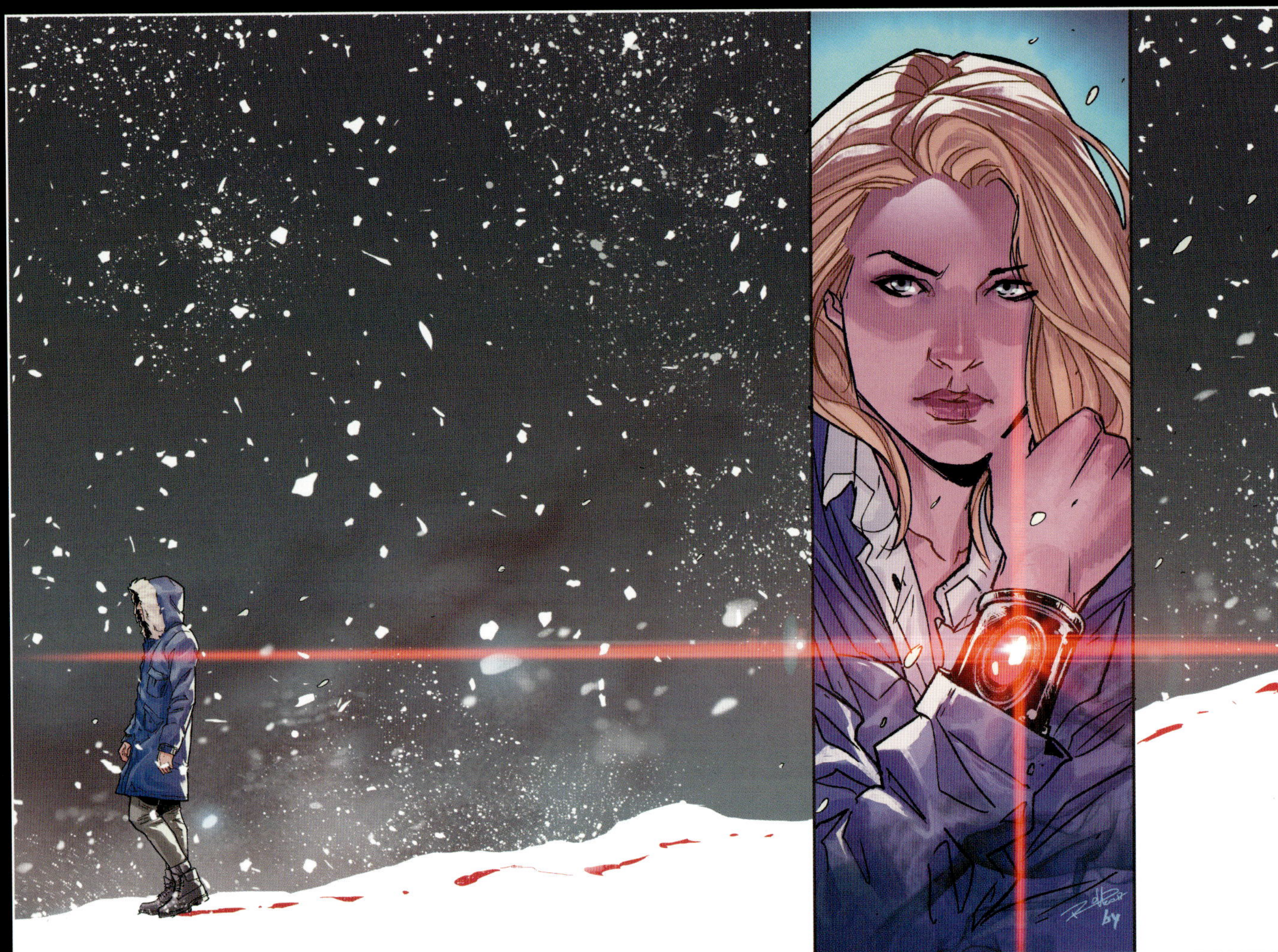

At left. *Witchblade* #7 [2017] cover,
art by: Roberta Ingranata and Bryan Valenza

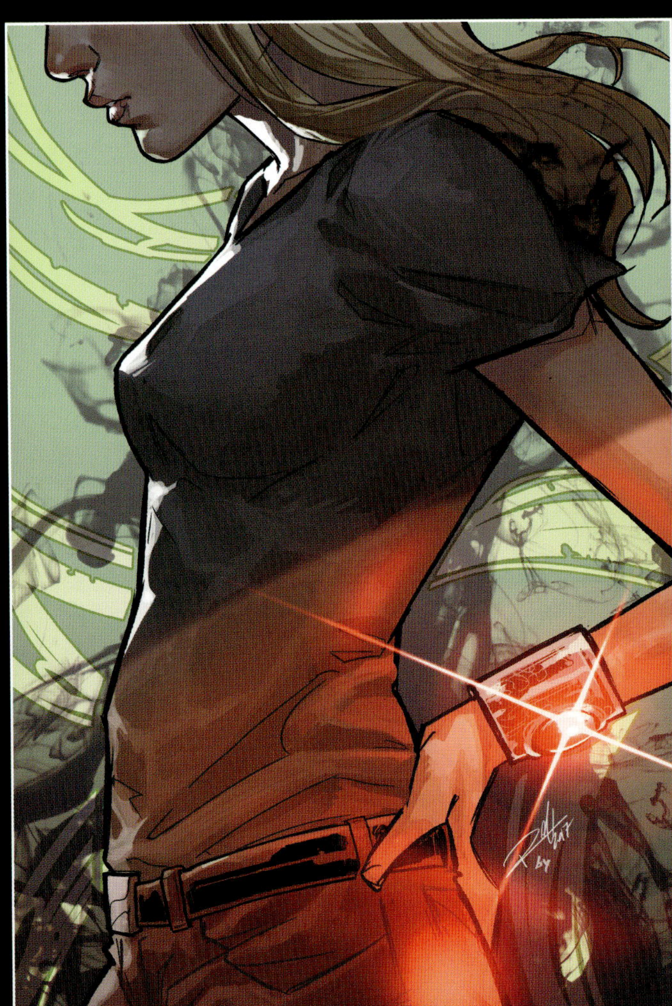

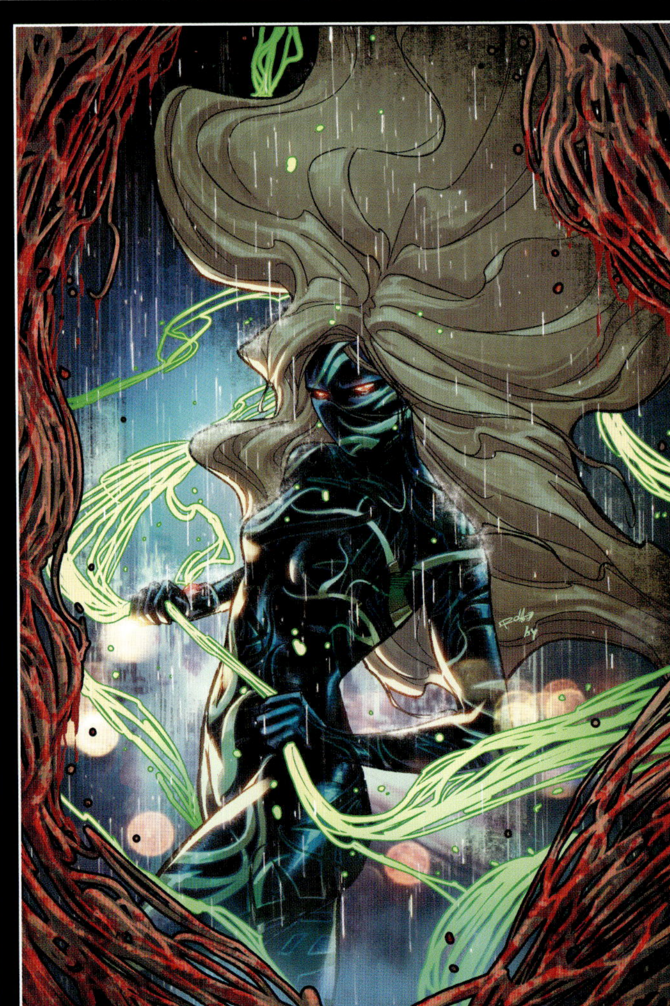

Far left. *Witchblade* #8 [2017] cover,
art by: Roberta Ingranata and Bryan Valenza

At left. *Witchblade* #9 [2017] cover,
art by: Roberta Ingranata and Bryan Valenza

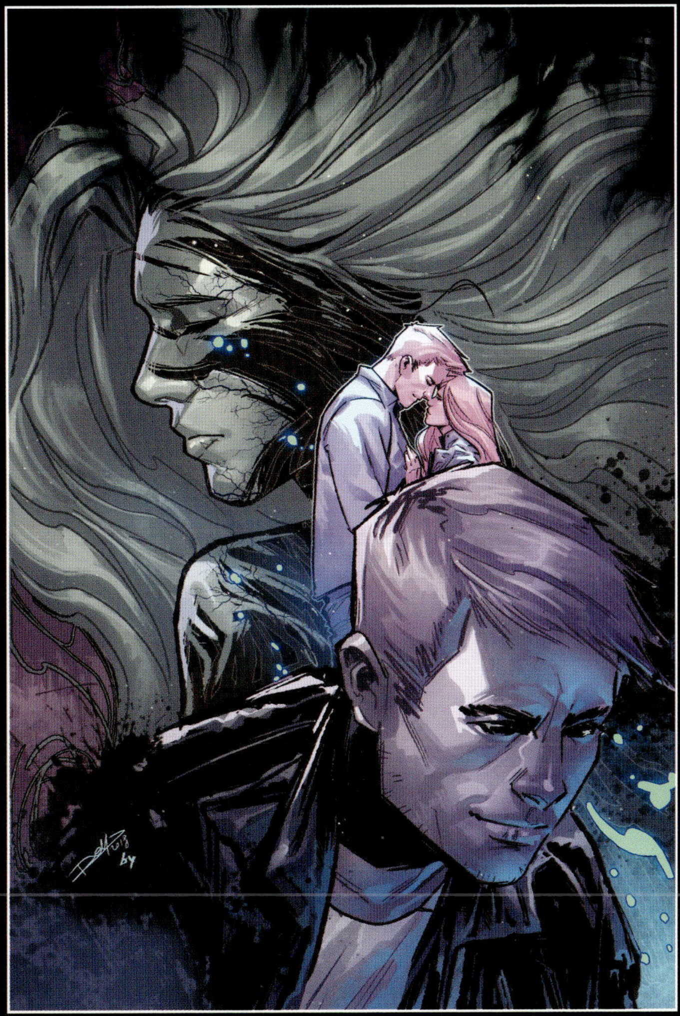

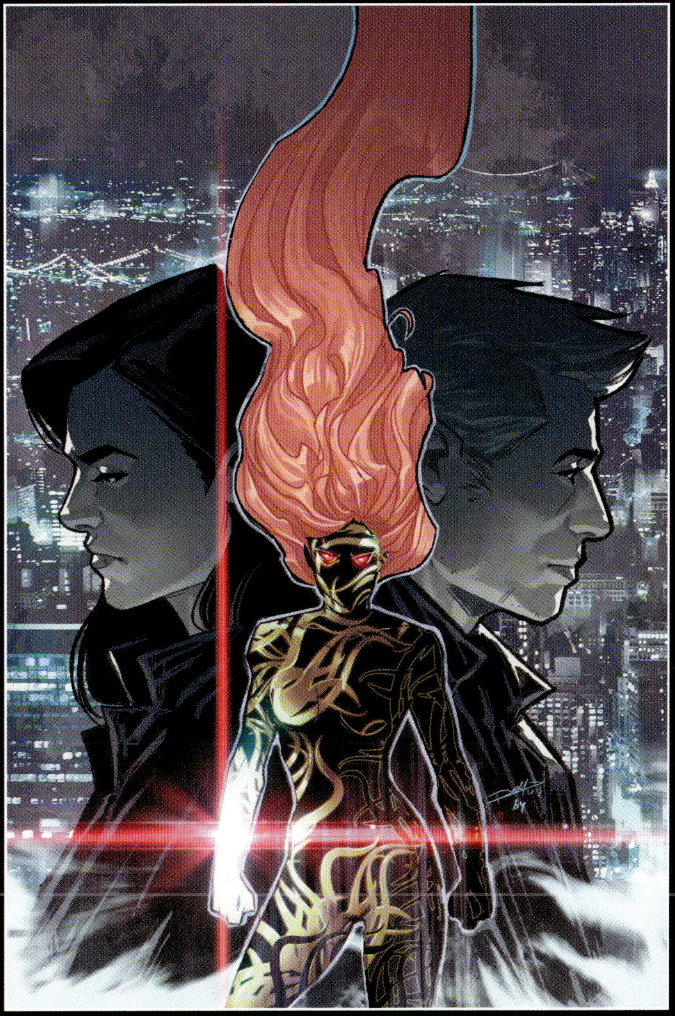

At right. *Witchblade* #10 [2017] cover,
art by: Roberta Ingranata and Bryan Valenza

Far right. *Witchblade* #11 [2017] cover,
art by: Roberta Ingranata and Bryan Valenza

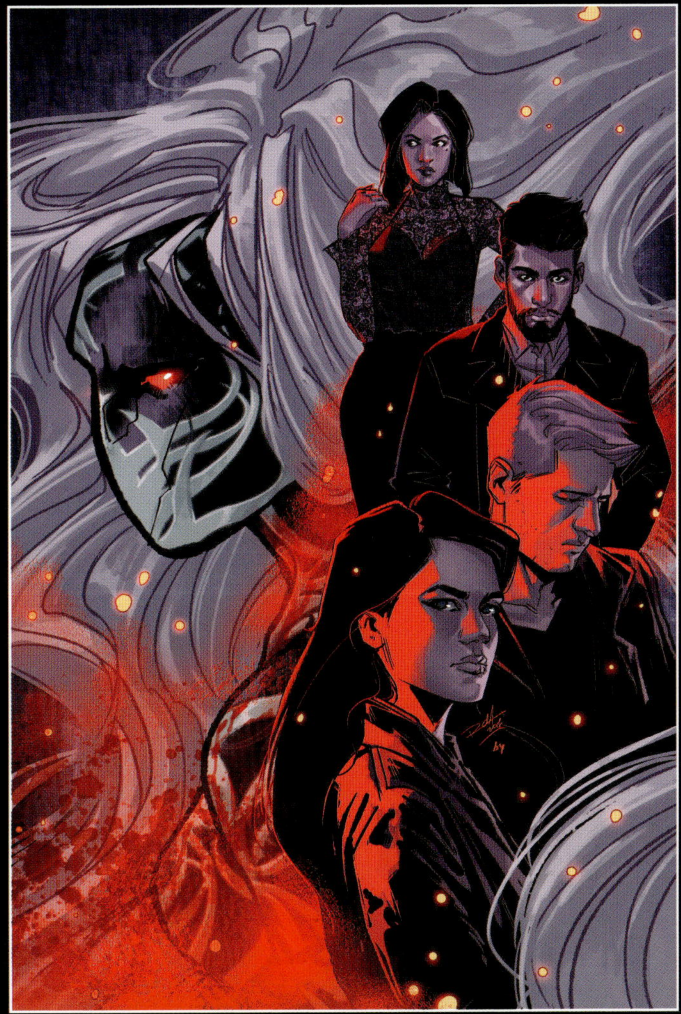

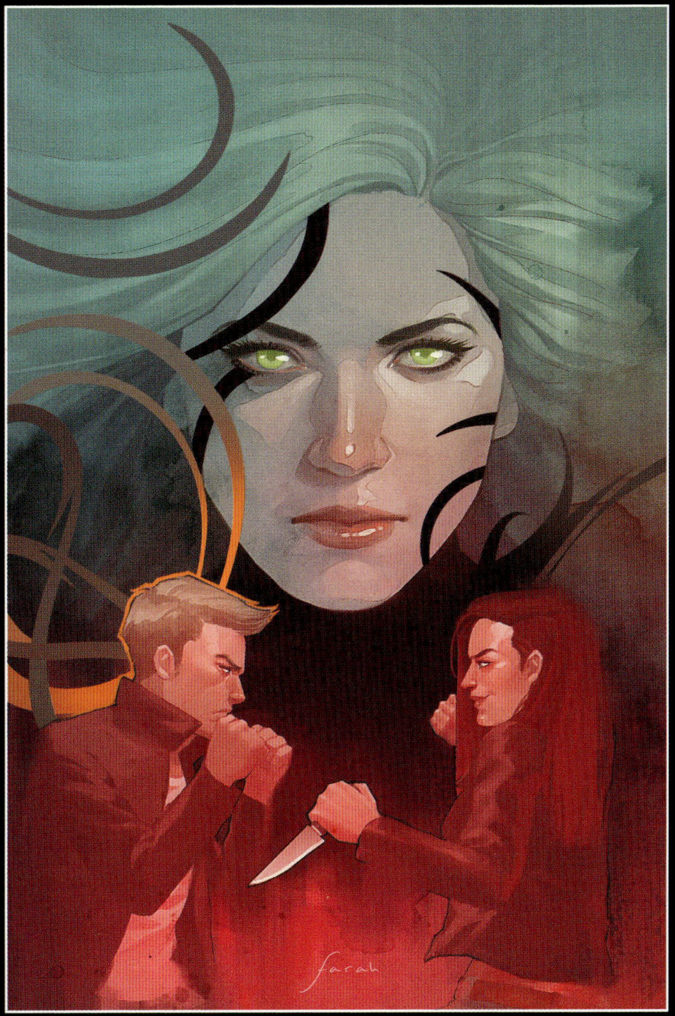

At right. *Witchblade* #12 [2017] cover A,
art by: Roberta Ingranata and Bryan Valenza

Far right. *Witchblade* #12 [2017] cover B,
art by: Farah Nurmaliza

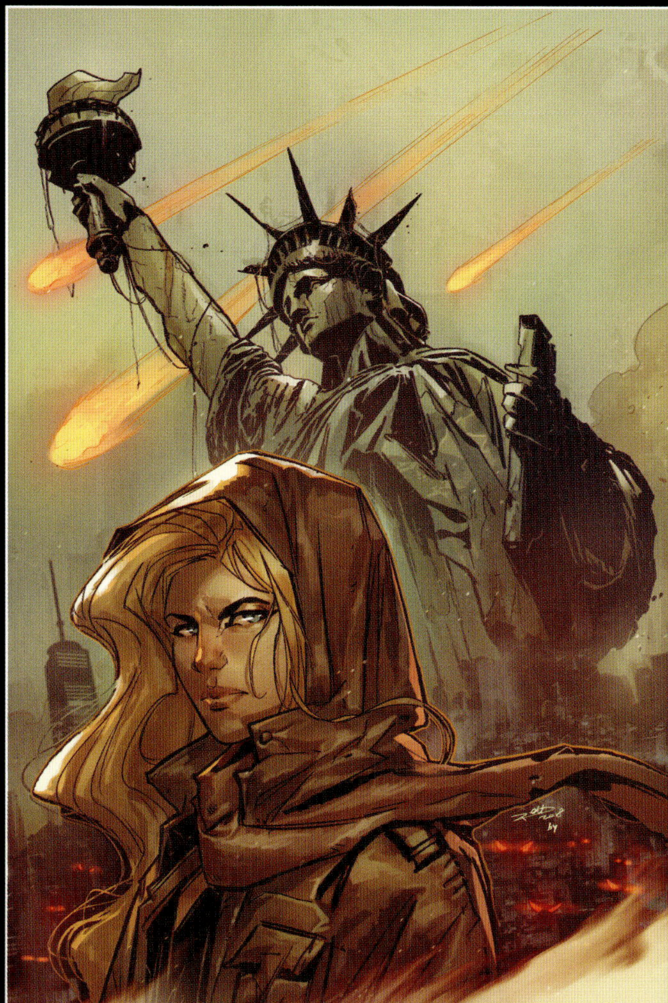

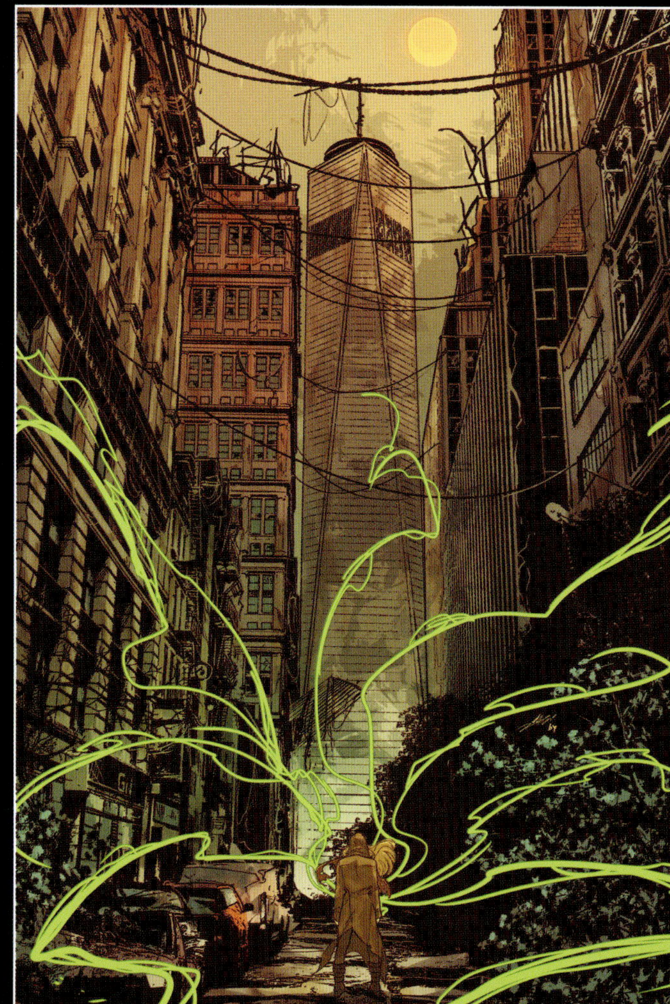

Far left. *Witchblade* #13 [2017] cover, art by: Roberta Ingranata and Bryan Valenza

At left. *Witchblade* #14 [2017] cover, art by: Roberta Ingranata and Bryan Valenza

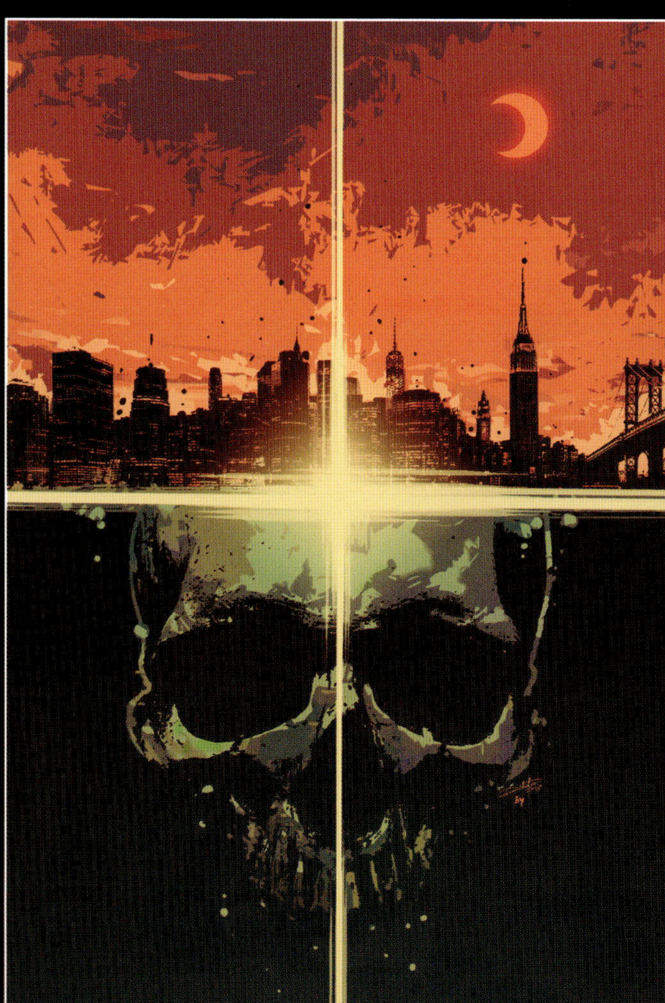

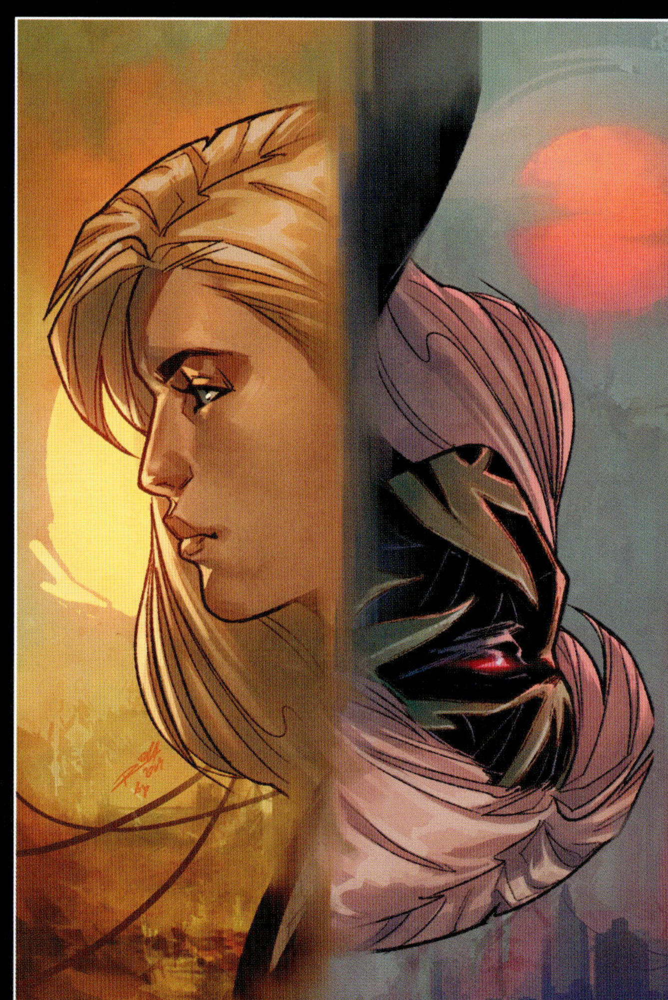

Far left. *Witchblade* #15 [2017] cover, art by: Roberta Ingranata and Bryan Valenza

At left. *Witchblade* #16 [2017] cover, art by: Roberta Ingranata and Bryan Valenza

" **BRITTANY:** The story is still set in New York City, which holds true to the urban fantasy that *Witchblade* embodies. What is it about the city that makes it a fertile setting? What is it about the Witchblade and New York in particular that works for you?

CAITLIN: You kind of have to have New York City if you have the *Witchblade*. It's such a versatile and moody backdrop for a story with thick overtones of the supernatural like this one. The first story takes place in the dead of winter, so Roberta had a chance to draw these amazing, David Fincher-esque cityscapes with snow and shadows that embody the gothic feel of the setting perfectly.

ROBERTA: New York is an amazing city. Everyone has seen it in photos, in movies, on television shows. Everybody knows New York, even those who don't live there (Italians like me!). I visited it two years ago for New York Comic Con. When I walked for the first time in New York City, it was like seeing an old friend. I felt at home, like Hiro from *Heroes*, and his famous "YATTA!" in Times Square!

I believe that anyone can see themselves in this city, and that makes everything more realistic.

BRITTANY: Roberta, are you doing a down-to-earth, realistic take on the lore or something more fantastic? How are you approaching the setting and defining *Witchblade* for a new era?

ROBERTA: I think that this *Witchblade* is more realistic, with fantastic events inside it, but mostly realistic. The real-life city, apartments, offices, and all the environments are analyzed to be reproduced in the best possible way. If I need to draw a new place (a shop, a nightclub, a restaurant), I look on Google Maps to identify where it is and how to get there, locate the nearest subway, and design it exactly according to that path. Fans can follow Alex's itinerary in every issue if they want to!

BRITTANY: Top Cow has a reputation for stellar art dating back to the early Marc Silvestri days. What kinds of flourishes or storytelling techniques are y'all incorporating?

CAITLIN: I love writing comics because I can use shifting timelines, much like you would in an episodic TV show, to fill in and flesh out the main story. I deliberately tried to evoke a dreamlike, slightly unreal feeling in the first scripts to echo what Alex is going through, suddenly finding herself host to this mystical entity. There are a lot of visions, dreams, hallucinations, and flashes to the past. Everything blends together perfectly in the first two issues—I can't sing Roberta's praises enough.

ROBERTA: I can say that working on a Silvestri creation is a great honor and a great responsibility for me. We'll do our best to make it right![4] "

4 Matter, "Kittredge and Ingranata," 31.

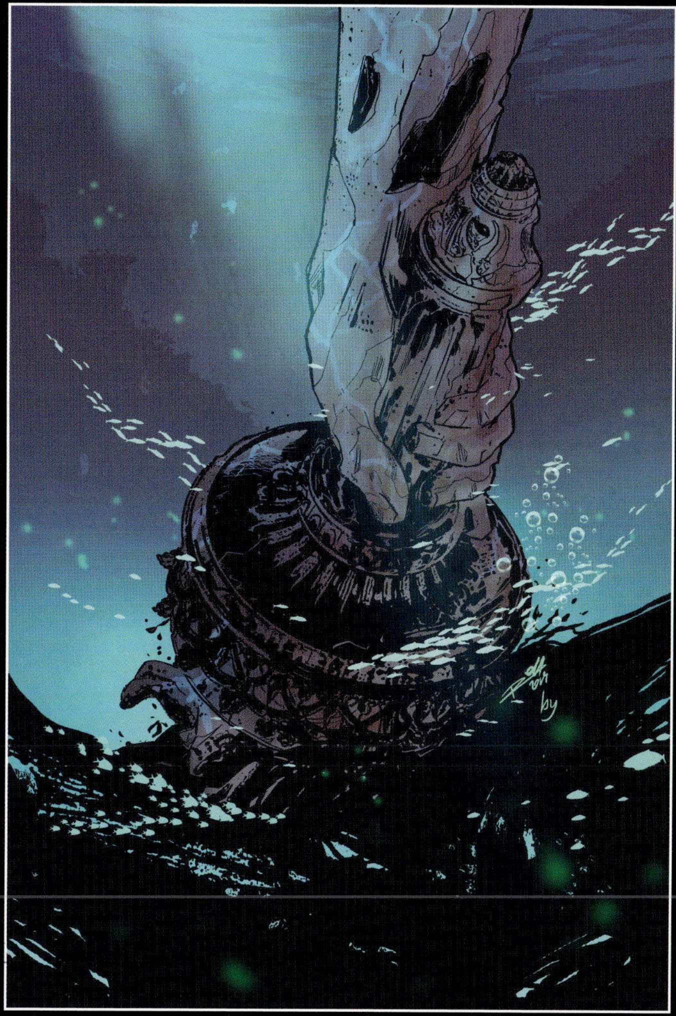

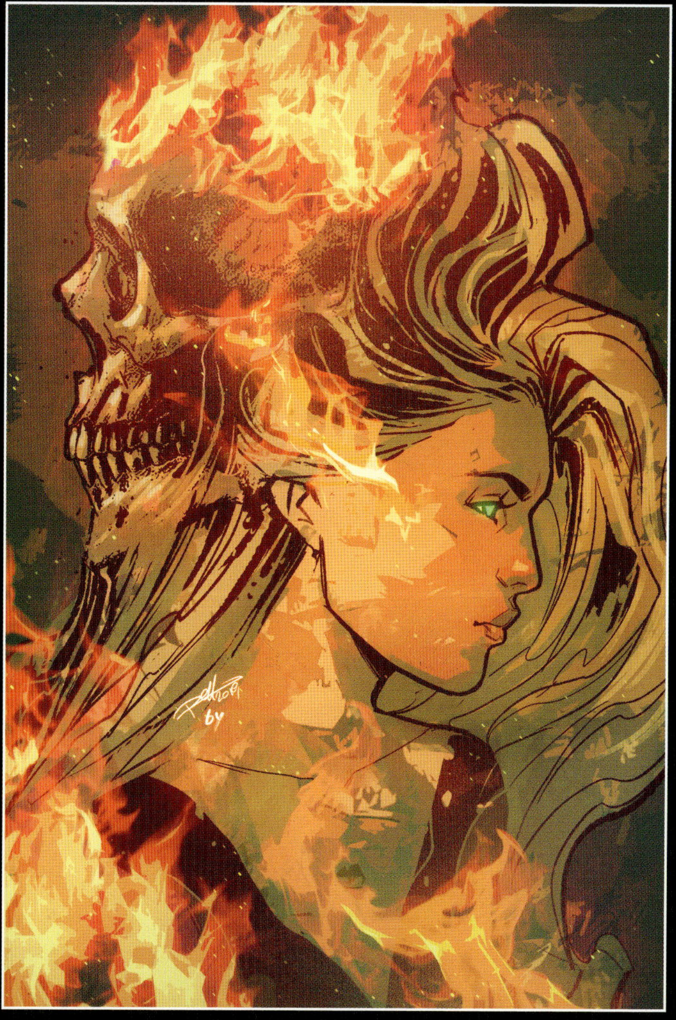

Above right. *Witchblade* #17 [2017] cover, art by: Roberta Ingranata and Bryan Valenza

At right. *Witchblade* #18 [2017] cover, art by: Roberta Ingranata and Bryan Valenza

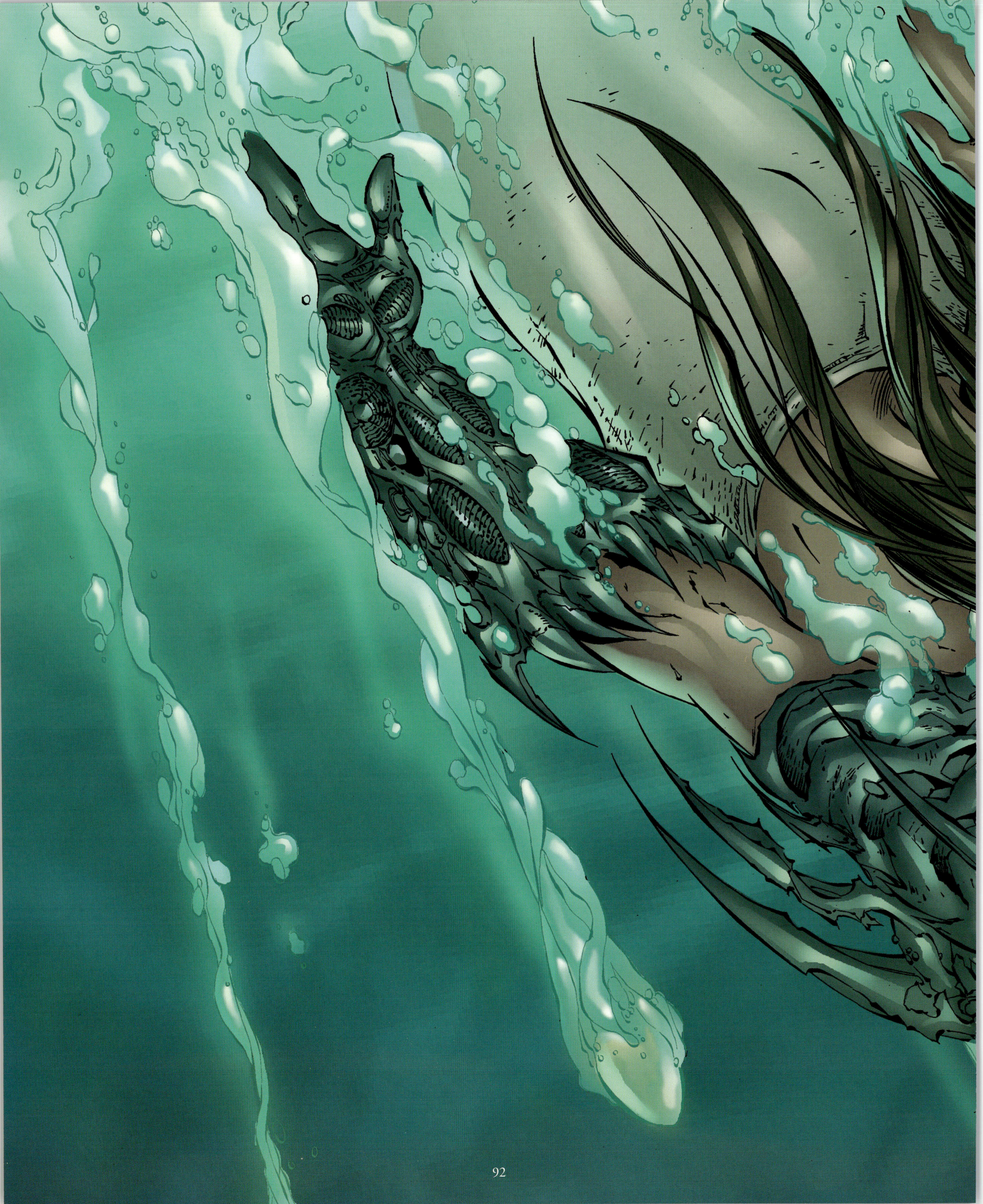

{WITCHBLADE}

First Series [c1995] Covers • Selected Works

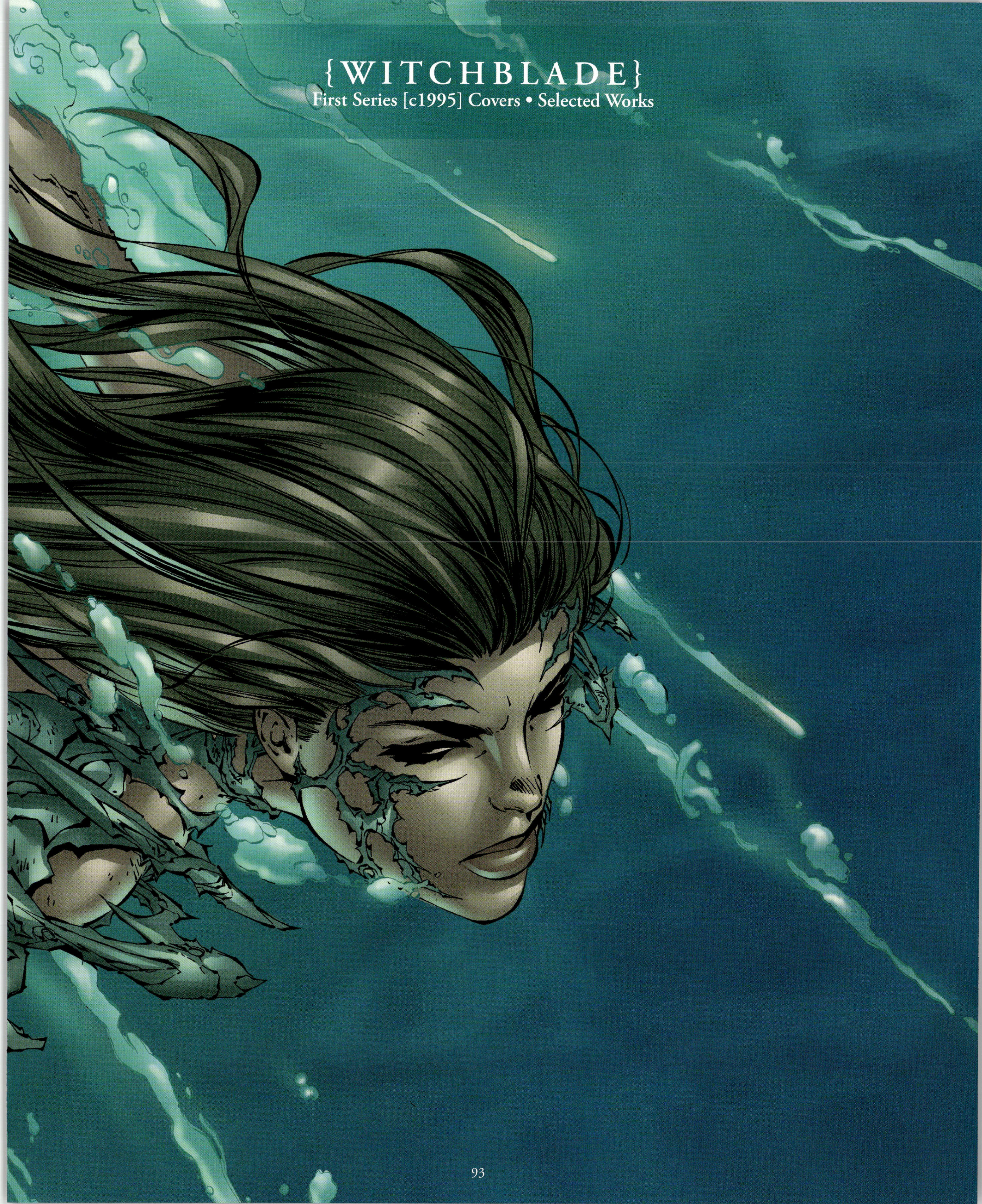

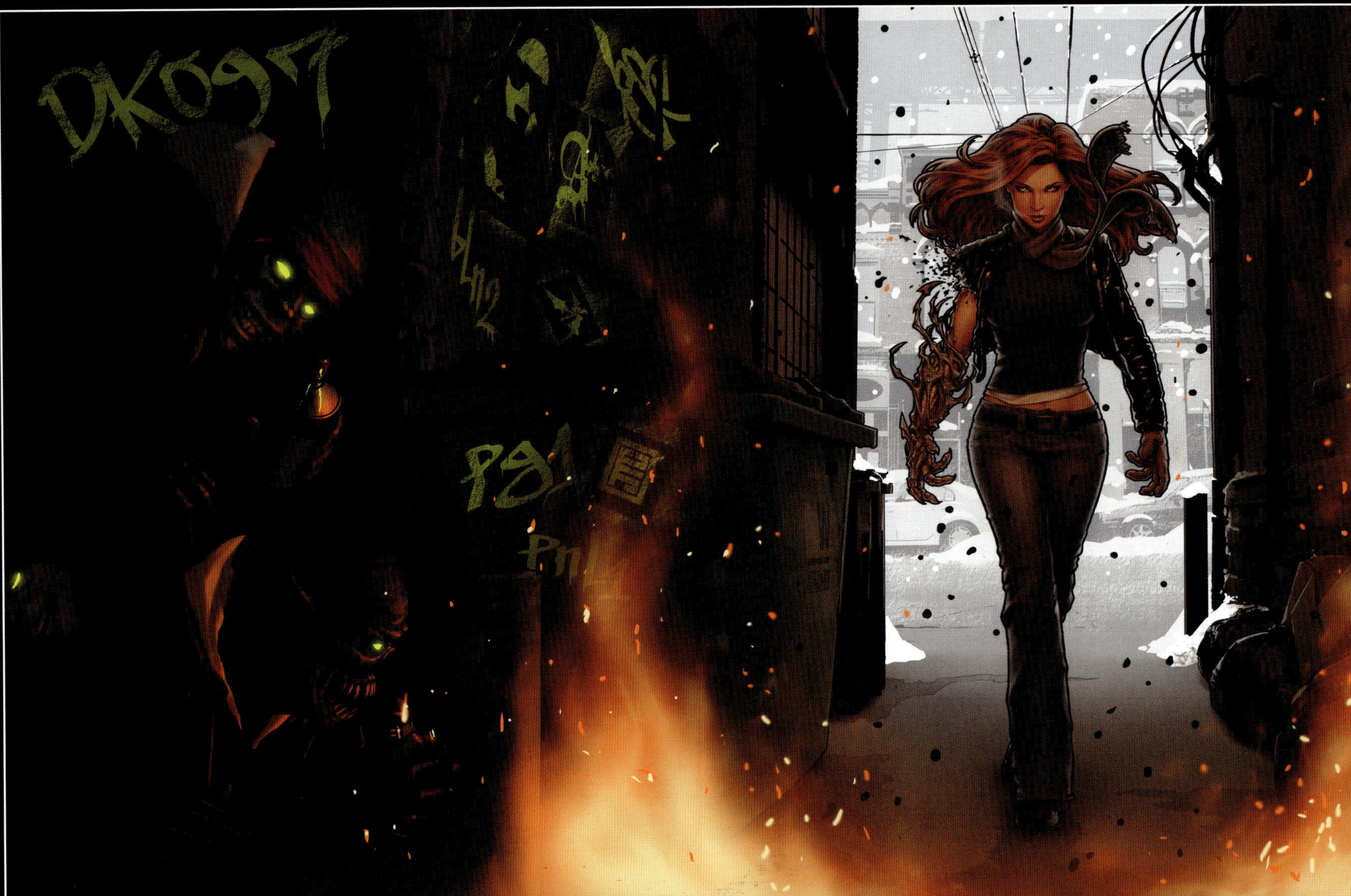

The Art of Top Cow [2009] included works up to the landmark *Witchblade* #129 and some preliminary artwork leading into the massive conclusion to the storyline, "The War of the Witchblades." It also included associated works from the *Witchblade: Anime* series, *Witchblade: Takeru* manga, *Tales of the Witchblade* and more.

In 2015 a deluxe hardcover book, *The Art of Witchblade, 20th Anniversary Edition*, celebrated the series anniversary and collected artwork up to the series finale with issue #185.

Following in the footsteps of artists like Michael Turner, Keu Cha, Francis Manapul, and many more, the series expanded the *Witchblade* legacy from #130 onward with superstar artists like Stjepan Sejic, John Tyler Christopher, Laura Braga, Diego Bernard, and more.

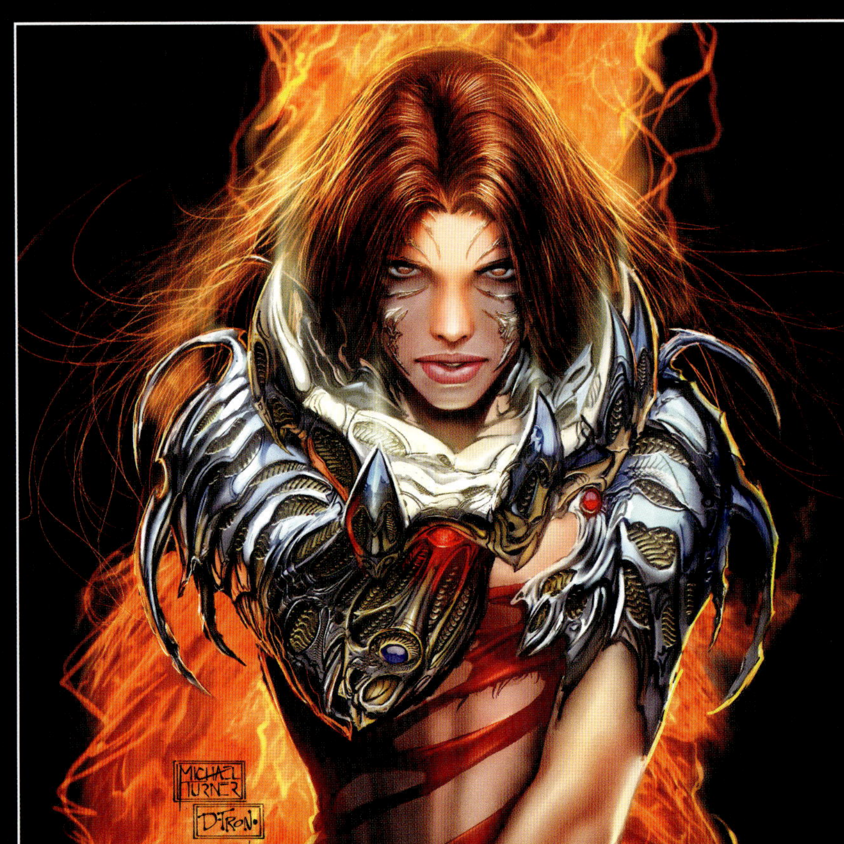

NOTE. On the following pages, *Witchblade* may be abbreviated to [WB] for various citations. - T.C.T.

Above. *Witchblade* #151 cover A, art by: John Tyler Christopher

Ar right. *The Art of Witchblade* [2008] cover, art by: Michael Turner and Stjepan Sejic

Previous page. *Witchblade* issue #3 pages 17-18, art by: Michael Turner, D-Tron and Jonathan D. Smith

On the following pages, please enjoy selected works that show the series' evolution and a few classic images from the Top Cow library.

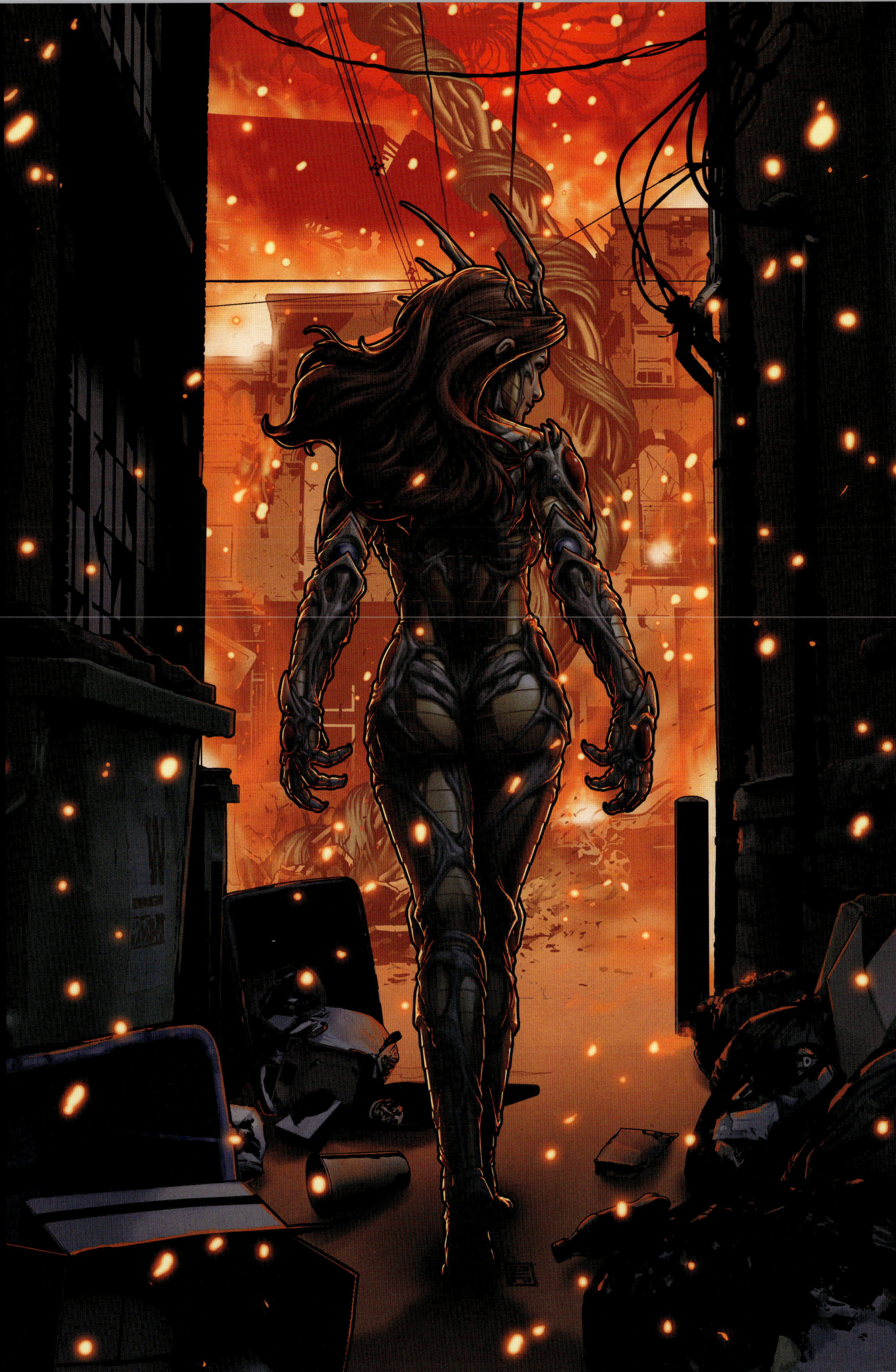

Witchblade #169 cover A,
art by: John Tyler Christopher

Below. WB #130 cover

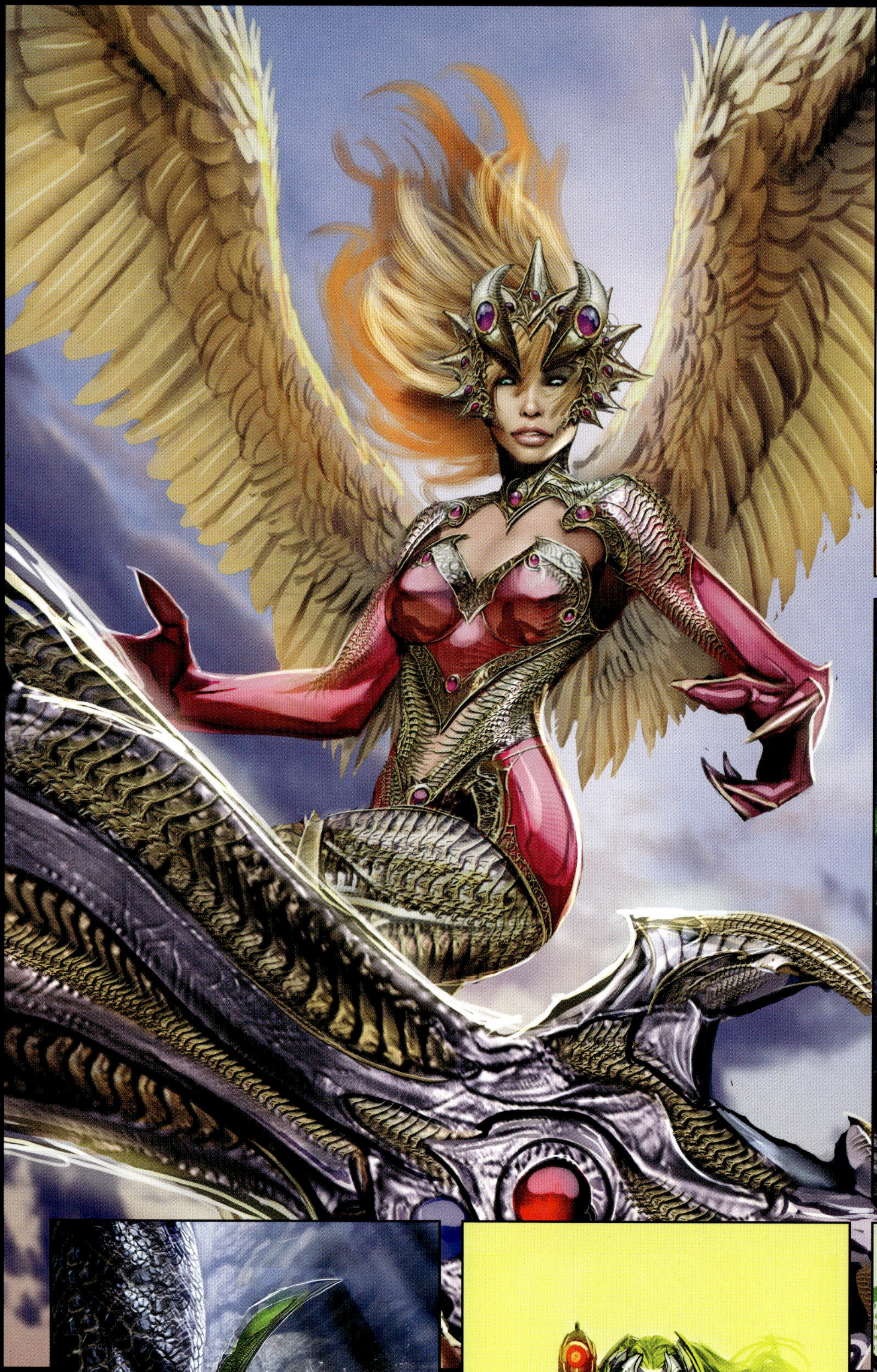

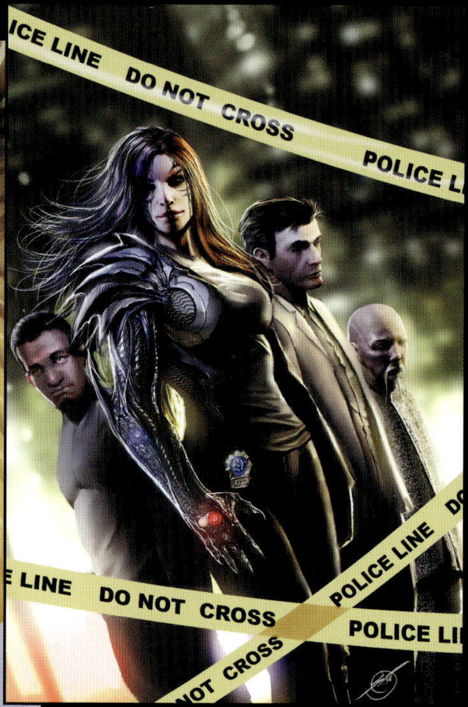

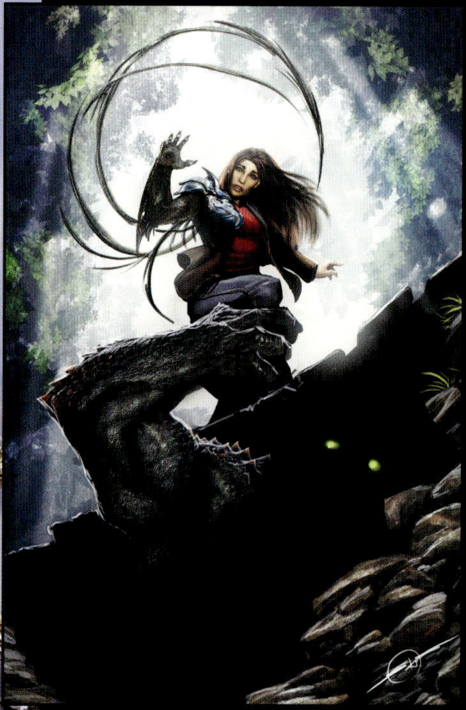

Witchblade #130-135 cover A's,
art by: Stjepan Sejic

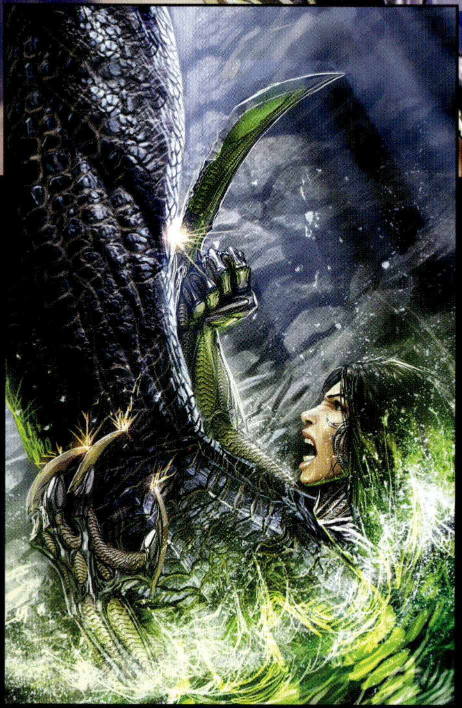

Above. WB #133 cover

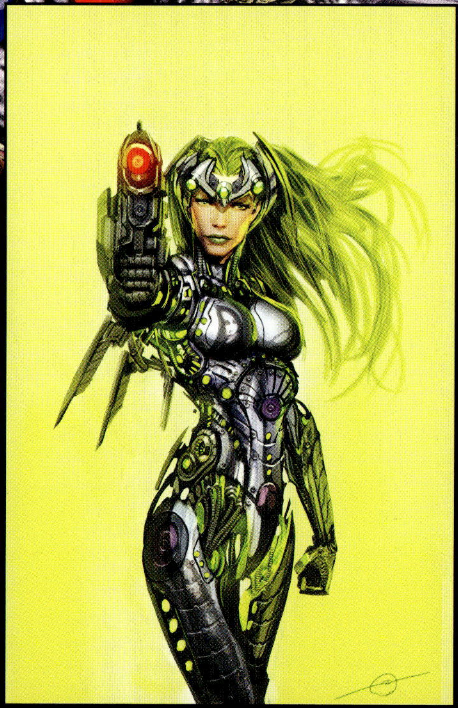

Above. WB #134 cover

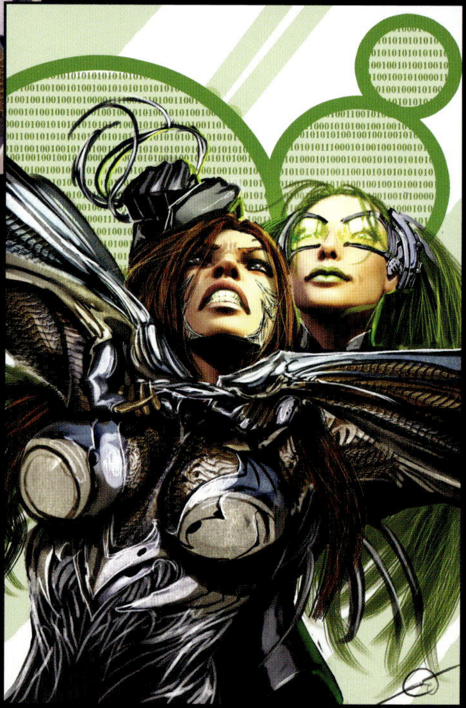

From the top, this row. WB #131, 132 and 135 covers

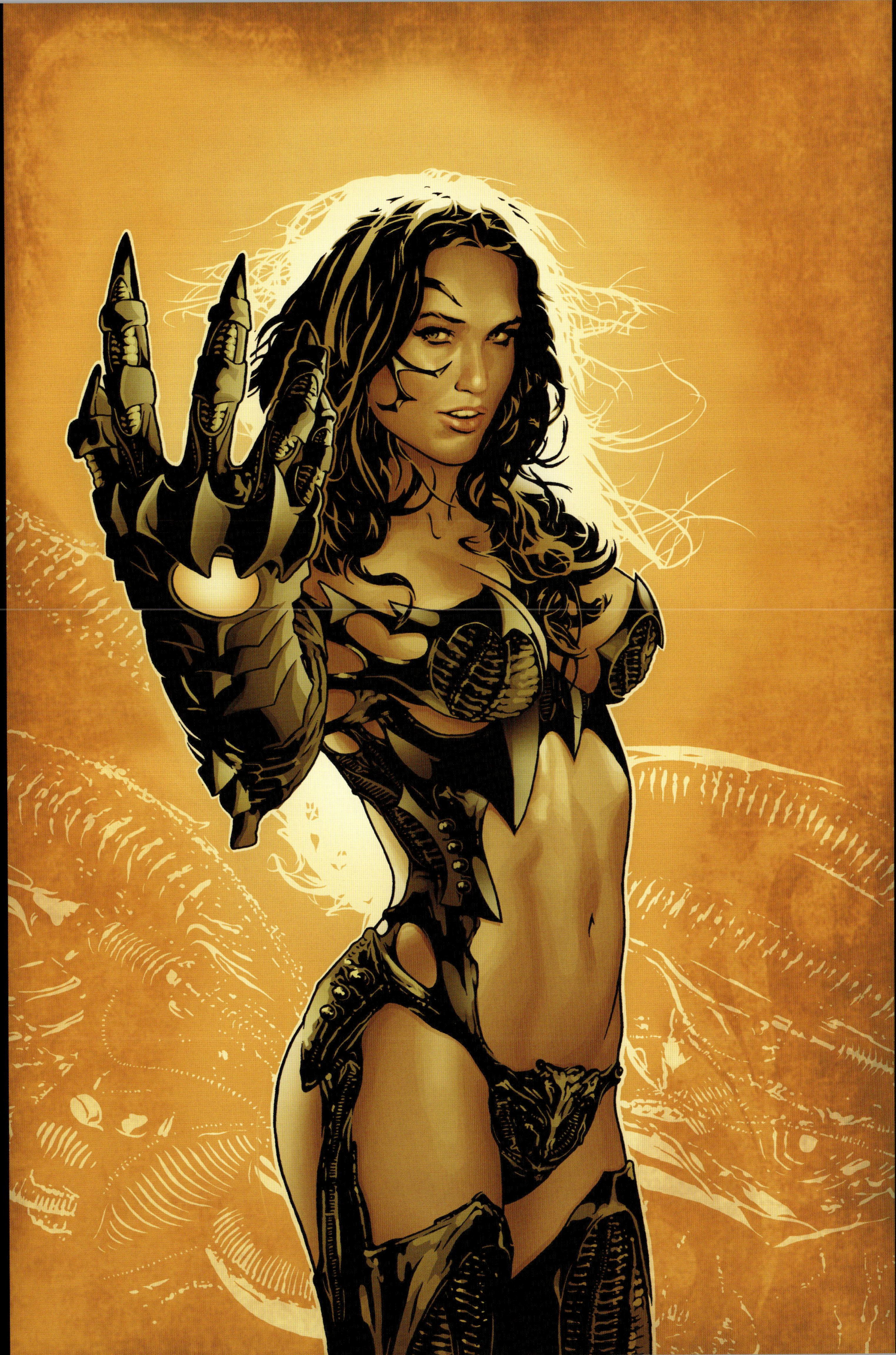

Witchblade #133 cover B,
art by: Jeffrey Spokes

Below. WB #136 cover

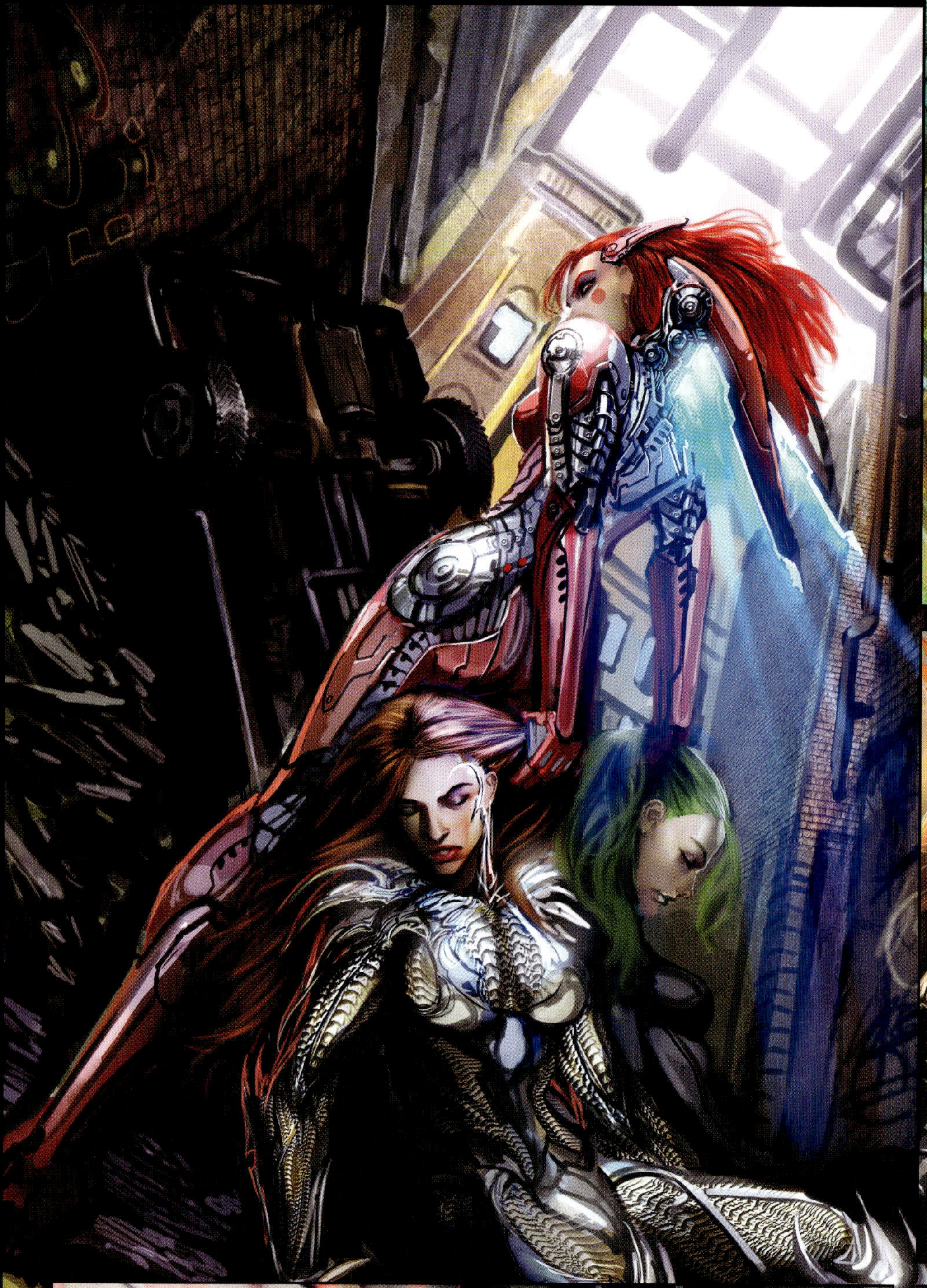

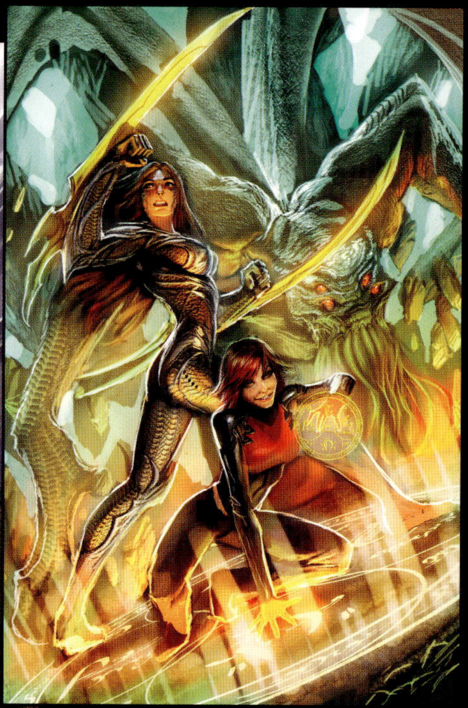

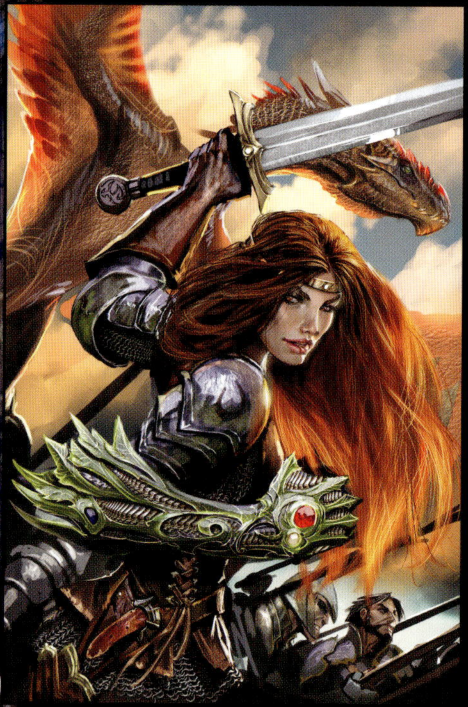

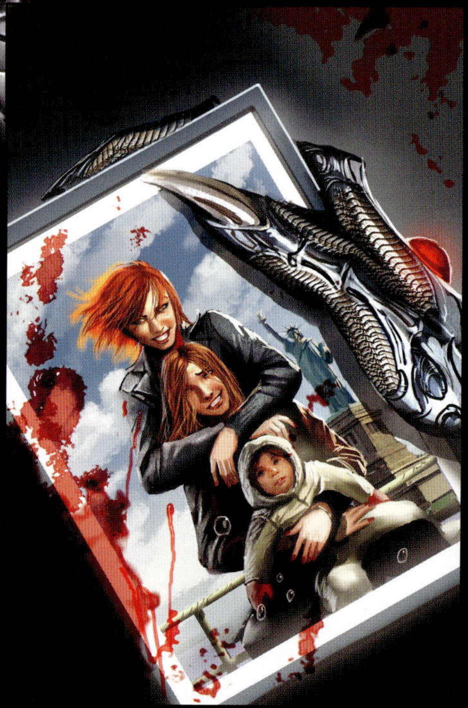

Witchblade #136-141 cover As,
art by: Stjepan Sejic

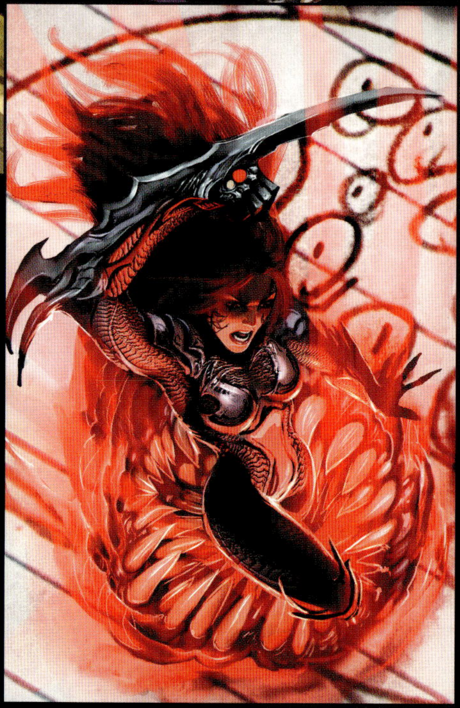

Above. WB #141 cover

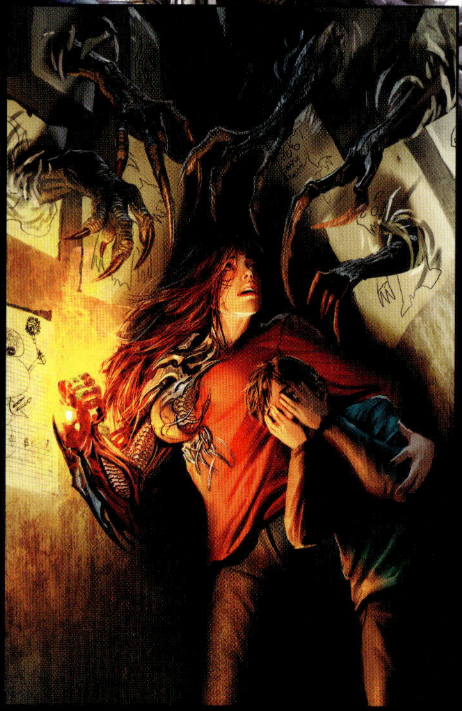

Above. WB #140 cover

From the top, this row. WB #137, 138 and 139 covers

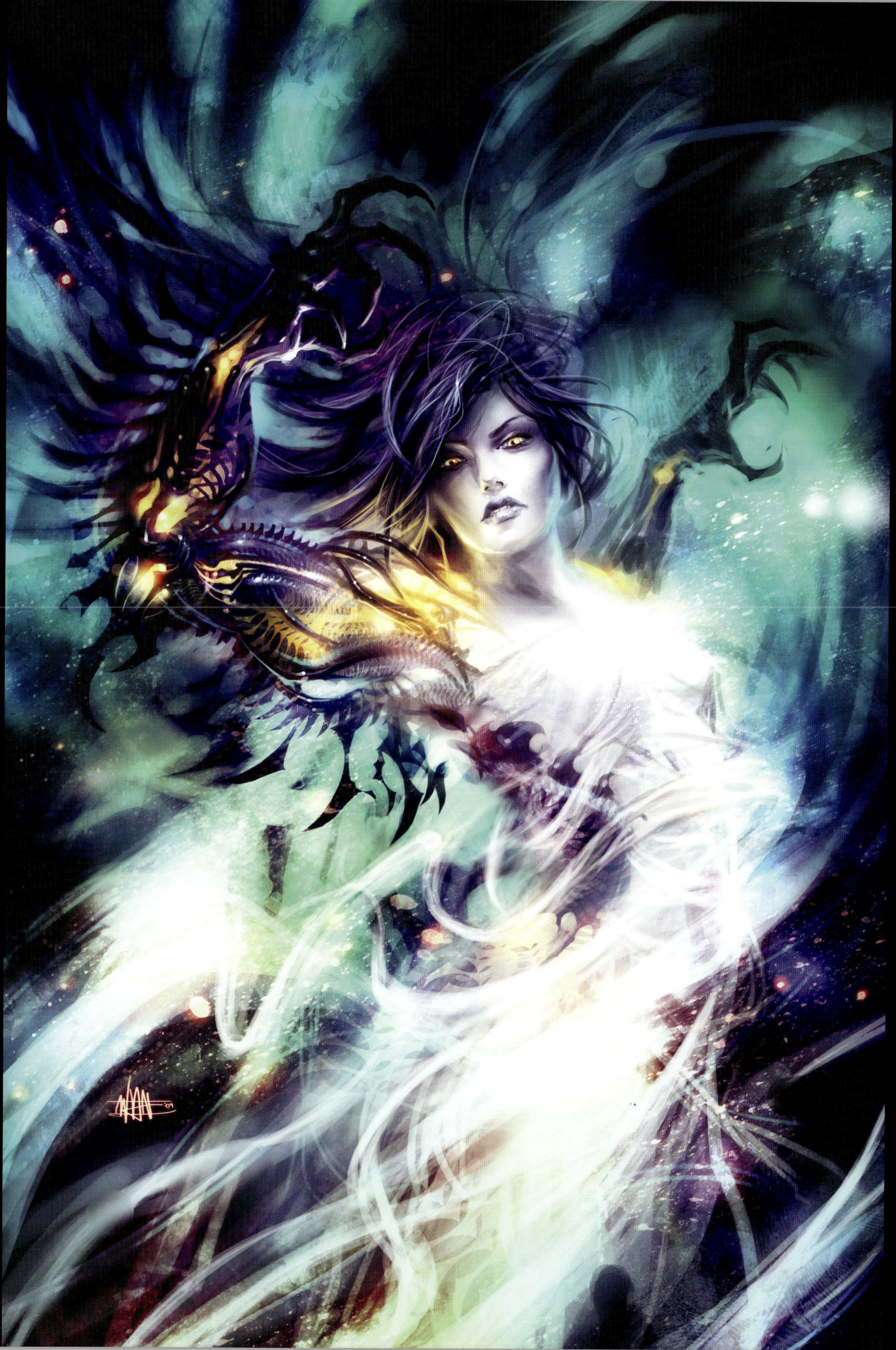

Witchblade #134 cover B,
art by: Michal Ivan

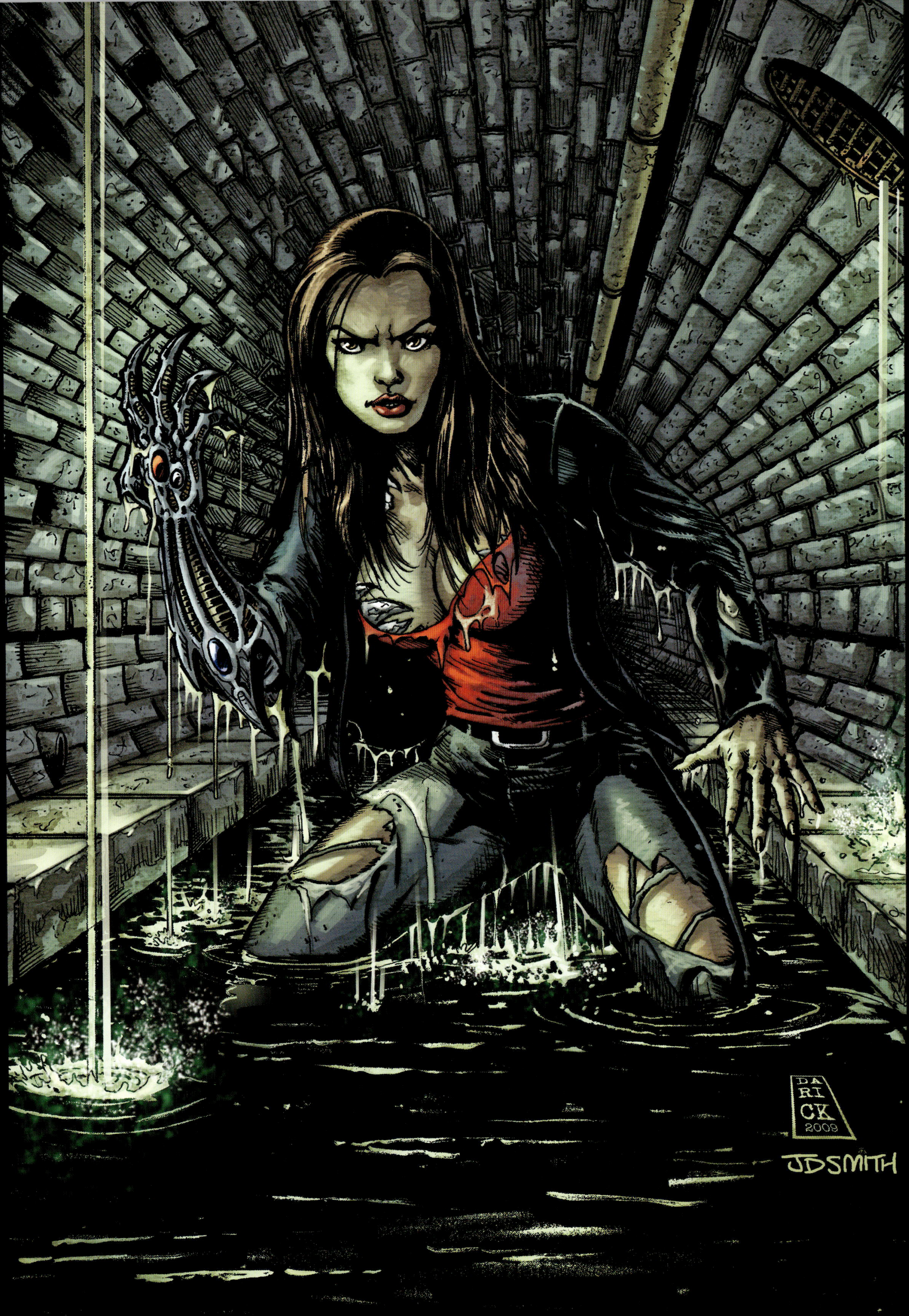

Witchblade #136 cover B,
art by: Derrick Robertson and Jonathan D. Smith

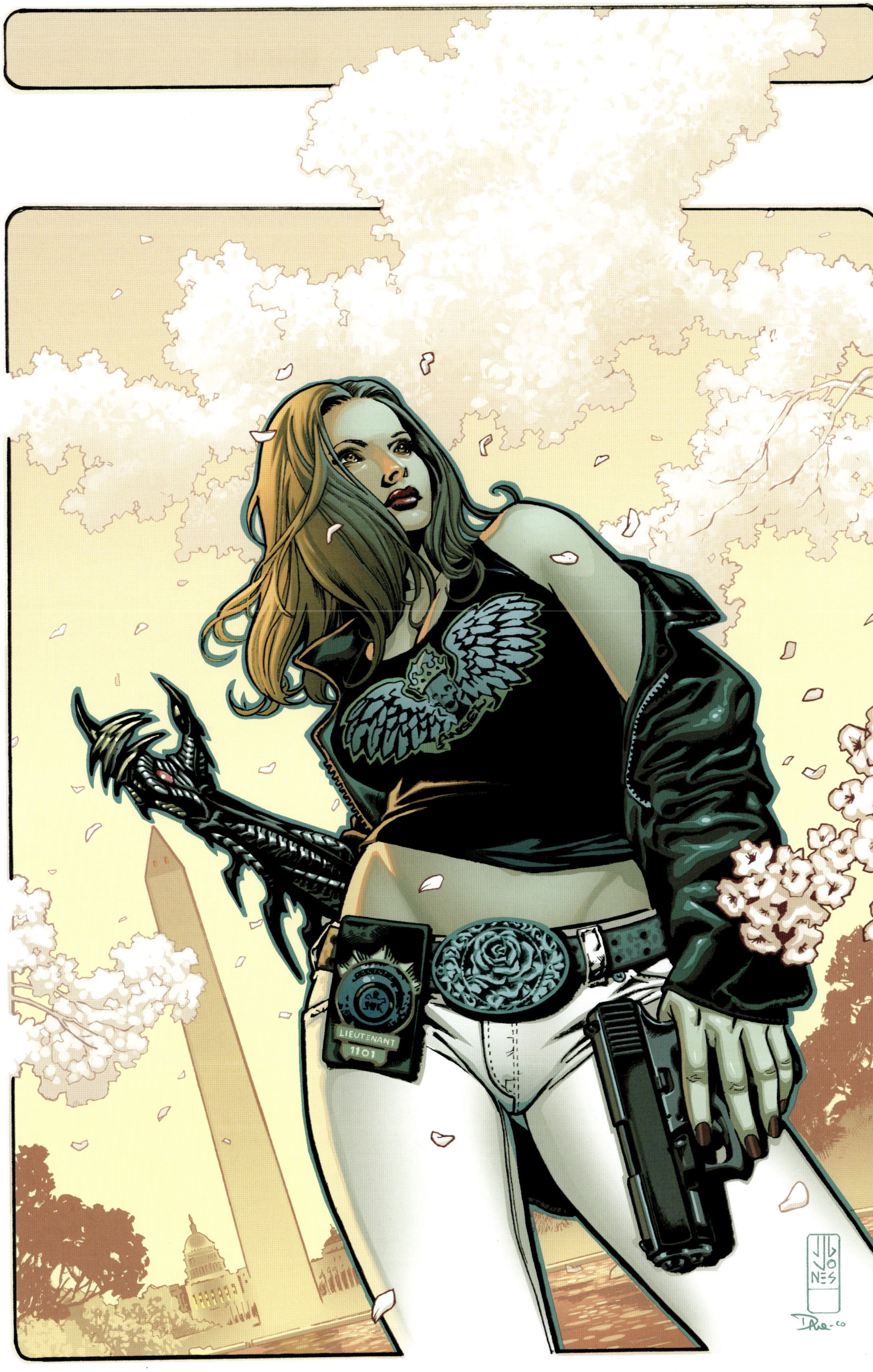

Witchblade #136 cover B,
art by: J.G. Jones and Dave McCaig

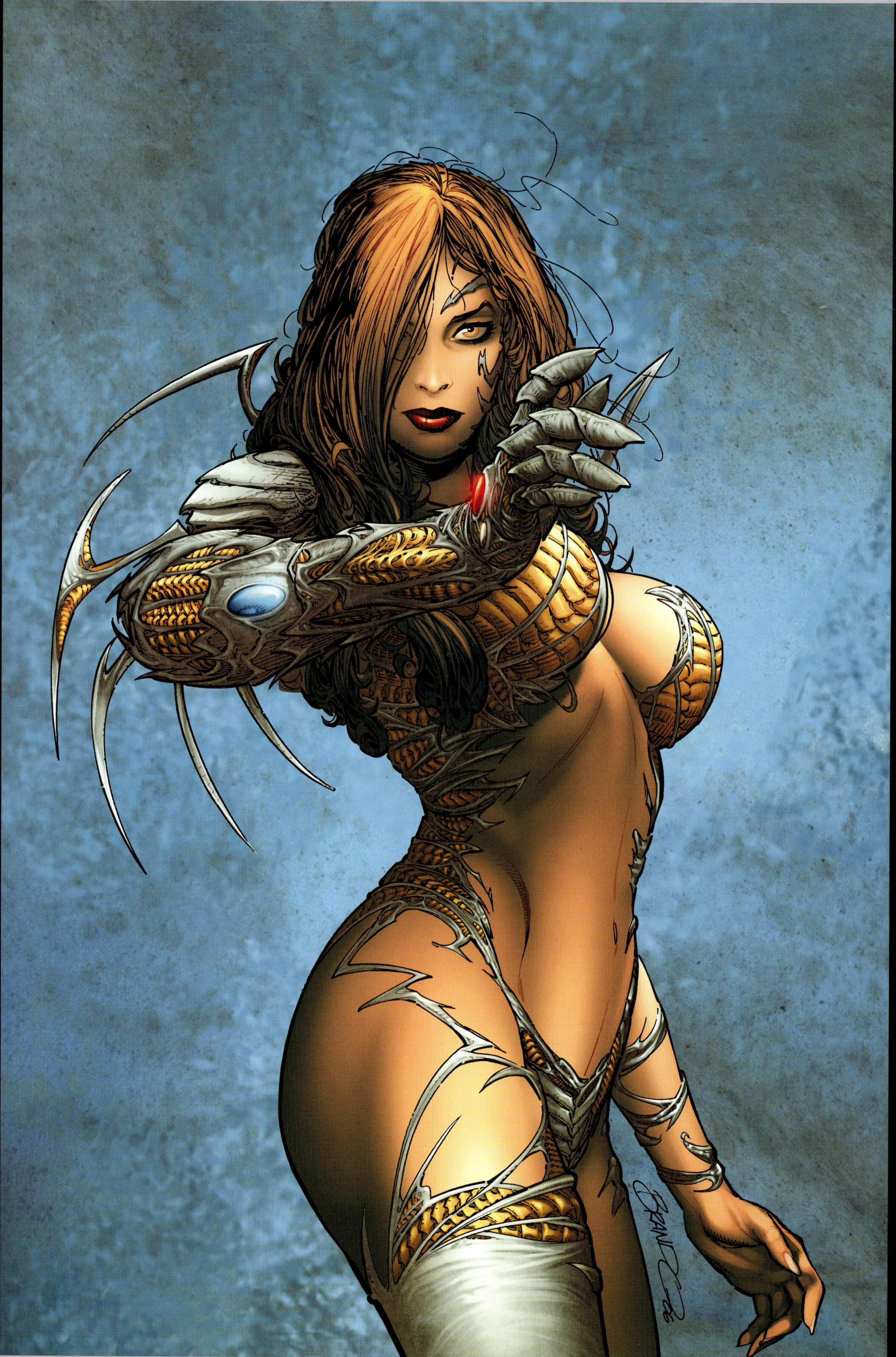

Witchblade #140 cover B,
art by: Brandon Peterson

Witchblade #142-147 cover A's, art by: Stijepan Sejic

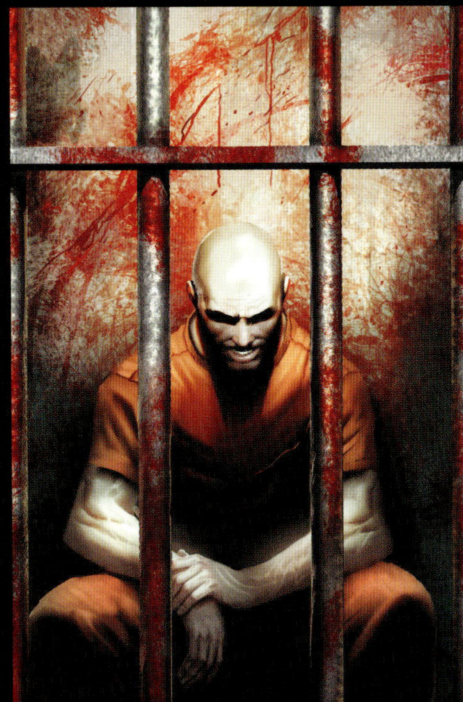

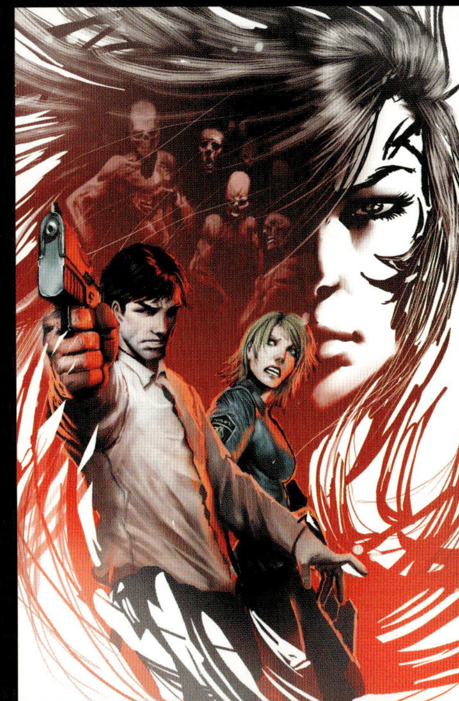

From Left. WB #142 and 143 covers

Below. WB #144 wraparound cover

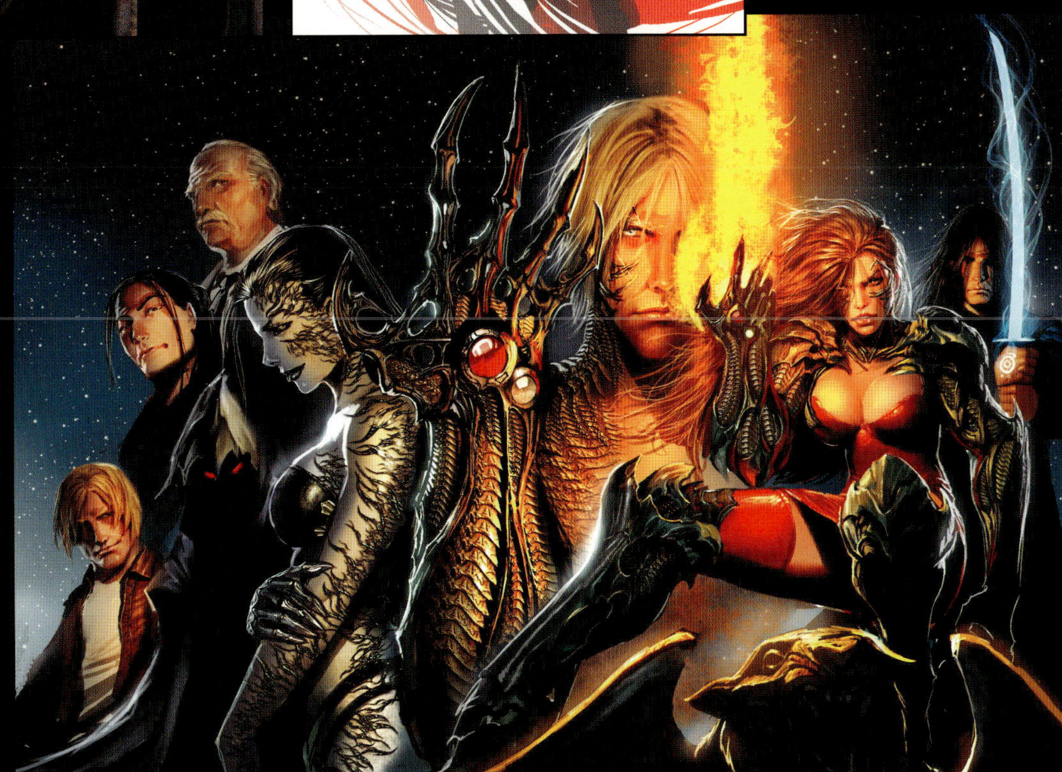

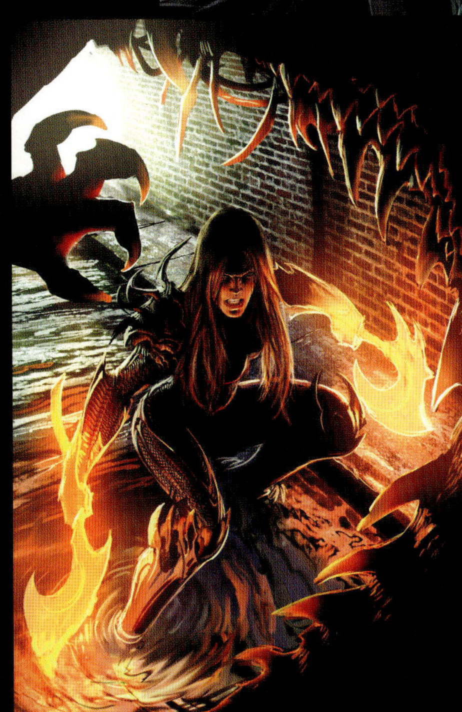

Above. WB #145 cover

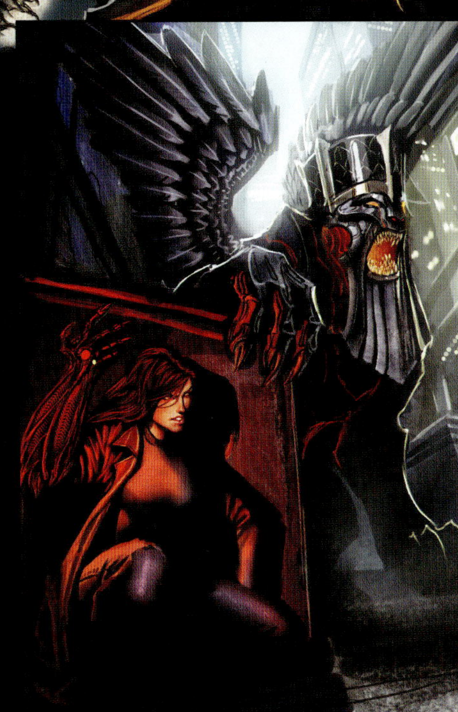

Above. WB #146 cover

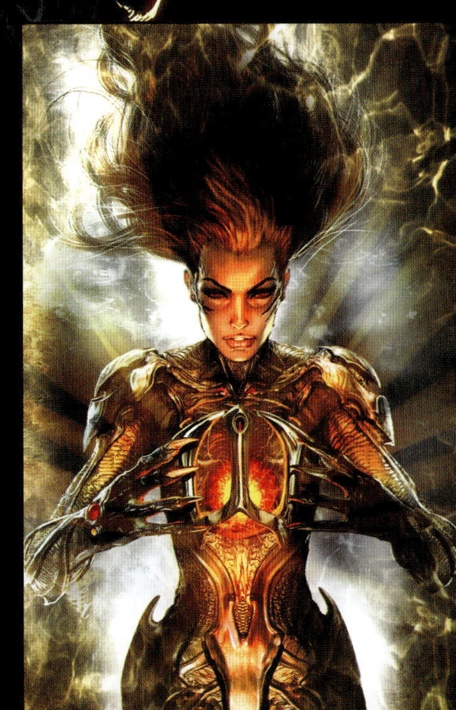

Above. WB #147 cover

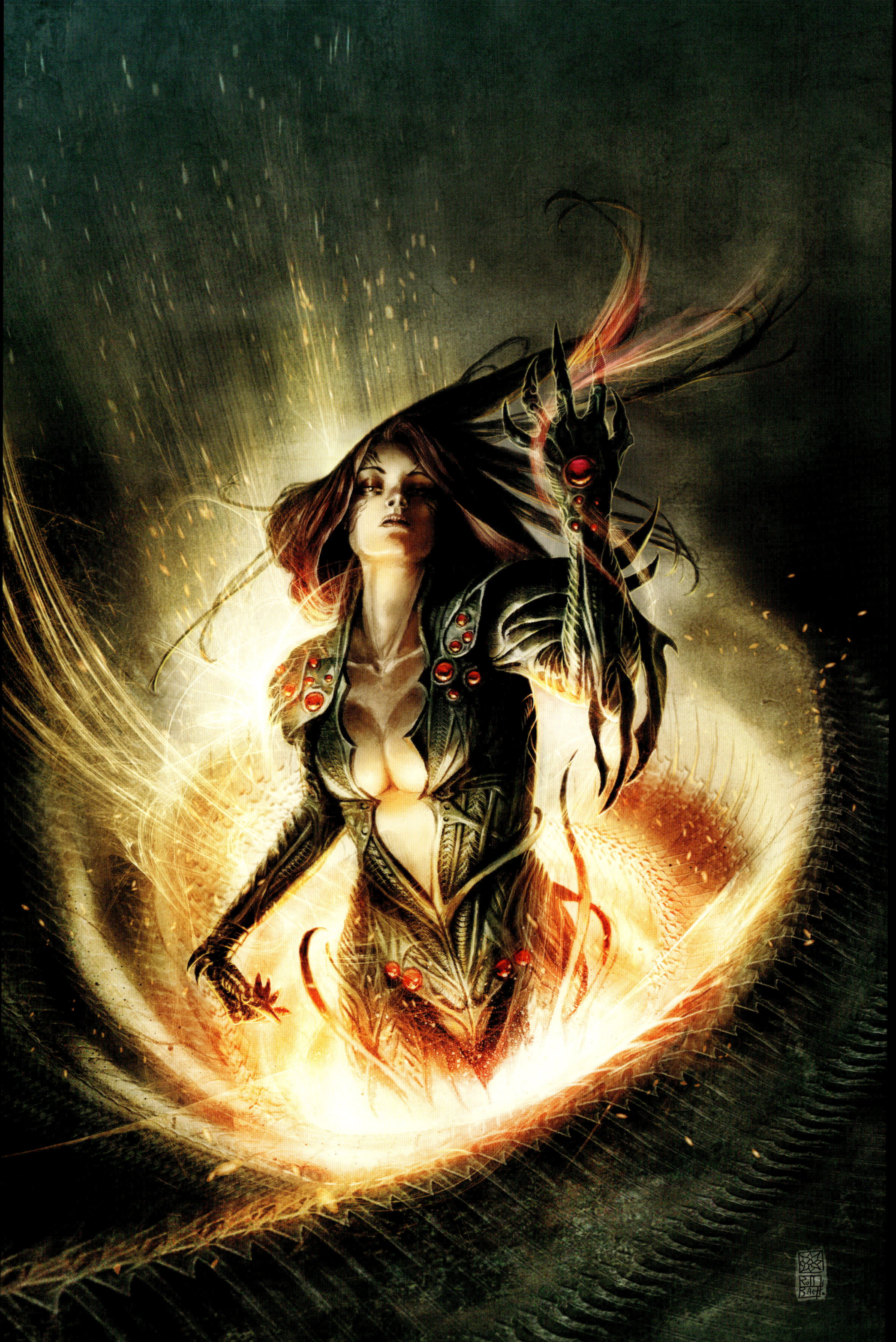

Witchblade #144 cover B.
art by: Jean-Sebastien Rosbach

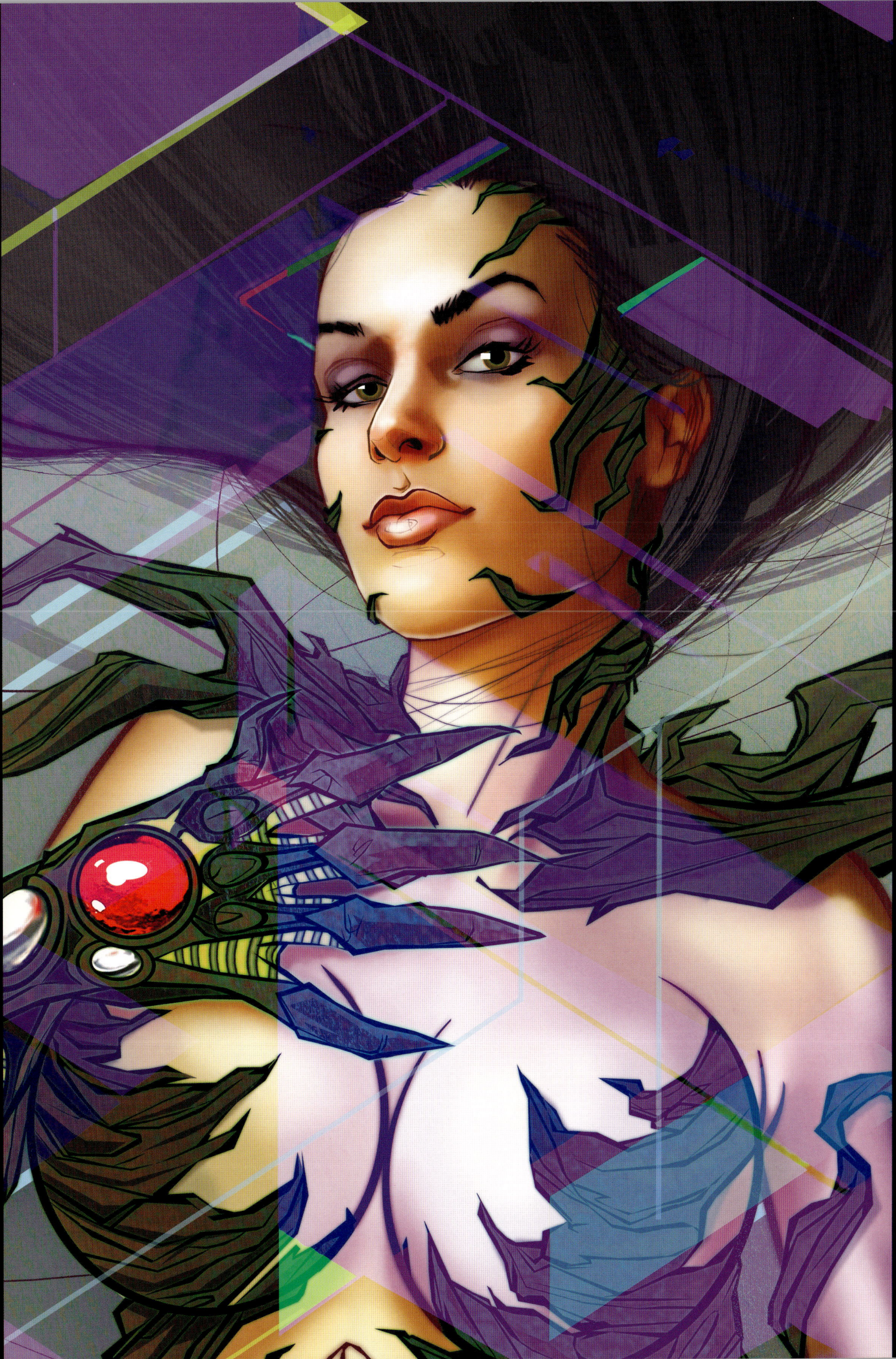

Witchblade #145 Heroes Con Variant,
art by: Erik Jones

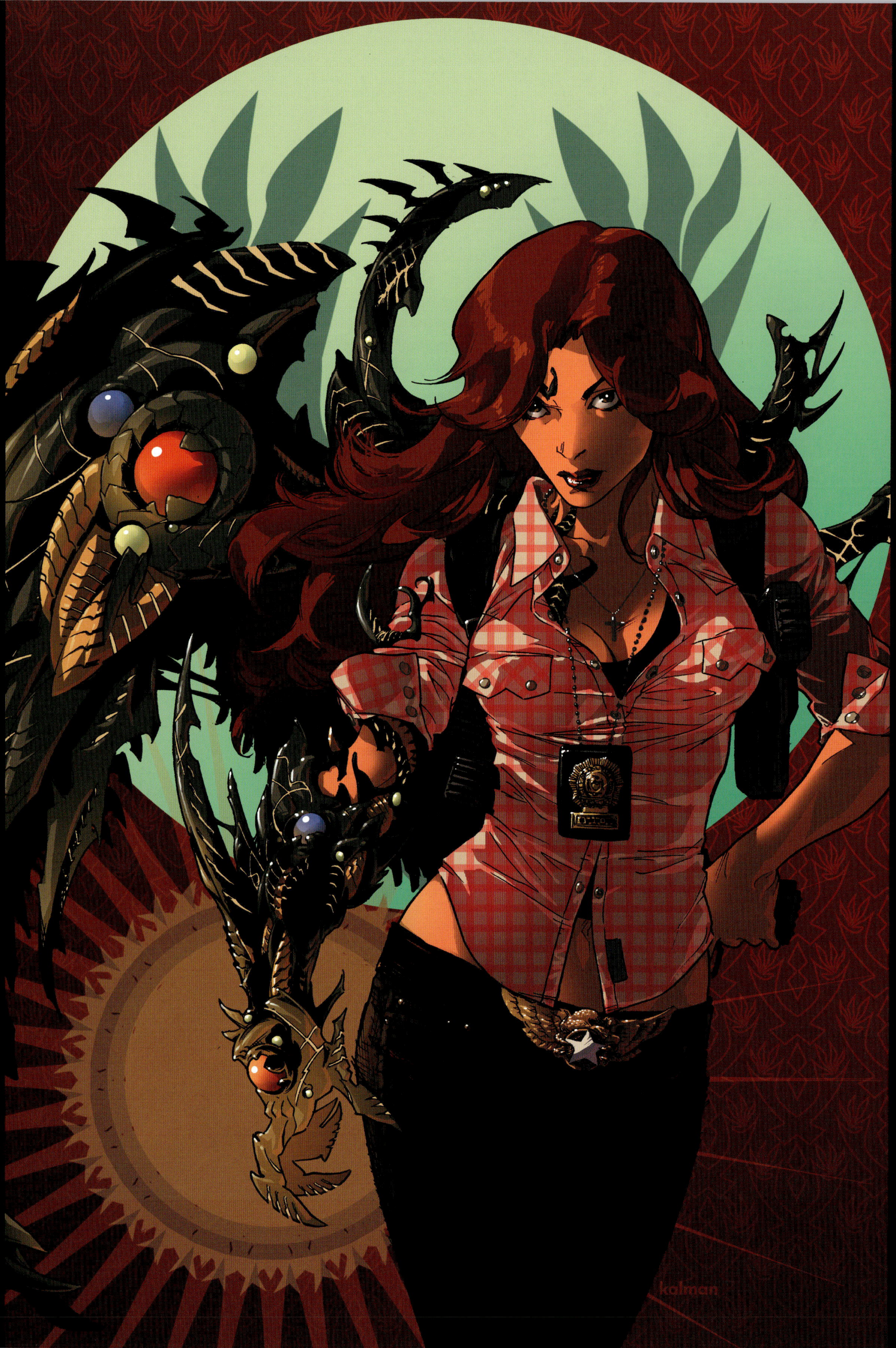

Witchblade #146 SDCC variant,
art by: Kalman Andrasofszky

Witchblade #148-149 cover A's and 149 cover D, art by: Stjepan Sejic, Diego Bernard and Sunny Gho

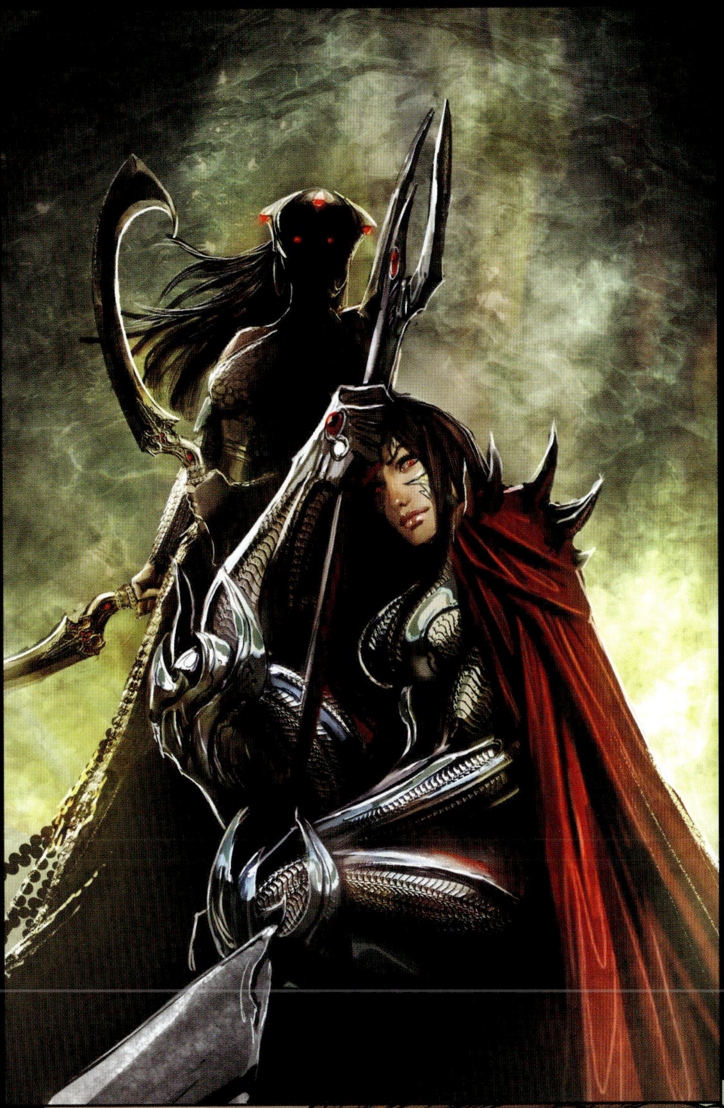

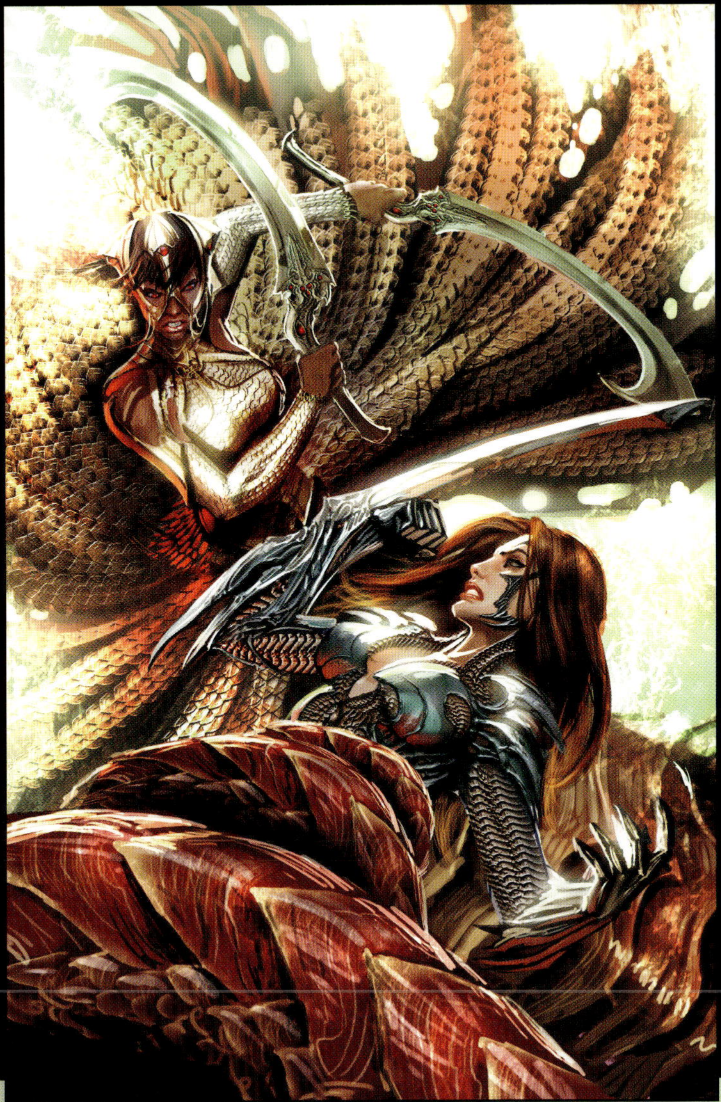

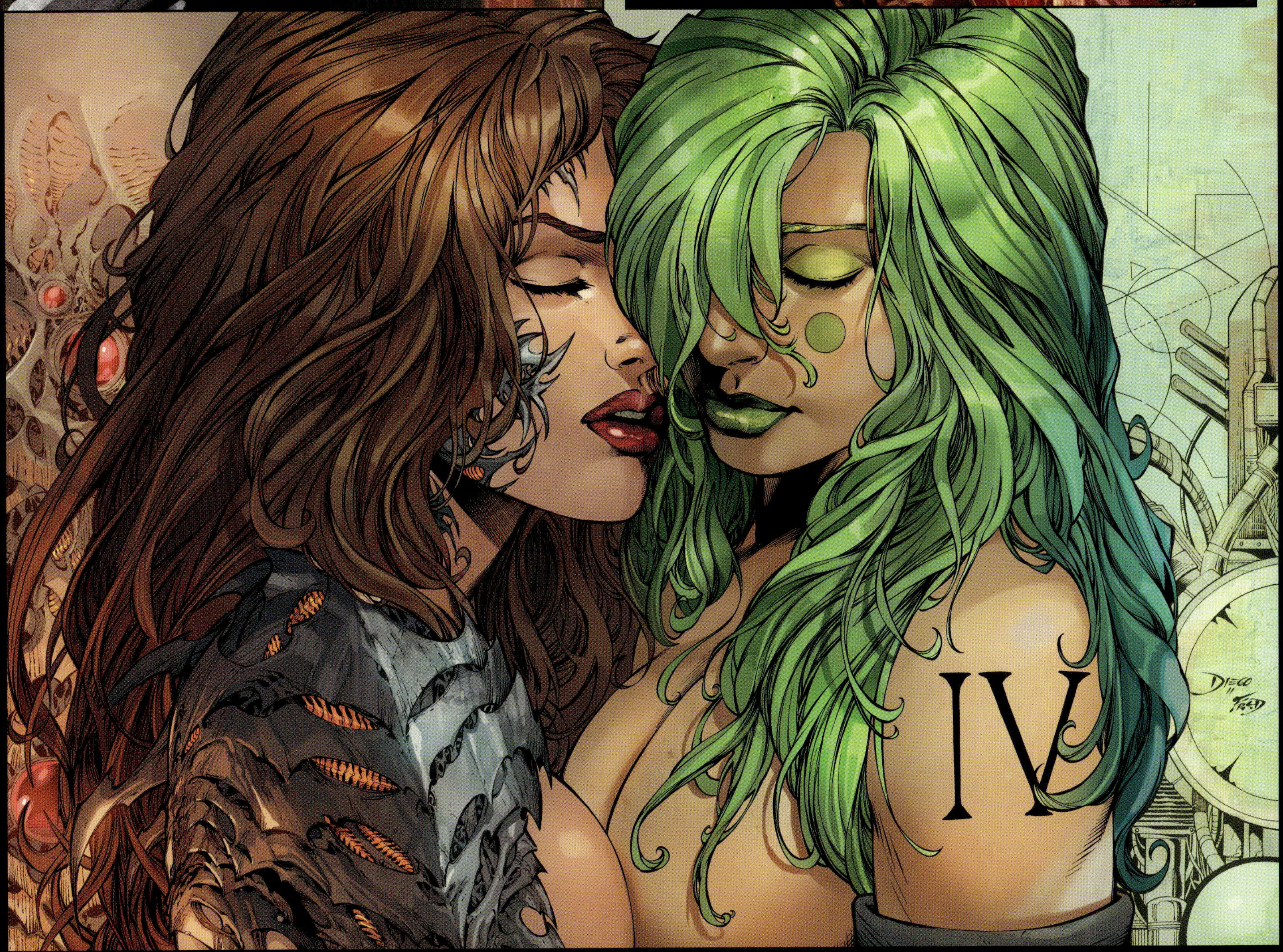

Top. WB #148 and 149 cover A's by Sejic

Above. WB #149 cover D, Virginia Comic Con Variant, cover by Bernard and Gho

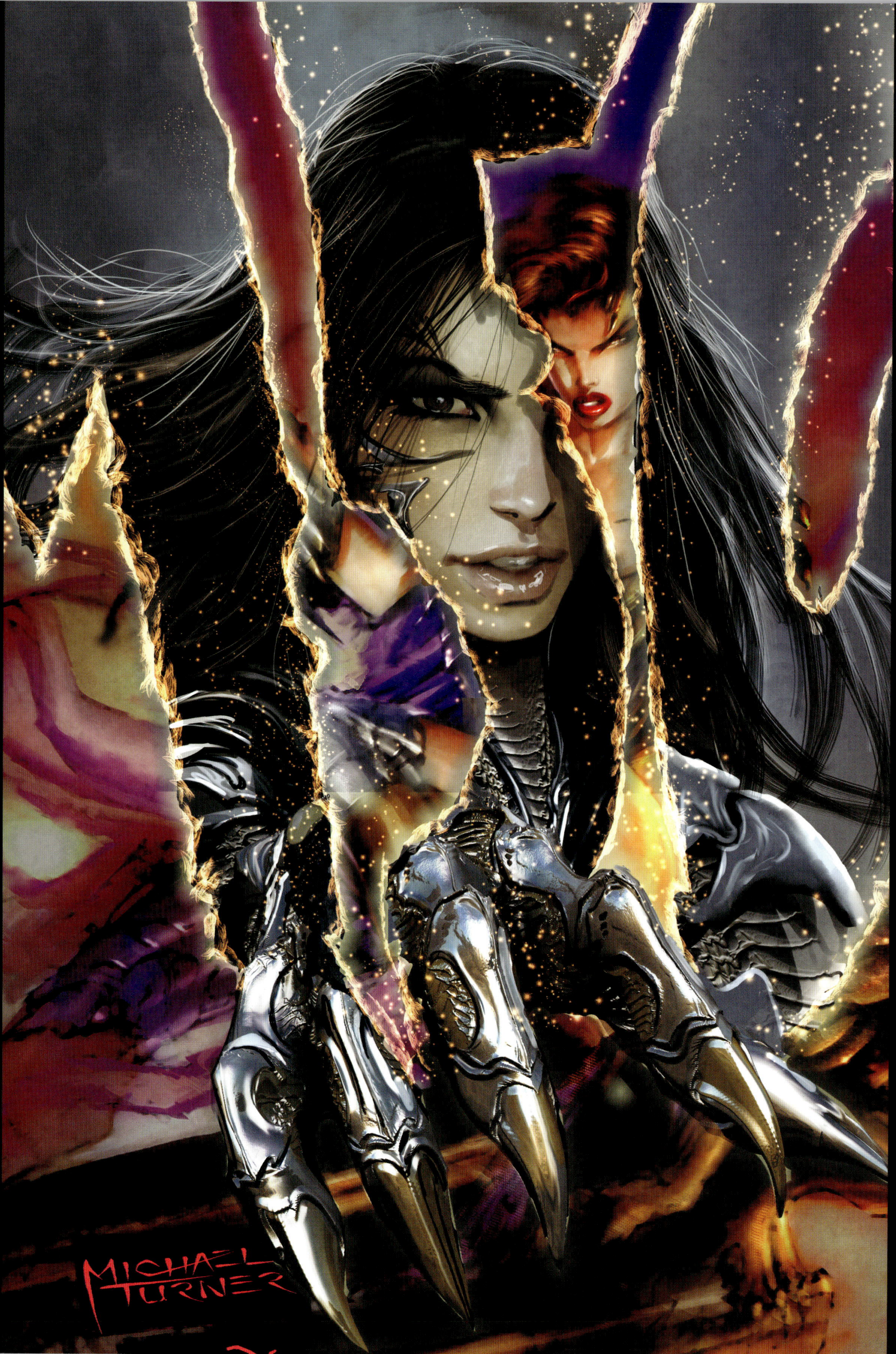

Witchblade #150 cover A,
art by: Stjepan Sejic, Michael Turner, and Brian Haberlin.

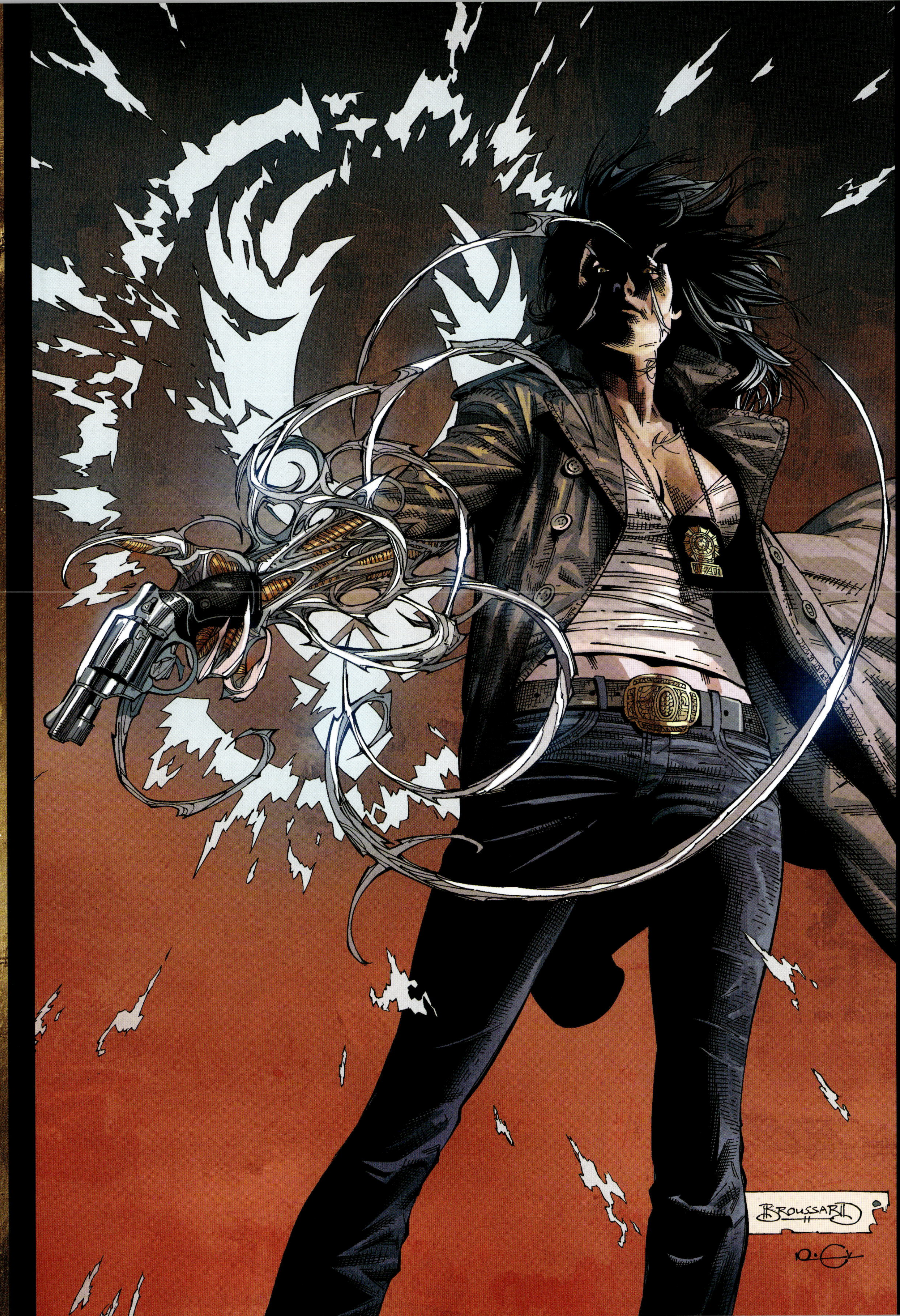

Witchblade #150 cover B,
art by: Michael Broussard, Rick Basaldua, and Sunny Gho

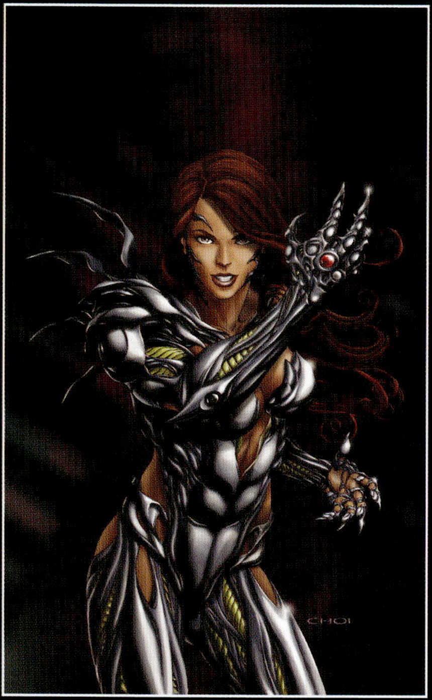

Above. WB #150 cover C, art by: Mike Choi

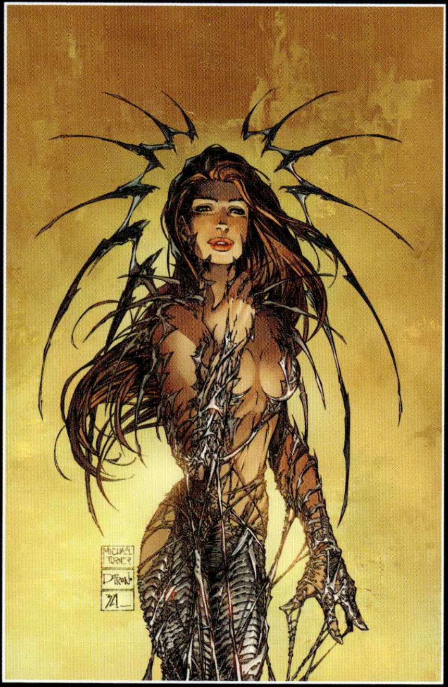

Above. WB #150 cover D, art by: Michael Turner, D-Tron, and Sunny Gho

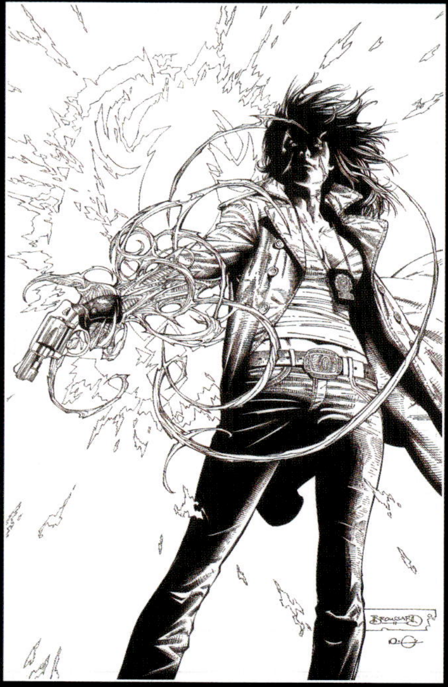

Above. WB #150 cover E, art by: Michael Broussard and Rick Basaldua

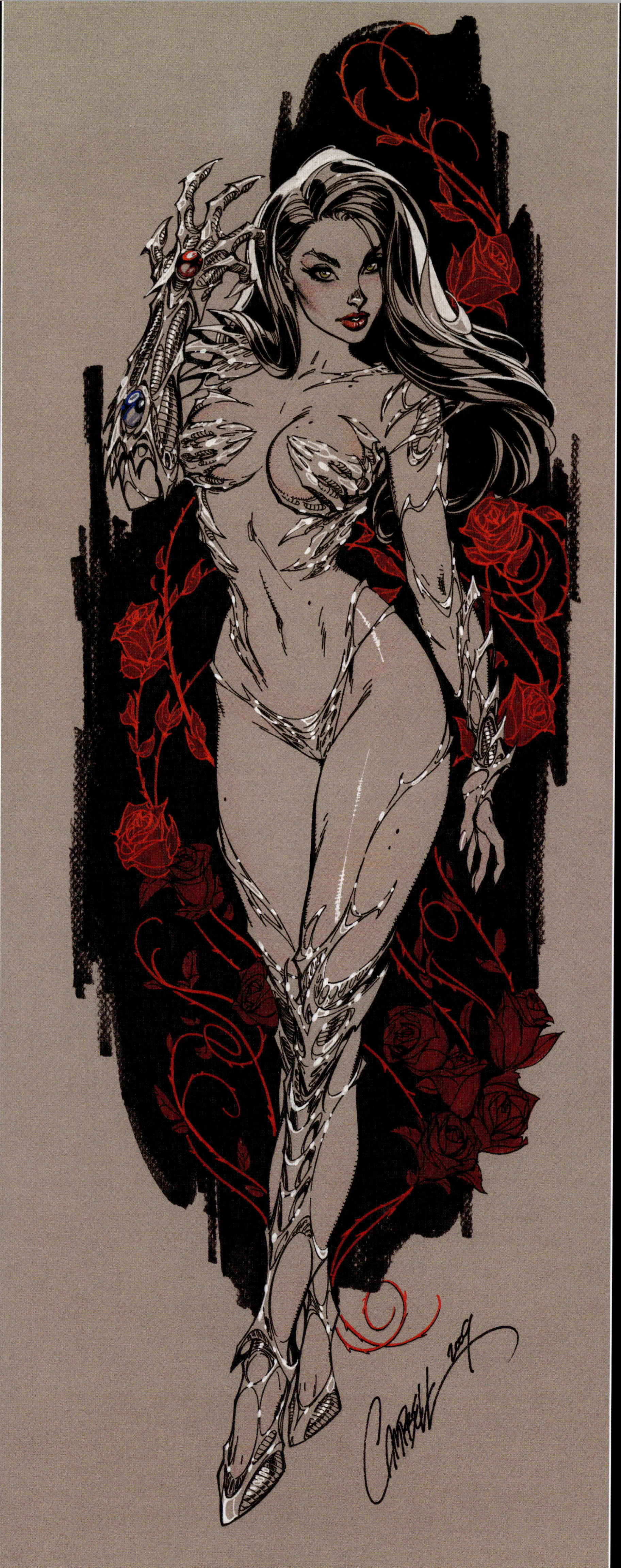

At left. WB#150 cover F art by: J. Scott Campbell

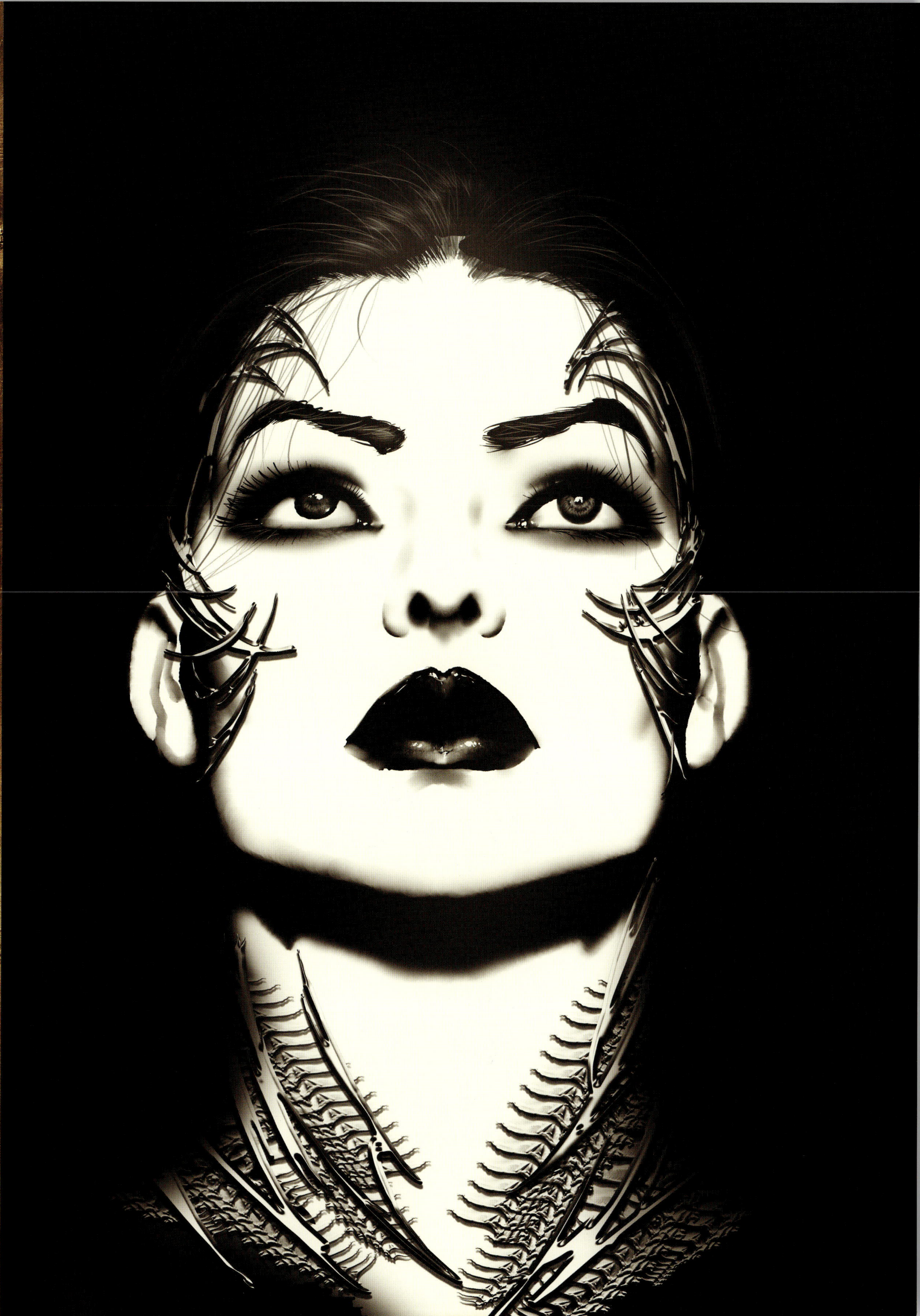

Witchblade #150 cover G,
art by: Stjepan Sejic

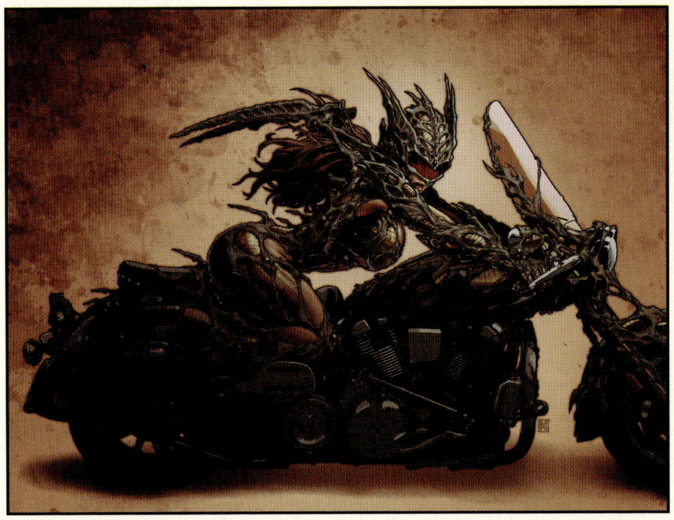
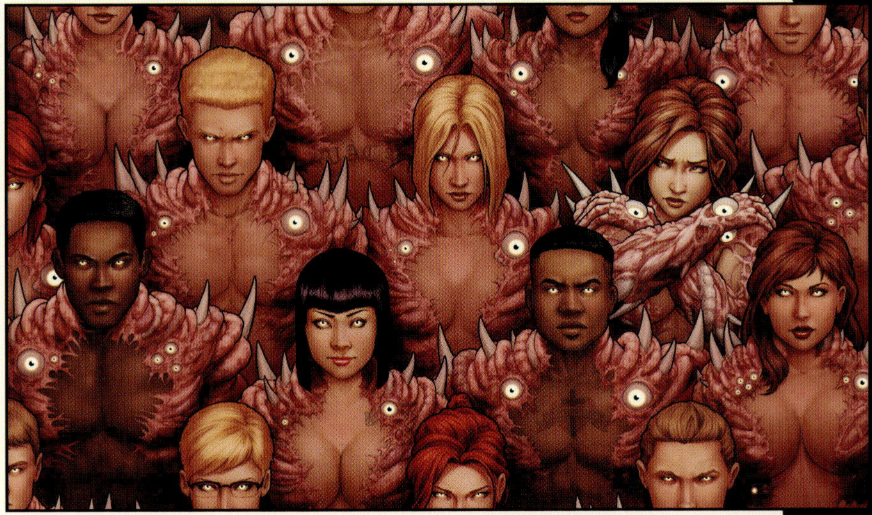
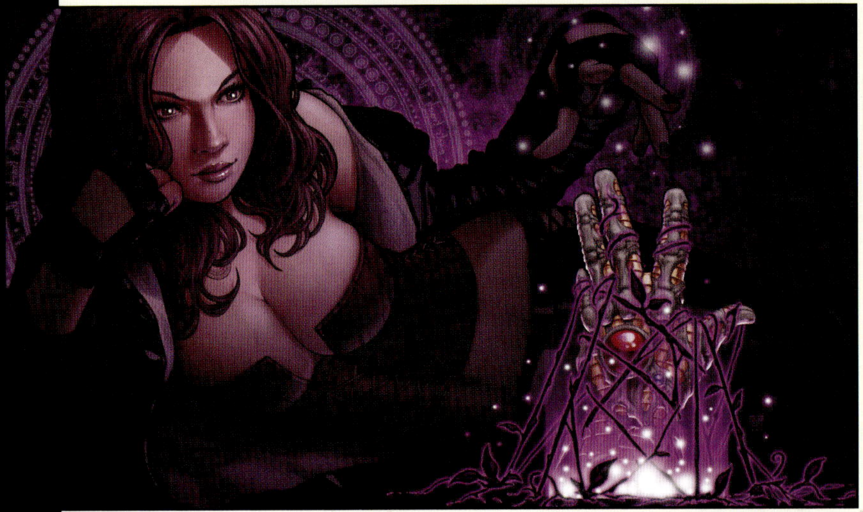
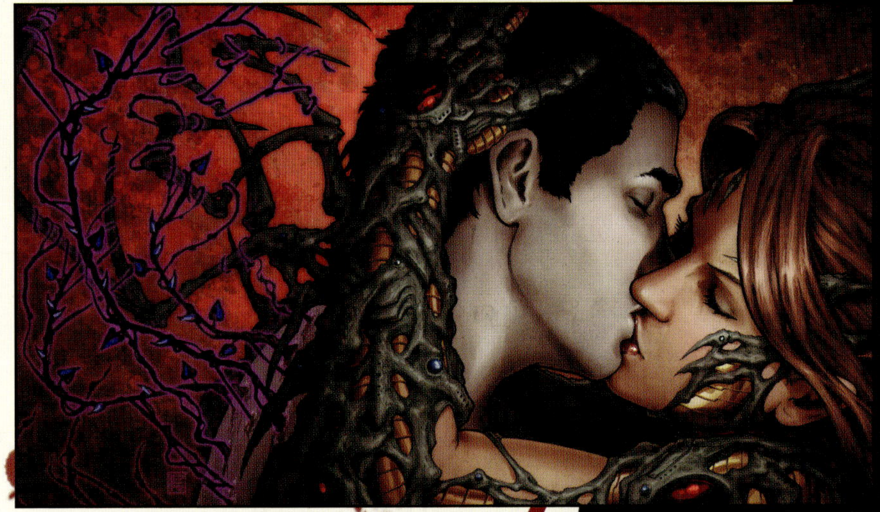
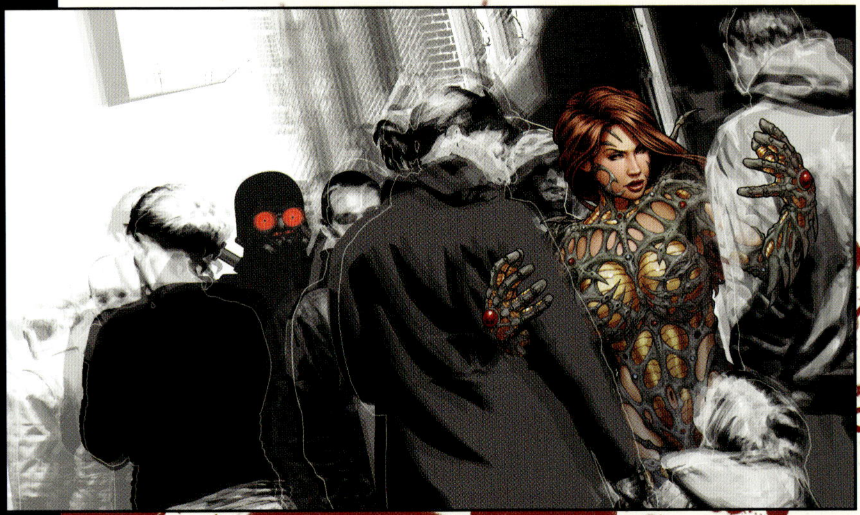
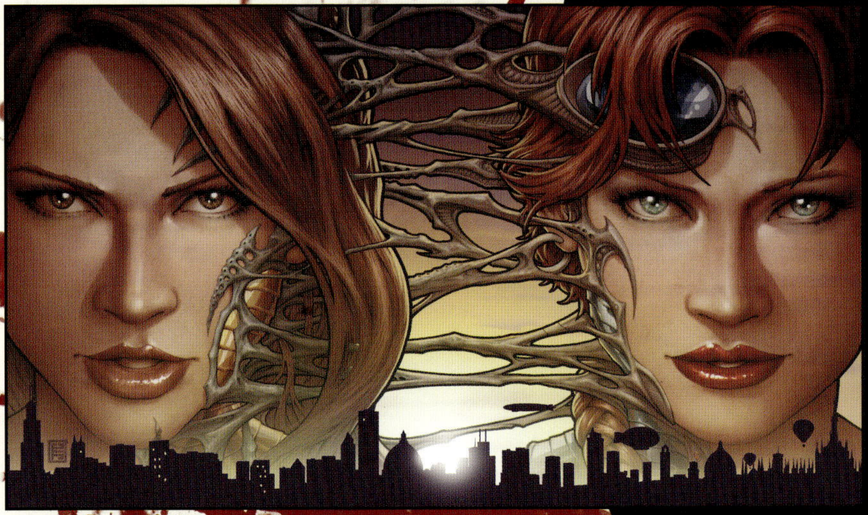
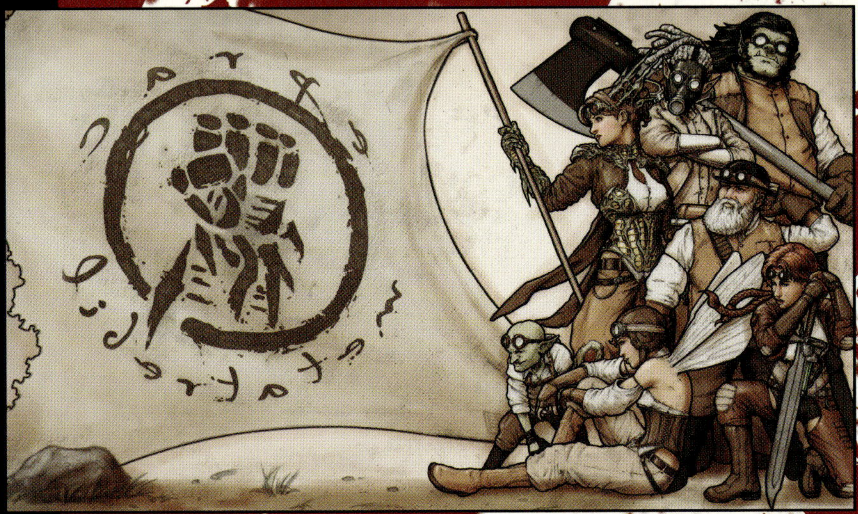
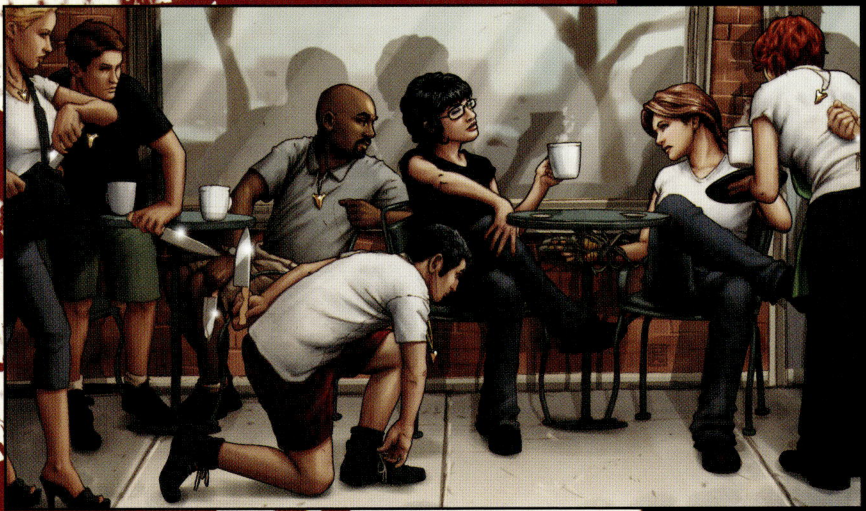

Starting from the top this page. *Witchblade* #151 cover B followed by WB #153-159 cover A's, art by: John Tyler Christopher

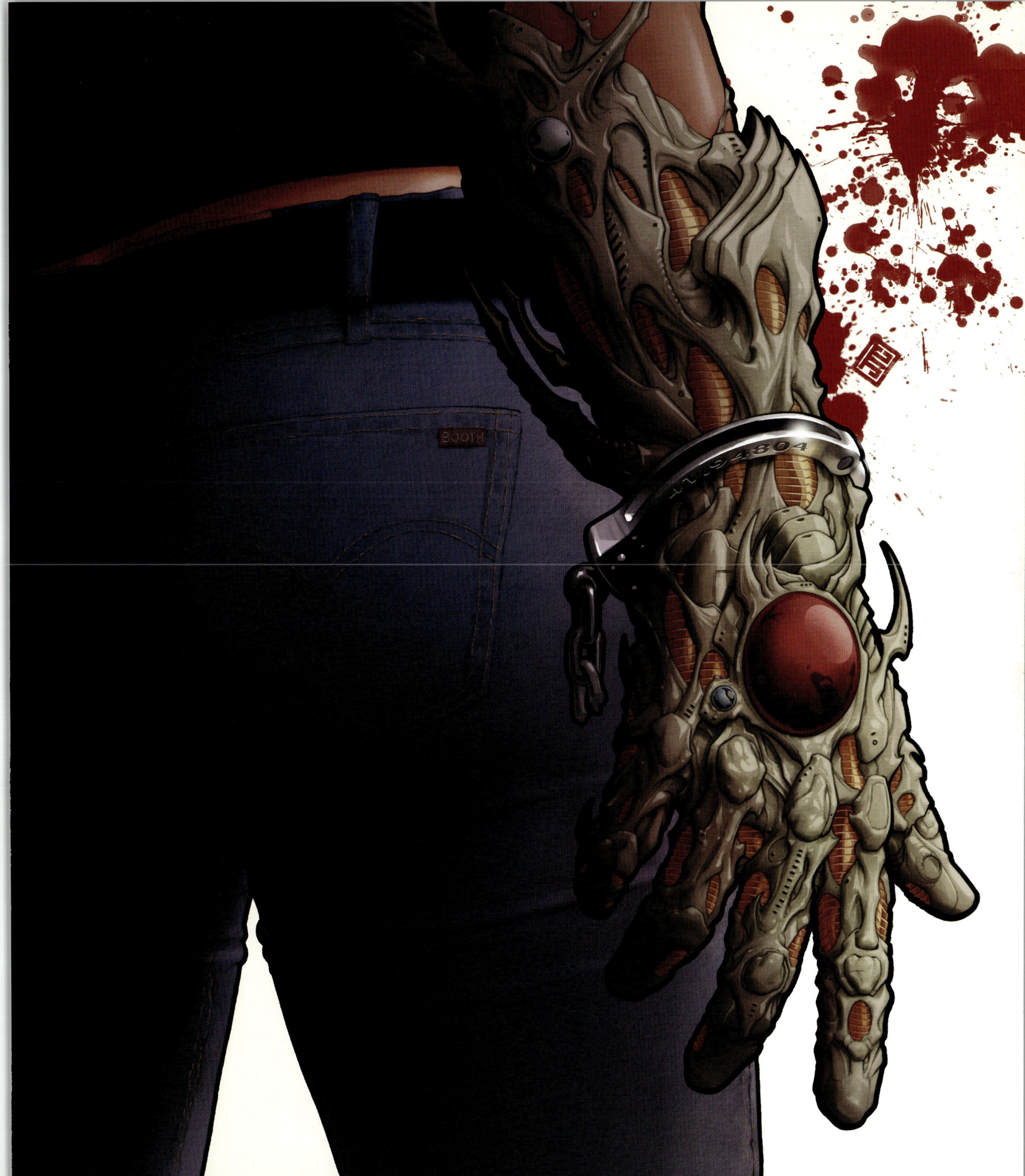

This page and underlying across the facing page. *Witchblade* #152 cover A, art by: John Tyler Christopher

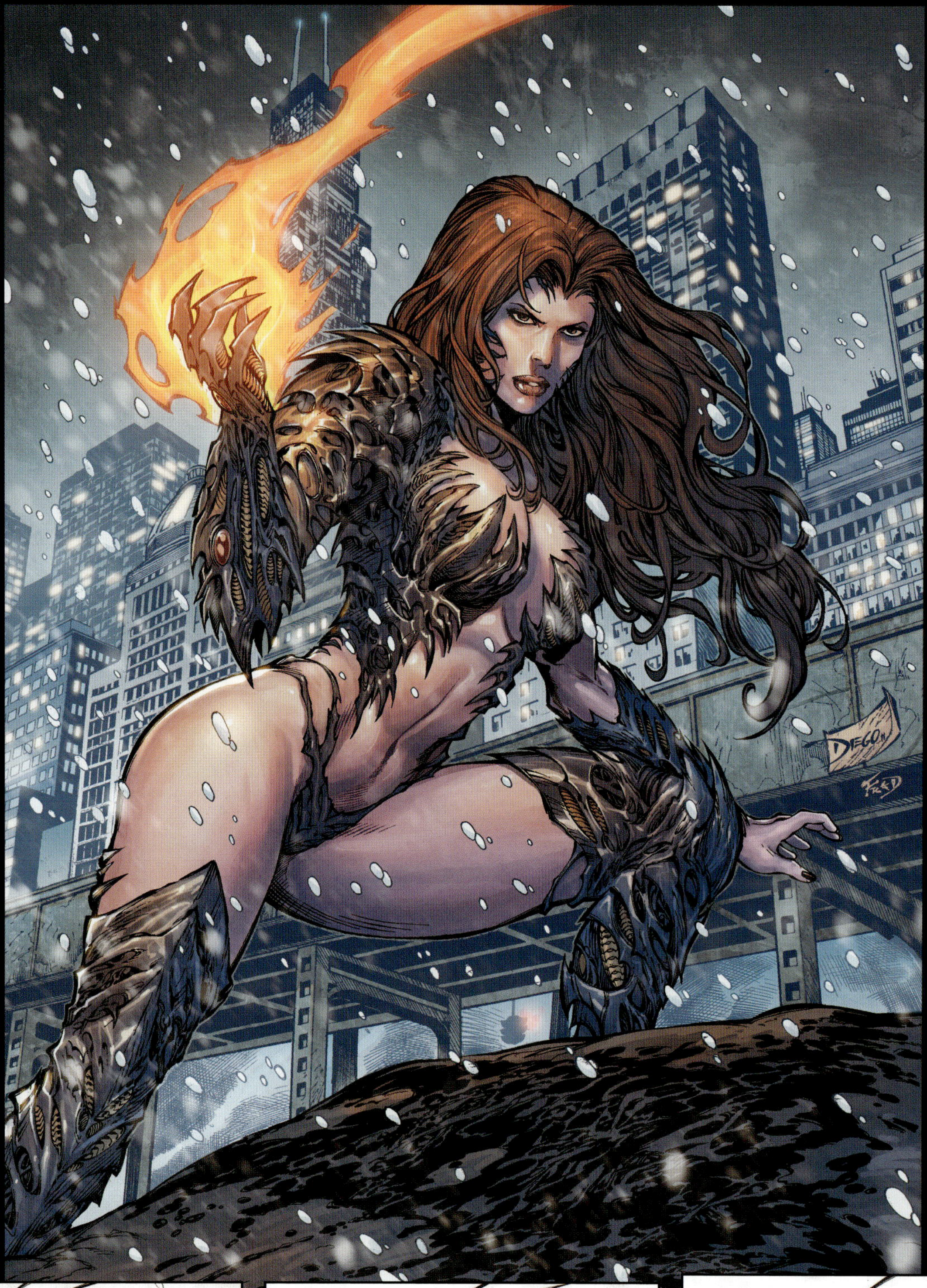

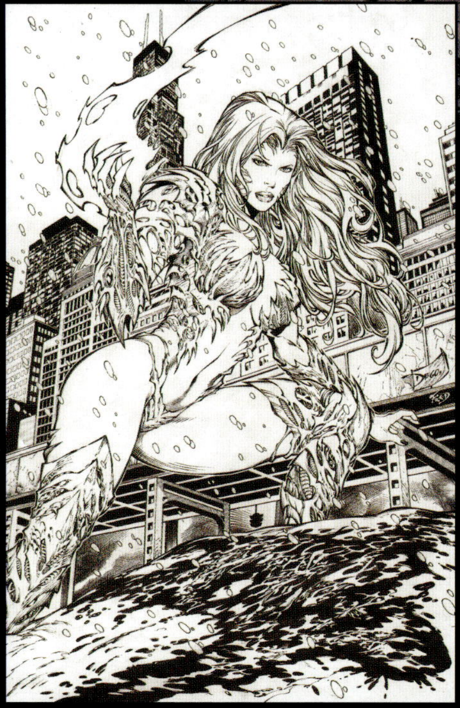

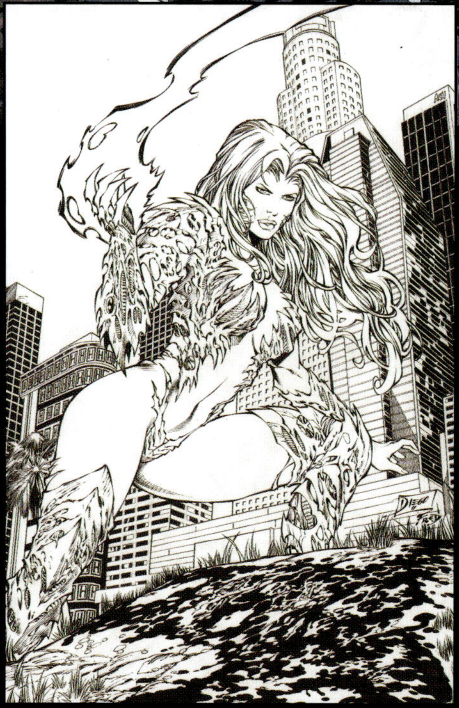

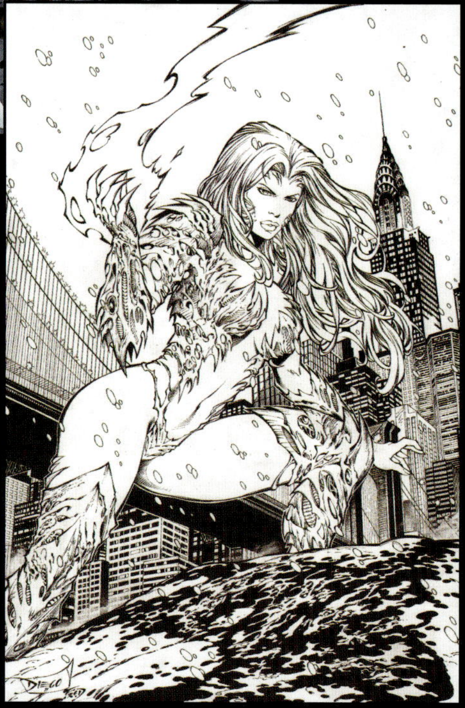

Witchblade #151 ComicsPRO variant,
art by: Diego Bernard, Fred Benes, and Arif Prianto

From the top, this row. Chicago, Los Angeles and New York variations.

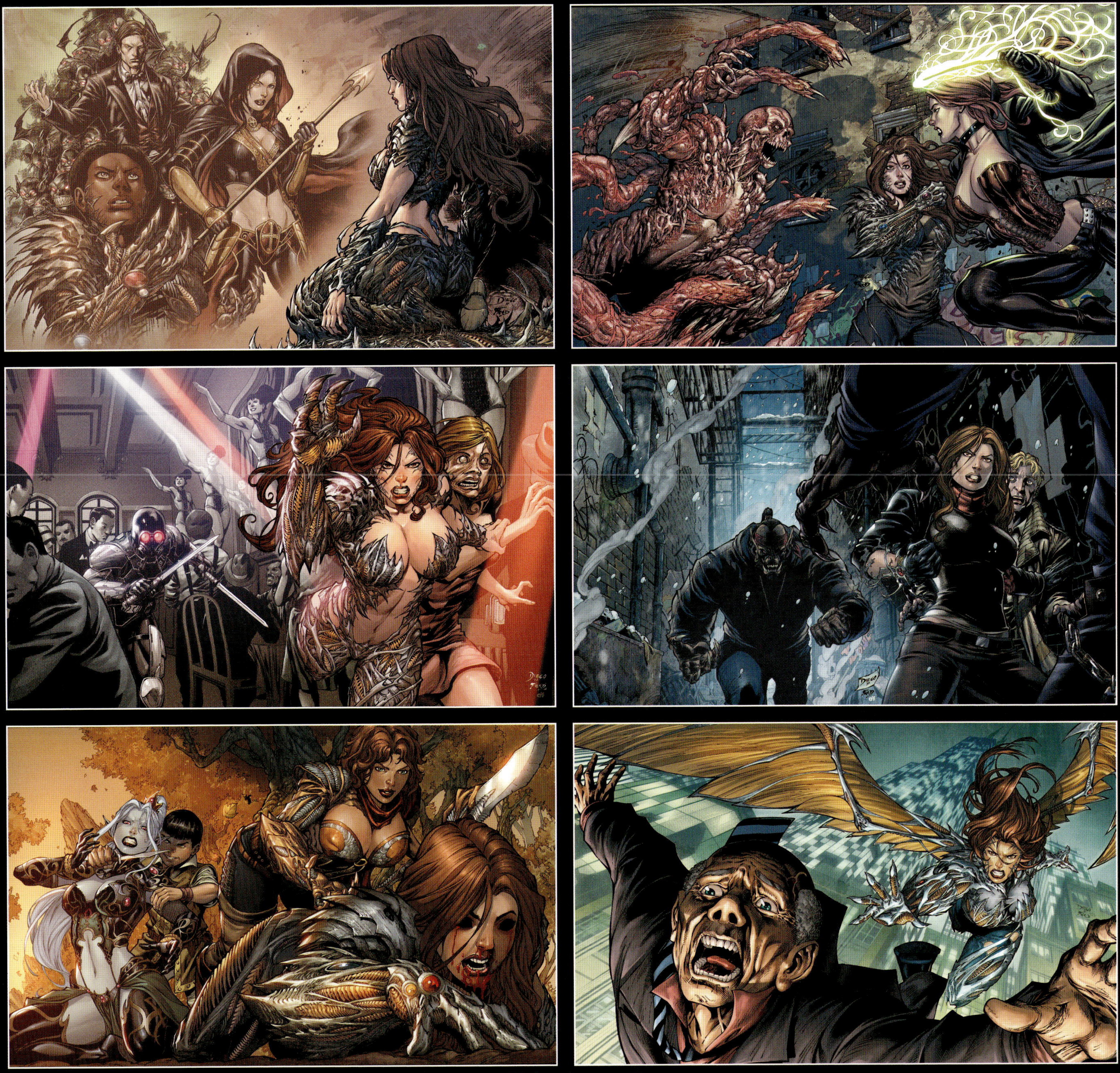

Witchblade #154-159 cover B's,
art by: Diego Bernard, Fred Benes, and Arif Prianto

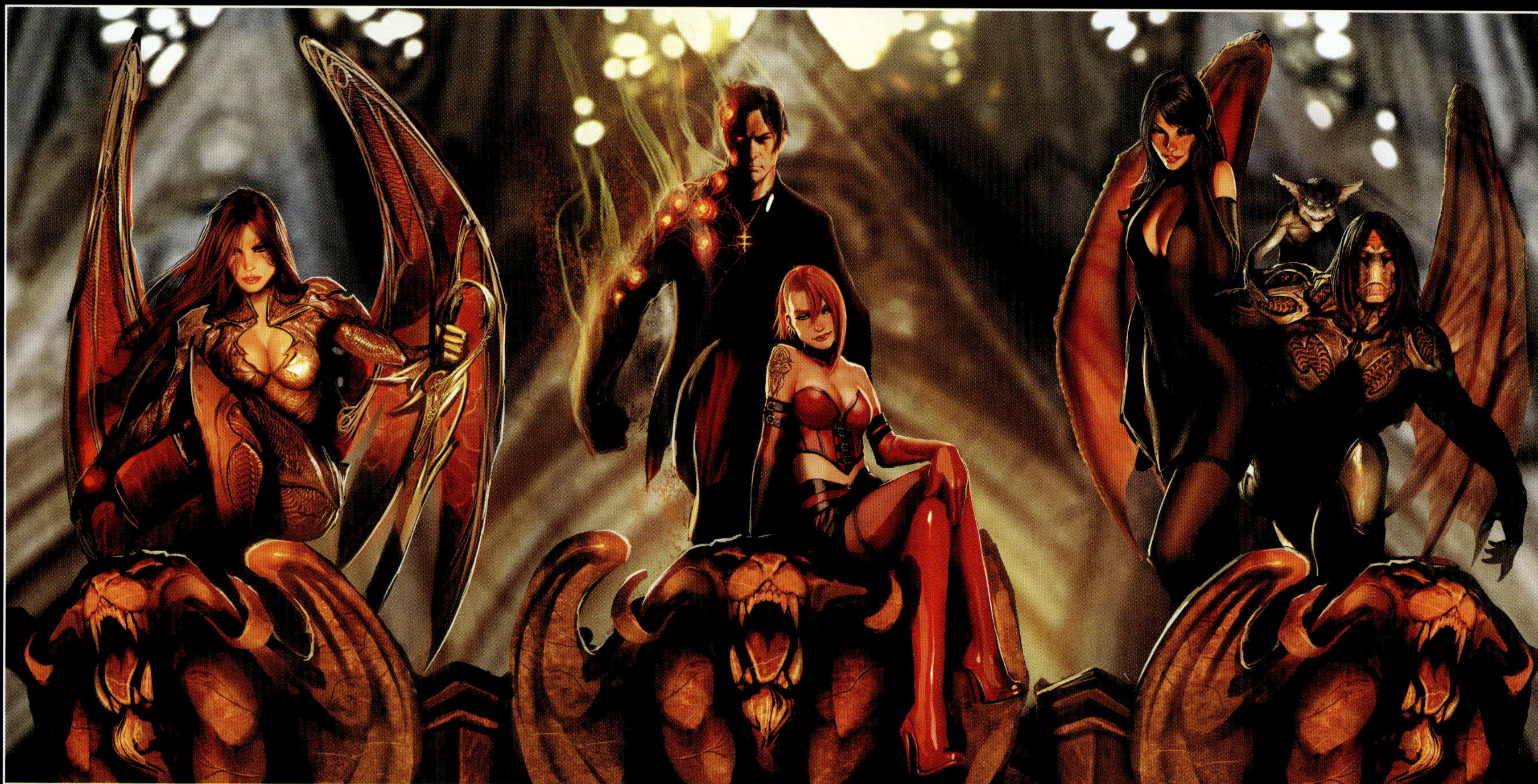

Witchblade #160, *Artifacts* #21, and *The Darkness* #107, New York Comic-Con & Long Beach Comic Con Exclusive Variants, art by: Stjepan Sejic

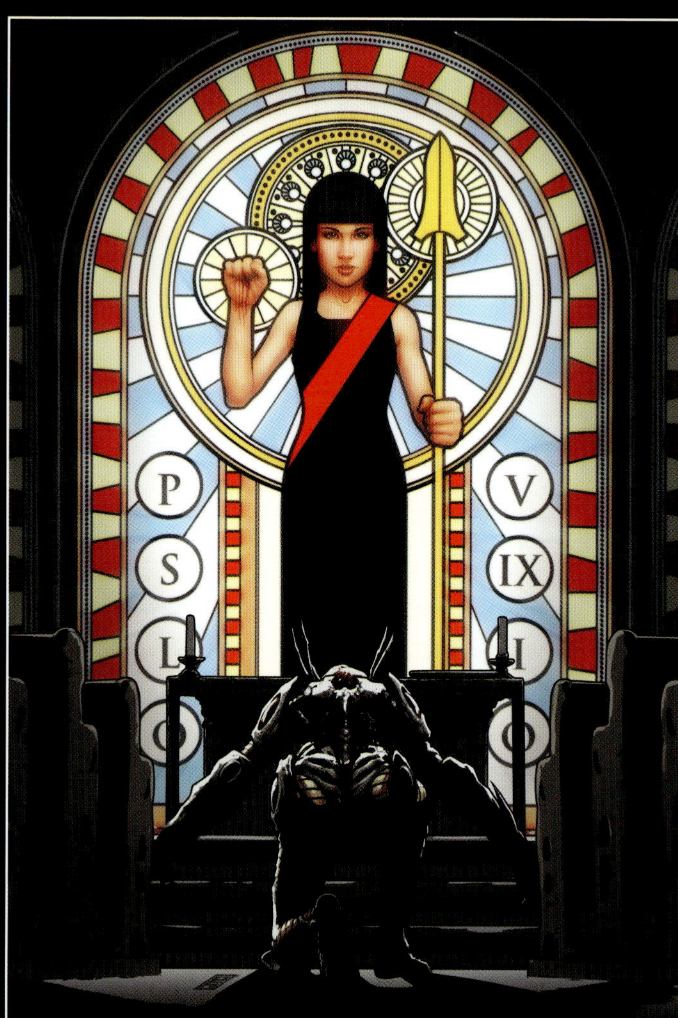

Witchblade #160, cover A, art by: John Tyler Christopher

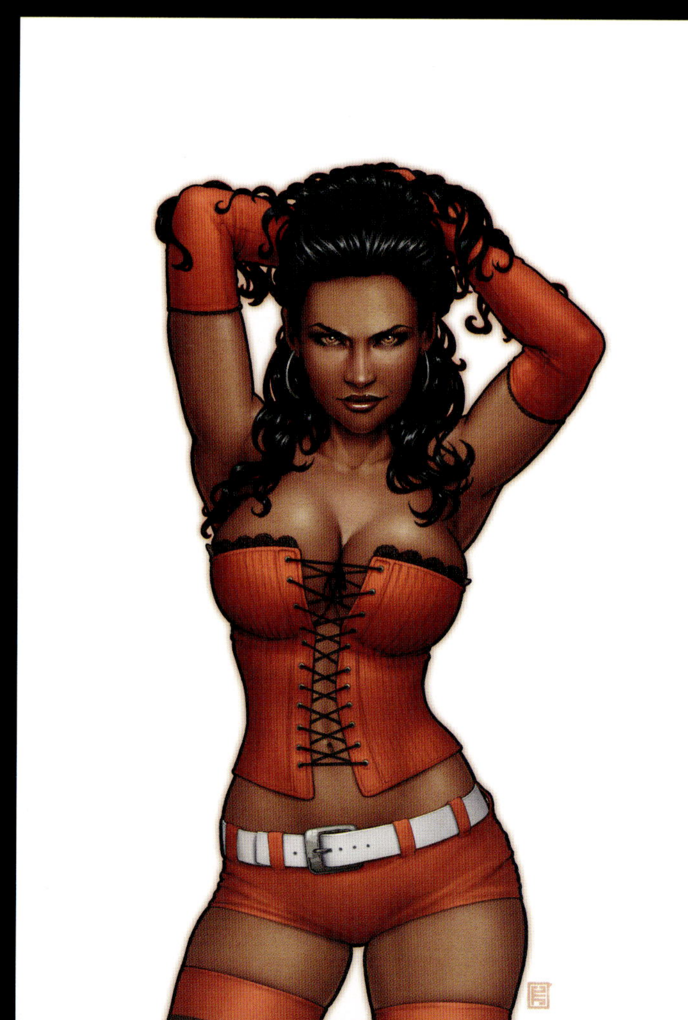

Witchblade #161, Top Cow Store Exclusive cover, art by: John Tyler Christopher

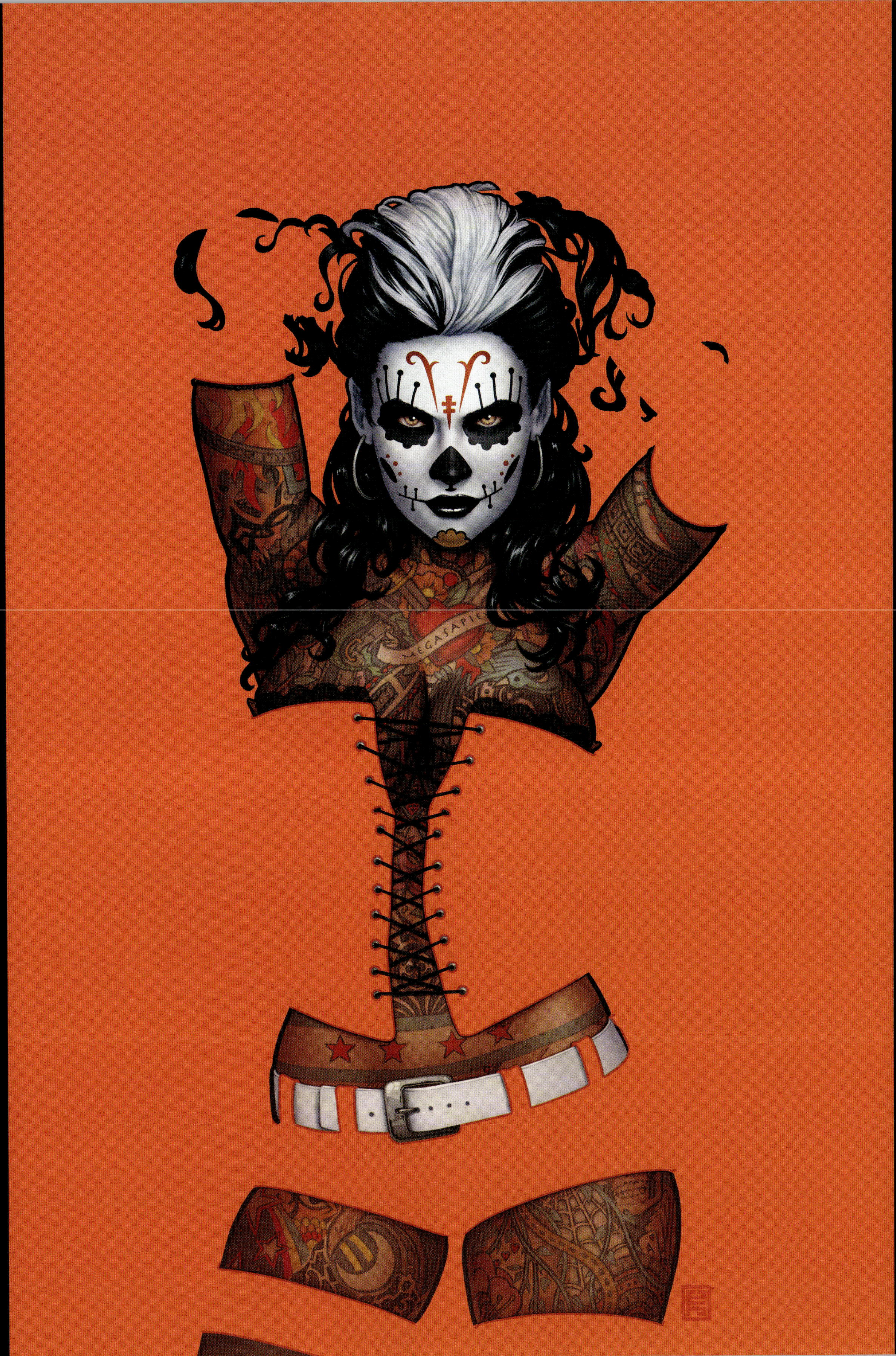

Witchblade #161 cover A,
art by: John Tyler Christopher

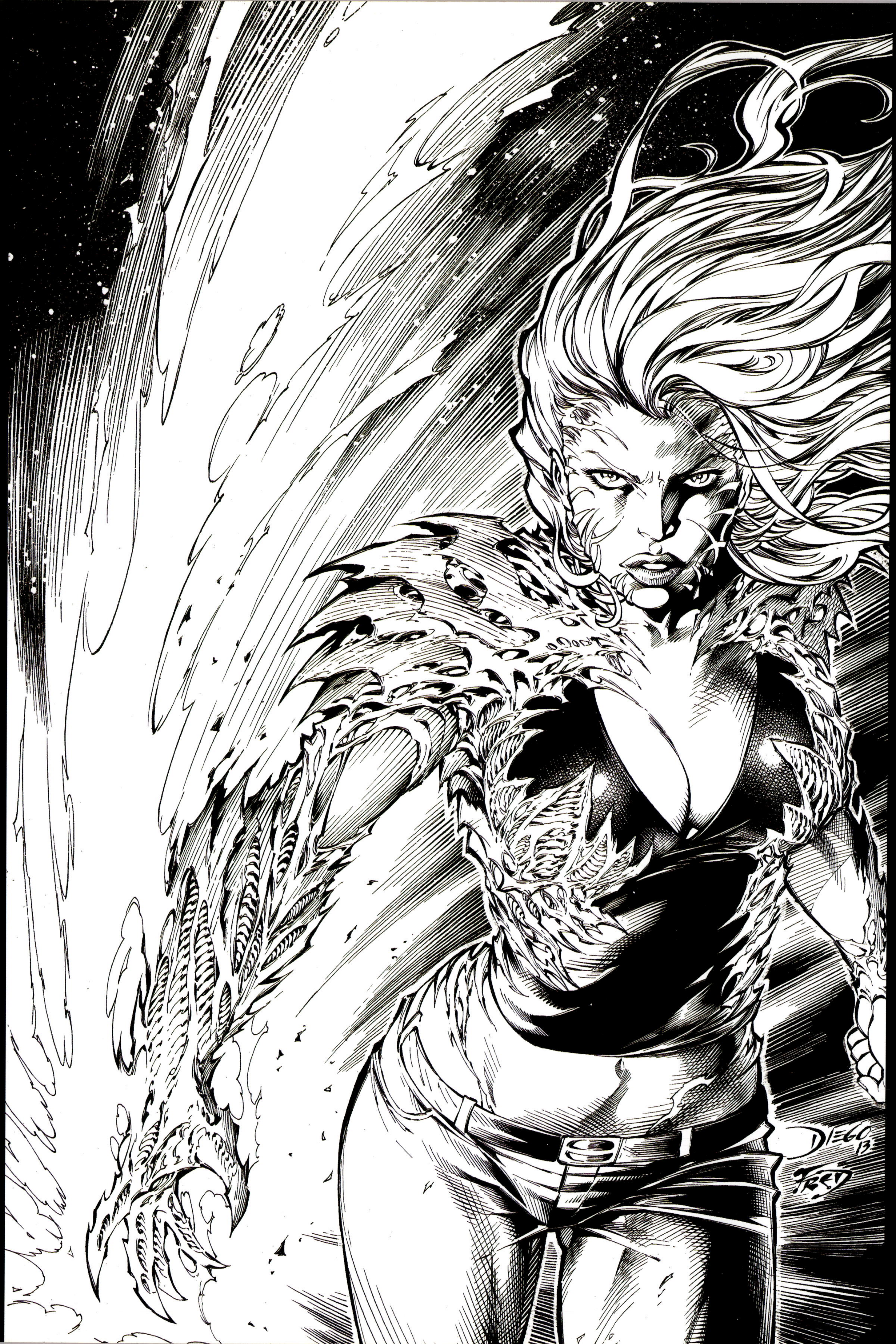

Witchblade #165 cover B,
line art by: Diego Bernard and Fred Benes

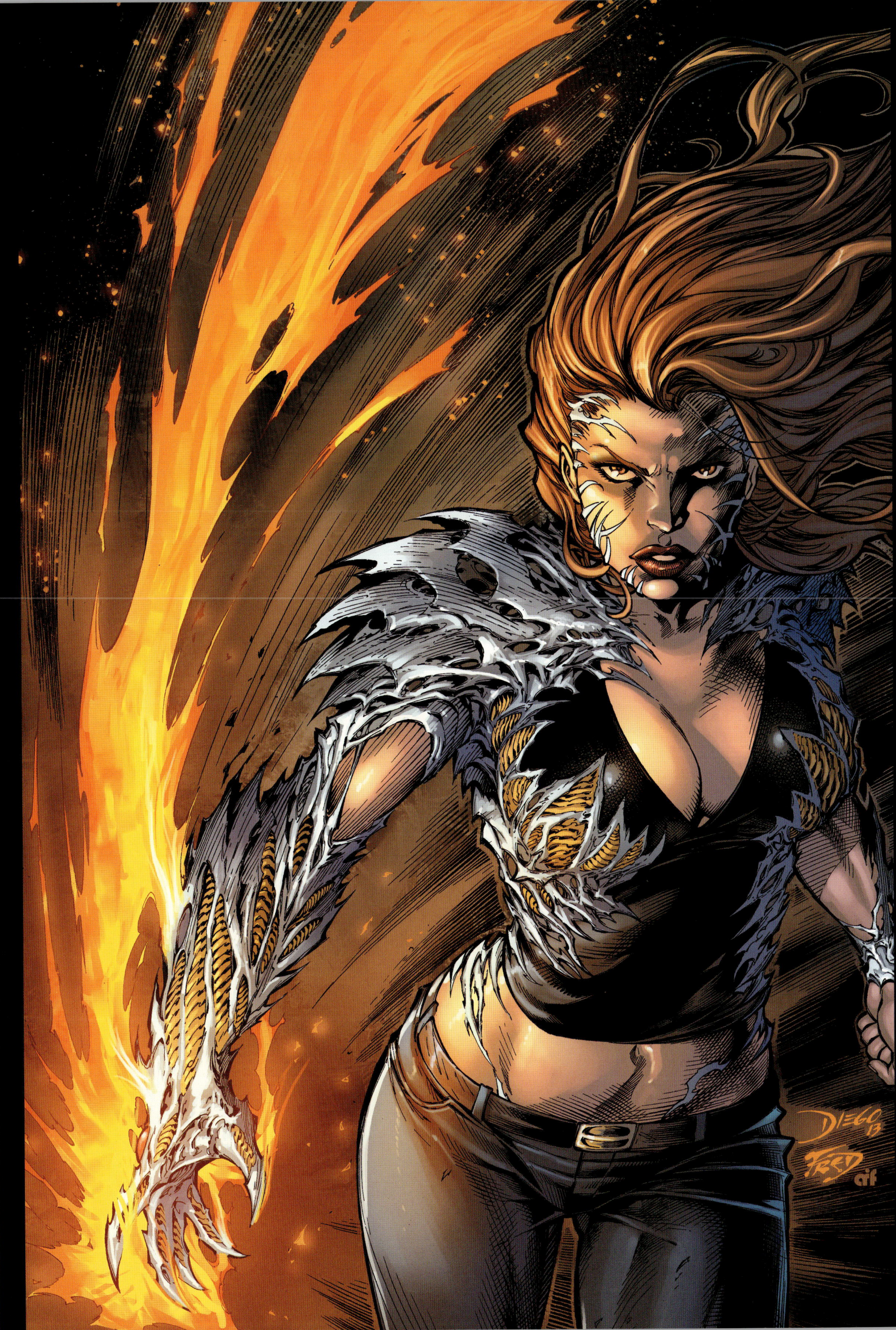

Witchblade #165 cover B,
art by: Diego Bernard, Fred Benes, and Arif Prianto

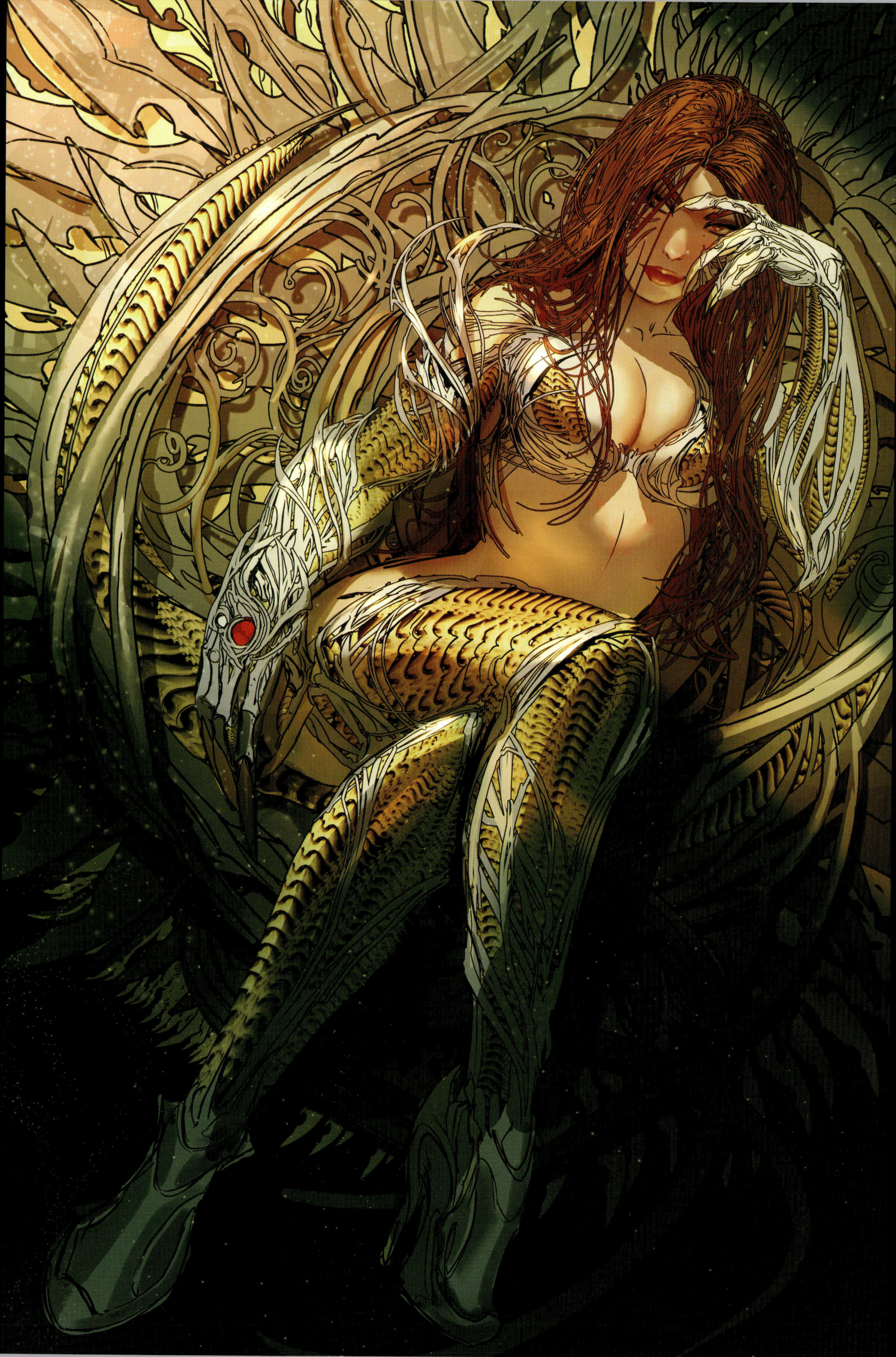

Witchblade #165 Wonder Con Exclusive cover,
art by: Stjepan Sejic

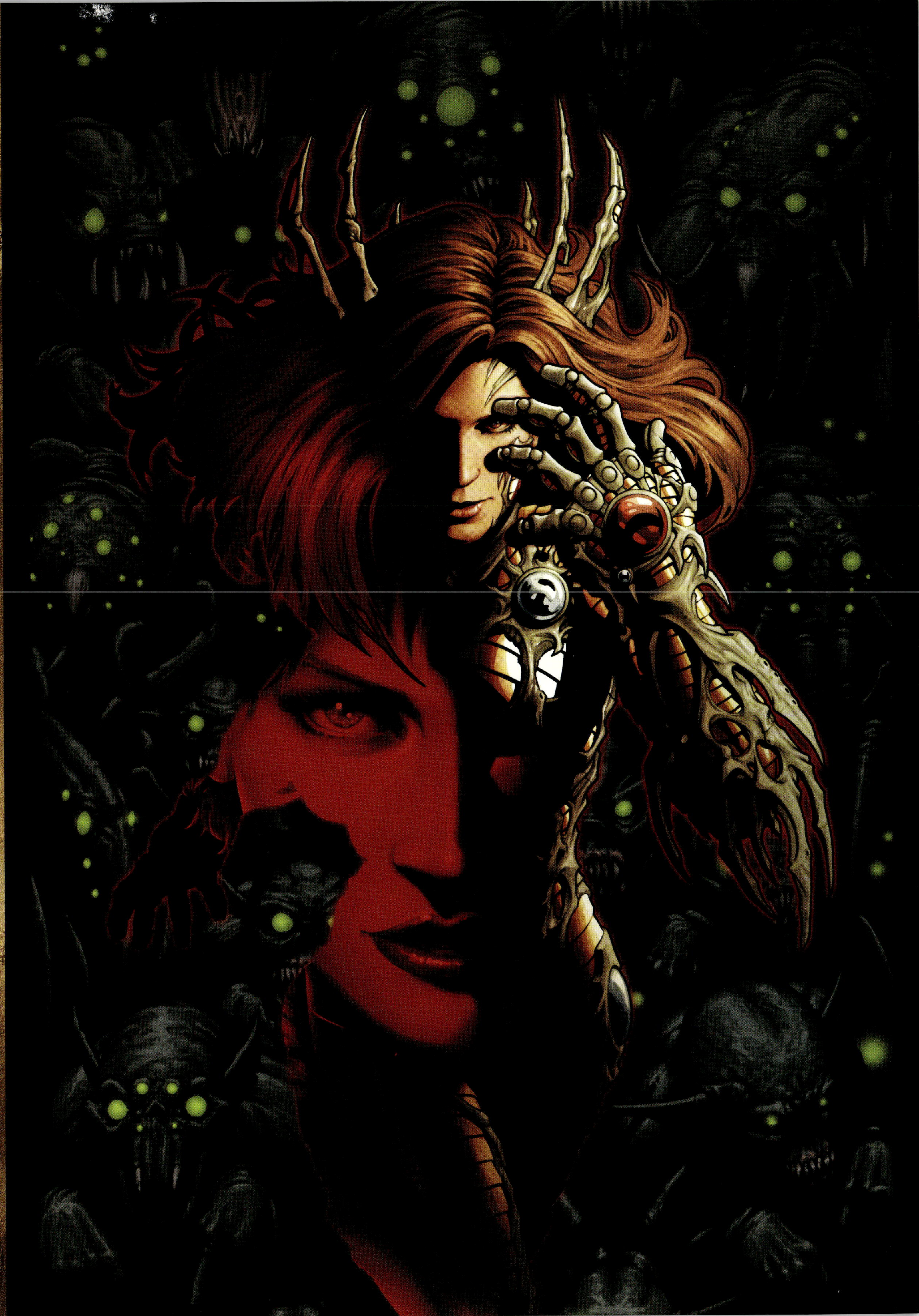

Witchblade #167 cover A,
art by: John Tyler Christopher

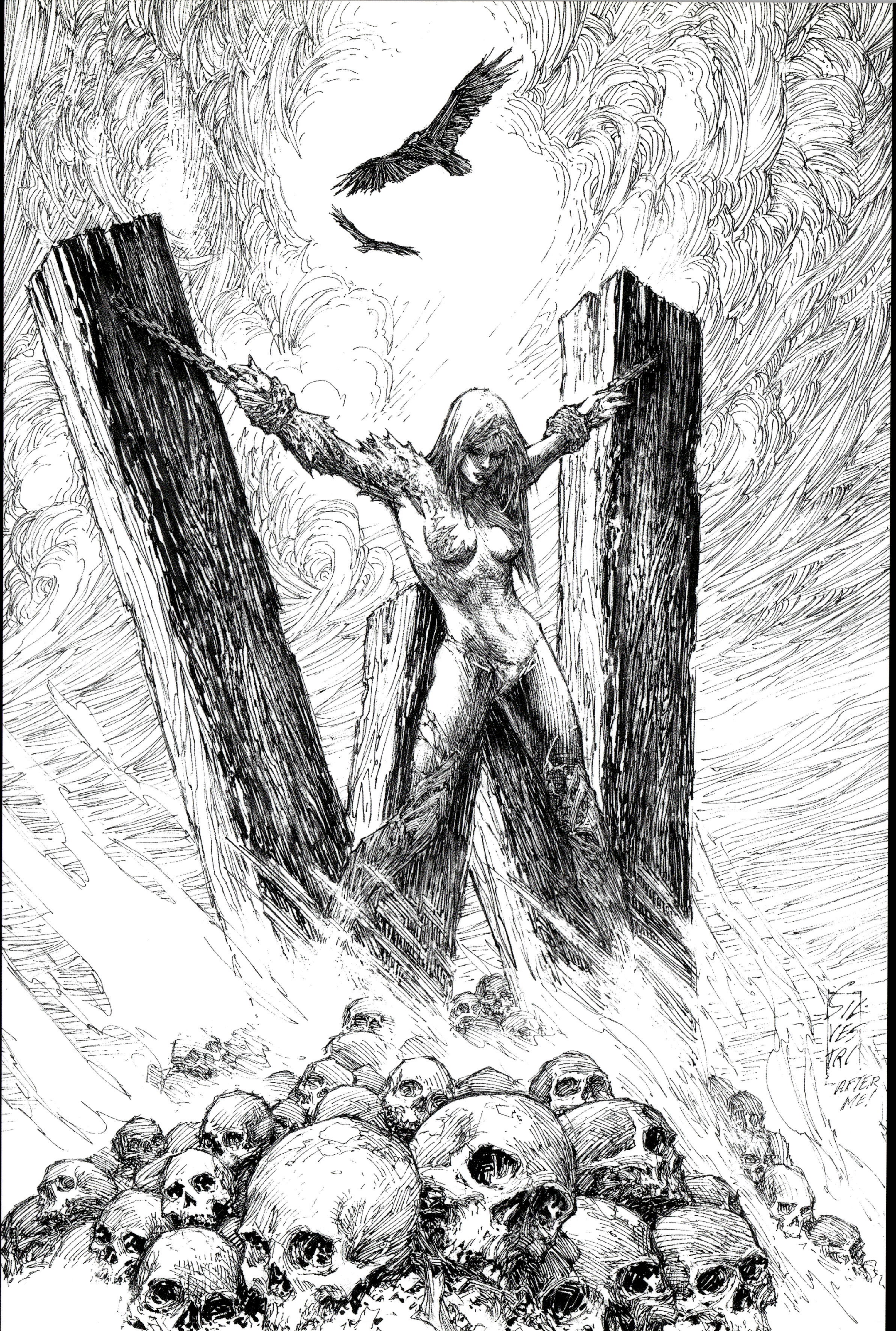

Witchblade #170 cover B,
line art by: Marc Silvestri

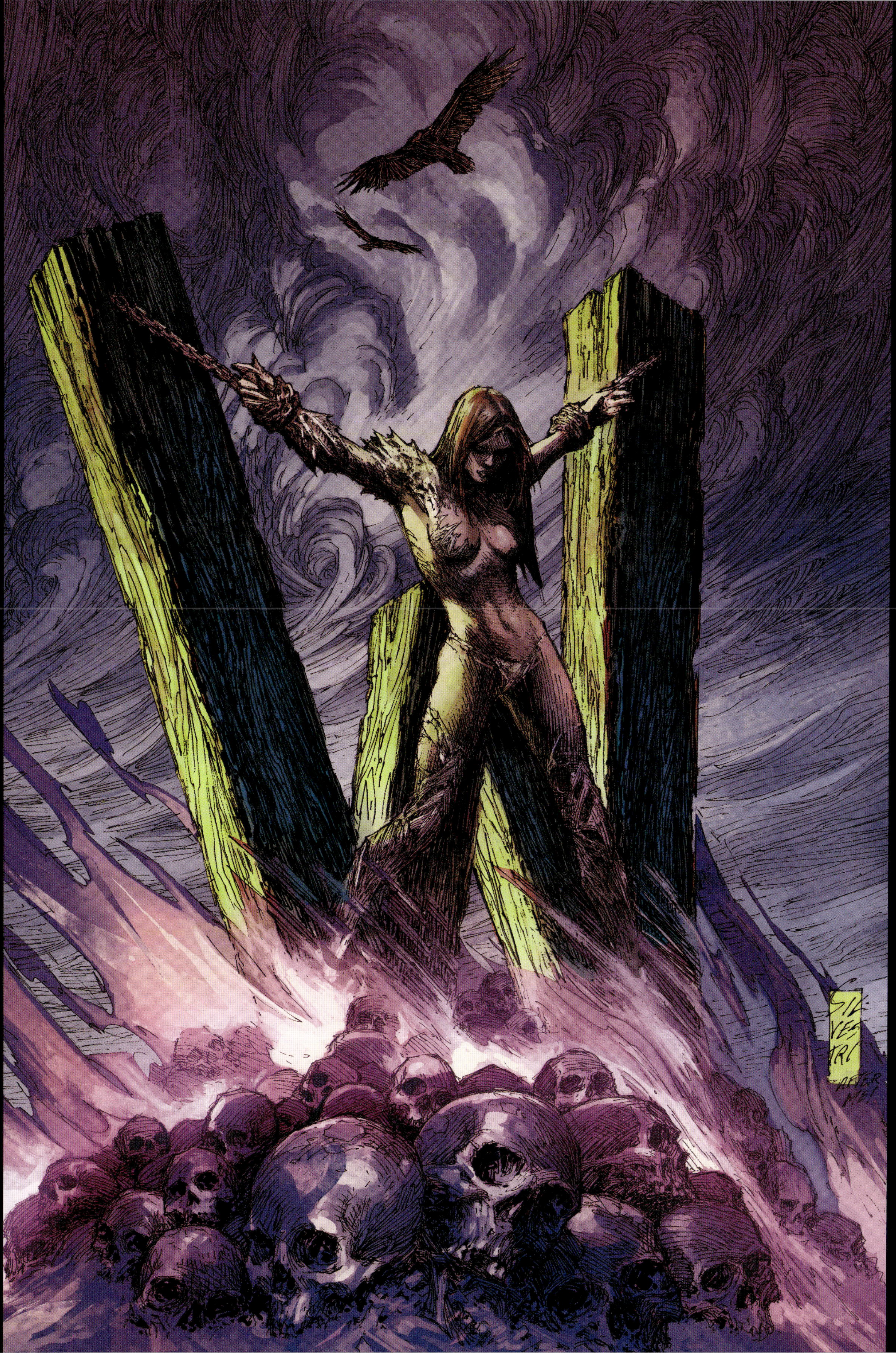

Witchblade #170 cover A,
art by: Marc Silvestri and Sunny Gho

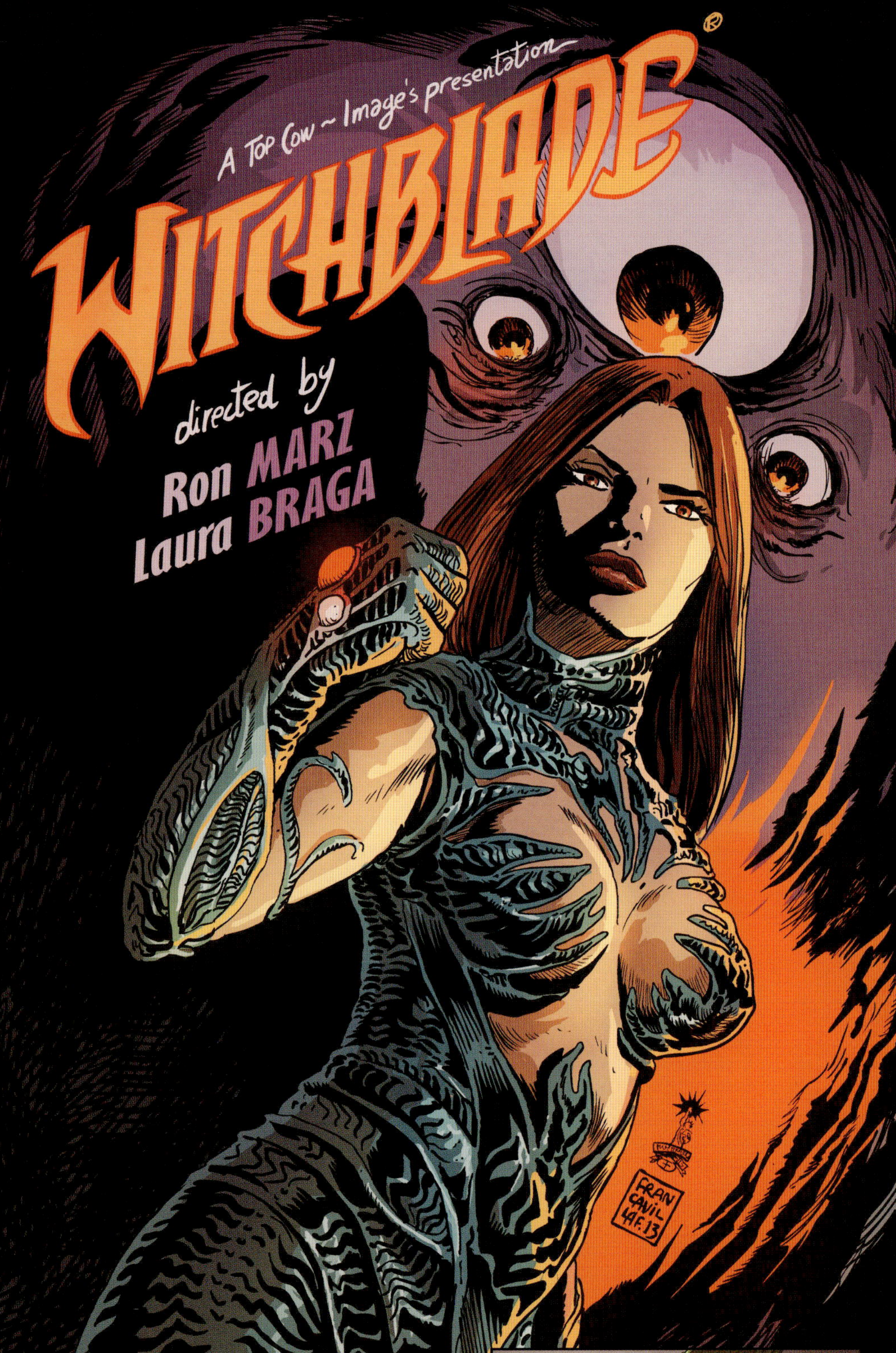

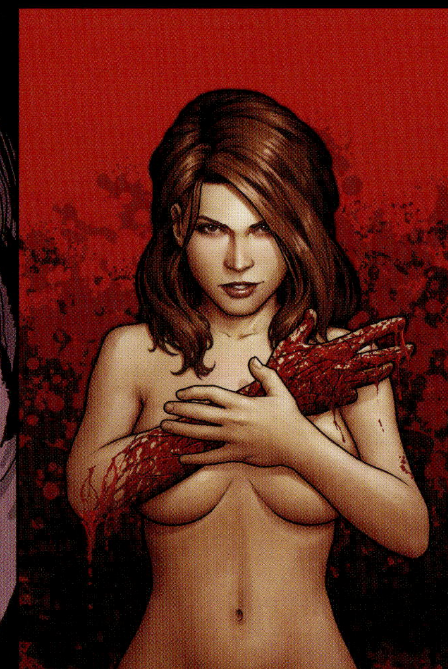

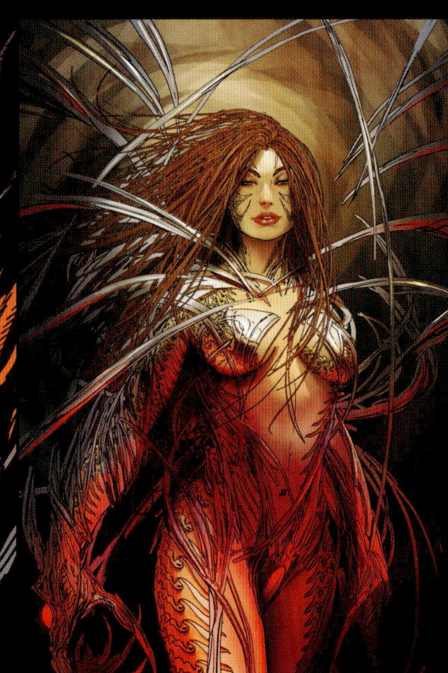

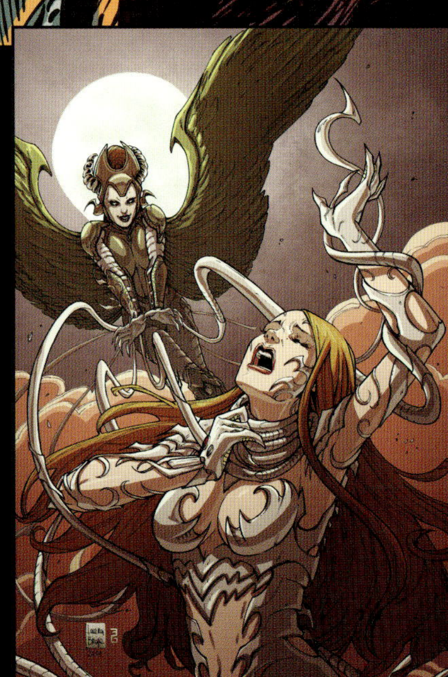

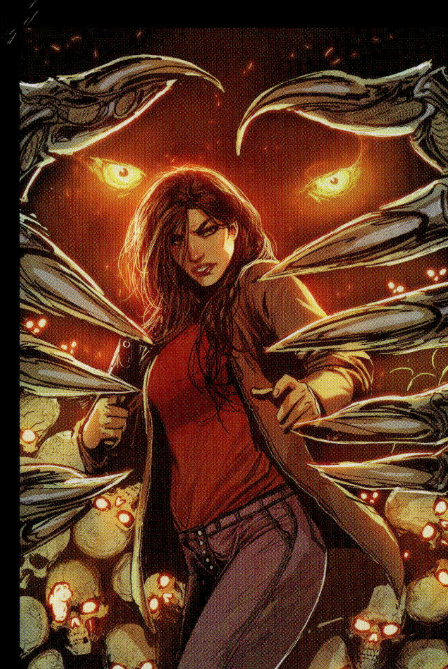

This page, clockwise from above.

Witchblade #170 Third Eye Comics variant,
art by: Francesco Francavilla

Witchblade #171 cover A,
art by: John Tyler Christopher

Witchblade #171 cover B,
art by: Stjepan Sejic

Witchblade #173 cover B,
art by: Stjepan Sejic

Witchblade #174 cover B,
art by: Laura Braga and Betsy Golden

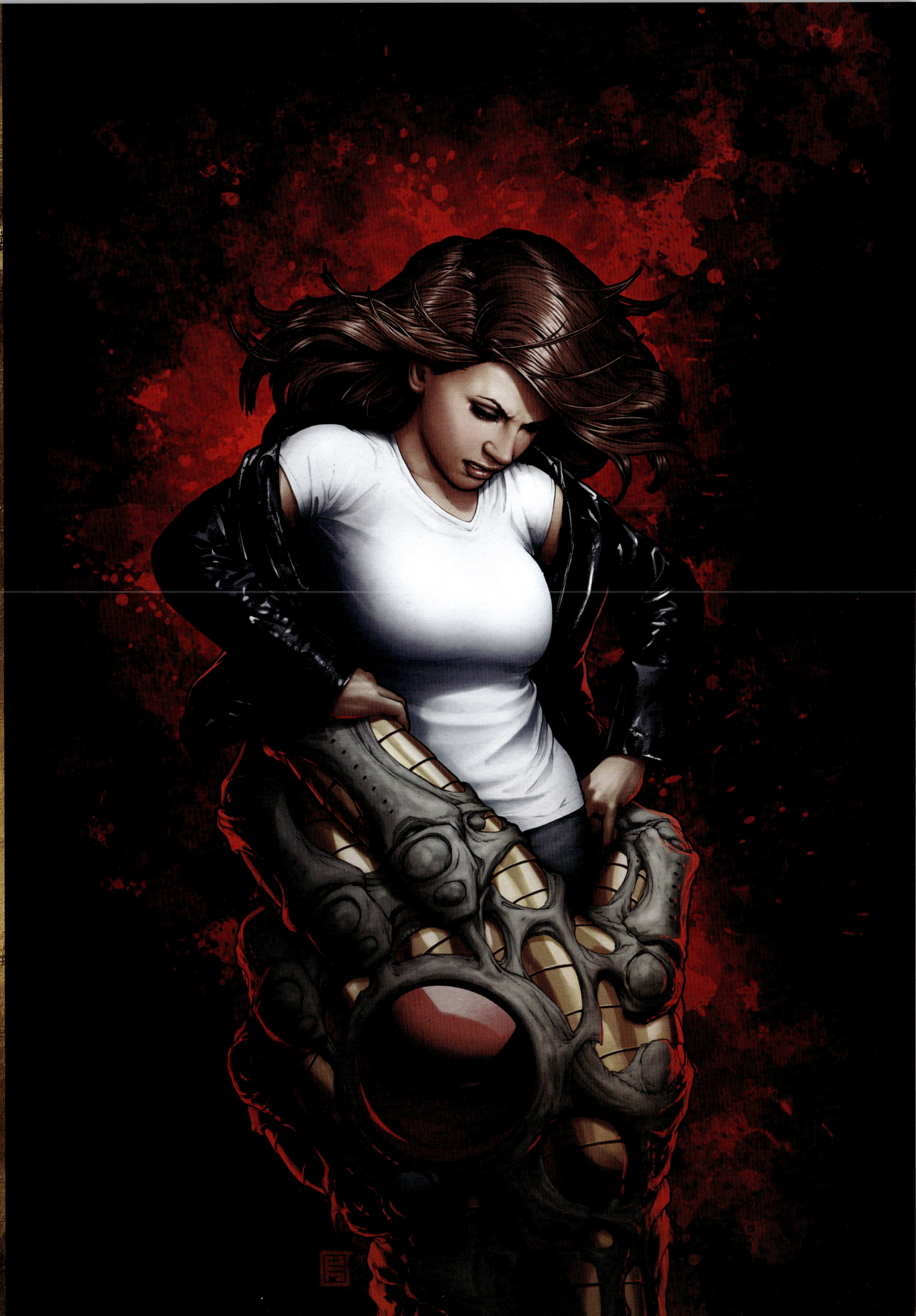

Witchblade #175 cover B,
art by: John Tyler Christopher

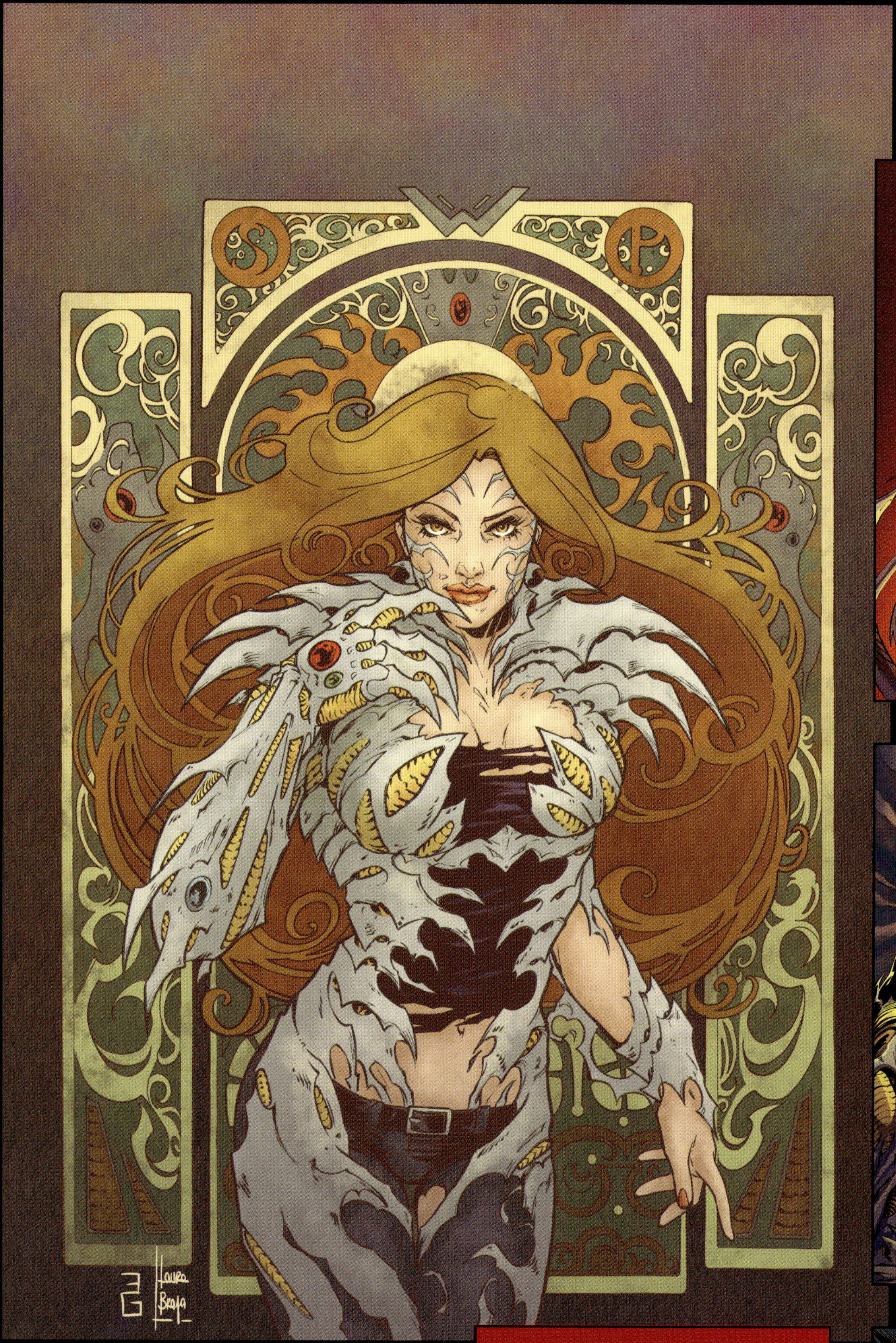

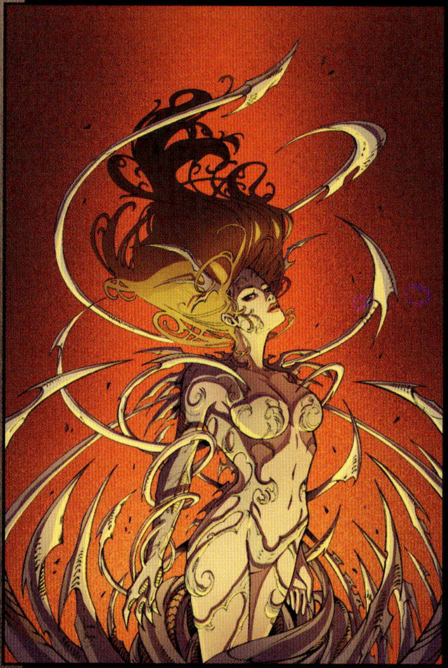

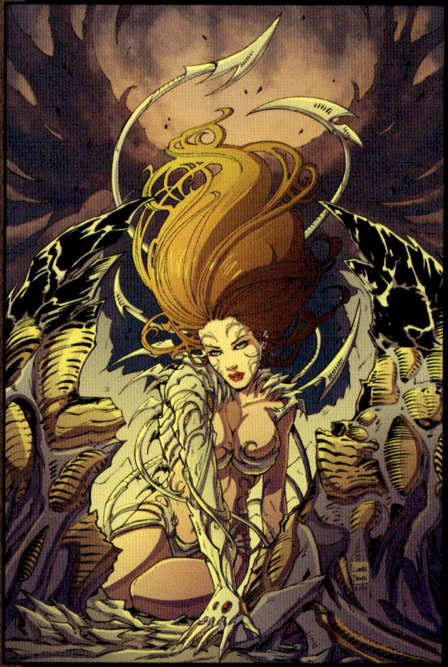

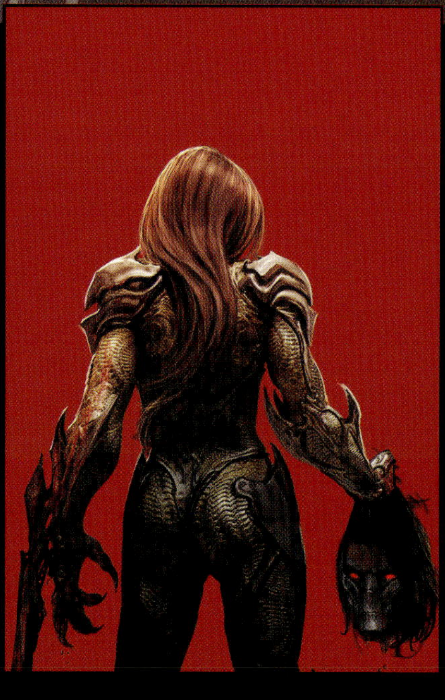

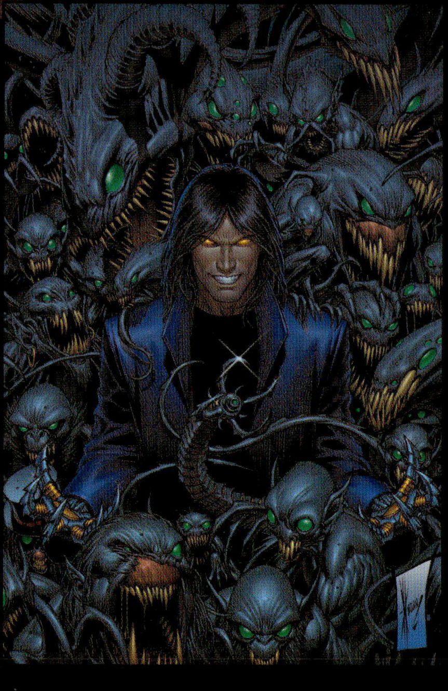

This page, clockwise from above.

Witchblade #175 cover A,
art by: Laura Braga and Betsy Golden

Witchblade #176 cover A,
art by: Laura Braga and Betsy Golden

Witchblade #179 cover A,
art by: Laura Braga and Betsy Golden

Witchblade #180 cover A,
art by: Dale Keown

Witchblade #180 cover B,
art by: Stjepan Sejic

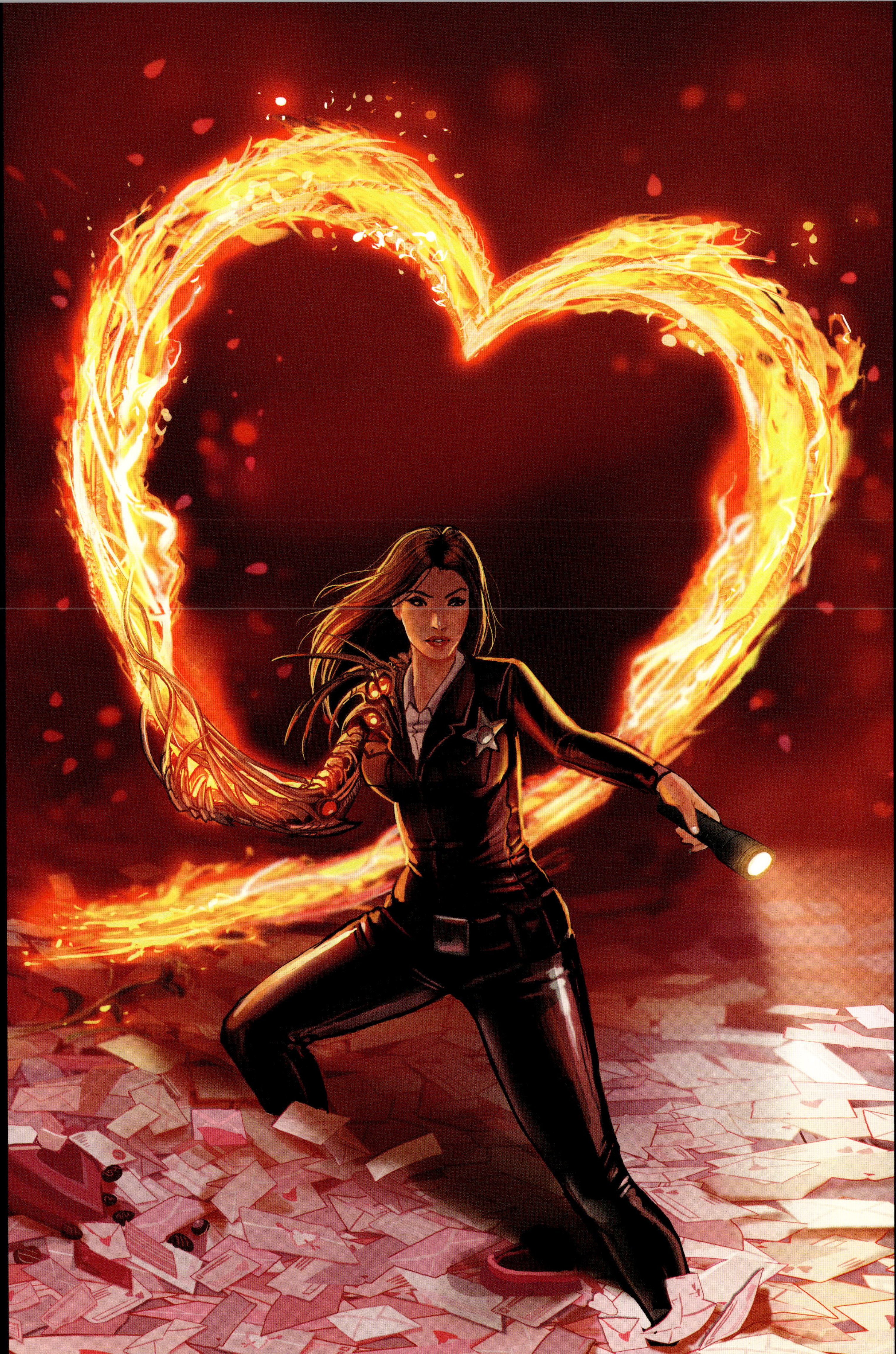

Witchblade #180 cover C,
art by: Linda Sejic

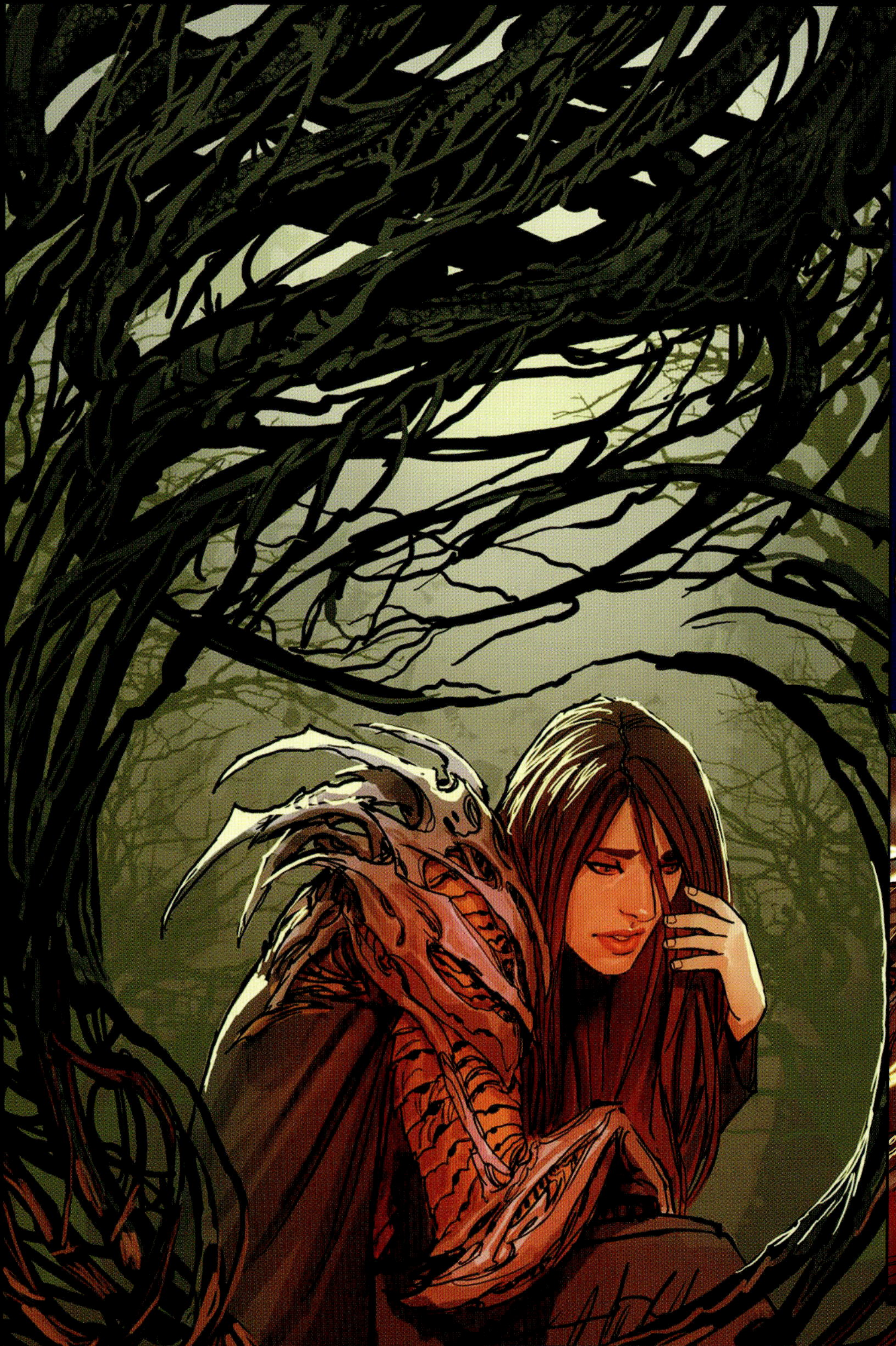

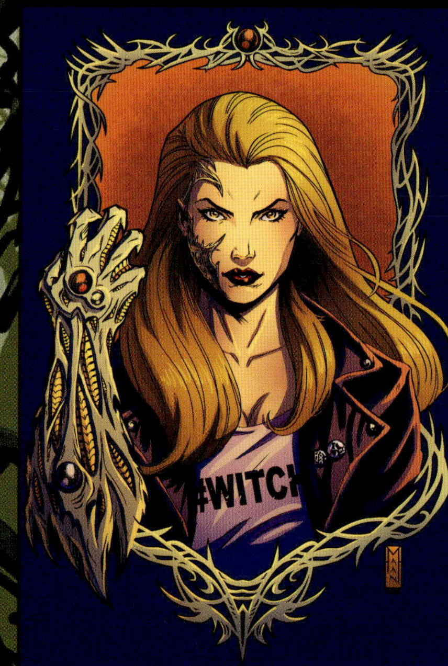

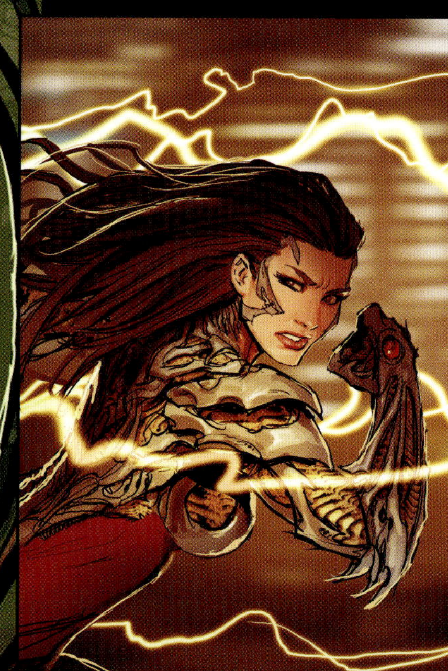

This page, clockwise from above.

Witchblade #181 cover B,
art by: Stjepan Sejic

Witchblade #182 cover A,
art by: Maan House and Betsy Golden

Witchblade #182 cover B,
art by: Stjepan Sejic

Witchblade #183 cover B,
art by: Stjepan Sejic

Witchblade #184 cover B,
art by: Stjepan Sejic

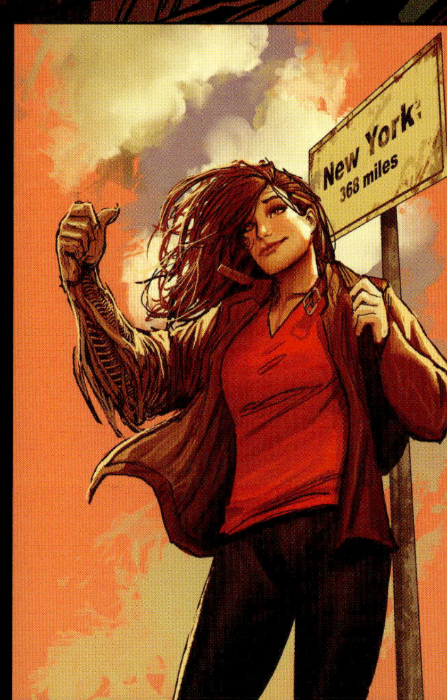

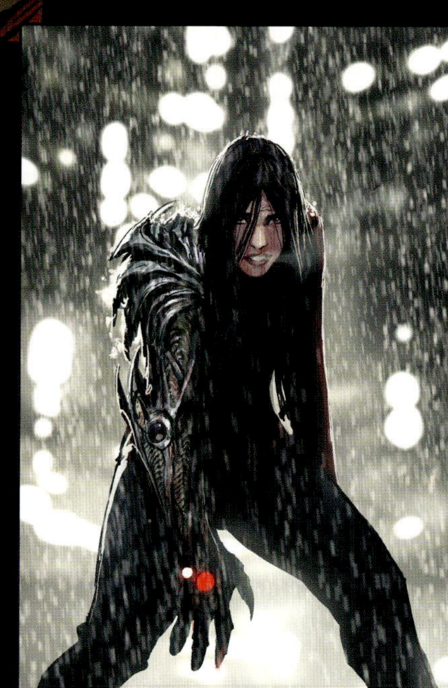

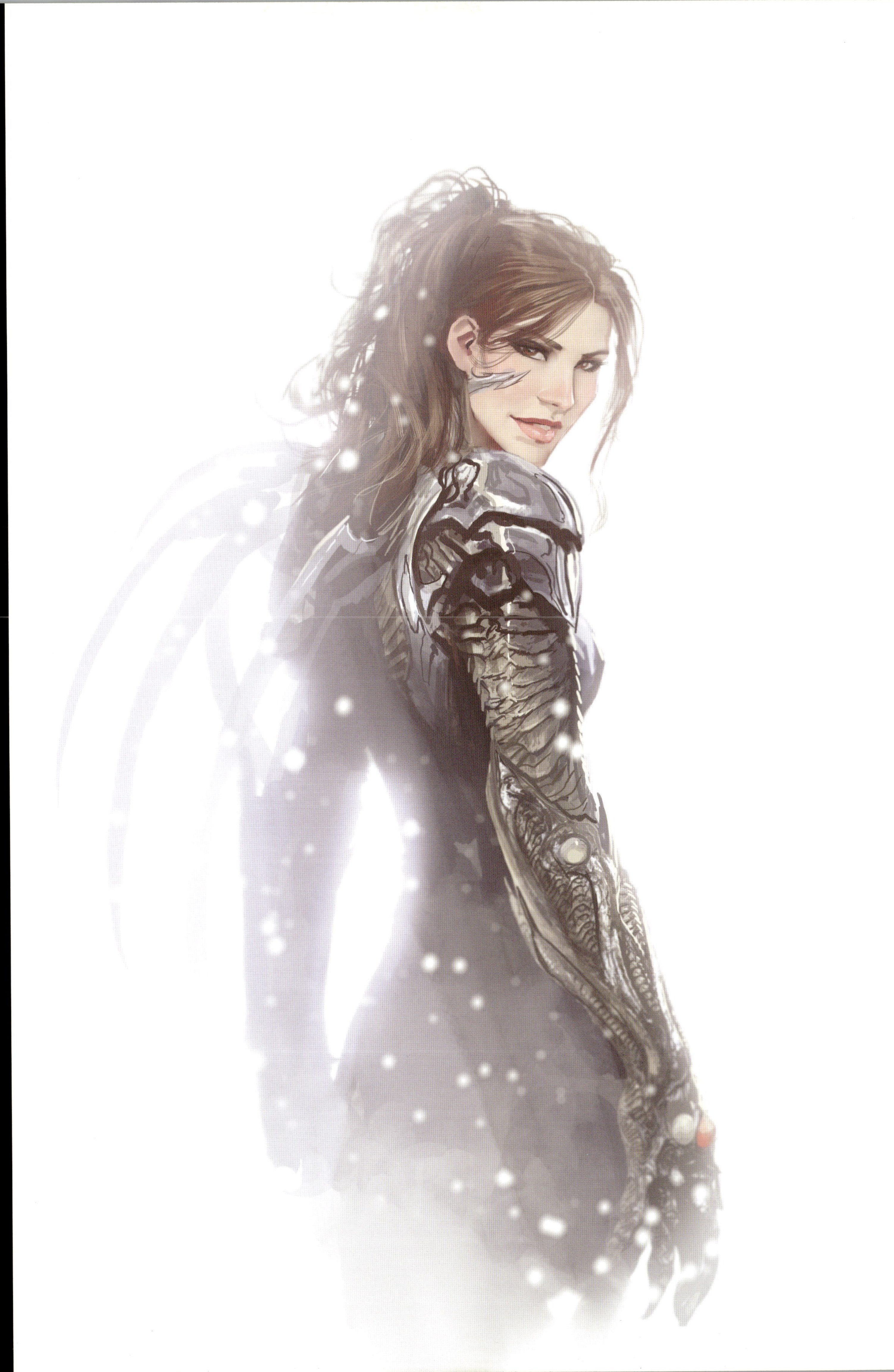

Witchblade #185 cover C,
art by: Stjepan Sejic

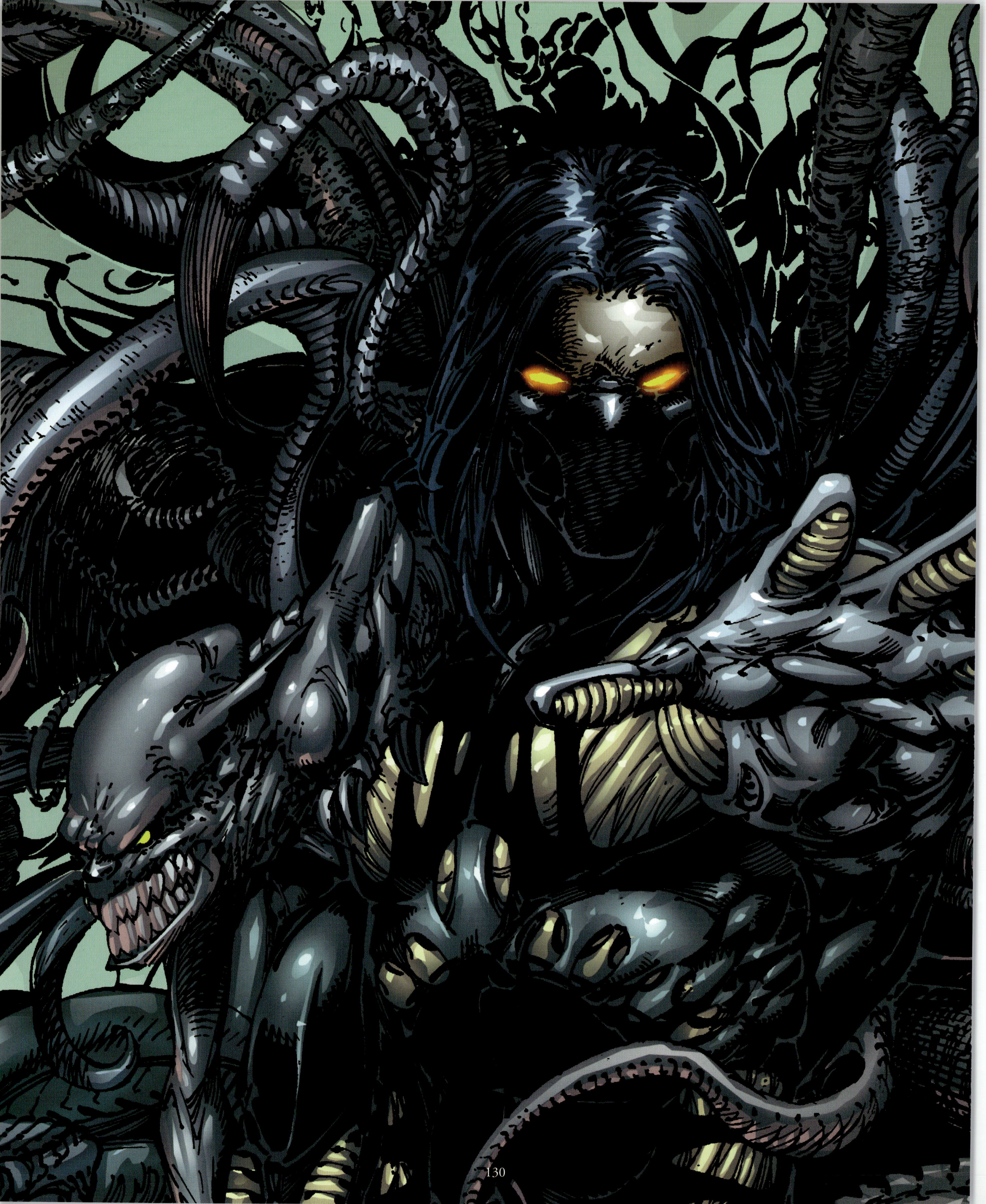

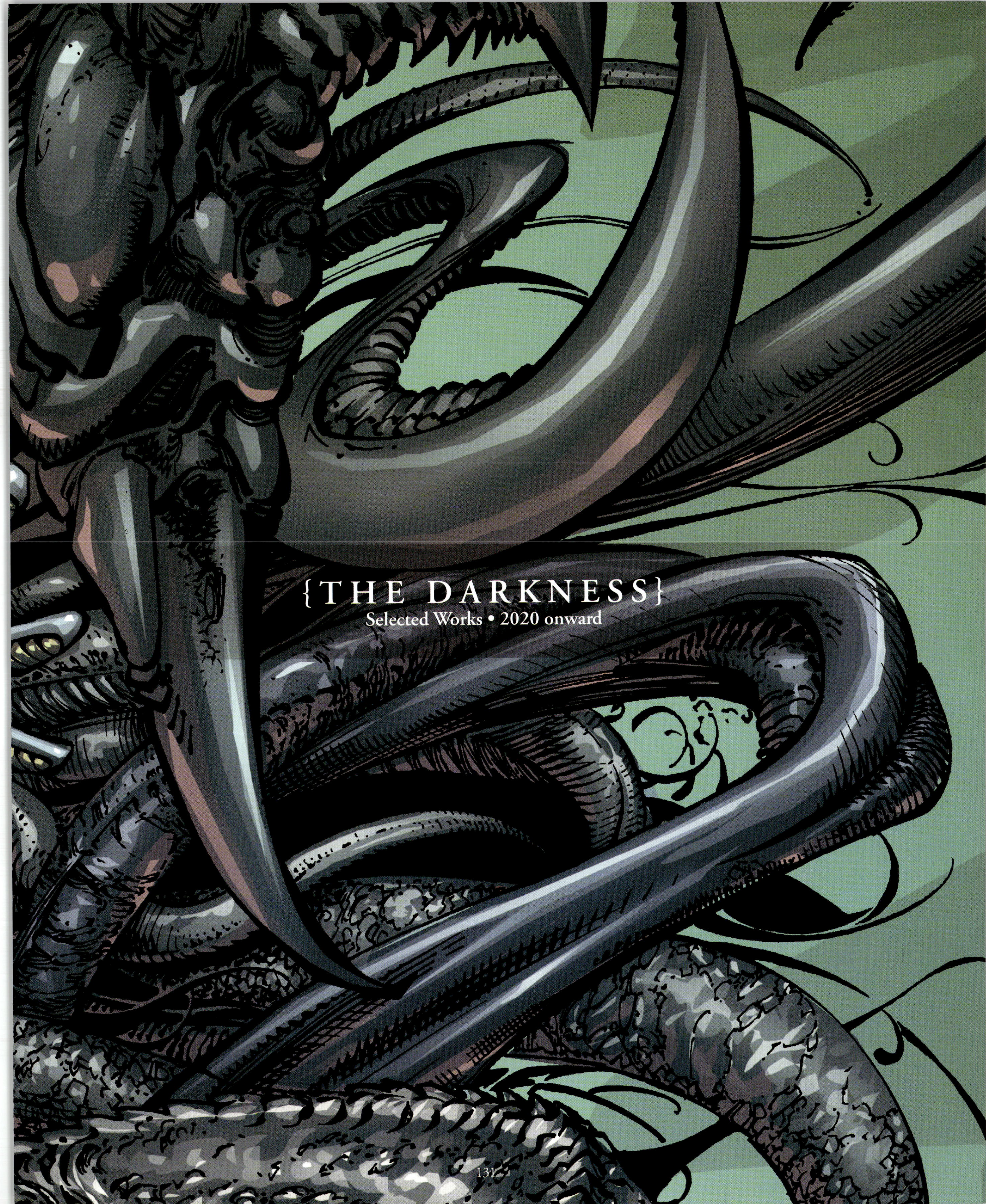

{THE DARKNESS}

Selected Works • 2020 onward

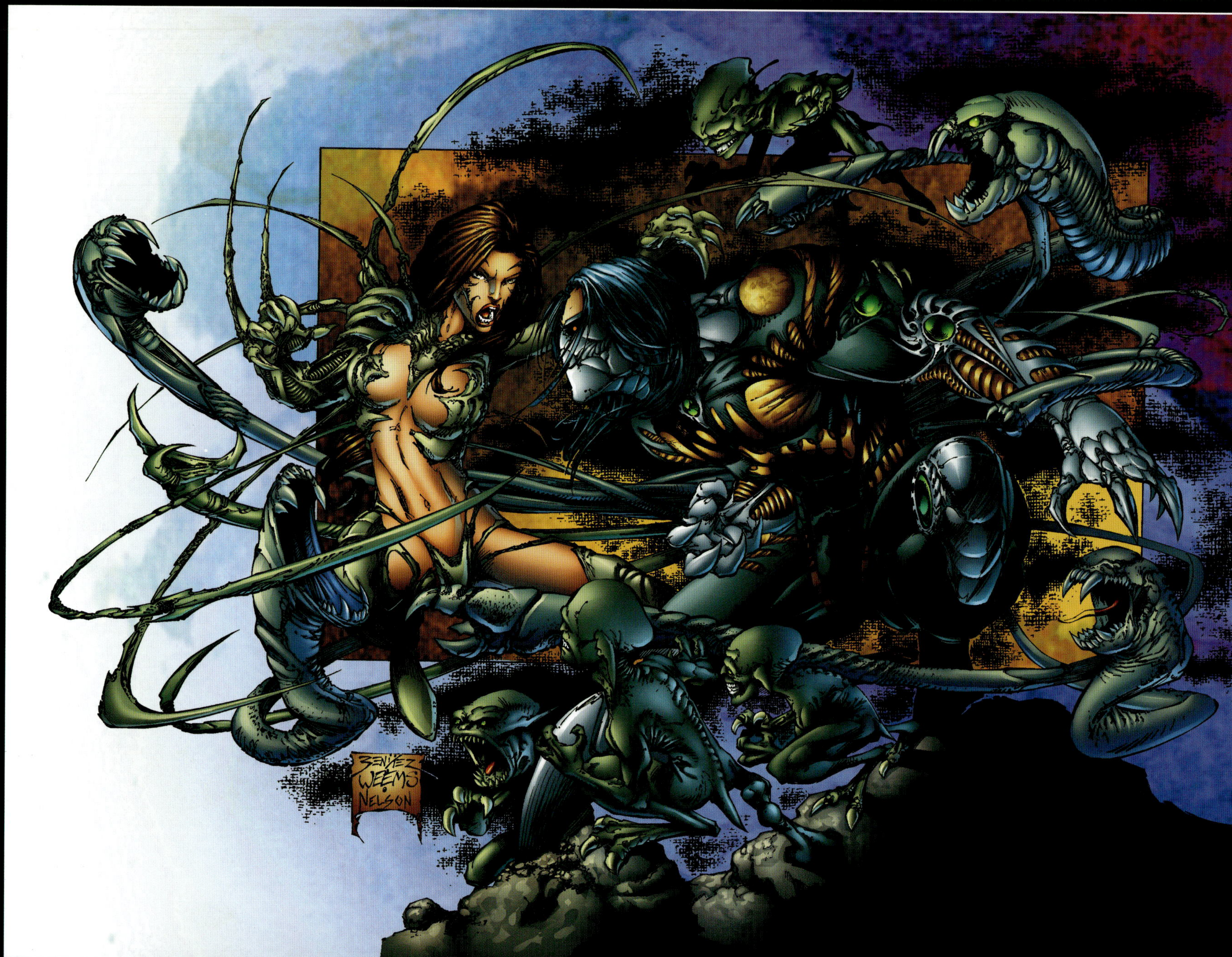

The Darkness created by
Garth Ennis, Marc Silvestri, and **David Wohl**

The Darkness was first published from December 1996 to August 2001, returned in December 2002, and relaunched in December 2007 for a third series, which concluded in December 2013. Along with *Witchblade* and *Cyberforce,* it continues to be one of the core titles of the Top Cow Universe.

If this is your first time hearing about *The Darkness,* in a nutshell: Mafia hitman Jackie Estacado was both blessed and cursed on his 21st birthday when he became the bearer of The Darkness, an elemental force that allows those who wield it access to an otherworldly dimension and control over the demons who dwell there. Forces for good in the world rise to face Jackie and the evil his gift represents, but there is one small problem. In this story, they are the bad guys.

Above. *Witchblade vs. The Darkness,* Wizard (#1/2) #1 pin-up
art by: Joe Benitez, Joe Weems V, and Matt Nelson

Previous page. *The Darkness* poster #3
art by: Joe Benitez, Joe Weems V, and Tyson Wengler

Facing page. *The Darkness* #1 25th Anniversary Commemorative Edition [2020] cover C,
art by: Marc Silvestri

Since 2013, *The Darkness* has been collected in the comprehensive *Complete Edition* line of trade paperbacks, currently coming up on their volume 4 edition, as well as various single issues including *The Darkness* 25th Anniversary #1, Commemorative Edition [2020], *The Darkness* #1/2 [2021], and *The Darkness: Sourcebook* [2024]. On the following pages, we look at recent works and a peek at what is coming.

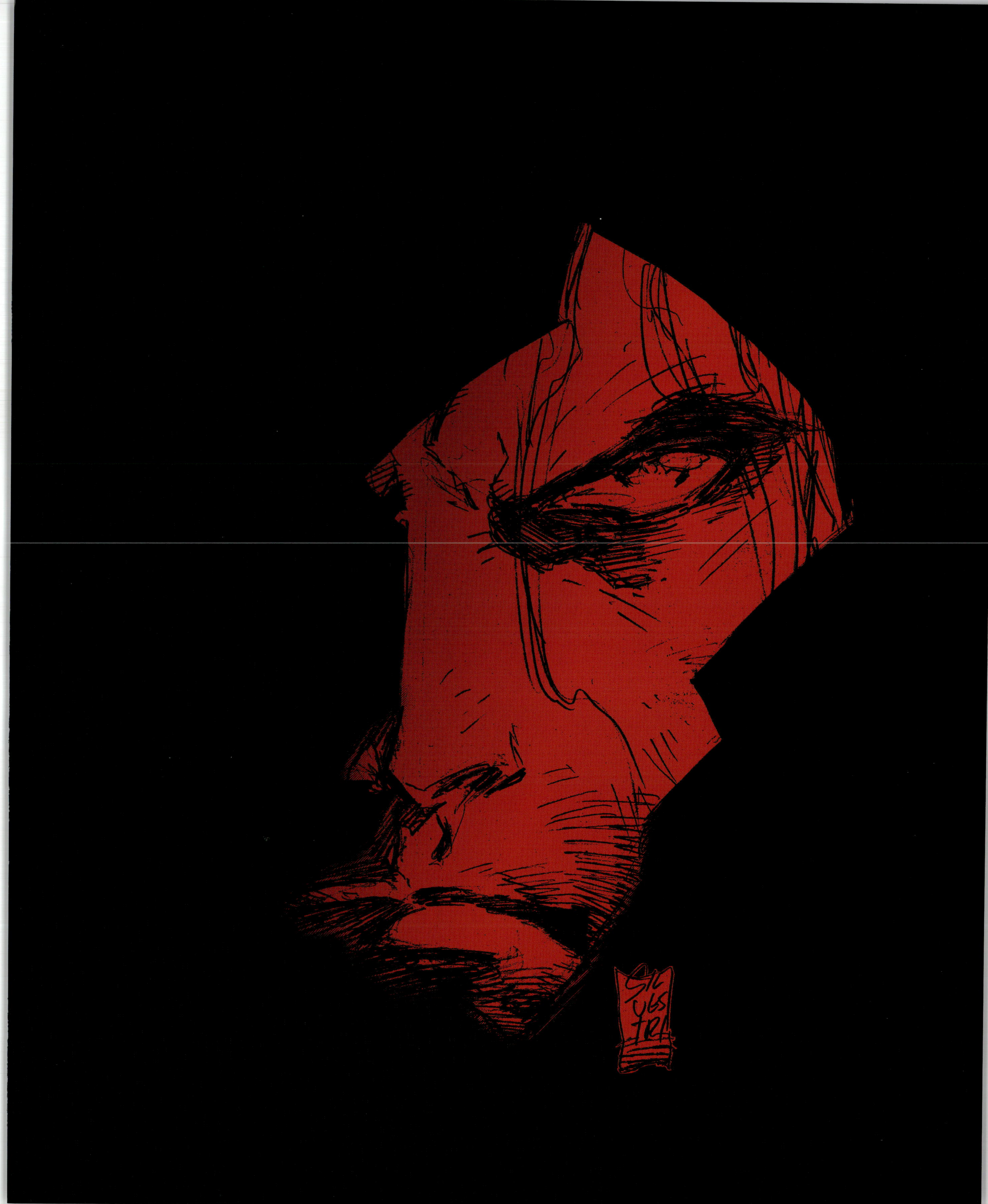

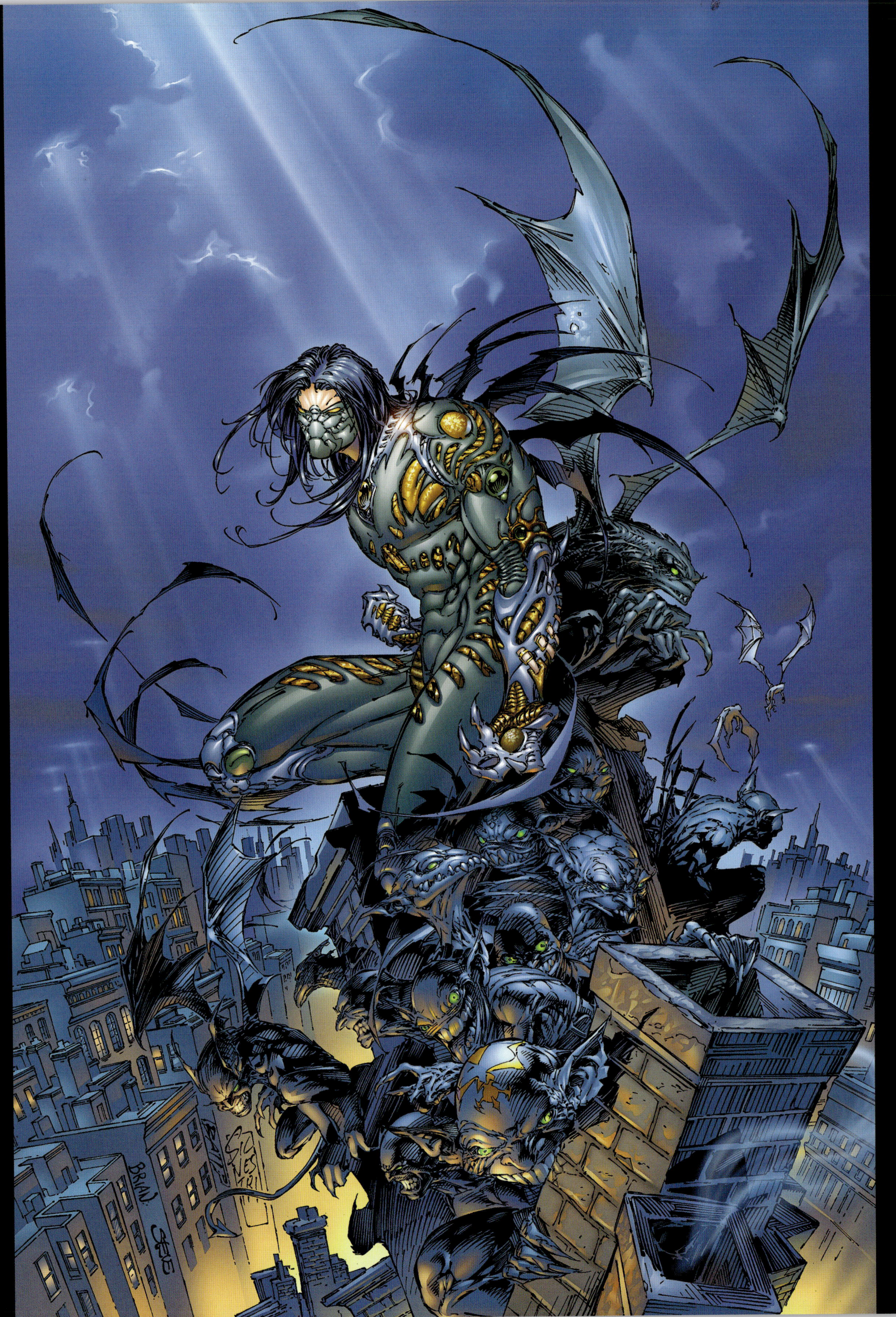

The Darkness #1 25th Anniversary Commemorative Edition [2020] cover A (reprint), art by: Marc Silvestri, Matt "Batt" Banning, Brian Haberlin, and Steve Firchow

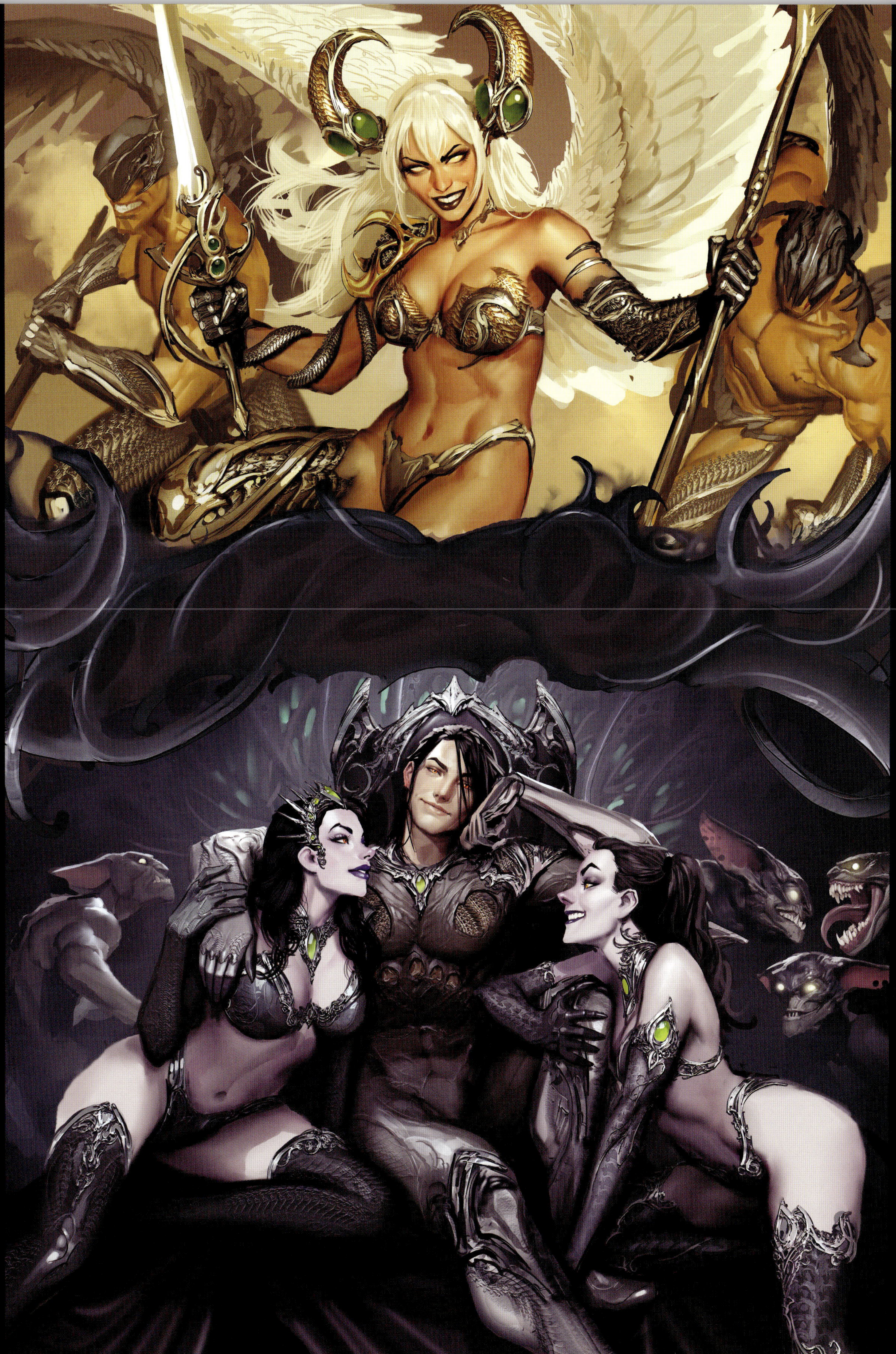

The Darkness #1 25th Anniversary Commemorative Edition [2020] cover B,
art by: Stjepan Sejic

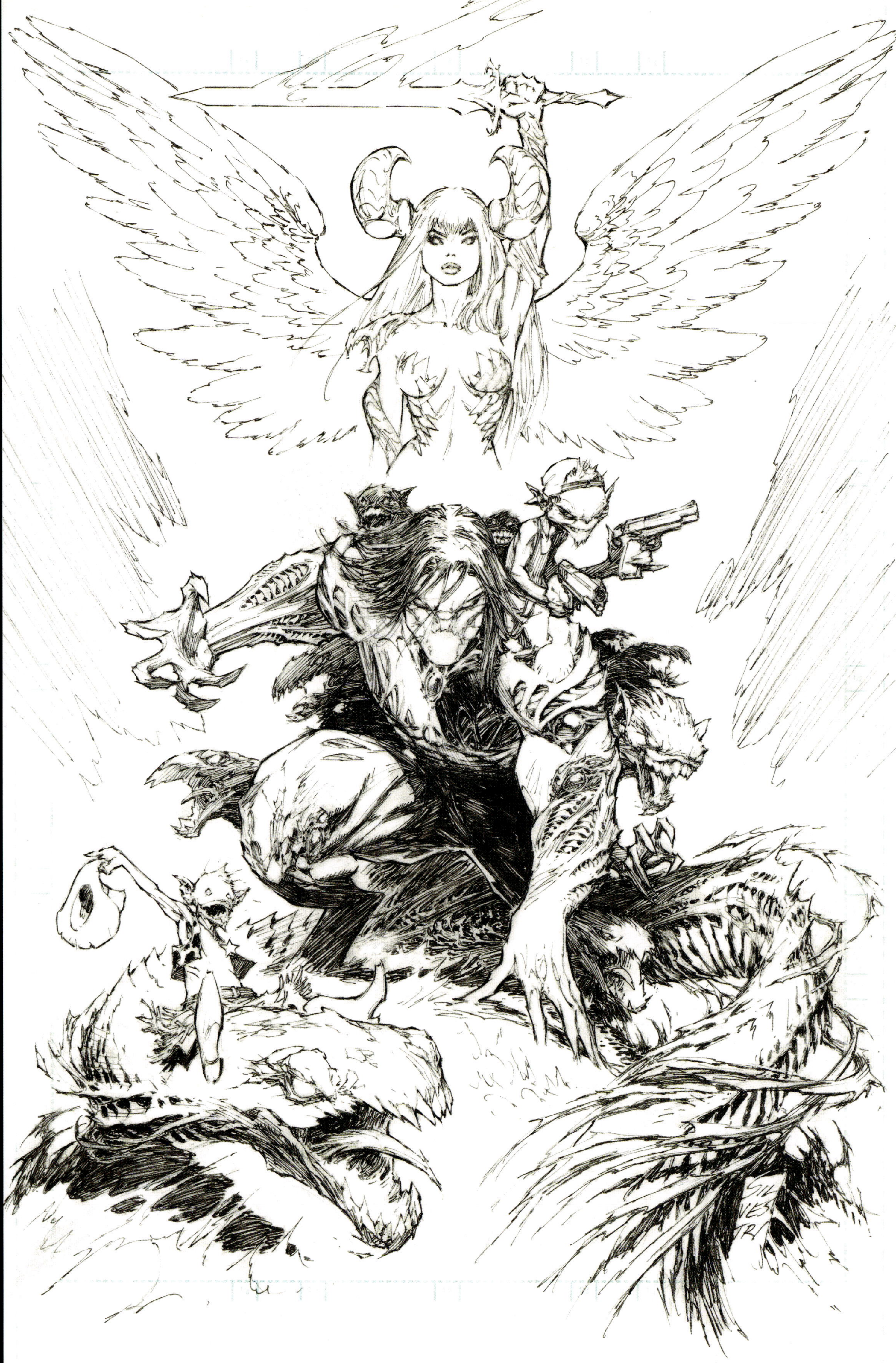

The Darkness #1 25th Anniversary Commemorative Edition [2020], "Stay At Home Edition" convention variant cover, line art by: Marc Silvestri

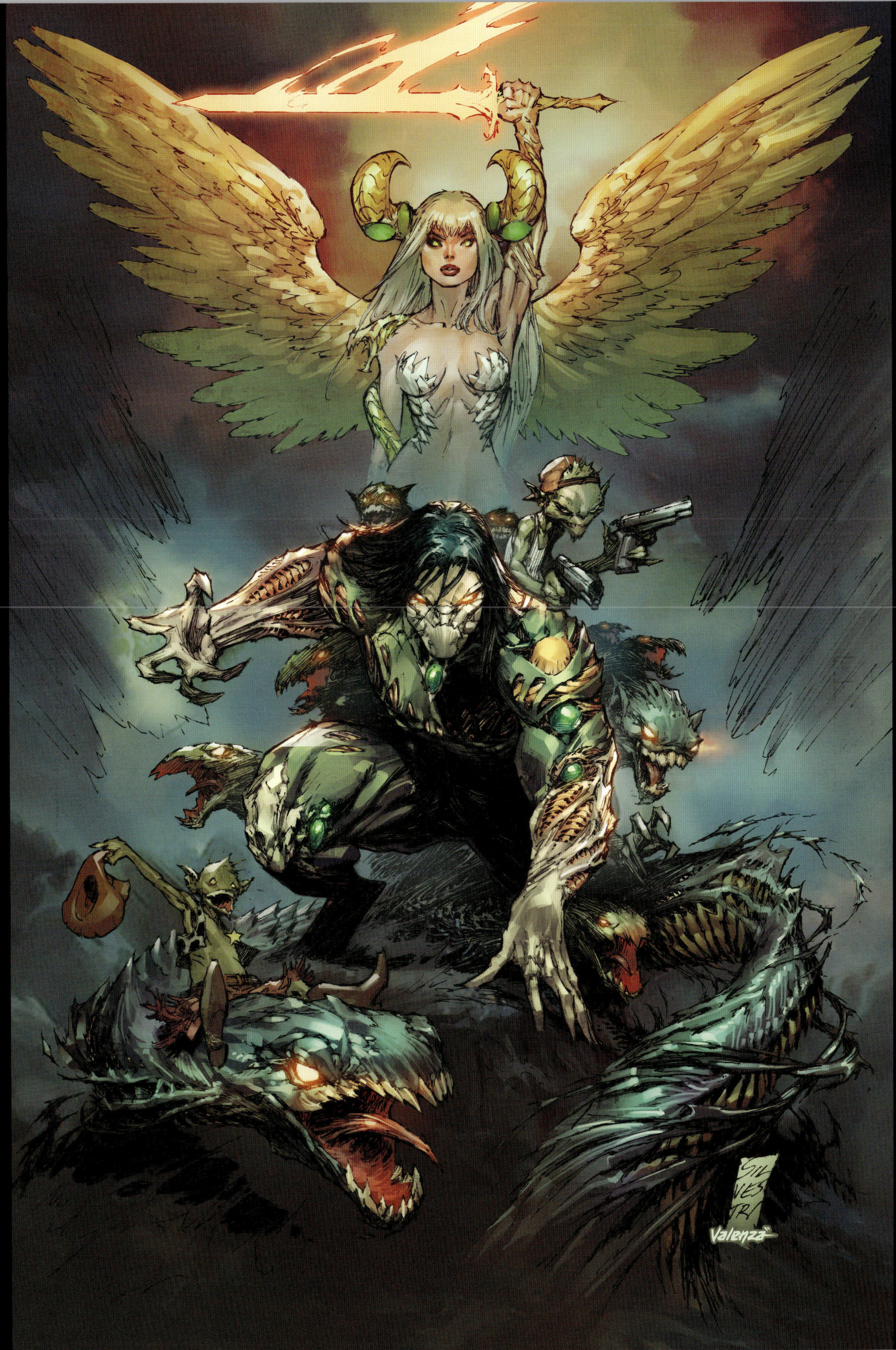

The Darkness #1 25th Anniversary Commemorative Edition [2020], Kickstarter Exclusive cover, art by: Marc Silvestri and Bryan Valenza.

Below are excerpts from the Editorial and interview presented in *The Darkness* #1, 25th Anniversary Commemorative edition. Editorial by **HENRY BARAJAS** & **CLAIRE NAPIER**.

“ SAY GOOD NIGHT TO THE “GOOD GUY”
A look back on everyone’s favorite anti-hero: Jackie Estacado, aka “The Darkness”
BY **HENRY BARAJAS** & **CLAIRE NAPIER**

“The Darkness is the ID that we all have buried deep inside, that our empathy and humanity keeps in check.”
– Marc Silvestri

Jackie Estacado was never the “good guy.” The teaser that preceded his solo debut, *The Darkness* #0, made a feature of it: he lists all the wickedness and aesthetic sleaze in his life, the sexy girls he couldn’t name, the mob murders he’s casual about, the power he has to produce vile and wicked outcomes. Then he finishes with can-you-believe-it rhetoric—and he’s the hero. It didn’t mean hero like, “good role model.” It meant hero as in protagonist and glamorised agent. Jackie was there to be admired as he did horrible stuff for the worst reasons. The Darkness offers “darkness” as a vibe. A true definition of an anti-hero.

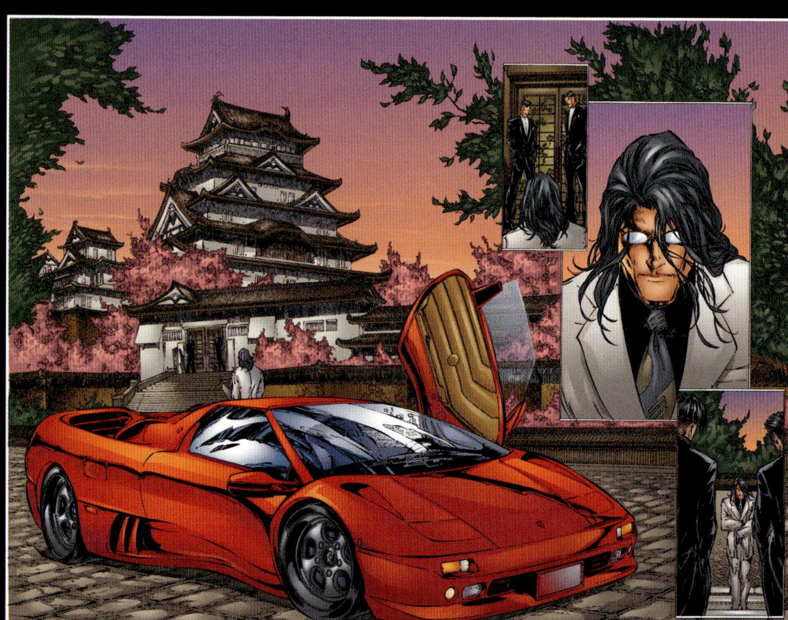

Above. *Witchblade* #10, pages 2-3,
art by: Michael Turner , D-Tron, and Jonathan D. Smith

Debuting as he did in *Witchblade* (issue #10, first series), The Darkness is unsurprisingly tied to visions and revisions of sexual masculinity. Introduced as a sex addict whose impulses are curbed by the “death or chastity” roulette, The Darkness plays with its host until he’s ready to pass it off to his next kind like his forefathers. He’s a victim of violent childhood abuse who grows into a violently abusive man. He’s an orphan who tears his found family apart at least twice. But Jackie is one of the few characters in the Top Cow Universe that evolves and changes for the better or worse.

While it makes perfect sense that a character spun off from a core title would return to that title later—Jackie and Sara Pezzini do visit each others’ books with regularity, with more or less lasting impact depending on the event at hand—it’s rarer that a crossover between two publishing companies will have an inescapable influence on a successful monthly comic. But Jackie Estacado turned the biggest corner in his moral development in 1999, that one time he met Batman. Before this Dark Knight of the soul, Jackie was happy to ram his car into someone’s legs and shoot him in the head — and laugh it off without the reader asking themselves “But isn’t that sort of evil, though?”—it was expected that everything he did would be; basically, distressing. After Bruce Wayne provided the active template for orphan playboys who get freaky in the night and also save people, Jackie would discover an apparent desire for adding the latter to his own CV as well. This more conflicted version of *The Darkness* would remain into the 21st century and inspire the storytelling in both Darkness video game outings—and Jackie would return the favour by sending many of his artists over to become recent and current architects of Gotham.

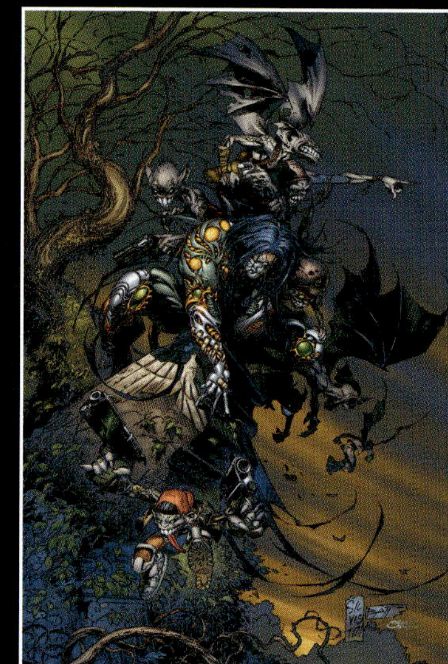

Above. *The Darkness* #1/2 [1996] cover,
art by: Marc Silvestri, Matt “Batt” Banning,
and Steve Firchow

The Darkness is responsible for ushering some of the most premier comic book art talent over the last two decades. Everyone from Stjepan Sejic, John Tyler Christopher, Dale Keown, Francis Manapul, Joe Benitez, Michael Broussard, Phil Hester, Tyler Kirkham, Mike Choi, Jeremy Haun, and so many others. It’s fair to say that the comic book industry’s superhero art style we know now wouldn’t have the same look or vibe if it weren’t for *The Darkness*.

Over the last two and half decades the character has been an inspiration to not only the comic book medium, the people that make them, devoted fans all over the world, but to everyone that doesn’t feel like they’re good enough to think they’re the “good guy” in their story because of all their flaws and what makes them human.

The truth is we’ve all got a little Darkness in us.[5] ”

5 Barajas, Henry and Claire Napier. “SAY GOOD NIGHT TO THE “GOOD GUY,” in *The Darkness* #1 25th Anniversary Commemorative Edition [2020] (November 2020): 26-31.

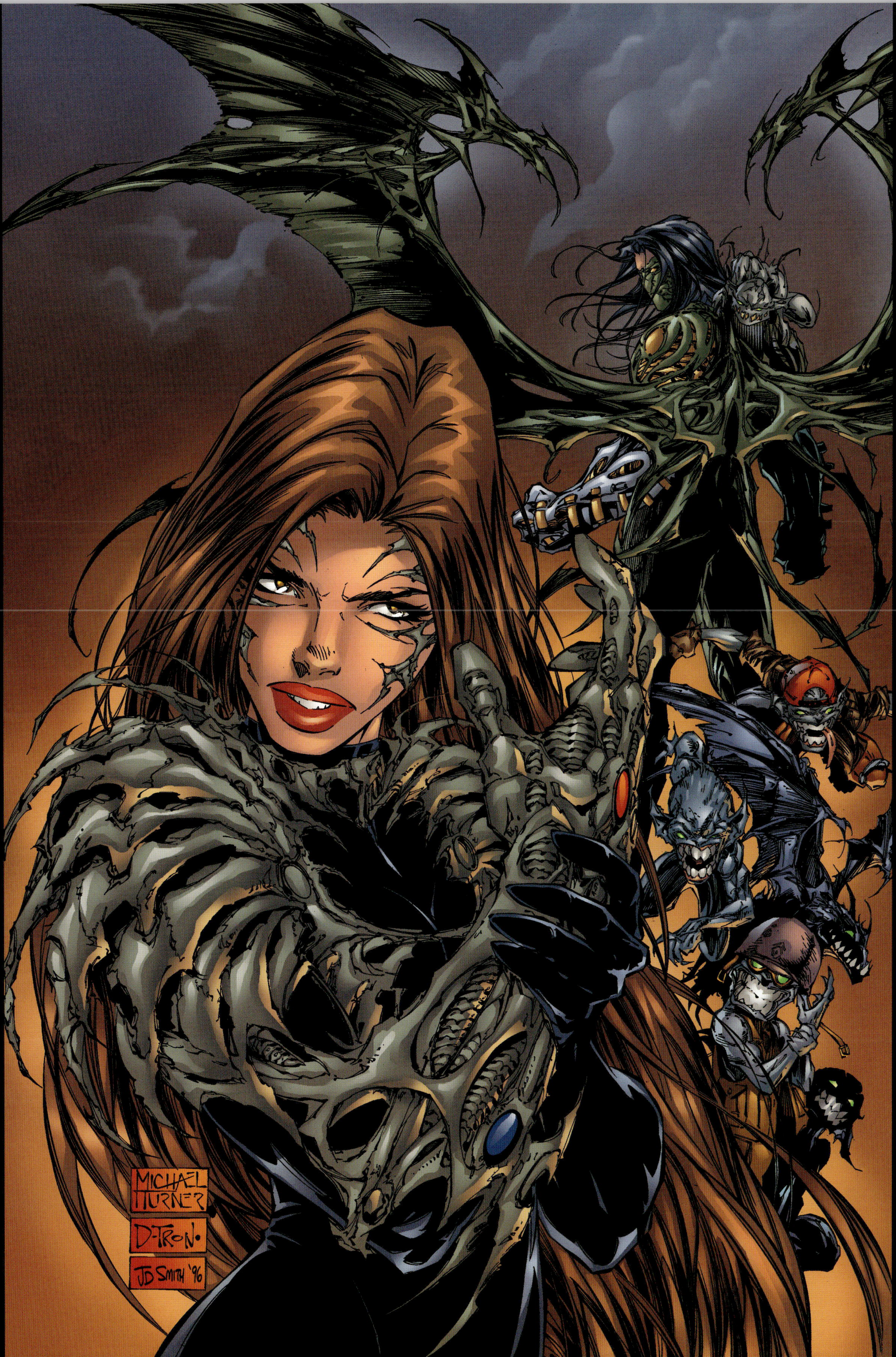

Witchblade #10 cover A,
art by: Michael Turner, D-Tron, and Jonathan D. Smith

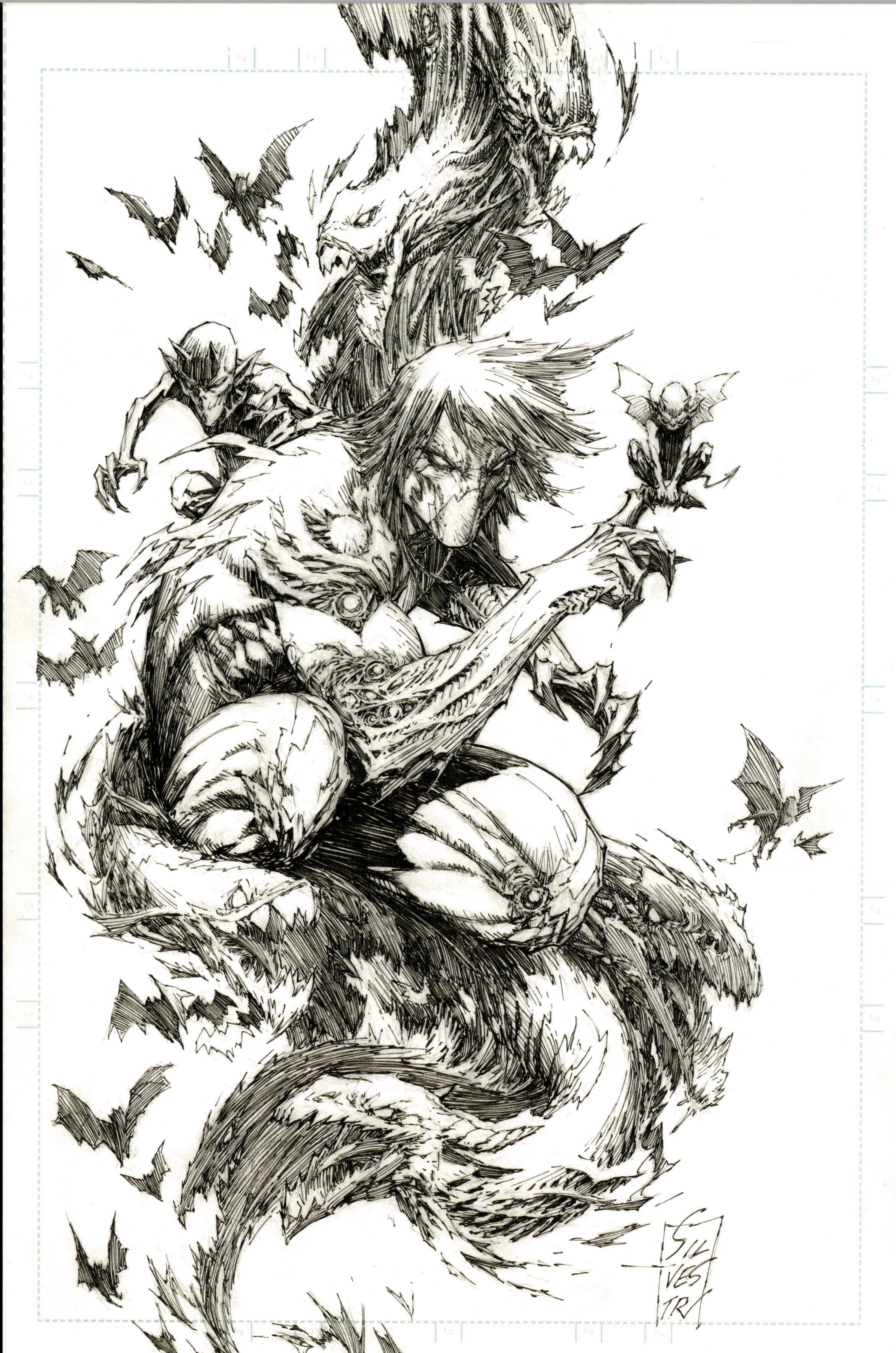

The Darkness #1/2 [2021] cover A,
line art by: Marc Silvestri

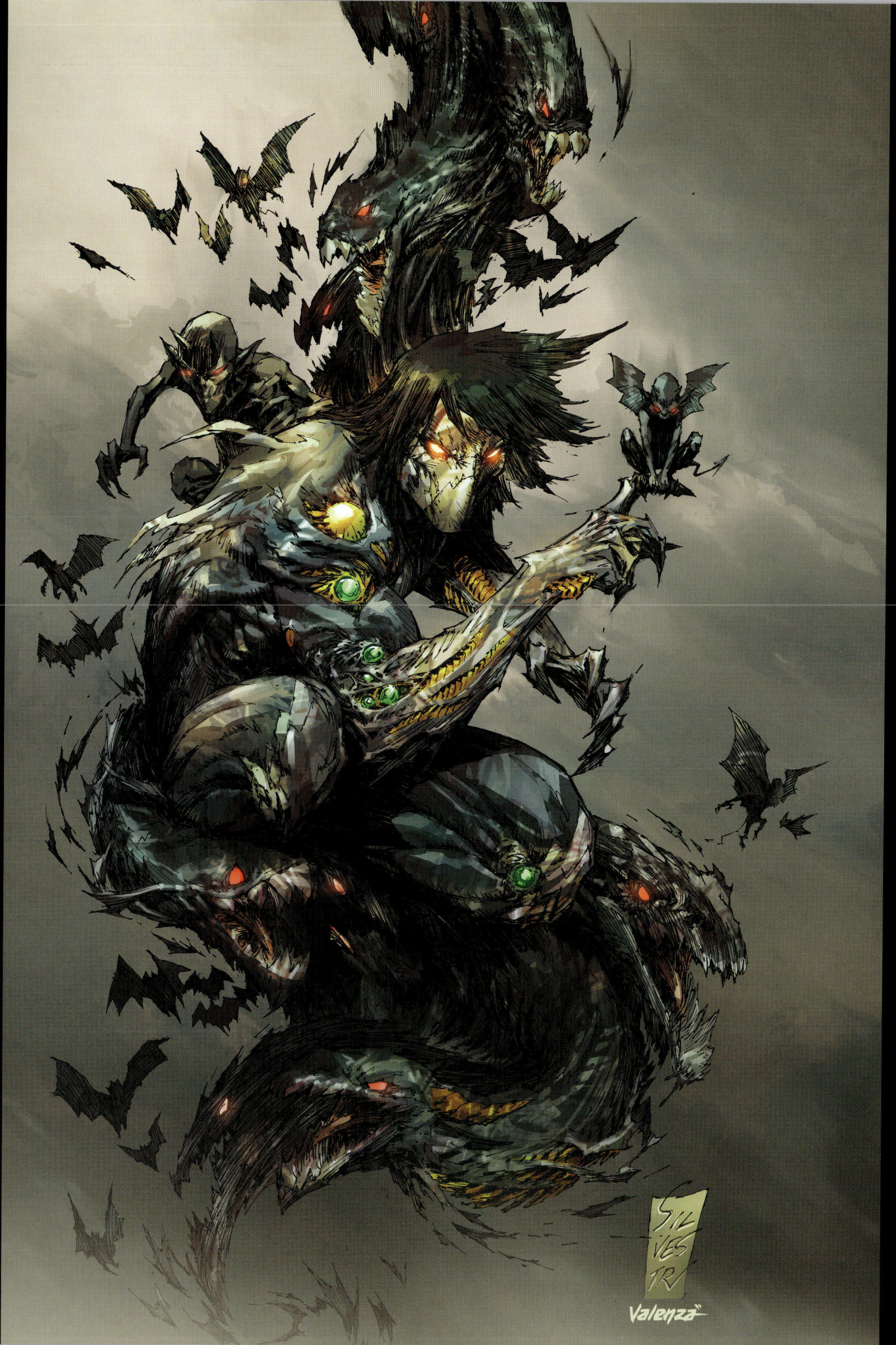

The Darkness #1/2 [2021] cover A,
art by: Marc Silvestri and Bryan Valenza

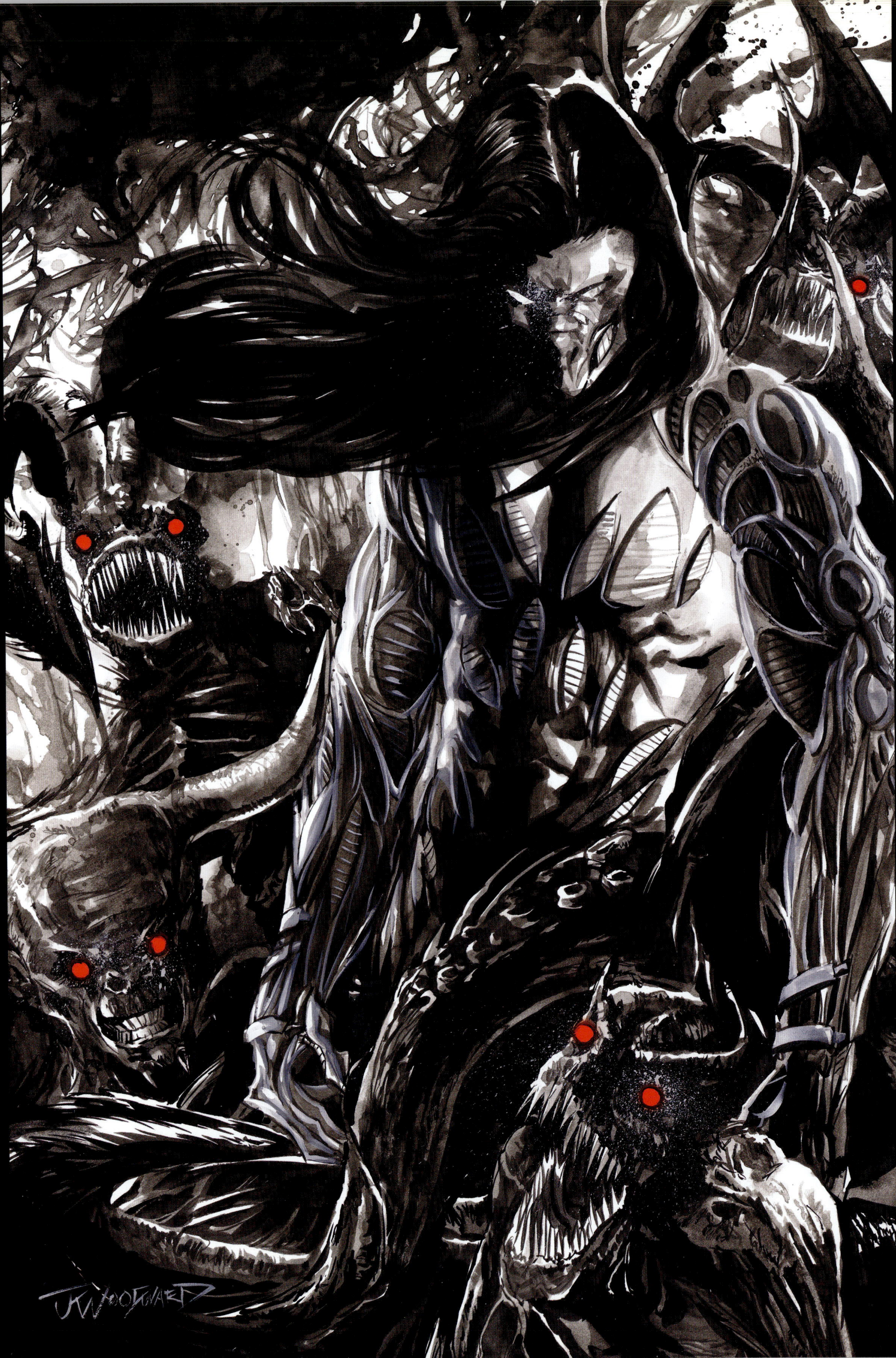

The Darkness #1/2 [2021] cover B,
art by: JK Woodward

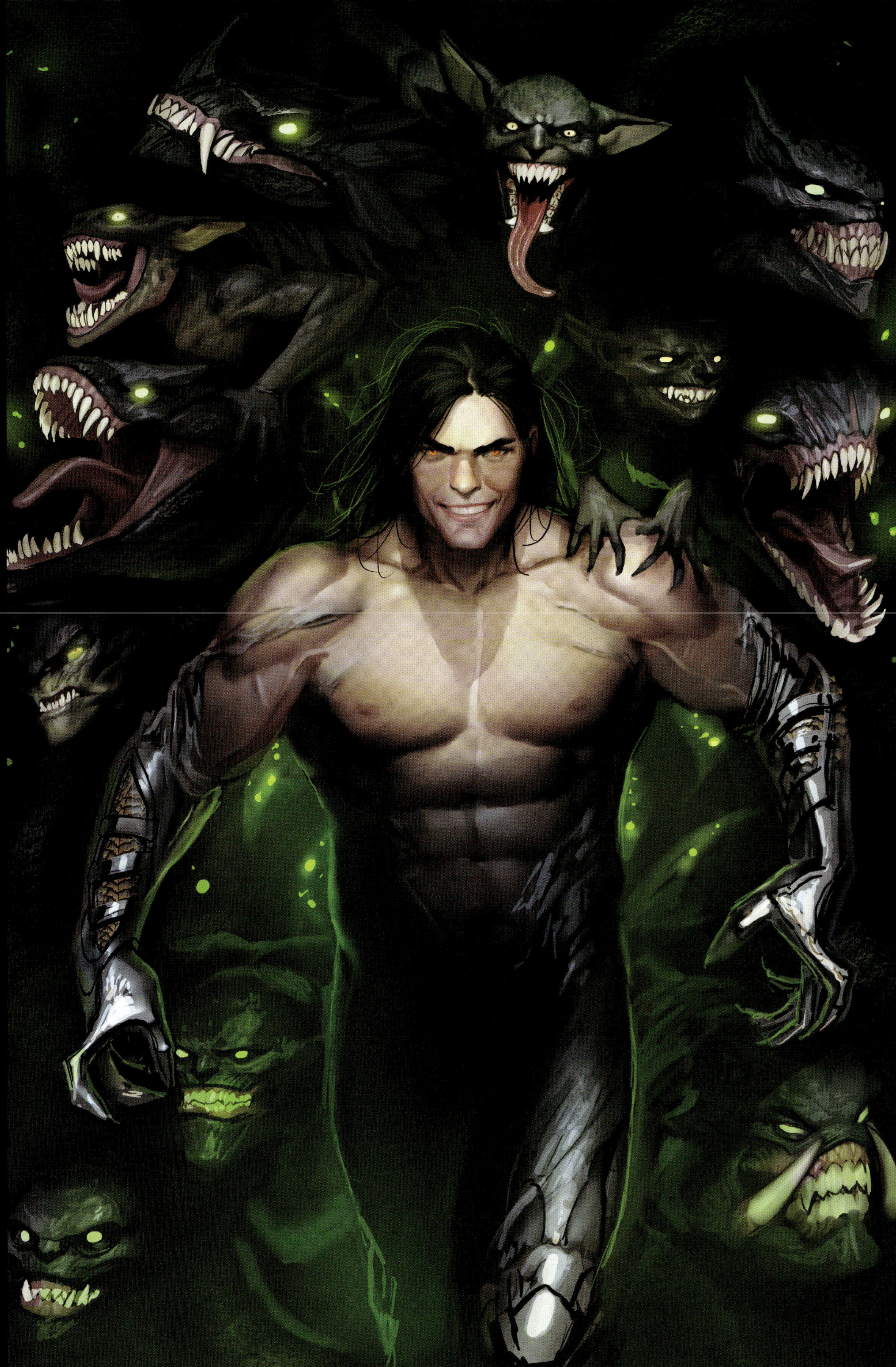

The Darkness #1/2 [2021] cover D,
art by: Stjepan Sejic

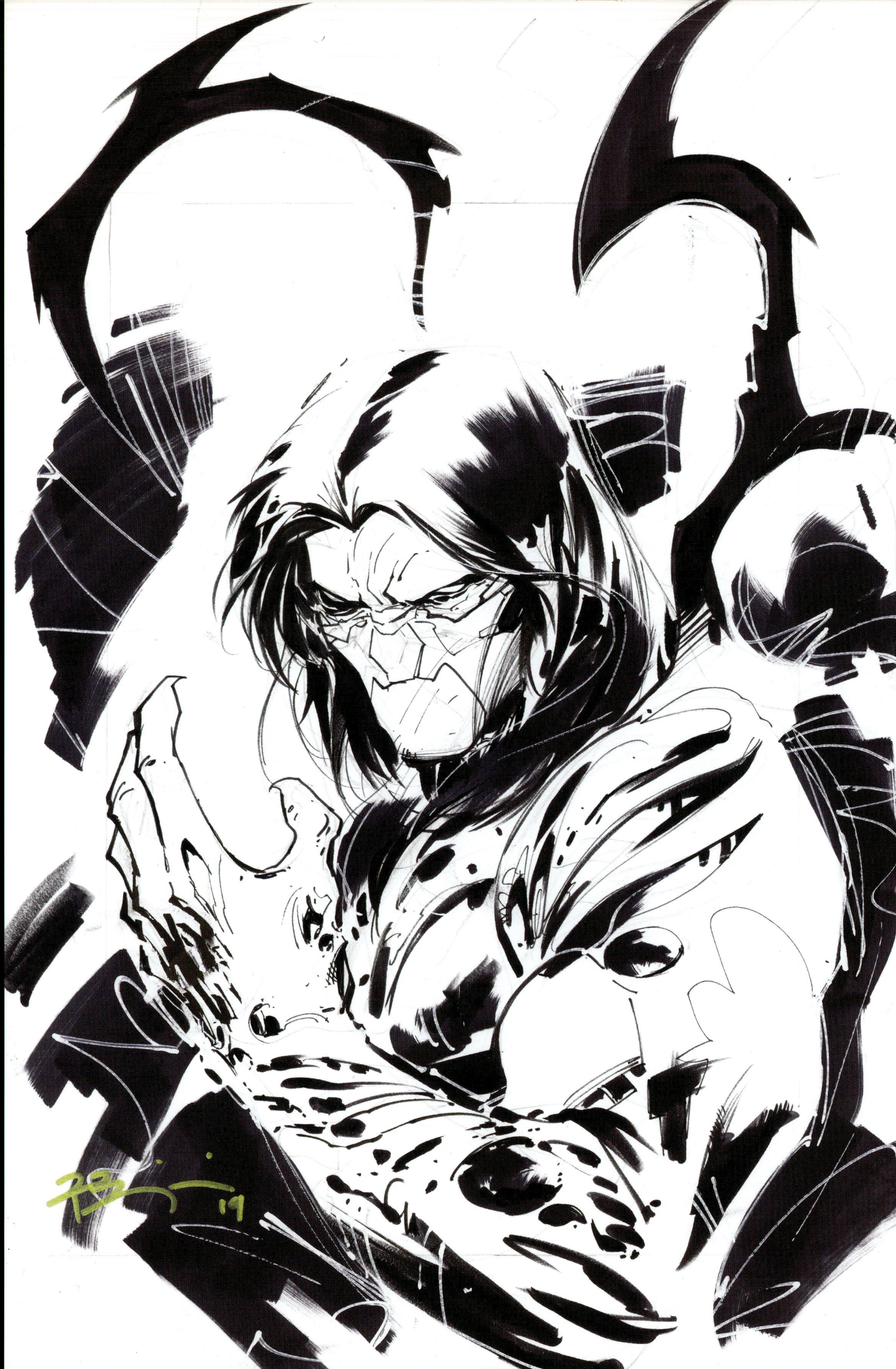

The Darkness #1/2 [2021] cover C,
line art by: Ryan Benjamin

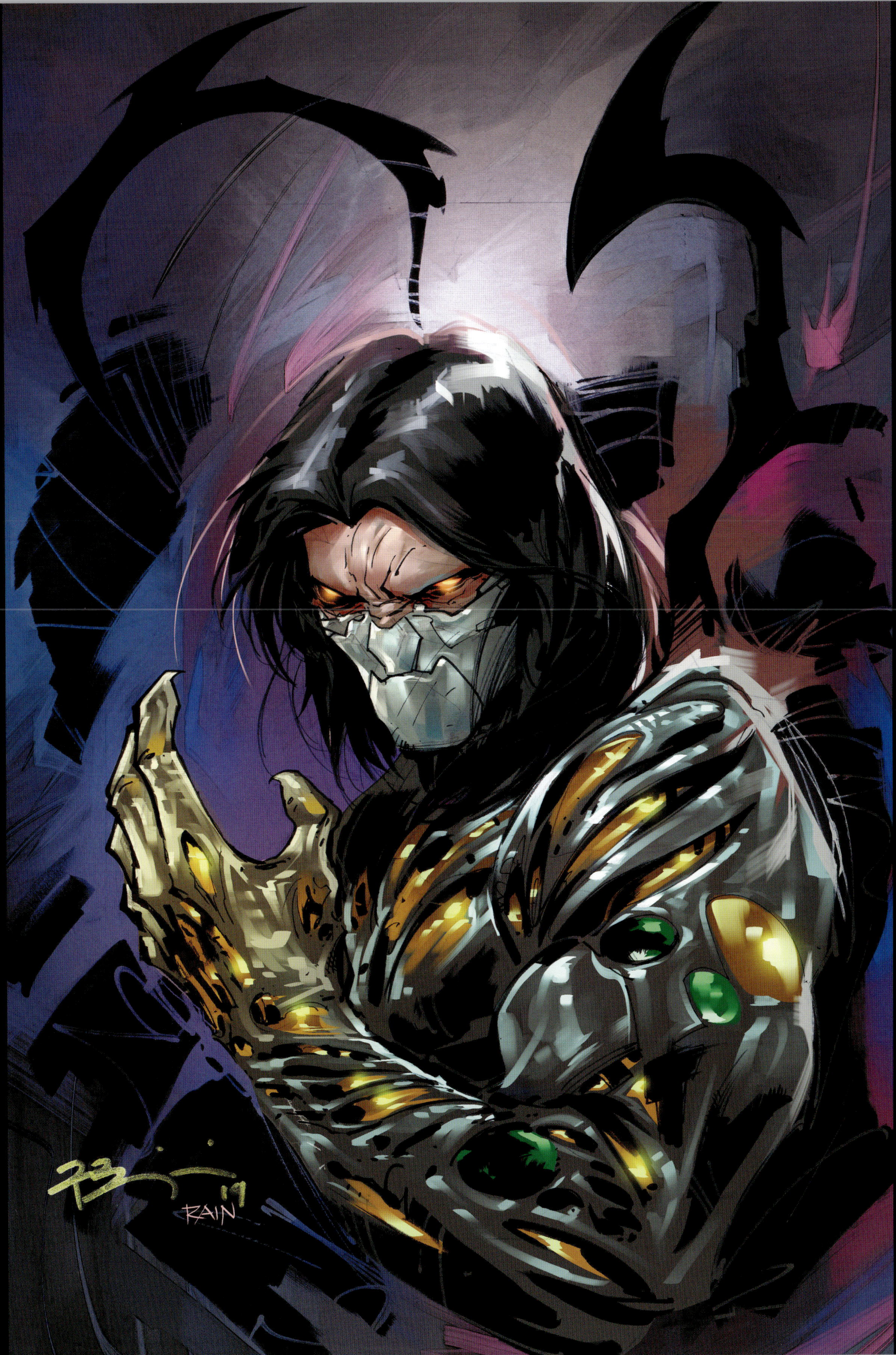

The Darkness #1/2 [2021] cover C,
art by: Ryan Benjamin

"To celebrate nearly 25 years of *The Darkness*, series co-creators Marc Silvestri and David Wohl reminisce on how they shaped the character that men want to be and women wished would leap off the page like in A-ha's *"Take On Me"* music video.

Henry Barajas: People love Jackie. There isn't a day that goes by where someone isn't asking for the series to come back. What do you think it is that people loved about him?

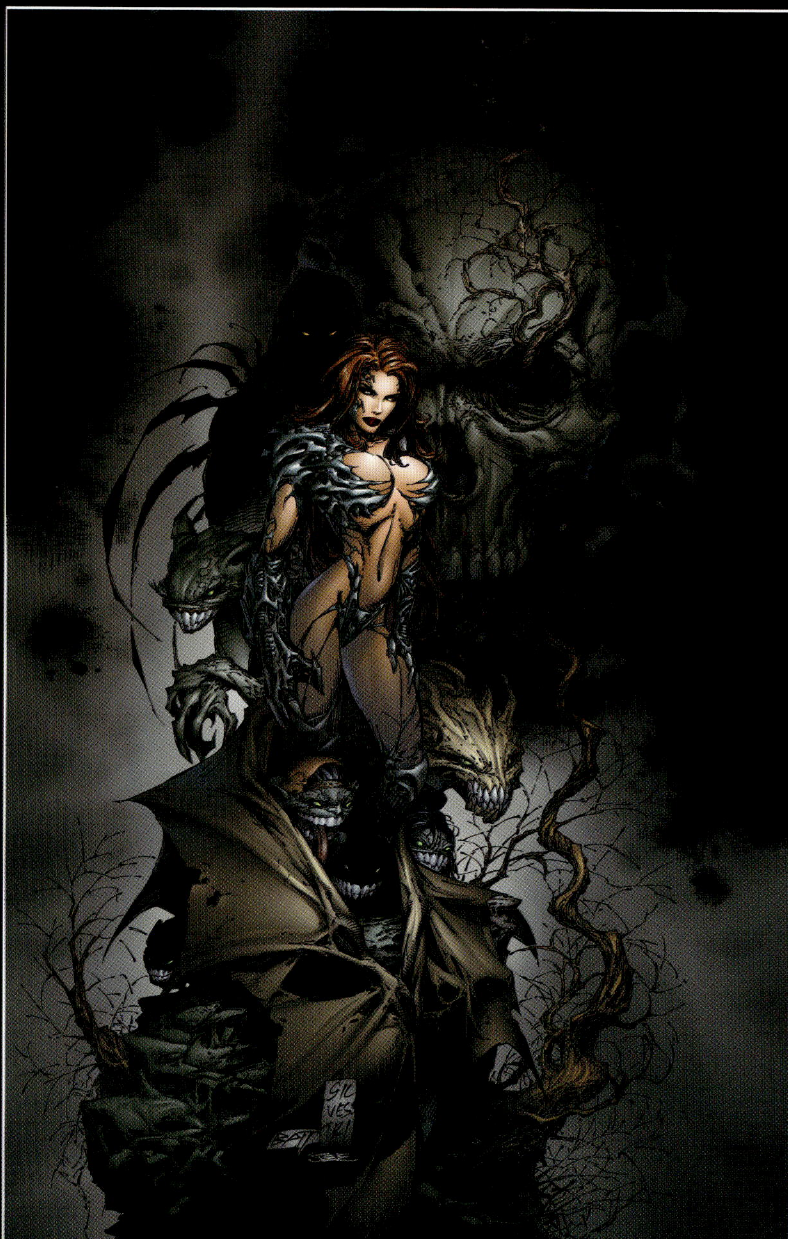

Above, *Witchblade* #10 cover B, art by: Marc Silvestri, Matt "Batt" Banning, and Steve Firchow

Marc Silvestri: On the surface, being a creature of the night brings with it a certain allure and mystery that has a built-in wish fulfillment. Just look at how popular vampires are. For their part, vampires are rarely portrayed as horrifying monsters. More often than not, they are powerful, (charming when they need to be) and magnetic. Jackie draws his power from the night and from the shadows like some super-powered Dracula. He has a unique, semi-Gothic vibe to his costume that isn't all that common in comics, so he stands out a bit from the rest. Plus, his power is supernatural, which is also unusual for a superhero. But mostly I think it's because he's an anti-hero that kicks ass and messes thing up in horrifying ways!

Looking deeper, Jackie is unique in that his greatest power is also his greatest weakness. In order to use The Darkness, he must first acknowledge that it is part of him. The Darkness is the ID that we all have buried deep inside that our empathy and humanity keeps in check. The Darkness power combined with Jackie's mob upbringing have conspired to make him a remorseless killer. Those are hard odds stacked against him, so you root for him to succeed. Jackie has to fight literal demons that have been hardwired into him just to do the right thing. This act alone makes him sympathetic and — at times in spite of himself — heroic. We as humans often cringe at having to look inside ourselves at the bad parts, and in Jackie's case, those bad parts manifest physically. That's a hard reality for Jackie, and I think this idea resonates on a deep level with people.

David Wohl: Well, there's no denying that Jackie is a cool guy. At Top Cow, we always had a philosophy that when you create heroes, they need to be someone who our readers wished they could be or be with. And Jackie definitely checks those boxes. He's charming, cool, and might not be the best educated, but he's very smart. He receives an incredible power and is thrust into an incredibly strange, supernatural world, but he never loses his sense of humor about it and has trouble taking his situation and the characters within it too seriously. And no matter how cavalier or rough he seems, he always has a soft spot for Jenny. She humanizes him. I think the fans really appreciate Jackie and the cast of characters around him. I know I do!

HB: What came first? The Darkness or Jackie? How did you guys come up with the character? There seems to be a lot of Marc's persona and hometown that made it to the page, but what were those early conversations like?

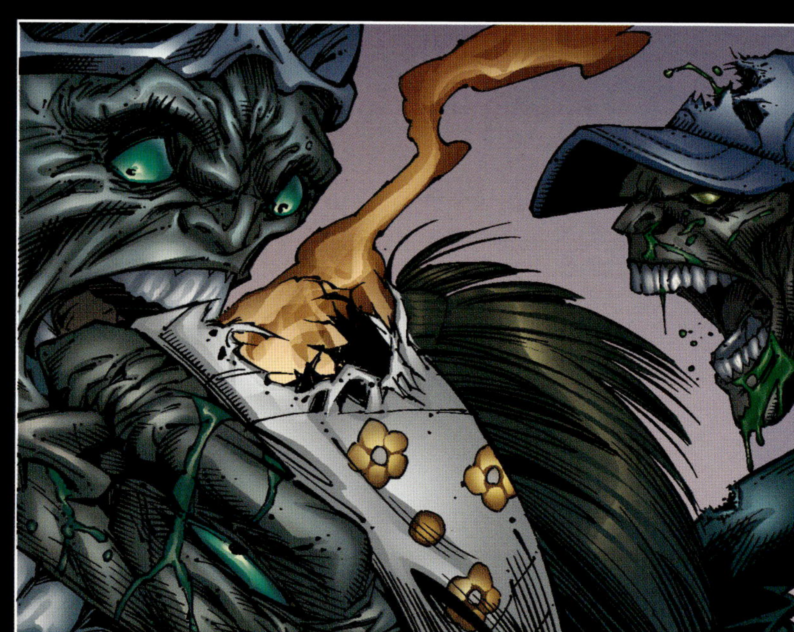

Above, *The Darkness* #8 page 7, panel 1, pencils by: Joe Benitez

Marc: The Darkness came first. I grew up as a fan of horror, sci-fi, and fantasy, and I wanted to bring those elements into Top Cow's comic universe. I loved vampires and werewolves when I was a kid, and the idea of this power that summoned demons and could only be used in the dark really appealed to me. Plus I always loved the fact that Dracula had to do his evil deeds before the sun came up or he was screwed. The concept of The Darkness as a character/power leaned heavily into this idea pretty much from day one. Light, as a way of negating Jackie's massive power, always struck me as a great Achilles' heel. I pitched the basic concept to David Wohl, and he dug it, but the idea was put on a shelf for a couple of years. After we came up with the idea for *Witchblade* and it became such a huge success, going back to *The Darkness* and developing it for it's own series was a no-brainer.

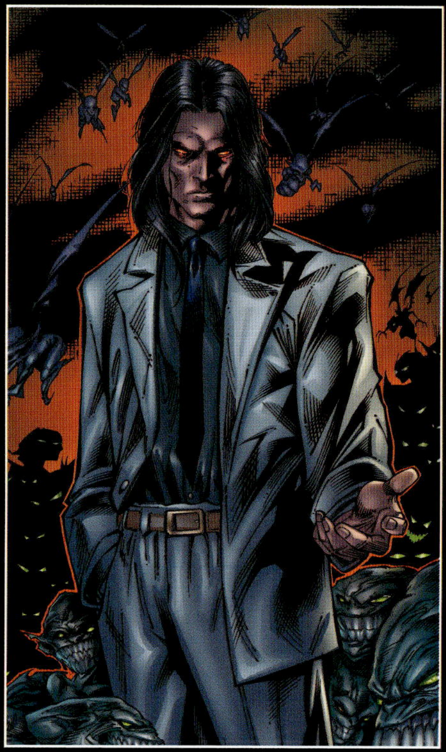

Above. *The Darkness* #8 page 7, panel 4, pencils by: Joe Benitez

Garth Ennis was doing some great edgy stuff in comics, and he seemed like the perfect choice as a writer. Once we brought him on board, he really fleshed Jackie out and gave the character a great voice. Making Jackie part of a crime family/syndicate was a perfect way to set him up as a man betrayed by nurture and doomed/blessed to be the master of unimaginable horrors. As for there being any of me in Jackie's persona, I'm gonna plead ignorance (or at least plead the 5th)!

David: The Darkness came first. I think we first started talking about it in 1994 during my early time at Top Cow. He was supposed to be an eccentric, Tim Burton-like character who lived in some Gothic mansion in the shadows. He created the Darklings as his only company. That was the genesis of *The Darkness*, but once we started working with Garth, he began to transform into the Jackie Estacado version that we all know and love. Once we started heading that way, there was no turning back!

HB: Do you have a favorite Jackie/Darkness moment you created and another artist came up with?

David: As a co-creator, a sometime writer, and a reader of *The Darkness*, my favorite moments of the book usually revolve around the Darklings. I feel like Marc and Joe Benitez created my favorite Darkling moments, giving them unique, wonderful personalities that Jackie was able to feed off of, and they'd make even the most grisly scenes funny.

Marc: Too many great moments and too many great artists and writers for me to pick just one to be honest!

HB: *The Darkness* Video game's success still resonates with gamers to this day. How did that change how you approach the character and series after the game?

Marc: Since the game followed the comic pretty closely, we really didn't change anything in the books. Having writer Paul Jenkins, who wrote some great *The Darkness* stories, write the actual game was a pretty unique idea back then. I think Paul was key to how the game resonated on such an emotional level with players. There are some incredible cinematic character bits in there that gamers still talk about. The first *The Darkness* game shocked a lot of people with how emotionally invested you could get with well-developed characters that drive the game's story.

David: I loved the video game. 2K and Starbreeze did some amazing work on it and were so into the character and the world of *The Darkness*. Teaming up with Paul Jenkins definitely helped as well. I think their creation of the Otherworld, controlled by The Darkness power, added a whole new element to the mythology that definitely still resonates.

HB: The series had the best artists working in this industry today. Do you think *The Darkness* had a lasting impact on how we look at superhero comics today?

David: I think one of the reasons that *The Darkness* has gathered so many quality artists to it (and continues to) is that Marc created a kind of Wonderland for them to be part of. They loved to draw *The Darkness,* and that love comes out on the page. To this day, I hear so many artists talk about how much they admire *The Darkness* and its place in the comic pantheon. And with Marc Silvestri at the helm, doing some of the best work of his career, I think we pushed the limits of a superhero book to new places, incorporating elements of horror, action, suspense, fantasy, and humor all together.

Marc: We've been very fortunate to have the level of writing and drawing talent that we've had over the years, and I think that's the real test to the viability of the character. Jackie's very complex, so he's fun to write, and he and his dark world are visually interesting, so he's fun to draw. I think the fans respond to the same things. Jackie is a kind of perfect storm between the creators that give him life and the readers that share that life with him.[6] ”

6 Barajas, Napier. "SAY GOOD NIGHT TO THE "GOOD GUY," 26-31.

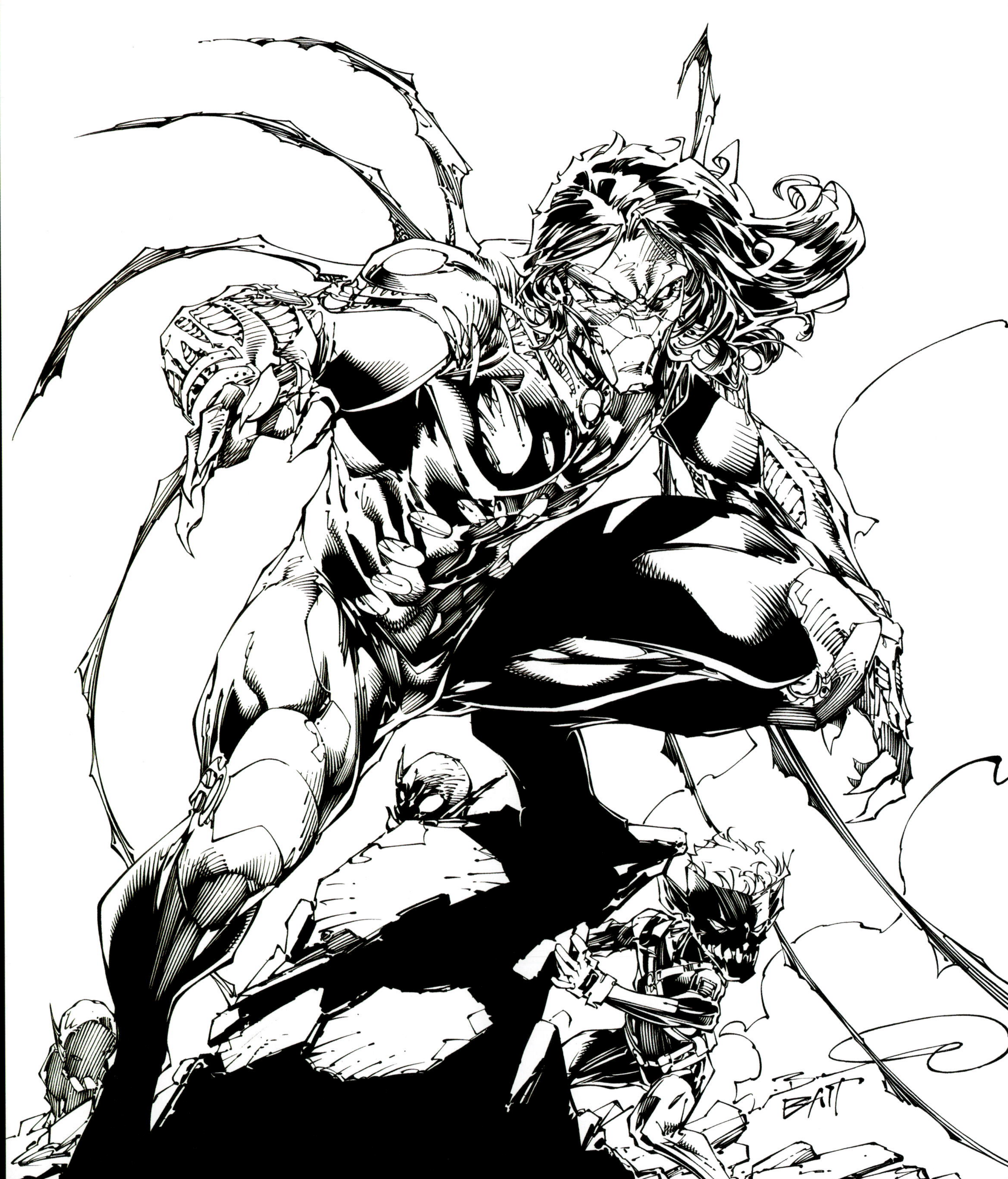

The Darkness: Sourcebook [2024] cover A,
line art by: Brett Booth and Matt "Batt" Banning

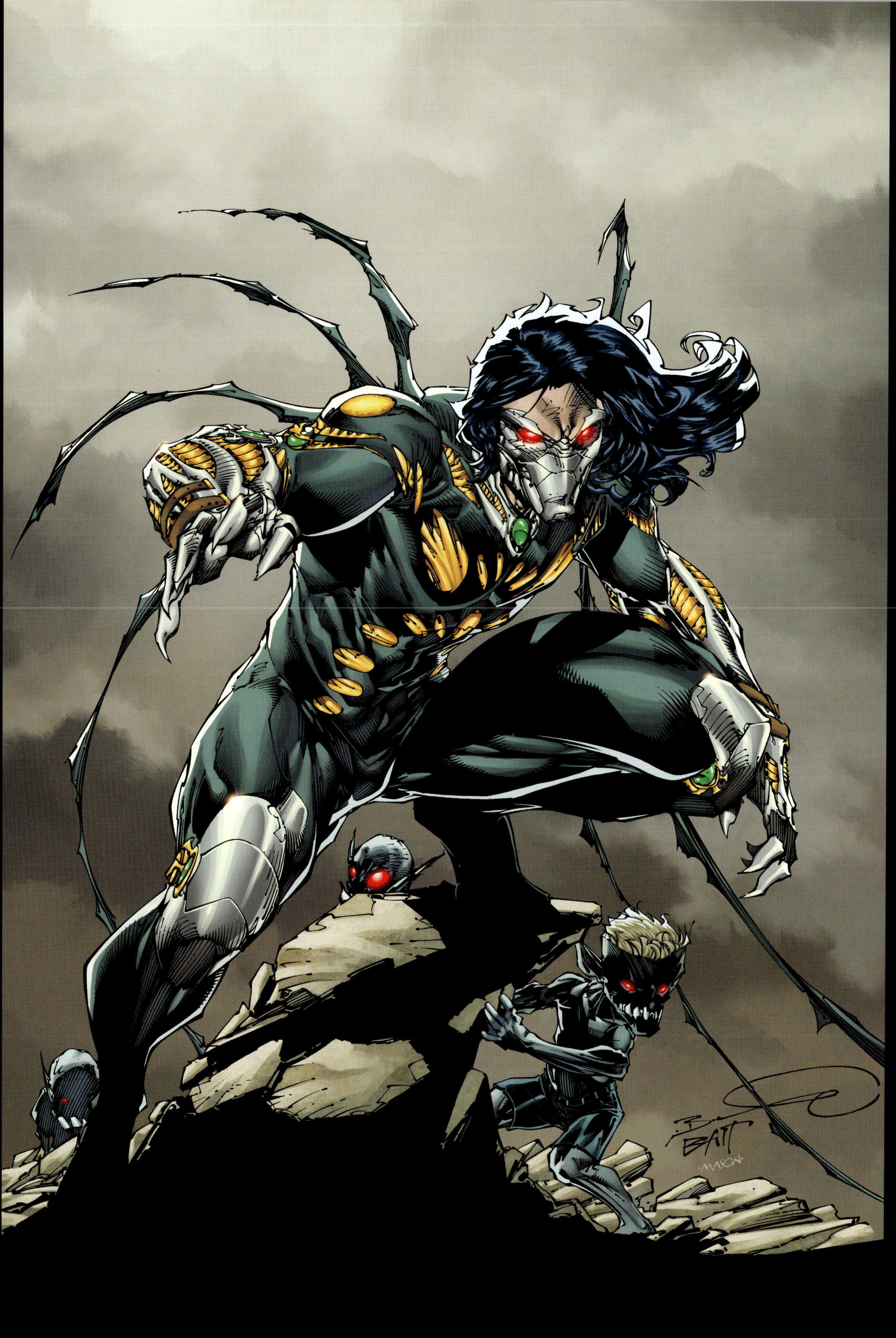

The Darkness: Sourcebook [2024] cover A,
art by: Brett Booth, Matt "Batt" Banning, and Thomas Mason

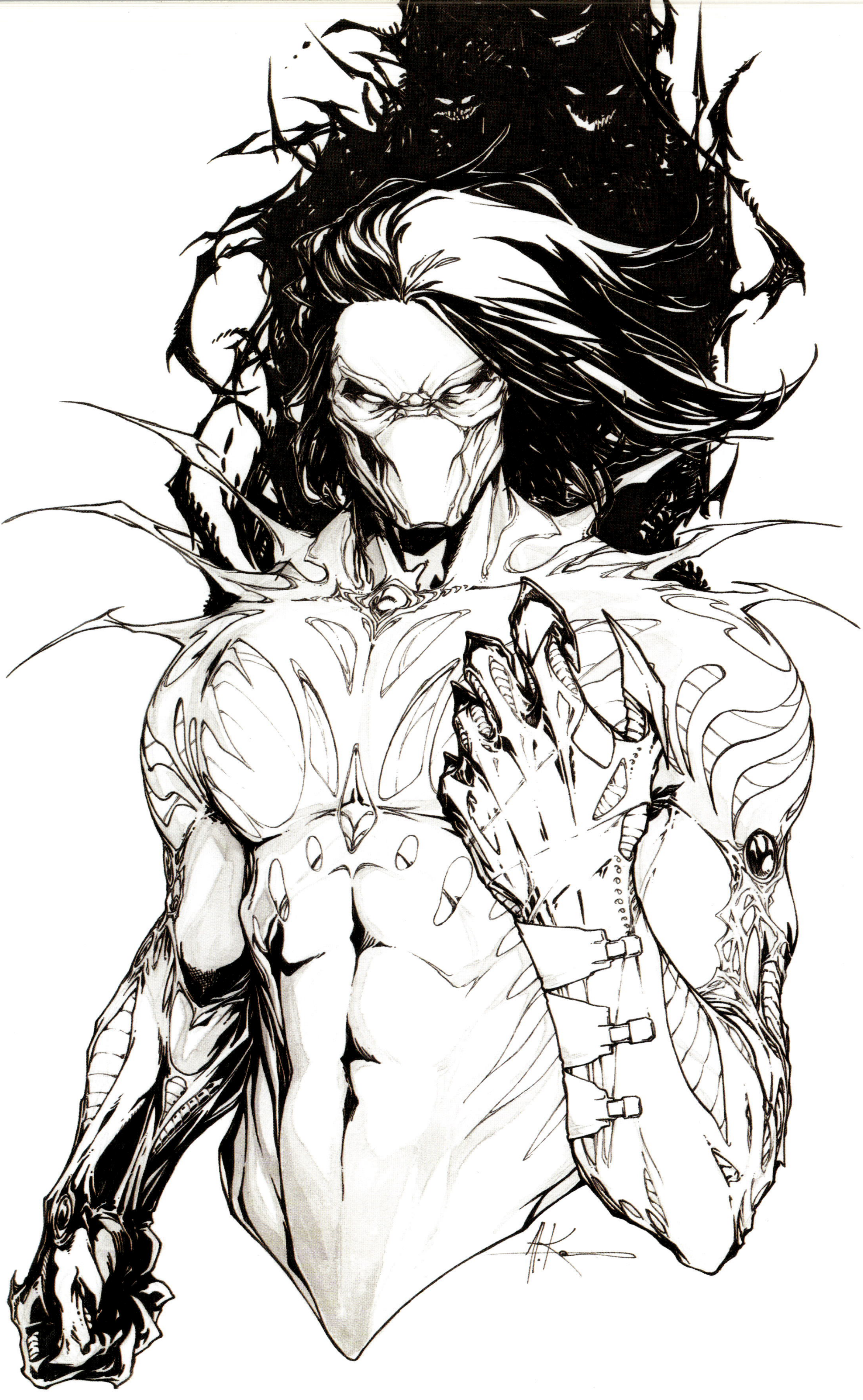

The Darkness: Sourcebook [2024] cover B, line art by: Alex Konat

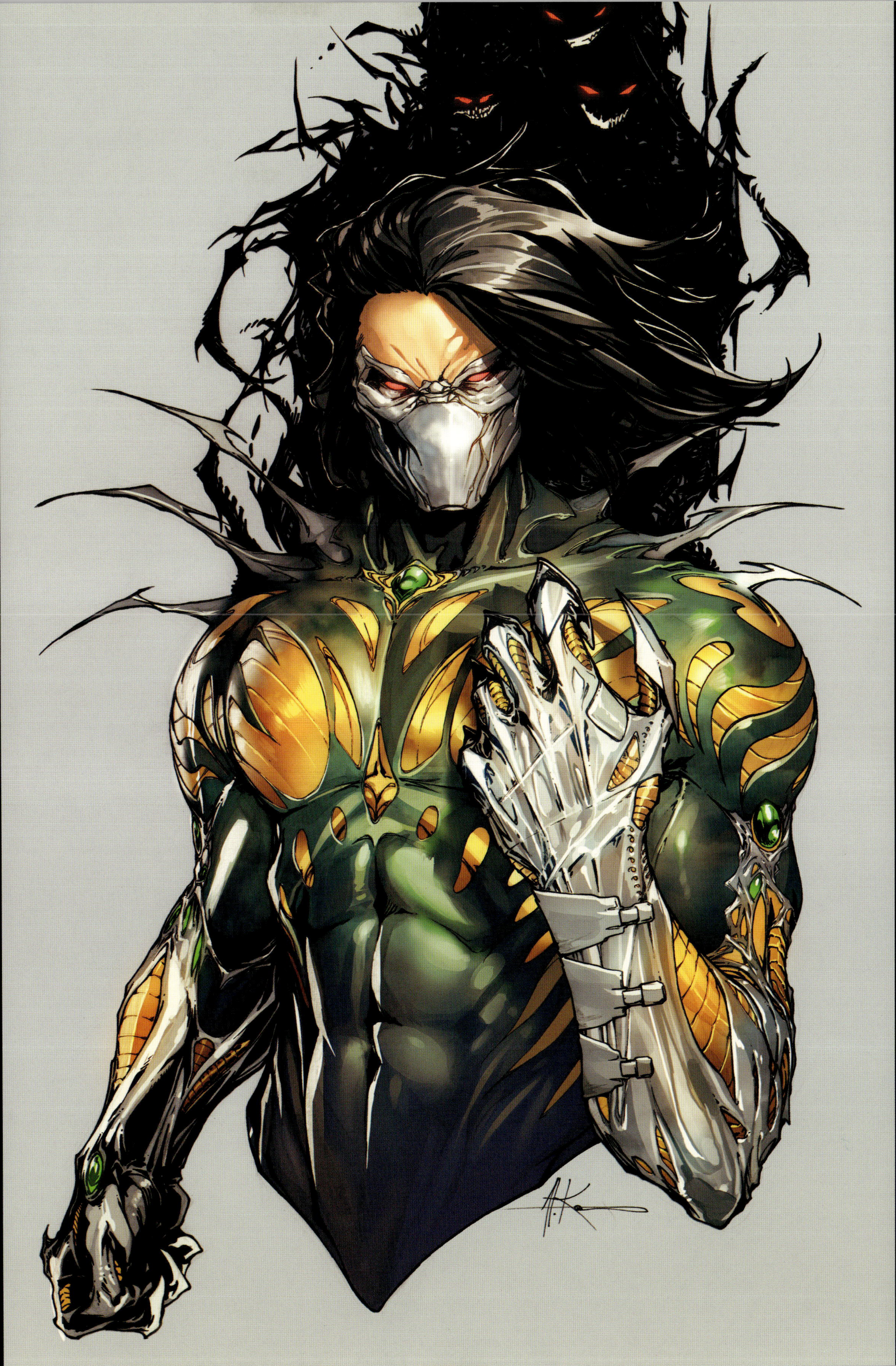

The Darkness: Sourcebook [2024] cover B,
art by: Alex Konat and Sunny Gho

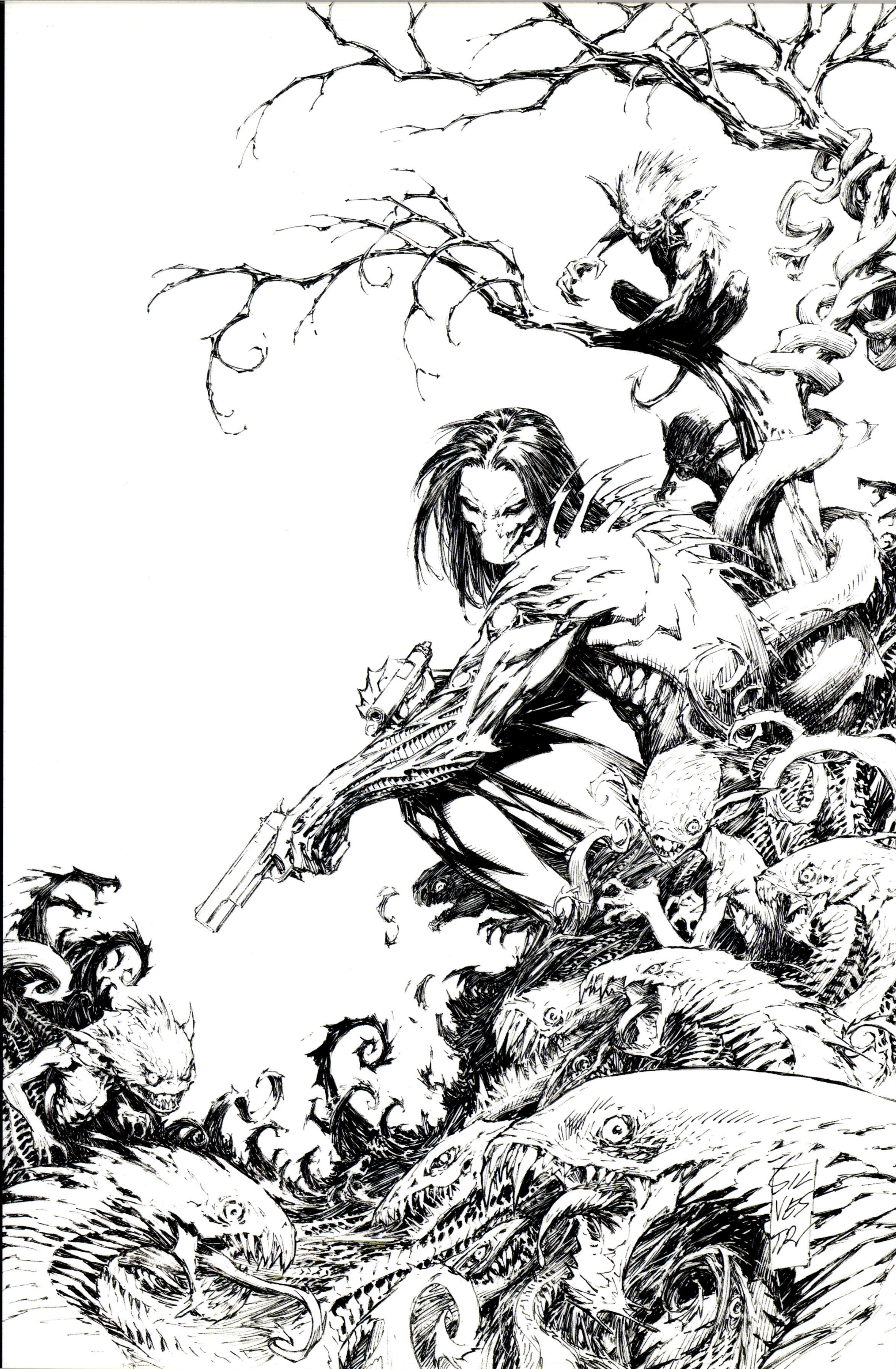

The Darkness: Sourcebook [2024] cover D,
line art by: Marc Silvestri

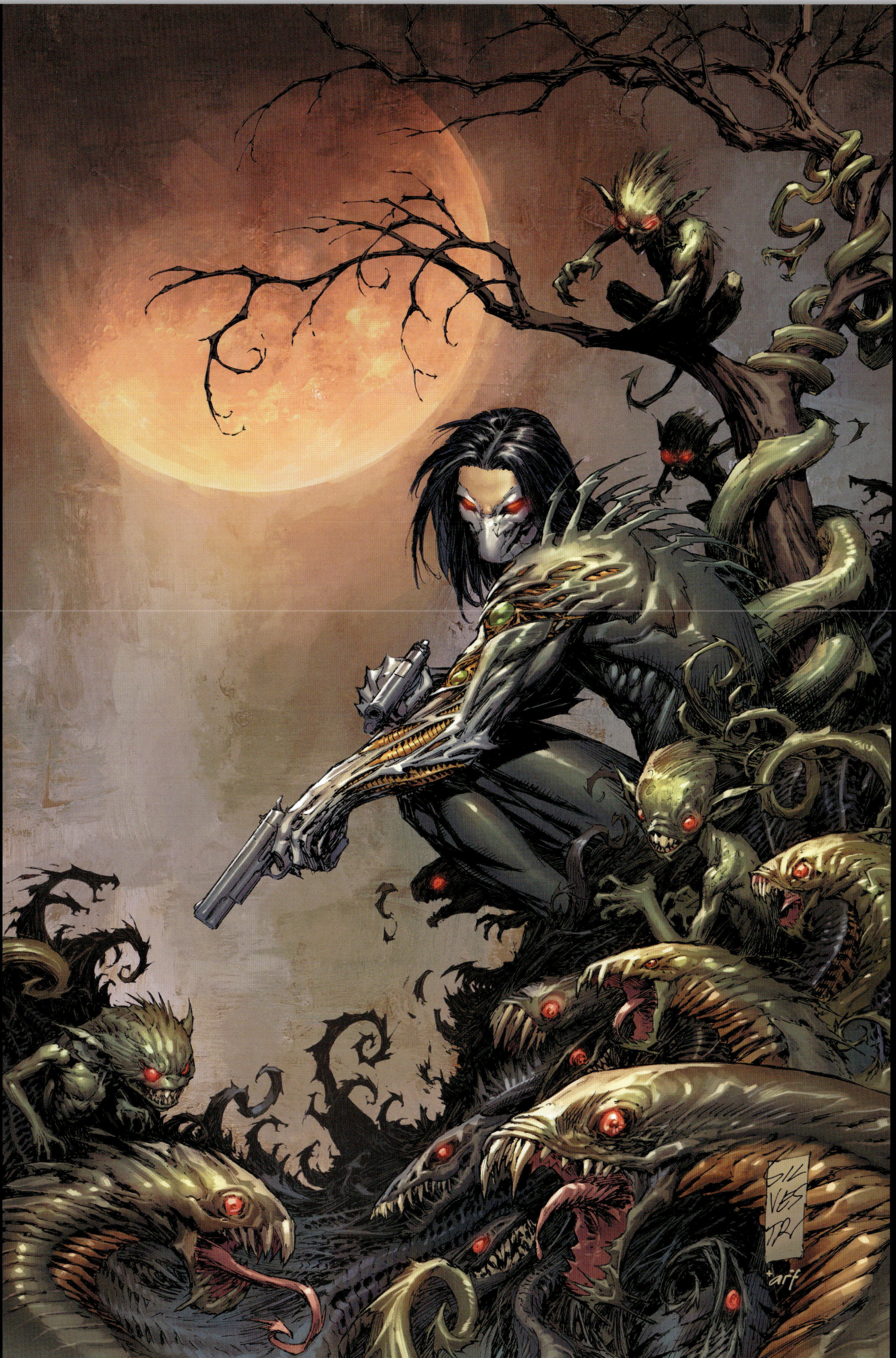

The Darkness: Sourcebook [2024] cover C,
art by: Marc Silvestri and Arif Prianto

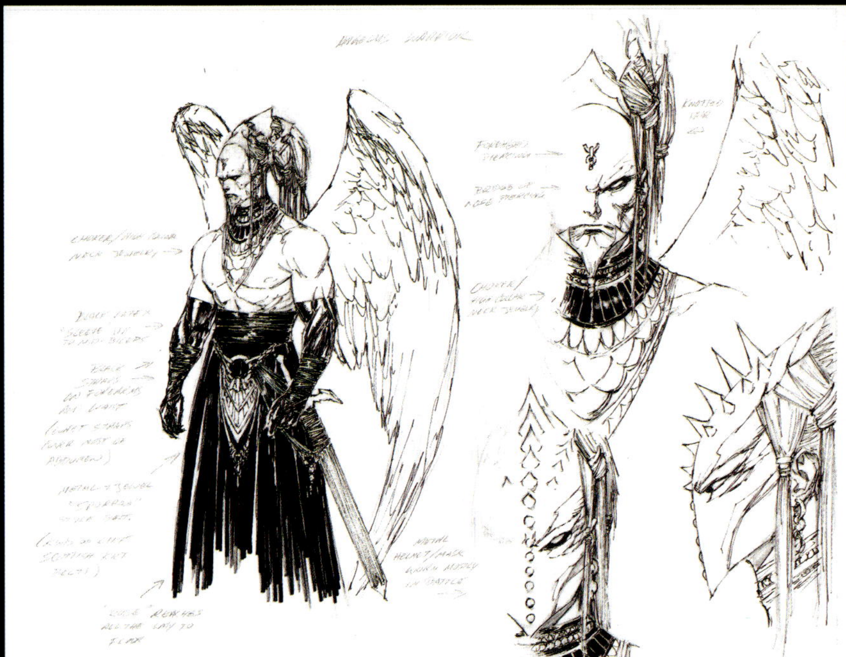
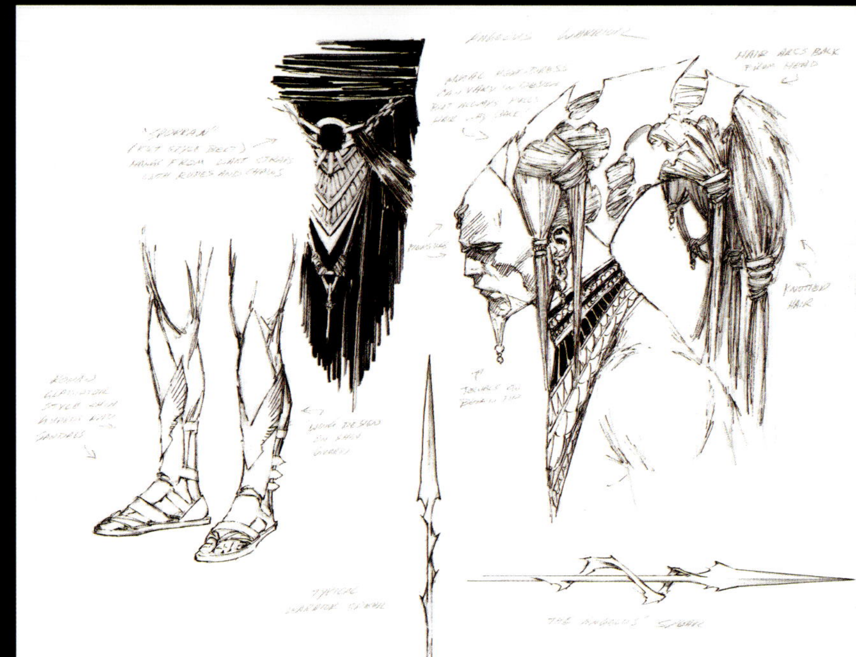

Early Angelus warrior redesign sketches for the next *The Darkness* series, art by **Marc Silvestri**

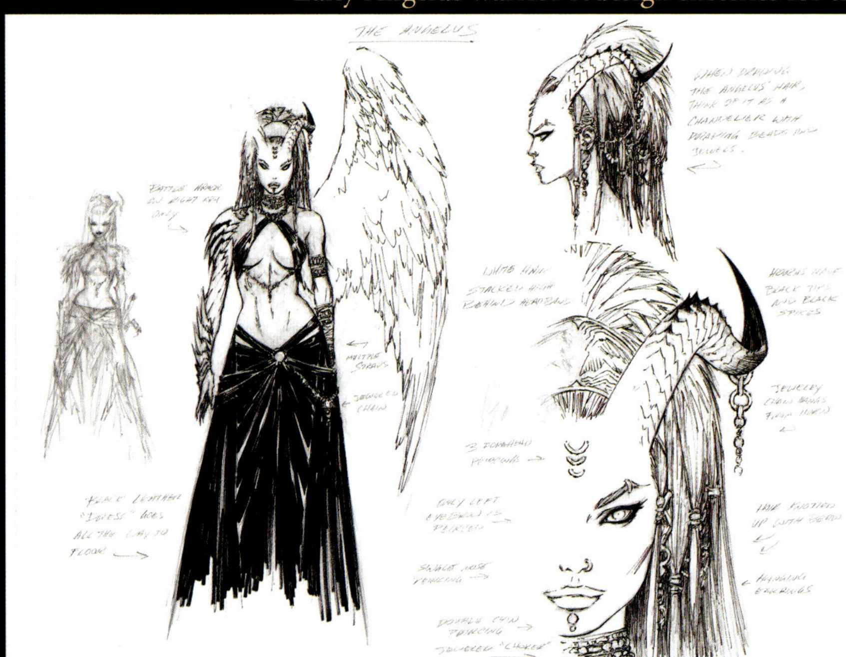
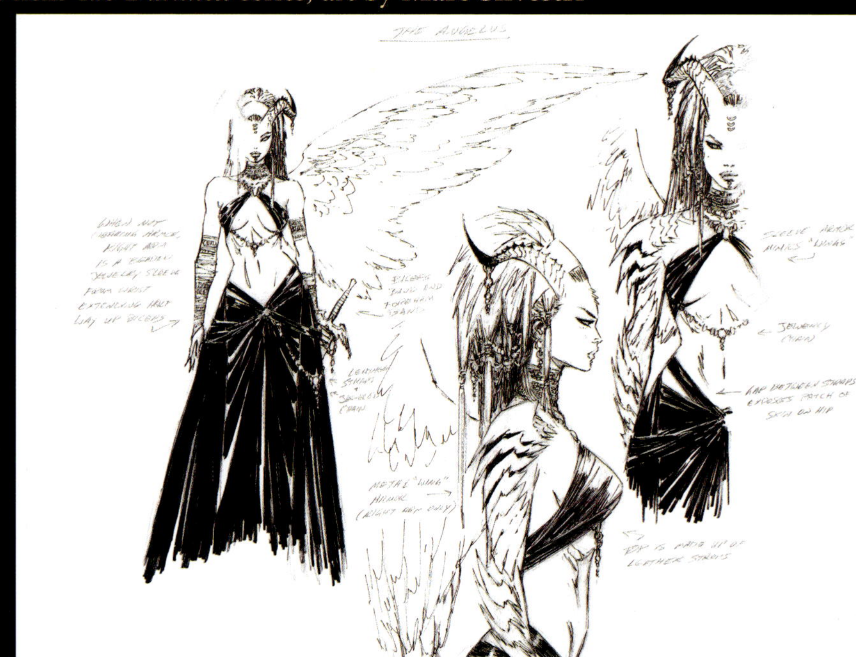

Early Angelus redesign sketches for the next *The Darkness* series, art by **Marc Silvestri**

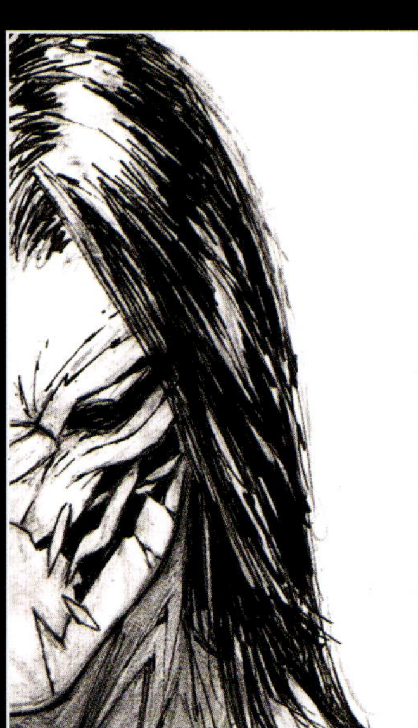
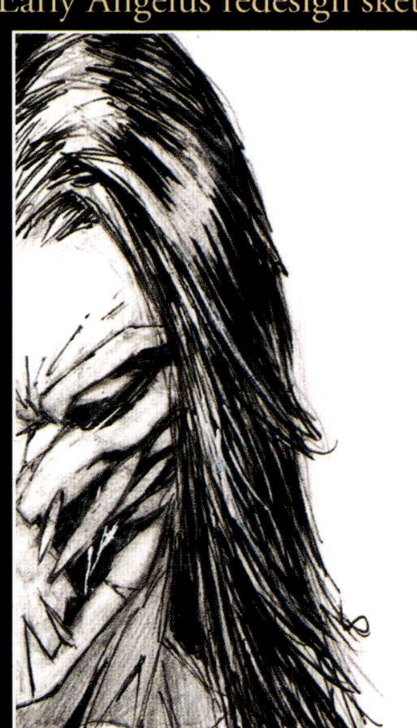
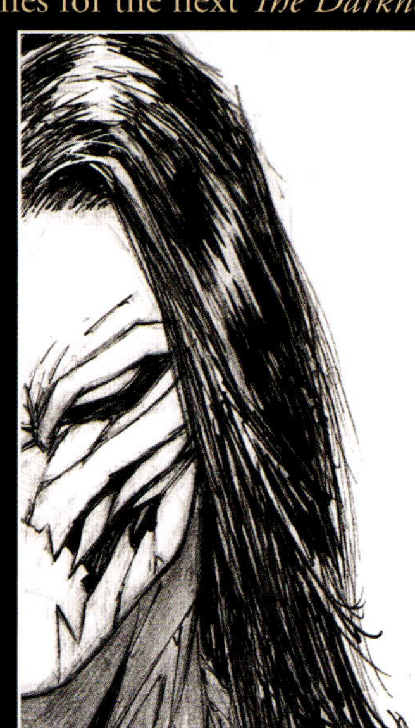
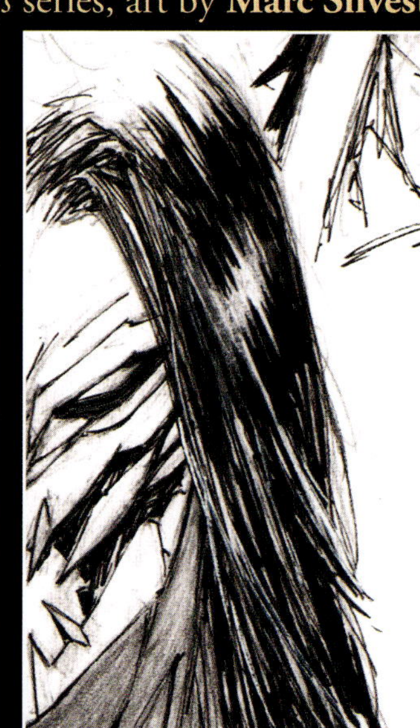
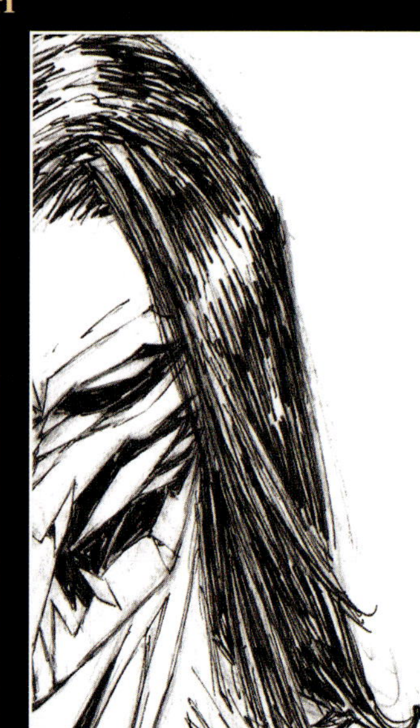

Early Darkness armor redesign sketches for the next *The Darkness* series, art by **Marc Silvestri**

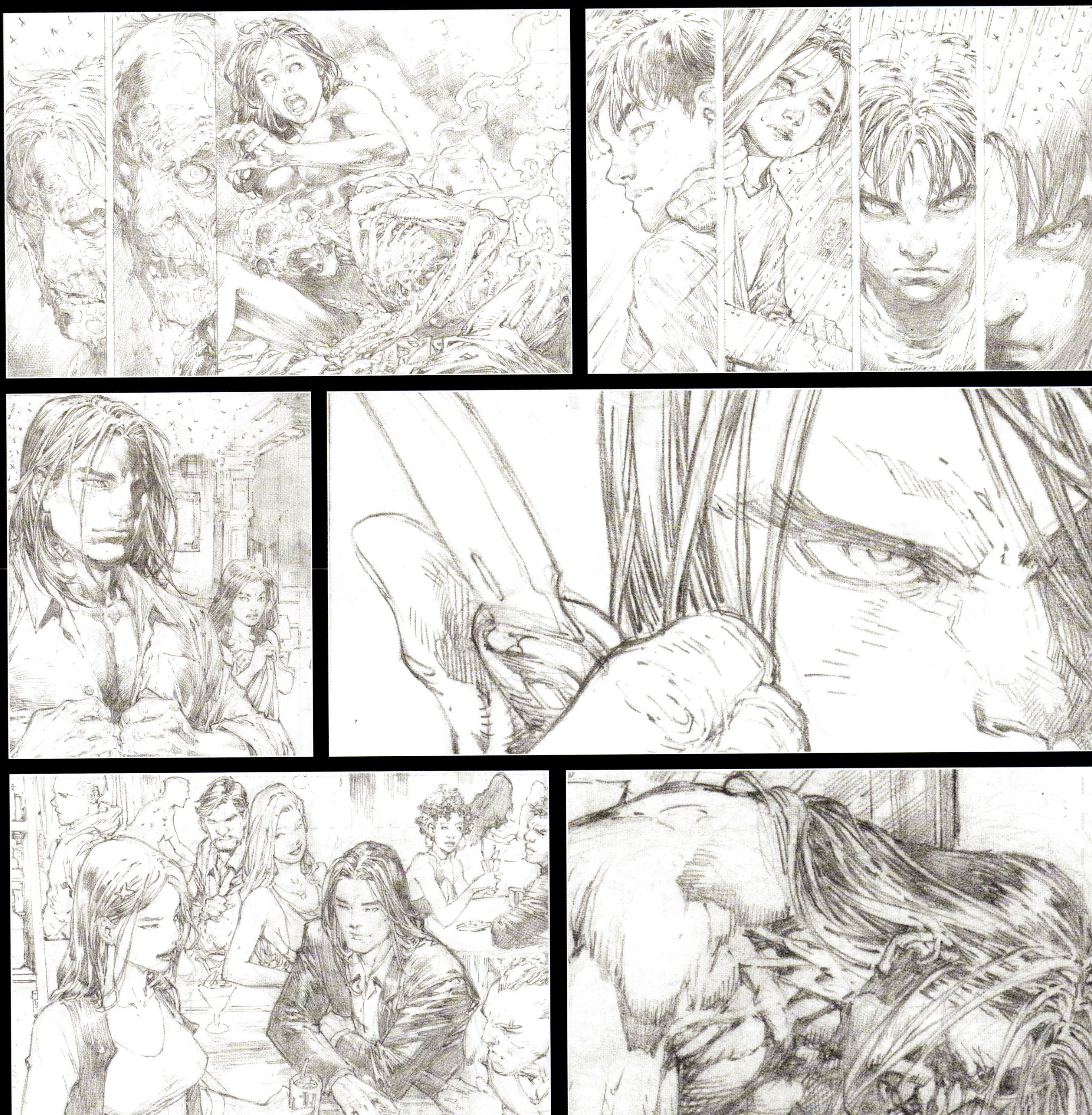

The Darkness #1 relaunch, early pencil panel snapshots, art by **Ed Benes**

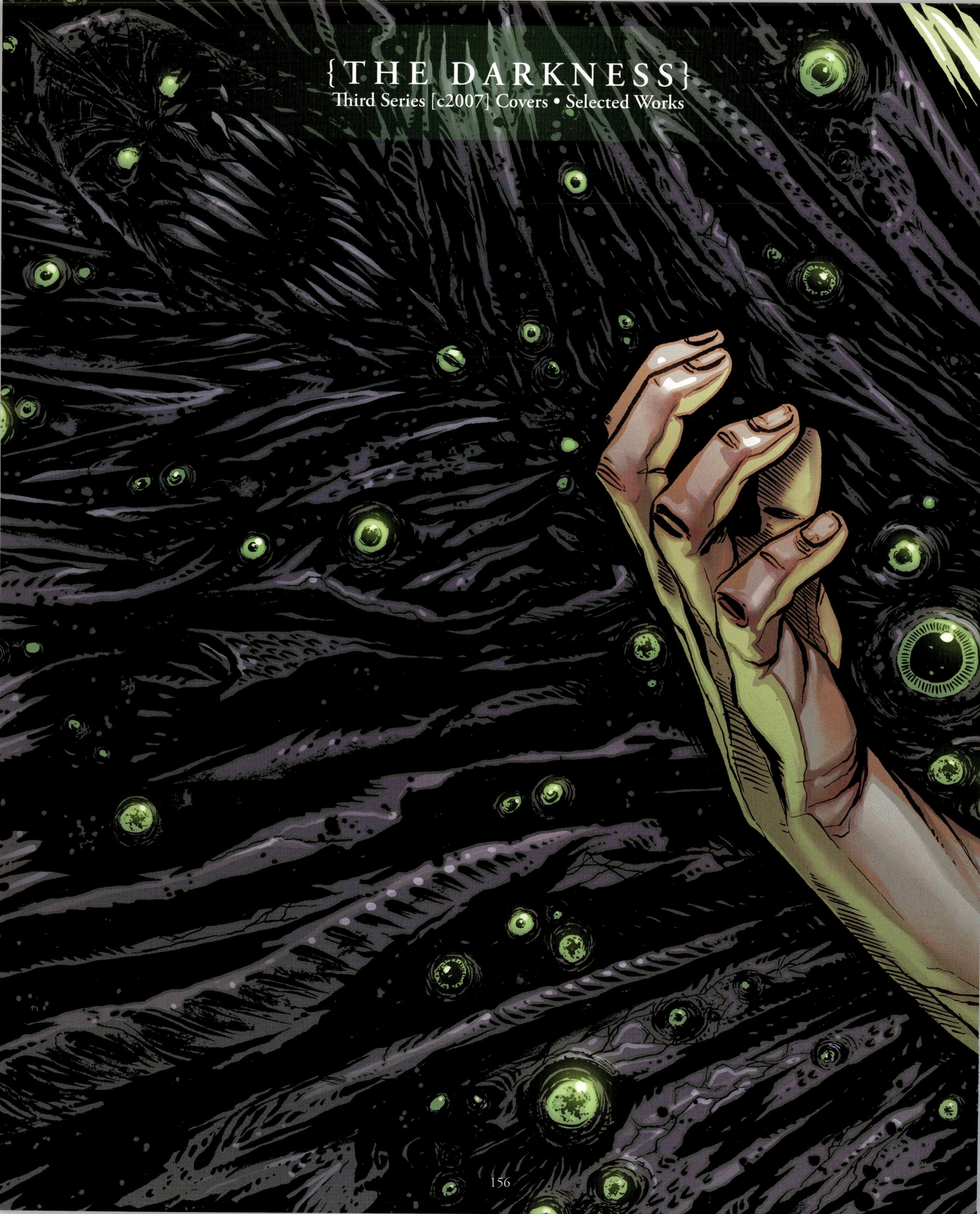

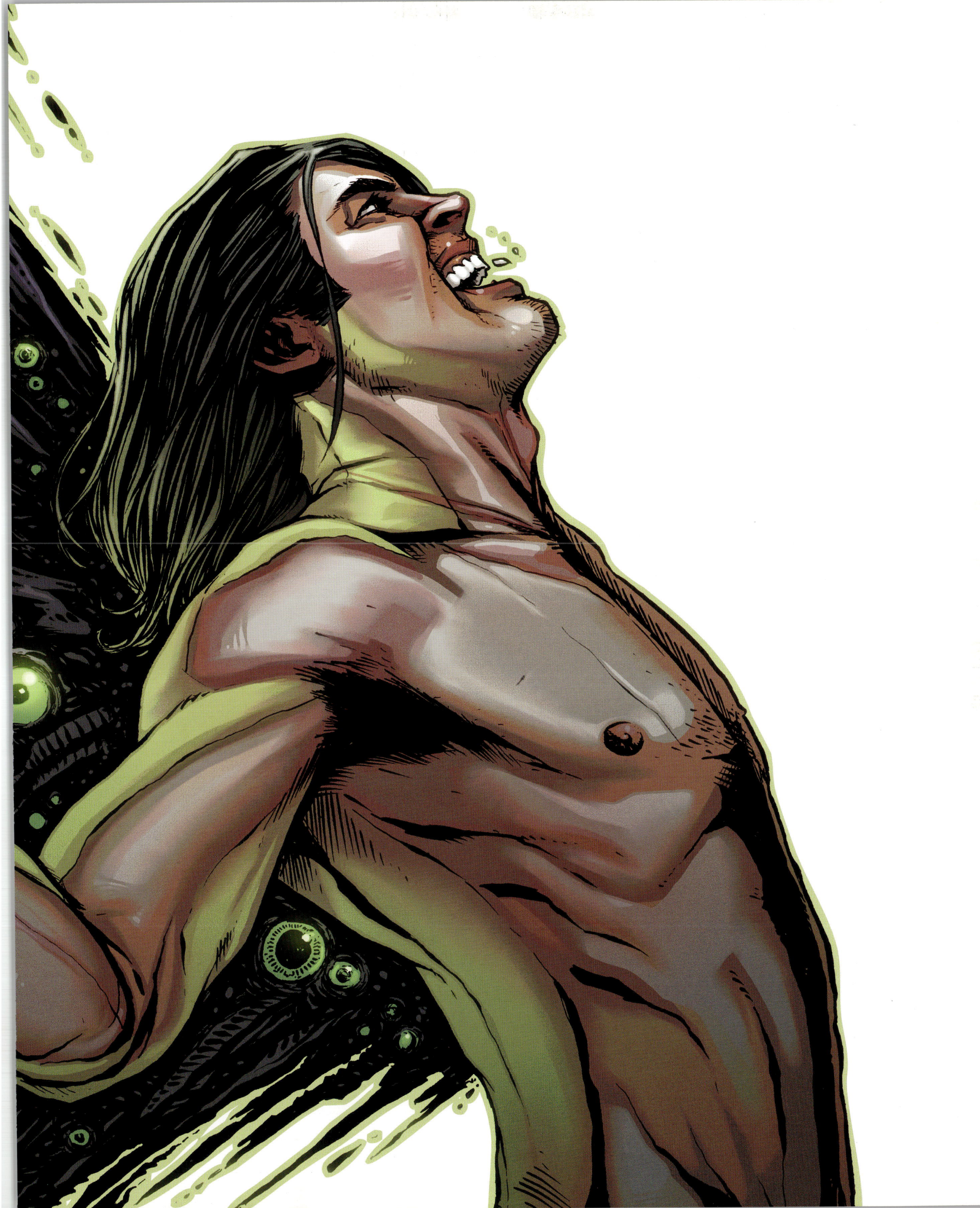

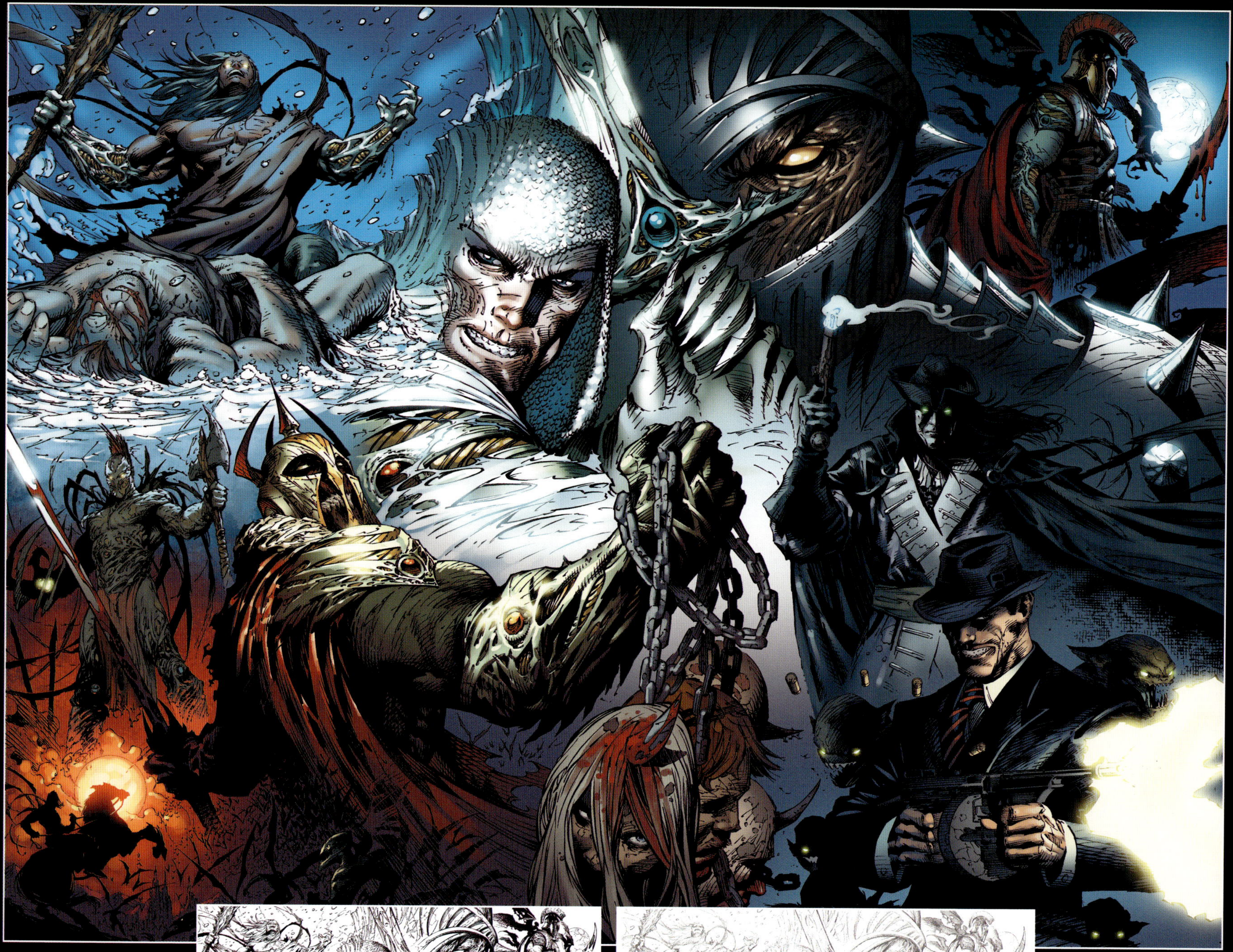

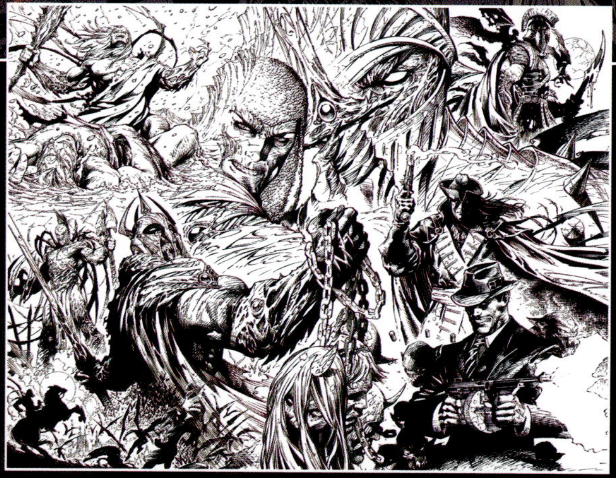

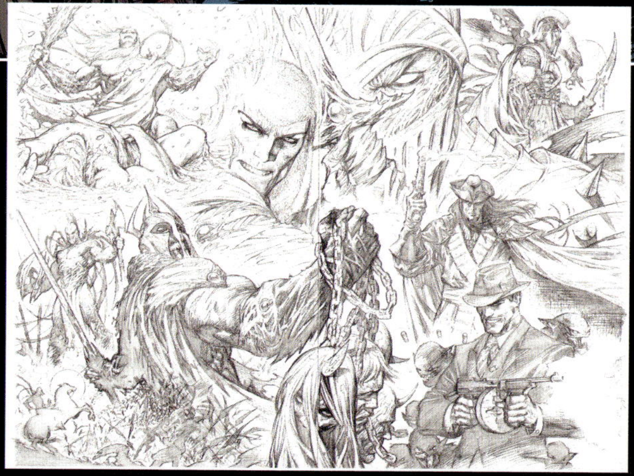

NOTE. On the following pages, *The Darkness* may be abbreviated to [DK] for various citations. - T.C.T.

Above. *The Darkness* #1 [2007]/Legacy #65 pages 2-3, art by: Michael Broussard, Ryan Winn, and Matt Milla

Previous page. *The Darkness* #101 cover A, art by: Jeremy Haun and John Rauch

Facing page. *The Darkness* #1 [2007]/Legacy #65 cover A, art by: Marc Silvestri, Joe Weems V, and Frank D'Armata

During the third series, after issue #10 starting with issue #11, the issues adopted a legacy numbering system making issue #11, the legacy issue #75. The legacy number reflects the total number of issues of the overall title, consolidating the issue numbers in one sequence from the first series #1 onward.

On the following pages, we pick up where *The Art of Top Cow* [2009] left off with a little overlap, of the art from the third series. This series featured not only great art but great writing from fan-favorite writers Phil Hester and David Hine.

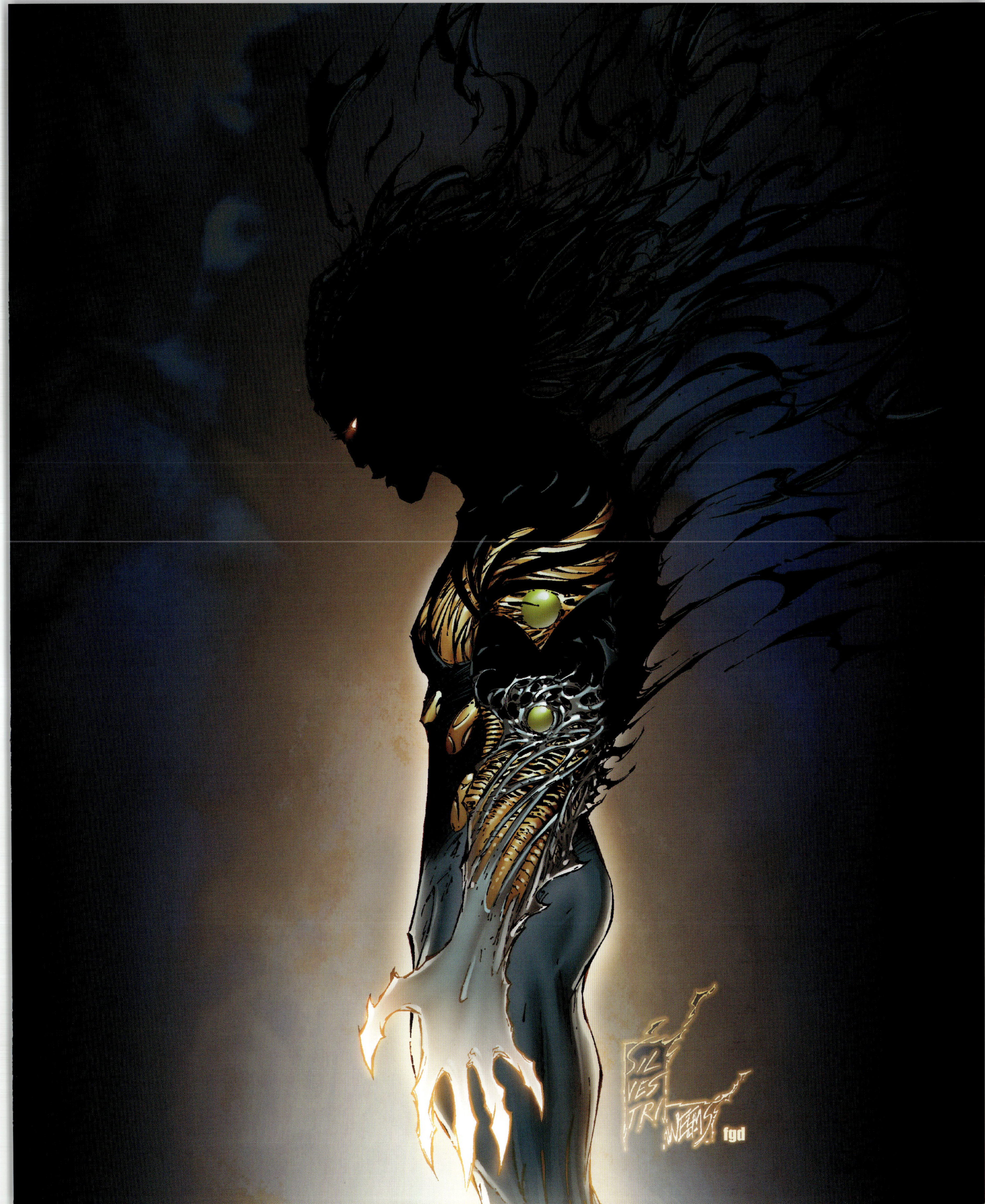

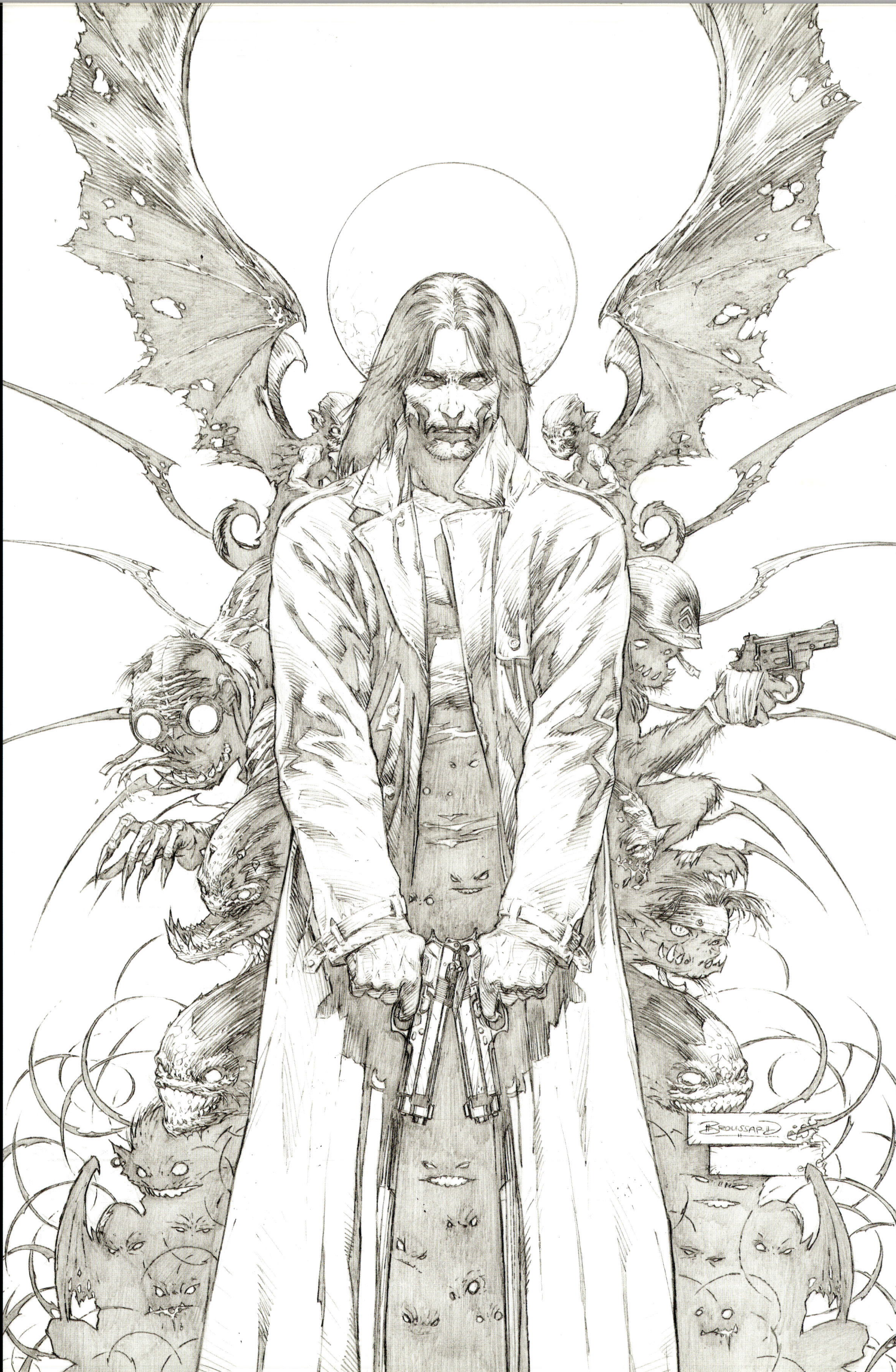

The Darkness, First Look [2007] cover,
line art by: Michael Broussard

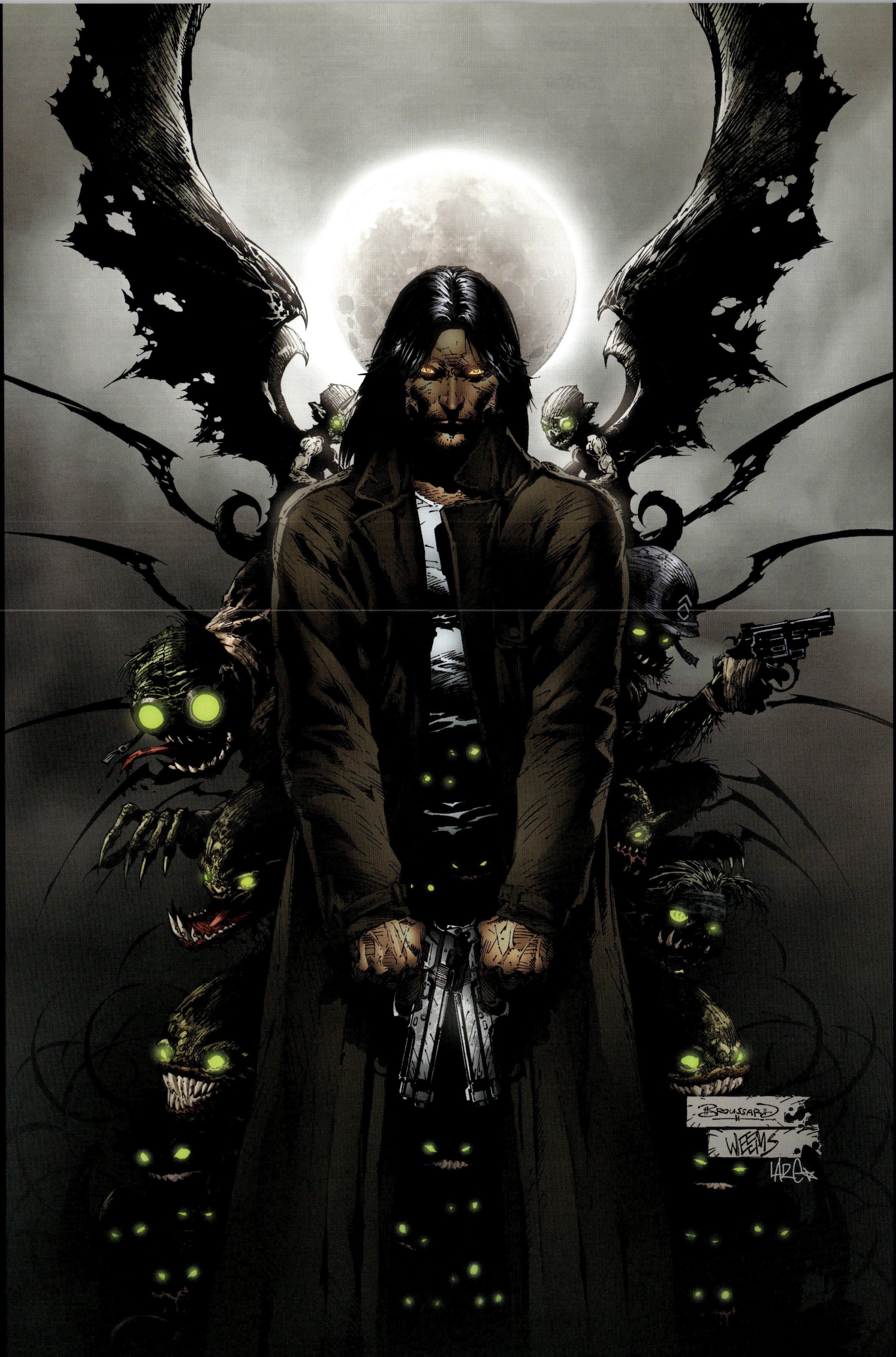

The Darkness, First Look [2007] cover,
art by: Michael Broussard, Joe Weems V, and Larry Molinar

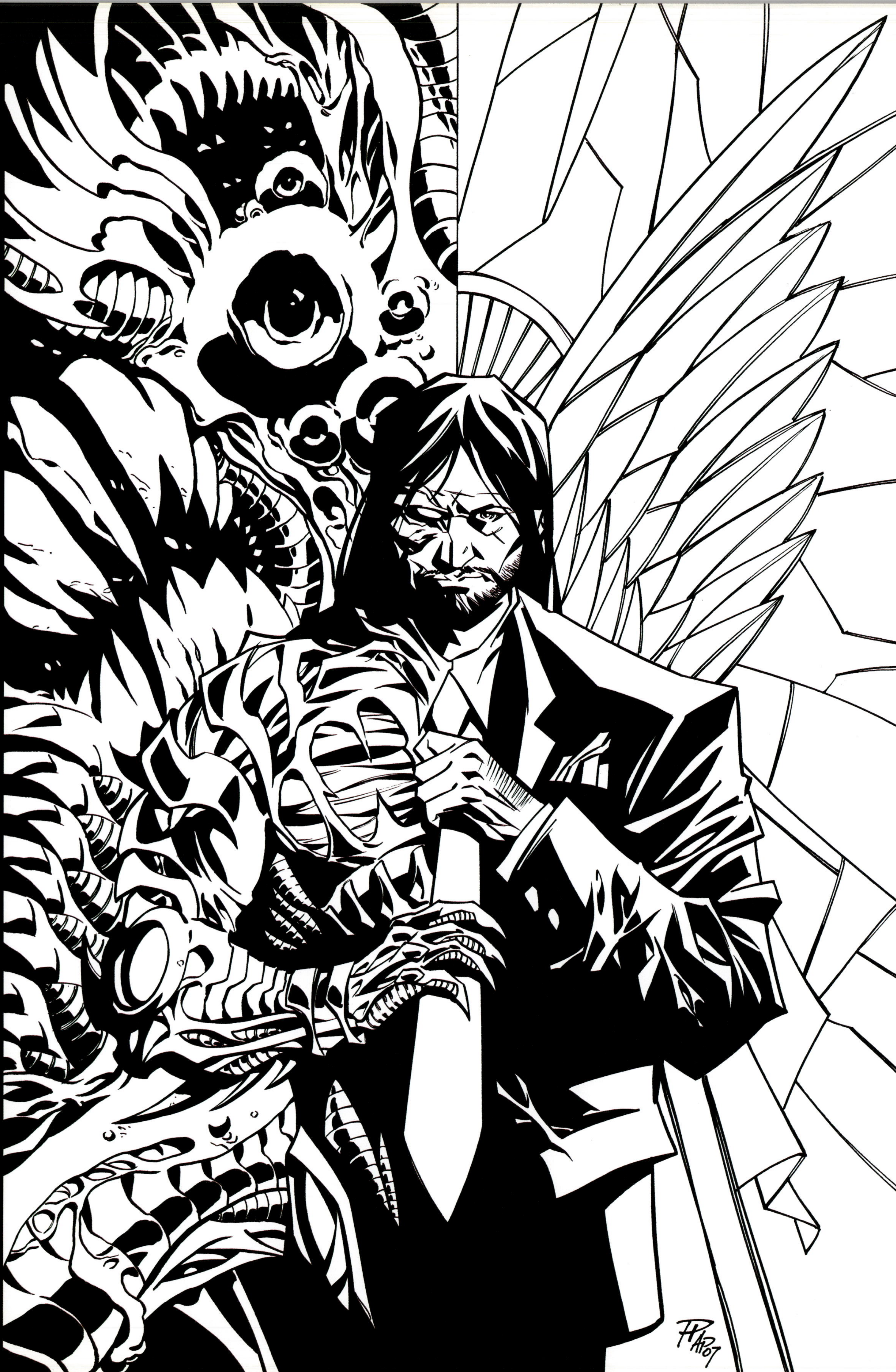

The Darkness #1 [2007] Top Cow Store Exclusive cover,
line art by: Phil Hester and Ande Parks

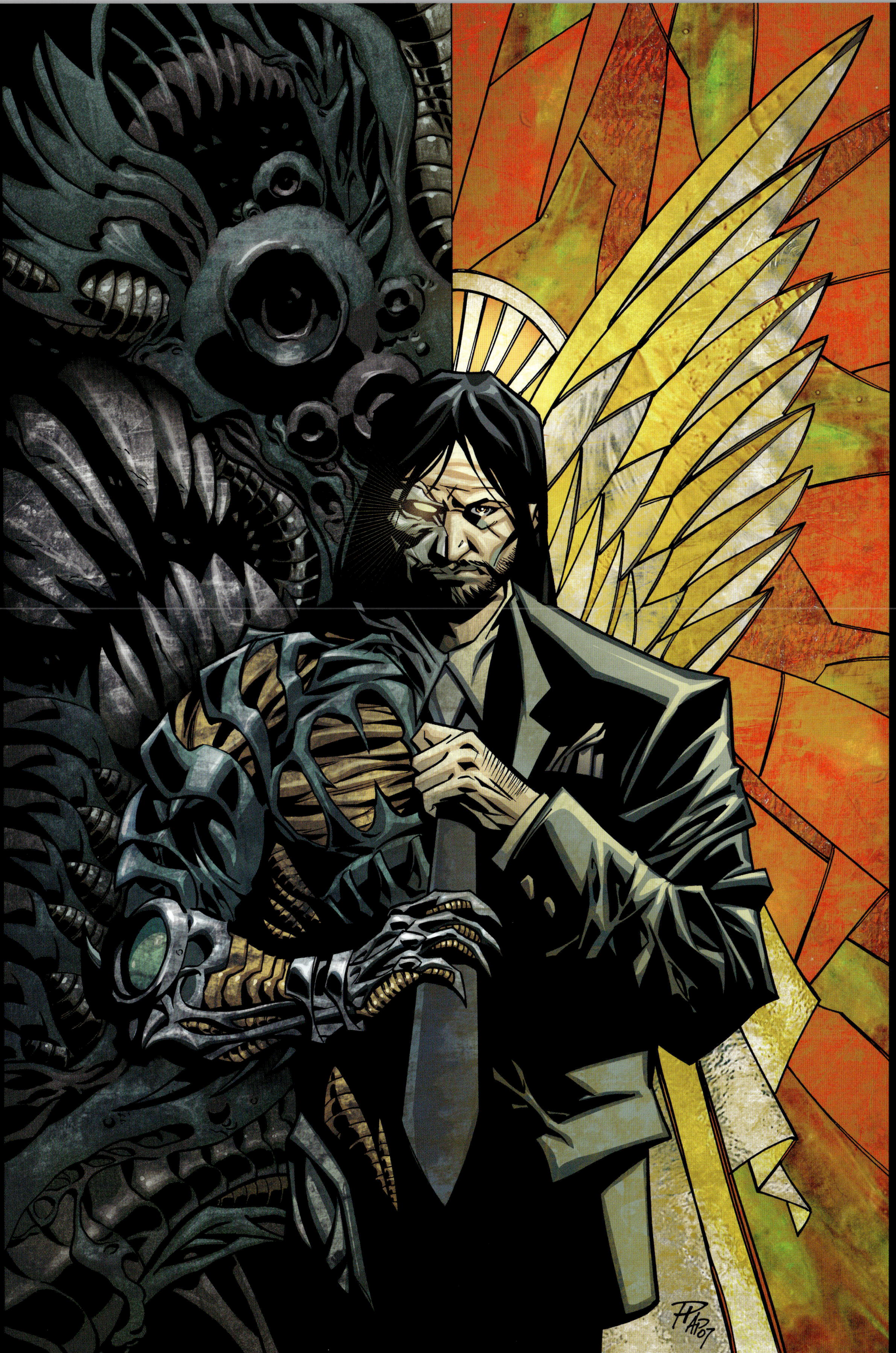

The Darkness #1 [2007] Top Cow Store Exclusive cover,
art by: Phil Hester, Ande Parks, and Dave McCaig

Below. DK #1 [2017] cover B

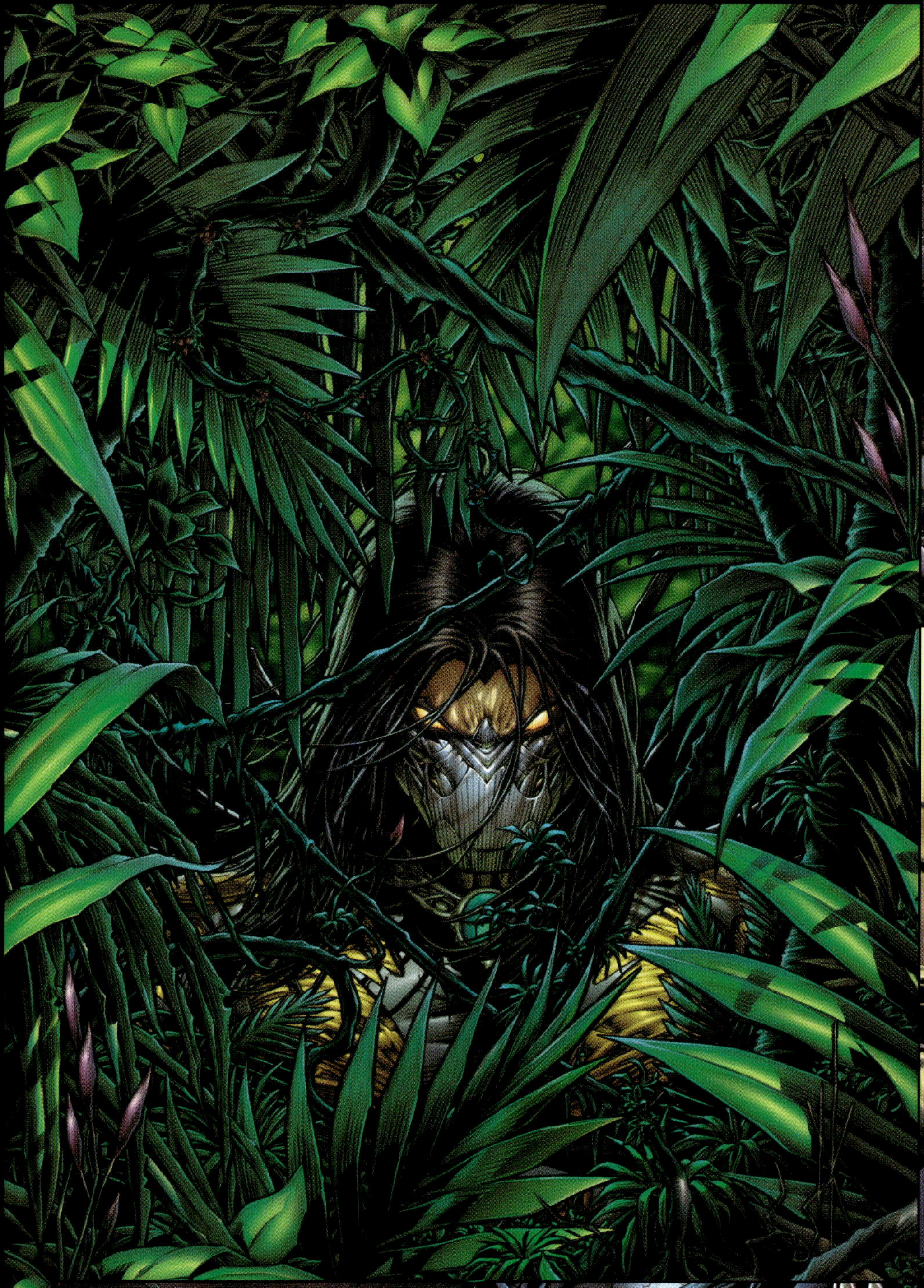

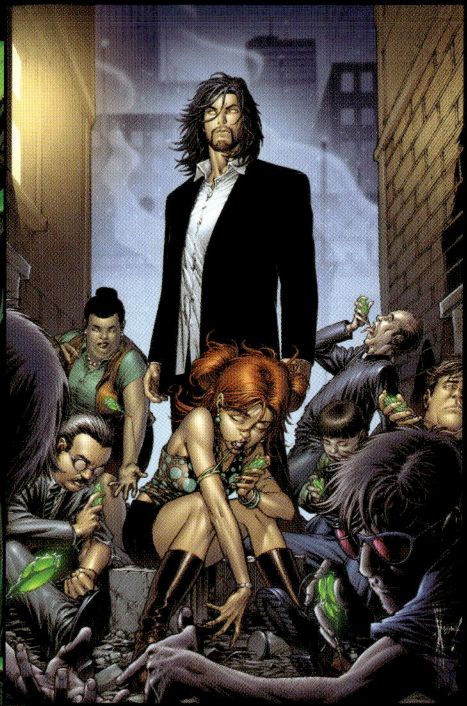

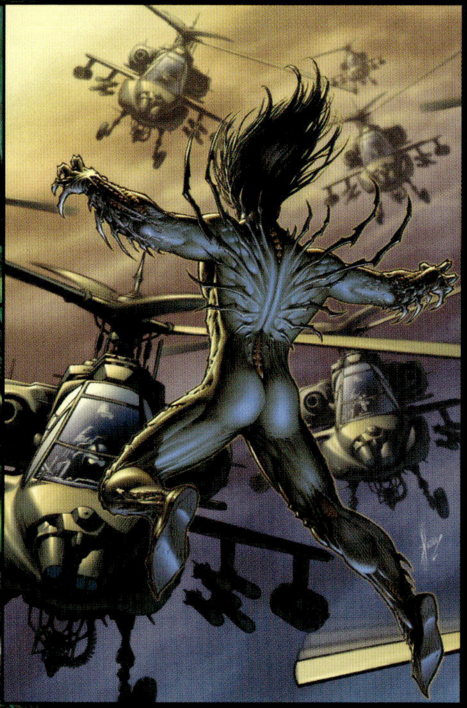

The Darkness #1-6 [2007] covers,
art by: Dale Keown

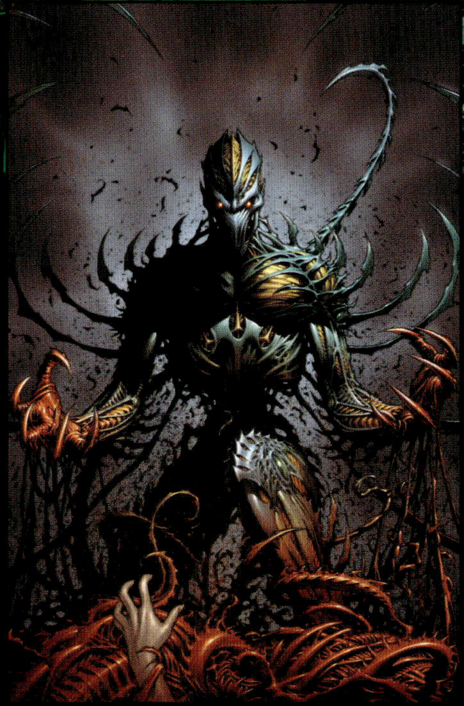

Above. DK #6 [2007] cover A

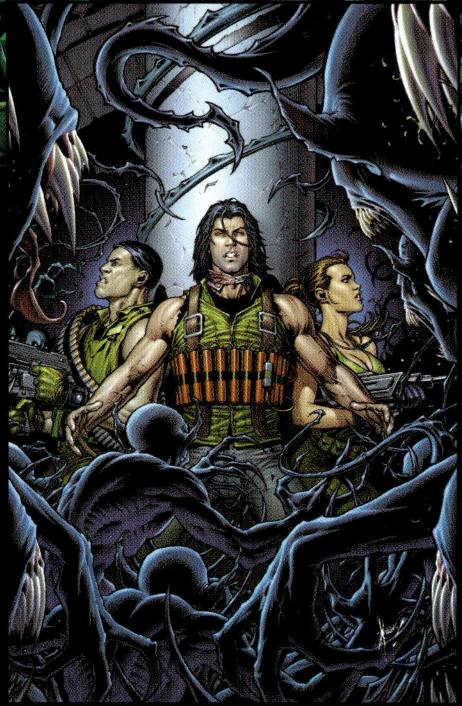

Above. DK #5 [2007] cover A

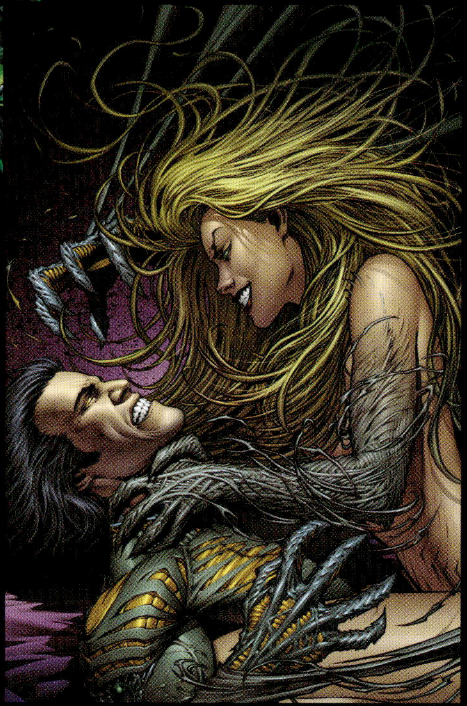

From the top, this row. DK #2, 3 and 4 cover A's

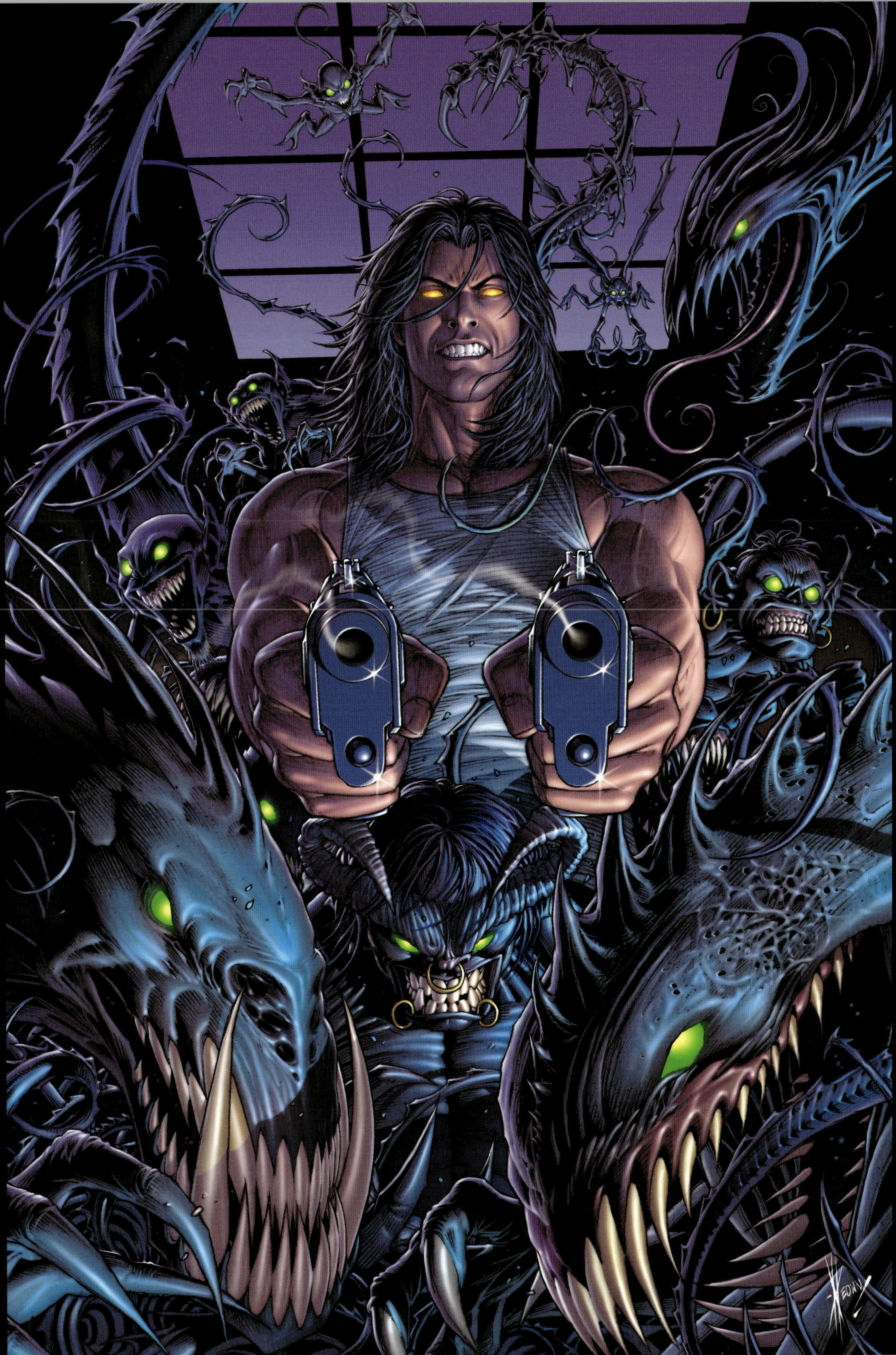

The Darkness #75 [2007] cover B,
art by: Dale Keown

Below. DK #1 [2017] cover C

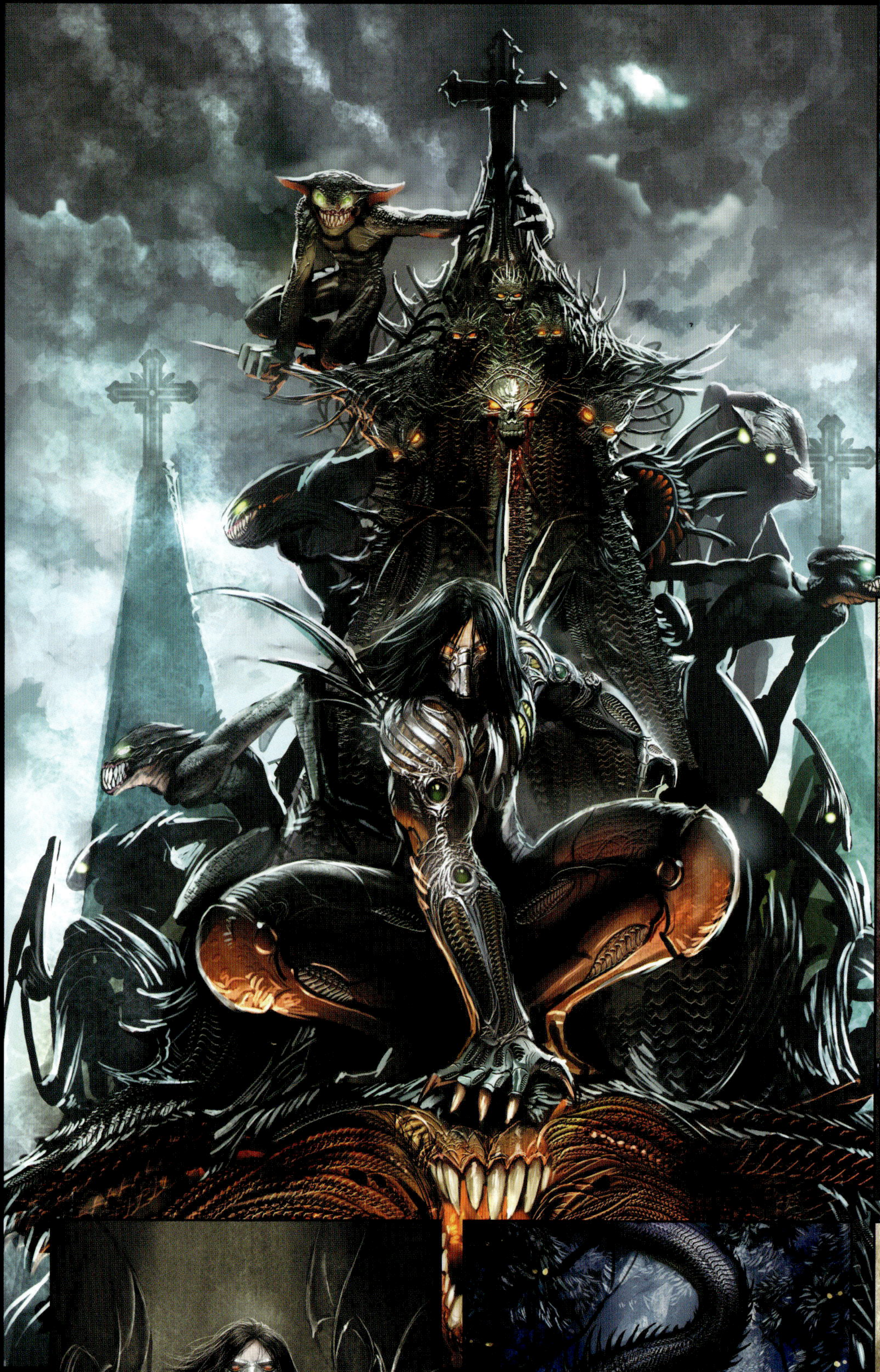

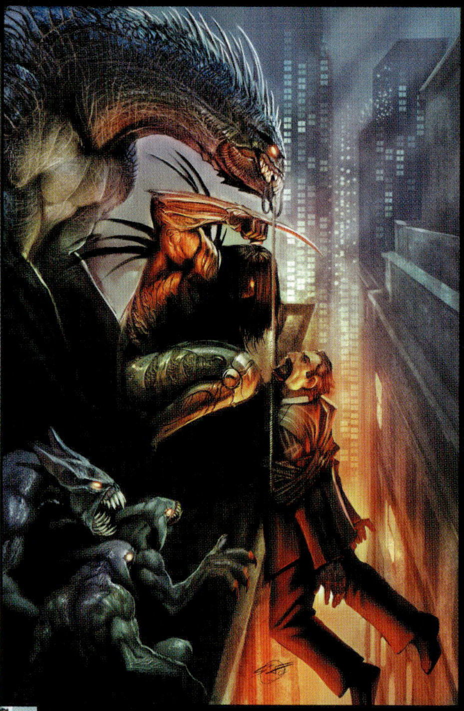

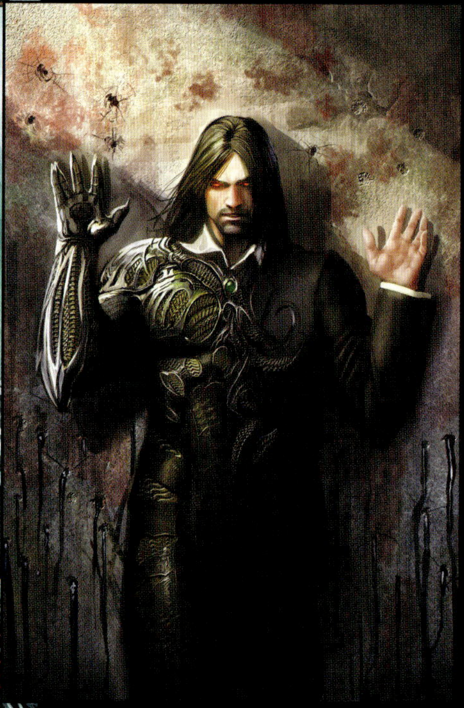

The Darkness #1-6 [2007] covers,
art by: Stjepan Sejic

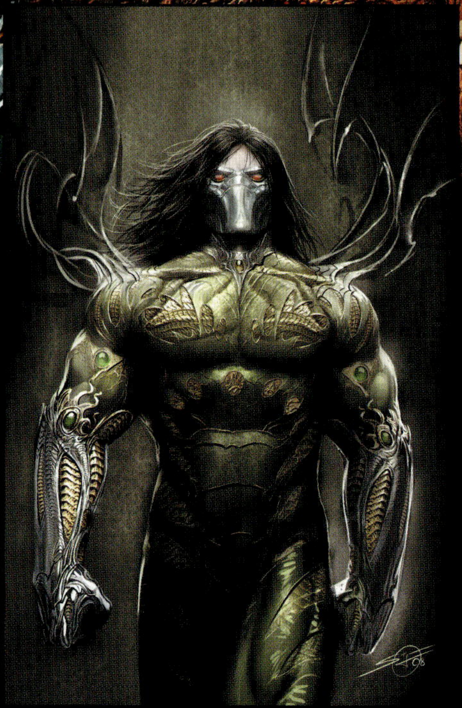

Above. DK #6 [2007] cover B

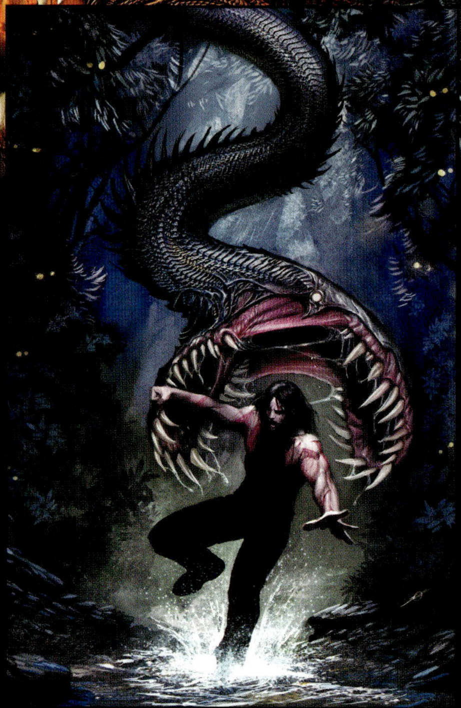

Above. DK #5 [2007] cover B

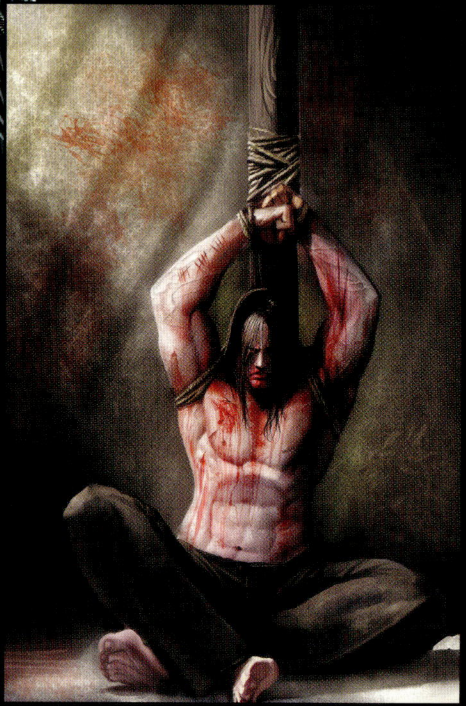

From the top, this row. DK #2, 3 and 4 cover B's

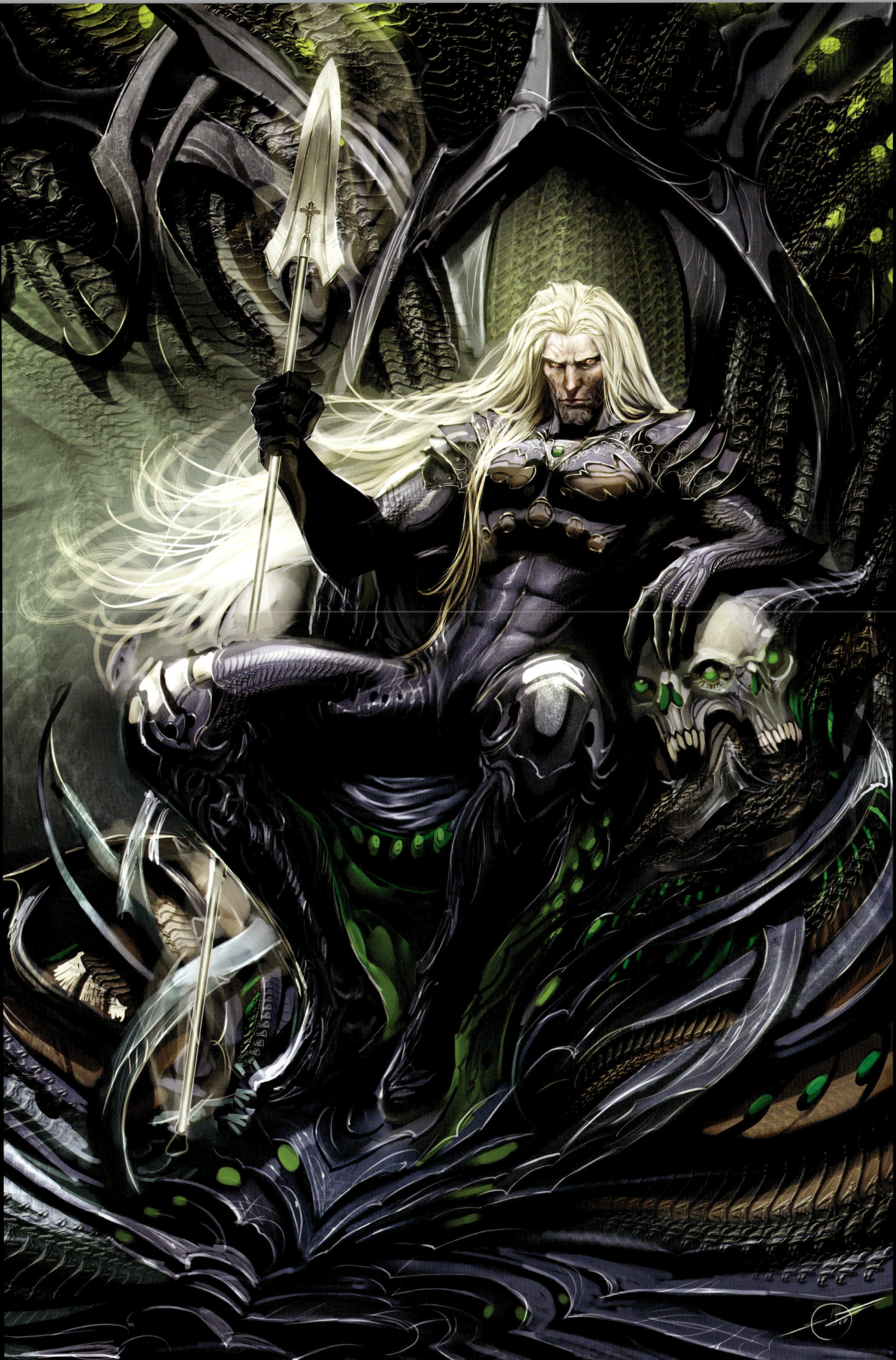

The Darkness #75 [2007] cover C,
art by: Stijepan Sejic

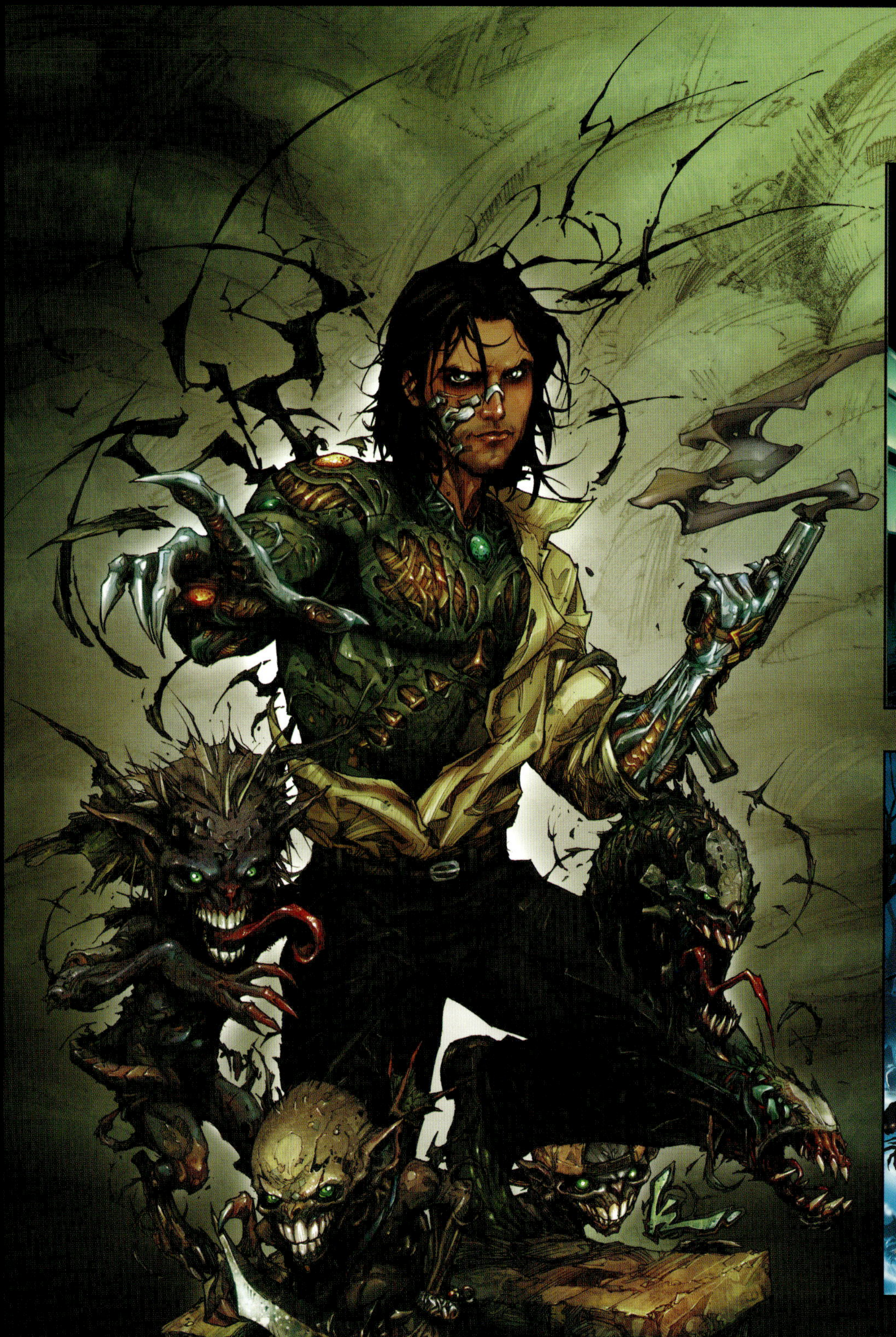

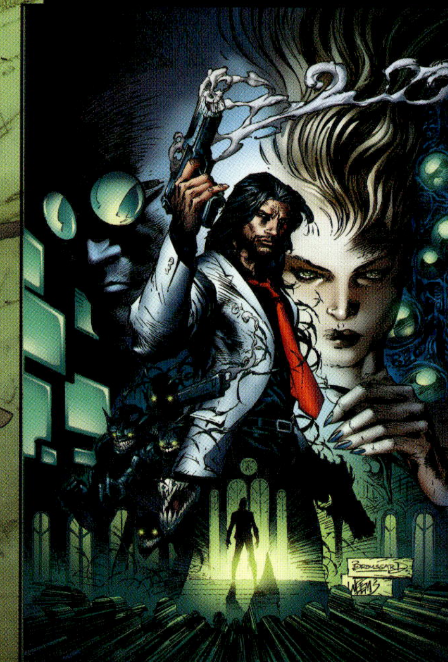

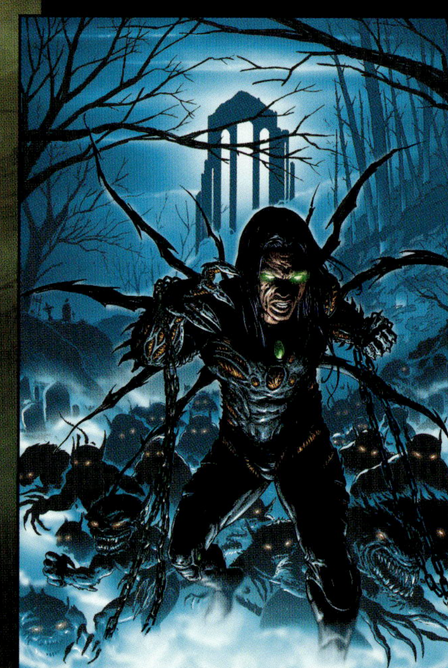

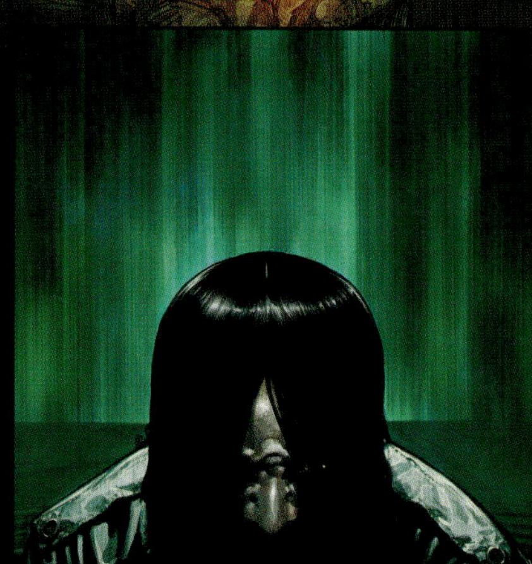

This page, clockwise from above.

The Darkness #4 [2007] Wizard World Chicago variant cover,
art by: Kenneth Rocafort

The Darkness #3 [2007] NYCC variant cover,
art by: Michael Broussard, Joe Weems V, and Matt Milla

The Darkness #7 [2007] cover A,
art by: Jorge Lucas and Lee Loughridge

The Darkness #9 [2007] cover B,
art by: Matt Timson

The Darkness #10 [2007] cover,
art by: Frazer Irving

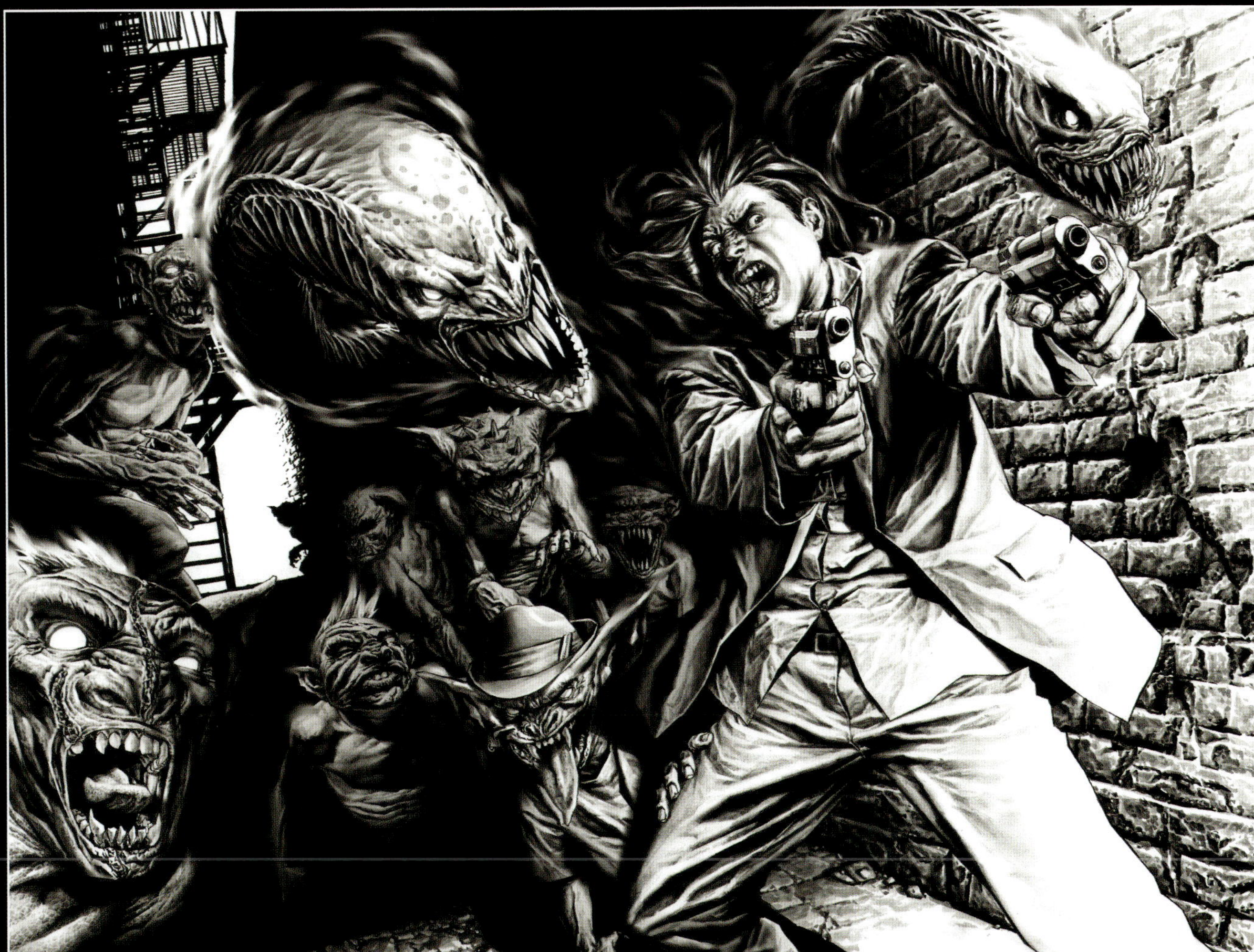

The Darkness #75 cover A, art by: Lee Bermejo and Grant Goleash

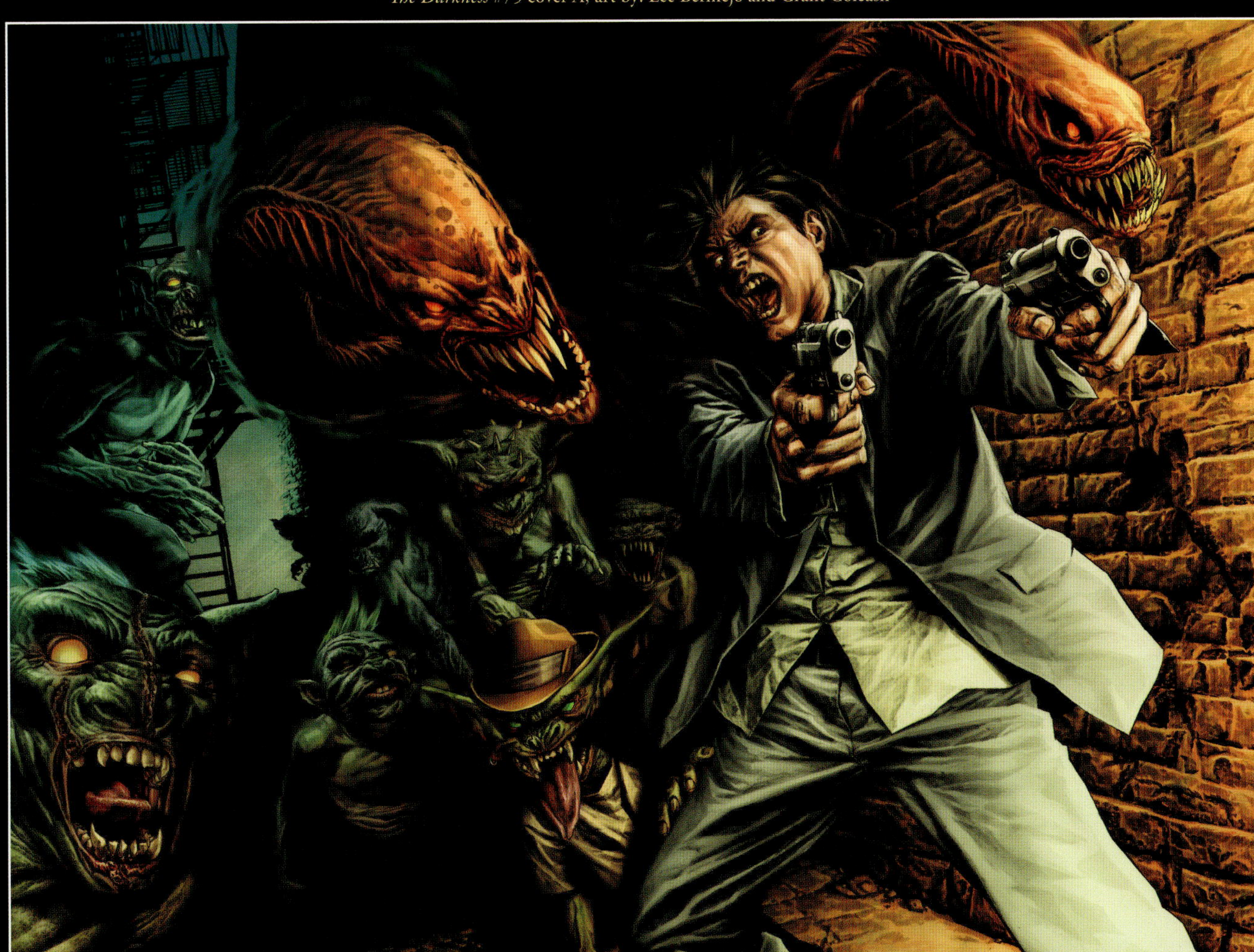

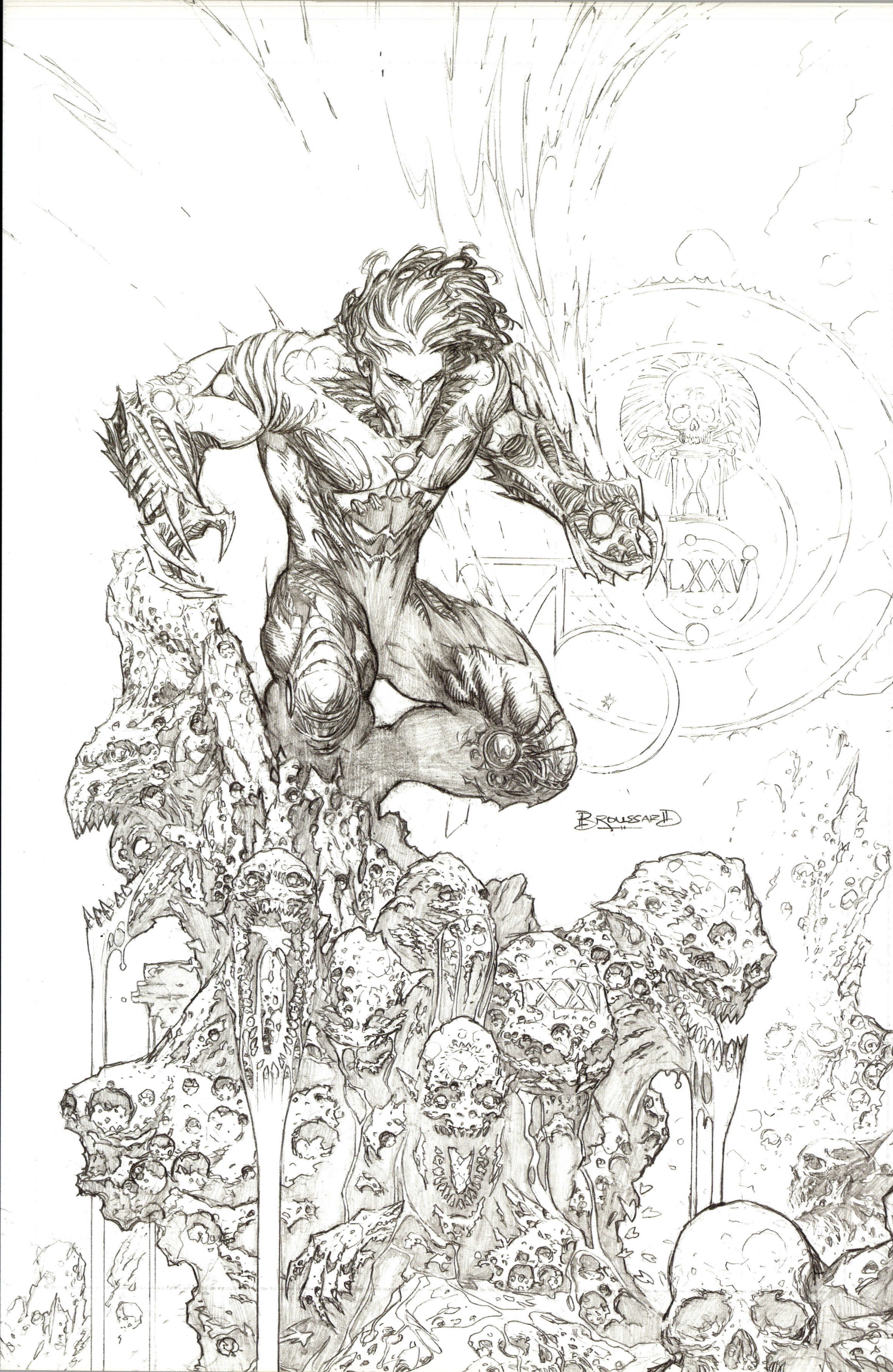

The Darkness #75 cover E, limited edition sketch variant,
line art by: Michael Broussard

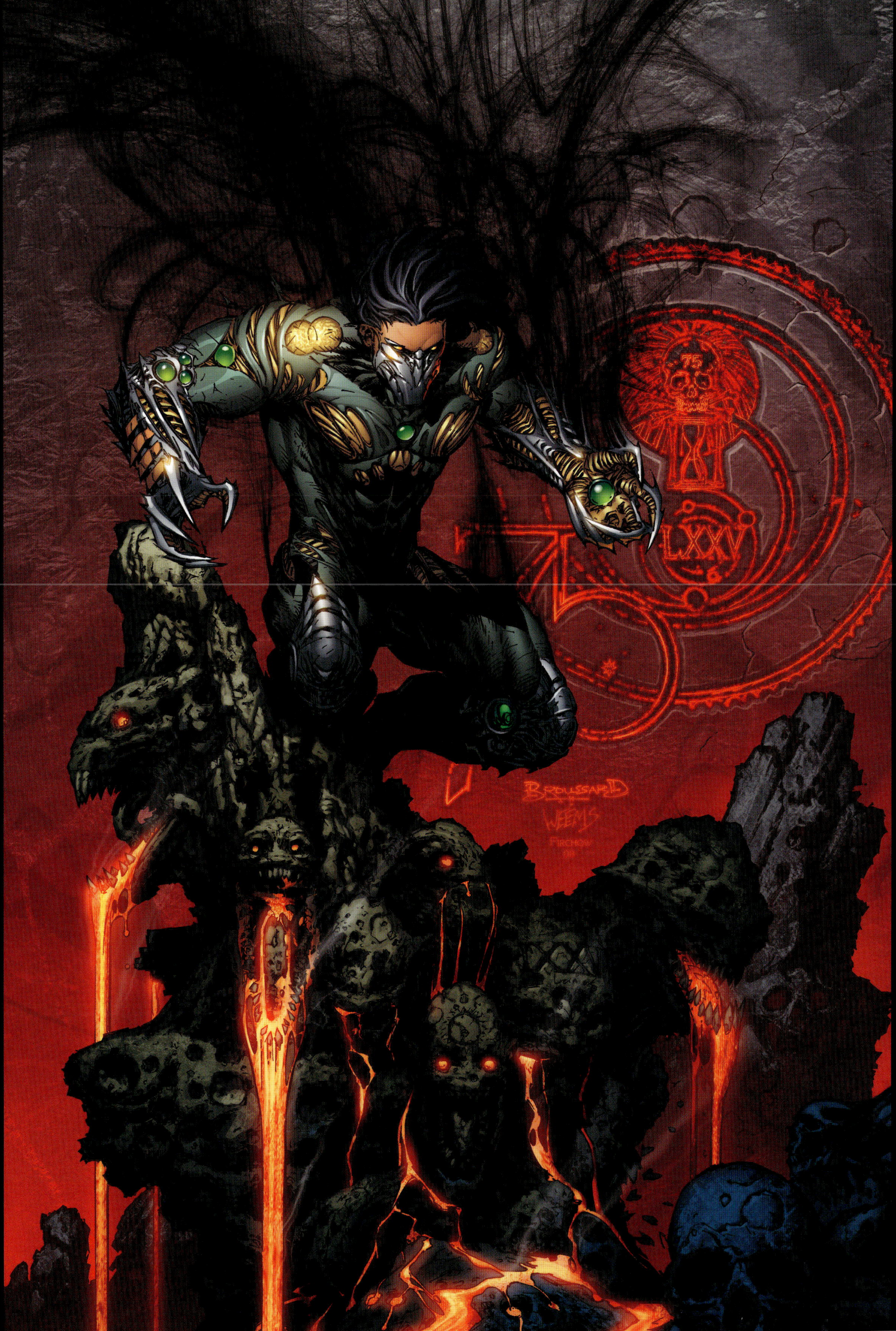

The Darkness #75 cover D,
art by: Michael Broussard, Joe Weems V, and Steve Firchow

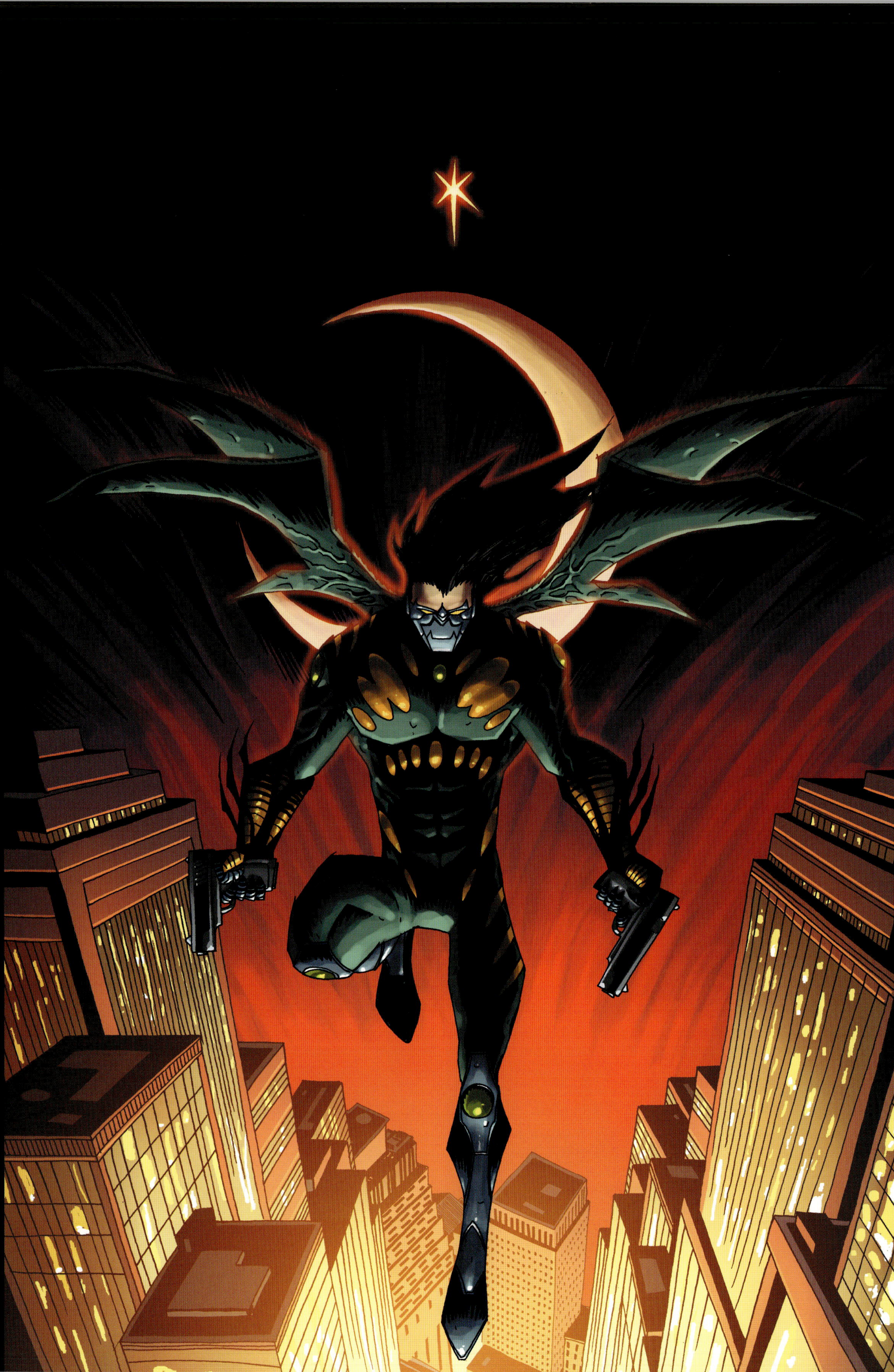

The Darkness #78 cover,
art by: Michael Avon Oeming and Val Staples

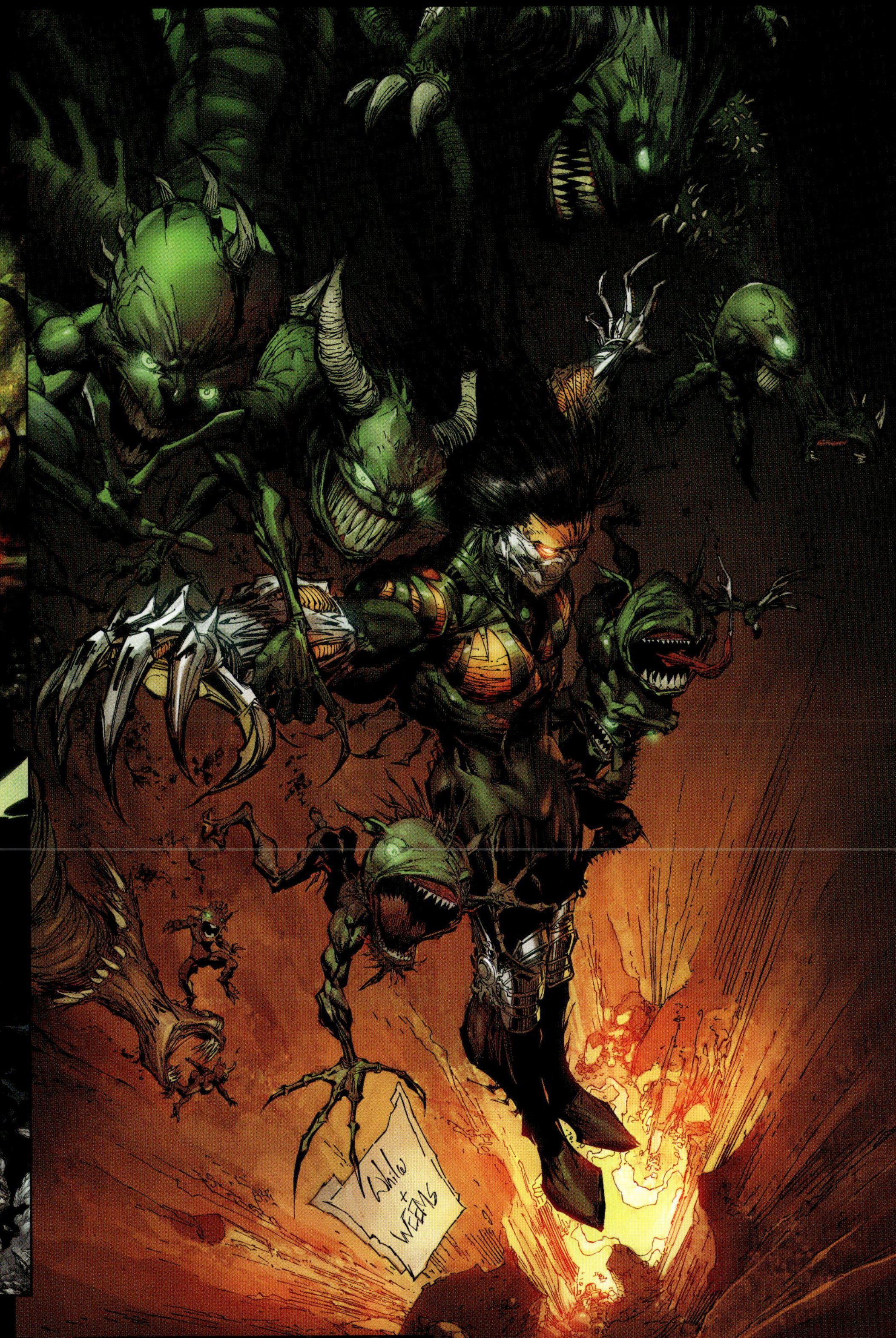

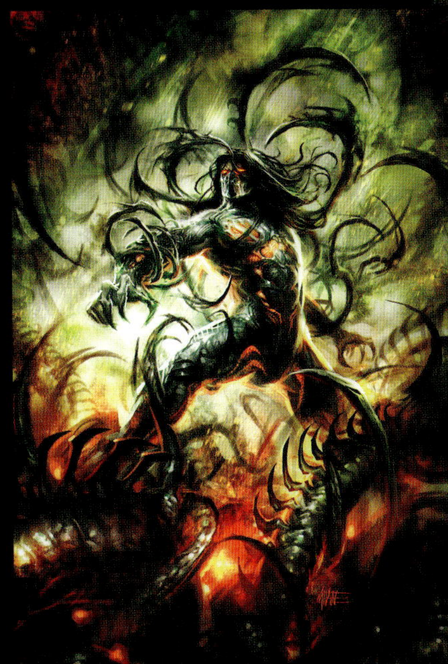

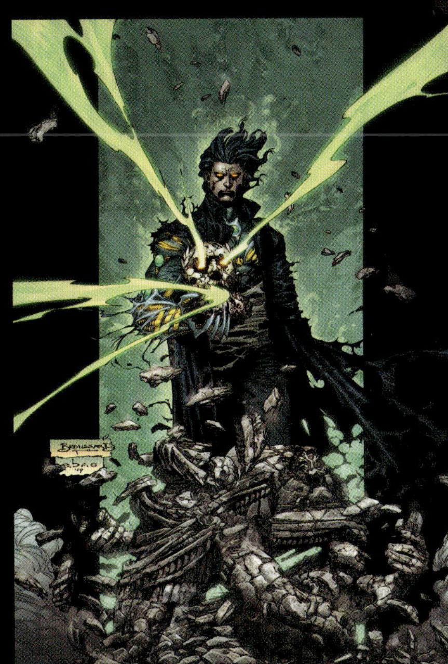

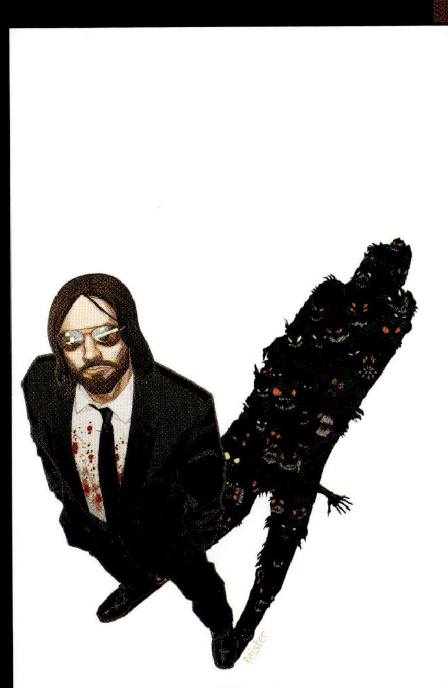

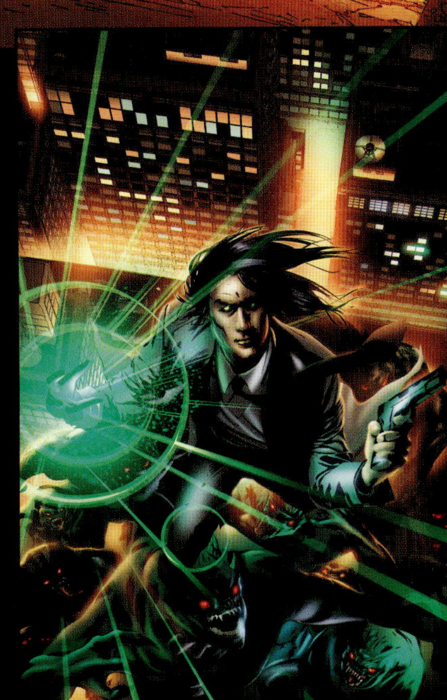

This page, counterclockwise from above.

The Darkness #79 cover B,
art by: Whilce Portacio, Joe Weems V, and Sunny Gho

The Darkness #80 cover B,
art by: Michal Ivan

The Darkness #81 [2007] cover,
art by: Michael Broussard, Eric Basaldua, and Arif Prianto

The Darkness #82 [2007] cover,
art by: Tom Feister

The Darkness #83 [2007] cover A,
art by: Dennis Calero

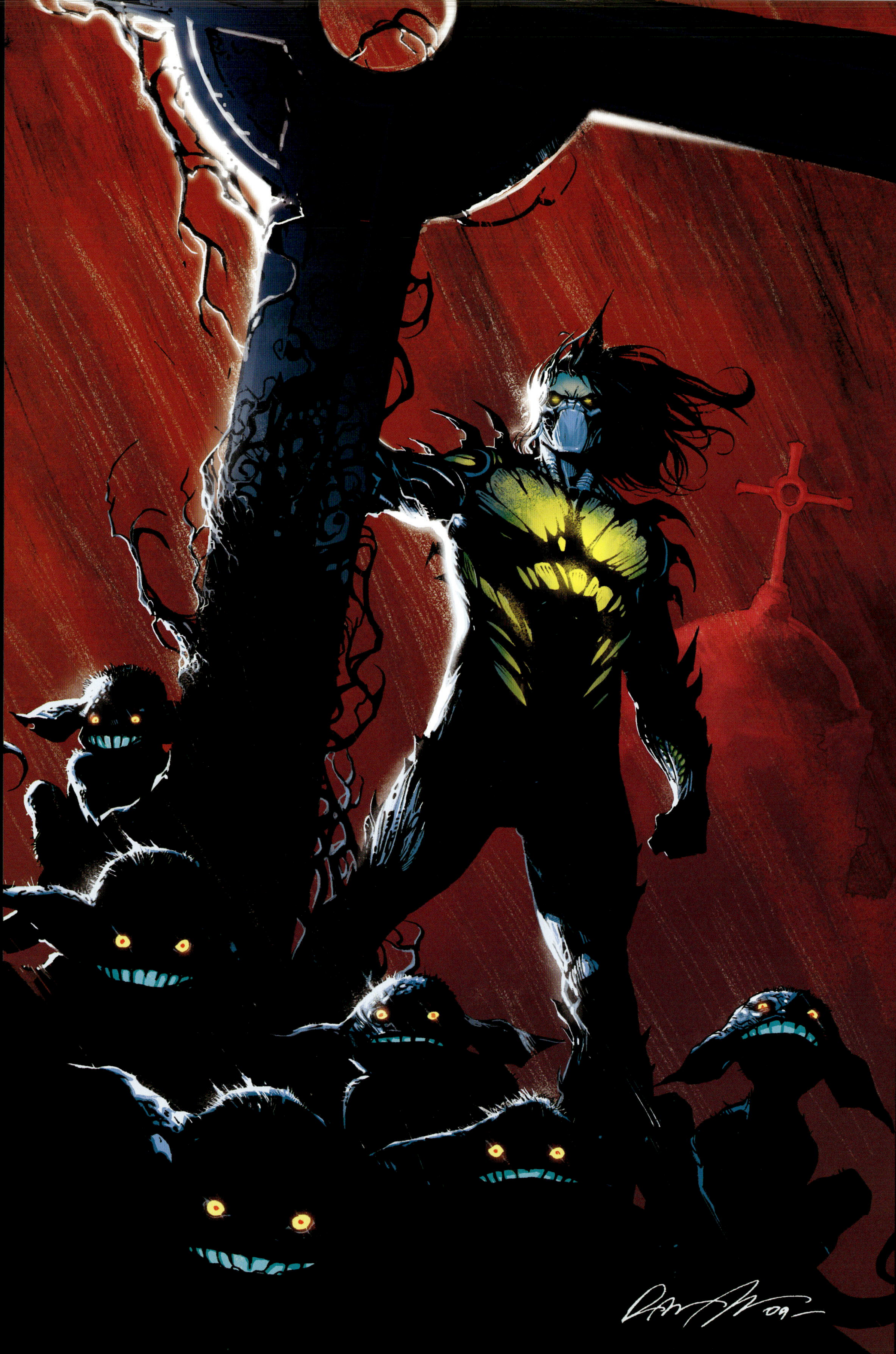

The Darkness #86 cover,
art by: Rafael Albuquerque

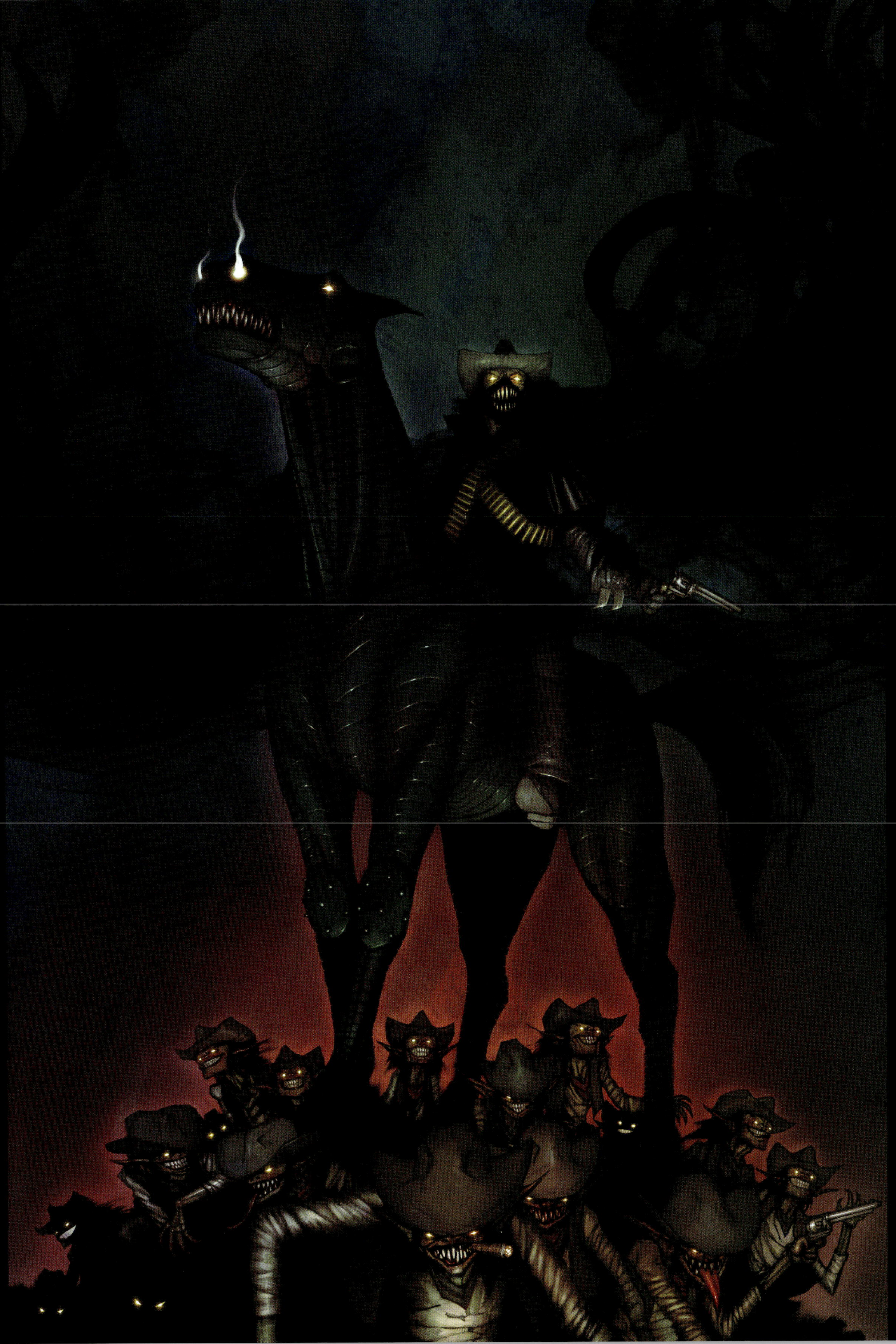

The Darkness #89 cover A,
art by: Matt Timson

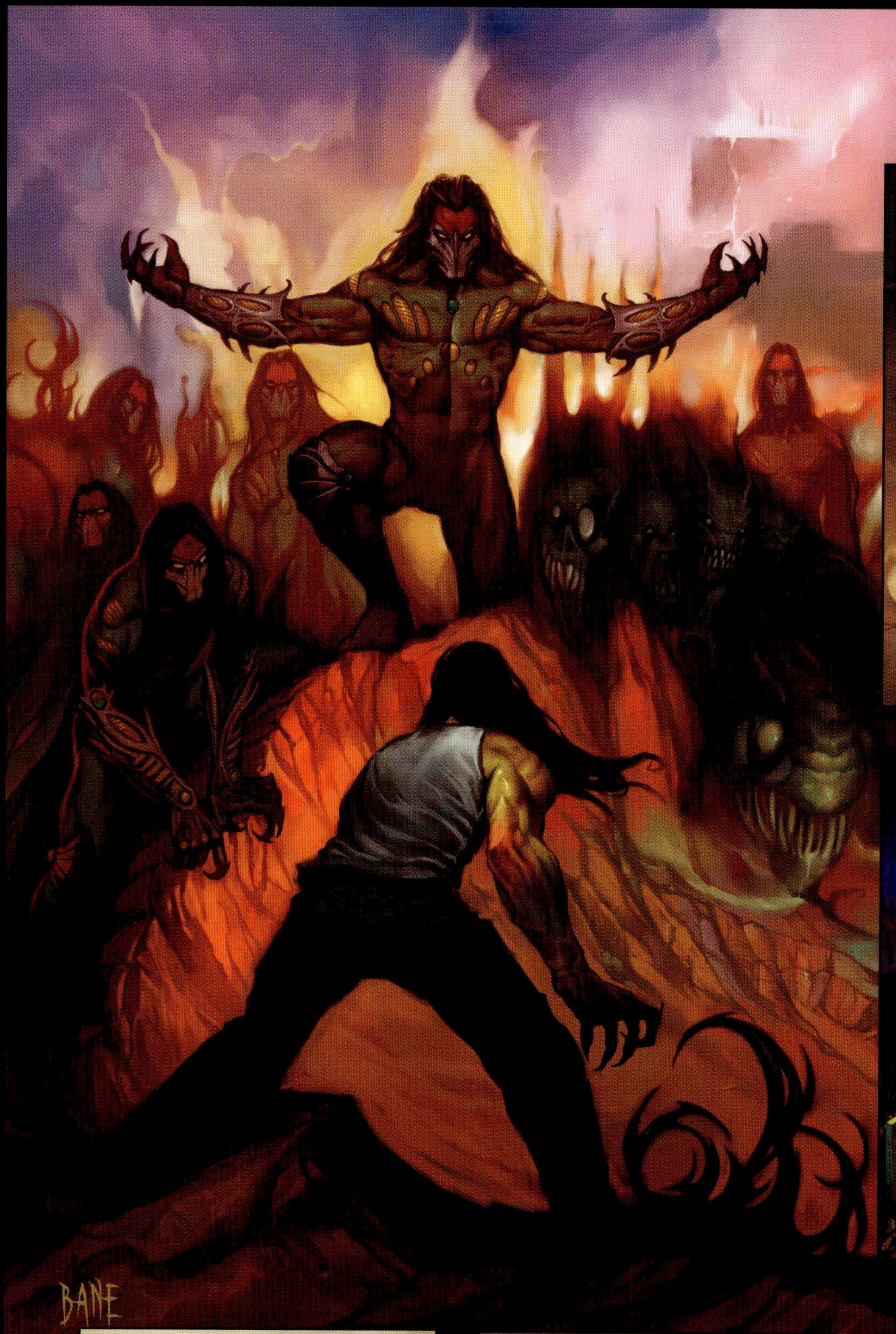

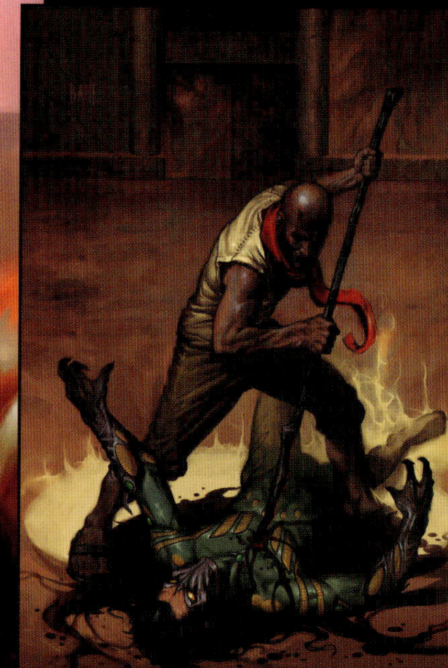

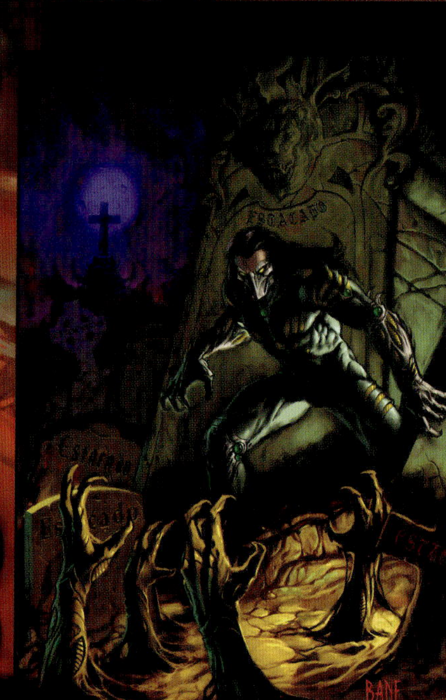

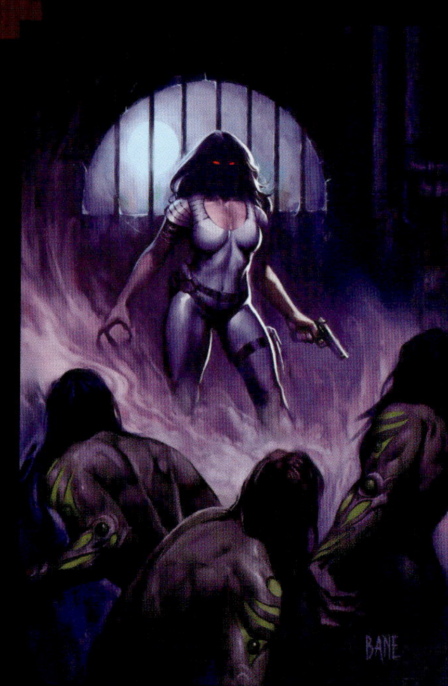

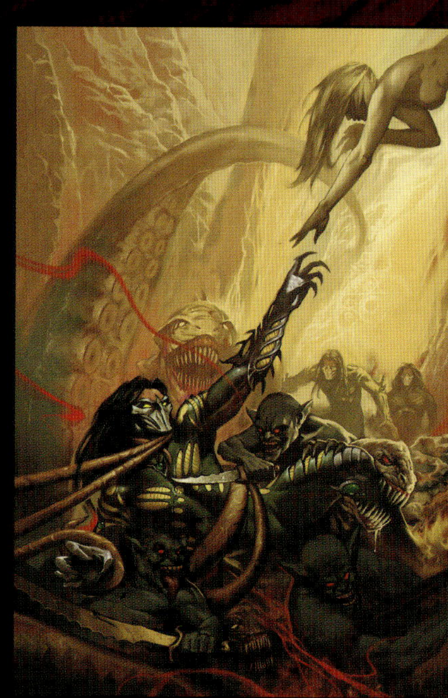

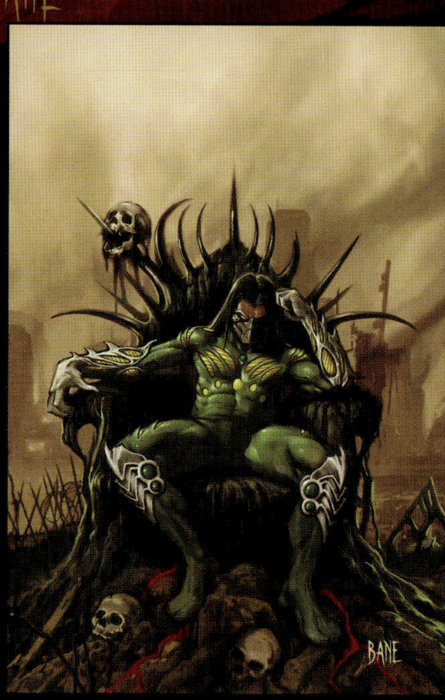

This page, clockwise from top left. • *The Darkness* #90-95 cover A's, art by: Bane

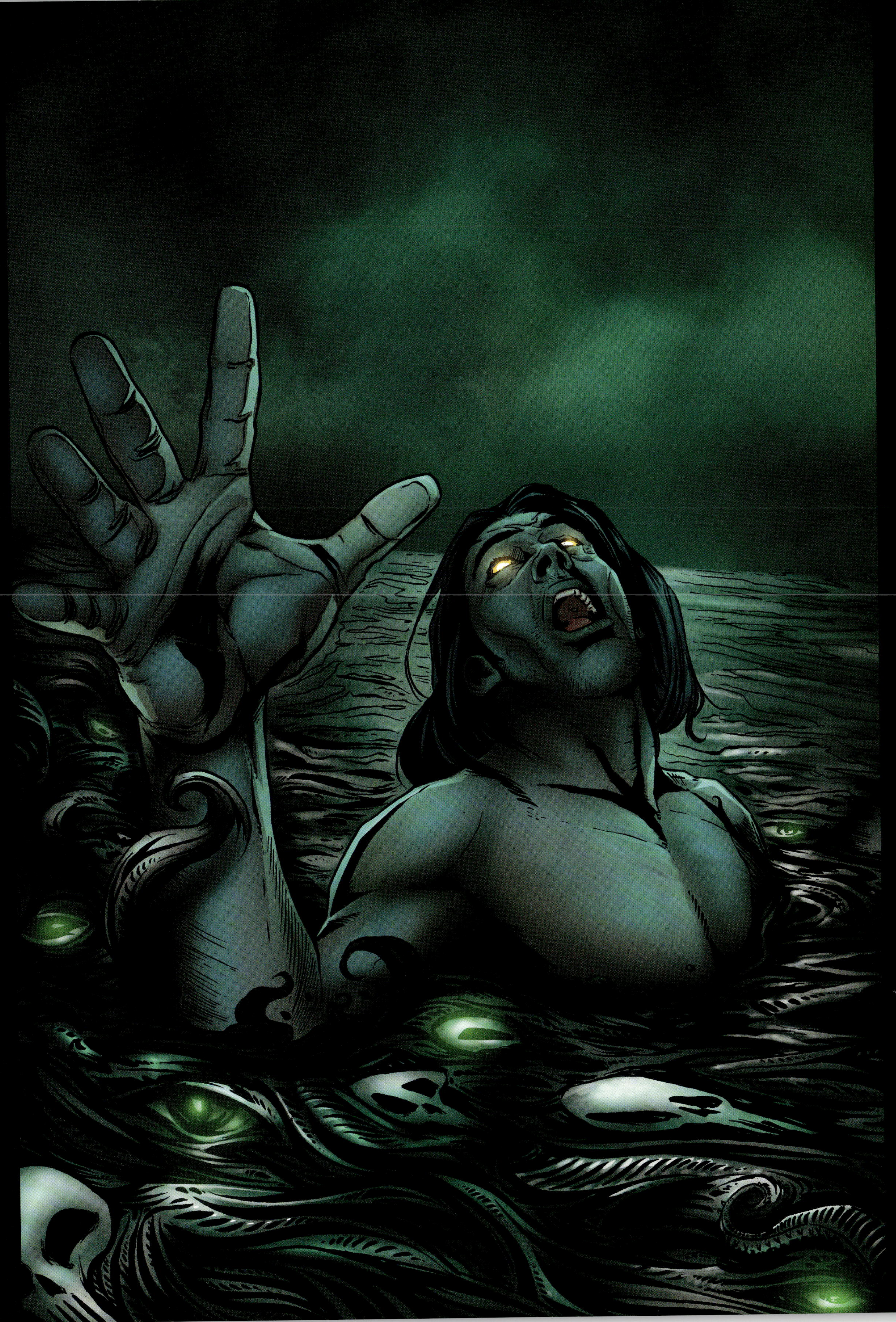

The Darkness #96 cover A,
art by: Jeremy Haun and Felix Serrano

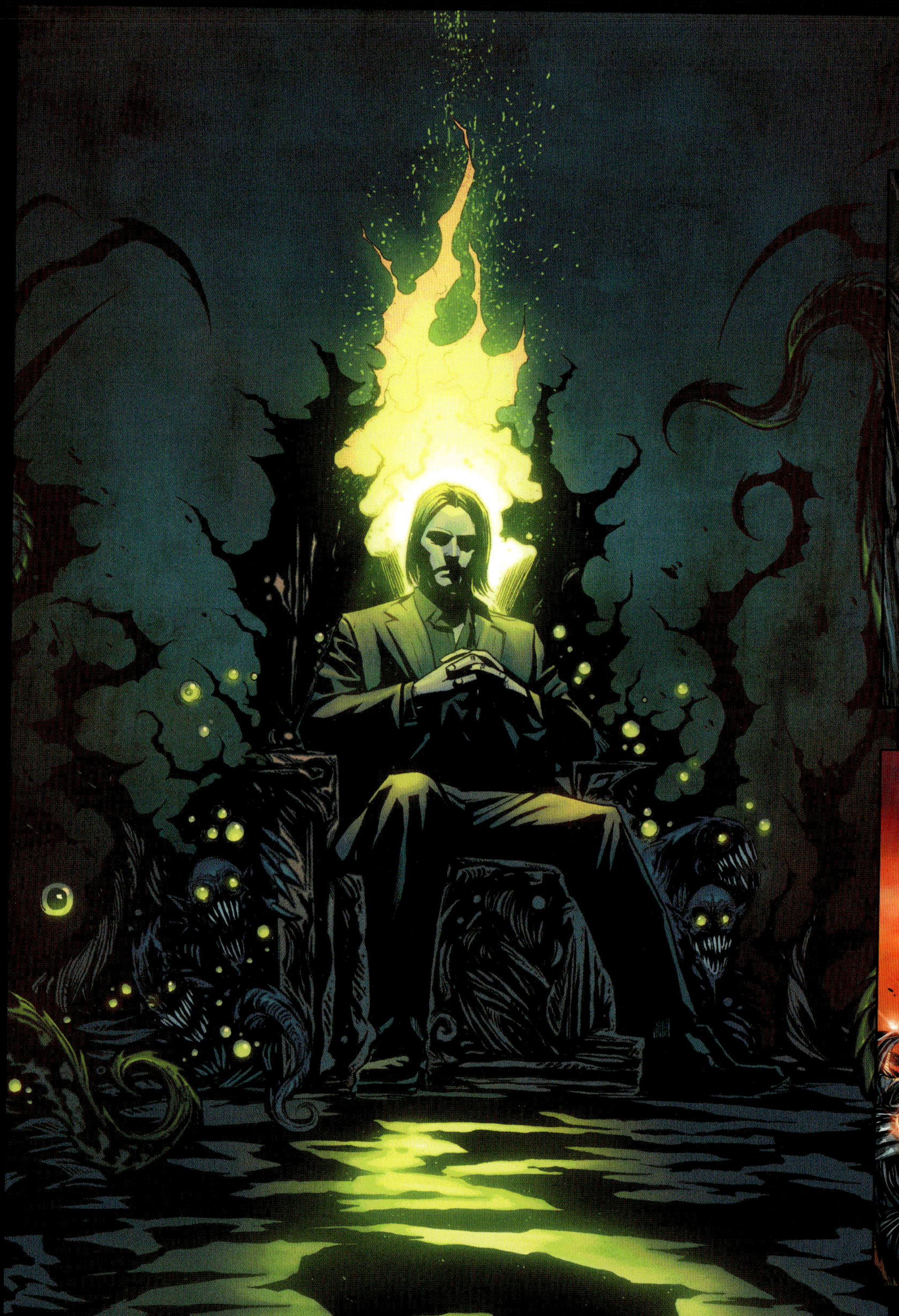

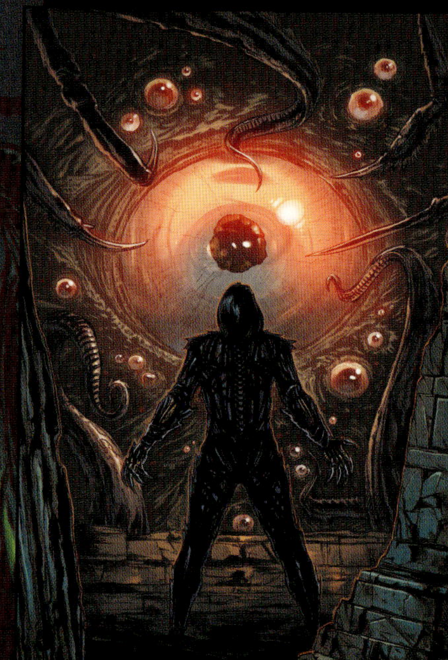

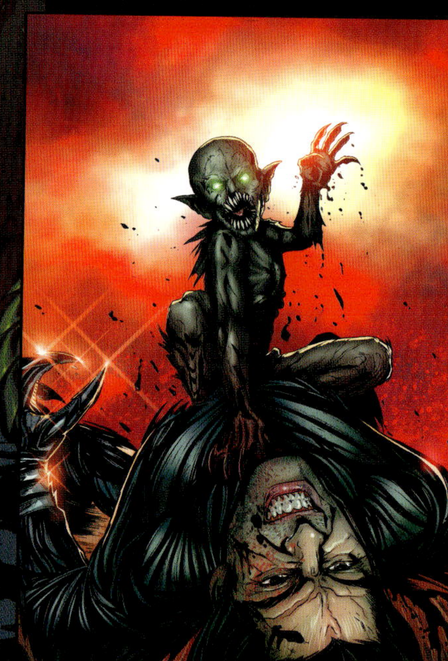

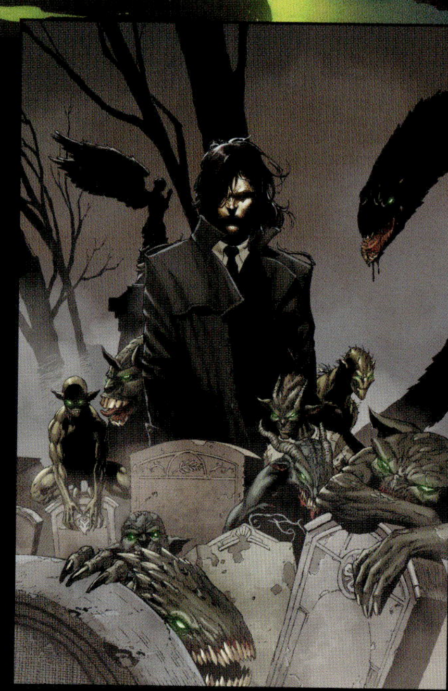

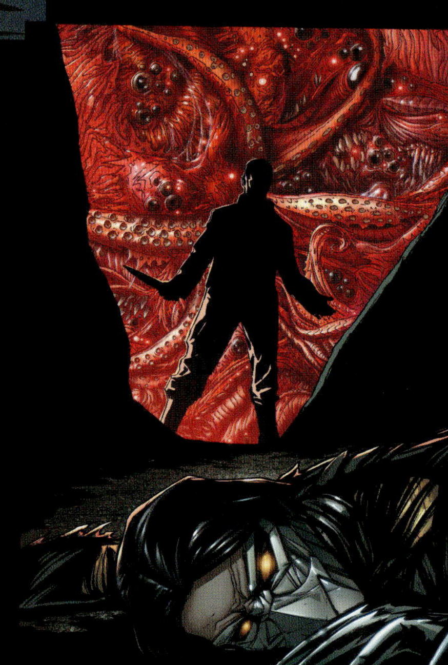

This page, counterclockwise from right.

The Darkness #96 cover B,
art by: Sheldon Mitchell, Rick Basaldua, and Brian Reber

The Darkness #97 cover,
art by: Jeremy Haun and Felix Serrano

The Darkness #98 cover,
art by: Jeremy Haun and Felix Serrano

The Darkness #99 cover A,
art by: Jeremy Haun and Felix Serrano

The Darkness #100 cover A,
art by: Jeremy Haun and Felix Serrano

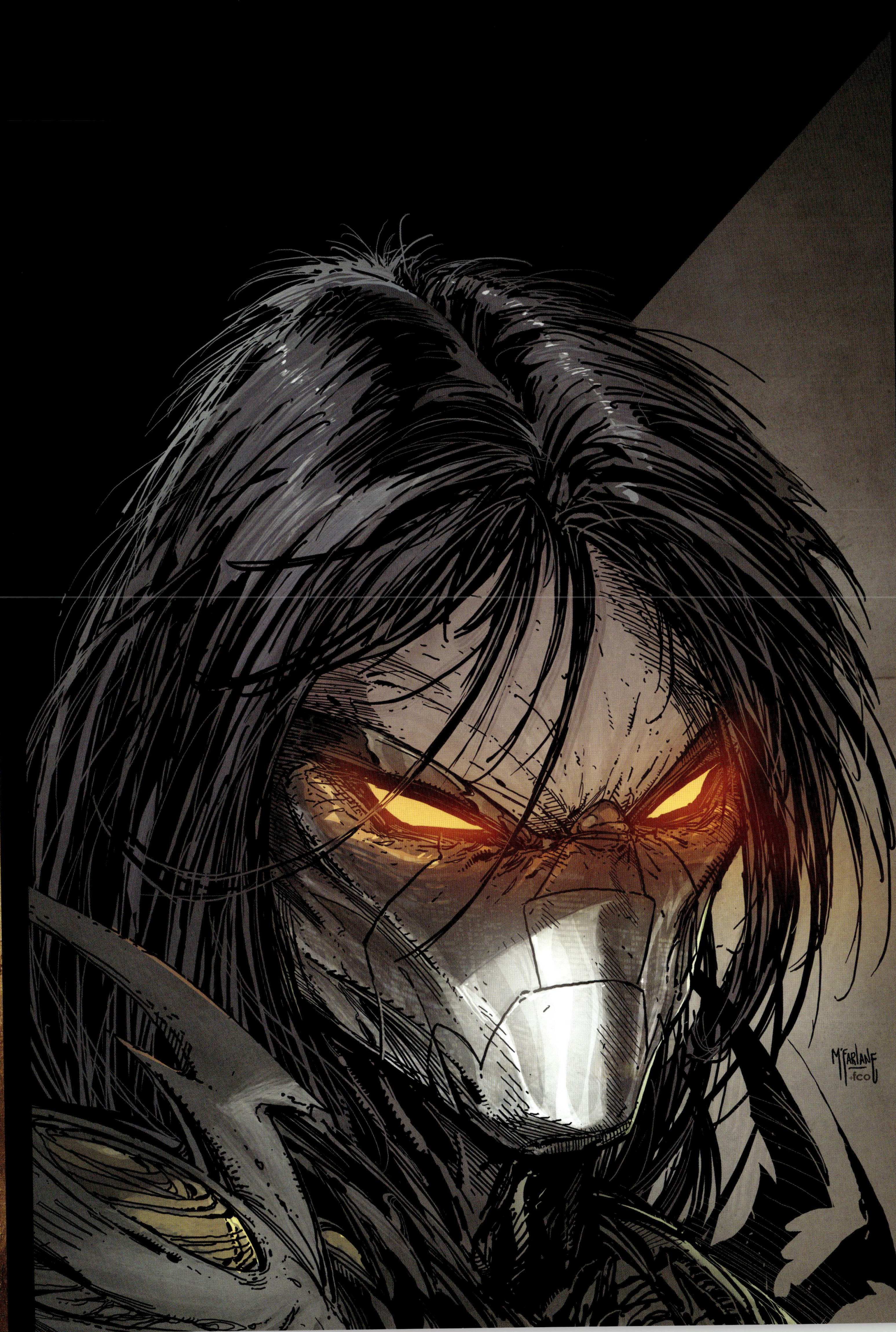

The Darkness #100 cover B,
art by: Todd McFarlane and FCO Plascencia

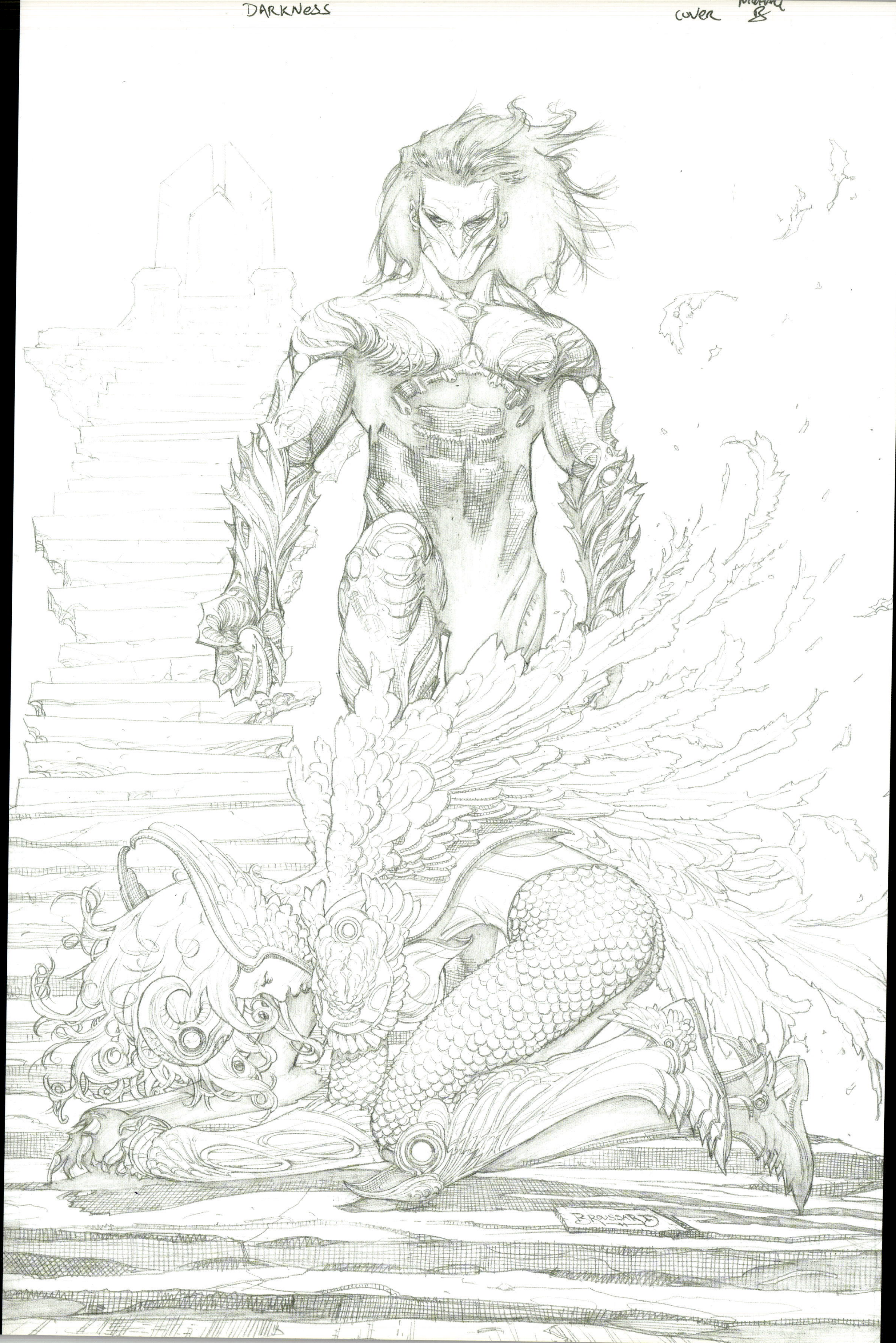

The Darkness #100 cover D,
line art by: Michael Broussard

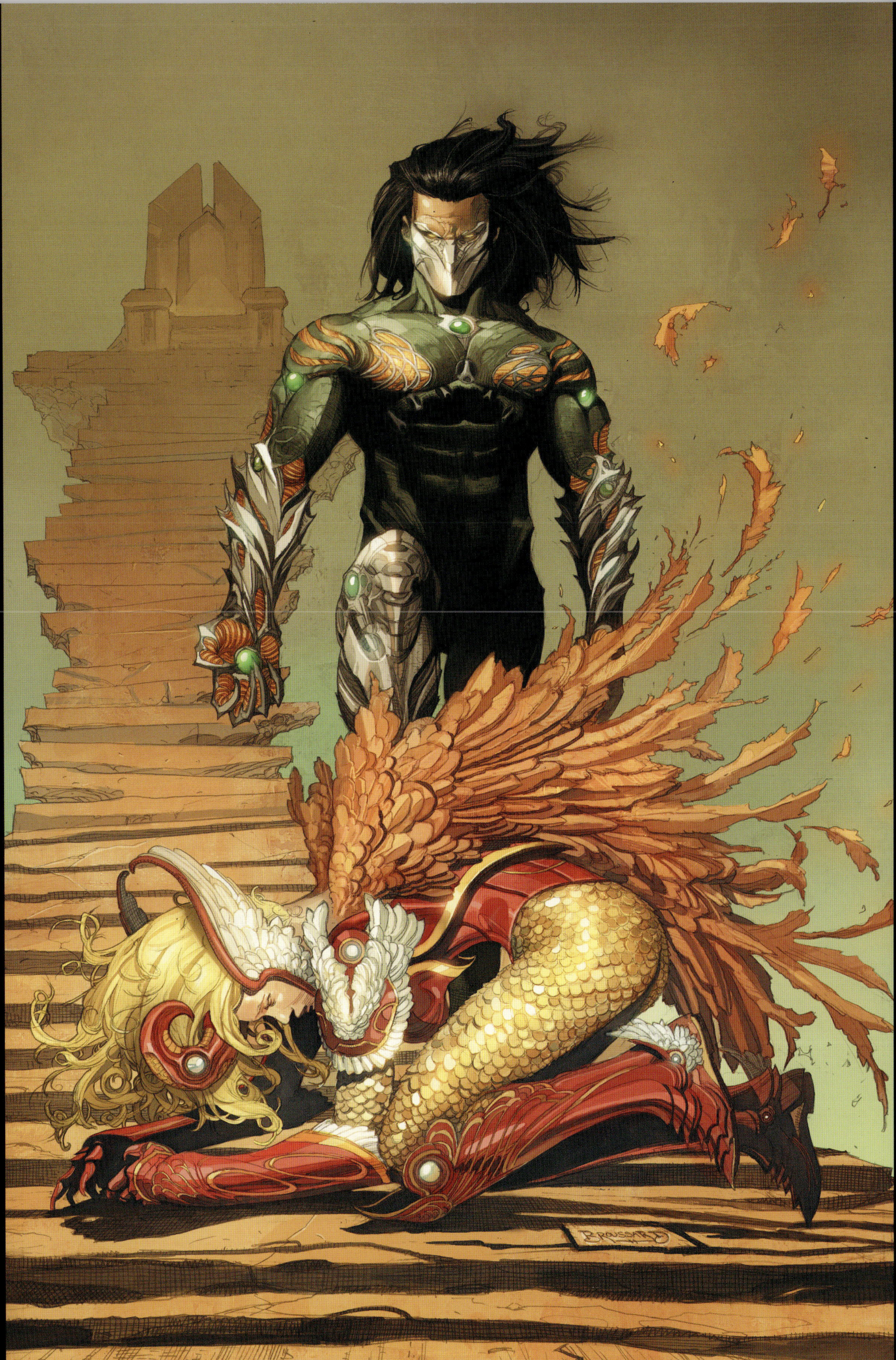

The Darkness #100 cover D,
art by: Michael Broussard and Sunny Gho

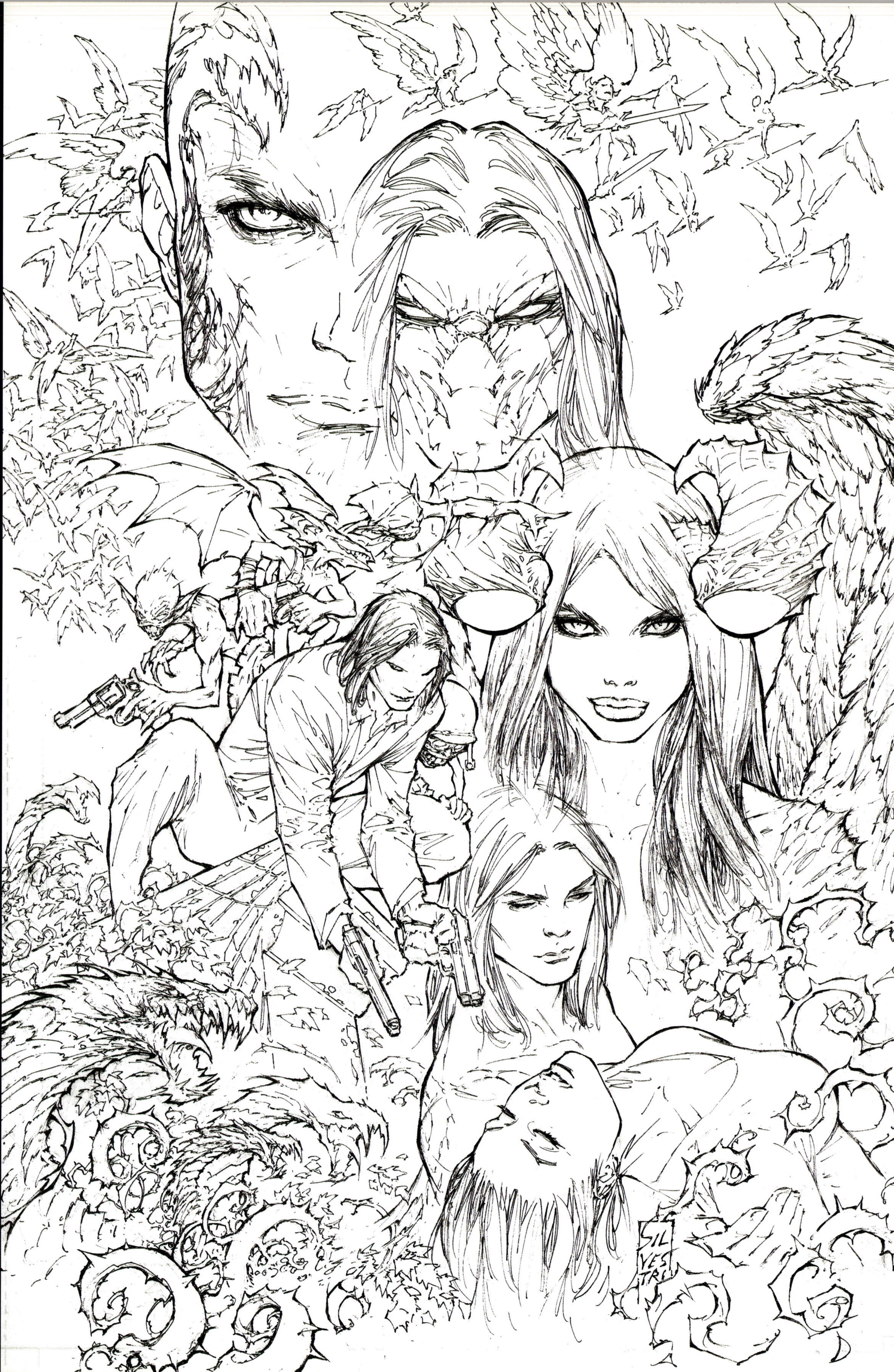

The Darkness #100 Emerald Knights variant cover F,
line art by: Marc Silvestri

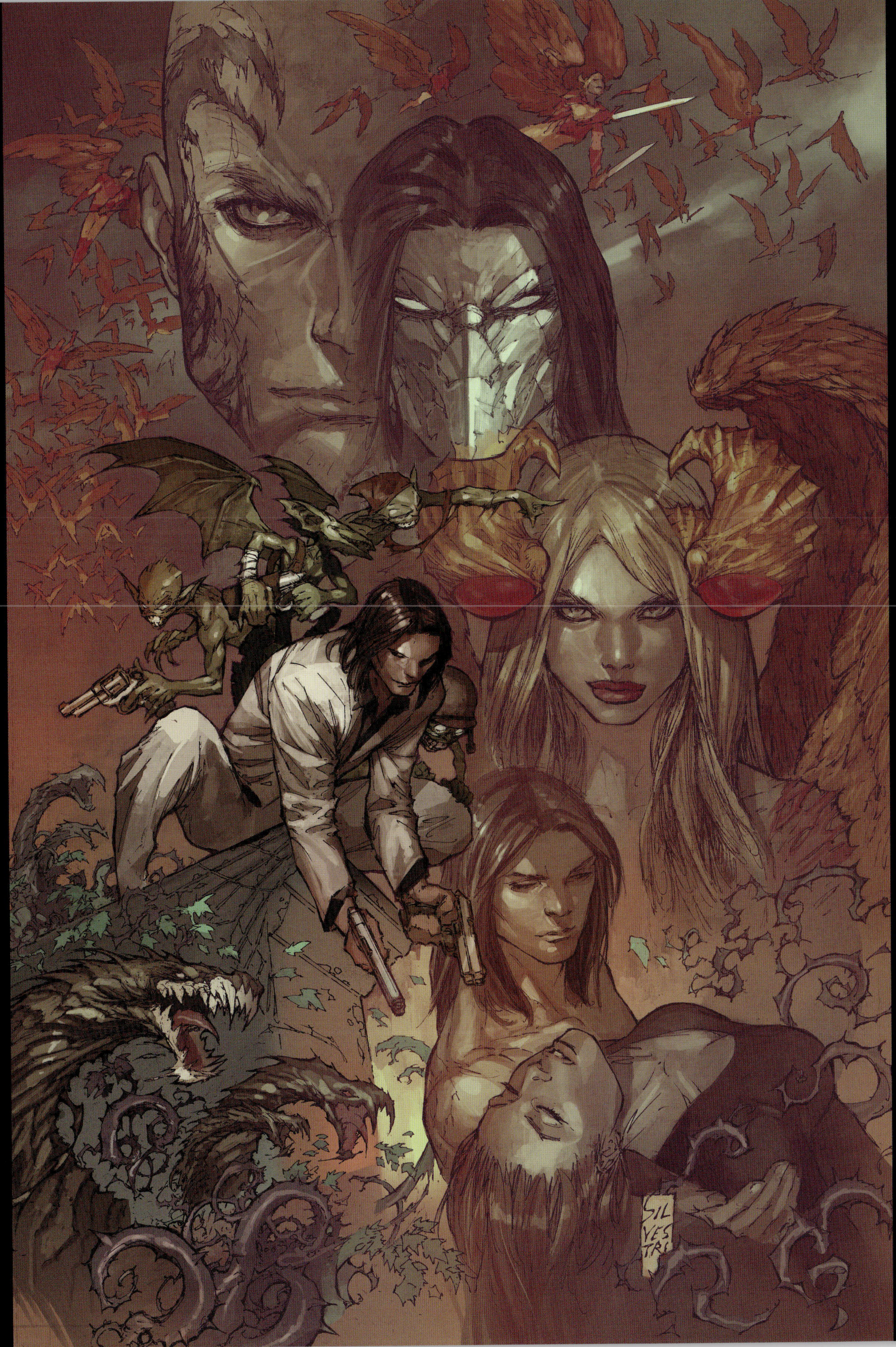

The Darkness #100 cover E,
art by: Marc Silvestri and Sunny Cho

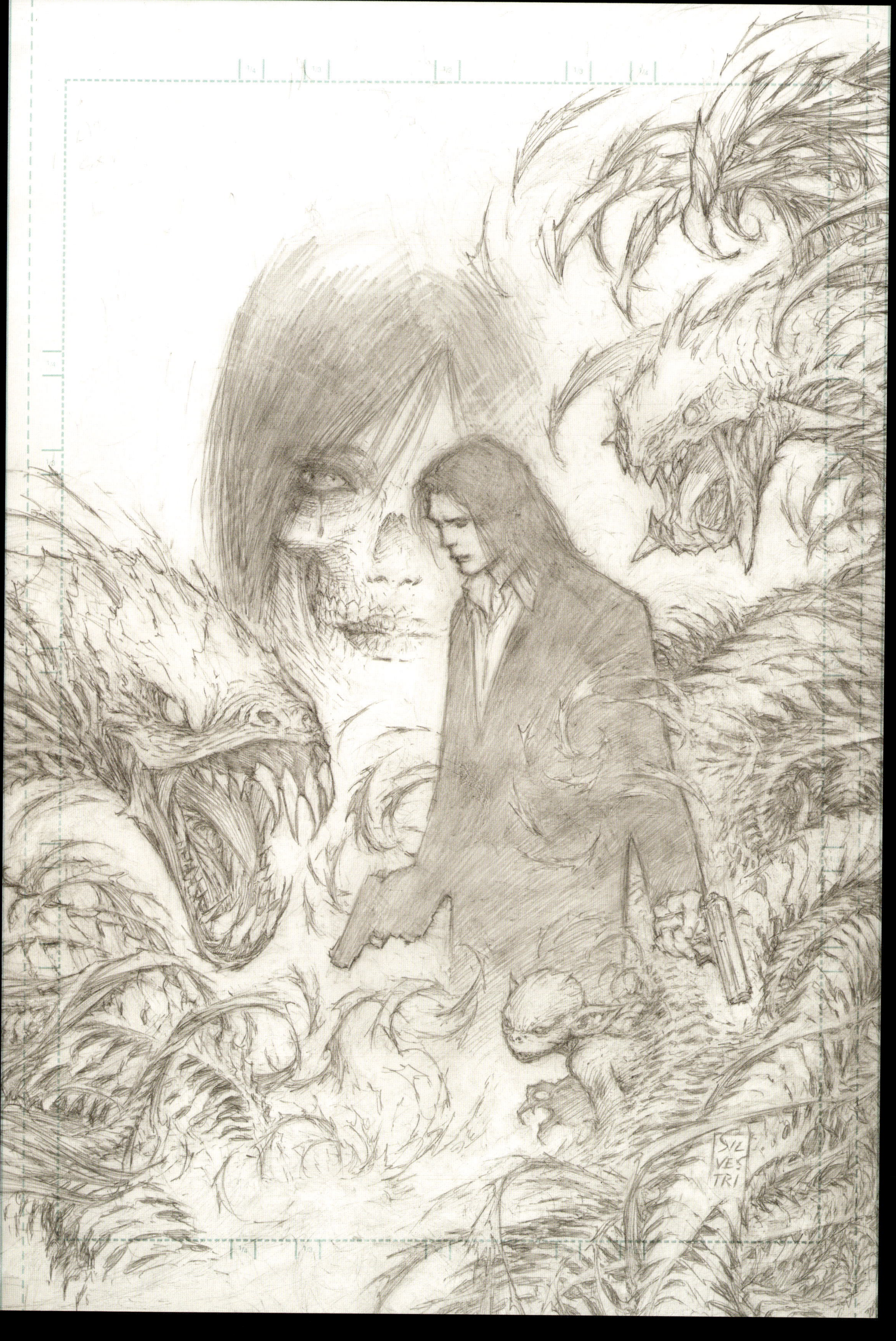

The Darkness #100 Image Expo Sketch variant.
line art by: Marc Silvestri

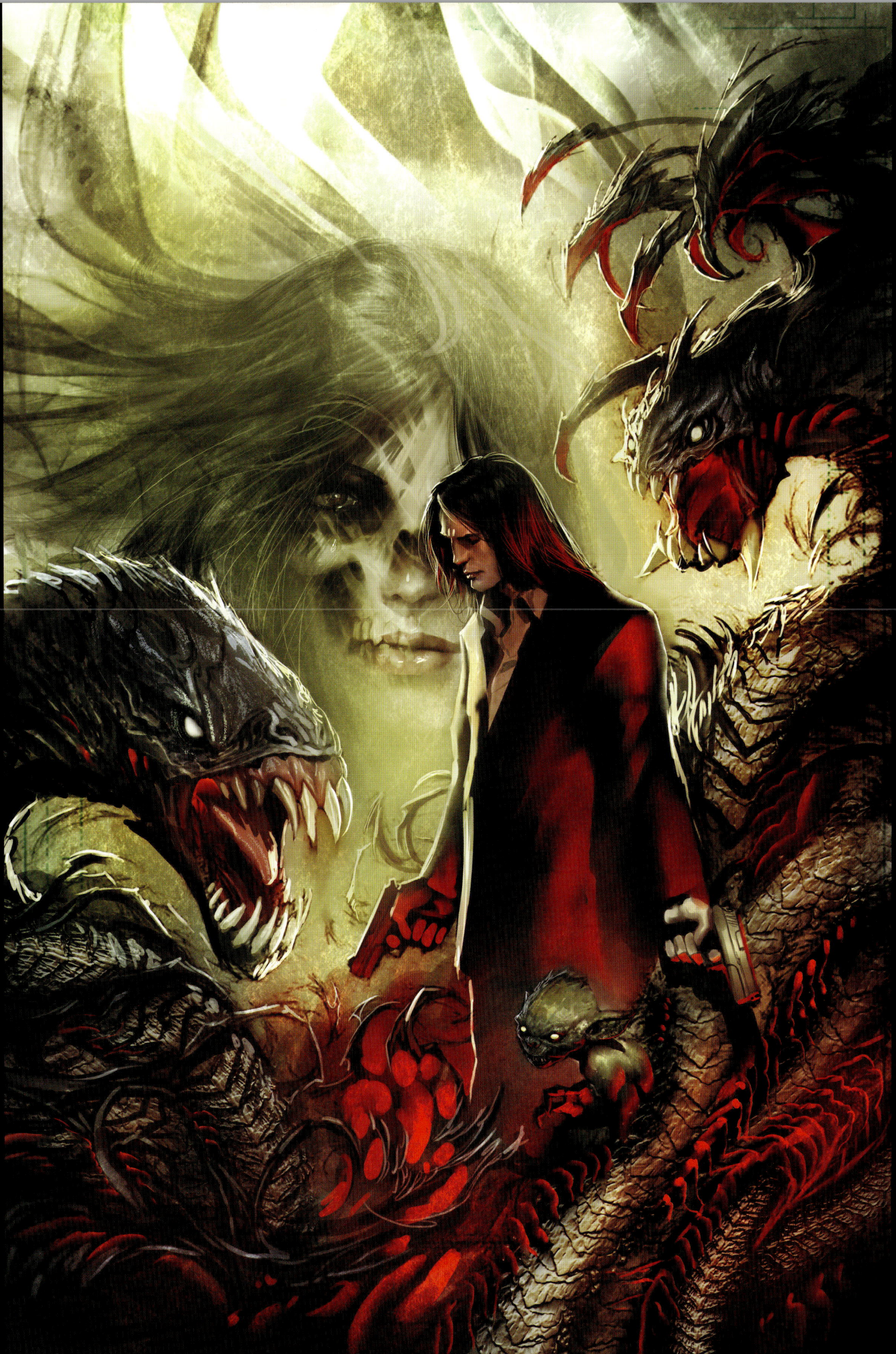

The Darkness #101 cover B,
art by: Marc Silvestri and Stjepan Sejic

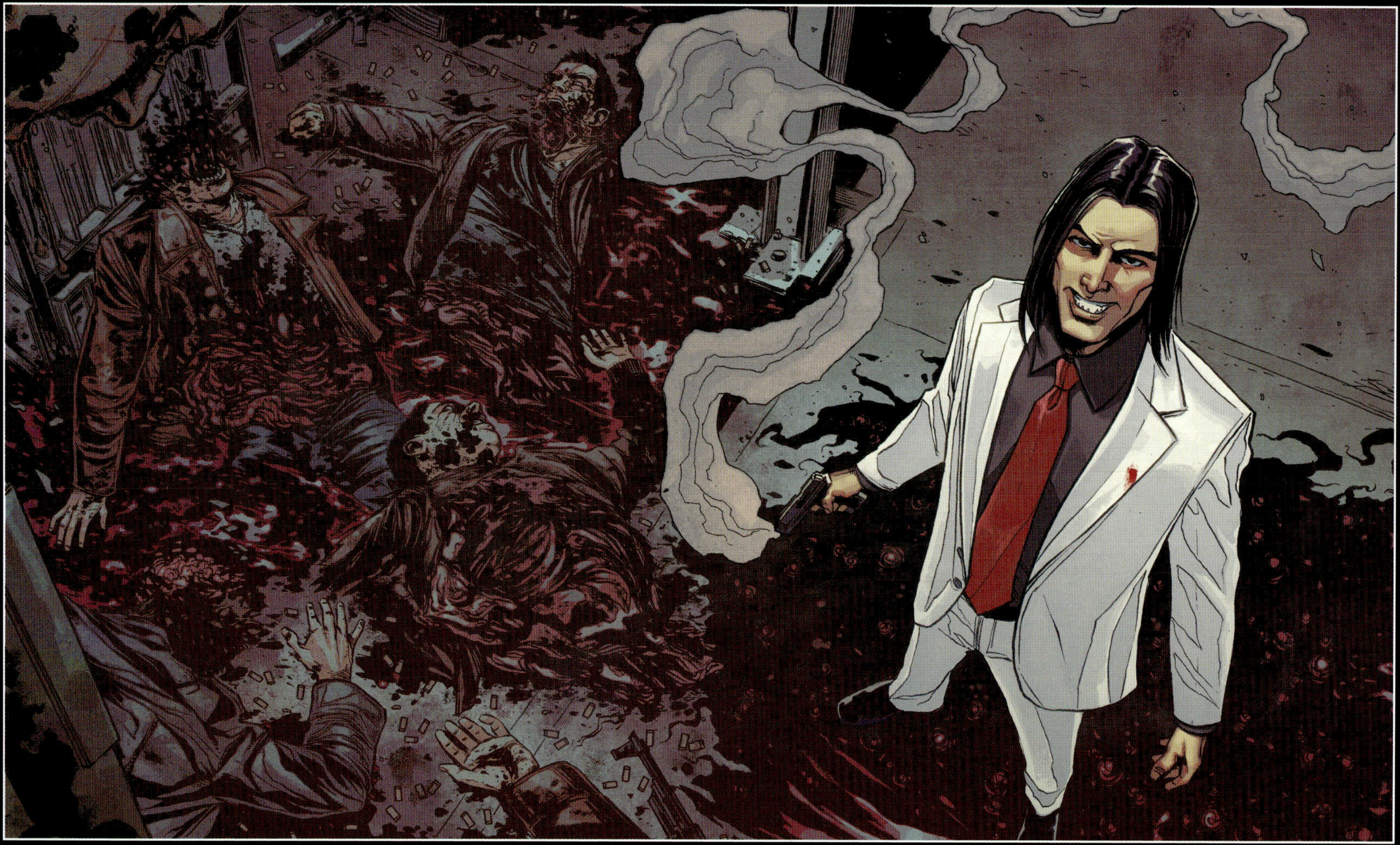

Above. *The Darkness* #102 cover A, art by: Jeremy Haun and John Rauch • Below. *The Darkness* #103 cover A, art by: Jeremy Haun and John Rauch

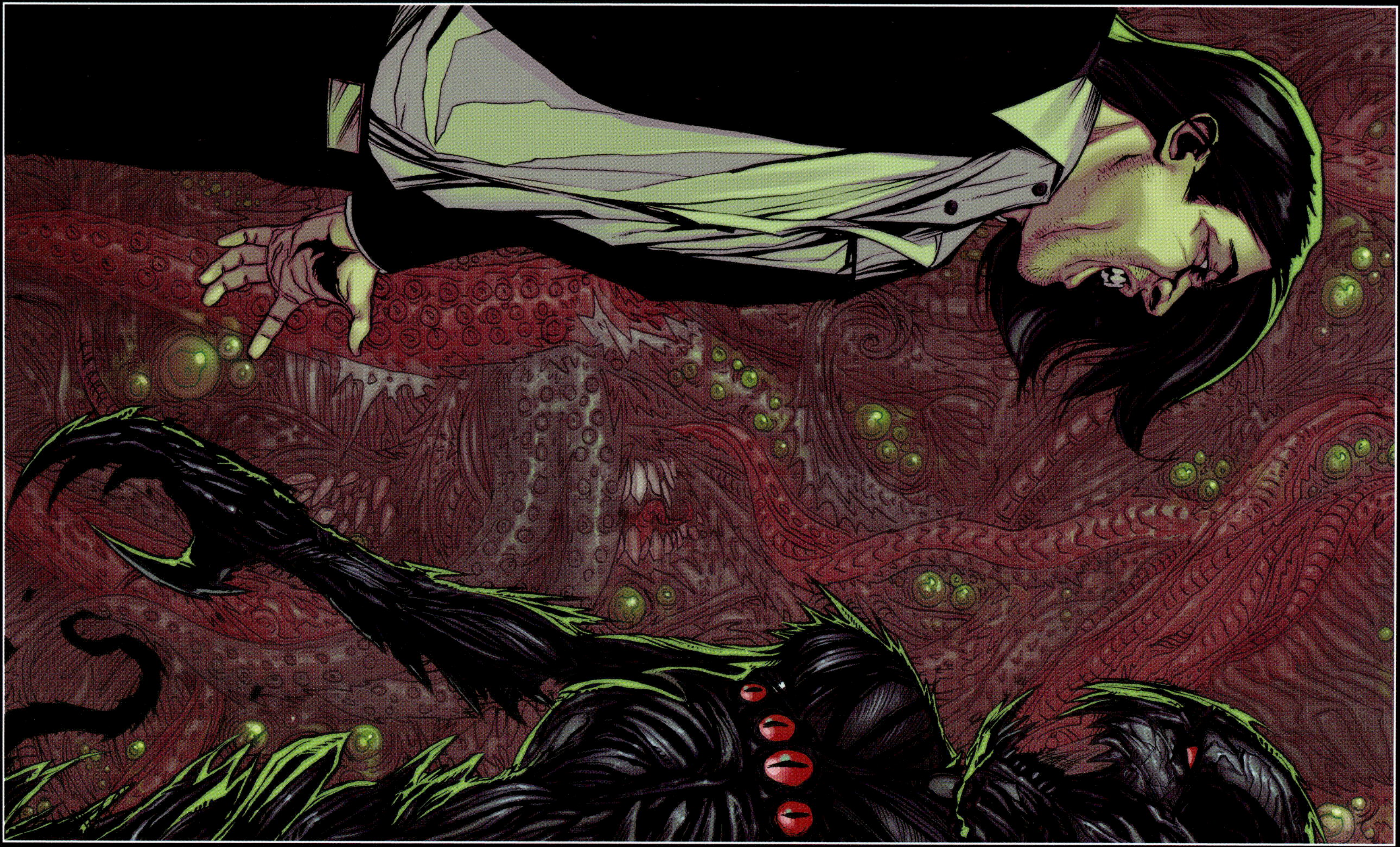

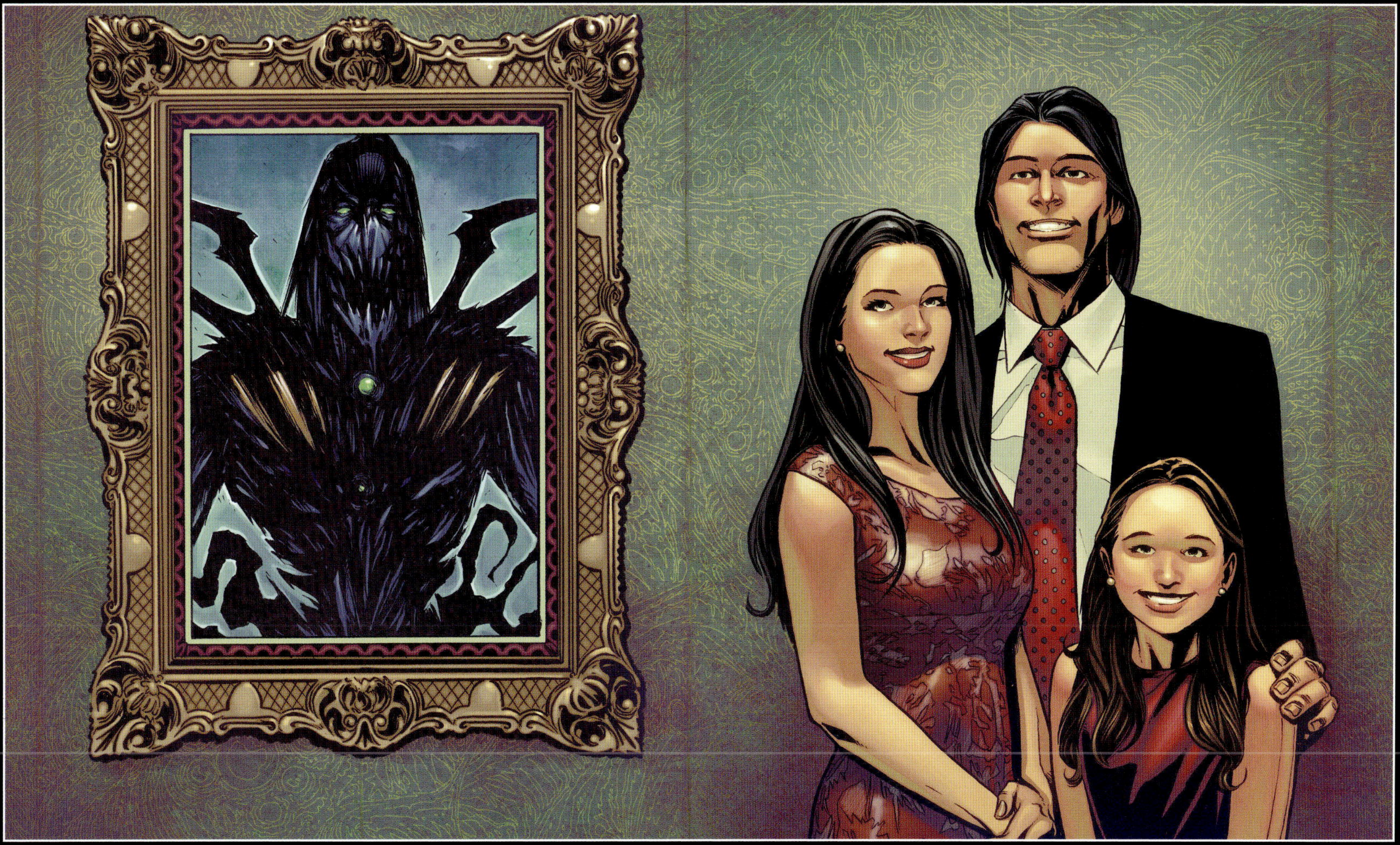

Above. *The Darkness* #104 cover A, art by: Jeremy Haun and John Rauch • Below. *The Darkness* #105 cover A, art by: Jeremy Haun and John Rauch

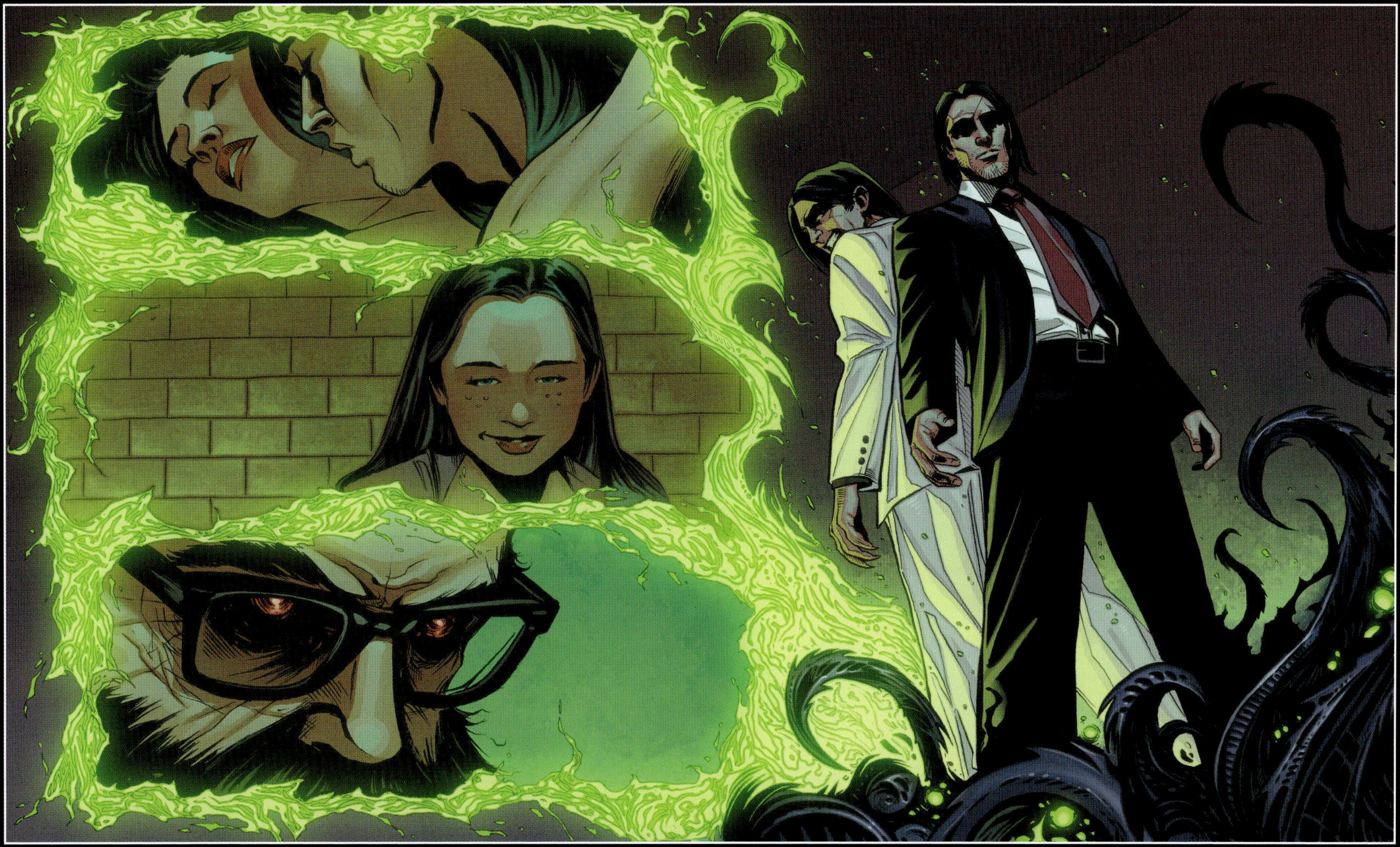

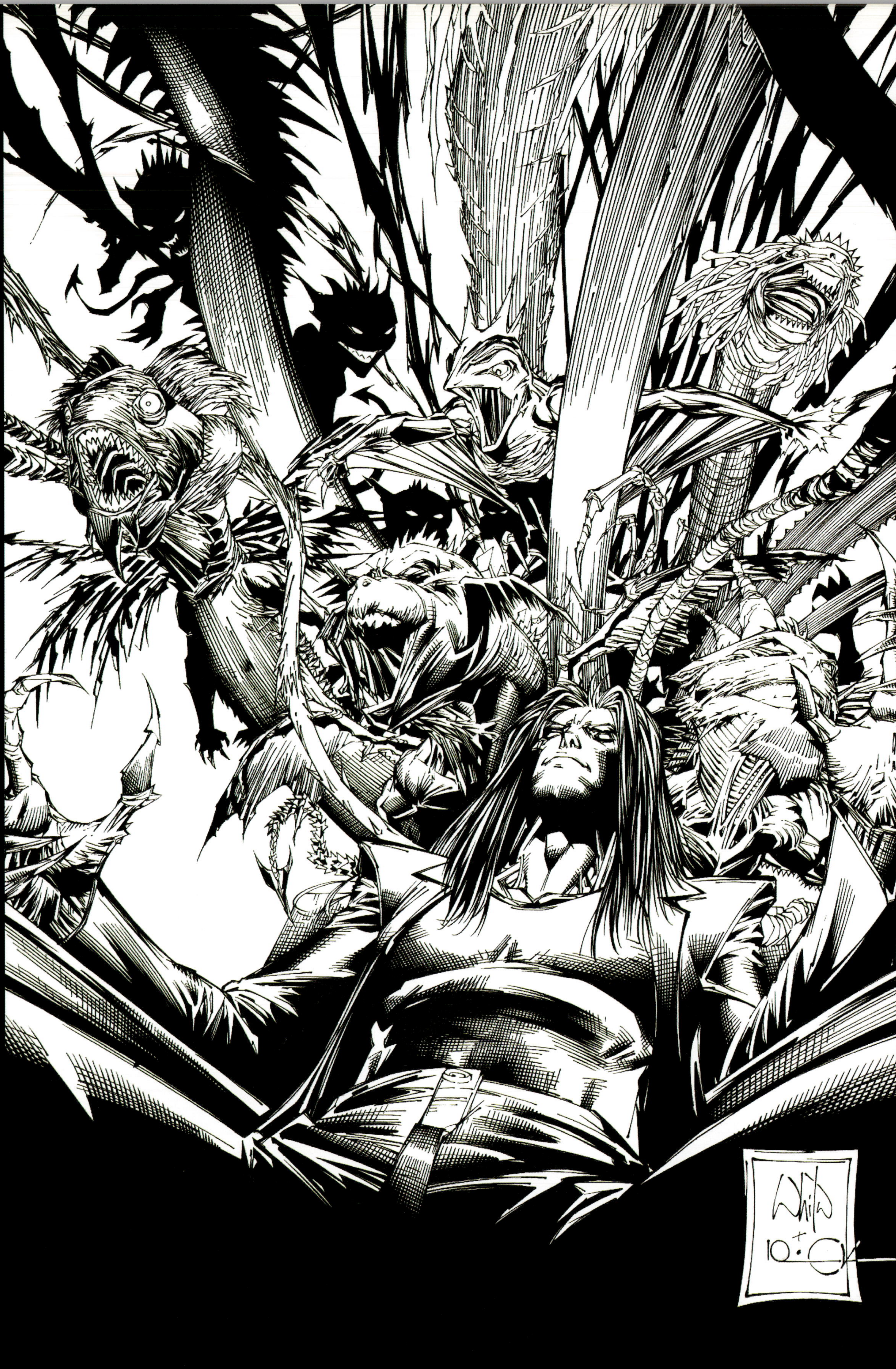

The Darkness #105 cover B,
line art by: Whilce Portacio and Rick Basaldua

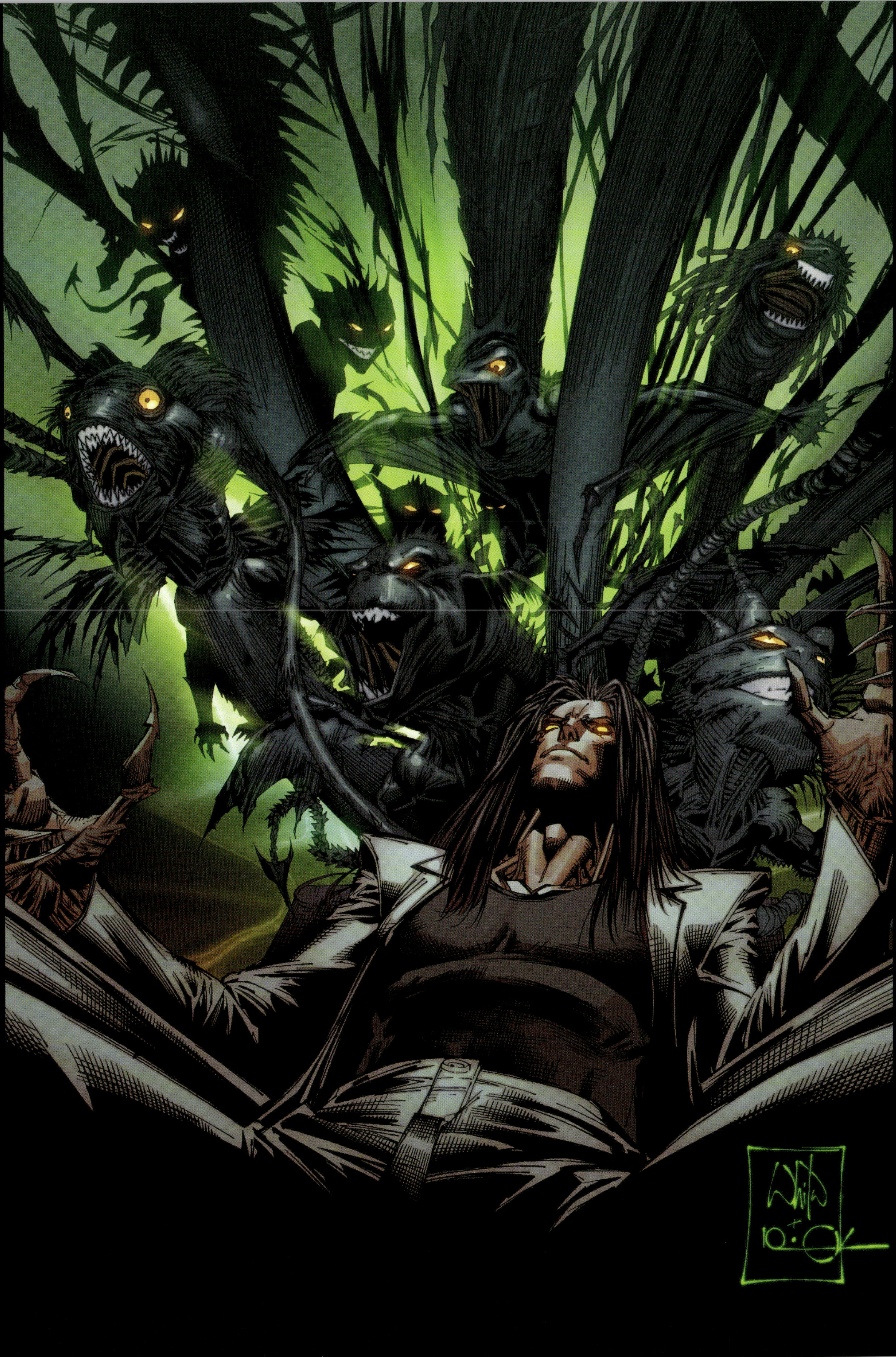

The Darkness #105 cover B,
art by: Whilce Portacio, Rick Basaldua, and John Rauch

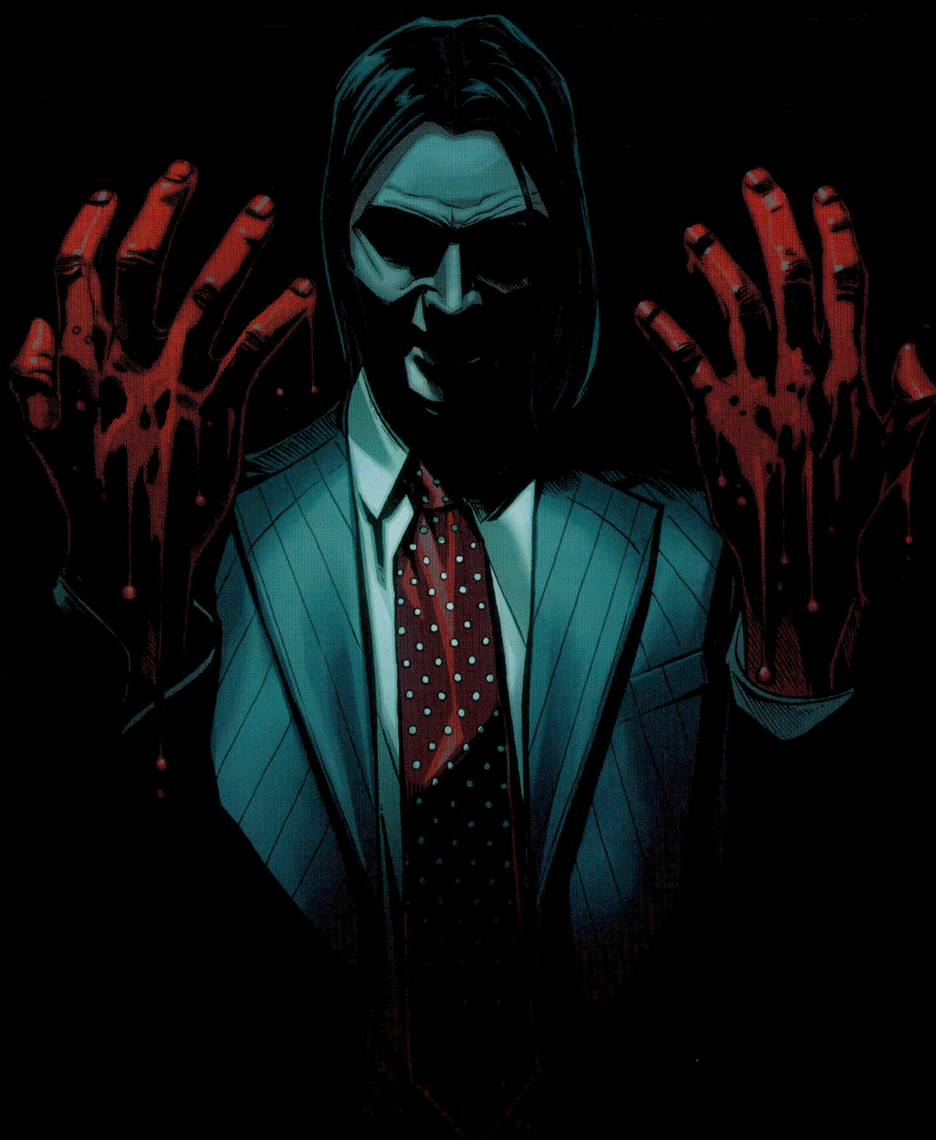

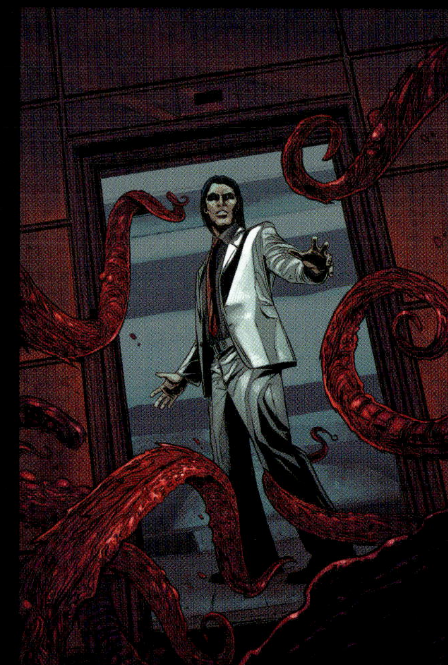

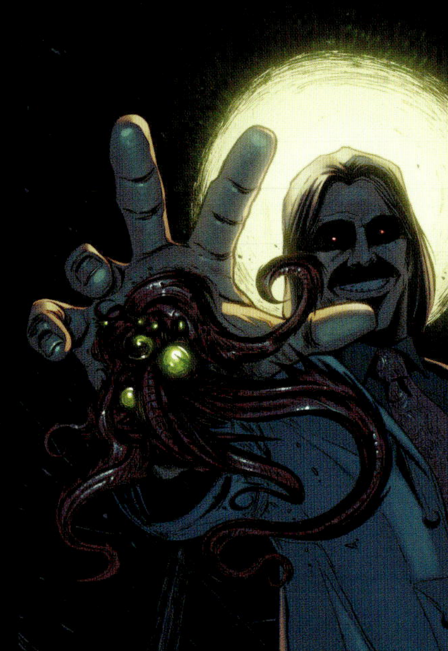

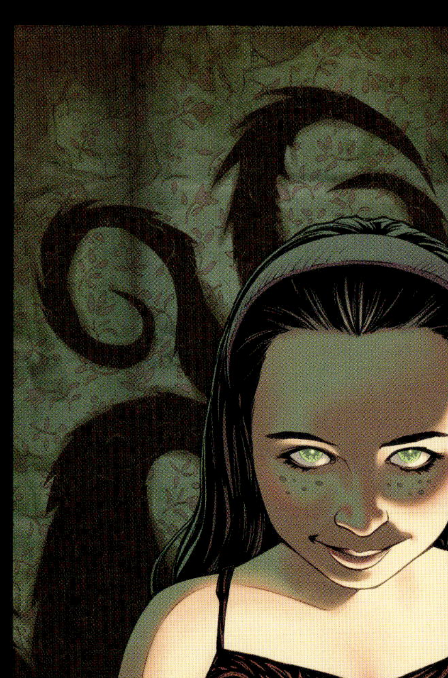

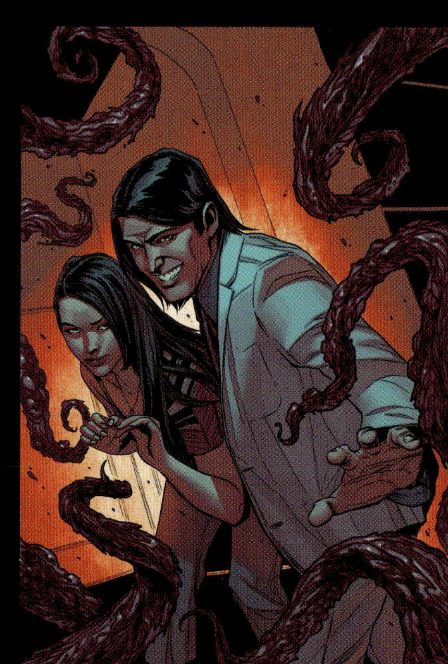

This page, clockwise from above.

The Darkness #106 cover A,
art by: Jeremy Haun and John Rauch

The Darkness #107 cover A,
art by: Jeremy Haun and John Rauch

The Darkness #108 cover A,
art by: Jeremy Haun and John Rauch

The Darkness #109 cover A,
art by: Jeremy Haun and John Rauch

The Darkness #110 cover A,
art by: Jeremy Haun and John Rauch

At right. *The Darkness* #112 cover A,
art by: Stjepan Sejic

Counterclockwise from below.
The Darkness #112 cover B, and 113-116 cover A's,
art by: Jeremy Haun and John Rauch

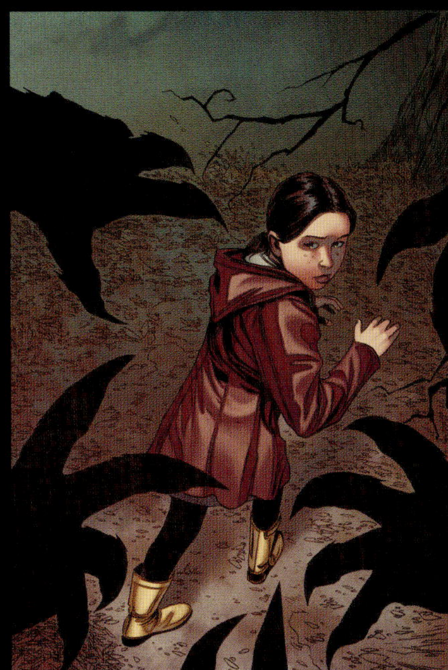

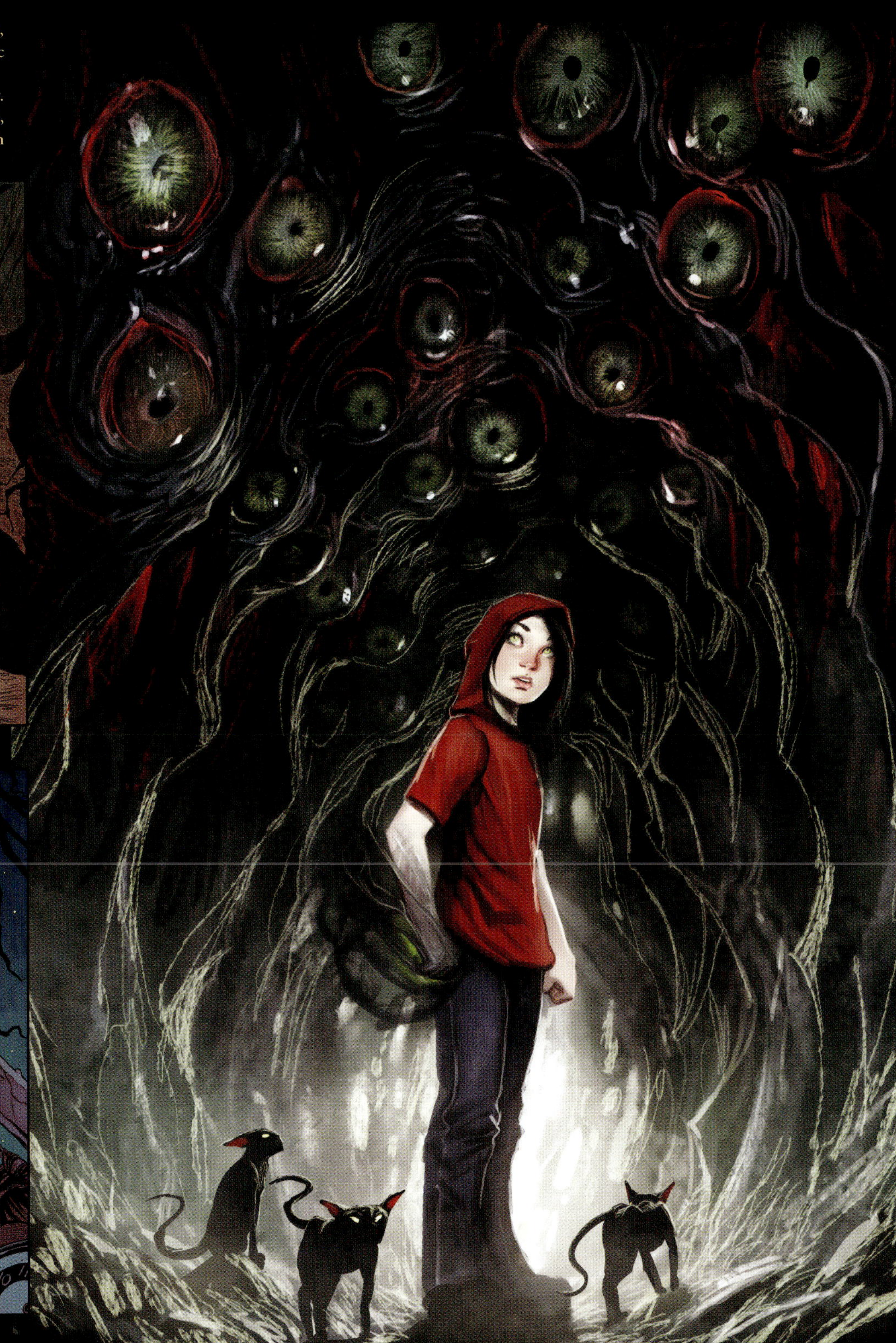

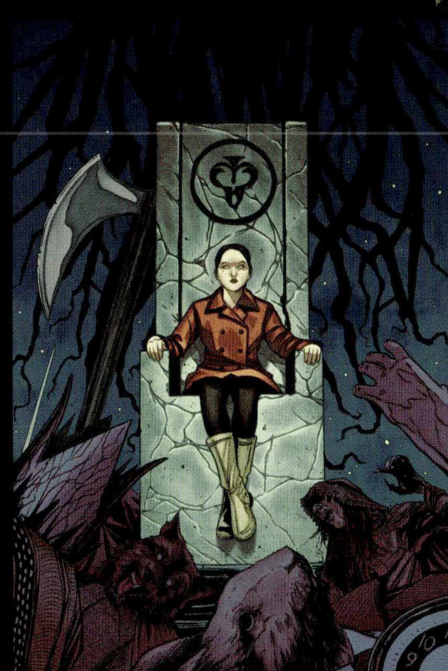

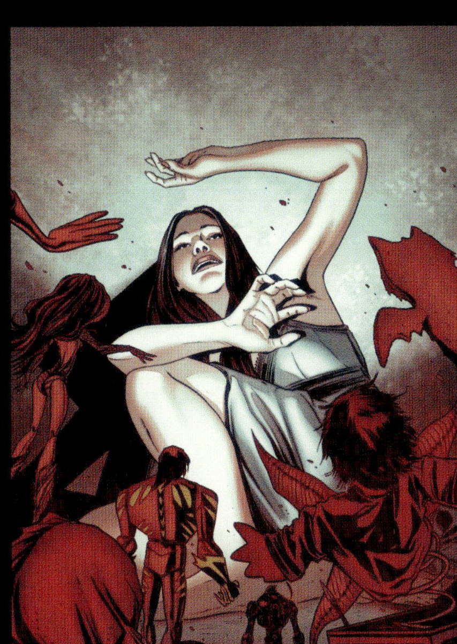

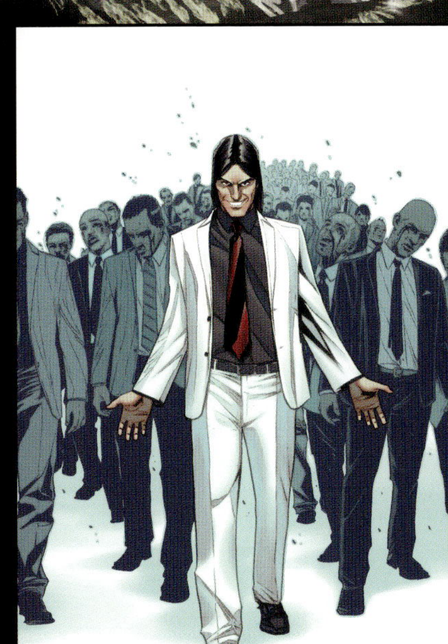

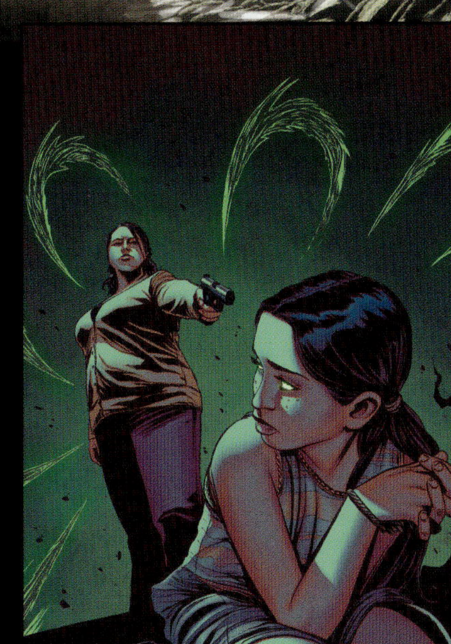

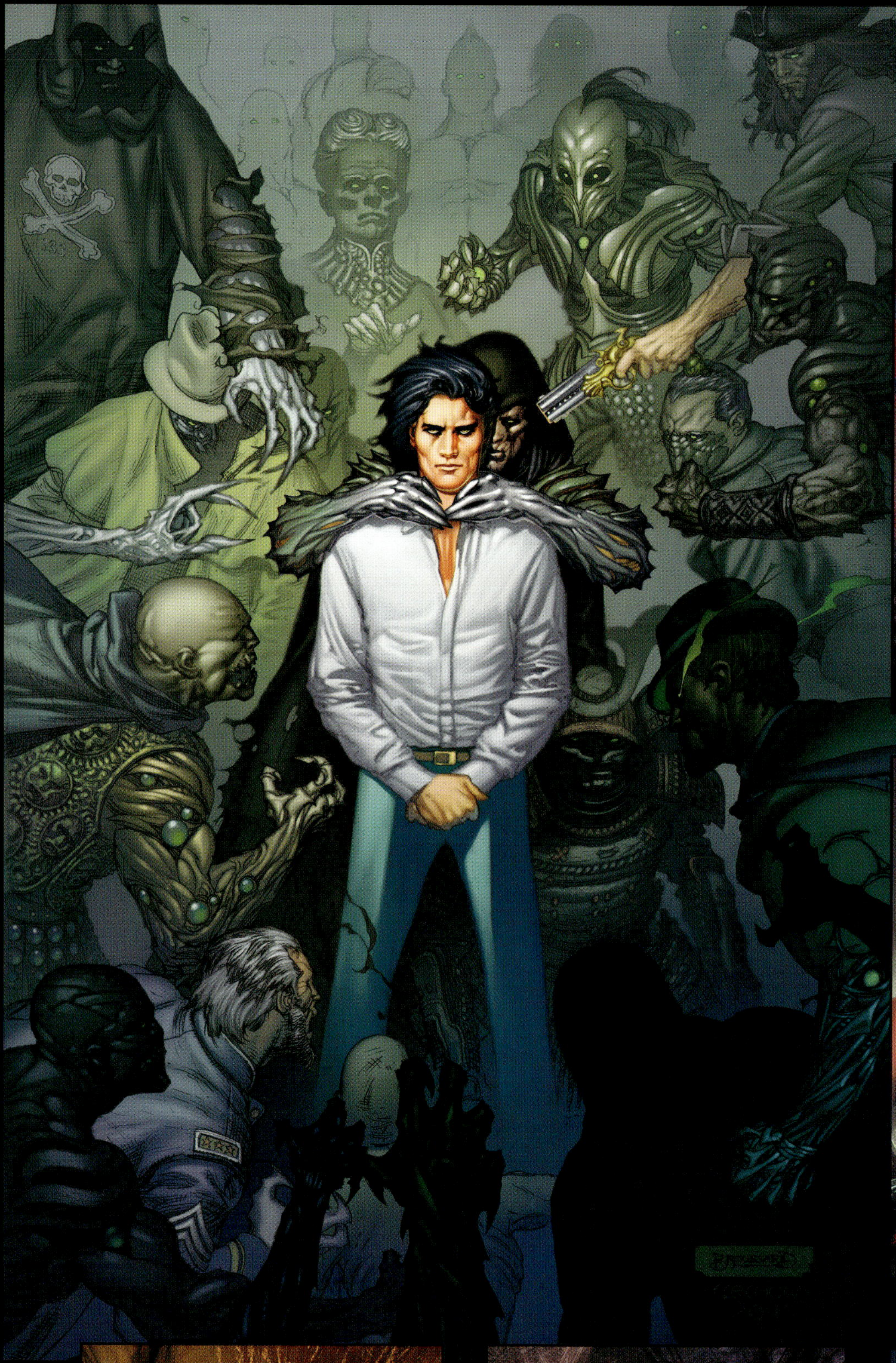

At left. *"Accursed"* volume 6 cover,
and bottom row from left. *"Accursed"* volume 1-3 covers, colors by: Steve Firchow

Clockwise from below and ending at the bottom.
The Darkness: Accursed volume 5-1 covers

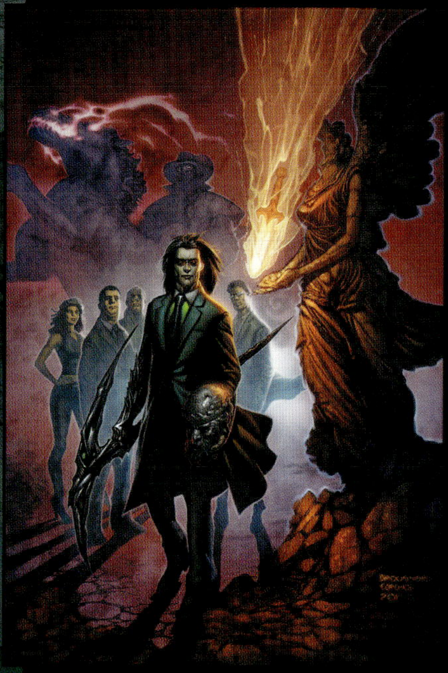

Above. Colors by: Steve Firchow

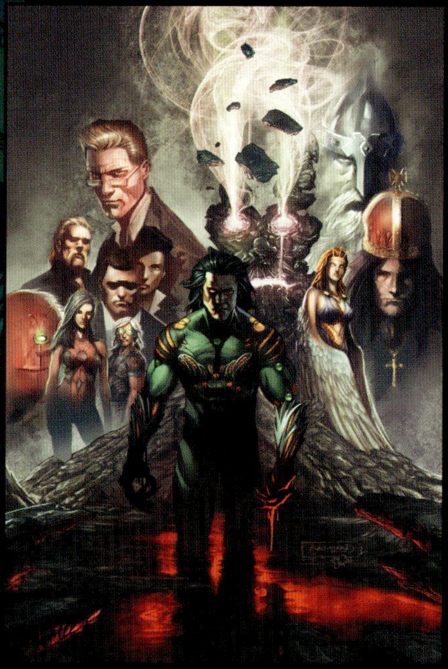

Above. Colors by: Sunny Gho and Eko Puteh

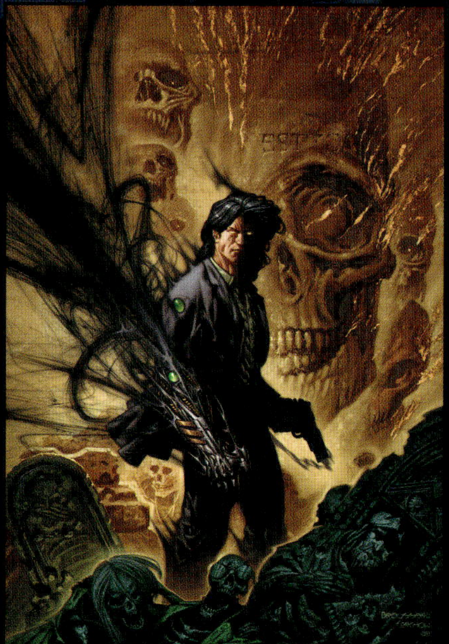

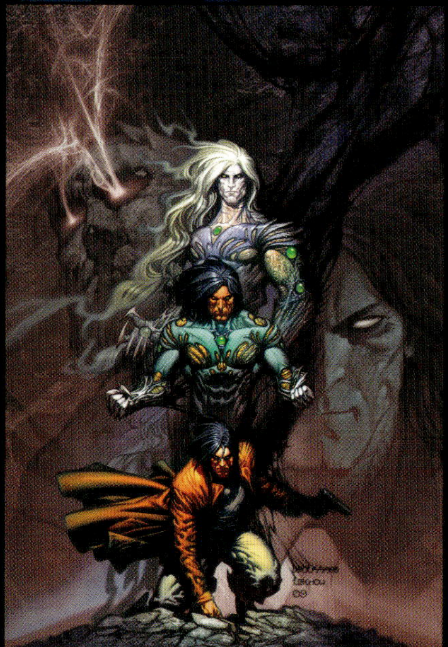

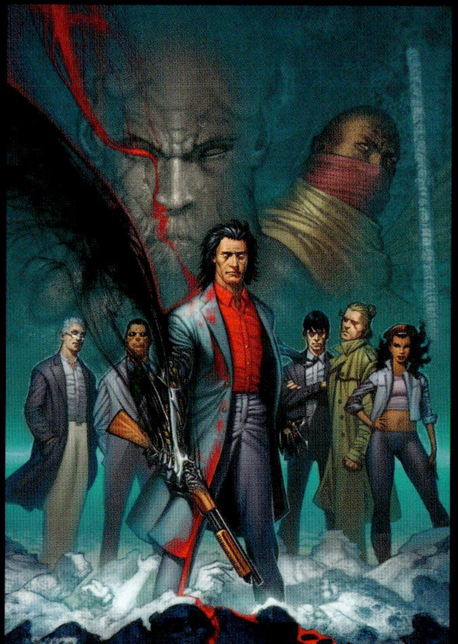

The Darkness: Accursed trade paperback volume 1-6 covers,
lin art by: Michael Broussard

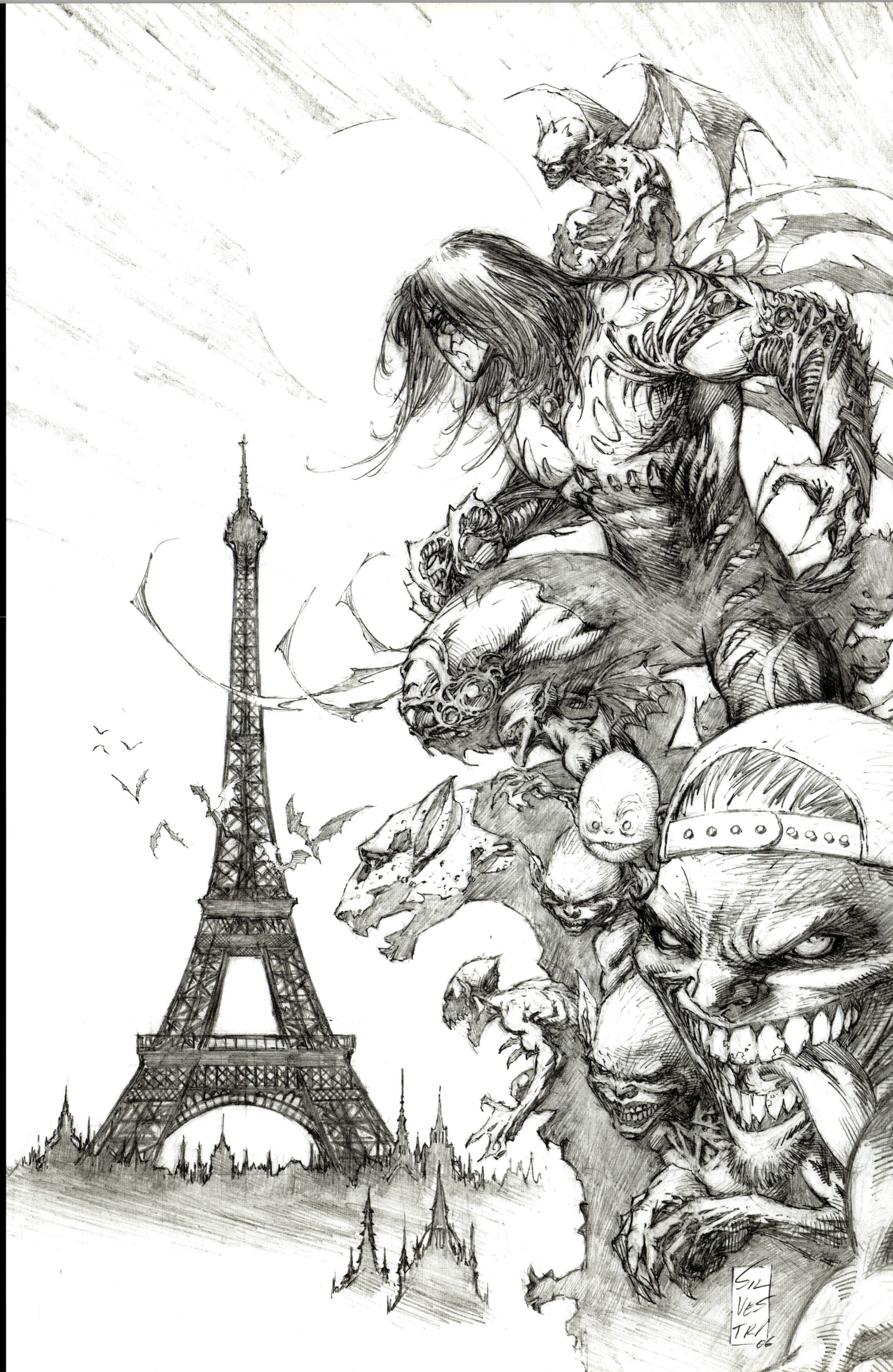

The Darkness #114 cover B,
line art by: Marc Silvestri

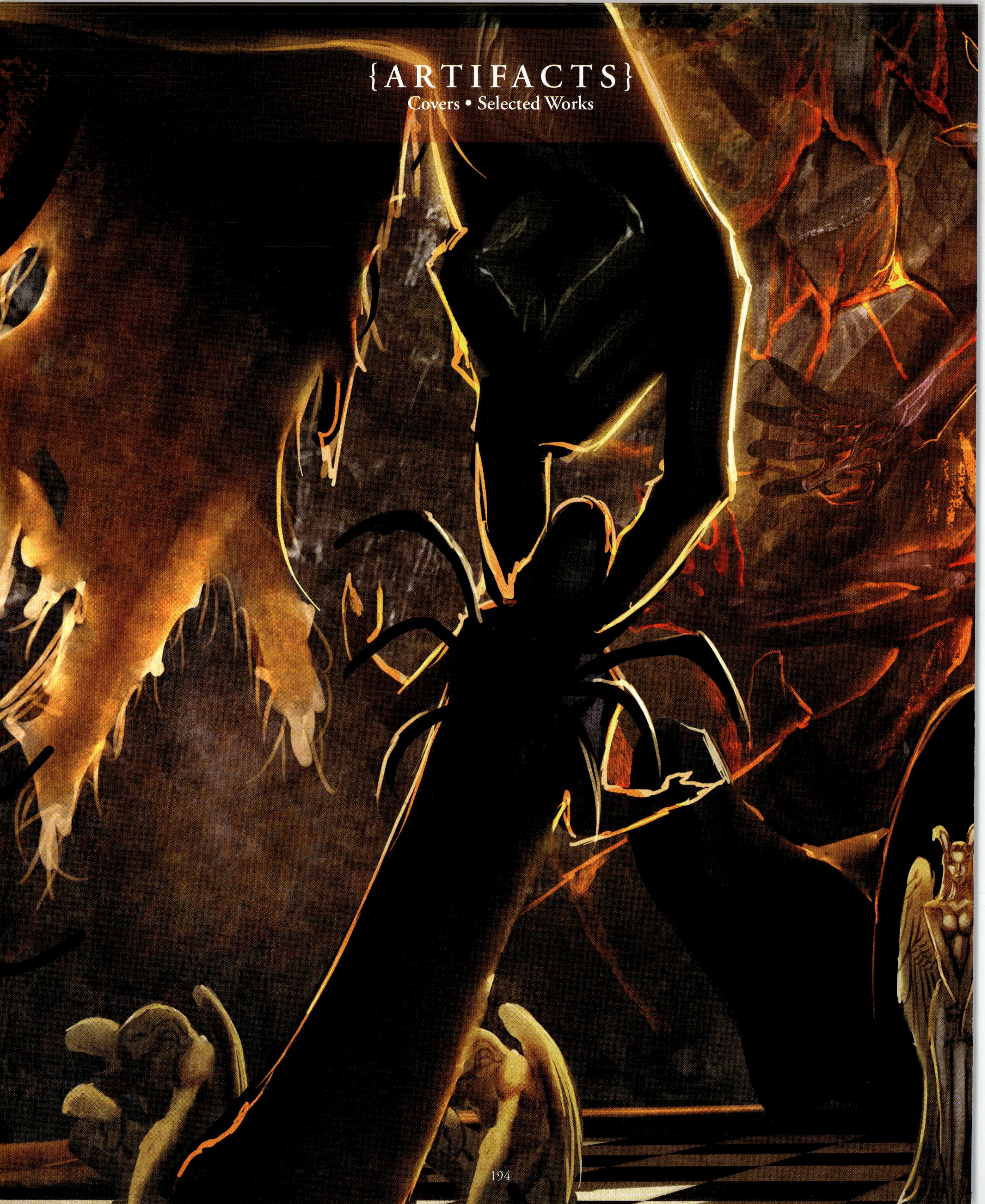

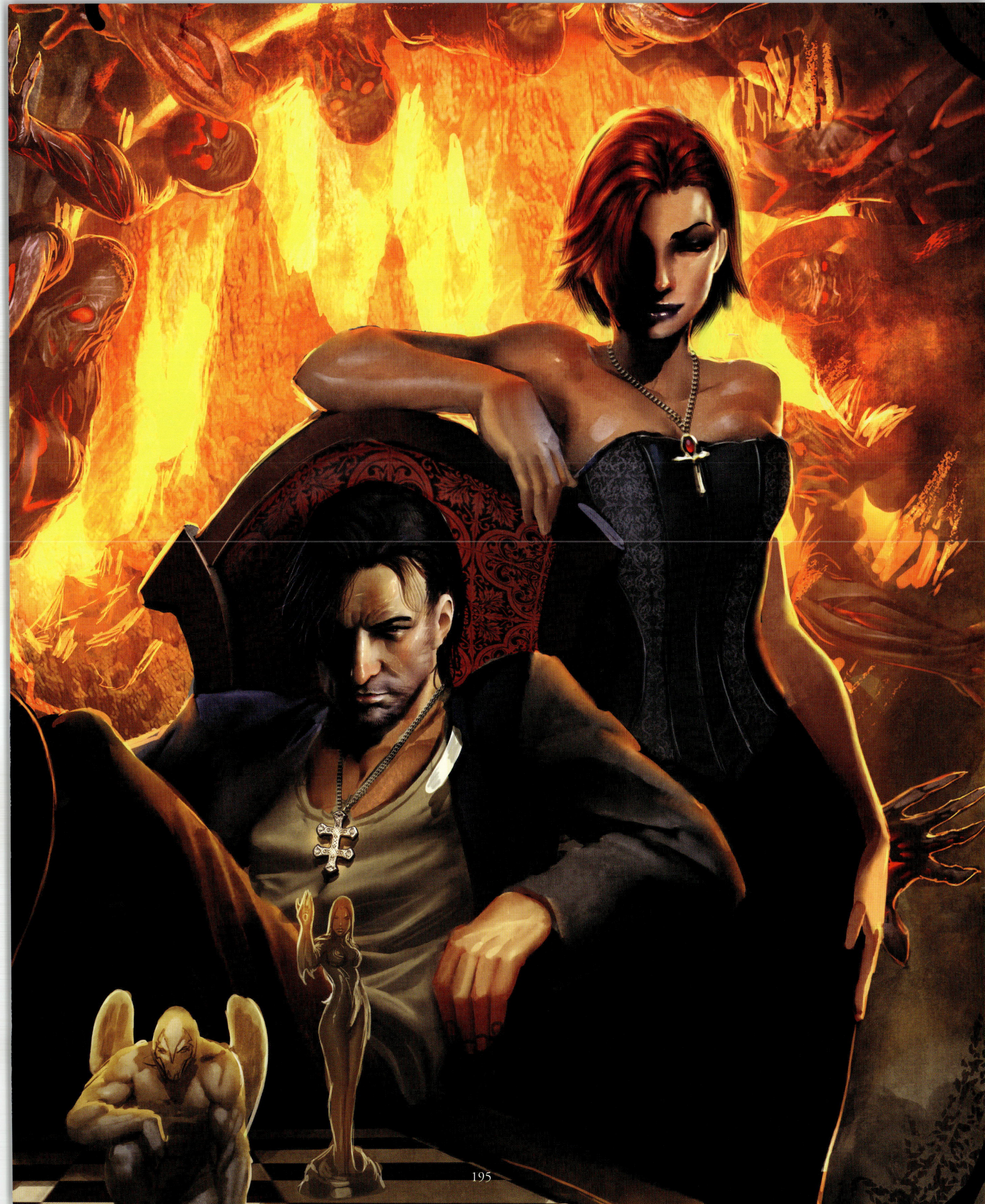

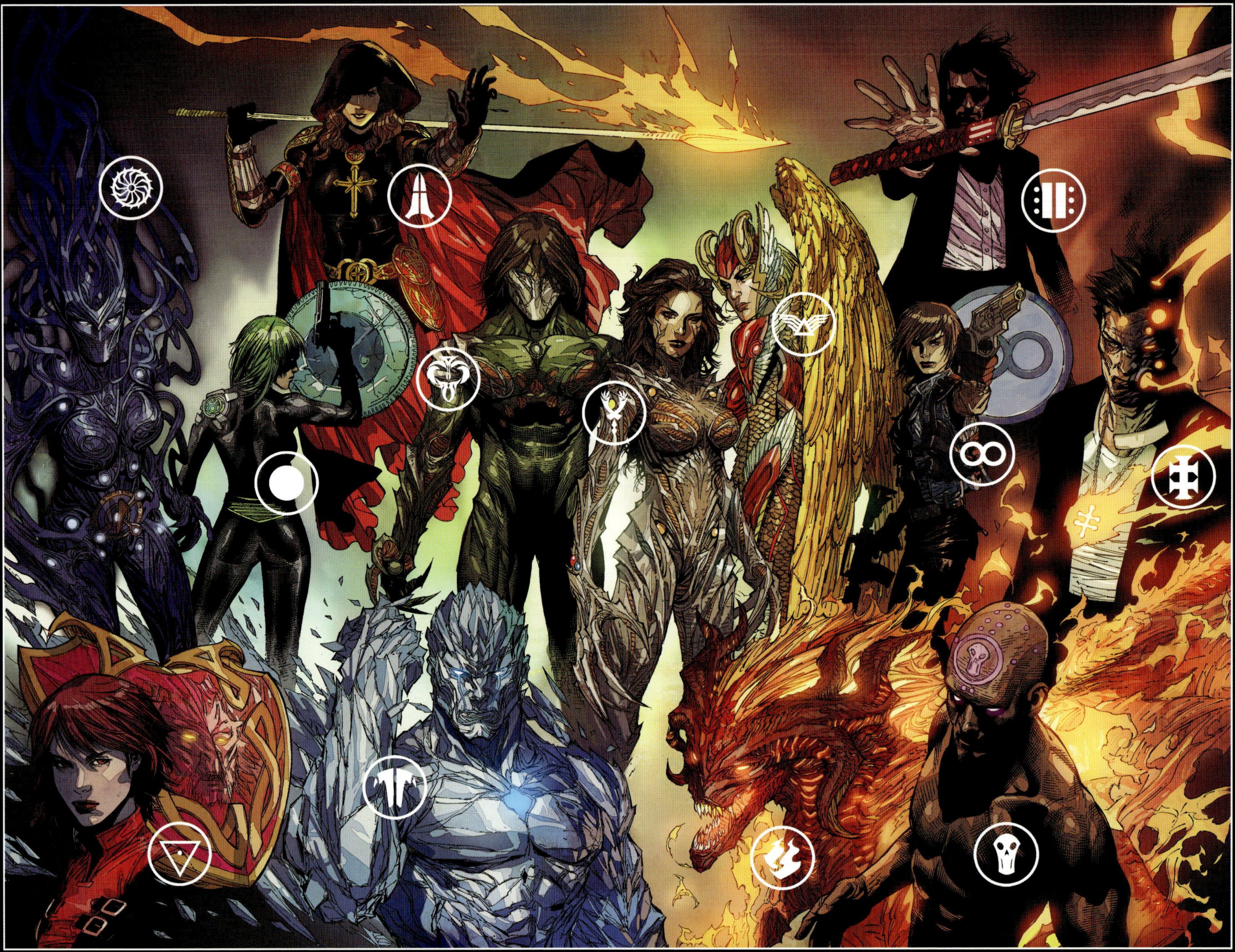

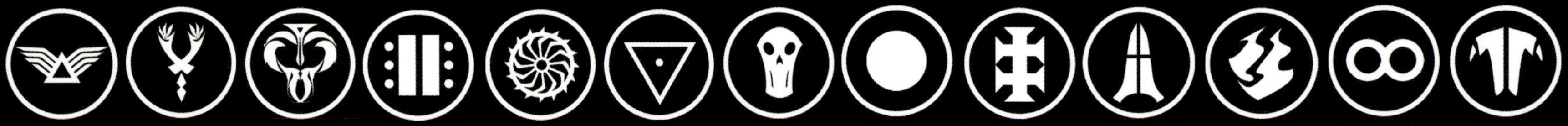

Artifacts was first published from December 2010 to November 2014 and ran for 41 issues, including the #0 Free Comic Book Day issue, and had spin-offs and crossovers into other Top Cow titles. *Artifacts* was a perpetual universe-spanning event series bringing together both the supernatural and science fiction sides of the Top Cow Universe.

Above. *Artifacts* #1 pages 14-15, art by: Michael Broussard, Rick Basaldua, and Sunny Gho, with supplemental overlay of Artifact icons.

Previous page. *Artifacts* #14 cover A, art by: Stjepan Sejic

Facing page. *Artifacts* #0 Free Comic Day cover, art by: Stjepan Sejic

If this is your first time hearing about *Artifacts*, in a nutshell: Thirteen mystical Artifacts, including the Witchblade, the Darkness, and others, guide the fate of the Top Cow Universe. For centuries, it's been whispered that bringing together all 13 Artifacts would herald mankind's destruction. But a mysterious figure has been manipulating events, laying plans to put Armageddon into motion. The final phase begins here, with the abduction of Hope, the daughter of Sara Pezzini and Jackie Estacado. What ensues will remake the entirety of the Top Cow Universe, from the Witchblade and the Darkness to the Angelus, Magdalena, Tom Judge, Aphrodite IX, the members of Cyberforce and more.

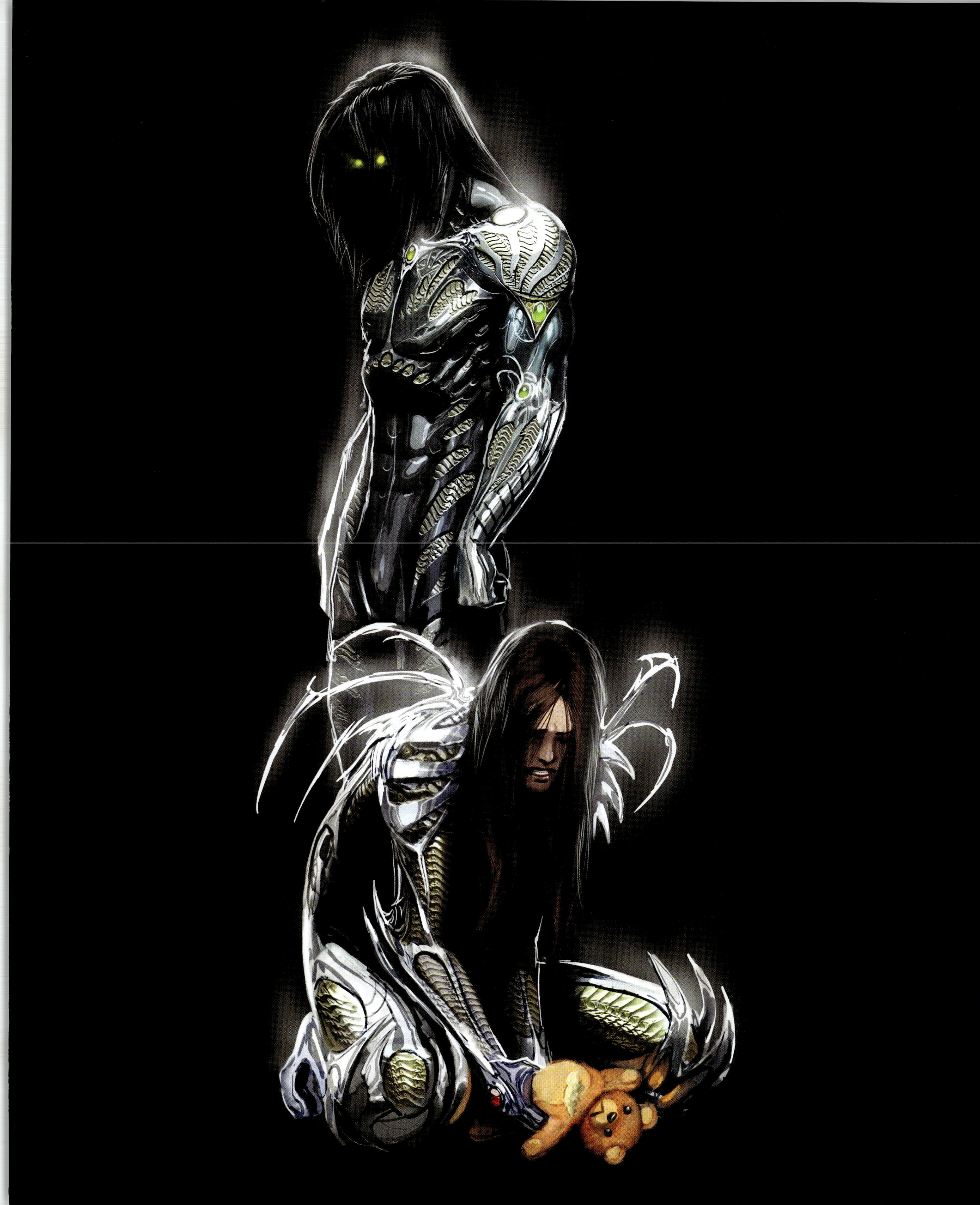

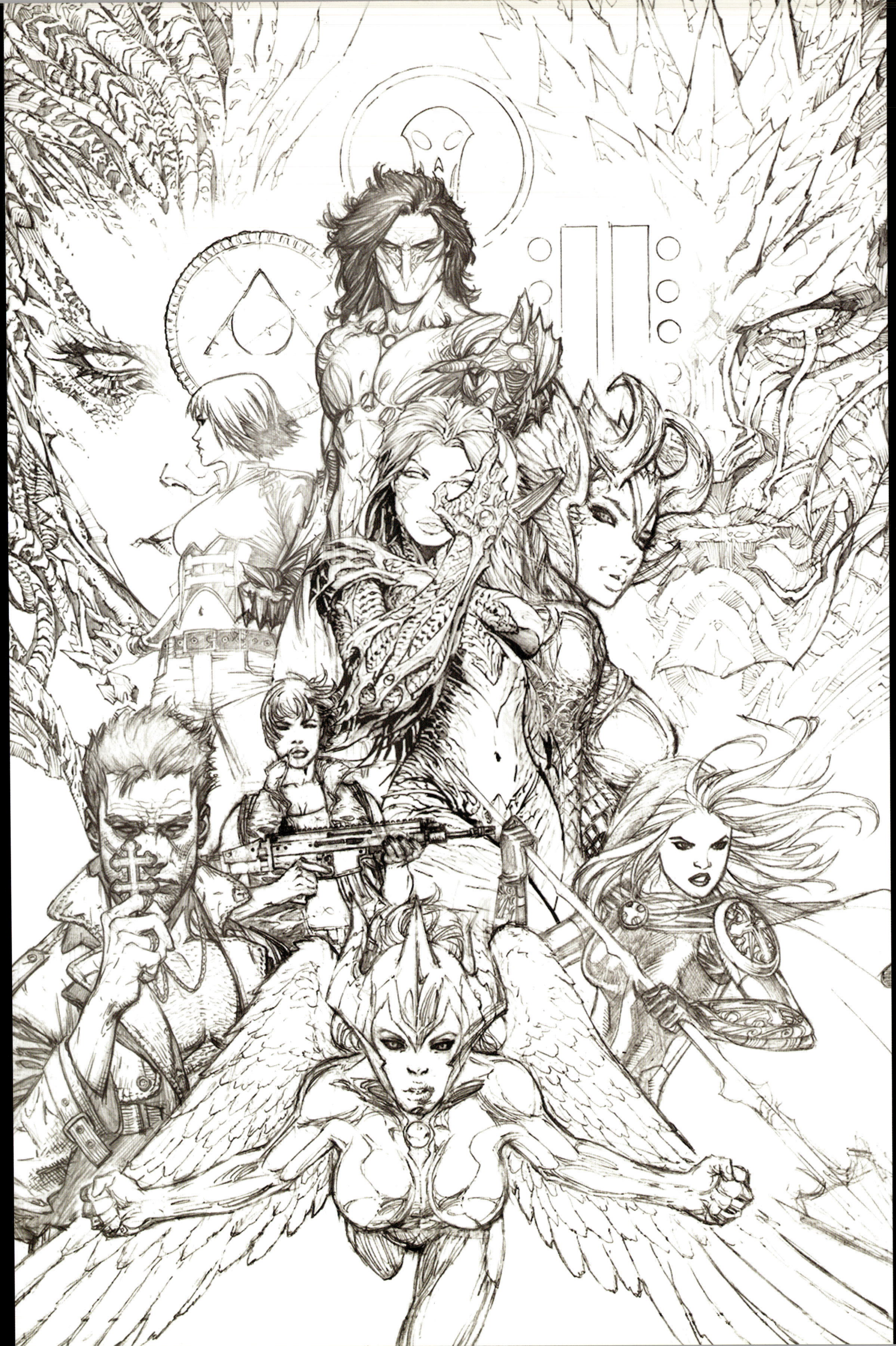

Artifacts #1 "Jan" cover D, line art by: Michael Broussard, Marc Silvestri, Stjepan Sejic, Kenneth Rocafort, Nelson Blake II, Sheldon Mitchell and, Rick Basaldua

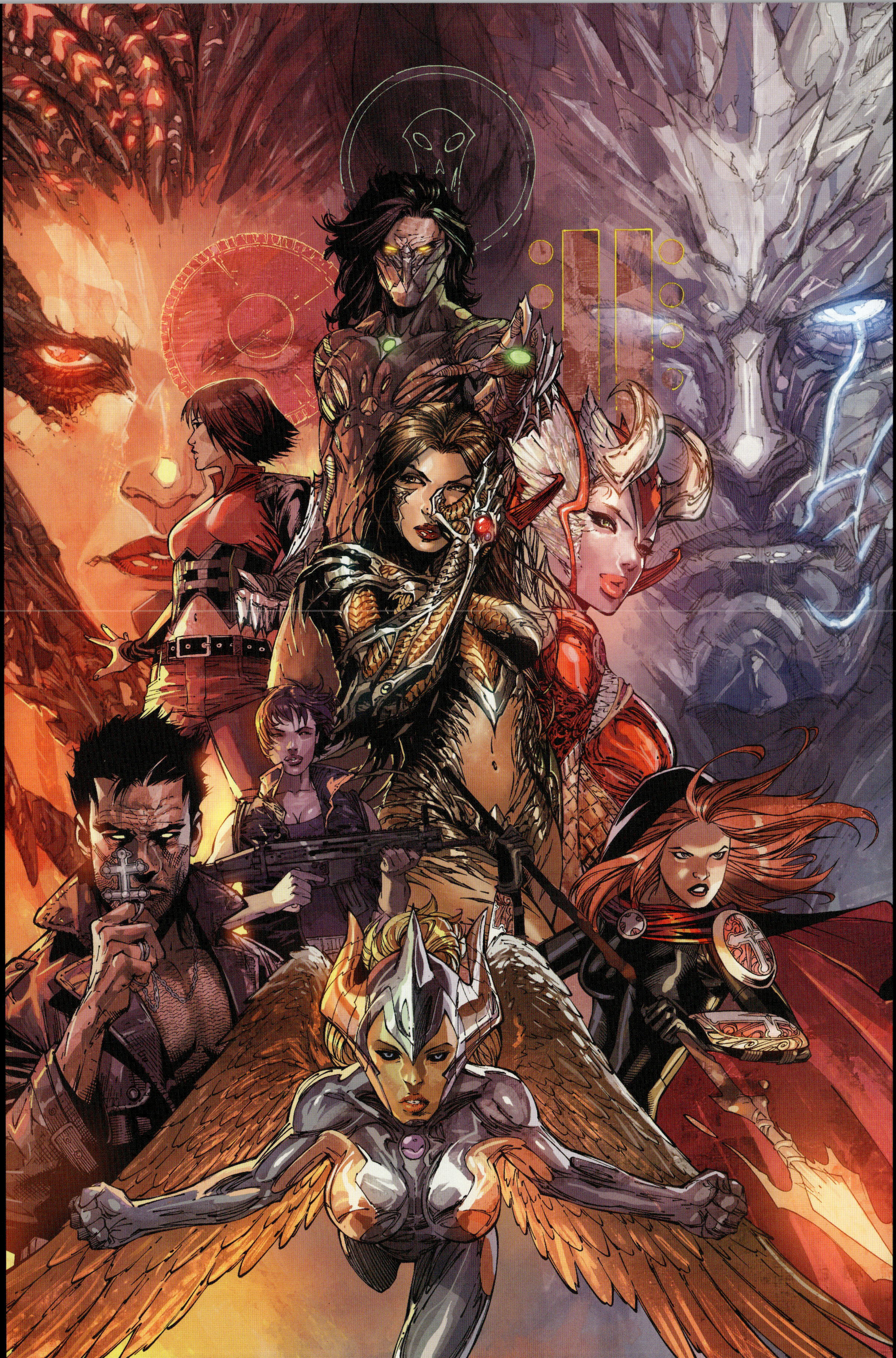

Artifacts #1 "Jam" cover A, art by: Michael Broussard, Marc Silvestri, Stjepan Sejic, Kenneth Rocafort, Nelson Blake II, Sheldon Mitchell, Rick Basaldua, and Sunny Gho

Artifacts had two consistent variants across the first thirteen issues relating to each bearer and artifact. Each cover "B" was illustrated by **John Tyler Christopher** and portrayed an Artifact bearer. There were also retailer incentive variants (1:100) featuring a hot gold foil stamp of that Artifact's icon corresponding to the cover B Artifact bearer showcased for that issue. The same artwork was used for the *Artifacts Playing Card Deck*, shown below. The deck was created as a retailer incentive with cards distributed in batches. A lot of research went into the deck's design to promote *Artifacts* and also serve as a legitimate poker deck complete with a "Suicide King" and additional elements for normal play. Complete decks had to be compiled by hand by the staff, who are resentful to this day. The complete suit of Clubs is shown below.

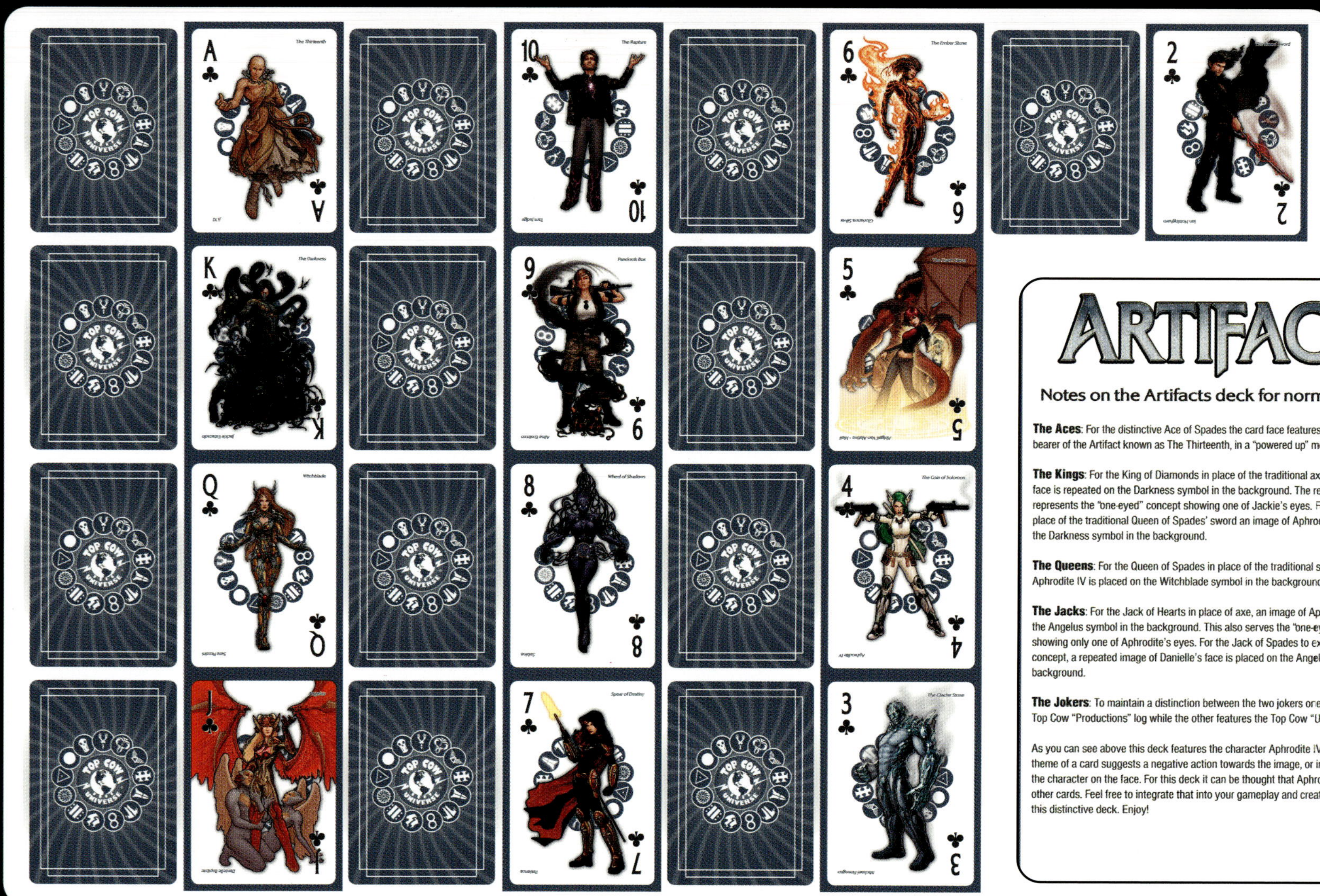

ARTIFACTS™

Notes on the Artifacts deck for normal gameplay

The Aces: For the distinctive Ace of Spades the card face features the Artifact bearer Ji Xi, bearer of the Artifact known as The Thirteenth, in a "powered up" mode.

The Kings: For the King of Diamonds in place of the traditional axe, an image of Jackie's face is repeated on the Darkness symbol in the background. The repeated face image also represents the "one-eyed" concept showing one of Jackie's eyes. For the King of Hearts, in place of the traditional Queen of Spades' sword an image of Aphrodite IV's face is placed on the Darkness symbol in the background.

The Queens: For the Queen of Spades in place of the traditional scepter, an image of Aphrodite IV is placed on the Witchblade symbol in the background.

The Jacks: For the Jack of Hearts in place of axe, an image of Aphrodite IV is placed on the Angelus symbol in the background. This also serves the "one-eyed" function of the card showing only one of Aphrodite's eyes. For the Jack of Spades to express the one-eyed concept, a repeated image of Danielle's face is placed on the Angelus symbol in the background.

The Jokers: To maintain a distinction between the two jokers one features the company Top Cow "Productions" log while the other features the Top Cow "Universe" logo.

As you can see above this deck features the character Aphrodite IV whenever the history or theme of a card suggests a negative action towards the image, or in the case of this deck, the character on the face. For this deck it can be thought that Aphrodite is "hunting" the other cards. Feel free to integrate that into your gameplay and create new games based on this distinctive deck. Enjoy!

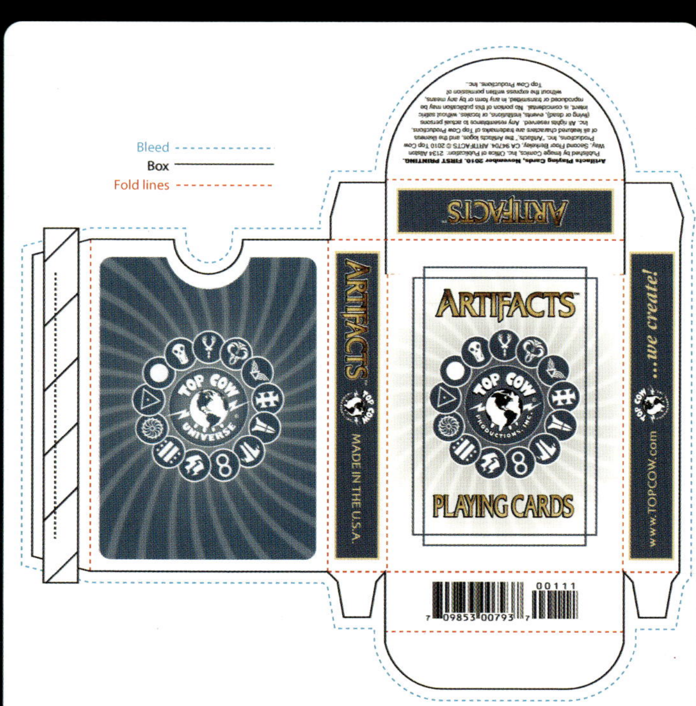

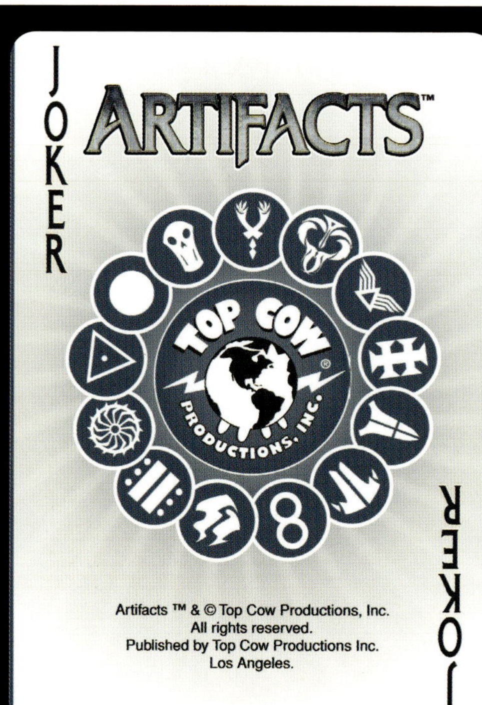

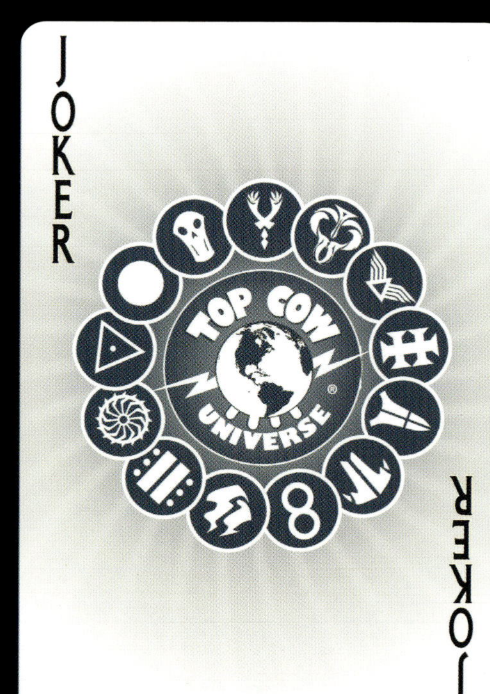

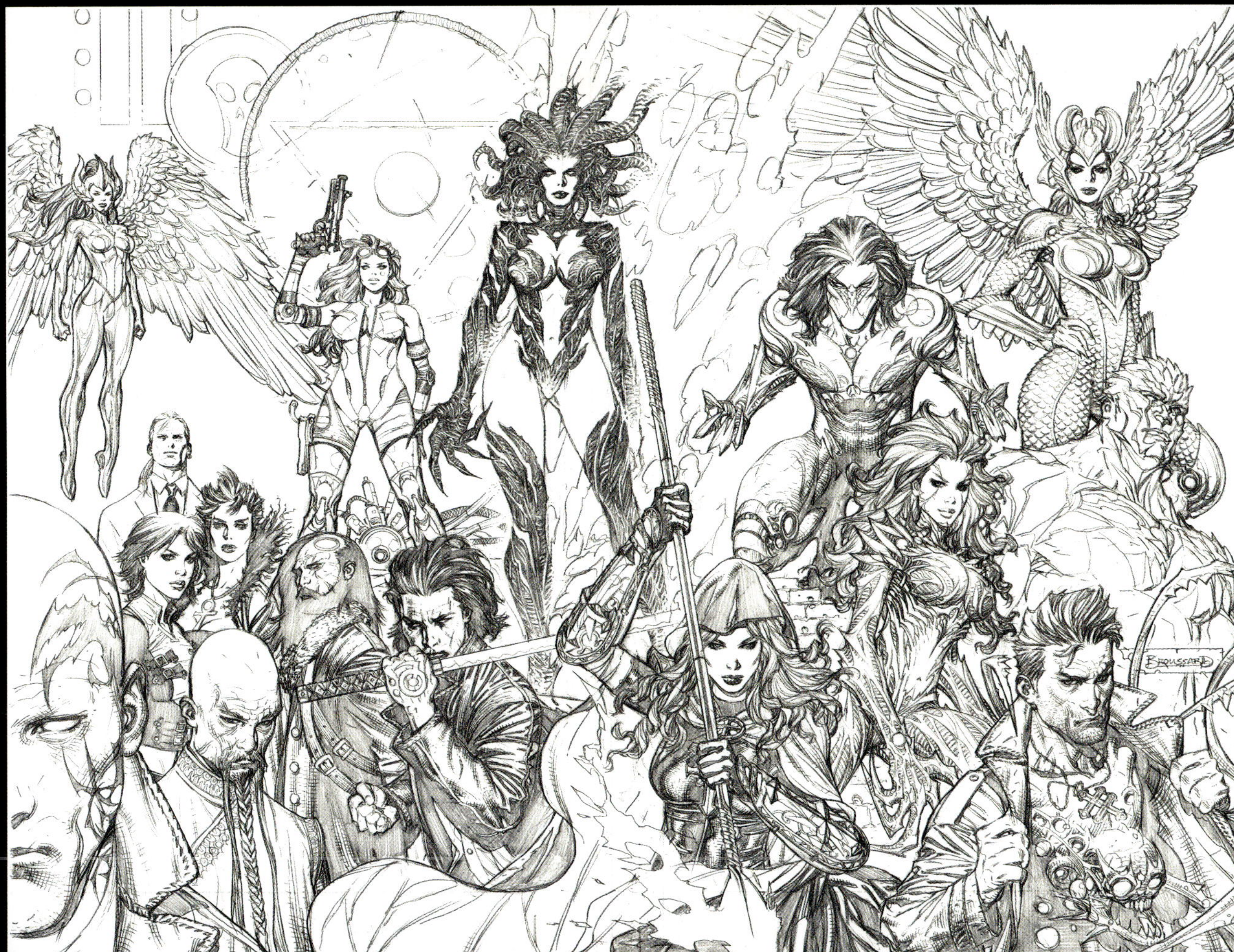

Artifacts #1 cover H (above), and cover G (below), art by: Michael Broussard and Sunny Gho

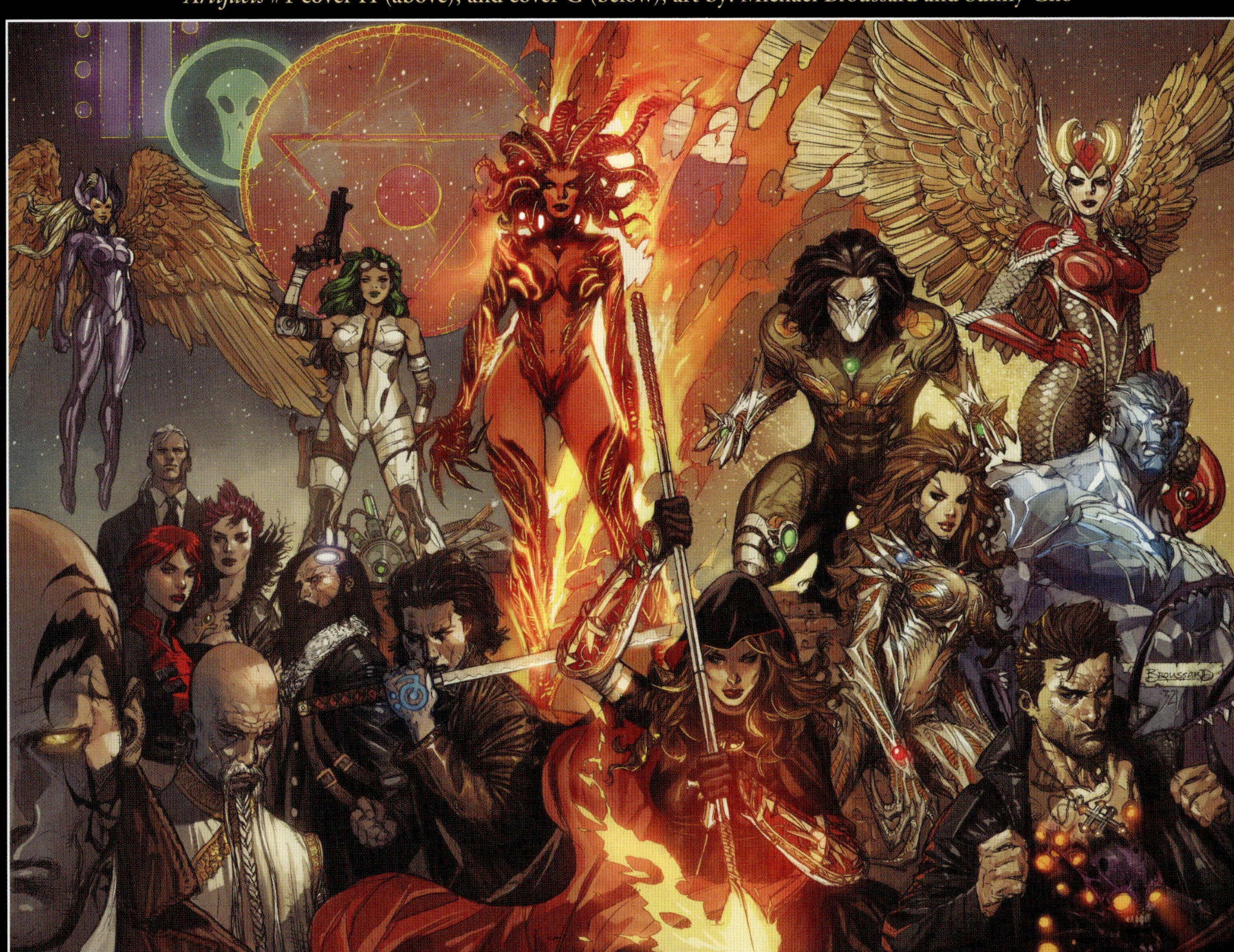

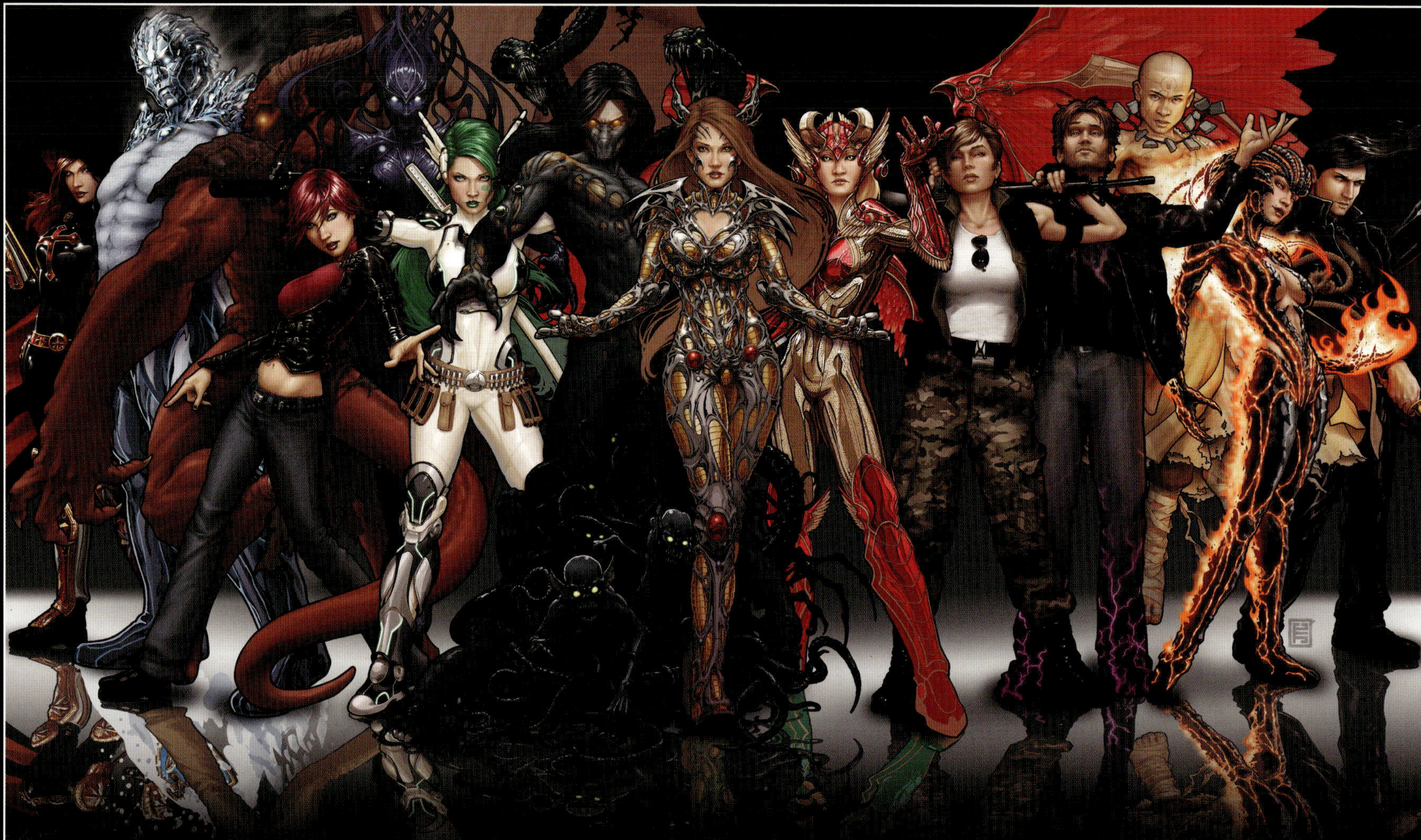

Artifacts: Origins #0 cover, art by: John Tyler Christopher

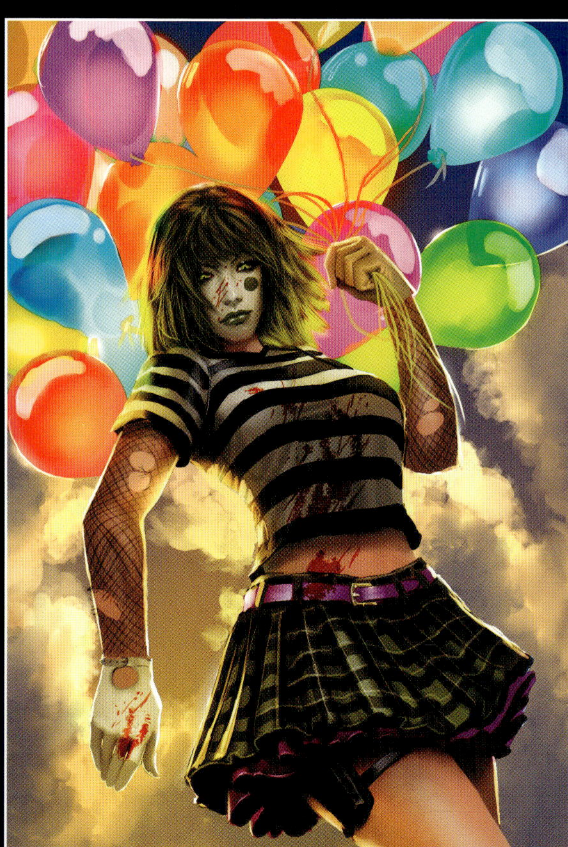

Artifacts #2 cover E, New York Comic Con Exclusive, art by: Stjepan Sejic

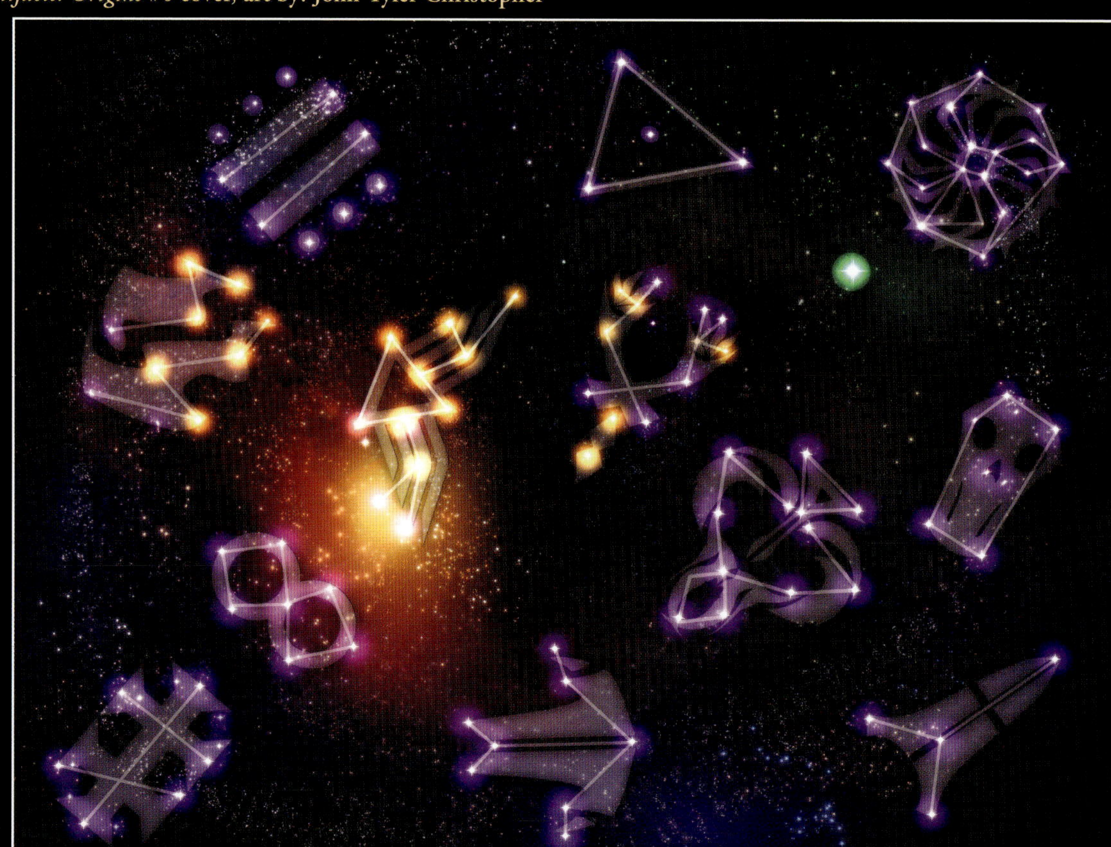

Artifacts: Lost Tales #1 cover, art by: Linda Sejic

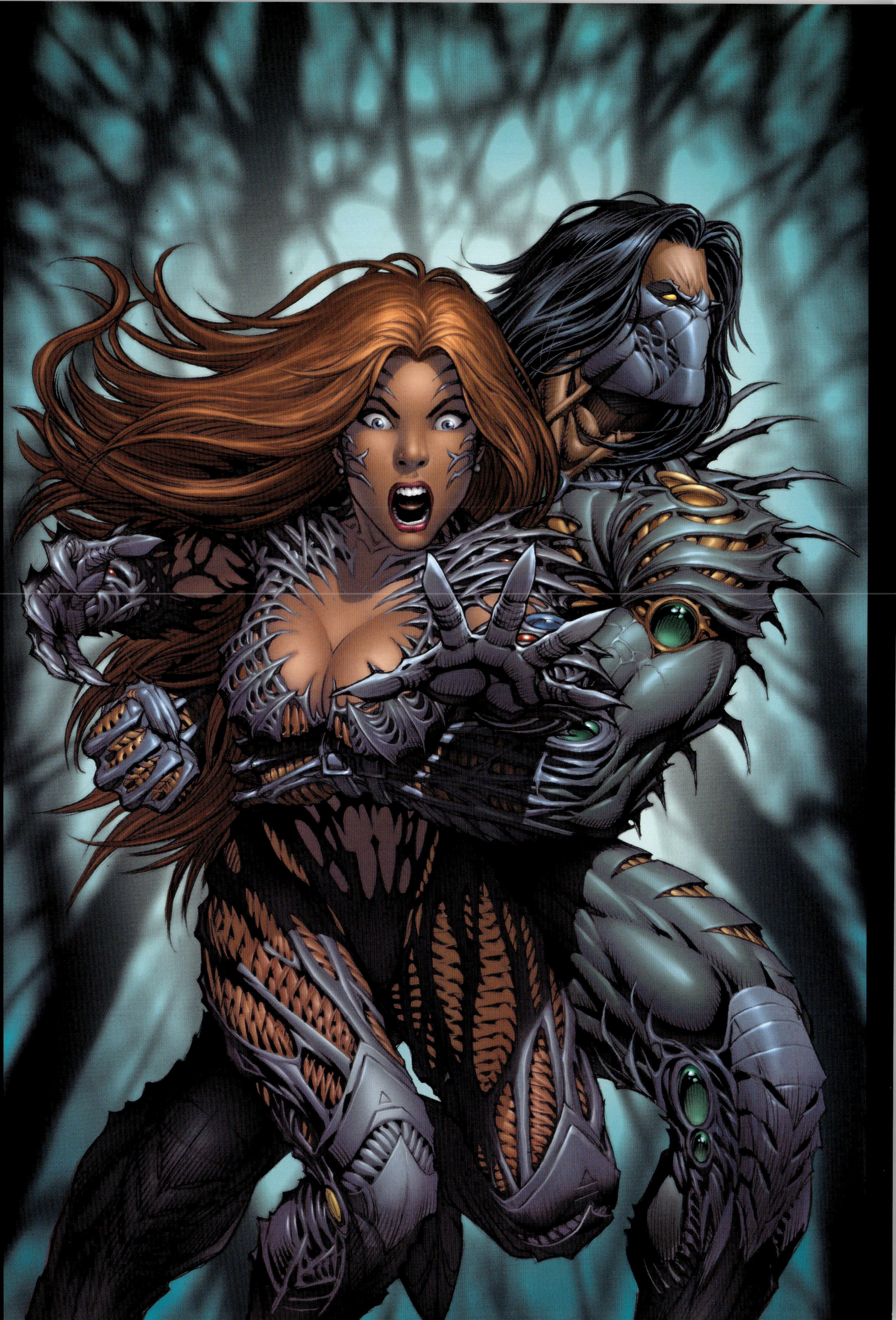

Artifacts #1 cover C,
art by: Dale Keown

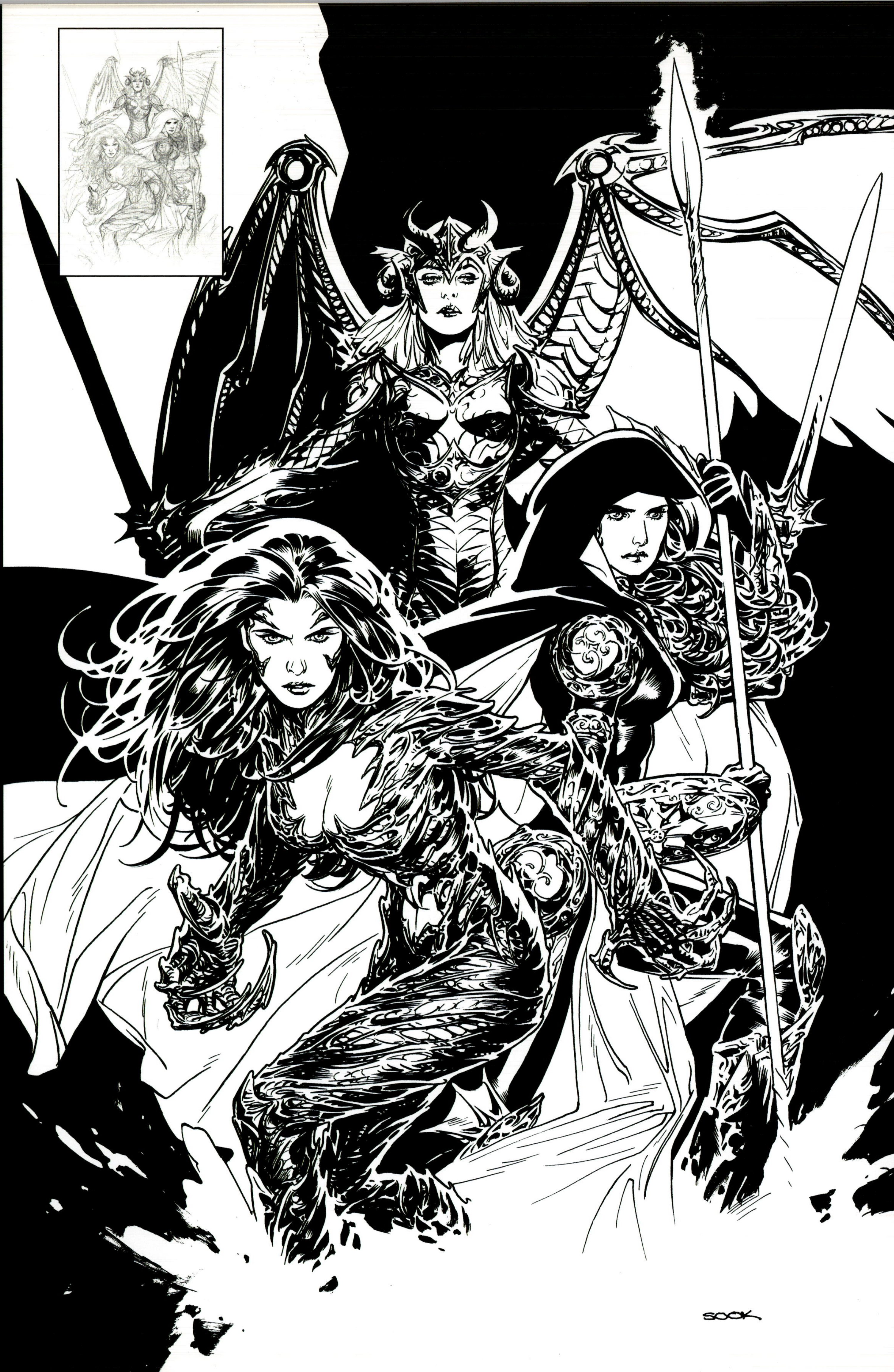

Artifacts #2 cover E, Cover C inset,
line art by: Ryan Sook

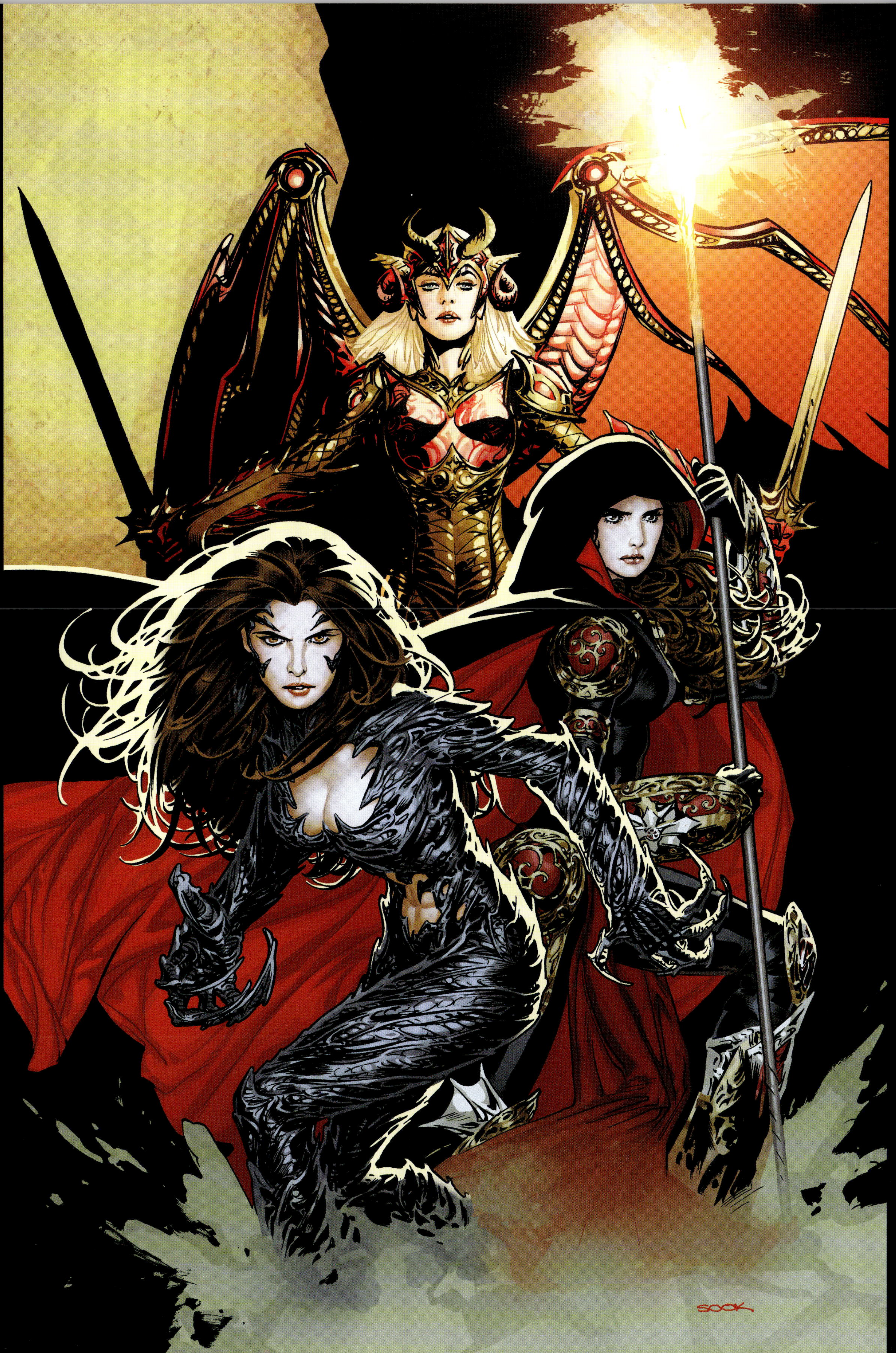

Artifacts #2 cover A,
art by: Ryan Sook

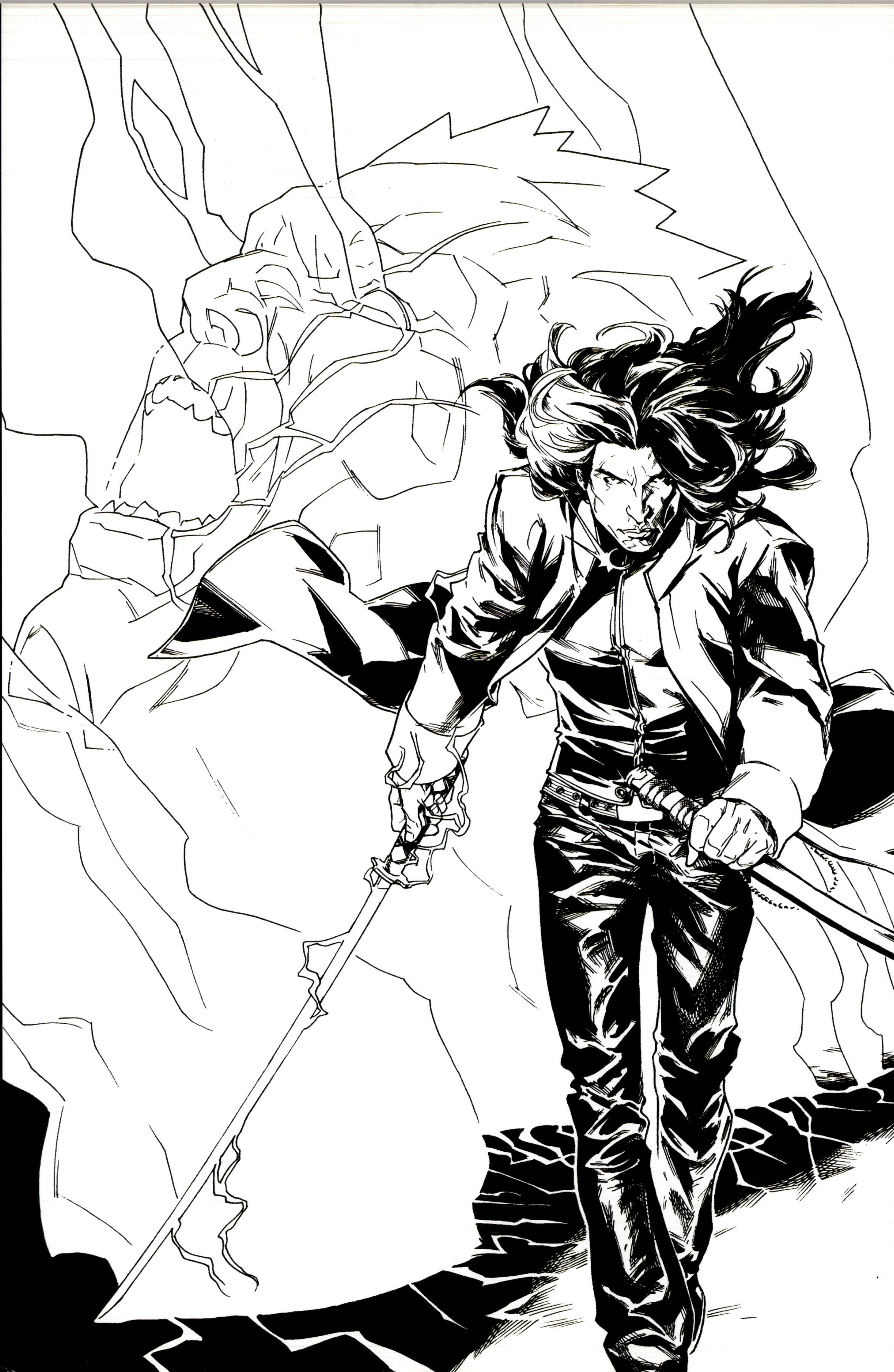

Artifacts #3 cover C,
line art by: Kalman Andrasofszky

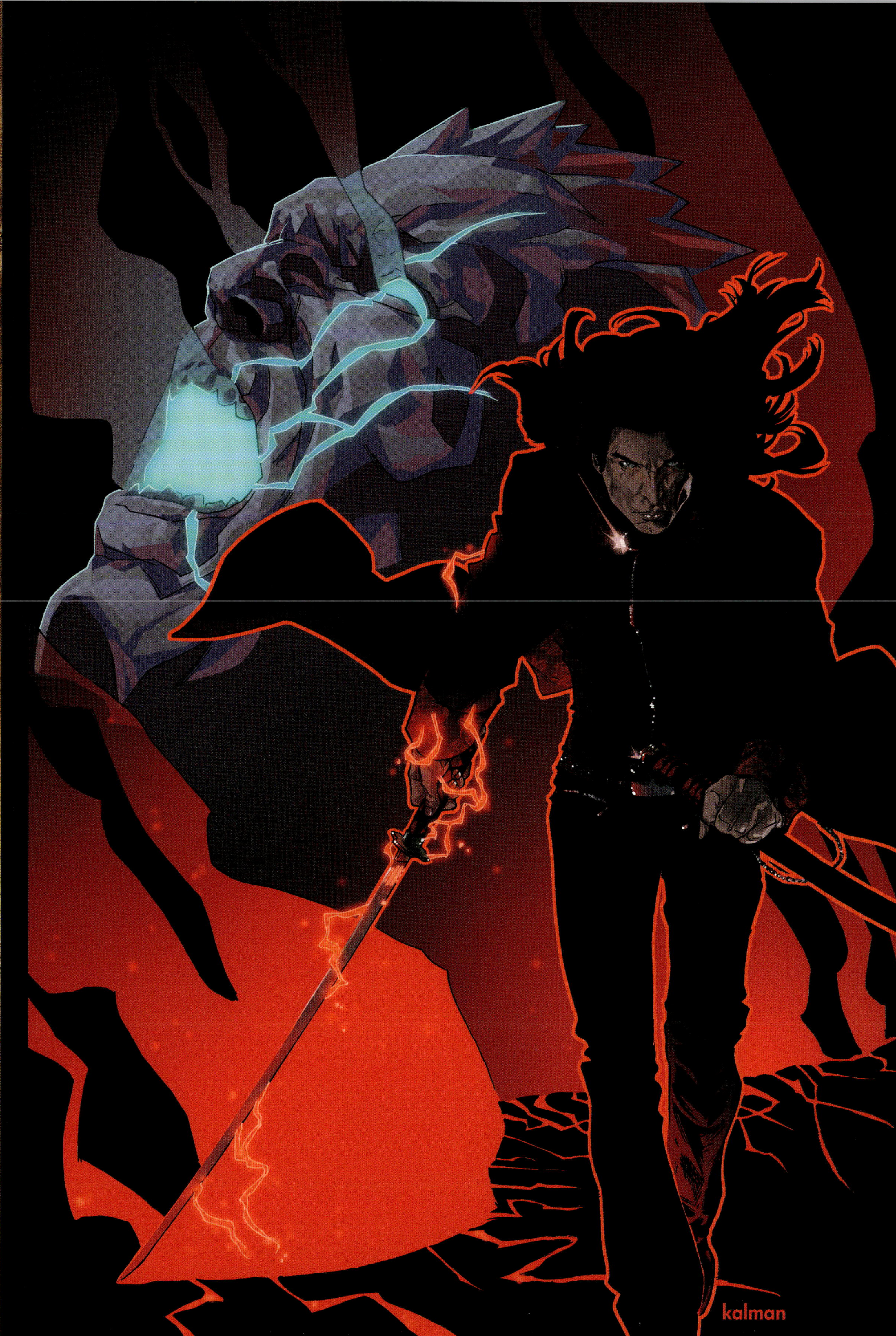

Artifacts #3 cover A,
art by: Kalman Andrasofszky

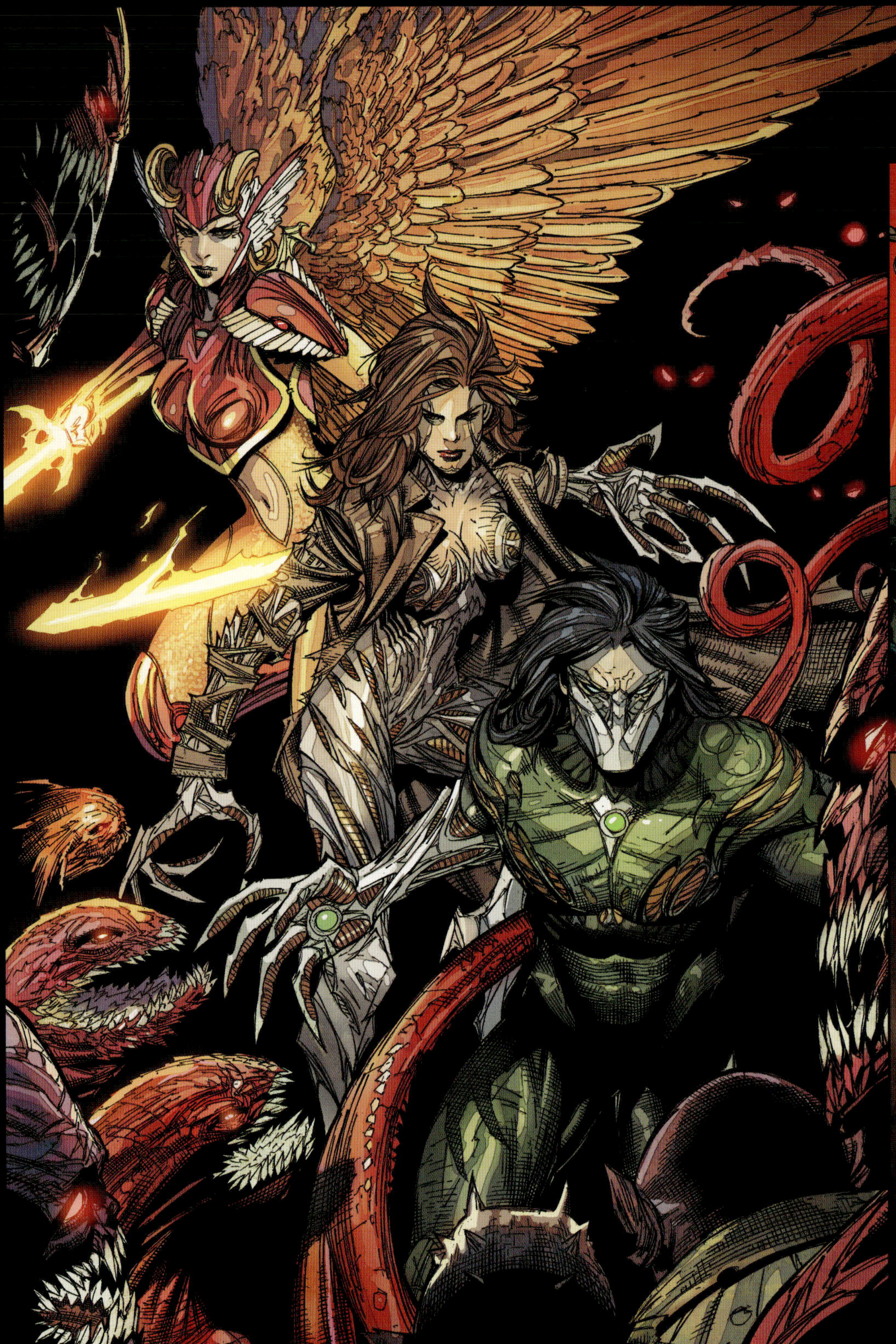

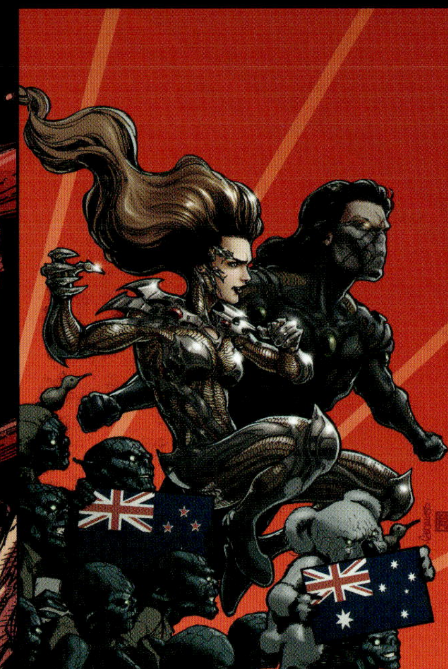

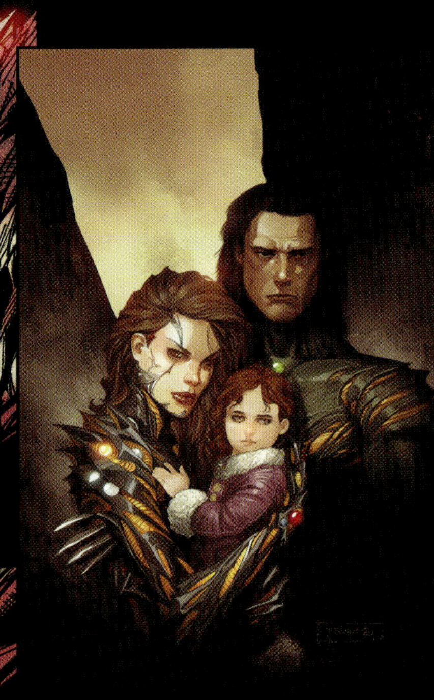

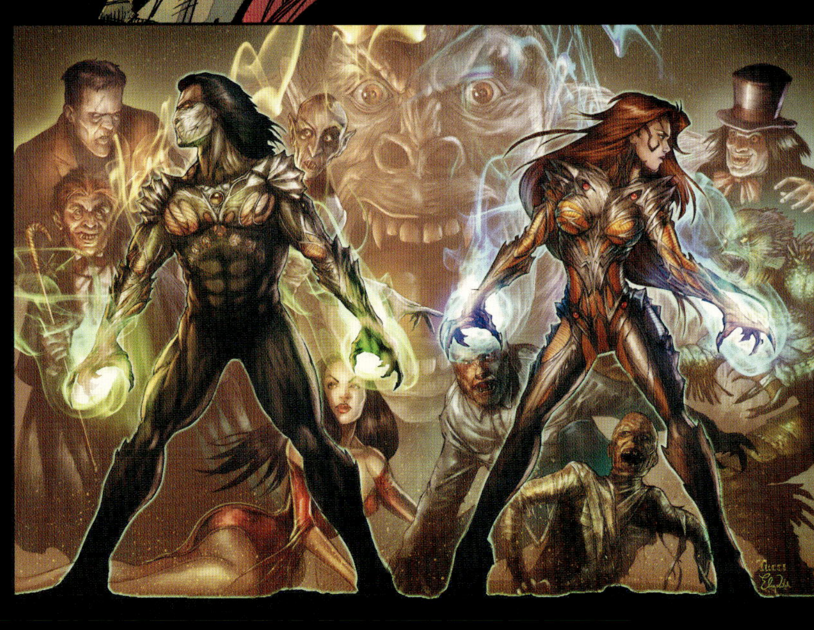

This page, clockwise from above.

Artifacts #3 cover H,
art by: Michael Broussard, Rick Basaldua, and Sunny Gho

Artifacts #3 cover F, Armageddon Expo variant,
art by: Georges Jeanty & John Tyler Christopher

Artifacts #4 cover A,
art by: Michael Broussard and Sunny Gho

Artifacts #3 cover E and G,
Virginia Comic-Con Exclusive covers,
art by: William Tucci and Eko Puteh

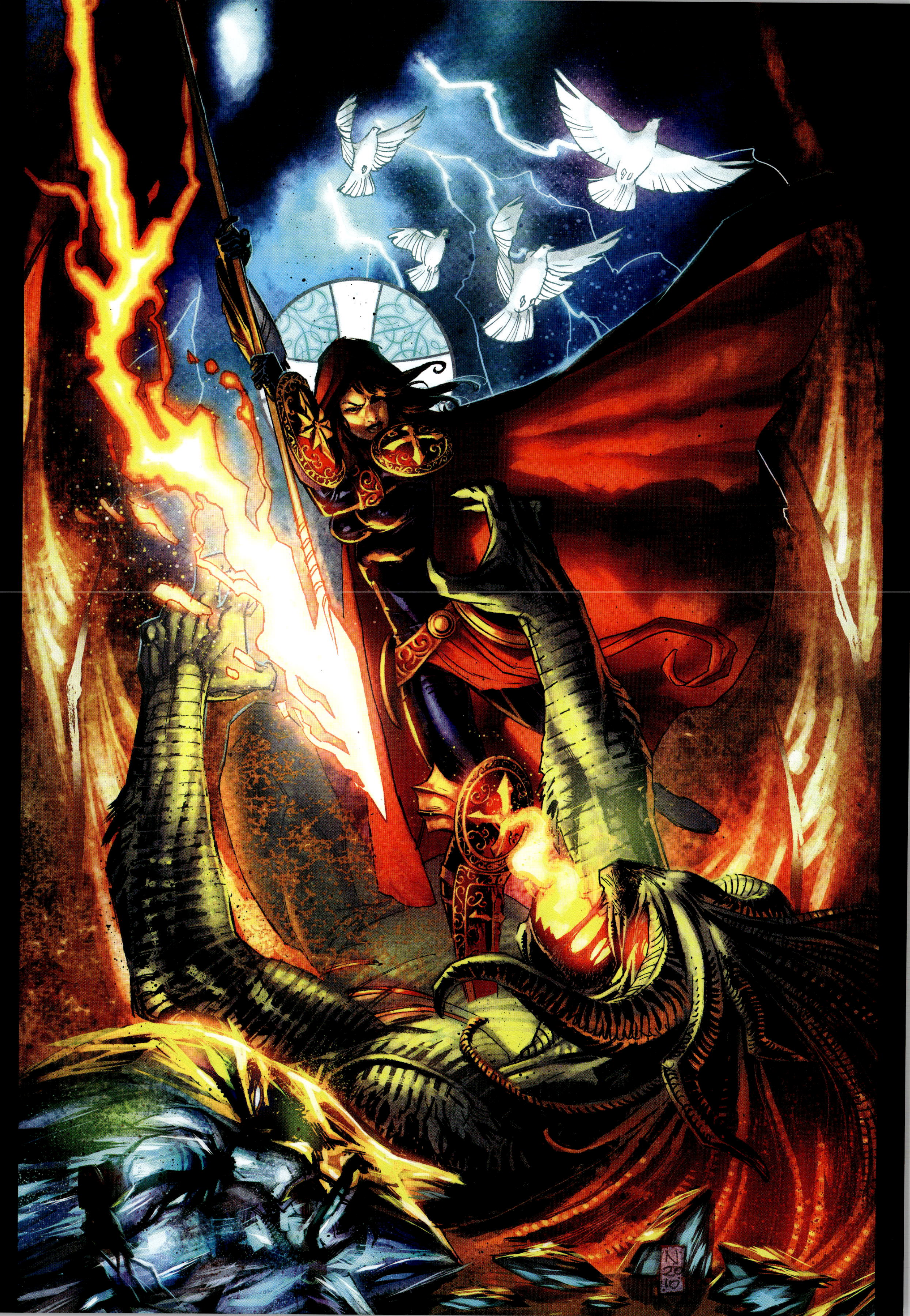

Artifacts #5 cover A,
art by: Nic Klein

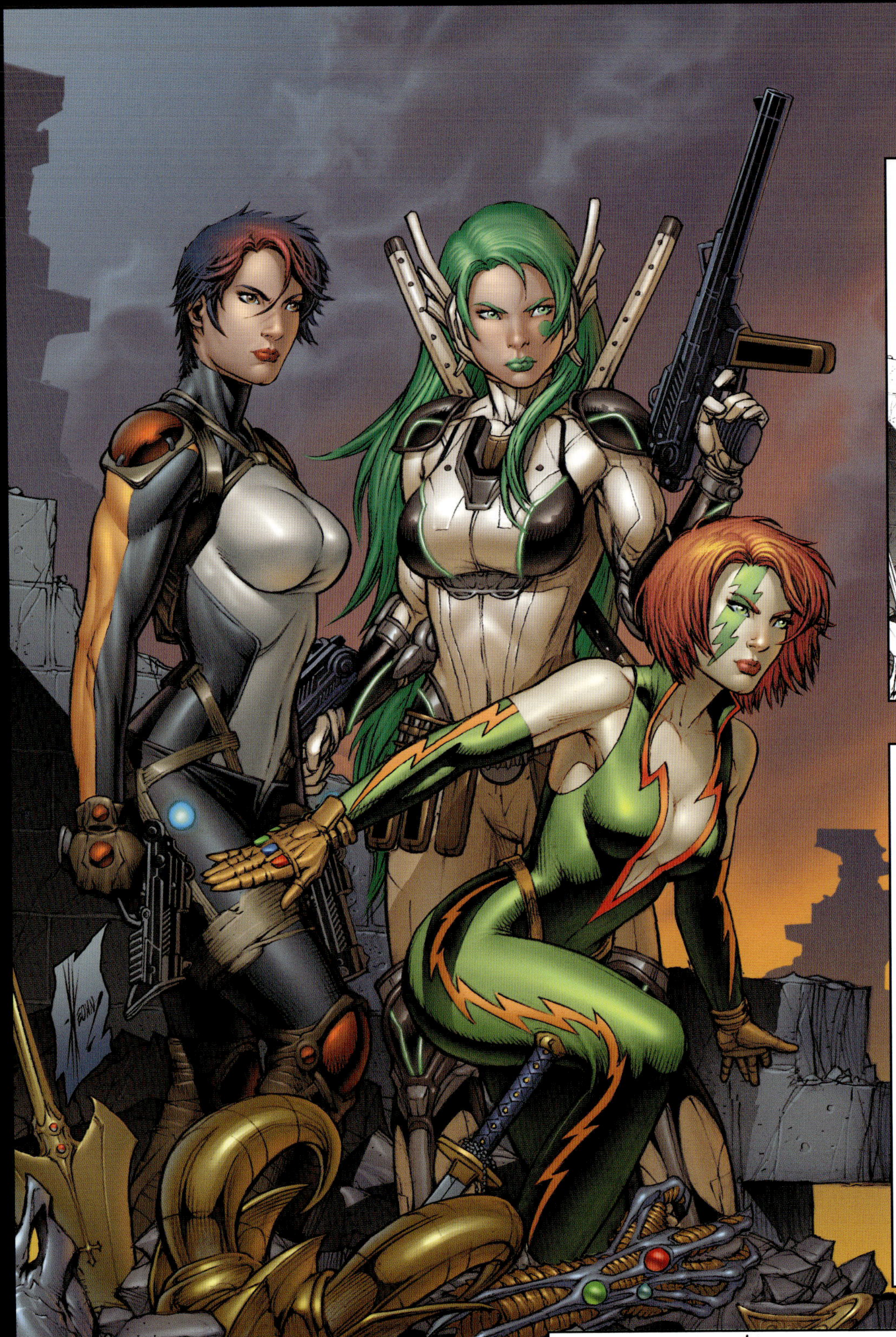

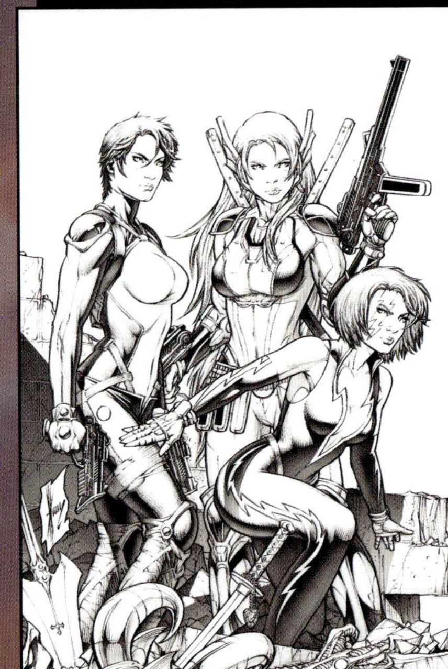

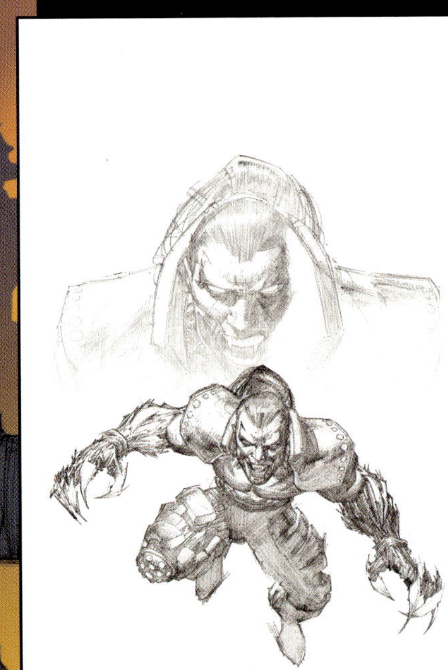

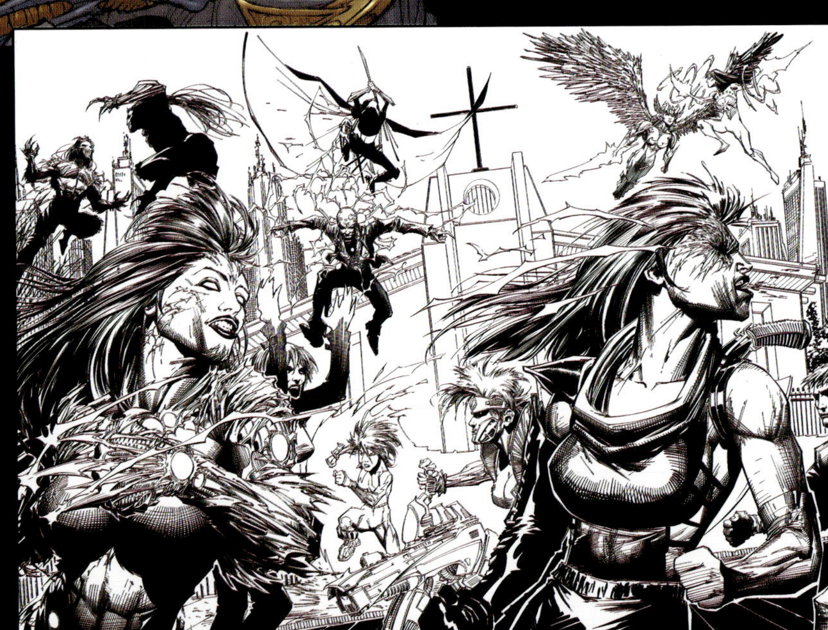

This page, clockwise from above.

Artifacts #5 cover C,
art by: Dale Keown

Artifacts #5 cover D,
art by: Dale Keown

Artifacts #5 cover F, Top Cow Store Exclusive,
art by: Whilce Portacio

Artifacts #5 cover G, second printing,
art by: Whilce Portacio

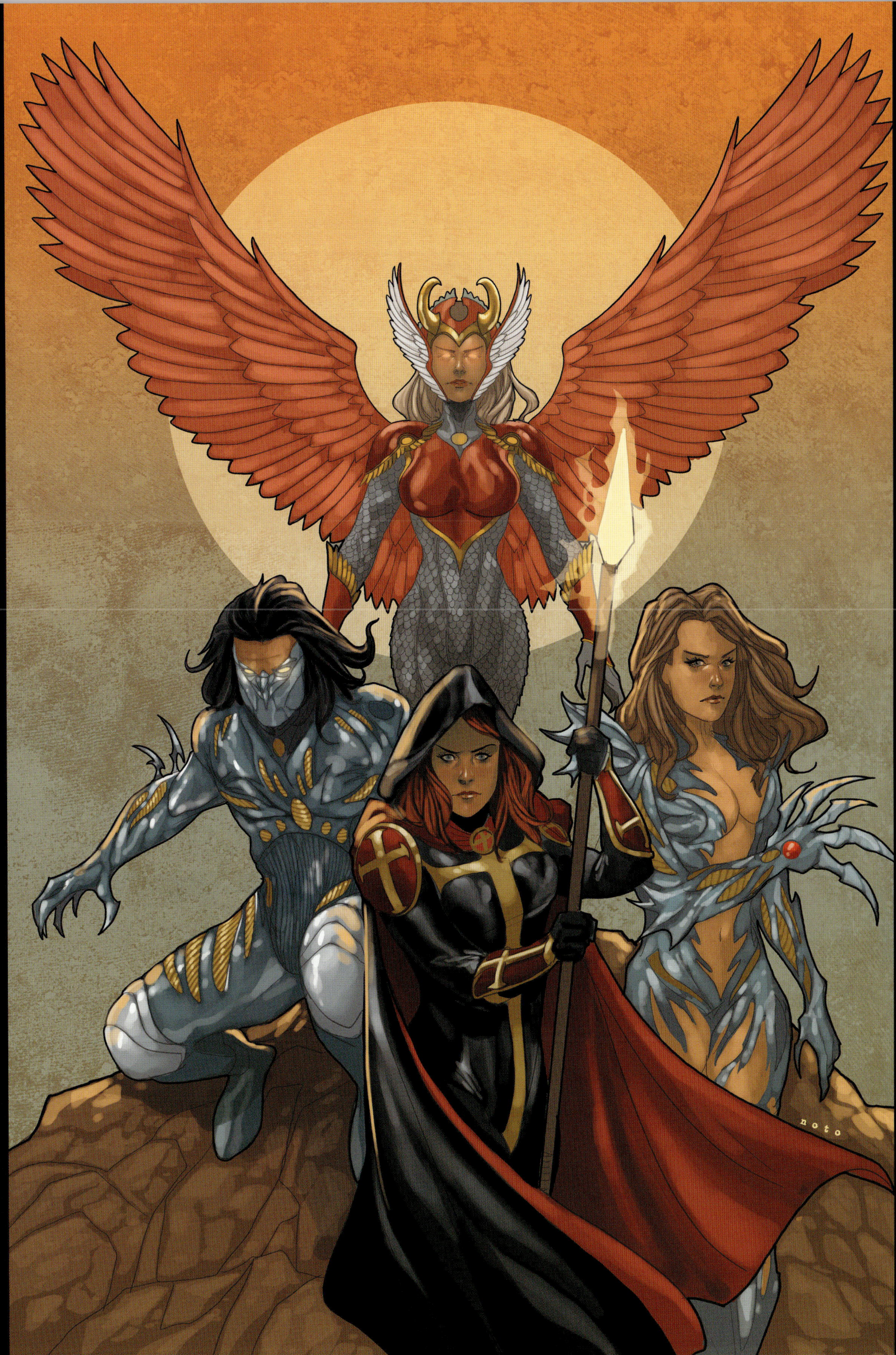

Artifacts #6 cover A,
art by: Phil Noto

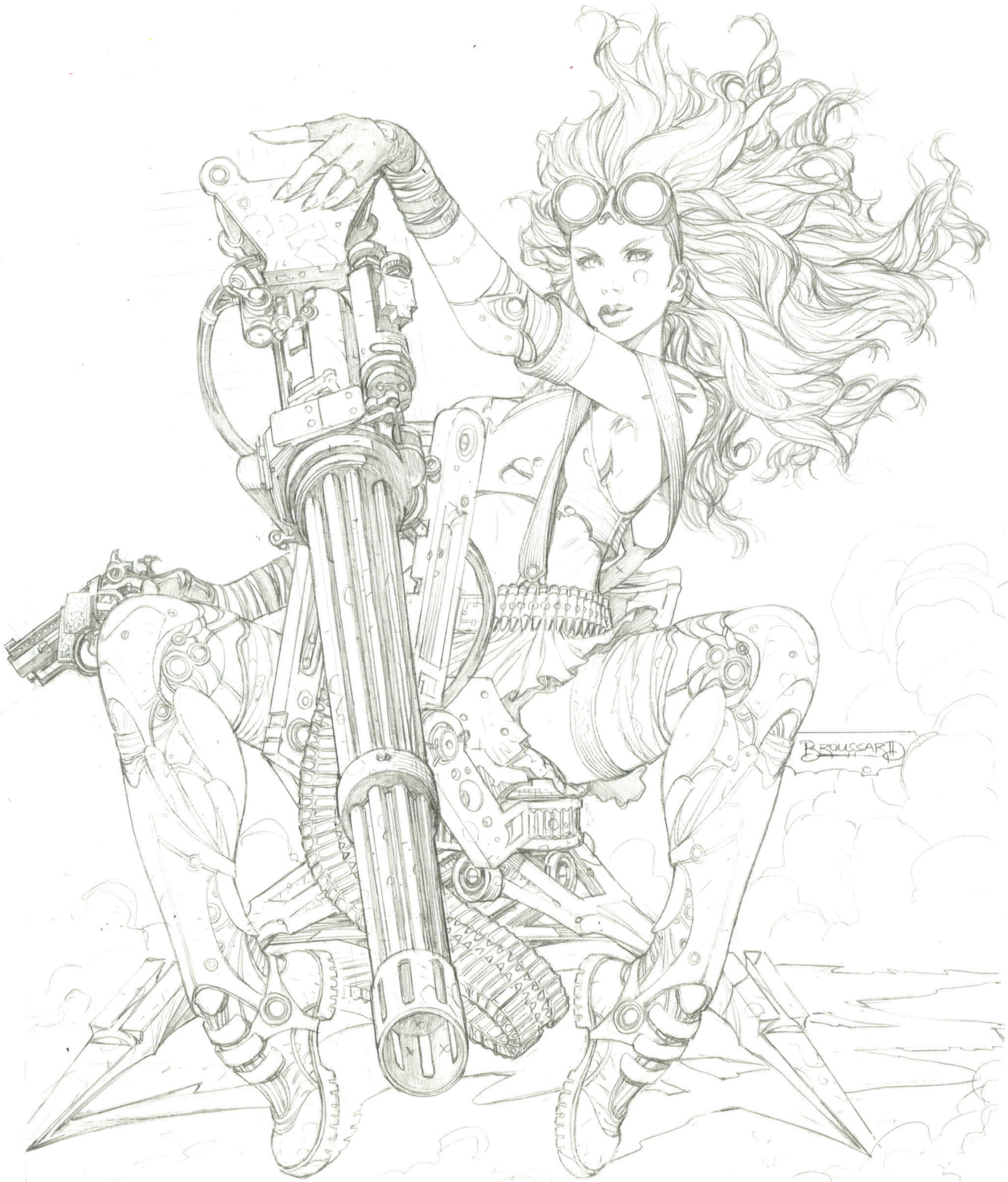

Artifacts #6 cover E, C2E2 variant,
line art by: Michael Broussard

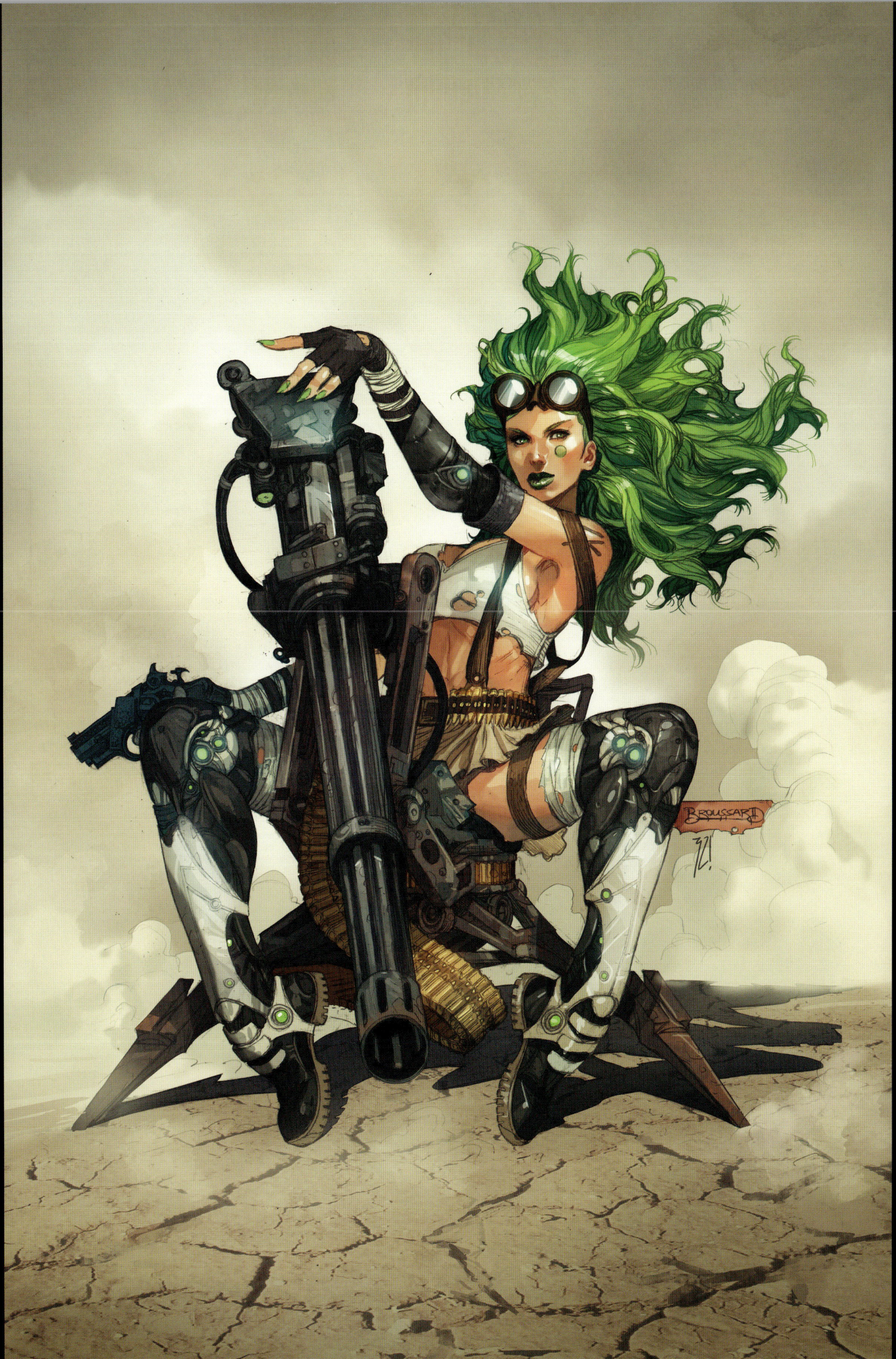

Artifacts #6 cover E, C2E2 variant,
art by: Michael Broussard and Sunny Gho

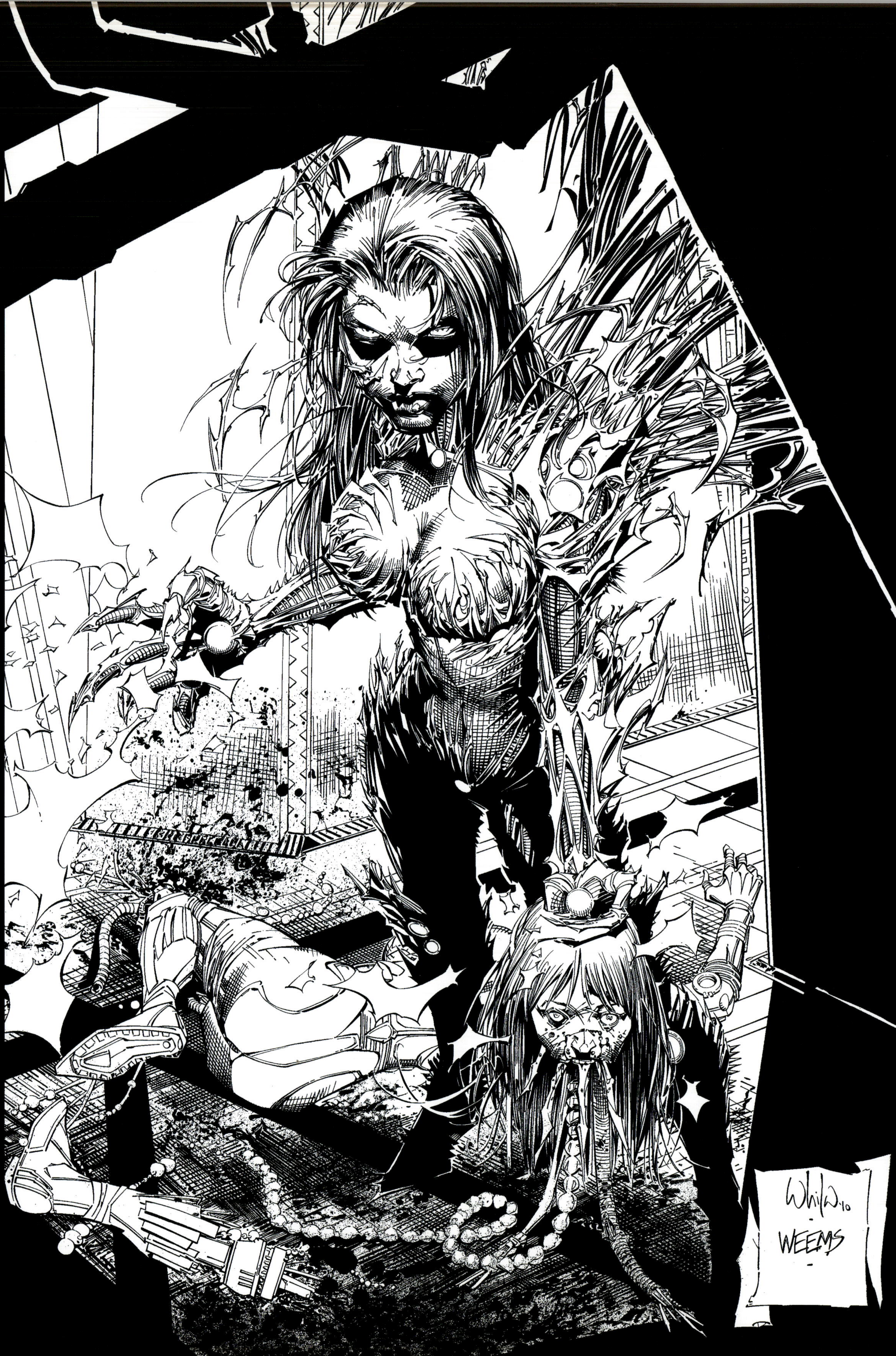

Artifacts #7 cover C,
line art by: Whilce Portacio and Joe Weems V

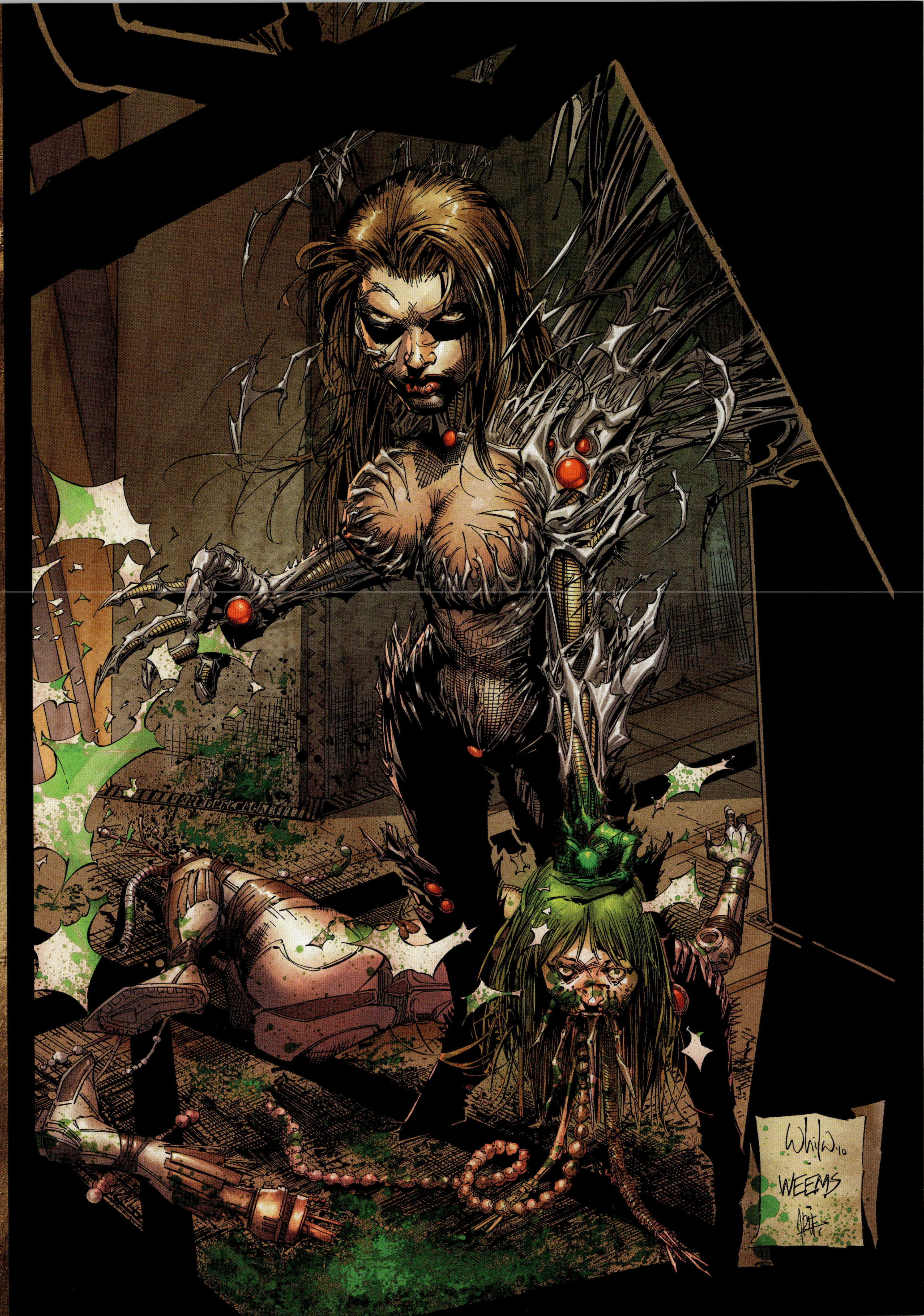

Artifacts #7 cover C,
art by: Whilce Portacio, Joe Weems V, and Arif Prianto

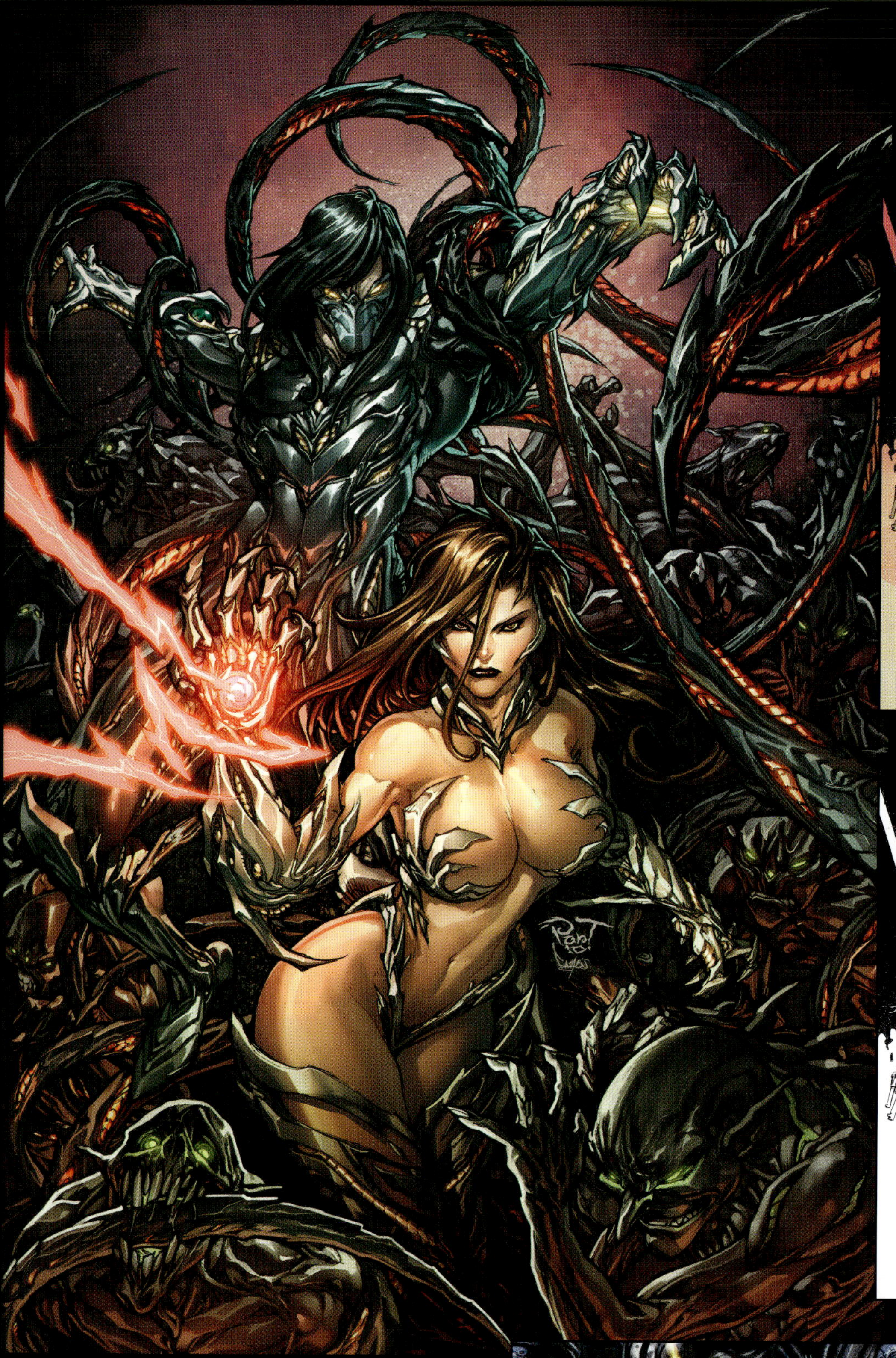

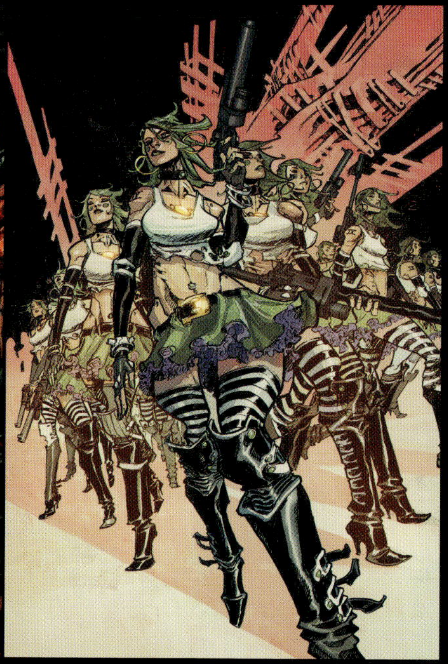

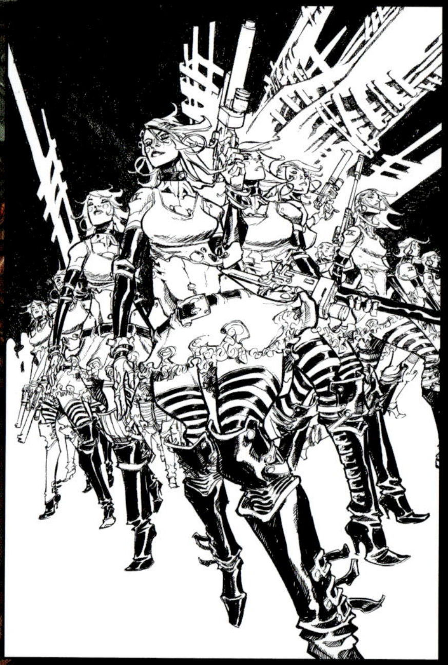

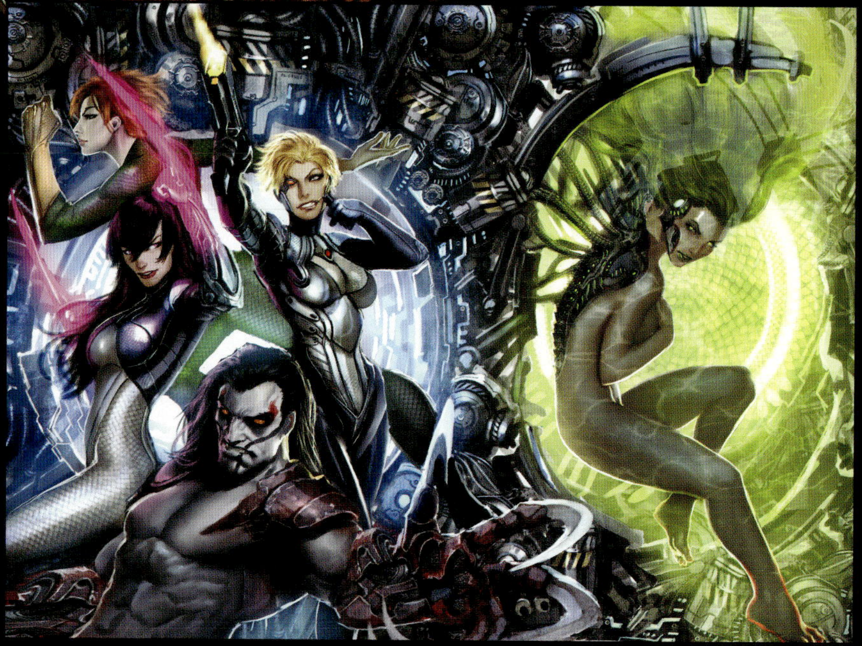

This page, clockwise from above.

Artifacts #7 cover E, Top Cow Store Exclusive,
art by: Paolo Pantalena and Jorge Fares

Artifacts #8 cover A,
art by: Eric Canete

Artifacts #8 cover C,
line art by: Eric Canete

Artifacts #8 cover E, SDCC variant
art by: Stjepan Sejic

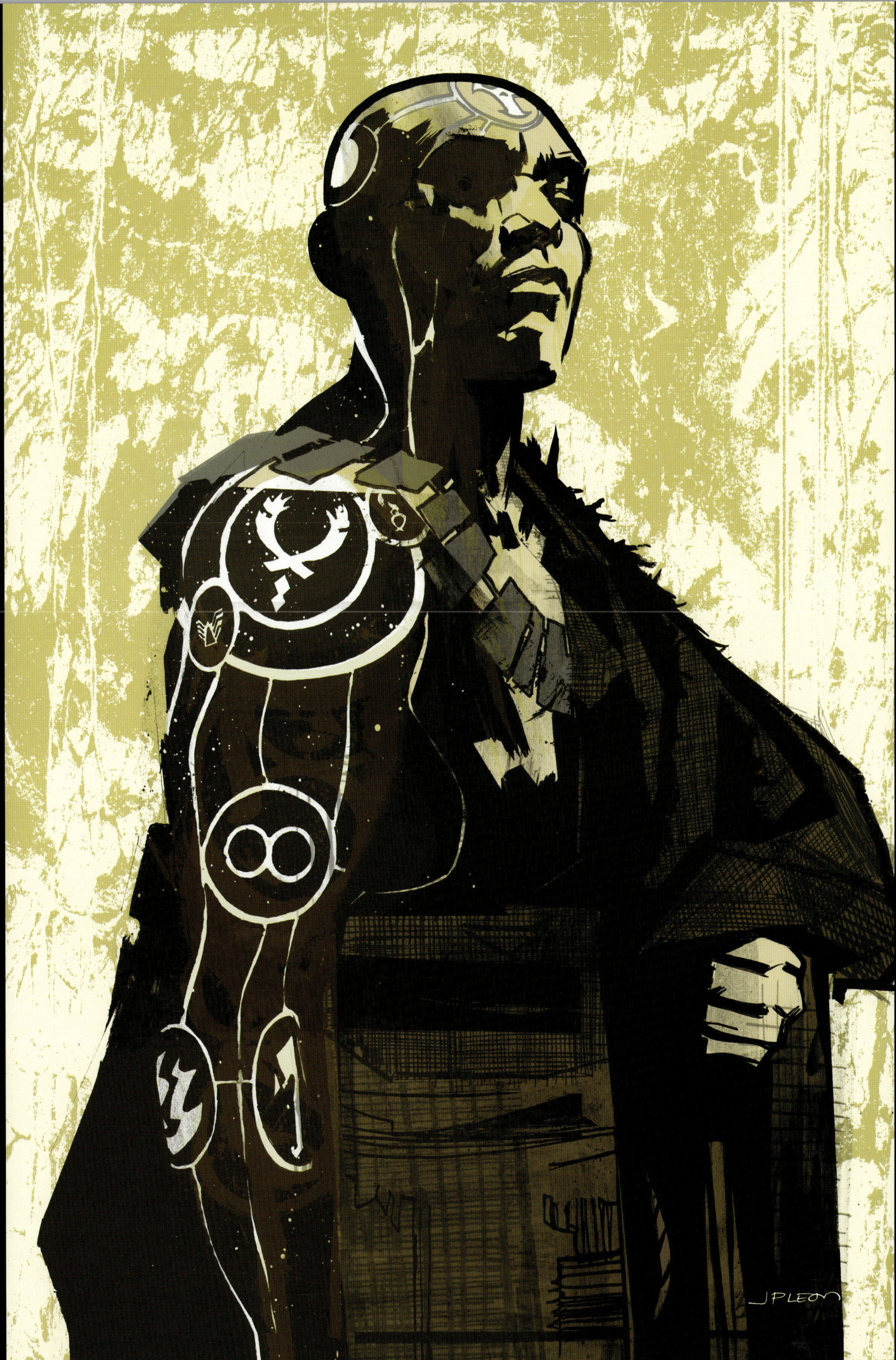

Artifacts #9 cover A,
art by: John Paul Leon

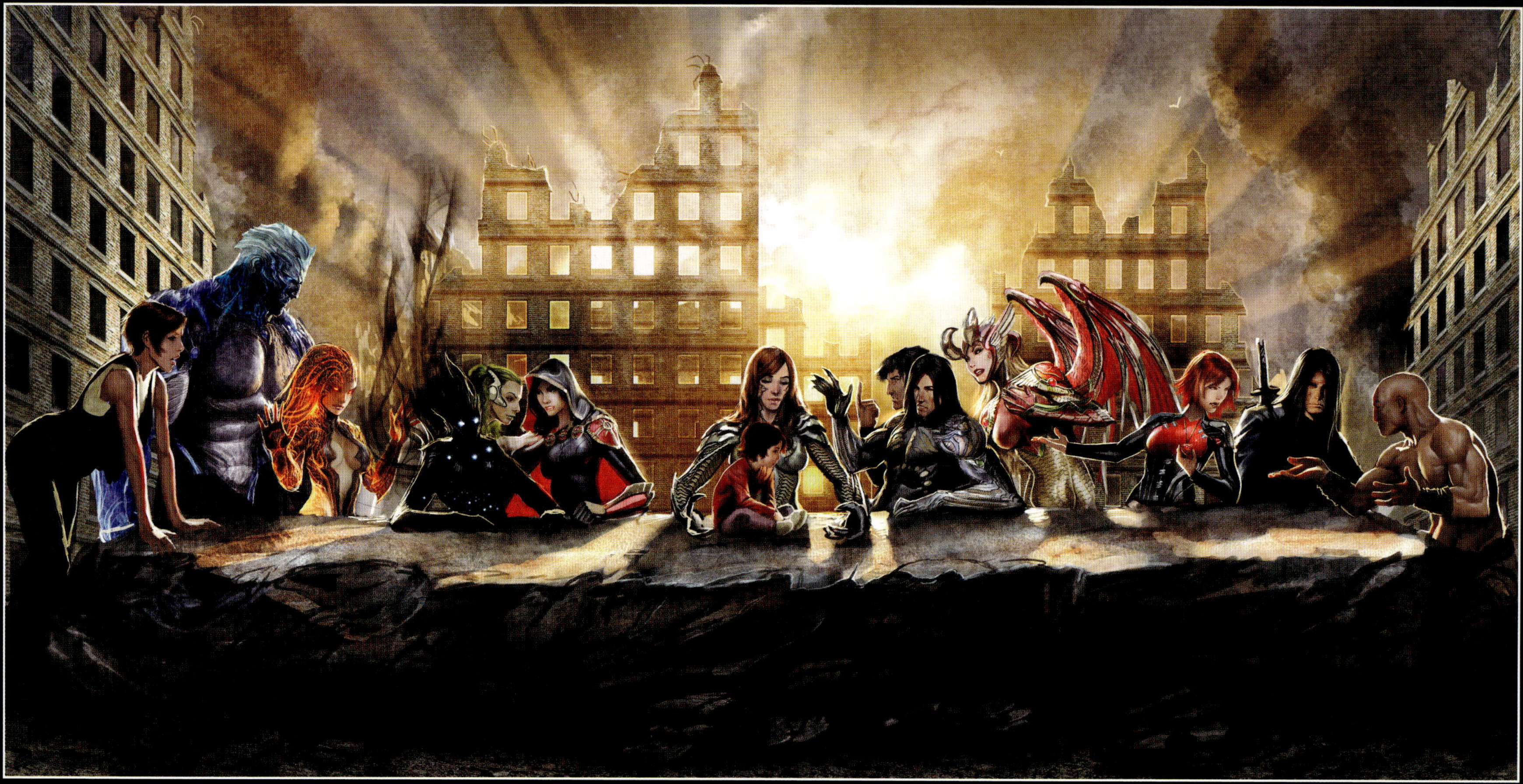

Artifacts #10 cover A, art by: Stjepan Sejic

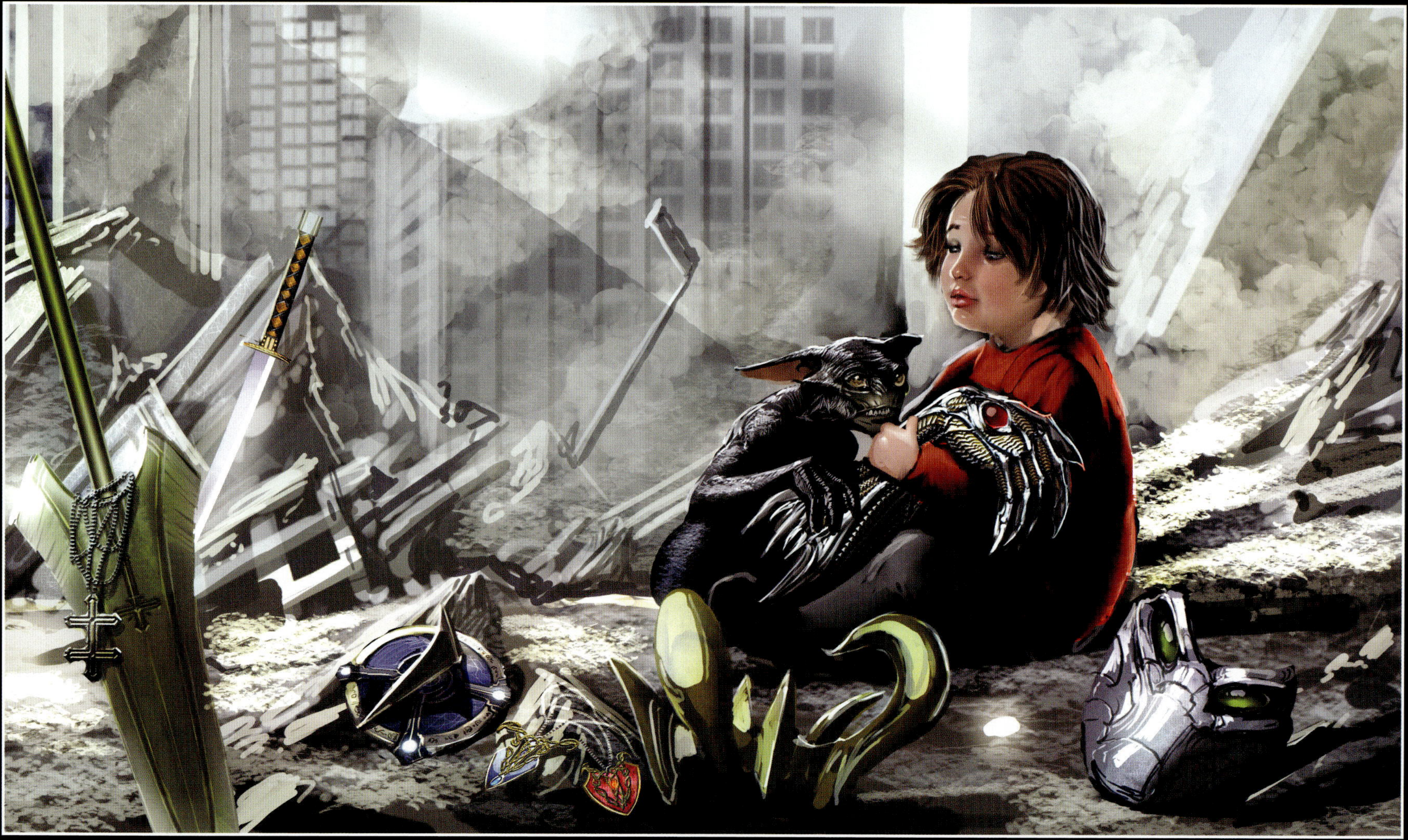

Artifacts #10 cover C, art by: Stjepan Sejic

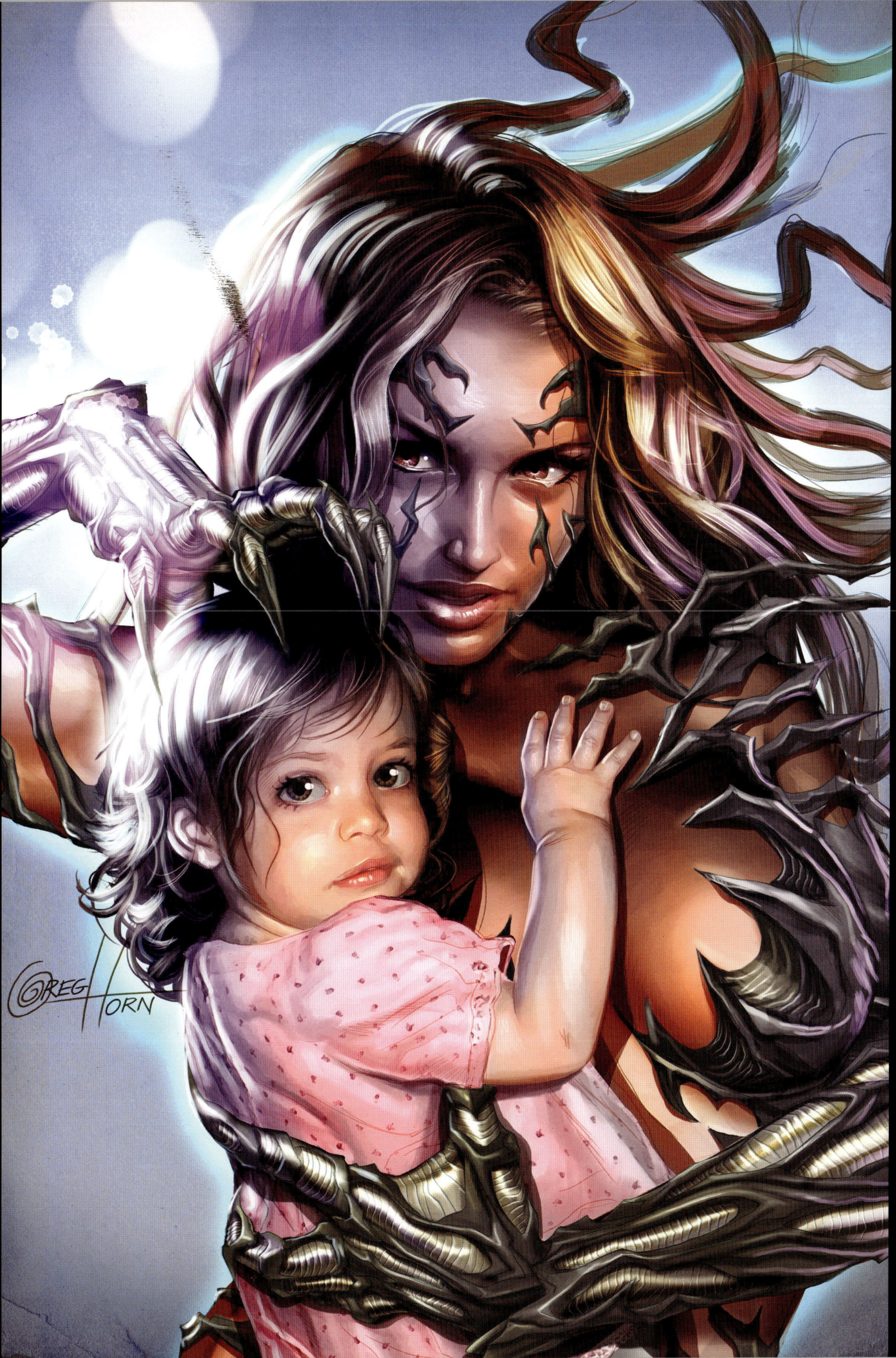

Artifacts #12 cover A,
art by: Greg Horn

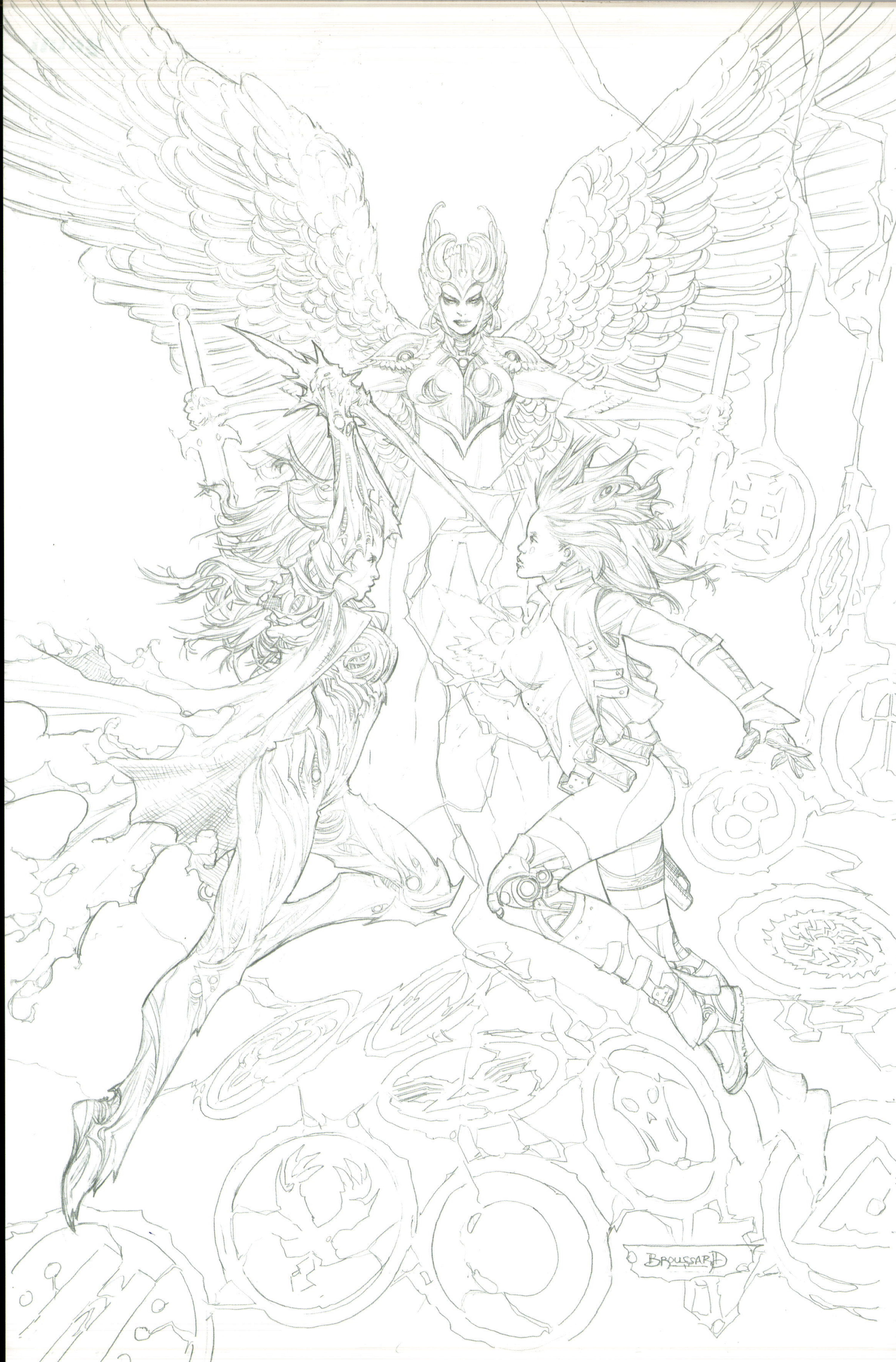

Artifacts #12 cover C,
art by: Michael Broussard

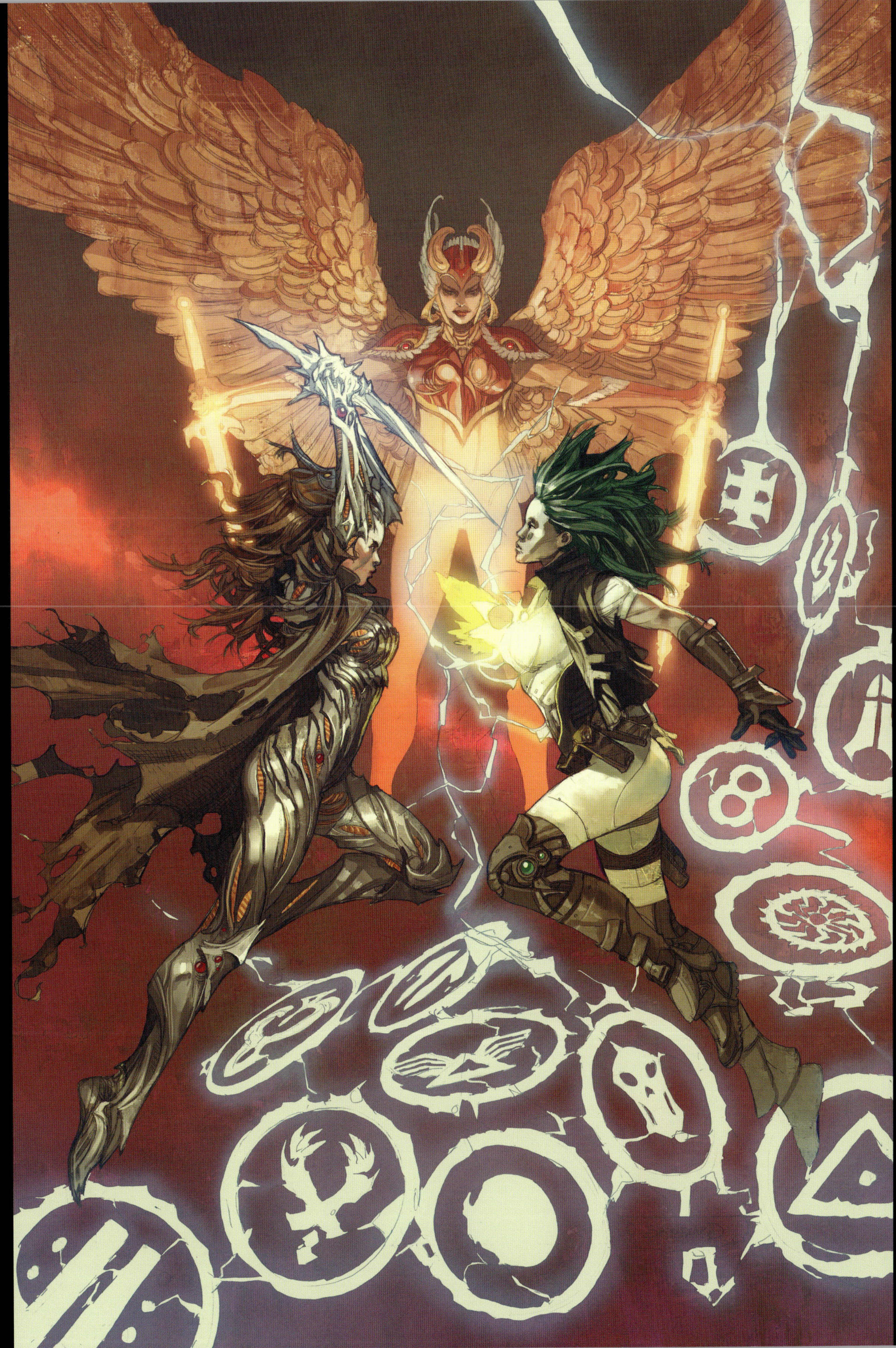

Artifacts #19 cover B, SDCC variant,
art by: Michael Broussard and Sunny Gho

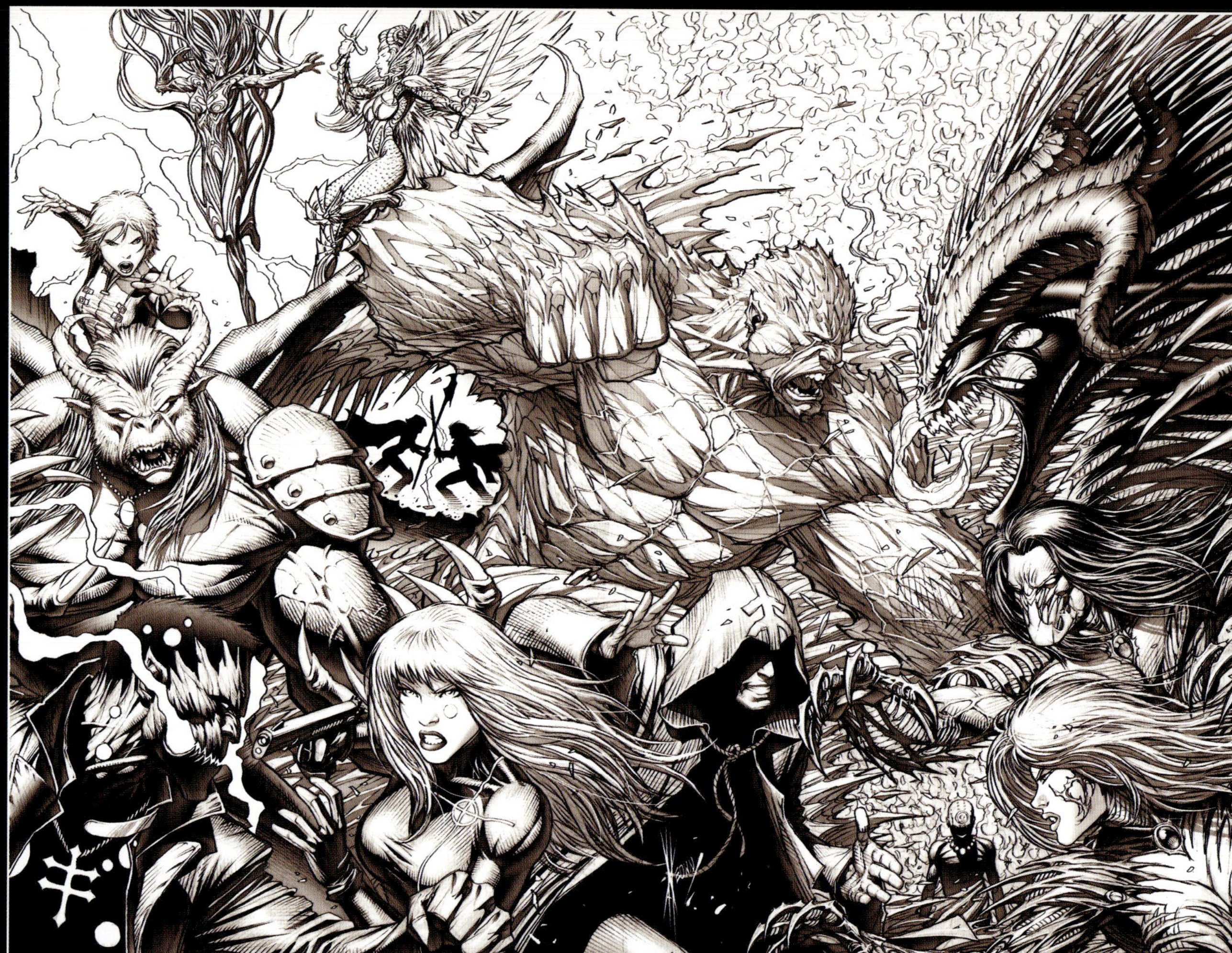

Artifacts #13 cover C (above), and cover A (below), art by: Dale Keown

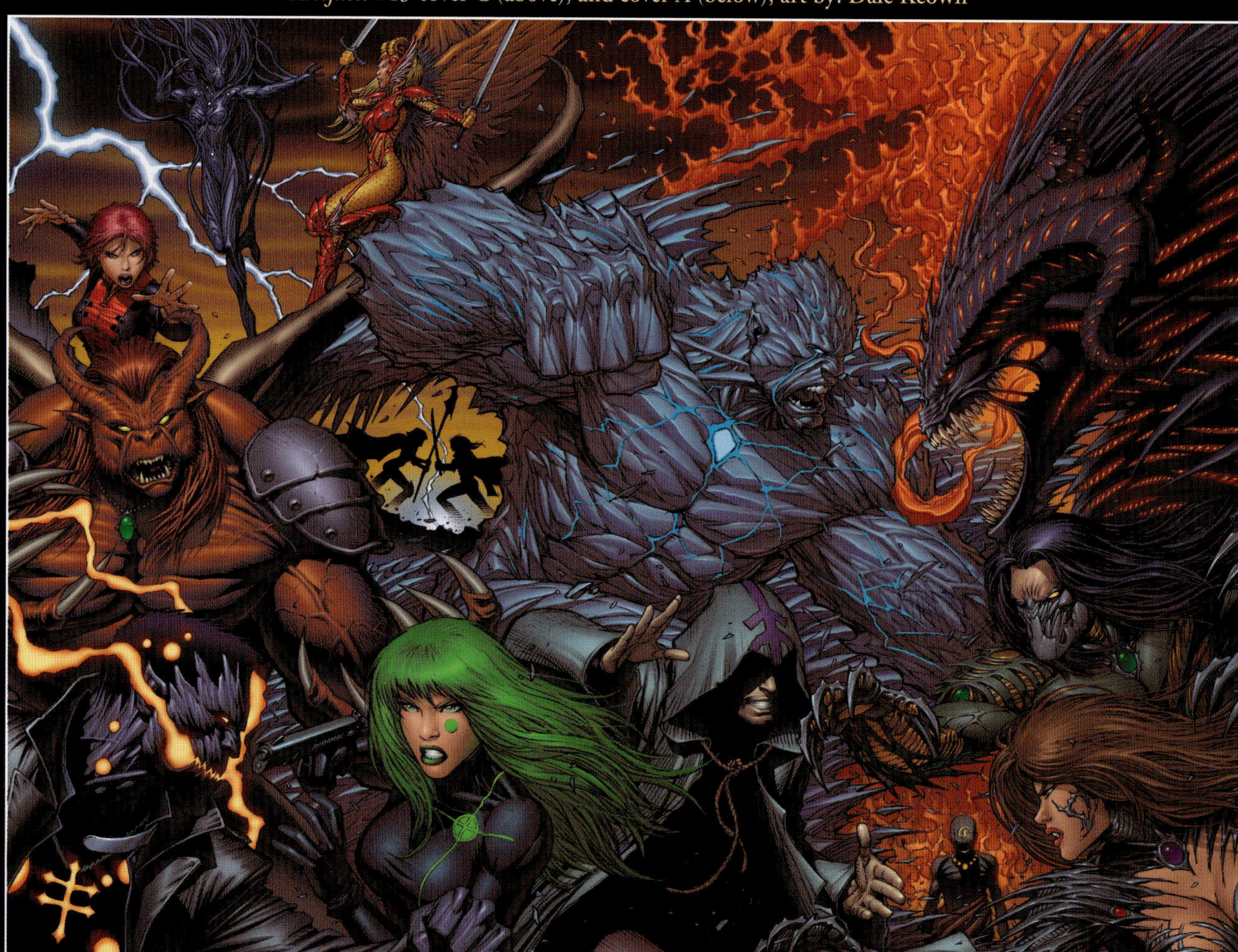

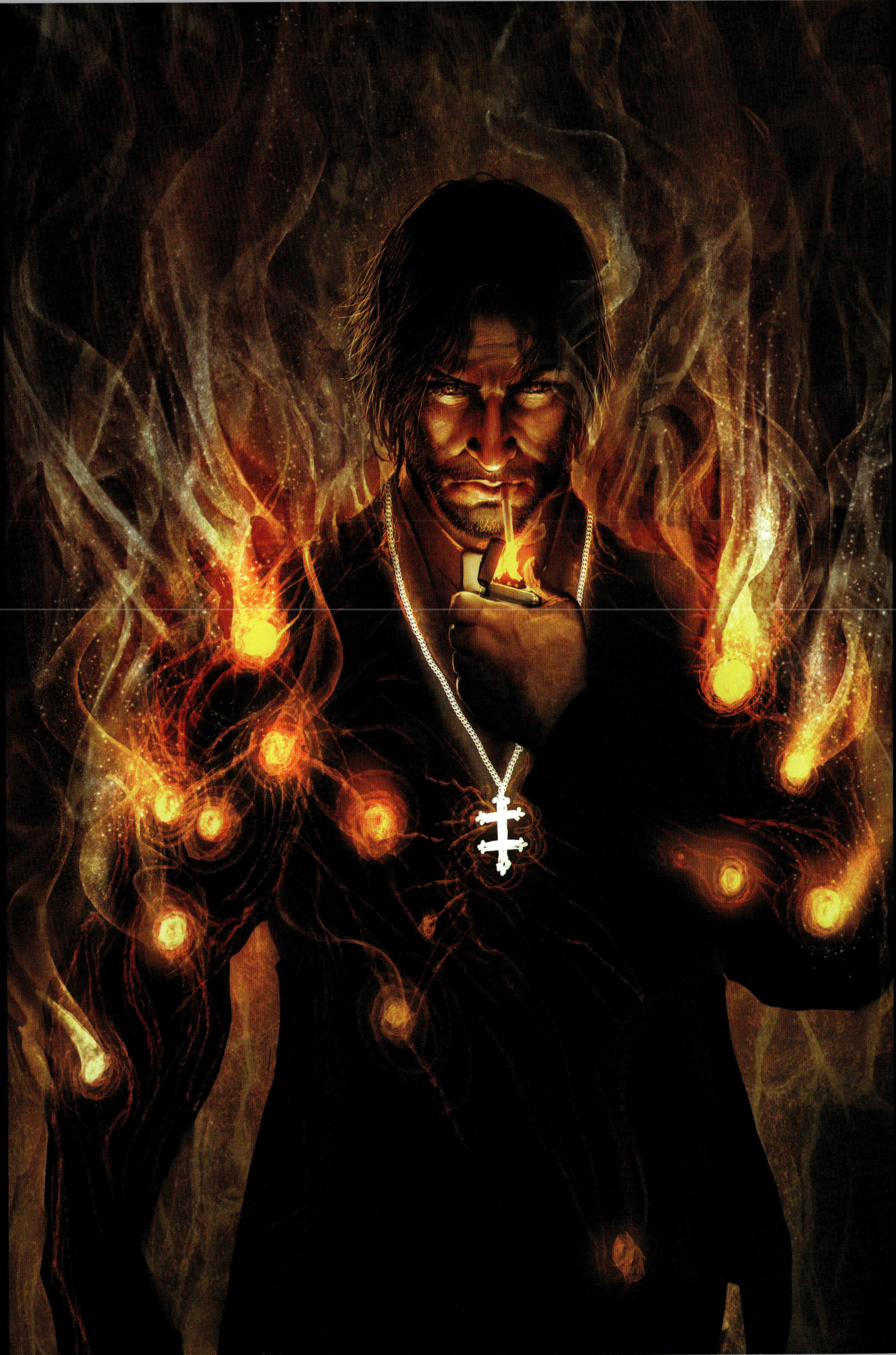

Artifacts #13 cover F, ComicsPro variant,
art by: Stjepan Sejic

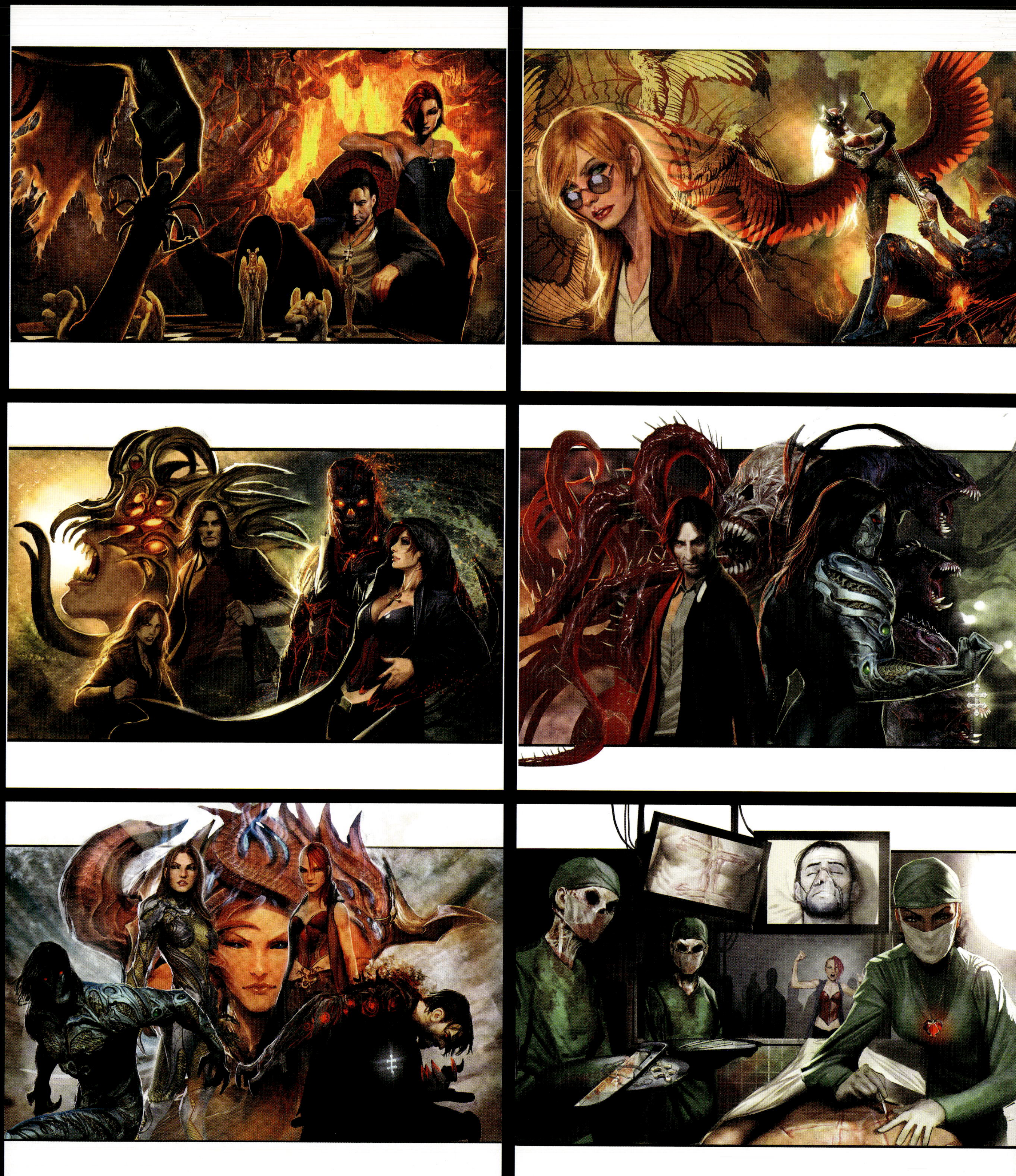

Artifacts #14-19 cover A's, art by: Stjepan Sejic

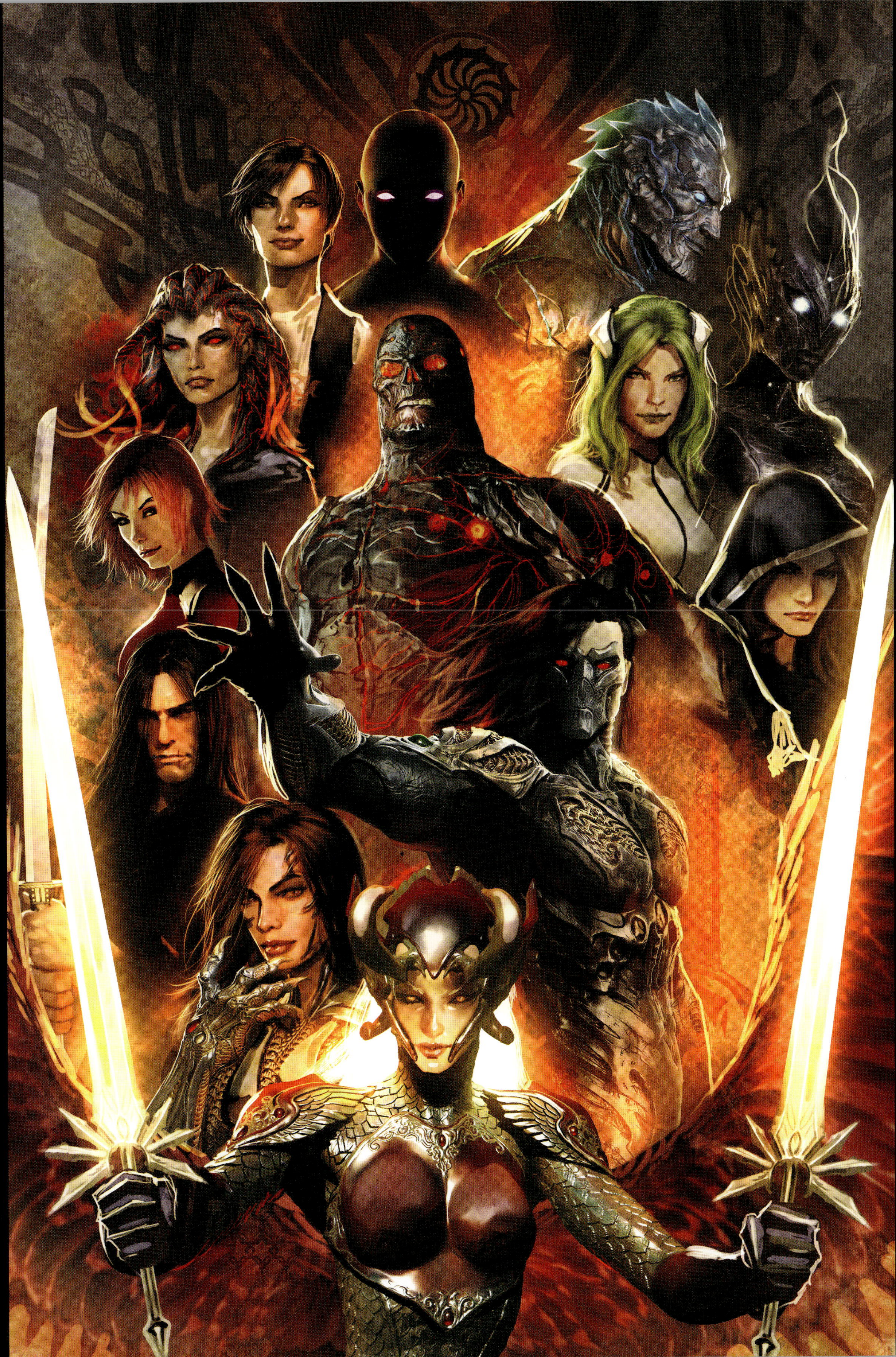

Artifacts #14 cover B,
art by: Stjepan Sejic

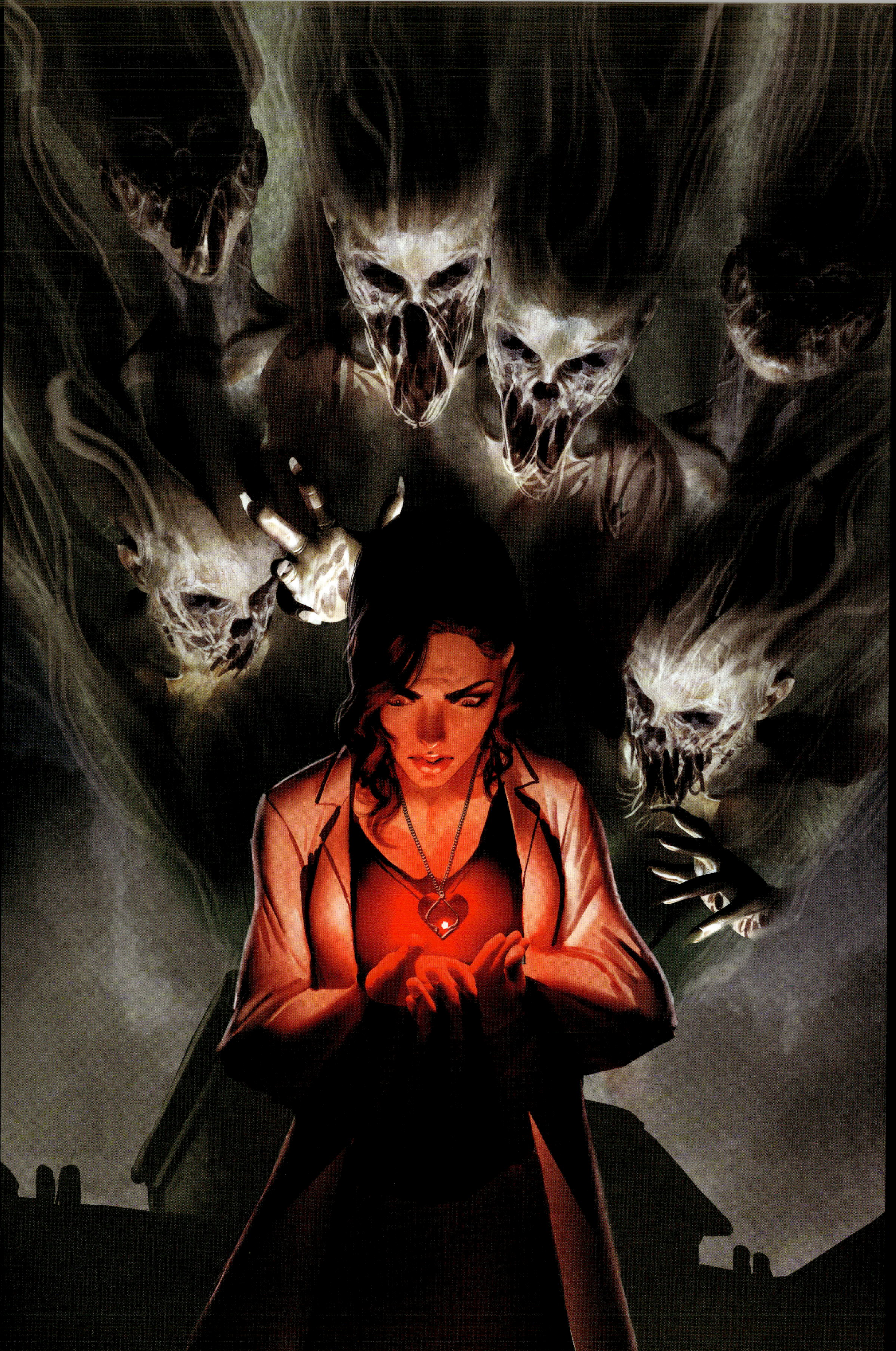

Artifacts #20 cover A,
art by: Stjepan Sejic

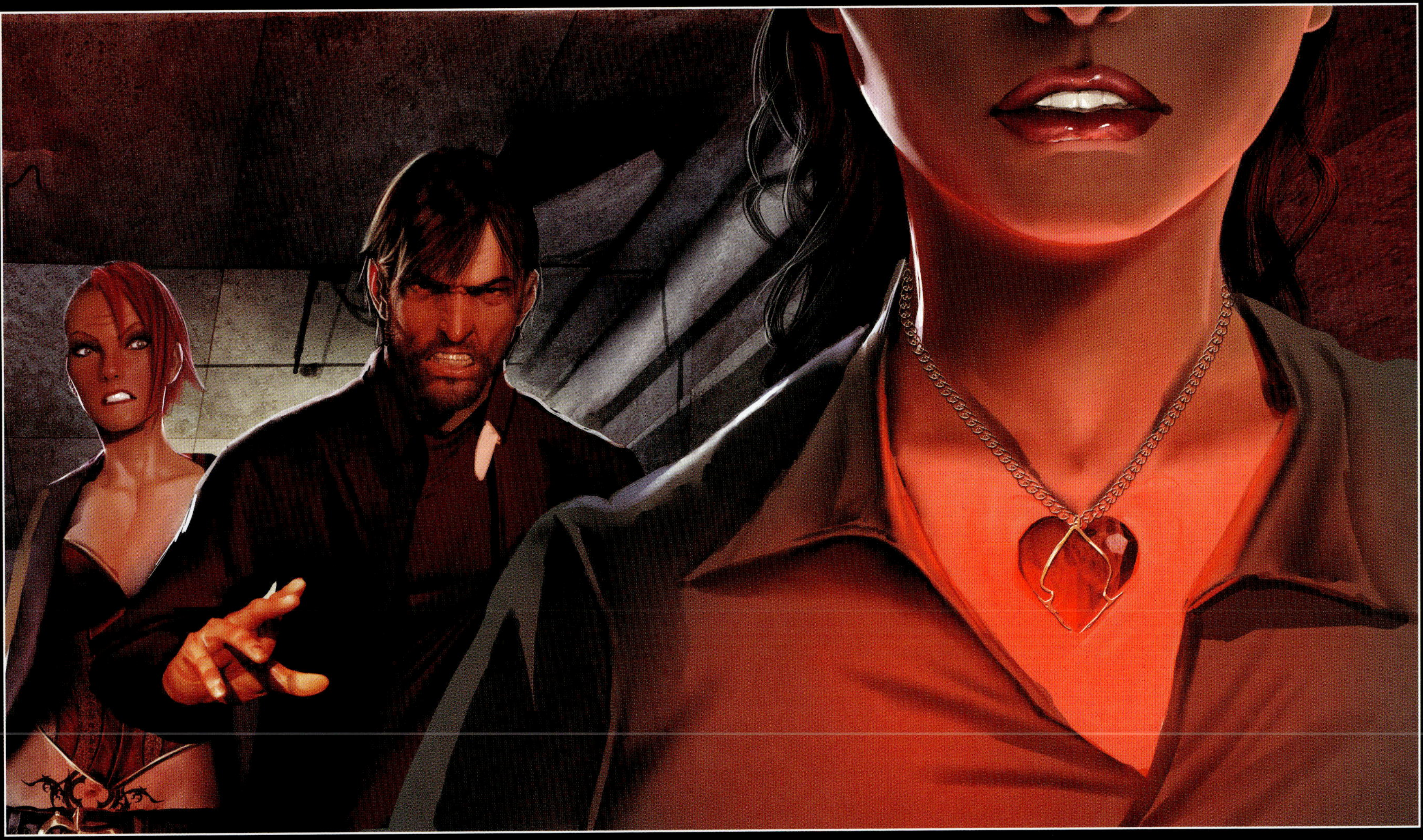

Artifacts #21 cover A, art by: Stjepan Sejic

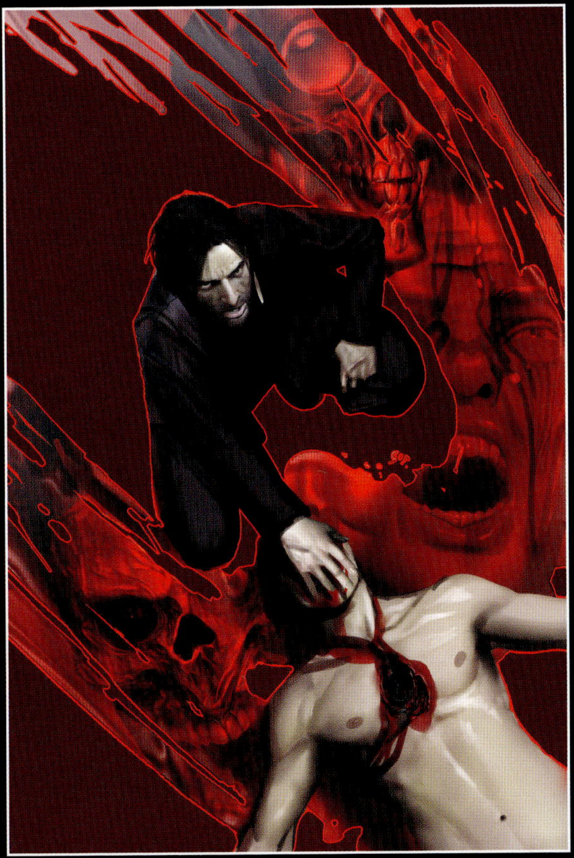

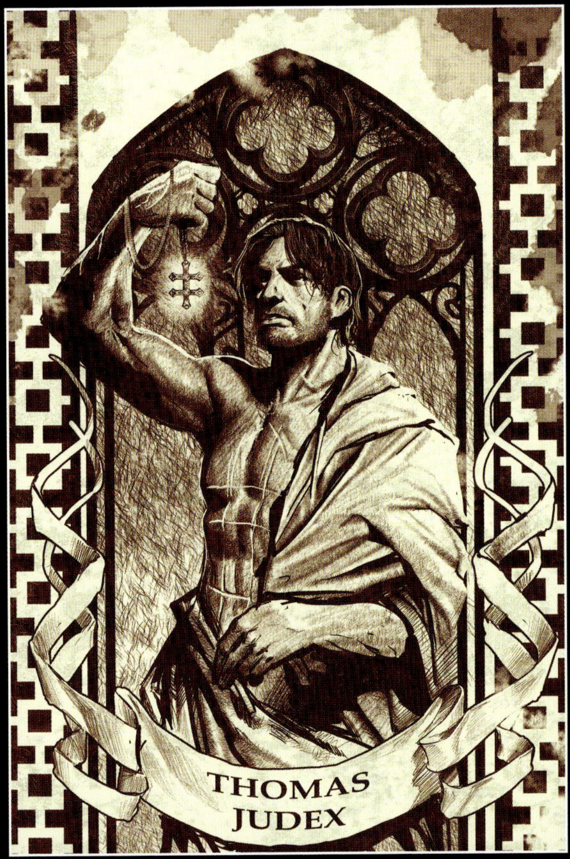

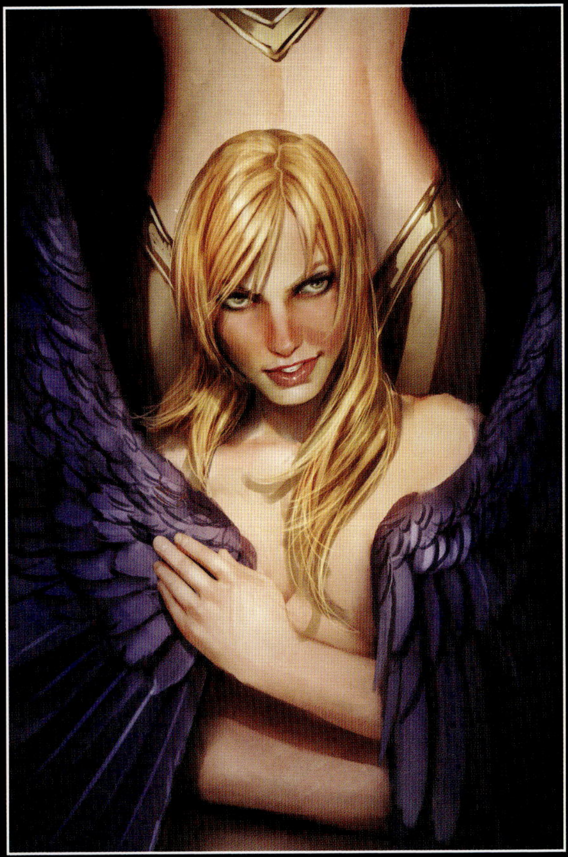

Artifacts #22-24 cover A's, art by: Stjepan Sejic

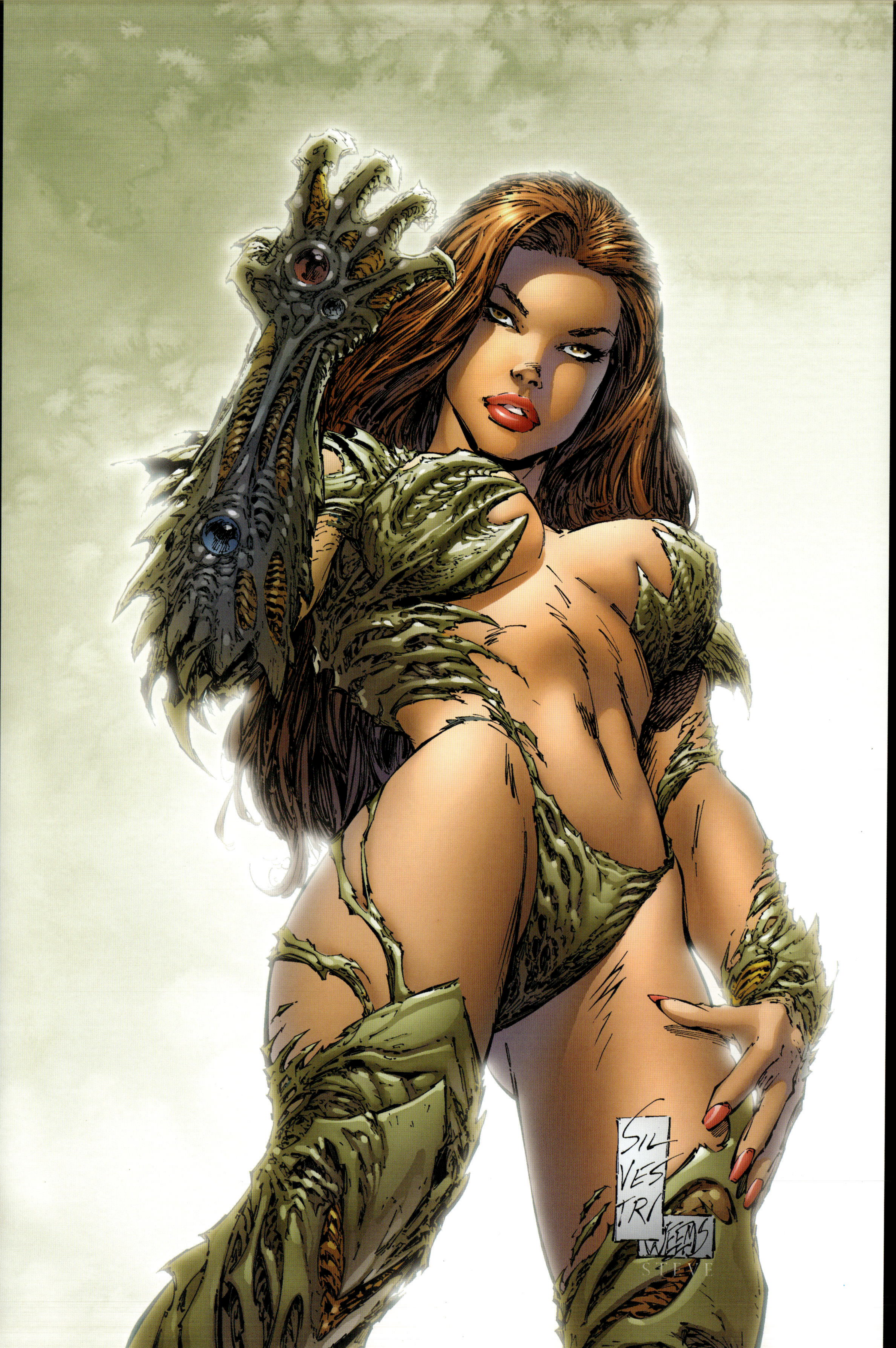

Artifacts #25 cover A,
art by: Marc Silvestri, Joe Weems V, and Steve Firchow

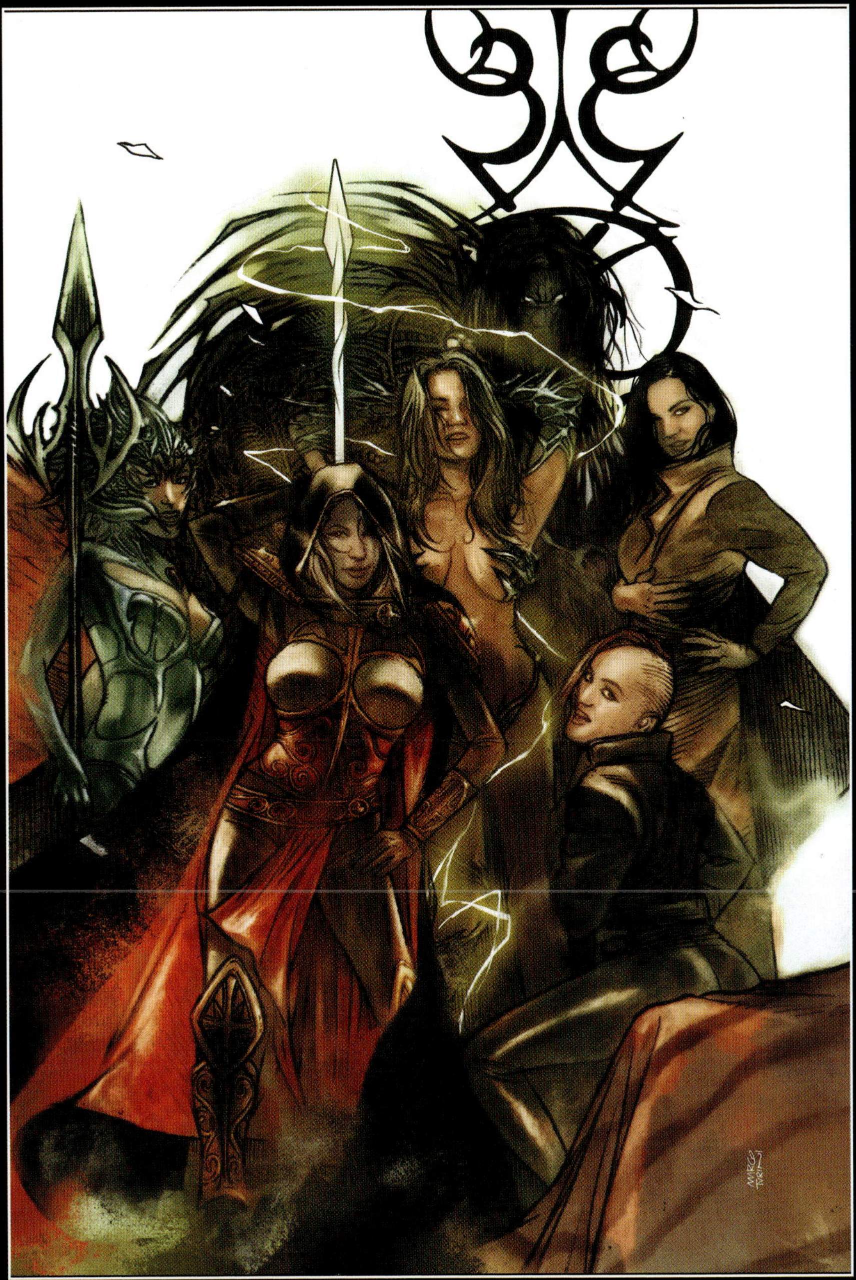

Artifacts #25 London Super Comic Con variant, art by: Marco Turini

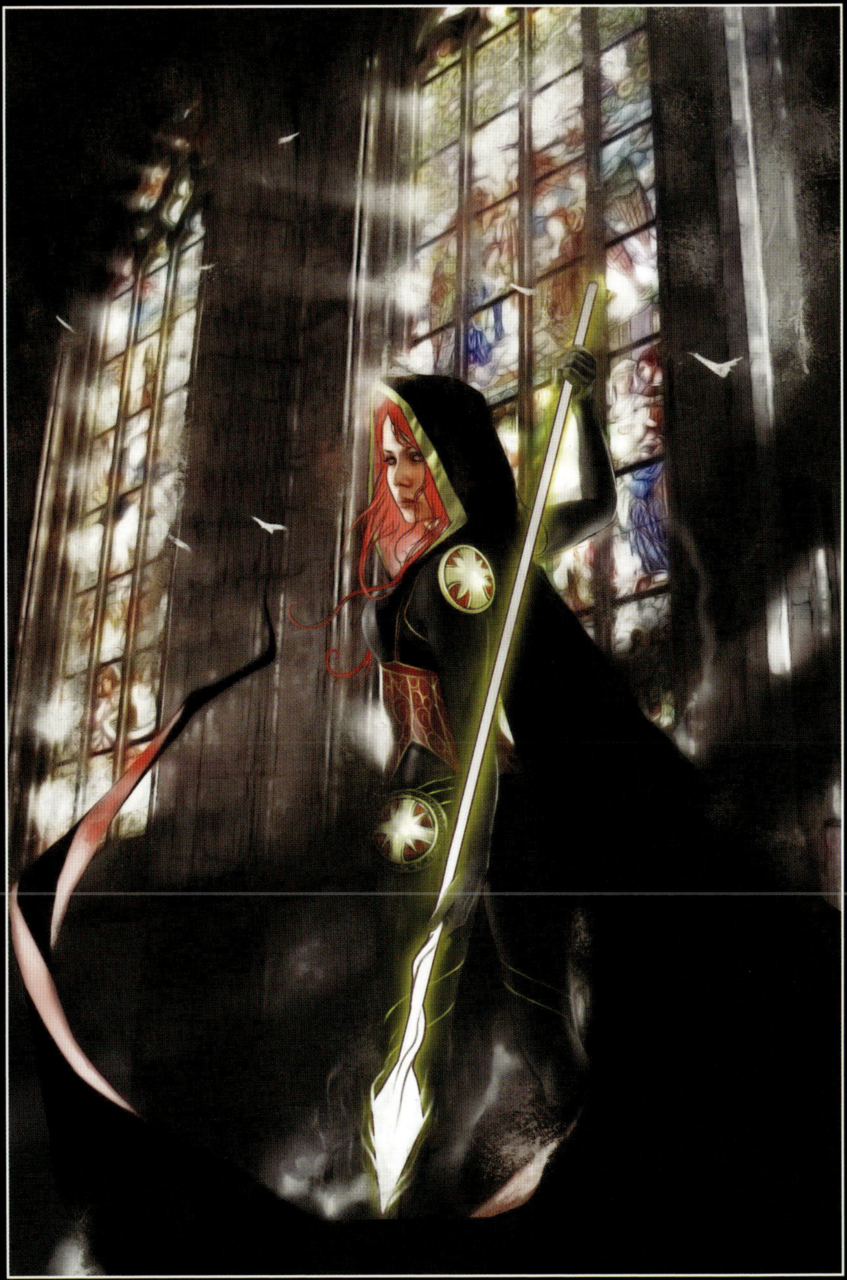

Artifacts #27 cover B, art by: Marco Turini

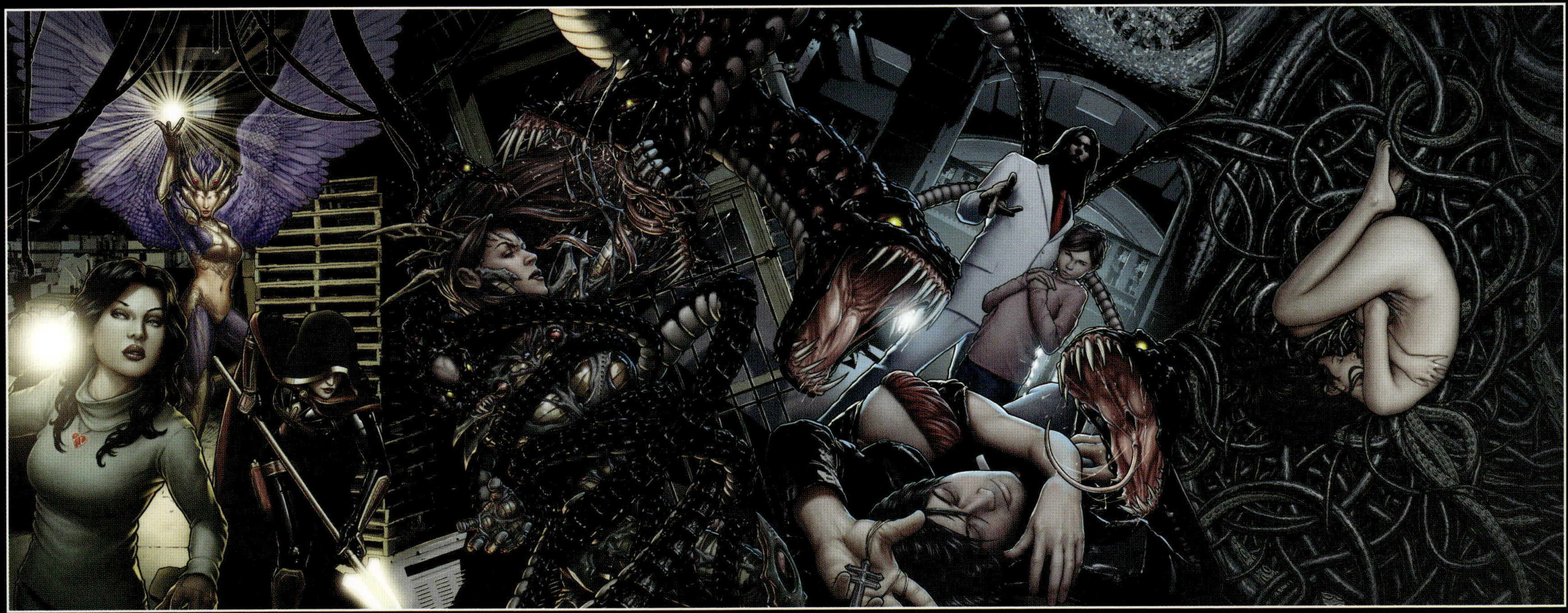

Artifacts #25 cover B, *Witchblade* #164 [1995] cover A, *The Darkness* #111 cover, and *Artifacts* #26 cover, *"Progeny"* connected covers, art by: John Tyler Christopher

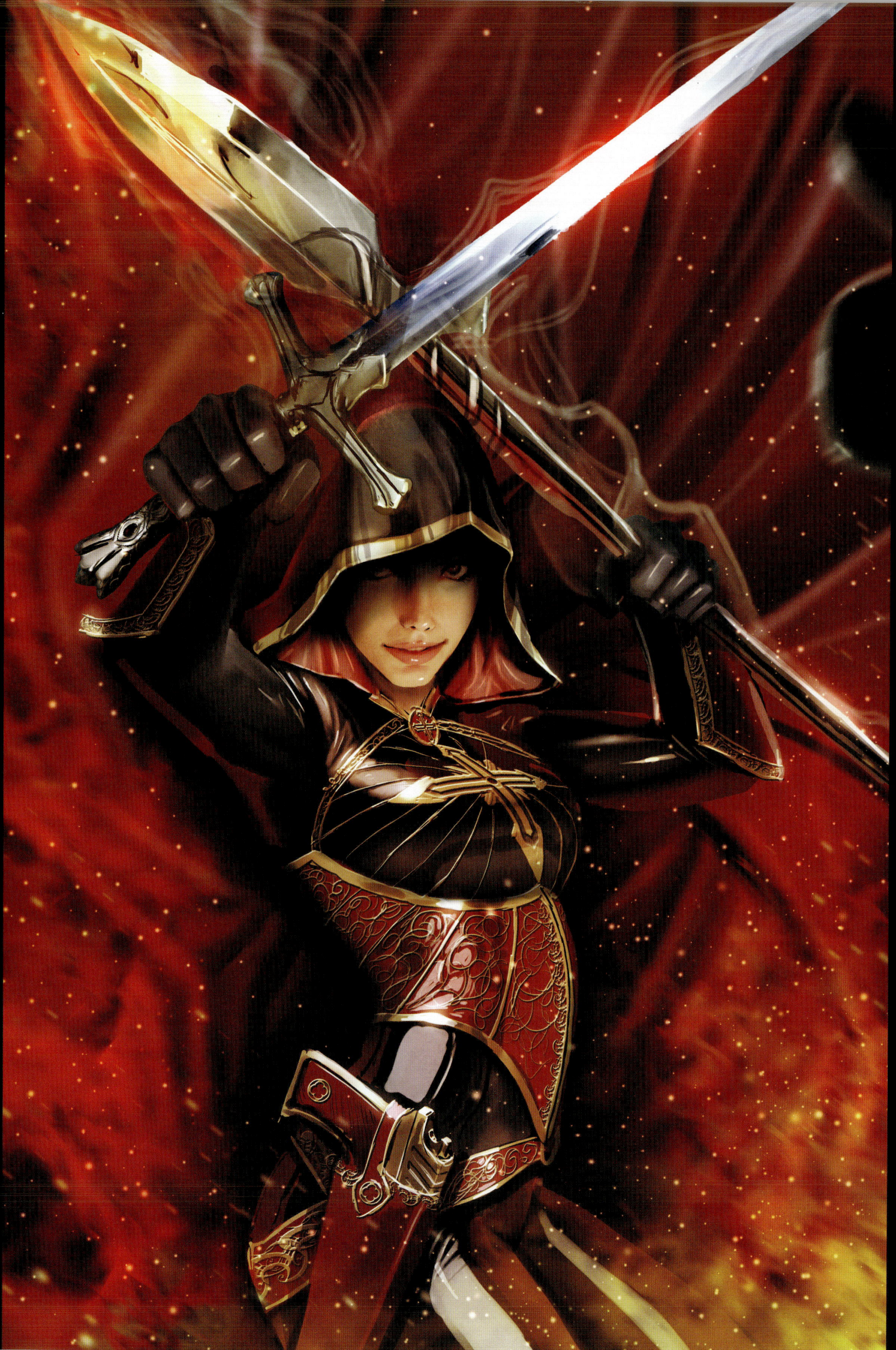

Artifacts #27 cover A,
art by: Stjepan Sejic

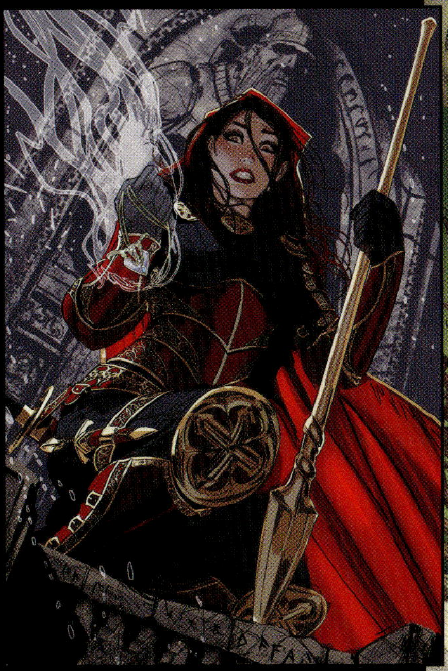

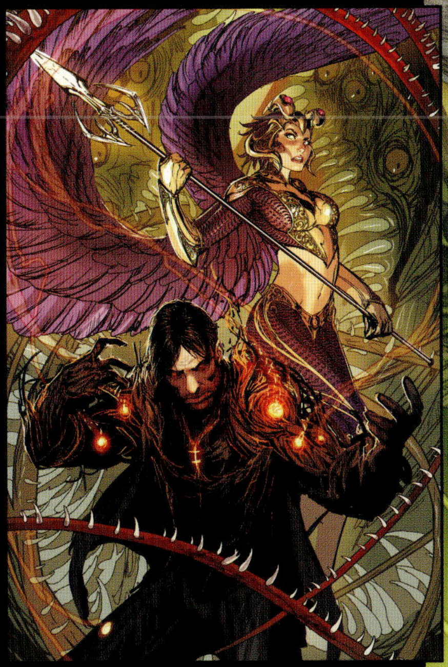

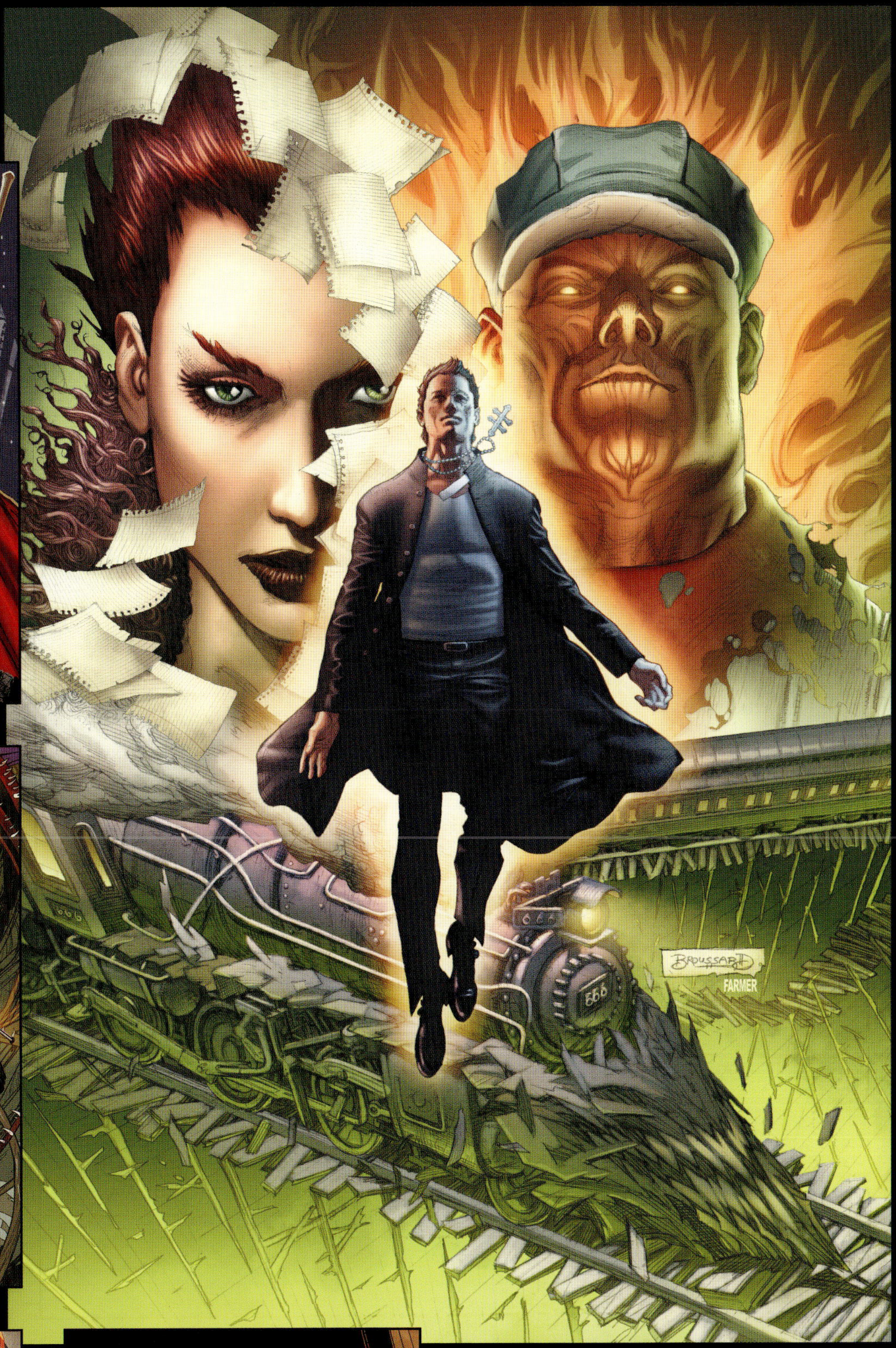

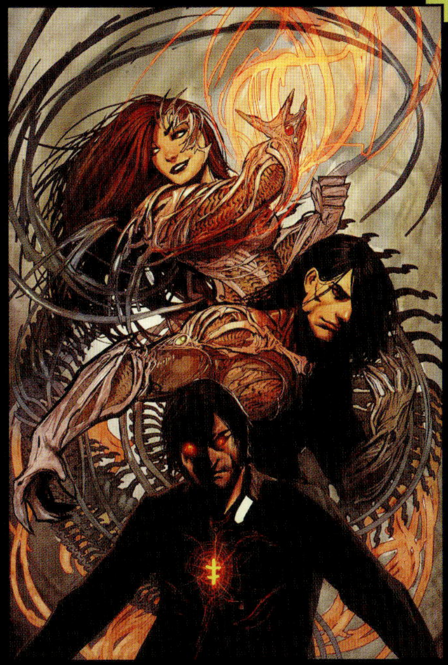

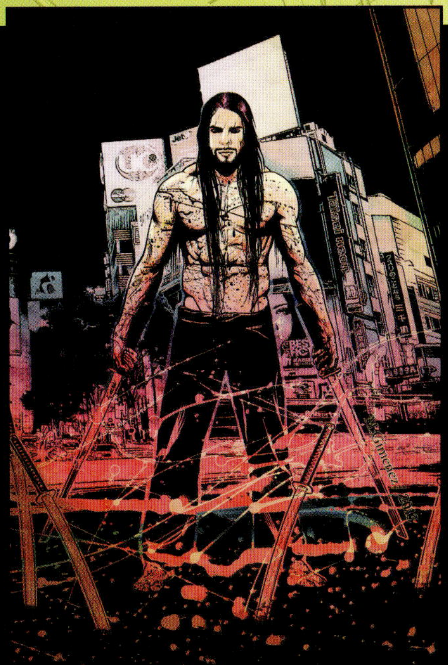

This page, counterclockwise from above.

Artifacts #29 cover,
art by: Michael Broussard and Bill Farmer

Artifacts #28 cover,
art by: Stjepan Sejic

Artifacts #30 cover,
art by: Stjepan Sejic

Artifacts #31 cover,
art by: Stjepan Sejic

Artifacts #34 cover,
art by: Martin Gimenez

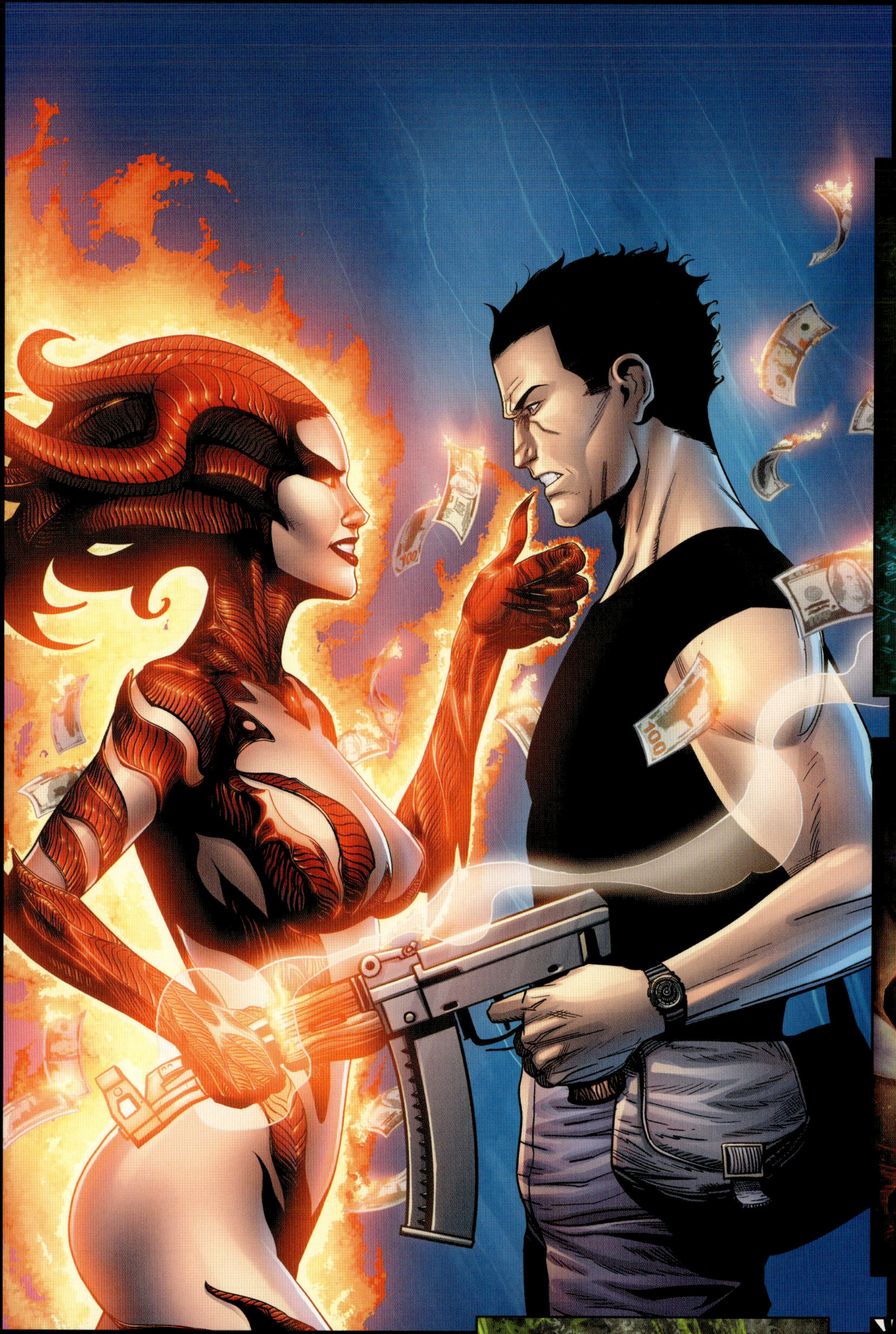

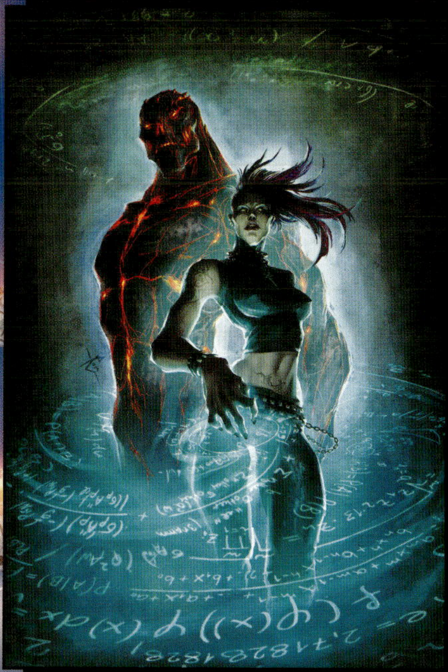

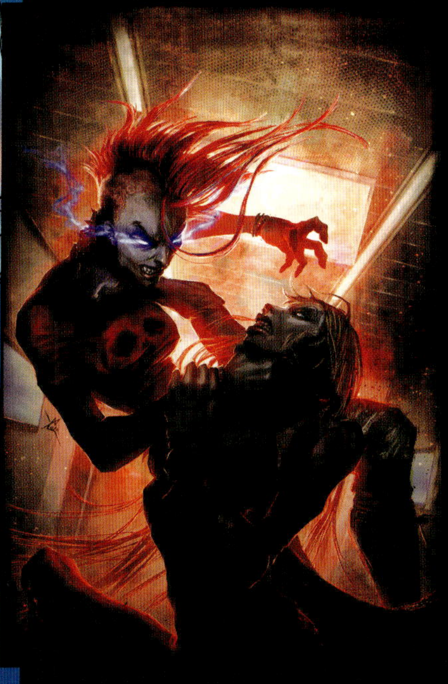

This page, clockwise from above.

Artifacts #35 cover,
art by: Nelson Blake II and Bill Farmer

Artifacts #36 cover,
art by: -ROM- Darkness.et.Folly

Artifacts #37 cover,
art by: -ROM- Darkness.et.Folly

Artifacts #38 cover,
art by: Stjepan Sejic

Artifacts #39 cover,
art by: Stjepan Sejic

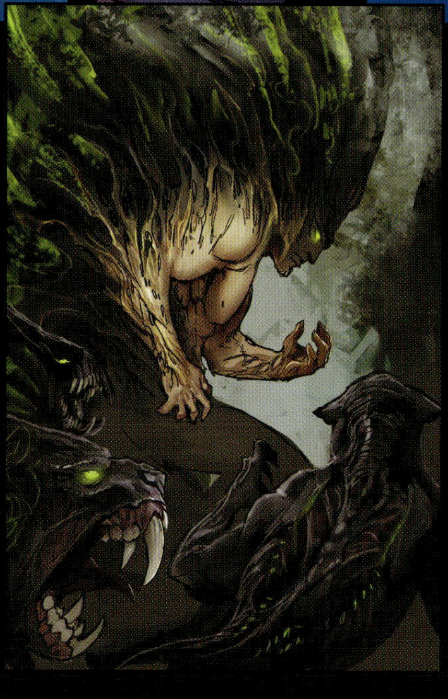

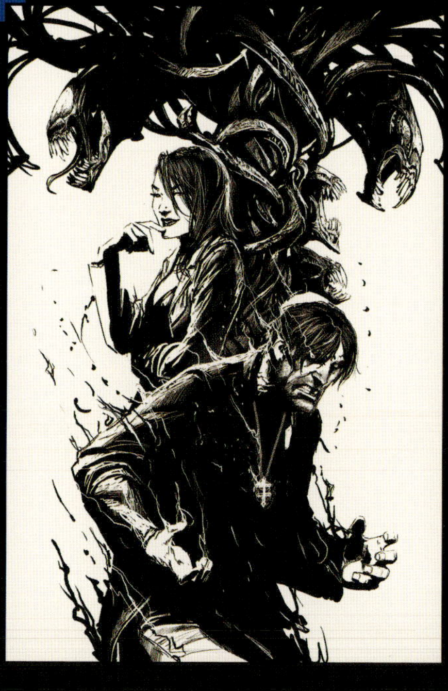

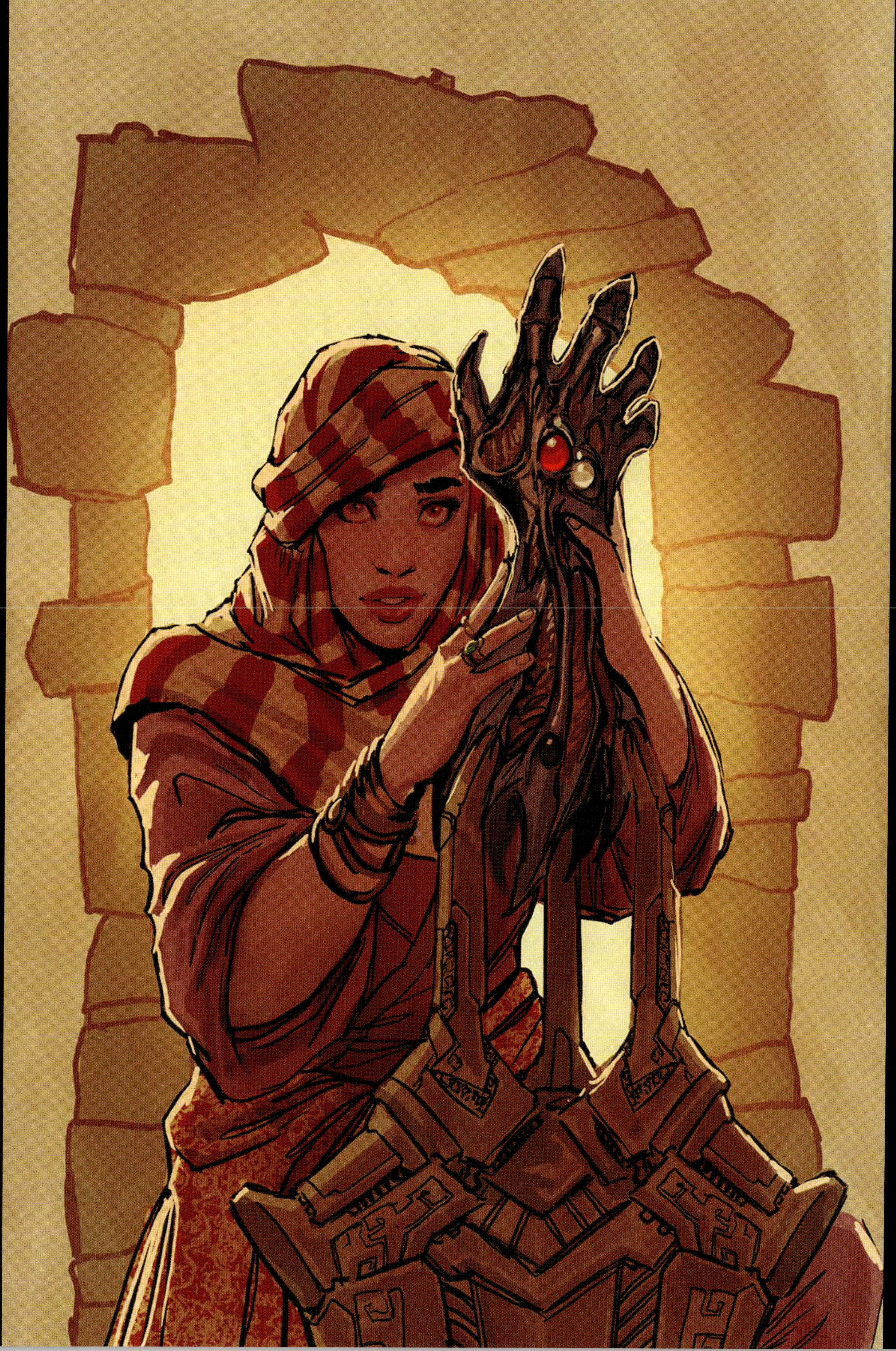

Artifacts #40 cover,
art by: Stjepan Sejic

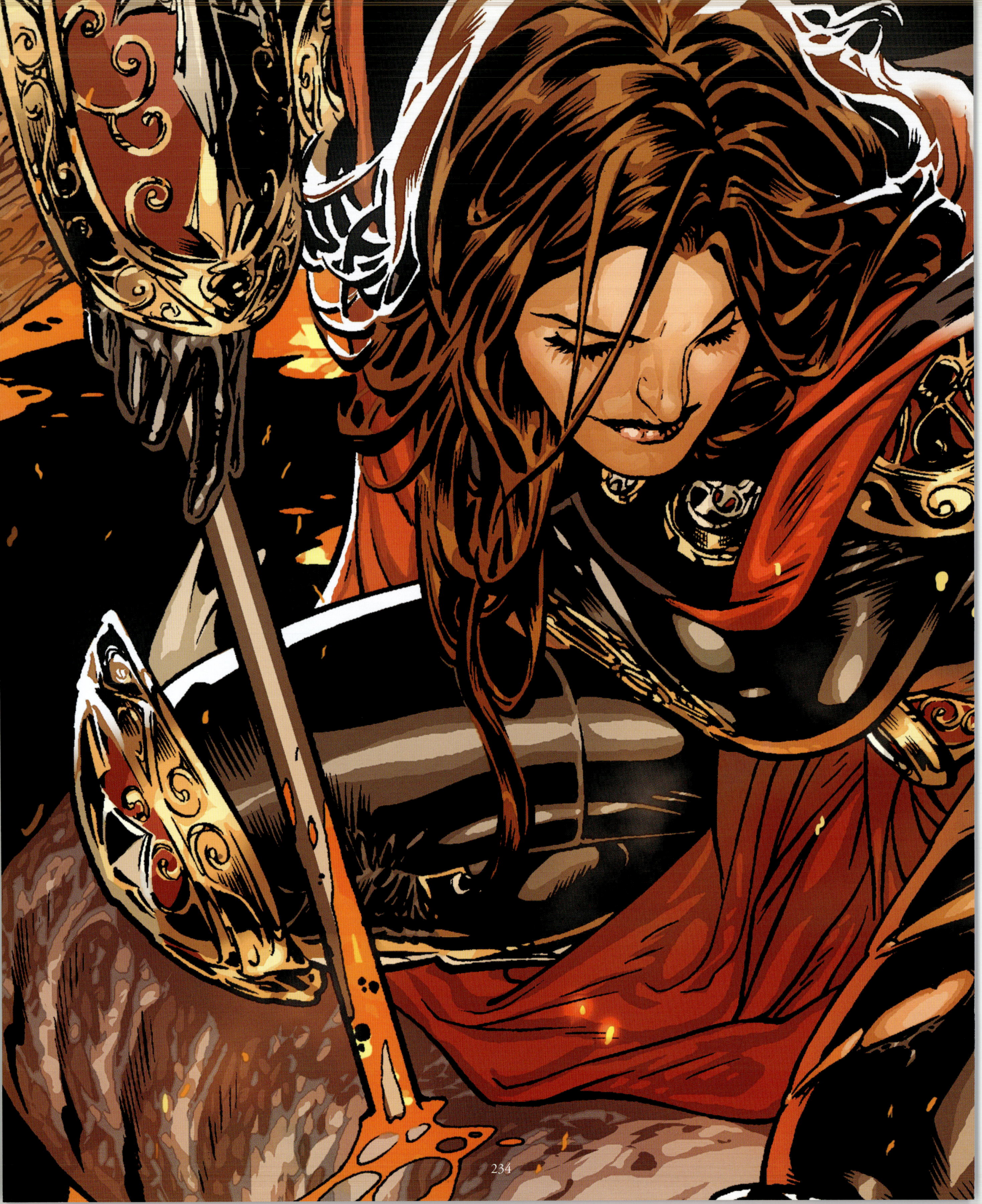

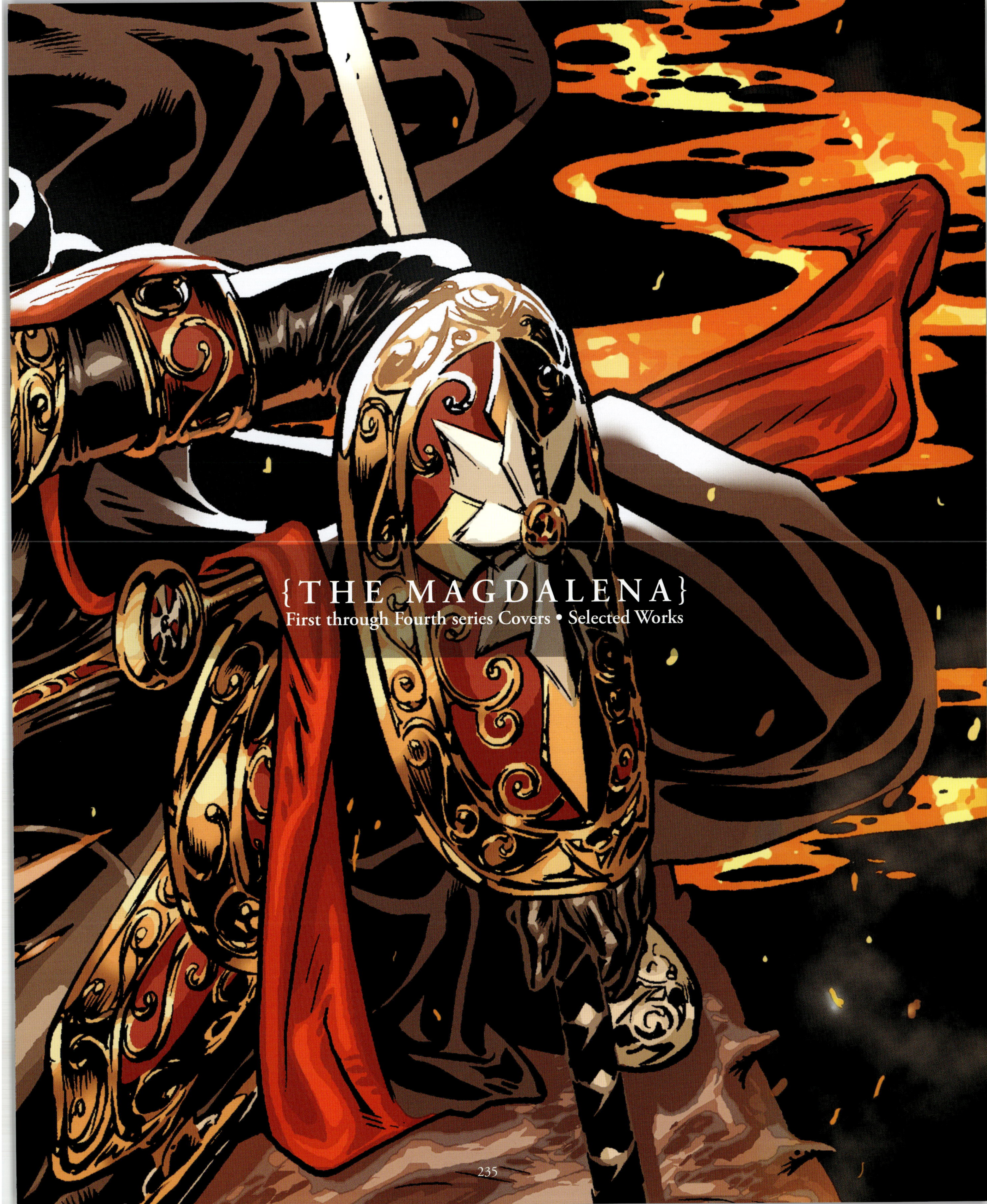

{THE MAGDALENA}

First through Fourth series Covers • Selected Works

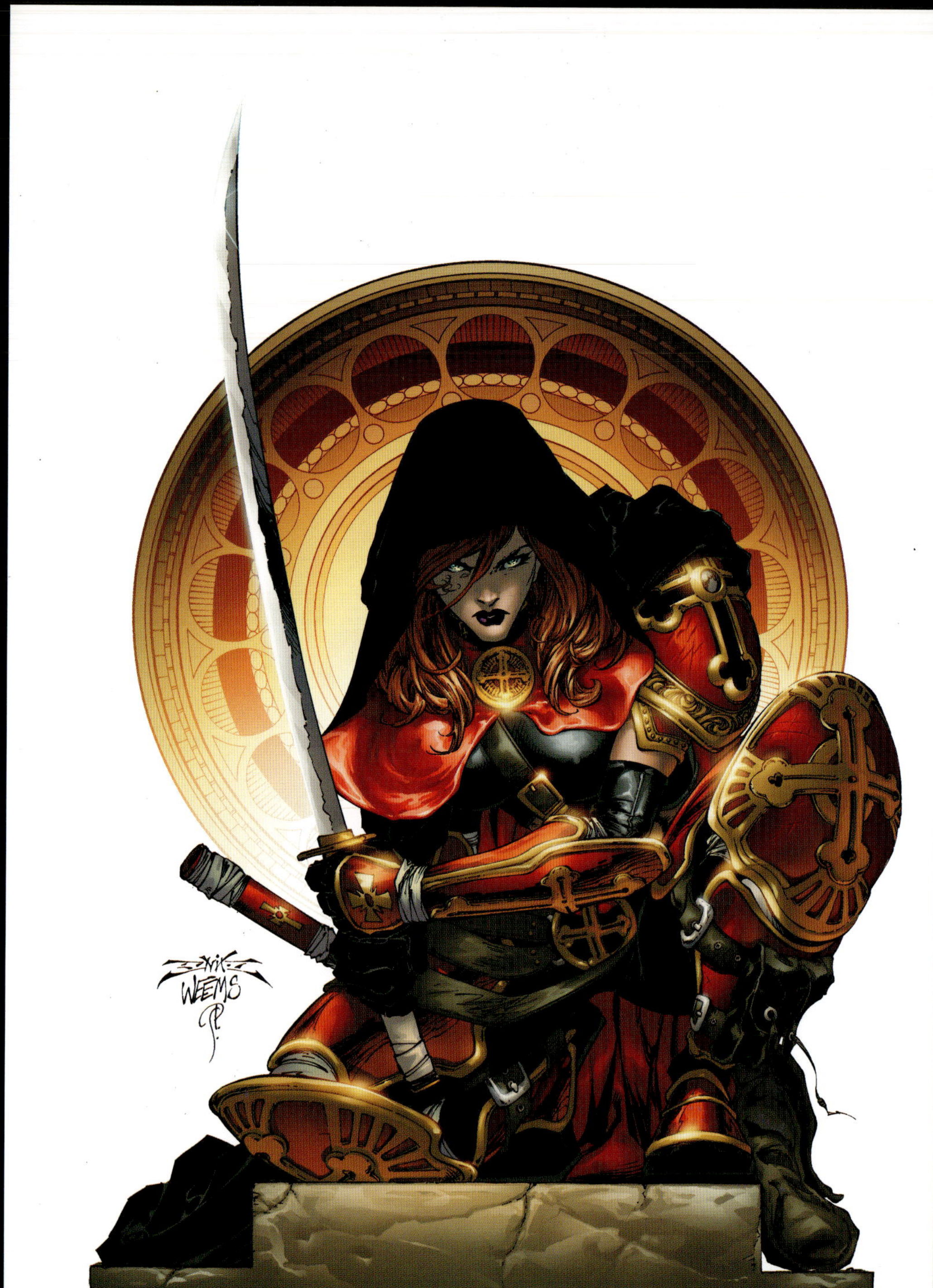

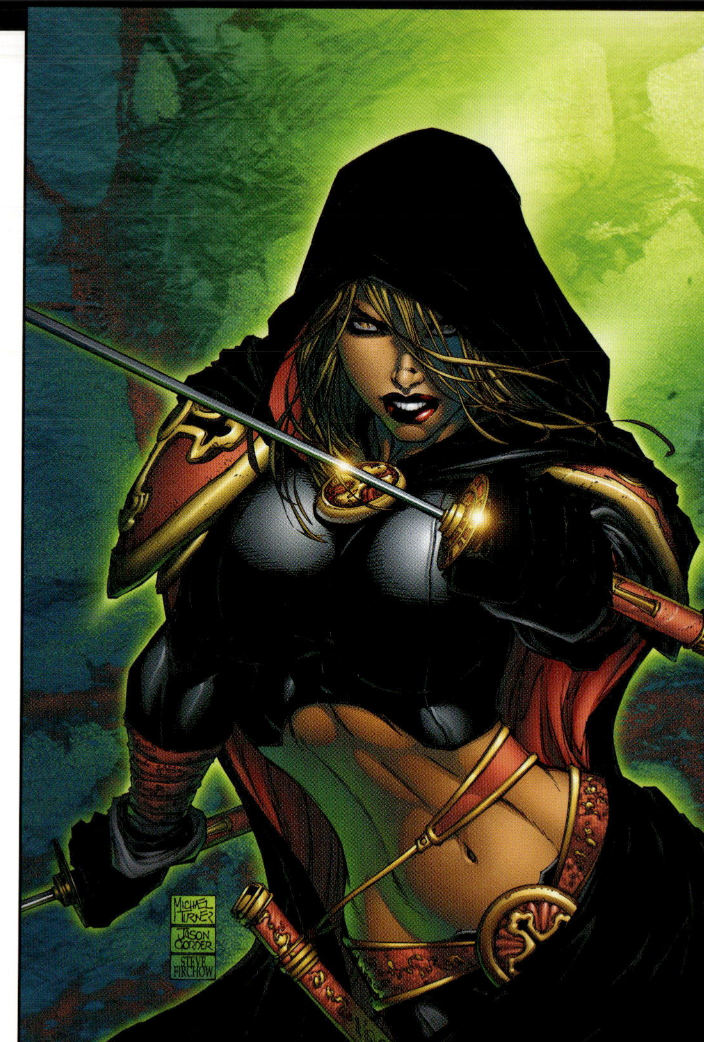

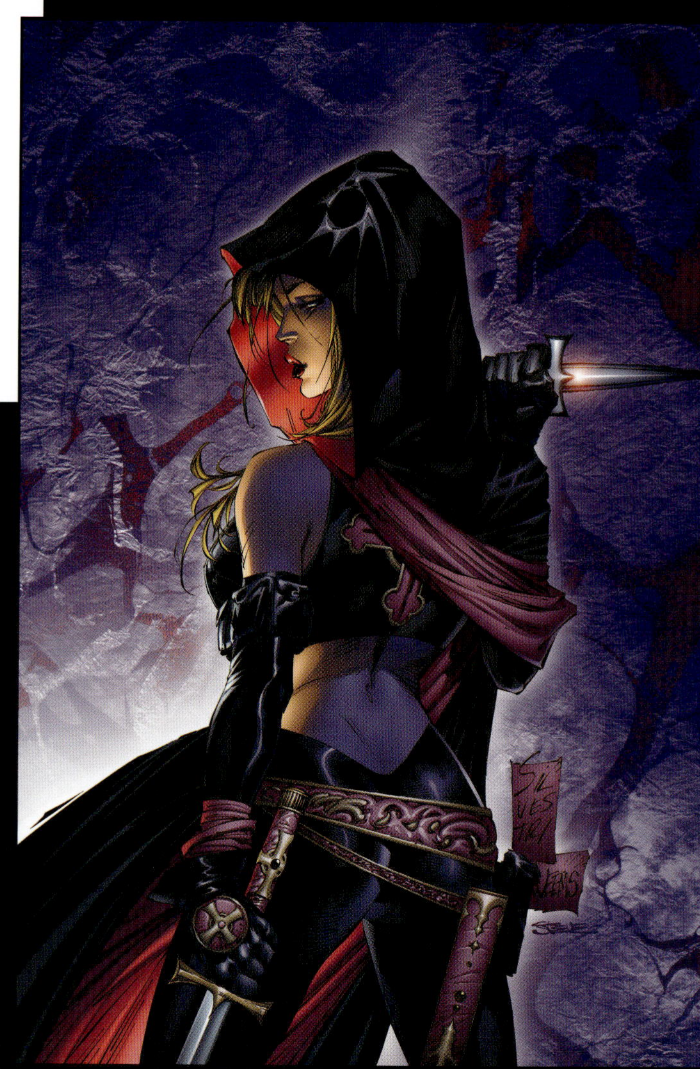

The Magdalena

The Magdalena was first released in April 2000 and spawned three series spanning up to June 2017 as well as appearances throughout the Top Cow Universe.

If this is your first time hearing about *The Magdalena,* in a nutshell: Descending from the bloodline of the King of Kings and trained within a Sacred Order of the Catholic Church, one woman is selected in each generation to serve as The Magdalena. Entrusted with the Spear of Destiny, one of the thirteen Artifacts, The Magdalena is the Church's protector and monster hunter. Her order has existed since the founding of the Catholic Church. The Magdalena is trained to be the Church's instrument of justice and, if need be, vengeance, fighting an endless silent war against the evils that would tear our world apart.

Above. *The Magdalena* #1 [2000] preview cover, art by: Joe Benitez, Joe Weems V, and Peter Steigerwald

Above right. *The Magdalena* #1 [2000] cover A, art by: Michael Turner, Jason Gorder, and Steve Firchow

At right. *The Magdalena* #1 [2000] cover B, art by: Marc Silvestri, Joe Weems V, and Steve Firchow

Previous page. *The Magdalena* #2 [2010] cover A, art by: Ryan Sook

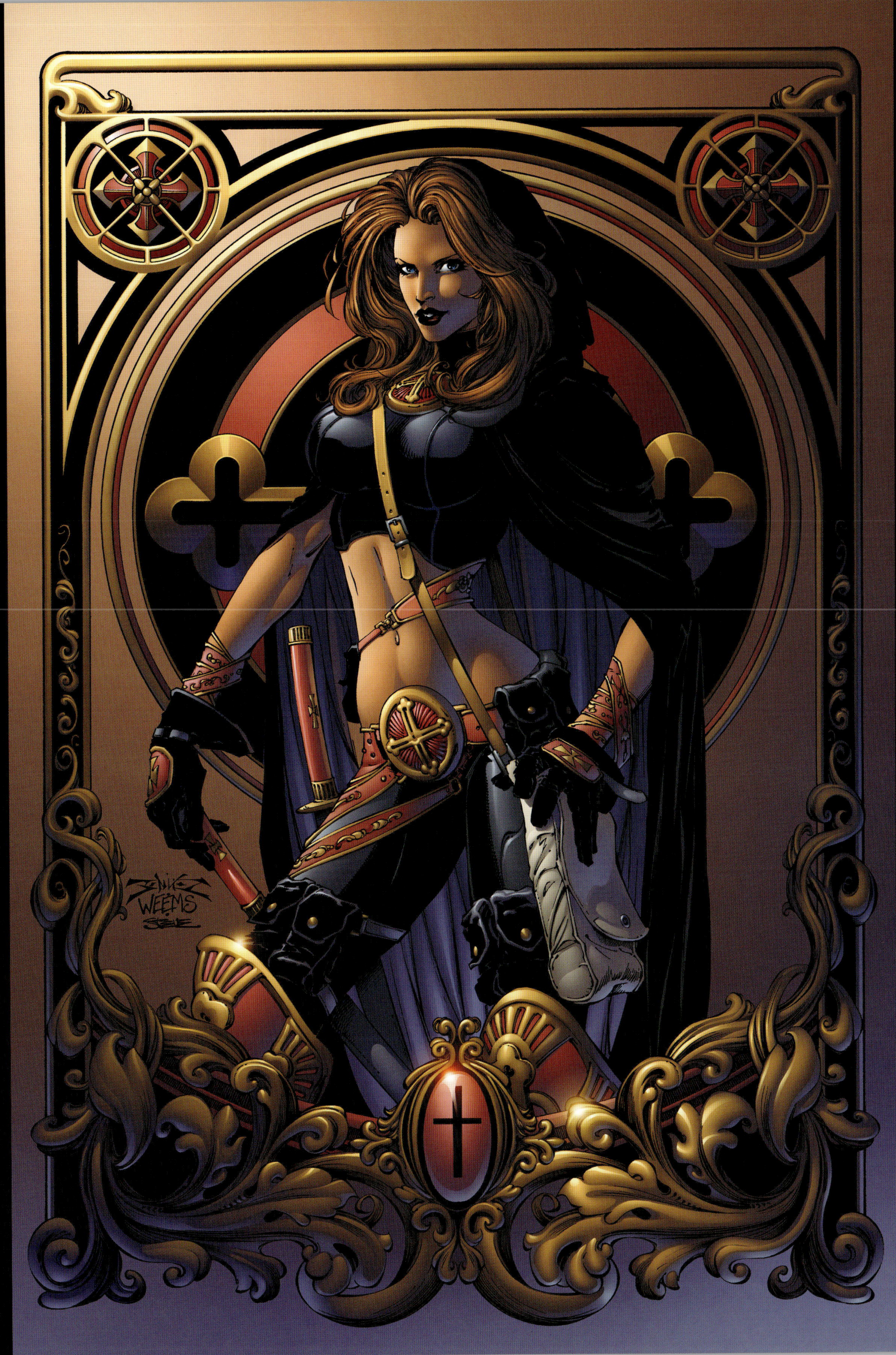

The Magdalena #1 [2000] cover C and poster art,
art by: Joe Benitez, Joe Weems V, and Steve Firchow

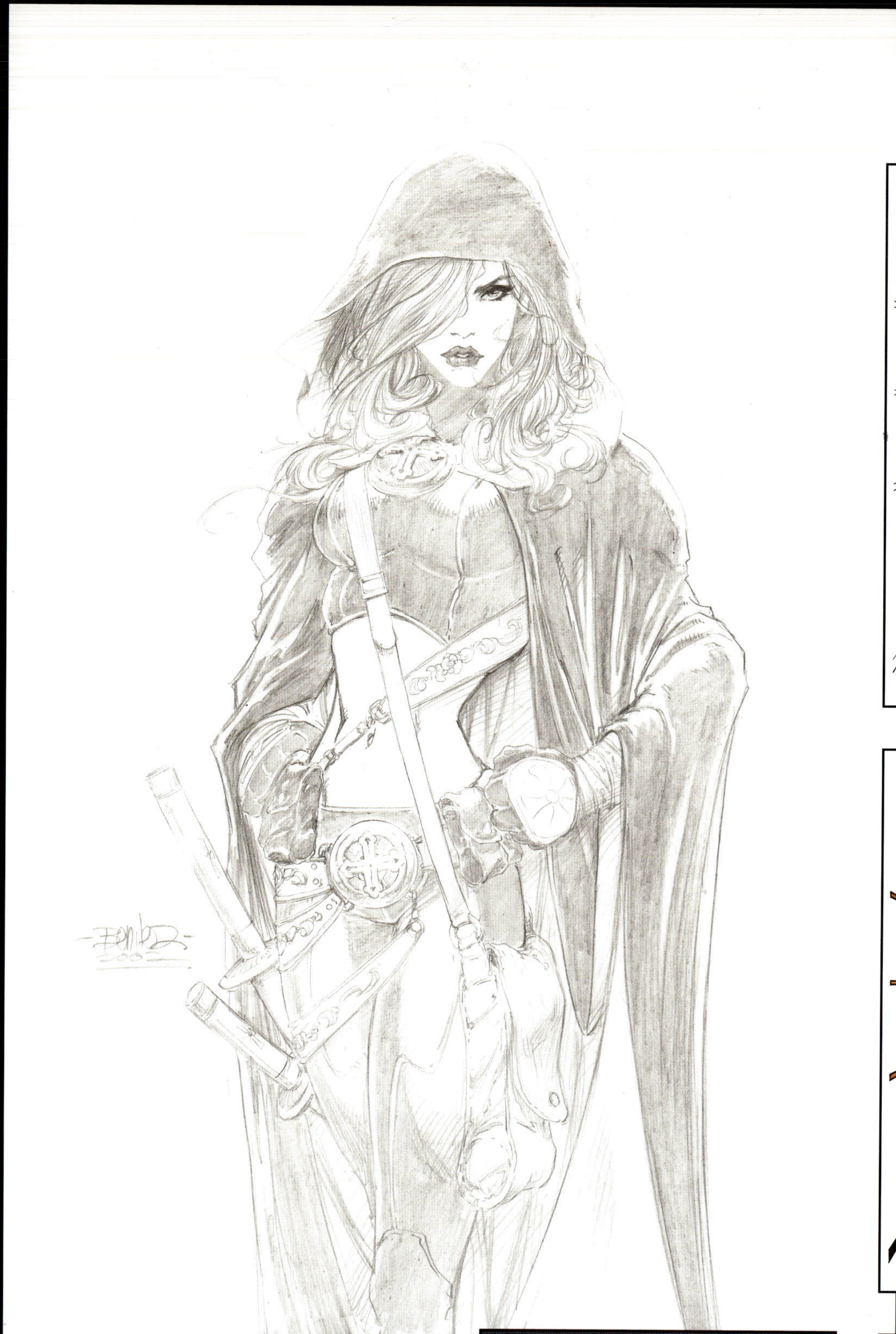

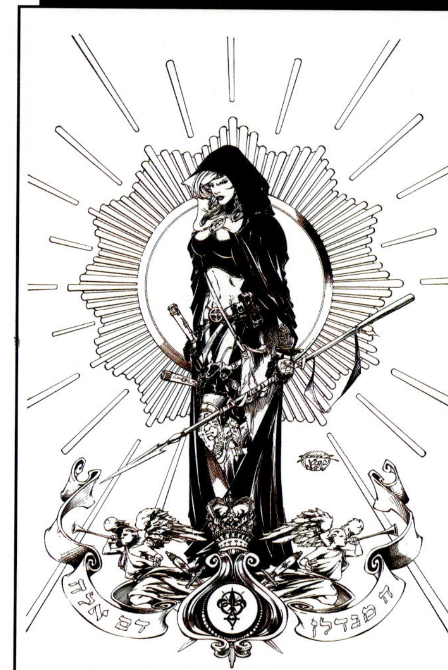

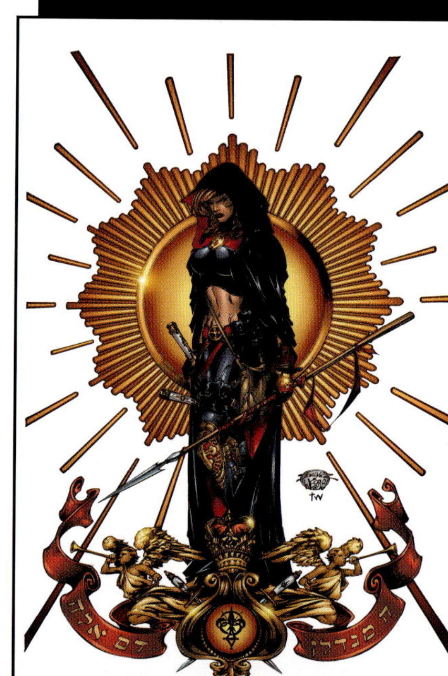

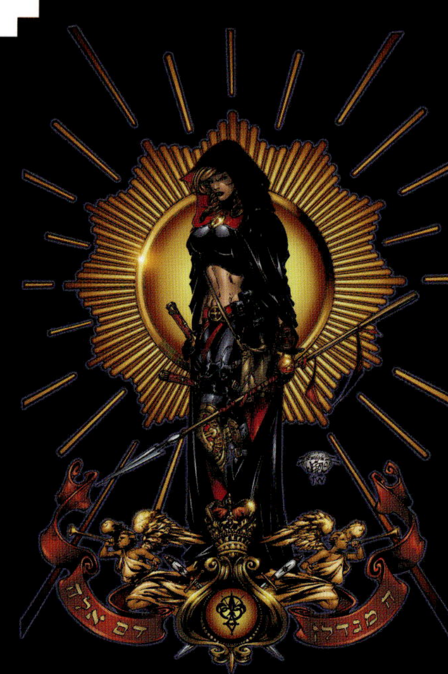

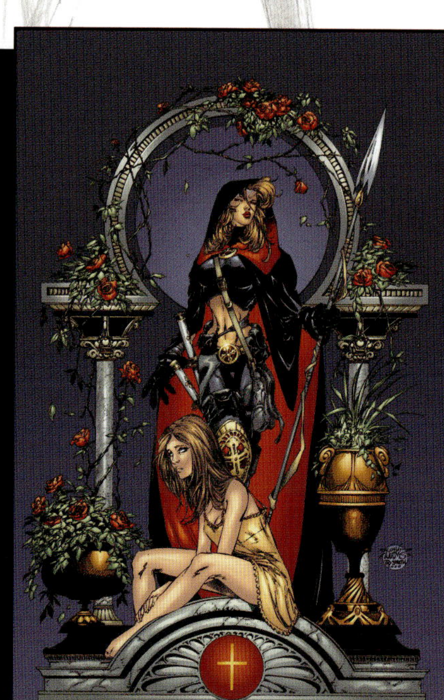

This page, clockwise from above.

The Magdalena #1 [2000]
Top Cow Classics In Black and White cover,
art by: Joe Benitez

The Magdalena #1 [2000] Fandom and Megacon covers,
line art by: Joe Benitez and Joe Weems V

The Magdalena #1 [2000] Fandom Exclusive cover,
art by: Joe Benitez, Joe Weems V, and Tyson Wengler

The Magdalena #1 [2000] Megacon Exclusive cover,
art by: Joe Benitez, Joe Weems V, and Tyson Wengler

The Magdalena #2 [2000] cover A,
art by: Joe Benitez, Joe Weems V, and Tyson Wengler

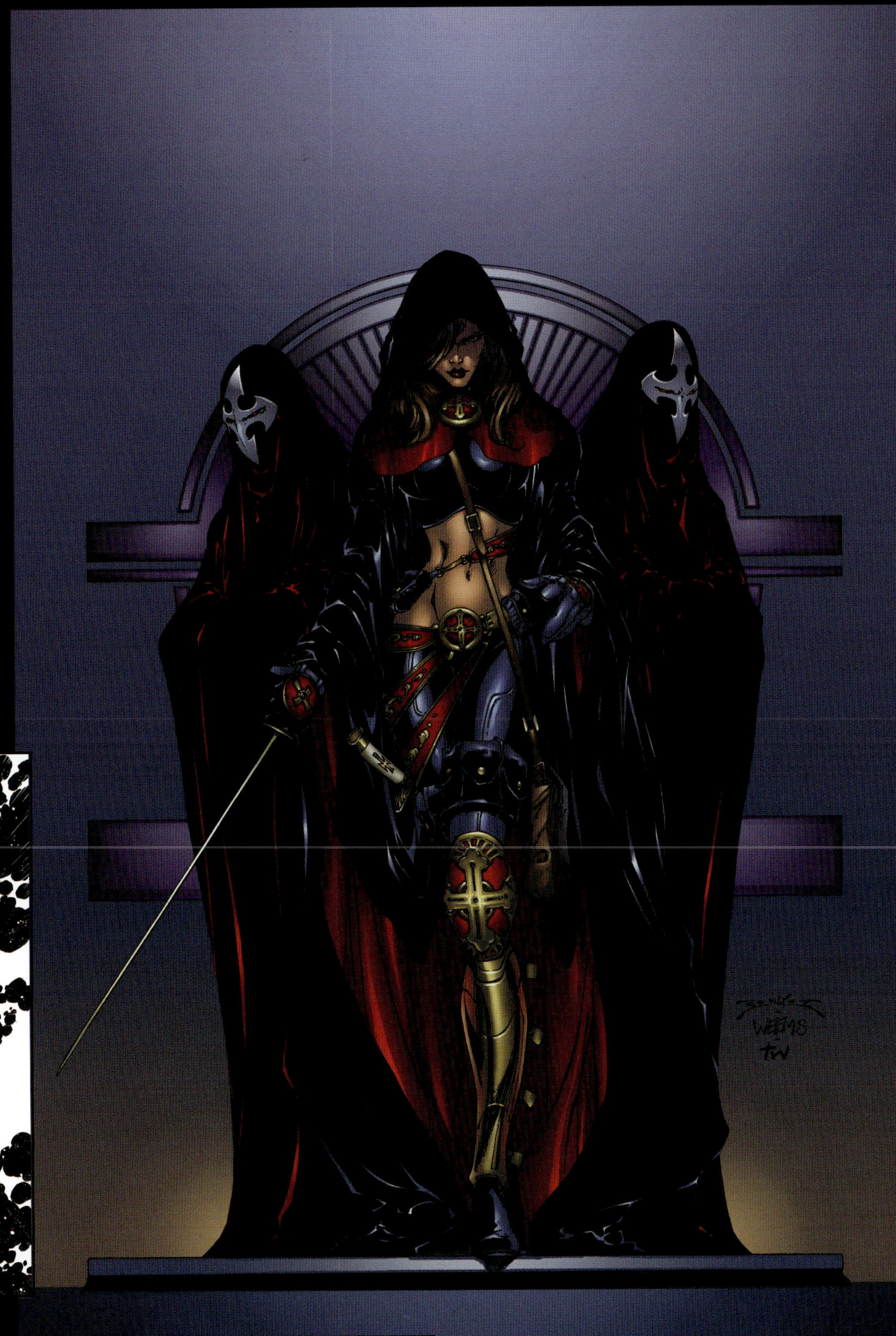

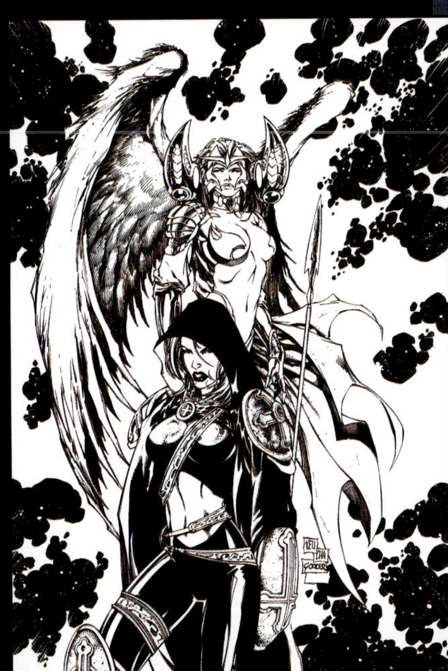

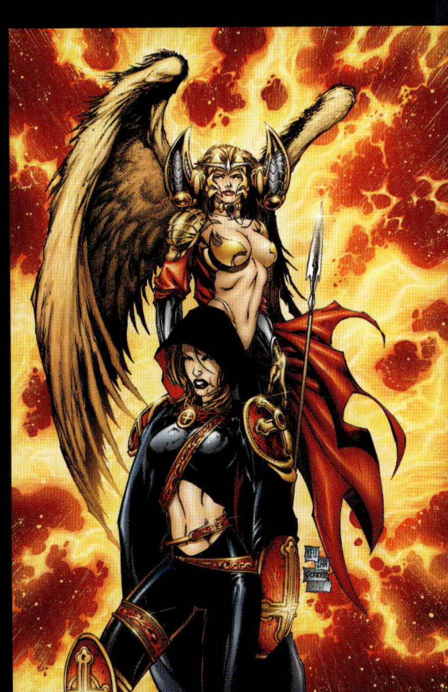

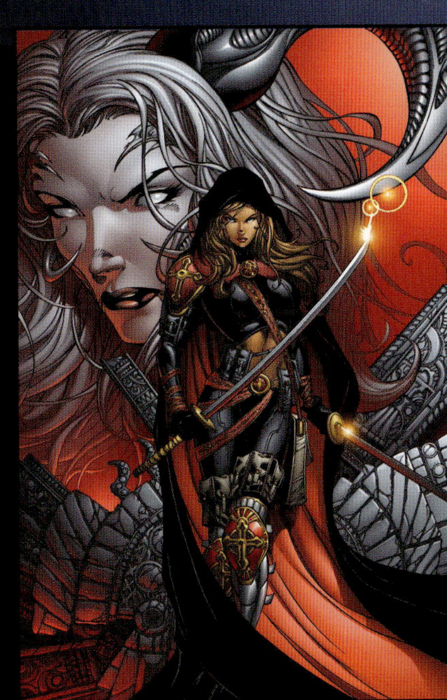

This page, counterclockwise from above.

The Magdalena #3 [2000] cover A,
art by: Joe Benitez, Joe Weems V, and Tyson Wengler

The Magdalena/Angelus #1/2 [2010] Wizard cover,
line art by: Keu Cha and Jason Gorder

The Magdalena/Angelus #1/2 [2010] Wizard cover,
art by: Keu Cha, Jason Gorder, and Matt Nelson

The Magdalena/Angelus #1/2 [2010] Wizard cover variant,
art by: Brian Ching, Marlo Alquiza, and Steve Firchow

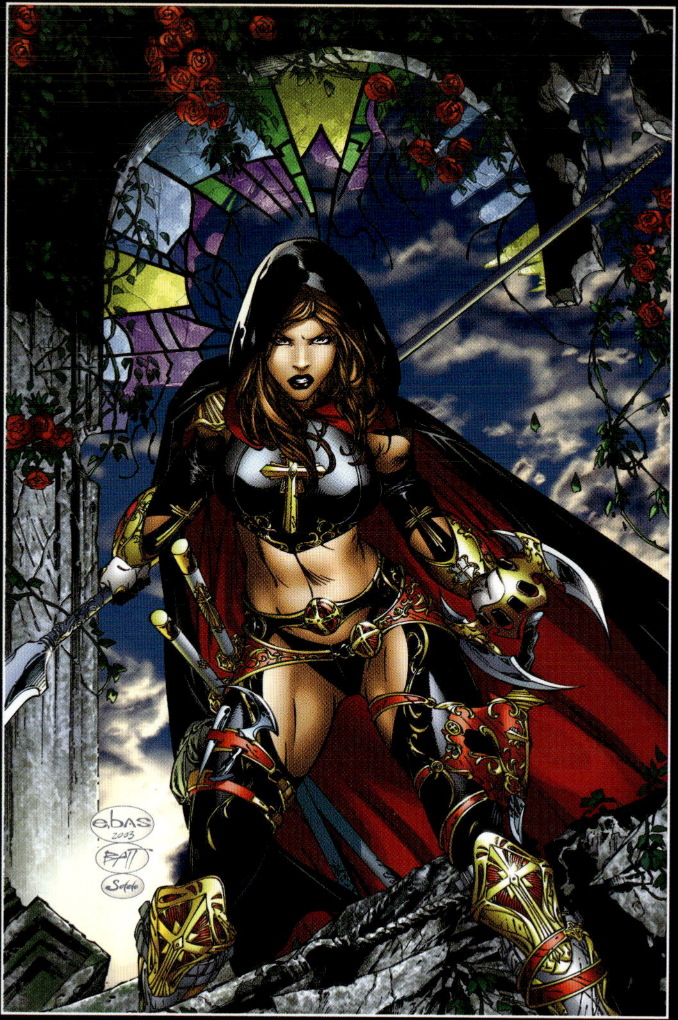

The Magdalena #1 [2003] cover A,
art by: Eric Basaldua, Matt "Batt' Banning, and Beth Sotelo

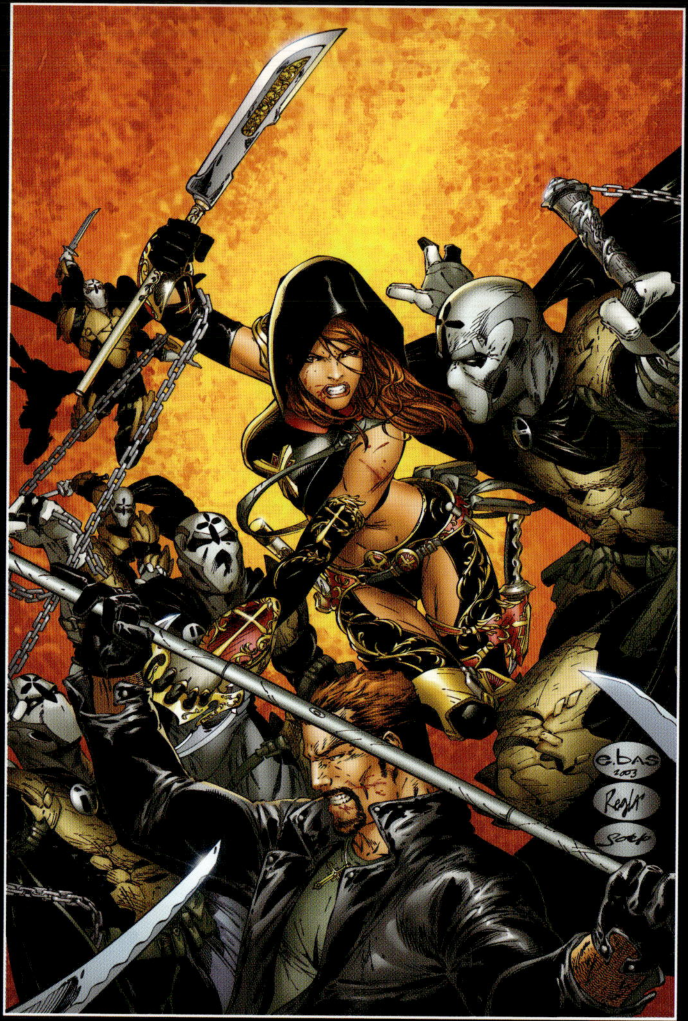

The Magdalena #2 [2003] cover A,
art by: Eric Basaldua, Sal Regla, and Beth Sotelo

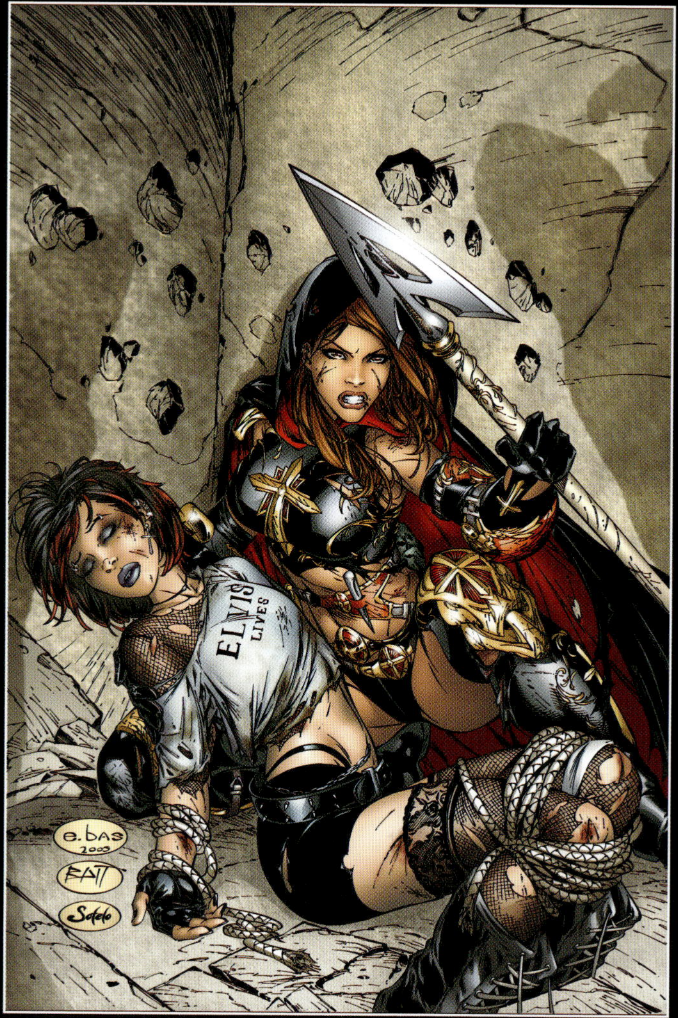

The Magdalena #3 [2003] cover A,
art by: Eric Basaldua, Matt "Batt' Banning, and Beth Sotelo

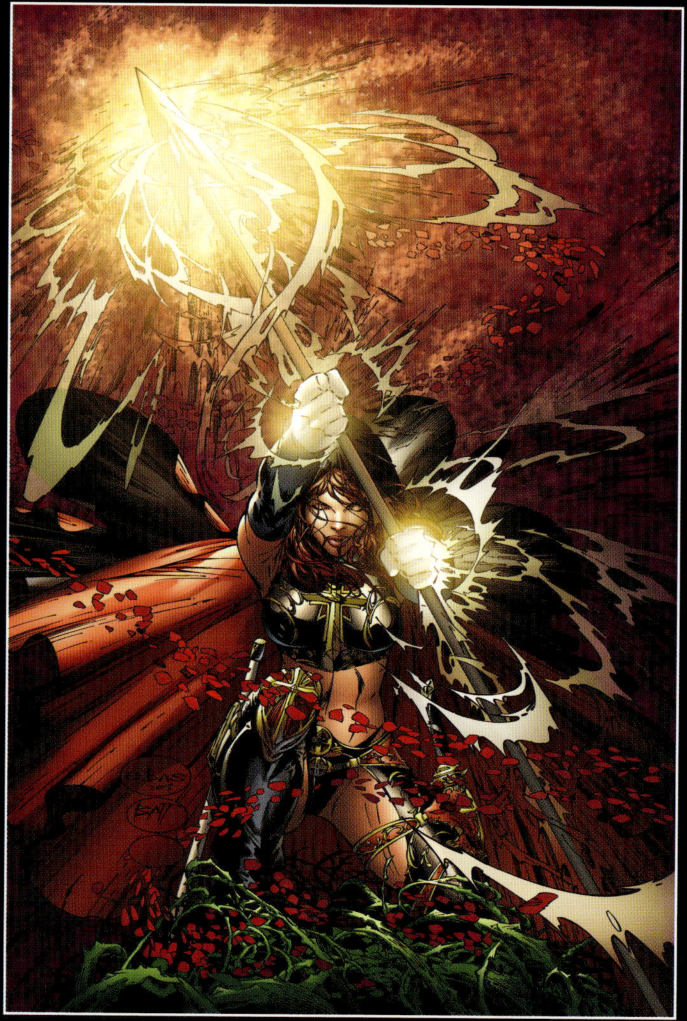

The Magdalena #4 [2003] cover A,
art by: Eric Basaldua, Matt "Batt' Banning, and Beth Sotelo

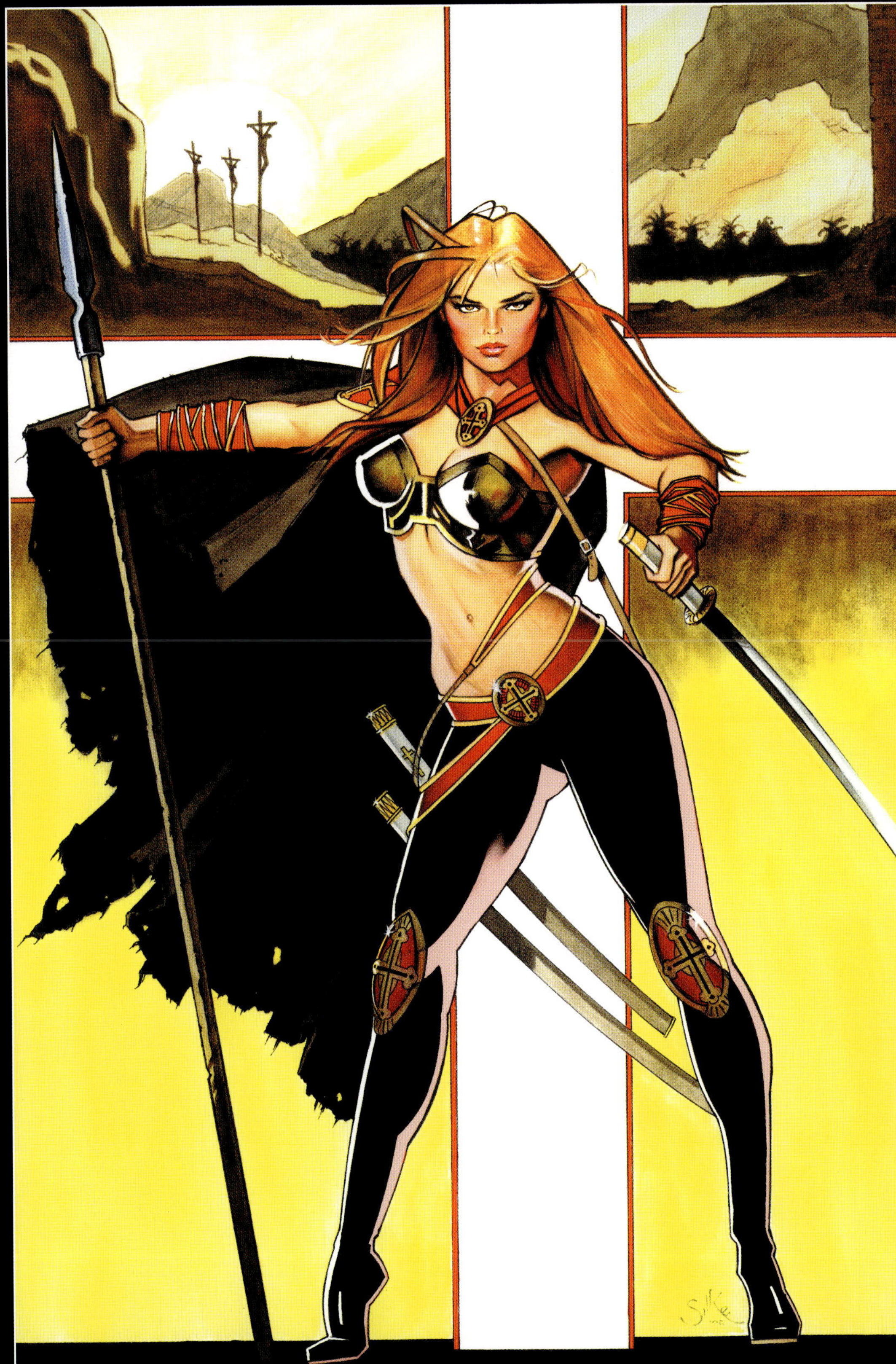

The Magdalena #1 [2003] cover C, ACTOR variant,
art by: Jim Silke

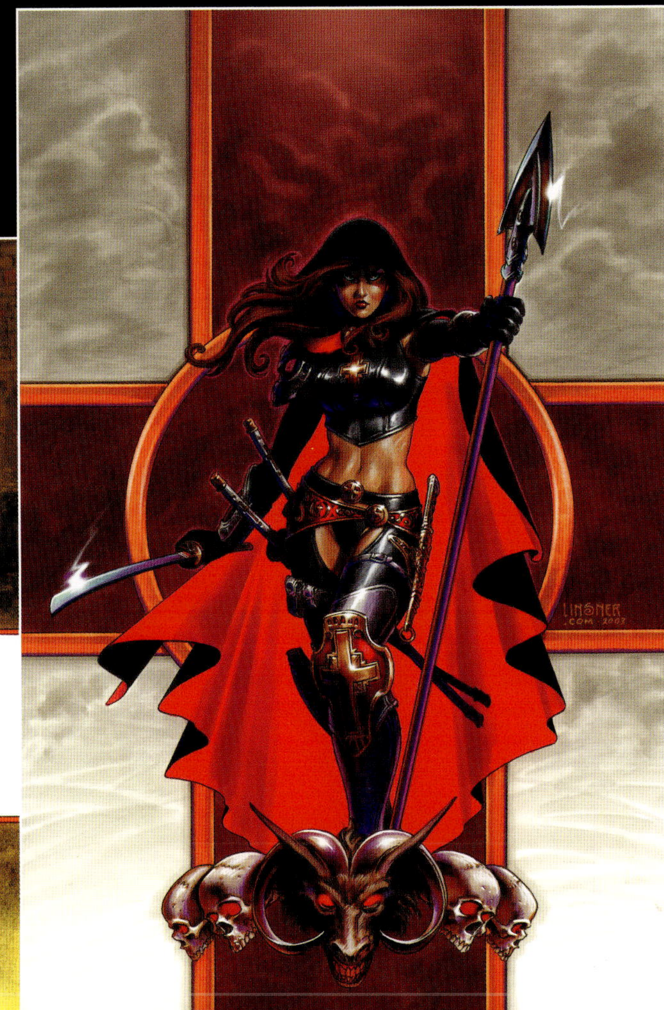

The Magdalena #1 [2003] cover B,
art by: Joseph Michael Linsner

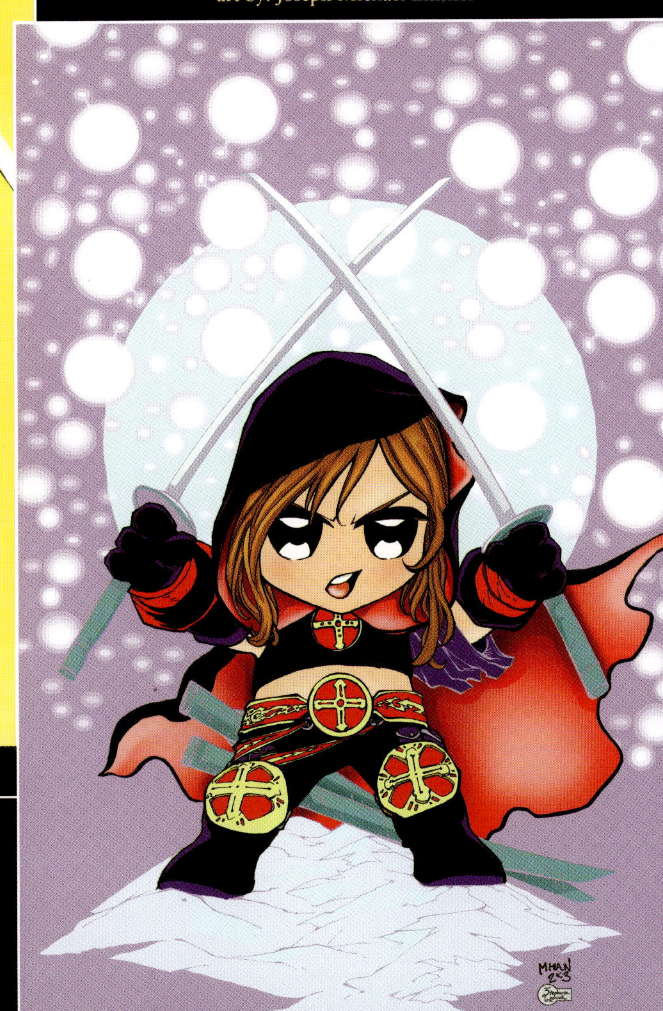

The Magdalena #2 [2003] cover B,
art by: Pop Mhan and Stephanie Lesniak

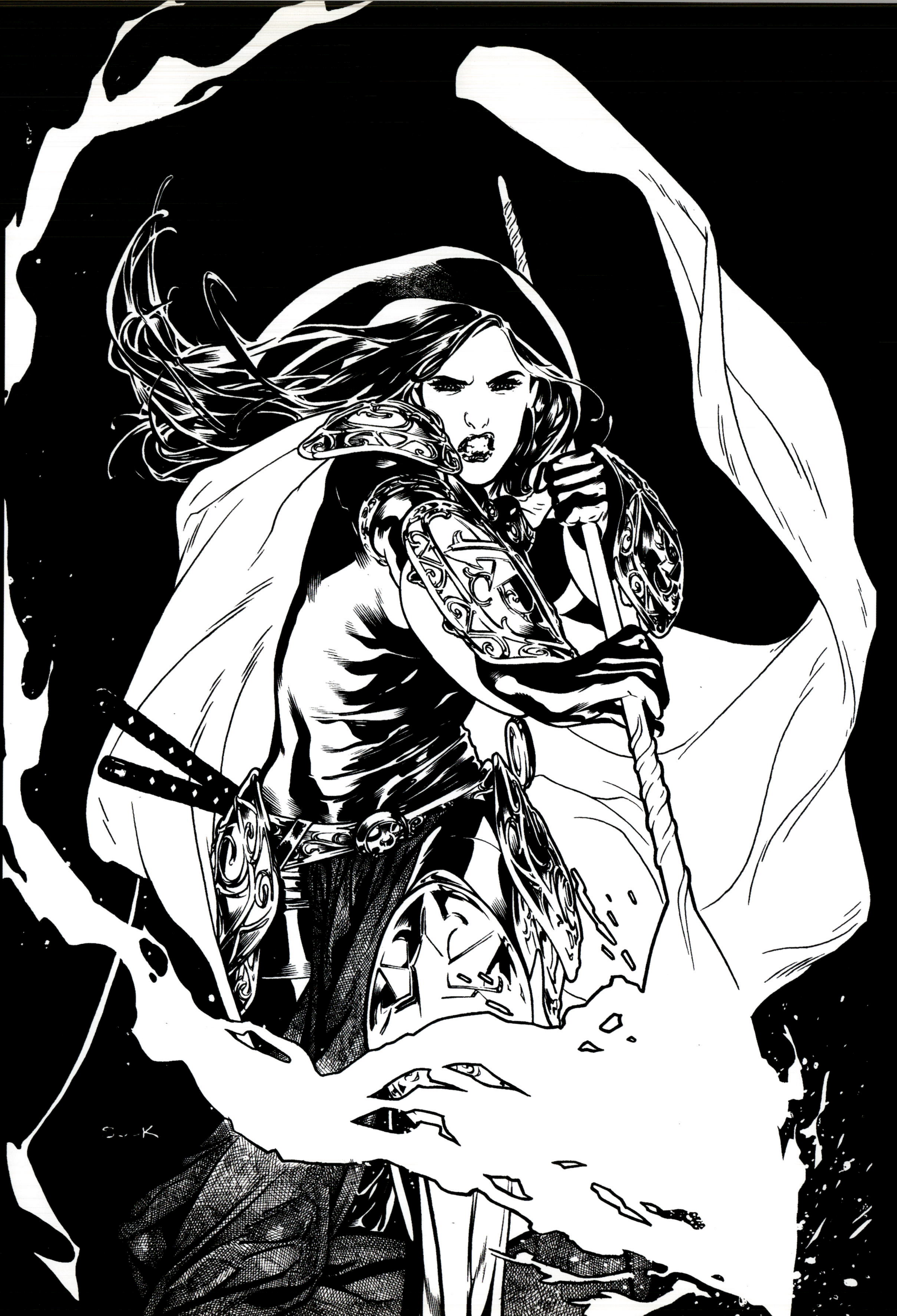

The Magdalena #1 [2010] cover D,
line art by: Ryan Sook

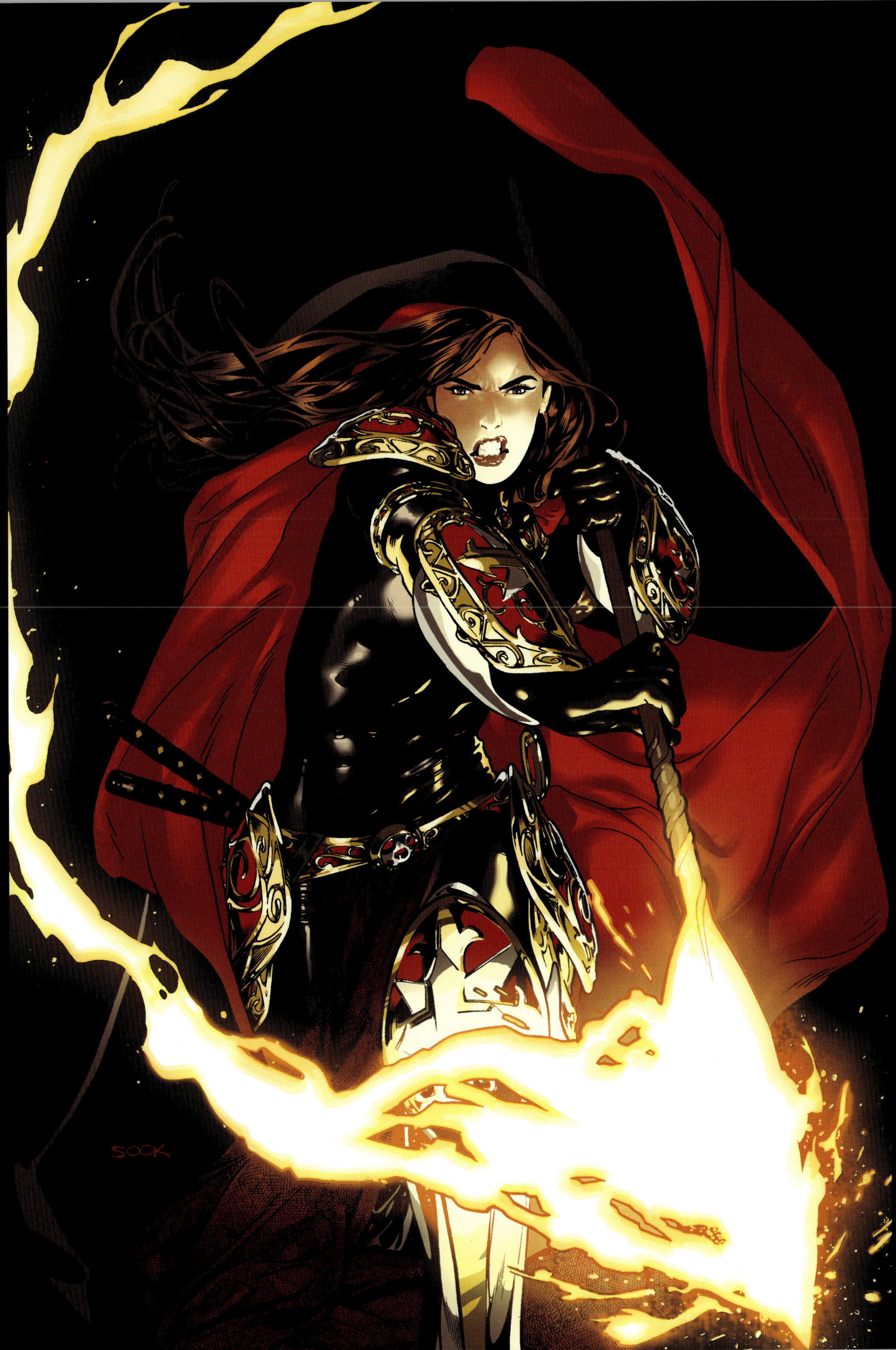

The Magdalena #1 [2010] cover A,
art by: Ryan Sook

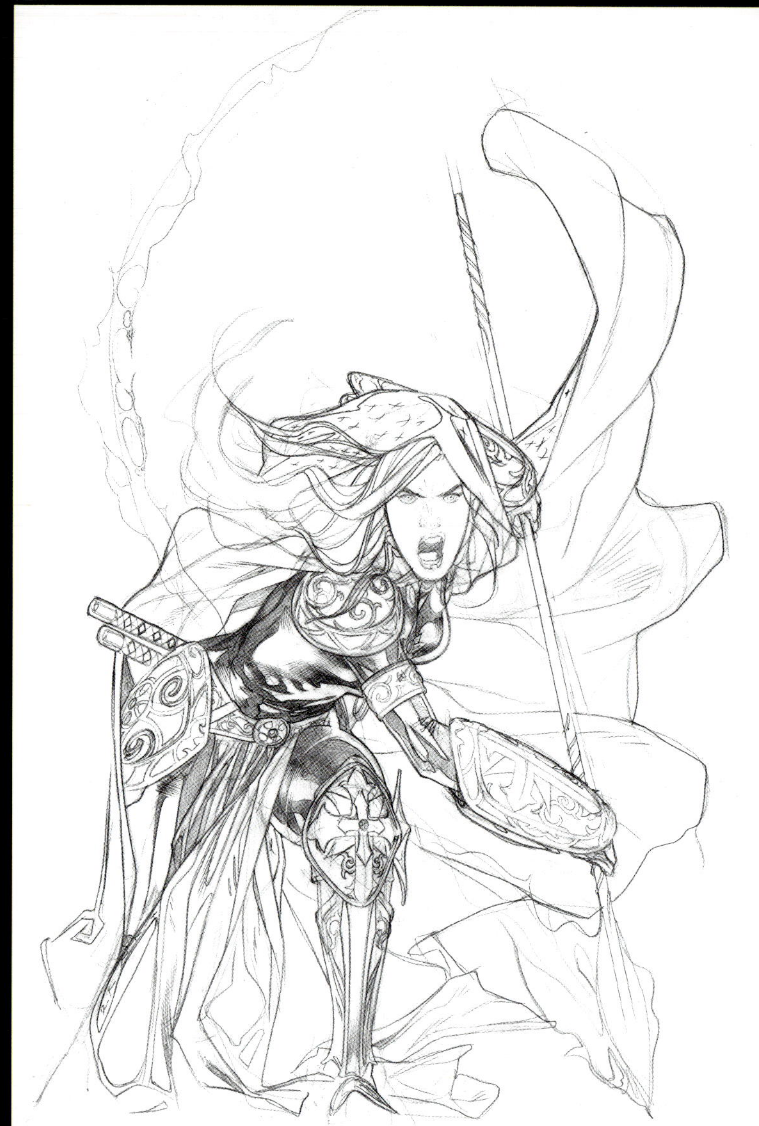

The Magdalena #1 [2010] cover C,
art by: Ryan Sook

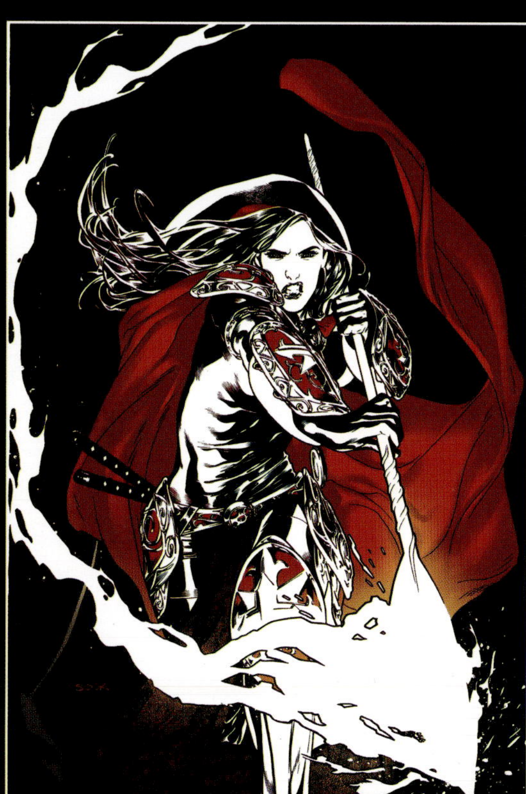

The Magdalena #1 [2010] cover B,
art by: Ryan Sook

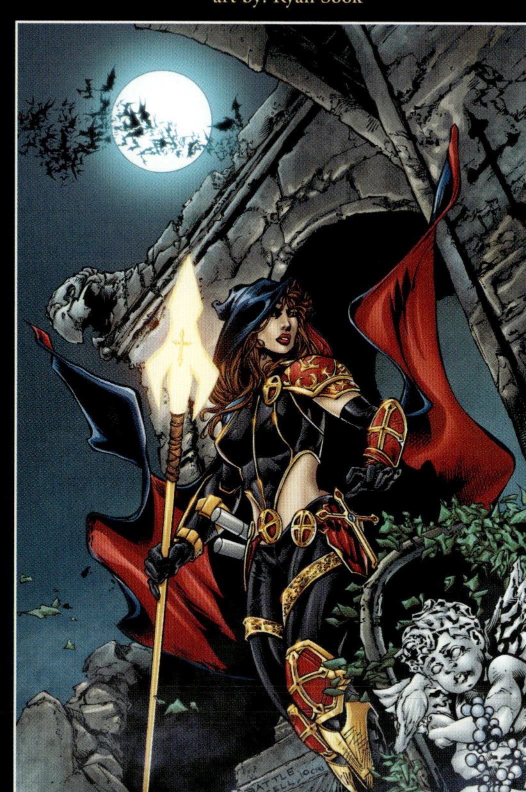

The Magdalena #1 [2010] cover E,
art by: Eric Battle, Jack Purcell, and Thomas Chu

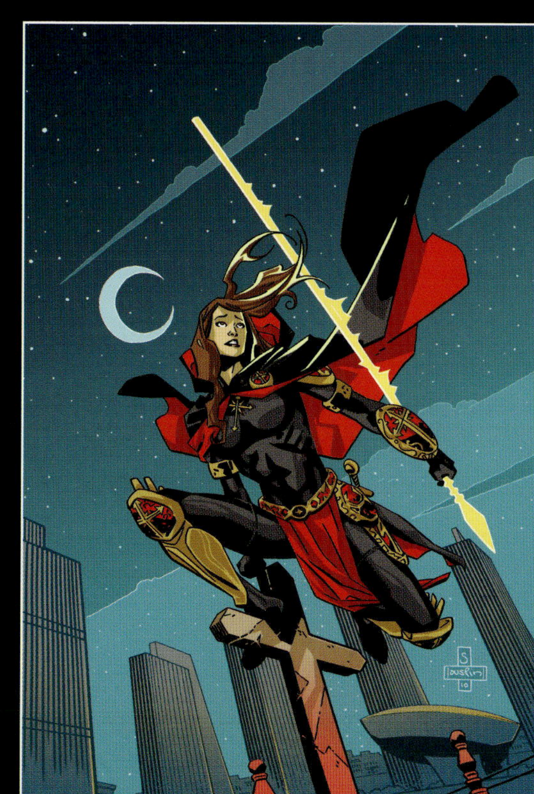

The Magdalena #1 [2010] cover F,
art by: Matthew Dow Smith, Terry Austin, and Saumin Patel

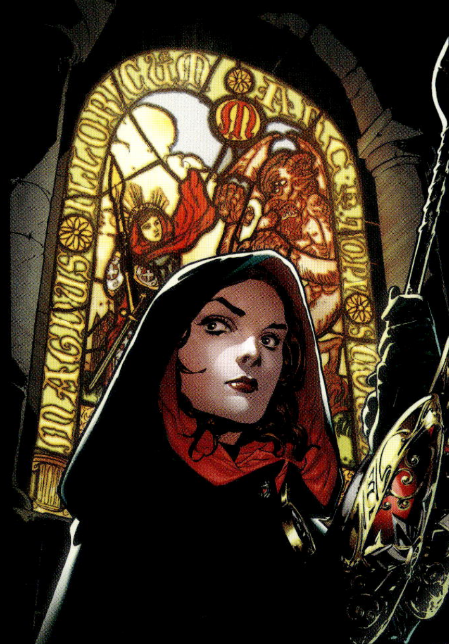

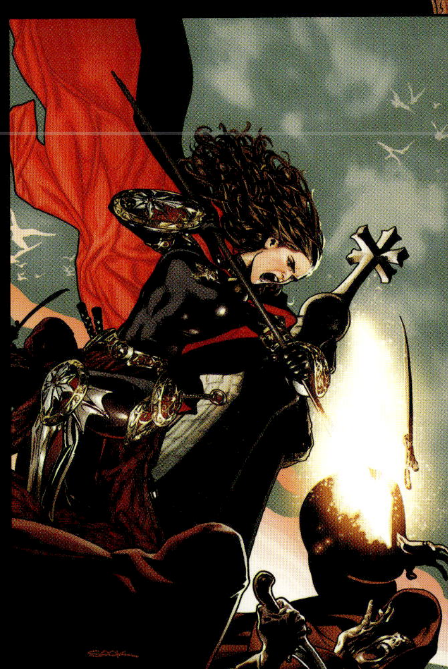

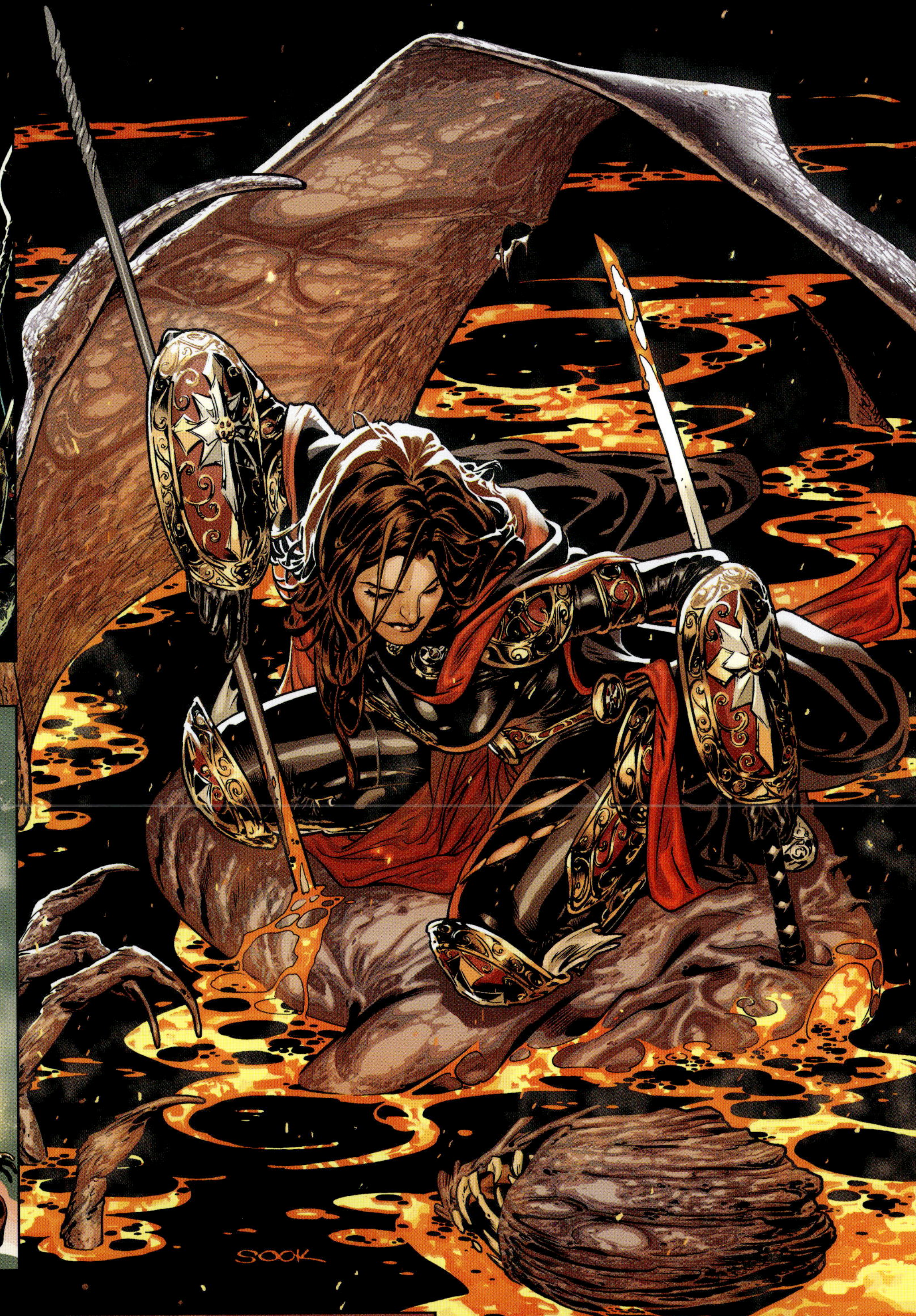

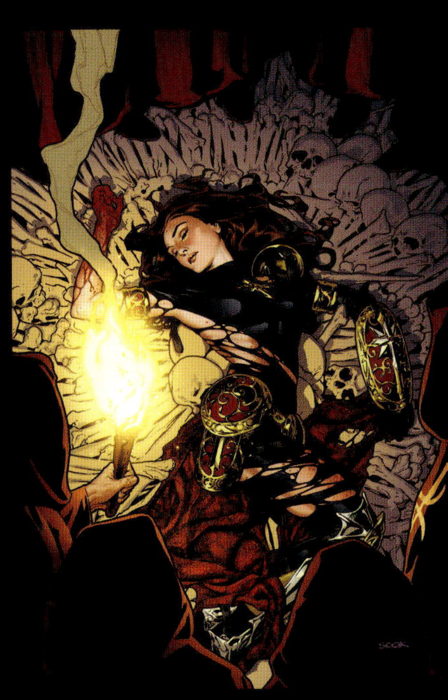

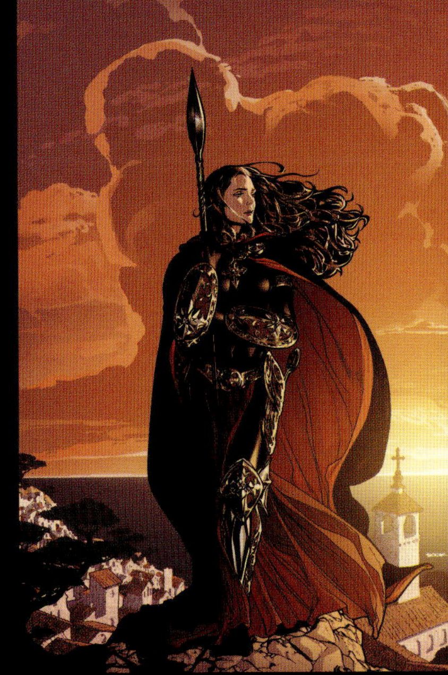

This page, ccounterlockwise from above.

The Magdalena #2-6 [2010] cover A's,
art by: Ryan Sook

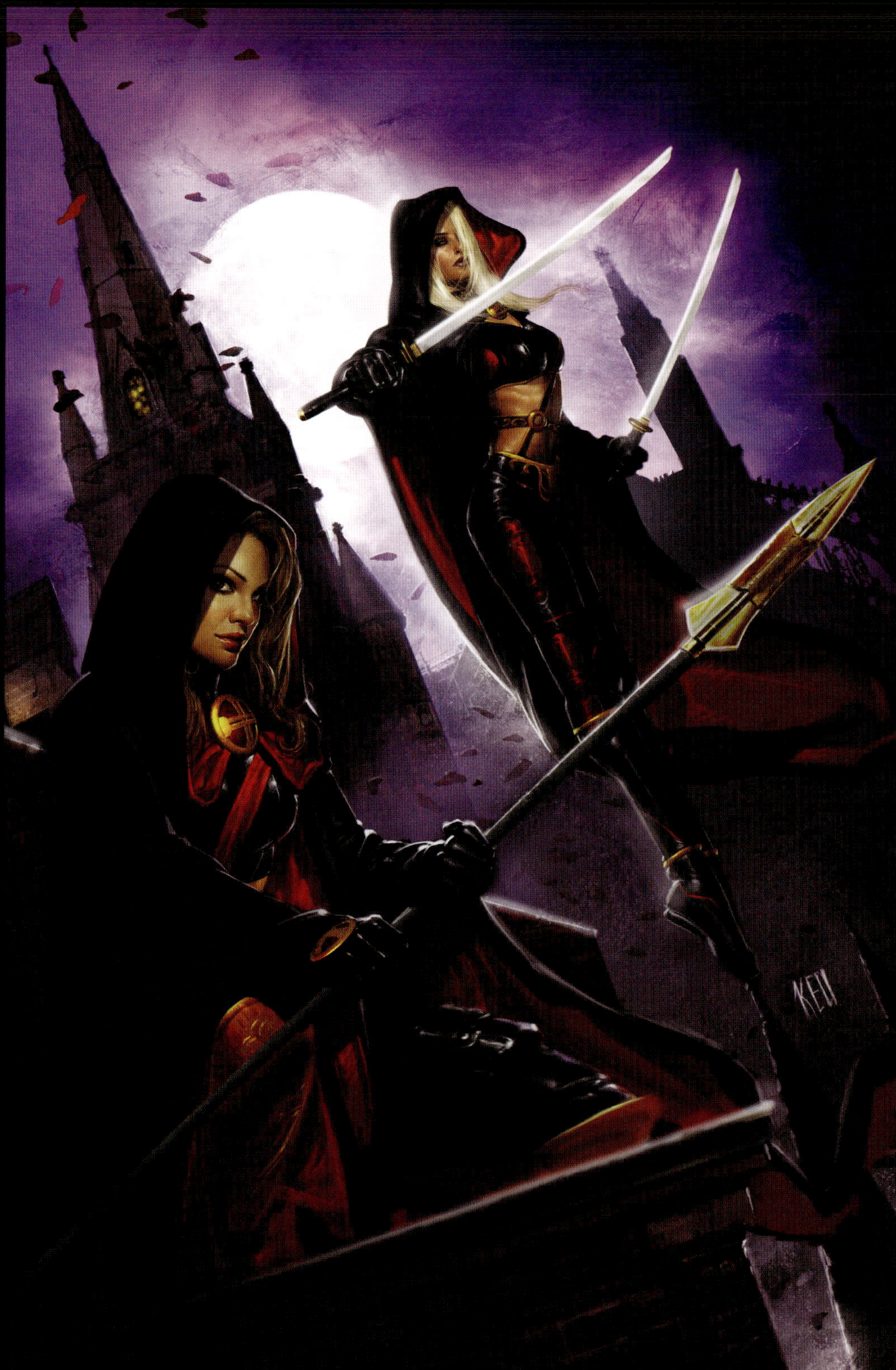

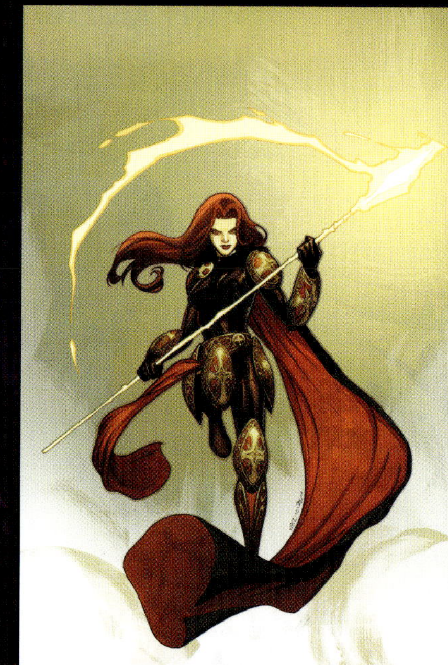

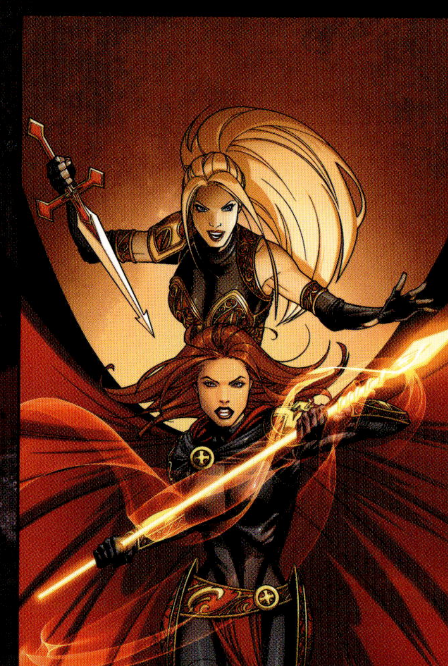

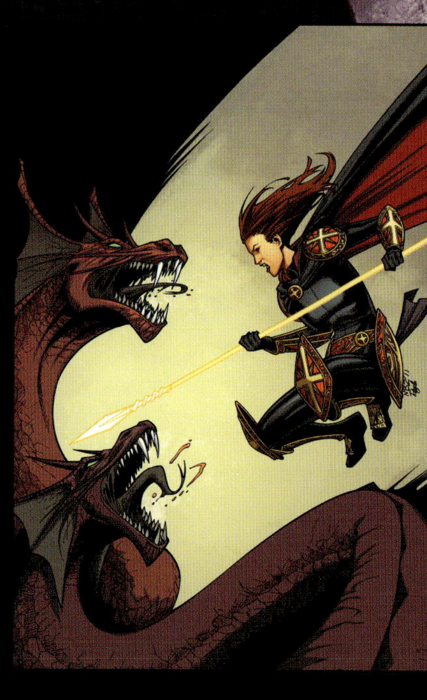

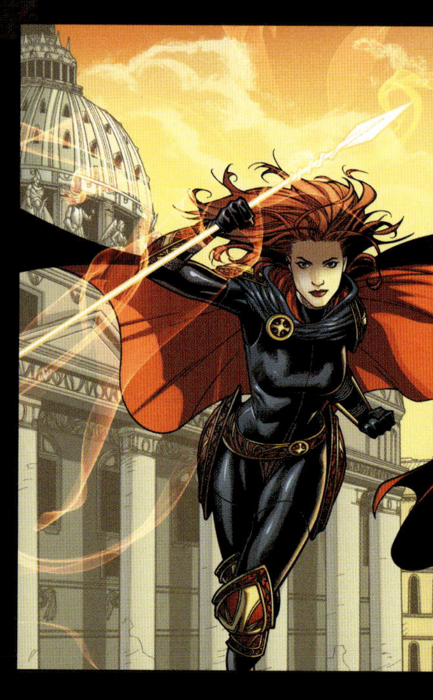

The Magdalena #7-10 [2010], selected covers

This page, clockwise from above.

The Magdalena #7 [2010] cover A,
art by: Keu Cha

The Magdalena #7 [2010] cover B,
art by: Nelson Blake II and Dave McCaig

The Magdalena #8 [2010] cover B,
art by: Nelson Blake II, Sal Regla, and Dave McCaig

The Magdalena #9 [2010] cover A,
art by: Nelson Blake II, Sal Regla, and Dave McCaig

The Magdalena #10 [2010] cover A,
art by: Nelson Blake II, Sal Regla, and Dave McCaig

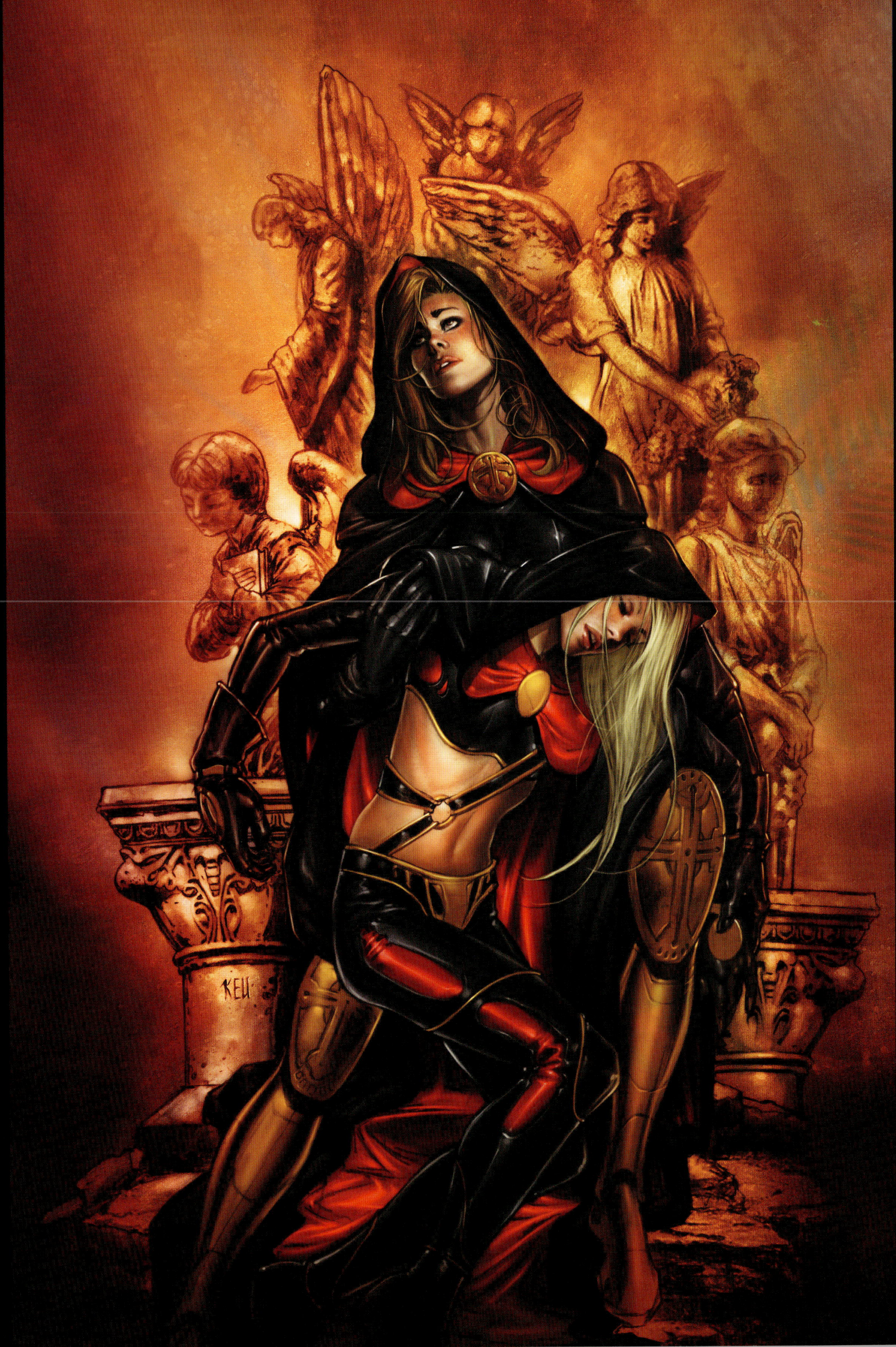

The Magdalena #8 [2010] cover A,
art by: Keu Cha

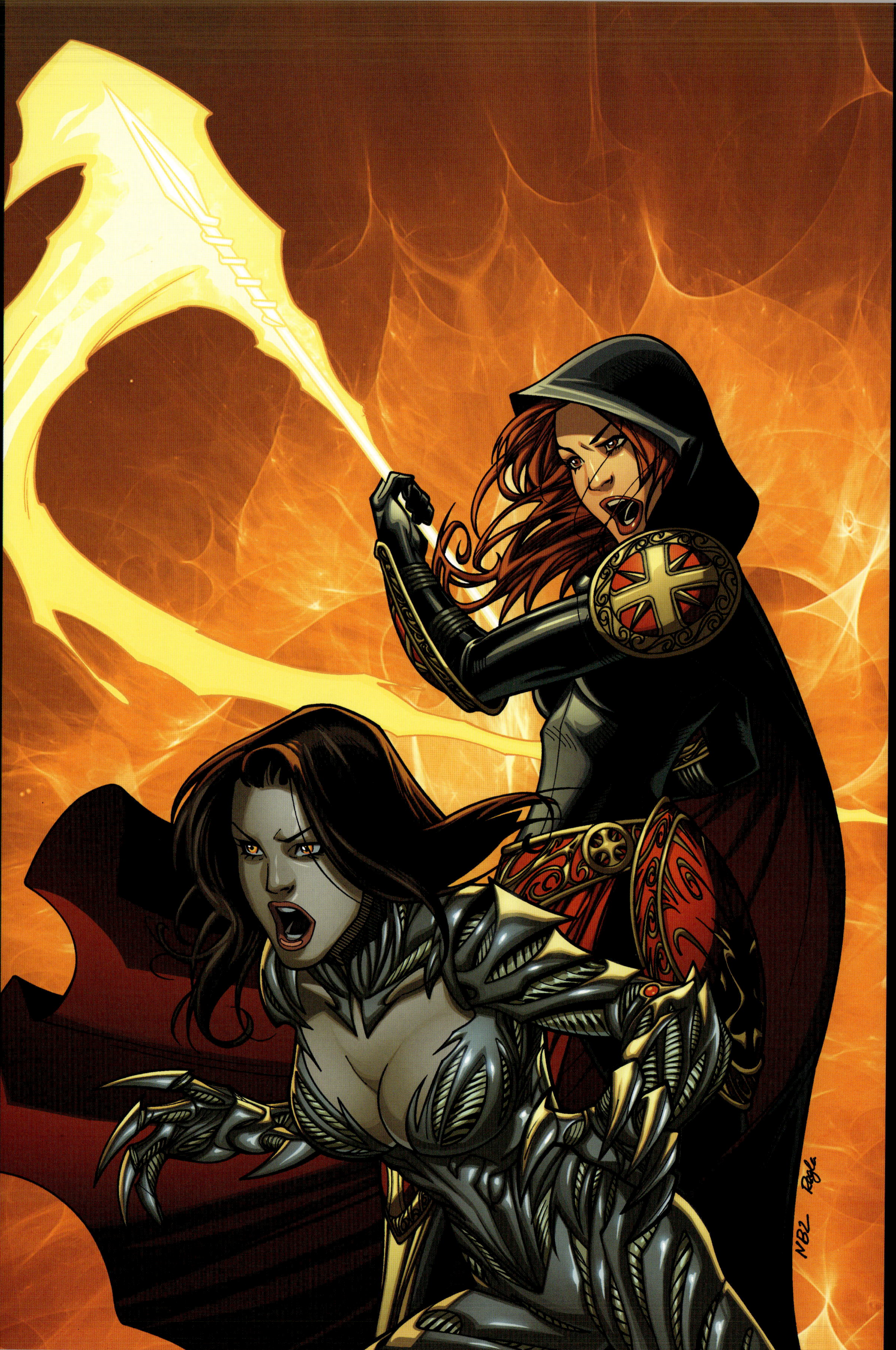

The Magdalena #11 [2010] cover A,
art by: Nelson Blake II, Sal Regla, and Dave McCaig

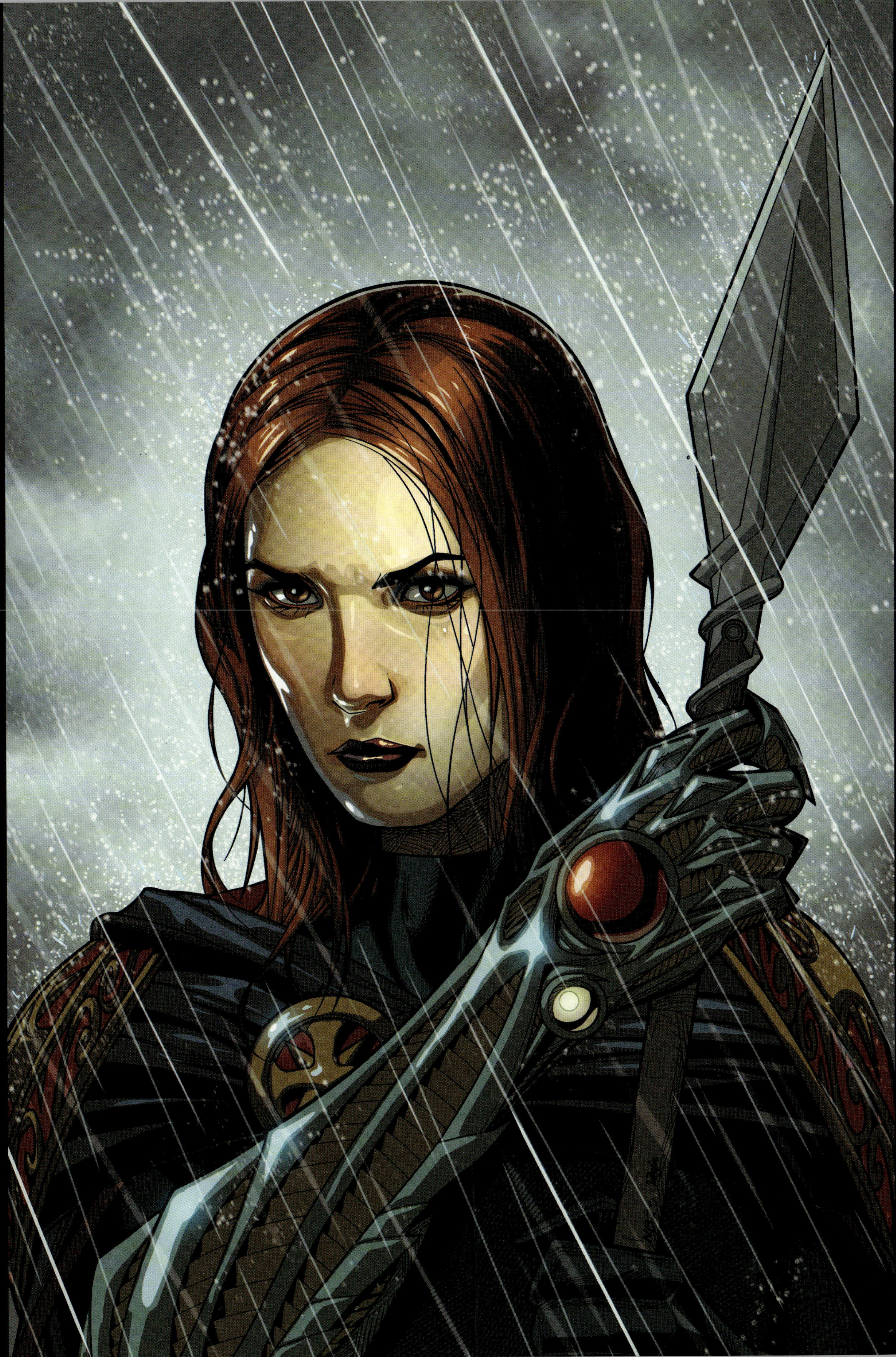

The Magdalena #12 [2010] cover A,
art by: Nelson Blake II, Sal Regla and Dave McCaig

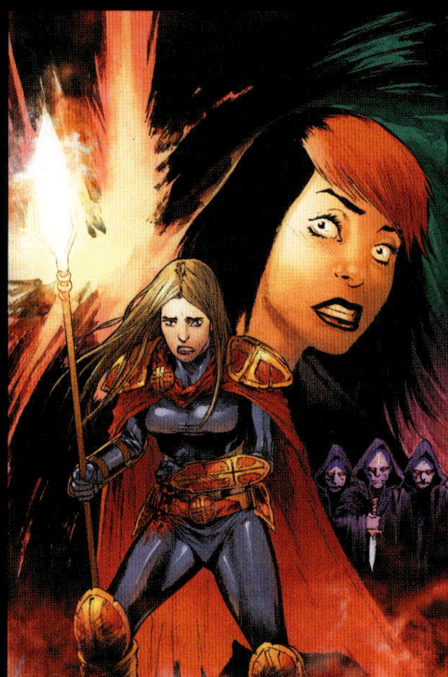

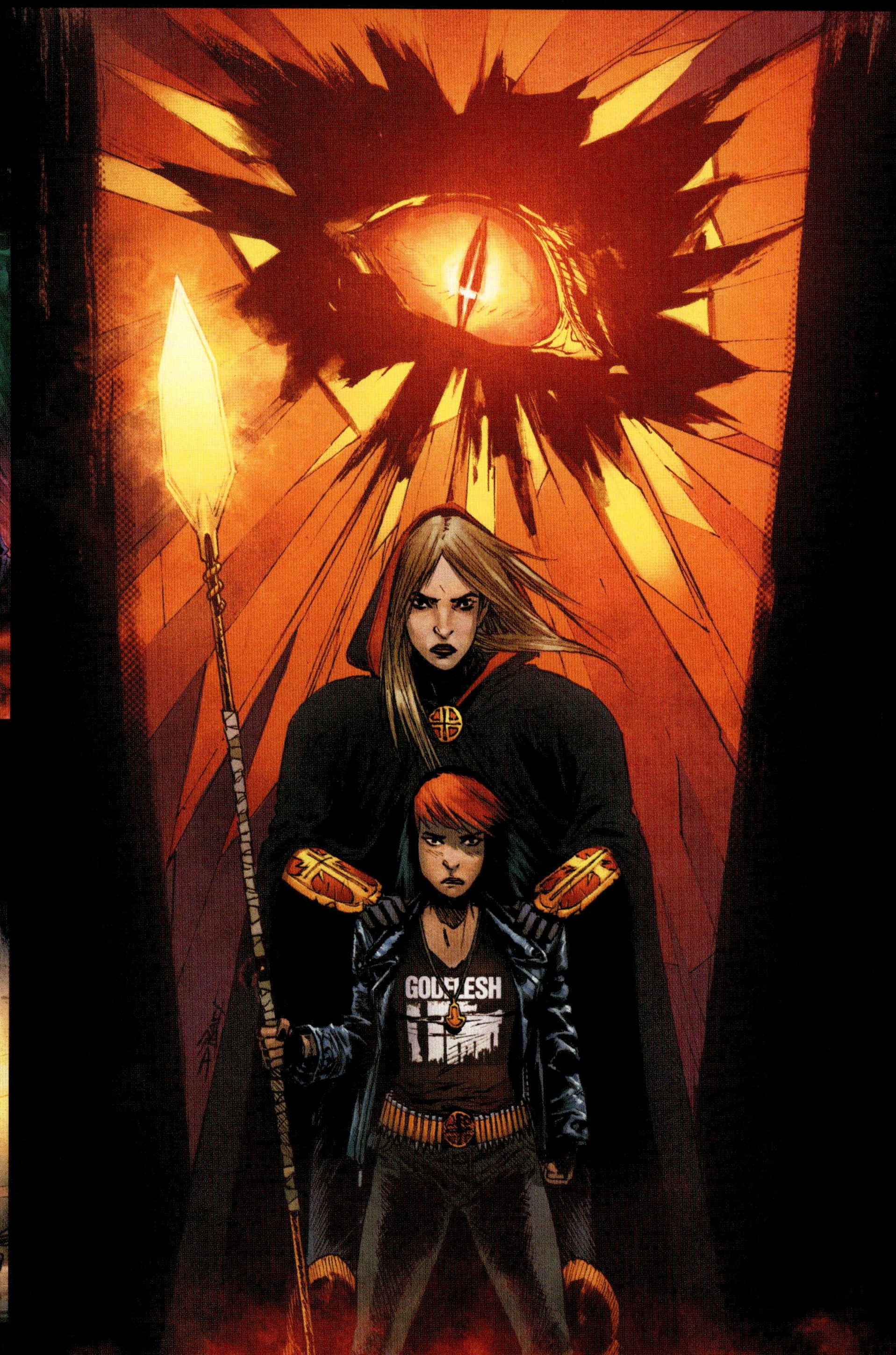

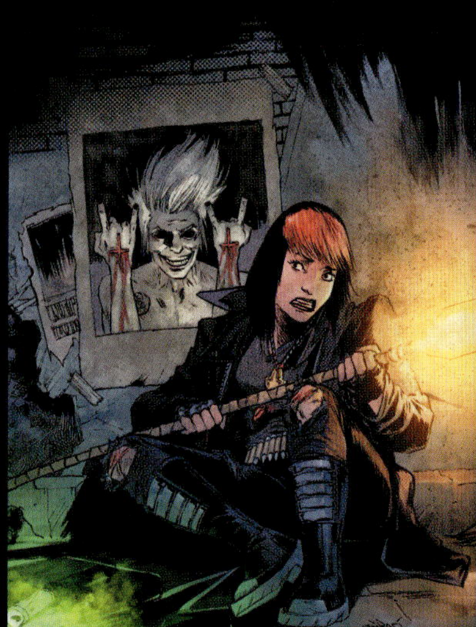

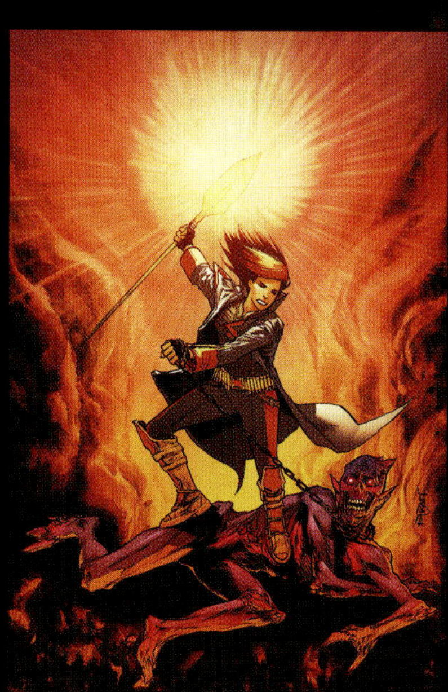

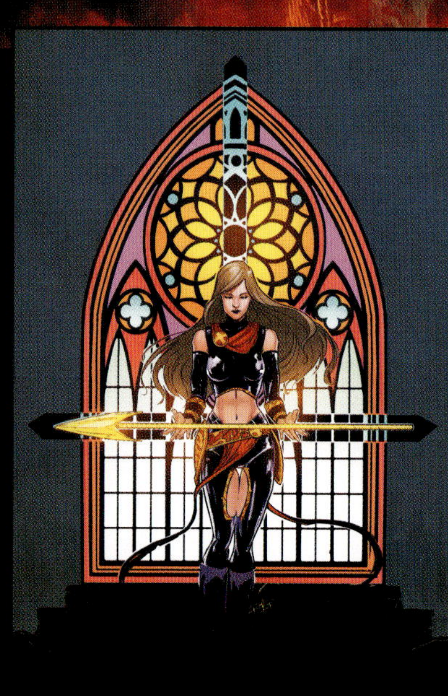

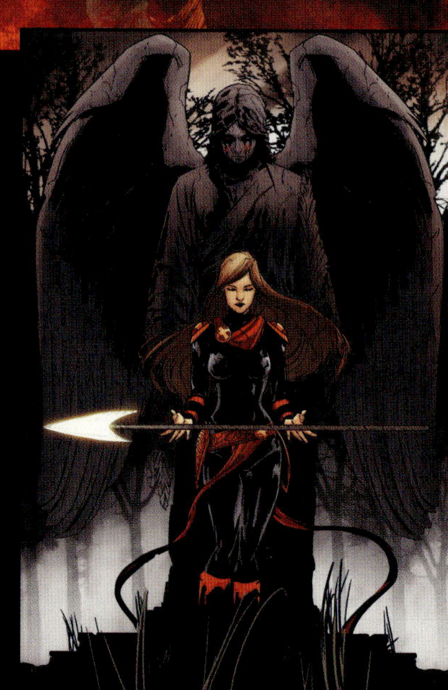

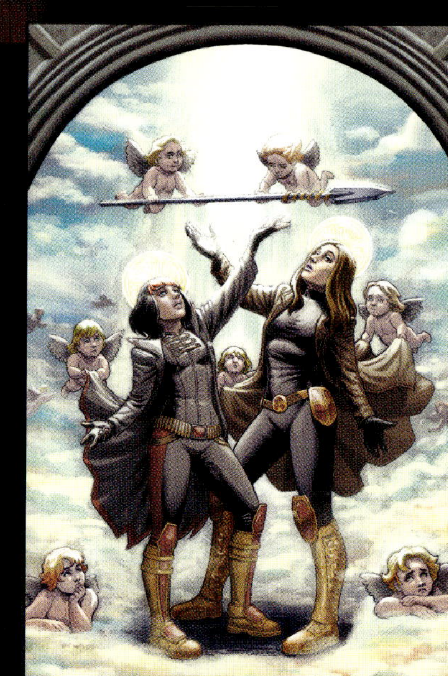

This page, counterclockwise from left.

The Magdalena #2 [2017] cover A,
art by: Chris DiBari and Mike Spicer

The Magdalena #1 [2017] cover A,
art by: Chris DiBari and Mike Spicer

The Magdalena #3 [2017] cover A,
art by: Chris DiBari and Mike Spicer

The Magdalena #4 [2017] cover A,
art by: Chris DiBari and Mike Spicer

The Magdalena #1 [2017] cover B,
art by: Roberta Ingranata

The Magdalena #2 [2017] cover B,
art by: Roberta Ingranata

The Magdalena #4 [2017] cover B,
art by: Atilio Rojo

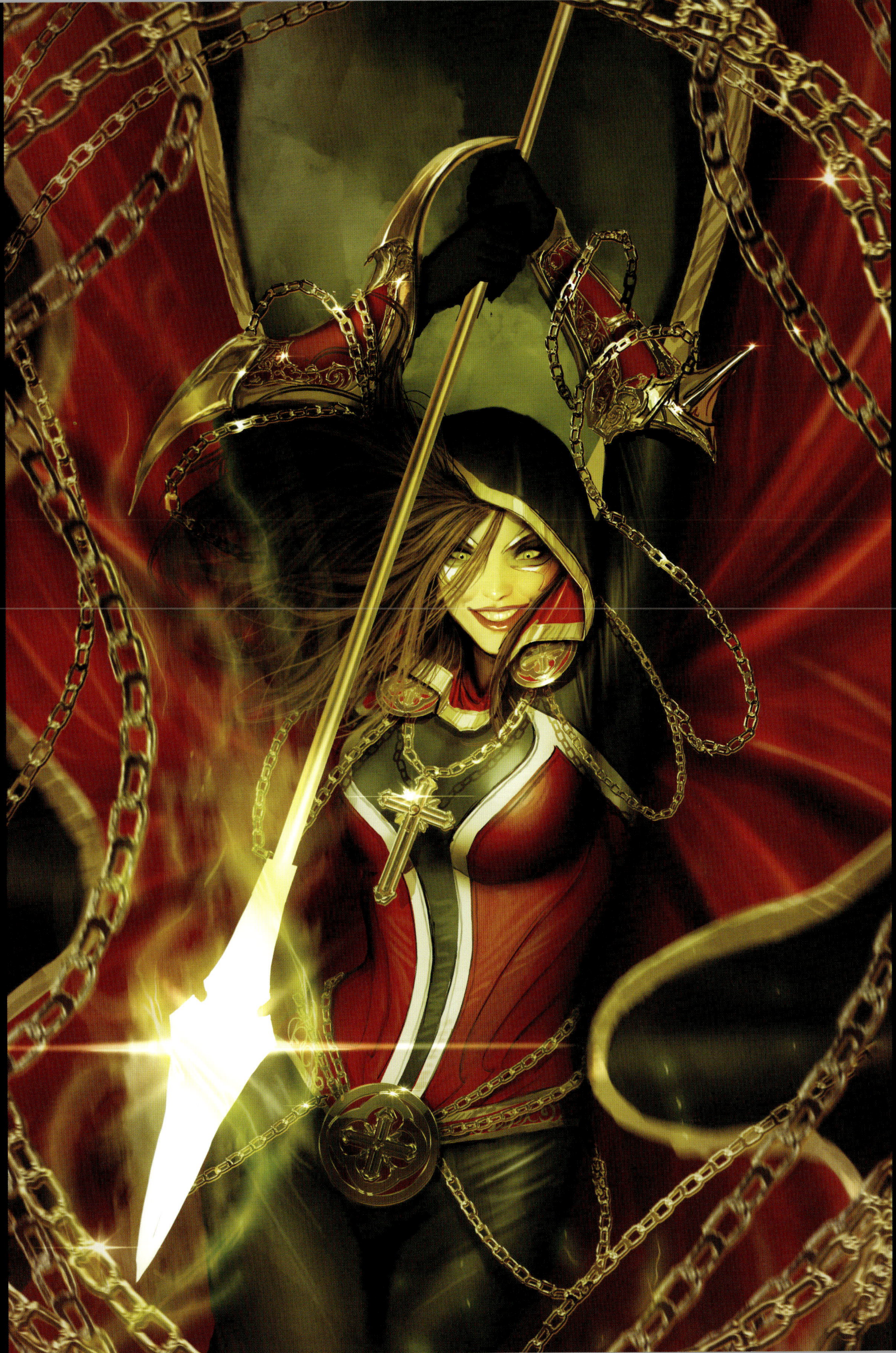

The Magdalena #3 [2017] cover B,
art by: Stjepan Sejic

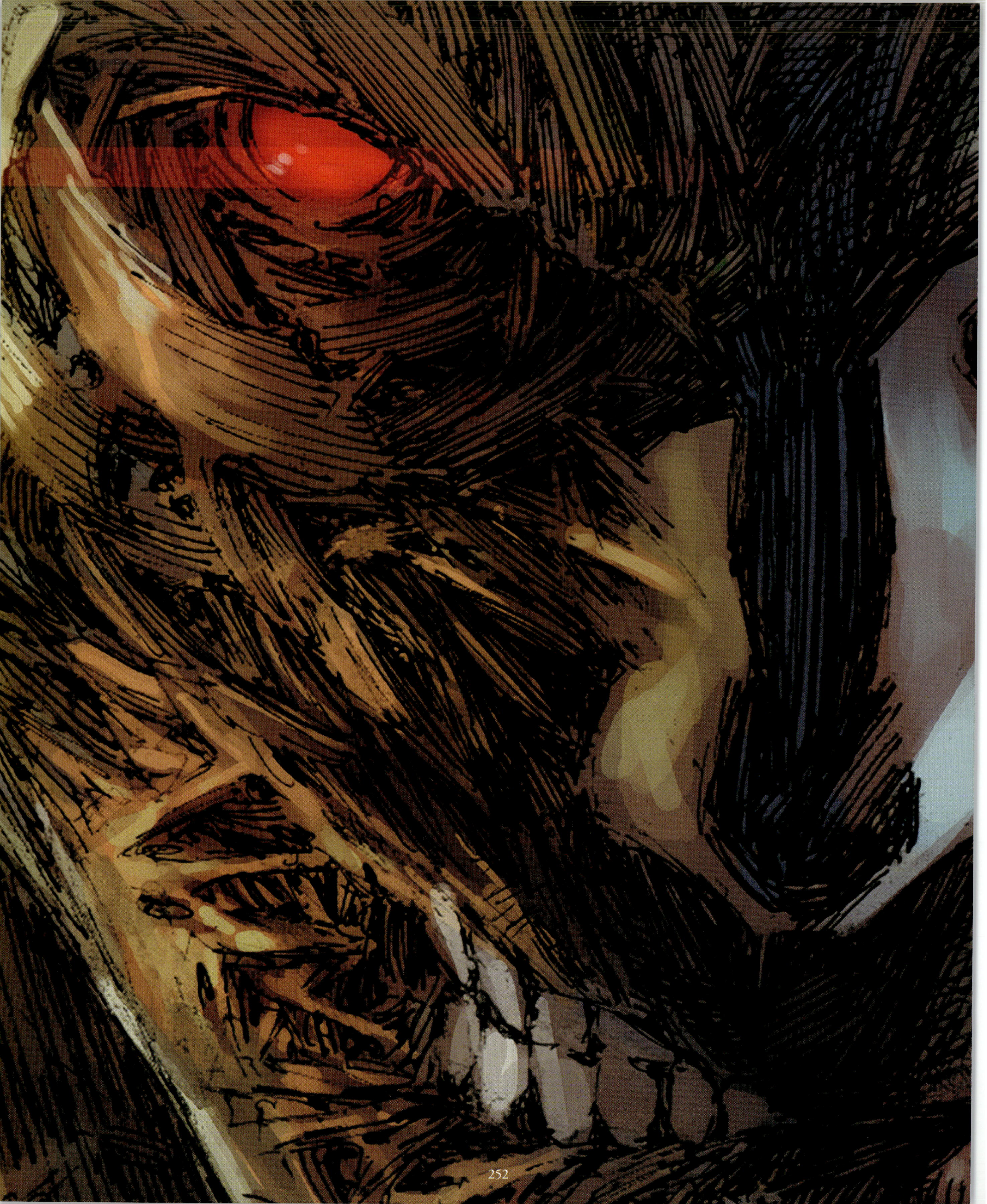

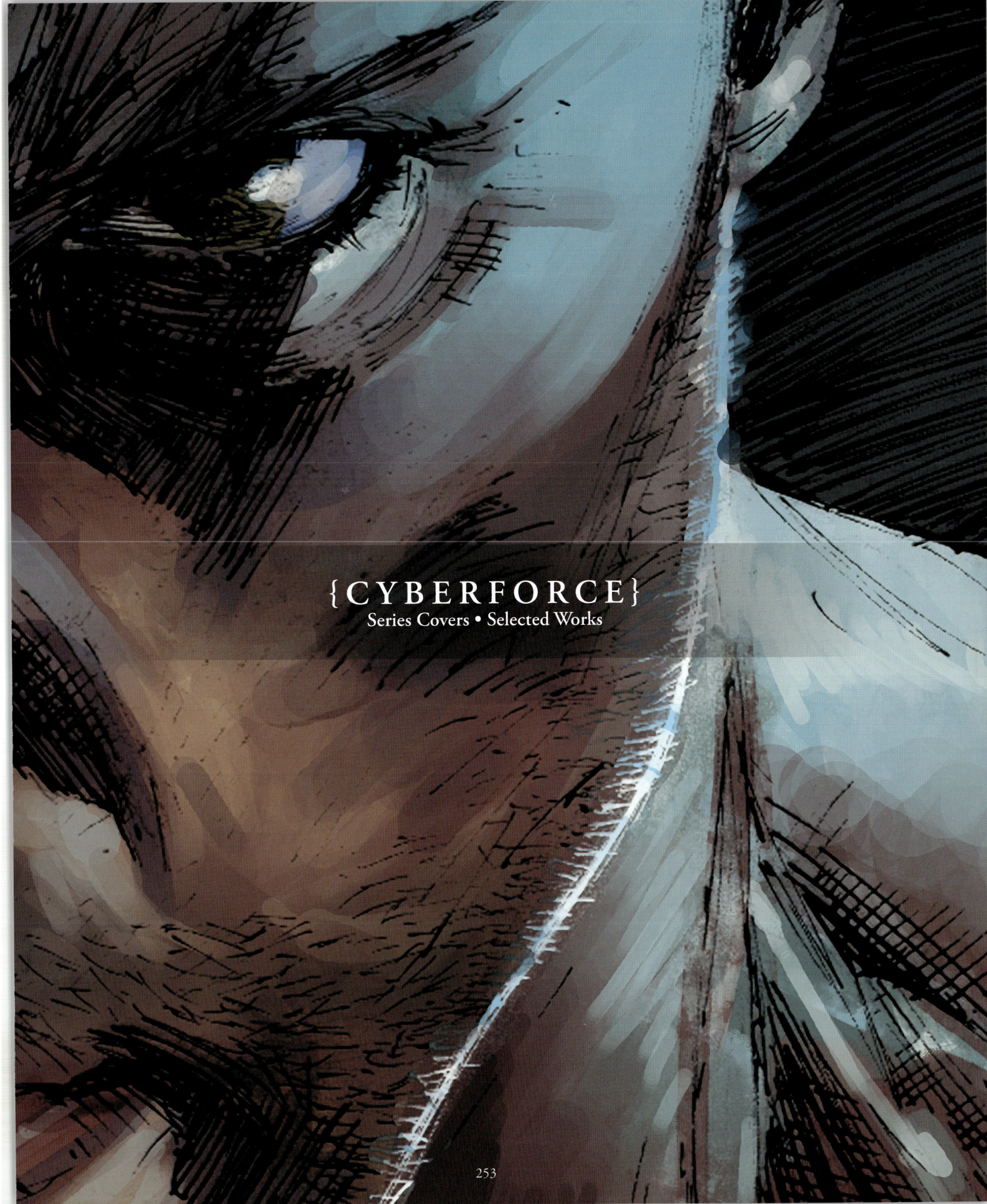

{CYBERFORCE}

Series Covers • Selected Works

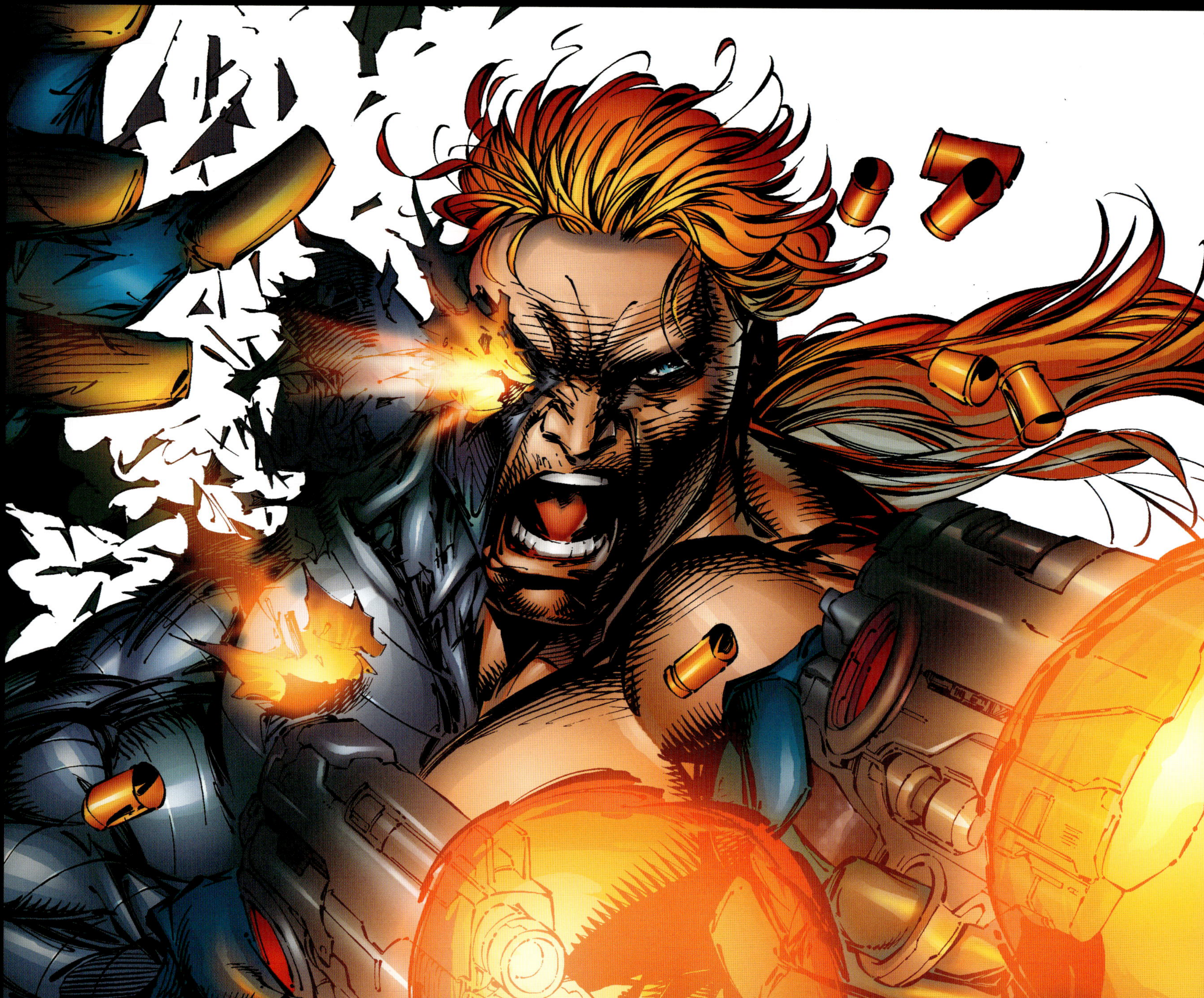

Above. *Cyberforce* #15 [1993] cover, art by: Marc Silvestri, Matt "Batt" Banning, and Steve Firchow

Cyberforce created by **Marc Silvestri**

Cyberforce was first released in October 1992 and spawned five series, last released July 2017, and celebrated its 30th anniversary with the launch of the *Cyberforce Complete Edition*, kicking off the Complete Edition line of trade paperbacks from Top Cow.

Cyberforce is about a group of cybernetically enhanced resistance fighters on the run from CYBERDATA, the monolithic multinational conglomerate that created them.

Cyberforce has evolved with the times. The most recent iteration places the team in a modern world where humanity is defined by the technology it creates, global biotech company CDI (Cyber Data Incorporated) pursues the goal of transhumanism by converting humans into powered soldiers. A small number of these "supersoldiers" escape and form a rebellion to actively fight against CDI and its objectives. The classic heroes Ripclaw, Stryker, Ballistic, Cyblade and more returned in 2017, and who knows...The next series may be right around the corner.

Previous page. *Cyberforce* #10 [2012] cover, art by: Marc Silvestri and Sunny Gho • At right. *Cyberforce* #12 [1993] cover, art by: Marc Silvestri, Matt "Batt" Banning, and Steve Firchow

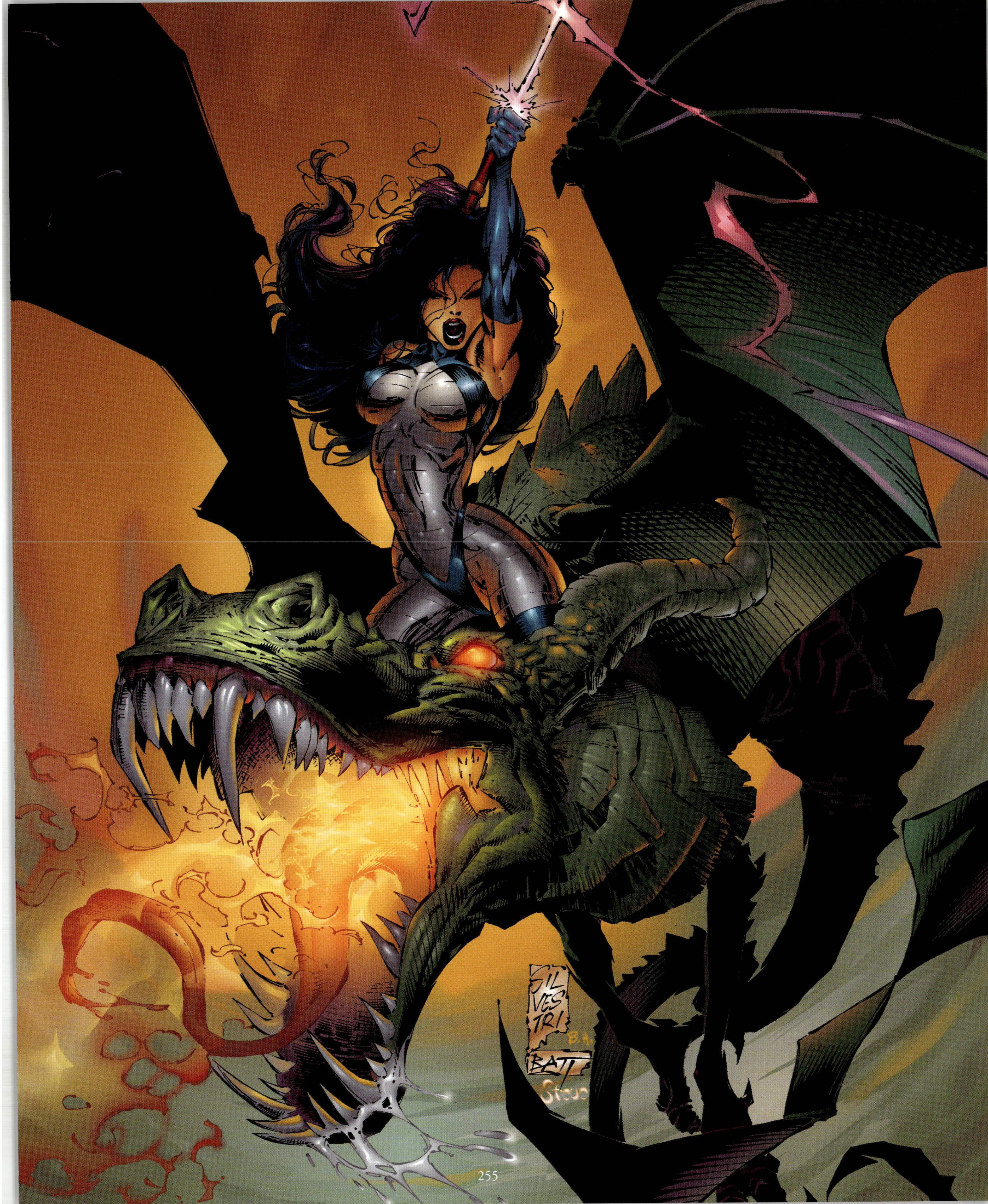
SILVESTRI
B.A.
BATT

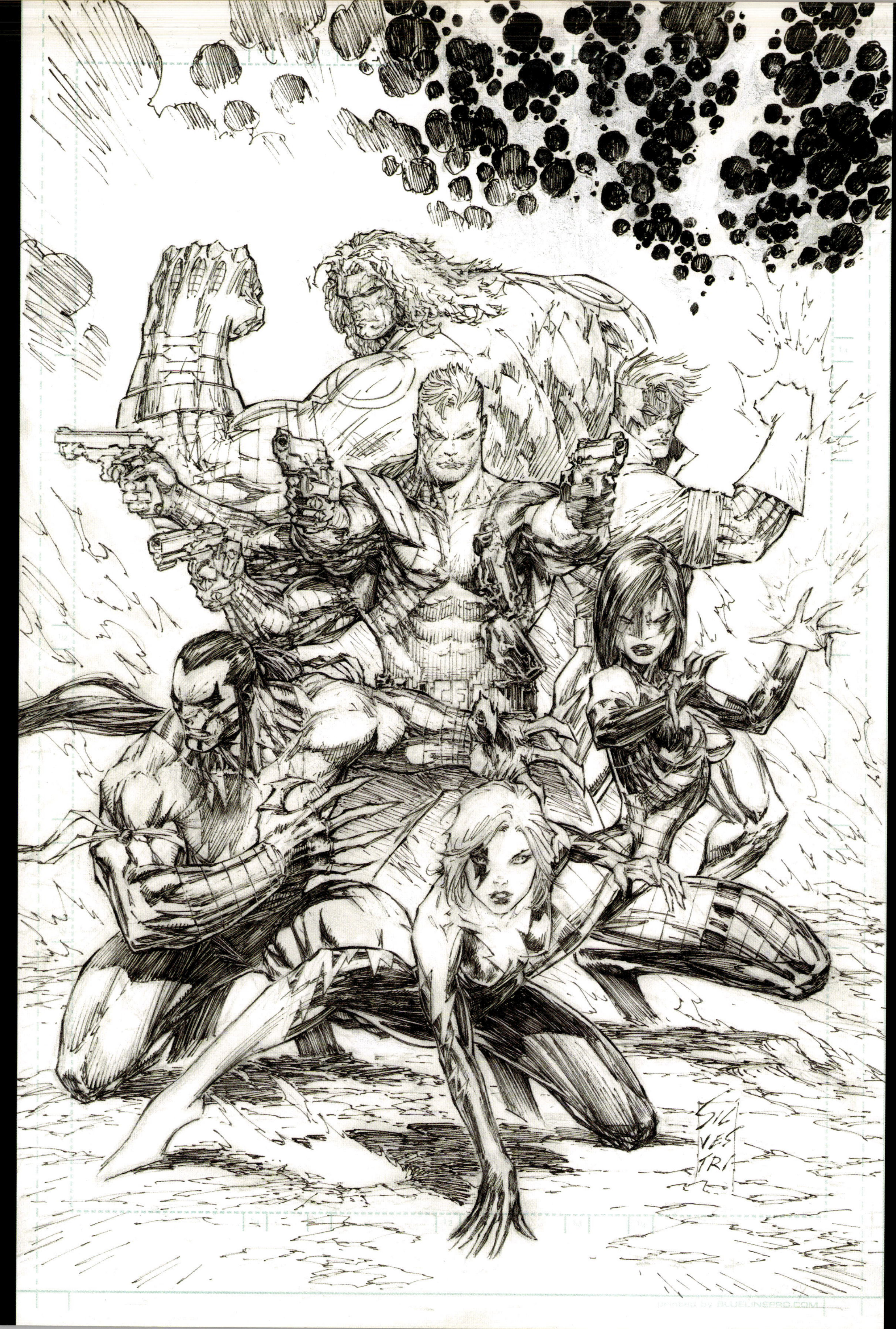

Cyberforce #1 30th Anniversary Edition [2022], Convention Exclusive cover, line art by: Marc Silvestri

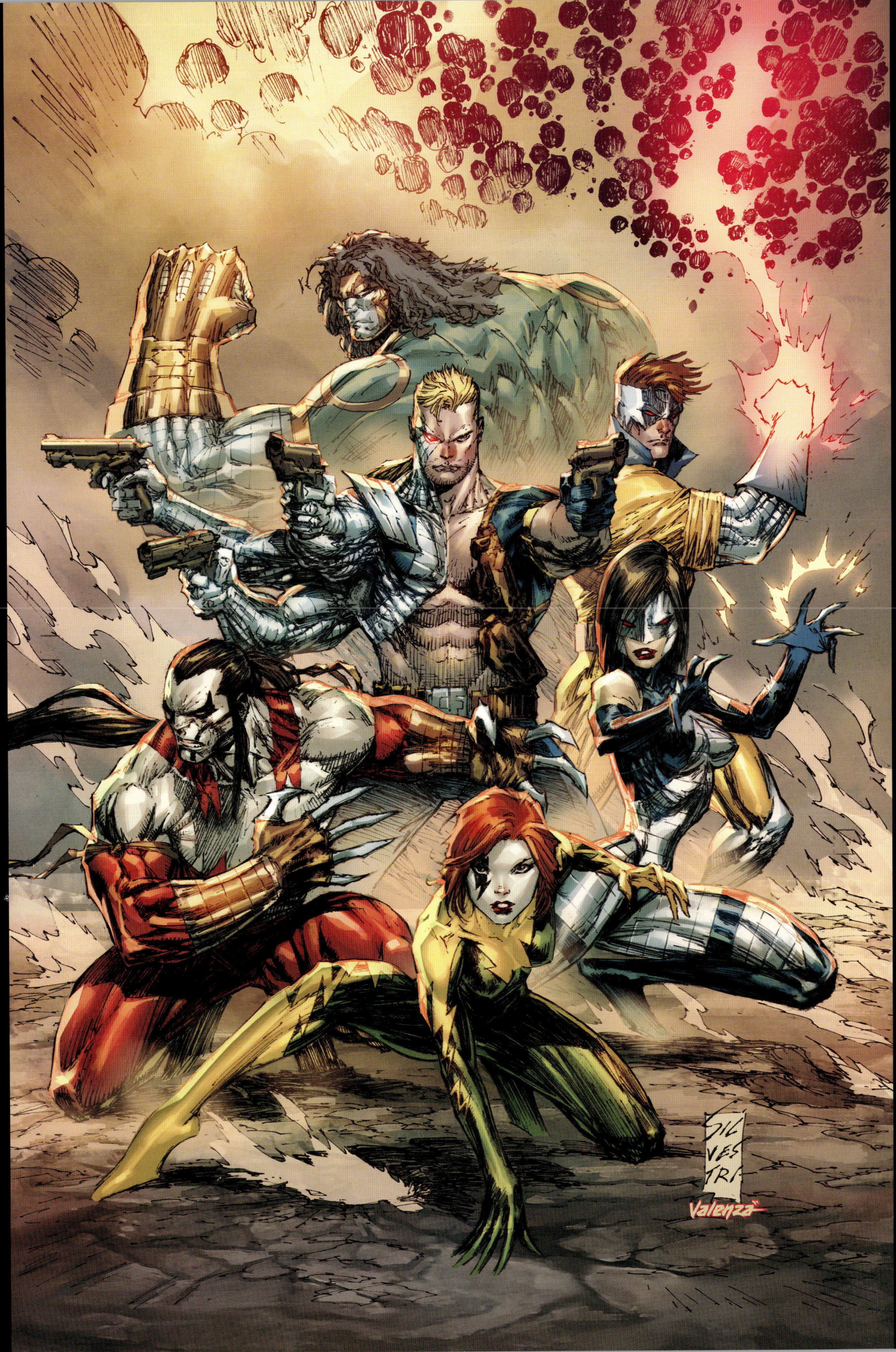

Cyberforce #1 30th Anniversary Edition [2022], Kickstarter Exclusive cover,
art by: Marc Silvestri and Bryan Valenza

Excerpt from "30 YEARS OF CYBERFORCE"

A look back on the early days of Top Cow and Image Comics By **LISA Y. WU**
Color Guide & Ink images courtesy of **BRIAN HABERLIN**

"*Cyberforce* was one of the founding books for Image Comics during a pivotal time in comic book history when Marc Silvestri, Rob Liefeld, Todd McFarlane, Jim Lee, Erik Larsen, Jim Valentino, and Whilce Portacio left Marvel Comics at the height of their popularity and decided to open new opportunities and creative freedom for comic book creators everywhere.

Created by writer and artist Marc Silvestri through his publishing studios, Top Cow Productions, in October 1992 and published through Image Comics as a mini-series, the success of the series launched an ongoing series a year later with *Cyberforce* #0 as Silvestri added creators such as Brian Haberlin, David Wohl and Scott Williams.

After 30 years, these legendary creators came together to reminisce on the classic series and the groundbreaking time of creativity that was '90s comics with a comic book fan of that time turned Top Cow Marketing Manager Lisa Y. Wu.

Lisa Y. Wu: Wow, 30 years since the first issue of *Cyberforce* came out. How does it feel?

Scott Williams: It is hard to wrap my head around it. I'm sure all you guys are feeling the same way. It's just it can't possibly be 30 years, but the calendar says it is.

Marc Silvestri: The calendar says it is. The fact that there are kids and parents coming to the shows and you know these kids weren't even born for another probably 10 years and, in some cases, 20 or 25 years. 30 years, it's unbelievable. Thinking back on essentially this group right now, we were all together you know 30 years ago down at Homage Studios in San Diego.

Williams: Physically together in a way that's pretty unusual… especially in the era of COVID. Many artists and creative people tend to work alone. We actually got to share studio space which is a whole different vibe and way better.

Silvestri: Definitely way better and that was one of the appeals really, when I went down to join you guys. Homage was already up and running. You (Scott), Jim, and Whilce.

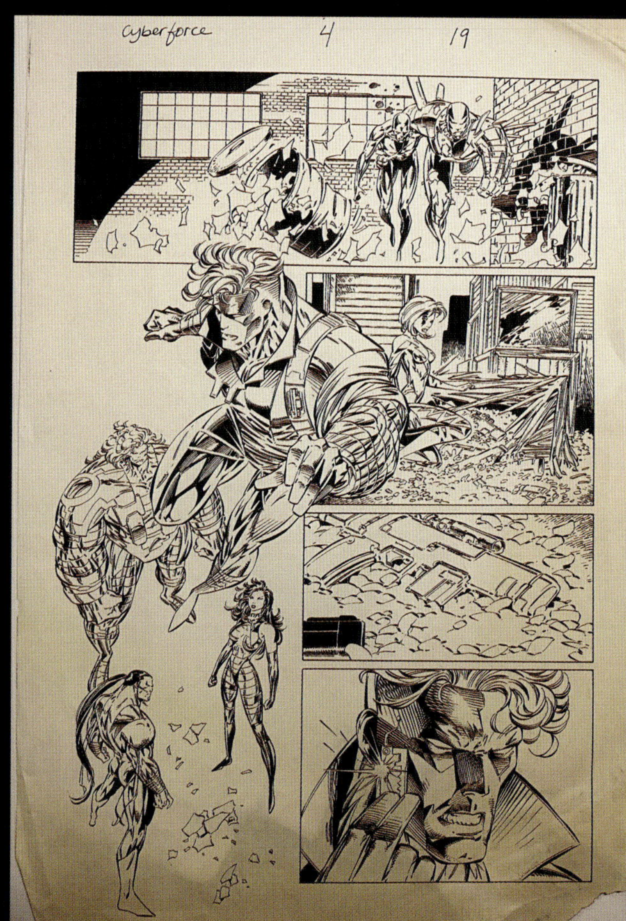

David Wohl: By the time that Brian started, there was you all… and all the Wildstorm artists were there in the summer of '93. I came down when we were working on *Cyberforce* #0… the Walt Simonson issue. Mike Heisler had called me to see if I wanted to work with you guys.

Williams: The funny thing is I don't even remember specifically what the impetus was for Marc to come down to join us.

Silvestri: I just wanted to screw with you. No, honestly when Image blew up, there was mad panic everywhere. I was living a freelancer life after I got into comics in 1981. We had no email. It was FedEx and the phone. So, to be able to hang out with people who did what I did, that I respected. That, combined with the fact that Image was just getting started, I absolutely think the exchange of ideas back then, specifically between me and Jim, we could pick each other's brains to kind of make this stronger.

Williams: Beyond the social implications, you also get the creative push from fellow artists. It's nice to have other artists in the same place, doing high quality work, it pushes you, it inspires you. There is the camaraderie, but you also get friendly competition, which is not a bad thing.

Silvestri: Homage Studios grew so fast and we had so much talent just walking through the door. Young new guys were all growing and evolving as they came in as they were sort of being absorbed into the studio… and everybody was evolving because everybody was around new ideas, fresh perspectives… David Finch and Travis Scott and J. Scott Campbell and they just kept coming through the door and it's like wow this is great and it was good for us old timers.

Brian Haberlin was at the forefront of what we all enjoy today with computer colors. He was working on a freaking Apple's Abacus back then. I remember that you know maybe moving those little balls over the sides and just figuring out how to do this stuff.

Brian Haberlin: I gotta give credit to John and Clydene Nee on the technical side. It was all three of us working together that made it work.

Wohl: I feel like that for the early issues of *Cyberforce*, it was Joe Chiodo reinventing coloring in a color guide. Haberlin wanted to remove that step by bringing in painters to work on the computer.

Haberlin: I had a hell of a crew. I was befuddled when I first got there and people were doing color guides. I didn't know color guides even existed at that point. Joe Chiodo hands me a color guide. I'm like "Why don't we scan these? What's my job again?"

Silvestri: I remember we tried that and it didn't work. I don't have the originals, I don't know if Joe still has them, but those color guides were a thing of beauty. It was weird because on the one hand you were thinking "Oh my God, I love looking at these things," and, in the back of your mind, saying most of that is not going to translate.

Haberlin: If you looked at a lot of the old color guides at that time, they were like almost four ups. So if you look at the ones from Malibu Comics, who had a touted coloring department, they were small four ups, like four on a 8 x 11 sheet.

Wohl: I remember at Marvel… I'm not going to say who… but he didn't think that coloring would even work out. He said it was too complicated and thought it was going to be the downfall of Image Comics.

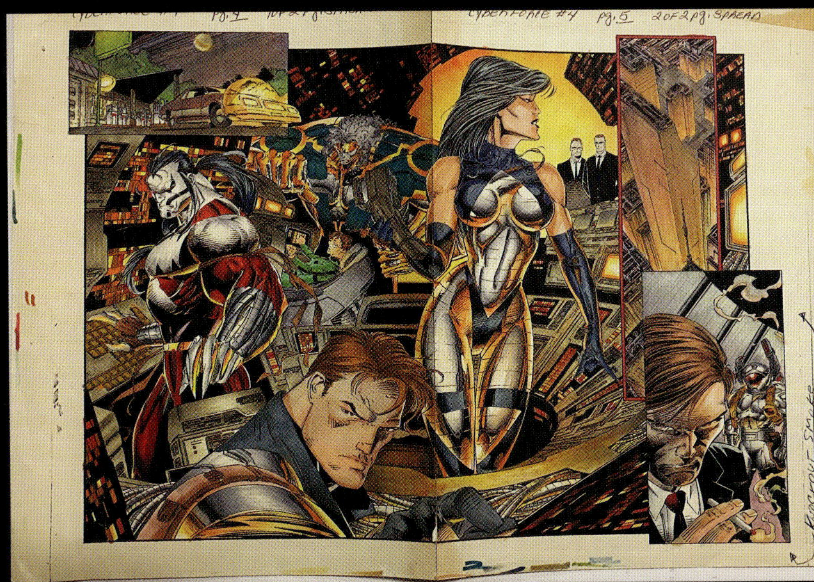

Silvestri: Because he wasn't looking ahead like Brian and his team were to the future. The future happened real fast. I mean Olyoptics was a good partner for us too because they understood Brian's language. They could at least get close.

Williams: It was a game changer. It's like those moments you'll never forget because we all lived and breathed comics and then somebody put something out that's revolutionary… it stays with you forever.

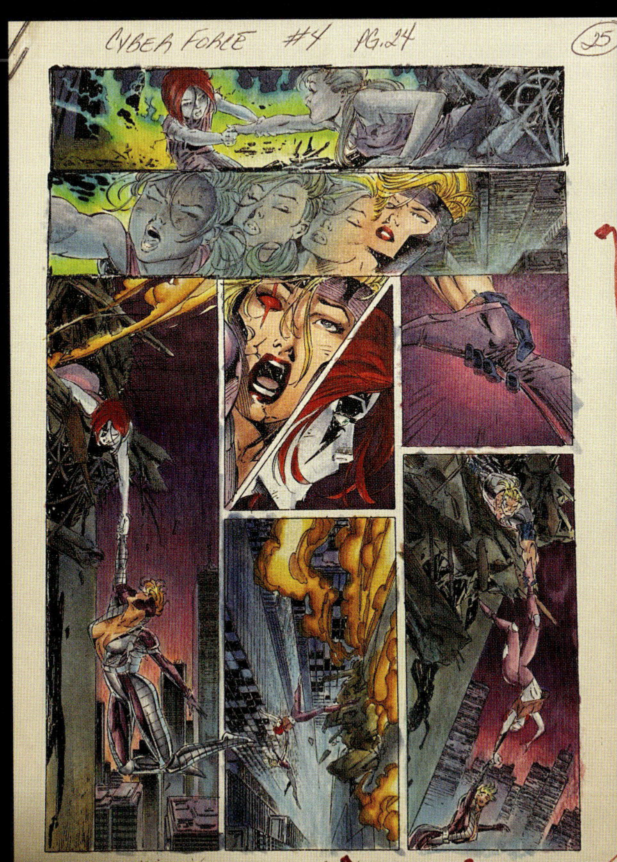

Silvestri: All the real changes were happening in Brian's sphere because those are all technological.

Haberlin: It would take 24 hours for us to do a CMYK conversion of pages once they were done and trapping them. We were stupid enough to work on full size 11 by 17 at 300 DPI banks.

That was when Jim did the five gatefolds, and they were still doing five pages at 11 x 17 on those old slow computers. To have a computer that could actually do it, we had to spend $10,000. Olyoptics existed because they used the Cod Barrett system, so they could run on PCs for maybe $1000 or $2000 bucks. The Cod Barrett system would cost whatever, so you could have a whole bunch of guys in the studio without having a whole bunch of money to fund that studio. It was like coloring by numbers. You couldn't see the representation of what the page looked like, you just knew this was a color ramp from 286 to whatever. In the Cod Barret system, you couldn't see it until you printed it out somehow for approval.

Williams: I chose to just stay in analog, man… just pieces of paper.

Haberlin: But now, I can draw my character and then print it out.

Silvestri: The enthusiasm. Everyone was part of this new club. Love Image or hate Image… everyone knew about Image. The pressure was pretty immense… but that pressure and chaos was what got our adrenaline going. There was so much insanity back then. I look back and think "How did we get any comics out?"

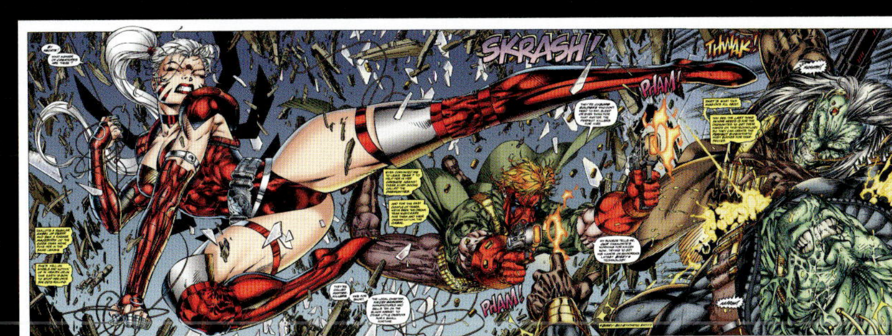

Williams: Well, we were 30 years younger first of all. Comics are a young man's game. But Marc was also having to learn the hard knocks of business life. How do you pay people on time and set up publishing schedules? I know you had a support staff, but you have to OK stuff, and sit in on the meetings and think where was I going to get the next Michael Turner?

Silvestri: It was never-ending.

Wohl: But when you are selling a million copies, you know that made the choices a lot easier, right?

Silvestri: And, it also ratchets up the pressure… the numbers. You always have to stay ahead. The only reason we existed so long was that the numbers were so high back then that we could make all those mistakes. There was a moment in time when suddenly the sales for everyone were not jiving with the costs… all future talent heard the stories of what the original talent was making and expected the same, and it's like, well that's not how reality works… but that's the game we had to play… so it was a very dangerous time there, but *Cyberforce*, for me, the fact that we're still talking about it today and we're doing this Kickstarter to celebrate 30 years, it was really an amazing time.[7]

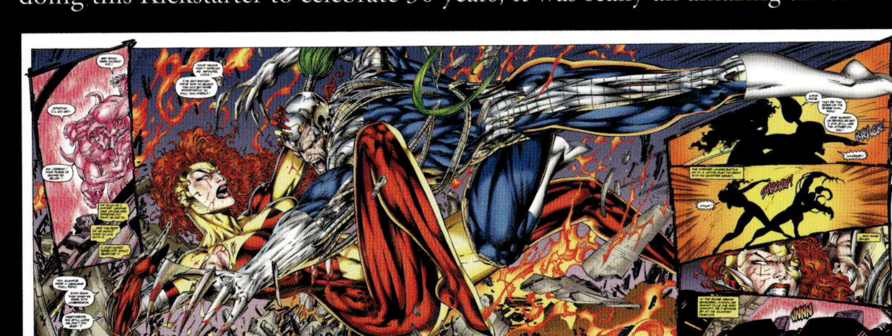

”

7 Wu, Lisa, with Elena Salcedo and Vincent Valentine, eds. "30 YEARS OF CYBERFORCE," in *Cyberforce* #1 30th Anniversary Edition (June 2022): 31-37.

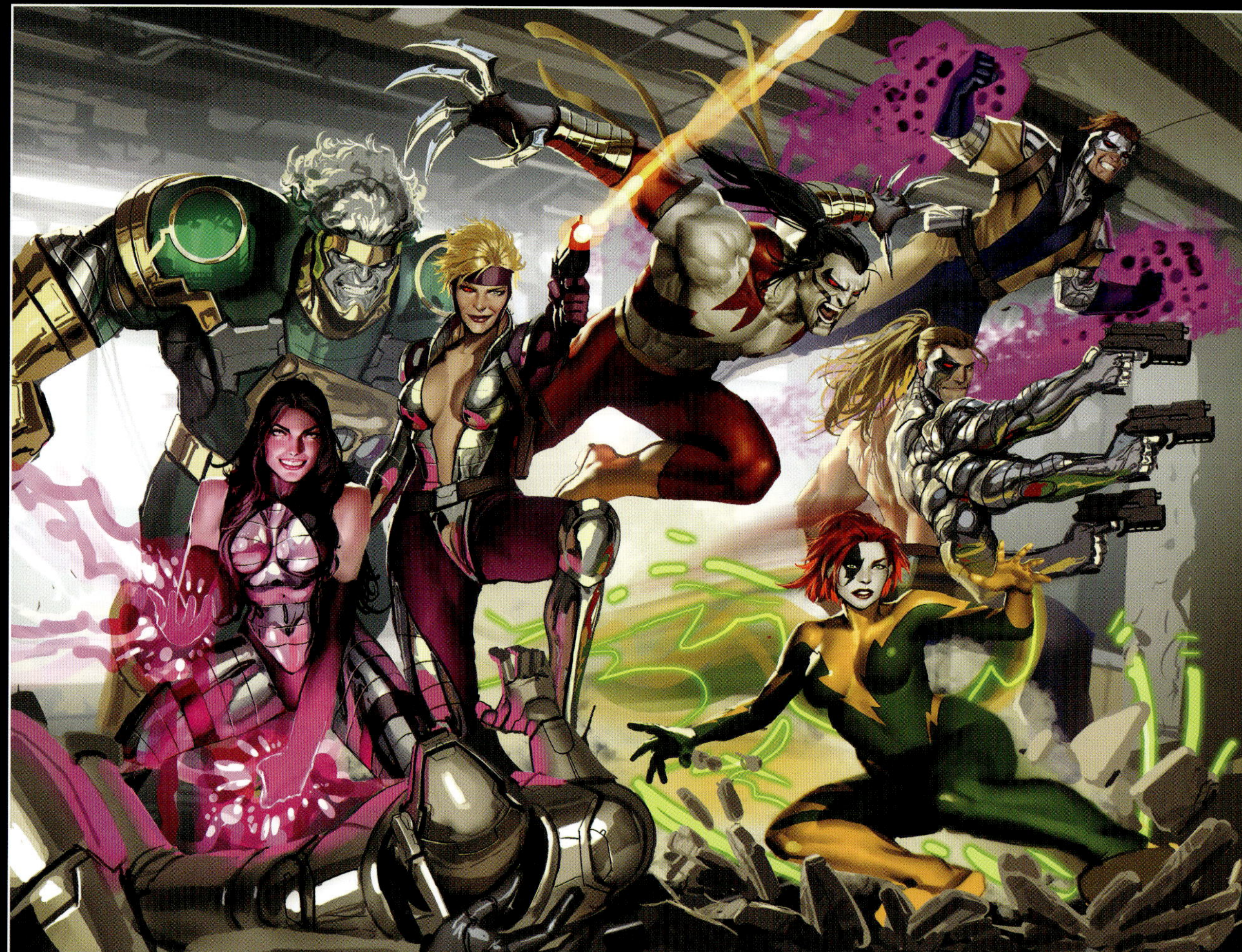

Above. *Cyberforce* #1 30th Anniversary Edition [2022]
Kickstarter variant cover, art by: Stjepan Sejic

Below. *Cyberforce* #1 30th Anniversary Edition [2022]
Top Cow Store Exclusive variant cover, art by: Brett Booth and Thomas Mason

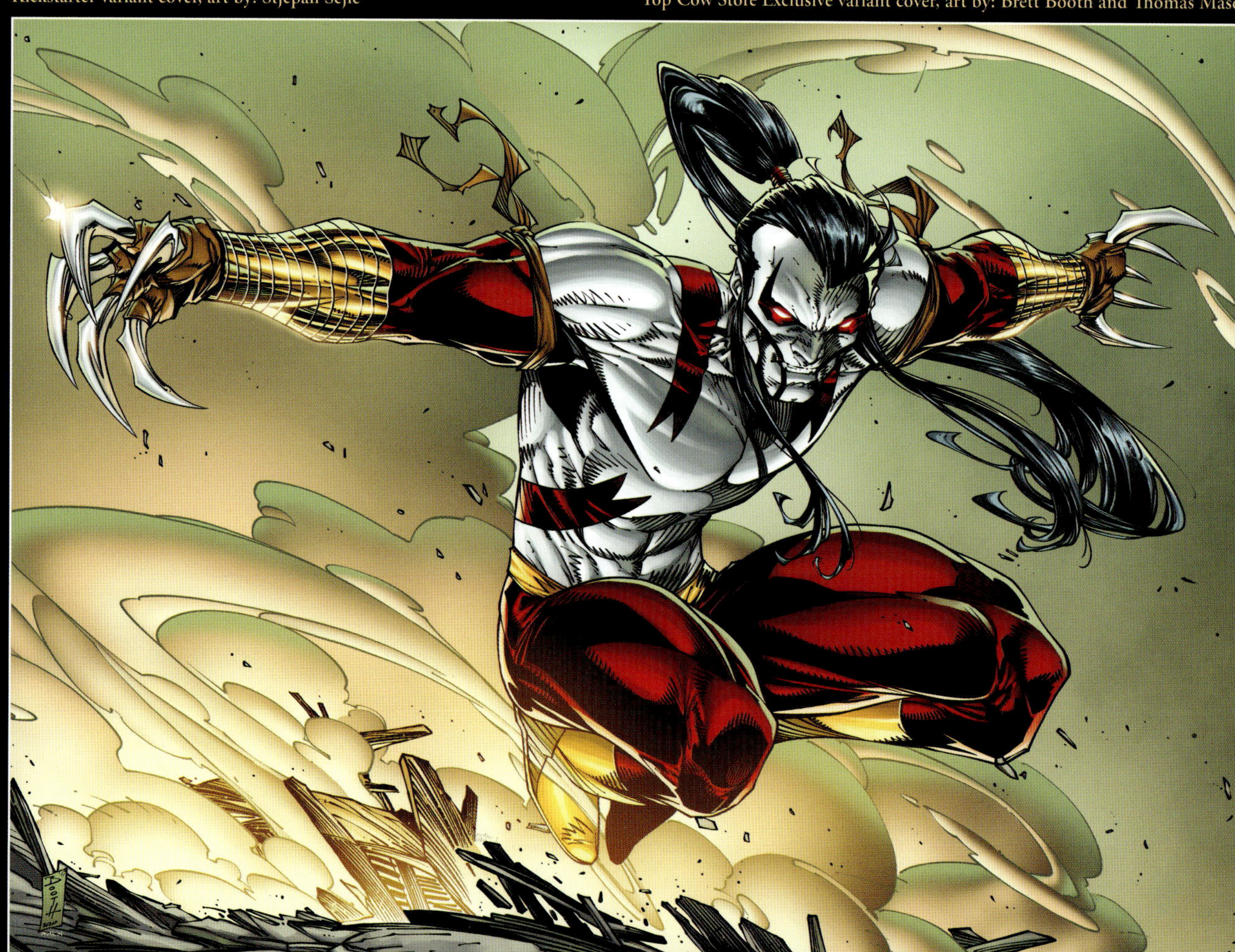

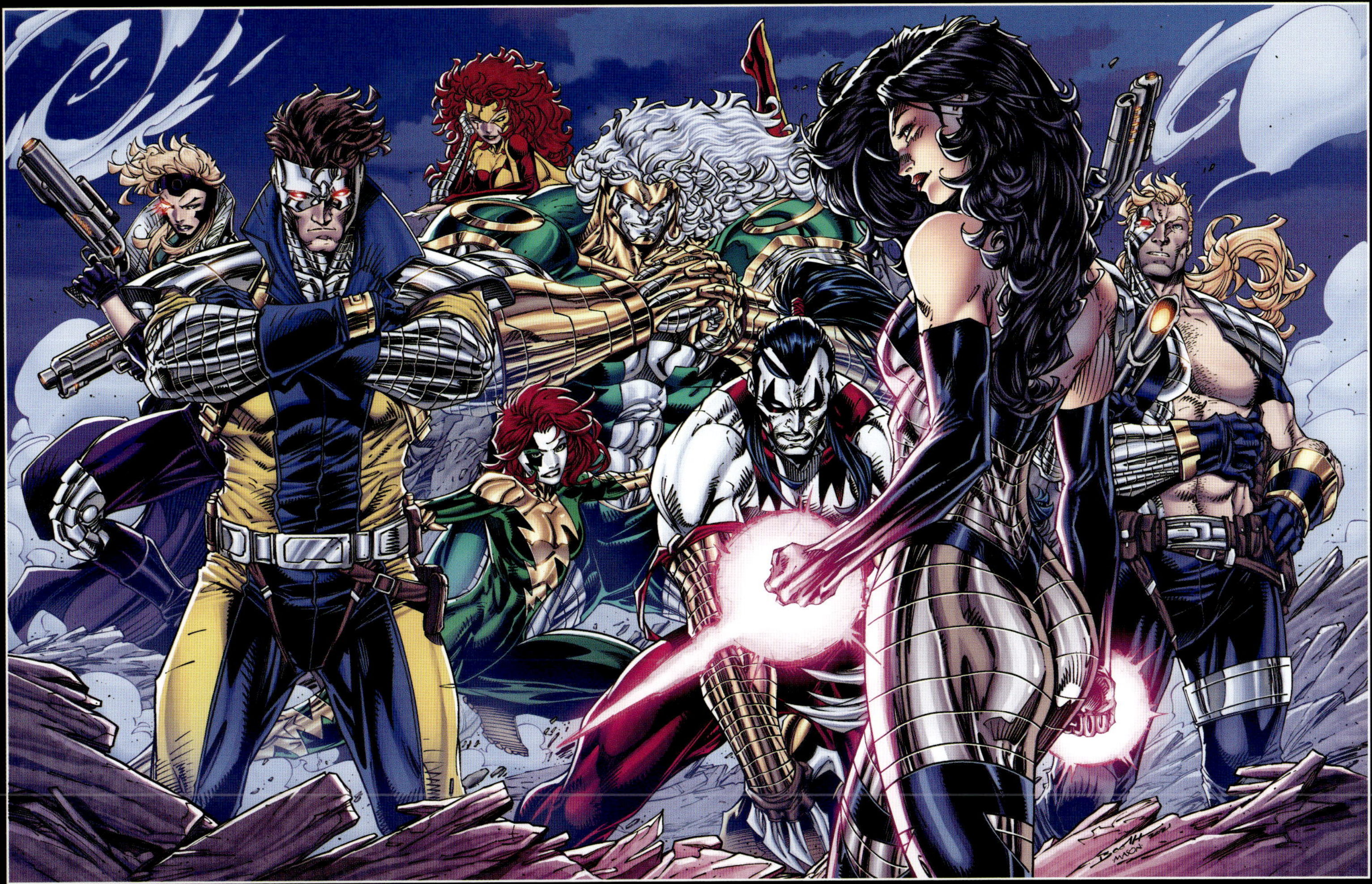

Above. *Cyberforce* #1 30th Anniversary Edition [2022] cover C, art by: Brett Booth and Thomas Mason
Below. line art by: Brett Booth

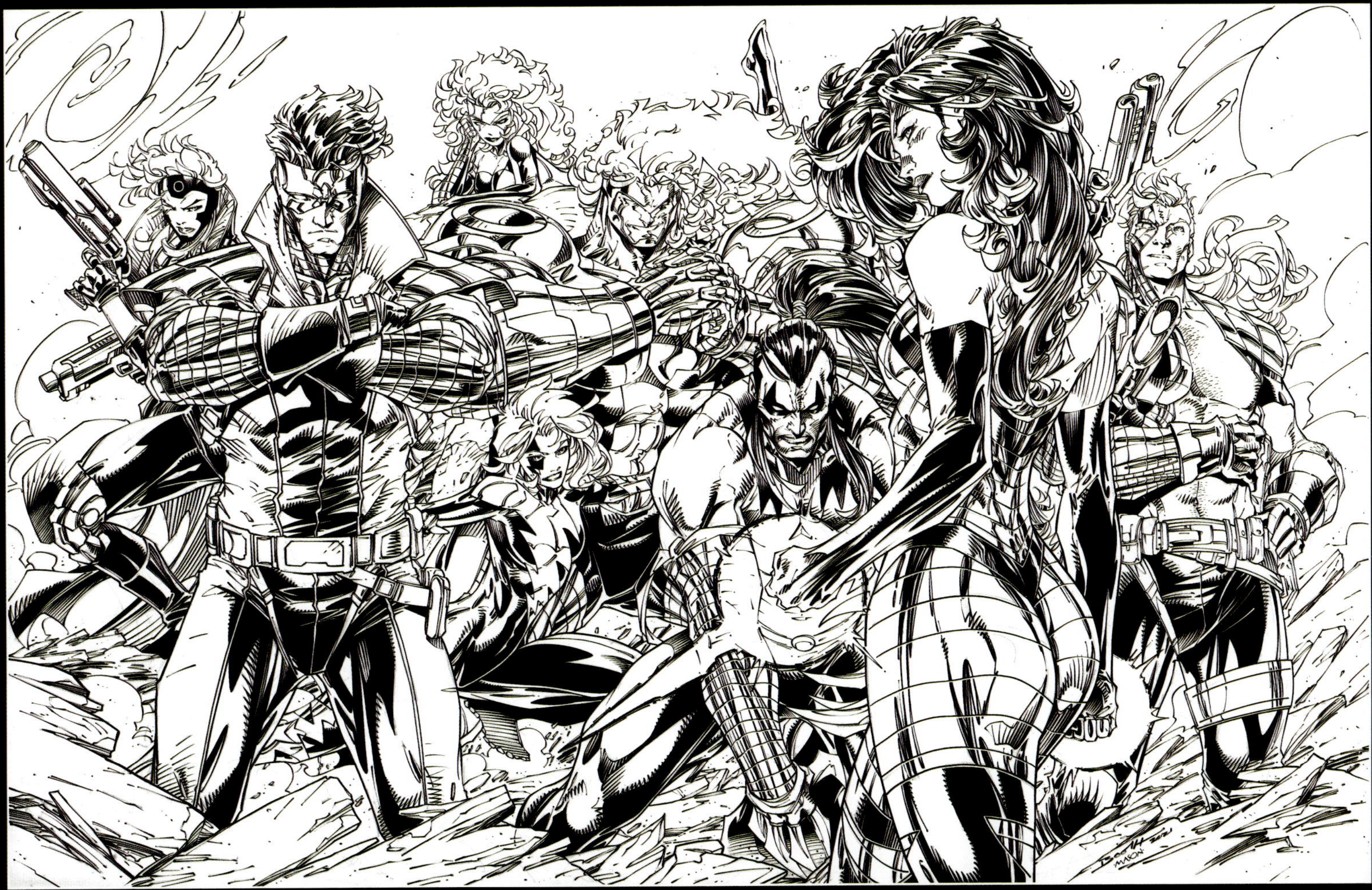

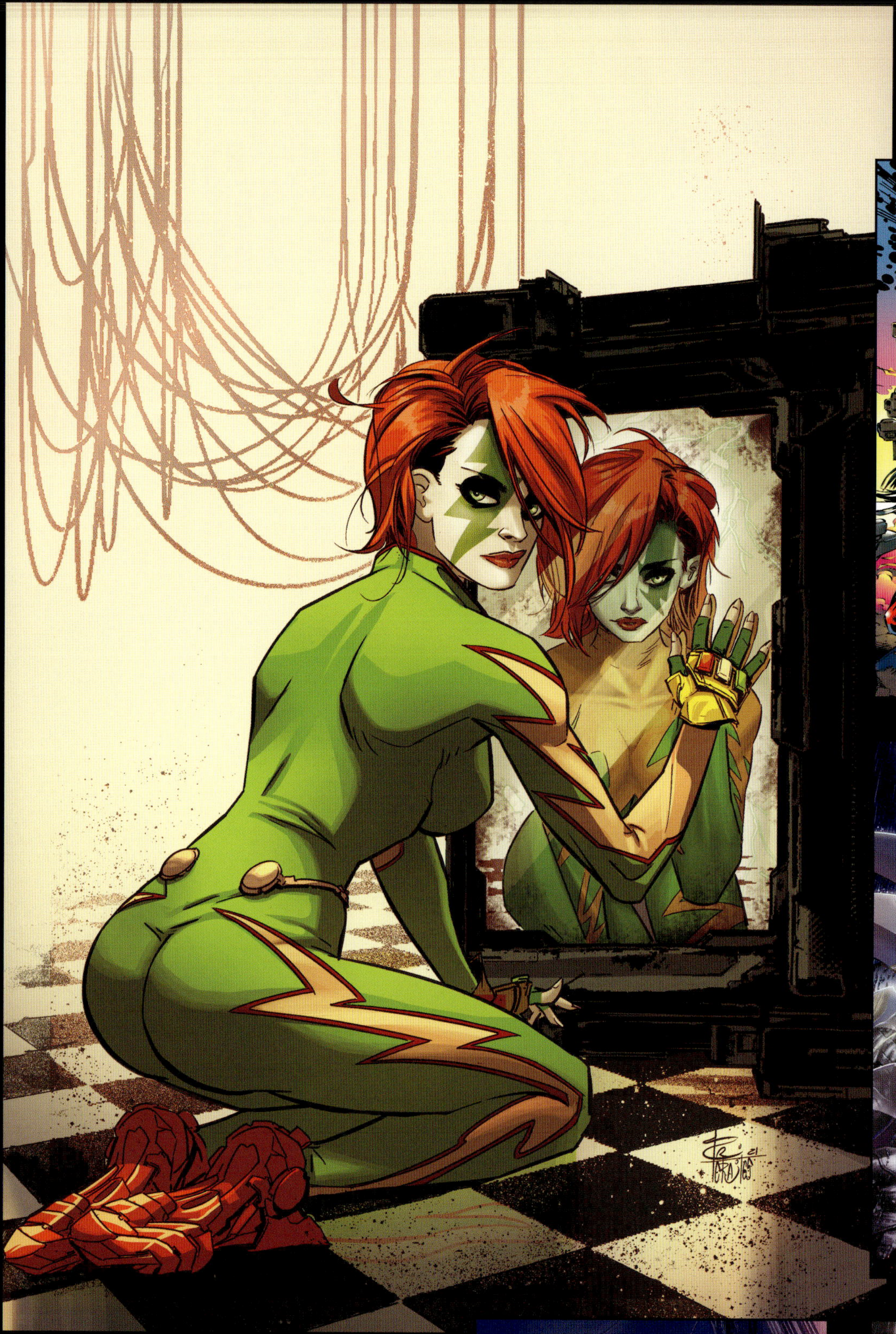

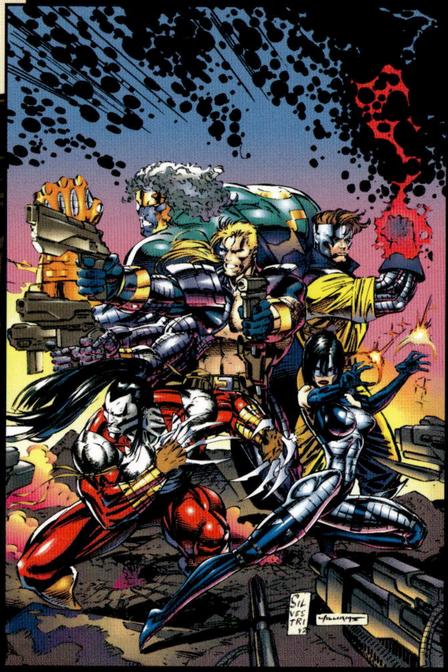

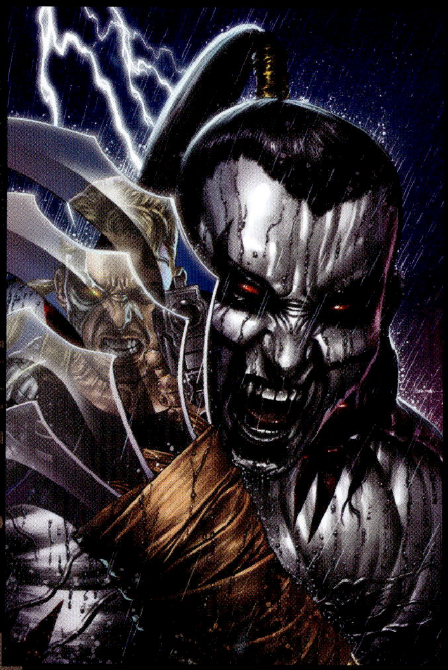

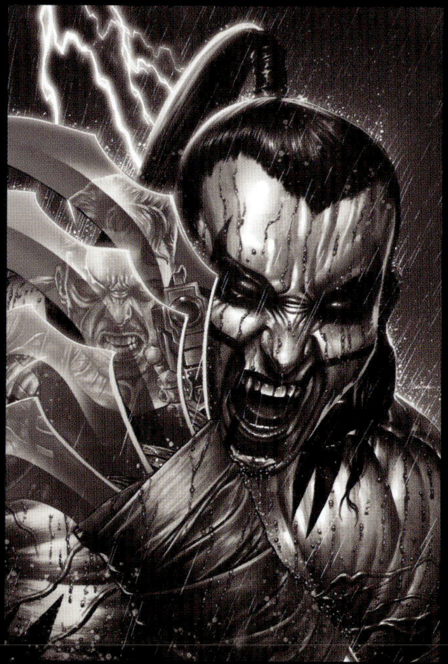

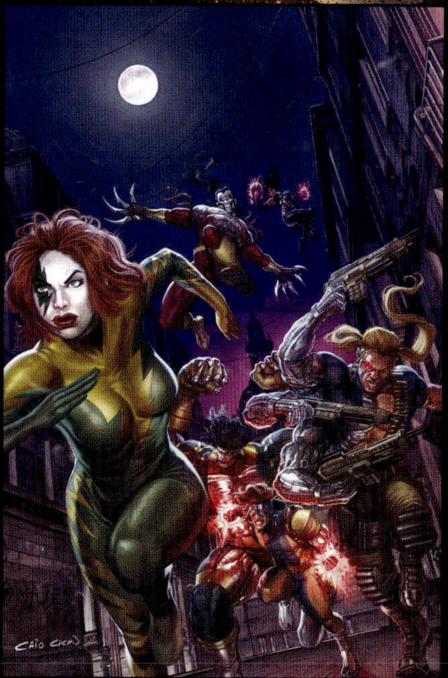

This page, clockwise from above.

Cyberforce #1 30th Anniversary Edition [2022] cover B,
art by: Priscilla Petraites

Cyberforce #1 30th Anniversary Edition [2022] cover A,
art by: Marc Silvestri, Scott Williams, Joe Chiodo,
and restored by Vincent Valentine

Cyberforce #1 30th Anniversary Edition [2022]
Big Time Collectibles variant cover,
art by: Mico Suayan

Cyberforce #1 30th Anniversary Edition [2022]
Big Time Collectibles and WhatNot variant cover,
art by: Mico Suayan

Cyberforce #1 30th Anniversary Edition [2022]
The Comic Mint variant cover,
art by: Caio Cacau

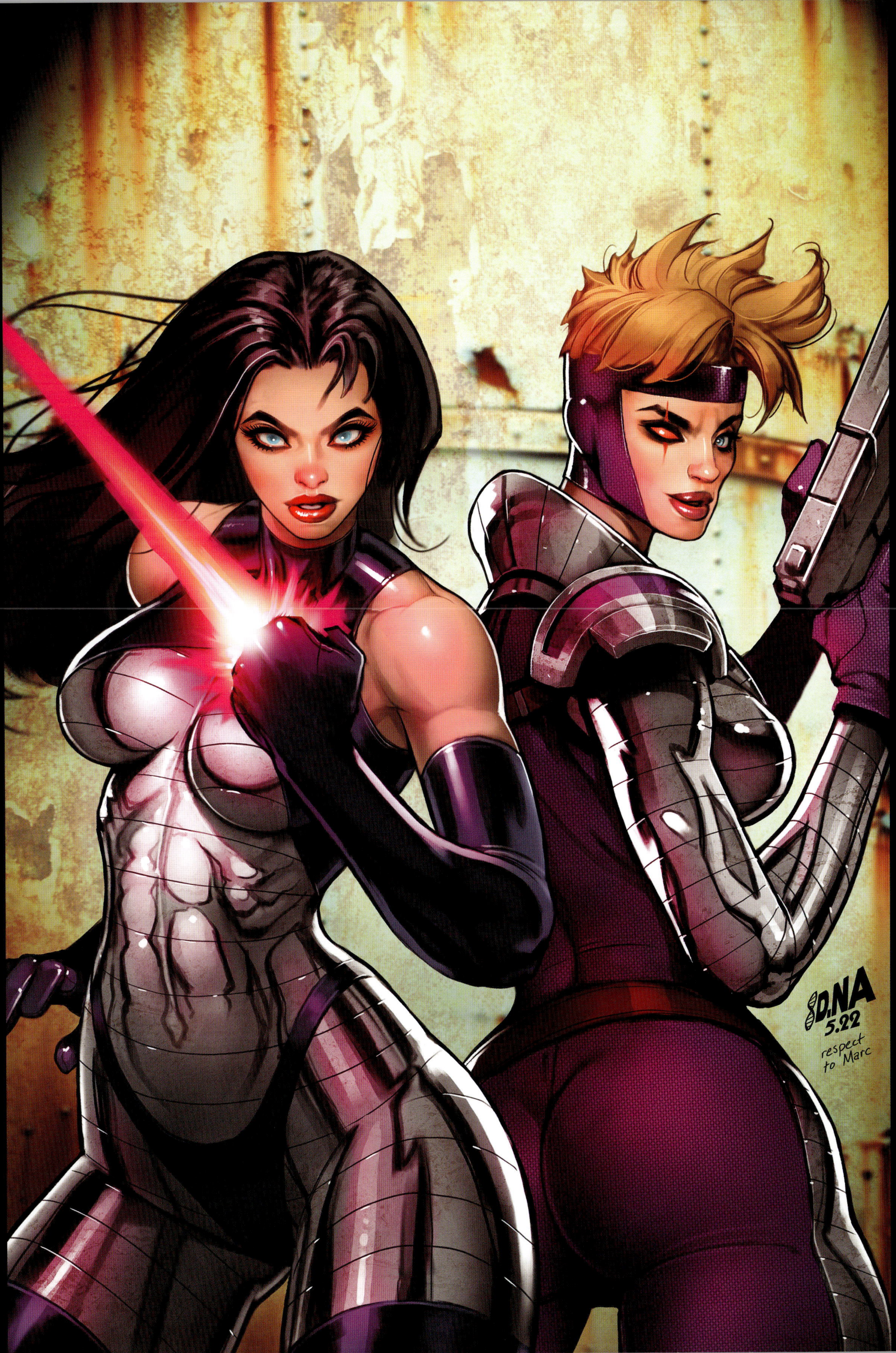

Cyberforce ##1 30th Anniversary Edition [2022] Big Time Collectibles variant cover,
art by: David Nakayama

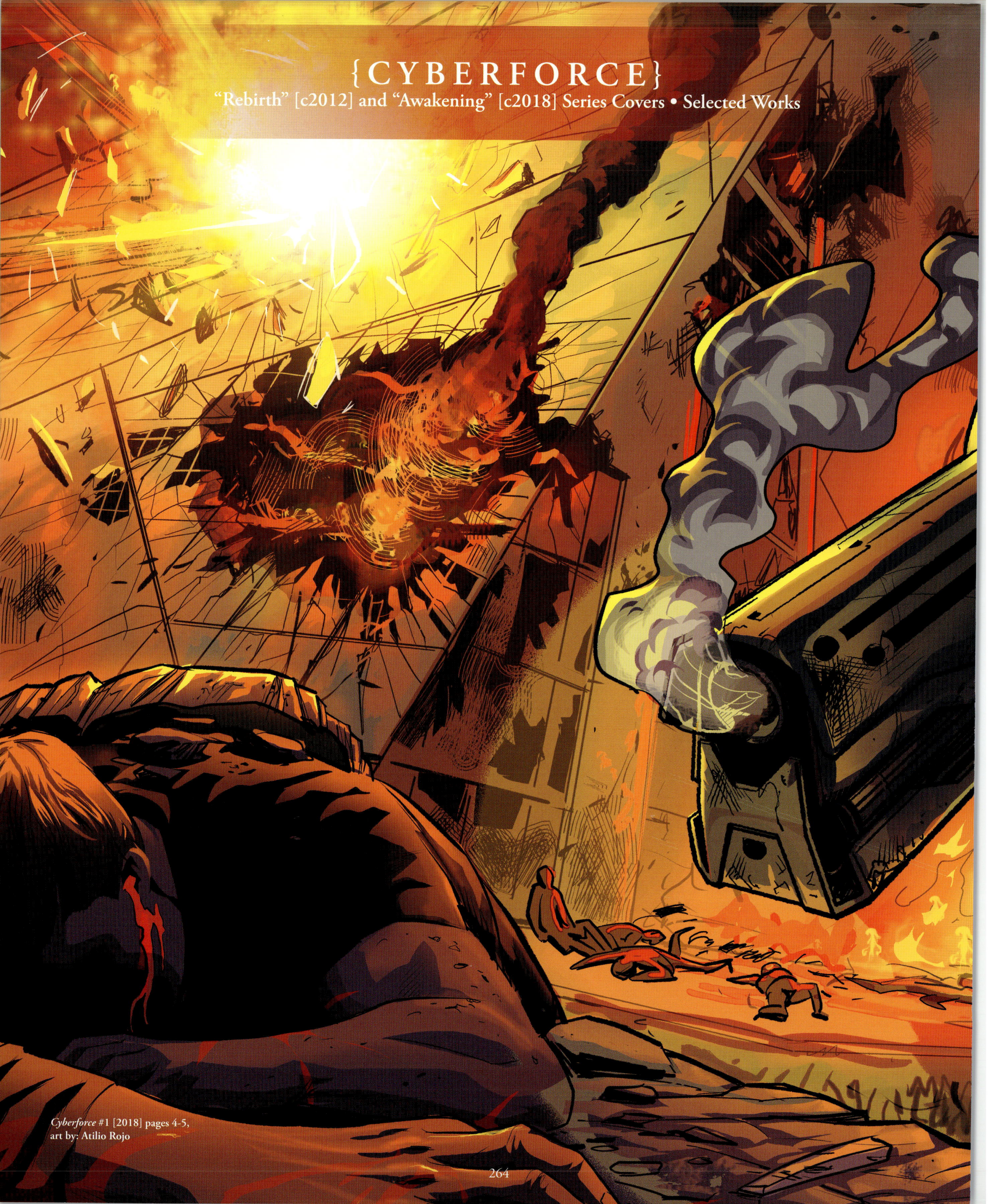

Cyberforce #1 [2018] pages 4-5, art by: Atilio Rojo

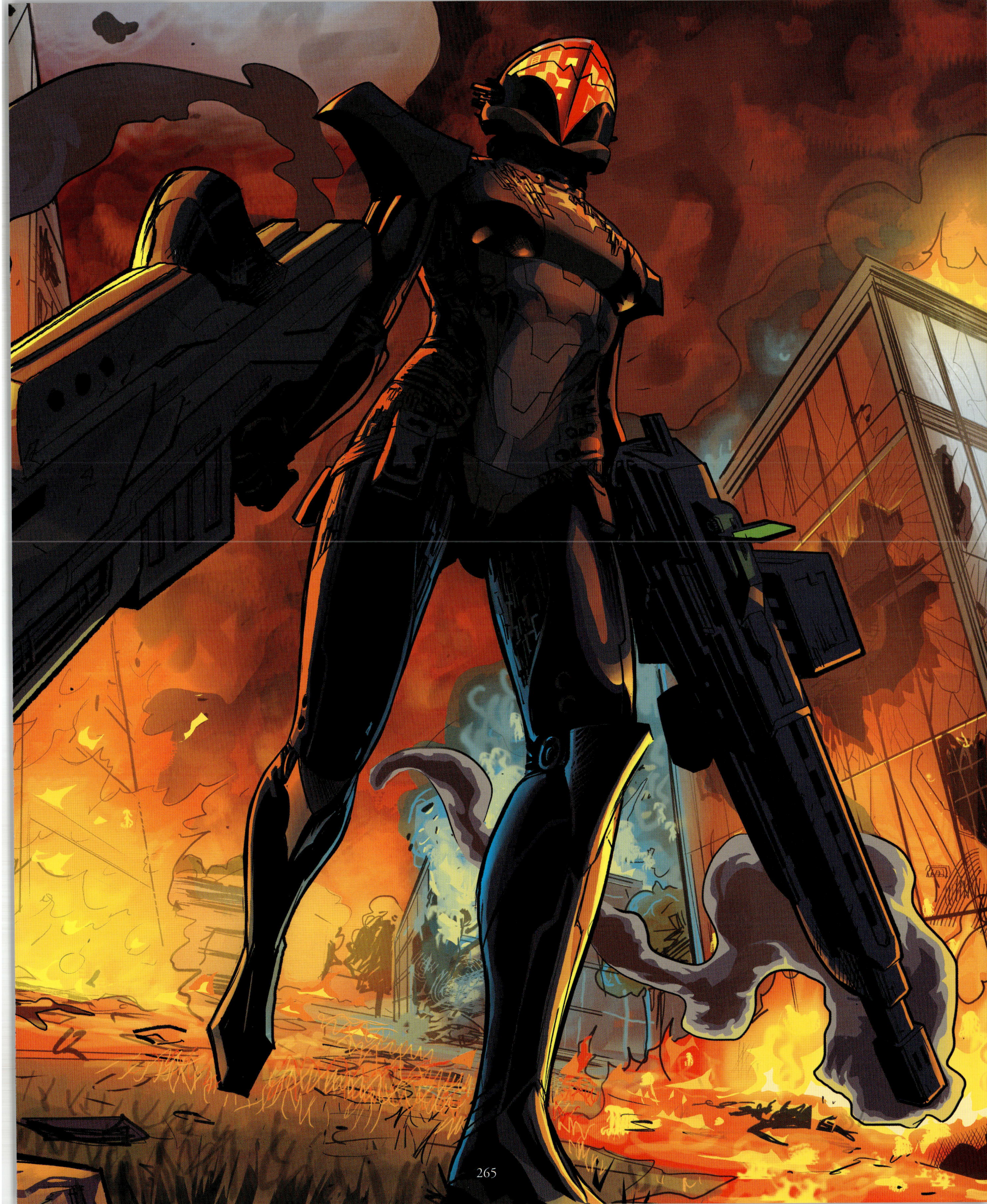

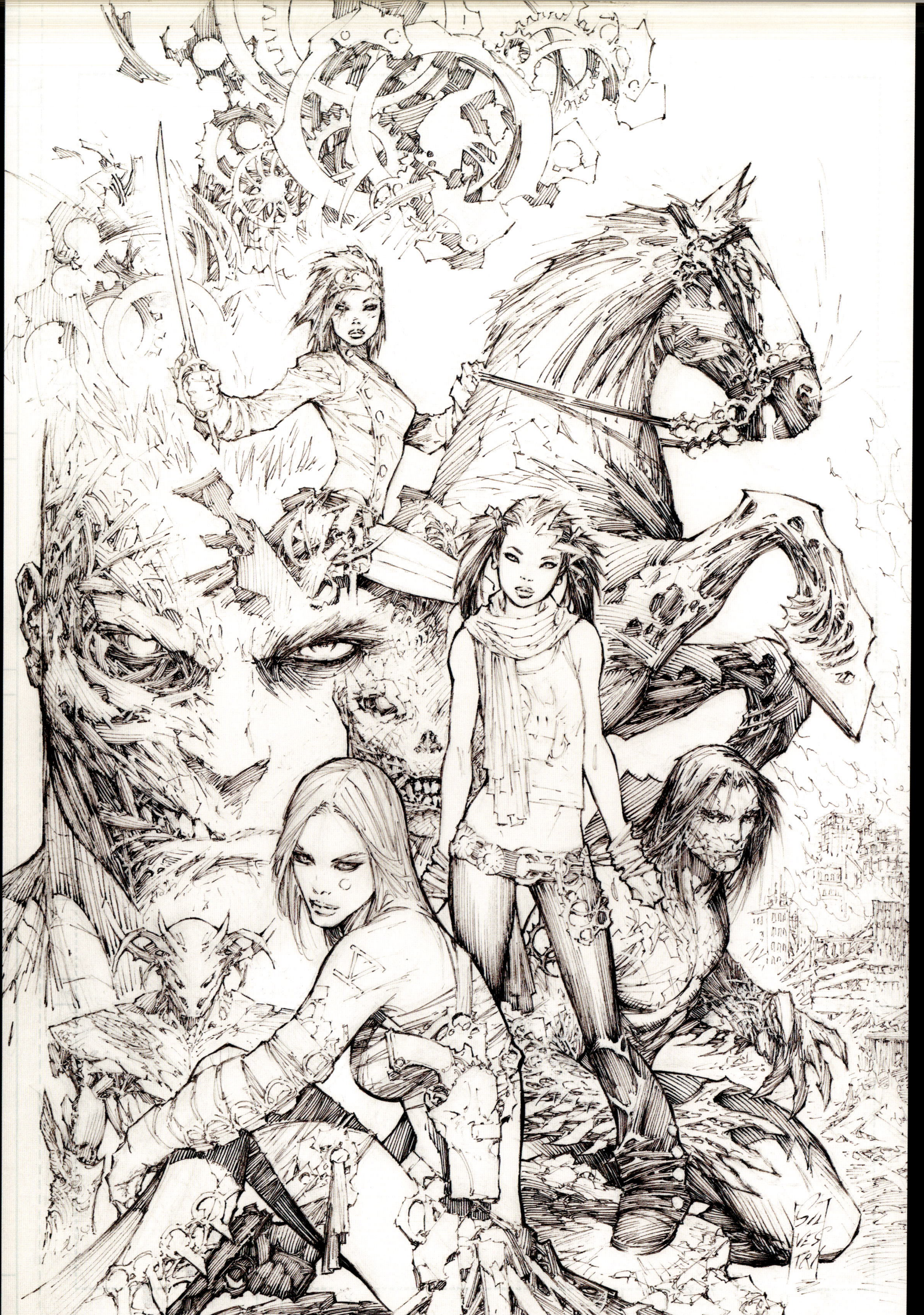

Cyberforce #1 [2012] cover B,
line art by: Marc Silvestri

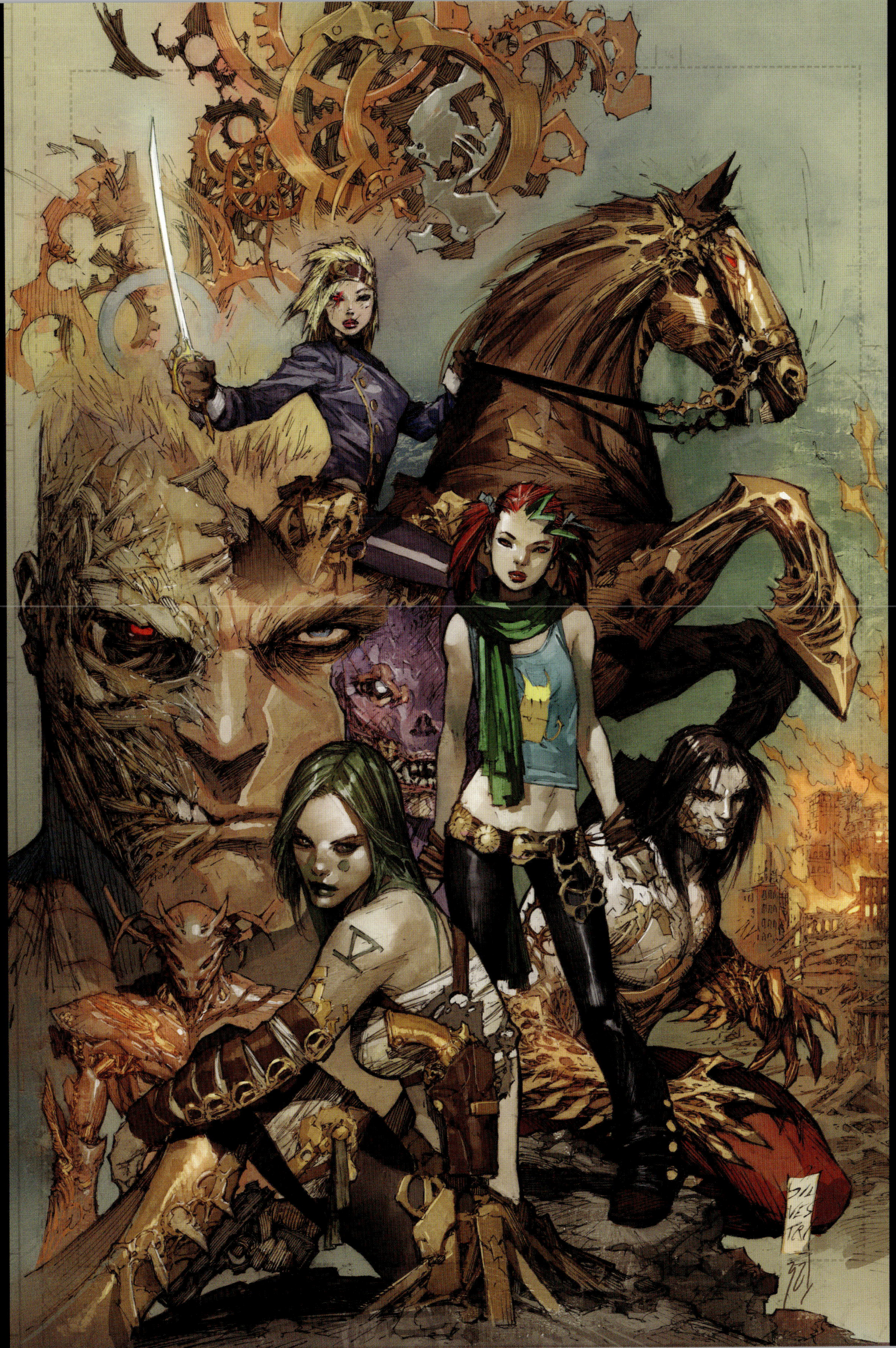

Cyberforce #1 [2012] cover A,
art by: Marc Silvestri and Sunny Gho

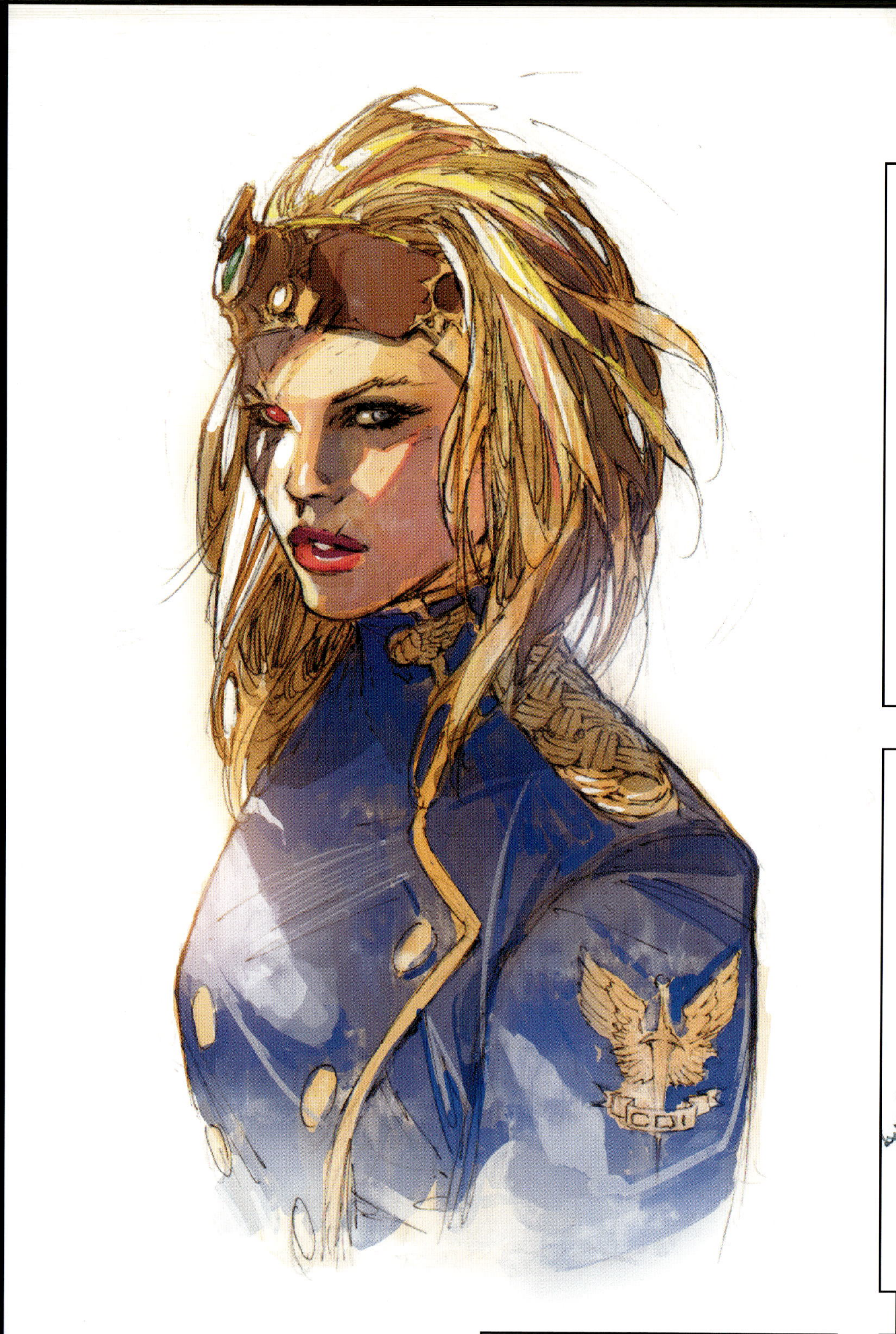

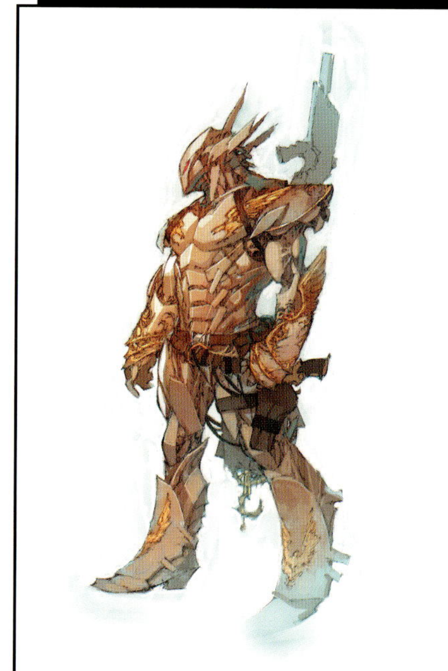

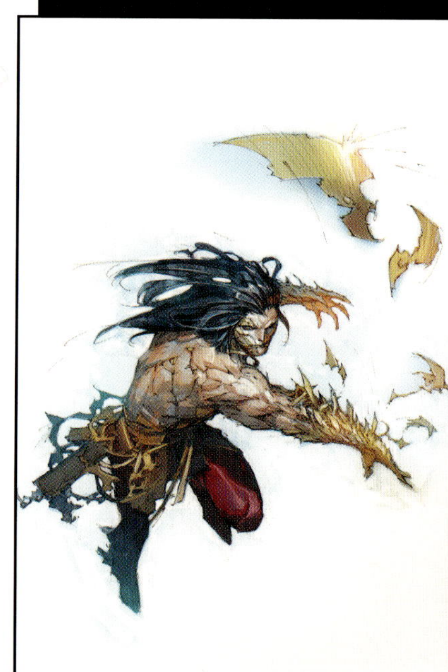

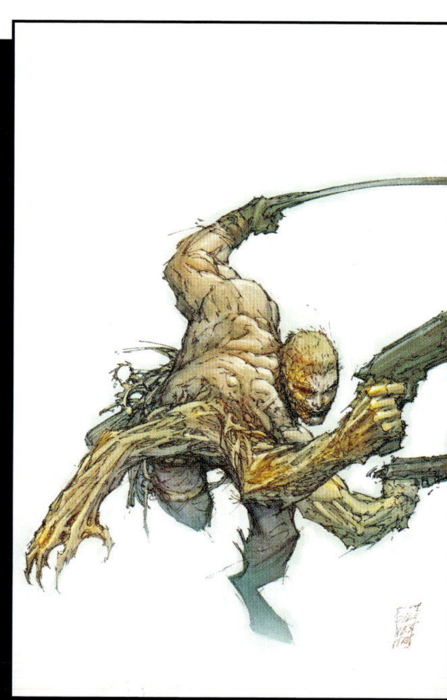

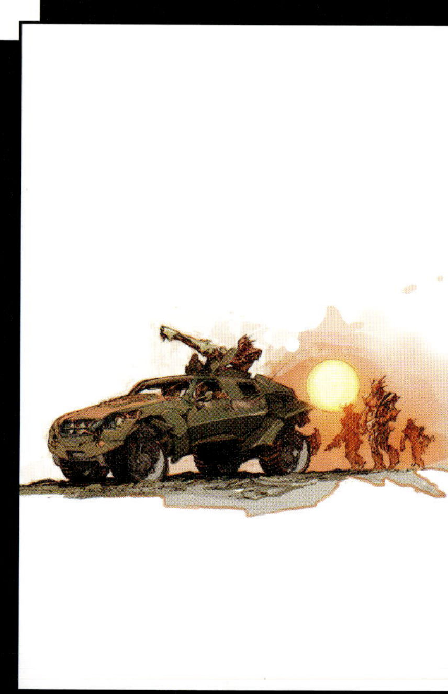

This page, clockwise from above.

Cyberforce #1 [2012] cover C,
art by: Marc Silvestri and Sunny Gho

Cyberforce #2 [2012] cover C,
art by: Marc Silvestri and Sunny Gho

Cyberforce #3 [2012] cover C,
art by: Marc Silvestri and Sunny Gho

Cyberforce #4 [2012] cover C,
art by: Marc Silvestri and Sunny Gho

Cyberforce #5 [2012] cover C,
art by: Marc Silvestri and Sunny Gho

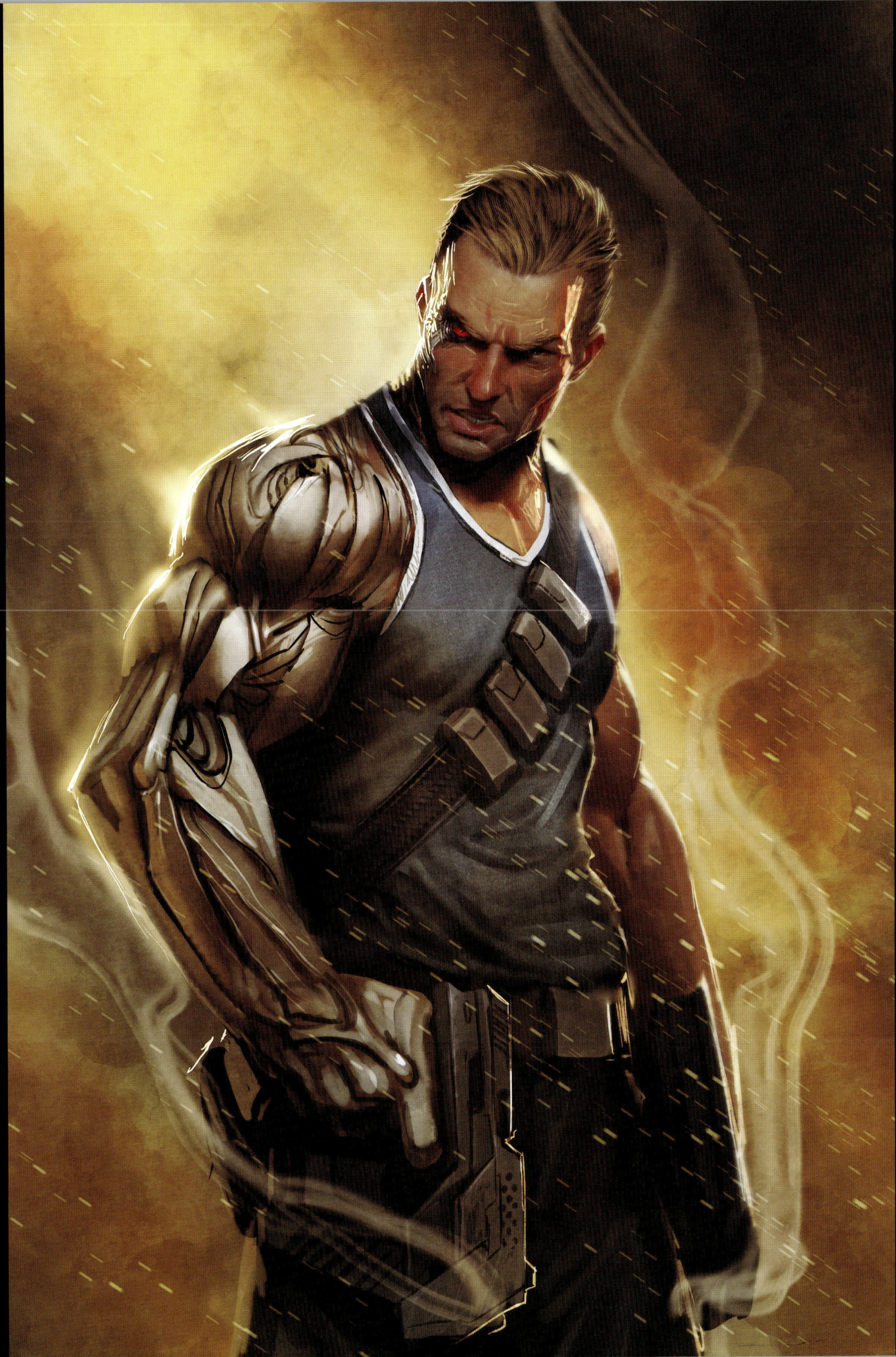

Cyberforce #3 [2012] cover D,
art by: Stjepan Sejic

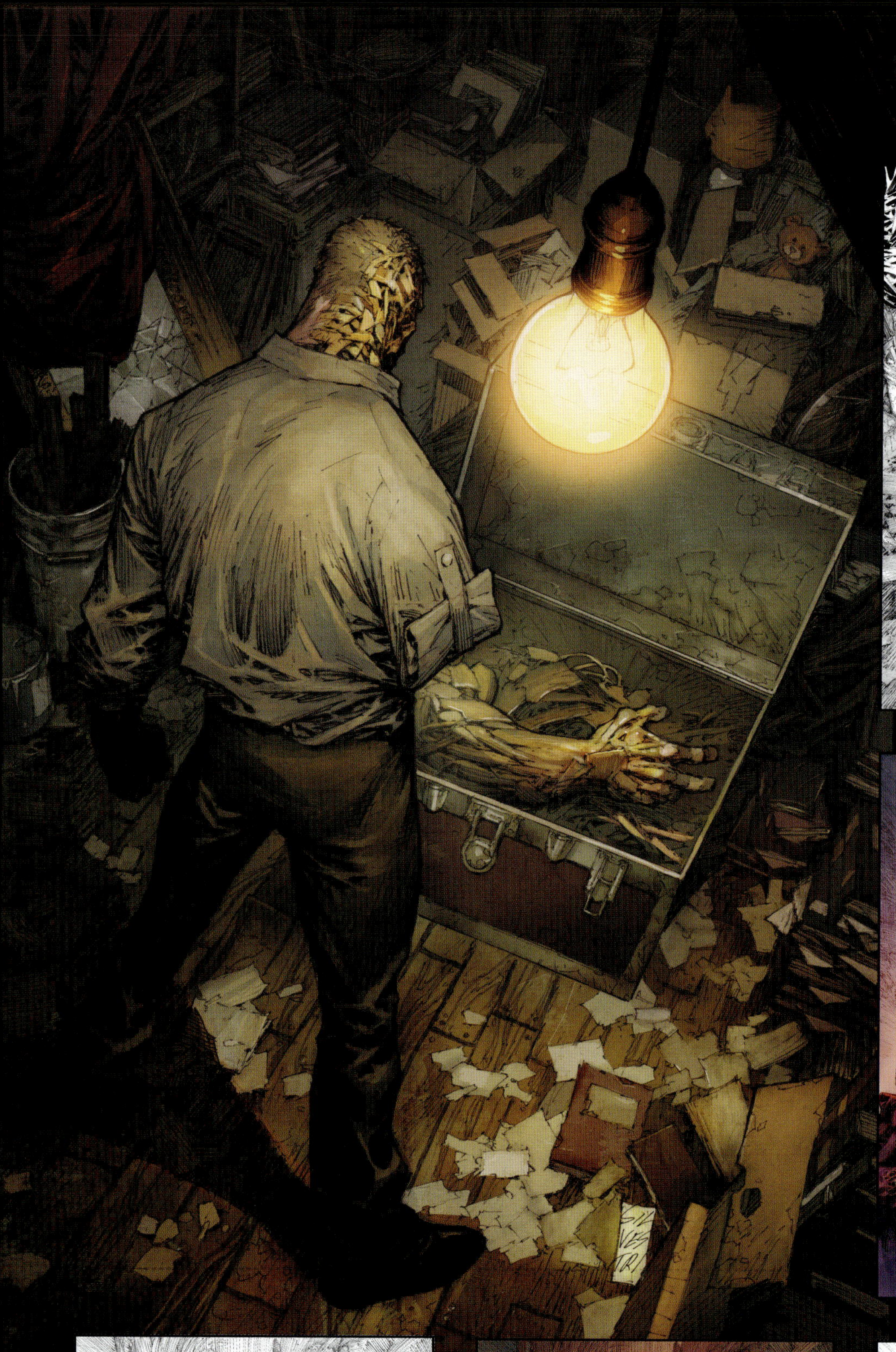

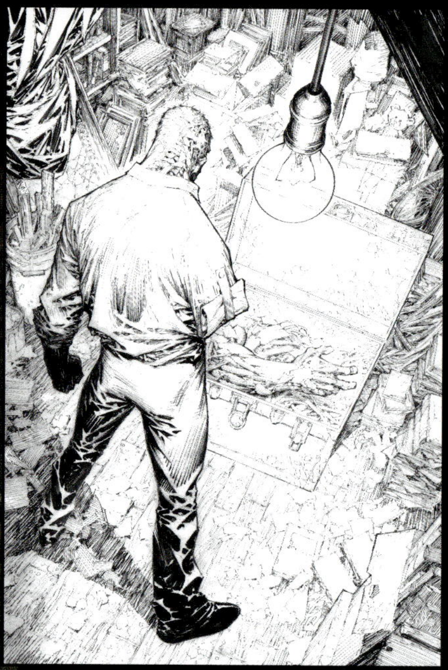

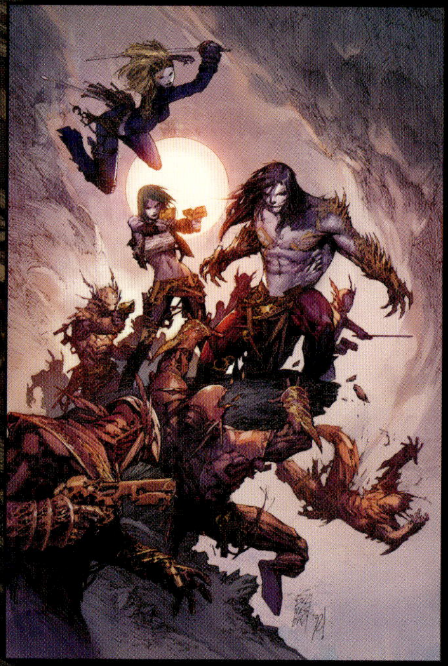

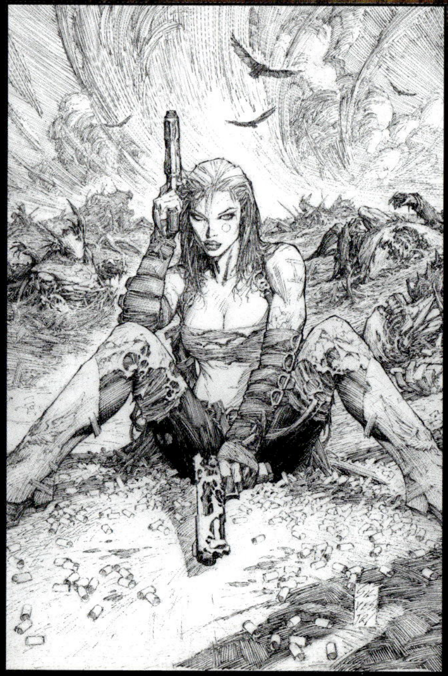

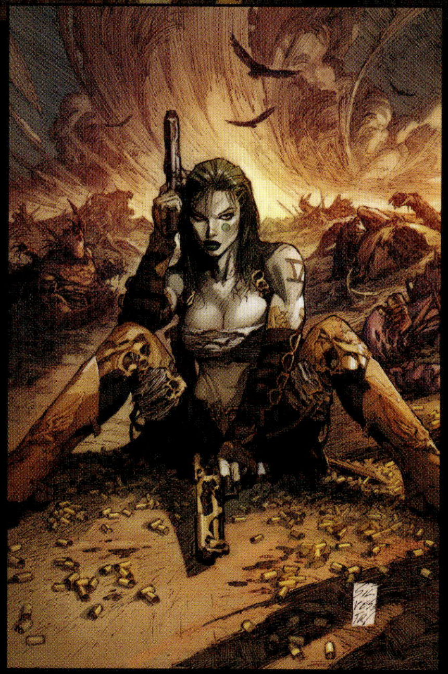

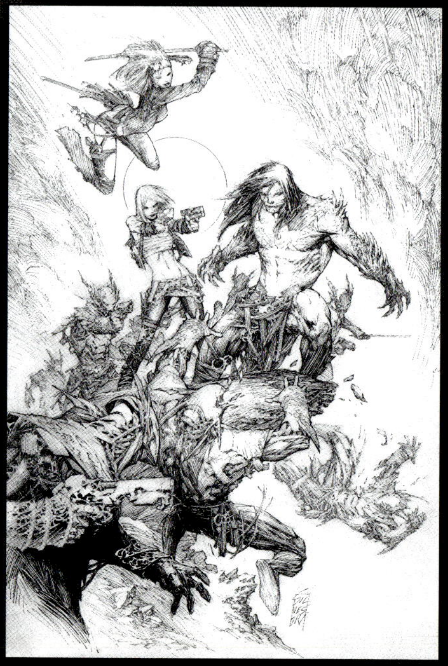

Clockwise from top left: *Cyberforce* #2A, 2B, 3A, 3B, 4A, and 4B [2012] covers, art by: Marc Silvestri and Sunny Gho

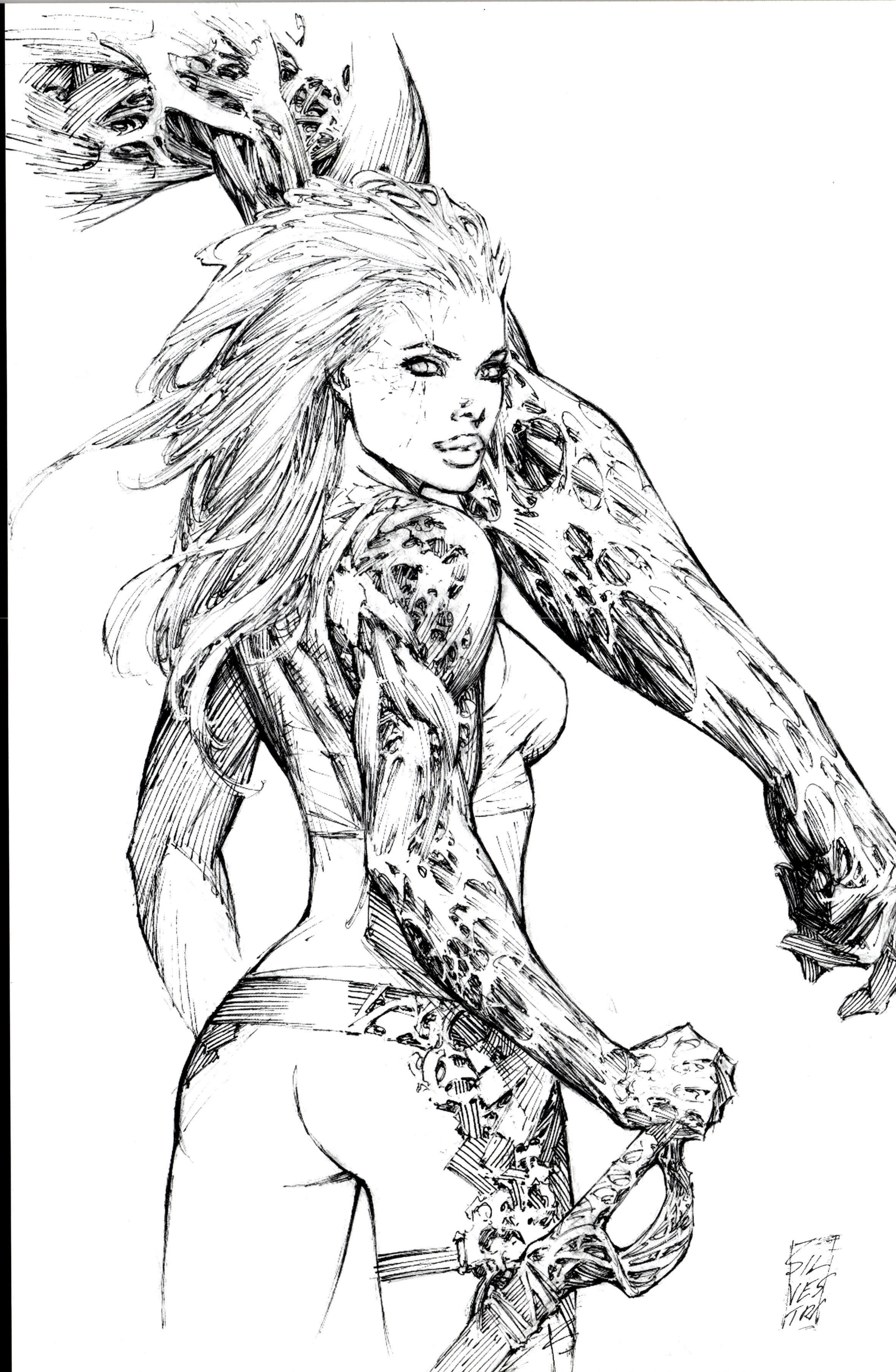

Cyberforce #5 [2012] cover D,
line art by: Marc Silvestri

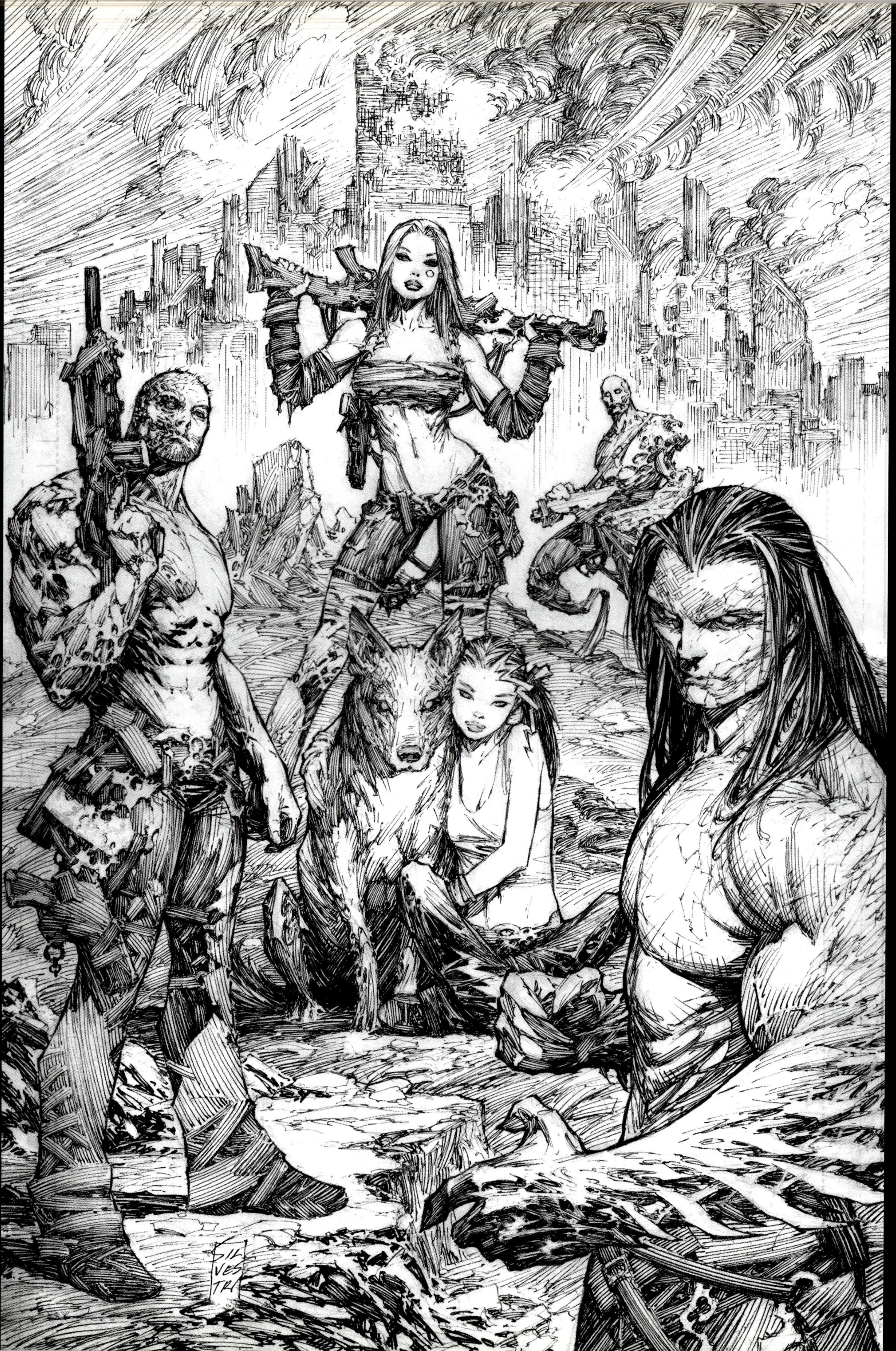

Cyberforce #5 [2012] cover B,
line art by: Marc Silvestri

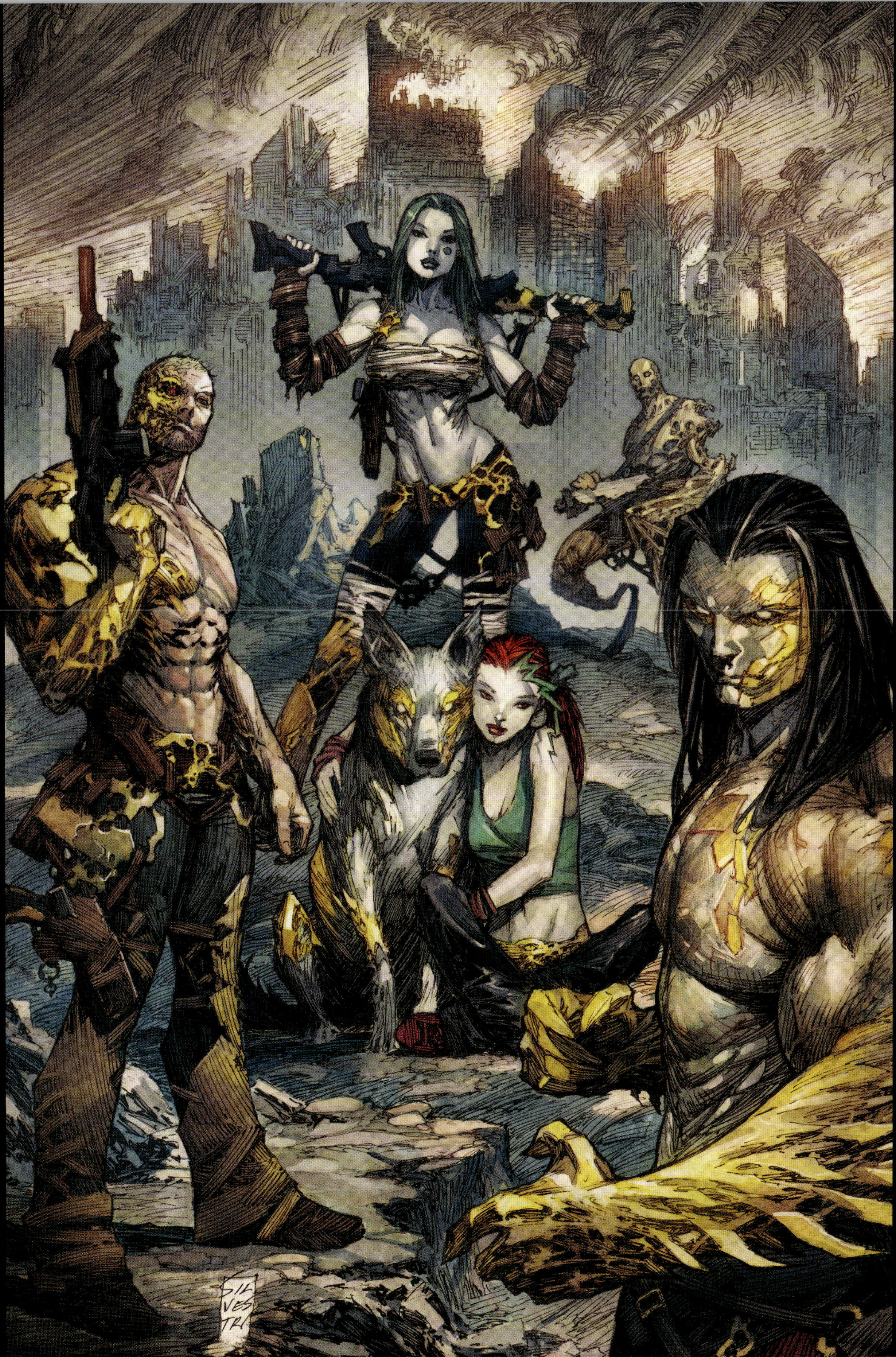

Cyberforce #5 [2012] cover A,
art by: Marc Silvestri and Sunny Gho

Cyberforce #6-7 [2012] covers

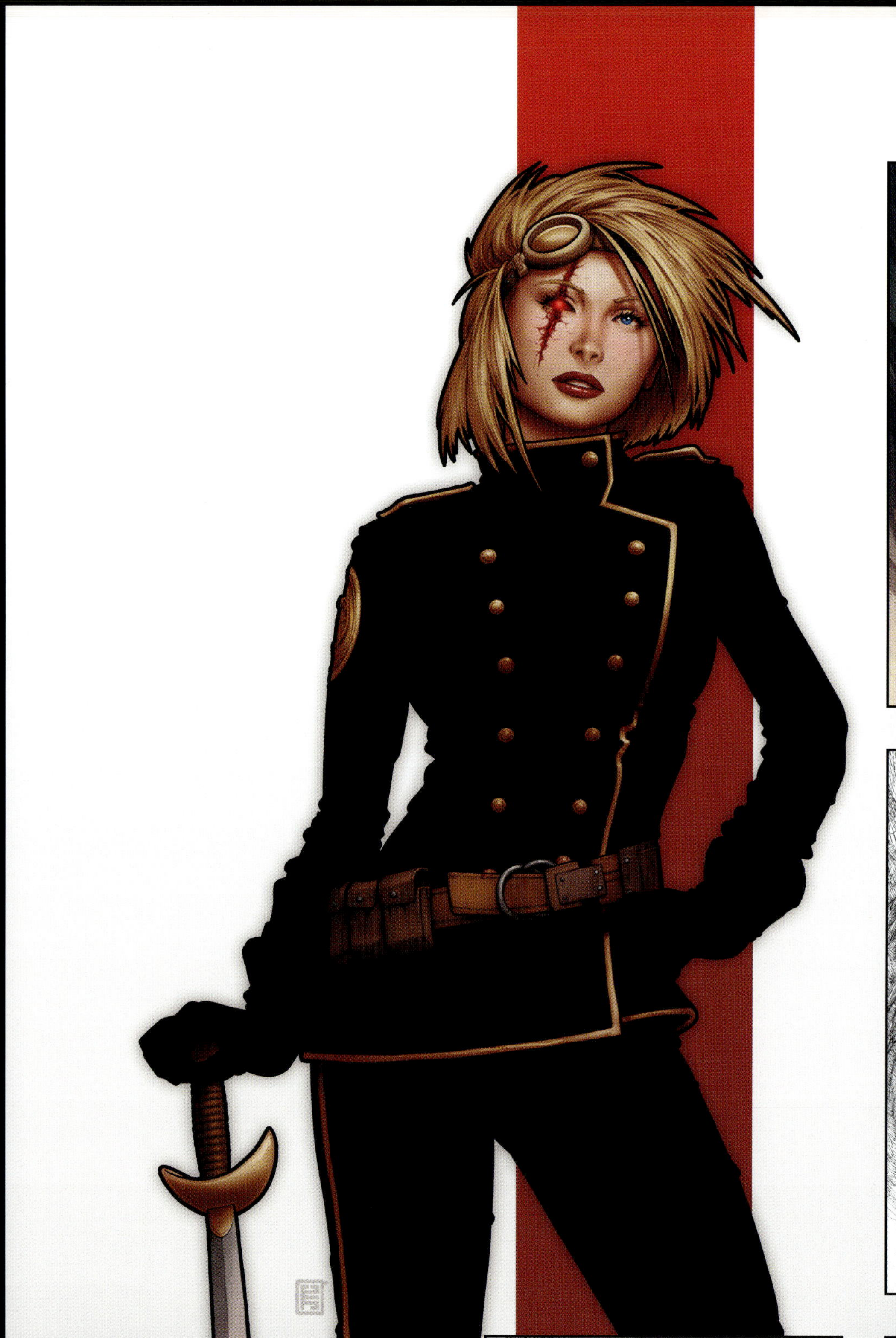

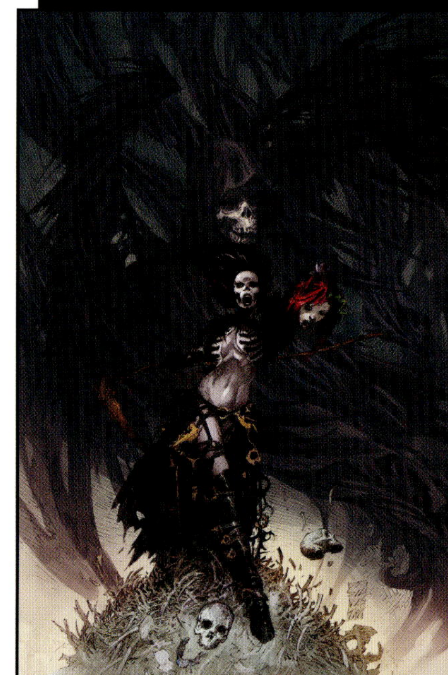

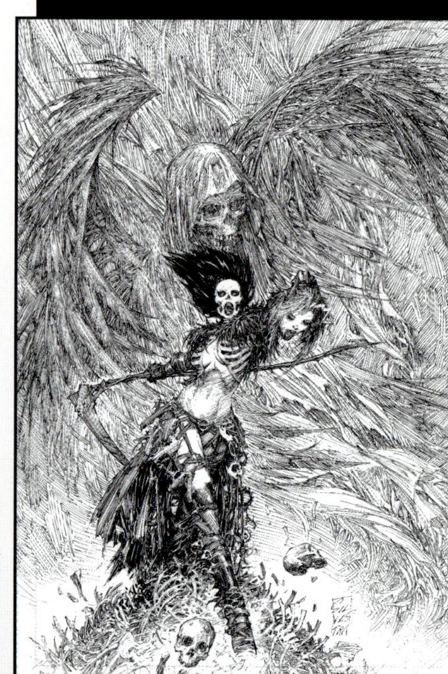

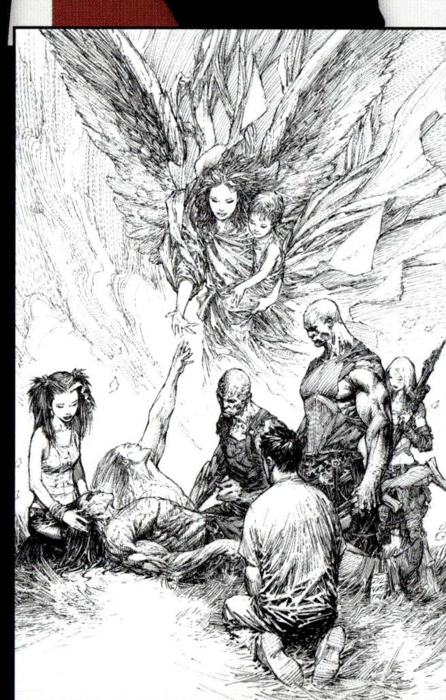

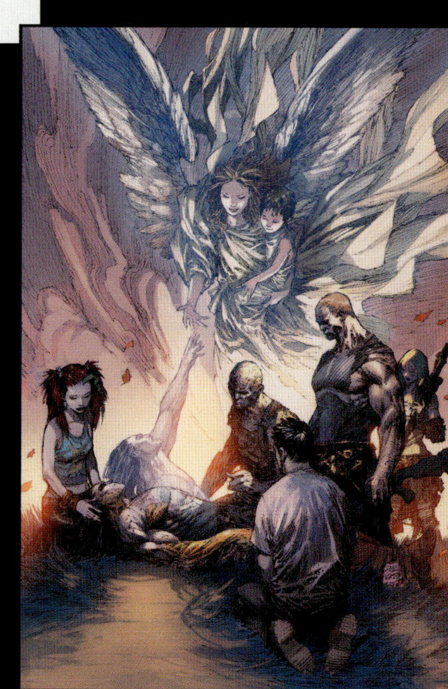

This page, clockwise from above.

Cyberforce #6 [2012] cover C,
art by: John Tyler Christopher

Cyberforce 6 [2012] cover A,
art by: Marc Silvestri and Sunny Gho

Cyberforce 6 [2012] cover D,
line art by: Marc Silvestri

Cyberforce 7 [2012] cover A,
art by: Marc Silvestri and Sunny Gho

Cyberforce 7 [2012] cover A,
line art by: Marc Silvestri

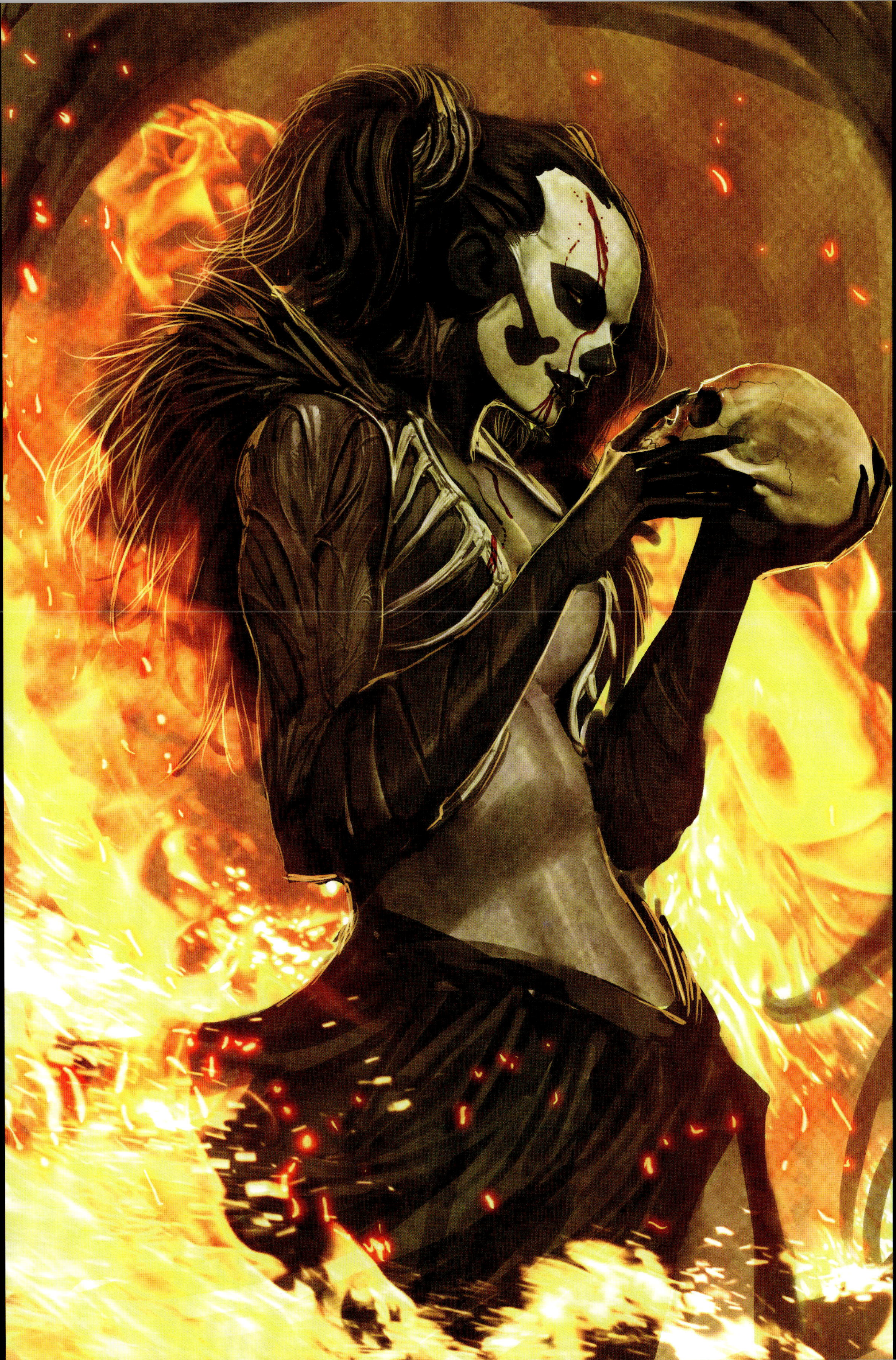

Cyberforce #6 [2012] cover B, art by: Stjepan Sejic

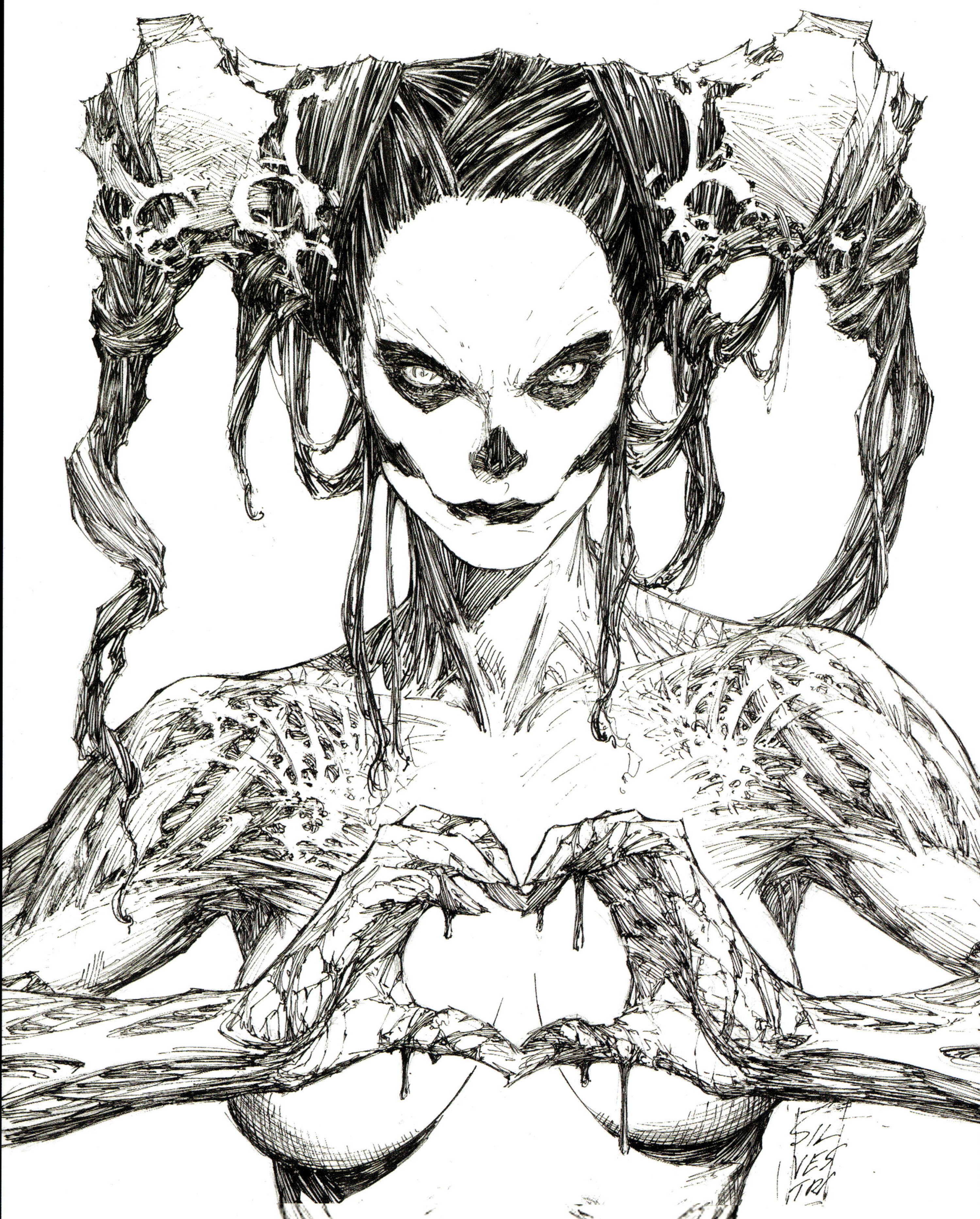

Cyberforce #8 [2012] cover A,
line art by: Marc Silvestri

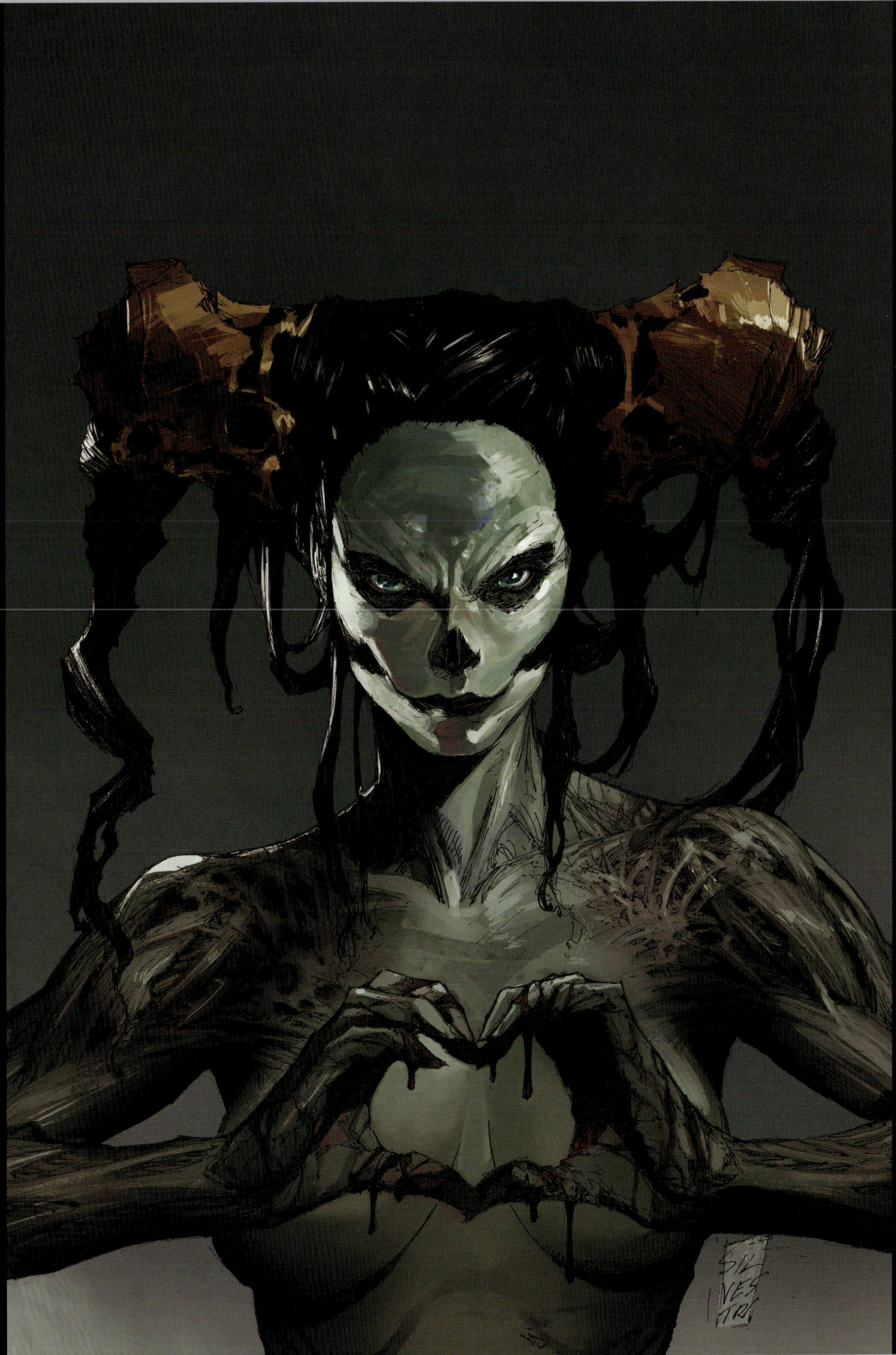

Cyberforce #8 [2012] cover A,
art by: Marc Silvestri and Sunny Gho

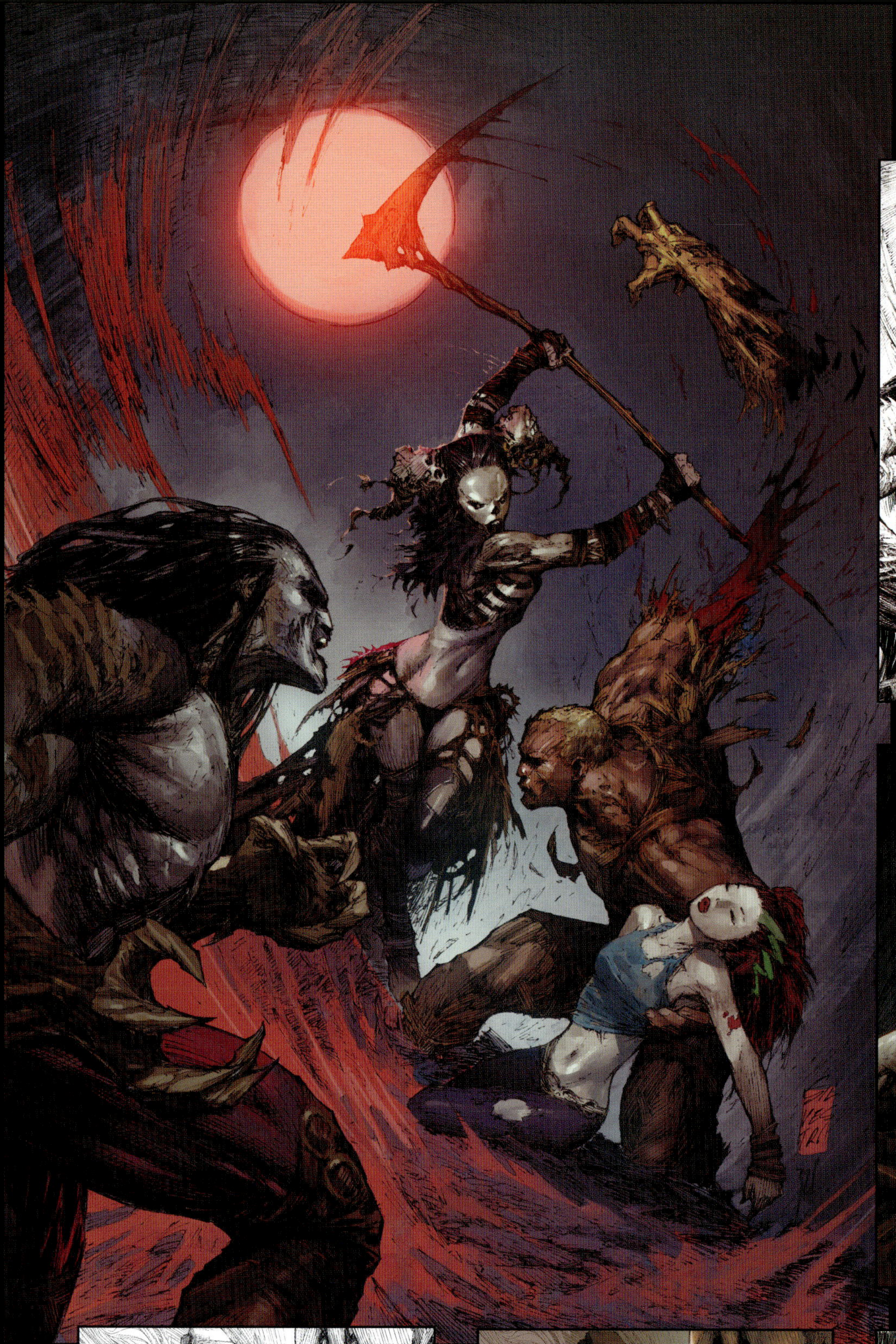

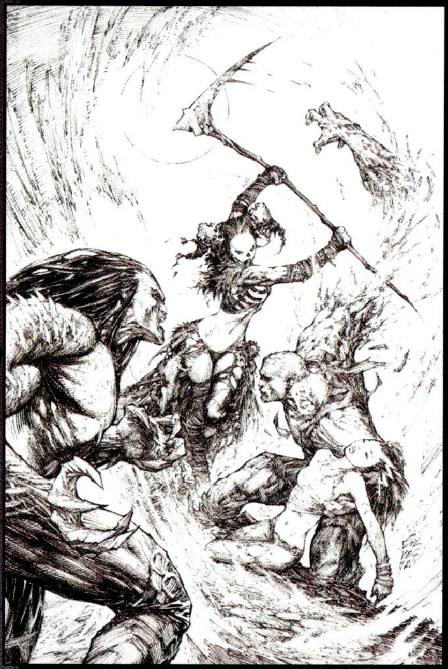

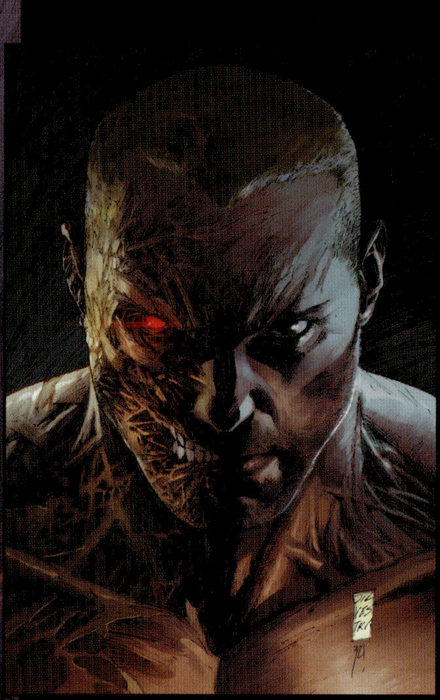

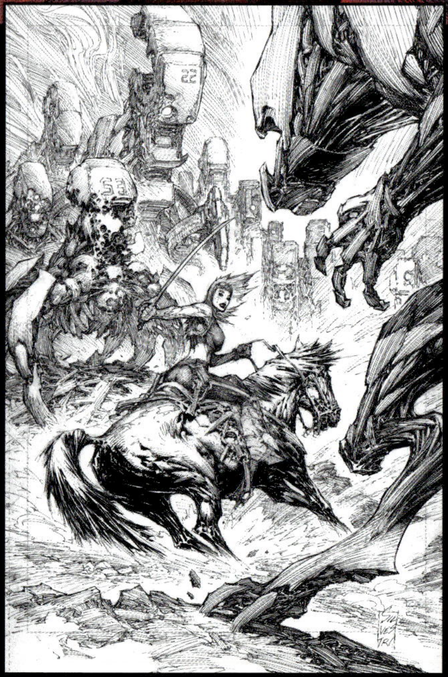

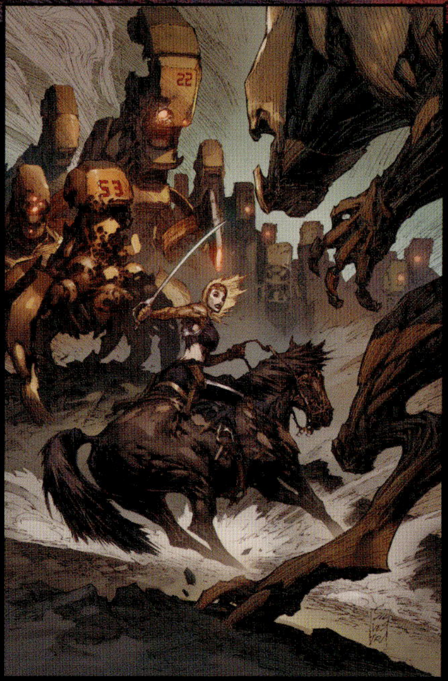

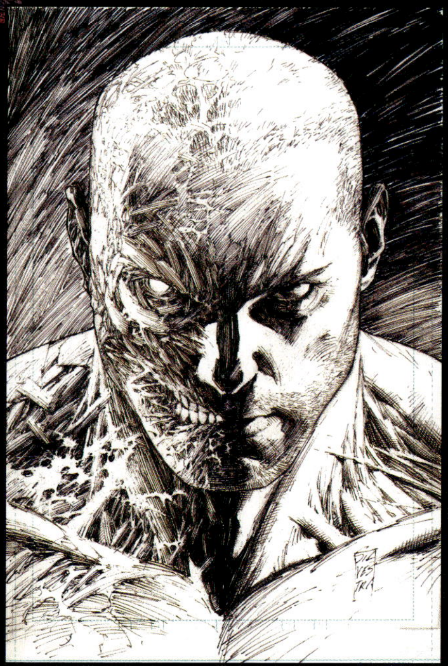

Clockwise from top left, *Cyberforce* #9A, 9 inks, 10A, 10 inks, 11A, and 11B [2012] covers
art by: Marc Silvestri and Sunny Cho

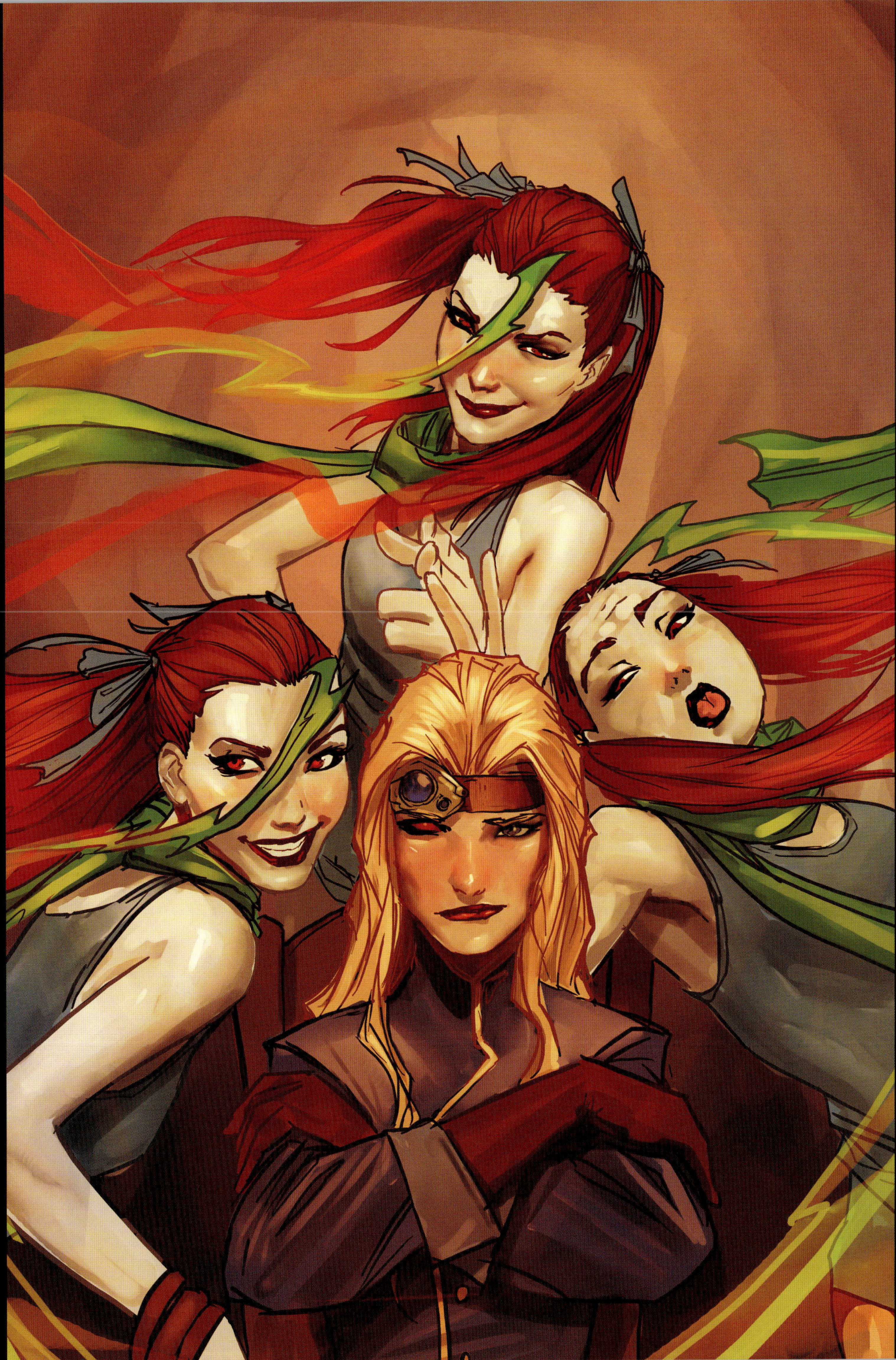

Cyberforce #4 [2012] cover D,
art by: Stjepan Sejic

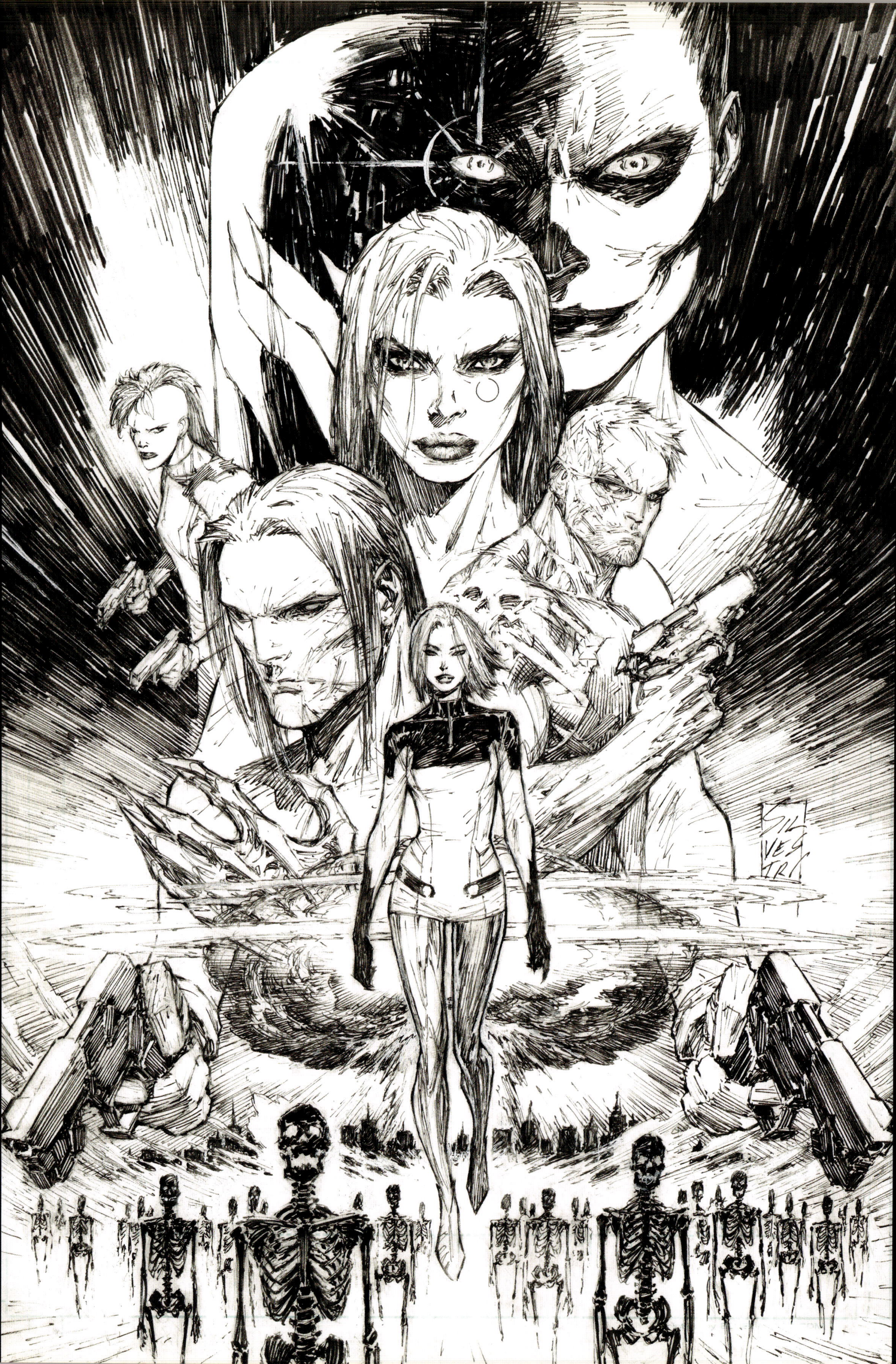

Cyberforce #1 [2018] cover A,
line art by: Marc Silvestri

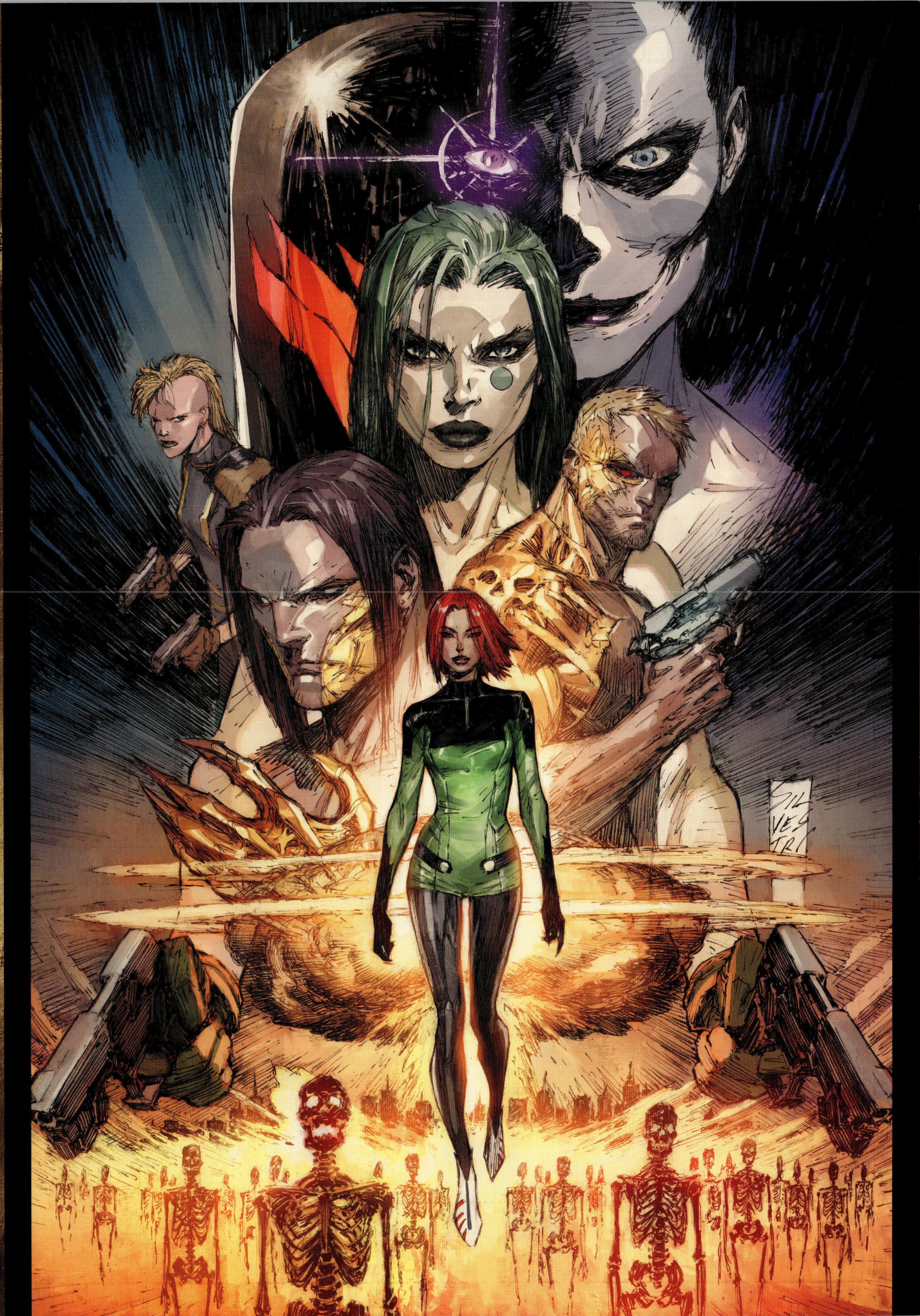

Cyberforce #1 [2018] cover A,
art by: Marc Silvestri and Sunny Gho

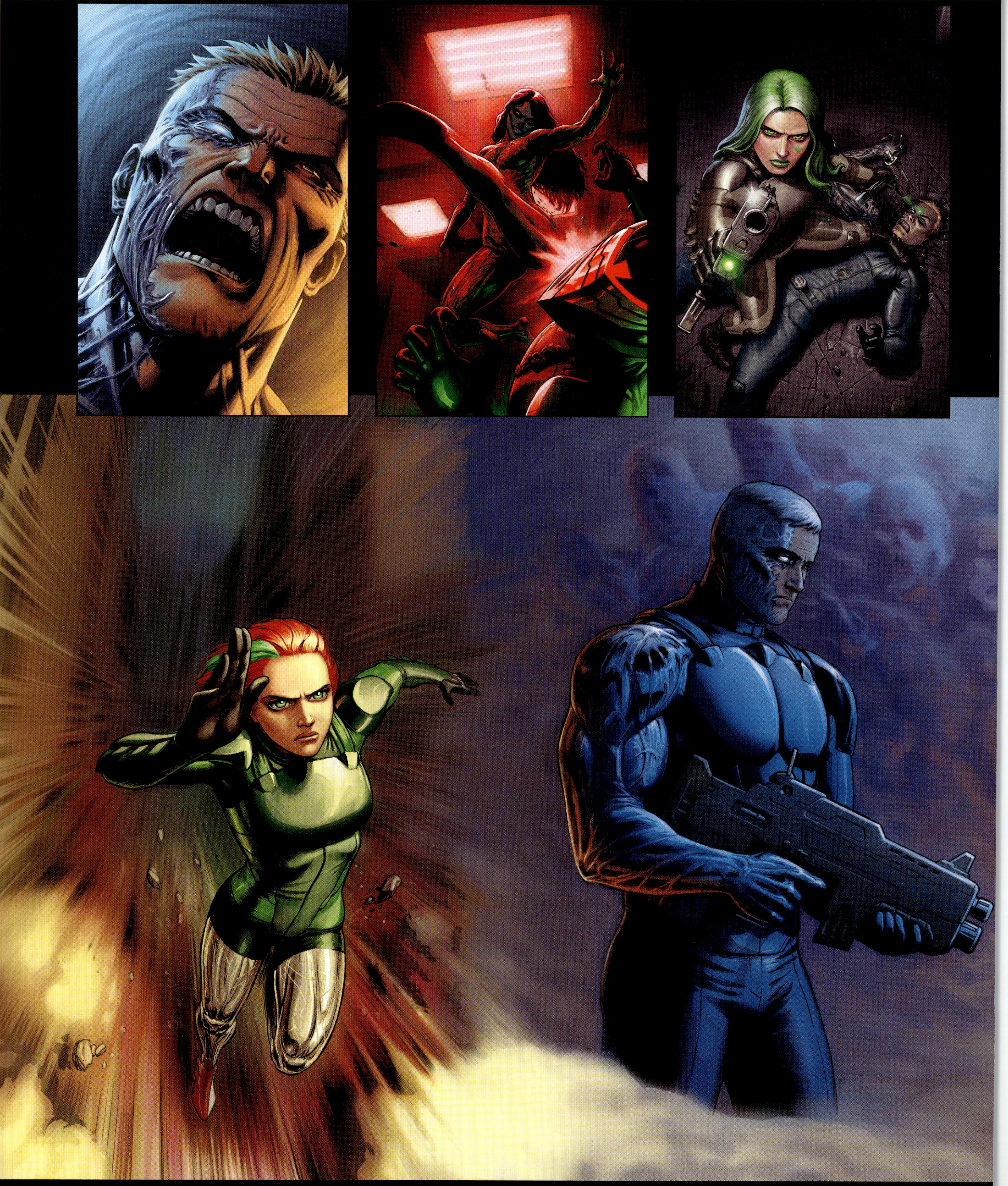

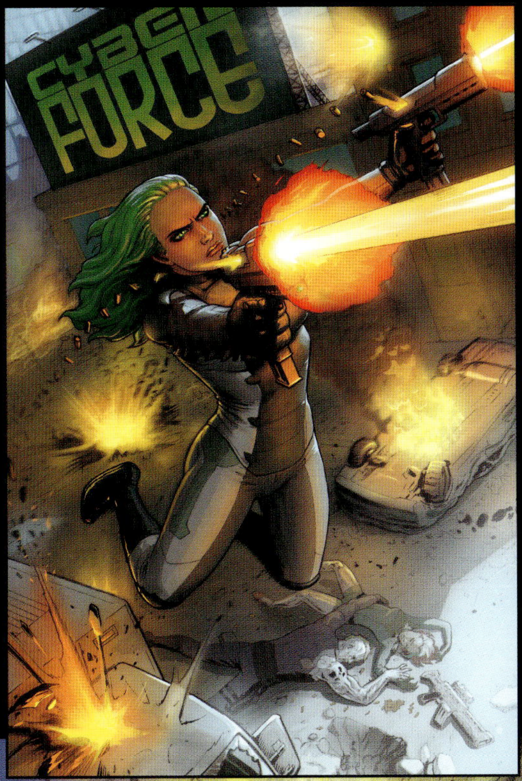

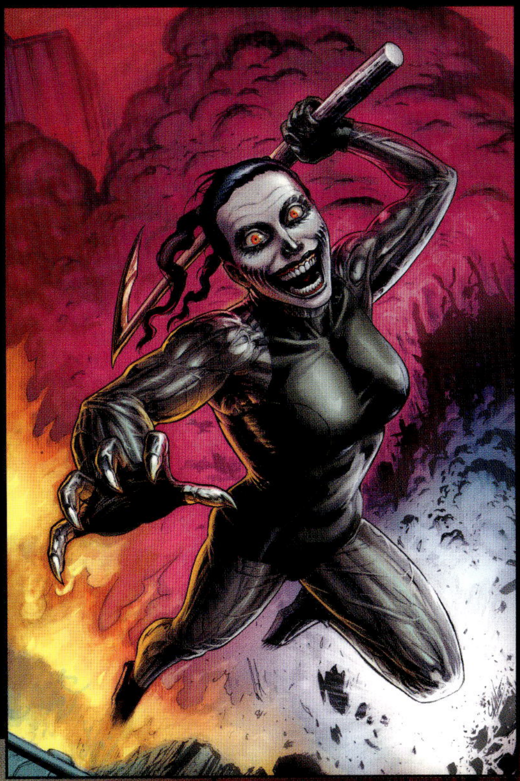

Top Row.

Cyberforce #1 [2018] cover B,
art by: Atilio Rojo

Cyberforce #2-4 [2018] covers,
art by: Atilio Rojo

Cyberforce #9 [2018] cover,
art by: Atilio Rojo

Bottom Row.

Cyberforce #5-8 [2018] connecting covers,
art by: Atilio Rojo

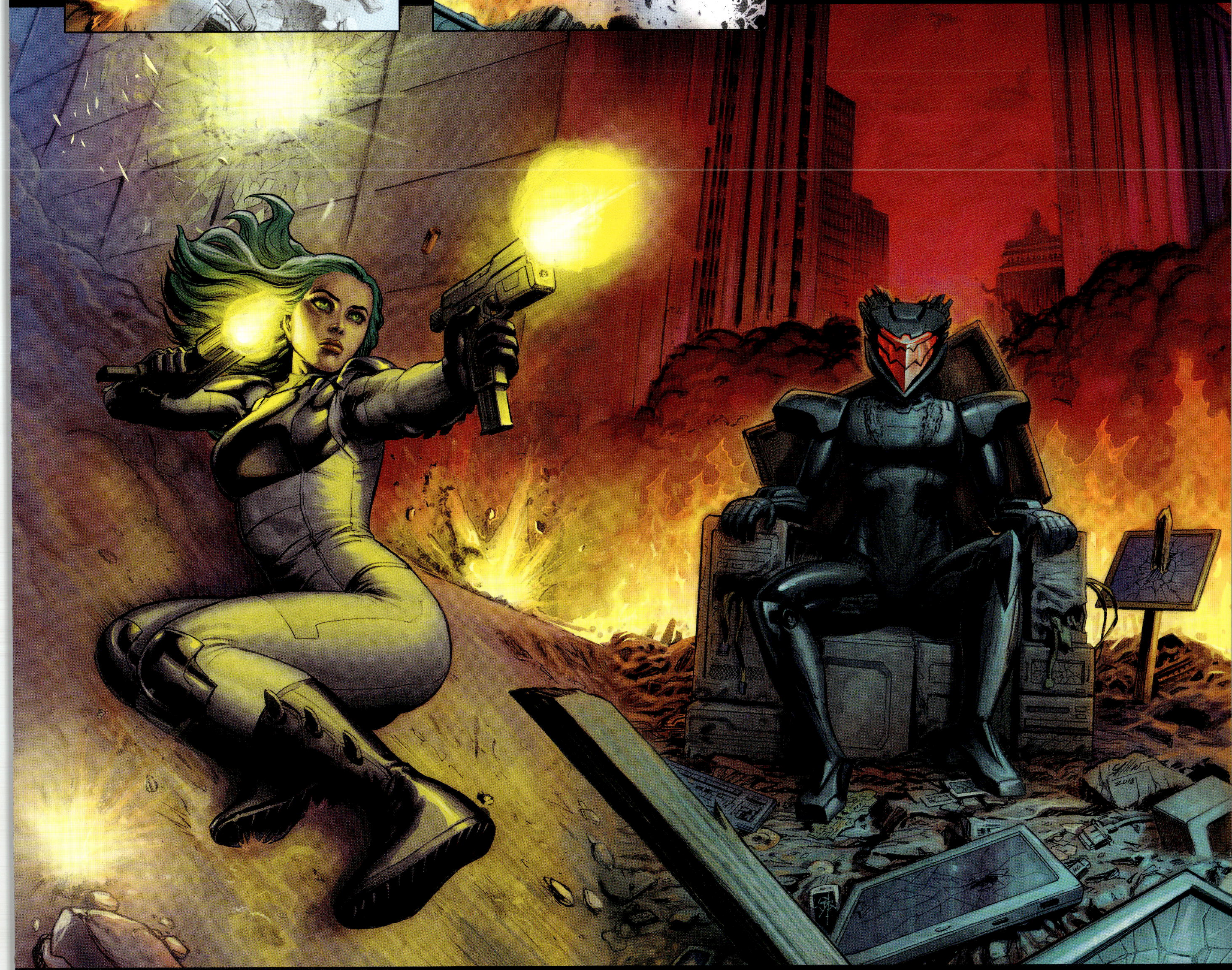

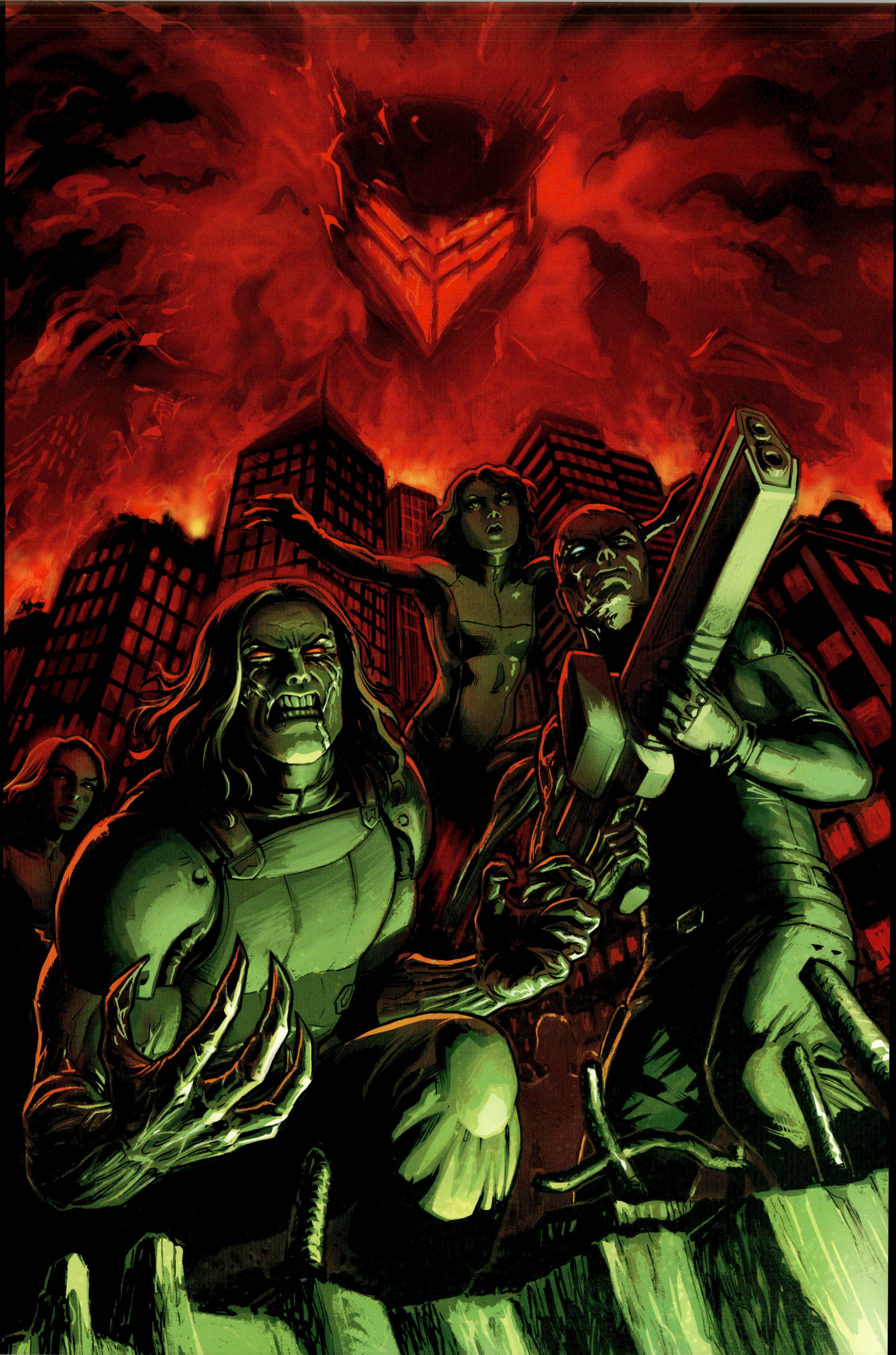

Cyberforce # 10 [2018] cover,
art by: Atilio Rojo

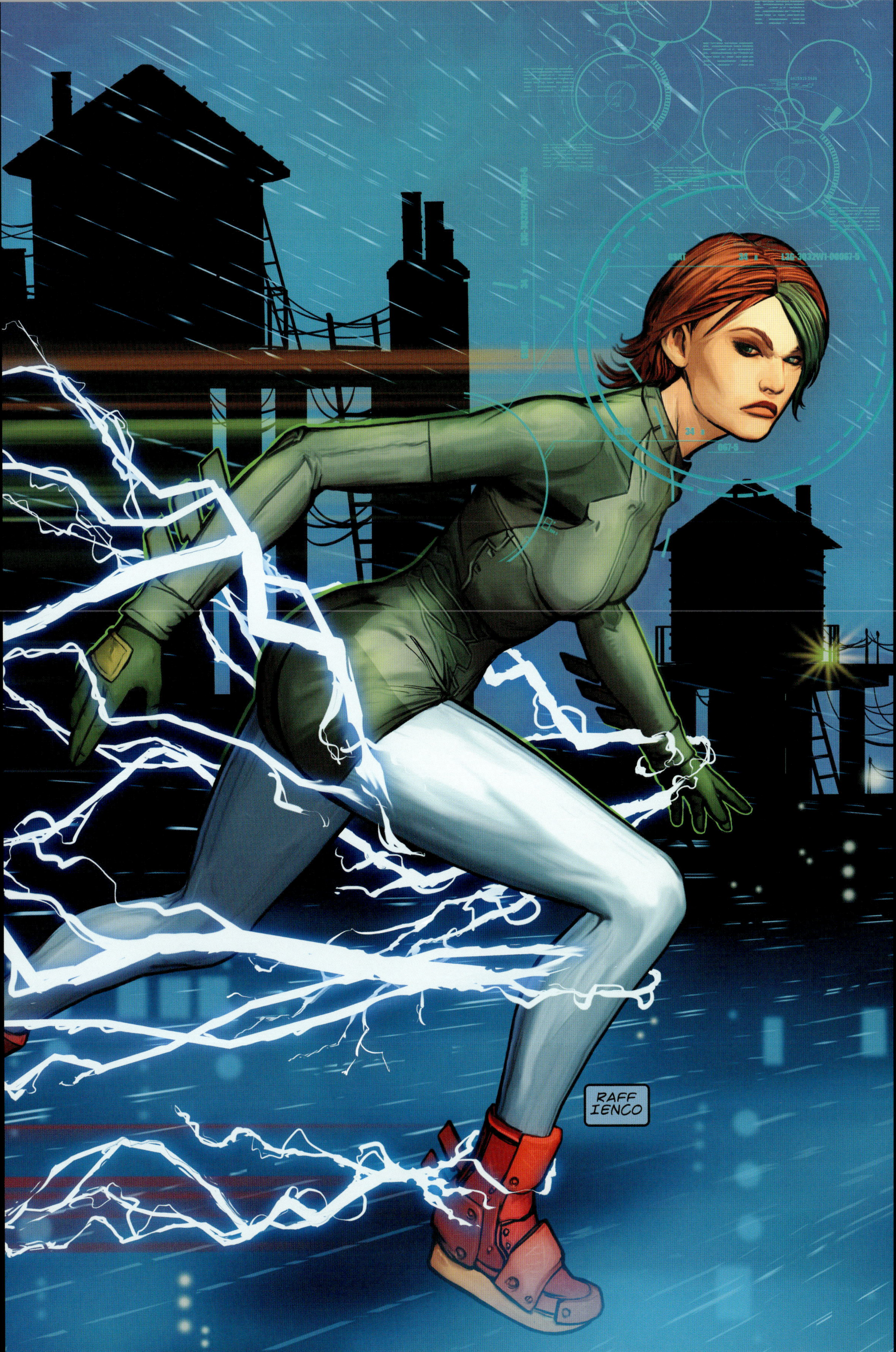

Cyberforce #11 [2018] cover,
art by: Raffaele Ienco

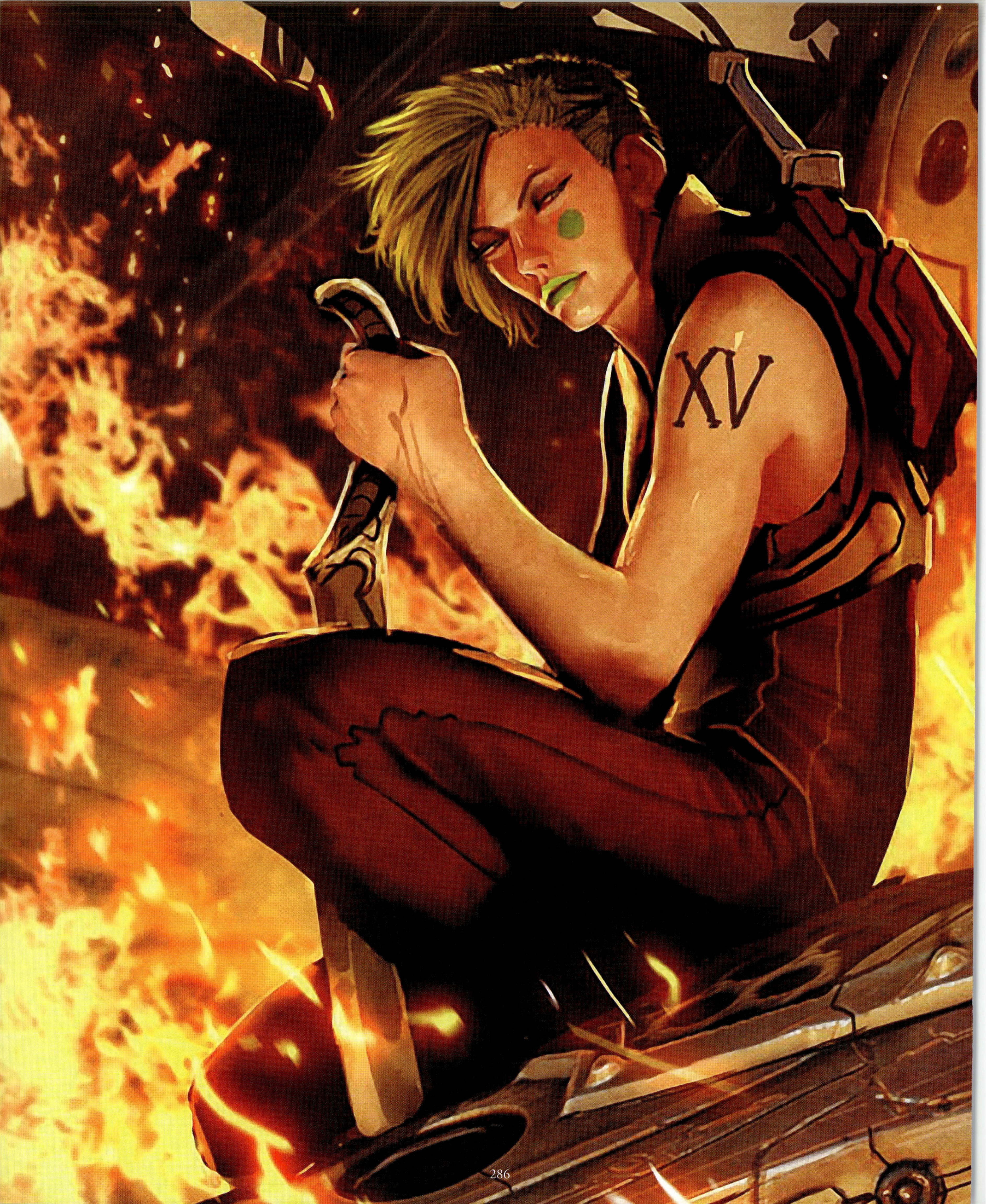
XV

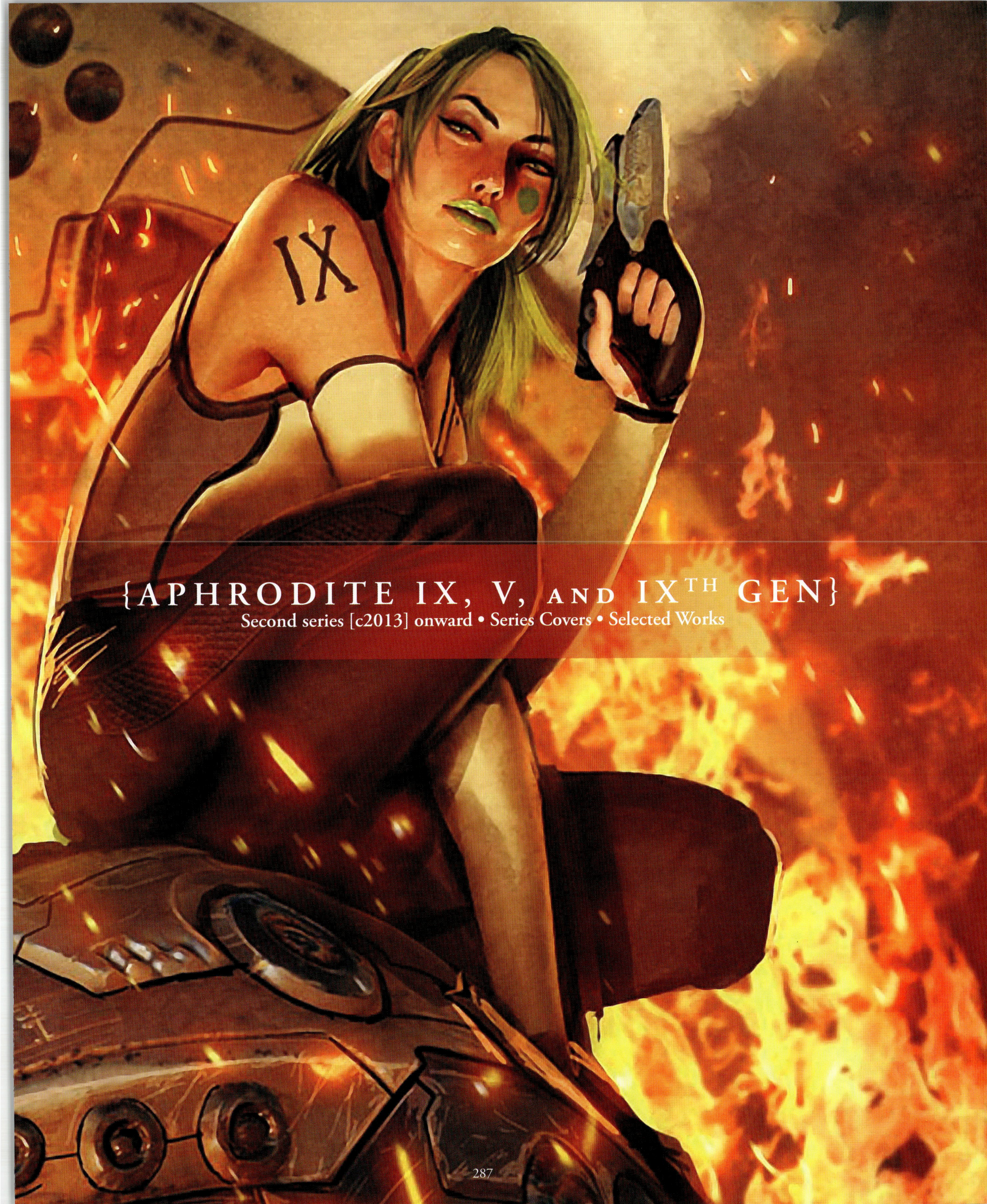

{APHRODITE IX, V, AND IXTH GEN}

Second series [c2013] onward • Series Covers • Selected Works

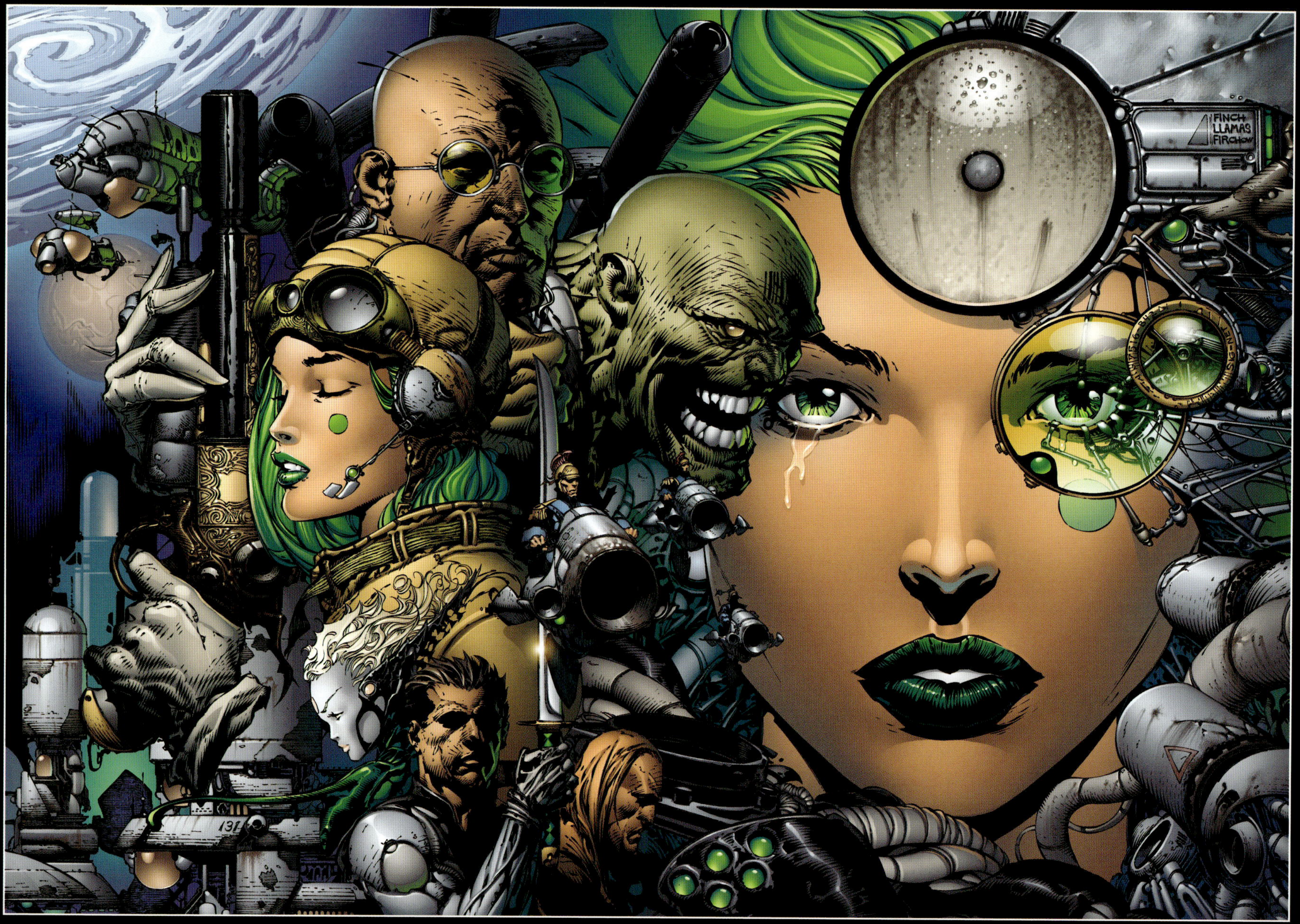

Above. *Aphrodite IX* #2 [2000] Dynamic Forces/Graham Cracker Comics variant covers, art by: David Finch, Victor Llamas, and Steve Firchow

Aphrodite IX created by **David Finch and David Wohl**

Aphrodite IX was first released in August 2000 and ran for 4 issues. The original premise had the story set in a decadent future, where mankind had transcended into a new renaissance of technology and prosperity. It was a future of gluttony and vanity in which towering monuments of metal and ornate glass were erected merely to satisfy our burgeoning egos. Our evolution had come at the price of our humanity as we replaced that which is flesh and bone with synthetic upgrades, all in an effort to defy the fate of our bodies, the finite absoluteness of our lives. Yet, despite our greatest efforts and advances, we still aged. We still died.

Everything changed with Aphrodite IX. A synthetic human, Aphrodite IX was designed to never age, to never die and more importantly, to be the ultimate covert killing machine.

The 2013 reboot, almost a sideways timeline, of *Aphrodite IX* wildly reimagined the series, now set hundreds of years after a cataclysmic event scorched the surface, Earth and its inhabitants have been forever altered and a new landscape and political struggle has taken hold with three distinct factions fighting for control. Aphrodite IX is both anachronism and advanced technology in a world that she no longer recognizes. No aliens, just humans and their genetically and technologically altered descendants in a mixture of the best sci-si and fantasy has to offer.

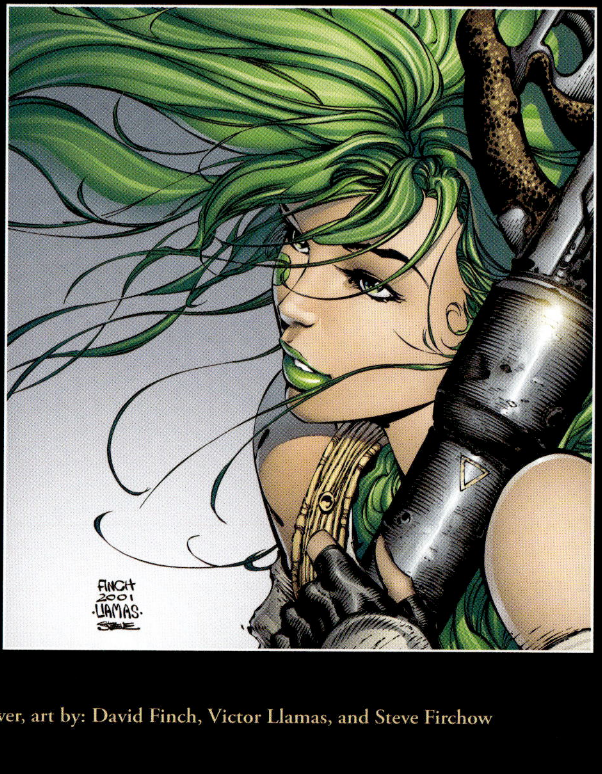

Previous page. *Aphrodite IX* #6 [2013] covers A and B, art by: Stjepan Sejic • At right and above. *Aphrodite IX* #3 [2000] cover, art by: David Finch, Victor Llamas, and Steve Firchow

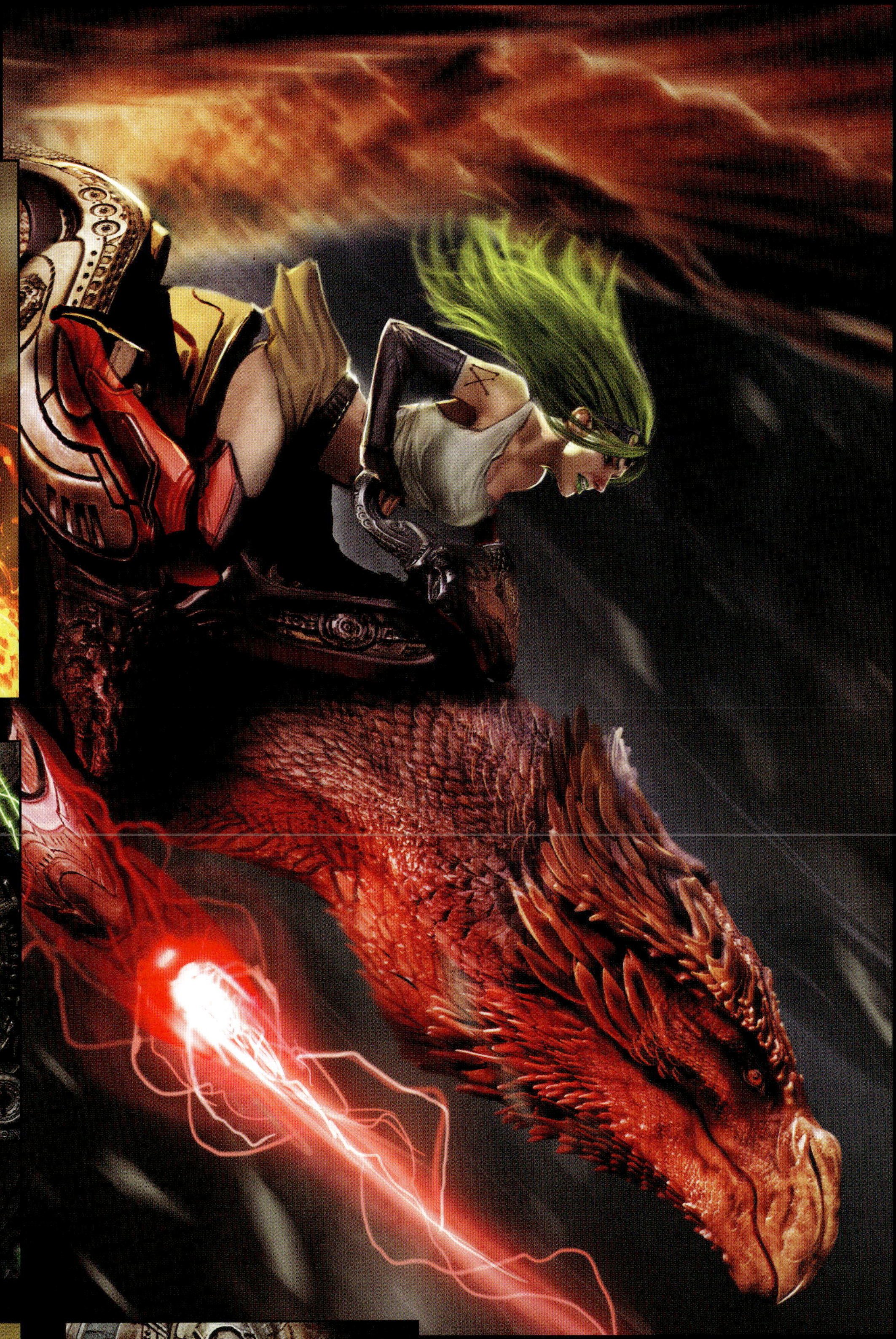

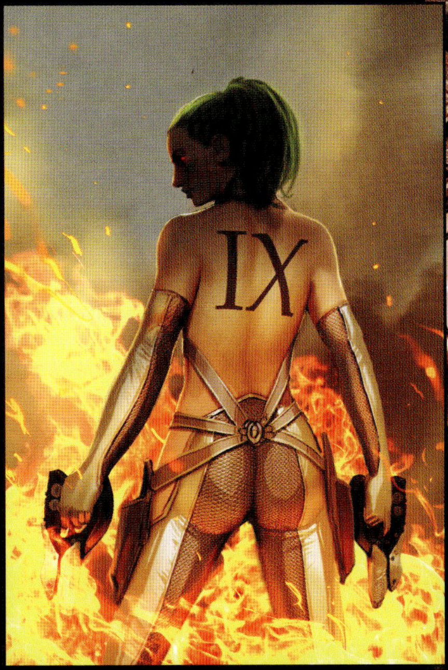

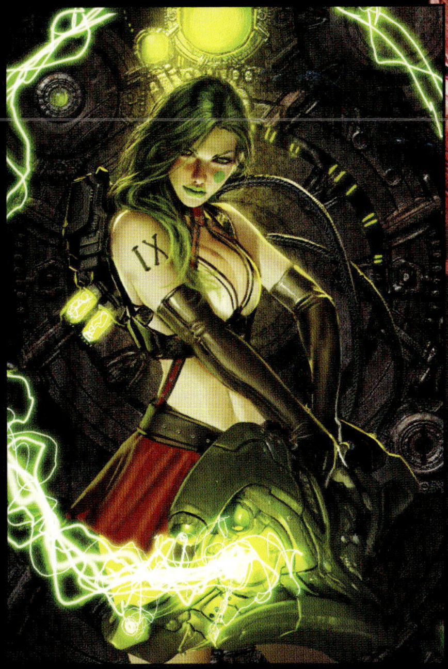

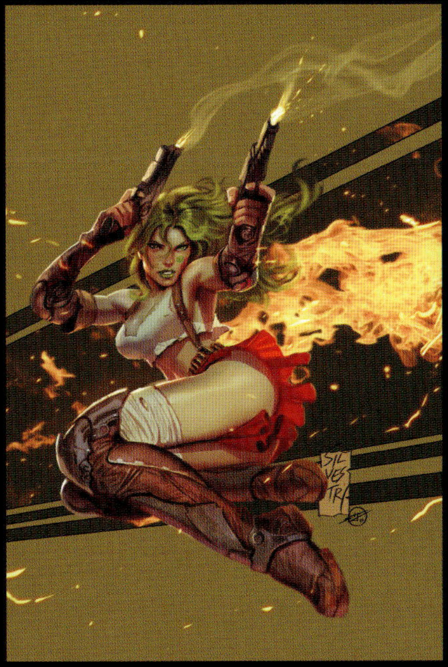

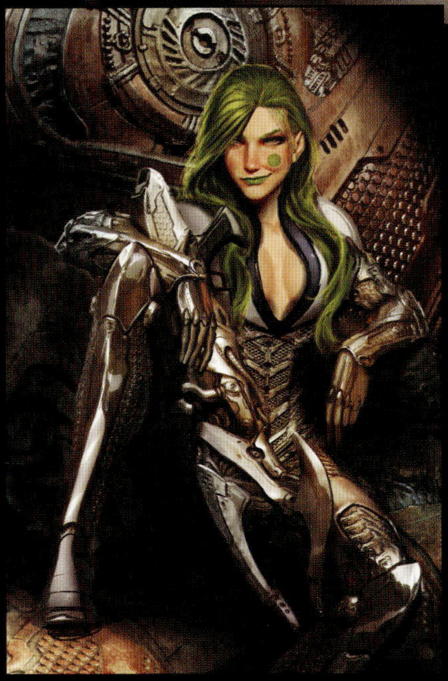

This page, counterclockwise from above.

Aphrodite IX #1 [2013] Free Comic Book Day cover,
art by: Stjepan Sejic

Aphrodite IX #1 [2013] 2nd Printing cover,
art by: Stjepan Sejic

Aphrodite IX #2 [2013] cover A,
art by: Stjepan Sejic

Aphrodite IX #2 [2013] cover B,
art by: Marc Silvestri and Stjepan Sejic

Aphrodite IX #2 [2013]
Amazing Las Vegas Comic Con variant cover C,
art by: Stjepan Sejic

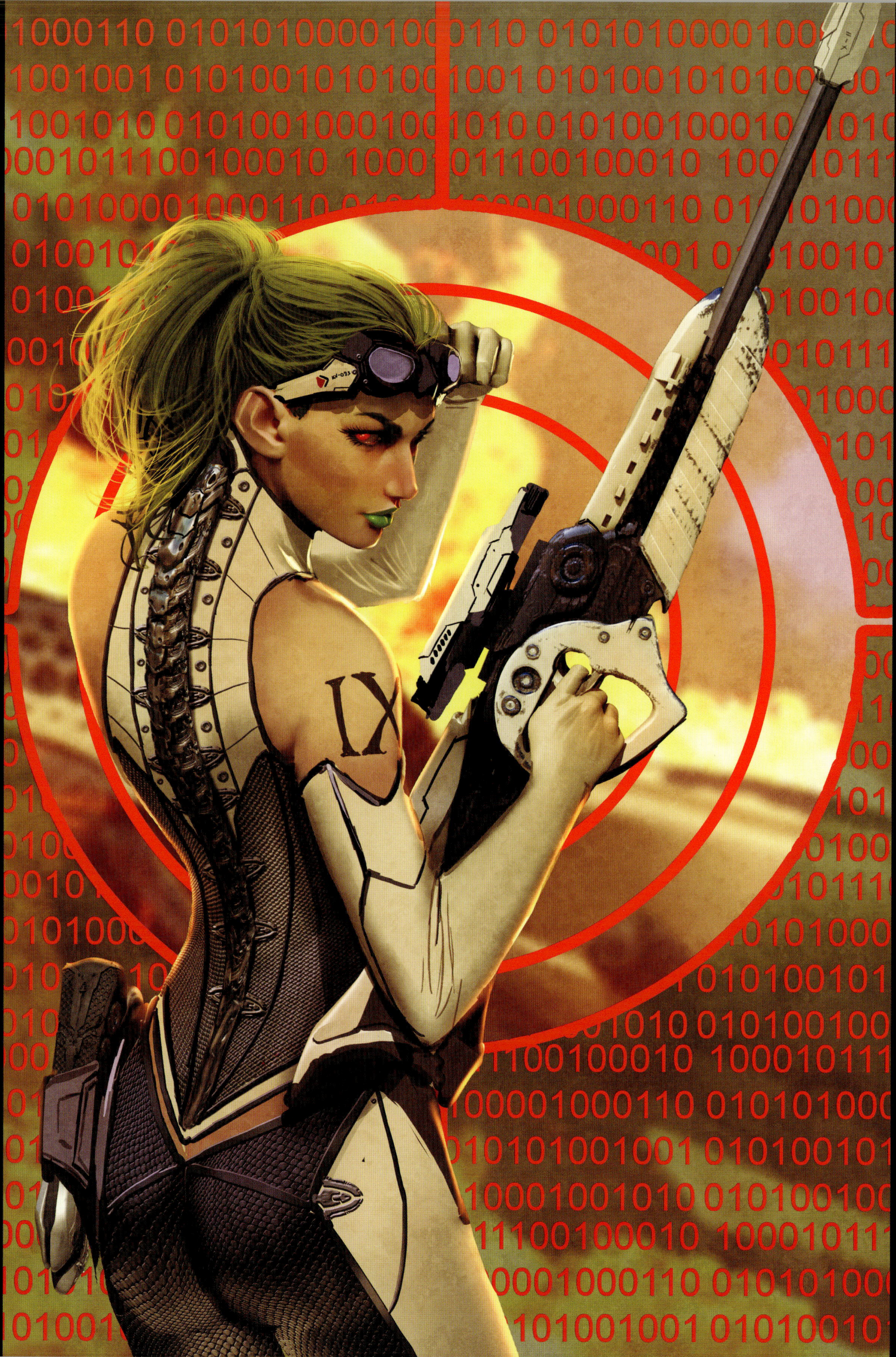

Aphrodite IX #3 [2013] cover A,
art by: Stjepan Sejic

Aphrodite IX #3-4 [2013], selected covers

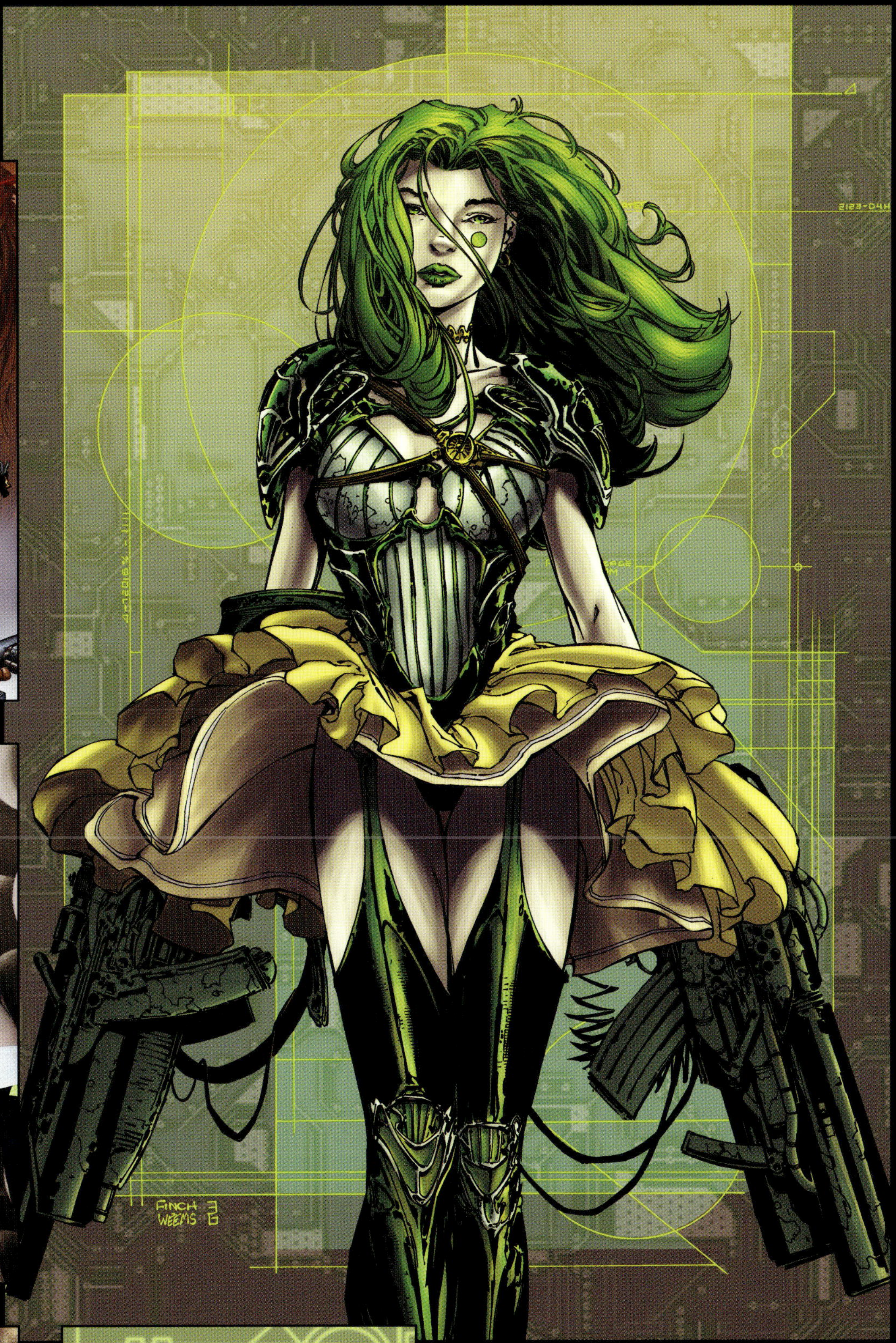

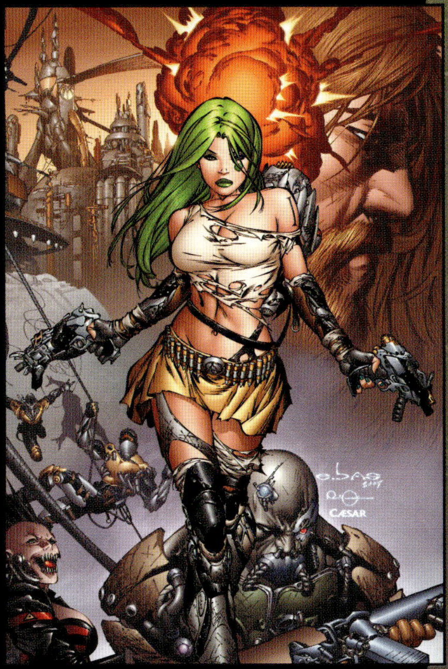

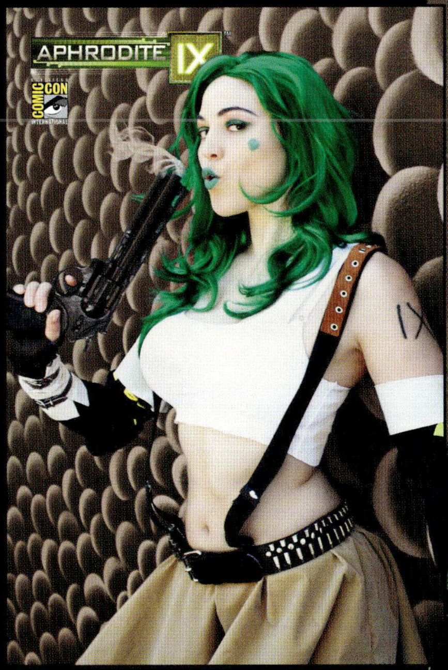

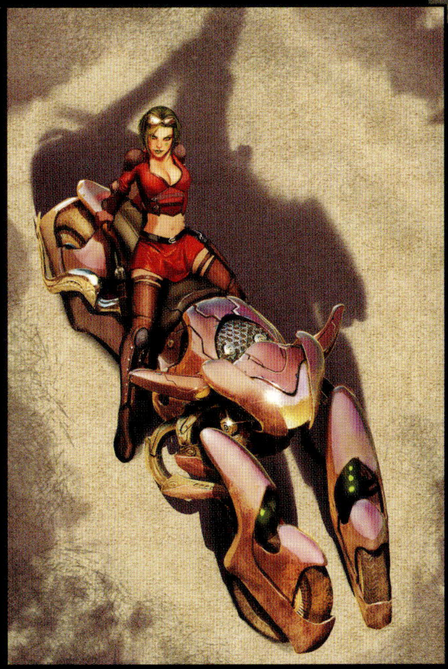

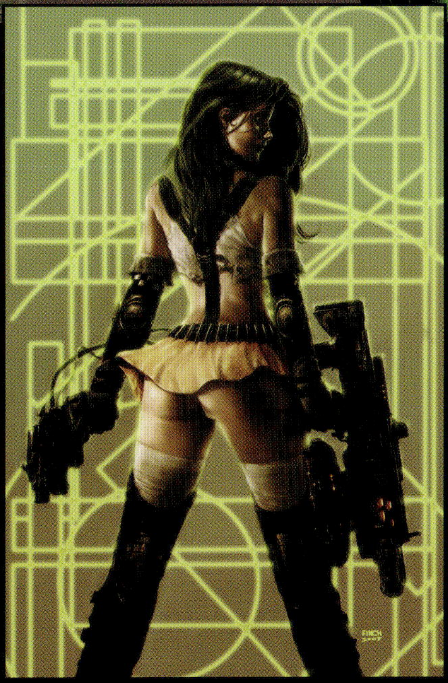

This page, counterclockwise from above.

Aphrodite IX #3 [2013] cover B,
art by: David Finch, Joe Weems V, and Betsy Golden

Aphrodite IX #3 [2013] cover C,
art by: Eric "E.Bas" Basaldua, Rick Basaldua,
and Caesar Rodriguez

Aphrodite IX #3 [2013] SDCC Cosplay cover D,
Model: Jennifer Lengerich for JENNIVY Creative Studios
Photographer: Amilie Turner for Dommino Inc. Photography

Aphrodite IX #4 [2013] cover A,
art by: Stjepan Sejic

Aphrodite IX #4 [2013] cover B,
art by: David Finch

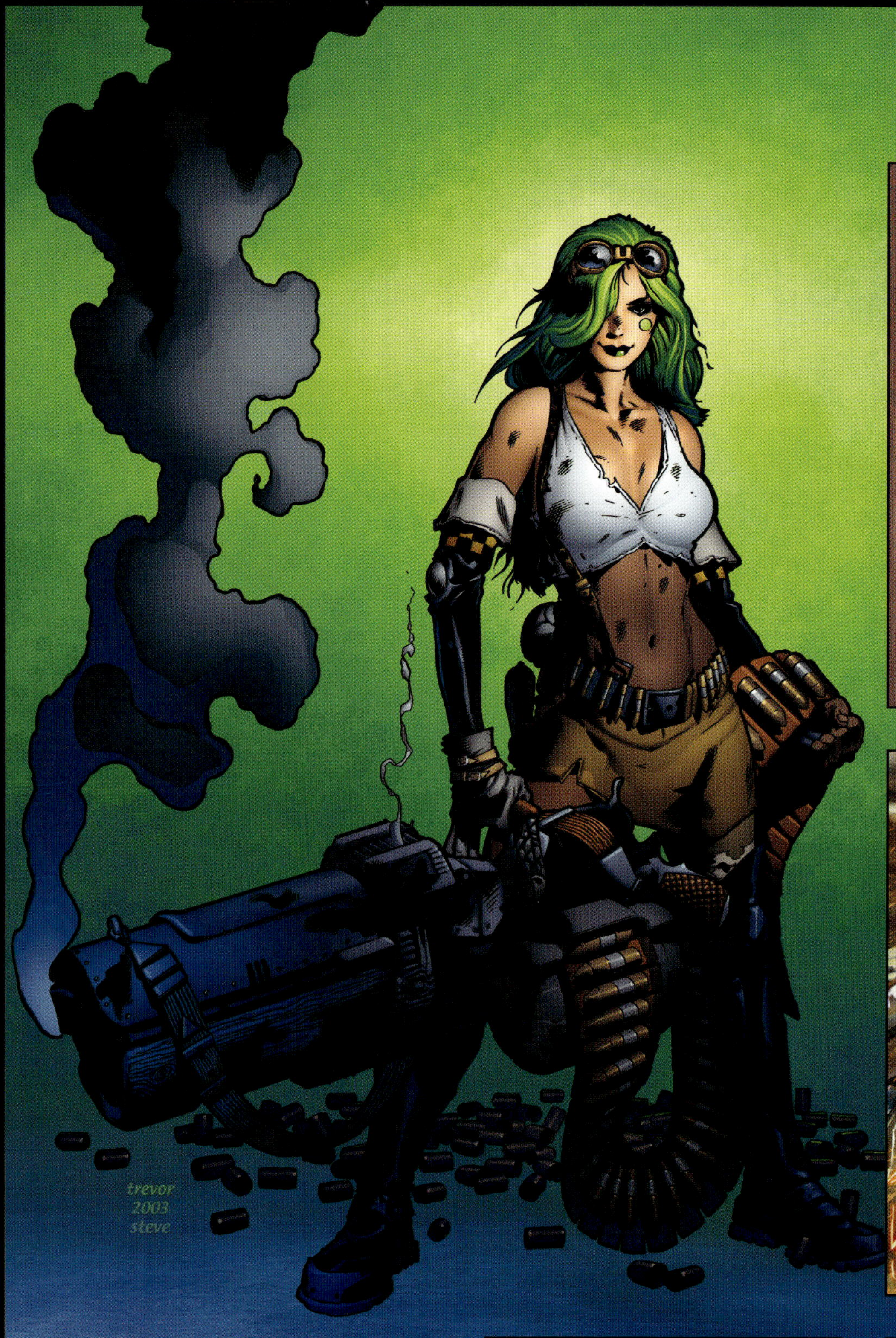

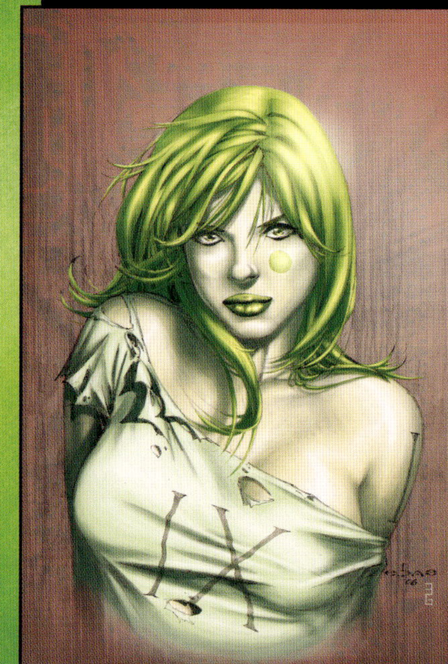

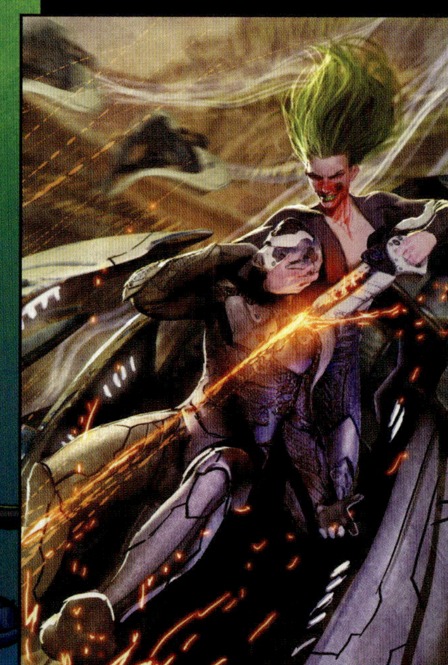

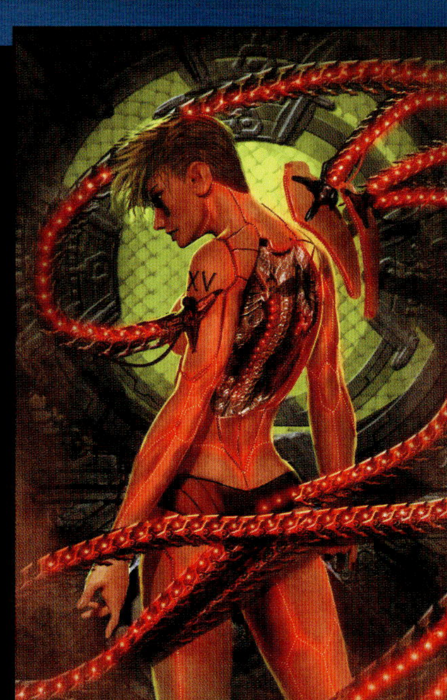

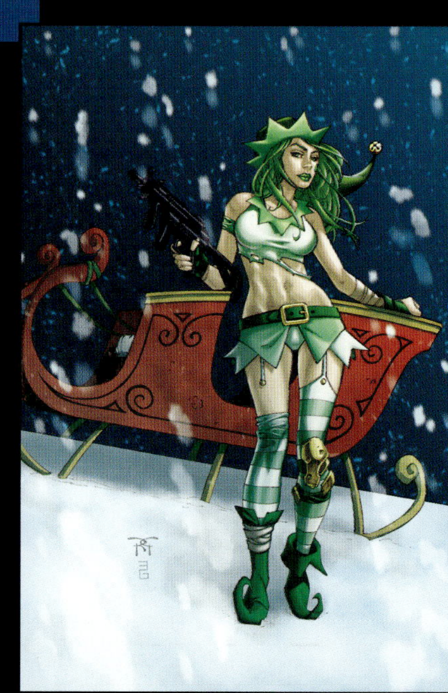

This page, clockwise from above.

Aphrodite IX #4 [2013] cover D,
art by: Trevor Hairsine and Steve Firchow

Aphrodite IX #4 [2013] cover C,
art by: Eric "E.Bas" Basaldua and Betsy Golden

Aphrodite IX #5 [2013] cover A,
art by: Stjepan Sejic

Aphrodite IX #6 [2013] cover C,
art by: Randy Green and Betsy Golden

Aphrodite IX #7 [2013] cover A,
art by: Stjepan Sejic

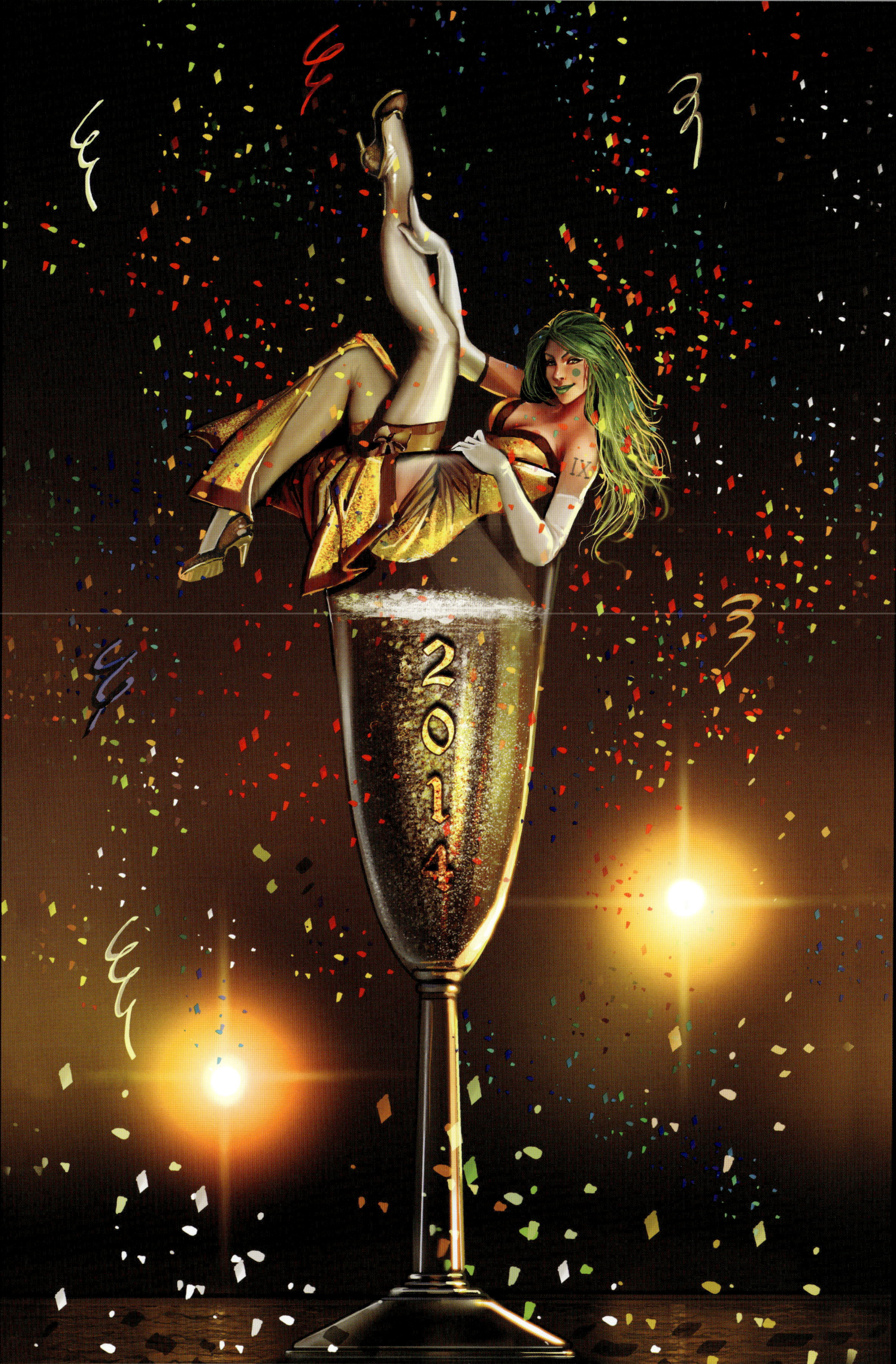

Aphrodite IX #7 [2013] cover B,
art by: Linda Sejic

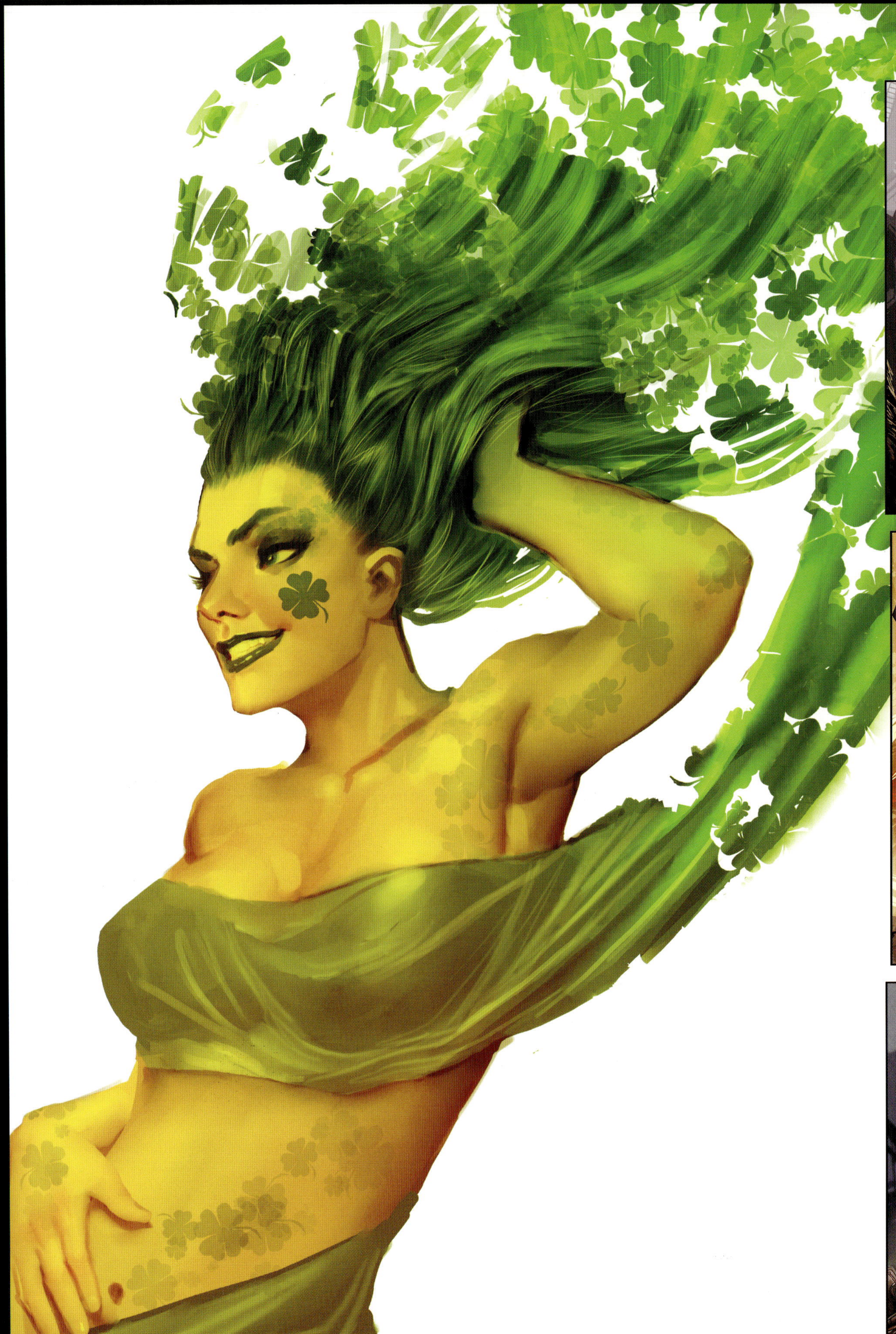

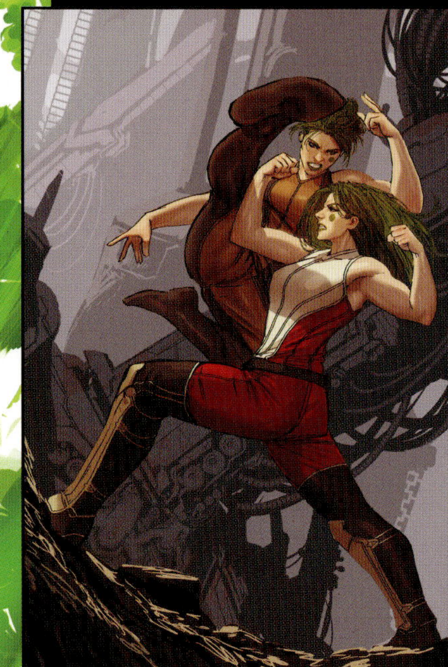

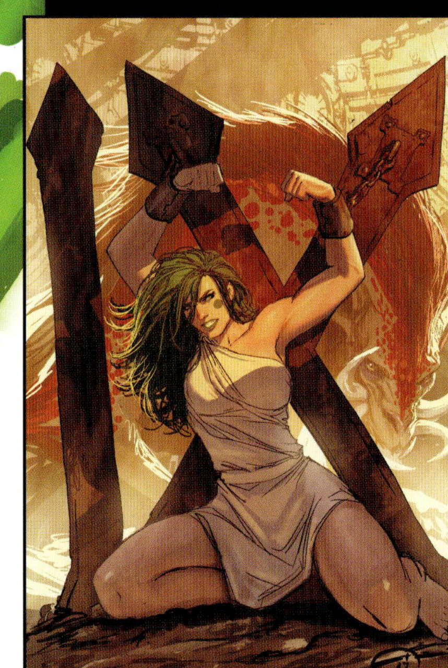

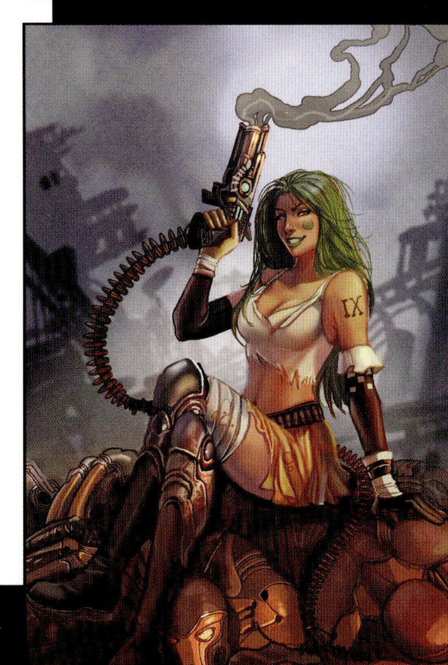

Clockwise from above. *Aphrodite IX* #9 [2013] cover C, art by: Stjepan Sejic

Aphrodite IX #8 [2013] cover, art by: Stjepan Sejic

Aphrodite IX #9 [2013] cover A, art by: Stjepan Sejic

Aphrodite IX #9 [2013] cover B, art by: Linda Sejic

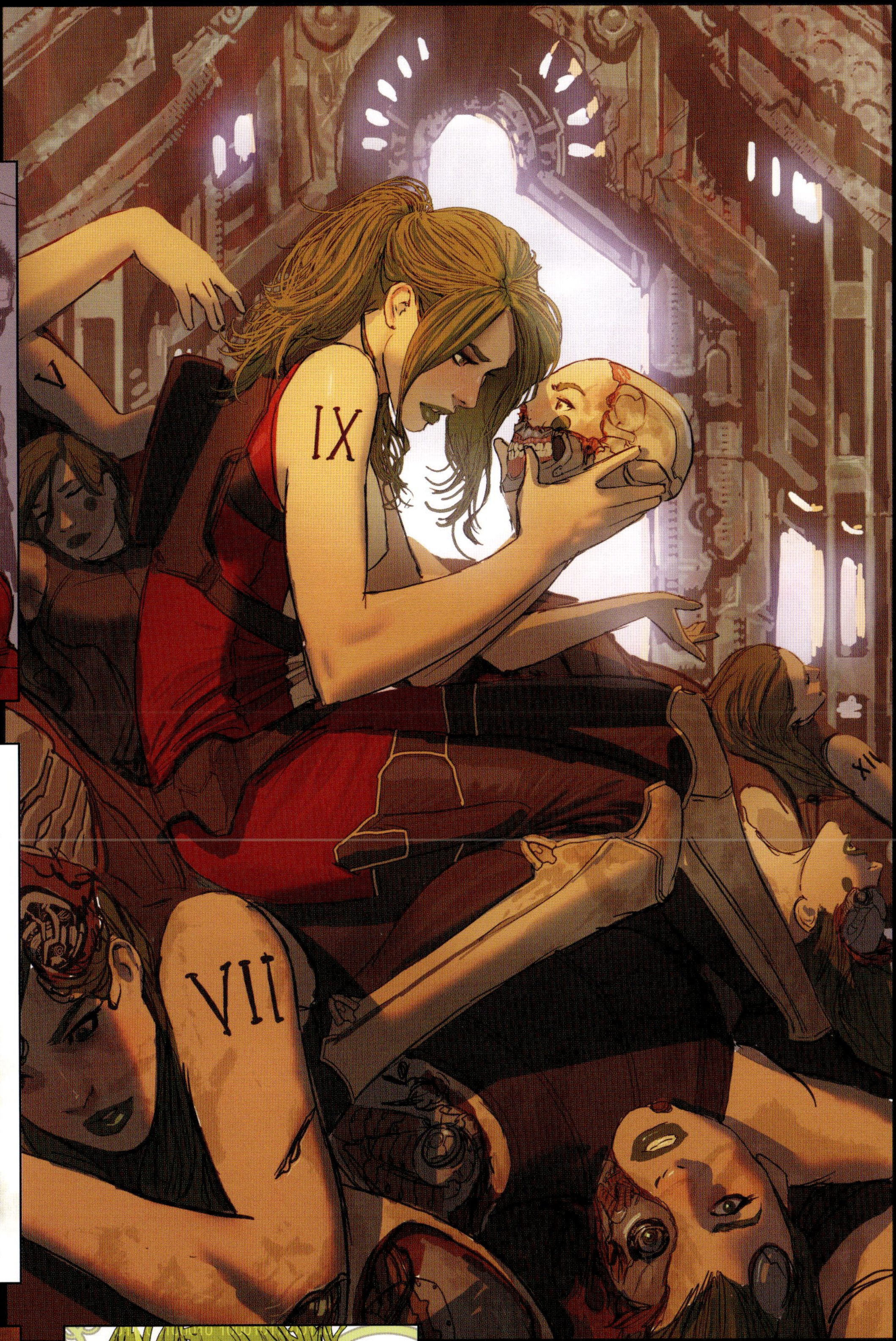

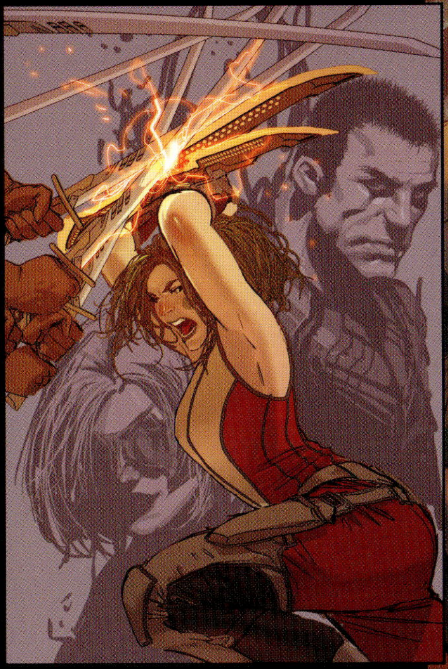

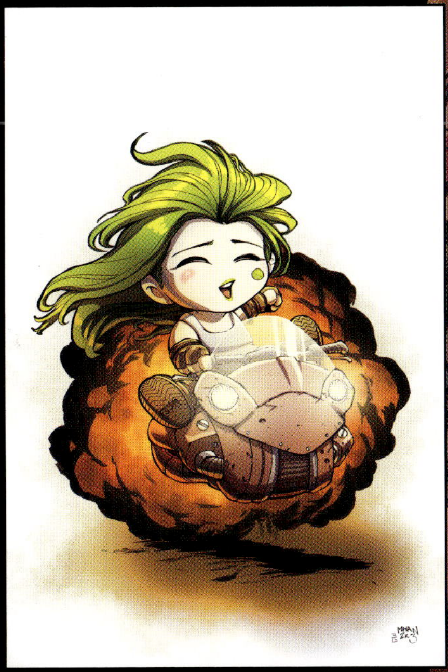

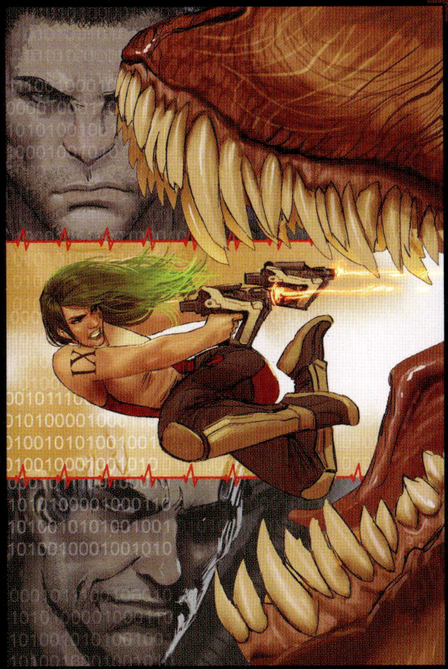

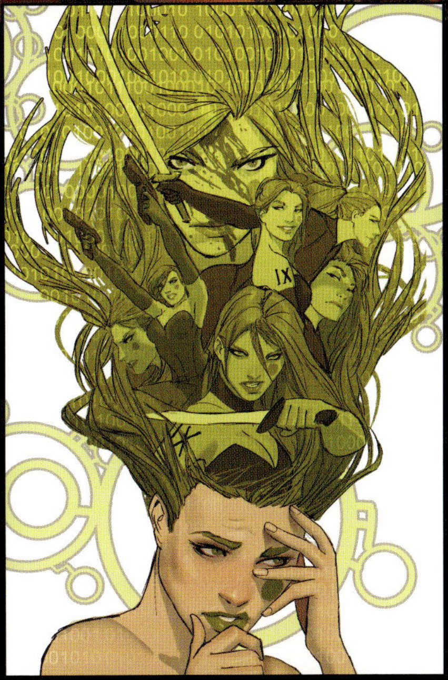

This page, counterclockwise from above.

Aphrodite IX #10 [2013] cover A,
art by: Stjepan Sejic

Aphrodite IX #10 [2013] cover B,
art by: Stjepan Sejic

Aphrodite IX #10 [2013] cover C,
art by: Pop Mhan and Betsy Golden

Aphrodite IX #11 [2013] cover,
art by: Stjepan Sejic

Aphrodite IX #1 [2013] Hidden Files cover,
art by: Stjepan Sejic

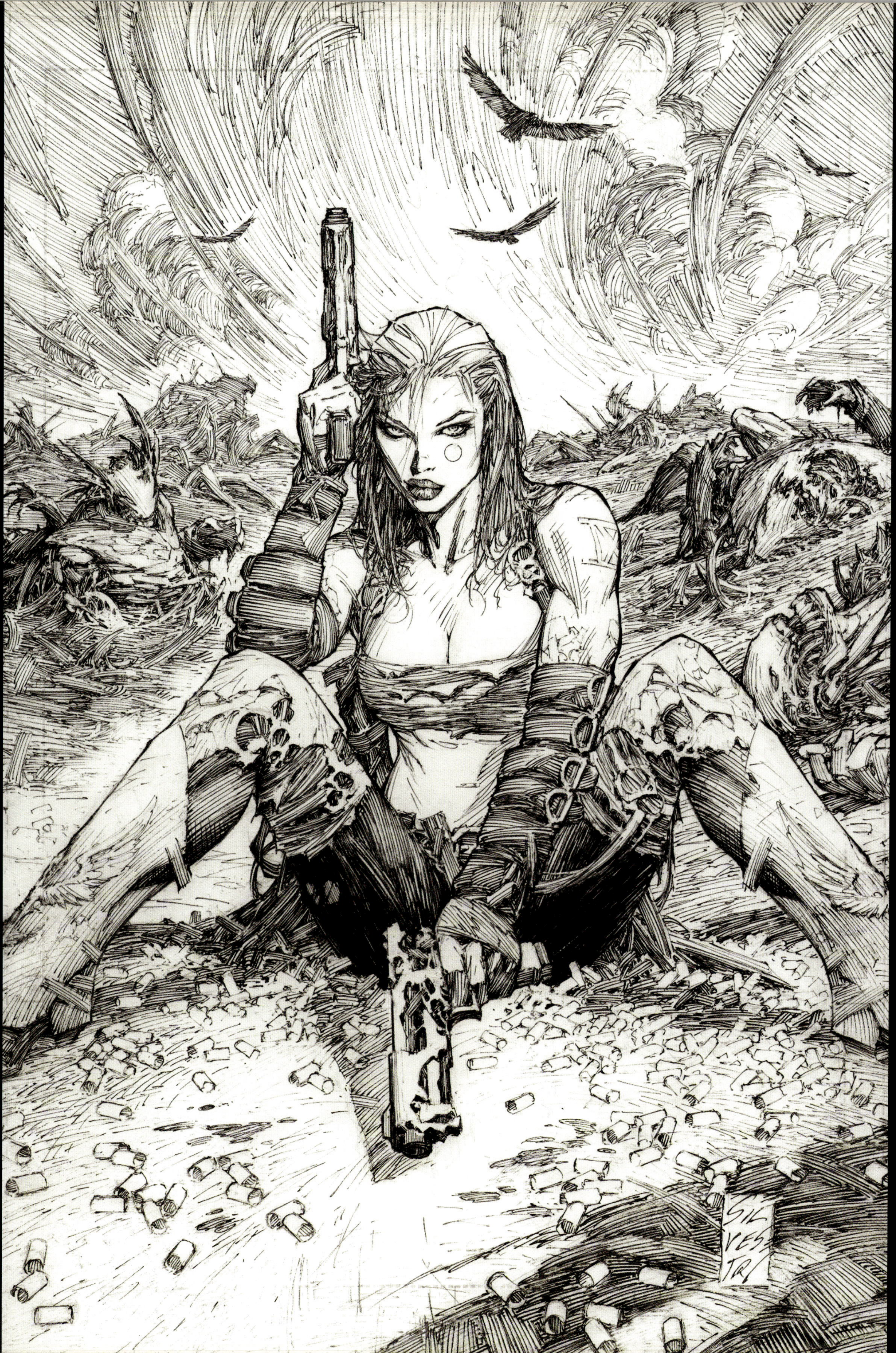

Aphrodite IX Cyberforce #1 [2014] cover D-E,
line art by: Marc Silvestri

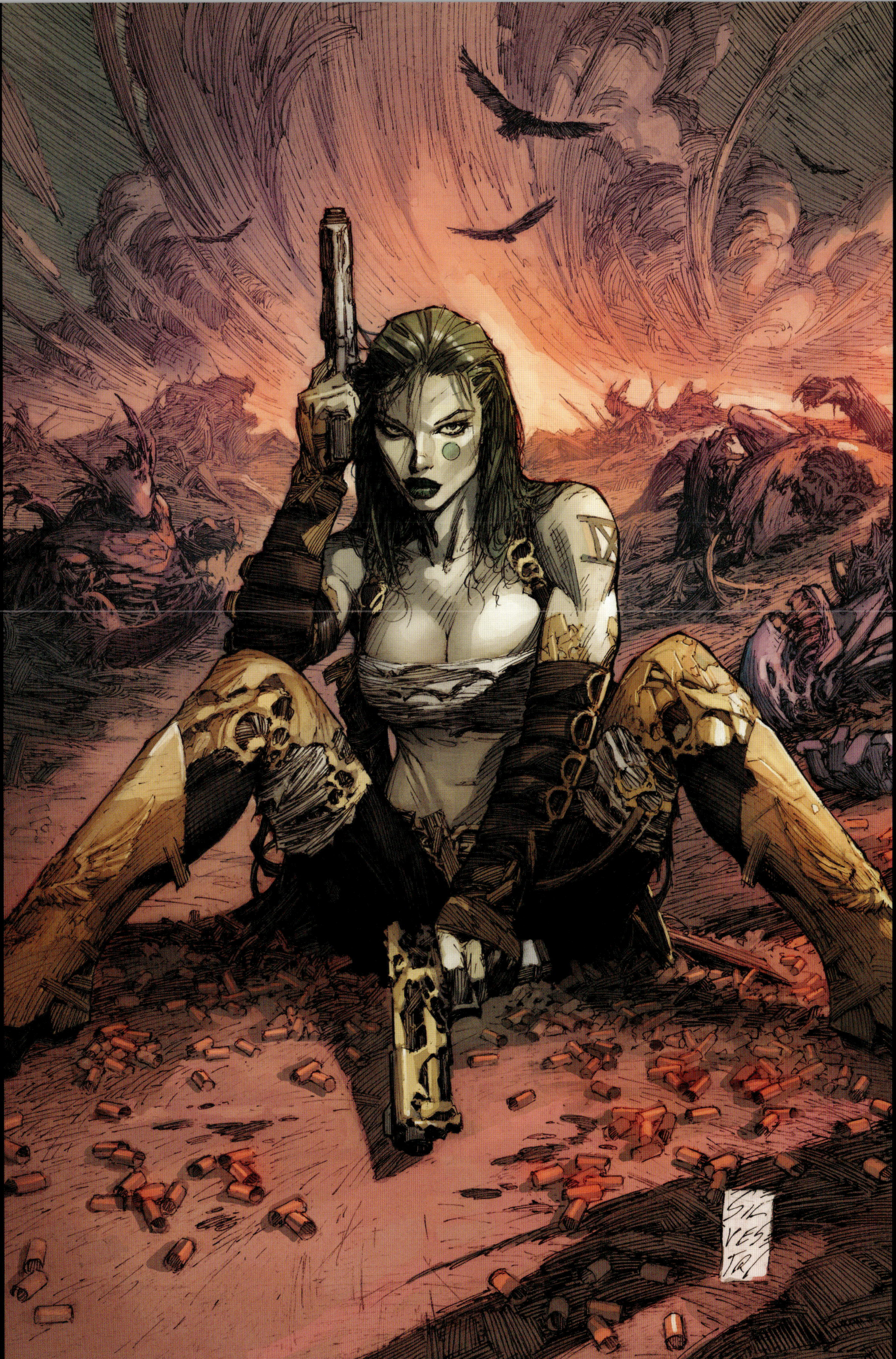

Aphrodite IX Cyberforce #1 [2014] cover C,
art by: Marc Silvestri and Sunny Gho

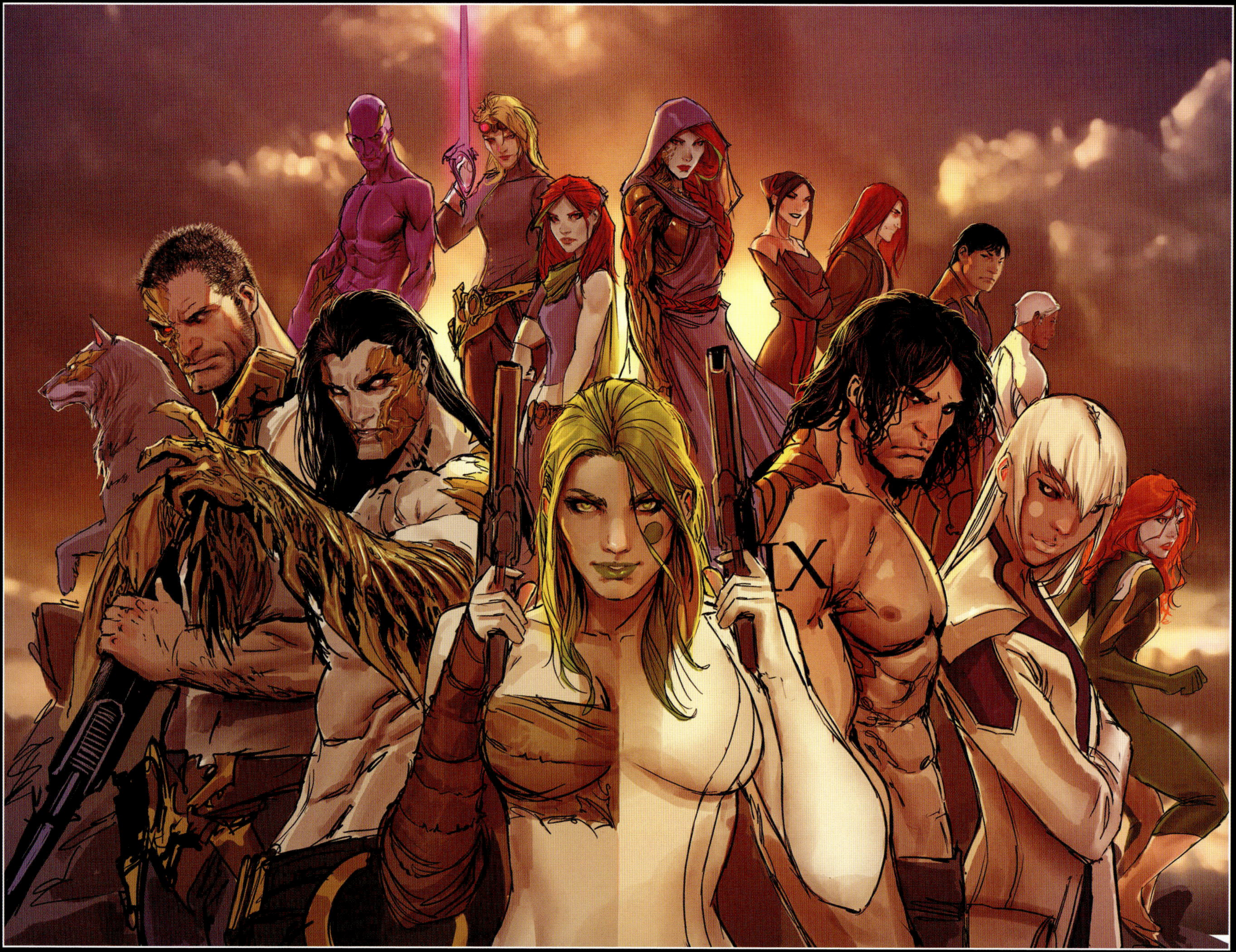

Aphrodite IX Cyberforce #1 [2014] cover A-B, art by: Stjepan Sejic

*** Series and one-shots in the future. ***

Aphrodite IX Cyberforce [2014] one-shot
Two teams, seven centuries apart, united by one woman's diabolical plan. The Chairwoman from the pages of *Cyberforce* and Aphrodite IX had a plan to recreate the world in her children's image. Things didn't go as planned. This double-sized one-shot featured the present day team of Cyberforce and the 28th century Aphrodite IX, and laid the foundation for the new comic series *IXth GENERATION*.

IXth GENERATION [2015] 8 issues, plus one-shot character-focused issues
In the future there is no more natural death, no needs unfilled and everything you could ever want is yours… as long as you're chosen to live in this new Utopia and you're willing to subjugate yourself to these new self-proclaimed gods with 'IX's emblazoned on them. This series raised the question: do the ends truly justify the means? Is a utopia built on genocide worth the price? Aphrodite, Velocity, Hades, and the other Nines establish fiefdoms in this new world and attempt to rule. Their internal clashes have escalated, but they are forced to put that aside as they face off against the relentless hordes of the Darkness. The sins of the past come to claim those who would pretend to be Gods. The cybernetic future established in *Aphrodite IX* and *Cyberforce* finally comes face-to-face with the supernatural *Artifacts* side of the Top Cow universe.

Aphrodite V [2018] 4 issues
In the near future, Los Angeles is a city on the brink of evolution, struggling with a new wave of terror fueled by black-market technology. Enter Aphrodite V: a fugitive from her masters, seeking individuality and purpose. She is the bleeding edge of biomechanics, and L.A.'s best hope against a new enemy-one that seeks to become a god among machines. One machine wants to destroy the city. Another has come to save it. Only one will survive.

Talent Hunt one-shots
- *Aphrodite IX Ares* #0 [2018]
- *Ares IX Darkness* [2018]

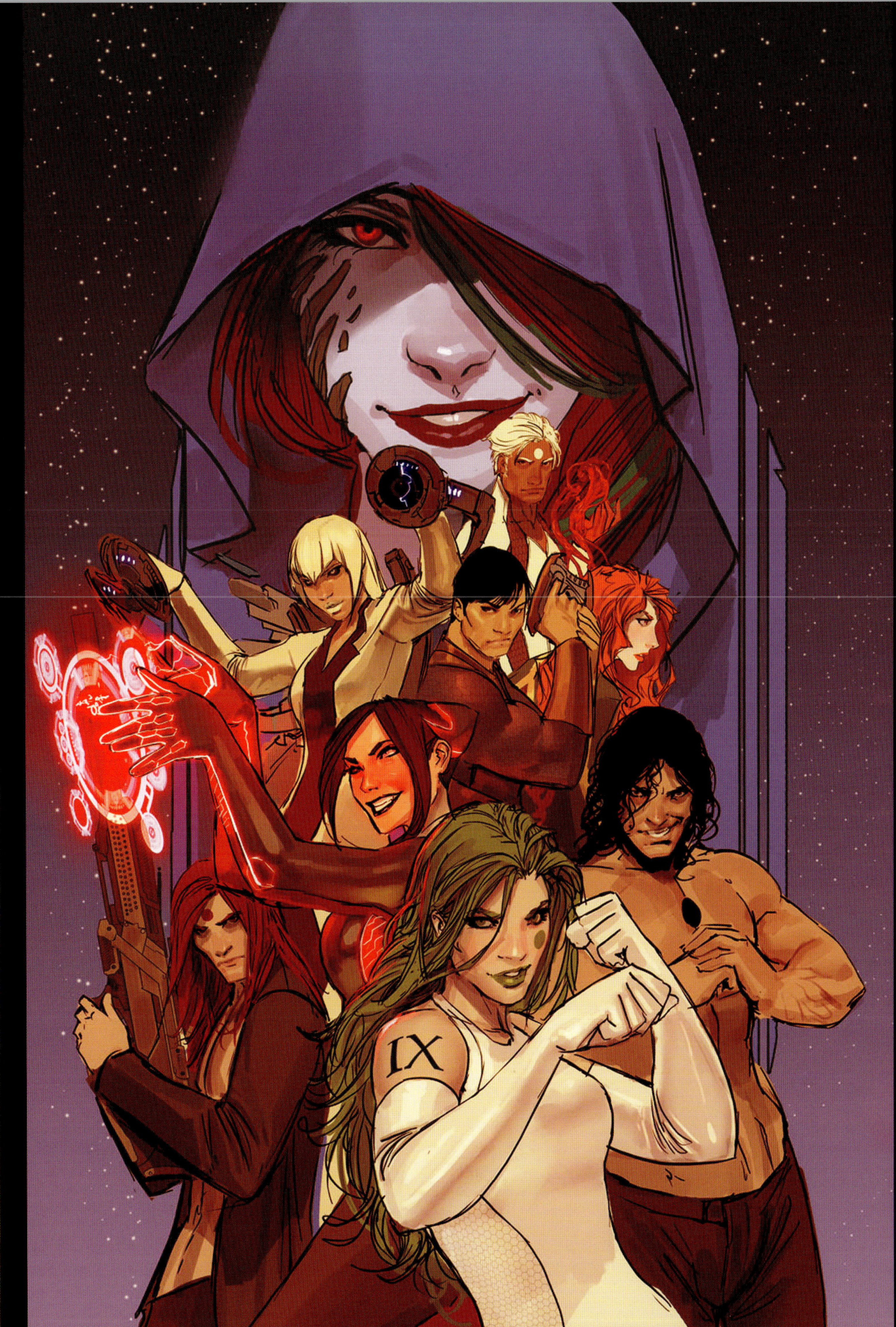

IXth Generation #1 [2013] cover B,
art by: Stjepan Sejic

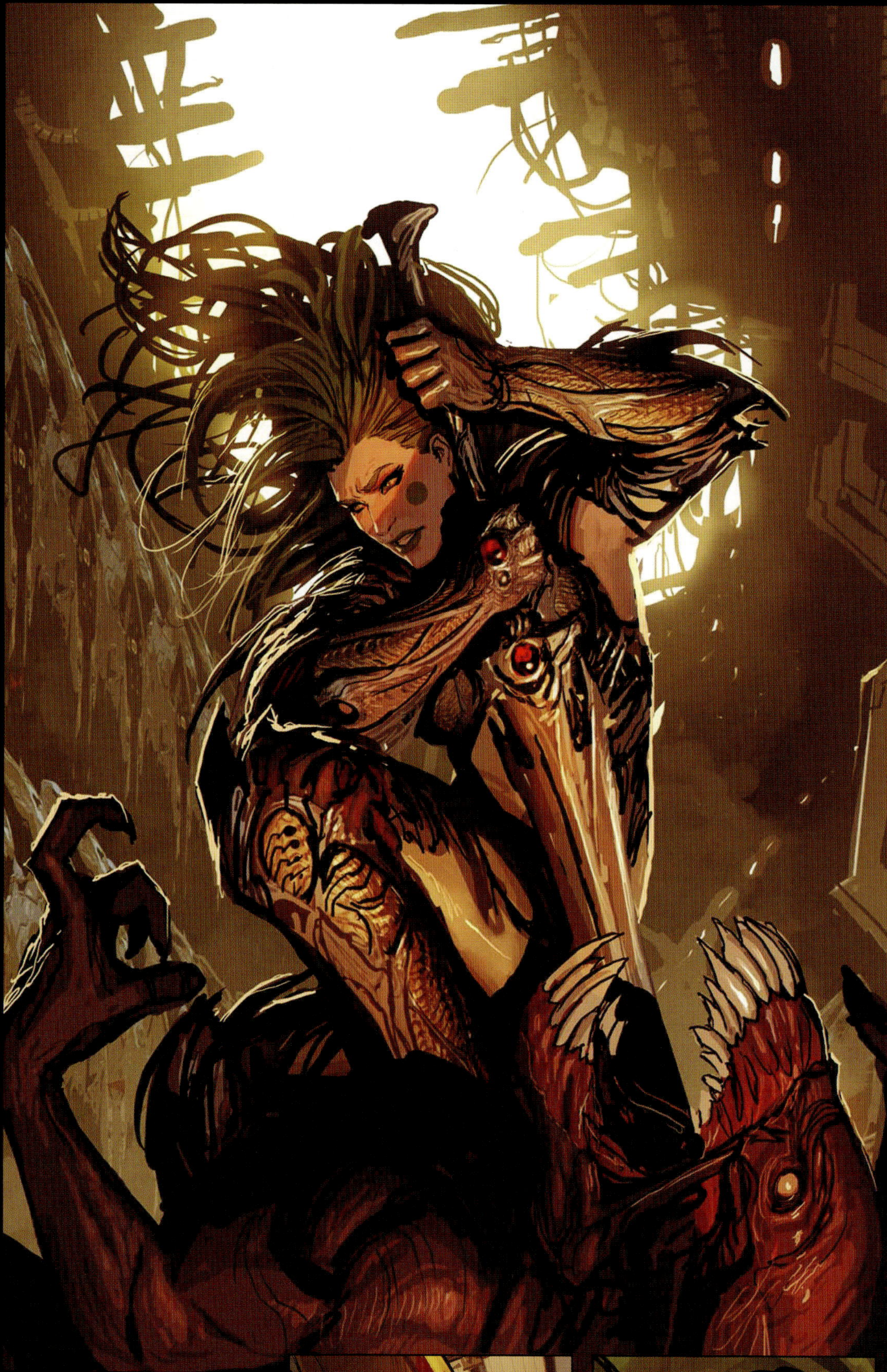

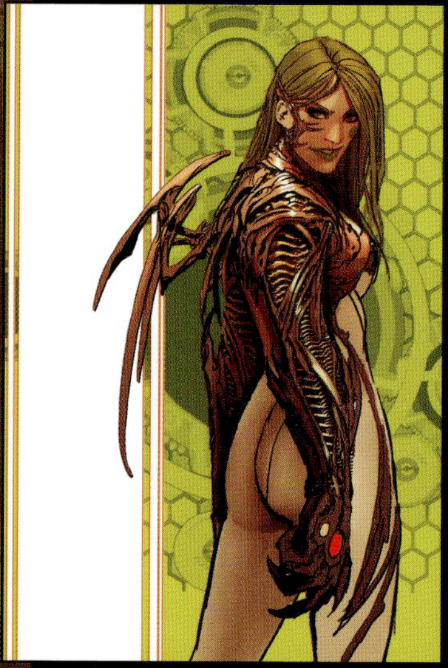

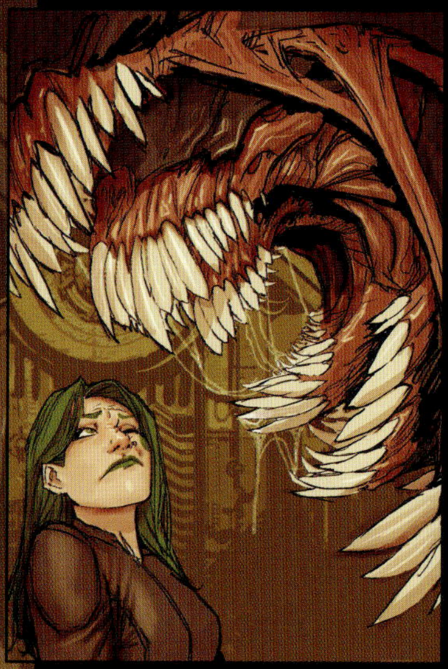

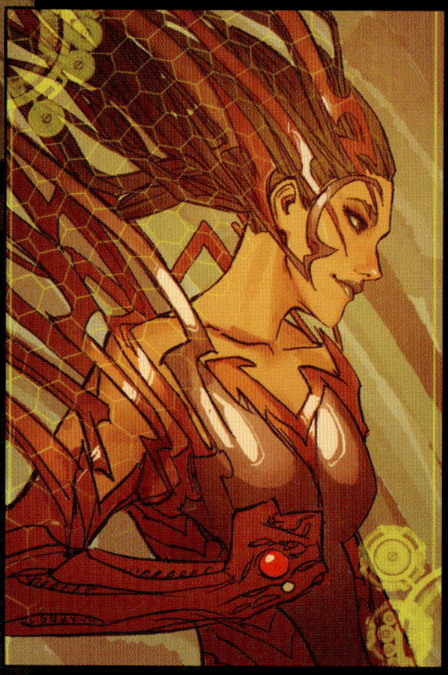

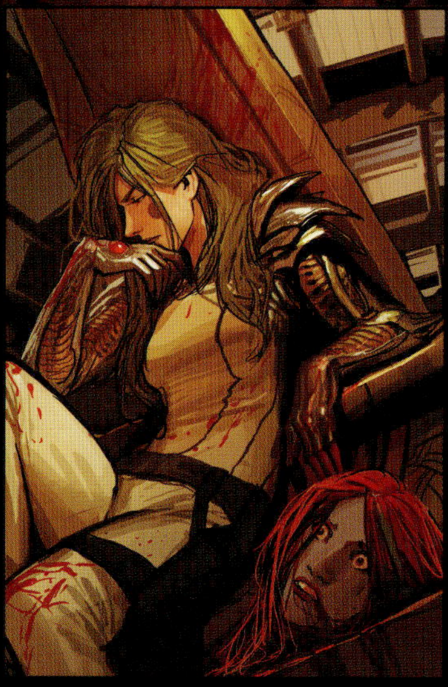

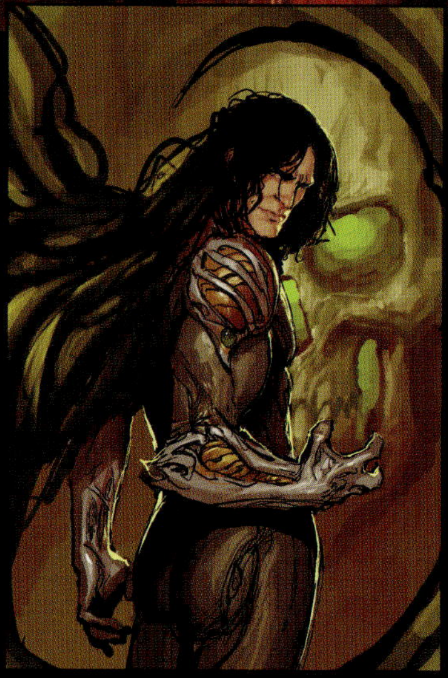

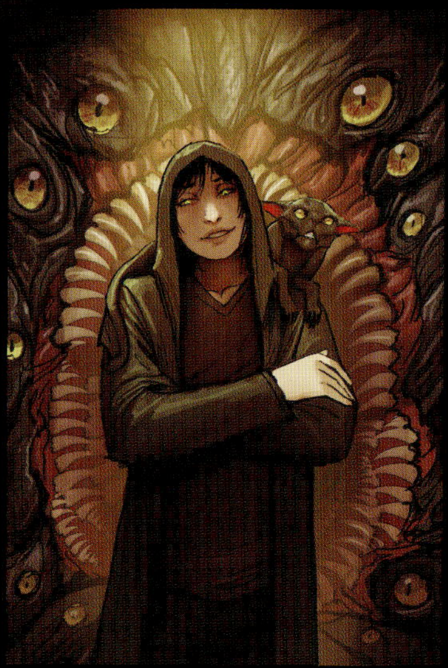

IXth Generation #2-8 [2013] cover A's
art by: Stjepan Sejic

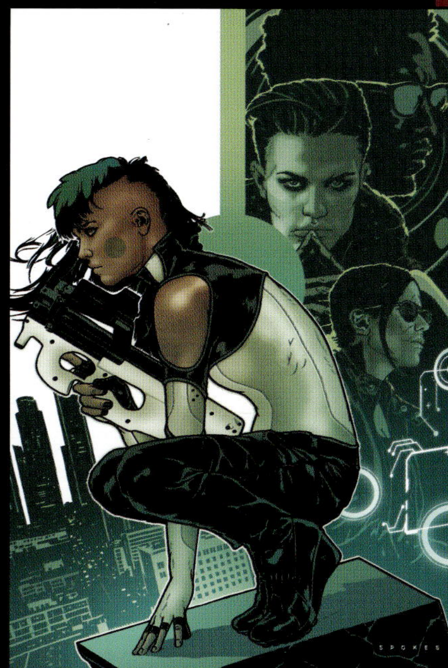

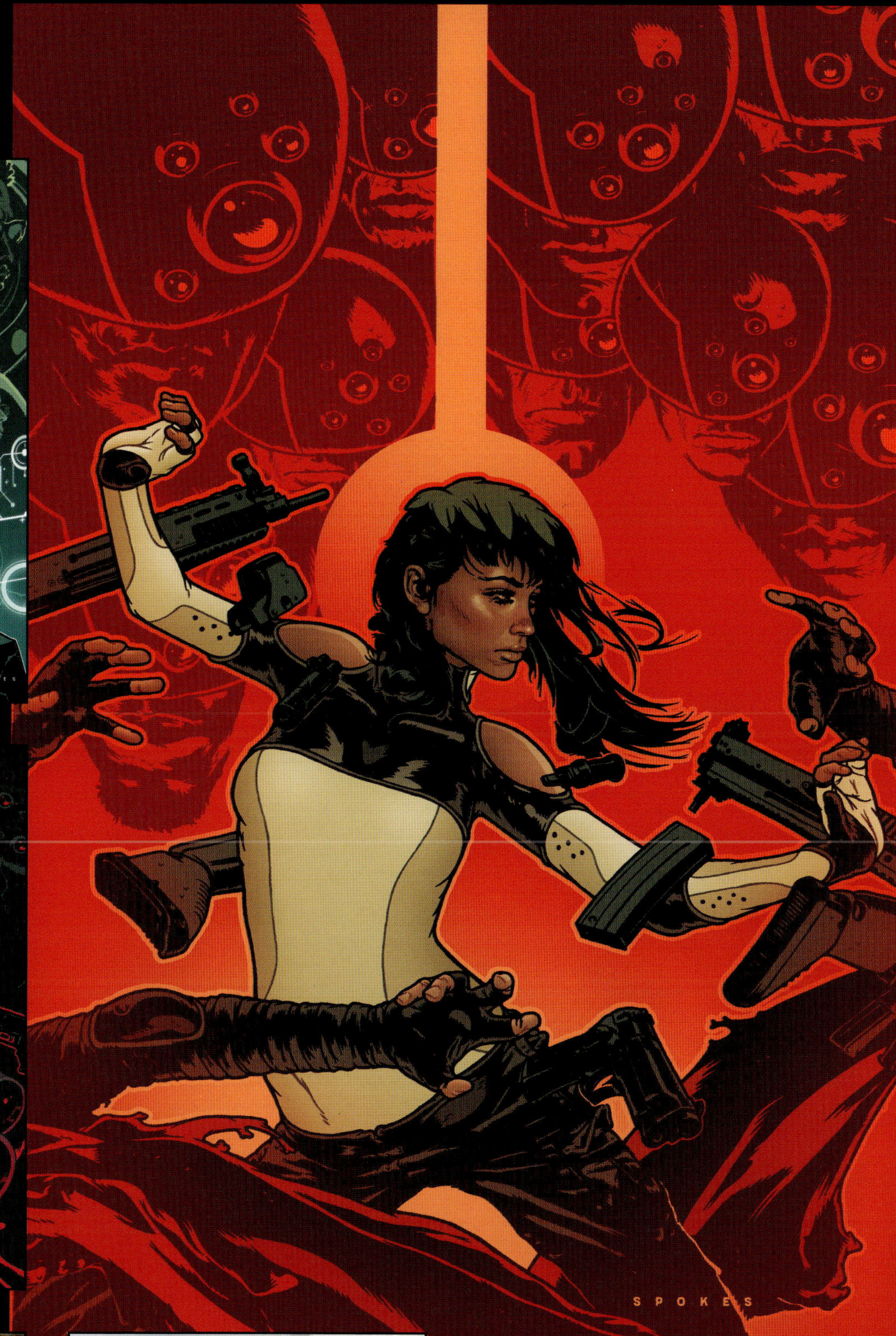

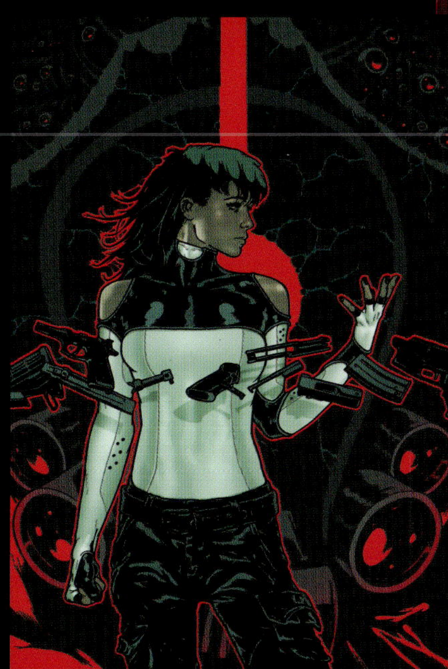

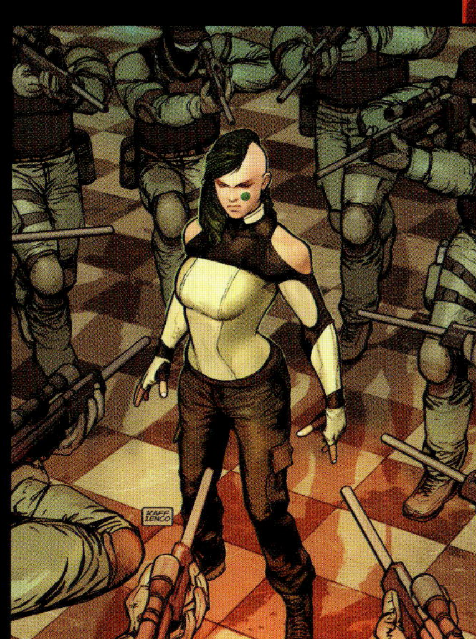

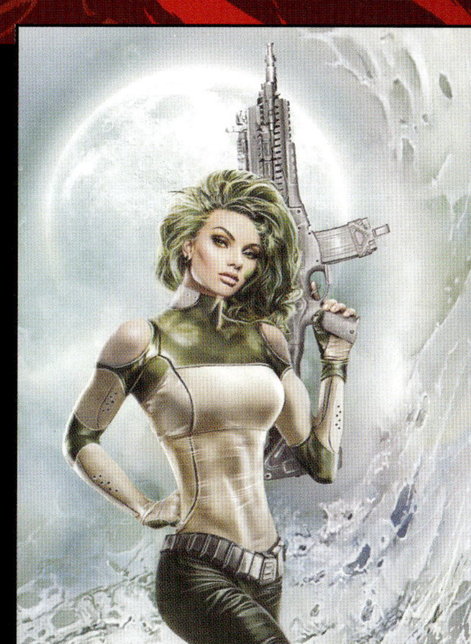

This page, counterclockwise from above.

Aphrodite V #2 [2018] cover,
art by: Jeff Spokes

Aphrodite V #3 [2018] cover,
art by: Jeff Spokes

Aphrodite V #4 [2018] cover A,
art by: Jeff Spokes

Aphrodite V #4 [2018] cover B,
art by: Raffaele Ienco

Aphrodite V #2 [2018] Convention Exclusive cover B,
art by: Natali Sanders

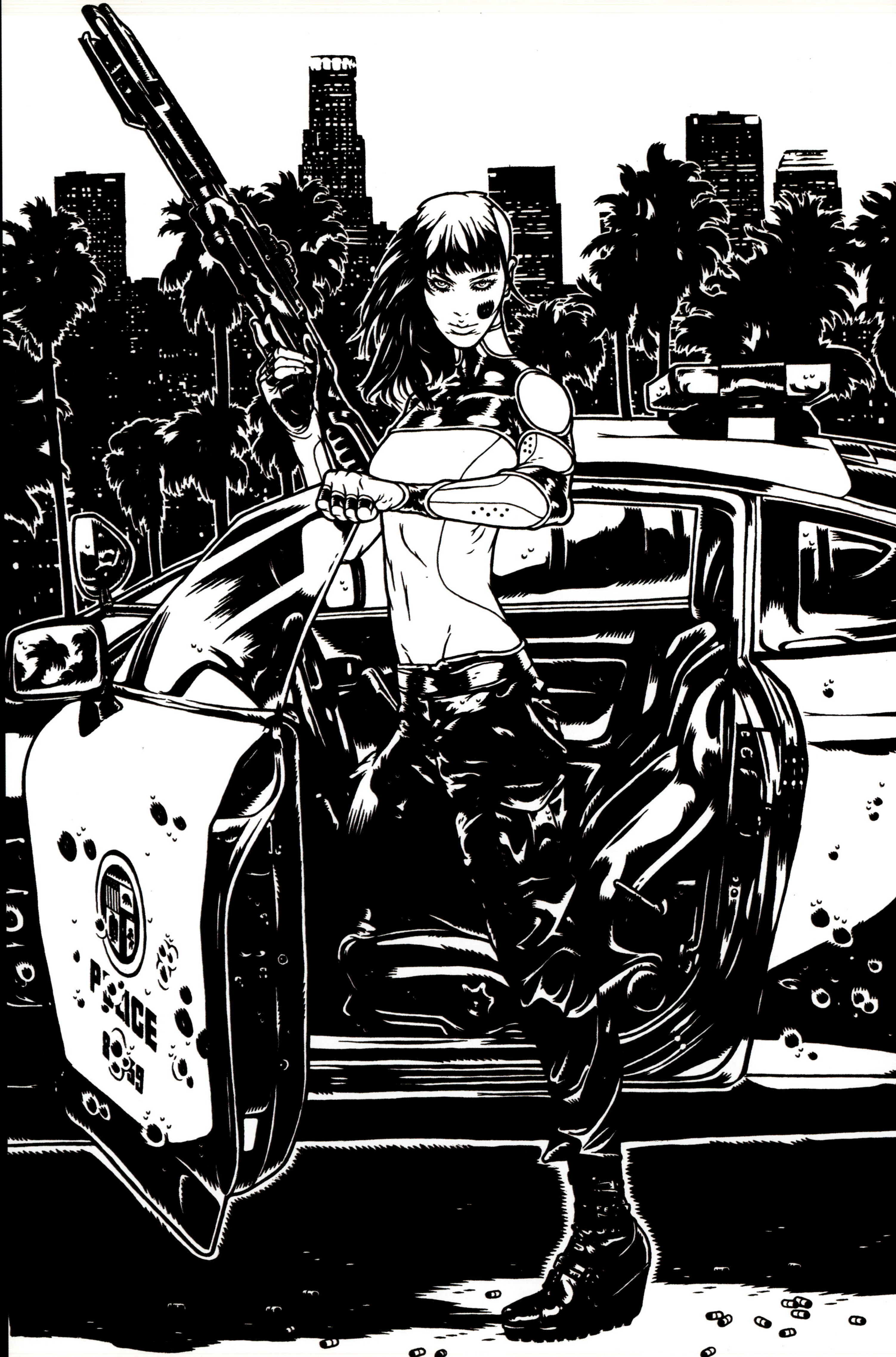

Aphrodite V #1 [2018] cover,
line art by: Jeff Spokes

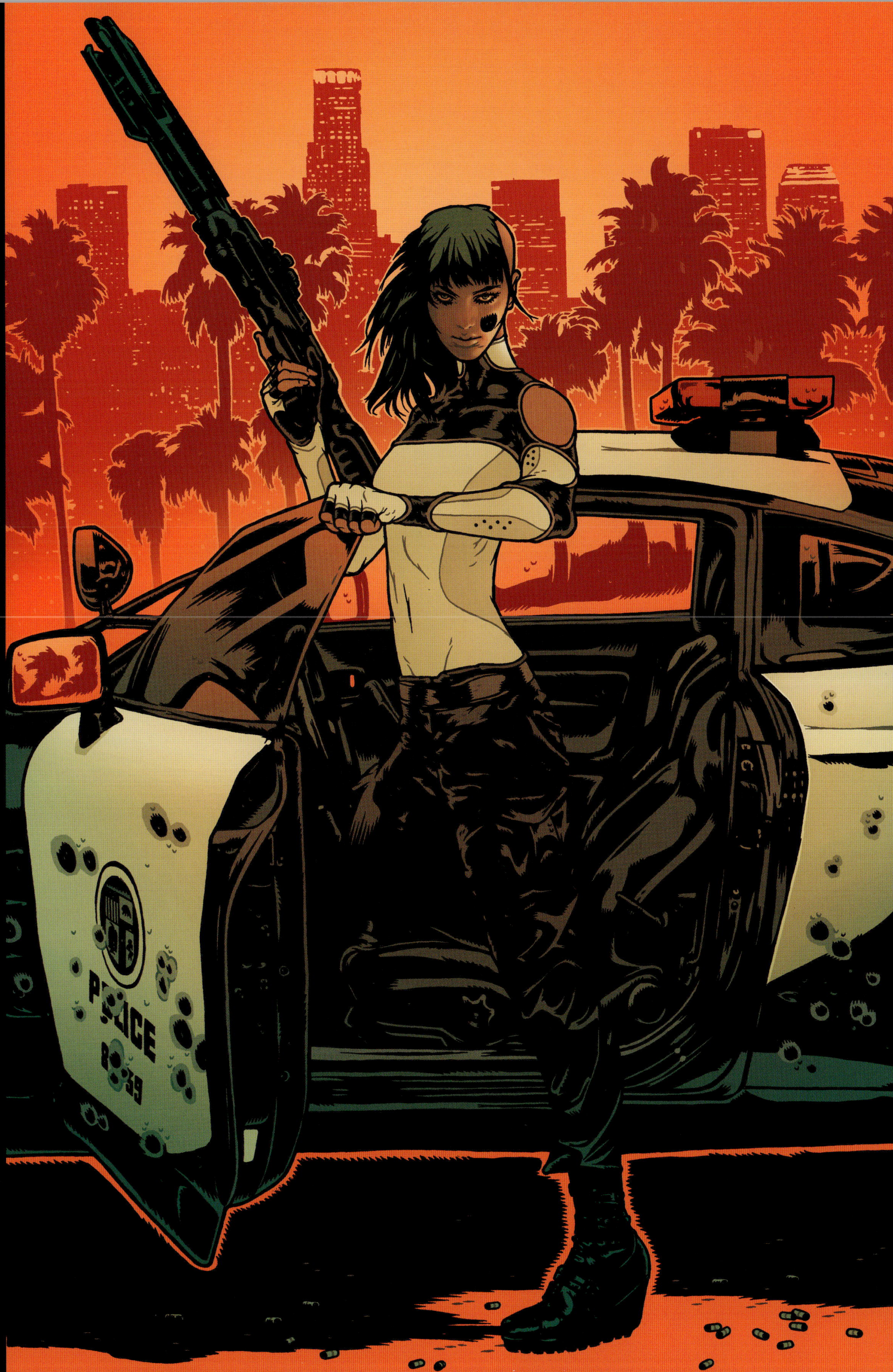

Aphrodite V #1 [2018] cover,
art by: Jeff Spokes

{CREATOR SPOTLIGHT}

Linda and Stjepan Sejic • Covers • Selected Works

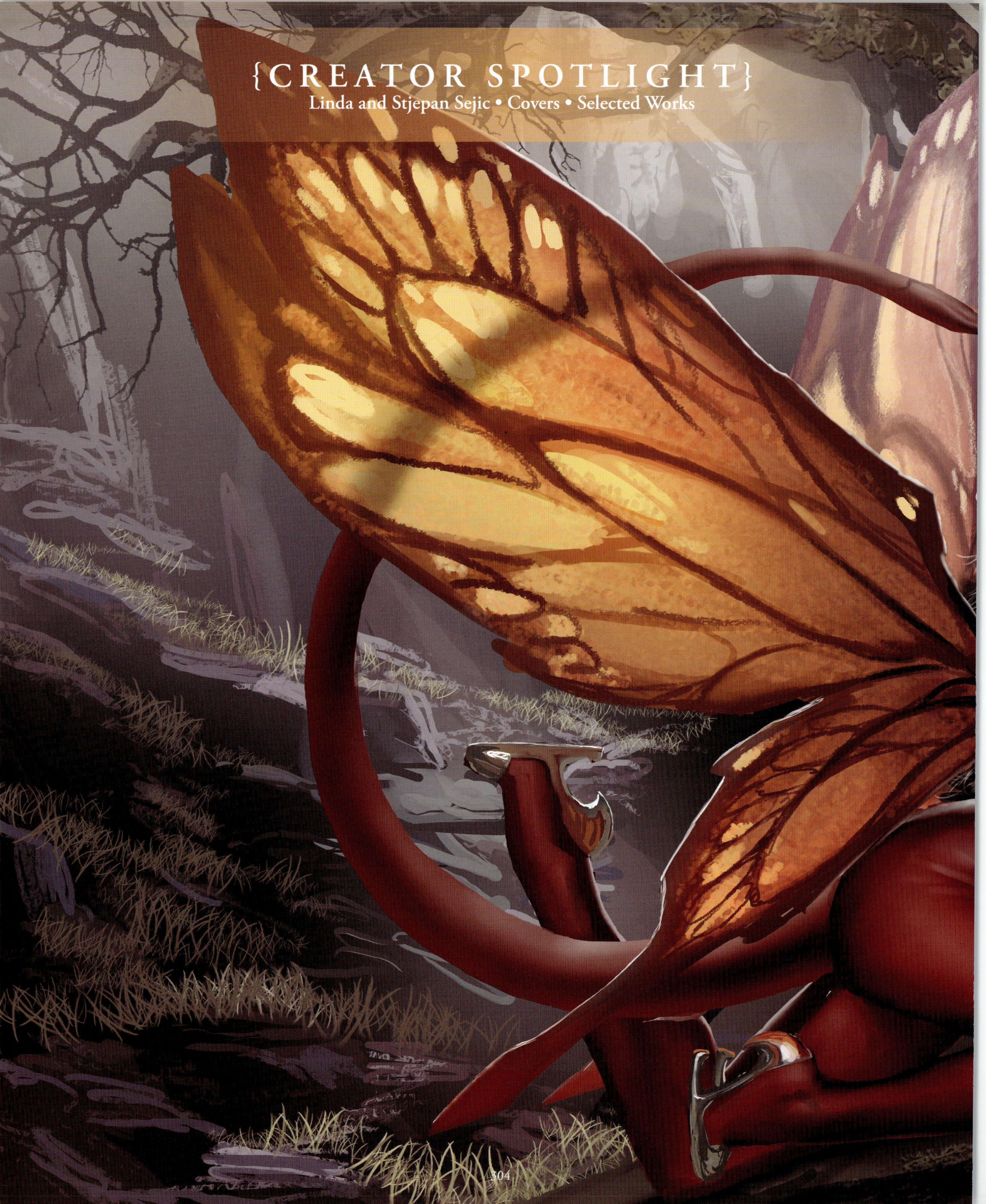

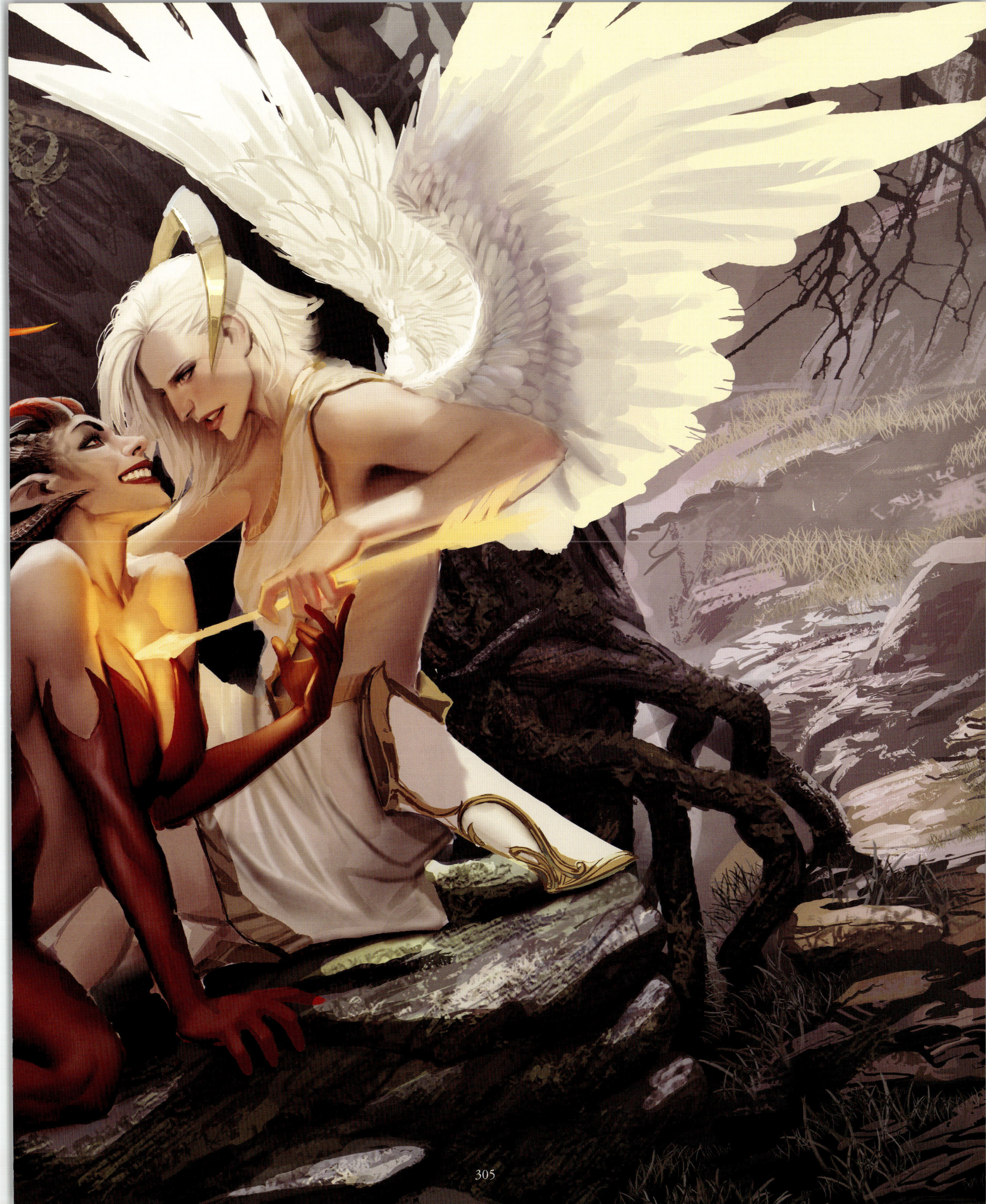

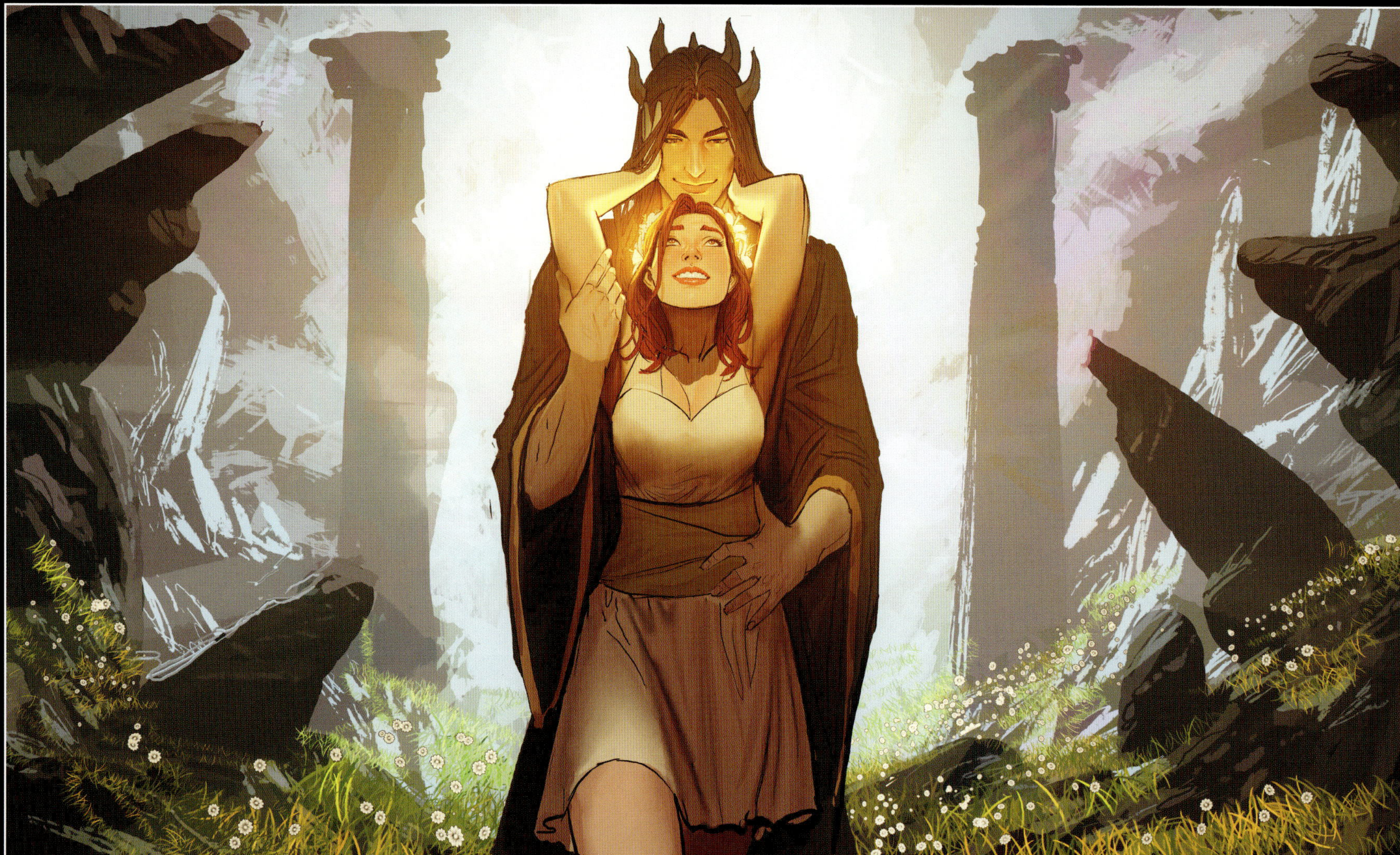

Above. *"...fanart piece I did of my wife's comic Punderworld. A reimagining of the tale of Hades and Persephone with some extremely cool narrative angles..."* - Stjepan

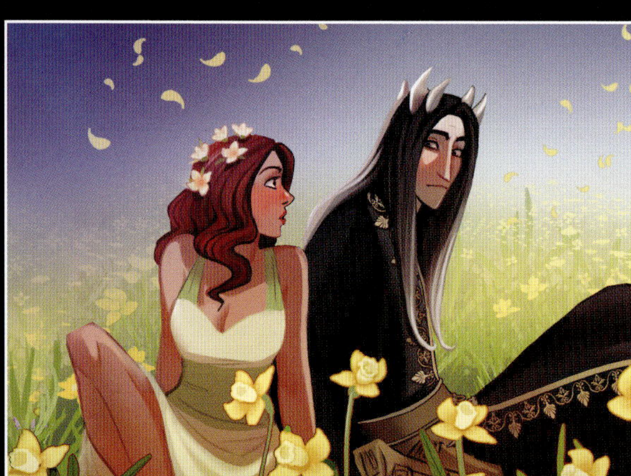

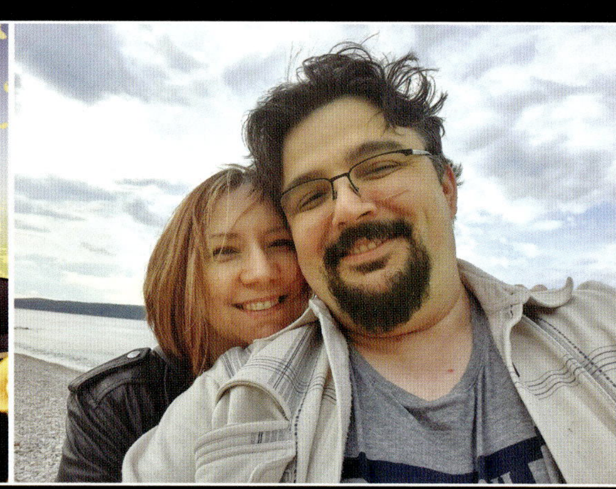

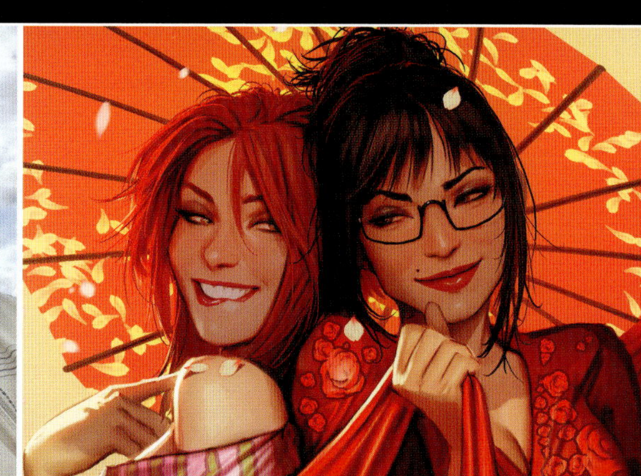

The Sejics are equally talented, prolific, and kind. Their impact on the comics industry and Top Cow, as you may have gathered from this book, is profound. On the following pages, please take a look at some of their creator-owned works and a Top Cow gem or two.

Linda Sejic
(*Punderworld, Blood Stain* and more)

Linda Sejic is best known for her creator-owned comics *Blood Stain* and *Punderworld*, which garnered massive popularity on the webcomic site Webtoons and is one of the industry's best-selling collections. Currently, she is working on the continuation of *Punderworld*, which is planned to have three volumes in total.

Stjepan Sejic
(*Ravine, Sunstone, Fine Print, Death Vigil* and more)

Stjepan is known for his years-long run on *Witchblade* alongside other Top Cow titles. He writes and draws his creator-owned series mixing science-fiction, the supernatural, and sexiness with *Sunstone, Fine Print, Death Vigil*, and his upcoming series, *Achilles Shield Maidens* and *The Queen and the Woodborn.*

Previous page. *Leliah and Heureca* from Fine Print, art by: Stjepan Sejic

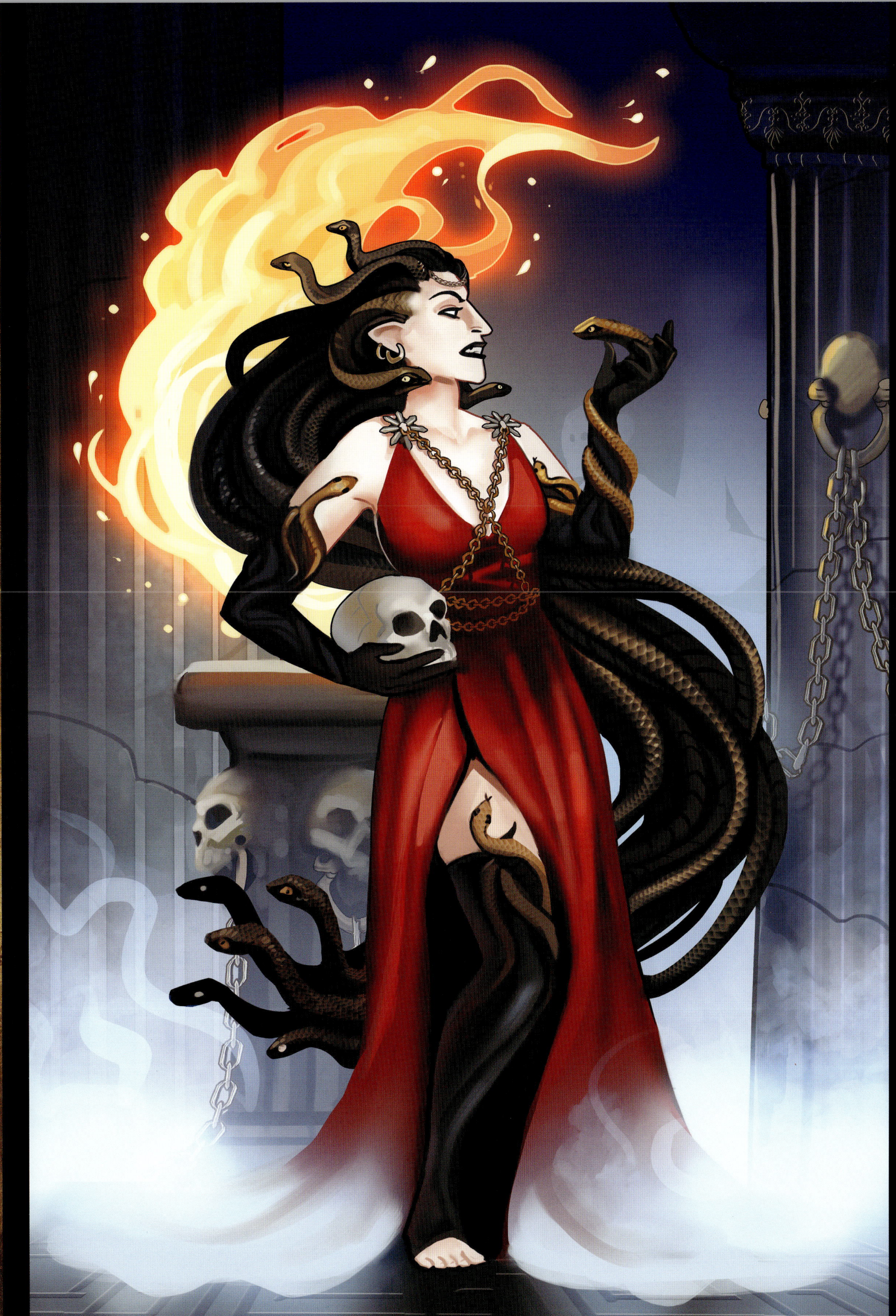

Punderworld "Alecto" Top Cow Store/Convention Print,
art by: Linda Sejic

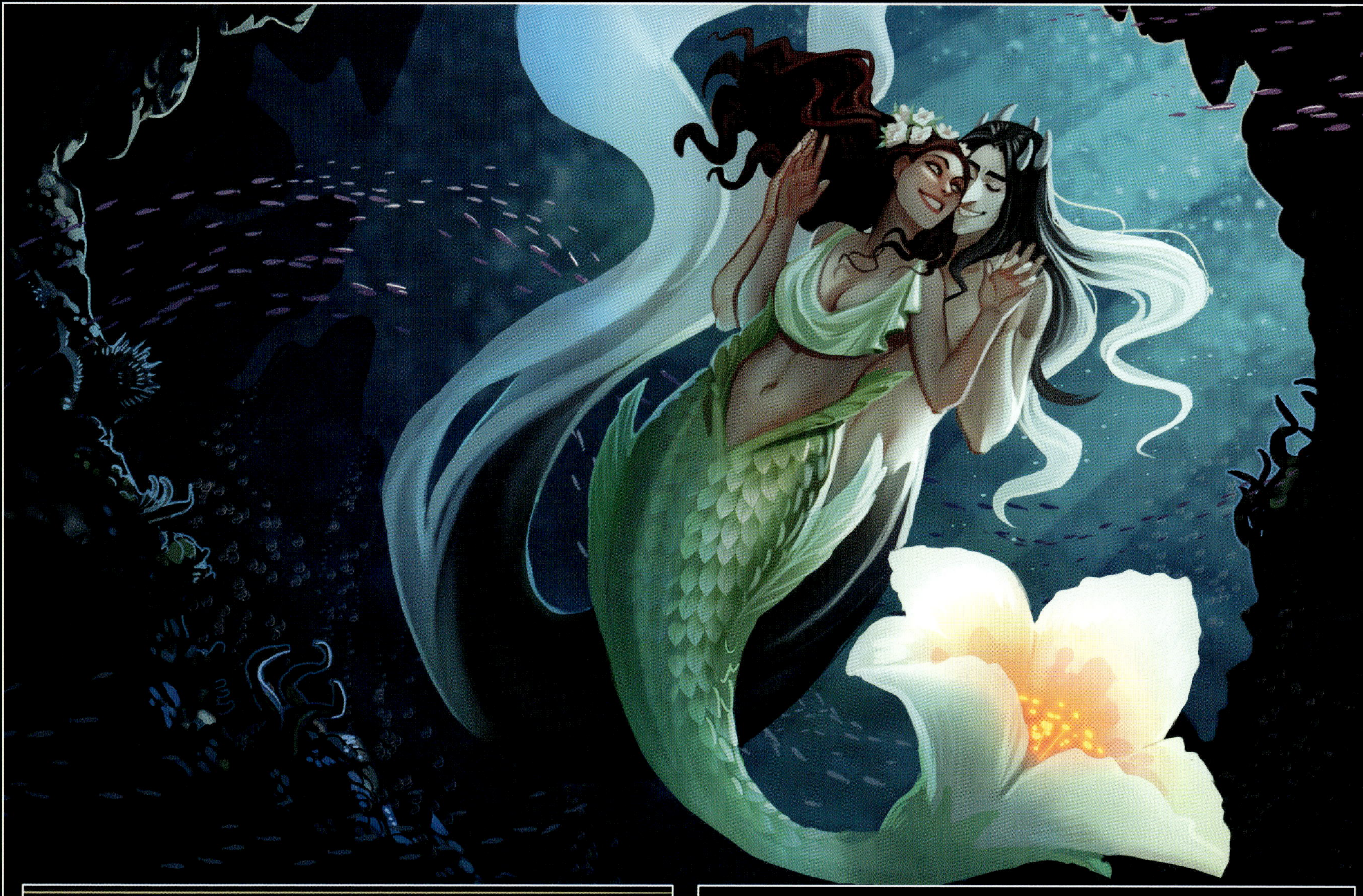

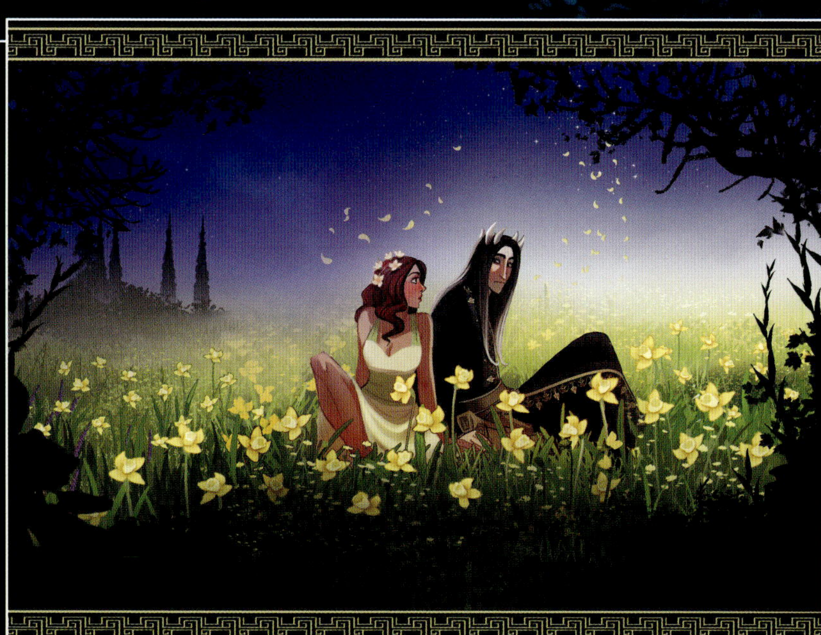

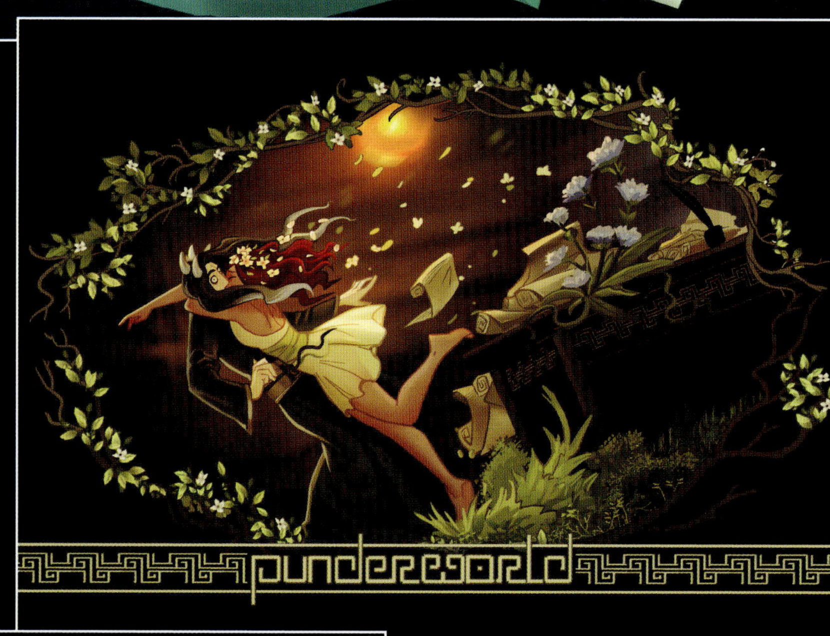

This page, left to right from top.

Punderworld Top Cow Store/Convention Prints

"Punderwater," art by: Linda Sejic

Punderworld volume 1 cover, art by: Linda Sejic

"Missed You," art by: Linda Sejic

"Cerby," art by: Linda Sejic

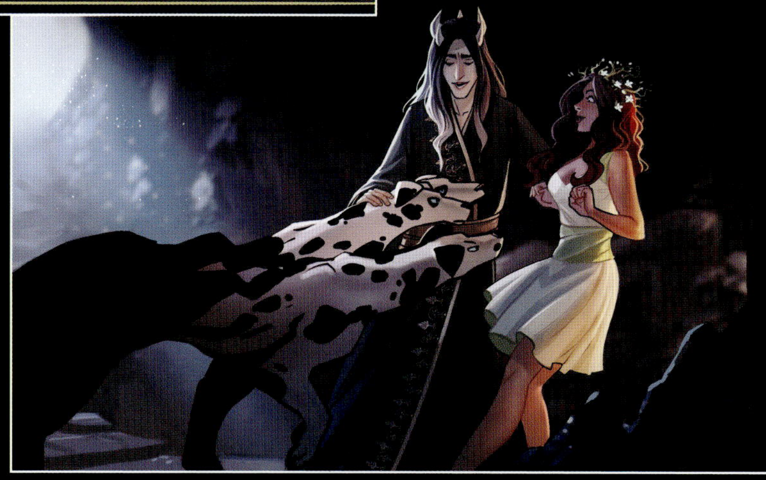

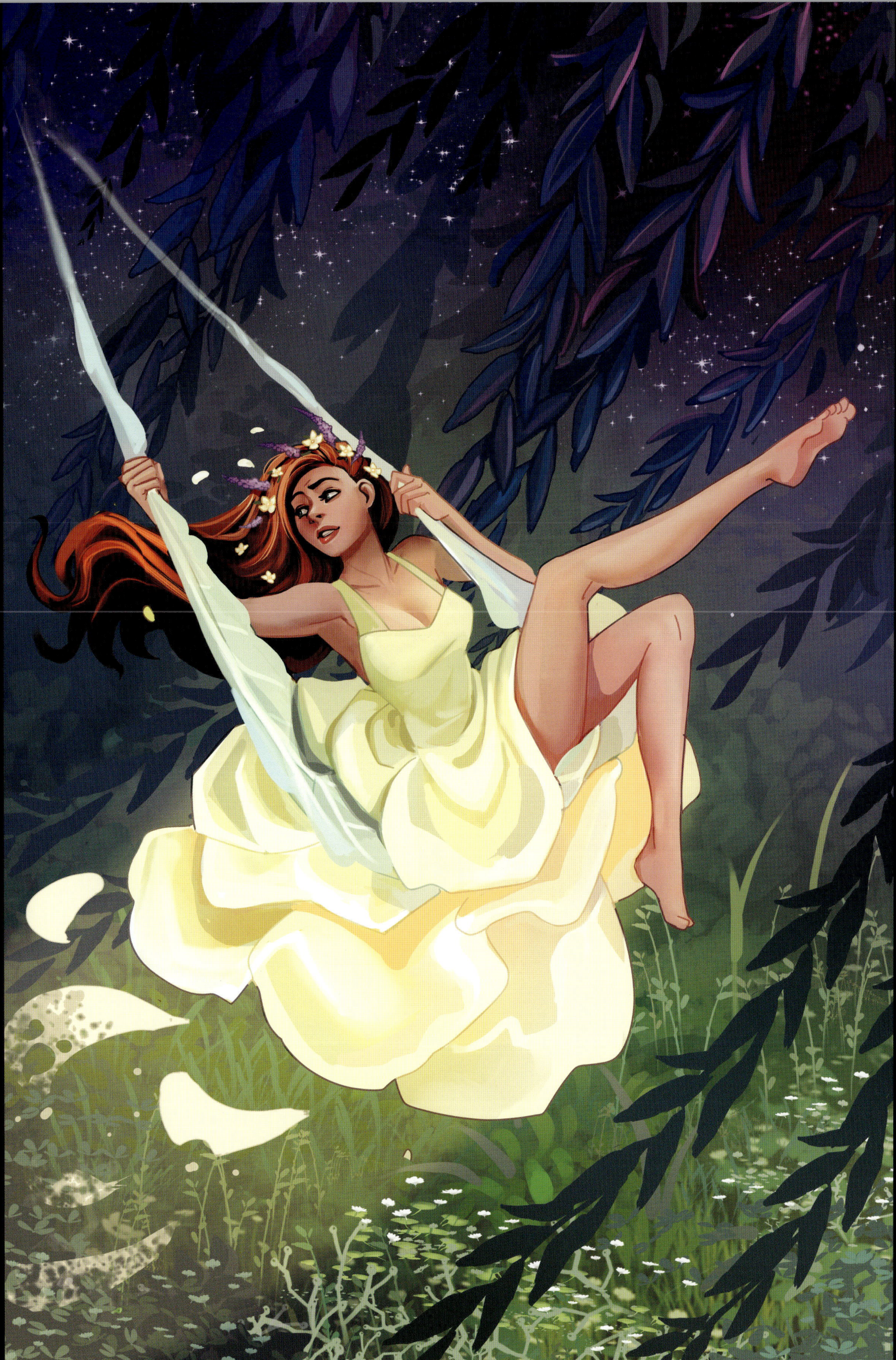

Punderworld volume 2 cover,
art by: Linda Sejic

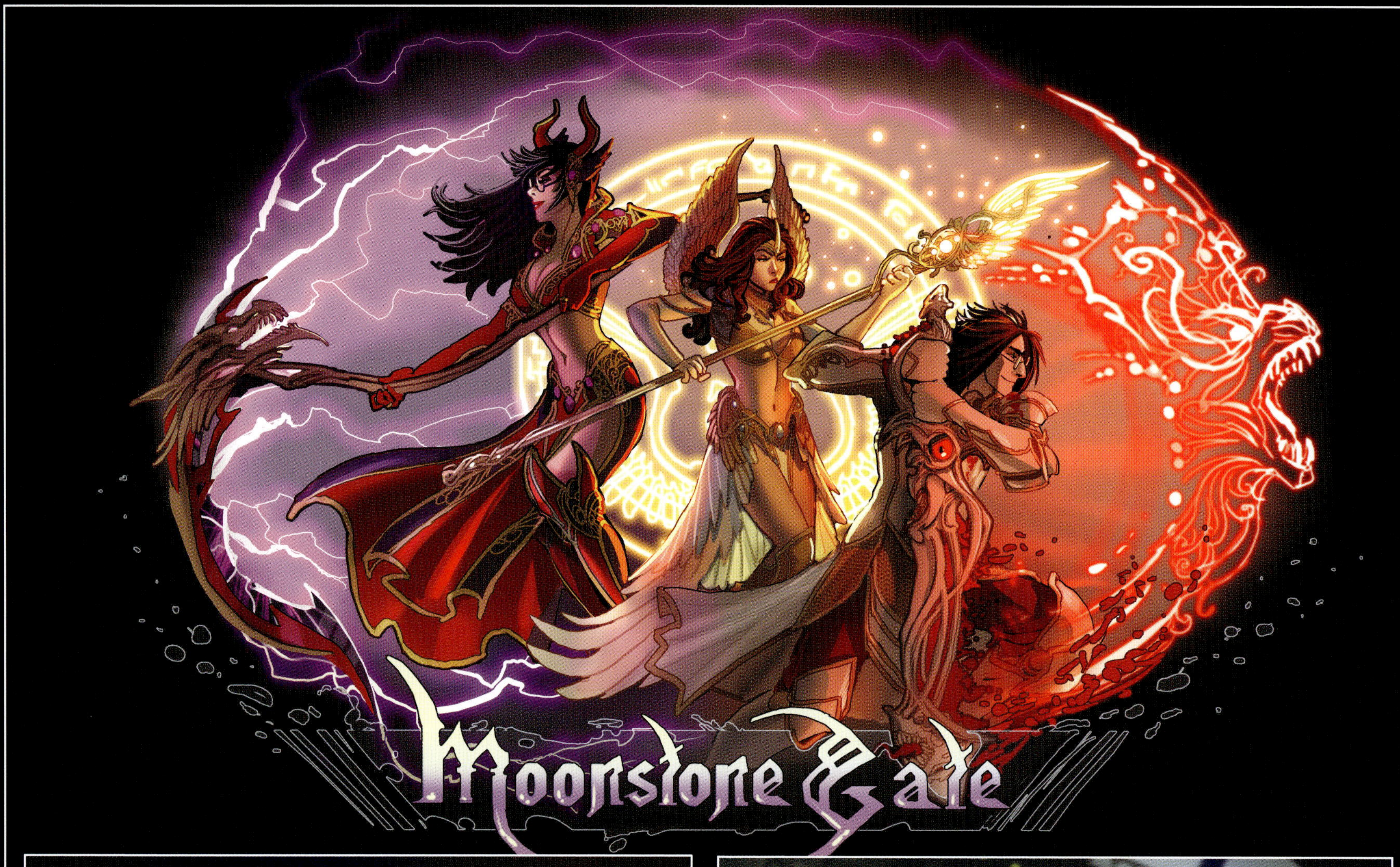

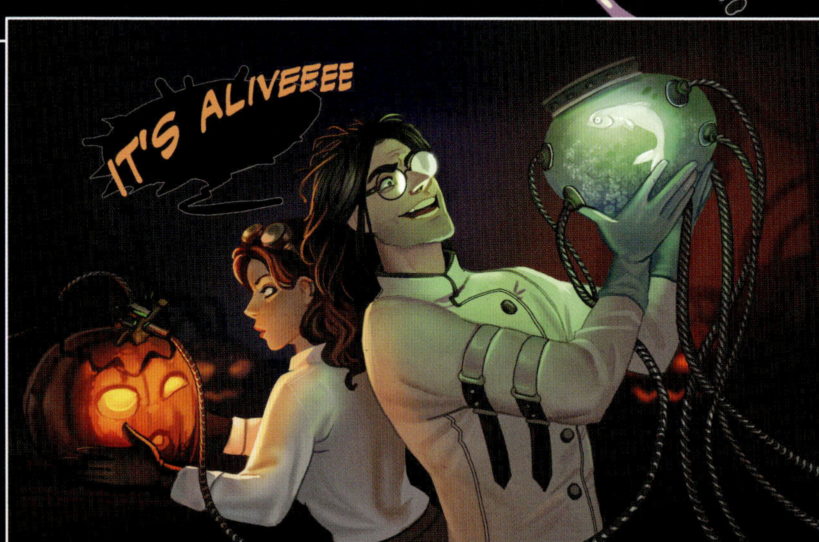

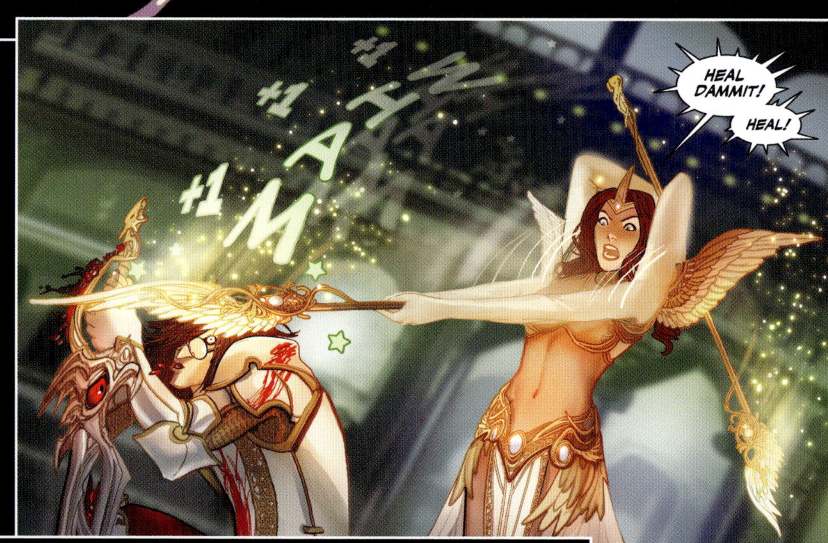

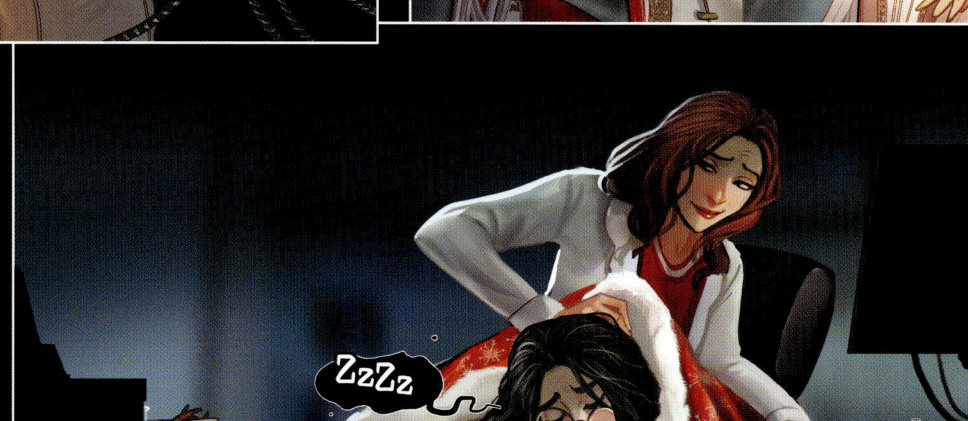

This page, left to right from top.

Blood Stain Top Cow Store/Convention Prints

"Moonstone Gate 500," art by: Linda Sejic

"Mad Science," art by: Linda Sejic

"Heal Damnit!," art by: Linda Sejic

Blood Stain Book 1 cover,
art by: Linda Sejic

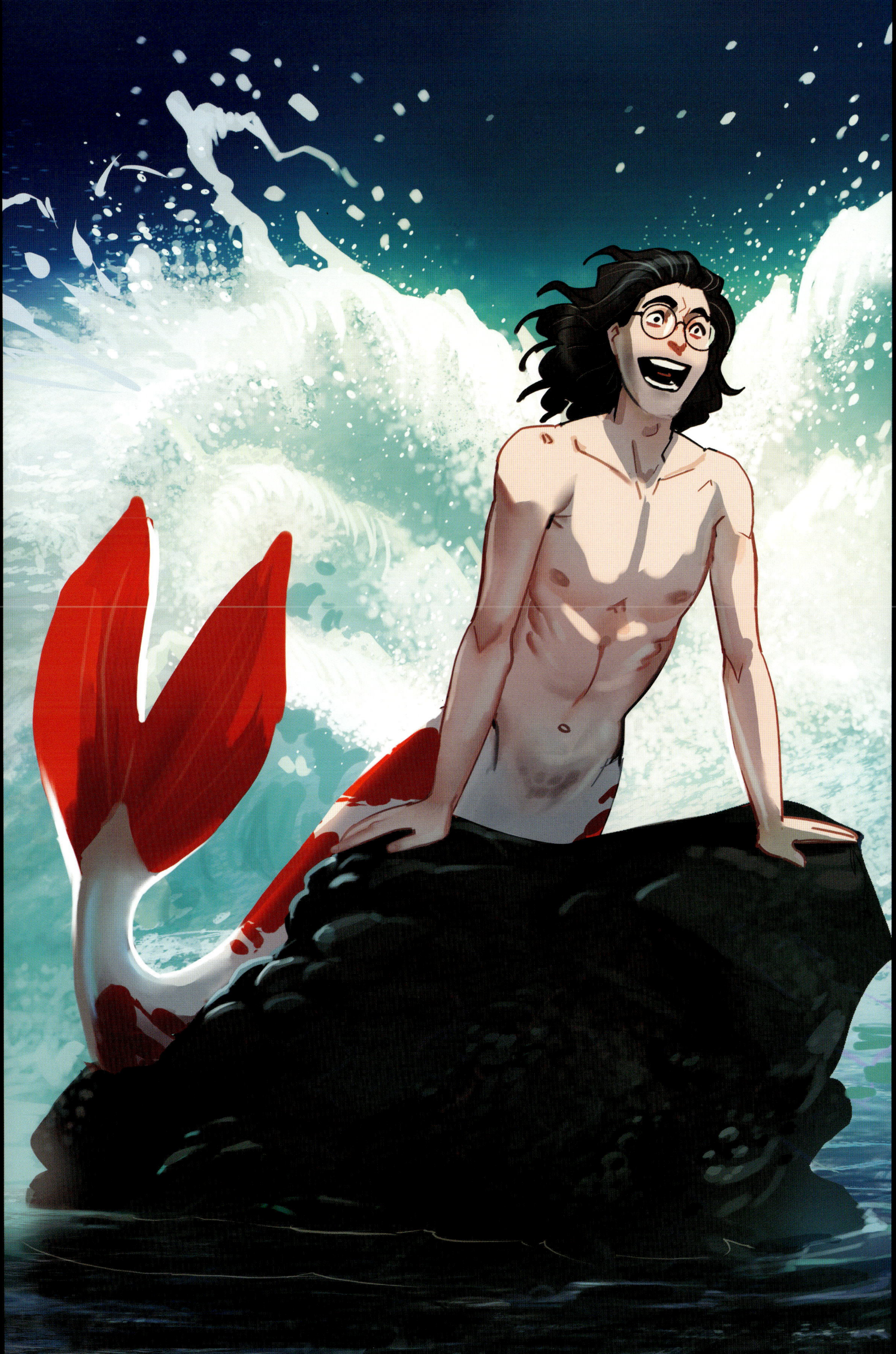

Blood Stain *“Vlariel”* Top Cow Store/Convention Print, art by: Linda Sejic

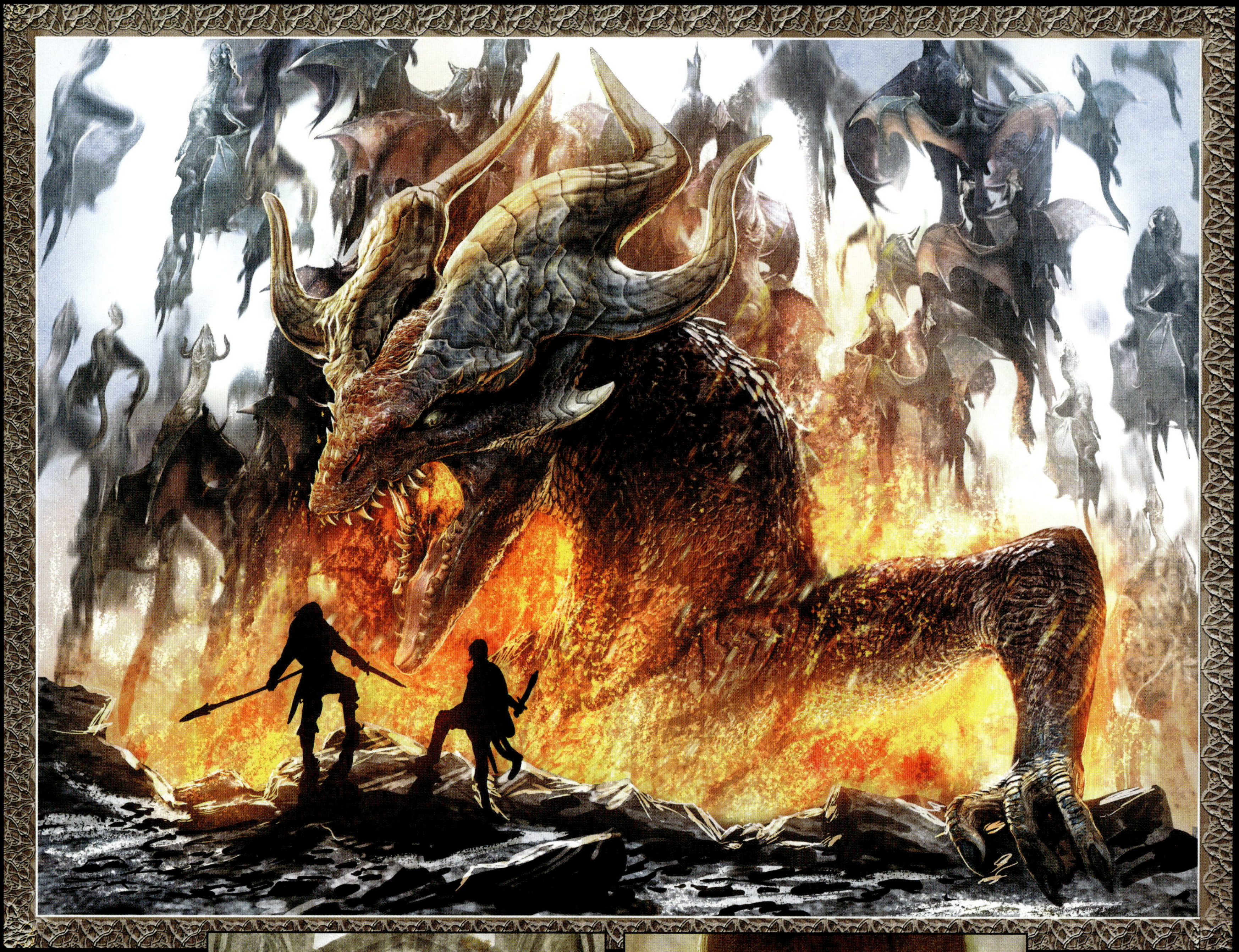

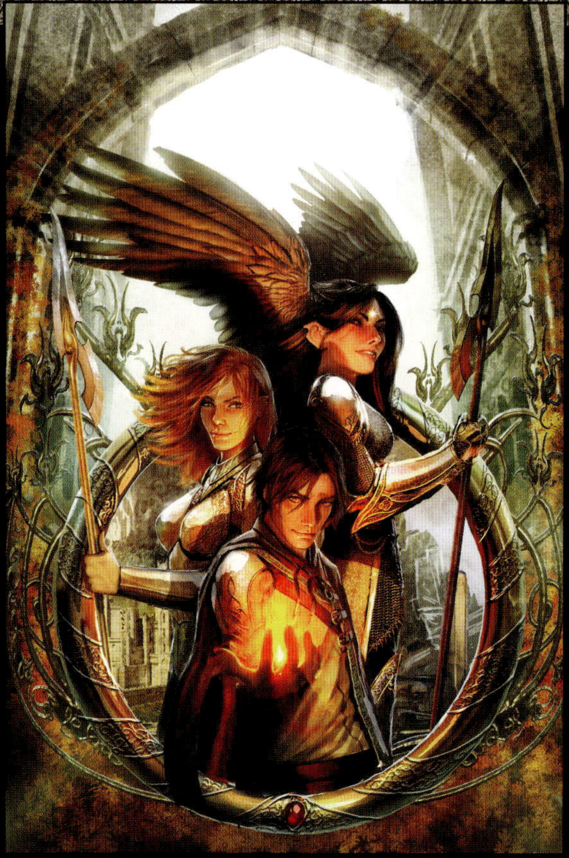

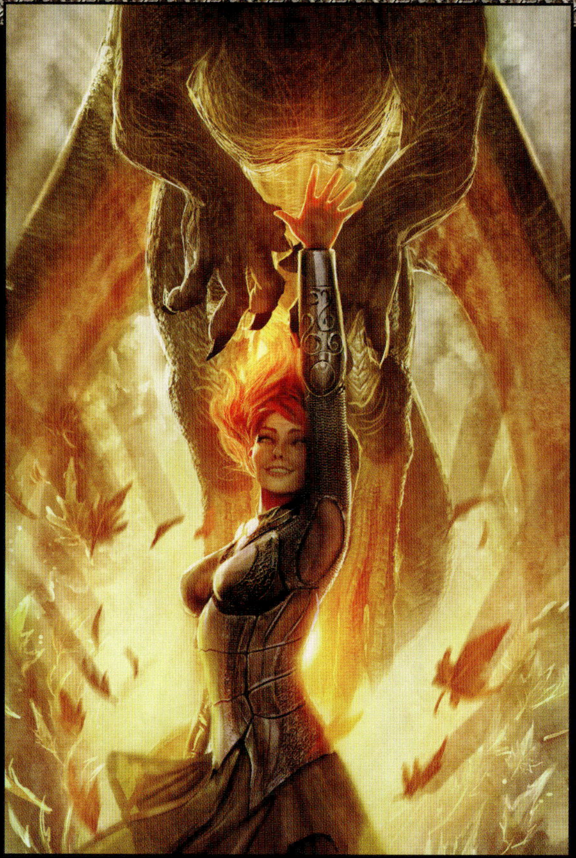

Top. Artwork from *Ravine* volume 1 pages 126-127 • Above. *Ravine* volume 1 covers A and B, art by: Stjepan Sejic

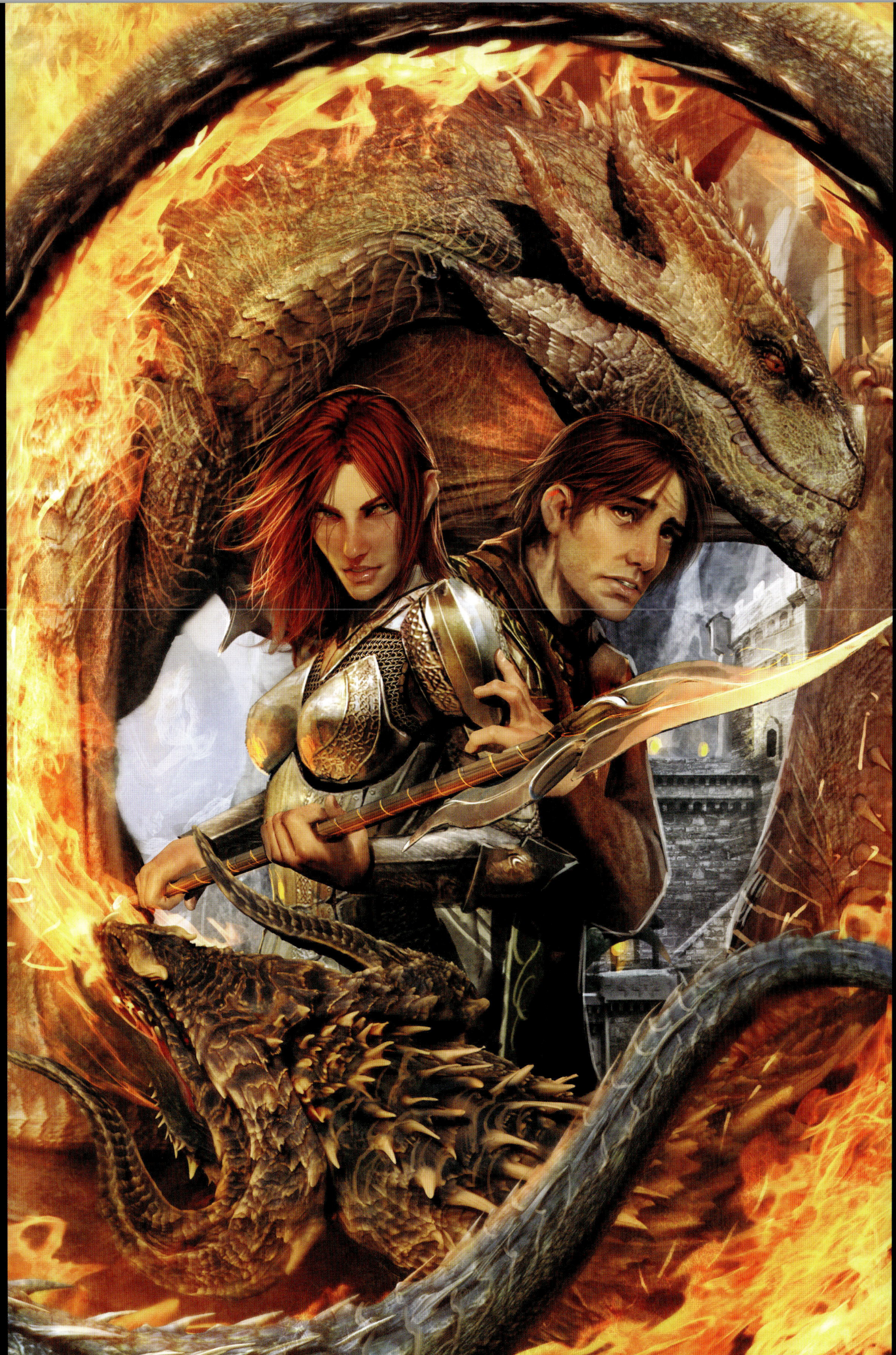

Ravine volume 2 cover,
art by: Stjepan Sejic

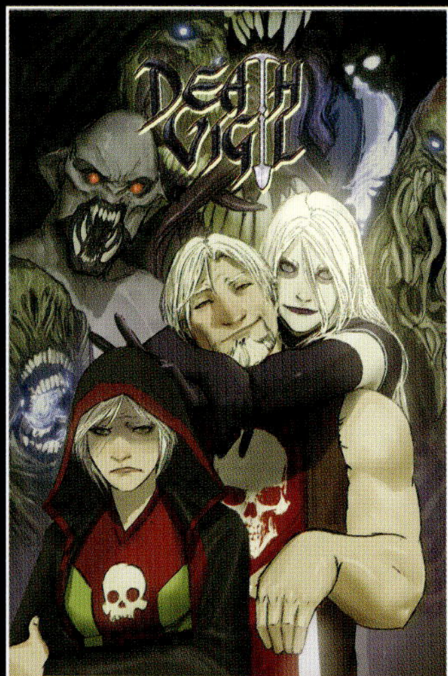

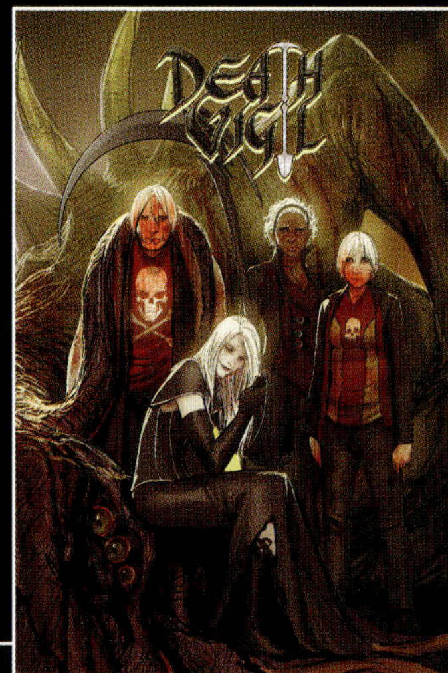

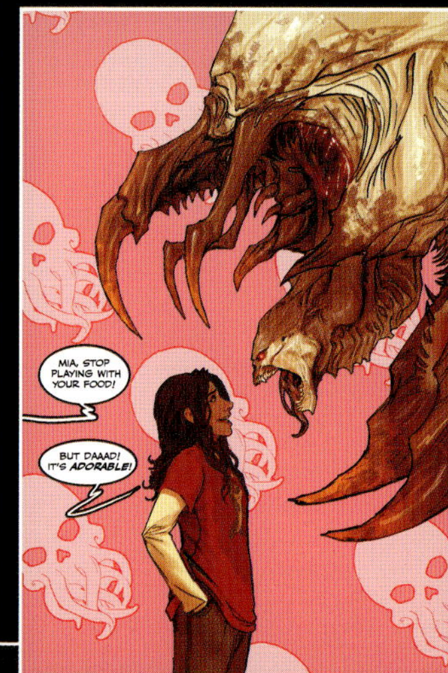

Top row, from left. *Death Vigil* #1-3 covers,

Center row, from left. *Death Vigil* volume 1 first printing and new printing,

Bottom row, from left. *Death Vigil* #4-8 covers,

art by: Stjepan Sejic

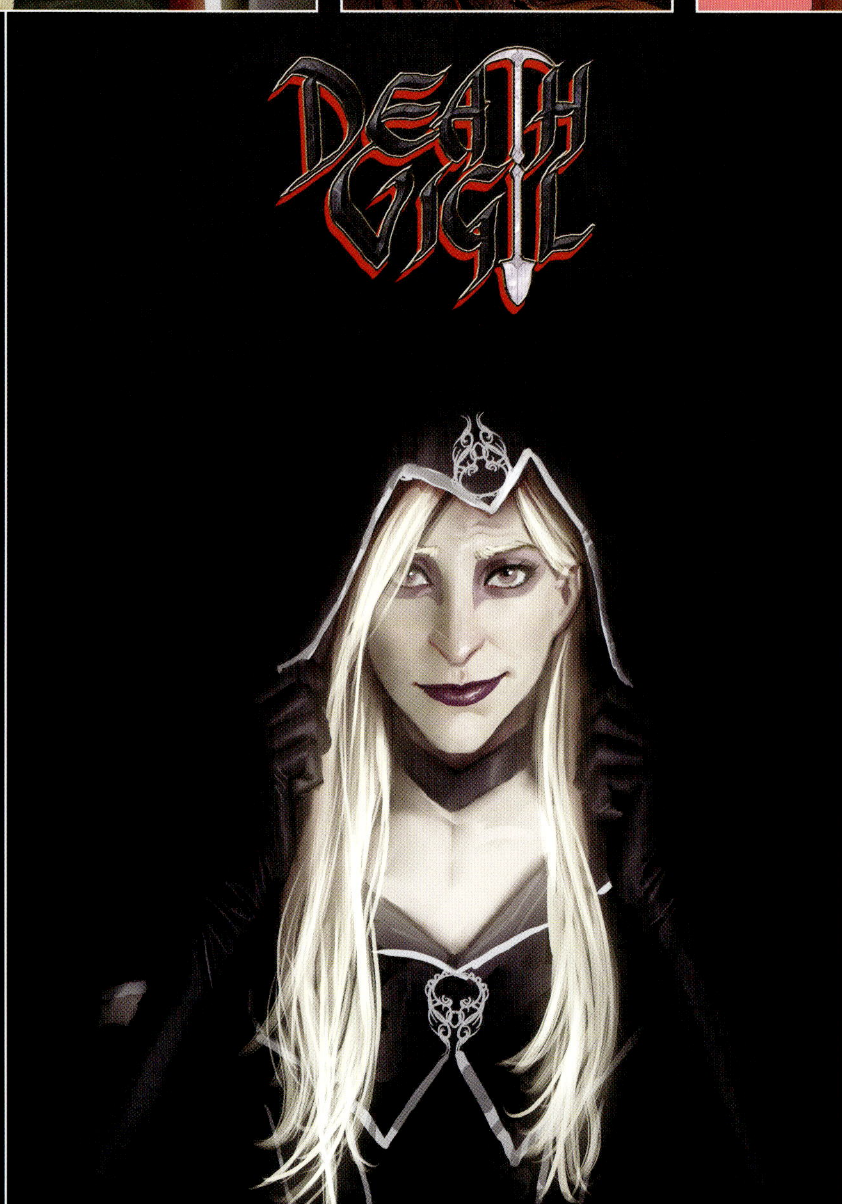

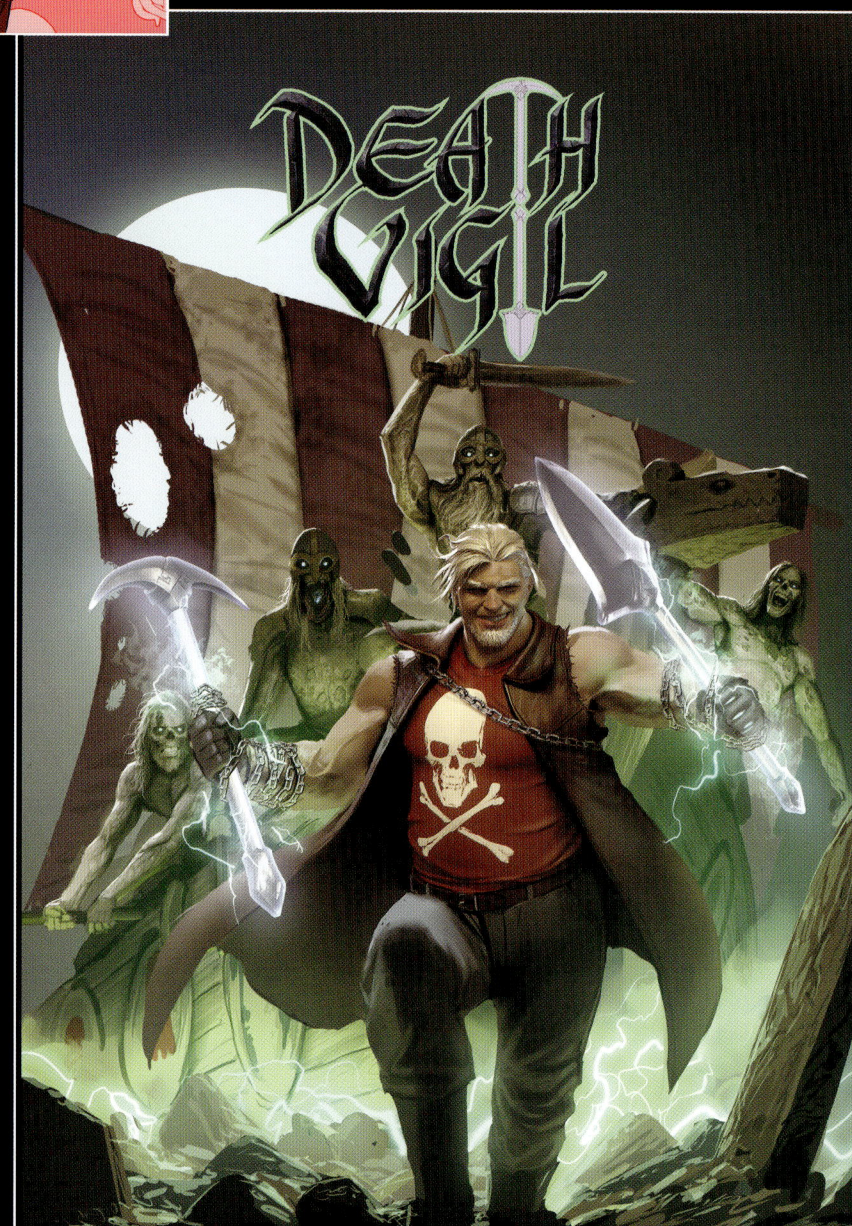

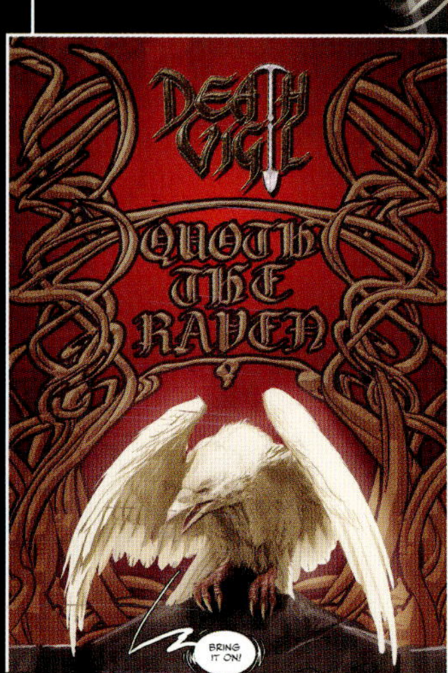

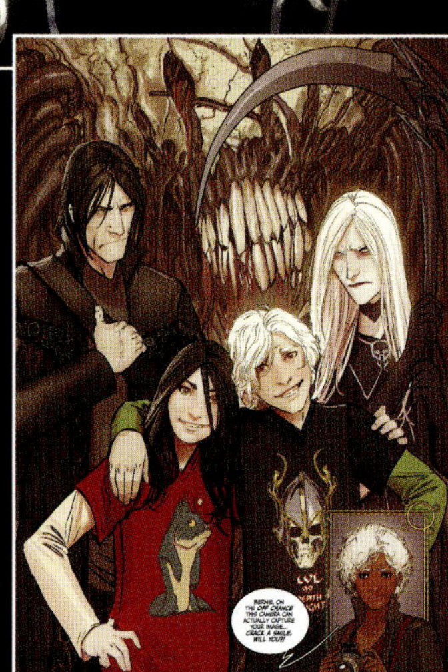

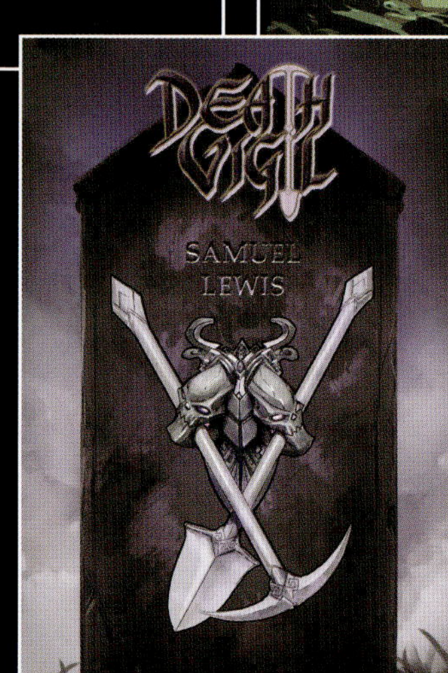

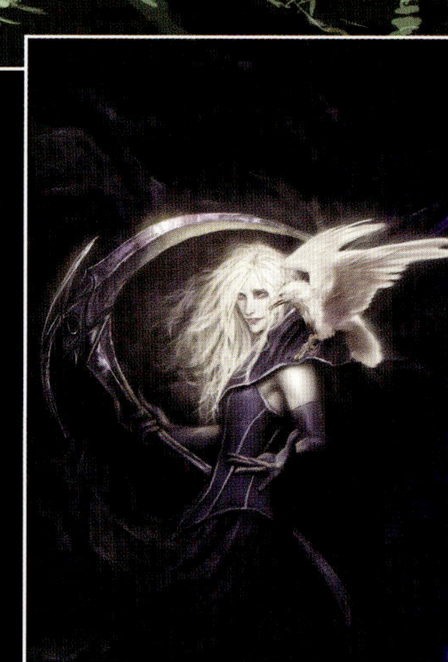

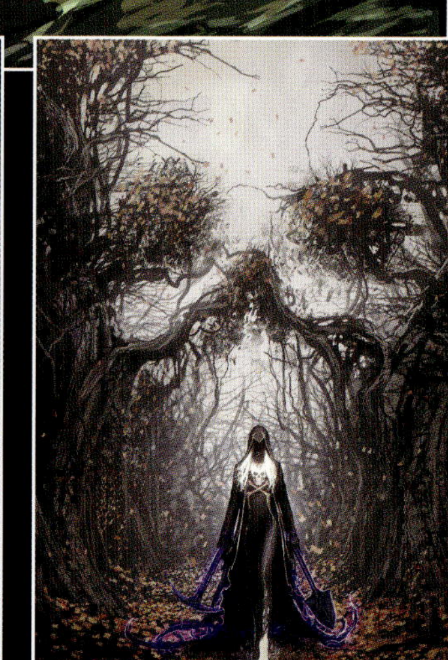

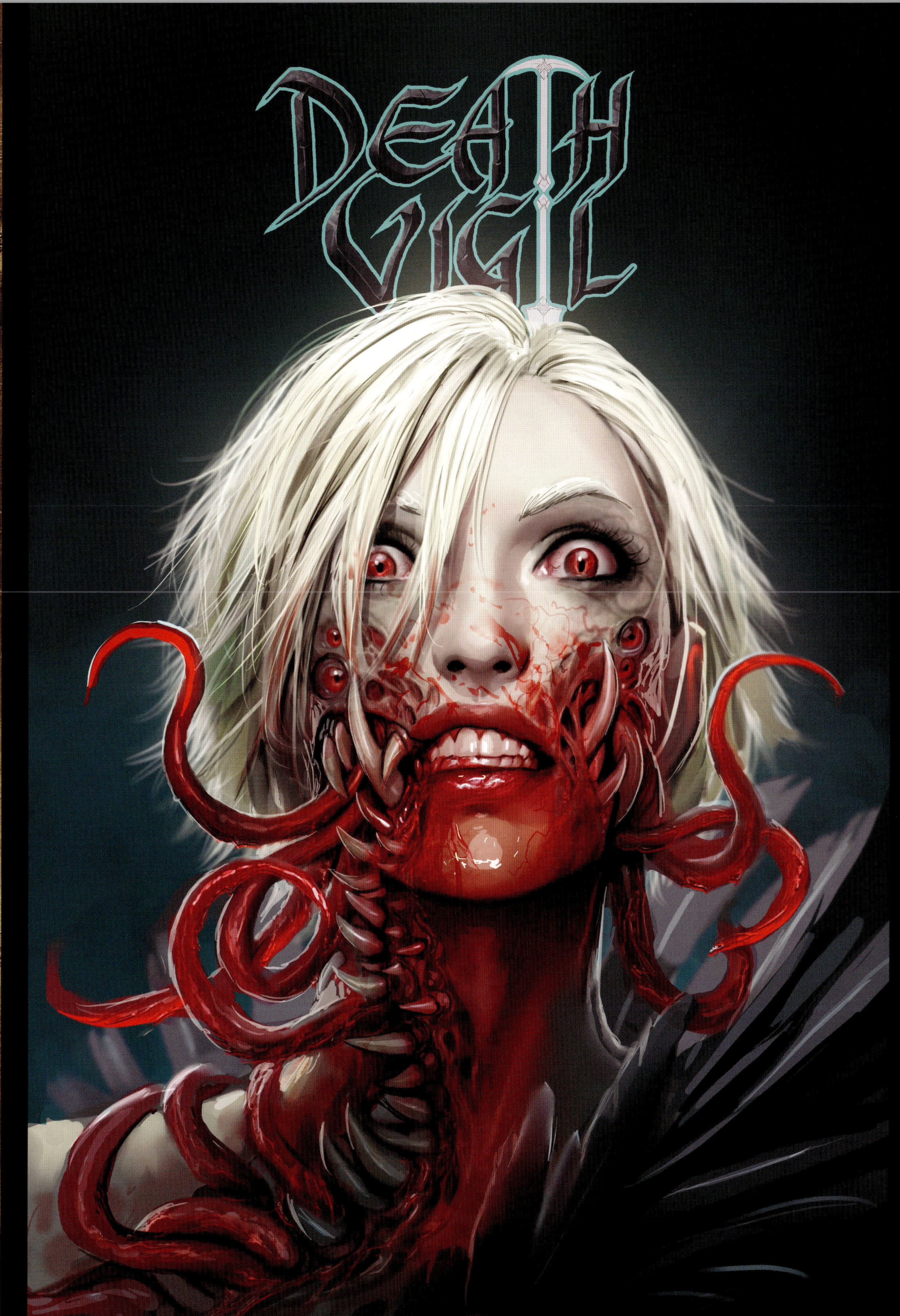

Death Vigil volume 2 advance cover,
art by: Stjepan Sejic

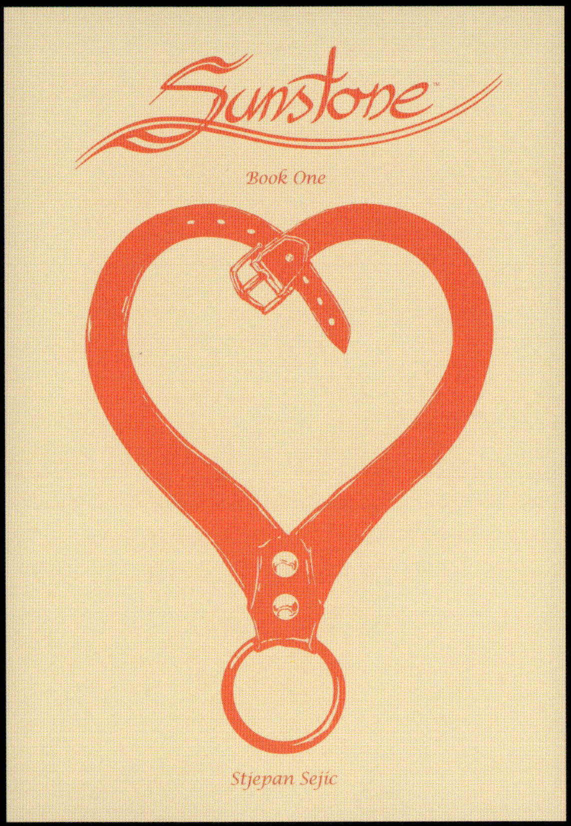

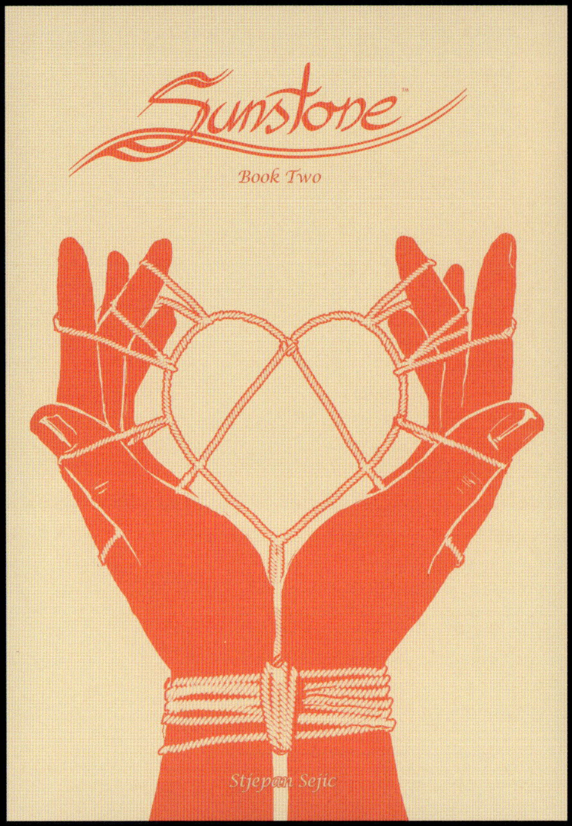

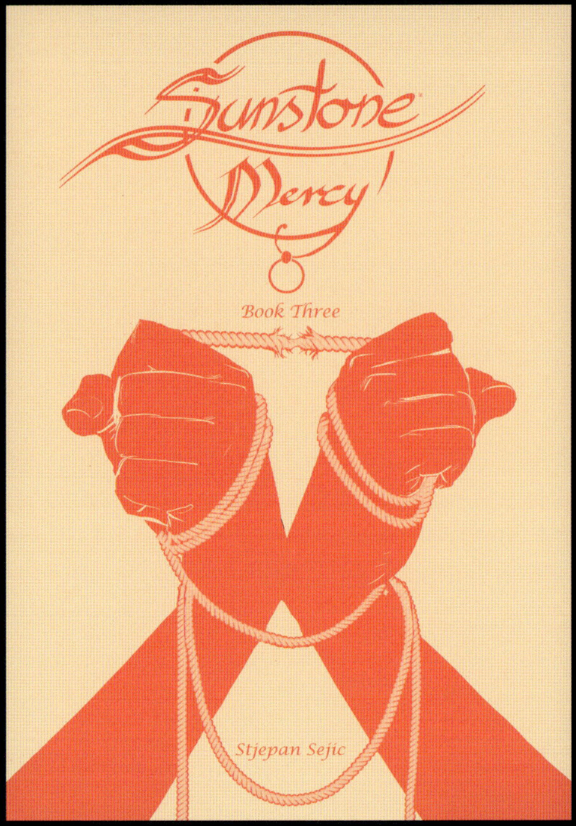

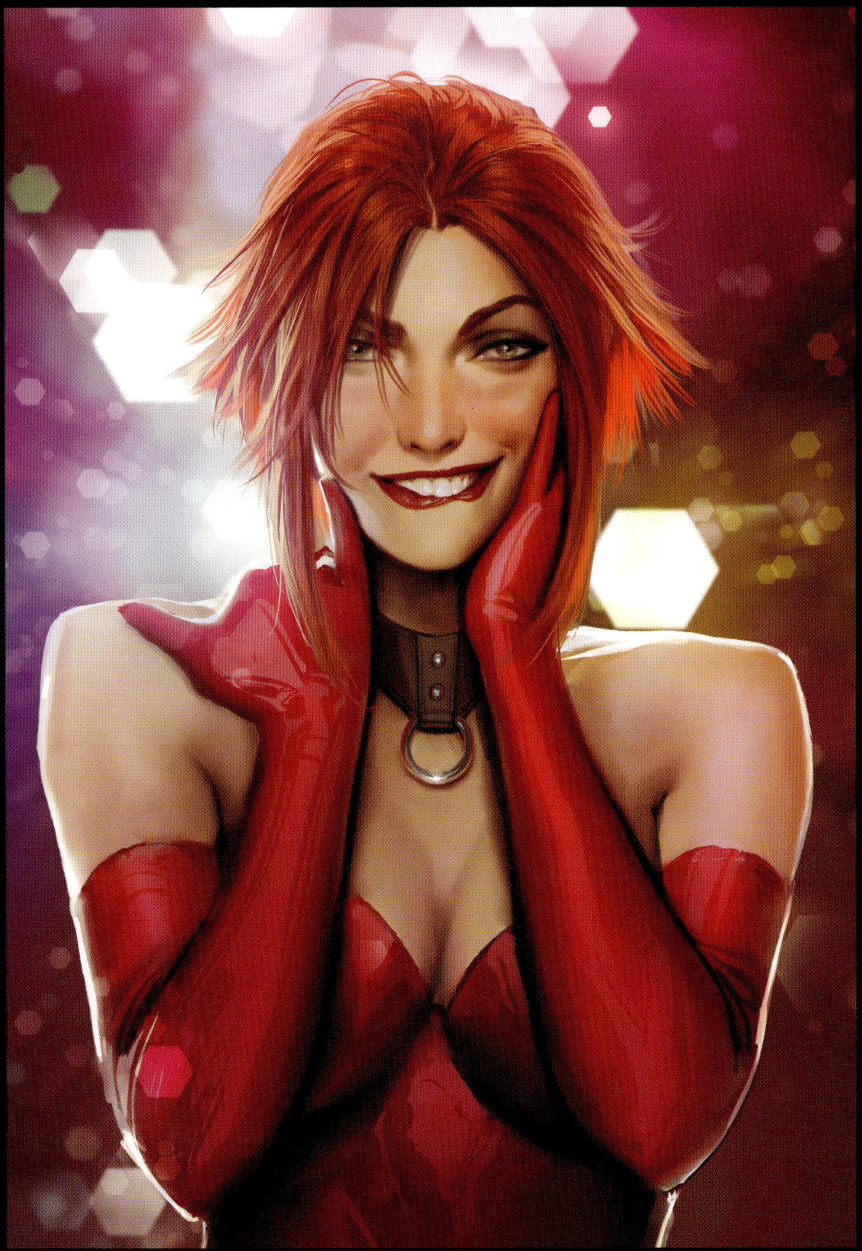

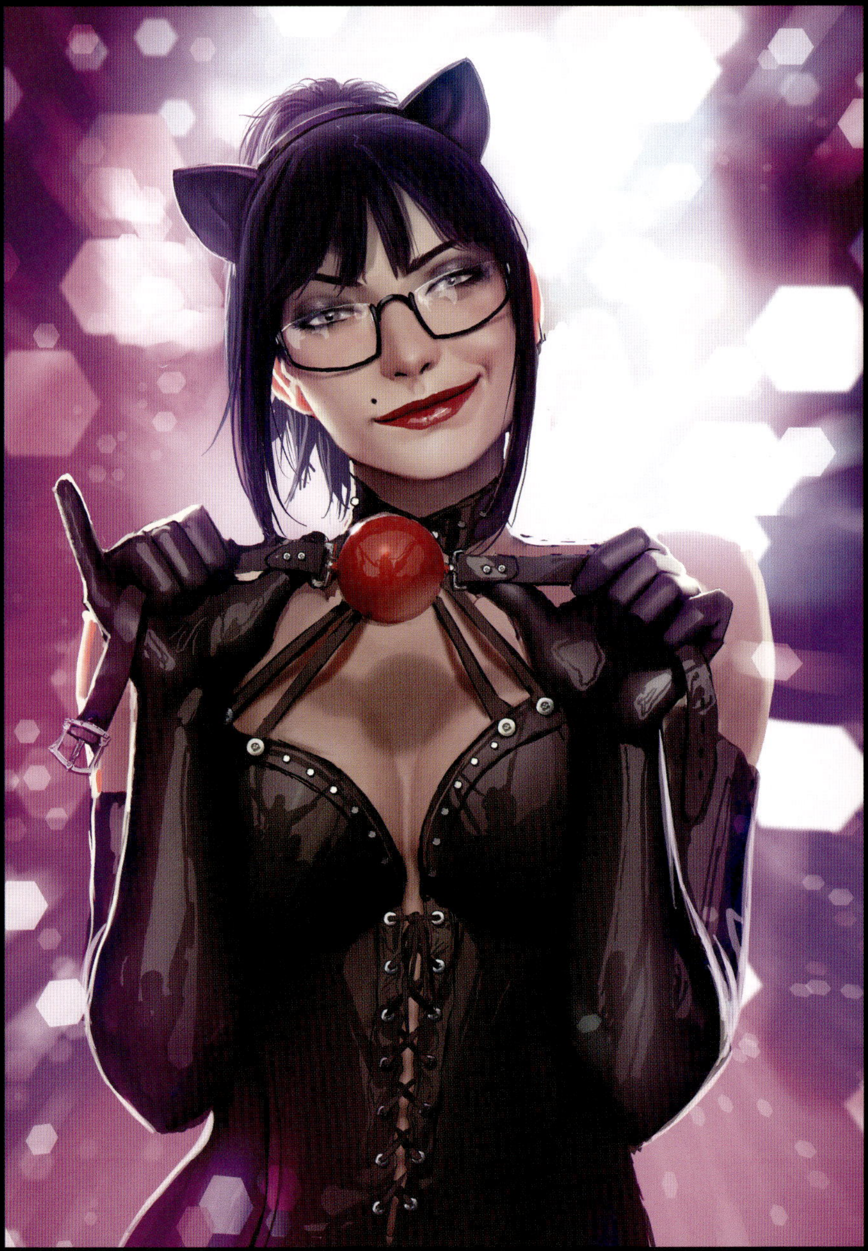

Top Row. *Sunstone* Books 1-3 first printing covers • Bottom row. *Sunstone* Books 1-2 second printing covers. Facing page. Ally and Lisa "Kimono" print, art by: Stjepan Sejic

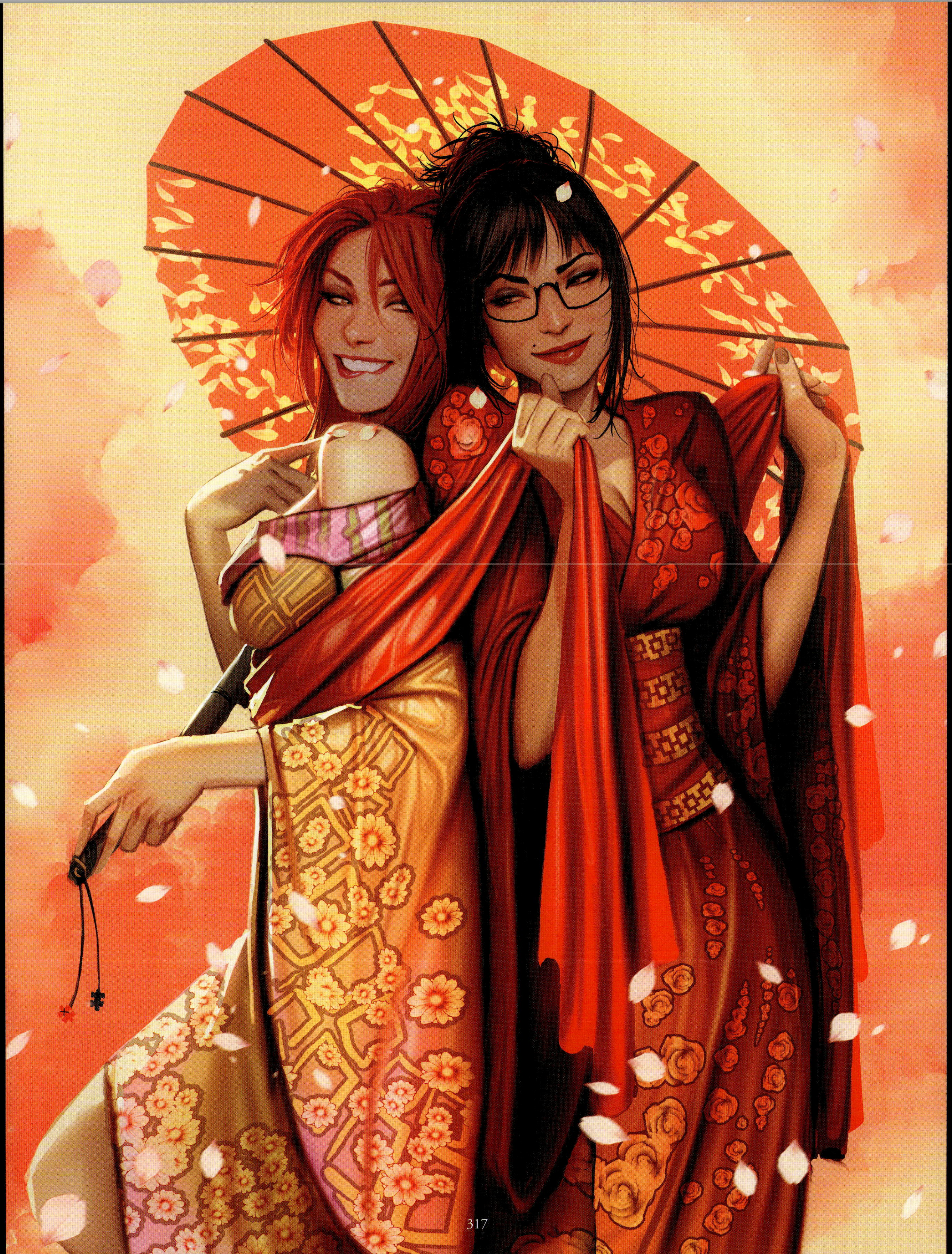

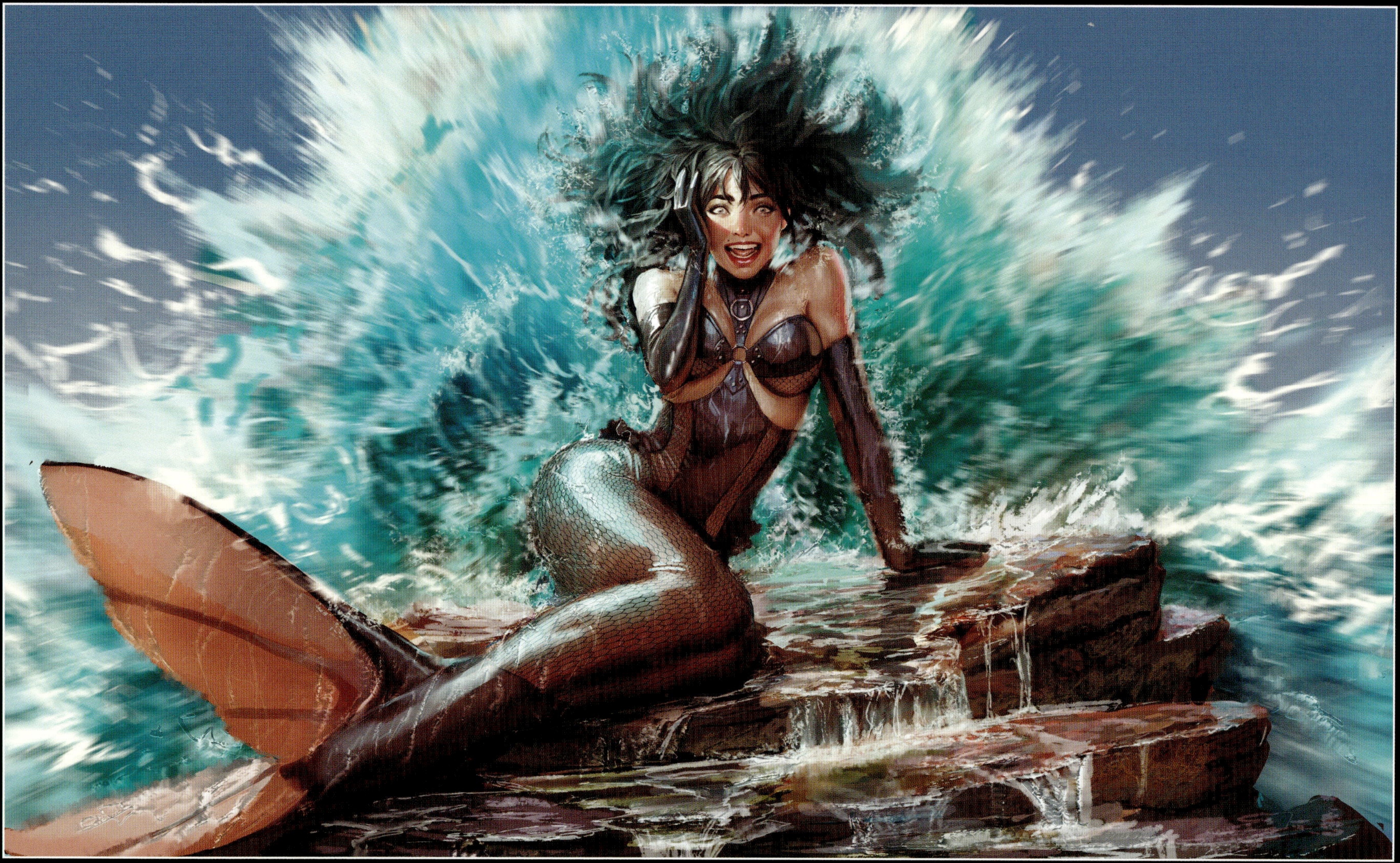

Sunstone: Ally "Splash" Top Cow Store/Convention print, art by: Stjepan Sejic

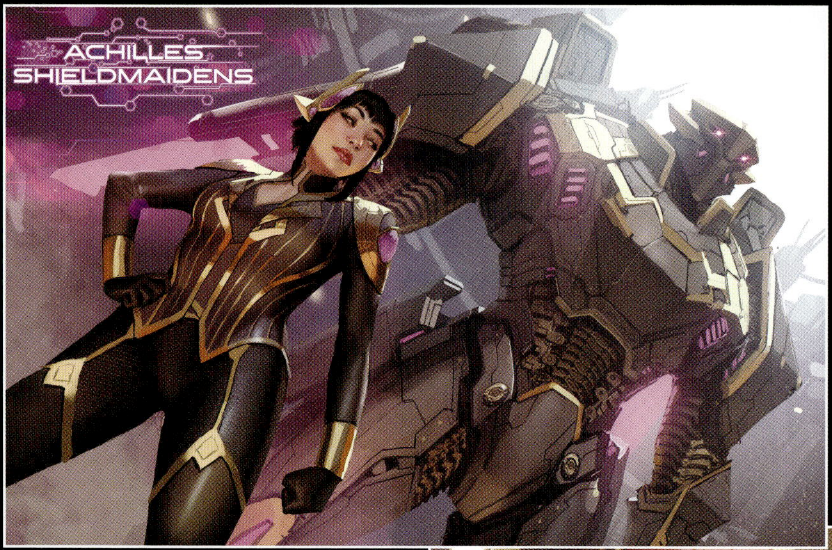

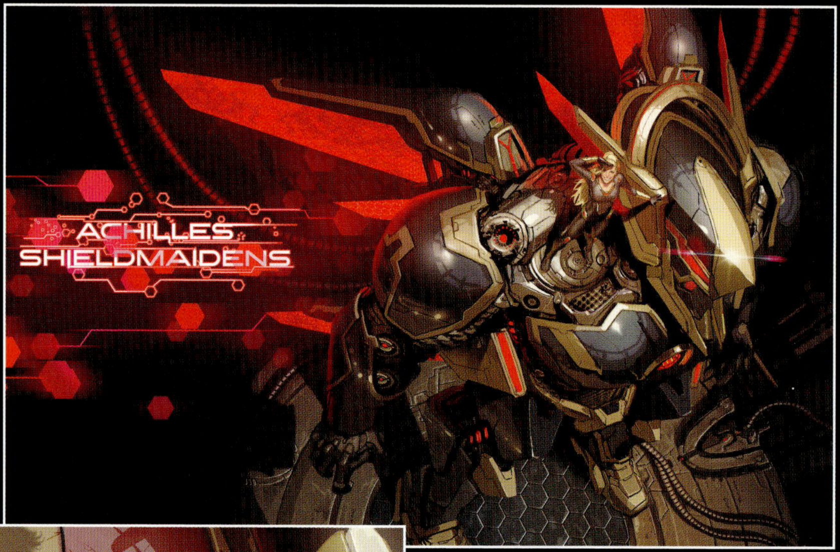

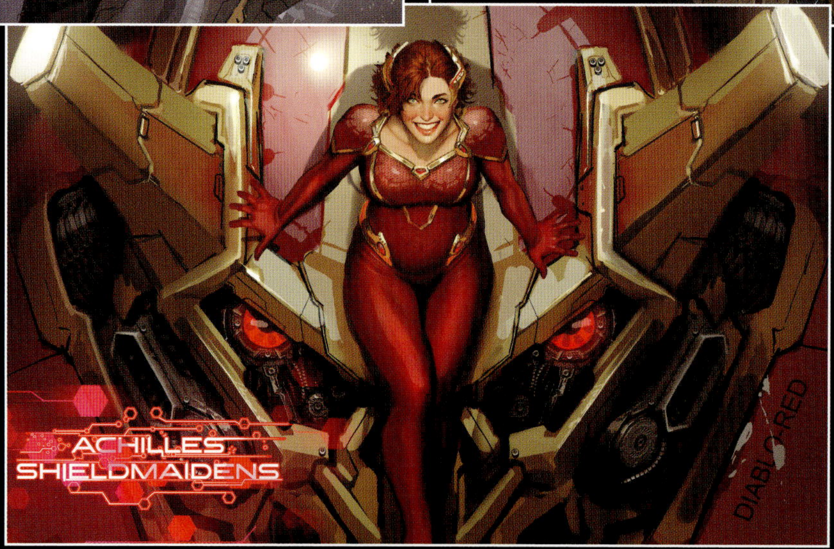

Clockwise from above.

Achilles Shieldmaidens
Top Cow Store/Convention Prints

"Lucy Dreamer," "Jane," "Emily Doyle,"
art by: Stjepan Sejic

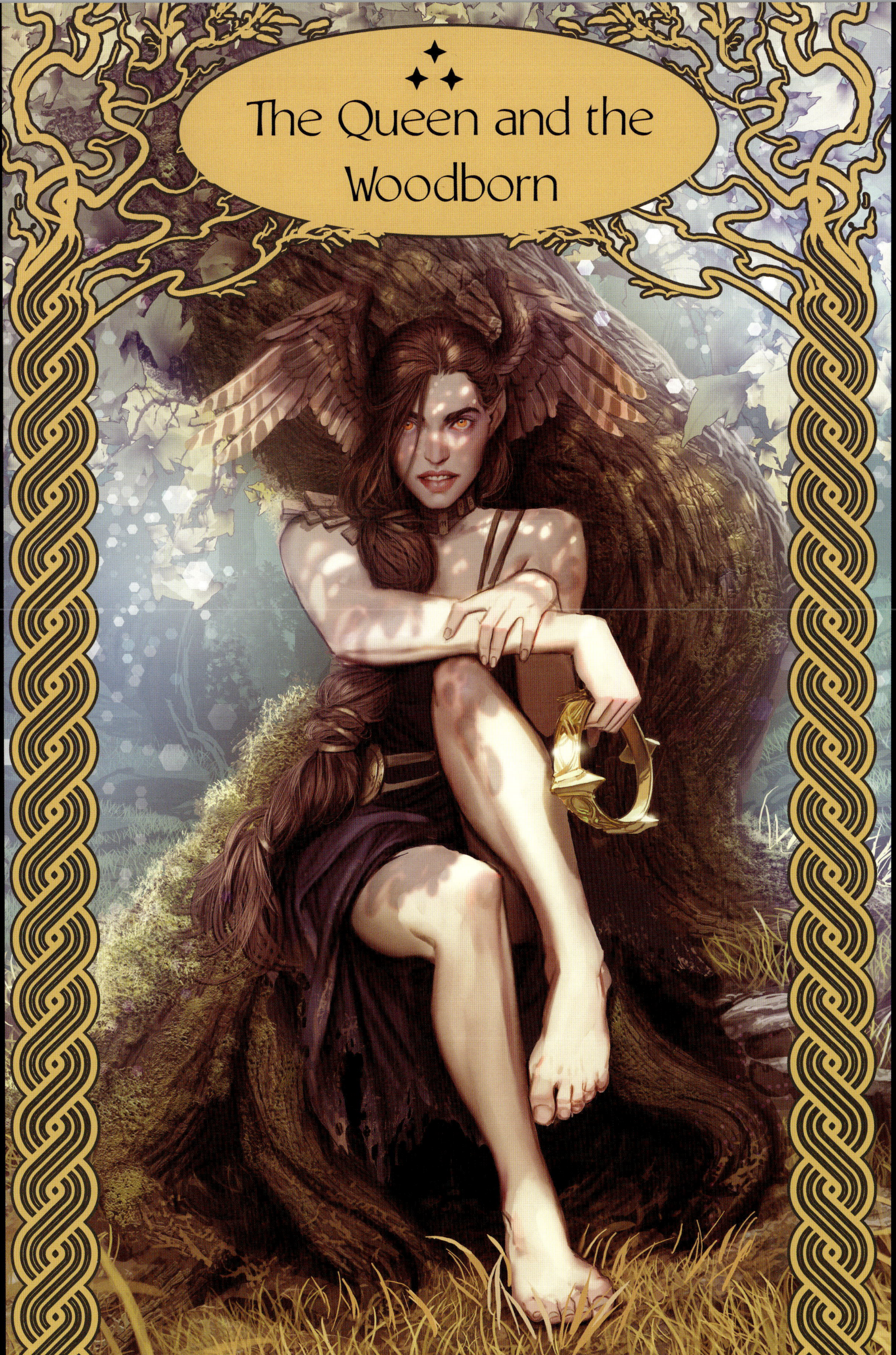

The Queen and the Woodborn volume 1 cover,
art by: Stjepan Sejic

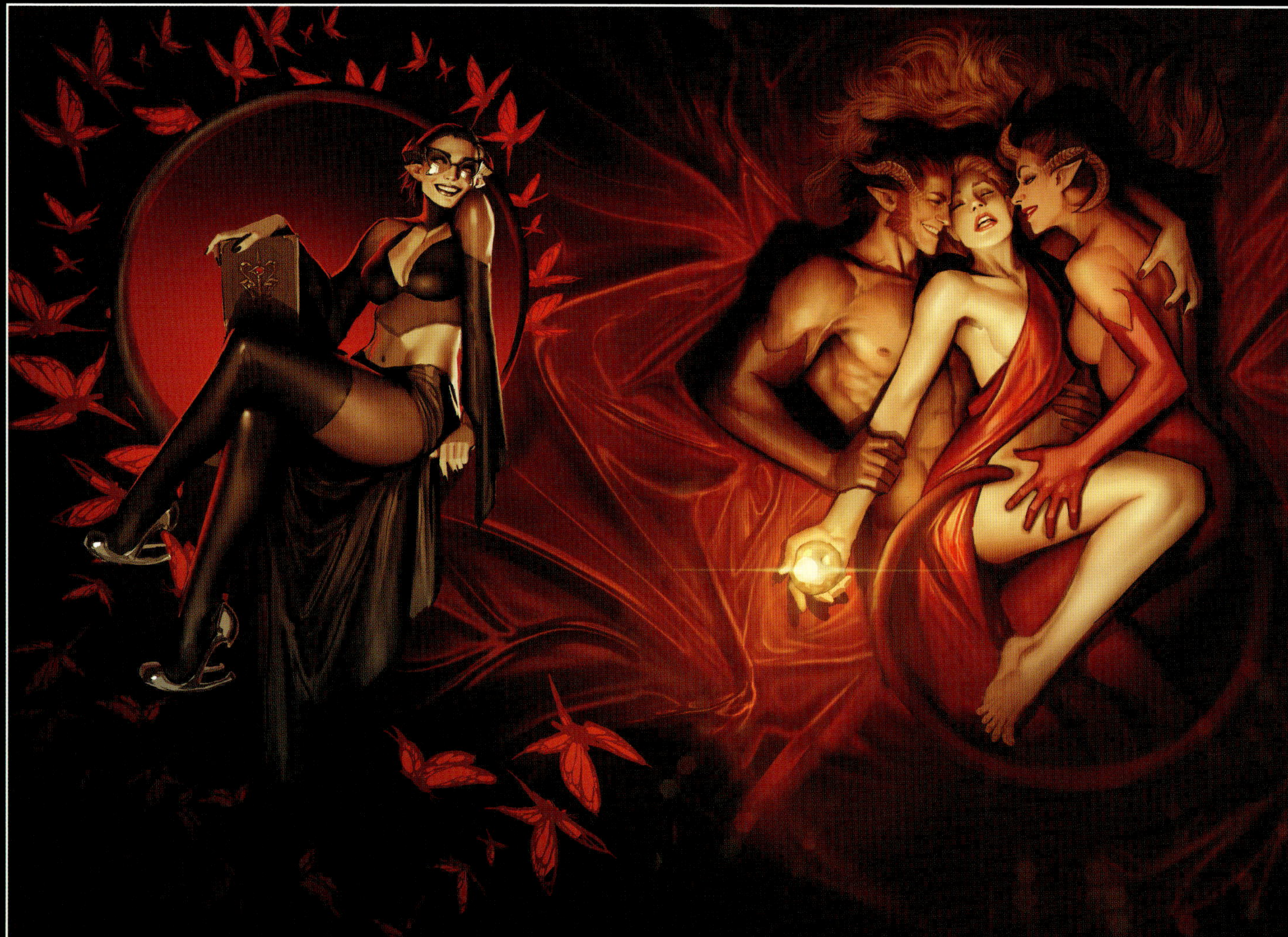

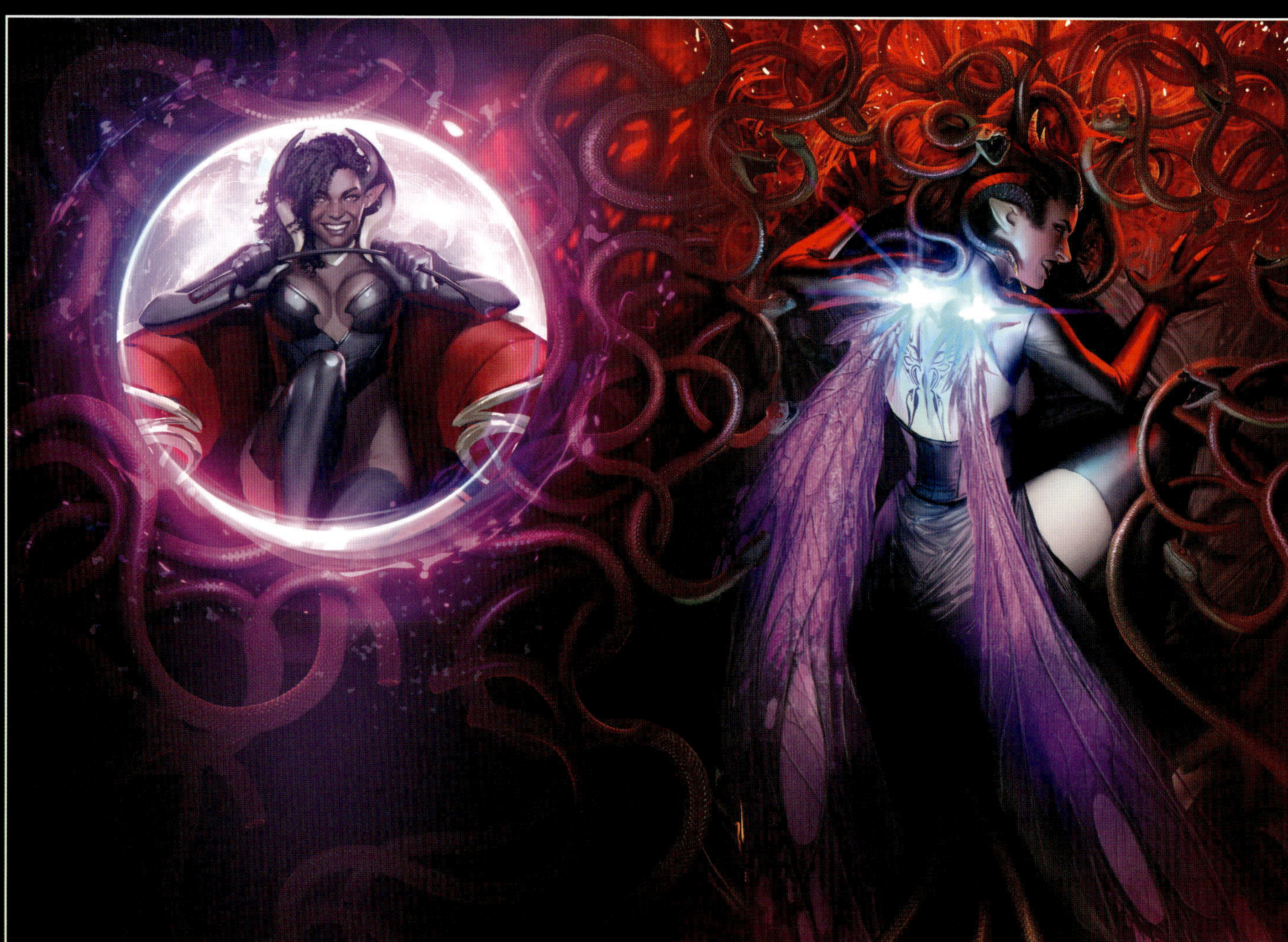

Fine Print volume 1 and 2 covers with wraparound, art by: Stjepan Sejic

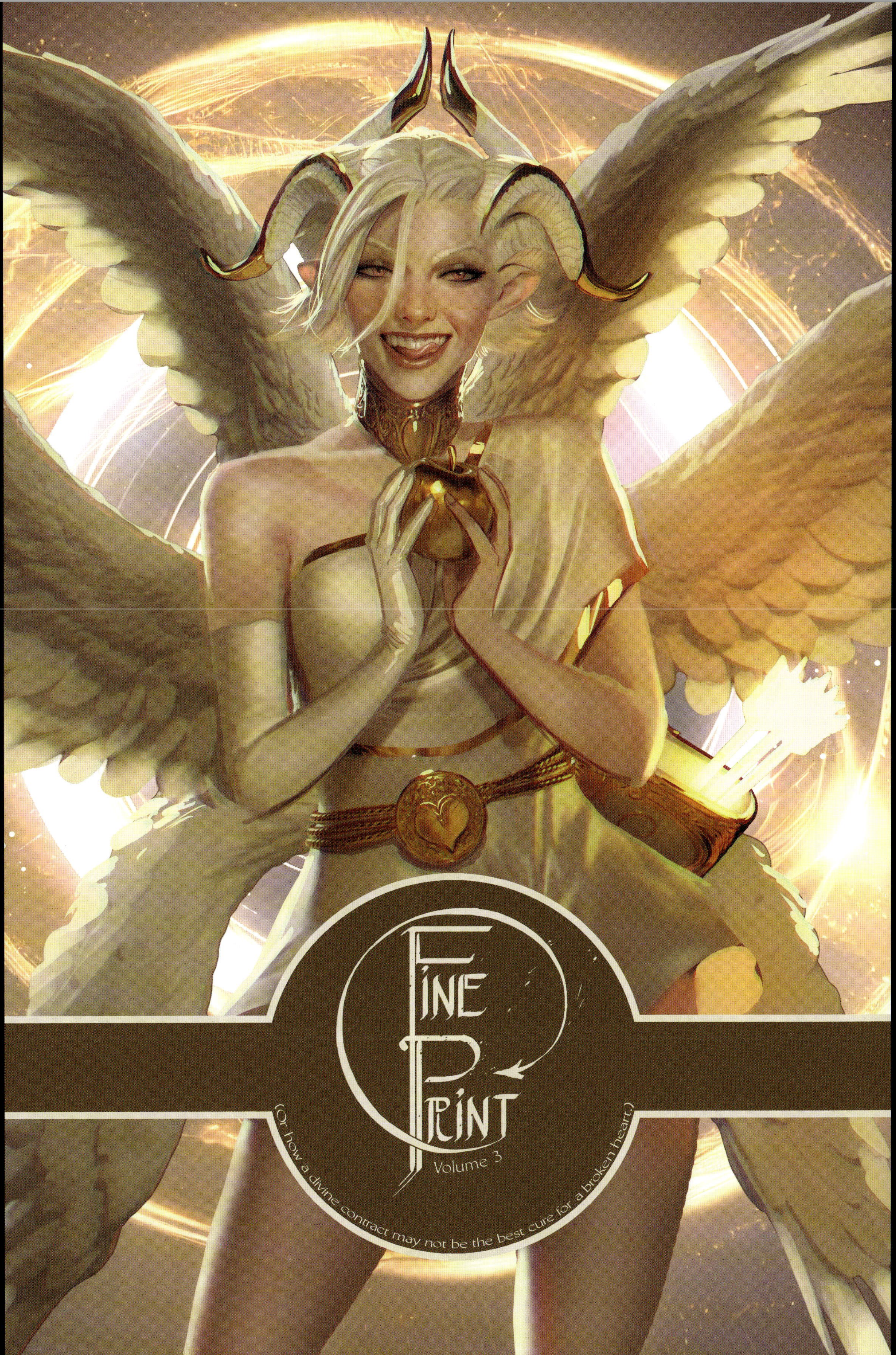

Fine Print volume 3 cover with trade dress,
art by: Stjepan Sejic

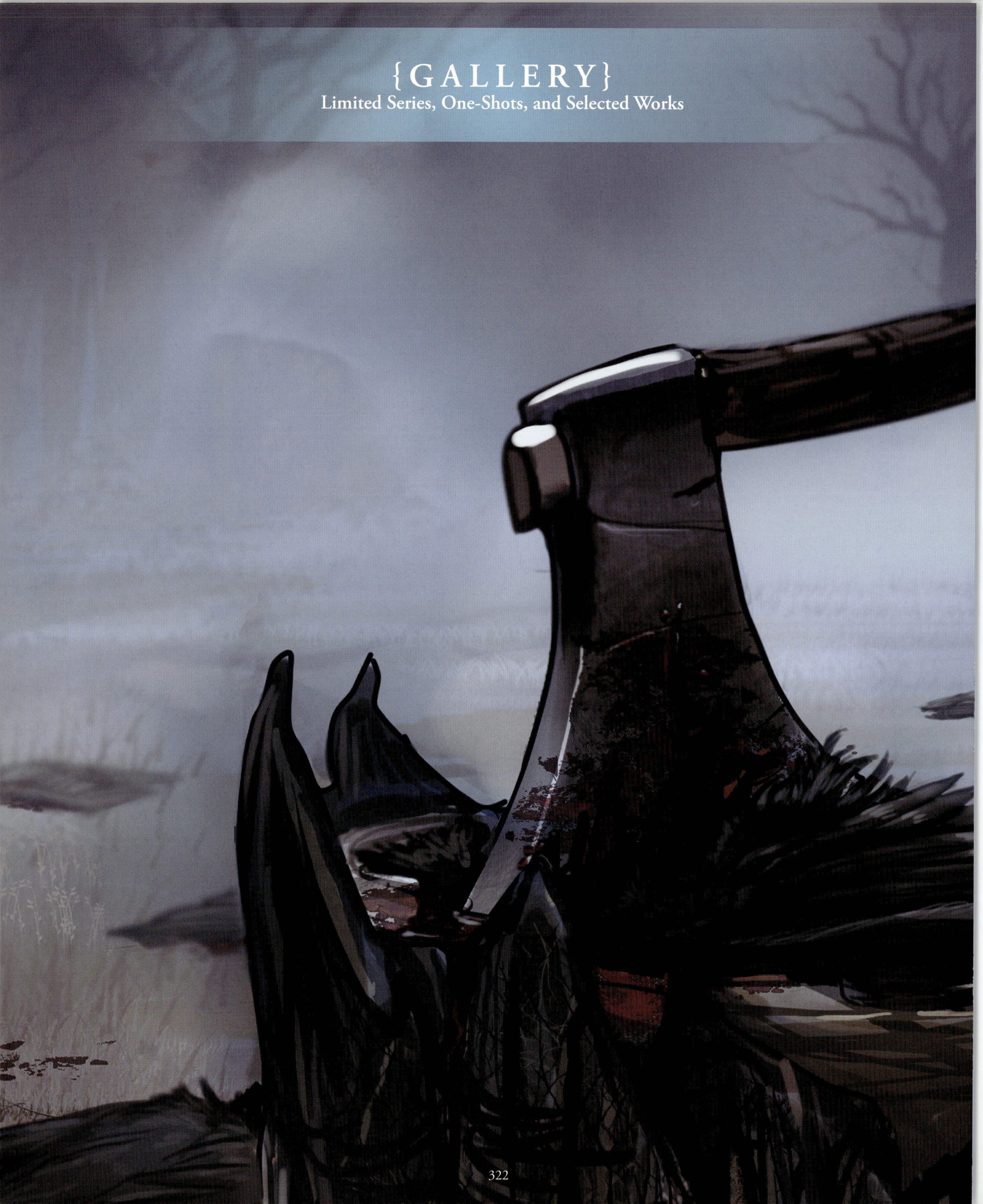

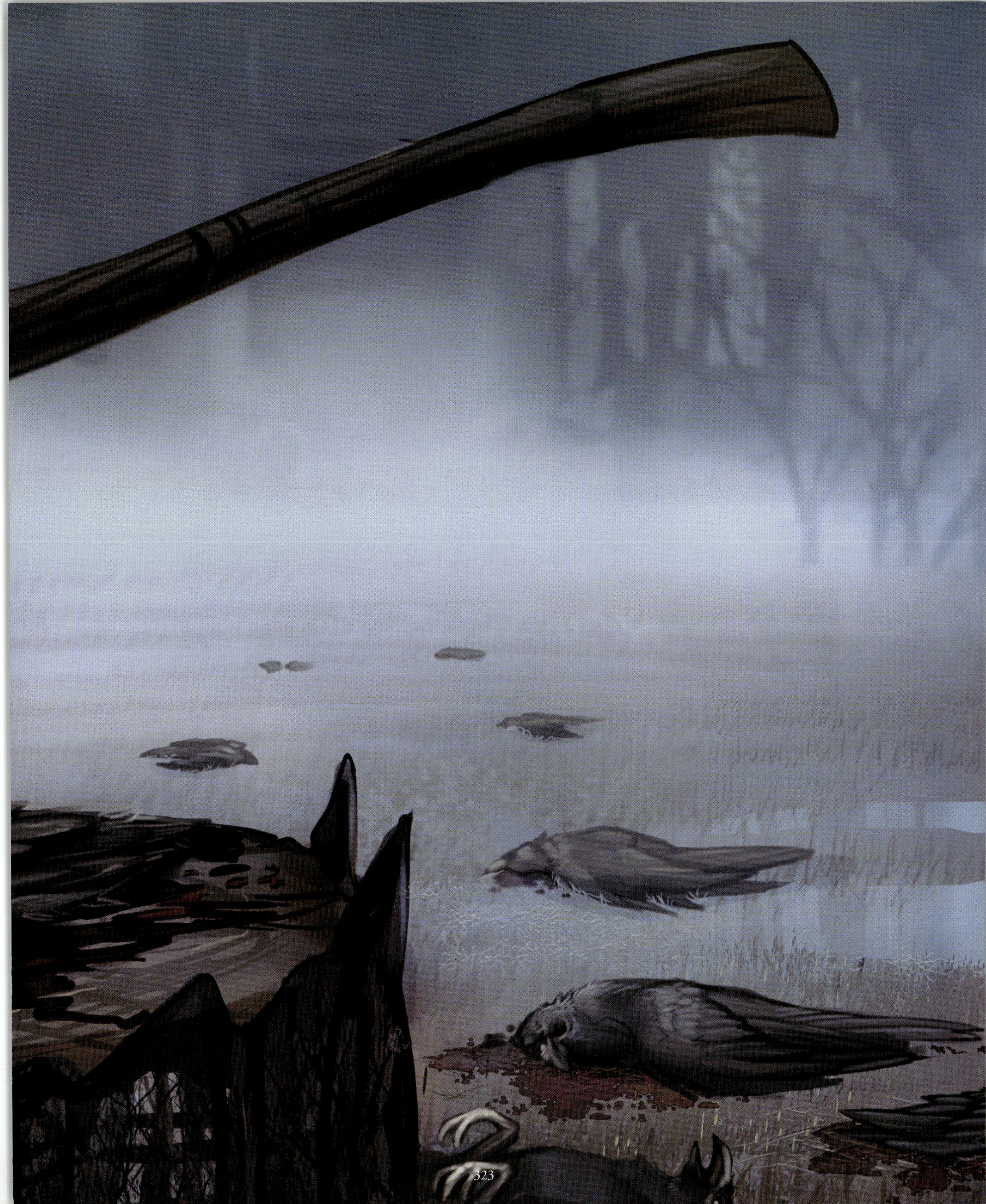

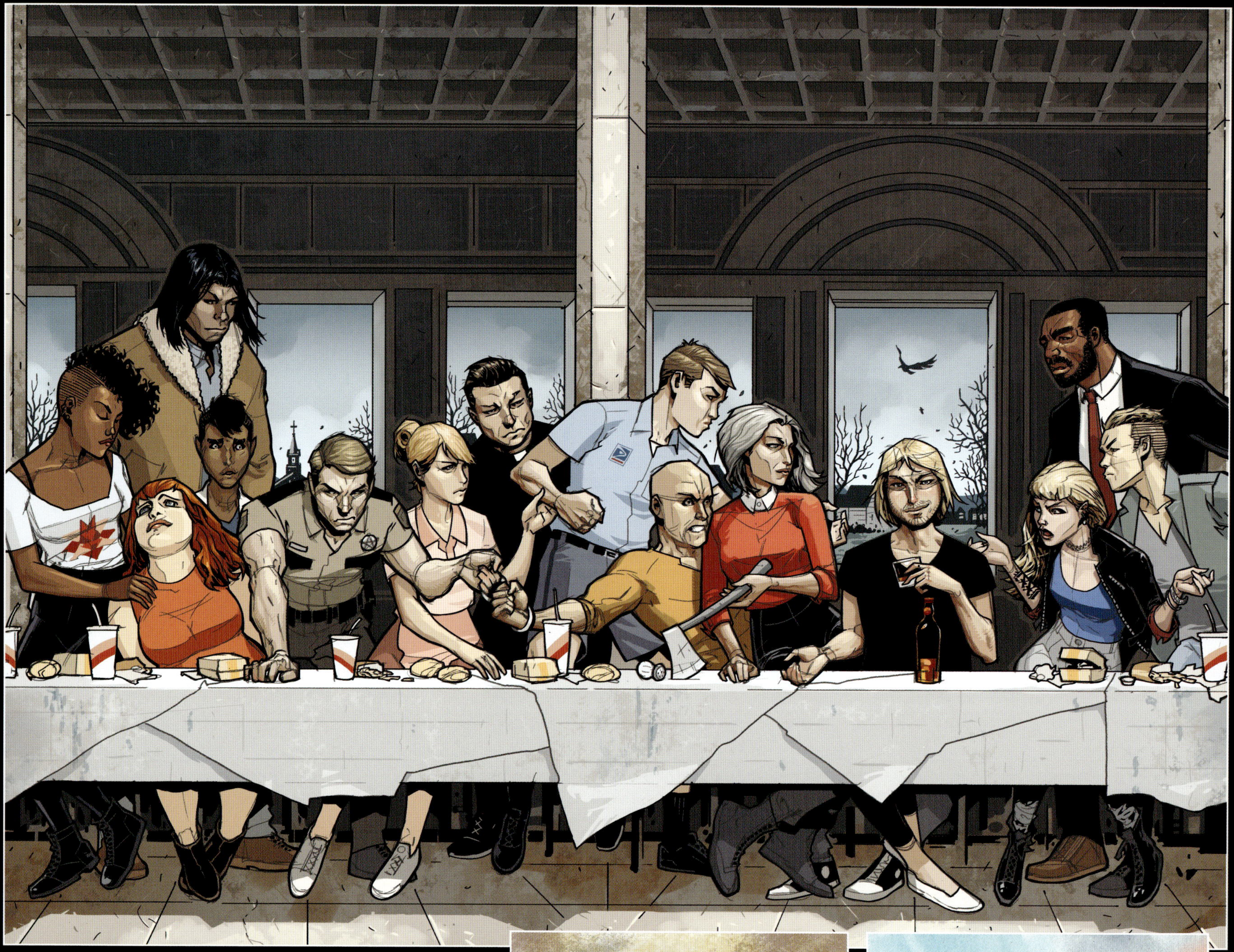

Above. *Eden's Fall* volume 1 trade paperback cover, art by: Rosa Ekedal

From the gritty and grounded *Postal*, combined with the cerebral *Think Tank*, and *The Tithe* in the event series *Eden's Fall* to the science fiction epics *Antarctica*, *Infinite Dark*, *Port of Earth*, and the supernatural *Rise of the Magi*, and more, Top Cow excels at hard-hitting limited series presented with the usual Top Cow flair.

On the following pages we take a look at only a small sampling of some of the limited series Top Cow has been proud to produce from outside it's established universe and a few series and gems from within.

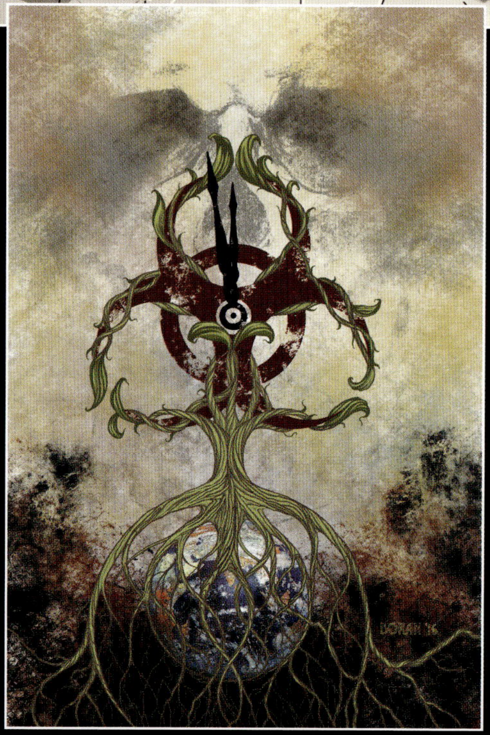

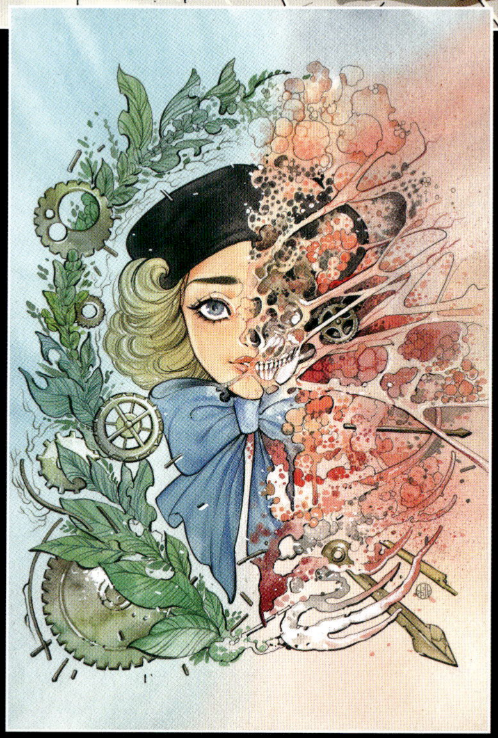

Previous page. *Postal* art by: Linda Sejic

At right. *The Clock* #1 cover art by: Colleen Doran

Far right. *The Clock* #1 Comics & Oddities exclusive variant art by: Peach Momoko

Facing page. *Postal* #7 cover A, art by Linda Sejic

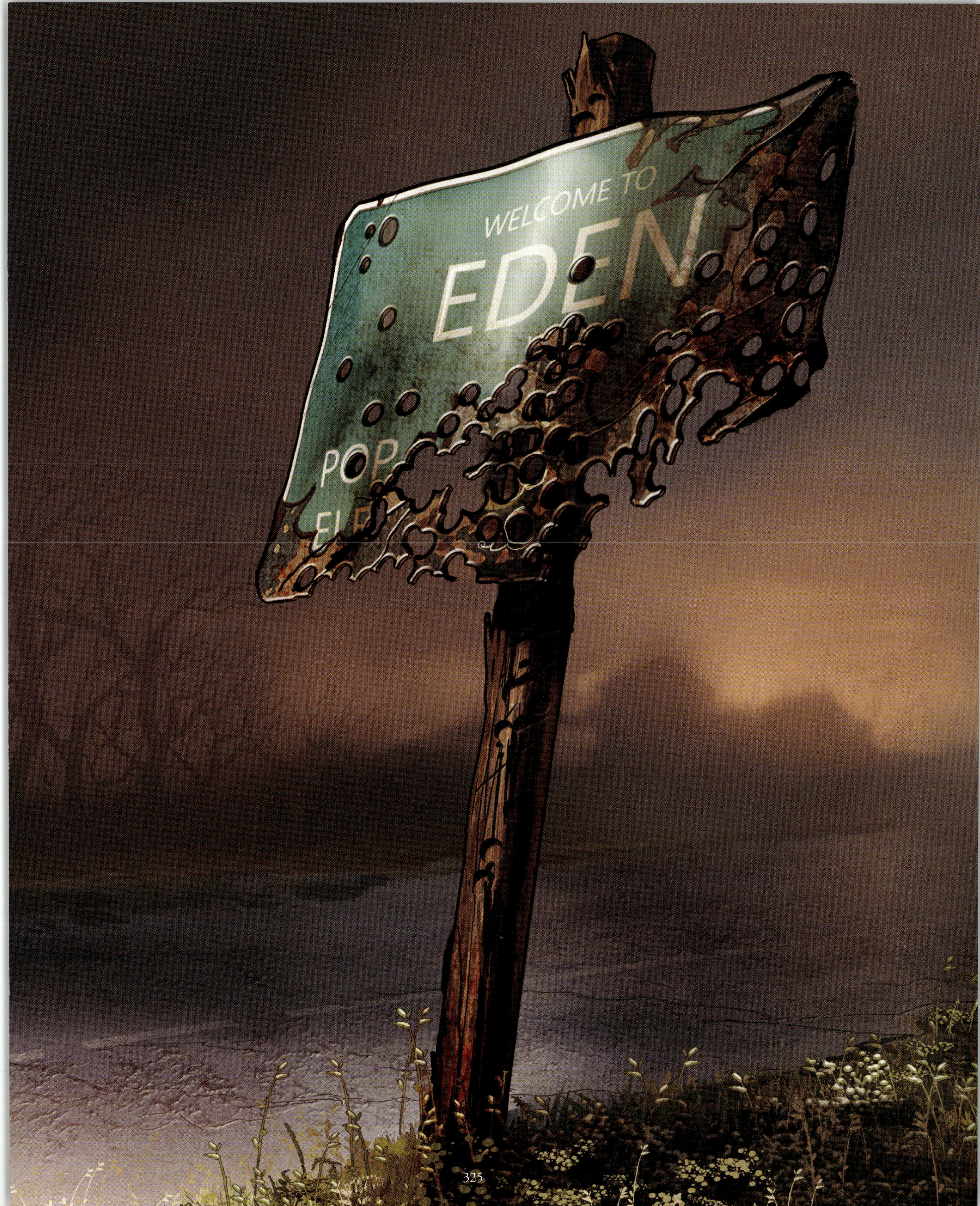
WELCOME TO
EDEN

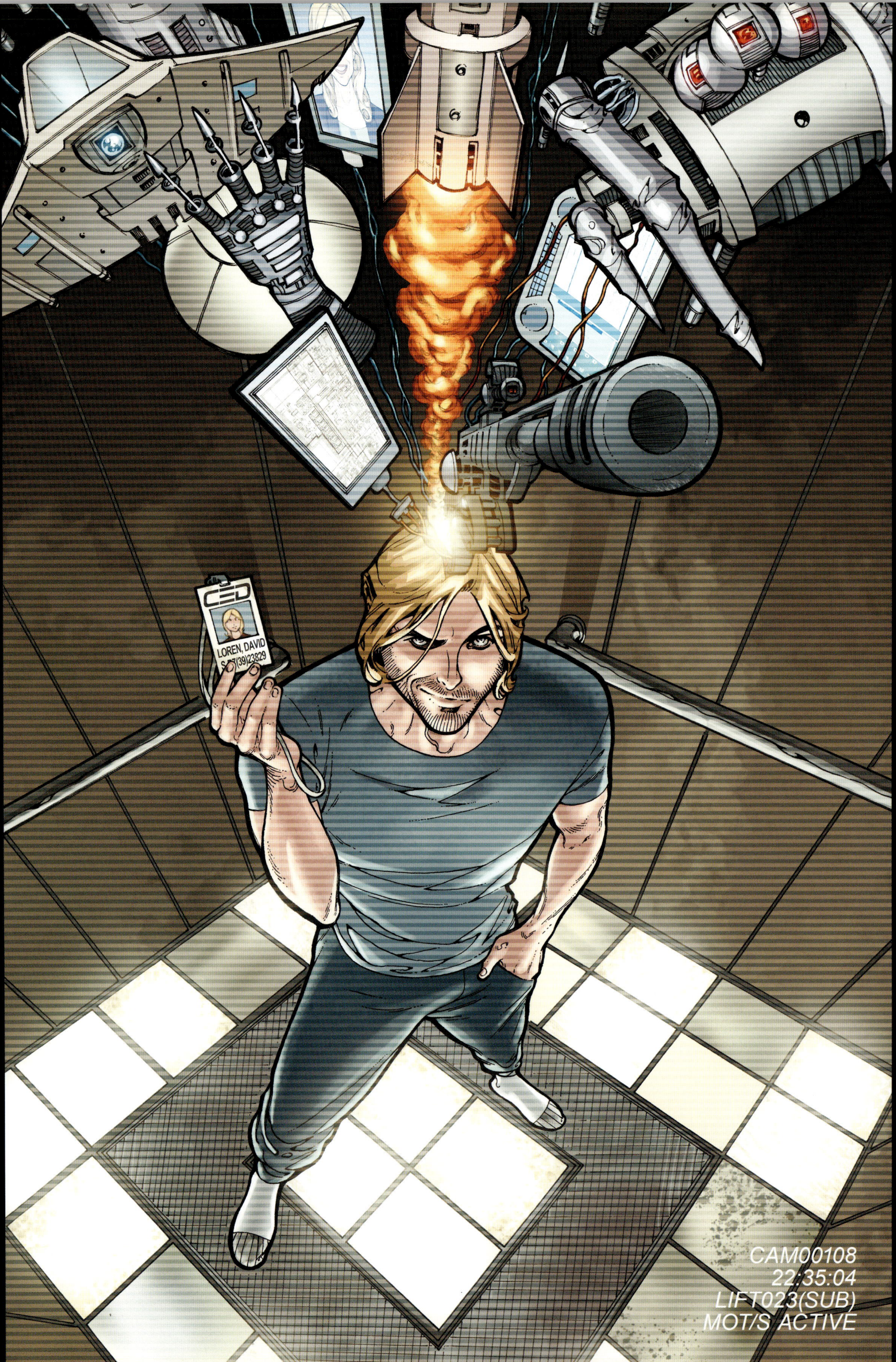

Think Tank #1 cover A,
art by: Rosa Ekedal and Brian Reber

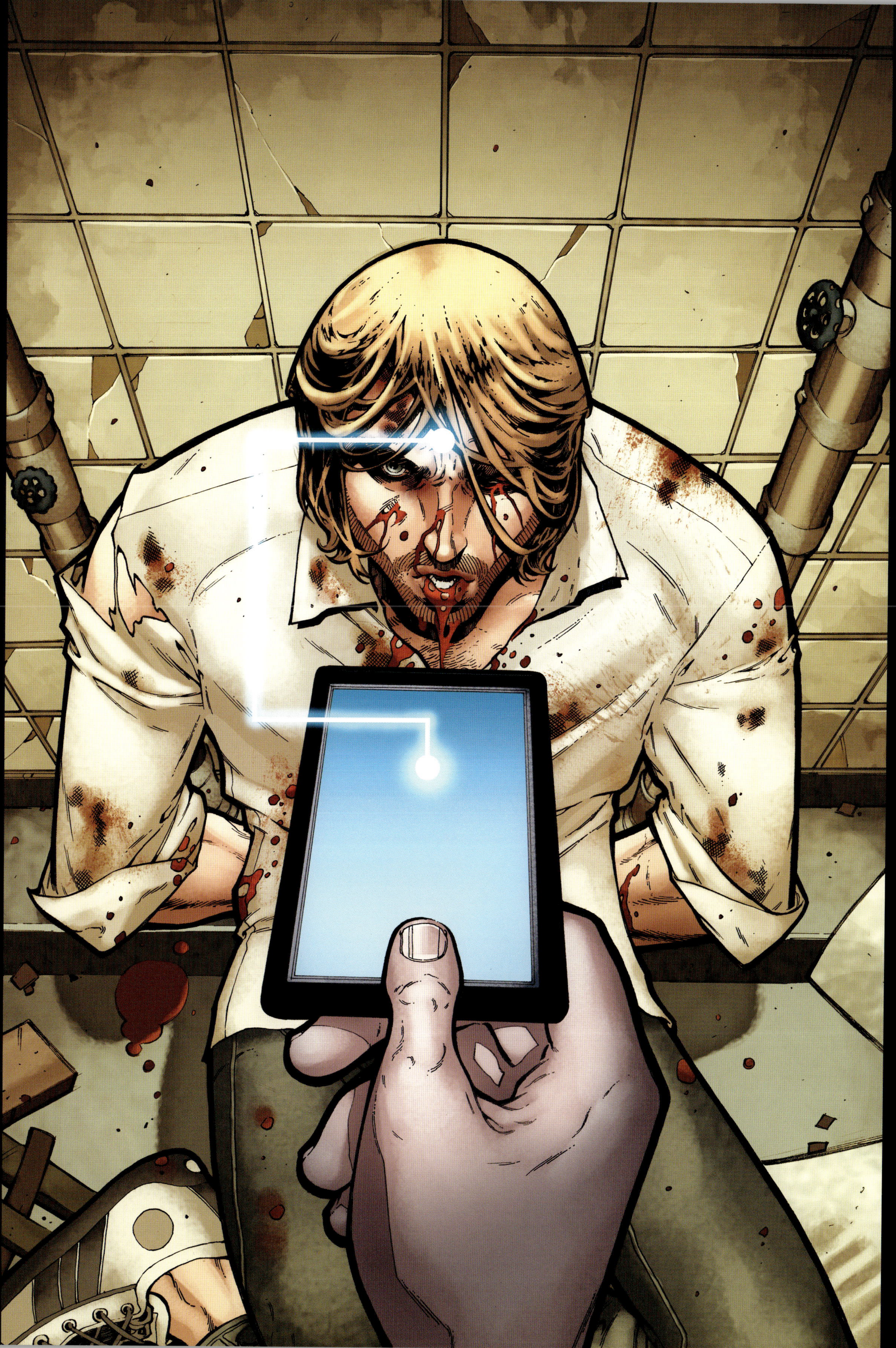

Think Tank #3 cover,
art by: Rosa Ekedal and Brian Reber

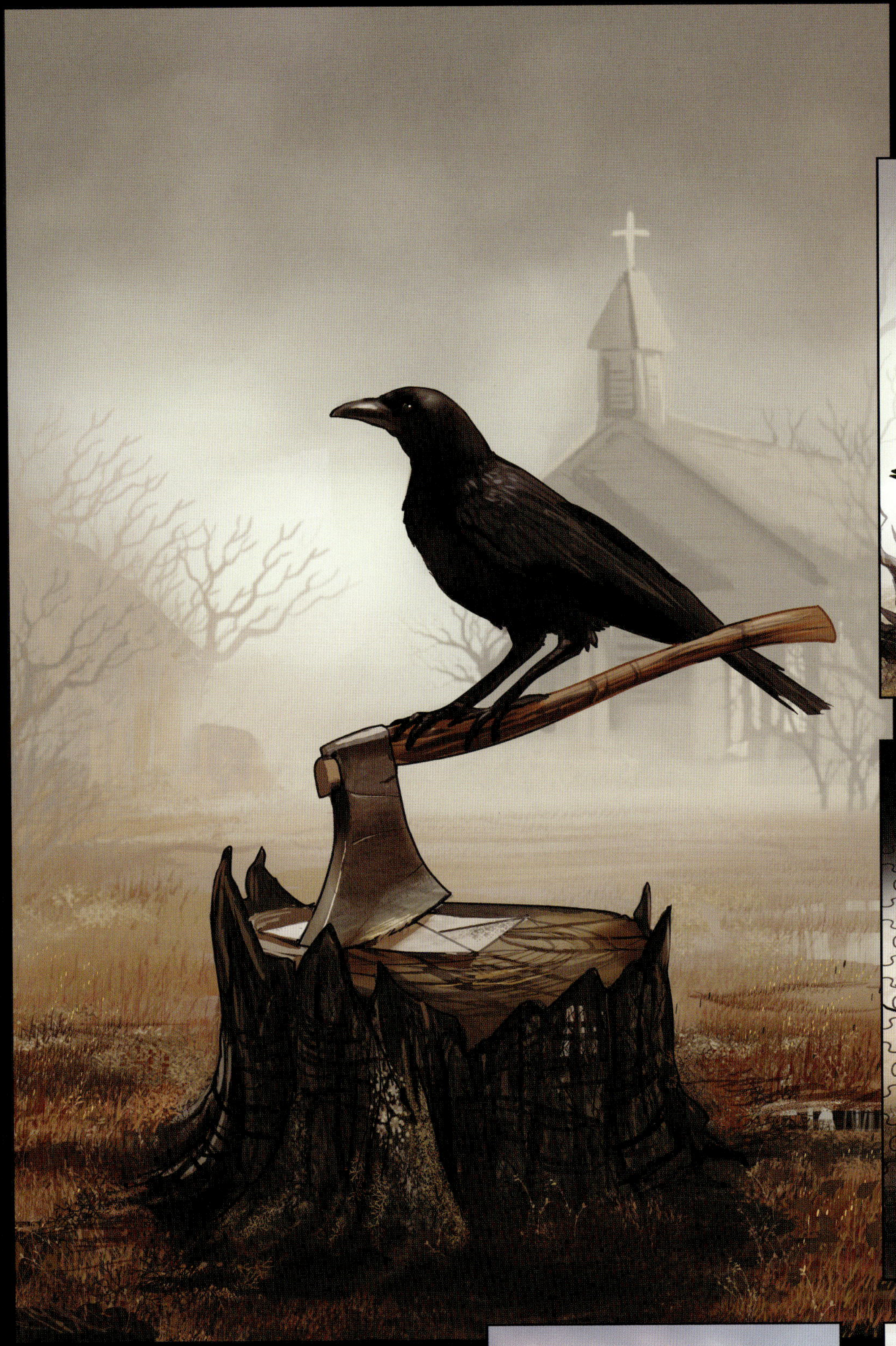

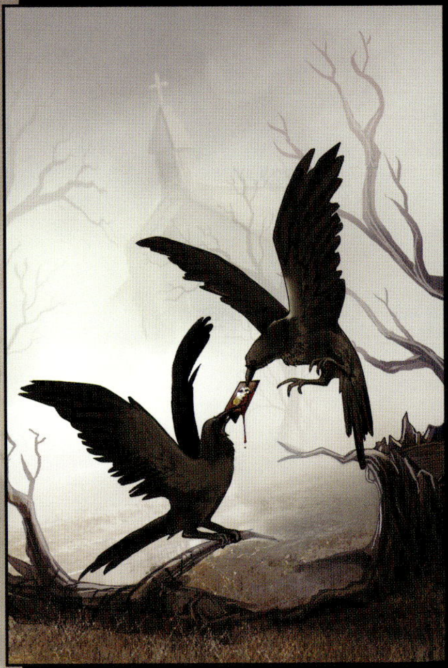

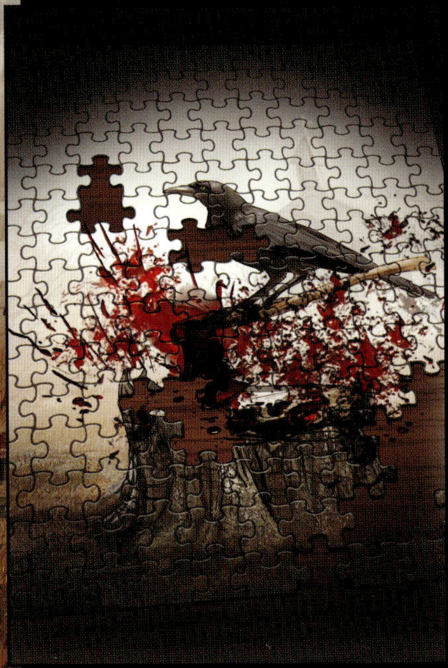

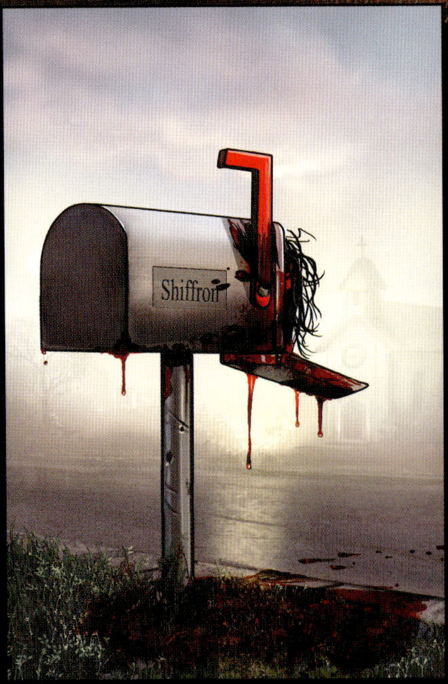

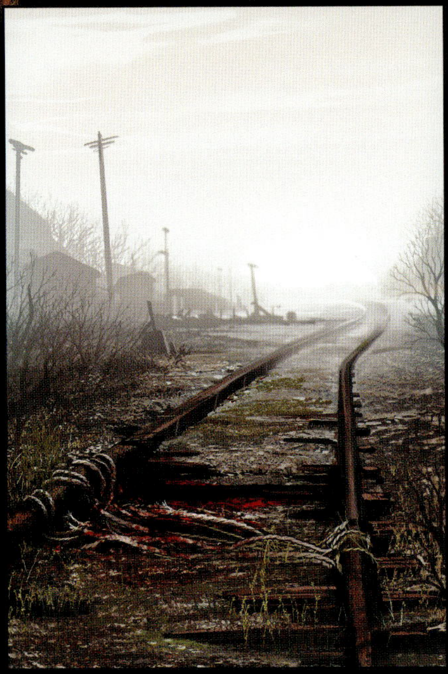

This page, clockwise from above.

Postal #1 cover C,
art by: Linda Sejic

Postal #9 cover A,
art by: Linda Sejic

Postal #10 cover A,
art by: Linda Sejic

Postal #11 cover A,
art by: Linda Sejic

Postal #21 cover A,
art by: Linda Sejic

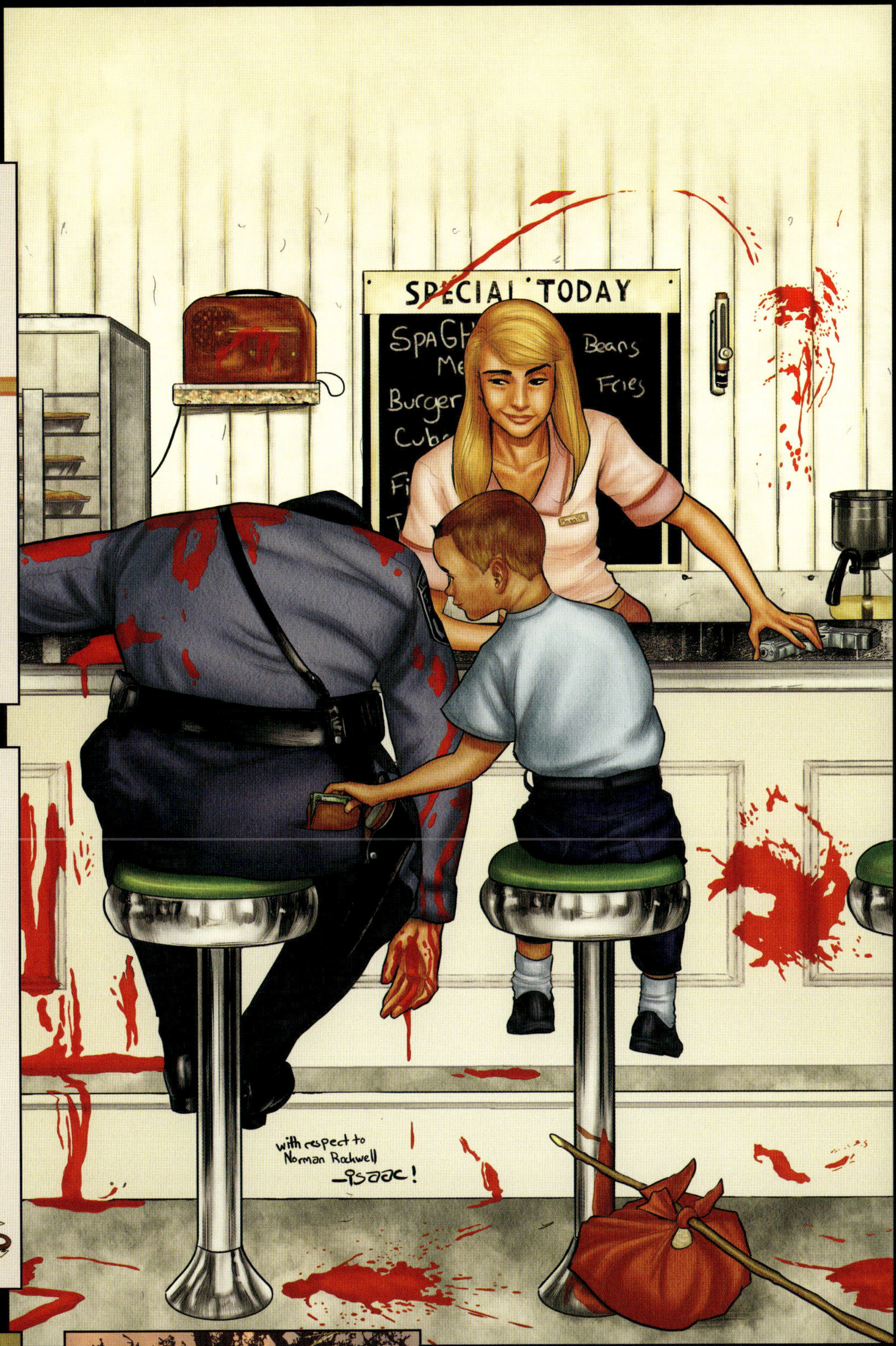

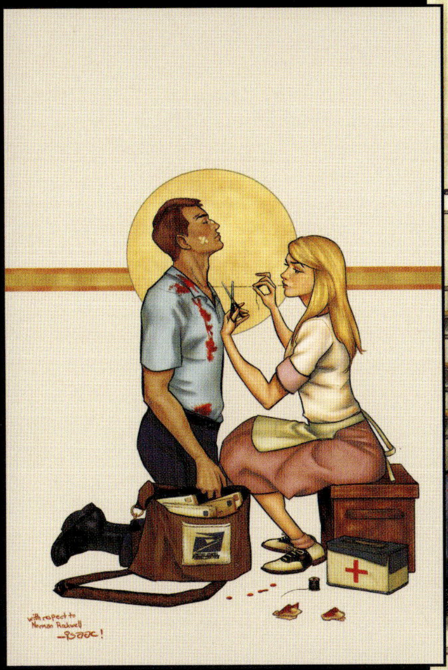

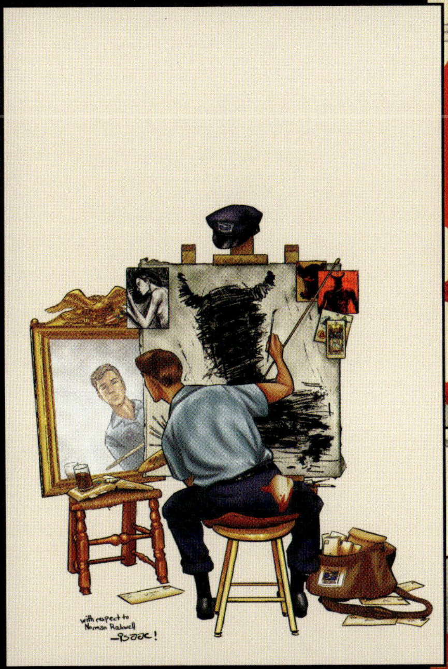

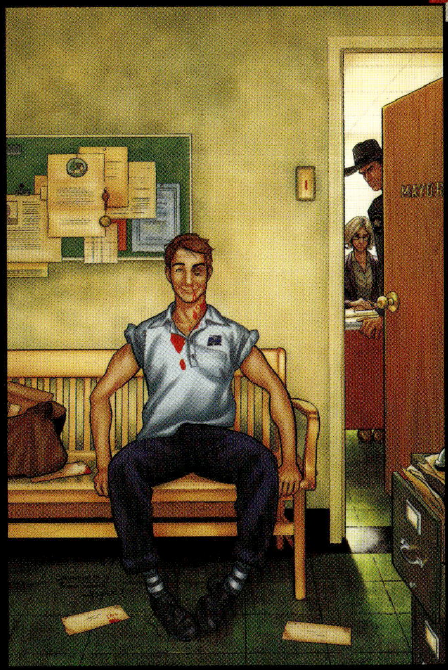

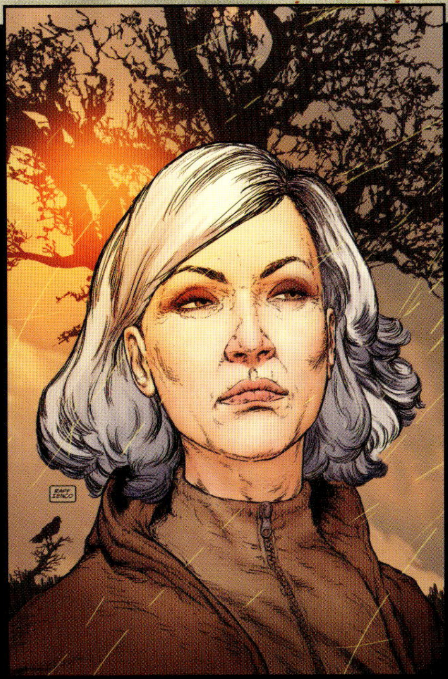

This page, counterclockwise from above.

Postal #9 cover B,
art by: Isaac Goodhart and Betsy Golden

Postal #10 cover B,
art by: Isaac Goodhart and Betsy Golden

Postal #11 cover B,
art by: Isaac Goodhart and Betsy Golden

Postal #12 cover B,
art by: Isaac Goodhart and Betsy Golden

Postal: Laura cover,
art by: Raffaele Ienco

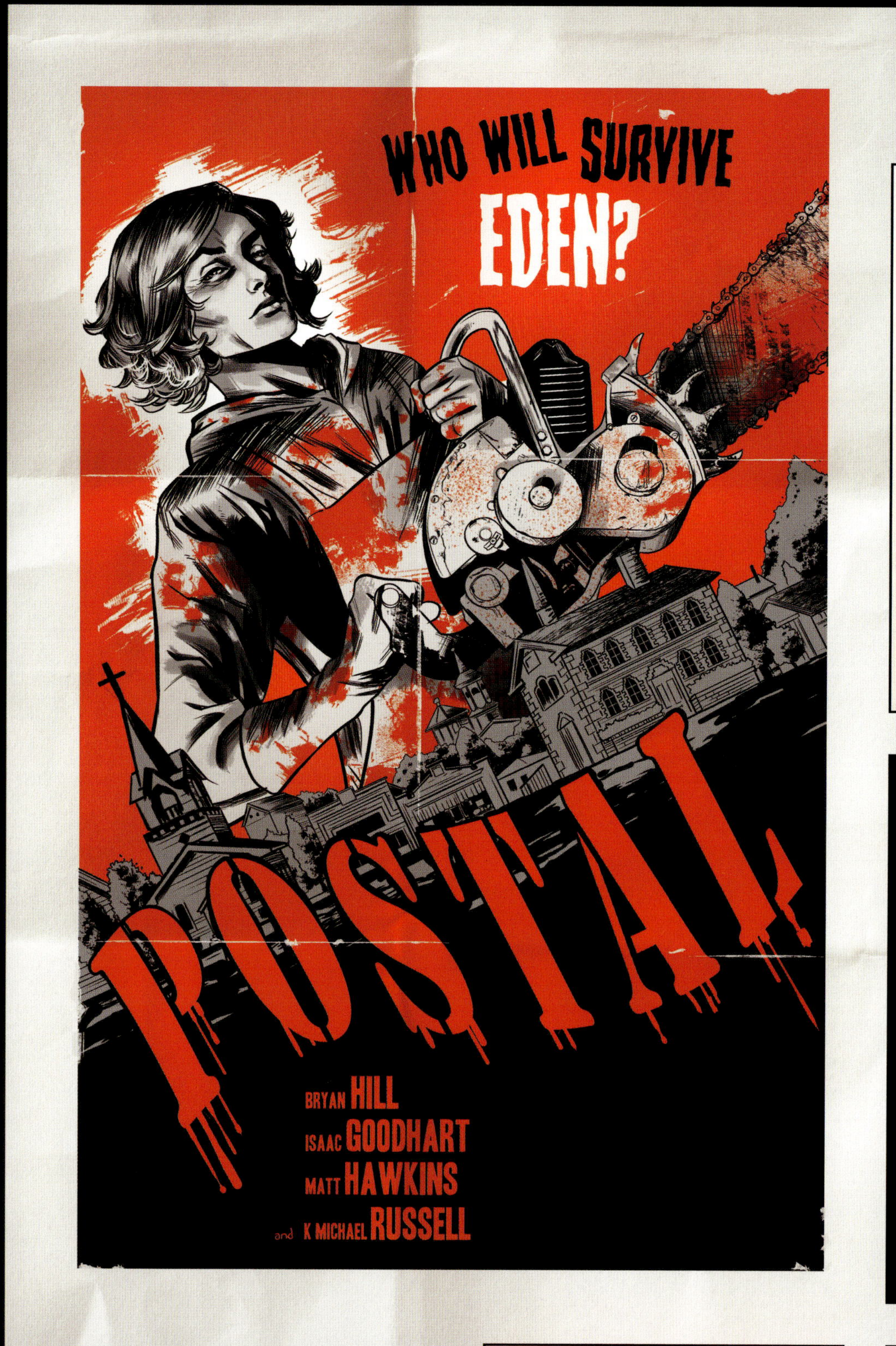

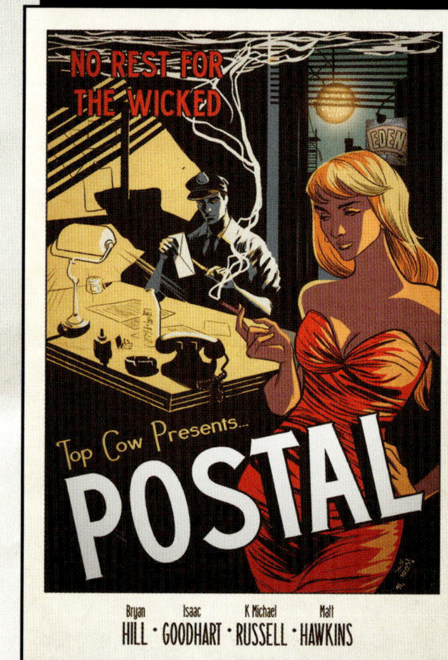

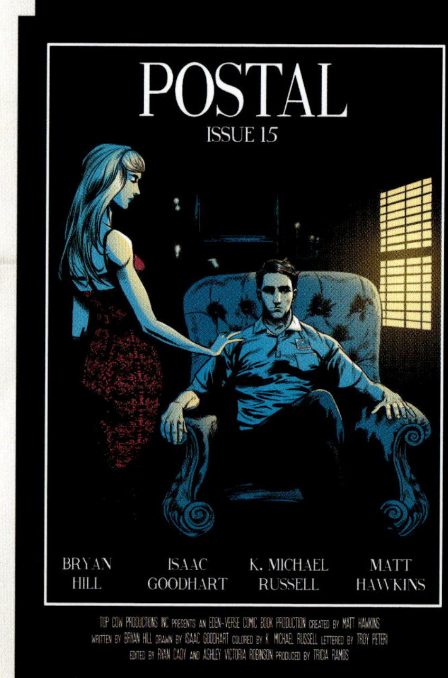

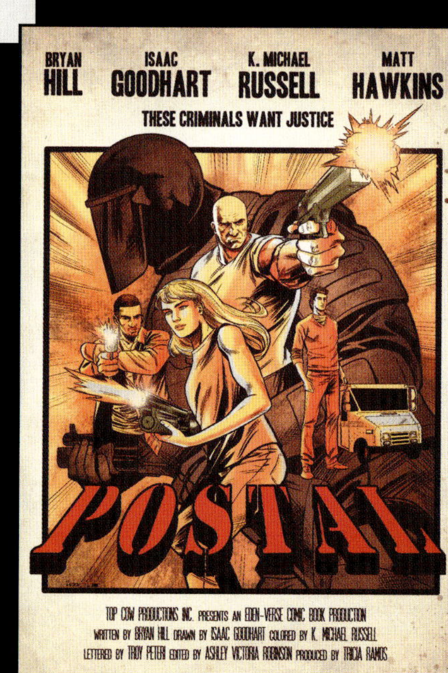

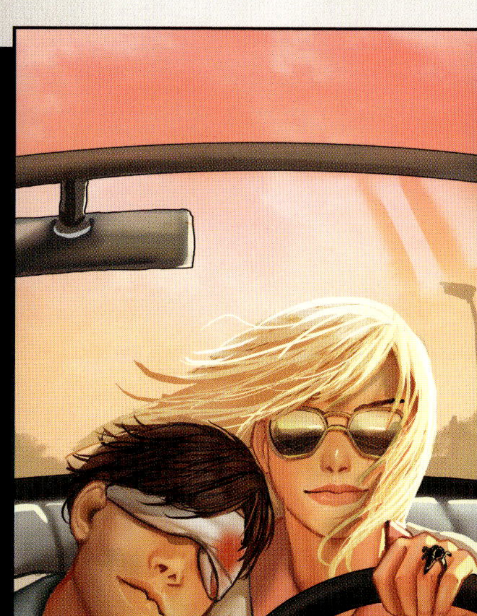

This page, clockwise from above.

Postal #13 cover B,
art by: Isaac Goodhart and K. Michael Russell

Postal #14 cover B,
art by: Isaac Goodhart and K. Michael Russell

Postal #15 cover B,
art by: Isaac Goodhart and K. Michael Russell

Postal #16 cover B,
art by: Isaac Goodhart and K. Michael Russell

Postal #16 cover A,
art by: Linda Sejic

Helm Greycastle selected covers

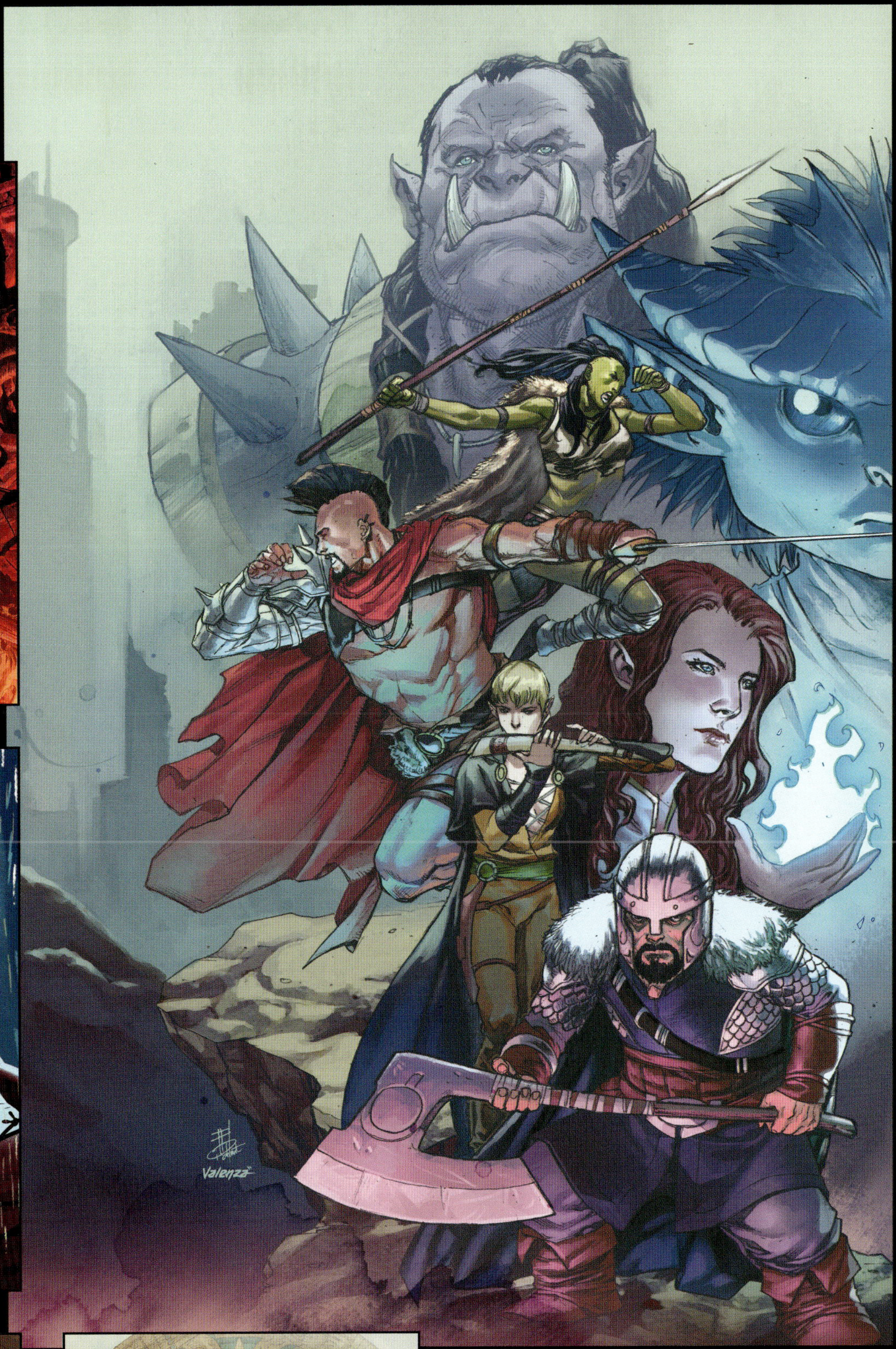

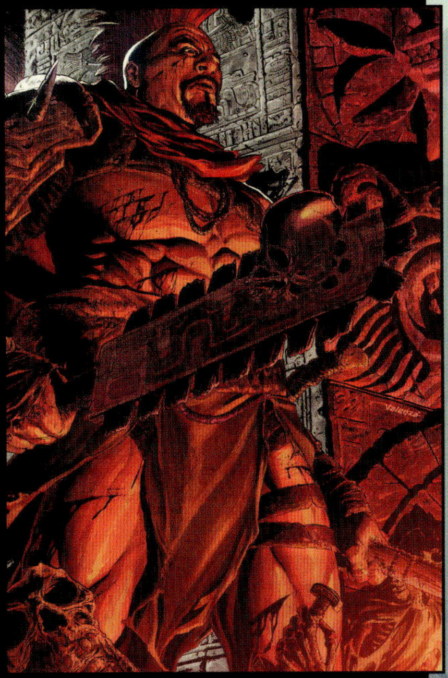

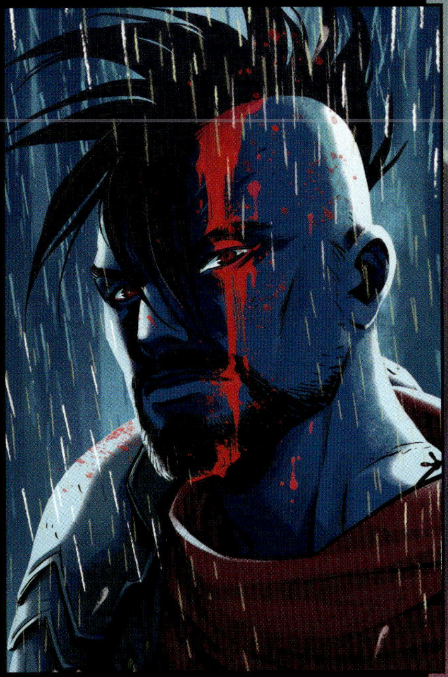

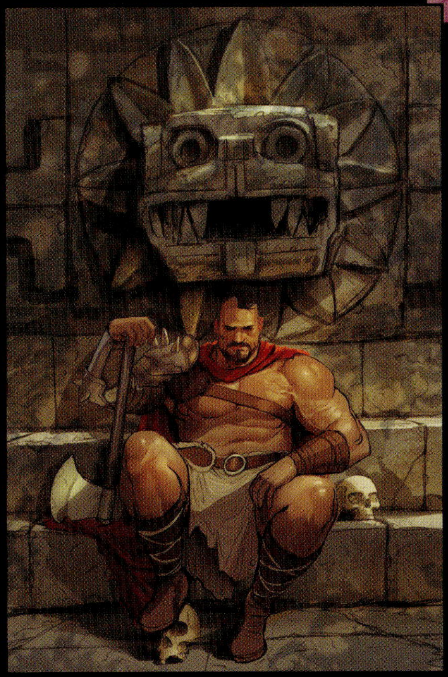

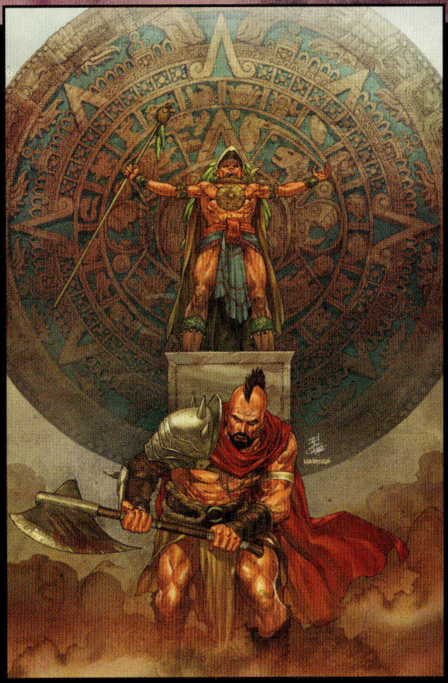

This page, counterclockwise from above.

Helm Greycastle #1 cover A,
art by: Rahmat M. Handoko and Bryan Valenza

Helm Greycastle #1 cover C,
art by: Tony Parker and Bryan Valenza

Helm Greycastle #1 cover D,
art by: Becky Cloonan

Helm Greycastle #2 cover B,
art by: Stjepan Sejic

Helm Greycastle #4 cover B,
art by: Rahmat M. Handoko and Bryan Valenza

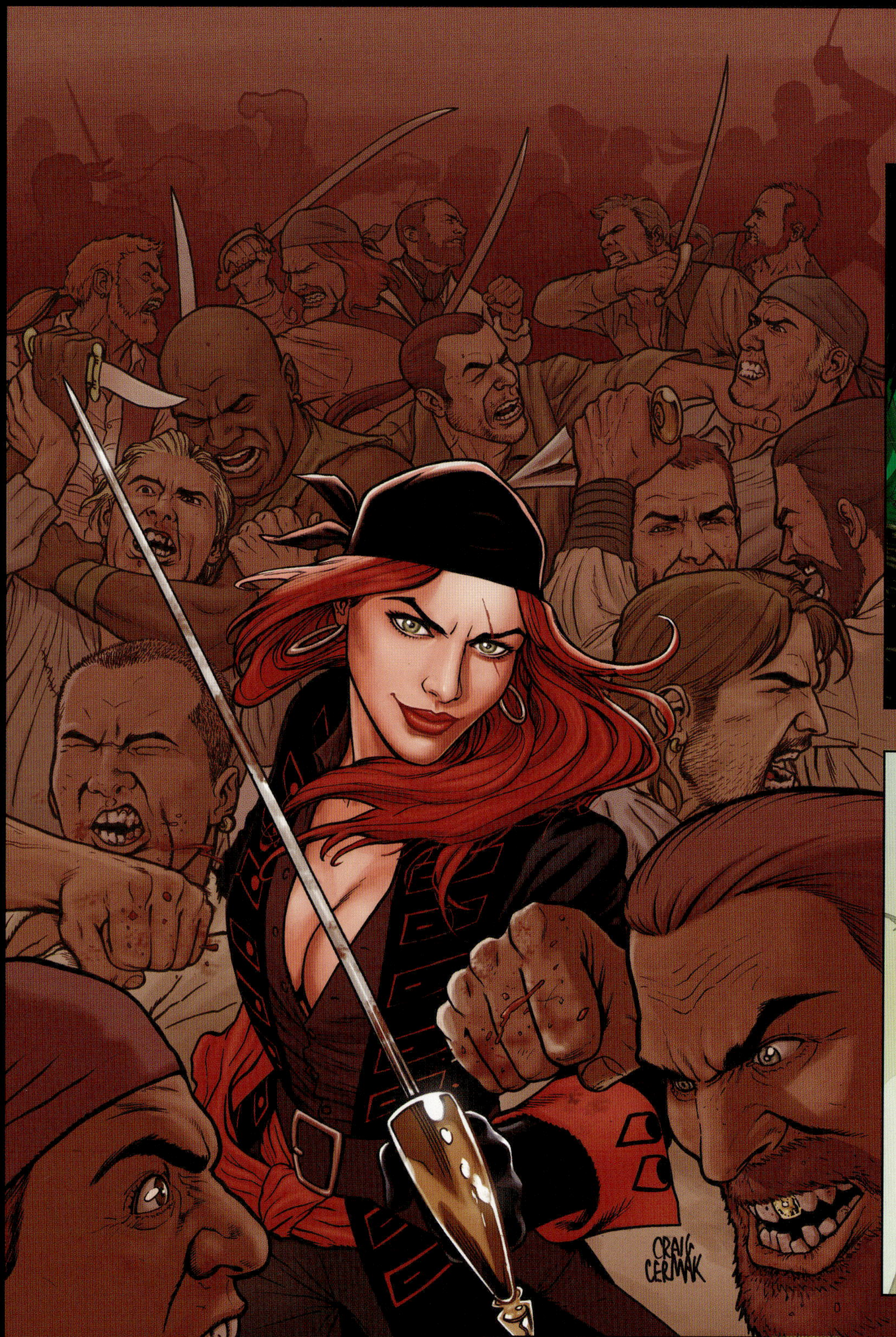

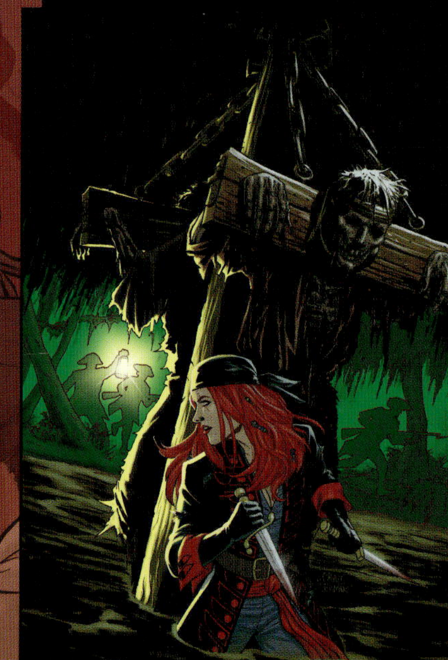

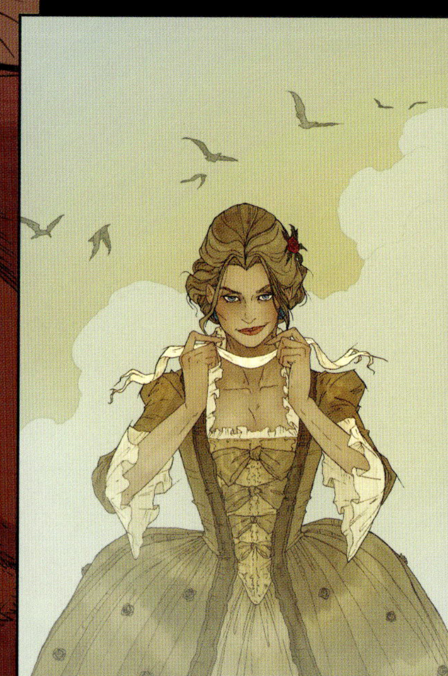

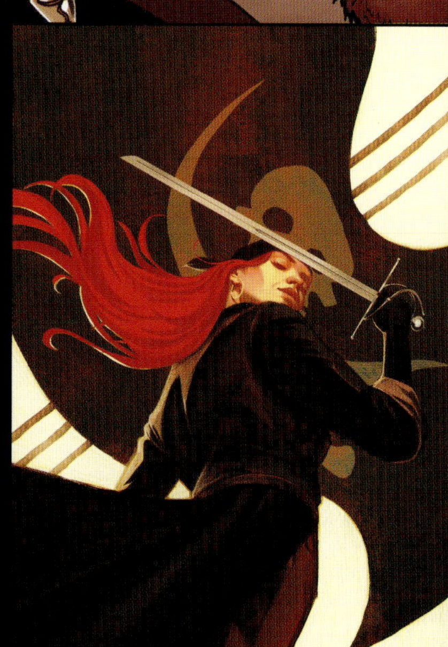

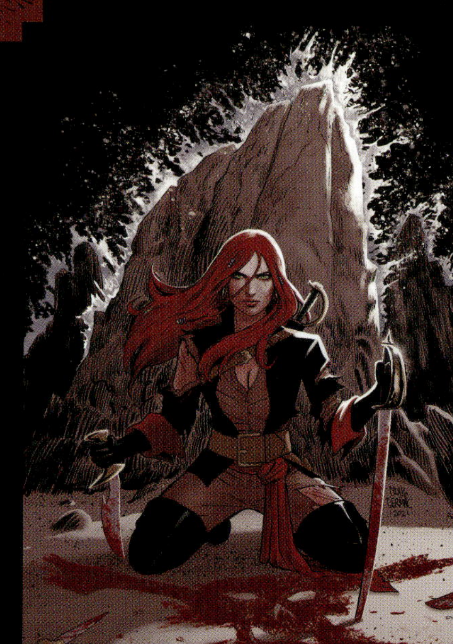

This page, clockwise from above.

A Man Among Ye #1 cover A,
art by: Craig Cermak

A Man Among Ye #3 cover,
art by: Craig Cermak

A Man Among Ye #5 cover B,
art by: Abigail Larson

A Man Among Ye #5 cover C,
art by: Craig Cermak

A Man Among Ye #6 cover B,
art by: Qistina Khalidah

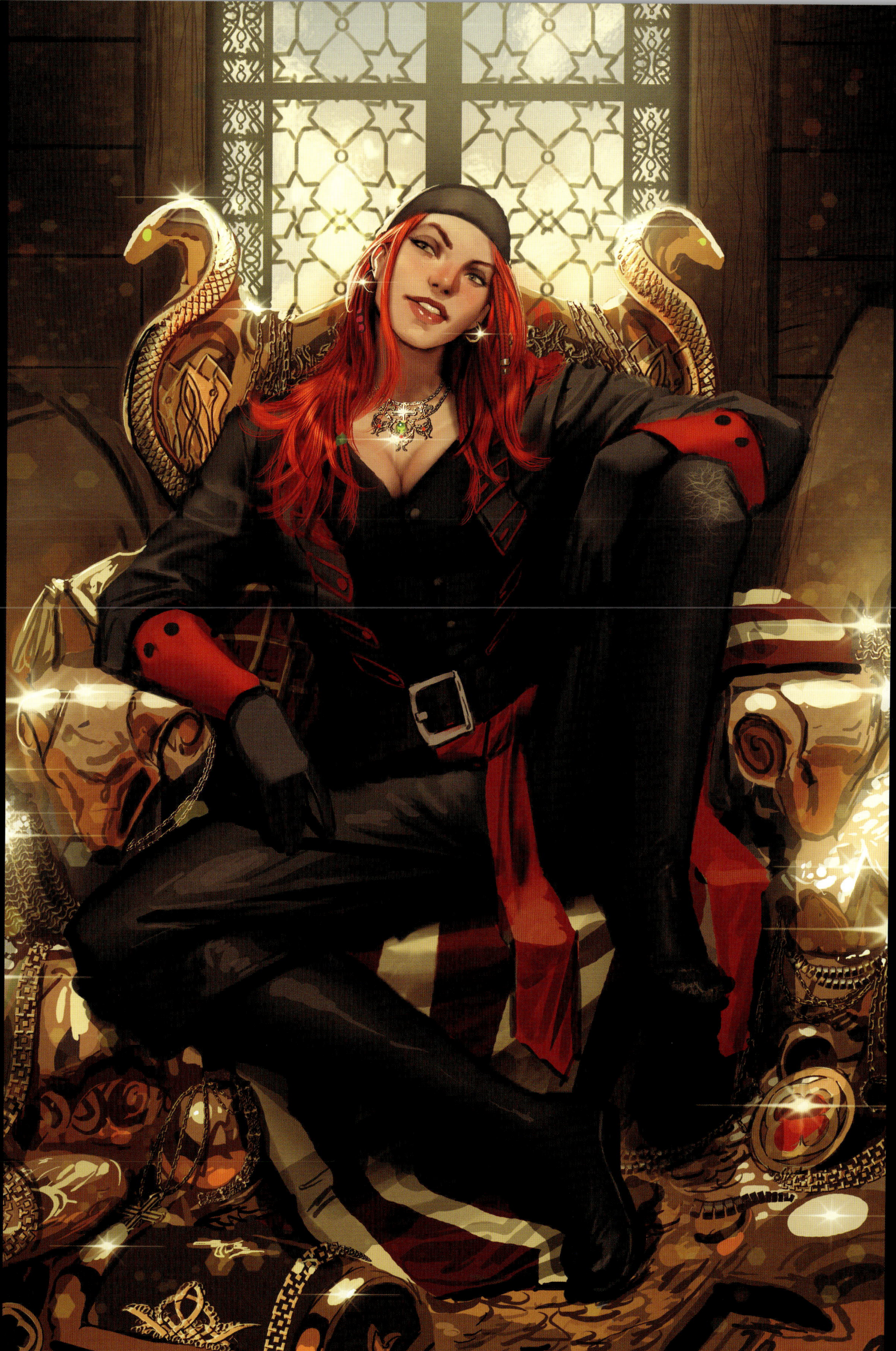

A Man Among Ye #1 cover B,
art by: Stjepan Sejic

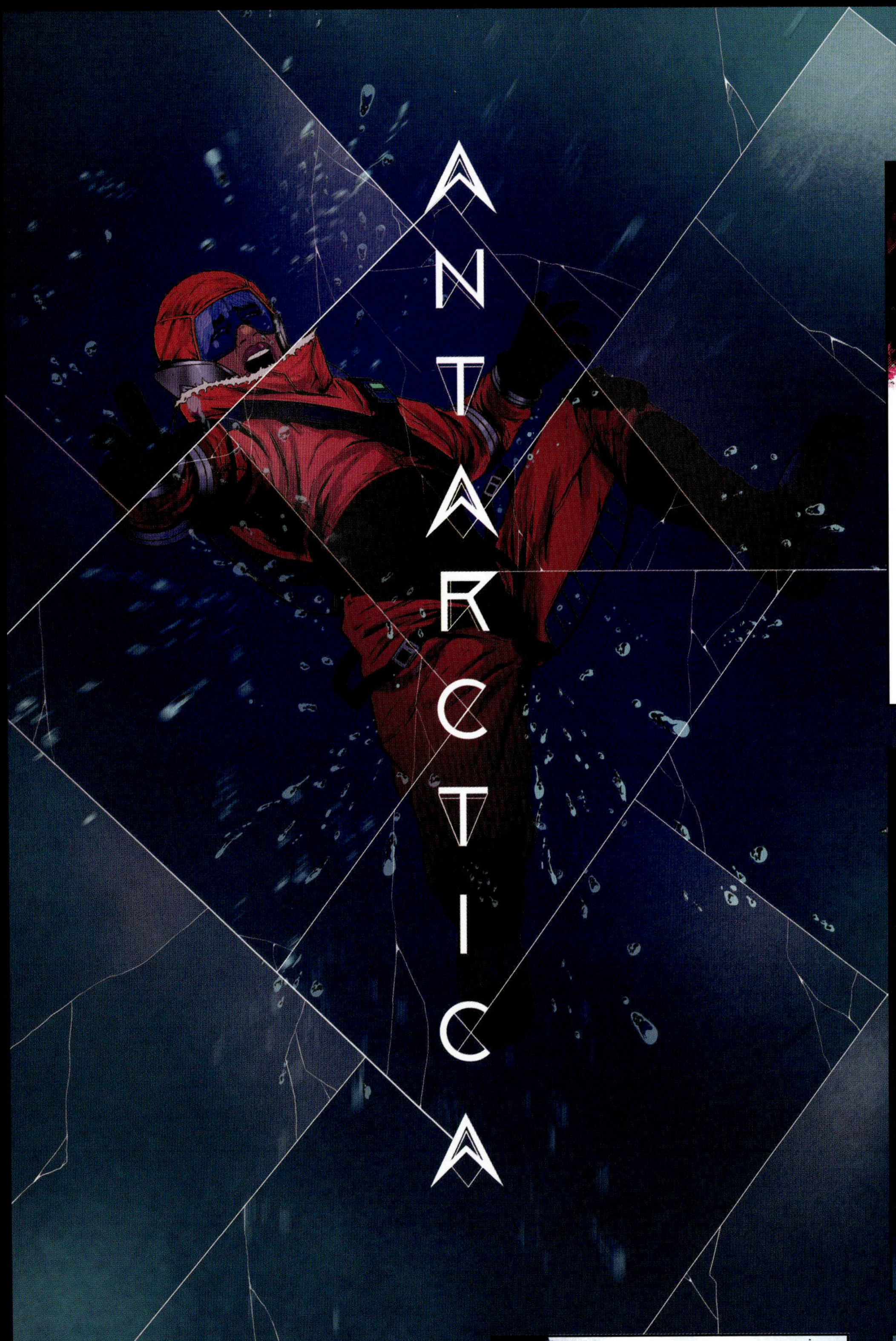

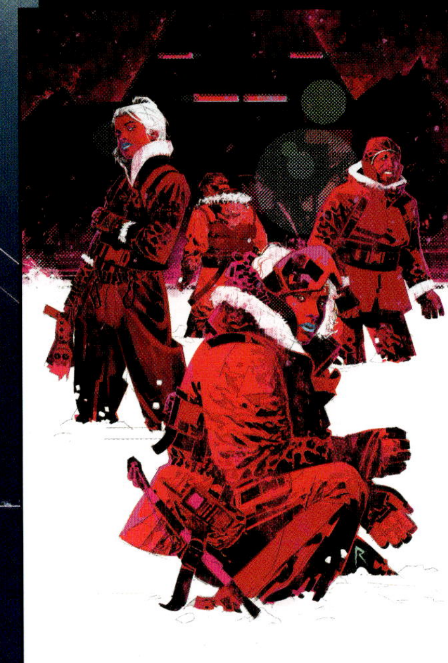

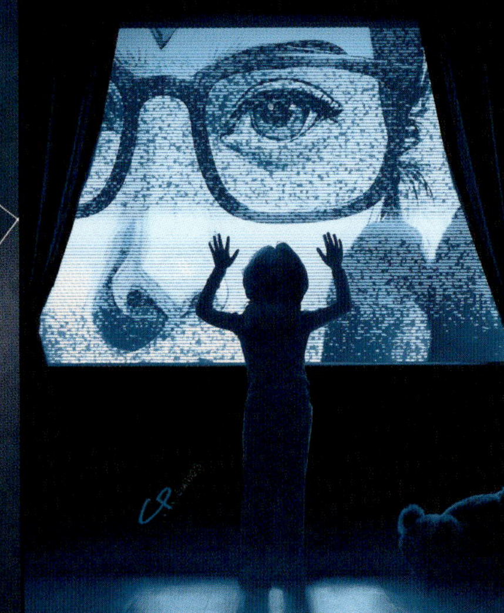

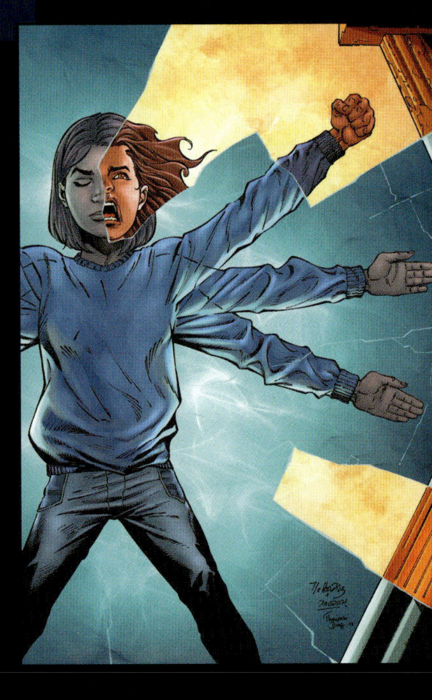

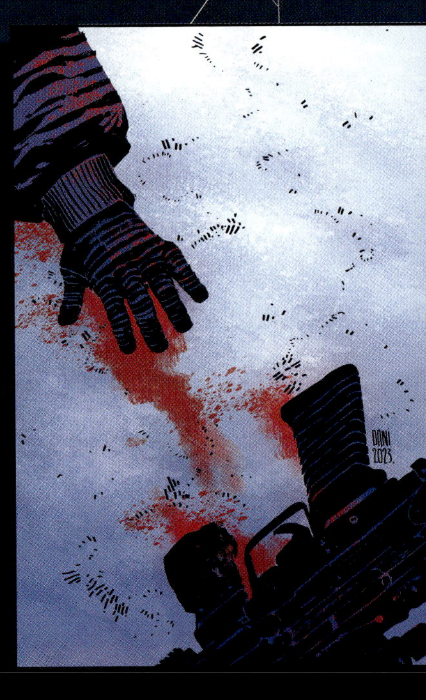

This page, clockwise from above.

Antarctica #1 cover A,
art by: Willi Roberts

Antarctica #2 cover B,
art by: Rosa Ekedal

Antarctica #3 cover B,
art by: C.P. Smith

Antarctica #8 cover B,
art by: Netho and Thaíssa Diaz

Antarctica #10 cover B,
art by: Dani and Brad Simpson

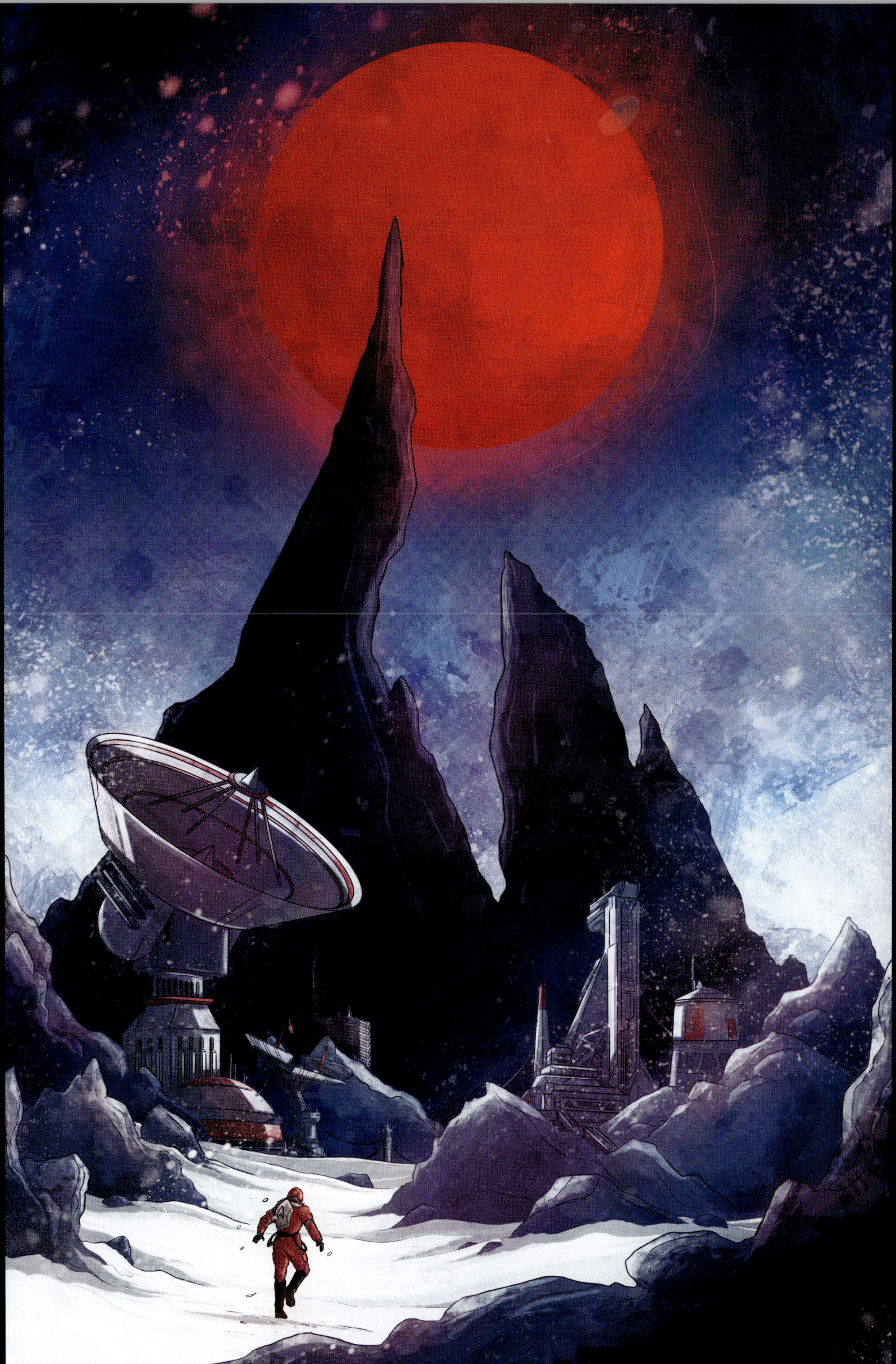

Antarctica #2 cover B,
art by: Lyndon White

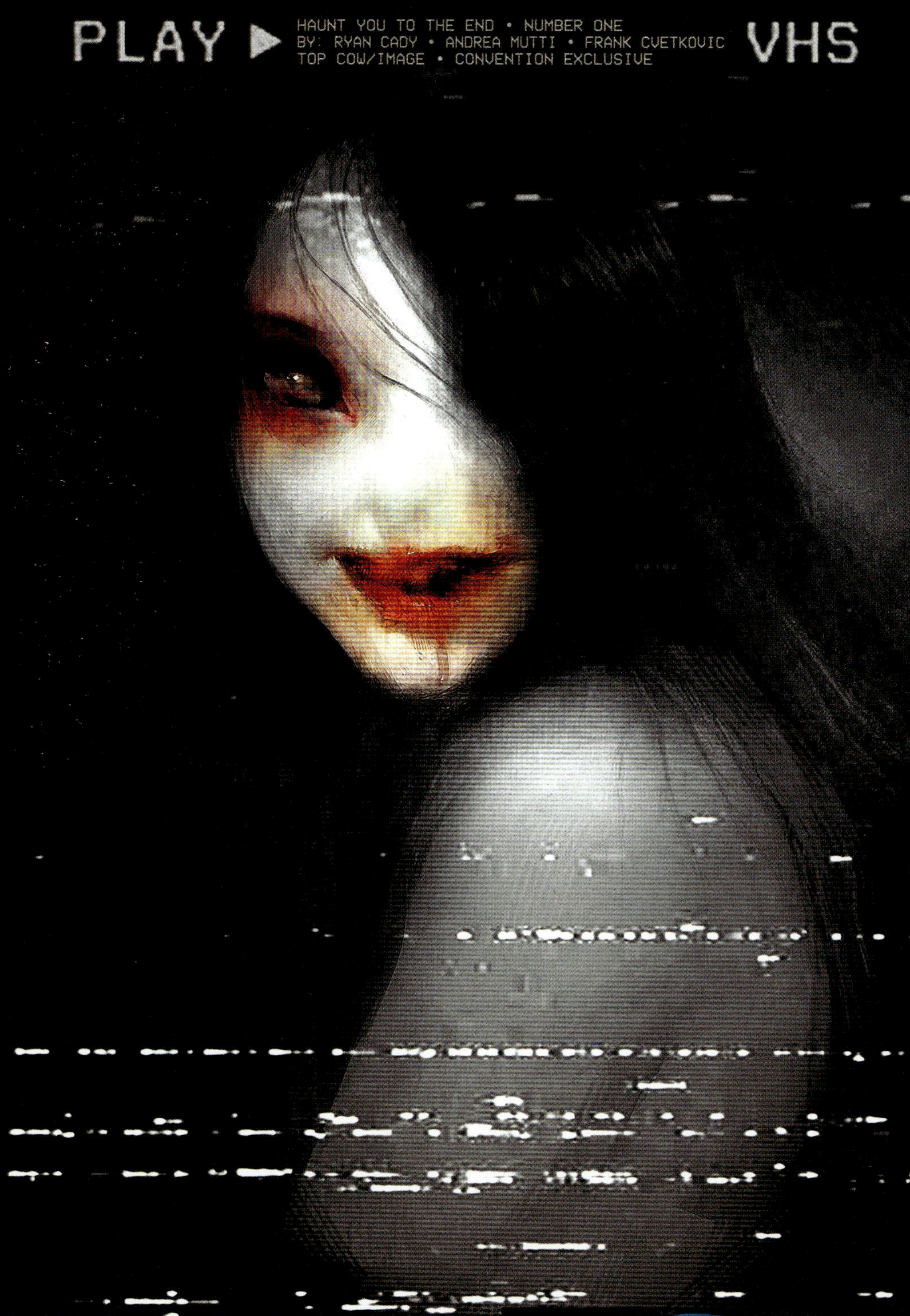

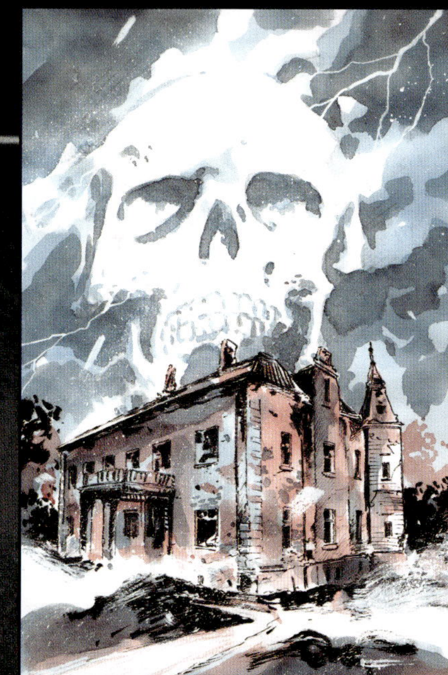

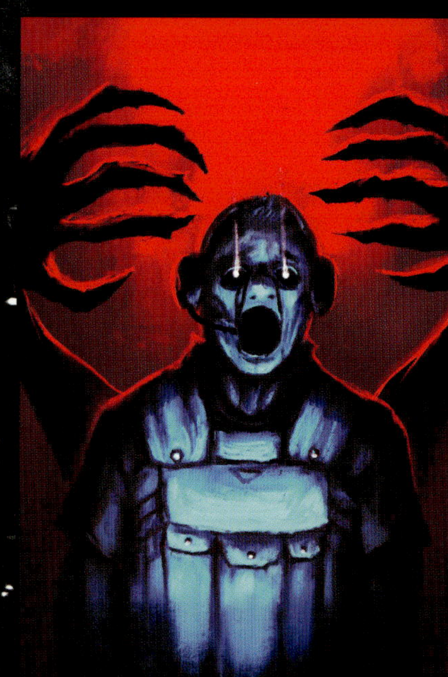

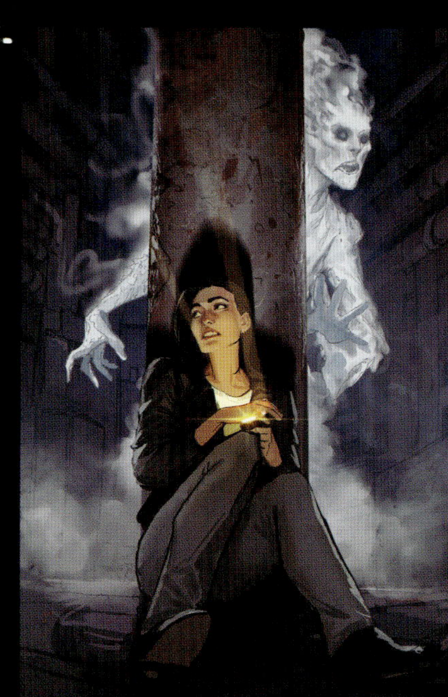

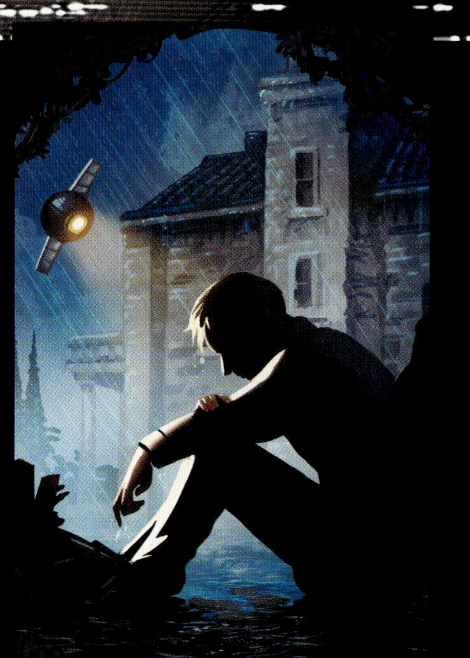

This page, clockwise from above.

Haunt You to the End #1 Convention Exclusive cover C, art by: Sozomaika

Haunt You to the End #1 cover A, art by: Andrea Mutti

Haunt You to the End#2 cover B, art by: Trevor Henderson

Haunt You to the End #3 cover B, art by: Stjepan Sejic

Haunt You to the End #4 cover B, art by: Linda Sejic

Selected works

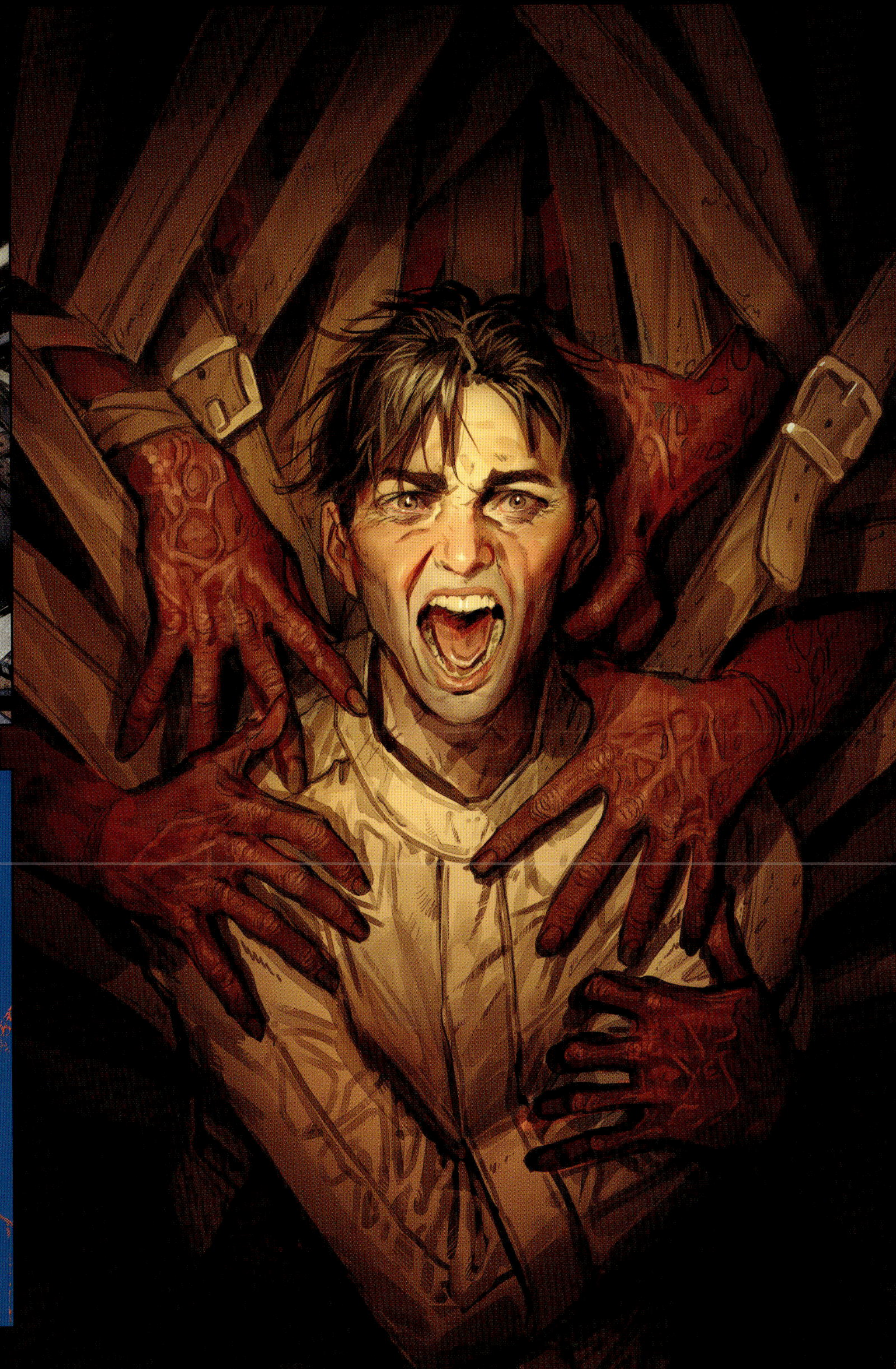

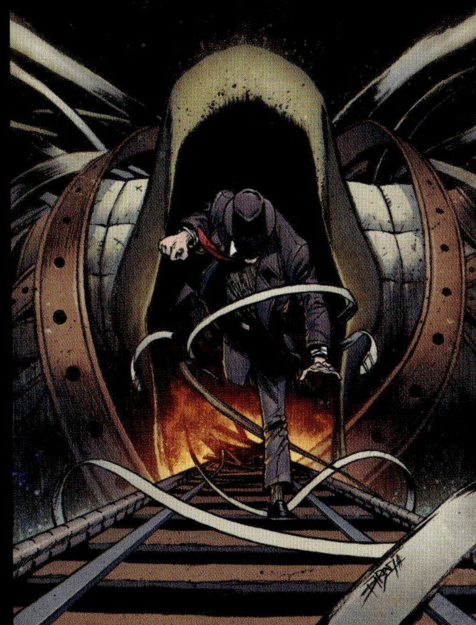

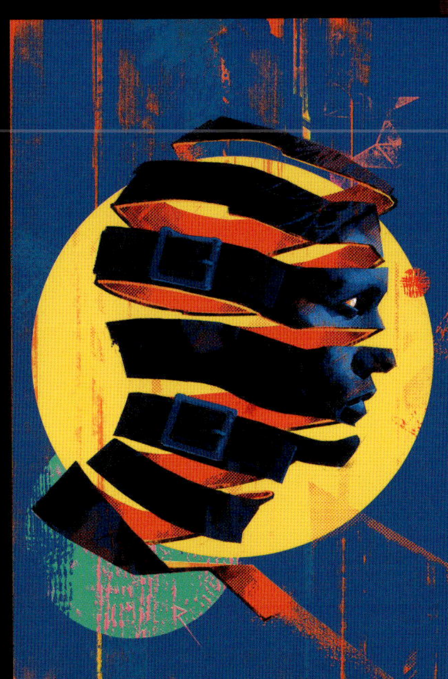

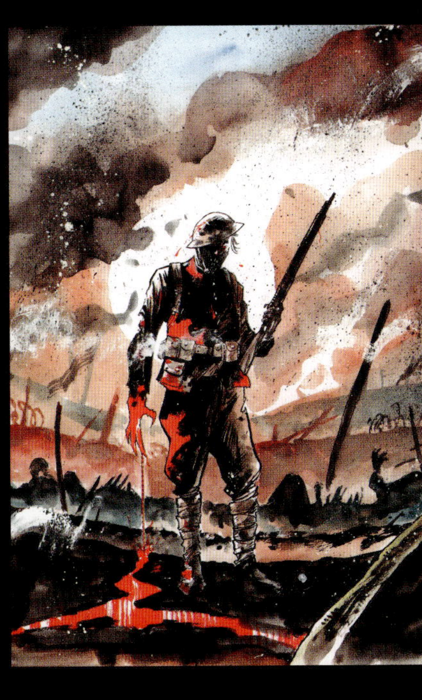

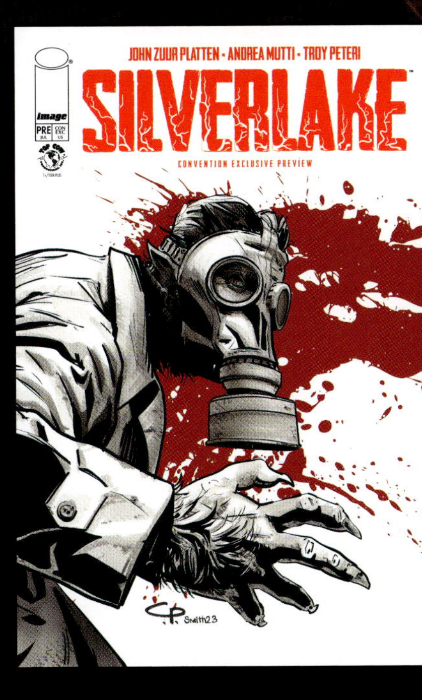

This page, counterclockwise from above.

Destiny Gate #1 Convention Exclusive cover,
art by: Stjepan Sejic

Destiny Gate #1 cover A,
art by: Chris DiBari and Simon Gough

Destiny Gate #1 cover B,
art by: Rosa Ekedal

Silverlake volume 1 cover,
art by: Andrea Mutti

Silverlake Convention Preview cover with trade dress,
art by: C.P. Smith

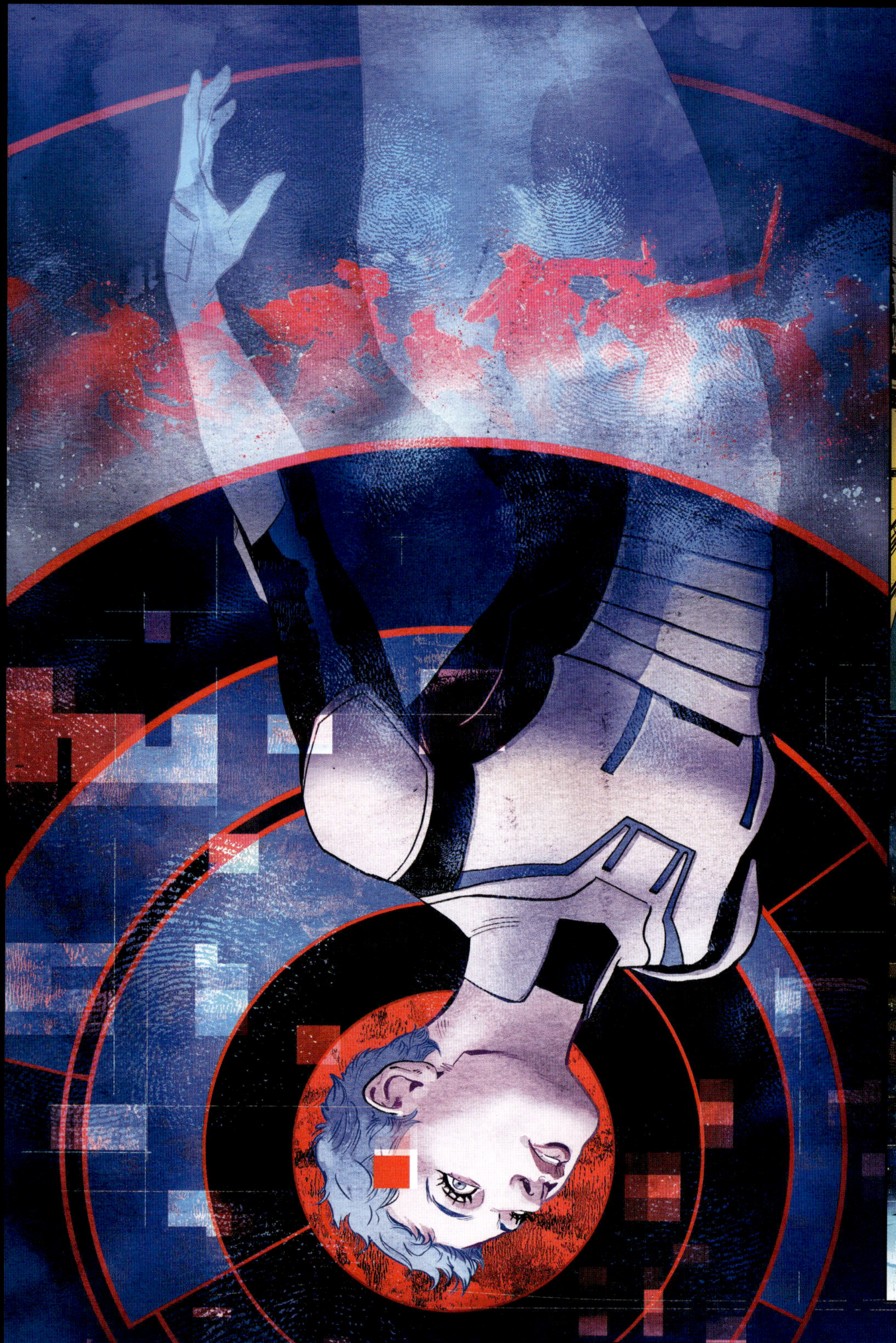

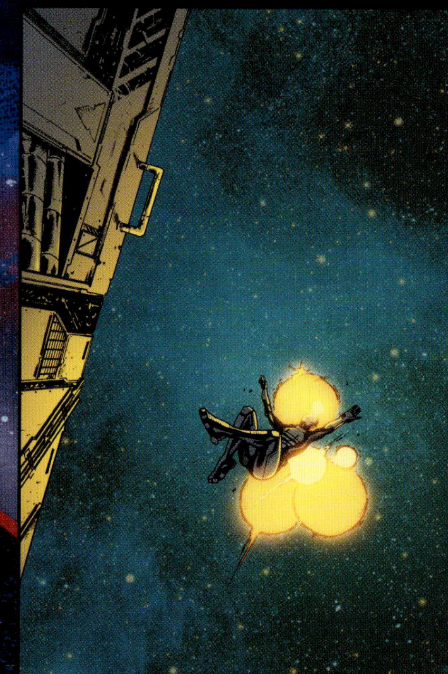

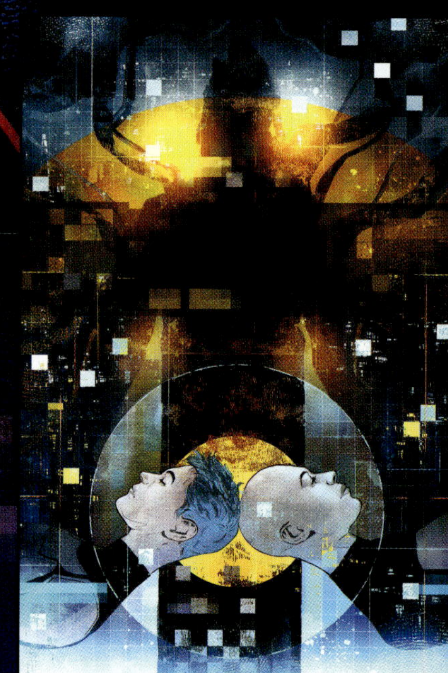

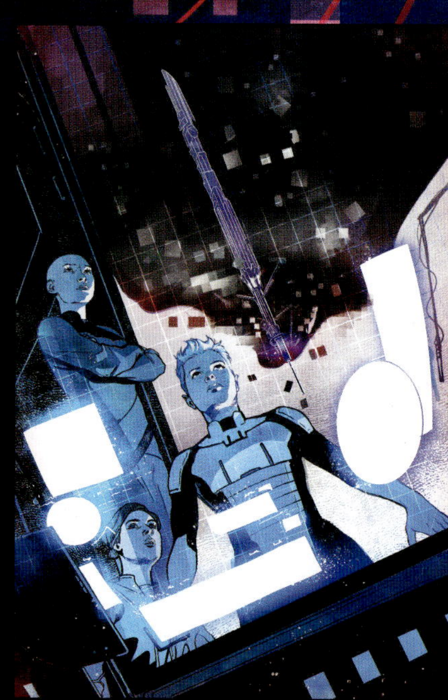

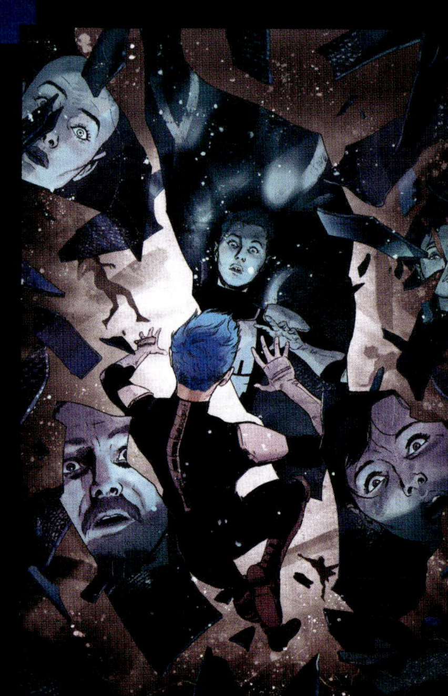

This page, clockwise from above:

Infinite Dark #7 cover,
art by: Nick Robles

Infinite Dark #1 cover,
art by: Andrea Mutti and K. Michael Russell

Infinite Dark #5 cover,
art by: Nick Robles

Infinite Dark #6 cover,
art by: Nick Robles

Infinite Dark #8 cover,
art by: Nick Robles

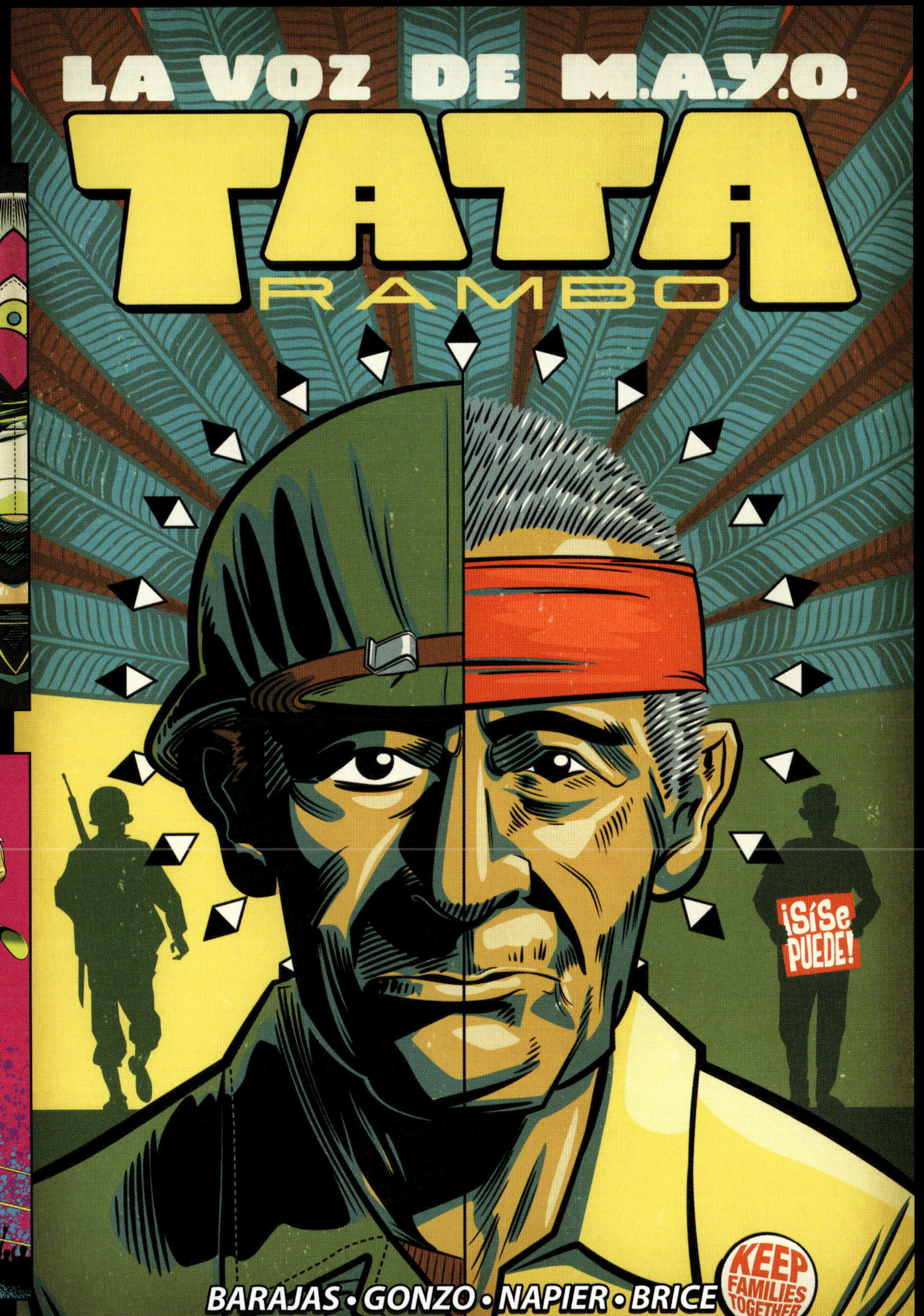

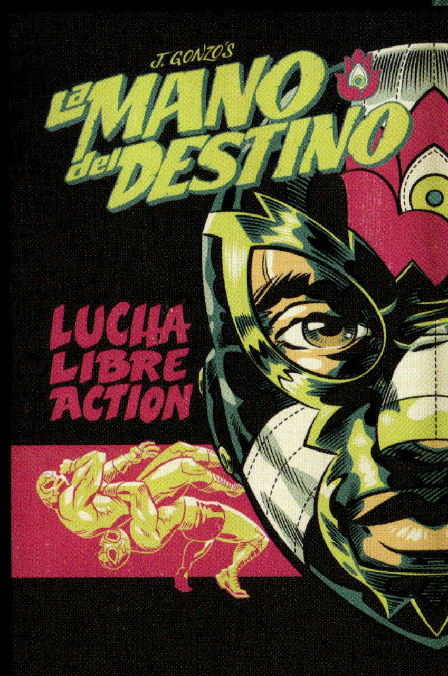

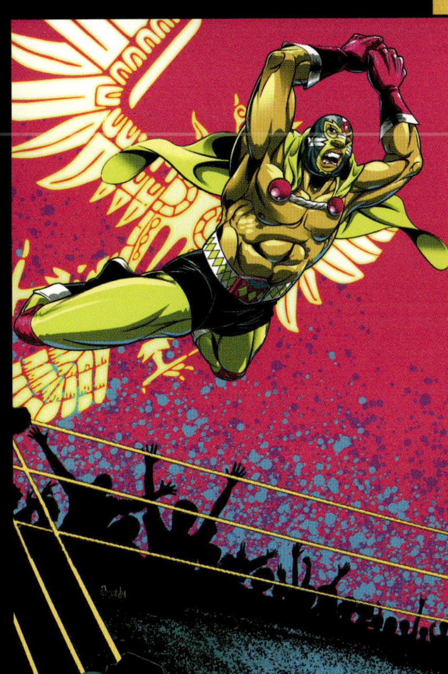

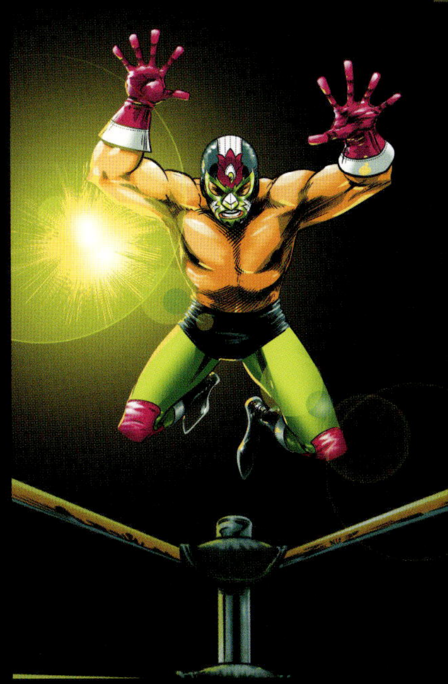

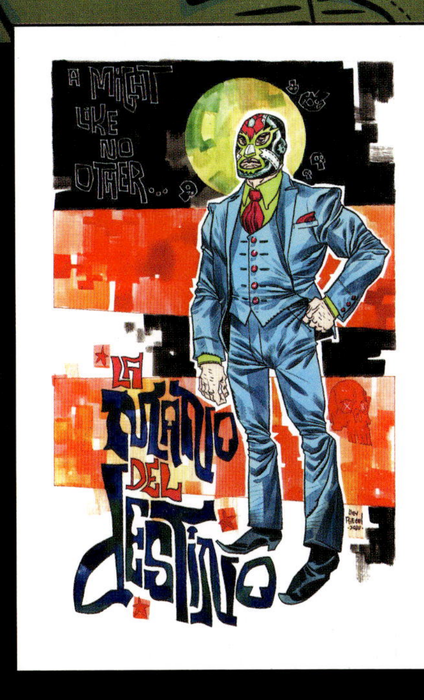

This page, counterclockwise from above.

La Voz de M.A.Y.O.: Tata Rambo volume 1 cover, art by: J. Gonzo

La Mano del Destino volume 1 cover, art by: J. Gonzo

La Mano del Destino pin-up, art by: Jiba Molei Anderson

La Mano del Destino pin-up, art by: Joe Benitez

La Mano del Destino pin-up, art by: Alex Riegel

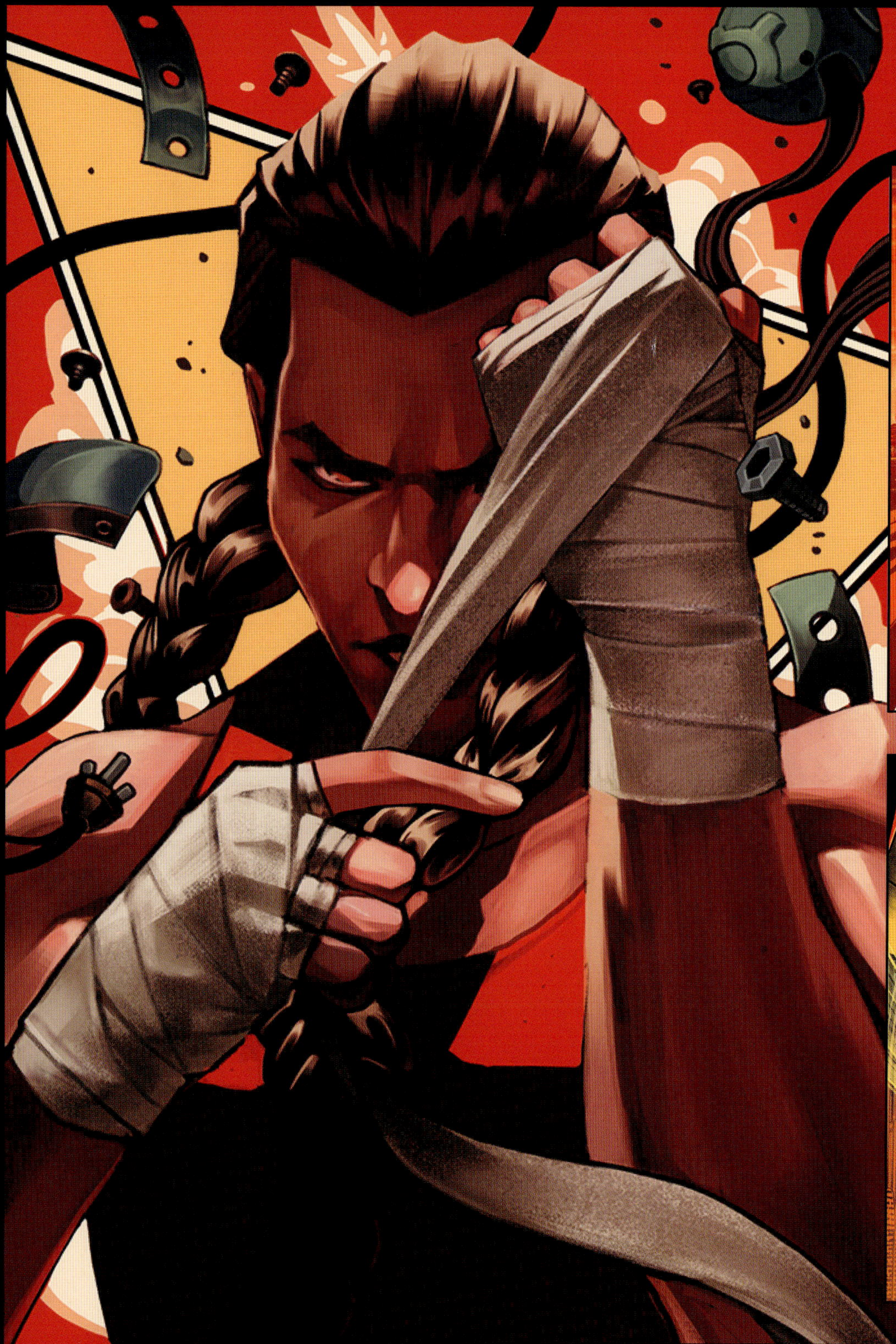

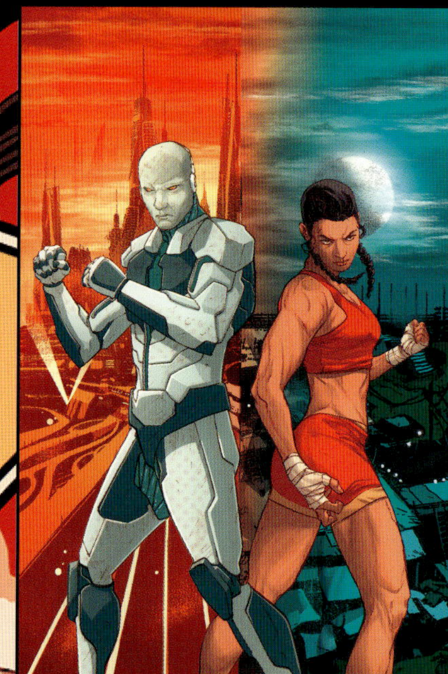

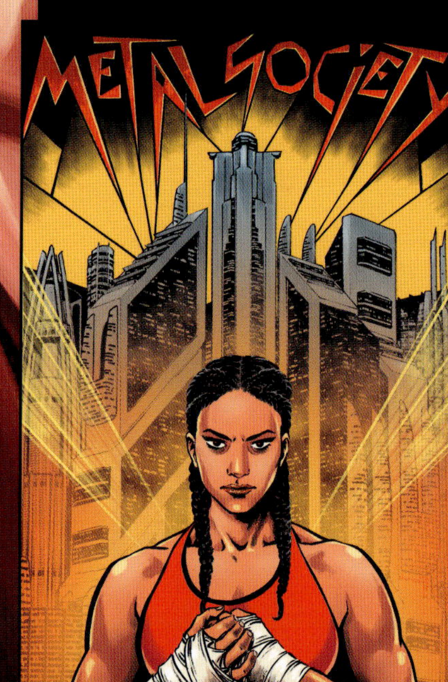

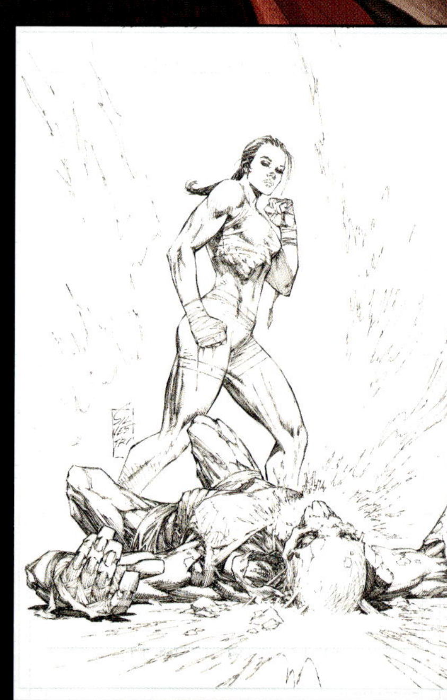

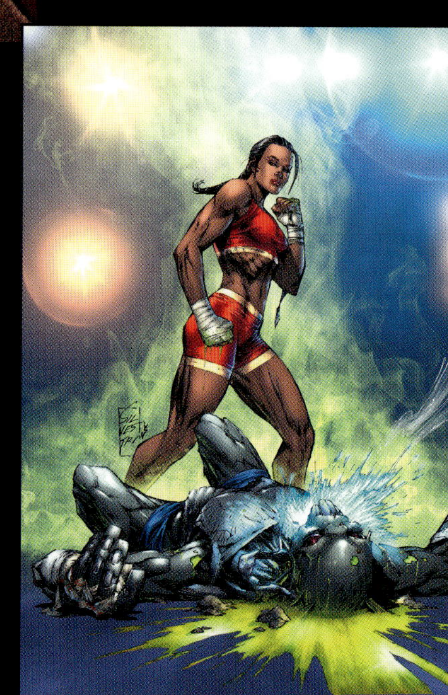

Metal Society selected covers

This page, clockwise from above.

Metal Society #1 cover B,
art by: Qistina Khalidah

Metal Society #1 cover A,
art by: Guilherme Balbi

Metal Society #1 cover E,
art by: Fernando Blanco

Metal Society #1 cover F,
art by: Marc Silvestri, and Alex Sinclair

Metal Society #1 cover F,
line art by: Marc Silvestri

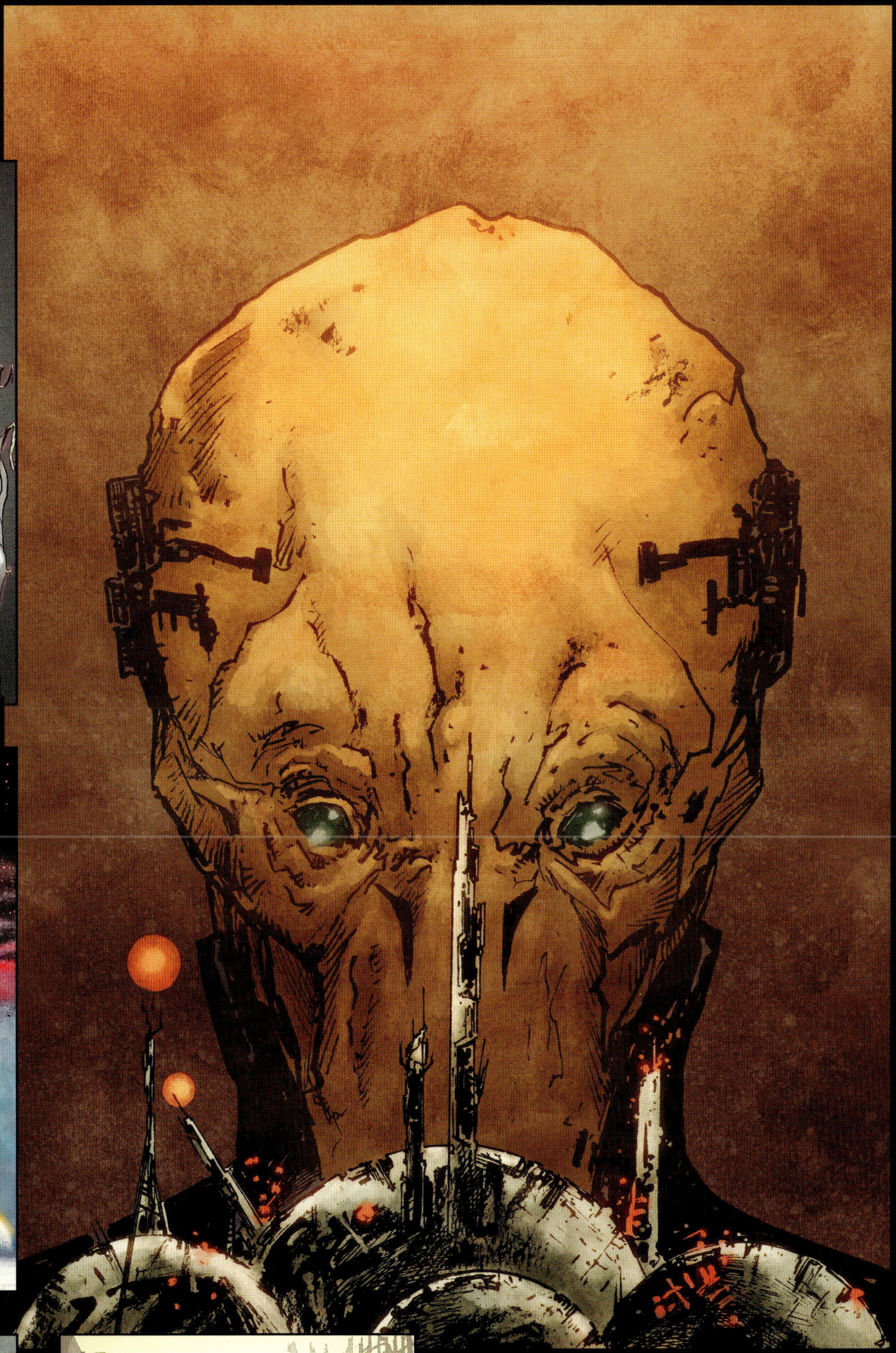

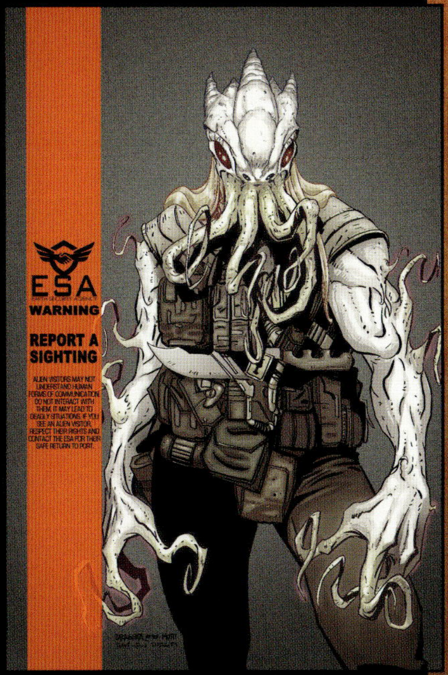

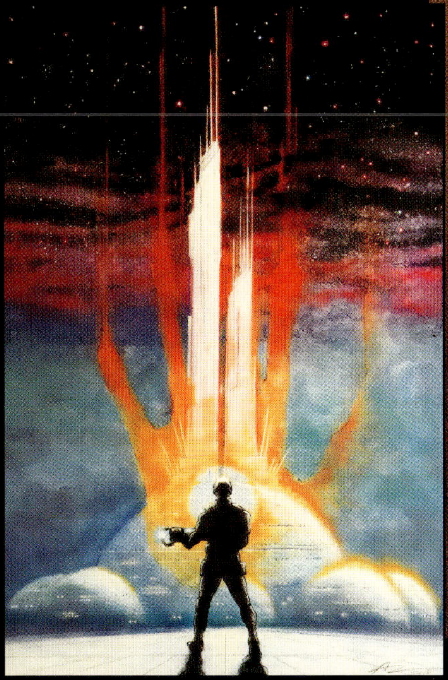

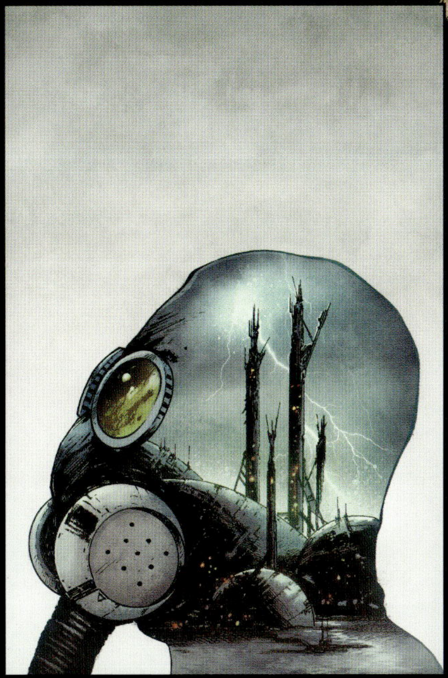

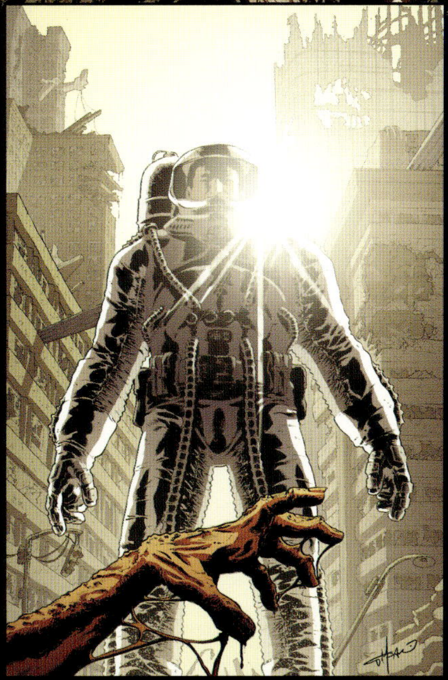

This page, counterclockwise from above.

Port of Earth #12 cover,
art by: Andrea Mutti and Jordan Boyd

Port of Earth #1 cover B,
art by: Nick Dragotta and Vladimir Popov

Port of Earth #9 cover B,
art by: Aaron Campbell

Port of Earth #10 cover,
art by: Andrea Mutti and Jordan Boyd

Eclipse #1 cover,
art by: Giovanni Timpano

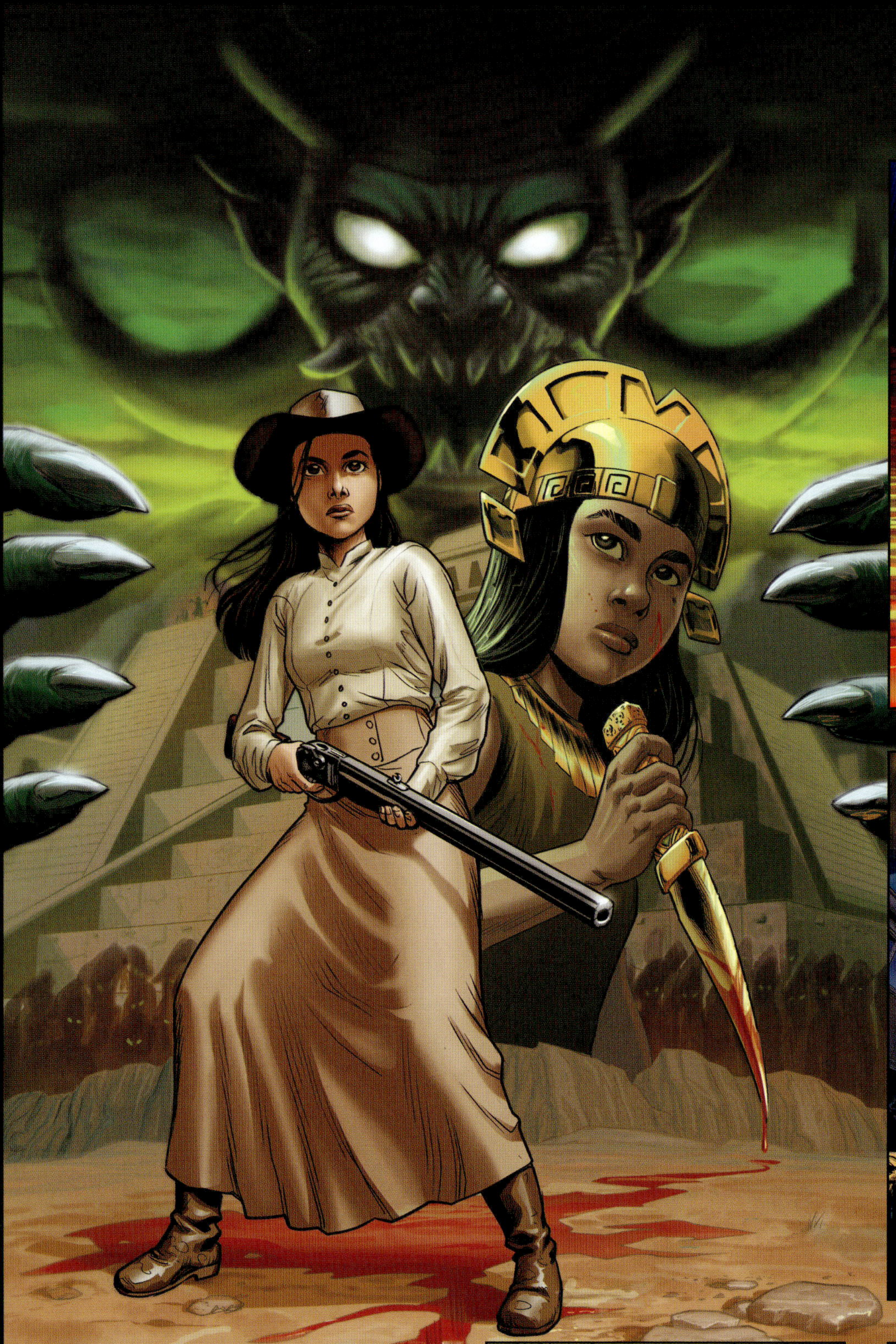

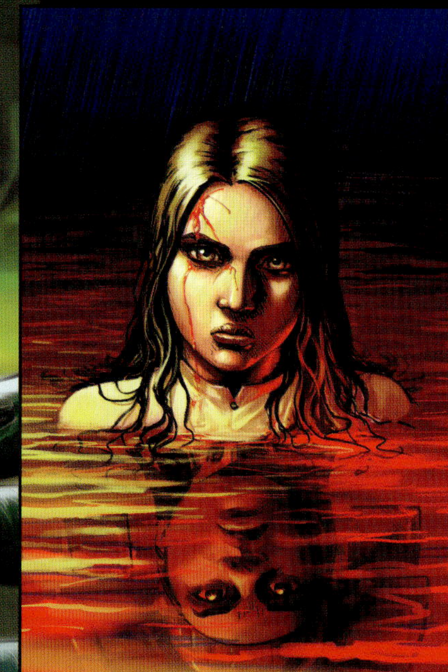

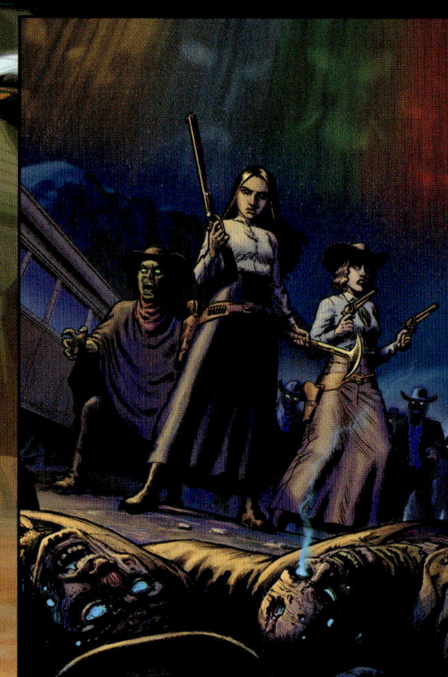

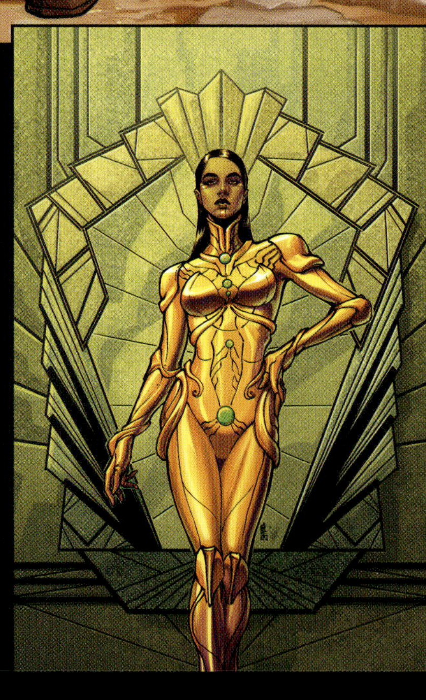

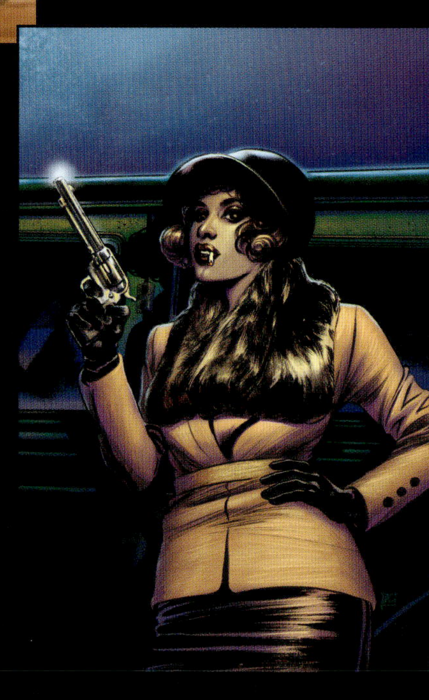

This page, clockwise from above.

St. Mercy volume 1, #1 cover A,
art by: Atilio Rojo

St. Mercy volume 1, #1 cover A,
art by: Atilio Rojo

St. Mercy volume 2, #1 cover A,
art by: Atilio Rojo

St. Mercy volume 2, #1 cover B,
art by: Francesca Ciregia and Atilio Rojo

St. Mercy volume 2, #3 cover B,
art by: Giuseppe Cafaro and Atilio Rojo

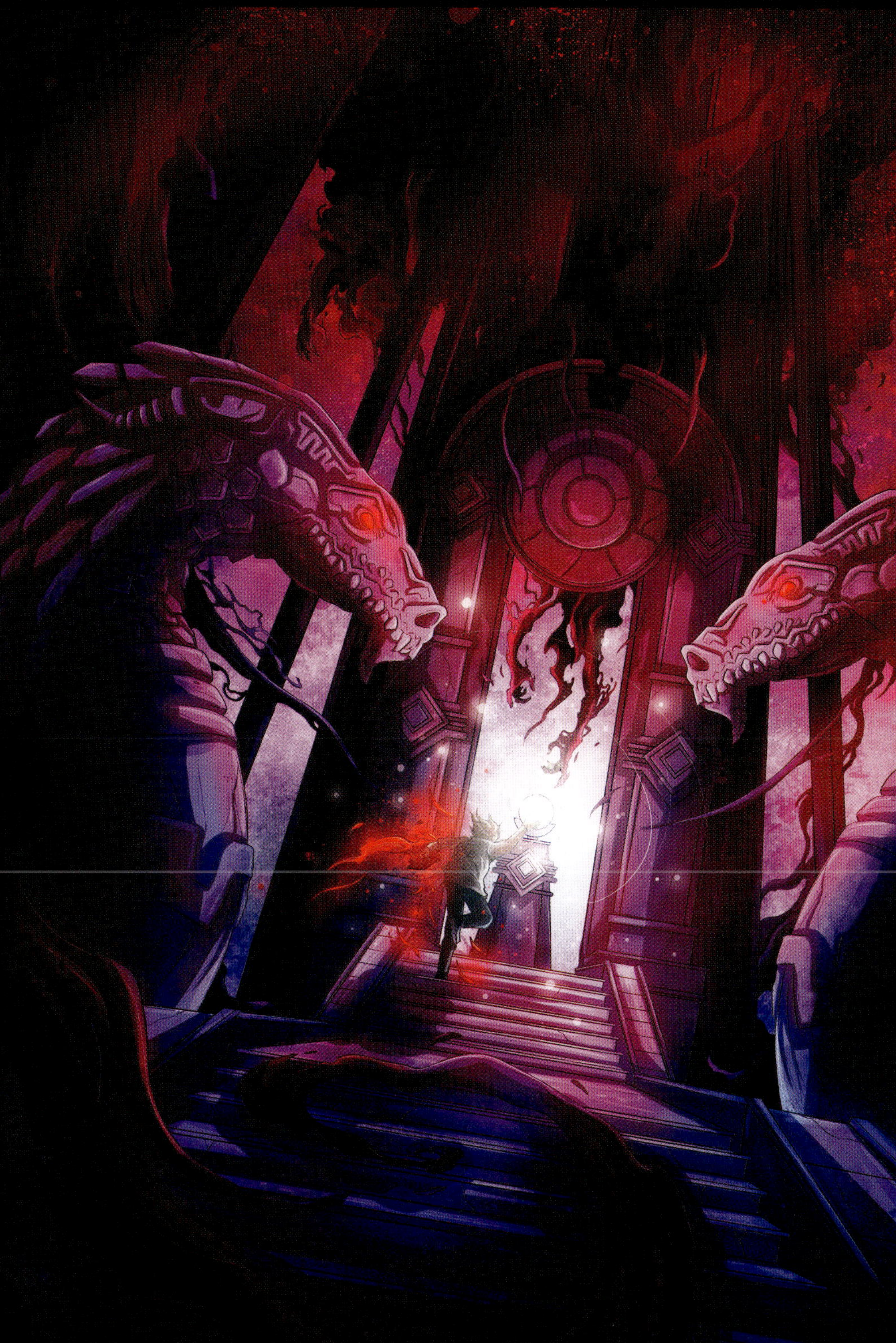

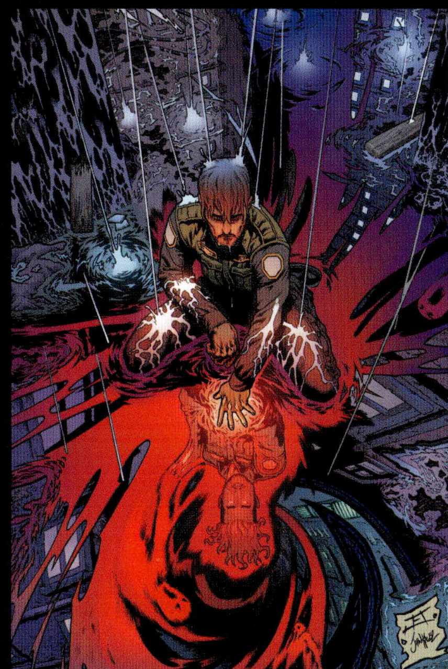

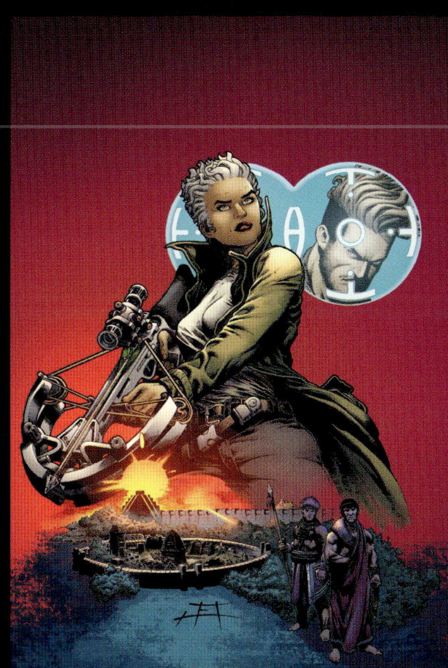

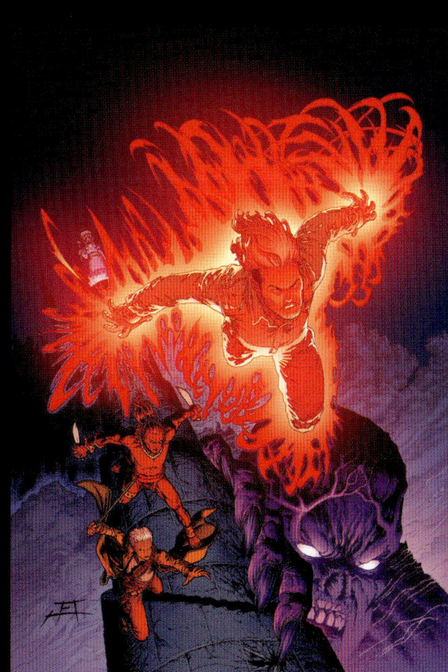

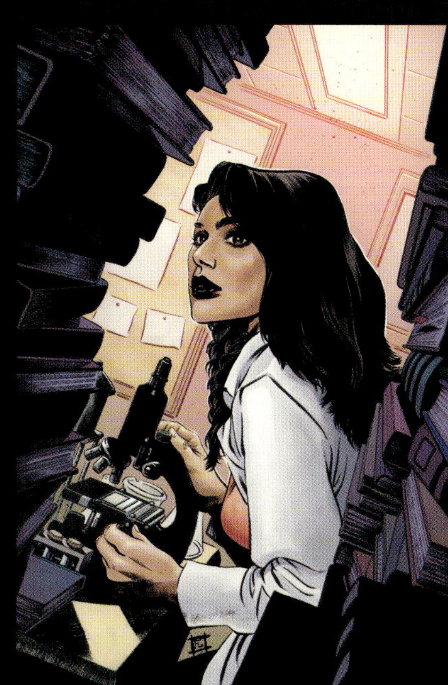

This page, counterclockwise from above.

Syphon volume 2, #3 cover B,
art by: Lyndon White

Syphon volume 1, #1 cover A,
art by: Jeff Edwards and John Kalisz

Syphon volume 2, #2 cover B,
art by: Jeff Edwards and John Kalisz

Syphon volume 2, #3 cover A,
art by: Jeff Edwards and John Kalisz

Syphon volume 2, #4 cover B,
art by: Francesca Ciregia and John Kalisz

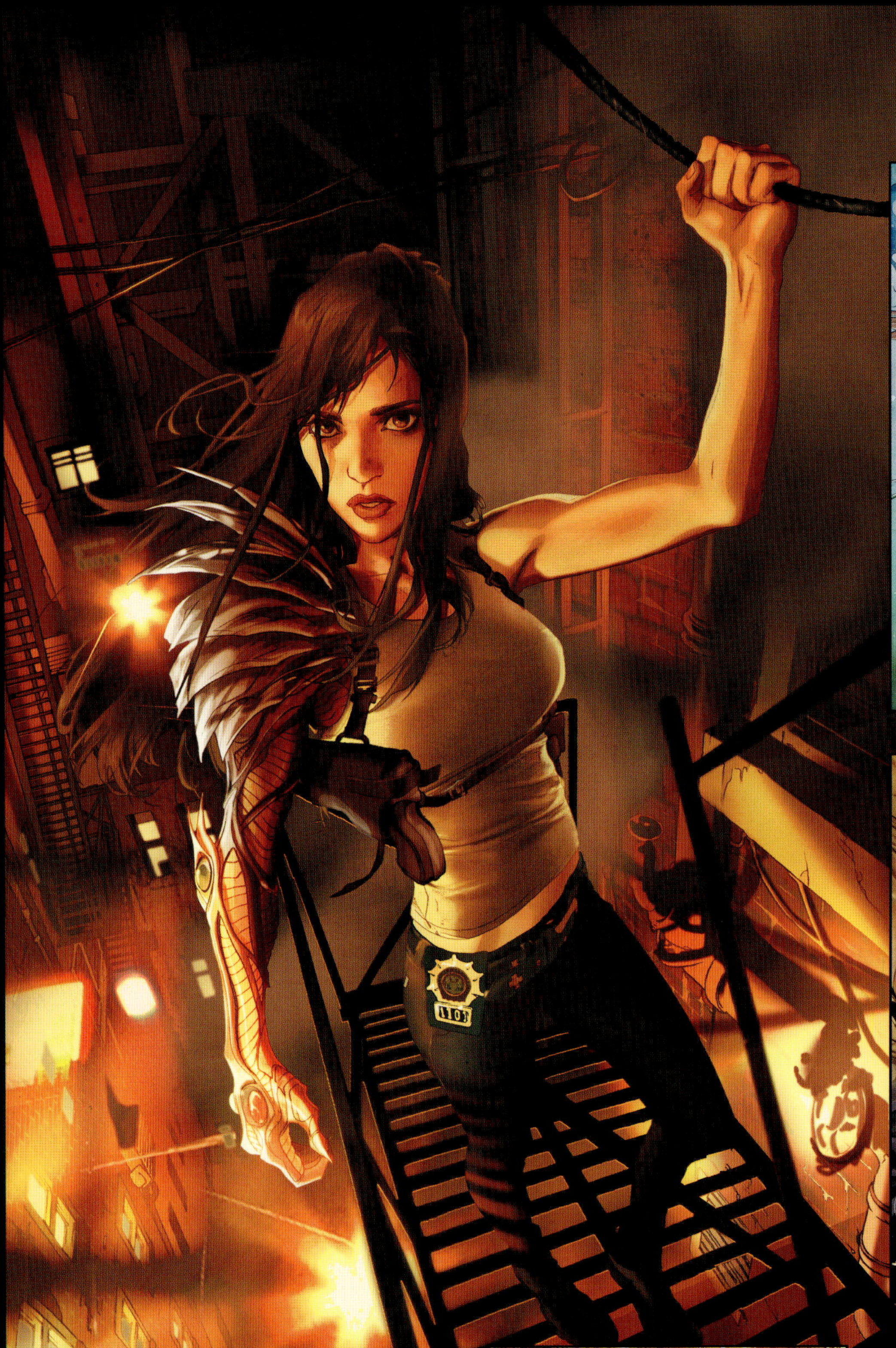

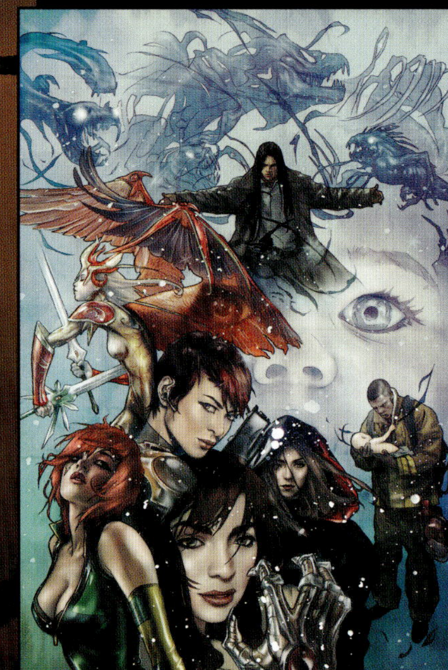

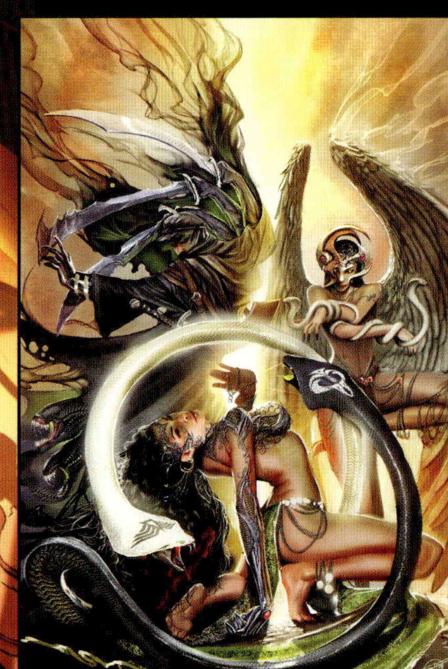

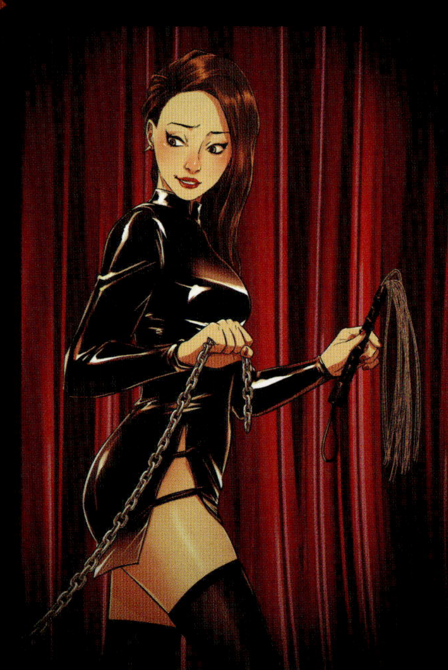

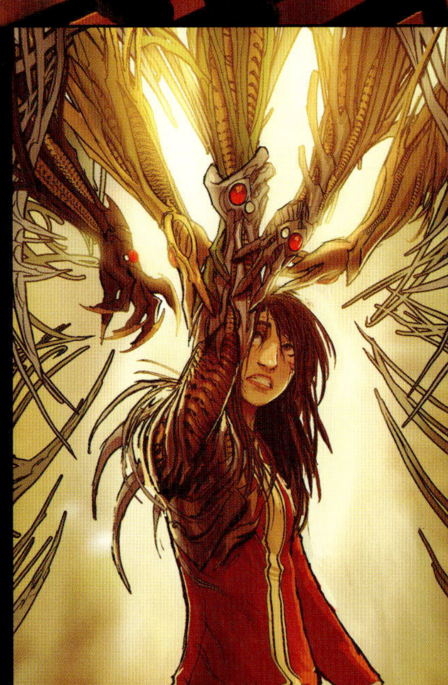

This page, clockwise from above.

Witchblade: Due Process #1 one-shot cover, art by: Alina Urusov

Top Cow Holiday Special [2010] one-shot cover, art by: Alina Urusov

Trinity: Blood on the Sands #1 one-shot cover, art by: Stjepan Sejic

Swing volume 4 cover, art by: Yishan Li

Switch volume 1 cover, art by: Stjepan Sejic

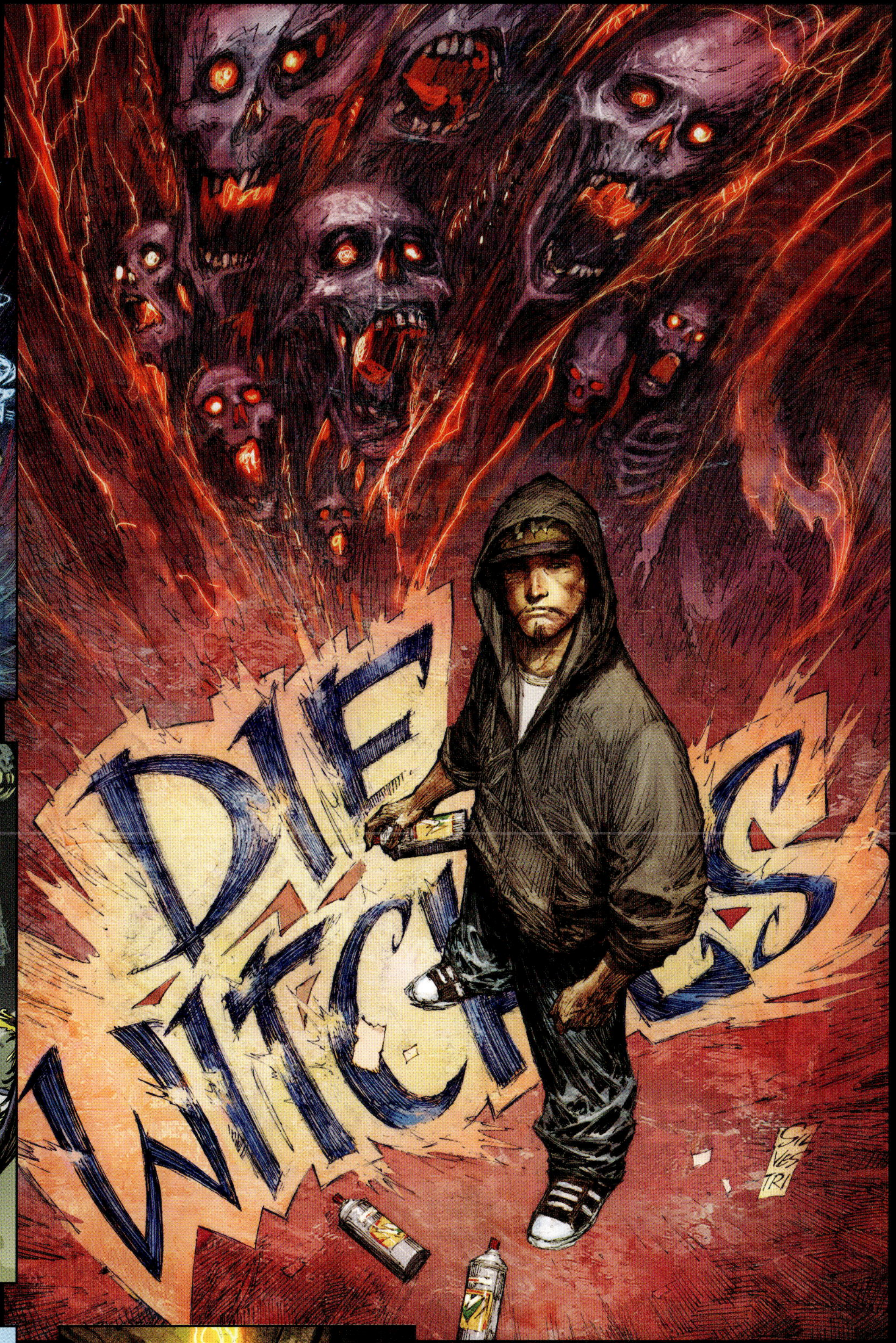

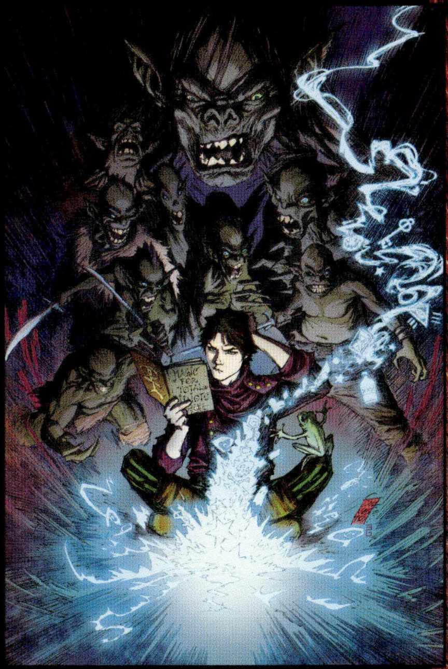

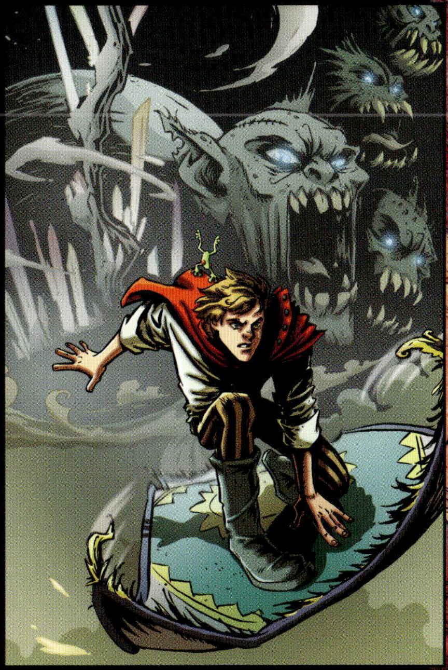

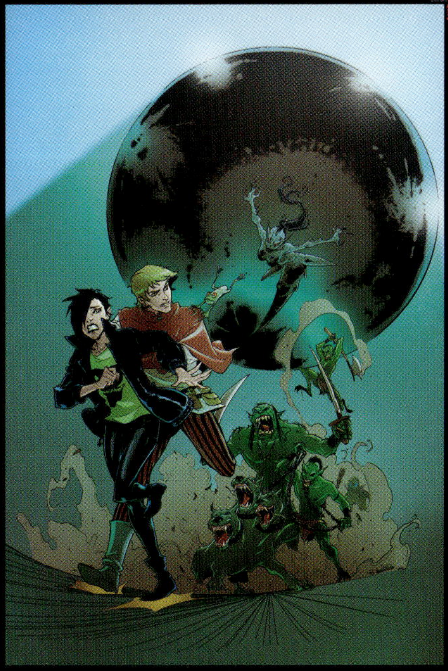

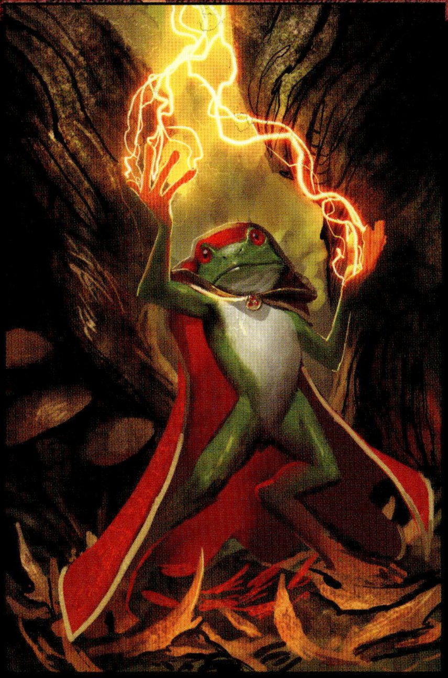

This page, counterclockwise from above.

Rise of the Magi #0 Free Comic Book Day cover,
art by: Marc Silvestri and Andy Troy

Rise of the Magi #1 cover A,
art by: Marc Silvestri and Betsy Golden

Rise of the Magi #1 cover C,
art by: Sumeyye Kesgin

Rise of the Magi #3 cover A,
art by: Tina Valentino and Betsy Golden

Rise of the Magi #3 cover B,
art by: Stjepan Sejic

The Walking Dead 20th Anniversary

To celebrate the 20th anniversary of Robert Kirkman's *The Walking Dead*, Image Comics brought everyone together to create a line of exciting team-up variants. These variant covers infected Image Comics titles all through October 2023 and featured Image artists' unique interpretations of the iconic horror series' characters.

All three of Top Cow's October titles participated, featuring our series' characters on the covers fighting side by side with some of your favorite *The Walking Dead* heroes and villains from across the series.

To get the ball rolling, Top Cow Editorial put their heads together, then commissioned artist Giuseppe Cafaro and colorist John Starr to get to work creating an epic connecting triptych. Here are the details of how it came together.

***DESTINY GATE* #1 cover C.** This cover features *The Walking Dead's* Negan wielding the mighty Lucille as he struggles with *Destiny Gate* protagonist Mitchell Slate while the demonic character "Madness" Looms. Zombies claw at their figures. Negan however is looking past Mitchell far across…

***ANTARCTICA* #4 cover C** …To Michonne, sword drawn with *Antarctica* heroine Hannah, as they fight back to back while Zombies claw at them. If you got this cover alone you would think Michonne was engaging eyes with Negan, but look further across to…

***HAUNT YOU TO THE END* #5 cover C**… A *Haunt You to the End* character, the tough as nails mercenary Gersh, struggling in the foreground while behind her the *The Walking Dead's* Maggie fights for her life against ravenous Zombies. There are tears of shock and surprise in her eyes as next to her, she sees the mangled, broken ghost corpse of her deceased love, Glenn, who does not see her, his eyes locked across the spread at Negan. The man who killed him.

The covers are as follows. *DESTINY GATE* #1 cover C (left), *ANTARCTICA* #4 cover C - (center), *HAUNT YOU TO THE END* #5 cover C - (right)

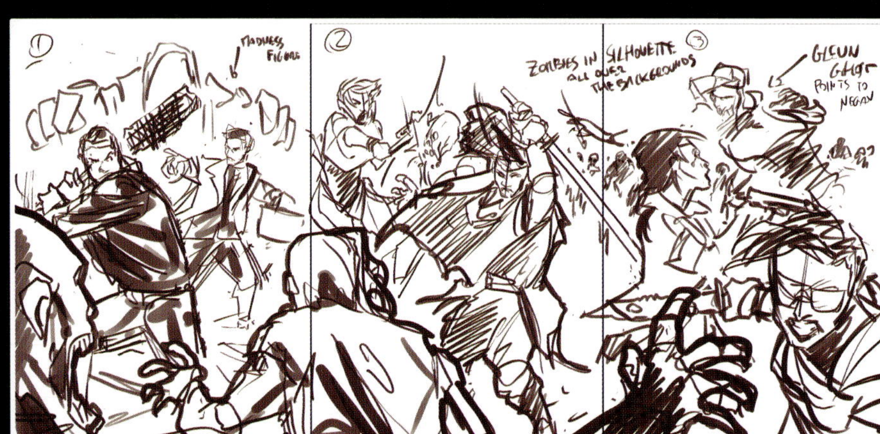

Thumbnails

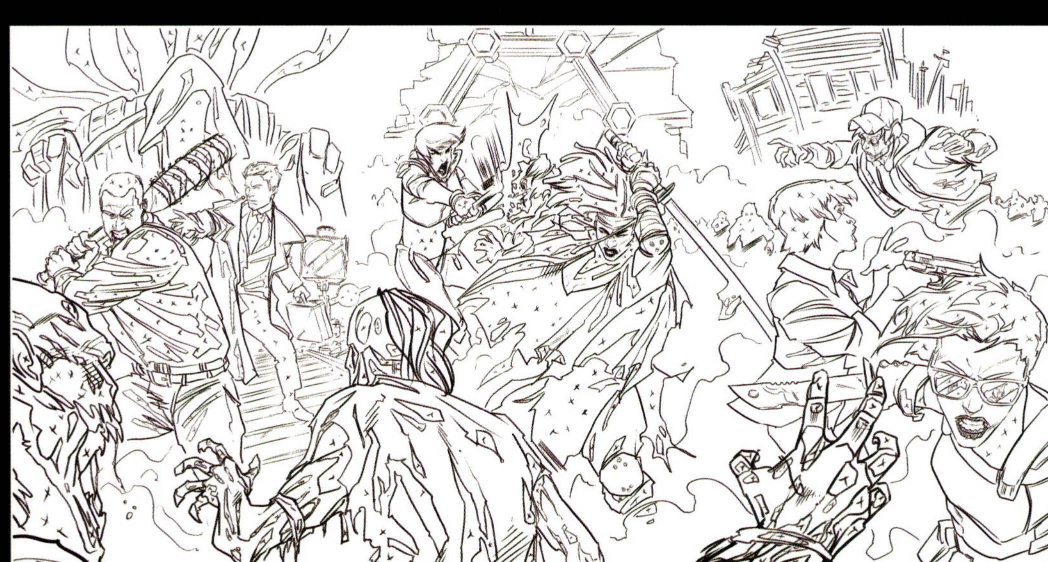

Pencils

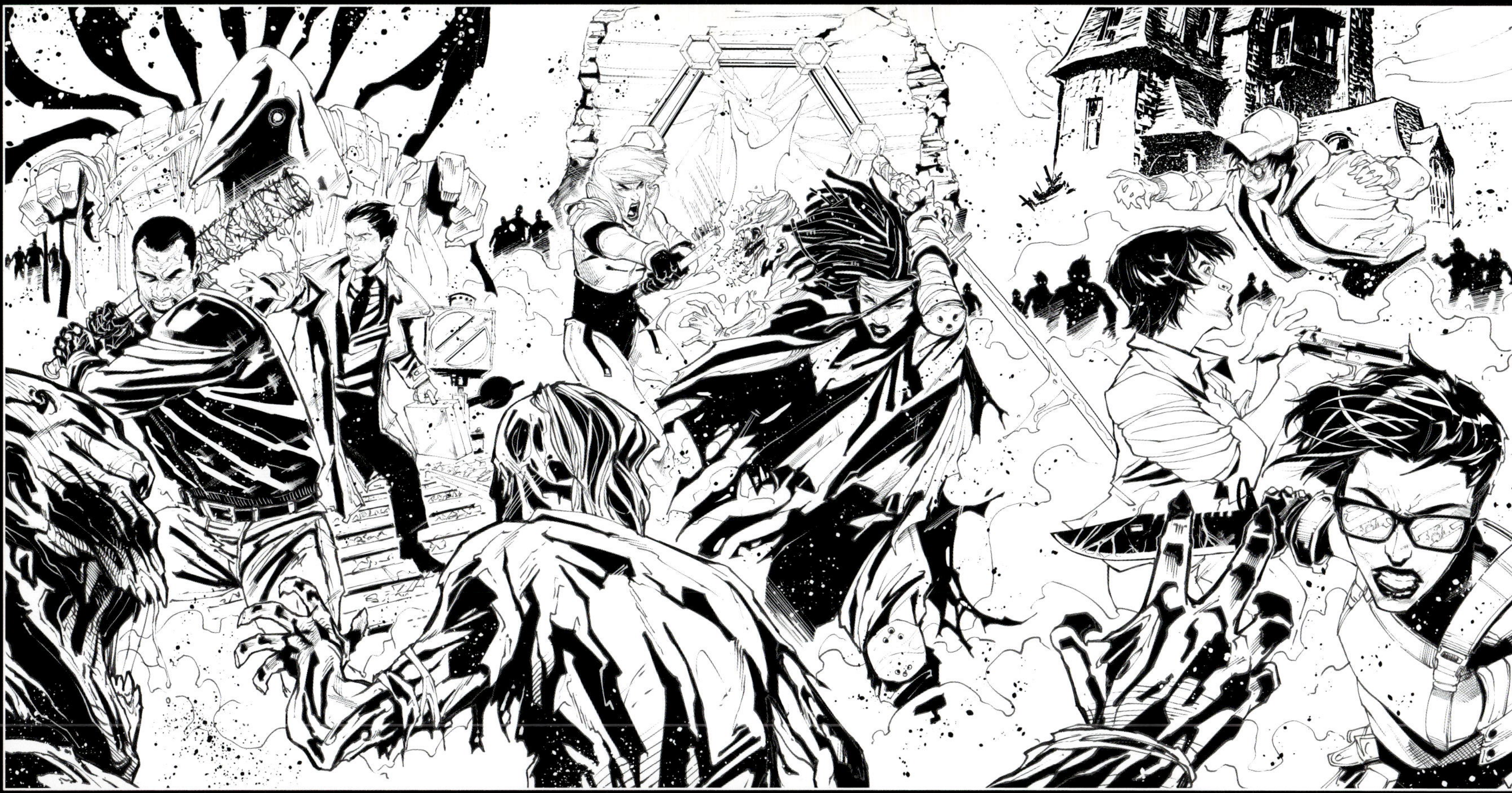

Inks

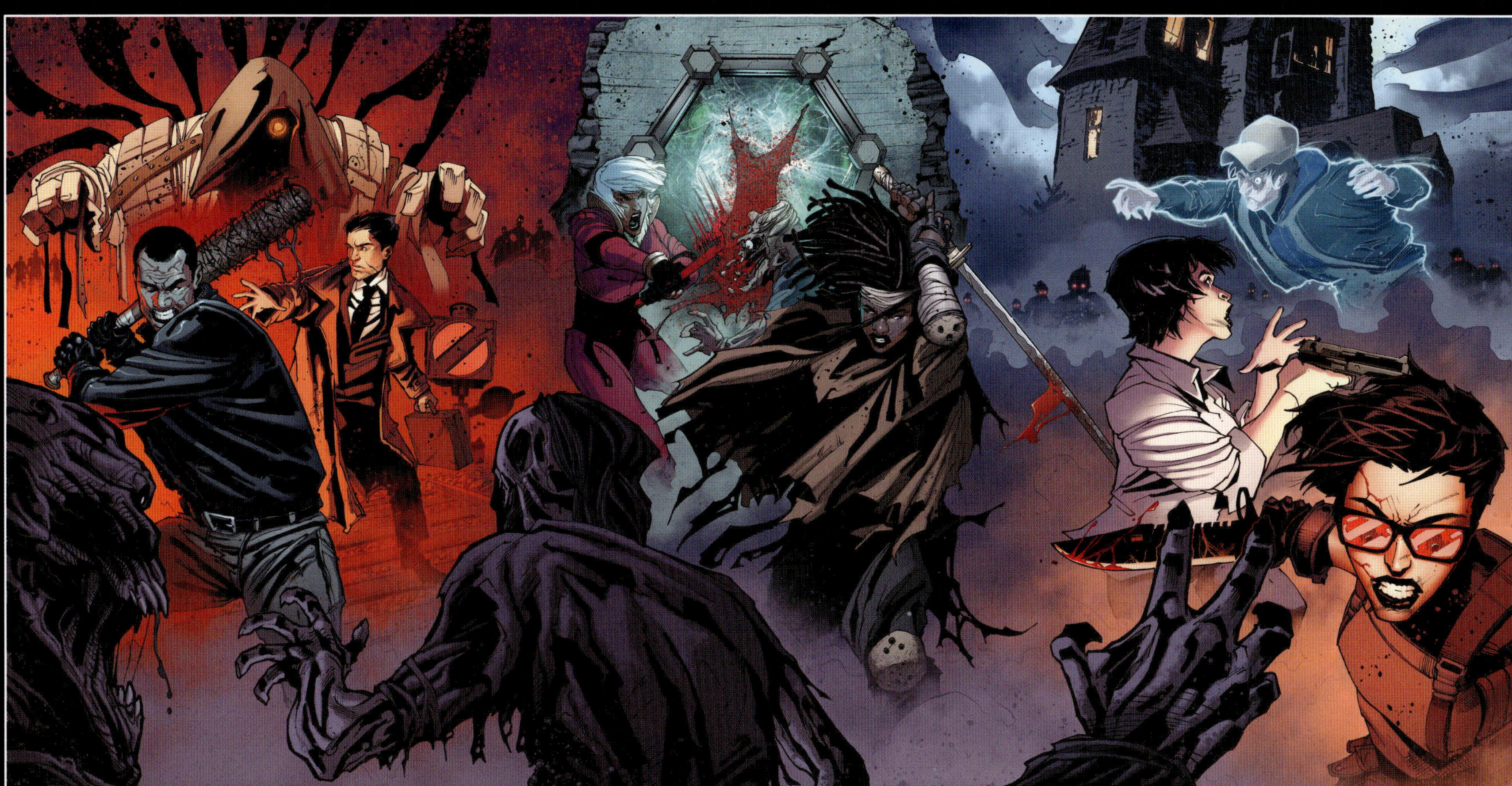

Colors

Selected gems from the *Witchblade* 1996 trading card set.

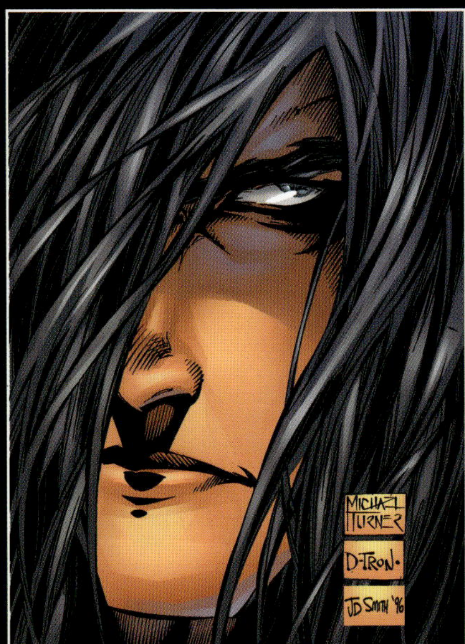

Card #2, art by Michael Turner, D-Tron, and Jonathan D. Smith

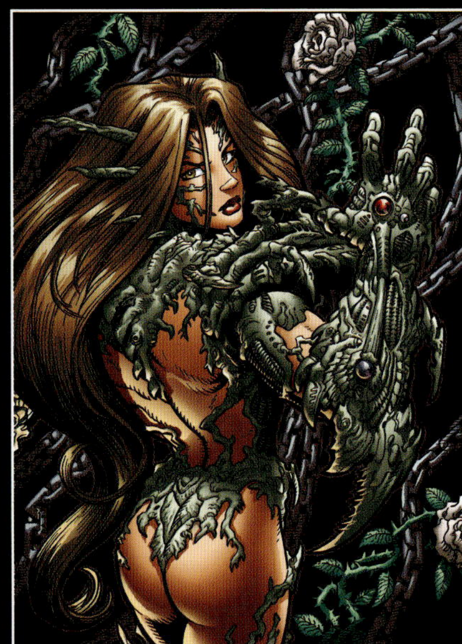

Card #28, art by Arthur Adams

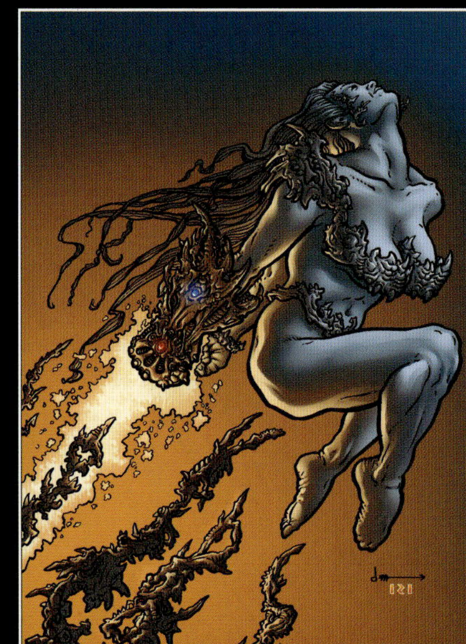

Card #30, art by Geof Darrow and Richard Isanove

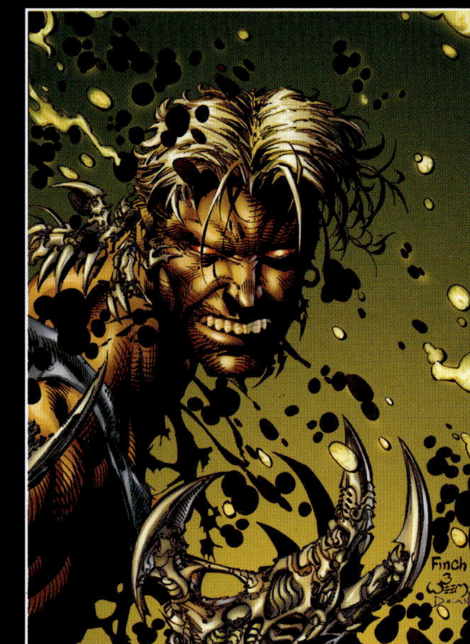

Card #46, art by David Finch, Joe Weems V, and Dean White

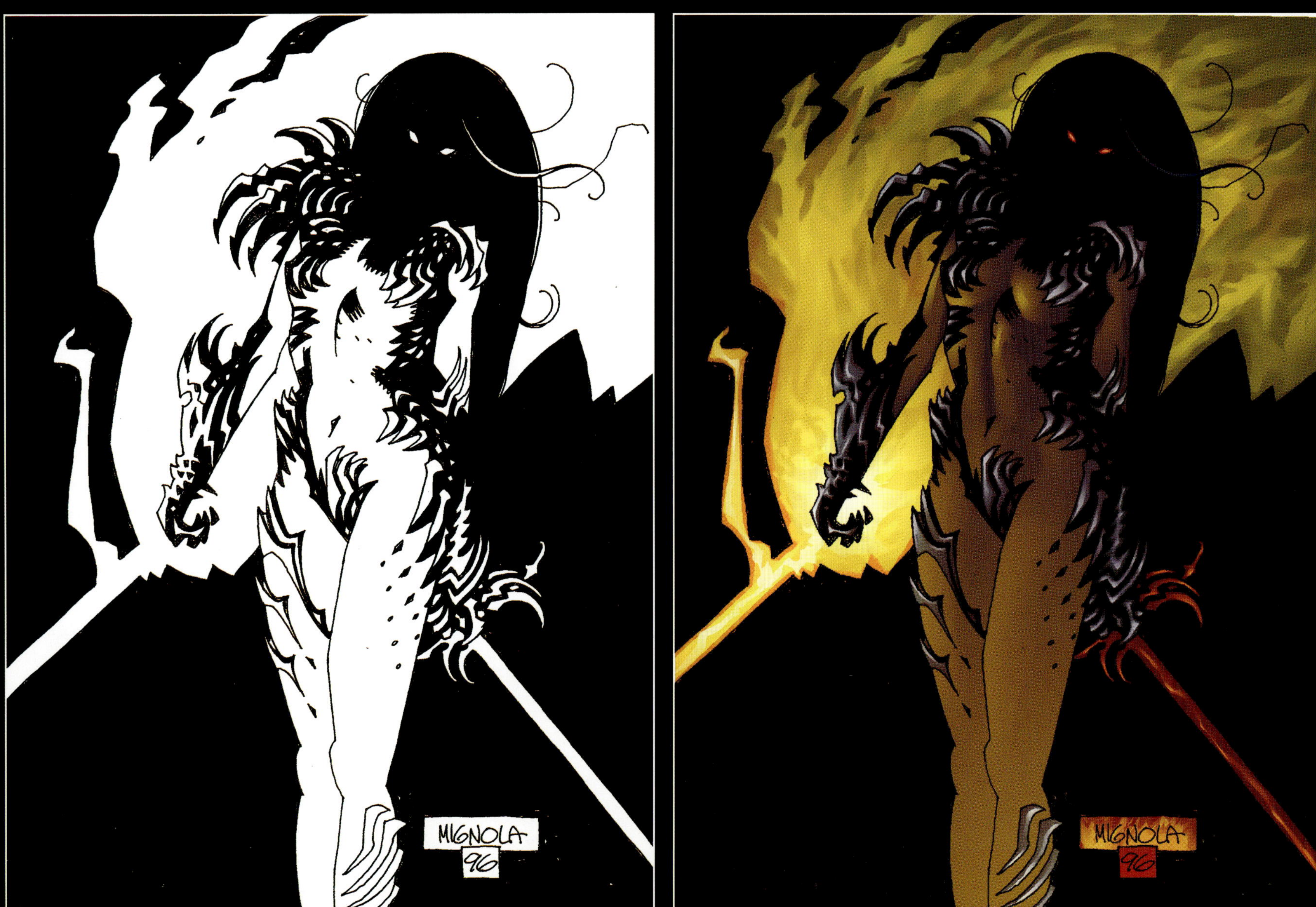

Card #33, line art by Mike Mignola with colors by Dean White

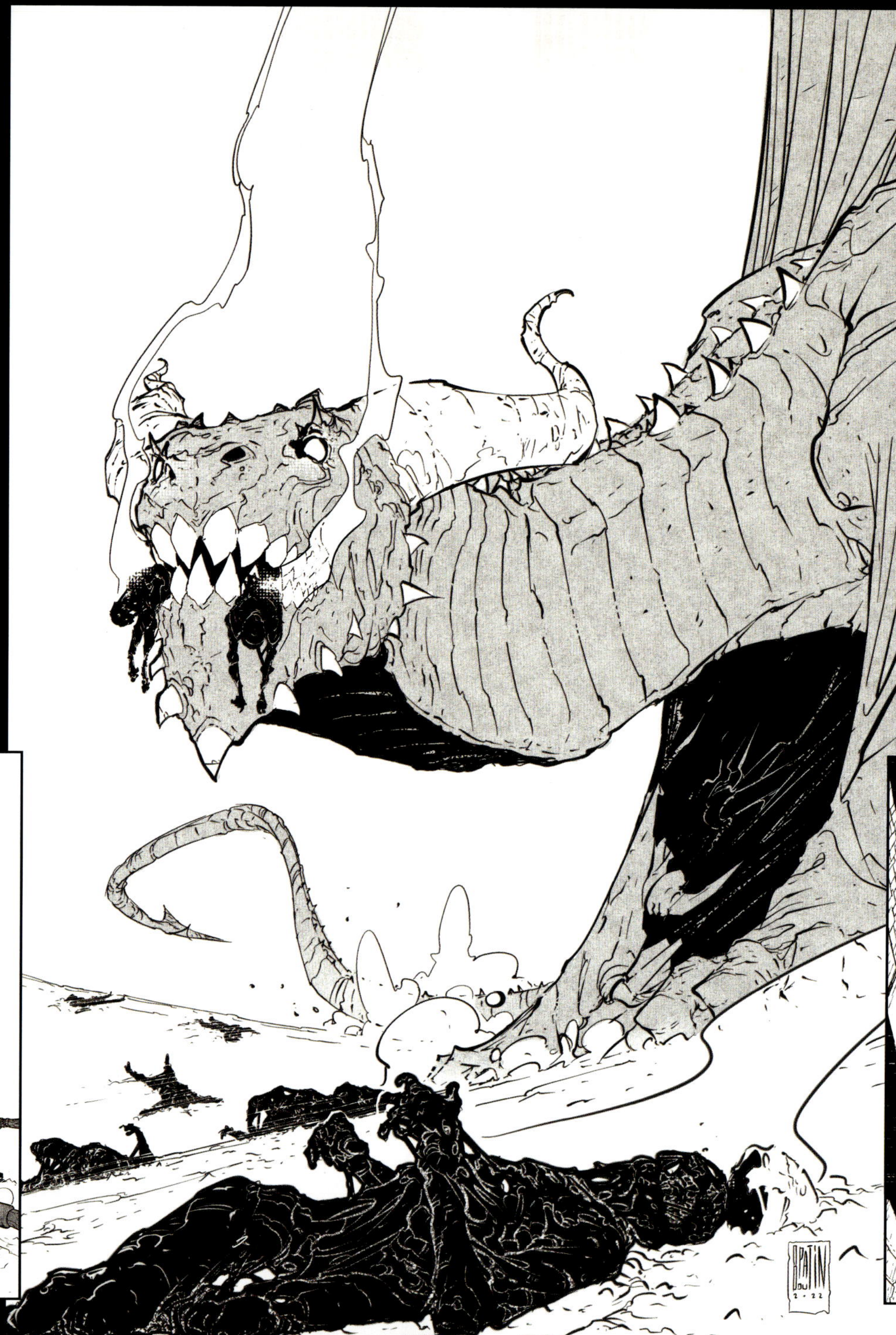

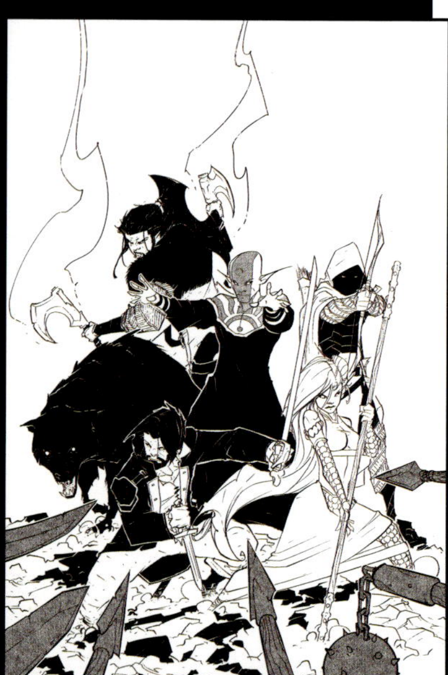

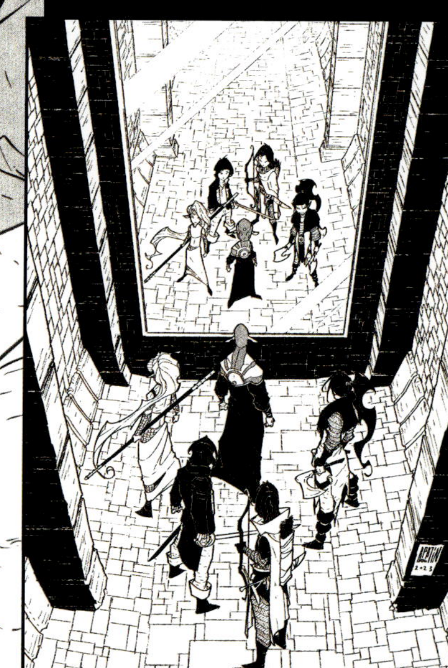

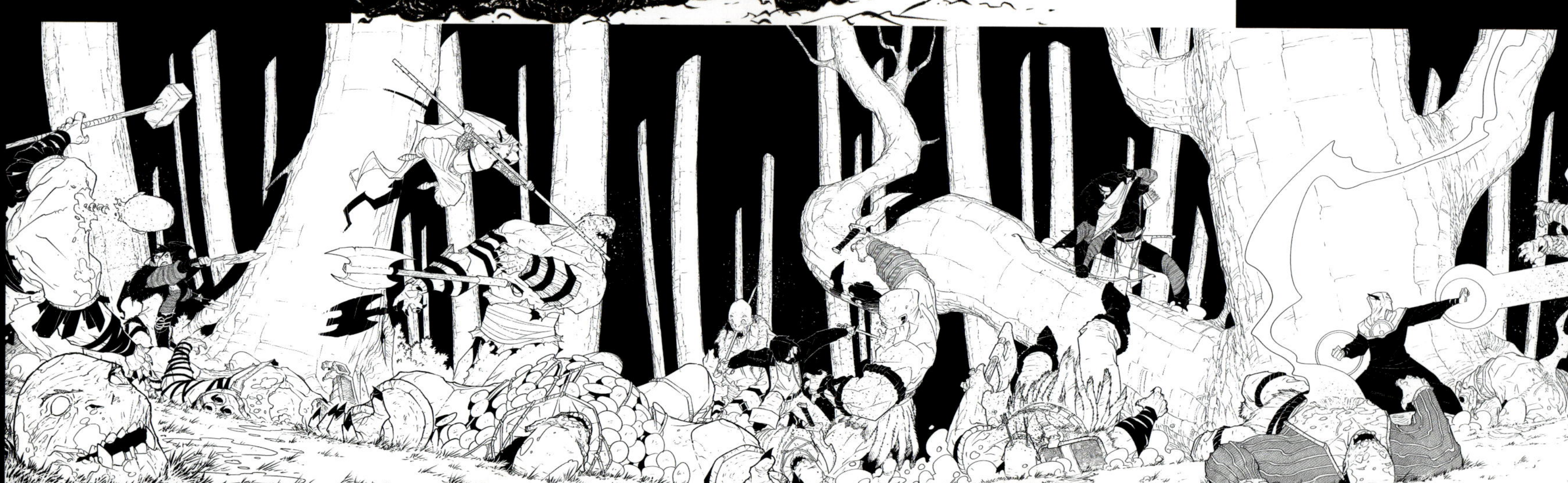

The Swords of Wintersea volume 1 covers and concepts, art by: Pat Boutin

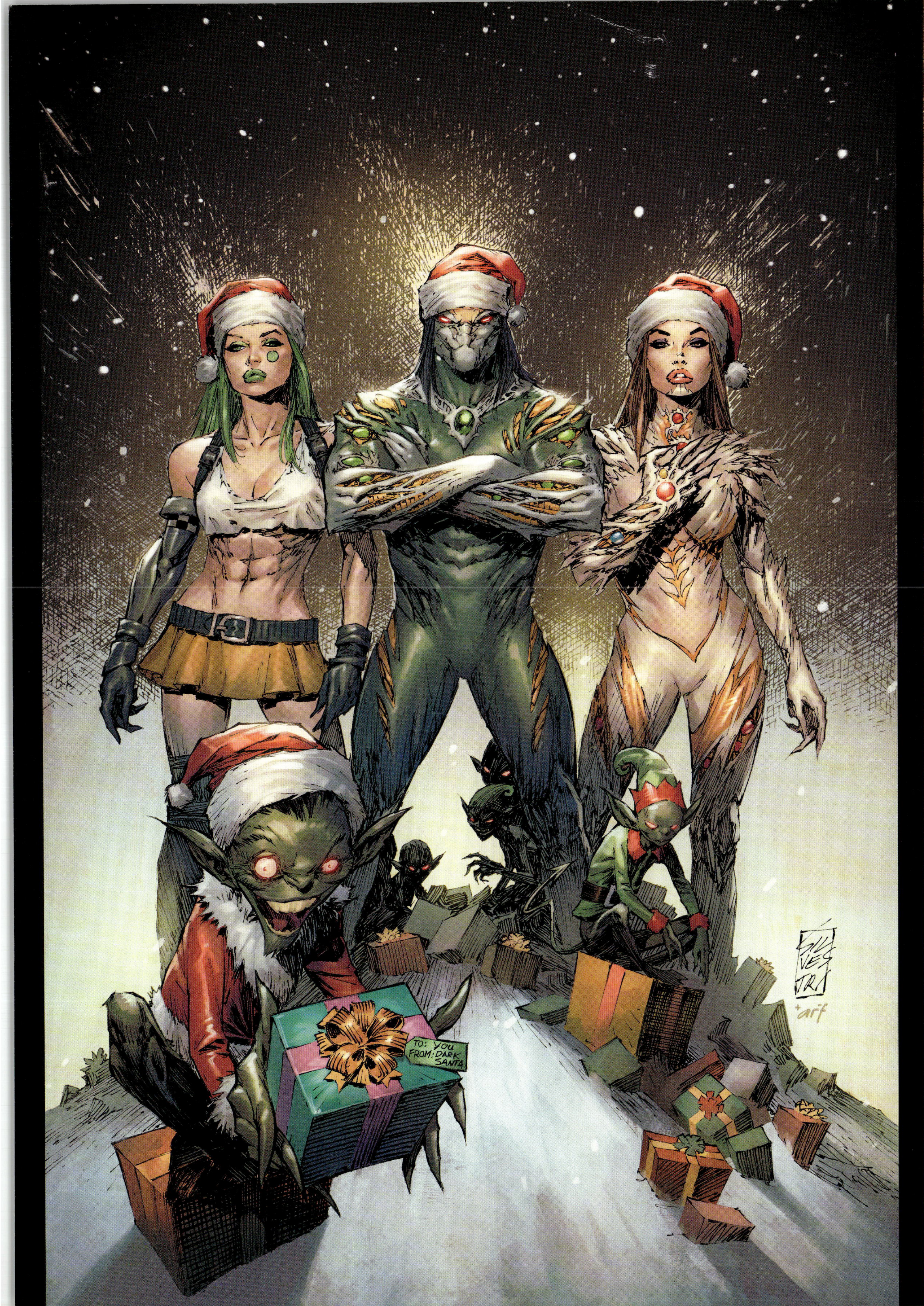

Top Cow Holiday Special "All Through the House..." [2024] cover.
art by: Marc Silvestri and Arif Prianto

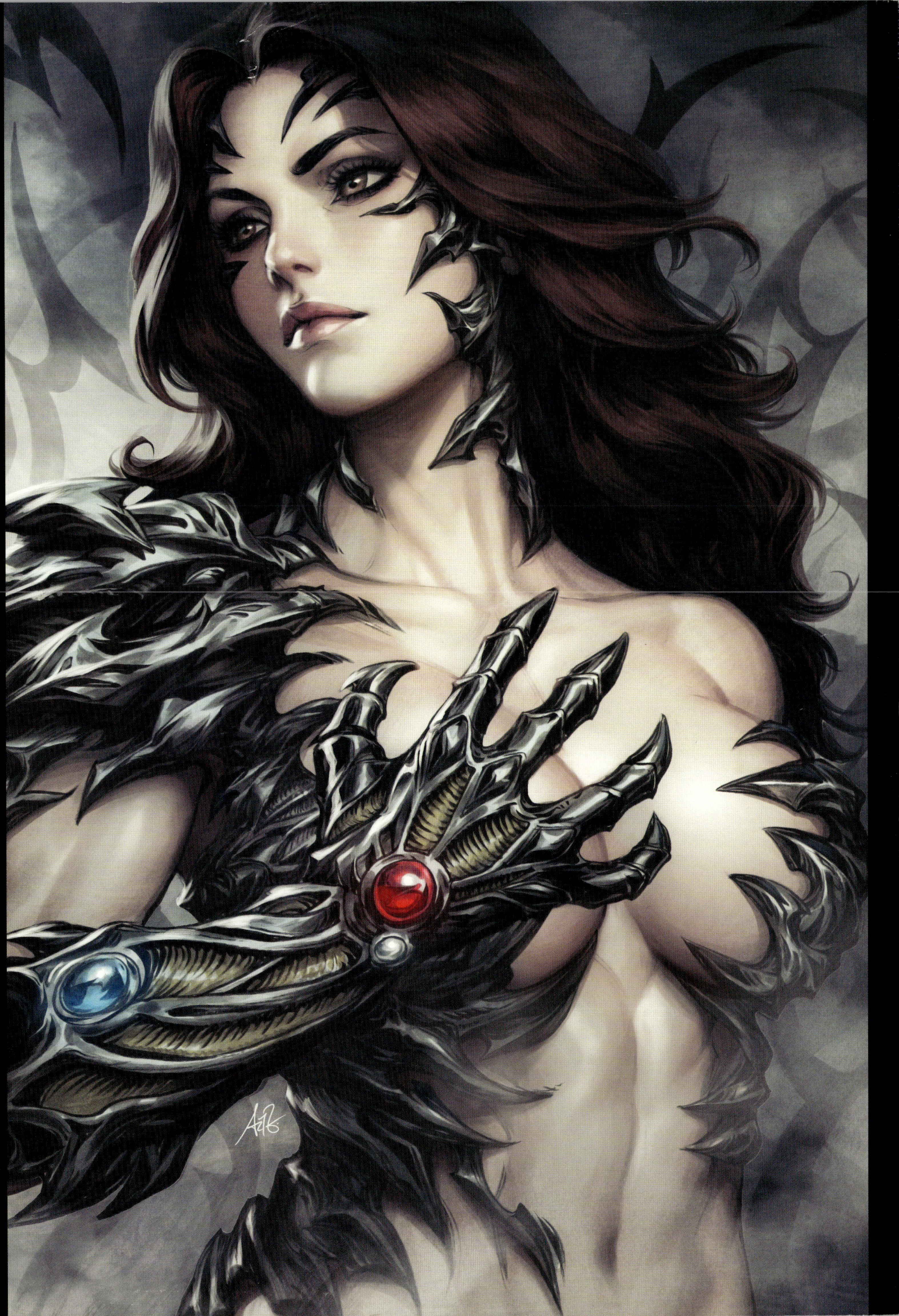

Witchblade #12 [2024] Convention Exclusive cover,
art by: Artgerm

Works Cited...

Wu, Lisa, with Elena Salcedo and Vincent Valentine, eds. "30 YEARS OF CYBERFORCE," in *Cyberforce* #1 30th Anniversary Edition (June 2022): 31-37.

Matter, Brittany. "Kittredge and Ingranata Raise Witchblade's Gauntlet," in *Witchblade* #1 [2017] (December 6, 2017): 28-31.

Salcedo, Elena, ed., and Matt Hawkins ed., "Witchblade Fan Questions," in *Witchblade* #1 Preview (May 2023): 16-17.

Salcedo, Elena, ed., "Witchblade, interview with Marguerite Bennett," in *Witchblade* #1/2 (August 2021): 16-17.

Barajas, Henry and Claire Napier. "SAY GOOD NIGHT TO THE "GOOD GUY," in *The Darkness* #1 25th Anniversary Commemorative Edition [2020] (November 2020): 26-31.

Notes...

In the 2009 edition of *The Art of Top Cow*, there is a typo on page 144. On that page, *Cyberforce* on the second line is spelled *Cybderforce*. I never got to explain. While producing the 2009 edition with the SDCC deadline looming, my wife went into labor. I brought my computer and three external drives and worked on the book in the delivery room. While working on page 144, the nurse tapped me on the shoulder and asked if I could hold my wife's leg, my child was coming. I hit [save as], and my daughter was born. In the rush, I made a typing error. I always wanted to come clean on that.

This is an art book, but comics are a collaborative medium. Thank you to the writers, letterers, editors, staff, and personnel who have contributed to Top Cow's successes over the years, and here's to more.

Special thanks to Drew Fitzgerald for his eagle eyes.

Live Long and Prosper
-Phil